ACCOUNTANCY

ACCOUNTANCY

A textbook
for the professional accountancy and
advanced commercial examinations

WILLIAM PICKLES

BCOM FCA FRSA

*Late Senior Lecturer in Accountancy and Allied Subjects for the
Professional Accountants' Examination Classes at the
Municipal High School of Commerce, Manchester
(now College of Commerce)*

FIFTH EDITION

by

JAMES L LAFFERTY

CA ATII

*Senior Administrative Officer,
The University of Edinburgh,
Edinburgh*

PITMAN

PITMAN BOOKS LIMITED
128 Long Acre, London WC2E 9AN

PITMAN PUBLISHING INC
1020 Plain Street, Marshfield, Massachusetts 02050

Associated Companies
Pitman Publishing Pty Ltd, Melbourne
Pitman Publishing New Zealand Ltd, Wellington
Copp Clark Pitman, Toronto

© William Pickles 1960
© Agnes Pickles and James L. Lafferty 1974
© James L. Lafferty 1982

Fourth edition 1974, reprinted 1977, 1980, 1981
Fifth edition 1982

British Library Cataloguing in Publication Data
Pickles, William
   Accountancy.—5th ed.
   1. Accounting
   I. Title   II. Lafferty, James L.
   657   HF5635

ISBN 0-273-01256-8

Typeset in Northern Ireland at
The Universities Press (Belfast) Ltd and
printed and bound in Great Britain
at The Pitman Press, Bath

Preface to the fifth edition

IN preparing the fifth edition the original main aim of the text was constantly borne in mind, namely, to assist students reading for the examinations of the leading professional accountancy bodies.

The revision work entailed: replacing obsolete legislation with current legislation—in particular the chapters on Limited Company Accounts and on Holding Companies have been revised to take account of the provisions of the Companies Act 1976 and of the provisions of the Finance Act 1972 concerning Advance Corporation Tax; inserting data on the main provisions of the Companies Act 1980 and of the Companies Act 1981; eliminating obsolete data; replacing certain topics with more relevant matters; deleting the articles on Capital Gains Tax and National Insurance Contributions, now considered inappropriate for a text book of this nature; incorporating certain Statements of Standard Accounting Practice—issued by associated approval of the leading accountancy bodies—where considered appropriate; reproducing, with kind permission, a brief extract from the annual report and the full published accounts of Lindustries Limited, a joint winner of The Accountant Annual Award 1977; in the chapter on Partnership Accounts amending figures to more realistic amounts bearing in mind that students will, I am sure, appreciate that on any topic the principles involved, not the figures, are of paramount importance.

Finally I wish to acknowledge with great pleasure the very able and much appreciated assistance afforded me in the revision work by my brother Rodney G. Lafferty C.A., a senior accountant with Strathclyde Regional Council

James L. Lafferty
August 1982

Preface to the first edition

As tutor, lecturer, and examiner for many years, I have observed that most students for the professional accountants' examinations enter the examination hall ill-prepared for the work they are expected to perform to the reasonable satisfaction of the examiners. To a great extent the fault lies solely, or largely, with themselves—lack of consistent and careful preparation throughout the whole period prior to the examination being the most usual fault. One of the most consistently presented excuses is that the textbook employed contains an insufficient number of illustrations and too profuse a display of extraneous matter.

With a view to affording the maximum assistance available by the medium of a textbook in the form that, after extensive inquiry, I am convinced beyond all doubt the student requires, I have attempted in the following pages to explain and illustrate the fundamental principles calling for application in the examinations.

The work is intended for one section of the accountancy profession, viz. for students reading for the Intermediate and Final examinations of the Institute of Chartered Accountants, the Society of Incorporated Accountants and Auditors, the Association of Certified and Corporate Accountants, the Institute of Certified Public Accountants, and kindred bodies.

In order to deal as adequately as space will permit with Accountancy proper, the subjects of Executorship and Costing are omitted, as an attempt to deal with them in a few cursory pages would be both dangerous and futile. With the same considerations in mind, discussions of purely legal and economic subjects are almost entirely excluded, and where introduced are done so only in so far as they relate to Accountancy. The same reasons are the justification for the brief chapter on Income Tax.

It may occur to the reader—and certainly would strike the practitioner forcibly—that certain topics absorb more space, illustrations, and comment than others. To the practitioner, the matter briefly dealt with may appear—and doubtless very properly—much more vital to him than a topic which occupies several pages. The reply is that the book is for the examination candidate, and from close observation I have learned that certain types of question cause difficulty to the student; and wherever a repetition of type appears in this work, it is on the ground of special difficulty to the student, or in one or two instances because of the partiality of the examiner for the type of problem in question.

It is my pleasure to acknowledge the assistance afforded me in the preparation of this work by my clerk, Mr C. E. Ruddin, B.A.(Com.), A.C.A.

WILLIAM PICKLES

48 Mosley Street
Manchester 2

Statements of Standard Accounting Practice

STATEMENTS of Standard Accounting Practice ('accounting standards') are issued periodically by and with the associated approval of the Councils of The Institute of Chartered Accountants in England and Wales, The Institute of Chartered Accountants of Scotland, The Institute of Chartered Accountants in Ireland, The Association of Certified Accountants and The Institute of Cost and Management Accountants. Members of these bodies are expected, under possible penalty of disciplinary action, to observe where practicable the accounting standards when producing U.K. financial accounts so as to present a true and fair financial position. Indeed, where financial accounts depart significantly from accounting standards this fact should be stated and explained in the accounts and material effects disclosed. Members acting as auditors or reporting accountants should not only ensure disclosure of significant departures from accounting standards but must also, where applicable, justify any concurrence, stated or implied, with such departures.

New accounting standards are produced and existing ones altered in the light of changes in business and economic needs.

Extracts of certain accounting standards are reproduced with kind permission at relevant points in this book.

Note. In so far as they are not replaced by Statements of Standard Accounting Practice the 'Recommendations of Accounting Principles' (issued by the Institute of Chartered Accountants in England and Wales) continue as guidance statements and indicators of best practice.

Contents

Note. The pages in this edition have been numbered in a decimal system. The chapters are numbered 01 to 32, and each chapter is paged independently from 01. The first page is therefore 0101, the second 0102, and so on. This system gives the author and publisher greater flexibility in keeping the book up to date, as any chapter may be revised without disturbing the entire pagination.

Preface to the fifth edition	v
Preface to the first edition	vi
Statements of Standard Accounting Practice	vii
Book-keeping to the trial balance	0101
Bank reconciliation statements and petty cash	0201
Arithmetic of accountancy	0301
Accounts current and average due date	0401
Trading and profit and loss account—balance sheet	0501
Bills of exchange	0601
Depreciation, reserves, and provisions	0701
Capital and revenue expenditure	0801
Containers, goods on approval, C.O.D., voyage accounts, value added tax, and P.A.Y.E.	0901
Self-balancing ledgers and sectional balancing	1001
Single entry	1101
Receipts and payments, and income and expenditure accounts	1201
Tabular book-keeping	1301
Correction of errors	1401
Royalty accounts	1501
Joint venture accounts	1601
Consignment accounts	1701
Departmental accounts	1801
Branch accounts	1901
Hire purchase accounts	2001
Income tax in relation to accounts	2101
Partnership accounts—	
A General principles and division of profits	2201
B Admission of a partner	2260
C Amalgamations and acquisitions of businesses	2281
D Retirement of partner	2293
E Retirement and admission	22120
F Continuance of personnel with revised profit-sharing ratio	22137

G Annuities   22147
H Dissolution   22158
I   Limited partnership   22189
J   Miscellaneous   22200

Limited company accounts—
A Introduction   2301
B Accounting period, accounting records, duties of directors etc. 2310
C Company taxation—corporation tax, advance corporation tax
      (ACT), treatment of taxation in limited company accounts,
      close companies   2353
D Share capital   2375
E Debentures   23108
F Alterations of share capital   23144
G Acquisition entries   23155
H Divisible profits and final accounts   23211
I   Dividends   23251
J   Reconstructions, amalgamations, and absorptions 23274
K The Companies Acts 1980 and 1981   23333
L Other Statements of Standard Accounting Practice 23351
Holding companies   2401
Double account system   2501
Stock exchange transactions, investment accounts, valuation of
   shares, investment trusts and unit trusts   2601
Insurance claims   2701
Bankruptcy   2801
Liquidation   2901
Manufacturing accounts   3001
Management accounting, aids and techniques
A Introduction   3101
B Interpretation of accounts   3108
C Balance-sheet criticism and accounting ratios 3138
D Takeover bids   3153
E Budgetary control   3157
F Marginal costing   3165
G Mechanical aids in accounting   3171
H Electronic data processing (E.D.P.)   3174
I   Investment appraisal   3179
J   Operational research (O.R.)   3187
Miscellaneous   3201
Index

CHAPTER 01

BOOK-KEEPING TO THE TRIAL BALANCE

THE system of book-keeping which is almost universally employed is that whereby 'every debit has a credit.' This is known as the Double Entry System, to distinguish it from the Single Entry System, a much less detailed and less accurate method now very little used. The principles of Single Entry and its disadvantages, a knowledge of which is essential for examination purposes, are dealt with in Chapter 11.

The Double Entry System seeks to record every transaction in money or money's worth in its double aspect—the receipt of a benefit by one account and the surrender of a like benefit by another account, the former entry being to the DEBIT of the account receiving, the latter to the CREDIT of the account surrendering. The fact that every debit has a credit does not necessarily entail the task of literally entering a separate credit for each debit, as, by the employment of special books, and the utilization of the totals of all entries contained therein, certain debits will be reflected, not in a series of separate credits but in a composite or collective item. Following the same principle, certain credits will be reflected in a composite or collective debit entry.

The student should find no difficulty in the entries in the Ledger accounts if he remembers the 'three cardinal rules' of double-entry book-keeping, viz:

1. **Real Accounts.** Accounts relating to tangible things, such as Cash, Fixtures, and Goods. 'Debit what comes in: Credit what goes out.'
2. **Personal Accounts.** Accounts relating to transactions with persons necessitated by 'Credit' transactions, i.e. where goods are sold and services rendered, payment being made at a subsequent date, or in the case of 'Debit' transactions where the converse position arises, i.e. payment is made at once for the future delivery of goods or rendering of services. 'Debit receiver: Credit supplier.'
3. **Nominal Accounts.** Accounts relating to gains or losses, e.g. Rents, Discounts. 'Debit losses (or expenses): Credit gains.'

As the first principle of double entry is that every entry in the **Ledger** shall be the subject of an originating entry in a book or Journal of prime or original entry, it is necessary as a preliminary to outline briefly the books or Journals of prime entry usually met with. These are as follows:

1. The General Journal.
2. Purchases and Sales Day Books or Journals.
3. Purchases and Sales Returns Books or Journals.

In addition may be included the Cash Book, which though strictly part of the Ledger, is, in practice, employed as a book of prime entry.

The books or journals will be considered separately.

1. The General Journal

This is employed for (a) opening entries, (b) closing entries and (c) transactions of a special nature. It should be borne in mind that *every* transaction is capable of entry in the General Journal, but in order to economize labour, other books are almost invariably employed in place of the General Journal.

The rule to be employed in writing up the General Journal is to enter in the debit column thereof the amount which is to be entered on the debit side of the Ledger, and in the credit column the amount which is to be entered on the credit side of the Ledger. The title of the appropriate account will be entered against each item. It is thus necessary to visualize the entry as it will appear in the Ledger, and to enter the items accordingly in the General Journal. The amount in the debit column must equal that in the credit column either in separate items or in a composite item.

At the foot of each entry a note, called the narration (or narrative), must be appended, showing the nature of and, where necessary, the authority for, the entry.

The entries made upon the inauguration of a business are—Debit assets: Credit liabilities and CAPITAL. These initial entries must balance simply because Capital is the excess of Assets over Liabilities. This rule is only a modified expression of the rules outlined on p. 0101, as Assets are usually Real Accounts, and as they come into the business are therefore debited. If some of those Assets consist of Debtors, they are personal accounts and are consequently debited as the persons in question have received goods and/or services from the proprietor at some time; as regards the credit entries, liabilities and capital are Personal Accounts and are credited in accordance with the rule appropriate thereto, i.e. credit supplier.

2. Sales and Purchases Day Books or Journals

Each sale (ignoring Cash Sales) will be entered in the Sales Day Book or Journal with such details as are required, e.g. date, name, reference to duplicate invoice, and posted to the debit of the buyer's account in the Ledger (Personal Accounts: debit receiver). At the end of a suitable period, weekly, monthly, or in fact at any interval, provided that it does not overlap the period for which the final accounts are to be prepared, additions of all the entries in the Sales Day Book or Journal will be made, and the total posted to the credit of Sales Account. (Real Accounts: credit what goes out.)

When this has been done the double entry in the Ledger has been effected in that the individual debits to the Personal Accounts are balanced by the total credit to the Sales Account.

Purchases will be similarly recorded but posted to the *credit* of the supplier's account in the Ledger (Personal Accounts: credit supplier). The total of the Purchases Day Book or Journal will be posted periodically to the *debit* of Purchases Account (Real Accounts: debit what comes in).

Particular attention must be paid to the method of dealing with trade discounts. These are adjustments of the listed price of goods, and should be deducted *before* the sale or purchase is entered in the Day Book or Journal in order that this entry may represent the true sale or purchase price. Any *cash* discount allowed will be based upon the true figure, i.e. after deducting trade discount.

With regard to Cash Sales and Purchases, three alternative methods are usually met with, viz:

(*a*) To enter them in the Cash Book, debiting Cash and crediting Cash Sales Account, or crediting Cash and debiting Cash Purchases Account. By using a separate column in the Cash Book, posting to Cash Sales (or Purchases) Account can be made in total.

(*b*) To enter the transaction in the appropriate Day Book or Journal in the same way as a credit sale or purchase, and to post the amount to the debit or credit respectively of Cash.

(*c*) To enter the transaction in the appropriate Day Book or Journal and post to the debit (sales) or credit (purchases) of a ledger account called Cash Sales (or Purchases) (Personal) Account, exactly as if it were a credit transaction.

3. Sales and Purchases Returns Books or Journals

These books or Journals occupy the converse position to the Day Books or Journals all postings being made, in respect of Sales Returns, to the *credit* of the account of the customer who returns goods (Personal Accounts: credit supplier), and in respect of Purchases Returns, to the *debit* of the account of the supplier to whom the goods are returned. The respective totals are posted periodically to the debit of Sales or Sales Returns Account, and to the credit of Purchases or Purchases Returns Account.

In these books or journals the treatment of trade discounts will be similar to that in the case of Sales and Purchases; that is, the amount to be entered will be the net figure *after* deduction of trade discount.

Cash Book. It will be recollected that one of the fundamental rules of double-entry book-keeping is that all entries must originate in a subsidiary book—a book of prime or original entry—and be posted therefrom to the Ledger. In practice, however, expedience and convenience dictate a departure from this rule in the case of cash and bank entries.

The Cash Book is a LEDGER, but the use of a subsidiary book in this connection is often dispensed with, and the double entry is completed by direct transfer from the Cash Book to the other ledgers.

The type of Cash Book employed depends largely on the circumstances, but for the purpose of exposition of principles the usual 'three-column' type will be taken. It should be noted that the three columns which appear on each side of the Cash Book represent the three types into which accounts are classified:

1. Discount, which is a NOMINAL ACCOUNT.
2. Cash, which is a REAL ACCOUNT.
3. Bank, which is a PERSONAL ACCOUNT.

The principal rules are as follows:

Receipts. (*a*) On receipt of cash from debtors, the amount actually received is entered in the Cash column *debit* (Real Accounts: debit what comes in) or if the money is paid direct into the Bank, into the Bank column *debit* (Personal Accounts: debit receiver). The credit in each case is to the debtor's Personal Account (Personal Accounts: credit supplier).

(*b*) On receipt of an amount in respect of Cash Sales, the entry is made in the Cash or Bank column *debit*, the *credit* in this case being either to the Cash Sales Account, or as a posting to the Sales Day Book or Journal, or to the credit of Cash Sales (Personal) Account. (See p. 0103.)

(*c*) On receipt of an amount from the sale of an Asset, the entry will be to the debit of Cash or Bank as outlined above, whilst the credit will be to the Asset Account (Real Accounts: credit what goes out).

In all the above cases, if a CASH DISCOUNT is allowed, such amount is entered in the Discount Allowed column *debit*, this column being totalled periodically, and the total *transferred* to the *debit* of Discounts Allowed Account (Nominal Accounts: debit loss or expense).

Payments. (*a*) On payment of an amount by cash to a creditor, the amount is entered in the Cash column *credit* (Real Accounts: credit what goes out); if the payment should be made by cheque, the amount is entered in the Bank column (instead of Cash) *credit* (Personal Accounts: credit supplier), the *debit* in each case being to the creditor's Personal Account (Personal Accounts: debit receiver).

(*b*) On payment of an amount in respect of Cash Purchases, the entry is made in the Cash or Bank column *credit* (rule as above), the *debit* in this case being either to Cash Purchases Account, or as a posting to the Purchases Day Book or Journal or to the *debit* of Cash Purchases (Personal) Account. (See p. 0103.)

(*c*) On payment of an amount for the purchase of an Asset, the *credit* will be to Cash or Bank, whilst the *debit* will be to the Asset Account (Real Accounts: debit what comes in).

In all the above cases, if a CASH DISCOUNT is received, such amount is entered in the Discount Received column *credit*, this column being totalled periodically, and the total *transferred* to the *credit* of Discounts Received Account (Nominal Accounts: credit gains).

Bank. Where Cash is paid into the Bank, the entries will be: *Credit* Cash column (Real Accounts: credit what goes out) and *debit* Bank column (Personal Accounts: debit receiver) unless on receipt it was paid into Bank and entered direct into the Bank column debit. If Cash is drawn out of the Bank for use in the business the entries will be exactly opposite, viz. *debit* Cash column (Real Accounts: debit what comes in), and *credit* Bank column (Personal Accounts: credit supplier).

The Ledger. The Ledger is the most important book of account and is the destination of the entries made in the subsidiary books or journals. It is essentially a collection of the three types of accounts already enumerated—Real, Personal and Nominal. Real Accounts record transactions which deal with material things. Assets such as Cash and Stock are typical examples.

Personal Accounts record transactions of a personal nature. It should be noted that while Cash is a real account, Bank is a personal account.

Nominal accounts relate, on the one hand, to all gains, and on the other hand, to all losses, costs, and expenses connected with the particular business. Examples of nominal accounts are: Wages, Rent, Rates, Insurance, Carriage, Discount, Telephone, Depreciation and Interest. The debits (i.e. losses, etc.) will usually have their original entry in the Cash or Bank column of the Cash Book, Purchases Day Book or Journal or the Expenses Day Book or Journal the latter book being used to record expenses on similar lines to the Purchases Day Book or Journal.

In concerns of any magnitude, the Ledger is divided up into many separate books. There will be Sales Ledgers and Purchases Ledgers containing the accounts of Debtors and Creditors respectively, which in turn may be subdivided alphabetically, geographically or otherwise, in accordance with the requirements of the particular business.

In addition, a separate Ledger, known as the Nominal (or General) Ledger, will be utilized, containing the accounts relating to Sales, Purchases, and Expenses. In practice a Private Ledger is employed in order to ensure privacy in regard to such accounts as Capital, Drawings, Deposit Accounts at the Bank, and the like.

Drawings. Where, as is usual, the proprietor withdraws cash or goods from the business for his personal use, such amounts are in effect withdrawals of Capital. In order to free the Capital Account from a large number of small entries a Drawings Account is generally opened.

(*a*) *Cash Withdrawals.* The entries will be: *debit* Drawings Account (Personal Accounts: debit receiver); *credit* Cash (Real Accounts: credit what goes out), or Bank (Personal Accounts: credit supplier).

(*b*) *Goods Withdrawals.* The entries will be: *debit* Drawings Account; *credit* Purchases Account (Real Accounts: credit what goes out).

The balance of Drawings Account will be transferred periodically by means of a Journal entry, thus: debit Capital Account; credit Drawings Account.

Not infrequently does a payment out partake of both a nominal and a private character, e.g. entertainment expenses, and, consequently, the correct proportions (often necessarily approximated) should be charged to their appropriate accounts. It is immaterial whether the whole composite item is first debited to the Nominal or to the Drawings Account, so long as the correct adjusting transfer is made. Suppose £10 is paid out representing £6 entertainment expenses and £4 drawings, it may be treated in two ways, viz:

JOURNAL

	Date			£	£
(1)		Drawings		4	
		Entertainment Expenses		6	
		Cash[1]			10
		Being Drawings and Entertainment Expenses			
(2)		Drawings		10	
		Cash[1]			10
		Being Drawings.			
		Entertainment Expenses		6	
		Drawings			6
		Being transfer of the amount of Entertainment Expenses included in Drawings.			

Dishonoured Cheques. It frequently occurs that a cheque received in respect of a debt on which cash discount has been allowed is dishonoured (i.e. not paid), thus necessitating an adjusting Journal entry in order to restore the original position. On receipt of the cheque the following entries will have been made:

JOURNAL

		£	£
Bank[1]	(say)	9	
Discounts Allowed	(say)	1	
Debtor			10
Being receipt of cheque and discount allowed in settlement of debt due.			

When the cheque is dishonoured these entries must be written back, care being taken that the discount is written back to the credit of Discounts Allowed Account and *not* to the credit of Discounts Received Account through the discount column credit in the Cash Book, as it is not a discount received but the cancellation of a discount allowed. The entries will therefore be:

JOURNAL

	£	£
Debtor	10	
Bank		9
Discounts Allowed		1
Being the writing back to Debtor in respect of cheque dishonoured and discount allowed.		

Bad Debts. If it becomes necessary to consider a debt as bad (whether a cheque has been dishonoured or not) a transfer must be made through the

---

[1] In practice cash transactions are not usually journalized.

Journal, as follows:

JOURNAL

		£	£
Bad Debts		10	
Debtor			10
Being debt due by debtor written off as bad.			

Amounts Received from Debts Written Off. Where debts have been written off, and amounts are received subsequently in respect thereof, the entries are: (1) Debit customer, credit Bad Debts Account, (2) debit Cash, credit customer.

Illustration 1

A debt for £100 owing by J. Jones is written off. £50 is subsequently received.

J. JONES

		£			£
Balance . . .	b/d	100	Bad Debts . . .		100
Bad Debts . . .		50	Cash . . .		50

BAD DEBTS

		£			£
J. Jones . . .		100	J. Jones . . .		50

Alternatively, cash may be debited and Bad Debts Account credited without the record in the personal account. In the foregoing illustration the posting from the Cash Account would be direct to the credit of Bad Debts Account.

THE TRIAL BALANCE

It has already been seen that in the double-entry system, every debit has its corresponding credit and *vice versa*. If follows, therefore, that at any given time, the postings from the General Journal, Day Books or Journals and Cash Book being completed, the debit balances standing in all the Ledgers (including the Cash Book) will equal the credit balances.

At the end of the financial period (or at some other date) these balances are extracted, and a schedule prepared in Journal form to test whether, in fact, the total debits equal the total credits. Such a schedule of balances is called a Trial Balance.

With the totals duly agreeing a *reasonably* reliable check on the *total* ARITHMETICAL accuracy of the book-keeping entries is afforded; otherwise it is obvious that some error exists either in the actual execution of the double entry or in the extraction of the balances.

Illustration 2

On 1st January 19.., A commenced business with:

		£
Cash at Bank	. . . .	600
Stock	. . . .	300
Furniture and Fittings	. . .	100
He owed B	. . : .	150

The following were his transactions for January:

19..

Jan. 1. Withdrew £35 from bank for petty cash purposes.
       Sold Y goods on credit £50.
       Paid for business stationery by cheque £20.
     3. Sold L goods on credit £30.
     5. Sold Q goods for cash £17, paid direct into bank.
     6. Sold Y goods on credit £40.
     8. Y returned goods to value of £5.
    12. Bought typewriter by cheque £60.
    13. Received cheque from Y in payment for goods purchased on 1st Jan., *less* 10% cash
        discount, paid direct into bank.
    14. Bought goods on credit from D £120.
    17. Bought goods from G £150, *less* 10% trade discount.
    18. L pays cash £30, paid direct into bank.
    20. Returned goods to G £50 (list price value).
    23. A drew out of bank £40 to pay premium on his life policy. He was allowed 2½%
        commission by the assurance company. The net premium was paid in cash on this
        date.
    25. Bought goods by cheque from R £15.
    26. Withdrew from stock £15 goods for private purposes.
        Sold to L goods on credit £20.
    27. Paid B £10 cheque on account of loan, plus £2 for interest.
    28. Paid electricity for month by cheque £5.
        Received from L cheque for £19 in settlement of his account, paid direct into bank.
    30. Cheque dishonoured and debt written off as bad.
    31. Acquired second-hand car £50, cheque £350.
        Drew £100 from bank to pay monthly wages.

At the end of the month the expenses paid out of Cash were:

Sundry Expenses	.	£13
Carriage	. . .	£14

Write up the books and prepare Trial Balance as at 31st January, 19...
(Ignore tax.)

The following abbreviations will be used in the illustration:

C.B. = Cash Book.	P.L. = Purchases Ledger.
J. = Journal.[1]	S.J. = Sales Journal.
L. = General Ledger.	P.J. = Purchases Journal.
S.L. = Sales Ledger.	S.R.J. = Sales Returns Journal.
	P.R.J. = Purchases Returns Journal.

[1] It should be noted that the General Journal is more commonly referred to simply as the Journal.

The opening entries and those for transactions of a special nature will be passed through the Journal:

JOURNAL

19..			£	£
Jan. 1	Sundries			
	Sundries			
	Cash at Bank	C.B.	600	
	Stock	L.	300	
	Furniture and Fittings	L.	100	
	B. Loan	L.		150
	A. Capital	L.		850
	Being Assets, Liabilities and Capital[1] at this date.			
26	A Drawings	L.	15	
	Purchases	L.		15
	Being Withdrawal of Goods from business for private use.			
30	L	S.L.	1	
	Discounts Allowed	L.		1
	Being Discount written back.			
	Bad Debts	L.	20	
	L	S.L.		20
	Being Debt written off as bad.			
31	Motor Car	L.	400	
	Sales	L.		50
	Bank	C.B.		350
	Being second-hand car acquired in exchange for assets as above.			

SALES JOURNAL

19..			£
Jan. 1	Y	S.L.	50
3	L	S.L.	30
6	Y	S.L.	40
26	L	S.L.	20
			£140
			L.

SALES RETURNS JOURNAL

19..			£
Jan. 8	Y	S.L.	5
			L.

Capital, being the excess of Assets over Liabilities, is found by subtracting the latter (£150) from the former (£1,000).

PURCHASES JOURNAL

19..				£
Jan. 14	D	P.L.		120
17	G £150			
	Less 10% Trade Discount . . 15			
	————	P.L.		135
				£255
	.	.		L.

PURCHASES RETURNS JOURNAL

19..				£
Jan. 20	G £50			
	Less 10% Trade Discount 5			
	————	P.L.		45
				L.

CASH BOOK

Date		Fol.	Discount Allowed	Cash	Bank	Date		Fol.	Discount Allowed	Cash	Bank
19..			£	£	£	19..			£	£	£
Jan. 1	Sundries .	J.			600	Jan. 1	Business				
	Bank: Contra .	C.		35			Stationery	L.			20
5	Q: Cash Sale .	L.			17		Cash: Contra	C.			35
13	Y . . .	S.L.	5		45	12	Typewriter	L.			60
18	L . . .	S.L.			30	23	Cash: Contra	C.			40
23	Bank: Contra .	C.		40			Drawings .	L.		39	
28	L . . .	S.L.	1		19	25	R: Goods .	L.			15
31	Bank: Contra .	C.		100		27	B: Repayment				
							of Loan .	L.			10
							B: Interest	L.			2
						28	Electricity .	L.			5
						30	L: Cheque Dishonoured	S.L.			19
						31	Sundry Expenses .	L.		13	
							Carriage .	L.		14	
							Sundries .	J.			350
							Cash: Contra	C.			100
							Wages .	L.		100	
							Balances . c/d	C.		9	55
			£6	£175	£711					£175	£711
			L.								
Feb. 1	Balances . b/d	C.		9	55						

GENERAL LEDGER
STOCK

19..			£				
Jan. 1	Sundries . . .	J.	300				

CAPITAL

				19..				£
			\	Jan. 1	Sundries . . .	J.		850

A—DRAWINGS

19..				£				
Jan. 23	Cash: Life Assurance Premium . . .	C.B.		39				
26	Purchases[1] . . .	J.		15				

B—LOAN

19..			£	19..				£
Jan. 27	Bank	C.B.	10	Jan. 1	Sundries . . .	J.		150

FURNITURE AND FITTINGS

19..				£				
Jan. 1	Sundries . . .	J.		100				
12	Bank: Typewriter .	C.B.		60				

SALES

19..			£	19..				£
Jan. 31	Sundries . . .	S.R.J.	5	Jan. 5	Cash: Q . . .	C.B.		17
				31	Sundries . . .	S.J.		140
				"	. . .	J.		50

PURCHASES

19..			£	19..				£
Jan. 25	Bank: R . . .	C.B.	15	Jan. 26	Drawings[1] . .	J.		15
31	Sundries . . .	P.J.	255	31	Sundries . . .	P.R.J.		45

LOAN INTEREST

19..				£				
Jan. 27	Bank . . .	C.B.		2				

BAD DEBTS

19..				£				
Jan. 30	L.	J.		20				

BUSINESS STATIONERY

19..				£				
Jan. 1	Bank	C.B.		20				

[1] For tax purposes the withdrawal of goods (£15) would have to be regarded as at *selling* price, in which case, assuming selling price to be £18, the sum of £3 would be added to the profit. Instead of crediting Purchases with £15, credit Sales and debit Drawings with £18. (See p. 2212, note.)

SUNDRY EXPENSES

				£				
19.. Jan. 31	Cash	. . .	C.B.	13				

CARRIAGE

				£				
19.. Jan. 31	Cash	. . .	C.B.	14				

MOTOR CAR

				£				
19.. Jan. 31	Sundries	. .	J.	400				

ELECTRICITY

				£				
19.. Jan. 28	Bank	. . .	C.B.	5				

WAGES

				£				
19.. Jan. 31	Cash	. . .	C.B.	100				

DISCOUNTS ALLOWED

				£				£
19.. Jan. 31	Sundries	. .	C.B.	6	19.. Jan. 30	L.	J.	1

SALES LEDGER
Y

				£				£
19.. Jan. 1	Goods .	. . .	S.J.	50	19.. Jan. 8	Returns . .	S.R.J.	5
6	,,	. . .	S.J.	40	13	Cheque and Discount (£5) . . .	C.B.	50
					31	Balance . . .	c/d	35
				£90				£90
Feb. 1	Balance	. . .	b/d	35				

L

				£				£
19.. Jan. 3	Goods .	. . .	S.J.	30	19.. Jan. 18	Cash . . .	C.B.	30
26	Goods .	. .	S.J.	20	28	Cheque and Discount (£1) . . .	C.B.	20
30	Cheque Dishonoured . Discounts Allowed .	C.B. J.		19 1	30	Bad Debts . .	J.	20

PURCHASES LEDGER

D

				19.. Jan. 14	Goods	P.J.	£ 120

G

19.. Jan. 20	Returns . .	P.R.J.	£ 45	19.. Jan. 17	Goods	P.J.	£ 135
31	Balance. . . .	c/d	90				
			£135				£135
				Feb. 1	Balance. . . .	b/d	90

TRIAL BALANCE as at 31st January 19..

		£	£
Stock		300	
Capital			850
A: Drawings		54	
B: Loan			140
Furniture and Fittings		160	
Sales			202
Purchases		210	
Loan Interest		2	
Bad Debts		20	
Business Stationery		20	
Sundry Expenses		13	
Carriage		14	
Motor Car		400	
Electricity		5	
Wages		100	
Discounts Allowed		5	
Y	S.L.	35	
D	P.L.		120
G	P.L.		90
Cash	C.B.	9	
Bank	C.B.	55	
		£1,402	£1,402

Detection of Errors

Errors not Affecting Balance. Although the Trial Balance totals may agree, it is only the total arithmetical accuracy of the books that may be said to be correct, though even then perfect accuracy is not assured, for compensating errors may arise, e.g. both the Sales and Purchases figures may be undercast to the extent of £100 each. The types of errors that may remain undetected are as follows:

1. *Errors of Omission.* The omission of *both* debit *and* credit aspects of a transaction will not affect the agreement of the Trial Balance.

2. *Errors of Commission.* The posting of £100 to the credit of J. Robson instead of to the credit of J. Dobson will not affect the agreement of the Trial Balance. The total of the extract of Sundry Debtors will not in itself be incorrect, though two of its composite items will be wrong. The entries required to correct an error of this type would (in this case) be as follows:

JOURNAL

			£	£
19..	J. Robson		100	
	J. Dobson			100
	Being Transfer of item posted in error.			

3. *Compensating Errors.* One or more debit errors which happen to equal one or more credit errors will not upset the Trial Balance. Thus, a £90 error in the balance of an Asset account—the balance of £100 having been brought down as £10—and a £10 under-addition in the Purchase Day Book or Journal would be compensated by the omission of the corresponding credit in the Sales Ledger for a debit of £100 in the Cash Book.

4. *Errors of Principle.* The posting of a revenue expense to a Capital Account or *vice versa* will not affect the Trial Balance agreement. It can thus easily be seen that the books might be quite incorrect as far as the true position of the business is concerned and yet the Trial Balance agree. The student must therefore take the greatest care throughout all his studies to distinguish between capital and revenue receipts and payments. In broad outline it may be stated that capital payments are those incurred in acquiring Assets for the purpose of earning income, usually identifiable as assets of a permanent nature, thus increasing the earning capacity of the business or decreasing costs. Revenue payments are those incurred in the ordinary course of business, being necessary for its efficient running. It may be generally stated that capital receipts are moneys received from the sale of assets or by the raising of loans, and revenue receipts are moneys received in return for goods sold or services rendered. (See Chapter 08.)

A simple example is given here to illustrate such error—X is the owner of £10,000 3½ per cent War Loan and upon receipt of the regular half-yearly dividend of £175 he posts the sum to the credit of the Investment Account, whereas it should go to the credit of Income Account or, as will be seen later, to the Profit and Loss Account.

Errors Affecting Balance. Though the above types of errors may occur and remain undisclosed in the Trial Balance, those given below will always have the effect of causing a discrepancy in the agreement of the Trial Balance unless by chance the errors collectively eliminate each other. They may be divided broadly into two classes:

1. Book-keeping errors.
2. Extraction errors.

1. *Book-keeping Errors.* These include the following:

(i) Items posted to the wrong side of an account.

(ii) The Discount columns of the Cash Book transferred to the wrong sides of the Discount Account.

(iii) Items for which the double entry is not complete. These often occur in the case of small returns, discounts and allowances, which have been entered in the personal accounts and not in the Returns or Discount Account.

(iv) Omission to post the totals of one or more of the subsidiary books.

2. *Extraction Errors.* These include the following:

(i) Omission to extract one or more balances, either debit or credit (particularly the Cash and Bank Balances), or a duplication of an item.

(ii) Errors in additions. These are caused more often than not by careless alignment of figures and incorrect carrying forward of additions (e.g. figure 1 badly aligned would result in a difference of 9, 90, 900 according to actual misplacement).

(iii) The confusion of figures, e.g. £1·05 taken as £105.

(iv) The extraction of items on the wrong side (causing an error of double the sum of the items).

Illustration 3

The table shown on p. 0116 is an example of some of the common errors that are made by students when preparing a Trial Balance.

In practice the different items in the Trial Balance would be earmarked by a reference to their Ledger and folio for the sake of quick verification. In examination work such detail is quite unnecessary.

The aim in an examination paper, furthermore, is to avoid the opening of unnecessary accounts, so that where possible all simple accounts should be 'posted' direct to the Trial Balance.

Trial Balance as at 31st January 19..

		Incorrect		Correct	
		£	£	£	£
Capital			2,000		2,000
Furniture and Fittings	£520				
Less Depreciation, 10%[1]	52				
		468		520	
Stock, Opening	£880				
Stock, Closing[1]	1,020				
		1,900		880	
Drawings		450		450	
Goodwill		500		500	
Sales			7,600		7,600
Purchases		5,100		5,100	
Rent, Rates, etc.		210		210	
Discounts Received		260			260
Discounts Allowed			150	150	
Sales Returns			430	430	
Purchase Returns		490			490
Cash in Hand		20		20	
Cash at Bank		590		590	
Sundry Debtors		2,750		2,750	
Sundry Creditors			1,250		1,250
		£12,738	£11,430	£11,600	£11,600

[1] Neither depreciation nor closing stock would normally be in the books at the time of the Trial Balance.

CHAPTER 02

BANK RECONCILIATION STATEMENTS AND PETTY CASH

It very rarely happens in practice that the bank balance as shown by the Cash Book agrees with the balance as shown by the Bank Statement. The three factors which contribute to this difference are:

1. Unpresented cheques.
2. Uncredited cheques.
3. Errors and omissions.

1. **Unpresented Cheques.** These are cheques which have been dispatched to suppliers in payment of their accounts, but which have not been presented for payment to the payer's bank. According to the circumstances, a period of from one to three days will elapse before the cheque is presented for payment, even assuming that the recipient pays the cheque promptly into his own bank. In effect they are items which are entered on the credit side of the Cash Book, and have not as yet been entered in the Bank Statement, so that the latter will show a balance more in the customer's favour than that shown by the Cash Book to the extent of such unpresented cheques, i.e. a larger balance due to the customer or a smaller overdraft.

2. **Uncredited Cheques.** These may be considered as the reverse of unpresented cheques. As soon as cheques are paid into the bank the Bank column of the Cash Book is debited. The bank, however, may not give credit for these cheques immediately owing to the lateness of the hour or for other reasons, so that the Cash Book will show a balance more in the customer's favour than the Bank Statement.

3. **Errors and Omissions.** An error, either on the part of the customer, or the banker, will obviously create a discrepancy between the two balances; further, at the end of every half-year the bank will enter in the Bank Statement sums representing interest (in the event of the account having been overdrawn) and commission, the exact amounts of which are unknown to the customer until such time as he has seen the Bank Statement. In addition, receipts or payments against Banker's Orders, and dividends and Bills of Exchange collected or paid by the Bank may not have been entered in the Cash Book. Banks do not normally allow interest on current accounts nowadays, but the account may be credited with interest on a deposit account.

FORM OF THE BANK RECONCILIATION STATEMENT

Subject to these considerations, the balances shown by the Cash Book and the Bank Statement should agree. It is usual to draw up a statement which effects the adjustments necessitated by the unpresented and uncredited cheques. This statement is known as a Bank Reconciliation Statement, and is drawn up on the following lines.

The first requirement, which is of paramount importance, is that the date at which the statement is being drawn up shall always be stated at the head thereof in a clear manner. The balance as shown by the Bank Statement is then extracted and used as a starting point. The unpresented cheques are found by checking up the payments side of the Bank Statement with the credit side of the Cash Book. All the unticked items in the Cash Book (subject of course to any clerical errors) will be the unpresented cheques. The uncredited cheques will be found in a similar manner. The Bank Statement balance will then (a) be decreased by the amount of the unpresented cheques, or, in the case of an overdraft, increased by such amount, and (b) increased by the amount of the uncredited cheques, or, in the case of an overdraft, decreased by such amount. The figure now obtained (subject to errors) should be the same balance as shown by the Cash Book. If the student should at any time be at a loss as to which balance should be used as a base from which to start, he should remember that the balance as shown by the Cash Book, subject to any errors or omissions arising therein, is the true and correct figure which forms the natural conclusion to the Statement.

Illustration 1

The following particulars relate to the business of A at 31st December 19..

	£
Balance as shown by the Cash Book	1,000
Balance as shown by the Bank Statement[1]	1,200
Unpresented Cheques	300
Uncredited Cheques	100

BANK RECONCILIATION STATEMENT AT 31ST DECEMBER 19..

	£
Balance as per Bank Statement	1,200
Add Uncredited Cheques (detailed)	100
	1,300
Less Unpresented Cheques (detailed)	300
Balance as per Cash Book	£1,000

Many questions are set in which, in addition to particulars as to unpresented and uncredited cheques, the candidate is informed that there are various clerical errors in the Cash Book, e.g. incorrect figures, entries on incorrect sides or in wrong columns, omissions, etc. When dealing with a question of this type the true Cash Book balance should always be ascertained separately and the Reconciliation Statement prepared from the Bank Statement balance.

---

[1] It is assumed that the Bank Statement is headed 'Bank in account with A,' but in the accounting records of the bank the amount of £1,200 will actually be in credit, in which form Bank Statements are often written up, the heading then being 'Customer in account with Bank'.

For examination purposes, however, it is permissible to prepare one Reconciliation Statement only, in which event it is imperative to point out to the examiner that this procedure has been adopted to economize time—a very formidable factor in the professional Accountants' examinations—and, in addition, to indicate briefly that the bank balance will require adjusting in the financial books, and that only when so adjusted, will it represent the true position. However, if the Bank Statement shows a sum of £100 in favour of the customer, but according to the latter's Cash Book there is an overdraft of £20 (the difference arising by reason of a cheque of £120 having been sent to a Creditor and entered accordingly), it would clearly be inaccurate and dangerous to adjust the Cash Book figure to that shown by the Bank. The Cash Book figure, subject to errors and omissions, always shows the real position.

Where the unpresented and uncredited cheques are not given, it is necessary to see the Bank Statement subsequent to the close of the period and deduce the information by noting each of the subsequent entries in the Bank Statement that have been entered in the Cash Book in the period under review.

Illustration 2

BANK COLUMNS OF CASH BOOK (OF S. SMITH)

19..				£	19..				£
Dec. 4	Balance.	. . .	b/d	38	Dec. 3	Drawings . . .			20
8	Walters & Co.	. .		42	10	F. Murray . . .			119
17	Drummond Bros	. .		100	17	Cheque Book . .			1
22	F. Scarfe	. .		131	21	Carlill & Co. .			52
30	McEuen & Co.	. .		30	30	Howe & Co. .			38
31	Garners, Ltd.	. .		18	31	G. Atkinson . . .			11
						Commission . .			1
						Wages and Salaries	.		40
						Balance. . . .		c/d	77
				£359					£359
19..									
Jan. 1	Balance.	. . .	b/d	77					

BANK STATEMENT
STATEMENT OF CURRENT ACCOUNT

BRANCH	A/C NO.	S. SMITH	IN ACCOUNT WITH	X BANK
Date		Cheques	Pay-ins	Balance
19..		£	£	£
Jan. 1	Forward			92
2		(a) 52		40
3			(b) 30	70
4		4		66
4			7	73
5			(c) 18	91
6		30		61
7		35		26
8			49	75
8		(d) 11		64

Prepare Bank Reconciliation Statement at 31st, December 19. .

It is clear that items (a) and (d) refer to the preceding period on the one side, and (b) and (c) on the other. Hence the other items refer exclusively to the following year. Thus, the uncredited cheques are (eliminating names) £30 and £18, the unpresented cheques £52 and £11.

The statement is therefore:

BANK RECONCILIATION STATEMENT AT 31ST DECEMBER 19..

		£
Balance as per Bank Statement		92
Less Unpresented Cheques	£52	
	11	
	—	63
		29
Add Uncredited Cheques	£30	
	18	
	—	48
Balance as per Cash Book		£77

It will be observed that McEuen's cheque of £30 is dishonoured. This may be dealt with as if the cheque had not been paid in, seeing that it has really never been paid, so that it will be necessary to credit the Bank column of the Cash Book with £30, thus reducing the balance thereon from £77 to £47. (The amount will be debited to McEuen, and thence, if the facts warrant it, to Bad Debts Account.) The Reconciliation Statement will now be:

		£
As above		29
Add Uncredited Cheque . .		18
		—
Balance as per Cash Book	*Dr.*	£47

The Cash Book, as adjusted, will be thus:

BANK COLUMNS, CASH BOOK (OF S. SMITH)

19..				£	19..				£
Dec. 31	Balance. . . .	b/d		77	Dec. 31	McEuen & Co., Dis- honoured Cheque .			30
						Balance. . . .	c/d		47
				£77					£77
19..									
Jan. 1	Balance. . . .	b/d		47					

The debit and credit items in the Bank Statement appearing in the next year (in reference to McEuen) merely cancel themselves.

On the other hand, the non-payment may be considered as relating to the next year, so that the original Reconciliation Statement and the cash balance remain, and the credit entry in the Cash Book will be made in the following year to agree with that made in the Bank Statement. If this procedure is adopted, the Reconciliation Statement is entirely unaffected. Should it be desired to make provision for the possibility of the debt being bad, a Reserve may be made in the books. It is submitted that the former method is the more prudent, as it eliminates £30, which cannot be relied upon as being cash in bank.

Illustration 3

The entries of bank transactions effected by B. Brown during the months ended 31st January and 28th February 19.., are shown, omitting names, as recorded in the Bank Statement and in the Cash Book of B. Brown for those periods. It is required to prepare Bank Reconciliation Statements at those dates.

Bank Statement entries:

STATEMENT OF CURRENT ACCOUNT

BRANCH	A/C NO.	B. BROWN	Cheques	IN ACCOUNT WITH	XYZ BANK
Date			Cheques	Pay-ins	Balance
19..			£	£	£
Jan. 1		Forward			272
4			71		201
5				35	236
9			32		204
12			38		166
13				75	241
15			17		224
21				113	337
25			14		323
28				23	346
31		Chges.	1		345
Feb. 1				20	365
4			23		342
5			35		307
9				84	391
10			16		375
18			19		356
20				36	392
22			24		368
23			17		351
24			3		348
25				44	392
26				100	492
28			258		234
		Chges.	1		233
				33	266
				15	281
Mar. 1				75	356

Cash Book entries:

B. BROWN

CASH BOOK (BANK COLUMNS ONLY)

19..			£	19..			£
Jan. 1	Balance	b/d	272	Jan. 1	Sundries		71
5	Sundries		35	4			38
13			75	5			(c) 23
21			113	12			17
28			23	20			14
31			20	28			16
				29			24
				30			(b) 23
				31	Balance	c/d	312
			£538				£538
Feb. 1	Balance	b/d	312	Feb. 1	Corrected Error		(c) 9
9			84	1	Bank Charges		(a) 1
20			36	2			35
25			44	15			19
26			100	18			19
28			75	19			3
				20			17
				22			258
				28	Balance	c/d	290
			£651				£651
Feb. 28	Balance	b/d	290	Feb. 28	Bank Charges		(d) 1
			(e) 15	28	Balance	c/d	337
			(f) 33				
			£338				£338
Mar. 1	Balance	b/d	337				

1. **Bank Reconciliation at 31st January 19..:**

(a) Bank charges have not been entered in the Cash Book.

(b) Cheque for £23 returned from the bank for endorsement by customer not entered in the Bank Statement.

(c) Item entered in Cash Book in error as £23 vice £32.

CASH BOOK ADJUSTMENT £

Balance as per Cash Book *Dr.*		312
Less Bank Charges	£1	
Error adjusted	9	
		10
Adjusted Balance as per Cash Book. *Dr.*		£302

BANK RECONCILIATION STATEMENT AS AT 31ST JAN., 19.. £

Balance as per Bank Statement *Dr.*		345
Less Unpresented Cheques	£24	
	16	
		40
		305
Returned Cheque unentered		23
		282
Add Uncredited Cheque		20
Balance as per Cash Book (adjusted) *Dr.*		£302

It will be noticed that all these matters requiring adjustment automatically smooth themselves out in the entries of the succeeding month ended 28th February, e.g. the returned cheque £23 is debited up to the customer by the bank. The Bank Statement is here shown in the form: 'B. Brown in Account with the XYZ Bank' and not 'The XYZ Bank in Account with B. Brown' and so the transactions are shown from the point of view of the bank—it is in fact a replica of the customer's account in the ledger of the bank.

2. Bank Reconciliation at 28th February 19...:

(d) Bank Charges not entered in the Cash Book.

(e) Item of $36 dividend paid direct to bank—notified credited at $2.40 to the £—not in Cash Book.

(f) Item of £33 paid in at another branch—not entered as yet in Cash Book.

CASH BOOK ADJUSTMENT

		£
Balance as per Cash Book . . . . . Dr.		290
Add Dividend unentered	£15	
Cheque unentered	33	
	—	48
		338
Less Bank Charges		1
Adjusted Balance as per Cash Book . . Dr.		£337

It is immaterial whether additions precede deductions or, as in the Cash Book adjustment on p. 0206, the deductions precede the additions.

BANK RECONCILIATION STATEMENT AS AT 28TH FEBRUARY, 19..

	£
Balance as per Bank Statement . . . . . Dr.	281
Less Unpresented Cheque.	19
	262
Add Uncredited Cheque	75
Balance as per Cash Book (adjusted) . . Dr.	£337

It will again be noted that the items calling for adjustment are righted in the subsequent period.

PETTY CASH BOOK

In all large businesses there are numerous small expenses to be met by cash payments. If all these payments were entered in detail in the main Cash Book, which is usually written up by a senior official, much valuable time would be wasted. To obviate this, a separate Cash Book, termed a Petty Cash Book, is utilized, in which all these expenses are recorded.

The conventional system for recording petty cash is known as the Imprest System, the main features of which are as follows. At the start of each accounting period the petty cashier is supplied with a round sum in cash, often termed a 'float.' This amount should be sufficient to cover the estimated petty cash expenditure for a stated period, e.g. a week or a month. At the end of this period the petty cashier must ascertain the total amount spent, and he will be reimbursed out of the General Cash Book for such amount, the balance in hand being thus restored to the original starting figure. Hence opportunity for the accumulation of large sums of cash in the hands of the petty cashier is eliminated and the risk of fraud minimized, as a complete check on the petty cashier may be kept at all times, since the sum of the vouchers representing money spent plus the cash in hand should always equal the amount of the 'float'.

When this system is adopted the initial advance to the petty cashier is debited to Petty Cash Account in the ledger, and cash is credited. At the same time the amount is debited for practical purposes (this is a memorandum entry, the double entry having already been completed) in the Petty Cash Book. When the expenditure for the period is recouped, the petty cashier's balance is restored to the original figure. The entries in the double-entry books will be as follows:

Debit side: Expenses (per the detailed analysis of the Petty Cash Book).
Credit side: Cash (with details) in the General Cash Book.

All moneys paid out of petty cash are entered on the credit side of the Petty Cash Book, and extended into analysis columns, the totals of which are utilized for posting at suitable periods to the debit of the appropriate nominal accounts from the General Cash Book. It often happens in practice that Ledger accounts are settled through the Petty Cash. In such cases a special column must be opened in respect of Ledger accounts, and the amounts paid to creditors must be inserted therein and posted to the debit of the respective accounts in the Ledger. The total of the Ledger column will not be posted to any account since the items contained therein will have been posted individually to their separate accounts.

Illustration 4

A. & Co., who keep their Petty Cash on the Imprest System, and maintain a weekly floating balance of £35, have the following transactions for the week ending 27th January:

19..		£p
Jan. 22.	Postages	4·50
	H. C. Smith (who has an account in the Creditors' Ledger)	3·45
23.	Office Table	6·55
24.	Travelling Expenses	1·25
25.	Tip to Vanman	0·50
26.	Carriage	2·75
27.	Casual Labour (Wages)	8·75
	Notepaper	1·50

The Petty Cash Book will be as follows:

PETTY CASH BOOK

		Folio				Voucher No.	Total
19.. Jan. 22	Cash		£p 35·00	19.. Jan. 22 23 24 25 26 27	Postages H. C. Smith Table Travelling Tip to Vanman Carriage Casual Labour Notepaper Balance	c/d	£p 4·50 3·45 6·55 1·25 0·50 2·75 8·75 1·50 29·25 5·75
			£ 35·00				£ 35·00
Jan. 29	Balance. Cash	b/d	5·75 29·25				

Postages	Stationery	Carriage	Furniture	Wages	Travelling	Sundries	Led. Fol.	Ledger Account
£p 4·50	£p	£p	£p 6·55	£p	£p 1·25	£p	20	£p 3·45
		2·75				0·50		
	1·50			8·75				
£4·50	£1·50	£2·75	£6·55	£8·75	£1·25	£0·50		£3·45
Fol.	Fol.	Fol.	Fol.	Fol.	Fol.	Fol.		

Nominals

The £35 on 22nd January will have come from the Cash Book and the debit entry will be made therefore to the debit of Petty Cash Account in the Ledger representing the amount expended. At 27th January the Cashier will hand cash amounting to £29·25 to the petty cashier. The double-entry will be:

PETTY CASH BOOK

	£p	£p	£p
Dr. Postages	4·50		
Stationery	1·50		
Carriage	2·75		
Furniture	6·55		
Wages	8·75		
Travelling	1·25		
Sundries	0·50		
Ledger Account (Smith)	3·45		
		29·25	
Cr. Cash (detailed similarly)			29·25

In this way the Petty Cash Book merely acts by way of memorandum and provides the necessary data for the double-entry.

Alternative Methods

Alternatively, the Petty Cash Book could be used as a double-entry book, in which case the double-entry would be provided thus:

1. Dr. Petty Cash Account in Petty Cash Book.
   Cr. Cash (in General Cash Book).
2. When the Cash spent is recouped.
   Dr. Petty Cash Account in Petty Cash Book.
   Cr. Cash (in General Cash Book).
3. Dr. Expenses (detailed).
   Cr. Petty Cash Account in Petty Cash Book.

In this case the Petty Cash Book is regarded as an account just as the General Cash Book and is definitely an integral part of the double-entry.

As a further alternative the cash recoupment may be posted in one sum from the Cash Book to the Petty Cash Account in the Ledger, and from there the different amounts will be credited out to the Expenses Accounts, leaving eventually the same balance on Petty Cash Accounts as before.

There may be cases to which the Imprest System is not suited, as when sudden large balances of cash are necessary, or when there are only very occasional calls for petty cash expense, which are met by the cashier as they arise.

It should be observed that two of the systems described in connection with the Imprest System can be utilized also in a slightly modified form where no imprest system is enforced.

(a) **Where the Petty Cash Book is Part of the Double-entry System.** Periodical sums paid to the petty cashier will be debited to the Petty Cash Book and credited to the General Cash Book. The Petty Cash Book will be ruled in columnar form or will be analysed at the end of periods by other means, the totals of the columns or the analysed amounts being posted at suitable periods from the Petty Cash Book to the debit of Expenses Accounts.

(b) **Where the Petty Cash Book is a Memorandum Book Only.** A Petty Cash Account in the Ledger will be opened, thus supplying the integral link with the main accounting system.

Periodical sums paid to the petty cashier will be debited (1) to the Petty Cash Account and (2) (for memorandum purposes) to the Petty Cash Book. The Petty Cash Book will be analysed under different headings as above, and these items will be credited to the Petty Cash Account and debited to the various Expenses Accounts. It is important to notice, in this method, that the postings to the Expenses Accounts are made from the Petty Cash Account and not from the Petty Cash Book. In view of this fact it is desirable to make a Journal entry which will show concisely at a glance the details of the transfers recorded.

Illustration 5

The following payments were made to the Petty Cashier during the month of December 19..:

	19..		£
	Dec. 4.	Cash	5
	18.	Cash	6
	24.	Cash	2

The balance on hand on 1st December 19.., was £2·08.

The Petty Cash Book was written up by the petty cashier, and the details appear in the subjoined account.

The above book, as stated previously, may be memorandum only, in which case the double-entry will be compiled by having a Petty Cash Account in the Ledger, as follows:

PETTY CASH

19..				£p	19..				£p
Dec. 1	Balance.		b/d	2·08	Dec. 31	Expenses as per Petty			
31	Cash			13·00		Cash Book[1]—			
						Postages			3·00
						Cleaning			3·25
						Sundries			4·11
						Carriage			1·37
						Balance.		c/d	3·35
			£	15·08				£	15·08
19..									
Jan. 1	Balance		b/d	3·35					

[1] These expenses will be posted to the debit of the appropriate Ledger Accounts, the details of which will appear in the Petty Cash Book.

CHAPTER 03

ARITHMETIC OF ACCOUNTANCY

THE author has learnt, from long experience gained in coaching, that one of the contributory causes of failure in examinations is the lack of ability to compute commonplace arithmetical calculations quickly and accurately. The capacity to recognize at sight a simple arithmetical point should also be developed by accountancy students. In this chapter, therefore, an attempt is made to deal with the calculations which are frequently required in working out problems set in the modern accountancy examinations, and which, simple though they be, cause endless confusion and uncertainty in the minds of students.

A great deal of time—a factor of utmost importance in examinations— can be saved by working out calculations in a systematic manner. The average student will have many opportunities in the course of his everyday work of putting into practice a multitude of simple time-saving arithmetical devices, of which the following are examples—(a) dividing twice by two when dividing by four. (b) Multiplying by two and dividing by ten when dividing by five. (c) Simple interest calculations may be considerably facilitated at times by the application of the following rules, viz:

5% per annum Simple Interest is 1p on £2·40 per month.
6%   ,,   ,,   ,,   ,, 5p on £10 per month.
4%   ,,   ,,   ,,   ,, 1% per quarter.

Illustration 1

5% per annum on £129 for 7 months

$$= 7 \times \frac{129}{2·40} p = £3·76$$

4% per annum on £285 for 3 months

$$= 1\% \text{ of } £285 = £2·85$$

The student is generally inclined to note these simple devices with mild interest and subsequently to banish them entirely from his mind, but it is essential that he should endeavour to cultivate these 'short cut' arithmetic habits until they become spontaneous. As a result when the examination time arrives he will find himself armed with a most useful battery of time-saving weapons against the examinee's chief adversary 'lack of time.' Again the student must learn the use of simple algebra, which is called for particularly in the more difficult problems, examples of which will be found in the chapters on Partnership and Limited Companies. It must be realized that a fundamental knowledge of simple algebra is absolutely essential for the modern examinations, and it is only by constant practice that proficiency may be attained. Though the problems in this book calling for algebraic solution may be passed over at a first reading, they must eventually be faced and mastered, so that algebra may be called to hand with complete confidence, and without the fear of unfamiliarity and uncertainty, in the examination hall.

COST AND SELLING PRICE

Many problems are set in which either the selling price or the cost price of a certain line of goods is given, together with the rate of gross profit earned, this rate of gross profit to be computed on either the cost or the selling price, according to which is the unknown figure. If the selling price is given, the student may be required to find the cost price, and *vice versa*. This type of problem is met with very frequently in examinations, especially in questions on Cost Accounts.

Great care must be taken to see on which price the rate of gross profit is based.

Illustration 2

The gross profit is 25 per cent on cost; the selling price is £175. It is required to find the cost price. This may be obtained as follows:

$$
\begin{array}{lr}
 & £ \\
\text{Let the cost price} & = \ 100 \\
\text{The profit is 25\% thereof} & = \ \ 25 \\
\hline
\therefore \text{When the cost price is £100 the selling price} = & 125 \\
\end{array}
$$

$$\therefore \text{When the selling price is £175 the cost price} = \frac{100}{125} \times 175$$

$$= £140$$

In the above illustration the percentage of gross profit or 'Loading' on COST is given and the Selling price is the known figure. The terms may be interchanged, i.e. the percentage of Gross Profit or 'Loading' on SELLING price may be given and the COST price be the known figure. It will be noted, for example, that the percentage of Gross Profit on Selling price is 20 per cent, whilst the percentage on Cost price is 25 per cent.

As an illustration of the interchangeability of the percentage expressions the following may be appended:

$$
\begin{array}{llllll}
20\% & \text{of Cost} = 16\tfrac{2}{3}\% \text{ of Selling, or } \tfrac{1}{5} \text{ of Cost} = \tfrac{1}{6} \text{ of Selling.} \\
25\% & ,, \quad = 20\% & ,, & \tfrac{1}{4} \quad ,, & = \tfrac{1}{5} & ,, \\
33\tfrac{1}{3}\% & ,, \quad = 25\% & ,, & \tfrac{1}{3} \quad ,, & = \tfrac{1}{4} & ,, \\
\end{array}
$$

Similarly:

$$\tfrac{2}{5} \text{ of Cost} = \tfrac{2}{7} \text{ of Selling, i.e. } \frac{2}{5+2} \text{ of Selling.}$$

$$\tfrac{3}{11} \quad ,, \quad = \tfrac{3}{14} \quad ,, \quad \text{i.e. } \frac{3}{11+3} \quad ,,$$

$$\tfrac{7}{19} \quad ,, \quad = \tfrac{7}{26} \quad ,, \quad \text{i.e. } \frac{7}{19+7} \quad ,,$$

It should be appreciated that, once proficiency in making this conversion has been attained, valuable time will be saved in examination work. If a percentage of profit on Sales and the Cost figure are given in a question, by the proceeds of conversion the required figure can usually be obtained mentally, e.g. a profit of $\frac{2}{13}$ is made on Sales, and the Cost is £1,650. What are the Sales? The student will immediately think of the known factor, i.e. Cost, and secondly he will convert the $\frac{2}{13}$ profit on Sales into $\frac{2}{11}$ profit on Cost (the known factor).

$$\text{Profit} = \tfrac{2}{11} \times £1,650 = £300$$
$$\therefore \text{Sales} = £1,650 \text{ (cost)} + £300 \text{ (profit)} = £1,950$$

The profit thereon is £300, which is $\frac{2}{13}$ of Sales.

ALIQUOT PARTS

Where a certain amount has to be subdivided into smaller parts which themselves must be maintained in a certain ratio, students are often at a loss as to how the whole is to be divided at each subdivision. The rule is to take the total of all the ratios and divide it into each ratio; this will give the fraction of the whole represented by each share.

Illustration 3

A, B, C, and D, are to divide £1,000 in the ratio of $4:3:2:1$. How much does each receive?

$$4 + 3 + 2 + 1 = 10$$
$\therefore$ A will receive $\frac{4}{10} \times £1,000 =$ £400
$\therefore$ B ,, ,, $\frac{3}{10} \times £1,000 =$ £300
$\therefore$ C ,, ,, $\frac{2}{10} \times £1,000 =$ £200
$\therefore$ D ,, ,, $\frac{1}{10} \times £1,000 =$ £100

£1,000

Should at any time one or more of the dividing parties drop out and the remainder still wish to maintain as between themselves the same *ratio* as before, all that is required is to proceed as before, ignoring the share of any party who has dropped out.

Illustration 4

Assume that in the previous example B drops out; the ratios will then be A:C:D in the ratio of $4:2:1$.

$$4 + 2 + 1 = 7$$
$\therefore$ A will receive $\frac{4}{7} \times £1,000 =$ £571$\frac{3}{7}$
$\therefore$ C ,, ,, $\frac{2}{7} \times £1,000 =$ £285$\frac{5}{7}$
$\therefore$ D ,, ,, $\frac{1}{7} \times £1,000 =$ £142$\frac{6}{7}$

£1,000

The same principles exactly are involved in many instances which occur in business of a sum being received before it is earned, e.g. in hire purchase contracts, and discounting of bills of exchange. In these cases it is necessary to transfer a portion only to Profit and Loss Account in the first year.

An excellent illustration arises in hire purchase transactions when a Hire Purchase Reserve is created and transferred to Profit and Loss Account in fixed instalments over the period of the agreement. The matter will be treated in detail in its appropriate place and the sole point of its introduction at this stage is to deal with the arithmetical side.

Illustration 5

X deals with goods on Hire Purchase and creates a Reserve to cover risk, interest, etc., which is added to the price to the customer. The amount in four years is £1,000 and it is to be transferred to Profit and Loss Account over four years as follows:

(1) 15 per cent, (2) 45 per cent, (3) 30 per cent, and (4) 10 per cent. Thus the amounts to be written off in the respective years will be $\frac{15}{100}$, $\frac{45}{100}$, $\frac{30}{100}$, and $\frac{10}{100}$ of £1,000, i.e. £150, £450, £300 and £100. The question thus presented is simple enough, but it is sometimes presented in a form that causes difficulty.

Illustration 6

Using the same data the question states that at the end of the second year the balance of the Reserve is £400 (i.e. £150 and £450 have been transferred to Profit and Loss Account). The amounts remaining to be transferred to Profit and Loss Account are to be calculated on the written down figure of the Reserve £400. If the beginning figure is not given, but merely the written down figure of the Reserve (£400), and the percentages transferred or to be transferred in each of the four years, the proportions to be written off in the third and fourth year may be obtained similarly, viz:

3rd year	$\frac{30}{40} \times £400 = £300$
4th year	$\frac{10}{40} \times £400 = £100$

The point to watch is that in the third and fourth year the calculation is based upon the REMAINING Reserve, and not on the original, so that the proportions transferred must likewise be based on the remaining proportions.

Thus, if the Reserve had been given as at the beginning of the second year, i.e. £1,000 − 150 = £850, the proportions to be written off in the three succeeding years would have been 45, 30, 10, i.e.:

2nd year	$\frac{45}{85} \times £850 = £450$
3rd year	$\frac{30}{85} \times £850 = £300$
4th year	$\frac{10}{85} \times £850 = £100$

COMMISSION

In many questions it is stated that the manager is to receive a commission of a certain percentage of the profits *after* deduction of this commission and only the trading profits figure is given (i.e. profits before deduction of the commission) and it is required to find the amounts due to the manager under this head.

Illustration 7

A is to get 10 per cent of the profits of A.B. Ltd., after deducting his commission. Profits prior to charging commission are £2,200.

> If A gets £100 commission
> The *remaining* profits = £1,000
> ∴ Total profits = £1,100
> ∴ Commission = $\frac{1}{11}$ of the total profits
> ∴ If the total profits are £2,200, the commission
> $$= \frac{1}{11} \times £2,200 = £200$$

Hence A's commission is one-eleventh of the profits *prior* to charging the commission and one-tenth of the profits *after* charging the commission.

Similarly, if the commission is 5 per cent $\left(\frac{5}{100}\right)$ of profits after charging the commission, the calculation would be $\frac{5}{105} \times$ profits before charging commission; if 8 per cent, then $\frac{8}{108} \times$ profits before charging commission; if 20 per cent, then $\frac{20}{120} \times$ profits before charging commission.

Where the commission on profits prior to charging commission is stated in the form of a vulgar fraction, into which form a percentage may easily be changed, viz—8 per cent $\frac{8}{100}$, 15 per cent $\frac{15}{100}$, etc., the rule is to increase the denominator by the amount of the numerator, and the resultant fraction multiplied by profits PRIOR to charging the commission produces the required commission figure.

Illustration 8

A is to get $\frac{2}{45}$ of the profits of A.B. Ltd., after charging his commission. Profits prior to charging his commission are £9,400.

The same type of problem arises as below:

$$\text{Commission} = \frac{2}{45+2} = \frac{2}{47} \times \text{profits prior to charging commission}$$

$$\frac{2}{47} \times 9,400 = £400 \quad \left[\text{or } \frac{2}{45}(9,400 - 400) = £400 \right]$$

The same type of problem arises as below:

· In bankruptcy it frequently happens that the trustee is entitled to a remuneration based upon dividends paid to unsecured creditors. After all the other expenses have been paid, the cash left will provide both for the remuneration of the trustee and for the dividend to the unsecured creditors, and the remuneration will be a percentage based, not upon the total cash remaining, but upon that paid to the unsecured creditors.

Illustration 9

A trustee in bankruptcy is entitled to $2\frac{1}{2}$ per cent commission on the dividend paid to unsecured creditors: the cash available, subject to the above, is £3,280, and the unsecured creditors amount to £6,400.

The remuneration of the trustee will be $\dfrac{2\frac{1}{2}}{102\frac{1}{2}} = \dfrac{1}{41} \times £3,280 = £80$, leaving £3,200 for the unsecured creditors. The remuneration is thus $2\frac{1}{2}$ per cent of £3,200.

Care should be taken in the case where the resultant figure is *already* ascertained, as the computation will be simply $2\frac{1}{2}$ per cent upon the ascertained figure.

Illustration 10

Assuming that £6,800 cash was available in the above illustration, then, as the creditors can receive no more than £6,400 (i.e. £1 per £), the dividend is already ascertained, and the remuneration of the trustee will simply be $2\frac{1}{2}$ per cent of £6,400, i.e. £160. (The balance left will be handed over to the Debtor.)

STOCKS AND SHARES

The majority of students will have learnt, at some time in their studies, the arithmetic of stocks and shares, but the author has found that the following types of problems involve even advanced students in difficulties.

1. Where the rates of interest paid and the required yield are given, and it is required to find the market price of securities, the calculation is as follows:

$$\text{Market price} = \text{Nominal value} \times \frac{\text{Actual rate of Interest paid}}{\text{Required yield}}$$

Illustration 11

At a certain date the market considers 8 per cent per annum to be a fair return on $3\frac{1}{2}$ per cent Conversion Loan. Accordingly the market price will be:

$$£100 \times \frac{3\frac{1}{2}}{8} = £43.75 \text{ per £100 Nominal}$$

2. When the amount of money invested is given together with the market price of the investment, the nominal amount purchased is found as follows:

$$\text{Nominal amount} = \frac{\text{Amount invested}}{\text{Market price}}$$

Illustration 12

A invests £1,000 in buying £1 shares in X. V. Ltd., paying £2·50 per share. The nominal amount of his holding is therefore:

$$£\frac{1,000}{2·50} = £400$$

3. Where the market price of the investment is so much per hundred (i.e. Stock) the formula is:

$$\text{Nominal amount} = \frac{\text{Amount invested}}{\text{Market price}} \times 100$$

Illustration 13

A invests £1,000 in $3\frac{1}{2}$ per cent Stock at 40. The nominal amount of his holding is therefore:

$$£\frac{1,000}{40} \times 100 = £2,500$$

4. When the cost of the investment, the market price and the rate of interest are given, the gross amount of the dividend (or interest) can rapidly be obtained without ascertaining the nominal amount of the investment from the formula (where the investment is quoted per £100):

$$\text{Interest} = \frac{\text{Amount Invested} \times \text{Rate of Interest}}{\text{Market price}} \times 100$$

Illustration 14

A invests £2,400 in $3\frac{1}{2}$ per cent Stock at 42. The interest for a full year is therefore:

$$£\frac{2,400 \times 3\frac{1}{2}}{42} = £200$$

Proof. The Nominal amount of the Stock will be:

$$£\frac{2,400 \times 100}{42} = £\frac{40,000}{7}$$

$$3\frac{1}{2}\% \text{ per annum for one year on } £\frac{40,000}{7} = £\frac{40,000}{7} \times \frac{7}{200} = £200$$

The above formula is true only where the investment is stated as so much per hundred. Otherwise the nominal amount of the investment will be found simply by dividing the amount invested by the market price, as shown above. The gross amount of the interest may then easily be calculated.

5. Where the risk involved in a certain investment is given together with the estimated cash amount of the dividend, and it is required to find the market price:

$$\text{Market price} = \frac{\text{Amount of the dividend}}{\text{Percentage of risk}} \times 100$$

Illustration 15

The shares of no par value of the Yankee Bank Inc. are considered to involve a risk of 7 per cent, and the next dividend is estimated to amount to $10.50 per share. (As the shares are of no par value, the dividend cannot be expressed in terms of a percentage.)

The price of each share will therefore be:

$$\$\frac{10.50 \times 100}{7} = \$150.00$$

Proof. Price of each share = $150.00. Risk 7 per cent per annum. Dividend—$10.50 per share *and* 7 per cent of $150.00 = $10.50 dividend.

In all questions of the above type, no candidate can expect to earn full marks unless he deals with the question of the amount of dividend earned to date included in the price.

In all cases the amount of any dividend accrued will have to be added to the price found by the formula to get the actual market price.

The following example illustrates the working of a problem in which it is necessary to find the proceeds of an original investment which has been converted into another.

Illustration 16

A expends £1,000 on 7 per cent Stock at 95 which he sells at 105, investing the proceeds in 5 per cent Stock at 70, and sells at 68. How much does he receive on sale?

The amount purchased of 7% Stock = £1,000 × $\dfrac{100}{95}$, i.e. Nominal = x

which when he sells produces $x \times \dfrac{105}{100}$ = y

with the amount of y, he is able to make a purchase of 5% Stock $y \times \dfrac{100}{70}$ = z

which when he sells produces $z \times \dfrac{68}{100}$ = ?

This will equal

$$£1,000 \times \frac{100}{95} \times \frac{105}{100} \times \frac{100}{70} \times \frac{68}{100}$$

It will be seen that the four '100's' cancel, leaving the calculation as follows:

$$1,000 \times \frac{105}{95} \times \frac{68}{70} = 1,000 \times \frac{21}{19} \times \frac{68}{70} = 100 \times \frac{21}{19} \times \frac{68}{7} = \frac{100 \times 3 \times 68}{19}$$

$$\text{i.e. } £\frac{20,400}{19} = £1,073 \cdot 68$$

It is therefore, simpler to employ the rule of dividing the original sum by the purchase price (in the above example, 95), then multiplying such result by the selling price (in the above example 105) and so on till the final sale is reached.

Illustration 17

A expends £2,000 on a purchase of 4 per cent Stock at 75, which he sells for 72, and with the proceeds he buys 5 per cent Stock at 96, selling the latter at 100. The amount finally realized

$$= \frac{2,000}{75} \times \frac{72}{1} \times \frac{1}{96} \times \frac{100}{1}$$

$$= 2,000 \times \frac{72}{75} \times \frac{100}{96} = 2,000 \times \frac{3}{75} \times \frac{100}{4}$$

$$= £2,000$$

Actually the answer is obtainable at sight, because in the first instance he loses $\frac{3}{75}$ and in the second he gains $\frac{4}{100}$, i.e. in one-case he loses $\frac{1}{25}$ and in the second he gains $\frac{1}{25}$.

FLAT AND REDEMPTION YIELD

(a) The flat yield is the yearly return on an investment, ignoring any profit or loss accruing on redemption, e.g. a stock may be issued at 98 redeemable in 10 years' time at 108, thus giving a profit to the holder, so that:

(b) The redemption yield is the yearly return on the investment taking into account any profit or loss on redemption, i.e. the flat yield plus yearly profit arising from surplus of redeemable price over purchase or issue price; or the flat yield less yearly loss resulting from deficiency of redeemable price as regards purchase or issue price.

Illustration 18

A buys at the date of issue 8 per cent Stock at 95 redeemable in 10 years' time at 105. Ignore expenses.

Flat yield

$$\frac{8}{95} \times 100 = 8 \cdot 42\% \text{ per annum}$$

Profit on redemption

$$= \frac{10}{95} \times 100$$

$$= \frac{\frac{10}{95} \times 100}{10} \text{ yearly}$$

$$= \frac{1}{95} \times 100 = 1 \cdot 05\% \text{ per annum}$$

Redemption yield $= 9 \cdot 47\%$ per annum

It is clear that the holder gains 10 points in 10 years on every £100 of Stock, so that on an outlay of £95 he receives (or strictly his capital is augmented by) £1 each year, i.e. $\frac{1}{95} \times 100$ per cent yield per annum.

The same principle will apply in case of a loss on redemption; for instance if the redemption price at the end of 10 years is 85 then there will be a loss of $\frac{10}{95}$ in ten years, which calculated exactly as above, equals 1·05 per cent per annum.

Therefore the yield per annum on the Stock, taking into account loss on redemption, is

Flat yield	= 8·42% per annum
Loss on redemption	⁺= 1·05% per annum
Net yield	= 7·37% per annum

In practice two very important details will affect the results, viz.:

1. Cost of purchase or sale (not applicable in the above illustration as the circumstances postulate an application for the Stock on issue and the retention of the Stock till maturity).

2. Income tax.

The above-mentioned method, so far as ordinary requirements are concerned, is invariably adopted in practice, although theoretically the profit on redemption per annum so determined is inaccurate (the inaccuracy increasing with the length of the period lapsing between date of purchase or issue and date of redemption).

This arises in consequence of the fact that the one point (£1) profit is not received yearly, as is the dividend, but only upon the expiry of the 10 years. A sum of £10 payable in 10 years is certainly not worth £10 now. Hence the true worth now (i.e. the present worth) is such a sum which, invested at such a rate of interest as is considered desirable and allowed to accumulate with yearly rests, will amount at the end of the ten years to £10.

As this is a matter of actuarial science, it will not be considered here. In practice if the precise figure is required, tables supplying the information are available and, so far as examination work is concerned, the requisite figures would undoubtedly be supplied in the question paper.

AVERAGE

Weighted Average may be defined as the quotient of the sum of a series of items multiplied by their number, divided by the sum of their number; that is to say, it is the result achieved by multiplying each item in the series by its number (commonly called weight), such products being totalled, and then divided by the sum of the number of weights.

Illustration 19

Of 20 companies:

15 companies pay 10 per cent dividend;
5 companies pay 6 per cent dividend.

The average rate of dividend is 9 per cent, arrived at as follows:

$$15 \times 10 = 150$$
$$5 \times 6 = 30$$

$$20 \qquad 180$$

∴ Average rate of dividend per company:

$$= \frac{180}{20} = 9\%$$

Illustration 20

A company's wage bill comprises the following:

						£
1,000	employees at £15	per week	=	15,000
400	,,	,, £20	,,	,,	=	8,000
100	,,	,, £26	,,	,,	=	2,600
20	,,	,, £35	,,	,,	=	700
5	,,	,, £47	,,	,,	=	235
1,525			Total Wages = £26,535

Average weekly wage per employee:

$$= £\frac{26,535}{1,525} = £17 \cdot 40$$

It is clear that this average is no true criterion of the wages received by any specific employee, since 525 employees are receiving £20 or over per week. The average is weighted heavily by the large bulk of the £15 per week employees.

Where the sales of a period are given, e.g. a year, and it is stated that the sales for specified months are a certain number of times as heavy as those in others, then to ascertain the amount of the Sales or the Gross Profit apportionable to any particular month, it will be necessary to weight the months accordingly.

Illustration 21

The Total Sales for the year = £7,600.

(a) The average sales for the first three months, January, February, and March, are three times as high as those for the last five months, August to December.

(b) The average sales for the four months, April to July, are twice as high as those for the first three months, January to March.

Taking the sales average of the last five months as the basic unit = 1, the first period's sales per month are three times as great = 3, and the second period's twice as great = 6.

The ratios in order of time are 3:6:1.

The average sales per month are:

(a) Three months in ratio 3:1 = 9 units
(b) Four   ,,   ,,   ,,   6:1 = 24 ,,
(c) Five   ,,   ,,   ,,   1:1 = 5 ,,
                                         ——
                                         38 units
                                         ==

The average sales per month in the different periods will vary in the ratio, 3:6:1, as explained. The amounts of the various averages will be found as follows:

The total amount of sales effected in periods will be:

		Ratio
(a) $\frac{9}{38} \times £7,600 = £1,800$ (3 months) = £600 per month		3
(b) $\frac{24}{38} \times £7,600 = £4,800$ (4 months) = £1,200	,,	6
(c) $\frac{5}{38} \times £7,600 = £1,000$ (5 months) = £200	,,	1

It will thus be seen how it is necessary to weight the months in the proportion in which they contribute to the total sales in order to find the specific monthly or periodical figures for comparative purposes, etc.

INTEREST

Just as money is payable, called rent, for the use of someone's house so money is payable, called interest, for the use of someone's money. The money borrowed or lent is called the principal. The total obtained by adding to the principal the interest for any period of time is called the amount at the end of that period of time. The percentage payment per year is called the rate per cent per annum. Thus interest at 8 per cent per annum means that £8 is the interest on £100 for one year.

Simple Interest

Simple interest is interest which is payable each year on a fixed sum at a stated rate per cent.

Illustration 22

Find the simple interest on £P for T years at R per cent.

The interest on £100 for 1 year is £R
∴ The interest on £100 for T years is £R×T
∴ The interest on £P for T years is $£\dfrac{P \times R \times T}{100}$

From the foregoing the following formula may be derived:

If the simple interest on £P for T years at R per cent is £I, then

$$I = \frac{P \times R \times T}{100}$$

From this formula the following further formulae may be derived:

Since

$$I = \frac{P \times R \times T}{100}$$

or

$$\frac{I}{1} = \frac{P \times R \times T}{100} \quad \text{or} \quad \frac{PRT}{100}$$

then by cross-multiplying

$$PRT \times 1 = 100I$$

$$\therefore P = \frac{100I}{RT}$$

and

$$R = \frac{100I}{PT} \quad \text{and} \quad T = \frac{100I}{PR}$$

Hence,

If given I, R and T, we can find P
  ,,   ,,   I, P ,, T, ,, ,, ,, R
  ,,   ,,   I, P ,, R, ,, ,, ,, T

Illustration 23

1. Find the simple interest on £900 for 4 years at 6 per cent.

$$I = \frac{PRT}{100}$$

$$= \frac{£900 \times 6 \times 4}{100}$$

$$= £216$$

2. If £81 is the interest on a certain principal for $2\frac{1}{2}$ years at 6 per cent what is the principal?

$$P = \frac{100I}{RT}$$

$$= \frac{£100 \times 81}{6 \times 2\frac{1}{2}}$$

$$= £\frac{8,100}{15}$$

$$= £540$$

3. Find the rate per cent when the interest on £720 for 5 months is £24.

$$R = \frac{100I}{PT}$$

$$= \frac{100 \times 24}{720 \times 5/12}$$

$$= \frac{2,400}{300}$$

$$= 8\%$$

4. How long will £500 take to amount to £650 at the rate of $7\frac{1}{2}$ per cent per annum, simple interest?

$$\text{Interest} = £650 - £500$$
$$= £150$$

$$T = \frac{100I}{PR}$$
$$= \frac{100 \times 150}{500 \times 7\frac{1}{2}}$$
$$= \frac{100 \times 150 \times 2}{500 \times 15}$$
$$= 4 \text{ years}$$

Compound Interest

Compound interest is interest payable under an arrangement whereby the borrower retains the interest, which is added to the principal. The principal increases each year by the amount of interest and consequently the interest on the principal increases each year.

Illustration 24

Find the compound interest on £100 for $1\frac{1}{2}$ years at 6 per cent, payable half-yearly.

Since the interest is payable half-yearly the interest must be calculated, in this instance, at the end of three half-yearly periods. The rate of interest per period is therefore $\frac{6\%}{3} = 2\%$.

Principal at start	£100
Add interest for 1st period	2
Amount, 1st period	102
Add interest for 2nd period	2·04
Amount, 2nd period	104·04
Add interest for 3rd period	2·0808
Amount, 3rd period	106·1208
Deduct Principal at start	100
Compound interest for $1\frac{1}{2}$ years	£ 6·1208

The amount accumulated at compound interest may be calculated by substitution in the formula:

$$A = P(1 + r)n$$

where
- A = the amount at compound interest
- P = the principal
- r = the rate per cent
- n = the number of years

Illustration 25

Find the amount at compound interest of £2,500 for 3 years at 5 per cent per annum.

$$A = P(1+r)n$$
$$\therefore A = £2,500(1 + 5/100)^3$$
$$\therefore A = £2,500(1 \cdot 05)^3$$

The above amount may be evaluated by ordinary multiplication but it is very much simpler to use an electronic calculator.

CHAPTER 04

ACCOUNTS CURRENT AND AVERAGE DUE DATE

WHEN it is agreed that interest be charged in respect of transactions between parties it is usual, in order to facilitate calculations, to have a special column ruled adjacent to the ordinary column, on each side of the Ledger, this being purely 'Memorandum.' Such additional columns are employed merely on account of their usefulness in the calculation of interest, and having provided the amount thereof the columns have fulfilled their function. Hence the entry of interest into the ordinary columns of the Ledger must be posted to Interest Account, either through the Journal, or if the number of transactions of this kind should warrant it, through an Interest Journal or Day Book.

An Account Current, then, is a statement in account form of transactions of one person with another, duly set out in chronological order, with additional columns for the purpose of computing interest allowed or received, the net balance of which will be entered to the credit or debit of the account itself.

Before the methods employed in accounts current are dealt with, it will be necessary to observe the following points:

1. The Account, save for Interest, will be an ordinary account, but just as Bank Statements may contain the entries reverse to the sides in the bankers' book, i.e. to correspond with the entries on the customer's Statements, so the Account Current *may*, when rendered to a party, be reversed to correspond with the entries in the books of the person to whom it is sent.

Thus 'Jones in Account Current with Brown' would represent the state of account of Jones in Brown's books; in other words, Jones is the accounting party, so that his account will be in debit for goods sold to him, charges, etc., and in credit for payments, discounts thereon, allowances, etc.

If, for the convenience of Jones, these sides are reversed, the heading will be 'Brown in Account Current with Jones', and the entries will correspond to, and be on the same side as, those appearing in Jones's Ledger; that is, Brown will be in credit for goods he has supplied to Jones, and in debit for payments, discounts thereon, allowances, etc.

2. In calculations of interest, if computed according to the number of days, the opening date, if it is the date on which the balance, if any, is brought down will be *included*, but if it is the date of the first transaction it will be *excluded*.

3. Particular care is required in dealing with bills of exchange and forward-dated sales, as the due date of the bill and the forward date of the sale are the material dates for the purpose of interest.

The methods adopted vary, and from an examination point of view it is advisable to be quite clear on *one* method and ignore the others.

The various methods are:

0401

First Method

Each item is taken separately and the number of days from the date opposite such item to the *end* of the period is ascertained and interest calculated at the agreed rate of interest for the requisite number of days.

Second Method

A modification of the above method is to employ the products system, i.e. instead of making separate calculations, each item is multiplied by the number of days from its date to the end of the period, and one interest calculation only is made on the net products for *one* day. It should be clear to the student that if there is interest on £150 for 10 days, this, when made into a product and treated by the products method, will be—Interest on £150 × 10 = £1,500 for one day; and this principle is employed herein.

Third Method

The other method of importance is the *Époque* method. Broadly speaking, the procedure is the reverse of those already explained. Interest is computed from the *commencement* of the period to the date of each item. Thus *no* Interest must be charged on the OPENING BALANCE,[1] but interest for the *whole* period of the account will be charged on the CLOSING BALANCE.[1]

Where interest is computed at a higher rate for debits than credits, or vice versa, there will be two calculations, one for the total debits and another for the total credits. This applies to all the above methods.

RED INK INTEREST

Where transactions are passed through an Account Current it is essential to compute interest from the due date, and not from the date of entry. As has been seen, an invoice may be dated forward, and, analogous to this, a bill of exchange may be payable at a future date. No particular difficulty is likely to arise so long as such future date falls *within* the period under review. Where, however, such due date occurs after the period of the account has terminated, the intervening time (i.e. between the close of such period and the due date) must be brought into consideration.

1. **Ordinary Method.** Where an entry is made against the customer, and the due date arises after the close of the period, it can be seen that not only should no interest be charged, but CREDIT given for the time elapsing from the close of the period to the due date, because the item debited will be brought down as a balance for the new period, and consequently interest which should run from the due date will be charged as from the start of the new period.

The converse applies where the customer accepts (i.e. remits) a bill of exchange, due after the period in question has closed. The opening

[1] Debit balances are here assumed. On the same principle interest will be credited for credit balances.

balance for the new period on which interest is calculated, will be unduly small. Accordingly it will be necessary to charge interest on the bill from the date of the close of the period to the due date of the bill.

Thus the interest will be normally on the *reverse* side to the relevant item, but it is customary to show it in *red ink* on the same side, to denote that it really belongs to the opposite side, and to connect it with its appropriate item. These *red ink* entries will be calculated separately from the others: that is, *red ink* entries on the debit side will be counted as credits, and *vice versa*, and if there are a number of *red ink* entries on both sides the balance only may be used for the interest calculation, provided that the rate of interest for debits and credits is the same.

2. **Époque Method.** Under the *Époque* method, interest must be charged on the bill from the commencement of the period in which the bill is remitted to the due date of the bill, since the interest calculation for the whole period is made on the closing balance, and not on the opening balance, which is understated by the amount of the bill. Thus no *red ink* modifications are called for. The same principle applies to forward dated sales.

In order to prevent confusion it is submitted that it is preferable to avoid *red ink* interest, and always to insert the interest upon its correct side.

The rules may be formulated thus:

1. **Ordinary Method.** Where an entry is made within the period in question but having a due date SUBSEQUENT to the close of such period, interest must be calculated for the time elapsing between the close of the period and the due date of the transaction, and shown on the *opposite* side to the principal entry, or, if the *red ink* principle is to be followed, the interest entry will be in *red ink* on the same side as the principal entry, to denote that its true side should be on the reverse of the account.

Alternatively, interest may be computed from the nominal date (on the usual lines) and shown in the ordinary way, and on the opposite side of the account an entry for interest may be made, for the length of time elapsing between nominal date and due date.

Illustration 1

A owes B on 1st January 19.., £300 and on 31st March he remits a bill of exchange for £120 (seven months' date). Interest is charged at 5 per cent per annum (calculated in months), the Account Current running to 30th June 19...

It will be seen that the bill is not due till the end of October, and therefore the period elapsing from the end of June is four months; hence interest on £120 for four months will be debited to the account.

The various alternative methods which may be used are shown on pp. 0405 to 0406.

2. **Époque Method.** It must carefully be observed that under the *Époque* method the interest on the bill is calculated from the *commencement* of the period to the due date of the bill, and not from the date of the

giving of the bill. Thus, in the above case, 10 months is the period upon which the calculation is based.

The same principle applies when items are *charged* within the period of the Account Current, and the due date falls after the end thereof:

Illustration 2

	£
On 1st January 19.., A owes B	200
„ 1st March 19.., A remits cash	50
„ 1st April 19.., A buys goods from B (due date, 1st September)	120
„ 1st May 19.., A remits an 8 months' bill	100

Show Account Current rendered by B to A for half-year to 30th June 19.. calculating interest at 5 per cent per annum. See Account (1) on p. 0407.

Alternatively, the Account Current may be stated by taking the nominal date of the goods and the bill as the true date and calculating the number of months from the nominal date to the actual dates on the *contra*, as in Account (2) on p. 0407, i.e.:

(a) Instead of calculating *red ink* interest on the bill for six months, interest will be calculated as if the bill were due on the date given, i.e. 1st May—two months interest and *contra* interest for the period of the bill, i.e. eight months; thus the difference 'contra' is six months as in the previous example (see items *q* and *r* in Account (2) and *b* in Account (1)).

(b) Instead of calculating *red ink* interest on the goods for two months, interest will be calculated as if the invoice for the goods were dated 1st April—three months interest and *contra* interest for the period elapsing between 1st April and 1st September—five months; thus the difference is two months as in the previous example (see items *x* and *y* in Account (2) and *a* in Account (1)).

(1) FIRST METHOD
A in Account Current with B

Date	Details		Mos.	Interest	Principal	Date	Details		Mos.	Interest	Principal
19..				£p	£p	19..				£p	£p
Jan. 1	Balance	b/d			300·00	Mar. 31	Bill of Exchange, due 31st Oct.				120·00
June 30	Interest on Bill		6	7·50		June 30	Balance of Interest to Contra			9·50	
	Interest from Contra		4	2·00	9·50¹		Balance	c/d			189·50
				£9·50	£309·50					£9·50	£309·50
July 1	Balance	b/d			189·50						

NOTE. Interest at 5% per annum = 1p on £2·40 per month. E.g. Interest on £120 for 4 months at 5% = 200p = £2·00.
¹ The double entry will be effected by debiting the above account and crediting Interest Account through the Journal. The Interest columns in the above account are purely 'memorandum.'

(2) FIRST METHOD—Alternative
A in Account Current with B

Date	Details		Mos.	Interest	Principal	Date	Details		Mos.	Interest	Principal
19..				£p	£p	19..				£p	£p
Jan. 1	Balance	b/d			300·00	Mar. 31	Bill of Exchange due 31st Oct.		3	1·50	120·00
June 30	Interest on Bill		6	7·50		June 30	Balance of Interest to Contra			9·50	
	Interest from Contra		7	3·50	9·50		Balance	c/d			189·50
				£11·00	£309·50					£11·00	£309·50
July 1	Balance	b/d			189·50						

(3) PRODUCTS METHOD
A in Account Current with B

Date	Details		Mos.	Products	Principal	Date	Details		Mos.	Products	Principal
19..					£p	19..					£p
Jan. 1	Balance	b/d			300·00	Mar. 31	Bill of Exchange due 31st Oct.				120·00
June 30	Products on Bill		6	1,800		June 30	Balance of Products to Contra			2,280	
	Interest on Products from Contra of £2,280 for 1 mth. at 5% per annum		4	480	9·50		Balance	c/d			189·50
				2,280	£309·50					2,280	£309·50
July 1	Balance	b/d			189·50						

(4) ÉPOQUE METHOD
A in Account Current with B

Date	Details		Mos.	Products	Principal	Date	Details		Mos.	Products	Principal
19..					£p	19..					£p
Jan. 1	Balance	b/d			300·00	Mar. 31	Bill of Exchange due 31st Oct.		10	1,200	120·00
June 30	Balance of Products			2,280		June 30	Balance of Account [i.e. £300 less £120] £180		6	1,080	
	Interest on balance of Products of £2,280 for 1 month at 5% per annum				9·50		Balance	c/d			189·50
				2,280	£309·50					2,280	£309·50
July 1	Balance	b/d			189·50						

(1) A in Account Current with B

Dr.

Date	Details		Mos.	Interest	Principal
19..				£p	£p
Jan. 1	Balance	b/d			
April 1	Goods (dated 1st Sept.) (a)		6	5·00	200·00
	Interest on Bill (b)		6	2·50	120·00
June 30	Interest from Contra			5·67	5·67
				£7·50	£325·67
July 1	Balance	b/d			175·67

Cr.

Date	Details		Mos.	Interest	Principal
19..			£p	£p	£p
Mar. 1	Cash		4	0·83	50·00
May 1	Bill due 1st Jan. (b)		2	1·00	100·00
June 30	Interest on Goods (a)				
	Balance of Interest to Contra			5·67	
	Balance	c/d			175·67
				£7·50	£325·67

(2) A in Account Current with B

Dr.

Date	Details		Mos.	Interest	Principal
19..				£p	£p
Jan. 1	Balance	b/d			
April 1	Goods (dated 1st Sept.) (x)		6	5·00	200·00
	Interest on Bill (q)		3	1·50	120·00
June 30	Interest from Contra		8	3·33	5·67
				£9·83	£325·67
July 1	Balance	b/d			175·67

Cr.

Date	Details		Mos.	Interest	Principal
19..			£p	£p	£p
Mar. 1	Cash		4	0·83	50·00
May 1	Bill due 1st Jan. (r)		2	0·83	100·00
June 30	Interest on Goods (y)		5	2·50	
	Interest to Contra			5·67	
	Balance	c/d			175·67
				£9·83	£325·67

(1) A IN ACCOUNT CURRENT WITH B

Date	Details		Mos.	Interest	Principal
				£p	£p
19.. Jan. 1	Balance	b/d			
June 30	Interest on Bill		6	7·50	300·00
	Interest from Contra		4	2·00	7·50
				£9·50	£307·50
July 1	Balance	b/d		2·00	187·50
Dec. 31	Interest on £187·50 at 5% for 6 months		6	4·69	6·69
	Interest from Contra				
				£6·69	£194·19
19.. Jan. 1	Balance	b/d			194·19

Date	Details		Mos.	Interest	Principal
				£p	£p
19.. Mar. 31	Bill due 31st Oct.			7·50	120·00
June 30	Interest to Contra			2·00	187·50
	Balance	c/d			£307·50
				£9·50	
Dec. 31	Interest to Contra			6·69	194·19
	Balance	c/d			
				£6·69	£194·19

(2) A IN ACCOUNT CURRENT WITH B

Date	Details		Mos.	Interest	Principal
				£p	£p
19.. Jan. 1	Balance	b/d			
June 30	Interest on Bill		6	7·50	300·00
	Interest from Contra		4	2·00	9·50
				£9·50	£309·50
July 1	Balance	b/d		4·74	189·50
Dec. 31	Interest from Contra		6		4·74
				£4·74	£194·24
19.. Jan. 1	Balance	b/d			194·24

Date	Details		Mos.	Interest	Principal
				£p	£p
19.. Mar. 31	Bill due 31st Oct.			9·50	120·00
June 30	Interest to Contra				189·50
	Balance	c/d			£309·50
				£9·50	
Dec. 31	Interest to Contra			4·74	194·24
	Balance	c/d			
				£4·74	£194·24

transaction, this process being continued throughout the period of the account.

Thus interest is reckoned in stages, each being measured by the length of time the balance remains unchanged.

This method is particularly suitable for interest calculations in banking accounts, but it may also be applied to ordinary accounts. Its use will necessitate alteration in the form of the Account Current inasmuch as it entails the striking of a new balance on the occasion of any transaction relating to the account. It must be clearly observed that where in a banking account a higher rate of interest is charged on overdrafts than is allowed on amounts in credit this is quite different from the system of charging one rate on all debits and allowing another on all credits, because in calculating Bank Interest the TEMPORARY BALANCE is the material factor.

Illustration 5

		£
19..		
Jan. 1	Balance due to Brown	400
Mar. 31	Jones remits cash to Brown	250
Apr. 14	Brown sells goods to Jones (dated 15th May)	50
May 1	Jones sells goods to Brown	20

Show Account Current to 30th June in Brown's books.
Interest to be calculated at 5 per cent per annum.
Calculate in (a) days and (b) months.

JONES IN ACCOUNT CURRENT WITH BROWN

					(a)		(b)	
Date	Debits	Credits	Dr. Balance	Cr. Balance	Days Unchanged	Products	Months Unchanged	Products
19..	£	£	£	£				
Jan. 1			400		90	36,000	3	1,200
Mar. 31		250	150		31	4,650	$1\frac{1}{2}$	150
May 1		20	130		14	1,820	$\frac{1}{2}$	65
15	50		180		46	8,280	$1\frac{1}{2}$	270
					181	50,750	6	1,685

(a) Interest on £50,750 for 1 day at 5% per annum   £p

$$= £\frac{50,750 \times 10}{73,000} = 6\cdot95$$

(b) Interest on £1,685 for 1 month at 5% per annum

$$= £\frac{1,685 \times 10}{200 \times 12} = 7\cdot02$$

[or, being 1p on £2·40 per month, 702p]

The difference in the results of the different interest calculations is due to the fact of:

(*a*) 14 days being treated as $\frac{1}{2}$ month.
(*b*) Difference in the length of months.
(*c*) Six months are treated as $182\frac{1}{2}$ days, i.e. one half of 365 days.

Illustration 6

T. Jones, a customer, had the following transactions with the Central Bank during the half-year to 30th June 19...
He drew out as follows:

19..	£	19..	£
Jan. 6 . . .	100	April 2 . . .	950
18 . . .	180	May 1 . . .	110
Feb. 22 . . .	100	June 1 . . .	40
Mar. 14 . . .	300	10 . . .	80

And paid in as follows:

19..	£	19..	£
Jan. 31 . . .	80	April 30 . . .	160
Feb. 16 . . .	50	May 8 . . .	30
Mar. 2 . . .	500	24 . . .	80
12 . . .	400	28 . . .	30
31 . . .	150	June 25 . . .	520

His balance at 1st January 19.. was in credit to the extent of £300.
You are required to show T. Jones's account in the books of the bank having regard to the following:

1. $2\frac{1}{2}$ per cent per annum is allowed on credit balances.[1]
2. 5 per cent per annum is charged on debit balances.
3. Commission charged at rate of £0·05 per £100 on sums paid in.

---

[1] Interest is not normally allowed nowadays on current accounts.

T. Jones in Account with the Central Bank, Ltd.

Date	Particulars	Debits	Credits	Balances Dr.	Balances Cr.	No. of Days	Products Debits	Products Credits
19..		£p	£p	£p	£p			
Jan. 1	Balance		300·00		300	6		1,800
6		100·00			200	12		2,400
18		180·00			20	13		260
31			80·00		100	16		1,600
Feb. 16			50·00		150	6		900
22		100·00			50	8		400
Mar. 2			500·00		550	10		5,500
12			400·00		950	2		1,900
14		300·00			650	17		11,050
31			150·00		800	2		1,600
Apr. 2		950·00		150		28	4,200	
30			160·00		10	1		10
May 1		110·00		100		7	700	
8			30·00	70		16	1,120	
24			80·00		10	4		40
28			30·00		40	4		160
June 1		40·00				9		
10		80·00		80		15	1,200	
25			520·00		440	5		2,200
30	Interest		1·05				7,220	29,820
	Commission	1·00						
	Balance c/d	440·05						
	£	2301·05	2301·05					
19..								
July 1	Balance b/d		440·01					

The interest is ascertained as follows:

$$£p$$
Interest receivable = $2\frac{1}{2}$% p.a. on £29,820 for 1 day = 2·04
Interest payable   = 5% p.a. on £7,220 for 1 day = 0·99

∴ Net Interest receivable   = £1·05

The commission is ascertained as follows:

Total payments into bank = £2,000
£0·05 per cent of £2,000 = £1

Note. The £300 balance has already borne commission during the preceding year.

AVERAGE DUE DATE

This may be defined as the mean or equated date on which one payment may be made in lieu of several payments due on a series of dates.

It is used in connection with the settlement of *contra* accounts; accounts which are to be settled by a series of bills; the calculation of interest on partners' Drawings Accounts; the piecemeal realization of assets during a partnership dissolution; and other transactions of a similar nature.

The method of arriving at the average due date is as follows:

1. A certain convenient basic date is taken as a starting point from which all calculations have to be made. This starting point should preferably be the due date of the earliest transaction.

2. The number of days (or months) that the due date of each transaction is distant from the basic point must then be ascertained.

3. Each item (usually taken to the nearest £) is multiplied by its distance (measured in terms of days or months) from the basic point.

4. The products are totalled and divided by the total of the various amounts.

5. The result is the number of days (or months) that the average due date is distant from the chosen basic date.

Illustration 7

A owes B the following sums of money due on the dates stated:

```
         £
100 due 4th March
160  ,,  23rd April
 40  ,,  1st May
200  ,,  15th May
500  ,,  31st July
```

He desires to make one payment on the average due date, which will be ascertained as follows:

Date	Amount	Time from 4th March in days	Product
19..	£		
Mar. 4	100	0	
April 23	160	50	8,000
May 1	40	58	2,320
15	200	72	14,400
July 31	500	149	74,500
	£1,000		99,220

Calculation

$$\frac{99,220}{1,000} = 99 \text{ (to the nearest whole number)}$$

∴ The average due date is 99 days from 4th March = 11th June.

It is not, of course, compulsory to take as a base the date of the first amount due. In fact any date may be taken so long as it lies between the first and last dates.

Illustration 8

Using the previous illustration, but taking 5th May as the basic date:

Date	Amount	Time from 5th May in days		Product	
		Before –	After +	Before –	After +
19..	£				
Mar. 4	100	62		6,200	
April 23	160	12		1,920	
May 1	40	4		160	
15	200		10		2,000
July 31	500		87		43,500
	£1,000			–8,280	+45,500
					8,280
				Net Product	37,220

Calculation

$$\frac{37,220}{1,000} = 37 \text{ days } after \text{ 5th May (to the nearest whole number)}$$

$$= 11\text{th June}$$

Illustration 9

Similarly, the end date may be used as the basic date.

Date	Amount	Time from 31st July in days	Product
19..	£		
Mar. 4	100	149	14,900
April 23	160	99	15,840
May 1	40	91	3,640
15	200	77	15,400
July 31	500	0	
	£1,000		49,780

Calculation

$$\frac{49,780}{1,000} = 50 \text{ days } before \text{ 31st July (to the nearest whole number)}$$

$$= 11\text{th June}$$

As has been mentioned above, the ascertainment of the average due date is often the quickest method of ascertaining the interest that should be charged on a series of transactions which bear interest over a period (e.g. partners' drawings).

Illustration 10

A, a partner in the firm A. B. & Co., draws out from the business the following amounts during 19.. upon which he is to be charged interest at 7 per cent per annum.

19..	£	19..	£
Jan. 31 . . .	150	July 31 . . .	250
Feb. 28 . . .	100	Aug. 31 . . .	150
Mar. 31 . . .	160	Sept. 30 . . .	120
April 30 . . .	200	Oct. 31 . . .	100
May 31 . . .	140	Nov. 30 . . .	180
June 30 . . .	70	Dec. 31 . . .	316

The best way to deal with a question of this type is to ascertain the average due date working in months and then find the amount of interest at 7 per cent per annum on £1,936 (the total amount of drawings) for the period from the average due date to 31st December 19.. The average due date will be ascertained as follows:

	Amounts	End date being used as basic date		Commencing date being used as basic date	
		Months before 31st Dec.	Product	Months after 1st Jan.	Product
19..	£				
Jan. 31	150	11	1,650	1	150
Feb. 28	100	10	1,000	2	200
Mar. 31	160	9	1,440	3	480
April 30	200	8	1,600	4	800
May 31	140	7	980	5	700
June 30	70	6	420	6	420
July 31	250	5	1,250	7	1,750
Aug. 31	150	4	600	8	1,200
Sept. 30	120	3	360	9	1,080
Oct. 31	100	2	200	10	1,000
Nov. 30	180	1	180	11	1,980
Dec. 31	316	0	0	12	3,792
	£1,936		9,680		13,552

Therefore the average due date is:

$$\frac{9,680}{1,936}\text{ months prior to 31st December, i.e. 5 months}$$

$$= \text{31st July}$$

Alternatively, calculating from 1st January, the average due date is:

$$\frac{13,552}{1,936}\text{ months subsequent to 1st January, i.e. 7 months}$$

$$= \text{31st July}$$

Accordingly the amount of interest that must be charged to A is: interest at 7 per cent per annum on £1,936 for five months = £56·46.

If, however, the withdrawals are the same each month it is not necessary to 'weight'. The months are added together and divided by 12, i.e.:

(a) Months before 31st December total 66 divided by $12 = 5\frac{1}{2}$ months *prior* to 31st December, viz. 15th July.

(b) Months after 1st January total 78 divided by $12 = 6\frac{1}{2}$ months *after* 1st January, viz. 15th July.

(If weighted—
  (a) 6,600 divided by $1,200 = 5\frac{1}{2}$ months.
  (b) 7,800 divided by $1,200 = 6\frac{1}{2}$ months.)

Illustration 11

A owes B £400, due 31st January; A owes B £600 due 30th April; B owes A £300, due 31st March. Find the average due date for a settlement in one sum. Calculate in months.

		A TO B Amt. £	Mths.	Pro-ducts			B TO A Amt. £	Mths.	Pro-ducts
Jan. 31	.	400	0	0	Mar. 31	.	300	2	600
Apr. 30	.	600	3	1,800					
		£1,000		1,800			£300		600

Average due date: $1,800 - 600 \div 700 = \dfrac{1200}{700} = 1\frac{5}{7}$ months from 31st Jan., say, 22nd Mar.

If the average due date is required for a fixed amount, it is found by taking the aggregate of the number of days (or months, or years), divided by the sum of the number of days (or months, or years), such quotient being the number of days (or months, or years) from the commencement.

Illustration 12

£10,000 lent on 1st January 19.1, is repayable in five equal annual instalments commencing 1st January 19.2. Find the average due date.

$$\frac{1+2+3+4+5}{5} = \frac{15}{5} = 3 \text{ years from 1st January 19.1, i.e. 1st January 19.4.}$$

CHAPTER 05

TRADING AND PROFIT AND LOSS ACCOUNT—
BALANCE SHEET

MOST students will already have familiarized themselves to a greater or lesser degree with the nature of the items appearing in the Trading and Profit and Loss Account and the Balance Sheet. The following pages are devoted to the principles and difficulties of this topic; problems of an advanced nature will be dealt with as they arise in connection with Partnerships and Limited Companies in the chapters on those subjects.

DEFINITIONS

Gross Profit and Gross Loss. Gross profit is the excess of the sales (less returns) over the cost of the goods sold including the expenses directly attributable to putting the goods in a saleable condition. The cost of the goods sold is the amount of the opening stock plus purchases (less returns), less the amount of the closing stock—not merely the amount of goods *purchased*. A gross loss is the converse of a gross profit.

Net Profit and Net Loss. Net profit is the surplus remaining after charging against gross profit all the expenses, including depreciation and other necessary provisions, properly attributable to the normal activities of the particular business. A net loss is the converse of a net profit.

FUNCTIONS OF THE FINAL ACCOUNTS[1]

The final accounts consist of (*a*) Trading Account, (*b*) Profit and Loss Account, (*c*) Profit and Loss Appropriation Account and (*d*) Balance Sheet.

The aim of the Trading Account is to ascertain the gross profit or gross loss for a certain period, that of the Profit and Loss Account is to ascertain the net profit or net loss for the same period. The traditional two-sided form of Trading and Profit and Loss Account is nowadays largely being replaced by the vertical or columnar form. It is considered generally that the vertical or columnar form of presentation of such accounts is understood more readily by the persons for whom they are primarily intended, viz. business persons in the case of sole traders and partnerships, and shareholders in the case of limited companies. Such persons can understand accounts more easily when balances or figures are arrived at by means of comprehensibly narrated additions and subtractions than they can when balances are carried down from one side of an account to the other, and debits and credits are shown with little indication of the reasons.

In this chapter the vertical or columnar form, and in some instances the two-sided form, will be used unless the Trading and Profit and Loss

---

[1] For the present, attention is confined to Trading and Profit and Loss Accounts, so that all references to other methods of showing business activities, e.g. Manufacturing Accounts, are excluded.

Accounts are shown as they would appear in the ledger, in which case the normal debit and credit form will be used.

The aim of the Profit and Loss Appropriation Account is to show all dispositions, divisions and appropriations of the net profit. Thus, whereas all expenses incurred in the gaining of the net profit, such as loan interest, depreciation, rent, rates, wages and the like, are chargeable to the Profit and Loss Account, the Appropriation Account will be debited with such items as Manager's commission (where intended to be a *division* of profits), interest on capital of a partner, dividends to shareholders of a limited company, etc. Similarly all income properly attributable to the ordinary business activities will be credited to the Profit and Loss Account, and not to the Appropriation Account.

The vital distinction between the Profit and Loss Account and the Appropriation Account is particularly applicable to the accounts of limited companies and the topic receives attention in Chapter 23.

The Appropriation Account is not usually used in the accounts of a sole trader, non-business expenses, such as drawings, being debited direct to Capital Account, or, where it is desired to keep the capital figure intact, to a Current Account to which also the net profit is credited.

The aim of the Balance Sheet is to show in summary form the financial state of the concern as disclosed by the books, and to that end will be scheduled the assets, liabilities, reserves and capital as they exist upon a given date.

The Trading and Profit and Loss Account is (as its name implies) an ACCOUNT and its construction conforms to the rules of double-entry, whereas the Balance Sheet is quite definitely not an account, but a mere SUMMARY OF ACCOUNTS APPEARING IN THE LEDGER AFTER ADJUSTMENT OF THE PROFIT AND LOSS ACCOUNT. It will therefore be comprised of all items that are not transferred to the Trading and Profit and Loss Account, including the closing stock as introduced into the books. Hence, as the Trading and Profit and Loss Account absorbs, as it were, Nominal items, the Balance Sheet will be made up only of assets and liabilities, including closing stock and Capital.

Its form—that is, reverse to the actual side of the Ledger on which the particular item appears—should cause no difficulty so long as the student treats every item consistently. In accordance with British custom, assets are sometimes shown on the right hand of the Balance Sheet and liabilities and capital on the left hand. The modern trend, however, is, as in the case of Trading and Profit and Loss Accounts, to present Balance Sheets in vertical or columnar form.

Finally, as the Trading and Profit and Loss Account contains the results of operations over a period, the heading should be 'Trading and Profit and Loss Account FOR THE YEAR (or other period) ENDED . . .'; the Balance Sheet, on the other hand, is a statement of the financial position AT a stated date and hence should be headed 'BALANCE SHEET AS AT (or ON) (or AT) . . . . . .' For example, if final accounts are drawn up as a result of operations for the half-year to 30th April 19 . . , the Trading and Profit and Loss Account will be headed:

The Balance Sheet at the close of the period will be headed:

BALANCE SHEET AS AT 30TH APRIL 19 . .

RULES FOR CONSTRUCTION OF FINAL ACCOUNTS

1. **Trading Section of the Trading and Profit and Loss Account.** The items usually appearing in this account in the ledger are:

(a) DEBIT SIDE.	Opening Stock.
	Purchases.
	Carriage Inwards.
	Wages.
(b) CREDIT SIDE.	Sales.
	Closing Stock.

The Trial Balance will include opening, but not closing, stock; stock at the end of the period must therefore be 'taken' and valued and be incorporated in the accounts by means of the following Journal entry:

Stock . . . . . *Dr.*
    To Trading Account . . . .

When this entry is posted, the closing stock will appear on the debit side of the Stock Account and on the credit of the Trading and Profit and Loss Account.

Where the vertical or columnar form of presentation is used, the items could be shown as follows:

			£
Sales			x
Less Cost of Goods Sold:			
Purchases . .	£x		
Add Opening Stock* . .	x		
	—		
	x		
Deduct Closing Stock* .	x		
	—		
	£x		
Carriage Inwards . .	x		
Wages . . .	x		
	—	x	
		—	
Trading Profit (or Loss) . . .			£x
			=

* It is more common to show one amount only in respect of the stock adjustment. Thus where the value of closing stock exceeds that of opening stock the form of presentation is:

		£
Purchases	x
Deduct Increase in value		
of stock . . .	x
	—
	x

Where the value of opening stock exceeds that of closing stock:

	£
Purchases	x
Add Decrease in value of stock	x
	—
	x

With a little thought it will be apparent that the net effect of each of the above adjustments is the same as the respective double adjustment.

As many students experience great difficulty in dealing with the Stock entries, the following is given by way of illustration. The Trial Balance at 31st December 19.2, contains an item Stock (1st January 19.2) £1,000, and on taking stock at 31st December 19.2, the stock on hand is valued at £1,500. The opening stock (£1,000) will have been incorporated into the books at 31st December 19.1, and have been shown in the Balance Sheet at that date as an asset, and will accordingly be a debit balance in the books throughout 19.2. At 31st December 19.2, it will be transferred to the Trading Account by debiting that account and crediting Stock. The closing stock (£1,500) will be introduced into the books by debiting Stock and crediting Trading Account. The new stock will thus appear as an asset in the Balance Sheet and will remain as a debit balance throughout 19.3. The Stock Account will appear thus:

STOCK

19.1 Dec. 31	Trading A/c [19.1]	.	£ [1]1,000	19.2 Dec. 31	Trading A/c [19.2]	.	£ 1,000
19.2 Dec. 31	Trading A/c [19.2]	.	[2]1,500				

[1] An asset in the Balance Sheet at 31st December 19.1.
[2] An asset in the Balance Sheet at 31st December 19.2.

If, as occasionally happens in examination questions, the closing stock is given as part of the Trial Balance, the presumption is that the Trading Account has already been prepared prior to the extraction of the Trial Balance; that is, the opening stock, purchases and sales and the necessary double-entry for the inclusion of the closing stock, have already been disposed of in the Trading Account. Reference to the Trial Balance will normally confirm this supposition, in that it will include gross profit as a separate balance. In these circumstances the closing stock will be shown in the Balance Sheet as an asset without adjustment.

The Profit and Loss Account only will be shown; the commencing figure will be the Trading Profit or Loss as shown in the Trial Balance, subject to certain adjustments if required.

2. **Profit and Loss Section.** The expenses incurred in carrying on the affairs of a concern will vary in accordance with circumstances. The

following is a list of the usual expenses:

Wages and Salaries.	Heating and Lighting.
Rent and Rates.	Repairs and Renewals.
Insurance.	Telephone.
Discounts Allowed.	Accountancy and Legal Expenses.
Stationery.	Motor Expenses.
Postages.	Bank Charges.
Advertising.	Travelling Expenses.
Carriage Outwards.	Distributing Expenses generally.
Depreciation.	Royalties.
Bad Debts.	Selling Commission.
Loan Interest.	

Expenses of a special nature (e.g. those peculiar to Limited Companies, such as Directors' Fees, Debenture Interest) are not included here, but will receive mention in their appropriate place.

Certain items representing gains will be credited to the Profit and Loss Account. Such are:

Discounts Received.	Selling Bonuses.
Bank Interest.	Profit on the Sale of Assets.
Recoveries or Part Recoveries of Bad Debts.	Income from Investments.

The Profit and Loss balance, being Net Profit or Loss will be carried to Capital or Current Account (or Appropriation Account where applicable).

3. **Balance Sheet.** The balances remaining in the books, comprised of Assets, Liabilities and Capital, will be extracted to form the schedule or statement known as the Balance Sheet. They are not 'transferred' but merely extracted in the form of a statement and comprise the opening entries for the succeeding period.

The Balance Sheet may be looked upon as the 'Trial Balance' *after* the transfer into one combined account of Purchases, Sales and Expenses, including the incorporation of the closing Stock and the transfer to Capital Account of the net profit or loss for the period.

It is important to observe that the amount shown in Drawings Account is transferred to Capital Account (and NOT to Profit and Loss Account) so that the Capital Account will in normal circumstances be made up of (1) Capital at the commencement of the period, (2) less Drawings, (3) plus net Profit (or less net Loss) for the period.

The general rules are shown by the following illustration.

Illustration 1

The following balances have been extracted from the books of H. Jones, retail merchant, at 31st December 19 . ., and a TRADING and PROFIT and LOSS ACCOUNT and a BALANCE SHEET have been prepared from them. The closing stock at 31st December 19 . . was £450. The Ledger accounts are appended in detail to amplify and clarify the processes called for in the preparation of final accounts.

The balances remaining in the books agree with the items set out in the Balance Sheet below—except that in the Ledger accounts the assets are 'debits' and liabilities and capital are 'credits.'

H. JONES

TRIAL BALANCE AS AT 31ST DECEMBER 19..

	Folio	Dr.	Cr.
		£	£
Fixtures and Fittings	1	2,000	
Stock (as at 1st January 19..)	2	600	
Purchases	3	7,200	
Sales	4		10,800
Debtors	5	3,000	
Creditors	6		1,800
Expenses	7	500	
Drawings	8	450	
Cash	9	20	
Capital (as at 1st January 19..)	10		1,170
		£13,770	£13,770

H. JONES

TRADING AND PROFIT AND LOSS ACCOUNT FOR THE YEAR ENDED 31ST DECEMBER 19..

		£
Sales		10,800
Less Cost of Goods sold:		
Purchases	£7,200	
Add Decrease in value of stock	150	
		7,350
Trading (or Gross) Profit		3,450
Less Expenses		500
Net Profit transferred to Capital		£2,950

BALANCE SHEET AS AT 31ST DECEMBER 19..

	£
CAPITAL	
At 1st January 19..	1,170
Less Drawings	450
	720
Add Net Profit	2,950
	£3,670

EMPLOYMENT OF CAPITAL

Fixed Assets:
    Fixtures and Fittings   .   .   .   £2,000

Current Assets:
    Stock   .   .   .   £450
    Debtors   .   .   .   3,000
    Cash   .   .   .   20

                    £3,470

Current Liabilities:
    Creditors   £1,800

Working Capital[1]   1,670

                    £3,670

1

FIXTURES AND FITTINGS

19.. Dec. 31	Sundries . . .		£ 2,000				

2

STOCK

19.. Jan. 1	Balance. . . .	b/d	£ 600	19.. Dec. 31	Trading Account . .		£ 600
Dec. 31	Trading Account .		450				

3

PURCHASES

19.. Dec. 31	Sundries . . .		£ 7,200	19.. Dec. 31	Trading Account . .		£ 7,200

4

SALES

19.. Dec. 31	Trading Account .		£ 10,800	19.. Dec. 31	Sundries . . .		£ 10,800

5

DEBTORS

19.. Dec. 31	Sundries . . .		£ 3,000				

[1] Working Capital = Current Assets less Current Liabilities.

6   CREDITORS

				19..			£
				Dec. 31	Sundries . . .		1,800

7   EXPENSES

19..			£	19..			£
Dec. 31	Sundries . . .		500	Dec. 31	Profit and Loss Account .		500

8   DRAWINGS

19..			£	19..			£
Dec. 31	Sundries . . .		450	Dec. 31	Capital Account . .	10	450

9   CASH

19..			£				
Dec. 31	Sundries . . .		20				

10   CAPITAL

19..			£	19..			£
Dec. 31	Drawings . . .	8	450	Jan. 1	Balance. . .	b/d	1,170
	Balance . . .	c/d	3,670	Dec. 31	Profit and Loss Account .		2,950
			£4,120				£4,120
				19..			
				Jan. 1	Balance . . .	b/d	3,670

The elementary rules may now be formulated:

(A) Trading Account

1. Sales
   Debit Sales.   Credit Trading.
2. Purchases
   Debit Trading.   Credit Purchases.
3. Opening Stock
   Debit Trading.   Credit Stock.
4. Closing Stock (which is *not* in the Trial Balance)
   Debit Stock.   Credit Trading.

The Closing Stock so introduced will now appear as a balance in the Ledger and therefore as an Asset in the Balance Sheet.

5. Expenses (Trading)
   Debit Trading.   Credit Expenses.

Notice that in the vertical or columnar form of account the principle of debit and credit is still maintained and the rules here stated in journal form are still appropriate.

6. The balance of Trading is the opening figure for the Profit and Loss Account. Normally this will be a credit balance; if, however, it should be a debit balance as a result of Cost of Goods Sold exceeding Sales then this will be indicated by prefixing the resulting balance thus (*Dr.*)

(*B*) Profit and Loss Account

1. As already stated there will be a balance, being either Trading (or Gross) Profit (credit) or Trading (or Gross) Loss (debit) from Trading.

2. Expenses (Profit and Loss)

Debit Profit and Loss.   Credit Expenses.

3. Sundry income (e.g. Discounts received).

Debit the appropriate account   Credit Profit and Loss.
(e.g. Discounts Received).

4. The balance of Profit and Loss will be transferred to Capital Account. The Journal Entries would be:

(*a*) If a Profit.

Debit Profit and Loss.   Credit Capital.

(*b*) If a Loss.

Debit Capital.   Credit Profit and Loss.

ADJUSTMENTS

When preparing final accounts it will be necessary to consider the question of the period in respect of which an expense has been incurred. It is easy to realize that at any given date, an expense may have been paid, or charged if an Expenses Day Book or Journal is used, in respect of a period which is not co-extensive with the period of accounts, either falling short of, or stretching beyond such period, and as it is essential that the period for which accounts are prepared should bear the true expenditure—no more, no less—an adjustment is usually called for to give effect to this principle. Where a payment is made in respect of a period beyond the date of the accounts it is in the nature of an asset; that is, the benefit of the expenditure is still to be derived and by so treating it the subsequent period bears the incidence of the expenditure. Conversely, if a payment for expenditure does not cover the whole period in question, provision has to be made for accruals, and this will be in the nature of a liability, and by so treating it relief will be made to the subsequent period, which will have debited against it the payment of the expense which has arisen in the preceding period.

In order to ensure that the accounts of a period do contain all the expenses and gains properly attributable to that period, all or some of the following adjustments will usually be required:

1. Carry forward of payments in advance, e.g. Insurance, Rates, and in certain circumstances, Advertising (pp. 0510–0513).

2. Charges for accrued or accruing expenses, e.g. Rent, Heating, Lighting, Telephone (pp. 0513–0515).

3. Carry forward of income received but only PARTLY earned or accrued, e.g. Subscriptions or Rents Received in Advance: and its converse, entries for income earned or accrued, not yet wholly received (pp. 0515–0516).

4. Incorporation of stock into the accounts, e.g. Stationery Stock.

5. (a) Depreciation (pp. 0518–0521).
   (b) Bad and Doubtful Debts (pp. 0521–0523).
   (c) Discounts (pp. 0523–0525).
   (d) Loan Interest (pp. 0526–0528).

6. Transfers:

(a) Correction of errors of commission, as for instance, correction of posting to (i) wrong account, (ii) wrong side of an account, e.g. charging private withdrawals to Expenses Accounts.

(b) Correction of errors of omission, e.g. omission of returns, etc.

(c) (i) Special or abnormal charges against Profit and Loss Account.
    (ii) Appropriations of Profits, e.g. commissions based upon profits.

1. Expenses Prepaid

The book-keeping entry required to deal with prepayments or payments in advance is: debit Expenses Prepaid Account, credit Expense Account; and the effect of the entry is to reduce the expenses debited to Profit and Loss Account. The Expenses Prepaid Account is an asset and will appear on the Balance Sheet as such.

Illustration 2

A commenced business on 1st April 19.., and at the date of the Trial Balance extracted on 31st December 19.., has paid rates to 31st March next, the proportion of such prepayment, i.e. for the three months between 1st January and 31st March, being £30. Make the adjustment for the purpose of preparing final accounts in respect of the period ended 31st December 19...

JOURNAL

19..		£	£
Dec. 31	Expenses Prepaid	30	
	Rates		30
	Being transfer of Rates prepaid at this date.		

The item will be shown in the Balance Sheet at 31st December 19.., as an asset, and on the following 1st January 19.., it will be transferred back to Rates Account, thus throwing the charge therefor on to the following period.

This entry will be:

JOURNAL

19..		£	£
Jan. 1	Rates	30	
	Expenses Prepaid		30
	Being transfer of Rates applicable to three months ended 31st March 19..		

The Ledger Accounts will then be:

RATES

19.. Oct. 3 (say)	Cash	.	.	.	.		£ 120	19.. Dec. 31	Expenses Prepaid . Profit and Loss Account .		£ 30 90
							£120				£120
19.. Jan. 1	Expenses Prepaid	.	.				30				

EXPENSES PREPAID

19.. Dec. 31	Rates Prepaid[1]	.	.		£ 30	19.. Jan. 1	Rates	.	.	.	£ 30

[1] This would appear in the Balance Sheet on 31st December 19.., as an asset, and on the following 1st January, the first day in the new period, be re-transferred to Rates Account.

The same procedure will be followed in *all* cases of prepayments.

In practice, a simpler alternative method is generally adopted, whereby the adjustments are made within the one account. The method is as follows:

The amount prepaid is credited to the Expense Account and brought down as a balance on the account (in the same way as a cash balance is brought down). The balance of the Expense Account is then transferred to the Trading and Profit and Loss Account. The amount brought down on the Expense Account is shown in the Balance Sheet as an asset.

Illustration 3

The facts in the preceding illustration may be shown thus:

RATES

19.. Oct. 3 (say)	Cash	.	.	.		£ 120	19.. Dec. 31	Amount Prepaid . . Profit and Loss Account .	c/d	£ 30 90
						£120				£120
19.. Jan. 1	Rates Prepaid	.	.	b/d	30				

It is important to see that the final balance transferred to Profit and Loss Account shows a consistent result, e.g. if rates are £30 prepaid, the rates for the whole year should be £120, and this can be seen with reference to the account for the following year, which will appear as follows:

RATES

19.. Jan. 1 Oct. 3	Rates Prepaid Cash	. .	. .	b/d	£ 30 120	19.. Dec. 31	Amount Prepaid . . Profit and Loss Account .	c/d	£ 30 120
					£150				£150
19..[1] Jan. 1	Rates Prepaid	.	.	b/d	30				

[1] Succeeding year.

The above assumes that the rates payable for the rating year to the following 31st March are unaltered.

In order to make the principle clear the following example is given relating to insurance, which is usually payable in advance.

Illustration 4

A commences business on 1st May, and draws up his accounts on 31st December. He has paid insurance £36 in respect of Fire on 15th May covering the year to the following 30th April. In the next year he increases his cover and the new premium is to be £48. Show how these matters would be dealt with in the accounts for the eight months ended 31st December, and for the next year ended 31st December. As the form required for the Journal is precisely as before, only the Ledger Accounts are given.

First Method. (i.e. the employment of Expenses prepaid Account).

INSURANCE

19..		£	19..			£
May 15	Cash—Insurance for year ended 30th April, 19...	36	Dec. 31	Expenses Prepaid Account Profit and Loss Account .		12 24
		£36				£36
19.. Jan. 1 May 15	Expenses Prepaid Account Cash—Insurance for year ended 30th April, 19...	12 48	19.. Dec. 31	Expenses Prepaid Account Profit and Loss Account .		16 44
		£60				£60
19.. Jan. 1	Expenses Prepaid Account	16				

EXPENSES PREPAID

19..		£	19..		£
Dec. 31	Insurance Prepaid[1] .	12	Jan. 1	Insurance Account .	12
19.. Dec. 31	Insurance Prepaid[1] .	16	19.. Jan. 1	Insurance Account .	16

Second Method. (i.e. the making of the adjustment within the Expense Account).

INSURANCE

19..			£	19..			£
May 15	Cash . . .		36	Dec. 31	Amount Prepaid . Profit and Loss Account .	c/d	12 24
			£36				£36
19.. Jan. 1 May 15	Insurance Prepaid[1] . Cash	b/d	12 48	19.. Dec. 31	Amount Prepaid . Profit and Loss Account .	c/d	16 44
			£60				£60
19.. Jan. 1	Insurance Prepaid[1] .	b/d	16				

[1] These items will appear in the respective Balance Sheets as assets.

It will be observed that A has been insured in the first period for EIGHT months only (i.e. the period commencing 1st May 19.., and ending 31st December 19..), and as the Insurance is £36 per annum, it is equivalent to £3 monthly, therefore £3×8 should be the charge to Profit and Loss Account for the first period. As regards the second period, A is insured for FOUR months (i.e. from the following 1st January to 30th April) at £3 a month, and for EIGHT months (i.e. from 1st May to 31st December) at £4 a month; the amount of Insurance chargeable to the Profit and Loss Account should be, therefore, £44 [i.e. £3×4 (£12) plus £4×8 (£32)].

If A ceased to carry on business on 1st May in the year next following, there would be no further payment for Insurance, and the item of £16 would be transferred to the Profit and Loss Account for the four months ended 30th April, which is four months' insurance at £4 per month, i.e. £16.

2. Expenses Accrued and Accruing

The circumstances giving rise to adjustments under this heading are roughly the reverse to those relating to prepayments; that is to say, where an expense has been incurred, but not brought into the accounts. Where an expense has become a definite debt this is termed an accru**ED** expense, but where it has not become a definite debt it is designated an accru**ING** expense. The distinction from a legal point of view is important but for the purpose of elementary adjustments is quite immaterial. In order that the student may thoroughly appreciate the difference, an example may be given in relation to Rent. If a tenant draws up his accounts to 31st January 19.., and has not paid his rent since the September quarter (29th September) then his Rent ACCRUED is for the quarter to 25th December 19.., and his Rent ACCRUING is from that date to 31st January 19... Both must be dealt with in the accounts because the business has had the use of the premises for such period, but in point of law it is the accrued portion that actually constitutes a definitely enforceable debt, and the accruing rent will not become ACCRUED rent, and therefore an enforceable debt, till 25th March 19..; nevertheless both, as mentioned, must be the subject of a provision for Rent accrued and accruing in respect of the period ended 31st January.

Illustration 5

A draws up his accounts to 31st December 19.., and his Rent is £180 per annum payable on the usual quarter days,[1] the last Rent being paid to 29th September 19...

At 31st December 19.., there is:

		£
(a) Rent accrued to 25th December 19..	.	45
(b) Rent accruing from 26th December 19.., to 31st December 19.., i.e. 6 days, i.e. 6/90×£45	.	3

The amount to be provided therefore is £48.

[1] The usual quarter days are 25th March (Lady Day), 24th June (Midsummer Day), 29th September (Michaelmas), 25th December (Christmas).

The methods adopted for accruals will be founded upon the same principles as those adopted in dealing with prepayments; that is, a separate Accruals Account may be opened or the adjustment may be made within the Expense Account itself. ·

First Method. The Journal entry will be:

JOURNAL

		£	£
19.. Dec. 31	Rent . . . . Expenses Accruals . . . . . . Being transfer of Rent accrued and accruing at this date.	48	48
19..[1] Jan. 1	Expenses Accruals . . . . Rent . . . . Being transfer of Rent accrued and accruing at this date.	48	48

[1] Succeeding year.

Second Method. The amount accrued or accruing is debited to the Expense Account and brought down as a balance on the account, whereupon the balance of the Expense Account is transferred in the ordinary way to the debit of Profit and Loss Account. The amount brought down on the credit side of the Expense Account is shown in the Balance Sheet as a liability.

Illustration 6

A started business on 1st January 19.., and draws up his first accounts in respect of the year to 31st December 19... At this date he had not received the account in respect of his Gas and Electricity for the quarter ended 31st December 19... This account is estimated to be £30. The charges incurred for the first three quarters were:

		£
Quarter ended 31st March .	.	25
,, ,, 30th June .	.	20
,, ,, 30th September	.	15

The journal entries to record the creation of this provision and the subsequent transfer to Profit and Loss Account are as follows:

JOURNAL

		£	£
19.. Dec. 31	Electricity and Gas . . . . Expenses Accrued . . . . . . Being amount accrued due and unpaid.	30	30

	Profit and Loss Account . . . . .
	     Electricity and Gas . . . . . .
	 Being transfer to Profit and Loss Account of amount
	     applicable to the year ended this date.
		90	90

The accounts will therefore be as follows:

ELECTRICITY AND GAS

19.. Mar. 31 June 30 Sept. 30 Dec. 31	Cash . . . . . ,, ... ,, ... Expenses Accrued[1] . .	£ 25 20 15 30	19.. Dec. 31	Profit and Loss Account .	£ 90
		£90			£90

EXPENSES ACCRUED

			19.. Dec. 31	Electricity and Gas[2] .	£ 30

[1] Alternatively, the balance could be brought down below the line in the same account, thus dispensing with the Expenses Accrued Account.

[2] This amount is shown as a liability on the Balance Sheet drawn up at 31st December,

In dealing with accruals, the student should be aware that if an Expenses Day Book or Journal is employed all expenses ACCRUED will have been passed through the books and if the account, at the date of the completion of the accounting period, is still unpaid, it will **appear as a creditor** so that provision is required only for items ACCRUING. On the other hand, if no such book or Journal is employed, the expenses being entered upon payment direct from the Cash Book, then all expenses *unpaid* whether accrued or accruing must be provided for. **In other words, in *all* cases, 'accruings' will require to be brought into the adjustments, but not 'accrueds' where the invoice has already been passed through the books.**

Care, however, must be exercised in obtaining all invoices for accrued items even if a Day Book or Journal is employed, particularly where time must elapse before the invoice is received, e.g. Electricity Account. The meter may be read to 6th December, and the accounts of the consumer be drawn up to 10th December. At this date it is improbable that the invoice for the quarter to 6th December will have been received. The Expenses Day Book or Journal might be kept 'open' till its receipt but, if it is closed off promptly, provision will be required for (a) Electricity accrued to 6th December, and (b) Electricity accruing from 7th December to 10th December. If no Expenses Day Book or Journal is employed, the entries not being recorded till payment (neither of the above having been paid) both (a) and (b) will have to be provided for.

The above distinction, it should be emphasized, applies to all expenses.

3. Income

(a) **Unearned Income.** Where sums have been received during a period in respect of future service, only part of such sums will be applicable to service rendered in the period of accounts during which they were received. The part apportionable to future periods will be treated similarly to an 'accrued' expense. A debit entry above the line and a credit entry below the line in the income account will ensure that the Profit and Loss Account is credited with the correctly apportionable amount. The credit balance will appear as a liability in the Balance Sheet.

Illustration 7

A club receives £3,000 in subscriptions from members during the year ended 31st December 19.. but £240 is in respect of subscriptions for the ensuing year.

The 'Subscriptions' Account will appear:

SUBSCRIPTIONS

19.. Dec. 31	Profit and Loss Account . Balance.	c/d	£ 2,760 240	19.– Dec.	Cash	. . .		£ 3,000
			£3,000					£3,000
				19.. Jan. 1	Balance	. . .	b/d	240

(b) **Income Accrued and Accruing.** The principle involved under this heading is analogous to that of expenses accrued or accruing except that the adjustment will operate in the reverse manner. The accrual for expenses, it will be remembered, has the effect of increasing the charge to the Profit and Loss Account and increasing the liabilities. The effect, therefore, of the adjustment now under consideration is to increase the income in the Profit and Loss Account, and increase the amount of the assets.

The rule is: Credit above the 'line'; debit below the 'line.'

Illustration 8

The amount standing to the credit of Loan Interest at 31st December 19.1, is £100; an amount of £30 is *due* and unpaid by a borrower to 30th November 19.1, and £6 accruing.

Show Journal entries (ignoring narratives).

JOURNAL

19.1 Dec. 31	Loan Interest Accrued and Accruing . . . Dr. Loan Interest		£ 36	£ 36

Alternatively, the simple device of crediting above the 'line' and debiting below the 'line' may be, and usually is, adopted. The Ledger account is shown on p. 0517.

In examination work the precise words used in the Trial Balance should be carefully scrutinized because if the words 'Loan Interest RECEIVED' are employed, the accrued and accruing amounts given in the question are *not* part of the balancing figures; if, on the other hand, the words 'Loan Interest RECEIVED AND ACCRUED (and/or ACCRUING)' are employed, the account has already been adjusted and the accrual is a DEBIT in the books; hence it is part of the Trial Balance, calling for no further adjustment. In the former instance, where the loan interest shown is only the amount received, the adjustment must be made.

LOAN INTEREST

19.1			£	19.1			£
Dec. 31	Profit and Loss Account .		136	Dec. 31	(details) . . .		100
					Loan Interest Accrued to		
					30th Nov., 19.1 . . c/d		30
					Loan Interest Accruing . c/d		6
			£136				£136
19.2							
Jan. 1	Loan Interest Accrued	b/d	30[1]				
	Loan Interest Accruing	b/d	6[1]				

[1] Shown as an asset in the Balance Sheet.

4. Expenses Stock

When stock is held other than of goods for resale, e.g. advertising or stationery stock, it should always be dealt with in the account to which it relates. It will therefore be included in the particular expense figure in the Profit and Loss Account and *not* in the stock of goods figure in the Trading Account. Thus, if the Trial Balance shows:

	£
Opening Stock (Stationery) . .	100
Stationery Purchases . .	470

and as a note (not in the Trial Balance) closing stock of £70, the Profit and Loss Account will show a net debit of £500, i.e. £100 + £470 − £70, and the Balance Sheet, Stationery Stock £70 as an asset. If the closing stock is shown as part of the Trial Balance it presupposes that the Stationery Account has been fully dealt with, and in reference to the preceding illustration the Trial Balance would in these circumstances show:

	£	
Stationery Account . . .	500	(Profit and Loss Account)
Stationery Stock (Closing) . .	70	(Balance Sheet)

In the Expense Account itself, the entries for stock will be a credit 'above the line' and a debit 'below the line,' thus:

STATIONERY

19..			£	19..			£
Jan. 1	Stock . . . b/d		100	Dec. 31	Stock . . . . c/d		70
Dec. 31	Purchases . . .		470		Profit and Loss Account .		500
			£570				£570
19..							
Jan. 1	Stock . . . . b/d		70[1]				

[1] Shown as an Asset in the Balance Sheet.

5. Provisions for Depreciation, Bad Debts and Discounts

(a) **Depreciation.** In normal circumstances the question of providing for depreciation is deferred until the Trial Balance is extracted and hence will not have been dealt with prior to the preparation of the final accounts. In examination work a note will be appended to the question stating the rate of depreciation to be provided. As the purpose at present is to explain the methods of entry of adjustments detailed consideration of depreciation is dealt with in Chapter 07, but in order to present the student with a rough conception of its nature, it may be stated that depreciation is the inherent decline in the value of an asset from any cause whatever. The wearing out of a machine is a simple and obvious example, but it must be emphasized that this is but one of many causes. As with all other entries, there must be complete double-entry for the depreciation adjustment. The required entry is: debit Trading and Profit and Loss Account and credit the Asset, in respect of which depreciation is being recorded. This entry conforms with the principles already enunciated in that the debit to Trading and Profit and Loss Account is necessary because the amount written off represents an expense and the credit to the asset is required as the asset has, *pro tanto*, been reduced in value.

As there are usually several assets which must be treated in a similar manner it is not unusual to make the transfer for depreciation to a Depreciation Account and transfer the whole of that account representing the depreciation of several assets to the Trading and Profit and Loss Account.

The following would be the Journal entries for Depreciation, assuming that an amount of £100 is to be written off Plant.

JOURNAL

19..		£	£
Dec. 31	Trading and Profit and Loss Account	100	
	Plant		100
	Being Depreciation for the year ended this date.		

If the Depreciation Account is employed in preference to the direct transfer as above, the entries would be:

JOURNAL

19..		£	£
Dec. 31	Depreciation	100	
	Plant		100
	Being Depreciation for the year ended this date.		
	Trading and Profit and Loss Account[1]	100	
	Depreciation		100
	Being Depreciation transferred		

[1] See p. 0519 (end of first paragraph).

Depreciation dealt with before extracting the Trial Balance will appear among the accounts therein. The asset will already have been credited with the amount of depreciation and the necessary debit to depreciation made, so that only the formal transfer to Trading and Profit and Loss Account is required. Reverting to the above example the only entry required will be that marked ([1]).

These points may be further illustrated by an example:

Illustration 9

Fixtures Account at 1st January 19.., appears in the books at £500 and 5 per cent Depreciation is to be written off. If no depreciation has been written off for the year prior to the extraction of the Trial Balance, the amount standing in the books against Fixtures of £500 will appear in the Trial Balance at 31st December 19... In order to write off depreciation an entry to the debit of Trading and Profit and Loss Account and to the credit of Fixtures Account will be required; or, the depreciation may be first debited to Depreciation Account and credited to Fixtures, and then transferred to the Trading and Profit and Loss Account.

On the other hand, if depreciation has been dealt with *prior* to the extraction of the Trial Balance, the Trial Balance will not show Fixtures Account as £500 (for £25 has already been credited to it by way of depreciation), but as £475, and Depreciation Account will be part of the Trial Balance at the figure of £25. Hence, instead of Fixtures £500 there will be Fixtures £475 and Depreciation Account £25. Upon preparing the Trading and Profit and Loss Account the amount of £25 debited in the Depreciation Account will be transferred to the former account by the following entry: debit Trading and Profit and Loss Account, credit Depreciation Account.

If the asset is to stay in the books at cost, the entries are:

> Debit Depreciation Account (or Profit and Loss Account).
> Credit Depreciation Provision or Fund Account.[1]

Where cash is invested outside the business to ensure that when replacement is required, the necessary CASH will be available, the following additional entries will be made:

> Debit Depreciation Investment Fund.
> Credit Bank.

Depreciation is usually computed at a certain rate per annum, e.g. 10 per cent per annum. The student must exercise great care in the calculation, when the period covered by the accounts is not a year, for when the accounts are prepared half-yearly the depreciation would be 5 per cent actual. Examiners often omit the term 'per annum,' so that if the *actual* rate is given, the amount to be calculated for depreciation will require

---

[1] This may also be referred to as 'Depreciation Reserve.' The difference between the terms Provision and Reserve is dealt with in Chapter 07. The distinction is important in Limited Company accounts, but the student may find it useful to accustom himself to the terms by using them also in the accounts of sole traders and partnerships.

adjusting accordingly. For example, if accounts are prepared half-yearly, depreciation at 15 per cent per annum will mean $7\frac{1}{2}$ per cent for the half year; but if the words 'per annum' are omitted, depreciation in that half-year will be 15 per cent instead of $7\frac{1}{2}$ per cent, that is at the rate of 30 per cent per annum.

Where assets have been acquired during the period covered by the accounts, depreciation should be charged upon the new assets from the date of acquisition to the end of the accounting period. In the examination, if no indication is given as to the date of acquisition, depreciation should be calculated on the closing balance, and an explanatory note made at the foot of the answer. The newly acquired asset may be an ADDITION to the existing assets, or may be merely a REPLACEMENT. In the latter case the book value of the old asset must be completely eliminated by crediting it with:

(i) Loss on Sale (if a profit the entry will be a debit).
(ii) Depreciation to the date the asset ceases to be used.
(iii) Proceeds of Sale.

If any costs should be incurred, for example on dismantling plant, these also will appear as a debit to the old Asset Account. Thus:

PLANT

		£			£
Balance.	b/d	150	Sale		10
Cost of Dismantling		22	Depreciation (to date of ceasing to be used)		20
			Profit and Loss Account (Loss on Sale)		142
		£172			£172

If the sale realized, say £210 the account would be:

PLANT

		£			£
Balance	b/d	150	Sale		210
Cost of Dismantling		22	Depreciation.		20
Profit and Loss Account (Profit on Sale)		58			
		£230			£230

Illustration 10

Period of accounts 1st June 19.. to 31st December 19.. (i.e. **seven months**).

	£
Plant and Machinery Balance, 1st June 19.. .	8,000
Plant and Machinery purchased 1st October 19.. .	2,000

Depreciation to be calculated at 6 per cent per annum.

The amount of depreciation is:

		£
6% on £8,000 for 7 months	. . . . .	280
6% on £2,000 for 3 months	. . . . .	30
		£310

[6% per annum = £0·05 (or 5p) per £10 per month.]

Plant and Machinery Account will appear as follows:

PLANT AND MACHINERY

19..				£	19..				£
June 1	Balance . .	b/d		8,000	Dec. 31	Depreciation . . .			310
Oct. 1	Cash (or Creditor) . .			2,000		Balance. . . .	c/d		9,690
				£10,000					£10,000
19..									
Jan. 1	Balance. . .	b/d		9,690					

Depreciation is dealt with in more detail in Chapter 07.

(*b*) **Bad and Doubtful Debts.** The provision for bad and doubtful debts is usually made by taking a suitable percentage on Sundry Debtors[1] and when computed the amount will be entered twice in the Bad and Doubtful Debts Account:

(i) On the debit side above the 'line,' and
(ii) On the credit side below the 'line.'

The latter figure will be shown either as a liability, or as a *deduction from* **Debtors on the assets side of the Balance Sheet. The latter method is more frequently used in modern accounting.**

Where separate accounts for Bad Debts and Provision for Bad and Doubtful Debts are kept, and it is required to carry forward to the next period a revised provision based upon a percentage of Sundry Debtors, the following steps must be taken:

1. The balance of Bad Debts Account, that is bad debts actually WRITTEN OFF, less bad debts that have been recouped, is transferred to the debit of Provision for Bad and Doubtful Debts, or to the credit of that account if recoveries exceed amounts written off.

2. The new Bad and Doubtful Debts Provision will be debited above the 'line' and credited below it in the Provision Account.

3. The balance will be dealt with thus:

(*a*) if DEBIT, the transfer will be—Debit Profit and Loss Account and Credit Provision for Bad and Doubtful Debts.
(*b*) if CREDIT, the transfer will be—Debit Provision for Bad and Doubtful Debts and Credit Profit and Loss Account.

[1] Alternatively the Bad and Doubtful Debts Provision may be based on an estimate of the worth of each debt at the balance sheet date or be taken as a percentage on *credit* sales. (Usually the former is preferred, as it is more accurate, and being specific, will be allowed for taxation purposes.)

Illustration 11

The following figures relate to the books of a trader.

Bad and Doubtful Debts Provision at 1st January 19..   .   Cr. £800
Bad debts written off during the year to 31st December 19..   .   Dr. £900

The Provision is to be maintained at 5 per cent of Sundry Debtors, which at 31st December 19.., is £20,000.

The Bad and Doubtful Debts Provision will be:

PROVISION FOR BAD AND DOUBTFUL DEBTS

19.. Dec. 31	Bad Debts written off Balance. . . .	c/d	£ 900 1,000	19.. Jan. 1 Dec. 31	Balance. . . . Profit and Loss Account .	b/d	£ 800 1,100
			£1,900				£1,900
				19.. Jan. 1	Balance. . . .	b/d	1,000

BAD DEBTS

19.. Dec. 31	Debtors (detailed) . .		£ 900	19.. Dec. 31	Transfer to Provision for Bad and Doubtful Debts		£ 900

It will be apparent that the 'clearance' may be effected by transferring *from* Bad Debts Provision *to* Bad Debts Account and to this alternative no objection can legitimately be raised. Eliminating dates the accounts would appear:

PROVISION FOR BAD AND DOUBTFUL DEBTS

Balance. . . .	c/d	£ 1,000	Balance . . Transfer to Bad Debts Account . .	b/d	£ 800 200
		£1,000			£1,000
			Balance. . . .	b/d	1,000

BAD DEBTS

Debtors (detailed) . Transfer from Bad and Doubtful Debts Provision . .	£ 900 200	Profit and Loss Account	£ 1,100
	£1,100		£1,100

Alternative Treatment of Bad Debts. A consolidated account is often used whereby the provision is raised and adjusted in the Bad Debts

Account, thus dispensing with the separate account, as below:

BAD DEBTS

			£				£
(details, etc.) . . .			900	Provision . . .	b/d		800
Provision . . .	c/d		1,000	Profit and Loss Account .			1,100
			£1,900				£1,900
				Provision . . .	b/d		1,000

(c) **Discounts.** Where a Provision for Discounts is to be created on Sundry Debtors, the object is to charge against the current period the estimated cash discounts that will be ordinarily allowed to debtors on sales during the period, and which will involve a reduction in the Balance Sheet of the book value of debtors. Naturally, such a discount will be allowed only upon payment being made within the period stipulated expressly or impliedly in the contract, so that it is **usually not necessary to provide for discounts on all the debtors,** and further it is clear that if a debtor's account is written off as bad no provision for discount is required. It is therefore important that the discount provision be calculated on the proportion of debtors likely to be 'good', that is, not merely those who will pay 'sooner or later' but the prompt payers. As a matter of caution, it is the practice generally to assume that the proportion of debtors who are likely to pay will pay promptly and take advantage of the discount terms. **Therefore, before making the Discount Provision the estimate of bad and doubtful debts must FIRST be made and provided for, and the Discount Provision created on the** *balance* **of debtors; in other words, on the estimated 'good' debtors, being the debtors according to the ledger less the Provision for Bad and Doubtful Debts.**[1]

It is usual to confine the creation and adjustment of the *Discount* Provision to the last method shown in relation to bad debts, i.e. the consolidated account.

Illustration 12

	£
Discounts allowed during the year to 31st December 19.. .	1,200
Discount Provision at 1st January 19..	270
Debtors (none likely to be bad) at 31st December 19.. . .	6,000
Discount Provision to be 5%.	

DISCOUNTS ALLOWED

19..				£	19..				£
Dec. 31	Sundries from Cash Book			1,200	Jan. 1	Provision . . .	b/d		270
	Provision . . .	c/d		300	Dec. 31	Profit and Loss Account .			1,230
				£1,500					£1,500
					19..				
					Jan. 1	Provision . . .	b/d		300

[1] The same principle must be followed in respect of Goods out on Sale or Return (see p. 0529).

If, however, it is estimated that 20 per cent of the £6,000 are likely to be bad, the Bad and Doubtful Debts Provision would be adjusted to £1,200, leaving £4,800 as the BASIS of the Discount Provision; so that the Provision of £300 as computed above would be 5 per cent of £4,800 = £240, the account being as follows:

DISCOUNTS ALLOWED

19..			£	19..			£
Dec. 31	Sundries from Cash Book Provision	c/d	1,200 240	Jan. 1 Dec. 31	Provision . . Profit and Loss Account .	b/d	270 1,170
			£1,440				£1,440
				19.. Jan. 1	Provision . .	b/d	240

The Balance Sheet at 31st December 19.., would, as far as Debtors are concerned, appear:

	£	£
Sundry Debtors	6,000	
Less Provision for Bad and Doubtful Debts[1] (20%) .	1,200	
	4,800	
Less Provision for Discounts[1] (5% of £4,800) . .	240	
		4,560

Illustration 13

The following figures appear in the books of Y:

	£
19..	
Jan. 1. Bad and Doubtful Debts Provision	1,200
Discounts Allowed Provision	560
Dec. 31. Discounts Allowed during year	930
Bad Debts written off	470
Bad Debts recovered	25
Debtors (per Ledger)	10,060

Write off a further £240 (definitely bad).
Create a Discounts Allowed Provision of 3 per cent.
Create a Bad and Doubtful Debts Provision of 10 per cent. Show Accounts: calculate to nearest £.

The accounts are:

PROVISION FOR BAD AND DOUBTFUL DEBTS

19..			£	19..			£
Dec. 31	Balance. . . Bad Debts . .	c/d	982 218	Jan. 1	Balance. . .	b/d	1,200
			£1,200				£1,200
				19.. Jan. 1	Balance. . .	b/d	982

[1] These items are CREDITS in the books, and instead of being shown as liabilities are DEDUCTED from the asset.

BAD DEBTS

19.. Dec. 31			£	19.. Dec. 31			£
	(details)		470		(details) Bad Debts Re- covered[1]		25
	Sundry Debtors written off		240		Bad Debt Provision		218
	Profit and Loss Account		25		Profit and Loss Account		492
			£ 735				£ 735

[1] The debit is to cash; or alternatively the treatment is:

Debit cash; Credit Personal Account.
Debit Personal Account; Credit Bad Debts Account.

DISCOUNTS ALLOWED

19.. Dec. 31			£	19..			£
	Sundries		930	Jan. 1	Provision	b/d	560
	Provision	c/d	265	Dec. 31	Profit and Loss Account		635
			£1,195				£1,195
				19.. Jan. 1	Provision	b/d	265

SUNDRY DEBTORS

19.. Dec. 31			£	19.. Dec. 31			£
	Detailed Ledger Accounts		10,060		Bad Debts		240
					Balances	c/d	9,820
			£10,060				£10,060
19.. Jan. 1	Balances	b/d	9,820				

Notes. 1. The Bad and Doubtful Debts Provision would be created on the value of the debtors as shown in the books at 31st December 19.., i.e 10% of £9,820.
2. The Discount Provision is 3% on:

	£
Book Value of the Debtors	9,820
Less Bad and Doubtful Debts Provision	982
	£8,838
∴ 3% on £8,838 (taken to nearest £) =	£265

These Provisions will then appear in the Balance Sheet in the following manner:

ASSETS SIDE

	£	£
Sundry Debtors	9,820	
Less Provision for Bad and Doubtful Debts (10%)	982	
	8,838	
Less Provision for Discounts (3% of £8,838)	265	
		8,573

(*d*) **Loan Interest.** The lender of money usually requires a reward for the use by the borrower of the sum loaned, the amount of which varies with circumstances. Such a reward is termed Interest and it is customary in normal circumstances to stipulate for the payment of loan interest at stated periods, yearly or half-yearly. Hence, if accounts are drawn up at a date other than that of the due date of the payment of the loan interest (assuming that the borrower pays promptly), an adjustment is required to cover the loan interest accruing since the last due date.

The same principle applies in connexion with other expenses, viz. that a charge may be required in respect of an amount ACCRUED (unless this should happen to be paid on the due date) and an amount ACCRUING in respect of the period elapsing from the due date of the loan interest and the date to which the accounts are made up.

Illustration 14

Trial Balance at 31st January 19.., shows (*inter alia*):

	£
Loan Account (*Cr.*) at 6% per annum . . .	100,000
Loan Interest (*Dr.*)	3,000

It is quite evident that, assuming the loan was made at least a year ago, there is accrued a half-year's interest and consequently the required adjustment is:

	£
Debit Loan Interest Account above the 'line' . .	3,000
Credit Loan Interest Account below the 'line' . .	3,000

The latter being a credit balance in the books will be shown in the Balance Sheet at 31st January 19.., as a liability, either as a separate item or with the loan, thus:

	£	£
Loan Account	100,000	
Add Interest to date	3,000	
		103,000

The Loan Interest of £6,000 for the year will be transferred in the usual way to the debit of Profit and Loss Account.

Illustration 15

A borrowed £5,000 on 30th April 19.1, agreeing to pay interest at the rate of 4 per cent per annum, on the 31st October and the 30th April in each year. He prepares his accounts yearly on 31st December. Show Loan Interest Account in A's books for the years ended 31st December 19.1 and 19.2. It may be assumed that the payments are made promptly on the due dates.

LOAN INTEREST[1]

			£p				£p
19.1				19.1			
Oct. 31	Cash: Half-year's Interest to date		100·00	Dec. 31	Profit and Loss Account		133·33
Dec. 31	Interest accruing, 2 months	c/d	33·33				
			£133·33				£133·33
19.2				19.2			
Apl. 30	Cash: Half-year's Interest to date		100·00	Jan. 1	Interest accruing	b/d	33·33
Oct. 31	Cash: do.		100·00	Dec. 31	Profit and Loss Account		200·00
Dec. 31	Interest accruing, 2 months	c/d	33·33				
			£233·33				£233·33
				19.3			
				Jan. 1	Interest accruing	b/d	33·33

[1] In practice, Income-tax is deducted from each payment of Interest. This does not affect the principle above outlined and treatment of Income-tax in this connection is dealt with in Chapter 21.

If in 19.3 the borrower pays only the half-year's interest to 30th April, 19.3, the half-yearly amount due on 31st October, 19.3, being paid on 10th January 19.4, the account for 19.3 and 19.4 (assuming the 19.4 payments are met promptly) would be:

LOAN INTEREST

			£p				£p
19.3				19.3			
Apl. 30	Cash: Half-year's Interest to date		100·00	Jan. 1	Interest accruing	b/d	33·33
Dec. 31	Half-year's Interest to 31st October, 19.3, ACCRUED	c/d	100·00	Dec. 31	Profit and Loss Account		200·00
	Interest accruing, 2 months	c/d	33·33				
			£233·33				£233·33
19.4				19.4			
Jan. 10	Cash: Half-year's Interest to 31st Oct., 19.3		100·00	Jan. 1	Half-year's Interest to 31st Oct., 19.3, ACCRUED	b/d	100·00
Apl. 30	Cash: do. to date		100·00		Interest accruing	b/d	33·33
Oct. 31	Cash: do. to date		100·00	Dec. 31	Profit and Loss Account		200·00
Dec. 31	Interest accruing, 2 months	c/d	33·33				
			£333·33				£333·33
				19.5			
				Jan. 1	Interest accruing	b/d	33·33

Where repayments of the loan itself have taken place it will be necessary to ascertain the date of repayment as the adjustment for loan interest accrued or accruing will be modified accordingly.

Illustration 16

Reverting to the preceding example, on 1st August 19.5, the borrower repays £1,000 and the interest payments are made promptly at due dates.

The calculation of the accrual at 31st December 19.5, will be thus:

Two months' interest accruing on £4,000 at 4% per annum, viz.
£26·67

Moreover, the Loan Interest paid 31st October 19.5, will be:

	£
Three months' Interest on £5,000 at 4% per annum, that is, for the period between 1st May, 19.5, and 31st July, 19.5	50
Three months' Interest on £4,000 at 4% per annum, that is, for the period between 1st August, 19.5, and 31st October, 19.5	40
Payment of Loan Interest on 31st October, 19.5 . . .	£90

The account would be continued in 19.5, as follows:

LOAN INTEREST

19.5				£p	19.5				£p
Apl. 30	Cash: Half-year's Interest to date . . .			100·00	Jan. 1	Interest accruing . .	b/d		33·33
Oct. 31	Cash: do . . .			90·00	Dec. 31	Profit and Loss Account[1]			183·34
Dec. 31	Interest accruing, 2 months . .	c/d		26·67					
				£216·67					£216·67
					19.6				
					Jan. 1	Interest accruing . .	b/d		26·67

[1] i.e. Interest for 7 months on £5,000 (£116·67) plus Interest for 5 months on £4,000 (£66·67) at 4 per cent per annum.

The repayment of the principal would be debited to the Loan Account.

In the books of the lender the entries will be exactly opposite to the above.

If an Expenses Day Book or Journal is used the interest *accrued* will have passed through the books; hence an adjustment is required only for items *accruing*.

6. Transfers

As the correction of errors requires detailed treatment (see Chapter 14) all that need be stated here is that the transfer required will conform to ordinary double-entry principles, a simple illustration sufficing for the present.

Illustration 17

An amount of £10 is paid for decorations to the private house of a trader, such amount being paid by cheque on the business banking account and debited to General Expenses. The correcting entries are:

	£
Debit Drawings (or Capital) Account . . .	10
Credit General Expenses	10

It is important also that abnormal or exceptional items or expenses should be shown quite clearly and separately in the accounts and not merged with normal items or expenses.

CONSIDERATION OF INDIVIDUAL ITEMS

There is no uniform practice as to which items should be included in the Trading and which in the Profit and Loss section of the final account. Each case must be considered on its own merits. In manufacturing concerns, a Manufacturing or Working Account is often employed either in addition to or instead of a Trading Account: these will be considered later in Chapter 23. In non-manufacturing concerns where goods are purchased for resale, and in manufacturing concerns where no separate Manufacturing or Working Account is prepared, the Trading Account should include only those expenses which are directly attributable to putting the goods in a saleable condition: all selling, distribution and overhead expenses will be included in the Profit and Loss Account. The most important point is that treatment must be consistent so that the rate of Gross Profit may be compared from one period to another.

1. Stock. Opening and Closing Stock of goods held for sale will be included in the Trading Account as already described. It is important that these items be confined to stock of goods purchased for resale or for manufacturing into saleable condition. This will exclude the following:

(*a*) *Expenses Stock.* This has already been dealt with (see p. 0517).

(*b*) *Stock in Special Circumstances.* Goods which are in possession of the trader are not necessarily his property, e.g. they may be goods received on sale or return, on consignment for sale, or as agent. The treatment will vary according to circumstances, but it may be stated as a general rule that unless the goods have been definitely purchased they should be excluded from the stock; and if they have been definitely purchased a corresponding entry will be, or ought to have been, made in the Purchases Account, Conversely, when goods have been bought and the seller dates forward the invoice (e.g. goods bought on 15th July 19.., may be invoiced as on 15th August 19..) the purchase should be duly recorded in July and the goods included in stock (unless sold), as such arrangement is merely one whereby the purchaser obtains extended credit.

Thus, the following goods must *not* be included in Stock:

1. Goods held by the business as agent or consignee, or sold awaiting delivery to the purchaser.

2. Goods held by the business as security.

3. Goods out on Sale or Return, when the title thereto has passed to the sendee.

Conversely, the following *must* be included:

1. Goods purchased and entered, including goods in transit or stored.

2. Goods purchased and entered which are in the hands of agents and consignees, or held as security.

3. Goods purchased and entered which are out on Sale or Return unless the title thereto has passed to the sendee. [If already entered out as Sales, an entry must be made to eliminate the sale, e.g. by debiting Sales and crediting Goods out on Sale or Return, the latter being deducted from Debtors in the Balance Sheet (see Chapter 09).]

4. Goods at Branches, unless dealt with in separate Branch Accounts.

Stocktaking. Where practicable Stock should be taken on the expiry of the business accounting period. Often this is not possible and the actual stocktaking may have to be done during the last day of the year, or may extend into the next few succeeding days.

In many retail businesses the Stock is evaluated at the retail selling prices and reduced to cost by a deduction of the gross profit percentage on selling prices, otherwise the valuation will be at cost.

In all cases the necessary revision to net realizable value if lower than cost will be required.

The principles to be followed are:

(a) That the goods purchased and the invoices therefor are passed through the books in the same accounting period, so that the liability is taken into account in the same accounting period as the appropriate asset.

(b) That where goods are sold, although not actually delivered, they should be included in the Sales but excluded from stock.

(c) That where goods, although not in its physical possession, belong to the business they must be included in Stock (and Rule 1 observed).

(d) Where Stocktaking takes place during the time sales are being effected, care must be taken to avoid inclusion of goods as Stock on hand and in the Cash (or Debtors), e.g. if a retailer takes Stock during, say, the last day of the year the Cash received in respect of goods taken into Stock must be reduced to Cost and deleted from Stock; if the Stocktaking takes place during the *day after* the close of the accounting period the whole of the takings for that day must be added to Stock either at cost, or, if evaluations are based on retail selling prices less percentage deduction, then the cash takings augment the Stock at selling price and the deduction is taken from the total.

Illustration 18

X's financial year ends on the last Wednesday in September, but actual stock is not taken until the following Saturday, when it is ascertained at £33,500. You find that:

1. Sales are entered in the Sales Journal on the same day as despatched, and Returns Inwards in the Returns Journal the day the goods are received back.

2. Purchases are entered in the Purchases Journal as the invoices are received.

3. Sales between the Wednesday and Saturday per Sales Journal and Cash Sales Book were £1,720.

4. Purchases between the Wednesday and Saturday per the Purchases Journal were £120, but, of these, goods amounting to £40 were not received until after the stock was taken.

5. Goods invoiced during September (prior to the last Wednesday) but not received until after the Wednesday amounted to £100 of which £70 worth were received between the Wednesday and Saturday.

6. Goods sold in the previous week £60 were returned on the Monday but did not reach X until the Thursday.

7. The rate of Gross Profit to Sales is 25 per cent.

Ascertain the value of the stock at the end of the financial year, assuming that the net realizable value is higher than cost and that the Purchases and Sales Journals are not to be amended.

CALCULATION OF STOCK VALUE AT LAST WEDNESDAY IN SEPTEMBER

	£	£
Stock (Saturday following)		33,500
Add Sales (Wednesday–Saturday)	1,720	
Less Gross Profit (25%)	430	
		1,290
		34,790
Less Purchases entered (Wednesday–Saturday) . .	120	
Less received after stocktaking . . .	40	
		80
		34,710
Add Goods invoiced September prior to the last Wednesday not received until after stocktaking		30
		34,740
Less Returns Inwards not entered in current financial period		45
Stock value at close of current financial period . . .		£34,695

It will be observed that all the entries from the Journals except (6) (see below) had been made to the Wednesday when the year ended, so that no adjustments are required in the Ledgers.

As to (3), the addition to the stock is the goods sold since Wednesday to restore it to the position on that day.

As to (4), all these purchases relate to the *next* period, so that if any goods are received between Wednesday and Saturday they must be eliminated. This figure is £120 less £40 received *after* Saturday, i.e. £80.

As to (5), all these purchases belong to the financial period ended Wednesday, so that any 'late' deliveries must be added to stock. Those actually delivered between Wednesday and Saturday will automatically have been taken into stock, i.e. £70; but those which have been delivered after Saturday, i.e. £30, are not included in stock and so must be added.

As to (6), the goods returned are included in stock at a cost price of £45, so that they are included both in Stock and Debtors. Stock should therefore be reduced by £45, but as the amount in the Debtors is still at the selling price of £60, a provision of £15 should be made. The better treatment, however, which can be effected without amending the Sales Journal or the Returns Journal is to:

(1) make no amendment to the stock figure, so that the deduction above of £45 would not be required; and

(2) adjust the Sales Account for the returned goods at selling price in the same way as making an entry for an accrual, thus:

SALES

		£			£
Returns . . .			Sales		
Trading Account .					
Returns unentered .	c/d	60			
		£			£
			Returns unentered . .	b/d	60

The £60 would be deducted from the Debtors' total for Balance Sheet purposes. If the goods were returned by the purchaser on the Thursday, the deduction of £45 without any further adjustment would be correct.

Stock Valuation. The valuation of stock, which embraces stock in trade and work in progress, in the final accounts of business concerns requires careful consideration, and particularly so in the case of the published accounts of limited companies. The importance attached to valuation of stock is emphasized by paragraph 11 (8B) of Schedule 2 of the Companies Act 1967, which states that if the amount carried forward for stock in trade or work in progress is material for the appreciation by its members of the company's state of affairs or of its profit or loss for the financial year the MANNER IN WHICH THAT AMOUNT HAS BEEN COMPUTED MUST BE STATED. It should be appreciated that whilst the foregoing requirement applies to the published accounts of limited companies its importance regarding the final accounts of all other business concerns cannot be overstressed. However, circumstances vary so widely that no single basis of stock valuation is suitable for all types of business concerns, but unless the basis adopted is appropriate to the circumstances of the particular business concern and is used consistently from period to period, the final accounts will not give a true and fair view either of the state of affairs of the business concern at balance sheet date or of the trend of its trading results from period to period.

Statement of Standard Accounting Practice. Statement of Standard Accounting Practice 1/9 concerns Stocks and Work in Progress and is largely reproduced hereunder:

1. **Explanatory Note**

Introduction

1. The determination of profit for an accounting year requires the matching of costs with related revenues. The cost of unsold or uncon-sumed stocks and work in progress will have been incurred in the expectation of future revenue, and when this will not arise until a later year it is appropriate to carry forward this cost to be matched with the

revenue when it arises; the applicable concept is the matching of cost and revenue in the year in which the revenue arises rather than in the year in which the cost is incurred. If there is no reasonable expectation of sufficient future revenue to cover cost incurred, (e.g. as a result of deterioration, obsolescence or a change in demand), the irrecoverable cost should be charged to revenue in the year under review. Thus stocks and work in progress normally need to be stated at cost, or, if lower, at net realizable value.

2. The comparison of cost and net realizable value needs to be made in respect of each item of stock separately. Where this is impracticable, groups or categories of stock items which are similar will need to be taken together. To compare the total realizable value of stocks with the total cost could result in an unacceptable setting off of foreseeable losses against unrealized profits.

3. In order to match costs and revenue, 'costs' of stocks and work in progress should comprise that expenditure which has been incurred in the normal course of business in bringing the product or service to its present location and condition. Such costs will include all related production overheads, even though these may accrue on a time basis.

4. The methods used in allocating costs to stocks and work in progress need to be selected with a view to providing the fairest possible approximation to the expenditure actually incurred in bringing the product to its present location and condition. For example, in the case of retail stores holding a large number of rapidly changing individual items, stocks on the shelves have often been stated at current selling prices less the normal gross profit margin. In these particular circumstances this may be acceptable as being the only practical method of arriving at a figure which approximates to cost.

Net realizable value

5. Net realizable value is the amount at which it is expected that items of stocks and work in progress can be disposed of without creating either profit or loss in the year of sale, i.e. the estimated proceeds of sale less all further costs to completion and less all costs to be incurred in marketing, selling and distributing directly related to the items in question.

Replacement cost

6. Items of stock and work in progress have sometimes been stated in accounts at estimated replacement cost where this is lower than net realizable value. Where the effect is to take account of a loss greater than that which is expected to be incurred, the use of replacement cost is not regarded as acceptable. However, in some circumstances (e.g. in the case of materials whose price has fluctuated considerably and which have not become the subject of firm sales contracts by the time the accounts are prepared) replacement cost may be the best measure of net realizable value.

Long-term contract work in progress

7. Separate consideration needs to be given to work in progress arising from long-term contracts. Owing to the length of time taken to complete such contracts, to defer taking profit into account until completion may result in the profit and loss account reflecting not so much a fair view of the activity of the company during the year but rather the results relating to contracts which have been completed by the year end. It is, therefore, appropriate to take credit for ascertainable profit while contracts are in progress.

8. The profit, if any, taken up needs to reflect the proportion of the work carried out at the accounting date and should take into account any known inequalities of profitability in the various stages of a contract. Many businesses, however, carry out contracts where the outcome cannot reasonably be assessed before the conclusion of the contract and in such cases it is prudent not to take up any profit. Where the business carries out contracts and it is considered that their outcome can be assessed with reasonable certainty before their conclusion, then the attributable profit should be taken up, but the judgement involved should be exercised with prudence.

9. If, however, it is expected that there will be a loss on a contract as a whole, provision needs to be made (in accordance with the prudence concept), for the whole of the loss as soon as it is recognized. This has the effect of reducing the work done to date to its net realizable value. Where unprofitable contracts are of such magnitude that they can be expected to absorb a considerable part of the company's capacity for a substantial period, related administration overheads to be incurred during the period to the completion of those contracts should also be included in the calculation of the provision for losses.

10. Thus, the gross amount of long-term contract work in progress should be stated in accounts at cost plus attributable profits (if any) less foreseeable losses (if any). In arriving at a decision as to whether there are attributable profits, a company should consider whether, having regard to the nature of the contracts undertaken, it is reasonable to foresee profits in advance of the completion of the contracts.

Disclosure in accounts

11. A suitable description of the amount at which stocks and work in progress are stated in accounts might be 'at the lower of cost and net realizable value' or, in the case of long-term contract work in progress 'at cost plus attributable profit [if any] less foreseeable losses [if any] and progress payments received and receivable'.

12. In order to give an adequate explanation of the affairs of the company the accounting policies followed in arriving at the amount at which stocks and work in progress are stated in the accounts should be set out in a note. Where differing bases have been adopted for different types of stocks and work in progress the amount included in the accounts in respect of each type will need to be stated.

13. In the case of long-term contract work in progress, the terms of a contract usually involve progress payments which reduce the amount at which the contract is stated in the accounts. The financial position of a company may be materially dependent on the outcome of such contracts despite this lessening of their apparent significance. A related note should, therefore, indicate the amount of progress payments received and receivable separately from the net amount of cost plus attributable profit, less foreseeable losses as appropriate.

2. Definition of Terms

14. The following definitions of terms are used for the purpose of this Statement.

Stocks and work in progress

15. Stocks and work in progress comprise:
(a) goods or other assets purchased for resale;
(b) consumable stores;
(c) raw materials and components purchased for incorporation into products for sale;
(d) products and services in intermediate stages of completion; and
(e) finished goods.

Cost

16. Cost is defined in relation to the different categories of stocks and work in progress as being that expenditure which has been incurred in the normal course of business in bringing the product or service to its present location and condition. This expenditure should include, in addition to cost of purchase (as defined in paragraph 17) such costs of conversion (as defined in paragraph 18) as are appropriate to that location and condition.

Cost of purchase

17. Cost of purchase comprises purchase price including import duties, transport and handling costs and any other directly attributable costs, less trade discounts, rebates and subsidies.

Cost of conversion

18. This comprises:
(a) costs which are specifically attributable to units of production, i.e. direct labour, direct expenses and sub-contracted work;
(b) production overheads (as defined in paragraph 19); and
(c) other overheads, if any, attributable in the particular circumstances of the business to bringing the product or service to its present location and condition.

Production overheads

19. Production overheads comprise overheads incurred in respect of materials, labour or services for production, based on the normal level of activity, taking one year with another. For this purpose each overhead should be classified according to function (e.g. production, selling or administration) so as to ensure the inclusion in cost of conversion of those overheads (including depreciation) which relate to production, notwithstanding that these may accrue wholly or partly on a time basis.

Net realizable value

20. This is the actual or estimated selling price (net of trade but before settlement discounts) less:
   (a) all further costs to completion; and
   (b) all costs to be incurred in marketing, selling and distributing.

Long-term contract

21. A long-term contract is a contract entered into for manufacture or building of a single substantial entity or the provision of a service where the time taken to manufacture, build or provide is such that a substantial proportion of all such contract work will extend for a period exceeding one year.

Attributable profit

22. Attributable profit is that part of the total profit currently estimated to arise over the duration of the contract (after allowing for likely increases in costs so far as not recoverable under the terms of the contract) which fairly reflects the profit attributable to that part of the work performed at the accounting date. (There can be no attributable profit until the outcome of the contract can be assessed with reasonable certainty.)

Foreseeable losses

23. These are losses which are currently estimated to arise over the duration of the contract (after allowing for estimated remedial and maintenance costs, and increases in costs so far as not recoverable under the terms of the contract). This estimate is required irrespective of:
   (a) whether or not work has yet commenced on such contracts;
   (b) the proportion of work carried out at the accounting date; and
   (c) the amount of profits expected to arise on other contracts.

Standard Accounting Practice

24. The expressions used in this Statement of Standard Accounting Practice are defined in Part II of the Statement.

Stocks and work in progress other than long-term contract work in progress

25. The amount at which stocks and work in progress, other than long-term contract work in progress, are stated in periodic financial statements should be the total of the lower of cost and net realizable value of the separate items of stock and work in progress or of groups of similar items.

Long-term contract work in progress

26. The amount at which long-term contract work in progress is stated in periodic financial statements should be cost plus any attributable profit, less any foreseeable losses and progress payments received and receivable. If, however, anticipated losses on individual contracts exceed cost incurred to date less progress payments received and receivable, such excesses should be shown separately as provisions.

Disclosure in financial statements

27. The accounting policies which have been used in calculating cost, net realizable value, attributable profit and foreseeable losses (as appropriate) should be stated.

28. Stocks and work in progress should be sub-classified in balance sheets or in notes to the financial statements in a manner which is appropriate to the business and so as to indicate the amounts held in each of the main categories.

29. In relation to the amount at which long-term contracts are stated in the balance sheet there should be stated:

(*a*) the amount of work in progress at cost plus attributable profit, less foreseeable losses; and

(*b*) cash received and receivable at the accounting date as progress payments on account of contracts in progress.

In dealing with the application of the 'lower of cost or net realizable value' rule for example, there are two methods (to be applied consistently):

1. To list all the Stock and obtain the aggregate cost and aggregate net realizable value, taking the lower total into the final accounts, or

2. To take each item or batch at the lower of cost or net realizable value.[1]

---

[1] This method was approved for tax purposes in *C.I.R.* v. *Cock, Russell & Co., Ltd.*, and *Worthington* v. *Oceana Development Co., Ltd.*, when it was proved that it was the normal commercial practice.

Illustration 19

STOCK LIST

Item	Cost Price	Net Realizable Value
	£	£
1 . .	40	55
2 . .	62	23
3 . .	*131*	137
	etc.	etc.
	£233	£215

Under (1), the amount shown in the Net Realizable Value column would be taken as the valuation. Under (2), the value would be £194 (composed of each 'lower' item, shown above in italics).

2. Purchases. Goods purchased for sale, whether immediate or ultimate, are included under this heading. Returns Outward will be shown as a deduction from the Purchases Account, and it is of little consequence whether the Returns Outward are recorded in a Returns Outward Account and transferred separately to the Trading Account, or transferred to the Purchases Account and the net balance only of the latter account transferred to the Trading Account, so long as the Trading Account correctly discloses the net purchases.

The following adjustments are usually required in references to purchases (if the latter includes purchases of goods otherwise than for sale):

(*a*) *Purchases of fixtures, plant and other assets.* The adjusting entry is: debit Fixtures (or other assets), credit Purchases Account.

(*b*) *Purchases of goods for private use.* The adjusting entry is: debit Capital or Drawings Account, credit Purchases Account.

(*c*) *Purchases of stationery, advertising materials, and other 'Expense' stock.* Unless it has been separately recorded either by means of an Expenses Day Book or Journal, or a separate column in the Purchases Day Book or Journal, a transfer is necessary as follows:

Debit Stationery Account (or other expense item); credit Purchases Account.

Where the balances have been extracted and it is discovered that certain items of purchases have not been entered, it is usual to ascertain the total of such items and to pass an entry through on lines similar to those called for by an 'accrual item', i.e. debit above the 'line', credit below the 'line'. The former entry will augment the Purchases Account, and the latter will represent creditors and will be shown as such in the Balance Sheet. The detailed purchase items will be passed through the books on the first day of the new period.

Returns outward will be dealt with conversely.

Illustration 20

In the Trial Balance on 31st December 19.., are:

					Dr. £	Cr. £
Creditors	.	.	.	.		4,000
Purchases	.	.	.	.	12,000	

It is discovered after balancing off the books and preparing the Trial Balance that items to the sum of £500 have been omitted from the Purchases Journal. The adjustment will be as follows:

PURCHASES

19.. Dec. 31	Sundries (as per Trial Balance) . . . Purchases omitted from Purchases Journal .	c/d	£ 12,000 500	19.. Dec. 31	Trading Account . .		£ 12,500
			£12,500				£12,500
				19.. Jan. 1	Purchases omitted . .	b/d	500

The Balance Sheet will show Creditors:

				£	£
Per Ledger .	.	.	.	4,000	
,, Purchases Account	.	.	.	500	
					4,500

3. Carriage. It is customary to charge carriage inwards (i.e. carriage of goods purchased) to the Trading Account, and carriage outwards (i.e. carriage of goods sold) to the Profit and Loss Account. If the item represents an expense not connected with purchases or sales a transfer is required to the appropriate account; e.g. if carriage inwards includes carriage in respect of new fittings, an adjusting entry is made thus:

Debit Fittings Account; credit Carriage Inwards Account.

4. Wages. For the purpose of convenience, salaries will be dealt with hereunder. The terms are generally distinguished by their method of computation (i.e. a wage is calculated or paid in reference to a week, a salary to a month or year), but this distinction does not necessarily form the true criterion of the work performed.

Only those wages should be included in the Trading Account which are directly attributable to the purchase or production of goods for resale; selling, distribution, etc., wages are included in the Profit and Loss Account.

[1] See footnote on p. 0501.

The following points should be considered:

(*a*) **Wages and salaries, if incurred other than for the ordinary purposes of the business,** should be transferred to the account to which they really relate, e.g. wages paid to workmen, (i) for repairs, (ii) for construction of a machine, (iii) for private purposes. These should be transferred to (i) Repairs, (ii) Machinery Account, and (iii) Proprietor's Capital or Drawings Account, unless the business is that of executing repairs or constructing machinery and such work is done for customers.

(*b*) **Where employees,** owing to the nature of the employment, are **housed, fed and/or clothed** (as at a Club, Hotel or Hospital) a transfer should be made to the debit of Wages Account from the account to which the expense has in the first instance been debited. In many cases no entry whatever will have been made and hence an estimated figure will be taken and the result incorporated in the accounts; e.g. for meals of waiters: credit Provisions or Meals Account; debit Wages Account, unless it is desired to keep separate accounts for Staff Meals, etc.

(*c*) **Where wages or salaries are stated at a rate 'free of Income Tax,'** i.e. the employer pays the tax on behalf of the employee, the net amount payable to the employee must be 'grossed up' and it is this latter amount which must be debited to Wages Account. Such payments come under the system of P.A.Y.E. which is dealt with in Chapter 09 where a detailed illustration will be found.

(*d*) **Wages accruing** should be provided for.

(*e*) **Where wages are shown 'net' after deduction of National Insurance contributions borne by the employee,** a transfer should be made by debiting Wages and crediting the National Insurance Account. For example if the Trial Balance shows:

	£
Wages paid	17,250
National Insurance . . .	1,032

(the amount deducted from the employees being £516) a transfer will be made accordingly: debit wages £516; credit National Insurance, £516, the revised figures being:

	£
Wages	17,766
National Insurance . . .	516

5. Sales. This account will normally be made up of goods sold, less returns. The question of dealing with returns in the Trading Account is analogous to that relating to purchases. Where goods are out on consignment or sale or return, it is important to ascertain what part is really sold. That part sold and not paid for must be shown as DEBTORS (and not included in stock), that part unsold must be shown as STOCK at say, the lower of cost and net realizable value, and not as Debtors. Where a business sells goods on condition that the invoice shall be dated 'forward,' this is usually equivalent to giving the buyer extra credit, but so far as final accounts are concerned the transaction must be treated as a sale, hence passed through as sales and included in Debtors (but not included as Stock). Where the account includes realization of assets a transfer from Sales to the credit of the Asset Account will be required. It should be further observed in connection with the sale of an asset that a resultant transfer will be almost inevitable, i.e. writing off any profit or loss on sale of the asset, as well as depreciation to date of sale.

Illustration 21

Sales as shown in the Trial Balance are £3,000, which includes the sale of a car (effected half-way through the yearly accounting period) realizing £120. The book value of the car at the commencement of the period was £210, and in the past 20 per cent depreciation has been written off yearly.

The entries will be: debit Sales £120, credit Car Account £120; but as the car stands in the books at £210, there is still a debit of £90 therein to be disposed of, as follows: £21 (i.e. at 20 per cent per annum on £210 for half-year) and £69 for depreciation and loss on sale respectively.

The Car Account will be thus:

CAR

			£			£
Balance .	.	b/d	210	Transfer from Sales		120
				Depreciation . .		21
				Profit and Loss Account: Loss on Sale . . .		69
			£210			£210

The inclusion of the proceeds of the car in Sales Account, moreover, may convey the hint that the purchase of a new car (if any) has been included incorrectly in Purchases Account; thus involving a transfer from Purchases Account to debit of new Car Account. It may be mentioned further that in the purchase of a new car the vendor often makes an allowance for the old car, and pays the licence for the new car, charging the latter to the purchaser. Such a transaction may involve several adjustments.

Where goods are purchased and resold without profit the amount of such sale should be transferred to the credit of Purchases Account. Similarly, goods sent out on consignment or to branches should be credited to a separate account and not treated as sales. (These matters will be fully dealt with in the chapters on Consignment and Branch Accounts respectively.)

Where the balances have been extracted and it is discovered that a batch of sales has not been entered, it is usual to remedy the omission by ascertaining the total of such sales and passing an entry through on lines similar to prepayment items (i.e. credit above the line; debit below the line). The former will augment the Sales Account and the latter will represent and be shown as Debtors in the Balance Sheet. The detailed sales figures will be passed through the books on the first day of the new period.

Returns inward will be dealt with conversely.

Illustration 22

The following items appear (*inter alia*) in the Trial Balance on 31st December 19 . . :

	£	£
Debtors . . .	3,500	
Sales . . .		15,200

After ruling off the various Journals and extracting the Trial Balance it is discovered that invoices to customers amounting to £729 have been omitted.

The adjustment will be as follows:

SALES

19.. Dec. 31	Trading Account .		£ 15,929	19.. Dec. 31	Sundries (per Trial Balance) . . Sales omitted from Sales Journal .	c/d	£ 15,200 729
			£15,929				£15,929
19.. Jan. 1	Balance . . Sales omitted .	b/d	729				

The Balance Sheet will show Debtors:

	£	£
Per Ledger . . .	3,500	
Sales Account . .	729	
		4,229

Various terms are commonly used in relation to Sales. These are:

(*a*) **Cost of Goods Sold** or **Cost of Sales.** This term is employed frequently both in ordinary and cost accounting. It is simply the cost price of the goods sold, or the price at which goods would be sold to recover exactly their cost, that is, without either profit or loss. Hence, assuming that in arriving at gross profit no unusual items are included, the cost of goods sold equals the amount of sales (less returns) less gross profit.

Illustration 23

Goods are sold for £2,000 (no returns inwards): opening stock is £500. Purchases are £1,200 and closing stock is £300. Find the cost of goods sold.

	£
Gross Profit is £2,000 plus £300	2,300
Less £500 plus £1,200	1,700
Gross Profit	£600
Cost of Goods Sold is Opening Stock . . .	500
Add Purchases	1,200
	1,700
Less Closing Stock	300
Cost of Goods Sold	£1,400

This gives the same result as:

	£
Sales	2,000
Less Gross Profit . .	600
Cost of Goods Sold	£1,400

(*b*) **Turnover.** In addition to its simple meaning of Sales, this term is frequently used to mean the number of times the Stock is 'turned over'; in other words the speed of the 'turn-over' of the average stock.

The usual criterion is the money equivalent of the yearly sales as compared with that of the average stock, the former being divided by the latter. It is important to have the average stock converted into selling price for this purpose.

There are also two other modes of arriving at the speed of the turnover:

(i) The cost of goods sold divided by the cost of the average stock.

(ii) The quantity (as distinct from the money equivalent) of the goods sold divided by the quantity normally in hand.

When a wide range of goods is carried, it is usually necessary to calculate the turnover figure for each class of goods since the rate will vary considerably for each class. The turnover rate of, say, Motor Lorries or Grand Pianos will be much less, for instance, than that of Groceries, Tobacco, and Meat. The average stock on hand, too, may be greatly affected by bulk purchases made with a view to reducing the buying price.

How the various adjustments dealt with so far in this chapter affect the Final Accounts can be seen from the following illustration.

Illustration 24

J. WALTERS
TRIAL BALANCE AS AT 31ST DECEMBER 19..

	£	£
J. Walters: Capital		4,250
J. Walters: Drawings	710	
Plant and Machinery	950	
Stock, 1st January 19..	1,460	
Purchases	10,362	
Purchases Returns		291
Sales		12,906
Sales Returns	210	
General Expenses	1,440	
Rent	120	
Rates	200	
6% Loan		500
Bank Overdraft		240
Bad Debts	172	
Sundry Debtors	3,620	
Sundry Creditors		1,000
Cash in Hand	48	
Bad Debts Provision		105
	£19,292	£19,292

You are required to prepare Trading and Profit and Loss Account, for the year ended 31st December 19.., and Balance Sheet as at that date, showing the adjustments and closing entries in Journal form, having regard to the following:

1. Write off depreciation on Plant and Machinery at 10 per cent per annum.

2. The Bad Debts Provision is to be increased to 5 per cent on Sundry Debtors. A discount provision of $2\frac{1}{2}$ per cent on Sundry Debtors is to be created.

3. Walters has drawn out Goods for his own consumption amounting to £40, of which there is no record in the books.

4. £100 Plant and Machinery purchased on 31st December 19.., has been inadvertently included in Purchases.

5. Rent Accrued is £40.

6. Rates of £80 are paid in advance.

7. Stock-in-hand at 31st December 19.. is valued at £1,730 including stock of stationery £20.

8. £500 6 per cent Loan was received from a friend on 1st January this year. Interest on the Loan has not been paid.

9. General Expenses include:

(a) Purchases of stationery £50.

(b) Carriage inwards £80, including £20 on the Plant and Machinery purchased on 31st December 19...

(c) Wages £1,180, including £30 for installation of the new Plant and Machinery. There are £30 wages accruing on 31st December 19 . . .

10. Sales include £100 resale without profit. It is discovered that sales to the value of £200 have not been entered in the books at 31st December 19 . . .

J. WALTERS

JOURNAL

19..		£	£
Dec. 31	Depreciation	95	
	Plant and Machinery		95
	Being 10% per annum written off.		
	J. Walters, Drawings	40	
	Purchases		40
	Being Goods drawn out of the business for private consumption.		
	Plant and Machinery	150	
	Sundries:		
	Purchases		100
	General Expenses (Carriage) . .		20
	General Expenses (Wages) . .		30
	Being transfers from Purchases and General Expenses of items included therein in error.		
	Rent	40	
	Rent Accrued		40
	Being Balance carried forward.		
	Rates Prepaid	80	
	Rates		80
	Being Balance carried forward.		
	Loan Interest	30	
	Loan Interest Accrued		30
	Being Balance carried forward in respect of loan interest accrued.		

Journal—(contd.)

	£	£
Sundries		1,260
General Expenses		
Stationery	50	
Carriage Inwards	60	
Wages	1,150	
Being allocation of General Expenses to correct accounts.		
Wages	30	
Wages Accruing		30
Being Balance carried forward in respect of wages accruing		
Sales	100	
Purchases		100
Being transfer in respect of goods resold without profit.		
Sundry Debtors' Total Account (or Sales Account 'below the line')	200	
Sales		200
Being sales omitted from Sales Day Book.		

Journal (Closing Entries)

19..			£	£
Dec. 31	Trading Account		11,351	
	Sundries			
	Stock			1,460
	Purchases[1] . . .	£10,122		
	Less Returns[2] . . .	291		
				9,831
	Carriage Inwards . . .			60
	Being Balances transferred.			
	Sundries			14,506
	Trading Account . . .			
	Sales[3]	£13,006		
	Less Returns[4]	210		
			12,796	
	Stock		1,710	
	Being Balances transferred.			
	Trading Account		3,155	
	Profit and Loss Account . .			3,155
	Being Gross Profit transferred.			

[1] Purchases per Trial Balance £10,362, less transfers £240 (see the second, third, and eighth previous Journal entries).

[2] Alternatively, the Returns may be transferred by means of separate Journal entries.

[3] Sales per Trial Balance £12,906, plus net transfer £100 (see the ninth and tenth Journal entries, p. 0546).

[4] Alternatively, the Returns may be transferred by means of separate Journal entries.

JOURNAL (CLOSING ENTRIES)—(contd.)

	£	£
Profit and Loss Account	2,094	
Sundries:		
Wages [£1,150 plus accrual £30] . .		1,180
Rent [£120 plus accrual £40] . .		160
Rates [£200 less prepaid £80] . .		120
Stationery [£50 less Stock £20] . .		30
General Expenses[5]		130
Loan Interest		30
Bad Debts		172
Bad Debts Provision[6] . . .		86
Discounts Provision[7] . . .		91
Depreciation		95
Being Balances transferred.		
Profit and Loss Account	1,061	
J. Walters, Capital		1,061
Being Net Profit transferred.		
J. Walters, Capital[8]	750	
J. Walters, Drawings		750
Being Balance transferred.		

[5] General Expenses per Trial Balance £1,440, less transfers £1,310 (see the third and seventh Journal entries, pp. 0545 and 0546).

[6] Sundry Debtors per Trial Balance £3,620, plus transfer £200 (see the tenth Journal entry, p. 0546)—£3,820; 5 per cent of £3,820 is £191, less provision per Trial Balance £105, which leaves £86.

[7] Sundry Debtors	£3,820
Less Bad Debts Provision	191
	£3,629

$2\frac{1}{2}$ per cent of £3,629 is £91 (to the nearest £).

[8] Drawings per Trial Balance £710, plus transfer £40 (see the second Journal entry, p. 0545).

J. WALTERS

TRADING AND PROFIT AND LOSS ACCOUNT FOR THE YEAR ENDED 31ST DECEMBER 19..

	£	£
Sales	13,006	
Less Returns	210	
		12,796
Less Cost of Goods Sold:		
Purchases	£10,122	
Less Returns	291	
	9,831	
Less Increase in Value of Stock	250	
	9,581	
Carriage Inwards	60	
		9,641
Trading Profit		3,155
Less Wages	£1,180	
Rent	160	
Rates	120	
Stationery	30	
General Expenses	130	
Loan Interest	30	
Bad Debts:		
Written Off	£172	
Provision	86	
	258	
Discounts Provision	91	
Depreciation of Plant	95	
		2,094
Net Profit transferred to Capital		£1,061

J. WALTERS

BALANCE SHEET AS AT 31ST DECEMBER 19..

	£	£
CAPITAL		
At 1st January 19..		4,250
Less Drawings		750
		3,500
Add Net Profit		1,061
		4,561
6% Loan		500
		£5,061
EMPLOYMENT OF CAPITAL		
Fixed Assets:		
Plant and Machinery at		
1st January 19..	950	
Additions	150	
	1,100	
Less Depreciation	95	
		1,005
Current Assets:		
Stock in Hand:		
Goods	£1,710	
Stationery	20	
	1,730	
Sundry Debtors	£3,820	
Less Bad Debts Provision	191	
	3,629	
Less Discounts Provision	91	
	3,538	
Rates prepaid	80	
Cash in hand	48	
		£5,396
Current Liabilities:		
Trade Creditors	£1,000	
Accrual and Accrued Expenses	100	
Bank Overdraft	240	
	£1,340	
Working Capital		4,056
		£5,061

EXAMINATION PROCEDURE

As the types of questions on this subject-matter are illimitable, it is essential that students should make it a habit in the *early stages of their preparation of* working, under time conditions, exercises involving the compilation of final accounts.

It is neither practicable nor desirable to lay down dogmatically any precise method of approach to these problems, but the author has found the following methods adequate to meet the general requirements of students:

1. Take a rough preliminary survey of the question, carefully underlining dates, nature of business, and unusual items.

2. Obtain agreement of the Trial Balance.

3. Note against each individual item in the Trial Balance any adjustment required.

4. Proceed to build up in skeleton in the Trading and Profit and Loss Account and Balance Sheet ONLY those items that are 'straightforward', that is, those items that require no adjustments, ticking each item in the Trial Balance as it is disposed of.

5. Next deal with remaining items (i.e. those requiring adjustment), making sure that the double-entry has been completed; the Trial Balance item should be ticked up to the adjustment note.

6. Insert closing stock first in the Trading Account and then in the assets side of the Balance Sheet, ticking up the adjustment note.

7. Avoid, if possible, a 'piecemeal' treatment of adjustments and stock; that is to say, deal at one and the same time completely with the adjustments, and if several items are involved, open rough working accounts to avoid confusion.

8. Until the problem is complete it is advisable to insert totals in pencil.

9. In case of ambiguity in the question, think out the most reasonable and common sense view and proceed accordingly; state your assumptions, supporting them with reasons, and other possible assumptions.

10. Ascertain whether any self-evident adjustments are required in accordance with the facts given in the problem, e.g. where the Trial Balance shows a loan outstanding and there is a debit charge for loan interest for a period only. If, for instance, the accounts are for a year and the debit for loan interest is for the half-year, an adjustment is clearly required (provided that the loan did not arise halfway through the year) to increase the loan interest debit to a full year's charge, with a corresponding liability for the half-year's interest unpaid.[1]

In examination work it is usually unprofitable to spend much time attempting to discover the out-of-balance where such exists.

The following points are illustrative of common failings in this type of problem:

1. Failure to complete the double-entry of the adjustments, e.g. insertion of closing stock in the Trading Account, but its omission in the Balance Sheet; the increase of an expense in the Profit and Loss Account and omitting to show the accrual as a *liability* in the Balance Sheet.

2. Incorrect or incomplete treatment of Bad and Doubtful Debts and similar provisions; the most frequent error being the ADDITION of the Bad

---

[1] The same principle applies where Loan Interest is shown 'net', i.e. after deduction of Income Tax (see Chapter 21).

and Doubtful Debts Provision to the Debtors instead of DEDUCTION in the Balance Sheet.

3. Failure to carry out 'inset' items.

4. Failure to provide for interest on loans and depreciation where the facts in the question clearly indicate the necessity for so doing.

5. Failure to 'clear' all the Trial Balance figures or the careless insertion of amounts on the incorrect side of the Profit and Loss Account and Balance Sheet.

6. Failure to transfer to Capital Account the balance of the Profit and Loss Account.

7. Careless lack of observation of important details, e.g. the period of the accounts, nature of the business, distinction between capital and revenue and the like.

As the examination bodies frequently require the preparation of Final Accounts from a schedule of balances, illustrations are provided in the succeeding pages of the working of the final accounts both from the orthodox Trial Balance and from a schedule of the balances.

1. From the Complete Trial Balance

It should be noted that rough workings—this is imperative where the adjustments are complicated—should be submitted, as the examiner's purpose is to test knowledge of PRINCIPLES; and further, he is not oblivious to the fact that the examinee is working under what may be considered as very unfavourable conditions.

Illustration 25

The Trial Balance of A on 31st December 19.., follows:

	£	£	
Debtors	2,000		(i) Closing Stock, £1,470.
Creditors . . .		1,400	(ii) Stock destroyed covered by Insur-
Drawings . . .	420		ance (not yet paid), £150.
Capital . . .		2,500	
Stock, 1st Jan. 19.. .	1,200		(iii) Provide 20% on Debtors for Bad
Purchases . . .	6,200		Debts.
Sales . . .		7,302	(iv) Included in Sales is £50, being Sale
Sales Returns . .	60		of Fixtures, book value, £80;
Wages . . .	900		Depreciation thereon, to date of
General Expenses .	350		sale, £5.
Bank		290	
Fixtures and Equipment	400		(v) Expenses accruing, £25.
Bad Debts . . .	172		(vi) Included in Purchases is a new
Bad Debts Provision .		210	Typewriter, £63, bought on 31st
			December of the current year.
			(vii) Write 10% Depreciation off Fix-
			tures.
	£11,702	£11,702	

The items in italic type are straightforward and do not require adjustment.

The skeleton will first be prepared by the insertion of the items complete in themselves and not influenced by the required adjustments.

This will appear as follows:

TRADING AND PROFIT AND LOSS ACCOUNT FOR THE YEAR ENDED 31ST DECEMBER 19..

		£
Sales		
Less Returns		60
		£
Cost of Goods Sold:		
Purchases . . . . £		
Add Stock at 1st Jan. 19.. . .		1,200
Less Stock Destroyed . . £		
Stock at 31st Dec. 19.. .		
Wages		900
Trading Profit		£
Less General Expenses . . . £		
Bad Debts		
Depreciation: Fixtures and Equipment .		
Loss on sale of Fixtures . .		
Net Profit (or Loss) transferred to Capital .		£

BALANCE SHEET AS AT 31ST DECEMBER 19..

	£
CAPITAL	
At 1st Jan. 19..	2,500
Less Drawings	420
	2,080
Add Net Profit	
or	
Less Net Loss	
	£

EMPLOYMENT OF CAPITAL

Fixed Assets:
Fixtures and Equipment at
   1st Jan. 19..   £
   Less Sale   .   .   .   £
       Loss on Sale .   .
       Depreciation .   .   ——

   Add Purchases .   .
                    —— £

Current Assets:
  Stock   .   .   .   . £
  Debtors .   .   . £
   Less Bad debts provision . ——

Insurance Company .   .   . ——
                     £

Current Liabilities:
  Creditors £1,400
  Expenses accruing .   .
  Bank Overdraft .   .   .   290
                     £

Working Capital .   .   .   .
                     £

At this stage all the items that can be completely disposed of have been inserted in the appropriate place in the Trading and Profit and Loss Account or Balance Sheet; and in an exercise will have been duly ticked up.

In addition, it will be observed that other expenses and adjustment items, not in the Trial Balance itself but required by the question, have been inserted WITHOUT figures, thus facilitating the double-entry of the adjustments by avoiding the necessity of having to perform the 'writing' part at the time of insertion of the relevant figures.

It is now necessary to deal with each adjustment.

(*a*) **Closing Stock.** This will be deducted from Purchases in the Trading Account, i.e. credited and immediately after this entry in the Balance Sheet as a current asset.

(*b*) **Stock Destroyed.** The amount should be deducted from Purchases in the Trading Account, i.e. Trading Account credited, as if the stock actually existed and the amount should be charged, i.e. debited, to Profit and Loss Account as a separate item if not covered by insurance, or in the probable event of its being so covered, the amount will go to the debit of the Insurance Company. The adjusting Journal entries will therefore be:

Debit Profit and Loss Account ⎫
Credit Trading Account   ⎬ If not insured.

Debit Insurance Company ⎫
Credit Trading Account ⎬ If fully insured.

In the event of the loss being partly covered, the proportion insured against will be debited to the Insurance Company and the uninsured portion charged, i.e. debited to Profit and Loss Account, the total of the two being deducted from Purchases, in the Trading Account, i.e. credited to Trading Account.

It is quite conceivable that the insurance claim may have been passed through the books as a sale and the Insurance Company debited; in these circumstances a transfer should be made by debiting, i.e. reducing, Sales and crediting Trading Account, i.e. deducting the amount from Purchases in the Trading Account, the Insurance Company's account having already been debited.

The transfer required where there is no insurance of the goods, or if partly insured, then to the extent of the loss not covered, will not reflect itself in the Balance Sheet at all, and actually will not amend the NET profit, but will INCREASE the TRADING profit and INCREASE the amounts charged to, i.e. debit side of, the Profit and Loss Account.

(c) **Bad Debts Provision.** The following rough working account will be prepared, and although such working account would be attached to the written answer to the problem there is no necessity to embellish it so long as it is made perfectly clear to the examiner what accounting process or processes it contains. Thus:

Bad Debts A/c			Bad Debts Provision		
	£	£		£	£
T.B.		172	New Provision (in B.S.) 400	T.B.	210
B.D.P..		190		B.D. A/c.	190
		——362 Dr. P. & L.			

Hence £362 will be charged, i.e. debited to the Profit and Loss Account and the new Provision of £400 shown as a deduction from Debtors. Both of the above will completely dispose of the Bad Debts Account, and the Bad Debts Provision appearing in the Trial Balance. This is made clear by a comparison of the Trial Balance and the Final Accounts figures, i.e.:

> Trial Balance: Dr. £172 and Cr. £210; difference Dr. £38.
> Final Accounts: Dr. £362 and Cr. £400; difference Dr. £38.

(d) **Expenses Accruing £25.** This will merely increase the Expenses in the Profit and Loss Account and be shown in the Balance Sheet as a liability.

The next adjustment is of a composite nature because the adjustments called for are interwoven with more than one account, so that the appropriate accounts may be referred to by letter or some other special designation.

Adjustment for sales, fixtures, depreciation, etc., are referred to as 'A' in the final accounts on pp. 0556–0557.

Rough working accounts will be prepared:

Sales				Purchases			
	£		£		£		£
FIXTURES .	50	T.B. . .	7,302	T.B. . .	6,200	FIXTURES, etc.	63
Trading . .	7,252					Trading . .	6,137

Fixtures and Equipment				Depreciation			
	£		£		£		£
T.B. . . .	400	SALES . .	50	FIXTURES .	5		
		DEPN. . .	5	FIXTURES .	[1]32	P. & L. . .	37
		P. & L. . .	25				
PURCHASES .	63	DEPN. . .	32				
		Balance . .	351				

[1] On £400 − 80 = £320 at 10% per annum.

The transfers between the accounts themselves have been inserted in BLOCK letters for clearness.

After these adjustments have been effected, the balance of the Trading and Profit and Loss Account will be transferred to Capital Account or (as it is unnecessary formally to open the latter account), added to or subtracted from the Capital shown in the Balance Sheet, according to whether the result disclosed is a profit or loss.

The Final Accounts will then be as shown on pp. 0556–0557.

TRADING AND PROFIT AND LOSS ACCOUNT FOR THE YEAR ENDED 31ST DECEMBER, 19..

	£	£
Sales	7,252	
Less Returns (see A)	60	
		7,192
Cost of Goods Sold:		
Purchases (see A)	£6,137	
Add Stock at 1st Jan. 19..	1,200	
	7,337	
Less Stock Destroyed (see (b)) £150		
Stock at 31st Dec. 19..		
(see (a)) 1,470		
	1,620	
	5,717	
Wages	900	
		6,617
Trading Profit		575
Less General Expenses	375	
Bad Debts	362	
Depreciation: Fixtures and		
Equipment (see A)	37	
Loss on Sale of Fixtures (see A)	25	
		799
Net Loss transferred to Capital		£224

BALANCE SHEET AS AT 31ST DECEMBER, 19..

CAPITAL	£	£
At 1st January 19..		2,500
Less Drawings		420
		£2,080
Less Net Loss		224
		£1,856

EMPLOYMENT OF CAPITAL

Fixed Assets:

Fixtures and Equipment:

At 1st Jan. 19..	.	.		£400
Less Sale	.	£50		
Loss on Sale	.	25		
Depreciation	.	37		
			112	
			288	
Add Purchases (See A)	.		63	
				351

Current Assets:

Stock (see (a))	.	.	.	£1,470
Debtors	.	.	.£2,000	
Less Bad Debts Provision				
(see (c))	.	.	400	
				1,600
Insurance Company (see (b))	.	.		150
				£3,220

Current Liabilities:

Creditors	.	.	.	£1,400
Expenses accruing (see (d))		.		25
Bank Overdraft	.	.	.	290
				£1,715

Working Capital	1,505
	£1,856

Notes. 1. If the Stock had been insured for, say, £100 only, £50 would be charged, i.e. debited to Profit and Loss Account and £100 to the Insurance Company.

2. As the question is not clear as to whether the loss on Stock had already been adjusted prior to the Trial Balance, a footnote should be made to the student's answer.

3. It will be appreciated that in preparing final accounts under the method proposed, it is more appropriate to show separate entries in the Trading Account in respect of opening and closing stocks.

Illustration 26

The Trial Balance of A at 31st December 19.., is:

TRIAL BALANCE

	£	£
Capital		22,000
Drawings	10,000	
Sundry Creditors		10,401
Loan on Mortgage		9,500
Interest on Loan	300	
Goodwill	5,000	
Cash in Hand	50	
Sundry Debtors	20,100	
Bad Debts Provision		710
Stock, 1st January 19..	4,839	
Plant and Machinery	8,000	
Bank	2,555	
Land and Buildings	12,000	
Bad Debts	525	
Purchases	51,458	
Purchases Returns		1,346
Sales		116,246
Sales Returns	7,821	
Carriage Outwards	2,004	
Wages	15,485	
Salaries	6,097	
Carriage Inwards	929	
Rent and Rates	2,000	
Gas, Water, and Electricity	720	
Insurance	171	
Advertising	3,264	
Discounts Received		1,100
Discounts Allowed	560	
Trade Investment, at Cost	5,000	
General Expenses	3,489	
Bills Payable		2,614
Bills Receivable	1,800	
Dividends Received		250
	£164,167	£164,167

You are required to prepare Trading and Profit and Loss Account for the year to 31st December 19.., and Balance Sheet as at that date, after making provision for the following:

1. Depreciation—Plant and Machinery, 10 per cent per annum; Land and Buildings, 5 per cent per annum.

2. End Stock in hand—31st December 19.., £5,100.

3. The Investments at 31st December 19.., are worth £5,500 at market values.

4. £200 is outstanding in respect of Rent and Rates.

5. Insurances are prepaid, £50.

6. The Bad Debts Provision is to be maintained at 5 per cent of Sundry Debtors.

7. Loan Interest at 6 per cent per annum is to be charged for full year having regard to the fact that £500 was repaid on 30th June 19...

8. The Manager is to get a commission of 1/10th on the net trading profits **after** charging his commission.

9. Transfer £2,250 to Reserve.

10. 3/4ths of the Rent and Rates are to be charged against trading.

11. 17/24ths of Gas, Water, and Electricity are to be charged against trading.

TRADING AND PROFIT AND LOSS ACCOUNT FOR THE YEAR ENDED 31ST DECEMBER 19..

	£	£
Sales		£116,246
Less Returns . . .		7,821
		108,425
Cost of Goods Sold:		
Purchases	£51,458	
Less Returns . . .	1,346	
	50,102	
Less Increase in Value of Stock .	261	
	49,851	
Carriage Inwards . . .	929	
Wages	15,485	
Rent and Rates . . .	1,650	
Gas, Water and Electricity . .	510	
		68,425
Trading Profit		40,000
Add Discounts received . .		1,100
Dividends received . .		250
		41,350
Less Salaries	£6,097	
Rent and Rates . .	550	
Gas, Water and Electricity .	210	
Insurance . . .	121	
Carriage Outwards . .	2,004	
Advertising . . .	3,264	
Discounts Allowed . .	560	
Bad Debts . . .	820	
Loan Interest . . .	585	
General Expenses . .	3,489	
Depreciation in:		
Plant and Machinery £800		
Land and Buildings 600		
	1,400	
Manager's Commission . .	2,000	
		21,100
Net Profit.		20,250
Less Transfer to Reserve . .		2,250
Net Profit transferred to Capital . .		£18,000

<small>Balance Sheet as at 31st December 19..</small>

	£	£
CAPITAL		
At 1st Jan. 19..	£22,000	
Less Drawings	10,000	
	12,000	
Add Net Profit	18,000	
		£30,000
Reserve		2,250
Loan on Mortgage		9,500
		£41,750
EMPLOYMENT OF CAPITAL		
Fixed Assets:		
Goodwill		5,000
Land and Buildings	12,000	
Less Depreciation	600	
		11,400
Plant and Machinery	£8,000	
Less Depreciation	800	
		7,200
Trade Investments at cost . . .		5,000
(Market value £5,500) . . .		
		28,600
Current Assets:		
Stock	£5,100	
Sundry Debtors . . .	£20,100	
Less Bad Debts Provision .	1,005	
	19,095	
Expenses prepaid (Insurance) . .	50	
Bills Receivable	1,800	
Cash in hand	50	
Cash at Bank	2,555	
	£28,650	
Current Liabilities:		
Sundry Creditors:		
Trade	£10,401	
Rent and Rates . .	200	
Manager's Commission .	2,000	
Mortgage Interest due . .	285	
	£12,886	
Bills Payable	2,614	
	£15,500	
Working Capital		13,150
		£41,750

Notes. 1. The Loan Interest has been computed as follows:

	£	
6% per annum on £10,000 for 6 months .	300	(already paid)
6% per annum on £9,500 for 6 months .	285	(outstanding)
	£585	

2. Computation of Manager's Commission equals 1/11th of the profit of the business *before* the Profit and Loss Account has been credited with dividends and debited with the commission, viz:

	£
Net Profit	20,250
Add Commission	2,000
	22,250
Less Dividends (non-trading receipts) .	250
	£22,000

One-eleventh thereof = £2,000

Subject to agreement, depreciation should, for the purpose of calculating commission, be computed on the straight line method.

The commission is based, in the absence of an agreement otherwise (as in this problem) on the profits *before* charging commission.

2. Where the Items are Shown in Single Columnar Form

No difference in principle arises in these circumstances as compared with the presentment of a complete Trial Balance. The additional work involved is the separation of items, so as to form, prior to the preparation of the Final Accounts, the Trial Balance. The time entailed in rewriting is usually considerable and cannot easily be spared in examinations, so that a 'short cut' method should be employed.

The method usually adopted is to add the whole list (after ascertaining that the list or schedule comprises only Ledger Balances) and either extract the credits by the side of the schedule or on a separate sheet, and the total schedule less the credits extracted should equal the latter figure. There is no reason why credits instead of debits should be extracted, but from the point of view of expediency it is almost invariably better to extract credits inasmuch as they are comparatively few in number.

Many of the advanced problems require adjustments of errors or omissions before the list of balances is complete; that is, not infrequently the list of balances does not contain the whole story. In subsequent chapters will be found illustrations of this type.

When the Trial Balance is obtained the problem will be worked out on the usual lines.

Illustration 27

The following is the Schedule of balances on 31st December 19.., of X:

Ledger items	Balances	Debits	Credits
	£	£	£
Purchases	1,200	1,200	
Debtors	1,700	1,700	
Bank Overdraft	50		50
Loan	180		180
Fixtures	200	200	
Capital	1,500		1,500
Drawings	300	300	
Expenses	420	420	
Bad Debts Provision	90		90
Creditors	280		280
Sales	1,900		1,900
Sales Returns	50	50	
Stock	130	130	
	£8,000	£4,000	£4,000

The items are also shown in Trial Balance form for reference.
The procedure in a question of this nature will be:

	£	£
(1) Total of balances		8,000
(2) Credit items	50	
	180	
	1,500	
	90	
	280	
	1,900	
Deduct (2) from (1)		4,000
∴ Total Debit items		£4,000

Where items (e.g. Bank, Loans, Discounts) are ambiguous, the question will generally give some indication or hint as to the correct side of the particular item. For instance, Bank Interest (Dr.) would suggest a bank overdraft.

Illustration 28

The following are the balances which appeared in the books of X, who is an Hotel Proprietor, at 31st December 19..:

	£
Apartments and Attendance	23,000
Meals	16,000
Provisions	7,750
Stocks	510
Cash in Bank	5,000
Capital	110,000
Debtors	400
Creditors	4,800
Provision for Depreciation of Buildings . .	12,000
Buildings	105,000
Furniture and Equipment	30,000
Bank Interest	565
General Expenses	13,705
Wages	3,000
Income Tax	240
Drawings	760

Prepare Final Accounts after making adjustments as follows:

1. Increase Provision for Depreciation of Buildings to £15,000.

2. A sum of £400 representing accommodation £120, and meals £280 to be charged to X.

3. A sum of £800 representing accommodation £280 and meals £520 to be charged up in respect of Staff.

The 'Trial Balance' is:

		£
(1) Total of *all* the items	. . .	332,730
(2) Total of Credit items	. . .	166,365
∴ Total Debit items .	.	= £166,365

Note. In this instance the two-sided form of presenting final accounts is used. It should be noted that in professional accounting practice, particularly in respect of small traders, final accounts are by tradition often still prepared on the two-sided basis.

PROFIT AND LOSS ACCOUNT FOR THE YEAR ENDED 31ST DECEMBER 19..

	£		£
Provisions	7,750	Apartments, etc.	23,400
Wages	3,800	Meals	16,800
General Expenses . . .	13,705	Bank Interest	565
Depreciation of Buildings . .	3,000		
Net Profit transferred to Capital			
Account	12,510		
	£40,765		£40,765

BALANCE SHEET AS AT 31ST DECEMBER 19..

Capital—	£	£	Fixed Assets—	£	£
Balance at 1st Jan. 19.. .	110,000		Buildings . . .	105,000	
Less Drawings .	1,400		*Less* Depreciation .	15,000	
		108,600			90,000
Add Net Profit per Profit			Furniture and Equipm't. .		30,000
and Loss Account .	12,510		Current Assets—		
		121,110	Stocks . . .	510	
Current Liabilities— .			Debtors . . .	400	
Creditors . .		4,800	Cash at Bank . .	5,000	
					5,910
		£125,910			£125,910

Notes. The General Expenses (which should include the complete upkeep and renewals of furniture, crockery, linen, etc.) would be in more detail in an examination question.

The adjustments will be effected thus:

	£	Apartments		£	Meals		£
Debit Drawings	400	Credit	.	120	Credit	.	280[1]
Debit Wages	800	Credit	.	280	Credit	.	520
	£1,200	Increase of	.	£400	Increase of	.	£800

Income Tax, £240, will also be transferred to Drawings; hence total Drawings are £1,400, i.e. £760 + £240 + £400.

Stocks are Closing Stocks (the credits already having been made to the appropriate Nominal Accounts).

Illustration 29

From the following balances prepare Final Accounts in respect of the year ended 31st December 19..:

	£		£
Loan	500	Creditors	3,740
Sundry Expenses	398	Income Tax	203
Stock (1st January 19..)	5,470	Investments	2,000
Purchases	31,400	Fixtures and Fittings	600
Wages	2,000	Motor Vans	500
Discounts Allowed	126	Investment Provision	500
Rent and Rates	170	Bad Debts written off	20
Sales	37,000	Bad Debts Provision	320
Carriage Inwards	224	Bank Interest	15
Bank	3,247	Capital	9,150
Sundry Debtors	1,900	Dividends on Investments	107
Buildings	2,674	Drawings	400

1. Stock in hand at 31st December 19.., £3,517 (including Stationery Stock £17).
2. Sundry Expenses include stationery purchased, £37.
3. The Loan was made on 1st March of the current year; interest at the rate of 6% per annum, no provision for which has yet been made.
4. Investments valued at £1,420; adjust Investment Provisions accordingly.
5. Provide 5% on Debtors for Discounts and 20% for Bad Debts.
6. Write off 5% for Depreciation on Buildings.
7. Included in Sundry Expenses is £26 for Legal Charges in connection with the acquisition of certain buildings (included in the item of £2,674).
8. Dividends accruing, £27; Rates paid in advance £20 and Rent owing £30.
9. The opening stock included Stationery Stock £20.

TRADING AND PROFIT AND LOSS ACCOUNT FOR THE YEAR ENDED 31ST DECEMBER 19..

		£		£
Stock		5,450	Sales	37,000
Purchases		31,400	Stock	3,500
Carriage Inwards		224		
Wages		2,000		
Gross Profit	c/d	1,426		
		£40,500		£40,500

[1] Alternatively, the amounts representing meals may be credited to Provisions Account instead of being credited to Meals Account.

Rent and Rates	.	.	.	180	Gross Profit	.	.	. b/d	1,426
Sundry Expenses	.	.	.	335	Bank Interest	.	.	.	15
Stationery	.	.	.	40	Dividends	.	.	.	134
Loan Interest	.	.	.	25					
Bad Debts	.	.	.	80					
Discounts (net)	.	.	.	202					
Depreciation—									
Buildings	.	.	£135						
Investments	.	.	80						
				215					
Net Profit transferred to Capital									
Account	.	.	.	498					
				£1,575					£1,575

BALANCE SHEET AS AT 31ST DECEMBER 19..

Capital:	£	£	Fixed Assets:	£	£
Balance 1st Jan. 19.. . .	9,150		Buildings:		
Less Drawings . .	603		Balance 1st Jan. 19... .	?	
			Additions . . .	?	
	8,547			2,674	
Add Net Profit per Trading			Add Legal Charges on		
and Profit and Loss A/c .	498		Purchase . .	26	
		9,045		2,700	
Loan		500	Less Depreciation at 5%	135	
Current Liabilities:					2,565
Creditors . . .	3,740		Fixtures and Fittings . .		600
Rent owing . . .	30		Motor Vans . . .		500
Loan Interest . .	25		Investments . . .	2,000	
		3,795	Less Provision . .	580	1,420
					5,085
			Current Assets:		
			Stock: Goods . .	3,500	
			Stationery .	17	
			Sundry Debtors £1,900		
			Less Bad Debts Prov. 380		
				1,520	
			Less Discount Prov. 76		
				1,444	
			Add Rates paid in		
			Advance . 20		
			Add Dividends accru-		
			ing 27		
				1,491	
			Cash at Bank . .	3,247	8,255
	£13,340				£13,340

> In absence of date of purchase of new buildings, depreciation taken at 5% on the balance at 31st December 19..

Note. For illustrative purposes the foregoing final accounts have been prepared on the two-sided basis.

MISCELLANEOUS ADJUSTMENTS

Having grasped the principles relating to the preparation of final accounts with comparatively elementary adjustments, a student will now be the better able to advance a step further. Therefore, examples will now be given illustrating as many types of adjustment as are compatible with the degree of knowledge that, at this stage, the student is reasonably assumed to have attained.

It will be recognized that many adjustments call for a considerable knowledge of advanced accounting and these will be dealt with in Chapters 21 and 23.

The almost inexhaustible number of adjustments makes it impossible to illustrate them completely, but the following are typical:

1. Included in the accounts are Plant and Machinery, £2,000; Investments, £3,200; Loose Tools, £720.

Plant and Machinery are to be written down by 10 per cent; Investments are revalued at £1,950; Loose Tools at £780.

During the year certain investments have been sold for £750, realizing a profit of £170 and passed through Sales Account; sundry loose tools have been purchased for £240 in respect of which carriage of £5 has been expended, the items being charged respectively to Purchases and Carriage.

As no dates are given, the assumption is naturally that the figures given in the first sentence are those in the books at the commencement of the period.

The adjustments are:

		£	£
Re Plant:			
(a) Trading and Profit and Loss Account	Dr.	200	
Plant and Machinery . .			200
Re Investments:			
(b) Sales Account	Dr.	750	
Investment Provision . . .			170[1]
Investment Account . . .			580

	£
The book value of Investments now is	
£3,200 *less* £580	2,620
And as the revised value is . .	1,950
A Provision is necessary for . .	£670[1]

		£	£
Re Loose Tools:			
(c) Loose Tools	Dr.	245	
Purchases			240
Carriage			5

Assuming there had been no sales of Loose Tools or other transactions not disclosed, the amount of Loose Tools will now be:

	£	£
Per Accounts	720	
Add Purchases and Carriage . . .	245	
		965
As the revised value of Loose Tools is .		780
The required Depreciation is . . .		£185

Entries for Depreciation of Loose Tools:

		£	£
(c) Trading and Profit and Loss Account	Dr.	185	
To Loose Tools			185

---

[1] But assuming no other items appear in the Provision, e.g. a commencing figure or other profits or losses on realization, the Investment Provision already is in credit for £170, thus requiring a further £500 more to augment it to £670, that is:

		£	£
Profit and Loss Account	Dr.	500	
To Investment Provision . . .			500

Alternatively, Loose Tools may be treated exactly like Stock, i.e. the commencing figure of £720 would be debited to Trading Account; Purchases and Carriage (£245) transferred separately to Trading Account; and the closing figure £780 introduced into the Final Accounts by the familiar entries:

		£	£
Loose Tools	Dr.	780	
To Trading Account			780

Actually Loose Tools will be unlikely to appear in accounts other than those relating to manufacturing, but the adjustment is introduced here for purposes of illustration.

2. A acquired a business from C on 1st September 19.1, and included in his expenses was one quarter's rent to 29th September 19.1, to the amount of £60; he makes up his accounts to 31st January 19.2. September quarter rent paid 2nd October 19.1; December quarter 31st January 19.2.

When he acquired the business A would receive credit for the rent accruing up to the date of acquisition, viz. two months from 24th June 19.1, to 1st September 19.1. Actually the computation would be in days and there would almost necessarily be several other items to be allowed or charged as between A and C.

The entries would be as under:

C

19.1			£				
Sept. 1	Accruing Rent .	.	40[1]				

[1] This debit will have been settled up either against the cost of acquisition of the business, or against adjustments in favour of C, e.g. prepayments, or in cash.

If, by error, the £40 debit to C and credit to Rent had not been effected at the date of acquisition, it would probably be done at the date when A paid the quarter's Rent to 29th September, 19.1; or upon the preparation of the final accounts.

RENT

19.1			£	19.1			£
Oct. 2	Cash: One Quarter's Rent to 29th Sept., 19.1 . .		60	Sept. 1	C for Rent accruing to 1st Sept., 19.1 .		40
19.2	Cash: One Quarter's Rent to 25th Dec., 19.1 . .		60	19.2 Jan. 31	Profit and Loss Account .		100[1]
Jan. 31	One Month's Rent accruing to 31st Jan., 19.2 . .	c/d	20				
			£140				£140
				Feb. 1	Balance: . One Month's Rent accruing .	b/d	20

[1] As the Rent is £20 a month there should be a charge to Profit and Loss Account of £100, made up of five months from 1st September, 19.1, to 31st January, 19.2, at £20 a month.

3. The Trial Balance of X shows the account of the Z Building Society as credit £1,225.

It is ascertained that the balance due at the commencement of the year was £1,346.

From the records supplied by the Building Society it is found that the £121 paid (i.e. £1,346 – £1,225) is made up of:

	£
Repayment of Capital	34
Loan Interest	86
Fire Insurance	1
	£121

The required entries are:

		£	£
Fire Insurance	Dr.	1	
Loan Interest	Dr.	86	
To Z Building Society			87

The Ledger Account of the Z Building Society will be:

Z BUILDING SOCIETY

		£			£
Cash	c/d	121	Balance b/d		1,346
Balance		1,312	Interest $(a)^1$		86
			Insurance $(b)^1$		1
		£1,433			**£1,433**
			Balance^2 b/d		1,312

[1] Alternatively 'By Sundries £87'.

	£
[2] Beginning Balance	1,346
Less Repayments of Capital	34
Closing Balance	**£1,312**

(a) and (b) The postings will be made to the debit of the appropriate account, and the usual adjustment made for prepayment (Insurance) and for accruals (Interest) unless (as would be probably the case) the amounts were trivial.

4. A trader with property standing in his books at £12,300, sold a portion of it for £4,200. The latter represents a profit of 20 per cent on book value. The date of the sale was 30th June 19.., the accounting period ends on 31st December, and depreciation at 10 per cent has always been written off.

(a) If the phrase 'profit of 20 per cent on book value' means value left *standing in* the books at 1st January 19.., the entries, ignoring narrations, are:

JOURNAL

		£	£
Depreciation	Dr.	175	
Property			175
Cash	Dr.	4,200	
Property			4,200
Depreciation	Dr.	880	
Property			880
Property	Dr.	875	
Profit on Sale			875

LEDGER
PROPERTY

19..			£	19..			£
Jan. 1	Balance	b/d	12,300	June 30	Cash: Sale		4,200
June 30	Profit and Loss				Depreciation		
	Account: Profit on				5% on £3,500		175
	Sale		875	Dec. 31	Depreciation		
					10% on £8,800		880
					Balance	c/d	7,920
			£13,175				£13,175
19..							
Jan. 1	Balance*	b/d	7,920				

	£
* Book value of remaining Property (£12,300−£3,500)[1]	8,800
Less 10% Depreciation	880
Balance per Ledger	£7,920

It will be seen that if the sale had realized exactly the depreciated value
at 30th June 19.., it would have been £3,500 less 5 per cent depreciation.
Thus:

	£
Book Value	3,500
Less Depreciation	175
	£3,325

As the sale price is £4,200 the profit is £875, as shown below:

	£
Sale Price	4,200
Less Depreciated Value	3,325
=Profit on Sale	£875

(b) If the phrase 'profit of 20 per cent on book value' means the value
after depreciation on the part sold has been dealt with on 30th June 19..,
the entries ignoring narrations, are:

JOURNAL		£p	£p
Depreciation	Dr.	184·21	
Property			184·21
Cash	Dr.	4,200·00	
Property			4,200·00
Depreciation	Dr.	861·58	
Property			861·58
Property	Dr.	700·00	
Profit on Sale			700·00

[1] The book value of the property sold was five-sixths of sale price, i.e. £3,500, therefore the
profit must be:

	£
Sale Price	4,200
Less Book Value	3,500
	700
Add Depreciation	175
Profit on Sale	£875

LEDGER

PROPERTY

19..			£p	19..				£p
Jan. 1	Balance . .	b/d	12,300·00	June 30	Cash: Sale	. .		4,200·00
June 30	Profit and Loss				Depreciation			
	Account: Profit				5% on			
	on Sale . .	.	700·00		£3,684·21	.	.	184·21
				Dec. 31	Depreciation			
					10% on			
					£8,615·79	.	.	861·58
					Balance .	.	c/d	7,754·21
			£13,000·00					£13,000·00
19..								
Jan. 1	Balance (i)	.	b/d	7,754·21				

		£p
(i) Total Book Value of Property at 1st Jan. 19..	. . .	12,300·00
Less Book Value of Property Sold	. . .	3,684·21
		8,615·79
Less 10% Depreciation	. . . .	861·58
Balance per Ledger	. . .	£7,754·21

The January book value of the property sold must be $\frac{100}{95}$ of the written down value; and the latter must be $\frac{5}{6}$ of the sale price of £4,200 (equals £3,500).

Therefore:

£p

Book Value at 1st January 19.., of the property sold

$$=\frac{100}{95}\times£3,500 \qquad . \quad . \quad . \quad . \quad 3,684·21$$

which, after providing Depreciation at 10% per annum for half-year (i.e. 5%) . . . . . . 184·21

Leaves net Book Value at 30th June 19.. . £3,500·00

Proof: £

Sale Price 4,200

Book Value at 30th June 19.., as written down . . 3,500

∴ Profit £700

This is a profit of 20% of Book Value (as written down), i.e. $\frac{1}{5}\times£3,500=£700$

do. $16\frac{2}{3}$% of sale price   i.e. $\frac{1}{6}\times£4,200=£700$

5. Included in the Purchases Journal of a trader, who draws his accounts up to 31st December of each year, is the following item:

19..		£p
May 17	Dud & Co. (Machine)	508·25

On examining the invoice you find the following material facts:

19..		£p
April 30	Purchase of New Machine	650·00
	Accessories	40·00
		690·00
	Less Old Machine	100·00
		590·00
	Less 10% Trade Discount on £550	55·00
		535·00
	Less 5% Cash Discount on £535	26·75
		£508·25

Received Cash,
17th May 19..
(Signed) Dud & Co.

Assuming depreciation at 20 per cent per annum you are required to make the necessary adjustment.

The old machine stood in the books at £180.

ADJUSTMENTS STATEMENT

Particulars	Gross	Trade Discount	True Price	Cash Discount	Net
	£	£	£	£p	£p
Cost of New Machine .	650	65	585	29·25	555·75
Accessories . .	40		40	2·00	38·00
	690	65	625	31·25	593·75
Deduct Old Machine .	100	10	90	4·50	85·50
	590	55	535	26·75	508·25

JOURNAL

19..		£p	£p
April 30	New Machine	555·75	
	Accessories	38·00	
	Purchases		508·25
	Old Machine		85·50
	Being the necessary adjustments as per statement attached.		
Dec. 31	Depreciation	86·10	
	Old Machine		12·00
	New Machine		74·10
	Being depreciation at 20% on the Old Machine for 4 months, and on the New Machine for 8 months.		
	Profit and Loss Account . . .	82·50	
	Old Machine		82·50
	Being the loss on the Old Machine written off.		

Notes. 1. The information indicates that the Trade Discount would only be allowed on the machines.

2. The transaction was entered in the Purchases Journal on the day the receipt was given, namely, 17th May; this, however, is not correct, as the machine was actually purchased on 30th April.

3. The narratives are added for purposes of illustration, but are not necessary when working an exercise on the final accounts.

6. A company draws up its accounts half-yearly to 31st July and 31st January. On 1st October 19.1, it commences to occupy its own factory newly built.

The rating authorities assessed the company at a rateable value (net) of £800. The company on receipt of the assessment in December 19.1, appealed, which appeal at 31st January 19.2, had not been heard.

On 15th December 19.1, the company paid rates on account £220.

The appeal was heard and settled in February 19.2, the assessment being reduced to £600 net. On 10th May 19.2, the Company paid £210 on account of the following Demand Note:

	£
Rates for 19.2–.3, £600 at £0·80	480
Add balance of Rates 19.1–.2	80
	560
Less allowance for the over-assessment, £200 at £0·75 .	75
	£485

On 1st November 19.2, the whole of the balance due, viz. £275, was paid.

Write up the Rates Account of the Company in respect of the three periods ended 31st January 19.3.

RATES

			£				£
19.1 Dec. 15	Cash on account		220	19.2 Jan. 31	Rates prepaid Profit and Loss Account (4 months on £800 at £0·75 in £)	c/d	20 200
			£220				£220
19.2 Feb. 1 May 10 July 31	Balance: Rates prepaid Cash on account Rates Adjustment Account: over-payment of Rates for the half year ended 31st January, 19.2 on £200 at £0·75 in £ for 4 months (1)	b/d	20 210 50	July 31	Rates prepaid (3) Profit and Loss Account (2)	c/d	45 235
			£280				£280
Aug. 1 Nov. 1	Balance: Rates prepaid Cash balance of Rates	b/d	45 275	19.3 Jan. 31	Rates prepaid (5) Profit and Loss Account (4)	c/d	80 240
			£320				£320
19.3 Feb. 1	Balance: Rates prepaid (5)	b/d	80				

Notes. 1. This item should be shown separately as it is in effect a relief in respect of the preceding period. The true rates for the period to 31st January 19.2, are £600 at £0·75 in £ for 4 months = £150, which is the £200 above, less the relief in the following period.

2. This item is arrived at as follows—

	£
Rates for 2 months (1st February 19.2, to 31st March 19.2) on £600 at £0·75	75
Rates for 4 months (1st April 19.2, to 31st July 19.2) on £600 at £0·80	160
	£235

3. This item is arrived at:

The payment of £210 discharges £5 still owing to 31st March 19.2 (i.e. balance of [1]£80 less allowance £75) leaving £205 on account of the current rating period 19.2–.3. The rates in respect of the current rating period, i.e. 1st April 19.2, to 31st July 19.2, are 4 months on £600 at £0·80 in £ amounting to £160 as against £205, leaving £45 prepaid.

4. This item is half-year's rates, viz., £600 for 6 months at £0·80 in £ = £240.

5. This item is £600 for 2 months at £0·80 in £ = £80 being the prepayment of 19.2–.3 rates, i.e. paid up to 31st March, 19.3.

The identical result would ensue if the Rates expenditure were passed through an Expenses Day Book or Journal.

7. On 1st April 19.1, Hardcastle Ltd., whose financial year ends on the 30th June took out a policy with Crag Insurance Co., Ltd., to cover Employer's Liability for the year ended 31st March 19.2.

The premium was at the rate of £0·50 per cent of wages paid during the year covered. As the current wages cannot be ascertained till 31st March

---

[1] Half-year's Rates, £800 p.a. (i.e. £400) at £0·75 in £ = £300, less Cash paid £220.

19.2, the premium was to be calculated on the wages paid for the year ended 31st March 19.1, and an adjustment to the premium on current year's wages was to be effected by a balance payment to or by Crag Insurance Co., Ltd. on the 25th April 19.2.

On 1st April 19.2, the insurance was renewed under similar conditions (i.e. *pro tem.* on 19.1–.2 wages, adjusted on 25th April 19.3, to actual 19.2–.3 wages and cash paid to or by the Insurance Company) except that the premium was to be £1 per cent of wages paid for the year covered.

The wages paid were:

	£
Year ended 31st March 19.1 . . .	60,000
Three months ended 30th June 19.1 . .	15,000
Nine months ended 31st March 19.2 . .	41,000
Three months ended 30th June 19.2 . .	25,000

Journalize the entries (except cash) to record the transactions and the closing entries on 30th June, 19.1 and 19.2, in the books of Hardcastle Ltd.

JOURNAL

		£	£
19.1 Apr. 1	Employer's Liability Insurance Suspense . . Crag Insurance Co., Ltd. . . . Premium for 19.1–.2 on wages for year ended 31st March 19.1 : $\frac{1}{2}$% on £60,000.	300	300
June 30	Employer's Liability Insurance[1] . . Employer's Liability Insurance Suspense . Transfer of proportion of premium for 3 mos. ended 30th June, 19.1 : $\frac{1}{2}$% on £15,000.	75	75
19.2 Apr. 1	Employer's Liability Insurance Suspense . . Crag Insurance Co., Ltd. . . . Premium for 19.2–.3 on wages for year ended 31st March 19.2 : 1% on £56,000.	560	560
19.2 Apr. 25	Crag Insurance Co., Ltd. . . . Employer's Liability Insurance Suspense . Refund due in respect of premium for 19.1–.2 on adjustment to actual ($\frac{1}{2}$% on £56,000 as against provisional £60,000).	20	20

June 30	Employer's Liability Insurance[1] . .
	 Employer's Liability Insurance Suspense .
	Transfer of premium for year ended 30th
	 June 19.2:
	            £
	9 mos. to 31st March 19.2—$\frac{1}{2}$% on
	 £41,000 205
	3 mos. to 30th June 19.2—1% on £25,000 250
	           ——
	          £455
		455	455

[1] This item will be transferred to Profit and Loss Account.

It will be seen that the insurance suspense account will be cleared each 25th April, but on the 30th June of each year the balance thereon will be carried forward as an asset. If each year's suspense account is kept separate, the clearance will become more apparent:

E.L.I. Suspense (1)

19.1 Apr. 1	Crag Insurance Co.		£ 300	19.1 June 30	E.L.I. . Balance.	c/d	£ 75 225
July 1	Balance	b/d	225[1]	19.2 Mar. 31 Apr. 25	E.L.I. . Crag Insurance Co.		205 20

[1] See note [1] on previous page.

E.L.I. Suspense (2)

19.2 Apr. 1	Crag Insurance Co.		£ 500	19.2 June 30	E.L.I. . Balance.	c/d	£ 250 310
July 1	Balance.	b/d	310[1]				

[1] These items appear in the Balance Sheet as assets.

E.L.I.

19.1 June 30	E.L.I. Suspense (1) .		£ 75	19.1 June 30	Profit and Loss A/c		£ 75
19.2 Mar. 31 June 30	E.L.I. Suspense (1) . E.L.I. Suspense (2) .		205 250	19.2 June 30	Profit and Loss A/c		455

8. Included in the Trial Balance of Trader are the following:

Purchases (including Samples £1,050) at invoice price . £22,050
Sales (including £800 of goods out on Sale or Return) . 17,600

The arrangement between Trader and Supplier is that the latter finances the former and supplies him with all goods at ordinary price plus 5 per cent, no discount being allowed.

Trader decided that 25 per cent of the goods out on Sale or Return should be regarded as sold.

The Stock of goods and samples on hand at the date of the Trial Balance at invoice price was £5,208. £200 of the samples purchased have been used and it was decided to write down the remainder, i.e. those on hand, by 25 per cent.

The Gross Profit, before allowing for samples used and Cost of Finance, uniformly earned is 10 per cent of selling price.

Show Trading Account and accounts for Purchases, Sales, Samples and Cost of Finance all as they would appear in the Ledger.

TRADING ACCOUNT

	£			£
Purchases . . .	20,000	Sales . . .		17,000
Samples used . .	200	Stock		4,700[2]
Gross Profit[1] . .	1,500			
	£21,700			£21,700[2]

Note. In this instance the Trading Account is prepared in the form in which it appears in the Ledger.

[1] Gross Profit before charging samples and Finance = £1,700 = 10% of £17,000.

[2] Calculation of Stock:

	£	£		£	£
Goods and Samples at invoice price . . .		5,208	Goods and Samples at invoice price		5,208
Add Goods 'out':			Less Finance Cost:		
Selling price . .	600		5/105 × £5,208 . .		248
Less 10% G.P. . .	60				4,960
	540		Add Goods 'out' . .	600	
Add 5% Finance . .	27		Less 10% G.P. . . .	60	
		567			540
		5,775			5,500
Less Samples at invoice price:			Less Samples at ordinary cost (i.e. excluding Finance Cost) .		800
Ordinary cost . . .	800				
Add 5% Finance . .	40				
		840			
Goods at invoice price .	4,935				
Less 5/105 . . .	235				
		£4,700			£4,700

Generally speaking, this method takes slightly less time than the other.

PURCHASES

	£		£
Sundries . . .	22,050	Samples . . .	1,050
		Finance . . .	1,000
		Trading Account . .	20,000
	£22,050		£22,050

SALES

		£			£
Goods on Sale or Return . . . c/d		600	Sundries . . .		17,600
Trading Account . .		17,000			
		£17,600			£17,600
			Goods on S. or R. . b/d		600[1]

[1] Goods on Sale or Return.

SAMPLES

		£			£
Purchases . . .		1,050	Finance . . .		50
			Trading Account		200
			P. & L. Account .		200[1]
			Balance . . .	c/d	600
		£1,050			£1,050
Balance . . .	b/d	600			

FINANCE

		£			£
Purchases . . .		1,000	Balances		
Samples . . .		50	Goods:		
			5% of £4,700 .	c/d	235
			Samples:		
			5% of £600 .	c/d	30
			P. & L. Account .		785[2]
		£1,050			£1,050
Balances:					
Goods . . .	b/d	235			
Samples . . .	b/d	30			

[1] Profit and Loss Account.
[2] £785 is made up of:

	£
Ordinary cost of goods used: £20,000 − £4,700 . .	15,300
Ordinary cost of samples used and written off . . .	400
	£15,700
5% thereof	£ 785

Sub-division of the Profit and Loss Account. Various views are found as to the most suitable sub-division of the Profit and Loss Account. The most important methods of arrangement are set out below:

1. Separation of Trading from the Profit and Loss Account or Section.
2. As in (1), with a further sub-division of the Profit and Loss Account or Section into (a) Commercial and (b) Financial.
3. As in (1) or (2), with a further extension for the appropriation of the Profit.

Sequence of Items in the Profit and Loss Account. As regards the order of items to be charged, i.e. debited—the items to be shown as income, i.e. credited, will be built up similarly, substituting gains for charges and costs—the following alternatives are met with:

A. 1. Current Fixed Charges—usually comprising those charges that must necessarily be incurred whilst the business is being carried on.

2. Depreciation.

3. Losses—as distinct from Charges—incurred, e.g. Bad Debts, Exchange losses, etc.

4. Expenses arising in relation to Capital—e.g. Interest on Loans.

B. 1. Normal Charges, sub-divided into (a) Charges of an exact nature, (b) Charges of an approximate nature, and (c) Losses.

2. Abnormal Charges.

The above are often dealt with according to their being recurring or non-recurring.

C. 1. Charges common to *all* businesses.

2. Charges *common* to all businesses of the type that is under review.

3. Charges *peculiar* to the particular business that is under review.

4. Exceptional Charges.

5. Losses.

D. 1. Relating to Premises—e.g. Rent.

2. Administration.

3. Selling Wages and Commission of Travellers.

4. Distribution and Despatch.

5. Finance—Discounts, Interest.

Usually, capital expenses written off are placed either last in the Profit and Loss Account (or Section) or in the Profit and Loss Appropriation Account (or Section).

Whatever method of sub-division and sequence is adopted, it is of paramount importance that the treatment should be consistent, so that, for instance, the rates of Gross Profit may be compared from period to period; and that whenever items of an unusual nature appear in the accounts, their inclusion and amount can be readily seen.

BALANCE SHEET

The effects upon the Balance Sheet of the various adjustments have been shown during the progress of this chapter, and consequently it will be only necessary to deal with one other important matter, namely, the sequence of the items.

Sequence. The Balance Sheet lends itself much more readily than does the Profit and Loss Account to a natural sequence of presentation of items. No two Balance Sheets will follow precisely the same order, but it is usual to set out assets and liabilities either:

(a) In order of permanence, or

(b) In order of liquidity.

Generally speaking, (a) is most commonly used by industrial and commercial businesses, (b) by banks and concerns of a similar nature.

In order to comprehend the rule, a clear conception of the various terms applied to assets and liabilities is necessary.

Assets are designated under the following headings:

1. Fixed.   2. Floating or Current.   3. Fictitious.

Fixed Assets may be regarded as those assets of a business which are of a permanent nature, and are definitely held for the purpose of earning revenue and not with a view to resale, e.g. Plant and Machinery, Buildings. Assets of a wasting nature are sometimes included under a separate heading, but this distinction is hardly necessary, as they are really Fixed Assets, which by their nature depreciate rapidly in value or content. Assets may be further sub-divided into Tangible and Intangible, but it must be borne in mind that the latter are not necessarily fictitious. Goodwill, for example, provided it is represented by actual value, is definitely a fixed asset, notwithstanding its intangibility.

Floating or Current Assets may be regarded as those assets which are made or acquired and merely held for a short period of time, with a view to sale at a profit in the ordinary course of business; that is to say, they are easily convertible into cash, e.g. Cash, Debtors, Stock, Bills Receivable.

Fictitious Assets are merely debit balances not written off; that is, items of expenditure or losses of an unusual character which are not recoupable: Preliminary Expenses of a Limited Company, property lost through confiscation and not yet written off, Removal Expenses carried forward, etc.

The modern practice is to dispense with the general headings of 'assets' and 'liabilities' and to arrange the assets and liabilities in groups with appropriate headings and with sub-totals to show the amount of (a) fixed assets, (b) current assets, (c) current liabilities, (d) long-term liabilities, and (e) proprietor's interest. By making use of these arrangements the comparison of assets and liabilities is facilitated.

Where the order of permanence is chosen, the Fixed Assets will come first, usually commencing with Land and Buildings, Plant and Machinery, and so on (Goodwill, however, is often placed first), followed by the Current Assets in order of realizability ending with Cash. In the liquidity order, on the other hand, the reverse is followed, the most liquid (i.e. Cash) being taken first, the remainder following in descending order of liquidity. Fictitious Assets, which are obviously not assets at all but merely debit balances not yet written off, will in either case appear at the bottom of the list.

Liabilities should as far as possible be placed in the same order as the assets. Thus, where the permanence order is chosen, Capital, Reserves and undistributed profits—comprising the proprietor's interest—will come first, followed by Long-term Liabilities (Mortgages, Debentures, etc.) and Current Liabilities and Provisions.

BALANCE SHEET AS AT . . .[1]

	£	£		£	£
Capital		15,000	Fixed Assets—		
Current Account		3,350	Land and Buildings:		
		————	(1) Freehold	2,000	
		18,350	(2) Leasehold	3,000	
Loan on Mortgage		6,000		————	5,000
Current Liabilities—			Plant and Machinery	2,500	
Sundry Creditors	1,950		Less Depreciation at 10%	250	
Bills Payable	1,800			————	2,250
Accruals: Rent etc.	750		Furniture and Fittings	1,500	
Bank Overdraft	2,000		Less Depreciation at 5%	75	
Mortgage Interest accrued	150			————	1,425
		6,650	Goodwill	2,000	
			Secret Processes	2,000	
			Patents and Trade Marks	1,000	
				————	5,000
			Investments:		
			Quoted	2,750	
			Not quoted	1,000	
				————	3,750
			Current Assets—		17,425
			Stock:		
			Raw Materials	£2,250	
			Finished Goods	1,400	
			Work in Progress	725	
			Goods on Consignment	500	
			Stationery	125	
				———— 5,000	
			Sundry Debtors	£2,750	
			Less Bad Debts Provision	450	
				————	
				2,300	
			Less Discounts Provision	100	
				———— 2,200	
			Bills Receivable	575	
			Prepayments:		
			Advertising	£ 180	
			Insurance	108	
			Rates	12	
				———— 300	
			Cash in hand	£ 15	
			Cash at Bank:		
			Deposit	2,500	
			Current	485	
				———— 3,000	
			Fictitious Assets—	————	1,075
			Property in X land confiscated		
			but not written off		2,500
		£31,000			£31,000

The principles outlined on pp. 0578–9 relate to ordinary concerns and do not apply to certain companies whose Balance Sheets are required by law to conform with a set layout; in the case of limited companies, certain requirements are laid down by the Companies Acts 1948 to 1976[2] relating to the Balance Sheet, not so much in relation to sequence as to disclosure of specific details. These requirements are dealt with in Chapter 23. It will be realized that no such form is laid down for partnerships and sole traders, but it is considered that, as far as possible, their accounts should follow the same principles.

Set out above is an illustration of a two-sided Balance Sheet constructed on the 'Permanence' principle, but it should always be borne in mind that there are considerable variations and modifications according to the nature of the business, the particular purpose of the Balance Sheet, and the wishes of the proprietor.

[1] See notes on p. 0581.
[2] Comprising the Companies Acts 1948, 1967 and 1976.

Notes

1. The question as to whether investments are fixed or current assets is sometimes difficult to determine, but, generally speaking, investments in affiliated companies are classified as fixed assets. Short-term investments, however, may be regarded as current assets as they are merely a substitute for cash.

2. In the case of stock the basis of valuation should be clearly indicated; that is, whether it is taken at say the lower of cost and net realizable value.

3. Where prepaid expenses represent payment for services to be performed in the future, they may be treated as current assets.

4. It is usual to subdivide investments into those quoted on the Stock Exchange and those not quoted, the former being more easily realizable than the latter.

5. It will be noticed that whereas ordinary liabilities such as loans, creditors, etc., appear on the left-hand side of the Balance Sheet, certain credit balances in the nature of reserves or provisions, e.g. Bad Debts, are often deducted from the particular asset to which they refer.

6. Instead of deducting depreciation for the year from the fixed assets balance brought forward and carrying forward the new balance, as is done in this illustration, the fixed assets may be shown at cost (or valuation) less the aggregate of the provisions for depreciation to date (*vide* Chapter 23 for the requirements of the Companies Acts 1948 to 1976, in this respect.)

There are many alternative methods of presentation. In one method the proprietor's interest is shown on the left-hand side and the net assets, sub-divided, on the right-hand side. This method lends itself particularly to presentation in columnar form, as shown in the following abbreviated example:

BALANCE SHEET AS AT . . .

	£	£
Current Assets	7,000	
Less Current Liabilities	3,100	
		3,900
Add Fixed Assets		3,100
		7,000
Less Long-term Liabilities		2,200
		£4,800
Representing:		
Issued Share Capital		£4,000
Reserves and undistributed profits		800
		£4,800

General Survey. From the aspect of examination work the following matters are worthy of the most careful attention:

1. The *Nature* of the business; e.g. if an extractive business like a quarry, attention will be directed to depletion; if an exporter, to the question of foreign exchange.

2. The *Period* covered by the accounts. The matters most usually affected by the period are Depreciation, Loan Interest, Partners' Salaries and Interest on Capital, Investment Income; on the other hand, the Provision for Bad Debts will not be affected thereby as it depends upon the amount of Debtors at a particular date.

3. Provision should be made for expenses and charges accrued and accruing where possible. Should no information be disclosed in the question, a footnote should be made. On the other hand, appropriations of profit and 'prudent' (as distinct from compulsory) reserves should not be made, but the matters relegated to a footnote. For instance, Loan Interest paid for six months only in a twelve month period (or indeed any period longer than six months) will indicate the necessity for provision in the accounts for interest accrued or accruing; or in the less frequent instance an adjustment in respect of a payment in advance. Care must be taken to note any change in the amount of the Loan or in the rate of interest in respect of the period not covered exactly by the payment, e.g. by a repayment of principal. Depreciation will be provided for if the rate of depreciation is given, but not otherwise.

4. If an item paid in advance or accruing appears in the Trial Balance, that is if it is a BALANCE, the Double Entry will already have been made. Frequently the wording of the question will serve as a guide; thus 'Rent paid and outstanding' clearly indicates that the provision for Rent accruing has been made so that the latter item is a balance. Likewise Depreciation may be a balance if the Asset to which it relates is 'NET, after Depreciation'.

Otherwise adjustment items are not part of the Trial Balance or if inserted must appear twice, once as a debit and once as a credit.

Stock on hand (if closing) will, by the same rule, be (a) either a balance (after the Trading Account has been closed off), in which case the Trading Account balance—usually credit—will appear in the Trial Balance; or (b) an adjustment item requiring crediting to Trading Account and insertion in the Balance Sheet as an Asset. In this case the Opening Stock, Purchases, Sales and other Trading items will all appear in the Trial Balance as the Trading Account will not have been closed off.

5. Items which may properly appear either as a debit or as a credit must be carefully scrutinized, particularly as there may, notwithstanding errors, be agreement of the Trial Balance—Bank Interest, Discounts, Bank, Profit and Loss balance forward are typical.

On the other hand, certain items inevitably indicate incorrectness of accounting, e.g. credit balance on Cash Account, credit balance on Short Workings in Royalties (as will be noticed in Chapter 15). But a credit balance on an Investment (Asset) Account or a debit balance on a Bad Debts Provision Account indicates not so much incorrectness as incompleteness of the accounting, the former involving a profit on sale of investment and a consequential transfer; the latter an incurring of bad debts of an amount larger than the existing provision. A transfer to Bad Debts Account (usually after creating the new Bad Debts Provision) is required, but the fact of there being a debit balance on the old account will not necessarily mean that the provision was inadequate, because the account may include bad debts incurred since the date of the provision.

6. Goods acquired in connection with expenses—and similarly stock on

hand—must be dealt with in the appropriate account, and not in the Trading Account, which deals with goods bought for resale.

7. Goods withdrawn for private purposes are not SALES. The latter account should include goods sold at SELLING prices. When the proprietor takes goods for private use he reduces his BUSINESS purchases, so that the credit is to PURCHASES, not sales. Logically, any cash discount, if identifiable, is not a business profit, and a transfer should be made to the credit of drawings.[1]

8. Where 'no profit' sales take place they should be separately shown or deducted in an inset column from general purchases.

9. Particular care is required in 'placing' debits of a 'Profit and Loss' nature. It is of vital importance to distinguish between the CHARGE against, as distinct from APPROPRIATIONS of profit.

As to depreciation, where a Manufacturing Account is required there appears to be unanimity as to depreciation of machinery being charged in that account, but otherwise there appears to be a divergence of view as to whether depreciation should be charged in the Trading section or the Profit and Loss section. The proper course to adopt is to insert the charge in the latter account and state the alternative in a footnote.

10. Where ambiguities occur or essential dates are lacking any reasonable assumption (supported by reasons) may be made, e.g. if Interest on a Loan has to be charged, the Loan may be assumed to have been in existence at the commencement of the period; where interest on drawings has to be charged, the drawings may be assumed to have been made uniformly over the period.

11. Frequently an adjustment will require a consequential entry, e.g. if goods sent out on sale or return have been incorrectly treated as sales, in addition to the reduction of Sales and Debtors there will be an increase of Stock at cost or say, net realizable value in respect of the goods in hands of customers. In addition, such adjustment may affect the amount of Bad Debts Provision, because as a result of the correction the amount of debts is diminished. Again, if the question requires the writing off of a loss on sale of an asset, part of the debit balance on the account may be in effect depreciation.

12. In regard to the Balance Sheet, the important matters are:

(a) Sequence and grouping of Assets and Liabilities.
(b) Deduction of provisions from the appropriate assets.
(c) A Bad Debts Provision is computed upon the book debts *less* contra accounts of customers, whilst the provision for discounts on debtors is based on the book debts less the Bad Debts Provision.
(d) Contingent Liabilities should be dealt with at the foot of the Balance Sheet in a note.

[1] For position regarding income tax see notes on p. 0111 and p. 2212.

13. Finally, mere arithmetic balancing will not gain full marks, nor will failure to balance necessarily cause serious loss of marks, so long as the PRINCIPLES involved—always present in the mind of the examiner—be adequately and intelligently dealt with. Hence, supporting schedules and computations should be attached to the answer.

So far as balancing is concerned the most frequent sources of trouble are (a) that the Trial Balance is not in agreement; (b) errors in dealing with the adjustments either by reason of omission of the double entry or by making them both debits or both credits; (c) overlooking the carry out of inset items into the main column.

The Use of Percentages in the Trading and Profit and Loss Account. Much valuable information can often be gained by comparing the accounts of one year with those of another on a percentage basis, since comparisons are more easily made on this basis than between actual money values. Unless due care is exercised, however, particularly in regard to the basis on which the percentages are made, the results may be very misleading. Thus, the usual basis from which the percentages are worked is Sales (i.e. Sales are taken as 100 per cent) but it is obvious that there can be little interest in the percentage on Sales of Purchases alone, the real figure to be taken being the cost of the goods sold, that is, opening stock plus purchases, less closing stock. Similarly, wages should be related to output, carriage inwards to purchases, and so on.

A distinction must also be made between those items which may be expected to vary with Sales and those which may be expected to remain constant. Thus, whereas the percentage of Gross Profit will normally be related to Sales, standing charges generally bear no relation to them, so that the former will normally be variable in amount but constant in ratio, whilst the latter tend to be fixed in amount but variable in ratio. For this reason the use of percentages is often confined to the Trading Account. The term 'standing charges' is, of course, only relative, e.g. there may be rising costs, etc., but even so some will remain the same, such as Rent on a long lease.

A business will seek to earn the marginal gross profit needed to cover its fixed charges, so that gross profit beyond that amount will, broadly speaking, be net profit, e.g. if standing charges are £400 per annum and the rate of gross profit 20 per cent, then the minimum net annual sales should be £2,000. Hence, if the net annual sales (assuming the same rate of gross profit) are increased to £6,000, there will be an increase of gross profit of £800 and a corresponding increase, subject to additional selling and distribution expenses, in net profit. Actually there will be included in the Profit and Loss Account some items which do vary with sales, e.g. carriage out, and, where there are credit sales, discounts allowed and bad debts, so that for this purpose these items should be brought into account in arriving at gross profit, leaving only the fixed charges to be debited against it. Naturally these fixed or standing charges may themselves vary over a period—increases in salaries, rates etc.—but these increases are not caused by, nor have any relationship to sales.

Illustration 30

X intends to purchase a retail shop and has the choice of two similar ones, the comparative figures of which are:

	A Shop	B Shop
	£	£
Annual Sales	40,000	120,000
Fixed Charges	2,500	4,000

The percentage of Gross Profit is 15 per cent in both cases. Both shops are run by their owners but X intends to install a manager at £3,500 per annum for A or £3,750 for B.

Assuming that conditions remain the same and the fixed charges contain no proprietorship items, the comparative position is:

	A £		B £
Gross Profit: 15% of 40,000	6,000	15% of £120,000	18,000
Fixed Charges: £2,500+£3,500	6,000	£4,000+3,750	7,750
	Nil		£10,250

The marginal gross profit (i.e. sufficient only to cover fixed charges) of A is £6,000 and of B £7,750. Regard will be had to the price of goodwill, stock to be carried, and working capital required. If X has insufficient funds to cover these he will have to resort to borrowing and the cost thereof will increase the fixed charges and convert A into a losing proposition. The charge for borrowing in connection with the goodwill would be a fixed charge, whereas that in connection with stock and working capital would be a variable and should be first deducted in arriving at the marginal gross profit.

CHAPTER 06

BILLS OF EXCHANGE

It is not within the scope of this book to deal with the purely legal aspect of bills of exchange, promissory notes, and cheques, and reference will be made to the legal side only in so far as is necessary to enable the student to obtain a proper perspective of the subject.

A bill of exchange is defined in the Bills of Exchange Act 1882, as follows:

A bill of exchange is an unconditional *order* in writing *addressed* by one person to another, signed by the person giving it, *requiring* the person to whom it is addressed *to pay* on demand, or at a fixed or determinable future time, a sum certain in money to, or to the order of, a specified person, or to bearer. (*Sect.* 3.)

By the same Act a promissory note is defined as follows:

A promissory note is an unconditional *promise* in writing *made* by one person to another signed by the maker *engaging* to pay on demand or at a fixed or determinable future time, a sum certain in money, to, or to the order of, a specified person or to bearer. (*Sect.* 83.)

By the same Act a cheque is defined as follows:

A cheque is a bill of exchange drawn on a *banker*, payable on *demand*. (*Sect.* 73.)

The important distinctive words are put into italics for emphasis. Beyond stating that the law is generally similar for bills of exchange and promissory notes with certain essential differences, the present chapter will not consider the legal incidents of promissory notes, and will be exclusively confined to bills of exchange.

When a bill is drawn up it is known as 'drawing' a bill and the person who draws it is the creditor (or his agent) of the person to whom it is addressed, that is the debtor; they are known respectively as the drawer and drawee, the former being the creditor, the latter the debtor. When the drawee signifies his assent to the order in writing he becomes the acceptor, and as such is liable to a holder of the bill according to the tenor thereof. The creditor or drawer may make the bill payable either to himself or to another person. Under the Bills of Exchange Act, the acceptor is always liable to pay the bill, all other parties being in the position of sureties, so that if the document has already passed through several hands (the parties having endorsed it in the same way as a cheque), the holder in whose possession it is when the bill matures (that is to say, becomes due), must, in order to safeguard and preserve his rights against the parties other than the acceptor (who is always liable on the bill) comply with certain formalities should the bill fail to be paid at maturity.

The custom of drawing bills of exchange dates from the Middle Ages and carried, and still carries, two very important rights, viz.:

1. It enables the holder, who is technically in law an assignee, to sue in his own name, and:
2. It entitles the holder to enforce payment 'free from equities'.

These two characteristics are the essentials of a NEGOTIABLE instrument—which term is a term of LAW, not of COMMERCE. Confusion exists, unfortunately, by the common employment of the term NEGOTIA-TION in relation to bill transactions when persons deal with, transfer, buy or sell a bill; but whilst a TRANSFERABLE document is one which may be transferred from one person to another, that is quite a different matter from its being a NEGOTIABLE document. A common example may be cited by reference to a postal order. Such a document is freely transferable, but is not a NEGOTIABLE instrument.

With reference to the first characteristic, the importance of this privilege is not so great as in the past when the Common Law did not recognize assignments of certain things, usually *choses in action*—rights which depend not on possession, but on the court's willingness to enforce them—so that the assignee had to join the name of the assignor if it became essential to enforce his rights; but the law relating to bills of exchange was gradually moulded and shaped by the law merchant which contained much foreign law through its contact with the ideas and customs of other nations. This fact, together with the practical needs of the mercantile community, led from the very outset to the rule that the assignee of a bill had the right, without being at the mercy of a capricious assignor, to go ahead with his action. In short, whether his assignor objected or not, the assignee's right to sue was, in the absence of nullifying causes, absolute.

The second characteristic is, however, of the greatest importance. The right here, as in the preceding paragraph, owed its origin to the law merchant. Provided that the holder of a bill has become technically a 'Holder in due course', he may sue on the bill despite the lack, or deficiency of, title of his assignor. It is this more than any other charac-teristic that determines whether or not a document is a negotiable instrument. Where the assignor can bestow a better title to his assignee than he himself possesses, the instrument so passing is a negotiable instrument, subject always to the presence of good faith on the part of the assignee.

The use of bills of exchange is not confined to financing exports and imports, but extends to the home trade and the book-keeping entries follow the same principles quite irrespective of the particular purpose of the bill transaction.

The nature of a bill may be understood better by considering the following example. Suppose A owes B £1,000, the latter may draw up a bill, address it to A, and make it payable (say in three month's time) to himself (B) or even to a third party (C). After he has signed it B will in the ordinary way obtain A's acceptance. The document, as will be seen, may be transferred (very much like a cheque) or may be kept 'in hand' for the three months; or may be taken to the bank for discounting.

It will be seen that should A owe B £1,000 and B owe C £1,000, and all parties agree, the one bill settles the mutual debts; that is when A accepts the bill (i.e. signifies his assent in writing thereon) B will credit A's account in the same way as if a cheque had been received; at the same time B will debit C's account as if he had paid him a cheque. A will debit B's account when he accepts the bill; the fact that the payee is C is immaterial. So far as C is concerned he will credit B just as if a cheque had passed between them and the fact that the acceptor is A is immaterial. The word 'immaterial' is naturally meant to signify that the nature of the book-keeping entry is the same for C whether the acceptor is A or B. The bill comes (as between B and C) from B, and A is not one of the accounting parties: but in a business sense the standing and reputation of the acceptor of a bill is of prime importance, as C would not take the bill either as payee or as endorsee if there were doubts as to A's capacity and willingness to fulfil his written obligation, notwithstanding C's right against B should the bill be dishonoured by non-payment at its maturity.

Inland Bill. From the legal standpoint an inland bill is defined as one which is, or purports to be, drawn and payable in the British Isles, *or* drawn in the British Isles on a person resident therein. All other bills are considered to be foreign for this purpose.

From the viewpoint of the Stamp Act the conceptions of inland and foreign bills are considerably different. A foreign bill is defined as a bill which is drawn and payable outside the United Kingdom, but paid, endorsed, or negotiated in the United Kingdom. All other bills from the viewpoint of stamp duty are considered as inland bills.

The significance of the above definitions is that for the purposes of determining the legal incidents of a bill of exchange (English law applying to an inland bill and foreign law to a foreign bill), one criterion is employed, and for determining the rate of stamp duty to be paid another criterion is applied.

A good example of this is that bills drawn in the Channel Islands and the Isle of Man are 'legally' inland bills—within the British Isles; yet for the purposes of stamp duty they are foreign bills—outside the United Kingdom.

It is important to note that only one definition (i.e. of an inland bill) occurs in the Bills of Exchange Act 1882; the other (i.e. of a foreign bill) occurring in the Stamp Act 1891, and being applicable for stamp duty purposes alone. However, the stamp duty on bills of exchange, including cheques and promissory notes was abolished as from 1st February 1971 by the Finance Act 1970.

The following is a specimen of an inland bill.

£1,000   LONDON,

14th January, 19..

THREE MONTHS after date pay to me (or, if arranged to my order, the sum of *One thousand pounds* value received.

*Accepted payable at
Lloyds Bank,
King Street, Manchester*

B.

TO A, MANCHESTER.

It should be noted that B is the drawer, A the drawee (and upon acceptance, the acceptor), B (or C) is the payee.

The following are examples of foreign bills:

£342   MANCHESTER,

                               30th October, 19. .

TWO MONTHS after date pay this First of Exchange (Second and Third same date and tenor unpaid) to *Fritz Troppau*, or order, the sum of *Three hundred and forty-two pounds*, at the rate of exchange as per first London endorsement, value received.

                               M. SMITH.

To HERR F. LUDWIG,
     BERNE.

Exchange for £470   LONDON,

                               29th April, 19. .

SIXTY DAYS after sight pay the First of Exchange (Second and Third of the same date and tenor unpaid) to Messrs. *Dubois et Cie*, or order, *Four hundred and seventy pounds*, value in account.

                         L. F. THOMSON.

To MM. MARTIN ET CIE,
     CALAIS.

Both the above bills are inland bills for stamp duty purposes.

The following are the chief advantages of a bill of exchange:

1. It is a means of settlement of foreign debts and the financing of exports. It bridges, as it were, the gap between the date of shipment and receipt at destination. Naturally, the exporter does not wish to wait for, say, three weeks for payment in respect of his sale to a South African importer, nor does the importer feel it incumbent upon him to pay until receipt of the goods. By drawing the bill, accompanied usually by bills of lading and other documents, the exporter is able to obtain his money from his banker, who, on his part, forwards the documents to his South African agent, who will transfer the documents necessary to enable the South African importer to claim the goods upon his acceptance or payment, according to circumstances.

2. In all cases it permits a debtor to defer payment until maturity.

3. It is evidence of indebtedness.

4. It enables (as has been shown) the holder in due course to sue in his own name and 'free from equities'.[1]

5. It fulfils to a certain degree, in this country, the function of currency.

6. It enables a person to 'lend his name' and so finance another by means of an accommodation bill. This is not a truly legitimate and normal function of a bill of exchange.

BOOK-KEEPING ENTRIES

The position of the acceptor will first be dealt with. By his acceptance he engages to pay the required sum at the due date, but by the same act is relieved of liability to pay before such date. It is immaterial to him what the drawer does with the document during the interval; his retention of it in his safe, his endorsing it over to his creditor, or his obtaining a loan from the bank on its security do not interest the acceptor. The latter is concerned alone with meeting his obligation on the due date and not before.

Where bill transactions are extensive a Bills Payable Book and/or Bills Receivable Book will be used for dealing with bills accepted, and drawn or received respectively, which may be incorporated, if desired, in the double entry system. But as such a book will not dispense with Journal entries, if kept in non-double entry lines, and, if so kept, will be but a Journal in modified form, for the purpose of concise explanation the entries in the examples below will be shown in Journal form (without narratives).

Where thought necessary, Ledger Accounts will be appended to supplement the explanation.

Entries in the Books of the Acceptor [i.e. the DEBTOR]

JOURNAL

Dates		£	£
Date of Acceptance	Creditor (Drawer) . . . . . Bills Payable		
Date if and when Drawer discounts the Bill	No entry		
Due date *if paid* by Acceptor	Bills Payable* . . . . . . Bank		
Due date *if dishonoured* by Acceptor	Bills Payable* . . . . . . Creditor		

* Only one of these Journal entries will be made according to whether the bill is met or dishonoured.

[1] NOTE. A person cannot obtain a better title to goods, chattels, etc., than that possessed by the seller, subject to certain exceptions, the most important of which is a bill of exchange.

The first entry against the creditor is precisely the same as if a cheque had been given, so that, so far as this transaction is concerned, it balances the creditor's account, and consequently when the bill is met the acceptor will not debit the account of the creditor, but Bills Payable. If the acceptor fails to pay the bill, the original debit to the creditor must be reversed, as the acceptor has paid his creditor nothing; not only must the amount of the bill be credited back to the creditor, but with it any discount allowed to the debtor. It should be clearly grasped that whether the bill be paid or dishonoured, the original bill is dead; it has been either discharged in the normal way by payment or dishonoured by non-payment. Hence, the Bills Payable Account must be closed.

Illustration 1

A owes B £1,000. On 1st January 19.., A accepts a three months' Bill for £975 being in full settlement. At its due date the bill is met.

Entries in the acceptor's books are:

1. On acceptance:

A's JOURNAL

		£	£
19.. Jan. 1	B	1,000	
	Bills Payable		975
	Discounts Received		25

The payment will be recorded in the Cash Book, but in this entry and subsequent entries relating to Bills the Journal will be used.

2. On payment:

A's JOURNAL

		£	£
19.. April 1	Bills Payable	975	
	Bank		975

3. If dishonoured, instead of (2), the entry will be:

A's JOURNAL

		£	£
19.. April 1	Bills Payable	975	
	Discounts Received	25	
	B		1,000

Three days of grace used to be added to the term of all bills payable after date or after sight (but not at sight or on demand). These three days were, therefore, taken into account in calculating the due date, and also for discount and interest. Thus, the due date of this bill would have been the 4th and not the 1st April 19...

The Banking and Financial Dealings Act 1971, taking into account the fact that banks are now closed on Saturdays, amended the Bills of Exchange Act 1882 so that now:

(a) Saturday is deemed to be a non-business day;
(b) bills falling due on a non-business day are payable on the succeeding business day;
(c) the three days of grace are abolished.

The day of payment is found as follows:

(a) The day of payment is included and the day from which the term is to begin to run is excluded.
(b) 'Month' means calendar month.
(c) A bill payable on demand, at sight or on presentation, is payable on the day of demand.

Entries in the Books of the Drawer [i.e. the CREDITOR]

1. Where the drawer discounts the bill:

JOURNAL

Dates			£	£
Date of Acceptance	Bills Receivable . . . . . Debtor (Acceptor)			
Date if and when discounted	Bank[1] . . . . . Bills Receivable Discounting Charges Account . . Bank			
Upon its due date if *paid* by Acceptor	No entry[2]			
Upon its due date *if dishonoured* by Acceptor	Debtor . . . . . Bank[2]			

[1] It is important to keep the two entries separate, that is first the payment into the bank at its face value; and secondly the banker's charge for discounting.

[2] If the bill is met no further entry is required, because the bill has been temporarily considered as met by the preceding transaction; but if the acceptor fails to pay at the due date his account will be debited and the bank credited, as obviously the bank will debit its customer—the person who has received the bill and discounted it—hence the bank's customer will credit the bank and debit the acceptor.

When it is realized that the bank is lending money for the period between the date the bill is DISCOUNTED—not necessarily the date of acceptance—and its maturity date, the justification for the charge for discounting needs no further explanation. The charge made by the banker is called banker's interest or discount as distinct from true discount. It is simply explained by the fact that the banker in discounting a bill of £1,000 for three months at (say) 5 per cent per annum will give credit to the customer for the £1,000, and at the same time debit him with discount or interest on £1,000 at 5 percent for three months, which is £12·50; that is, the banker lends £1,000−£12·50 = £987·50 for which he charges £12·50 interest. If a true 5 per cent interest rate were charged that is to say on the amount which plus interest at 5 per cent per annum for three months would amount to £1,000, the charge would be £12·35, calculated as follows:

$$\frac{^1 1\frac{1}{4}}{101\frac{1}{4}} \times £1{,}000 = £12\text{·}35$$

Thus interest on £987·65 for 3 months at 5 per cent = £12·35.

Thus £12·50 is chargeable (banker's discount) instead of £12·35 (true discounts).

The difference is slight; in this case (on the £1,000 bill) the amount is £0·15 which is:

$$\frac{1\frac{1}{4}}{101\frac{1}{4}} \times £12\text{·}50 = £0\text{·}15$$

2. **Where the bill is 'paid' away:** when the bill receivable is transferred to a creditor of the drawer the entries are (after debiting the bills receivable account and crediting the customer upon the latter's acceptance):

JOURNAL

Dates		£	£
When transferred	Creditor . . . . . Bills Receivable . .). .		
Upon its due date *if paid* by Acceptor	No entry		
Upon its due date *if dishonoured* by Acceptor	Debtor (Acceptor of the Bill) . . Creditor		

For reasons already mentioned, an entry will be made only if the acceptor fails to pay, when the drawer (the creditor of the acceptor) will redebit the acceptor and recredit the person to whom he assigned the bill.

3. **Where the bill is held till maturity:** the bill will be presented at the bank, [in fact it will be paid in on a separate slip like a cheque], the entry

---

[1] 5 per cent per annum for three months equals $1\frac{1}{4}\%$.

for which is:

JOURNAL

Dates Due date whether Acceptor meets it or not	Bank . . . . Bills Receivable		£	£
If met by Acceptor	No entry			
If dishonoured by Acceptor	Debtor . . . . Bank			

Before proceeding with the illustration, students may, at this stage, observe:

1. That in the acceptor's books the important factors are the date of acceptance and the due date of the bill, in that any intervening transactions relating to the bill (whether discounting, or transfer, or payment into bank by the holder) are not of importance to the acceptor; nor, in the case of the bill being discounted, are the discounting charges.

2. That in the drawer's books, the important factors are the date of acceptance, date of transfer or discounting as well as the due date of the bill, but no book-keeping entries will be required in the drawer's books at the latter date, if, having disposed of the bill by discounting or transfer, he is not notified of its dishonour.

3. Whenever any one party has received discount (cash discount), and the bill of exchange in question is dishonoured, thus necessitating the recrediting of the Personal Account of the creditor, the cash discount must be reversed; conversely, when one party has allowed to an acceptor cash discount and the bill is dishonoured.

4. The phrase 'no entry' relates only to the ordinary books of account, so that if Bill Books are utilized suitable entries will be made therein.

Summarizing the chief points of (1) and (2) normally:

1. There is no entry in the **acceptor's** books when the drawer disposes of or discounts the bill during its currency, whilst:

2. There *is* an entry in the books of the **drawer** upon disposing or disposing of the bill, but no further entry at its due date, unless it is dishonoured.

Illustration 2

Entries in the drawer's books when the bill is discounted.

A owes B £1,000; on 1st January 19. ., A accepts a three months' Bill for £975, in full settlement. Discounting charges £12·50.

1. Where the bill is met.

B's JOURNAL

19..			£p	£p
Jan. 1	*On acceptance—*			
	Bills Receivable		975	
	Discounts Allowed		25	
	A			1,000
	On discounting (assumed same date as acceptance)—			
	Bank		975	
	Bills Receivable			975
	Discounting Charges		12·50	
	Bank			12·50
19..				
April 1	*On being met.* No entry			

2. Where the bill is dishonoured.

The entries will be the same as those just outlined, except as to 1st April 19..; instead of there being 'No entry' the following entry will be made:

B's JOURNAL

19..		£	£
April 1	*On being dishonoured:*		
	A	1,000	
	Bank		975
	Discounts Allowed . . .		25

Entries in the drawer's books when the bill is transferred to his (the drawer's) creditor.

Same facts (as before) except that the bill is transferred to C in complete settlement of an account of £985 (1st February).

B's JOURNAL

19..			£	£
Jan. 1	*On acceptance—*			
	Bills Receivable	L.	975	
	Discounts Allowed	L.	25	
	A	L.		1,000
Feb. 1	*On transferring bill to C—*			
	C	L.	985	
	Bills Receivable	L.		975
	Discounts Received . . .	L.		10
	[Should C discount the bill with his banker that concerns neither A nor B.]			
April 1	*On being met.* No entry.			

If, however, the bill is dishonoured at maturity, attention need only be given to the position at 1st April 19.., the entries in the preceding example having been made.

B's JOURNAL

19.. April 1			£	£
A[1]	L.	975	
C	L.		975
A	L.	25	
Discounts Allowed	L.		25
Discounts Received	L.	10	
C	L.		10

[1] See p. 0612 for posting to Ledger.

These entries have the effect of:

1. Debiting A back with £1,000.
2. Recrediting C with £985.
3. Cancelling the original discount received and allowed entries, resulting in a net credit of £15.

Entries in the drawer's books when the Bill is held by B till maturity:

B's JOURNAL

19.. Jan. 1	*On acceptance—*	£	£
	Bills Receivable	975	
	Discounts Allowed	25	
	A		1,000
April 1	*On paying bill into bank—*		
	Bank	975	
	Bills Receivable		975
April 1	*On being met.* No entry.		

If the bill is not met but dishonoured at maturity, instead of 'No entry' there will be the following:

B's JOURNAL

19.. April 1		£	£
A		1,000	
Bank			975
Discounts Allowed			25

The postings will be made in the usual way to the Ledger, e.g. taking the entries in the drawer's books when he passed the bill on to his creditor, the bill being dishonoured. (See top of page where Journal entries are folioed 'L'.)

B's LEDGER
A

19..			£	19..			£
Jan. 1	Balance . . .	b/d	1,000	Jan. 1	Bill due 1st April, 19...		975
					Discount . .		25
			£1,000				£1,000
April 1	Bill due this date dis-honoured[1] .		975				
	Discount allowed writ-ten back[1] . . .		25				

[1] The circumstances may require the balance to be written off as bad.

BILLS RECEIVABLE

19..		£	19..		£
Jan. 1	A: Bill due 1st April 19..	975	Feb. 1	C . . .	975

BILLS RECEIVABLE

19..		£	19..			£
Feb. 1	Bill due 1st April 19.. (Acceptor A) .	975	?	Balance . .	b/d	985
	Discount . . .	10				
		£985				£985
			April 1	Bill due this date dis-honoured by A .		975
				Discount received writ-ten back . .		10

DISCOUNT ALLOWED

19..		£	19..		£
Jan. 1	A	25	April 1	A: Discount allowed written back .	25

DISCOUNT RECEIVED

19..		£	19..		£
April 1	C: Discount received written back .	10	Feb. 1	C	10

Illustration 3

On 1st July 19.., Smith owes Jones £1,200 and accepts three bills of £400 each due respectively in one, two and four months. The first bill is retained by Jones and met in due course; the second is discounted (charges £2) and met in due course; the third is discounted (charges £2) and dishonoured, the noting charges being £0·50. (For an explanation of noting charges, see p. 0614.)

New arrangements are immediately made whereby Smith pays £100 cash immediately and accepts a bill due in two months for the balance of the account with interest at 6 per cent per annum. The bill is retained by Jones till maturity. On presentment the bill is dishonoured—noting charges £0·25. Smith is shortly afterwards made bankrupt, his trustee paying a first and final dividend of £0·25 in £. Write up the Ledger Accounts in Jones's books.

SMITH

19..			£p	19..		£p
July 1	Balance . . . b/d		1,200	July 1	Bills Receivable due:	
					1st Aug. . .	400
					1st Sept. .	400
					1st Nov. .	400
			£1,200			£1,200
Nov. 1	Bill due this date dis-			Nov. 1	Cash . . .	100·00
	honoured. .		400·00		Bill due 1st Jan. 19..	303·50
	Noting Charges .		0·50			
	Interest for 2 mos. on					
	£300·50 @ 6% per					
	annum . .		3·00			
			£403·50			£403·50
19..				19..		
Jan. 1	Bill due this date dis-			?	First and Final Divi-	
	honoured. .		303·50		dend of 25p in £ on	
	Noting Charges .		0·25		£303·75 . .	75·94
				?	Bad Debts . .	227·81
			£303·75			£303·75

BILLS RECEIVABLE

19..		£p	19..		£p
July 1	Smith: Bills due:		July 1	Bank: Bills due:	
	1st Aug. . .	400		1st Sept. . .	400
	1st Sept. .	400		1st Nov. .	400
	1st Nov. .	400	Aug. 1	Bank . . .	400
		£1,200			£1,200
			19..		
Nov. 1	Smith: Bill due 1st Jan.		Jan. 1	Bank . . .	303·50
	19.. . .	303·50			

BANK

19..		£p	19..		£p
July 1	Bill due:		July 1	Discounting Charges .	2·00
	1st Sept. . .	400		„ „	2·00
	1st Nov. .	400	Nov. 1	Bill due by Smith dis-	
Aug. 1	Bill due 1st Aug.. .	400		honoured . .	400·00
Nov. 1	Smith. . .	100		Noting Charges there-	
				on . . .	0·50
19..			19..		
Jan. 1	Bill due 1st Jan. 19.. .	303·50	Jan. 1	Bill due by Smith dis-	
?	First and Final divi-			honoured .	303·50
	dend, Smith .	75·94		Noting Charges there-	
				on . . .	0·25

DISCOUNTING CHARGES

19.. July 1	Bank ,,		£p 2 2				£p

IINTEREST

			£p	19.. Nov. 1	Smith		£p 3

BAD DEBTS

19.. ?	Smith		£p 227·81				£p

Where a bill is dishonoured, the bank will incur charges attendant upon the formalities required by the law, called noting charges, and as the bank has incurred the expense on behalf of its customer it will debit him with the sum so spent. The customer will then credit bank and debit the acceptor to whose fault are attributable the charges for noting.

It may be stated, then, that the effect of dishonour is that the account of the debtor will be readjusted to the position at which it stood *before* the acceptance was given, together with noting charges necessarily incurred by the drawer through his bank. New arrangements will now be required to discharge the debt and not infrequently the new arrangement will involve a payment of interest by the defaulting acceptor.

The position arising when the drawer transfers the bill to his creditor is similar as between themselves. The transferee has relied upon the acceptance passed on to him and naturally he looks to his transferor (not the acceptor) to reimburse him—just as if the transferor had himself accepted the bill instead of passing on another's acceptance. The drawer will consequently debit the acceptor (as before), credit transferee (his creditor).

So far as the acceptor is concerned, he will in the circumstances now discussed, simply debit expenses and credit his drawer's account irrespective of whether the bill had been retained till maturity, discounted or transferred.

The entries for noting charges thus may be summarized:

1. In *Acceptor's* books:
   Debit Expenses, Credit Drawer.

2. In *Drawer's* books:
   Debit Acceptor, Credit Bank or (if the Bill had been transferred) Transferee.

3. In *Transferee's* books:
   Debit Transferor, Credit Bank.

Illustration 4

If, reverting to the previous illustration (p. 0612) C had incurred noting charges £0·50 on the dishonour of A's acceptance, the entries would be:

1. In A's books.
   Debit Expenses, Credit B.

2. In B's books.
   Debit A (the acceptor), Credit C.

3. In C's books.
   Debit B (the transferor), Credit Bank.

From the outline given in the preceding pages, it will be perceived that even if the bill is discounted there is no certainty that it will be paid at maturity and hence the amount appearing in the bank, assuming that the bill has been discounted, is always subject to a possible reduction at any time in respect of unmatured bills, and this makes it necessary to have full records of such bills in order to know what risk is involved. This risk is an example of what is known as a Contingent Liability.

Retiring a Bill. If all parties agree, a bill may be withdrawn before maturity either because the acceptor desires its withdrawal to avoid its dishonour or because he is desirous of paying the amount without waiting till its due date. The entries are similar to those outlined where a bill is dishonoured substituting the words Bill Retired for Bill Dishonoured; except that no noting charges will be incurred. Interest may, as in the case of dishonour, be charged to the original acceptor where the latter accepts in place of the one retired an entirely new bill.

Illustration 5

On 1st January 19.., A accepts a three months' Bill for £1,000 for balance owing to B. On 28th March 19.., A finds that he will be unable to meet the bill and accordingly B agrees to A retiring the bill and new arrangements are subsequently agreed upon.

Entries in A's books are (ignoring narratives):

A's JOURNAL

19..		£	£
Jan. 1	B . . . . Bills Payable	1,000	1,000
Mar. 28	Bills Payable . . . . . . B	1,000	1,000

Entries in B's books are:

B's JOURNAL

19.. Jan. 1	Bills Receivable . . . . A		£ 1,000	£ 1,000

Mar. 28	A . . . .
	    Bills Receivable . . . . . .
	      Or (if the Bill had been discounted in the
	        meantime)—
	    Bank . . . .
	      Or (if the Bill had been transferred in the
	        meantime to C)—
	    C . . . .
			1,000	1,000

A's LEDGER
B

19.. Jan. 1	Bill Payable due 1st April 19.. .		£ 1,000	19.. ? Mar. 28	Balance . . Bill due 1st April 19.., retired . .	b/d	£ 1,000 1,000

BILLS PAYABLE

19.. Mar. 28	Bill due 1st April 19.., retired .		£ 1,000	19.. Jan. 1	B: Bill due 1st April 19.. . . .		£ 1,000

If B had discounted the Bill on 1st January 19.. (discounting charges £8) his Ledger would show:

B's LEDGER
A

19.. ? Mar. 28	Balance . . Bill due 1st April 19.., retired: Bank .	b/d	£ 1,000 1,000	19.. Jan. 1	Bill due 1st April 19.. . . .		£ 1,000

BILLS RECEIVABLE

19.. Jan. 1	Bill due on 1st April 19.., accepted by A		£ 1,000	19.. Jan. 1	Bank . .		£ 1,000

BANK

19.. Jan. 1	Bill Receivable .		£ 1,000	19.. Jan. 1 Mar. 28	Discounting Charges . Bill due 1st April retired . .		£ 8 1,000

DISCOUNTING CHARGES

19.. Jan. 1	Bank		£ 8				

The position is that, unless the bill is paid at maturity, the parties are back to the point where they started just as if no bill had originally been given; and even if the bill has been discounted the party discounting has obtained, in consideration of the charge made by the bank, the use of the proceeds in the meantime.

The entries subsequent to those made by reason of dishonour of retirement depend upon the nature of the new arrangements. In all probability the defaulting acceptor will be charged with **interest** and required to pay a proportion of the debt in **cash,** whilst the acceptor who desires to retire his Bill will usually be called upon to pay the whole of the Bill in **cash** to the holder as a condition precedent to its withdrawal.

The entry for Interest will be:

In the *defaulting Acceptor's* books:

(*a*) Debit Interest, Credit Drawer.

In the *Drawer's* books:

(*b*) Debit Acceptor, Credit Interest.

That is, using the parties previously named:

(*a*) Debit Interest, Credit B.
(*b*) Debit A, Credit Interest.

Should the bill have been transferred to C:
C will debit B and credit Interest, and B will debit Interest and credit C, at the same time debiting A and crediting Interest.

If the bill is retired because the acceptor wishes to pay the bill before maturity the entries will be similar to those arising in the case of payment on the due date (except as regards any rebate given by the Bank to the creditor, in the event of his having discounted the bill).[1]

Illustration 6

A discounted a bill on 1st January 19.., being a six months' bill for £1,000 accepted on the date of discount. The bill was retired on 1st May 19... If the bank makes an allowance of 1 per cent it will be calculated on £1,000 for the period between 1st May 19.. and 1st July 19... The computation then is:

$$1,000 \times \frac{1}{100} \times \frac{2}{12} = £1 \cdot 67$$

The entry in the bank's book will be:

Debit Discount on Bills.
Credit Customer (A).

[1] NOTE. When a bill is retired, some banks make no allowance for the period between date of retirement and maturity; others allow interest at a reduced rate on the face value of the bill for such period.

The entry in A's book will be:

Debit Bank, Credit Discounting Charges.

The other entries relative to the transaction above are not shown here, having already been fully explained.

Illustration 7

On 1st December, D sold goods to the value of £1,000 to A.B. and £1,000 to M. D draws on each of them at three months for £1,015 (i.e. plus interest at 6 per cent per annum) and received the bills duly accepted on the 6th December. (The acceptances were dated 1st December.)

The goods sold to A.B. and M had been purchased from X.Y for £1,600 and by arrangement with them D handed to X.Y on 31st December (when payment for the goods was due) A.B's bill for the credit of his account, which it was agreed should be debited with £7 representing interest from 31st December, to the date of the maturity of the bill, the balance of the account being paid in cash on the same day.

D, on the same date, asked his bank to discount the bill accepted by M. The bank declined, but offered as an alternative a loan at 5 per cent per annum to the full extent of the bill until it matured; the bill was to be endorsed and handed to the bank for collection. This transaction was carried out on 31st December.

Show the Ledger of D up to the 31st December, ignoring the question of bill stamps, and expenses, other than arising and given above.

A.B.

19..			£	19..			£
Dec. 1	Goods[1]	. .	1,000	Dec. 6	Bill Receivable due 1st March 19..	.	1,015
6	Interest at 6% per annum for 3 mos. on £1,000	.	15				
			£1,015				£1,015

M

19..			£	19..			£
Dec. 1	Goods[1]	. .	1,000	Dec. 6	Bill Receivable due 1st March 19..	.	1,015
6	Interest at 6% per annum for 3 mos. on £1,000	.	15				
			£1,015				£1,015

BILLS RECEIVABLE

19..			£	19..			£
Dec. 6	A.B; 3 mos. Bill	.	1,015	Dec. 31	Bill due 1st March 19.., by A.B. trans- ferred to X.Y.		
	M; 3 mos. Bill	.	1,015			.	1,015

[1] The items marked thus would be entered in and posted from the Day Books in the usual way.

X.Y.

19.. Dec. 31		£	19.. ? Dec. 31		£
	Bill Receivable due 1st March 19.., by A.B.. Cash	1,015 592		Goods[1] Interest on Bill . .	1,600 7
		£1,607			£1,607

[1] See footnote on previous page.

CASH

19.. Dec. 31		£	19.. Dec. 31		£
	Bank Loan at 5% per annum on Bill due on 1st March 19.., by M	1,015		X.Y .	592

BANK LOAN

			19.. Dec. 31		£
				Cash: Loan at 5% per annum on Bill due 1st March 19.., by M.	1,015

INTEREST

19.. Dec. 31		£	19.. Dec. 6		£
	X.Y	7		A.B.. . . . M	15 15

The above balances, except interest, would appear in the Balance Sheet at 31st December; the interest being transferred to the credit of Profit and Loss Account.

Ignoring all other entries and thus confining the position to the transactions enumerated, the summary of the result would be:

	£	£
Profit on Sales, £2,000−£1,600 . . .		400
Interest, £30−£7		23
Cash	423	
Bill Receivable	1,015	
Bank Loan		1,015

The profit would not appear as a distinct and separate figure because the purchases and sales would form part of the total purchases and sales as written up in and posted from the Day Book.

As the bank is making a *Loan* the interest will be charged up at the date of the maturity of the bill, i.e. 1st March, on £1,015 at 5 per cent per annum for *two* months. This amounts to £8·46.

If the bill had been *discounted* the Discounting Charge would be made immediately on discount.[1]

Accommodation Bills. An Accommodation Bill is a bill of exchange which has been accepted, drawn, or endorsed by a person not in the course of ordinary business transactions, but for the specific object of enabling another person to raise funds by discounting the bill on the strength of the first person's name. There is no value given to the accommodating party and hence there is no liability on his part unless the bill is sued upon by a third party who has either himself given value for the bill or has derived his title thereto from a person who has given value; but when the bill is discounted the banker gives value therefor, and as a consequence, is entitled to hold the accommodating person liable on his acceptance, drawing, or endorsement.

Sect. 28 of the Bills of Exchange Act 1882, provides:

1. An accommodation party to a bill is a person who has signed a bill as drawer, acceptor or endorser, without receiving value therefor, and for the purpose of lending his name to some other person.

2. An accommodation party is liable on the bill to a *holder for value*, and it is *immaterial* whether, when such holder took the bill, he knew such party to be an accommodation party or not.

The book-keeping entries follow the same rules as laid down in this chapter, but it must be remembered that the person who is 'accommodated' will reimburse the accommodating party for what is in effect a loan.

Illustration 8

A accepts a bill for the accommodation of B (say, £100), the latter discounting the bill. The entries in A's books are:

A's JOURNAL

	£	£
On acceptance:		
B	100	
Bills Payable		100
When the bill matures and is paid:		
Bills Payable	100	
Bank		100
When B recoups A:		
Cash or Bank	100	
B		100

[1] If true interest were charged, this would be $\frac{\frac{5}{6}}{100\frac{5}{6}} \times £1,015$, amounting to £8·39, which is interest on the net advance of £1,006·61 at 5 per cent per annum. The difference between the two charges of £0·07 is calculated as follows (see pp. 0607–0608)—

$$\frac{\frac{5}{6}}{100\frac{5}{6}} \times £8·46 = £0·07$$

The entries in B's books are:

B's JOURNAL

		£	£
On receipt of acceptance:			
Bills Receivable		100	
A			100
On discounting the bill:			
Bank		100	
Bills Receivable			100
Discounting Charges (say) . . .		1	
Bank			1
When B recoups A:			
A		100	
Bank			100

Where the accommodating party insists upon a bill being accepted in return for his accommodation bill, there will be in each set of books, (*a*) a series of entries for a Bill Receivable and (*b*) a series of entries for a Bill Payable. This type of problem causes trouble to students but confusion is easily avoided by keeping the two parts quite distinct and completely dealing with one bill before commencing upon the other.

Illustration 9

A accepts a bill for the accommodation of B, in return for which B accepts a bill in favour of A—both bills being for three months and for £1,000. A's bill only is discounted, the cost of which is to be borne solely by B. Show the Journal entries in the books of A and B, ignoring narratives.

A's JOURNAL

	£	£
Bills Receivable	1,000	
B		1,000
B	1,000	
Bills Payable		1,000
Bills Payable	1,000	
Bank		1,000
Bank	1,000	
Bills Receivable		1,000

		£	£
A		1,000	
Bills Payable			1,000
Bills Receivable		1,000	
A			1,000
Bank		1,000	
Bills Receivable			1,000
Discounting Charges (say)		5	
Bank			5
Bills Payable		1,000	
Bank			1,000

It may happen that the accommodating party DRAWS a bill upon the party to be assisted, instead of ACCEPTING a bill; in this case it will be obviously necessary for the drawer to REMIT cash to enable the acceptor to meet the bill at maturity.

Illustration 10

In order to accommodate B, A agrees to DRAW on B for £1,000 (the bank being willing to discount for A owing to his high standing—his name being on the bill as Drawer). A discounts the bill for £997 net and remits the proceeds to B. In order that B shall be in a position to meet his acceptance, A remits a cheque for £1,000.

Show abbreviated Journal entries.

		£	£
Bills Receivable		1,000	
B			1,000
Bank		1,000	
Bills Receivable			1,000
B (Discounting Charge)[1]		3	
Bank			3
B (Remittance)		997	
Bank			997
When the bill matures:			
B		1,000	
Bank			1,000

[1] The charge of £3 being for B's benefit should be debited to B.

B's JOURNAL

		£	£
A		1,000	
Bills Payable			1,000
Bank		997	
Discounting Charges		3	
A			1,000
When the bill due by B matures, he will receive a cheque from A:			
Bank		1,000	
A			1,000
He is then able to meet his acceptance thus:			
Bills Payable		1,000	
Bank			1,000

The Ledger Accounts (abbreviated) will be:

A's Ledger (items numbered in order of sequence).

BILLS RECEIVABLE

	£		£
B (1) .	1,000	Bank (2) . . .	1,000

B

	£		£
Charges (3) . .	3	Bills Receivable (1) .	1,000
Remittance (4) . .	997		

BANK

	£		£
Bills Receivable (2) .	1,000	Charges (3) . .	3
		B (4) . .	997

It will be observed that the foregoing entries cancel out, leaving the last entry when A forwards his cheque to B, which to avoid confusing the student will be shown below, but actually would be entered in the above accounts.

B

	£		
Cheque (5) . . .	1,000		

BANK

			£
		B (5) . . .	1,000

At the end of all these transactions B owes A £1,000.

B's Ledger (items numbered in order of sequence).

BILLS PAYABLE

	£		£
Bank (5) . . .	1,000	A (1) . . .	1,000

A

	£		£
Bills Payable (1) . .	1,000	Remittance (2) . .	997
		Charges (3) . .	3
		Cheque (4) . .	1,000

BANK

	£		£
A (2). . . .	997		
A (4). . . .	1,000	Bills Payable (5) .	1,000

DISCOUNTING CHARGES

	£		
A (3). . . .	3		

A is thus a creditor for £1,000, which is represented by cash in the bank, £997, and discounting charges, £3.

Sometimes a bill is drawn up for mutual accommodation whereby the proceeds after discounting are divided between the parties equally, the discounting charges being similarly apportioned. This may be effected by the entries already outlined, e.g. in the preceding illustration A would have remitted to B £997 × $\frac{1}{2}$ only, = £498·50 and debited B with discounting charges £1·50, the other £1·50 remaining charged against himself.

Illustration 11

X accepts a bill drawn by Y for their mutual accommodation on an equality basis; the bill is for £500, discounting charges £6. Upon maturity Y reimburses X for his proportionate part of the liability.

Entries in X's books:

X's Journal

	£	£
On acceptance:		
Y	500	
Bills Payable . . .		500
On receiving half net proceeds of discounting from Y:		
Bank	247	
Discounting Charges . . .	3	
Y		250
On payment of bill at maturity:		
Bills Payable	500	
Bank		500
On receipt of Y's reimbursing remittance:		
Bank	250	
Y		250

Entries in X's Ledger (abbreviated):

Bills Payable

	£		£
Bank (4) . . .	500	Y (1) . . .	500

Y

	£		£
Bills Payable (1) . .	500	Remittance (2) . .	247
		Charges (3) . .	3
		Cheque (5)[1] . .	250

Bank

	£		£
Y (2) . . .	247	Bills Payable (4) . .	500
Y[1] (5) . . .	250		

[1] Should Y fail to pay this, the above entry would not be made; and if the amount was irrecoverable from Y, a transfer would be made as follows:

Debit Bad Debts Account, Credit Y.

Y being one of the parties to the accommodation bill in *law* is not liable thereon, except to a holder for value.

Discounting Charges

	£		
Y (3). . . .	3		

Thus at the conclusion of the transactions, Y's bank balance is reduced by £3 reflected in discounting charges, representing the cost of accommodation on £250.

Entries in Y's books:

Y's JOURNAL

	£	£
On receipt of X's acceptance:		
Bills Receivable	500	
X		500
On discounting the bill:		
Bank	500	
Bills Receivable . . .		500
X	3	
Discounting Charges . . .	3	
Bank		6
On payment to X of half proceeds:		
X	247	
Bank		247
On discharge of his liability to X:		
X	250	
Bank		250

The entries in Y's Ledger (abbreviated):

BILLS RECEIVABLE

	£			£
X (1)	500	Bank (2) . . .		500

X

	£			£
Charges	3	Bills Receivable (1) .		500
Cheque (5) . . .	247			
,, (6) . . .	250			

BANK

	£			£
Bills Receivable (2) . .	500	X (3) . . .		3
		Charges (4) . .		3
		X (5) . . .		247
		X (6) . . .		250

DISCOUNTING CHARGES

	£			
Bank (4) . . .	3			

On conclusion, Y's position is precisely the same as X's, that is, his bank balance is reduced by £3 reflected in discounting charges of £3, representing the cost of accommodation on £250.

If X fails to meet the bill of £500, entry (6) will not appear and his account will be debited with £500 (or, as the case may be, Bad Debts Account) and the bank credited. This will result in X's account (unless written off) being in debit for £250, thus:

X

		£			£
Charges . . .		3	Bills Receivable . .		500
Cheque . .		247			
Bill dishonoured . .		500			

Illustration 12

On 1st January 19.1, A drew, and B accepted, a bill at three months for £1,000. On 4th January A discounted the bill at 6 per cent per annum and remitted half the proceeds to B. On 1st February 19.1, B drew and A accepted a bill at three months for £400. On 4th February B discounted the bill at 6 per cent per annum and remitted half the proceeds to A. A and B agreed to share the discounts equally.

At maturity A met his acceptance, but B failed to meet his, and recourse was had to A; A drew and B accepted a new bill at three months for the amount of the original bill plus interest at 5 per cent per annum.

On 1st July 19.1, B became bankrupt. A first and final dividend of £0·50 in the £ was paid by his Trustee in Bankruptcy on 31st October 19.1. B obtained his discharge on 5th December 19.1, and agreed to pay A the unsatisfied balance of his account; this was paid on 10th November 19.2.

Write up B's account in A's books and state how you would advise A to treat the balance on the account when preparing his Balance Sheet as on 31st December 19.1. Make calculations in months and compute discount on face value of bill. The answer appears on p. 0628.

Bill Books. Where the dealings in bills are frequent, separate books are employed to show complete details both of bills receivable and of bills payable.

The general form of the usual bill books is shown on p. 0629, but will be adapted to the particular needs of the business.

The bill when received will be entered in the relevant book, the sender of the bill being usually, but not necessarily, the acceptor; a drawer of a bill may endorse it over to his creditor so that it is necessary to have columns to note *all* parties according to their relation to the bill. When the bill is disposed of, by endorsement to a creditor, or by discount, or by presentment for payment at maturity, suitable entries will be made.

In the Books of A:

B

19.1		£p	19.1		£p
Jan. 4	Cash: Half Proceeds of Bill discounted	492·50	Jan. 1	Bill Receivable due 1st April 19.1	1,000·00
	Half Share of Discounting Charges on above	7·50	Feb. 4	Cash: Half Proceeds of Bill discounted	197·00
Feb. 1	Bill Payable due 1st May 19.1	400·00		Half Share of Discounting Charges on above	3·00
April 1	Bank: Bill Dishonoured	1,000·00	April 1	Bill Receivable due 1st July 19.1	1,012·50
	Interest thereon at 5% per annum for 3 months	12·50	Oct. 31	First and Final Dividend of £0·50 in £ paid by Trustee in Bankruptcy of B	356·25
July 1	Bill Dishonoured	1,012·50	Dec. 31	Bad Debts[2]	356·25
		£2,925·00			£2,925·00
19.2			19.2		
Nov. 10	Bad Debts[1]	356·25	Nov. 10	Cash	356·25

[1] At 31st October 19.1, when it is clear that nothing more will be received (a first *and final* dividend having been declared), A would write off the remainder of the debt to Bad Debts Account. He might postpone making this entry until preparing his accounts at the end of December and in the meantime receive B's agreement to pay the unsatisfied balance. Nevertheless, at 31st December the amount should be written off to Bad Debts Account or a provision should be created therefor, as B's agreement to pay is unenforceable, unless valuable consideration has been given or a deed executed by A, since the old debt has been extinguished in the bankruptcy. No reversing entry should be made until the amount is actually received.

[2] B's balance is £356·25 made up as follows:

				£
(1)	$\frac{1}{2} \times$ £1,000	.	.	500·00
(2)	$\frac{1}{2} \times$ £400	.	.	200·00
(3)	Interest	.	.	12·50
				712·50
	Less Dividend	.	.	356·25
				£356·25

The book may be used by way of memorandum only or as part of the double entry: in the latter case, the amounts of the bills will be posted to the CREDIT of the SENDER, not necessarily the ACCEPTOR, and the total of the 'amounts' column posted to the DEBIT of Bills Receivable. If desired, further columns may be employed for discounts allowed, and, on the disposal side, a discounting charges column, but as to whether these extra columns are justified depends to a great extent upon the uniformity or otherwise of the treatment of bills, e.g. *all* the bills as received may be sent for discounting.

BILLS PAYABLE BOOK

No. of Bill	Date Given	To whom sent	Drawer	Payee	Where Payable	Date of Bill	Tenor	Due Date	Folio	Amount	Remarks
										£	

BILLS RECEIVABLE BOOK

No. of Bill	Date Received	From whom received	Drawer	Acceptor	Endorser(s)	Where Payable	Date of Bill	Tenor	Due Date	Folio	Amount	Date of Disposal	To Whom Sent	Discounting Charges	Remarks
											£				

Columns for Discount and interest may be added, if necessary.

BILLS DISCOUNTED REGISTER

No. of Bill	Date	Name	Drawer	Payee	Acceptor	Date of Bill	Tenor	Due Date	Amount	Days to Run	Discount	Remarks
									£			

The remarks column is employed for insertion of necessary observations. It is customary to pass dishonoured bills through the Journal.

If the Bill Book is employed by way of memorandum only, the entries for bills will flow through the usual channel, viz. the Journal.

The following example will explain the principle of double-entry as applied to the Bills Receivable Book. (The 'record' columns will be eliminated.)

Illustration 13

BILLS RECEIVABLE BOOK

From whom Received	Cash Discount Allowed	Bills Received (1)	Bills Paid into Bank (2)	Discounting Charges
	£	£	£	£
A	3	50	50	2
B	2	20	20	1
D	4	106	106	4
A	2	38	38	2
R	5	95		
			214	9
			Bal. 95	
	£16	£309	£309	£9

The bill and discount items will be posted to the credit of the individual customers and the total discounts (£16) and bills (£309) will be posted to the debit of Discounts and Bills Receivable Accounts respectively. The payments to Bank will be posted separately to the debit of Bank and credited to Bills Receivable Account; the discounting charges will be credited separately to the Bank and the total thereof posted to the debit of Discounting Charges. The balance of columns 1 and 2 will be carried forward as bills on hand.

The Bills Payable Book will be ruled and employed similarly (except that no entries for discounting charges will be necessary). The headings are as given on p. 0629.

When bill transactions are numerous a special Bill Diary should be kept so that the amounts receivable and payable on any day can be readily ascertained.

Bills for Collection. A banker, in addition to discounting bills, collects proceeds or makes an advance to the customer representing a proportion of the face value of the bill. In these circumstances the Bank will be debited only when they have collected, in the meantime a special account called Collection Account being opened. Bills paid into a Bank for collection are sometimes termed 'Short Bills,' since they have only a short time to run.

Sometimes a banker retains a proportion of the proceeds of a bill as security for advances made against other bills. This proportion is credited to the customer's Special Margins Account and a Marginal Deposit

Receipt is issued. When all the bills have been met, the balance on the Special Margins Account is paid to the customer.

Illustration 14

A has £10,000 of bills. The Banker agrees to receive £4,000 for collection, and upon the remainder he is prepared to make an advance of 25 per cent. Assuming all the 'Collection' bills are met, except one for £200, and all the 'Advance' bills are likewise met except one for £1,000, show entries in A's books. Banker's Expenses on Collections are £40, and on Advances £50, Interest, £48.

BILLS RECEIVABLE

	£		£
(Details) . . .	10,000	Bills for Collection Account	4,000
		Bills for Collection (Advance) Account .	6,000
	£10,000		£10,000

BILLS FOR COLLECTION

	£		£
Bills Receivable. . .	4,000	Cash . . .	3,760
		Collection Expenses .	40
		Bills Uncollected .	200
	£4,000		£4,000

BILLS FOR COLLECTION (ADVANCE)

	£		£
Bills Receivable. . .	6,000	Advance Account . .	4,950
		Collection Expenses .	50
		Bills Uncollected .	1,000
	£6,000		£6,000

ADVANCE ON BILLS FOR COLLECTION

	£		£
Bills for Collection (Advance) . . .	4,950	Cash . . .	1,500
		Interest . .	48
		Cash, Balance of Bills Collected less Expenses	3,402
	£4,950		£4,950

BANK

	£		£
Advance on Bills . .	1,500		
Bills for Collection . .	3,760		
Advance on Bills . .	3,402		

COLLECTION EXPENSES

	£			£
Bills for Collection .	40			
Bills for Collection (Advance) . . .	50			

INTEREST

	£			£
Advance on Bills .	48			

BILLS UNCOLLECTED

	£			£
Bills for Collection[1] .	200			
Bills for Collection (Advance) . . .	1,000			

[1] This account would be dealt with according to the reasons for non-collection, but normally a transfer would be made to the debit of the drawee (as these transactions chiefly arise in connection with exports, the foreign importer not accepting until receipt of the goods at the destination).

The Bank or Discounting House. Upon the discounting of a bill for a customer the Discounting House will effect the following entries in its books—

1. Debit Bills Discounted Account.
2. Credit Customer's Account with 'proceeds.'
3. Credit Discount on Bills Account with discounting charges. On maturity (if bill met):

> Debit Cash, credit Bills Discounted Account.

On maturity (if bill dishonoured):

> Debit Customer, credit Bills Discounted Account.

Illustration 15

On 30th November 19 . 1, A discounts a bill of exchange for B. The bill matures on the following 1st March, interest is at 5 per cent per annum, and the amount of the bill is £1,000. Calculate interest in months. Show the Journal entries in A's books (ignoring narratives).

A's JOURNAL

19.1		£p	£p
Nov. 30	Bills Discounted	1,000·00	
	B		987·50
	Discount on Bills		12·50

If A is a banker he will make two distinct entries:

(a) Credit the gross amount of the bill to the customer.
(b) Debit the discounting charge to the customer.

A's JOURNAL

19.1		£p	£p
Nov. 30	Bills Discounted	1,000	
	B		1,000
B		12·50	
	Discount on Bills		12·50

In practice, the entries will not be journalized but passed through special subsidiary books. See ruling on p. 0629.

The total of Discount on Bills Account will, at the end of the customary accounting period, be transferred to the credit of Profit and Loss Account.

Rebate on Bills Discounted. Although on discounting a bill, the Discounting House debits the customer with the amount of the charge and credits, as a profit, the Discount on Bills Account, it would manifestly be imprudent to consider it as *earned* until the Bill had been finally cleared by a payment. At the end of the accounting period the correctly proportionate part of the total credits of Discount on Bills Account is taken as profit; in other words, the amount is divided in the same ratio as the EXPIRED portion of the period for which the Bill is under discount bears to the UNEXPIRED, the latter portion being carried forward as a 'liability.' This may be done by a transfer to a separate account bearing the imposing title of Rebate on Bills Discounted Account, or by the familiar entry, made in the Discount on Bills Account, debit above the 'line,' credit below the 'line.'

Illustration 16

Continuing illustration 15, the Ledger Accounts of A, whose year runs to 31st December, would now be:

DISCOUNT ON BILLS

19.1		£p	19.1		£p
Dec. 31	Transfer to Rebate on Bills Discounted Account[1]	8·33	Nov. 30	B	12·50
	Profit and Loss Account	4·17			
		£12·50			£12·50
			19.2 Jan. 1	Transfer from Rebate on Bills Discounted Account . . .	8·33

REBATE ON BILLS DISCOUNTED

19.2		£p	19.1		£p
Jan. 1	Transfer to Discount on Bills Account .	8·33	Dec. 31	Discount on Bills Unearned[1] . . .	8·33

[1] i.e. two-thirds of £12·50, being the proportion unexpired (two months) over the total period (three months) of £12·50. This item would appear in A's Balance Sheet at 31st December, 19.1, as a liability.

Alternatively:

DISCOUNT ON BILLS

19.1 Dec. 31	Discount Unearned Profit and Loss Account	c/d	£p 8·33 4·17	19.1 Nov. 30	B · · · ·		£p 12·50
			£12·50				£12·50
				19.2 Jan. 1	Discount Unearned	b/d	8·33

The latter method avoids the necessity for opening a separate account.

Actually there will not be a separate *Discount on Bills Account for each transaction*, any more than in ordinary trading there will be separate sales accounts for each sale; the 'carry forward' figure being constructed from the schedule of bills outstanding.

The same process will be carried out each year, so that the amount carried forward will benefit the succeeding year, e.g. in the example just given, if there were no alteration to the facts the amount of £8·33 would be transferred to the credit of Profit and Loss Account for the year ended 31st December 19.2.

The following example is given, showing a collective Discount on Bills Account.

Illustration 17

A bank has the following accounts in its books relative to bills discounted at 31st December, 19.1:

	£
Unearned Discount, 1st January 19.1	420
Discount on Bills—year to 31st December 19.1	6,200
Allowances thereon to customers during the year to 31st December 19.1	150

Unearned discount is to be calculated and the Discount on Bills Account closed off for the year ended 31st December 19.1.

There were the following discounting charges credited but not fully earned.

	Date of Acceptance	Term in Months	Date of Maturity	Date of Discounting
1. Sundry Bills (estimated carry forward, £220·25				
2. Bill for £500 at 5% p.a.	1 Aug., 19.1	6	1 Feb., 19.2	1 Aug., 19.1
3. Bill for £2,000 at 5% p.a.	1 Nov., 19.1	4	1 Mar., 19.2	1 Dec., 19.1
4. Bill for £1,200 at 6% p.a.	1 Nov., 19.1	5	1 April 19.2	15 Dec., 19.1
5. Bill for £600 at 5% p.a.	1 Dec., 19.1	3	1 Mar., 19.2	31 Dec., 19.1
			*	

* In the above, columns marked * are the important ones.

The proportion of profit on discounting to be carried forward is calculated as follows:

Bill No.	Period of Discounting	Months	Months prior to 31st Dec. 19.1	Months subsequent to 31st Dec. 19.1	Proportion to carry forward
2	1 Aug., 19.1, to 1 Feb., 19.2	6	5	1	1:5 (or $\frac{1}{6}$)
3	1 Dec., 19.1, to 1 Mar., 19.2	3	1	2	2:1 (or $\frac{2}{3}$)
4	15 Dec., 19.1, to 1 April, 19.2	$3\frac{1}{2}$	$\frac{1}{2}$	3	$3\frac{1}{2}$ (or $\frac{6}{7}$)
5	31 Dec., 19.1, to 1 Mar., 19.2.	2	0	2	Total

The amount to be carried forward is £262 as shown below:

Bill No.	Details	Total Discount	Proportion to carry forward	Amount to carry forward
		£p	£p	£p
2	£500 at 5% p.a. for 6 months =	12·50	$\frac{1}{6} \times 12·50$	2·08
3	£2,000 at 5% p.a. for 3 months =	25·00	$\frac{2}{3} \times 25·00$	16·67
4	£1,200 at 6% p.a. for $3\frac{1}{2}$ months =	21·00	$\frac{6}{7} \times 21·00$	18·00
5	£600 at 5% p.a. for 2 months =	5·00	$\frac{2}{2} \times 5·00$	5·00
				41·75
	Plus Sundries (No. 1)			220·25
	Total of carry forward			£262·00

It is of VITAL importance to see that the calculations are made by reference to the discounting period, viz. the period from the date of *discounting* to the date of *maturity*, so that the date of acceptance merely serves as a guide to the date of maturity and does not otherwise enter into the above calculations.

For instance, taking No. 3 Bill, it will be seen that the bank becomes interested on 1st December 19.1, and as the bill is a four months' bill it matures on 1st March 19.2; hence the bank in effect lends money on the security of the bill for the THREE months, 1st December 19.1 to 1st March 19.2, charging interest on £2,000 at 5 per cent for three months, which equals £25, that is £8·33 per month.

At 31st December 19.1, therefore, one month's interest (£8·33) has been earned but £25 has been credited, hence £16·67 must be carried forward, which is shown in the schedule, $\frac{2}{3} \times £25$. All the other calculations may be independently checked, e.g. No. 4 interest is earned for half a month, but interest (6 per cent) for one month is '5p per £10 per month,' which on £1,200 is 600p and therefore for half a month 300p, or £3. The total discount on the bill must be seven times £3, as the discounting period is 15th December 19.1 to 1st April 19.2, viz. $3\frac{1}{2}$ months. Hence the total discount is £21, of which £3 has been earned to 31st December 19.1, involving a carry forward of £18.

Entries in Bank Ledger:

DISCOUNT ON BILLS

19.1 Dec. 31	Allowances . . Discount Unearned Profit and Loss Account . .	c/d	£ 150 262 6,208	19.1 Jan. 1 Dec. 31	Balance: Discount Unearned . . . (Details) . . .	b/d	£ 420 6,200
			£6,620				£6,620
				19.2 Jan. 1	Balance: Discount Unearned[1] . . .	b/d	262

[1] Shown as a liability in Balance Sheet.

Bills as Security. Where a bill is deposited as security, there is no sale of the bill as in the case of a bill being transferred or discounted, so that the entries relating to transfers and discounting of bills do not apply. The ownership of the bill is still the borrower's, subject to his discharging his obligation to the lender at the due date.

A note will be required in the books as to the fact that the bill has been deposited as security and such other details as the circumstances require.

Illustration 18

On 1st March 19.., A receives a 3 months' bill for £2,000 from B in payment of his account, whereupon he forthwith deposits it with X as security for a loan of £1,500 at 8 per cent per annum. The bill is met at maturity and the lender remits to A the balance of the proceeds of the bill after deducting the total amount of indebtedness. Show the Journal entries in the books of the borrower, ignoring income tax.

JOURNAL

19..		£	£
March 1	Bills Receivable . . . . . . B . . . . Being 3 months' Bill in payment of account.	2,000	2,000
	Cash . . . . X . . . . Being Loan at 8% per annum for 3 months on security of B's Bill of £2,000.	1,500	1,500
June 1	X . . . . Bills Receivable . . . . . Being Bill collected by X.	2,000	2,000
	Cash . . . . Interest . . . . . . X . . . . Being proceeds of B's Bill collected by X after deducting repayment of Loan of £1,500 at 8% per annum; and Interest thereon for 3 months.	470 30	500

CHAPTER 07

DEPRECIATION, RESERVES, AND PROVISIONS

DEPRECIATION may be defined as the permanent and continuing diminution in the quality, quantity, or value of an asset. The purchase of an asset, generally, is nothing more than a payment in advance for an expense. A simple example of this is seen in the purchase of buildings. By such purchase the purchaser expends a certain sum in advance, as a result whereof he will save the cost of rent in the future, but at the end of a period of years the building will become valueless. Thus the purchase outlay is the equivalent to paying rent in advance for a period of years.

The reason for the non-permanency of an asset is merely that in consequence of natural laws it usually suffers from the effects of TIME. The infinite variety of operative causes superimposed upon the fundamental one—the effluxion or lapse of time—will cause unequal INCIDENCE in the depreciation burden; hence the amounts of depreciation will vary according to circumstances. Obviously the elements of destruction will, sooner or later, overcome the elements of resistance.

The question of depreciation must be differentiated from FLUCTUATION, not only because the latter is temporary, but because it may signify an *increase* in the value of an asset. Speaking generally, the question of fluctuation confines itself to the money value aspect.

The chief agents or causes of depreciation are:

1. Wear and tear.
2. Physical factors: evaporation of liquids, loss of potency of acids, erosion, dampness.
3. Obsolescence, due to invention or change of fashion.
4. Fall in market prices (including foreign exchange rates).
5. Effluxion of time.

All attachable and incidental revenue expenses *must* be provided for before the true profits can be computed, so that whether the particular expense is wages, repairs, or depreciation it follows that a proportion— exact or as approximately so as the circumstances permit—for the use or consumption of an asset must be included in the charge for running the business.

The provision for depreciation does not depend upon what the business 'can afford' as the debit therefor is an essential one, constituting not an appropriation of, but a *charge* against, profits for the period in question.

The distinction between *maintenance* and *depreciation* is important. A machine may be kept in a high state of efficiency, e.g. by constant overhauling and prompt replacement of parts, such being always necessary; but the expenditure on upkeep and preservation can never be a substitute for making provision for the time when the machine is merely a bundle of scrap-iron—ready to be sold to the scrap-metal broker. During the usual yearly period a year's life has been 'consumed,' however careful the activities of the engineer in maintaining the efficiency of machines, so that the cost of such consumption should be charged up against the profits of the appropriate period, however great may be the difficulty of measuring it.

Whatever method is adopted, the following principles are fundamental:

(*a*) Assets with certain possible exceptions, e.g. land, antiques, etc., suffer depreciation, although the process may be invisible or gradual.

(*b*) The provision for depreciation (unless excessive) is a *charge* against profits.

(*c*) Maintenance of assets in a state of efficiency is not a substitute for the depreciation provision.

(*d*) The building up of a CASH FUND (by deposit in a special Banking Deposit Account, or by insurance policy, or by outside investments) is not a provision for depreciation of an asset but a financial procedure for ensuring its replacement.

(*e*) The question of the replacement of an asset is incidental to, but not a fundamental question of, depreciation.

The more important methods of dealing with depreciation will now be considered.

1. **Straight Line Method.** By this method the original cost less the residual value, divided by the number of years of useful life, is the annual revenue charge, the amount thereof being equally divided (repairs being also charged to Revenue). The advantage of this method is its simplicity and the fact that it entirely eliminates the asset where no residual value will ensue by the end of its life, although it is often quoted as a disadvantage that the early years should be charged with the same depreciation as the later, when an asset, e.g. machine, may be losing its efficiency. This, as can clearly be seen, will tend to be levelled out when there are a number of machines bought in different years, as what is undercharged on the one is overcharged on the other. This method has been judicially recommended where, for the purpose of computing an employee's remuneration based on a share of profit, depreciation of fixed assets should be calculated on the straight line method (*Edwards* v. *Saunton Hotels*).

Illustration 1

Machine cost £1,000. Life 3 years. Residual value £125. Show Machine Account. Workings to nearest £.

MACHINE

			£				£
Year 1	Cash		1,000	Year 1	Profit and Loss Account:[1]		
					Depreciation		292
					Balance	c/d	708
			£1,000				£1,000
Year 2	Balance	b/d	708	Year 2	Profit and Loss Account:		
					Depreciation		292
					Balance	c/d	416
			£708				£708
Year 3	Balance	b/d	416	Year 3	Profit and Loss Account:		
					Depreciation	c/d	291
					Balance		125
			£416				£416
	Balance	b/d	£125		Cash		£125

[1] Where a Production Account is required, the depreciation of the machinery used in production will be debited thereto, otherwise the transfer is to Trading Account or Profit and Loss Account. The student is advised to charge depreciation to the latter account where no Production Account is required, making a footnote that some accountants debit the charge to Trading or Profit and Loss Account.

2. **Diminishing Balance Method.** By this method a fixed percentage is written off the **diminishing** balance of the Asset Account yearly. The chief advantage over (1) is that the charges in relation to the opening and closing years of the Asset Account are more scientifically provided for, the depreciation charge being heavy in the early years when the cost of repairs is light. The student will see that the percentage will have to be much greater than in (1). Theoretically, the asset can never be entirely written off.

Examination candidates often experience difficulty in computing the amount of depreciation to be provided in respect of additions to fixed assets made during the period of the accounts. Where dates of additions are given, it can be assumed that depreciation is to be provided on the additions on a time basis. Thus, if the rate is 5 per cent per annum and additions are made halfway through the year, the effective rate will be $2\frac{1}{2}$ per cent.

Occasionally the rate is given without the words 'per annum,' in which case the date of the additions is immaterial. Where no dates of additions are given but it is obvious that depreciation should be on a time basis, an average date halfway through the period should be taken. On the other hand, where insufficient information about the additions is given to enable depreciation to be calculated on a time basis, then the computation should be made on the final debit figure standing on the asset account.

Illustration 2

Machine cost £1,000. Life 3 years. Residual value £125. Show Machine Account.

MACHINE

		£			£
Year 1	Cash	1,000	Year 1	Profit and Loss Account: Depreciation . Balance c/d .	500 500
		£1,000			£1,000
Year 2	Balance b/d .	500	Year 2	Profit and Loss Account: Depreciation . Balance c/d .	250 250
		£500			£500
Year 3	Balance b/d .	250	Year 3	Profit and Loss Account: Depreciation . Balance c/d .	125 125
		£250			£250
	Balance b/d .	£125		Cash	£125

[1] The rate is 50 per cent on diminishing balance.

A modified form of the diminishing balance method is to employ the progressing or 'digit' method so that in the foregoing illustration the total depreciation (£875) will be in the annual ratio of 3:2:1.

Illustration 3

The following are the details of Motors Account at 31st December 19.7:

Dr.		
19.7		£
Jan. 1. Cost		19,500
Dec. 31. Additions at cost		4,000
		£23,500

Cr.		
19.7		£
Jan. 1. Depreciation provided		13,600
June 30. Sale proceeds .		7,000
		£20,600

The vehicles sold cost £10,666 on 1st July 19.4. They have been written down at 25 per cent on written-down values at end of each year.

Show how the above will be dealt with in the final accounts for 31st December 19.7.

Vehicles		Depreciation adjustment
	£	£
Cost	19,500	
Less Cost of motor sold written out	10,666	10,666
Carried forward (a)	8,834	Carried forward 10,666

	£		£
Brought forward	8,834	Brought forward	10,666
Less Depreciation 19.4.			2,666
			8,000
Depreciation 19.5			2,000
			6,000
Depreciation 19.6			1,500
(Total Depn. = £6,166)			
		Written down to	4,500
Additions at cost . . . (b)	4,000	Sale	7,000
	12,834		
Less Depreciation to 31st December, 19.6 . . . £13,600		Depreciation over provided	£2,500
Less Depreciation written off to 31st December, 19.6 for vehicles sold . . . 6,166 (c)	7,434	To Credit of Profit and Loss	
	5,400		
Depreciation 25% to debit of Profit and Loss . . (d)	1,350		
	£4,050		

In the Balance Sheet it will appear as follows—

Vehicles at Cost (a + b) . .	12,834
Less Depreciation to date (c + d)	8,784
	£4,050

3. **Annuity Method.** Under this system the capital sunk is assumed to earn a certain rate of interest, the asset being charged accordingly; the amount of depreciation to be written off yearly is calculated on the straight line method so that it eliminates the asset or brings it down to its residual value (if any) after charging it with interest on the value of the asset at the commencement of each year.

The book-keeping entries are:

Debit the asset each year with the interest charge at the rate chosen and credit Profit and Loss Account through Interest Account.[1] This charge will *diminish* each year.

Debit Profit and Loss Account direct or through a Depreciation Account and credit the asset with the depreciation charge. This amount will be the *same* each year.

The figure of depreciation will be obtained from Annuity Tables.

[1] Deduct from Depreciation in the Profit and Loss Account.

As the yearly interest diminishes whilst the depreciation charge is the same, the net charge to revenue increases annually.

The above procedure is usually confined to the writing off of leases. The following illustration shows the method as applied to a machine, so that comparison may be made with the other methods.

Illustration 4

Machine cost £1,000. Life 3 years. Residual value £125. Interest at 5 per cent per annum. Show Machine Account. Workings to nearest £.

MACHINE

			£					£
Year 1	Cash		1,000	Year 1	Profit and Loss Account: Depreciation			328
	Interest on £1,000 at 5% p.a.		50		Balance		c/d	722
			£1,050					£1,050
Year 2	Balance	b/d	722	Year 2	Profit and Loss Account: Depreciation			328
	Interest on £722 at 5% p.a.		36		Balance		c/d	430
			£758					£758
Year 3	Balance	b/d	430	Year 3	Profit and Loss Account: Depreciation			327
	Interest on £430 at 5% p.a.		22		Balance		c/d	125
			£452					£452
	Balance	b/d	£125		Cash			£125

4. **Sinking Fund Method.** By this method the cash necessary to replace the asset at the end of its effective life is provided. As with the annuity method, the sinking fund method also takes interest into account. An agreed amount is set aside each year and invested, which, with compound interest, will be sufficient to provide a sum equal to the cost of the asset, less residual value (if any). The advantage attaching to the employment of this method is that cash will be forthcoming to provide for the renewal[1], but it must also be remembered that it may be a disadvantage to take out of the business liquid capital which can be more conveniently and advantageously employed in the business. The book value of the asset remains unaltered during the period of the building up of the Sinking Fund, the depreciation being reflected in the credit balance of the Sinking Fund. At the end of such period the Sinking Fund balance will be transferred to the credit of the asset, leaving the balance of the latter at the figure computed for the residual value.

As it will be necessary to advert to the book-keeping entries at a later stage, the entries are shown on p. 0714 to avoid repetition.

[1] Assuming that replacement cost is the same as the original cost.

Illustration 5

Machine cost £1,000. Life 3 years. Residual value £125. Investment at 5 per cent. Show Accounts, assuming that the amounts to be set aside are £277 for the first year and £278 for the remaining two years. Workings to nearest £.

SINKING FUND

			£				£
Year 1	Balance	c/d	277	Year 1	Profit and Loss Account		277
Year 2	Balance	c/d	569	Year 2	Balance . . .	b/d	277
					Interest		14
					Profit and Loss Account .		278
			£569				£569
Year 3	Balance	c/d	875	Year 3	Balance . . .		569
					Interest		28
					Profit and Loss Account .		278
			£875				£875
	Machine Account . .		£875		Balance . . .	b/d	£875

MACHINE

			£				£
Year 1	Cash (Cost) . . .		1,000	Year 3	Sinking Fund Account .		875
					Cash[1]		125
			£1,000				£1,000

[1] The investments will be sold for £875, which together with £125 cash received for the scrap value of the old machine, will provide £1,000 towards the cost of a new machine.

SINKING FUND INVESTMENT—5% STOCK

Year				£	Year			£
1	Cash			277	1	Balance . . .	c/d	277
2	Balance . . .	b/d		277	2	Balance . . .	c/d	569
	Cash . . . £ 14							
	Cash . . . 278			292				
				£569				£569
3	Balance . . .	b/d		569	3	Balance . . .	c/d	875
	Cash . . . £ 28							
	Cash . . . 278			306				
				£875				£875
4	Balance	b/d		875				

The student will observe that the fund and its counterpart are always equal.

5. **Insurance Policy Method.** By this method steps are taken similar to those under the Sinking Fund method except that the investment takes the form of annual payments of premium to an insurance company, whilst no interest on investment is actually received.

Actually the policy does yield 'interest' as the policy moneys receivable normally exceed the total premiums, but as the premiums are payable in advance, the calculation of interest will be for a year longer than under the Sinking Fund method.

An endowment policy is taken out to produce the sum required at the end of the life of the asset. An Endowment Policy Account and an Asset Amortization Account will be opened as for the Sinking Fund method. Interest earned on the policy will be debited to the Endowment Policy Account and credited to the Asset Amortization Account.

The interest earned will be the excess of the policy moneys payable over the total premiums. As mentioned, the policy moneys will not be payable until one year *after* the payment of the last premium, so that it will be necessary to pay the first and each subsequent premium at the *commencement* of each year.

Illustration 6

The same facts as before except that an endowment policy for three years is taken out for £875, the annual premium being £275, which works out at 3 per cent compound interest. Show Endowment Policy Account and Asset Amortization Account. Workings to nearest £. (These accounts appear on p. 0709.)

Alternatively, the policy may be revalued yearly at the surrender value[1] either with or without taking into account interest, the 'loss' on revaluation being debited to the Sinking Fund or Asset Amortization Account and credited to the Endowment Policy Account. When the policy matures there will be a 'profit' as the full value of the policy will be payable, and this will be debited to the Policy Account and credited to the Sinking Fund or Asset Amortization Account.

Illustration 7

Same facts as in the preceding illustration except that no interest is taken into account, and that the surrender values are:

Year 1 (end) £30.   Year 2 (end) £225.

Show Endowment Policy Account and Asset Amortization Account. Workings to nearest £. (These accounts are shown on p. 0710.)

---

[1] The surrender value of a policy is the amount that the insurance company will pay the policyholder should he surrender the policy at any time before maturity. Such a course would involve the policyholder in a considerable loss which may be avoided by obtaining a loan from the insurance company.

ENDOWMENT POLICY

			£				£
Year 1 (commencement) (end)	Cash—Premium		275	Year 1 (end)	Balance . . .	c/d	283
	Interest on £275 at 3% per annum.		8				
			£283				£283
Year 2 (commencement) ,, (end)	Balance . . .	b/d	283	Year 2 (end)	Balance . . .	c/d	575
	Cash—Premium		275				
	Interest on £558 at 3% per annum.		17				
			£575				£575
Year 3 (commencement) (end)	Balance . . .	b/d	575	Year 3	Cash . . .		875
	Cash—Premium		275				
	Interest on £850 at 3% per annum[1]		25				
			£875				£875

[2] ASSET AMORTIZATION

			£				£
Year 1 (end)	Balance . . .	c/d	283	Year 1 (end)	Profit and Loss Account .		275
					Endowment Policy Account .		8
			£283				£283
Year 2 (end)	Balance . . .	c/d	575	Year 2 (commencement) (end)	Balance . . .	b/d	283
					Profit and Loss Account .		275
					Endowment Policy Account .		17
			£575				£575
Year 3 (end)	Transfer to Asset Account		875	Year 3 (commencement) (end)	Balance . . .	b/d	575
					Profit and Loss Account .		275
					Endowment Policy Account .		25
			£875				£875

[1] In practice, the Interest 'earned' will not necessarily be 3 per cent per annum.
[2] Alternatively the Account may be described as a Sinking Fund.

ENDOWMENT POLICY

			£					£
Year 1 (commencement)	Cash—Premium . .		275	Year 1 (end) "	Asset Amortization Account . . Balance (Surrender Value)	c/d		245 30
			£275					£275
Year 2 (commencement)	Balance . . . Cash—Premium . .	b/d	30 275	Year 2 (end) "	Asset Amortization Account . . Balance (Surrender Value)	c/d		80 225
			£305					£305
Year 3 (commencement) (end)	Balance . . . Cash—Premium . . Asset Amortization Account . .	b/d	225 275 375	Year 3 (end)	Cash			875
			£875					£875

ASSET AMORTIZATION

			£					£
Year 1 (end) "	Endowment Policy Account . . Balance . . .	c/d	245 30	Year 1 (end)	Profit and Loss Account			275
			£275					£275
Year 2 (end) "	Endowment Policy Account . . Balance . . .		80 225	Year 2 (commencement) (end)	Balance . . . Profit and Loss Account	b/d		30 275
			£305					£305
Year 3 (end)	Transfer to Asset Account		875	Year 3 (commencement) (end)	Balance . . . Profit and Loss Account Endowment Policy Account	b/d		225 275 375
			£875					£875

It will be seen that in both cases cash is available for £875, and the asset of £1,000 after making the transfer in the third year of £875 stands at £125.

6. **Revaluation Method.** By this method the asset is revalued each year, any diminution in value being charged to Profit and Loss Account.

Illustration 8

1st January 19.., stock of loose tools £500. Purchases during year £150. 31st December 19.., stock of tools £520.

LOOSE TOOLS

19..			£	19..			£
Jan. 1	Balance	b/d	500	Dec. 31	[1]Profit and Loss Account		
Dec. 31	Cash		150		(or Production Account: Depreciation		130
					Balance	c/d	520
			£650				£650
19..							
Jan. 1	Balance	b/d	520				

Loose tools are frequently treated exactly like stock, the purchases thereof being shown as a separate item. In this case the treatment of the preceding facts would be:

LOOSE TOOLS

19..			£	19..		£
Jan. 1	Balance	b/d	500	Dec. 31	[1]Profit and Loss Account (or Production Account)	500
Dec. 31	Profit and Loss Account: (or Production Account).		520			

LOOSE TOOLS PURCHASES

19..			£	19..		£
Dec. 31	Cash (or Sundries)		150	Dec. 31	[1]Profit and Loss Account (or Production Account)	150

[1] In practice, the employment of loose tools predicates manufacturing or production and the transfer would be to Manufacturing or Production Account, and shown thus:

Charge to, or Debit side of, Production Account:
  Loose Tools:

		£
Opening Stock		£500
Purchases		150
		650
Less Closing Stock		520
		£130

7. **Repairs, Maintenance and Depreciation Fund or Provision.**[2] The method of making a composite yearly charge to cover repairs, maintenance, and depreciation is frequently met with. The excess of the provision created over repairs and maintenance is in reality the provision for depreciation, and should by the time the asset has become merely scrap be adequate to meet the depreciation suffered. Hence, such provision must at

[2] In accounts not governed by the Companies Acts 1948 to 1976, this may be referred to as a Reserve (see p. 0717 and footnote on p. 0519).

the end of the life of the asset be equal to the difference between its cost price and its residual value. The book-keeping entries are:

(1) Debit Profit and Loss Account
    Credit Provision for Repairs, Maintenance and } with yearly charge
    Depreciation

(2) Debit Provision for Repairs, Maintenance and } for repairs and maintenance
    Depreciation
    Credit Cash

Illustration 9

A yearly sum of £400 is set aside to cover repairs, maintenance, and depreciation. The expenses for repairs and maintenance in the first two years are £30 and £47. Show Repairs, Maintenance and Depreciation Provision Account.

PROVISION FOR REPAIRS, MAINTENANCE AND DEPRECIATION

			£				£
Year 1	Cash—Repairs etc.		30	Year 1	Profit and Loss Account		400
	Balance	c/d	370				
			£400				£400
Year 2	Cash—Repairs, etc.		47	Year 2	Balance	b/d	370
	Balance	c/d	723		Profit and Loss Account		400
			£770				£770
				Year 3	Balance	b/d	723

8. **Depletion Method.** In the case of concerns owning wasting assets, provision for the depletion of such assets is sometimes made by means of a charge to Profit and Loss Account per unit of asset extracted.

Illustration 10

The cost of a mine is £30,000 and the estimated quantity of payable ore in tons is 300,000. The first and second years' output: 500 tons and 1,600 tons. Show Mine Account assuming residual value of the Land to be worth nothing. (This illustration appears on p. 0713.)

In reference to this topic it should be noted that the lessee of the mine will usually be liable to pay compensation to the lessor at the end of the lease for spoiling the land, and consequently will probably build up a compensation provision or fund.

[The same principle applies in the case of a machine, e.g. 2½p an hour where the estimated running hours of the machine's life are 50,000 and the cost of the machine £1,250 (machine hour rate): or instead of the rate being fixed at 2½p an hour, the first year may be charged with, say, 3½p an hour, the second with 2½p, and so on in subsequent years, the rate diminishing in ratio to the machine's loss of efficiency (efficiency hour rate).]

MINE

Year 1	Cash		£ 30,000	Year 1	Profit and Loss Account (or Production Account) Depletion: $\dfrac{500}{300000} \times £30,000$. Balance . . .	c/d	£ 50 29,950
			£30,000				£30,000
Year 2	Balance . .	b/d	29,950	Year 2	Profit and Loss Account (or Production Account) Depletion: $\dfrac{1600}{300000} \times £30,000$. Balance . . .	c/d	160 29,790
			£29,950				£29,950
Year 3	Balance . .	b/d	29,790				

9. **Renewals.** By this method the original asset remains in the books at the original cost and the cost of replacement is charged as an expense. The method does not conform to good accounting practice and is criticized on two grounds: (1) That the value of the original asset will by no means equal that of the one replacing it; and (2) that there is an uneven distribution of the burden of depreciation, as only in the year of replacement does revenue bear the renewal charge, entirely relieving most of the years and over-charging that in which the replacement takes place.[1]

Illustration 11

The cost of an original asset is £480. Three years later it is replaced by an asset costing £570. How are these dealt with on the Renewals system?

The former remains as an asset and the latter is debited to the Profit and Loss Account.

The Life of an Asset. The proportion to be written off in respect of depreciation depends, as has been seen, to a large extent on the estimated life of the asset, but it must be noted that certain assets, e.g. patents, copyrights, mining leases, etc., have, as it were, two 'lives,' viz. (a) legal life, e.g. the lease of a mine, and (b) commercial life, e.g. profitable working life of a mine. Depreciation must obviously be calculated on the shorter of the two 'lives.'

Statement of Standard Accounting Practice[2]. Statement of Standard Accounting Practice 1/12 concerns Accounting for Depreciation and the

---

[1] This criticism may, however, be overcome by setting up a Provision for Renewals with an annual charge to Profit and Loss Account, renewals being debited to the Provision.

[2] It will be realized that these apply particularly to companies rather than to partnerships and sole traders.

main extract therefrom is as follows:

1. Provision for depreciation of fixed assets having a finite useful life should be made by allocating the cost (or revalued amount) less estimated residual values of the assets as fairly as possible to the periods expected to benefit from their use.

2. Where there is a revision of the estimated useful life of an asset, the unamortized cost should be charged over the revised remaining useful life.

3. However, if at any time the unamortized cost of an asset is seen to be irrecoverable in full, it should be written down immediately to the estimated recoverable amount which should be charged over the remaining useful life.

4. Where there is a change from one method of depreciation to another, the unamortized cost of the asset should be written off over the remaining useful life on the new basis commencing with the period in which the change is made. The effect should be disclosed in the year of change, if material.

5. Where assets are revalued in the financial statements, the provision for depreciation should be based on the revalued amount and current estimate of remaining useful life, with disclosure in the year of change, of the effect of revaluation, if material.

6 The following should be disclosed in the financial statements for each major class of depreciable asset:

(a) the depreciation methods used;

(b) the useful lives or the depreciation rates used;

(c) total depreciation allocated for the period;

(d) the gross amount of depreciable assets and the related accumulated depreciation.

Plant Registers. Following on the last point above, it is essential in any large concern that adequate records should be kept in respect of Plant and Machinery. A separate record may be kept for each machine, the following information being shown:

1. Description—type, number, maker, etc.

2. Where situated.

3. Purchase—date, from whom, cost, cost of erection, etc.

4. Alterations and Additions, Repairs and Renewals.

5. Depreciation—basis, annual rate, amounts and aggregate.

6. Sale—date, to whom, price, profit or loss on sale.

7. Taxation—Rate of Capital Allowances, First-year and Writing-down allowances, Balancing Adjustments.

8. An engineer's report is sometimes included.

Sinking Fund for Depreciation and Redeeming Debenture. It may here be convenient to contrast the position arising in the case of a Sinking Fund created by way of amortization of an asset and that created when a liability is to be repaid. The latter arises chiefly in connection with debentures of a limited company, which will be dealt with fully in Chapter 23, but for the present the debenture may be considered in the light of a loan.

The positions are shown by means of the following table:

	SINKING FUND to write off asset	SINKING FUND to 'redeem' a liability
1. On setting aside the instalment annually	Debit Profit and Loss Account Credit Sinking Fund	Debit Profit and Loss APPROPRIATION Account Credit Sinking Fund
2. On investing the instalment	Debit Sinking Fund Investment Credit Cash	Same as Sinking Fund to write off Asset
3. On receipt and reinvestment of interest on investment	Debit Cash Credit Sinking Fund Debit Sinking Fund Investment Credit Cash	Same as Sinking Fund to write off Asset
4. On the expiry of the life of the asset	Debit Sinking Fund Credit Asset	Not applicable
4a. On the purchase of new asset	Debit Cash Credit Sinking Fund Investment Debit (new) ASSET Credit Cash	Not applicable
5. On the redemption of debentures	Not applicable	Debit Cash Credit Sinking Fund Investment Debit DEBENTURES Credit Cash Debit Sinking Fund Credit General Reserve

The essential differences are:

1. The amount set aside for the Sinking Fund for writing off the asset is debited to the Profit and Loss Account; for the redemption of debentures it is debited to the Appropriation Account.

The difference in treatment is explained by the fact that one is a definite charge for depreciation, and the other merely an appropriation to prevent the amount set aside from being distributed as dividends until the debt is repaid.

2. When the asset is written off, the fund and the asset disappear, and until purchase of the new asset is made the investment (or cash if the investment is realized) remains; but in the case of the repayment of the debenture the investment and the debenture disappear (as the investment is converted into cash which is used to repay the debt), but the fund remains and is now 'free,' i.e. it is available for distribution. As has been seen in (1), the fund was created solely to prevent the amount represented thereby being distributed in dividends until the repayment of the debentures. Although the expression 'redeeming by means of Sinking Fund' is convenient, it is not strictly accurate, as it is CASH that redeems the liability.

In practice, of course, it does not follow that the cash realized from the Sinking Fund investment (which equals the original value of the old asset) will be sufficient to defray the cost of the *new* asset.

Illustration 12

A company borrows £20,000 by debentures and agrees to redeem the whole sum at the end of five years by means of a Sinking Fund.

At the end of the period the relevant accounts will be:

DEBENTURES

	£				£
Cash	20,000	Balance. . . .	b/d	20,000

SINKING FUND

	£				£
Reserve. . . .	20,000	Balance. . . . (instalments debited to Profit and Loss Appro- priation Account)	b/d	20,000

SINKING FUND INVESTMENT

		£			£
Balance. . . .	b/d	20,000	Cash		20,000

CASH

	£			£
Sinking Fund Investment .	20,000	Debentures . . .		20,000

RESERVE

			£
		Sinking Fund . . .	20,000

It will be noted that the Debentures and Investment Account disappear, the Sinking Fund being transferred to Reserve.

If an asset is to be replaced at the end of five years by the utilization of a Sinking Fund, the relevant accounts will be:

ASSET

	£		£
Cost	20,000	Sinking Fund . . .	20,000

SINKING FUND

	£			£
Asset	20,000	Balance. . . . (instalments debited to Profit and Loss Account)	b/d	20,000

SINKING FUND INVESTMENT

		£			£
Balance. . .	b/d	20,000	Cash . . .		20,000

CASH

	£		
Sinking Fund Invest-ment . . .	20,000		

It will be perceived that the asset and fund accounts disappear, the cash (realized from the investment) remains, pending the acquisition of the new asset.

The question of profit or loss on the realization of the Sinking Fund Investment is dealt with in Chapter 23.

It will be clear that the Sinking Fund instalment in the case of debentures is an *appropriation* of profits; in the case of the amortization of an asset a *charge against* profits.

RESERVES AND PROVISIONS

The lack of uniformity and looseness in the past in the employment of the term 'reserve' have tended not only to create confusion in the mind of the student but to difficulties in the proper understanding of the financial position of businesses as shown in their Balance Sheets. The matter has now been considerably clarified by the Companies Acts 1948 to 1976, and although the requirements of the Acts (which will be stated in detail in a later chapter) apply only to limited companies, it is proposed in this chapter to deal with reserves and provisions on the lines of the definitions laid down in the Acts. The reader should, however, bear in mind that at this stage the matter is being considered more in broad principle than in regard to the specific requirements of the Acts which apply to the published accounts of limited companies.

As a preliminary to closer study, reserves and provisions may be defined as follows:

1. *Reserves* are amounts set aside out of profits and other surpluses which are not designed to meet any liability, contingency, commitment or diminution in value of assets known to exist at the date of the Balance Sheet.

2. *Provisions* are amounts set aside out of profits and other surpluses to provide for:

(a) depreciation, renewals or diminution in value of assets, or

(b) any *known* liability of which the amount *cannot* be determined with substantial accuracy.

It follows therefore that:

1. Any amount set aside for the purposes described in (2) (a) and (b)

(above) in excess of estimated requirements must be regarded as a reserve, and

2. Sums set aside to meet known liabilities of which the amount *can* be determined with substantial accuracy do not fall within the definition of a provision and should therefore be described as accruals or accrued liabilities.

Reserves are in effect part of the undistributed profits of the business and therefore part of the proprietorship, whereas provisions and accruals are a diminution of proprietorship in the form of a liability or diminution of an asset. The former are broadly appropriations of, the latter charges against, profits.

Reserves

By the Companies Act 1967, there is now no legal requirement as there was by the Companies Act 1948, to distinguish between capital and revenue reserves in the published accounts of limited companies. This change affects only what must be disclosed; it does not affect whether a reserve is legally distributable or what reserves Directors determine should not be distributed. Consequently it might still be considered appropriate in the published accounts of certain limited companies to distinguish the two kinds of reserves.

1. **Capital Reserves.** These are not, in limited company accounting, normally regarded as available for distribution as dividend; such reserves arise from:

(a) Sale of fixed assets at a profit.[1]
(b) Profit of a company accrued before incorporation or purchase.
(c) Premium on shares or debentures.
(d) Profit on redemption of debentures.
(e) Profit on forfeiture of shares.
(f) Surplus on revaluation of assets and liabilities.
(g) Capital Redemption Reserve Fund.

The matters are dealt with in more detail in Chapter 23, but it may be stated broadly that in certain circumstances some of these profits *may* be considered as revenue but the better practice is to regard them as capital; others are subject to special restrictions and treatment in accordance with the provisions of the Companies Acts 1948 to 1976.[2]

2. **Revenue Reserves.** These are normally regarded as available for distribution through the Profit and Loss Account, but are themselves divided into two classes—those immediately and those not immediately so available:

(i) *General Reserve.* This reserve is created by setting aside profits in order to strengthen the general financial position of the business. Such

---

[1] In practice, the surplus over book value is often taken to Capital Reserve, although strictly the capital profit is only the excess of sale proceeds over cost.
[2] Comprising the Companies Acts 1948, 1967 and 1976.

profits, however, remain available for distribution, and for this reason it is often described as a 'free' reserve. In this group should be included any undistributed balance of the Profit and Loss Account (by deduction, if a debit balance).

(ii) *Specific Reserve.* Under this heading are included amounts set aside out of profits for a specific purpose or because of a specific obligation, which, though still revenue, are not immediately available for distribution. The best example of this arises in the accounts of limited companies when a company engages to set on one side a portion of profits until debentures—which for this purpose may be considered the equivalent of a loan—are repaid; throughout the whole period of liability in respect of the loan, the reserve set aside is part of the undistributed profits and upon repayment of the loan may be transferred back to the Profit and Loss Account or to the General Reserve.

Share Premium Account and Specific Reserves should be separately stated in the Balance Sheet. In respect of all reserves sufficient detail should be given to show how increases and decreases have arisen and how the reserves have been utilized.

So far, consideration has been confined to reserves which are shown as such in the Balance Sheet. There may, however, be reserves which are not disclosed therein:

1. *Hidden Reserves*, where an item of profit is (including Revenue or Capital Reserve) described in such a manner as to indicate a liability, being included for instance in Sundry Creditors.

2. *Inner Reserves*, where a provision is made to cover exceptional and abnormal losses, and such provision is not openly disclosed, e.g. general contingencies reserve (in the case of a bank) included in creditors, usually under the heading of 'Deposit, Current and other accounts.'

3. *Secret Reserves*, where the net asset position is stronger than that disclosed by the Balance Sheet by reason of:

(a) Excessive depreciation of an asset (particularly Goodwill), or excessive valuation of a liability, or excessive provisions.

(b) Complete elimination of an asset; undervaluation or understatement of an asset.

(c) Charging capital expenditure to revenue, or crediting revenue receipts to an asset (e.g. dividends received and earned credited to the investment).

(d) Permanent appreciation in a fixed asset, or permanent diminution or extinction of liability not recorded.

(e) Showing a contingent liability as an actual liability or as a provision therefor; or an actual asset as a contingent asset.

(f) Grouping of 'free' reserves with creditors.

(g) Crediting exceptional or non-recurring profit to a Contingencies Reserve without proper disclosure.

(h) Allowing undistributed surplus in the hands of a subsidiary company.

An example of the creation of a secret reserve is seen where a bank provides for depreciation of investments, but does not re-credit a subsequent appreciation of investments.

From this it will be seen that secret reserves may
  (i) arise, as in (d),
  (ii) be created, as in the remainder of the examples given,
  (iii) be maintained, by allowing (i) to remain or by continuing the
practice in (ii).

It may here be noted that the Companies Acts 1948 to 1976, contain provisions which aim at preventing the creation of secret reserves; this is dealt with more fully in Chapter 23.

Reserve Fund. The word 'fund' is now frequently employed in substitution for the word 'account,' whether it is represented by specifically earmarked investments or not. It is recommended that the term 'Reserve Fund' should only be used where a reserve is in fact specifically represented by readily realizable and earmarked assets.

Provisions

Provision will be required in the final accounts for (1) Depreciation and diminution in value of assets, and (2) Estimated and anticipated liabilities which exist at the date of the Balance Sheet, e.g. claims for delay in delivery of goods, accident and employer's liability claims, estimated bad and doubtful debts (these may be regarded as coming under the heading in (1) of diminution in value of assets), etc.

These provisions will be normally either deducted from assets in the Balance Sheet (as in the case of depreciation and bad and doubtful debts) or grouped with liabilities under appropriate sub-headings, unless in the published accounts it would be detrimental to the company's interests for a provision to be openly disclosed, e.g. a provision against a disputed claim.

Where any provision is used for a purpose other than that for which it was created, this fact should be shown, and when any provision becomes redundant it should be credited back to the Profit and Loss Appropriation Account.

Contingencies

Amounts set aside in respect of contingencies may be in the nature of a reserve, or a provision, or what is termed a contingent liability.

1. **Contingency Reserve.** Amounts are sometimes set aside out of profits under this heading although there are no actual, probable or really possible contingencies at the date of the Balance Sheet. There is thus little or no difference between such a reserve and a General Reserve as already described, and the two may well be shown together.

2. **Contingency Provision.** As already stated provision should be made for all known contingencies, even if the amount can only be estimated, existing at the date of the Balance Sheet, e.g. under employer's liability, to cover possible claims against accidents which have already occurred.

3. **Contingent Liabilities.** Where there is a possibility that upon the

happening of a contingency an actual liability will arise, it is not usual to make any relevant provision in the accounts, but by way of a footnote in the Balance Sheet. Examples of contingent liabilities are bills under discount and calls on shares in limited companies.

If the contingency does arise it will involve a loss. The liability incurred may be reflected in an asset, e.g. the call on the share may arise because the company is in difficulties, in which case the liability incurred will probably be considered a loss; but if the calls are made in the ordinary course of events, the liability incurred will be reflected in an increase in the value of the assets.

As already stated any amount set aside in excess of a necessary provision is a *reserve* and should appear so in the Balance Sheet. For example, in regard to Stock, the amount required to cover the excess of cost over say, net realizable value is a provision; any further amount, e.g. in respect of a possible future fall in values, is a reserve.

In recent cases dealing with the ascertainment of Capital Transfer Tax valuation of shares the Court has taken the narrow view of the meaning of contingent liabilities—that a liability which already actually *exists in law* at a relevant date, though it might be payable in certain events only, is quite **different** from a *potential* liability, which from the business angle is almost a certainty but which does not become a liability *in law* until the happening of a *future* event, such as liability for future balancing charge which might arise on a sale of assets where Capital Allowances have in the past been given in excess assessments for Taxation.

Thus a contingent liability may be regarded from either of the following angles: (*a*) a 'negative' to a 'positive,' i.e. a possible to an actual liability (e.g. as in a guarantee), or (*b*) a 'positive' to a 'negative,' i.e. an actual to a possible or probable liability (e.g. as in future tax liability).

CHAPTER 08

CAPITAL AND REVENUE EXPENDITURE

BEFORE each term is discussed it is sufficient to say that revenue expenditure constitutes a charge against profits, and must be charged, i.e. debited to Profit and Loss Account, whereas capital expenditure is treated as a capital charge, and is shown as an asset in the Balance Sheet.

It is a matter of extreme difficulty to lay down a hard and fast rule as to what dividing line separates capital expenditure from revenue expenditure. There is much divergence of opinion and practice on this matter, and *inter alia* the following *indicia* have been laid down as establishing the fact that the expenditure is capital.

1. Any expenditure which is undertaken for the purpose of increasing profits either positively by way of INCREASING earning capacity, or negatively by DECREASING working expenditure, is capital expenditure. The formal acquisition of a tangible asset is not a necessary element in this rule. For example, owing to increased demand for seats, a theatre reconstructs the auditorium; such expenditure may be capitalized.

2. If the expenditure, whether increasing the earning capacity or not, produces an asset comparatively permanent in character, it is capital expenditure.

Capital expenditure, therefore, may be described as outlay resulting in the increase or acquisition of an asset or increase in the earning capacity of a business.

Revenue expenditure, on the other hand, is such outlay as is necessary for the MAINTENANCE of earning capacity, including the upkeep of the fixed assets in a fully efficient state, and the normal total cost involved in selling, including the cost of goods and services of the business to which it relates.

In short, if the purpose of expenditure is to MAINTAIN the business it is revenue; if it is to IMPROVE the business it is capital.

Improvements. The judicial view is that the cost of an improvement of an asset is a legitimate capital charge quite irrespective of whether it is by way of mere substitution or is entirely new. The accounting view is that in regard to the former, i.e. the substitution, the EXCESS of the value of the new over the old asset is the only amount that can properly be charged to capital. The former view is that the original asset was necessary before the improvement could be made. Although this view may be tenable in extreme instances, it is not supported by the vast majority of accountants. It is important, however, in that when the question of whether a dividend has been improperly paid out of capital arises in the case of limited companies, the procedure of capitalizing an improvement by way of substitution, contrary though it be to prudence, may be supported and justified on LEGAL grounds.

Capital Expenses. Certain expenses are recognized as being of a capital nature, although no tangible property may have been acquired as a result. The most important are:

1. Preliminary expenses of a limited company.

2. Cost of issuing shares and debentures: procuration and legal fees on loans and mortgages.

3. The initial outlay as well as the losses in the early years of concerns which by their very nature require a very long period of development, e.g. rubber and other plantations, mines, etc.

4. Cost of experiments.

5. Advertising where its nature is to INTRODUCE a line or 'boost' a new business.

6. Interest on construction capital.

7. Renewals in public utility companies, where, for instance, diesel engines of a railway are replaced by electrical equipment.

8. Legal expenses incurred in the acquisition of property.

9. 'Repairs' on purchase of a dilapidated asset to put it into workable condition.

10. Additions to property and other assets.

Capital and Revenue Receipts. Capital receipts may be said to consist solely of additional payments into the business, made either by shareholders of a company or by proprietors of a business, and receipts from the sale of any fixed assets of a business (not being in the nature of a normal sale). Most receipts, with comparatively few exceptions, may be treated as revenue receipts, e.g. sales, income from investments, transfer fees, commissions and discounts received, etc.

It should be noted that in taxation and double account questions the distinction between capital and revenue receipts and expenses is of extreme importance, and is based on principles that do not necessarily coincide with those already enumerated.

It is not always possible by mere inspection to distinguish between capital and revenue expenditure for many reasons, the chief being that:

1. Certain expenses are in the nature of capital for some businesses and of revenue for others.

2. Certain expenses may be said to be partly capital and partly revenue. If in doubt as to the nature of any item candidates should always make a note at the foot of their solution as to the method of treatment adopted, though the question should always be scrutinized for any information as to the nature and circumstances of the business.

Although in general it may be said that all expenditure laid out in the purchase of land, buildings, plant, and machinery and other assets of a similar type is in the nature of capital expenditure, the actual circumstances must be considered in each case. Taking the illustration of an engineering business, some plant and machinery may have been purchased with the object of earning profits (capital expenditure), and other amounts may have been purchased for the purpose of re-sale (revenue expenditure). Again, in the case of real estate business, most land and buildings purchased are revenue expenditure, as they may be considered as trading assets, subject to the obvious qualification that (a) purchases for own occupation; and (b) for permanent holding or for letting purposes, are in the nature of capital expenditure.

In certain cases the policy of those in charge of the business will decide whether certain expenditure may be classed as revenue or capital. Although expenditure will generally be capable of strict classification, yet where the true nature of such expenditure is doubtful, it is preferable to charge it to revenue, as the charging of revenue expenditure to capital may involve very serious consequences. If capital expenditure is wrongly charged to revenue the resulting effect is an understatement of profits; but if revenue expenditure is wrongly charged to capital, the profits will be overstated, resulting maybe in the withdrawal of such inflated profits by the proprietors.

Legal Expenses. These are nearly always a revenue expense, but legal charges incurred in connection with the purchase of property or other assets may be said to be merely an addition to the price of the asset and accordingly may be capitalized.

Wages. Wages which are paid to employees in the construction of the fixed assets of the business are in the nature of part of the cost of the asset and should be transferred from Wages Account to the debit of the asset account, e.g. if a firm of building contractors decides to enlarge its own premises, all the wages and the materials consumed for this purpose should be debited to the Premises Account. Such facts in an examination will readily suggest that *in addition* a transfer from purchases in respect of materials used is required. The business may, however, charge such expenditure to revenue, thus creating a secret reserve. The charging of capital expenditure of the above nature to revenue will not be allowed as a charge for TAXATION purposes.

Many questions are set involving the problem of a business constructing its own assets, e.g. suppose the cost of a new asset is £10,000, whilst the lowest outside quotation is £12,000; then the question to consider is 'should the latter amount be capitalized?'

In no case can it be considered a sound financial policy to charge up the asset with the additional £2,000, taking credit for profit of that amount, such money saved not being in the nature of profit, since a business cannot make a profit out of itself. On the other hand, if the outside quotation were £8,000, only this lower figure should properly be capitalized, the excess of the cost over this figure (£2,000) being written off as soon as possible.

Repairs. Repairs are usually in the nature of a revenue charge, though an instance of their being capital expenditure may be seen in the purchase of second-hand assets, and the subsequent repair by the purchaser to put them into an efficient state. Such an expense is capital, and must be transferred to the Asset Account, even if outside labour be employed. The problem often arises where plant and machinery which is still in good working order is sold at a considerable loss, and replaced by new machinery of a more modern type. Whether the loss should be written off or added to the cost of the new machinery is a very debatable point. There is no legal compulsion in the case above-mentioned to write off a loss of this type to revenue, though unquestionably the soundest policy is to write off such loss during the accounting period in which it is incurred, as the profits will have been previously overstated. If no balance remains on Profit and Loss Account (e.g. because all the profits have been withdrawn), the treatment is either to charge future years with the loss or to deduct the amount from capital.

DEFERRED REVENUE EXPENDITURE

There is a class of expenditure known as deferred revenue expenditure, i.e. revenue expenditure incurred during one accounting period which is applicable either wholly or in part to future periods.

There are four distinct types of deferred revenue expenditure:

1. Expenditure *wholly* paid for in advance, where no service has yet been rendered, necessitating its being carried forward, i.e. the showing of such outlay as an asset on the Balance Sheet as prepaid expenditure, e.g. telephone rental, rent in advance, etc.

2. Expenditure *partly* paid in advance where a proportion of the benefit has been derived within the period under review, the balance being as yet 'unused,' and therefore shown in the Balance Sheet as an asset, e.g. proportion of rates paid in advance or special advertising expenditure incurred in introducing a new line or developing a new market.

Most items paid in advance will fall either under head (1) or (2), according as the payment relates wholly or partly to future periods.

3. Expenditure in respect of service rendered which for any sound reason is considered as an asset, or more properly, is not considered to be allocable to the period in question, e.g. development costs in mines and plantations; discount on debentures in limited companies and cost of experiments.[1]

The practice which varies considerably in detail is to write off the amount over a period of years. If the expenditure can be earmarked as being in respect of a specific object, the expenditure should be written off during the life of that object, e.g. in the case of debenture discount at the latest by the time the debentures are redeemed.

4. Amounts representing losses of an exceptional nature, e.g. property confiscated in a foreign country, heavy loss of non-insured assets through, say, fire.

As a rule an item falling under this heading is a fictitious asset, i.e. although it is shown as an asset in the Balance Sheet, it is not really an asset at all but a capital or abnormal loss which has not been written off.

A few instances will now be given of expenses which, usually of a revenue nature, may occasionally be classed as capital expenditure.

Illustration 1

The sum of £1,000 has been spent on a machine as follows:

(*a*) £100 for repairs necessitated by negligence and lack of care and attention.

(*b*) £200 for replacements of worn parts.

(*c*) £700 for additions, incorporating new devices which enabled the output to be doubled.

---

[1] Usually the reason is that the expenditure is so heavy that it is right and proper to spread it over several years.

State how these items would be dealt with, as between Capital and Revenue.

Items (a) and (b) are Revenue, being necessary to keep the asset in efficient running order. They add nothing to the original value of the machine, nor to its proper functioning.

Item (c) is a Capital charge because it enhances the earning capacity of the business.

Illustration 2

Haworth & Co. remove their works to more suitable premises, incurring the following expenditure: (a) Cost of dismantling, removing and reinstalling plant, etc. £1,720.

(b) Certain old plant standing in the books at £750 was sold for £300 and replaced by new plant costing £1,200.

State how these items should be dealt with, as between Capital and Revenue.

	Capital £	Revenue £
(a) Removal Expenses.		1,720
(b) Plant:		
Loss on sale of old plant		450
Cost of new plant	1,200	
	£1,200	£2,170[1]

[1] The sum of £2,170 could be written off at once, but it would also be quite legitimate to write it off over a short period of years, say four or five.

Illustration 3

Carlo, Ltd., a company owning a greyhound racing track, incurs the following expenditure in its first year to 31st December.

1. Purchase of a totalisator costing £80,000, which, owing to legal actions pending, should not really be in operation. Fines have been incurred totalling £100 through continuing to use the machine, and £1,000 legal charges have been incurred to obtain the necessary licence to legalize the use of this totalisator.

2. The stand has been repainted by the track staff, and it is estimated that the wages under this heading, included in general wages, amount to £2,400.

3. The rates for the year to 31st March amount to £1,680. Nothing has yet been paid.

4. Preliminary expenses were £6,000.

5. Free tickets have been issued during the year to advertise the track. It is estimated that 40,000 of these tickets have been used on the popular side, the usual price being 25p.

6. Fire insurance was paid on 25th December for the year following amounting to £182·50.

7. When the track was being constructed several temporary sheds for workmen were built which were demolished upon the completion of the track, the cost being £290.

1. The cost of the totalisator is clearly a capital charge, as are the legal charges incurred. If, however, the totalisator can never be used the expenditure will be sheer loss, to be written off against profits (if any) as expeditiously as is practicable.

The fines incurred, £100, cannot be capitalized. They are a revenue loss, and must be borne in the current period.

2. It is evident that the stand (presumably as taken over by the company) was not newly painted, and this painting may be thus considered as part of the capital cost. A transfer of £2,400 should be made from Wages Account to the debit of the Stand Account.

3. Rates £1,680. Nine months' rates have accrued, and thus $\frac{9}{12} \times$ £1,680 = £1,260 must be charged to revenue, and shown in the Balance Sheet as a liability.

4. Preliminary expenses £6,000. This item will be capitalized but should be gradually written down, as it is unrepresented by tangible assets.

5. Free tickets £10,000. Although this represents advertising which will probably benefit future periods, it would be difficult to attach any figure of cost to it, it being rather a loss of revenue. It would therefore be imprudent to capitalize the £10,000 and write it off over several years. There will probably be no entry in the books in respect of the item but, if desired, the amount could be credited to Revenue Account to show a full gross profit and then written off to Profit and Loss Account.

6. Fire insurance £182·50. The major part of this item represents a prepayment, as only 6 days out of the 365 covered by the payment can be treated as current expenditure: $\frac{6}{365} \times £182·50 = £3$. The balance of £179·50 will be carried forward.

7. Temporary sheds £290. This item may be considered as part of the cost of construction of the track, and thus capitalized. The receipts (if any) in respect of the demolished sheds must be credited to the cost of construction.

Illustration 4

The following is a summary of the Alpha Brickyard Account for the years ended 31st December 19.1 and 19.2, in the books of Brickmakers, Ltd.

	19.1 Bricks	19.1 £	19.2 Bricks	19.2 £		19.1 Bricks	19.1 £	19.2 Bricks	19.2 £
Stock, 1st Jan.	250,000	450	100,000	175	Sales	1,600,000	3,280	850,000	1,785
Wages		1,500		2,320	Stock, 31st Dec.	100,000	175	100,000	170
Salaries		250		550	Bricks spoiled	50,000		50,000	
Coal, Stores, Plant, etc.		775		2,950	Used for New Kiln			700,000	
Royalties					Balance				4,394
Rates, Head Office Expenses and Sundries		225		354					
Profit		255							
		£3,455		£6,349			£3,455		£6,349

In 19.2 work began on building a new kiln by the company's own labour the expenditure being included in the above account. You ascertain:

(a) That no particulars have been kept of the wages incurred in the building; men were sometimes diverted to the work for part shifts, while the foundations were dug in clay, which was used for brick making in the existing kiln.

(b) That it may be taken that the wages-cost per *thousand* bricks in 19.2 was lower by 5 per cent than in 19.1.

(c) That £350 of the salaries, £2,100 of the plant, and £100 of the head office expenses should be capitalized.

(d) That sundries included Employer's Liability Insurance at a premium of £0·50 per cent of capital wages.

Show the amounts you would transfer to capital expenditure or elsewhere, and construct the Alpha Brickyard Account for the year 19.2.

It is first necessary to appreciate the significance of the question. The expenditures outlined are made up both of capital and revenue, so that the object is to separate them. In constructing the kiln, naturally, the bricks made by the company will be utilized instead of making a purchase.

The cost of making the bricks is made up of materials, labour, and expenses, hence the first objective is the cost per 1,000 bricks. Then it will be observed that some are sold, some retained in stock, and some transferred, as it were, to another department, i.e. the 'Construction' Department.

The cost of bricks is ascertained as follows:

1. Wages-Cost of Making Bricks:

(a) Cost per 1,000 bricks in 19.2—a reduction of 5 per cent on 19.1 cost. Cost per 1,000 bricks in 19.1:

$$= \frac{\text{Wages paid}}{\text{Bricks produced}} \times 1,000$$

$$= £ \frac{1,500}{(1,750,000 - 250,000)} \times 1,000$$

$$= £1.$$

∴   19.2 cost per 1,000 bricks = £1 less 5% thereof,

$$= £0·95.$$

(b) Bricks produced are 1,600,000 (i.e. 850,000 + 100,000 + 50,000 + 700,000 − 100,000).

(c) Bricks produced for sale are 1,600,000
     Less used for new kiln   700,000
                                   ——————— 900,000

		£
(d) The wages chargeable to production of bricks for sale are 900,000 at £0·95 per 1,000	. . . .	855
(e) The wages chargeable to production of bricks for new kiln are 700,000 at £0·95 per 1,000	. . . . .	665
		1,520
Total wages for bricks produced	. . .	
(f) ∴ Wages on construction of kiln (see par 4)	. .	800
Accounting for wages item of	. . .	£2,320

2. Cost of Making Bricks:

	Bricks	£
Stock at commencement	100,000	175
Wages (as above)		1,520
Salaries (£550−£350) (i) (see par. 4)		200
Coal, Stores, etc. (£2,950−£2,100) (ii) (see par. 4)		850
[1] Royalties, Rates, etc. (£354−£104) (iii) (see par. 4)		250
Bricks manufactured	1,600,000	
Total	1,700,000	2,995
Less Stock at end	100,000	170
Gross Production	1,600,000	2,825
Less Spoilage	50,000	
Net Production	1,550,000	£2,825

[1] The item of £104 is Head Office Expenses £100, plus Employer's Liability Insurance of £4 (being £0·50 per cent on capital wages of £800).

3. Transfer Cost of Bricks to Kiln.[1]
After having arrived at cost of bricks, it is now possible to charge out the 700,000 'sold' to the 'Construction' Department; i.e.:

$$\frac{700,000}{1,550,000} \times £2,825 = £1,276 \text{ [to nearest £]}$$

4. Cost of Kiln.
Inasmuch as the wages (as per 1 (f)), bricks (as per 3), and other capital costs are known, the compilation of the cost of construction of the new kiln is simply as follows:—

		£
Wages	(see par. 1 (f))	800
Bricks	(see par. 3)	1,276
Salaries, etc.	(see par. 2 (i))	350
Plant	(see par. 2 (ii))	2,100
Head Office Expenses	(see par. 2 (iii))	100
Employer's Liability Insurance	(see par. 2 (iii))	4
		£4,630

[1] See footnote[1] on p. 0809.

ALPHA BRICKYARD ACCOUNT (RECONSTRUCTED)
for the Year ended 31st December 19.2

	Bricks	£		Bricks	£
Stock (opening) . . .	100,000	175	Stock (closing) . . .	100,000	170
Wages.		1,520	Bricks Spoiled . . .	50,000	
Salaries		200	Cost of Usable Bricks pro-		
Coal, Stores, Plant, etc. .		850	duced . . . c/d	1,550,000	2,825
Royalties, Rates, Head Office					
Expenses and Sundries		250			
Bricks Produced . .	1,600,000				
	1,700,000	£2,995		1,700,000	£2,995
Cost of Usable Bricks Pro-			Bricks used for New Kiln at		
duced . . . b/d	1,550,000	2,825	Cost[1] . . .	700,000	1,276
			Cost of Sales of Bricks. c/d	850,000	1,549
	1,550,000	£2,825		1,550,000	£2,825
Cost of Sales of Bricks . b/d	850,000	1,549	Sales.	850,000	1,785
Profit		236			
	850,000	£1,785		850,000	£1,785

The above account discloses the results of the operations of the brick-yard so far as they relate to trading and entirely eliminates the entries relating to capital, viz. the cost of constructing the kiln.

In a question of this character the student should at the first perusal obtain a general idea of what is required and proceed to find the first clue, which in this particular illustration is the wages cost of brick making.

Ignoring quantities and intermediate balances carried down, the whole effect may be presented in abridged columnar form:

	Revenue	Capital	Total		Revenue	Capital	Total
	£	£	£		£	£	£
Stock	175		175	Sales . . .	1,785		1,785
Wages	1,520	800	2,320	Transfer . . .	1,276		
Salaries	200	350	550	Stock . . .	170		170
Coal, Plant, etc. . .	850	2,100	2,950	Cost of Kiln . .		4,630	[2]4,394
Royalties, Rates, Head							
Office Expenses and							
Sundries . . .	250	104	354				
Transfer of Brick Cost		1,276					
Profit	236						
	£3,231	£4,630	£6,349		£3,231	£4,630	£6,349
			[3]				[3]

[1] If the assumption is made that only the bricks actually produced during the year are transferred, i.e. leaving the opening stock of 100,000 still on hand, the transfer will be based on £2,820 instead of £2,825 as the difference in the value of the 100,000 old bricks (£175 − £170) will be eliminated: the transfer will be $\frac{700}{1550} \times £2,820 = £1,274$. Either assumption is valid.

[2] £4,630 − £236.

[3] As per question.

In order to obtain the desired results, transfers will be made to capital from the accounts presented in the original question, e.g. wages—debit Kiln Account and credit wages with £800, thus reducing the figure of £2,320 to £1,520.

The depletion cost of clay, if known, will be charged up like the other expenses and its due proportion charged to capital.

It is assumed that the spoiled bricks realize nothing.

SUMMARY OF CLASSIFICATION OF EXPENDITURE

The position relating to expenditure may be summarized as follows:

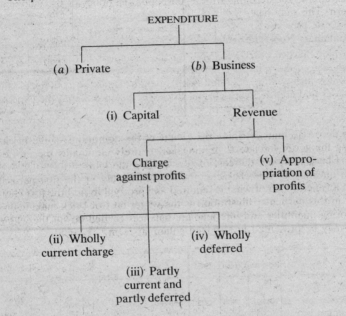

The debits will be as follows:

   (a) Proprietor's Capital Account.

   (b) (i) Asset.

      (ii) Profit and Loss Account.

      (iii) { Profit and Loss Account for current proportion.
            { Deferred Revenue item for carry-forward portion.

      (iv) Deferred Revenue item for the whole amount.

      (v) Profit and Loss Appropriation Account.

CHAPTER 09

CONTAINERS' GOODS ON APPROVAL, C.O.D., VOYAGE ACCOUNTS, VALUE ADDED TAX AND P.A.Y.E.

CONTAINERS

THE treatment of containers (sometimes termed cases, packages, empties, drums, etc.) in the accounts will depend upon the policy of the individual concern. This may be:

1. Containers Non-returnable

(a) **Not charged out.** The charge for the containers in this instance will be included in the sale price of the goods. A Containers Account should be kept which will be debited with opening stock of containers and purchases and credited with closing stock, the balance, being the expense of containers during the period of the accounts, being written off as a distribution expense to Profit and Loss Account, or, if desired, being charged to Trading or Manufacturing Account as part of the cost of putting the goods into a saleable condition.

(b) **Charged out.** Sometimes when containers are non-returnable, a separate charge is made for them. These charges should be entered in a separate column in the Sales Day Book or Journal, the total being credited periodically to a Containers Account as in (a) above, the balance of which account, being either a profit or loss on containers for the period of the accounts, being transferred to Profit and Loss Account.

2. Containers Returnable

(a) **Not charged out.** The double entry book-keeping will be similar to that in 1 (a) above, except that opening and closing stock will be divided between containers in the warehouse and those in the hands of customers. Stock must be brought into the accounts at cost, less adequate depreciation. Further entries will be necessary in the books, however, in order to keep a check on containers. Each container should have an identification number, and columns should be provided in the Sales Day Books or Journals and in customers' accounts for these numbers. When goods are sent to a customer, the container number will be entered in the special column in the Day Book or Journal and posted to the column on the debit side of the customer's account. When containers are returned, the number will be entered in a book kept for this purpose at the gate; from this book it will be posted to the column of the credit side of the customer's account. Periodical cancellation of numbers appearing on both sides of the account will reveal the numbers of the containers still in the hands of the customer.

(b) **Charged out.** Containers are sometimes charged at cost but more usually at a price in excess of cost in order to cover depreciation, cooperage, repairs, and bad debts. Similarly, credit given for returns is often less than the price at which the containers are charged out. A time limit is often imposed after which containers are not returnable. There are two methods of dealing with these transactions in the books:

(i) **Containers Trading Account.** A Containers Stock Account and a Containers Trading Account should be opened. Containers 'out' should be entered in a special column in the Sales Day Book or Journal and debited to customers' accounts, the total of the Sales Day Book or Journal column being credited periodically to Containers Trading Account Returns should be entered in a special column in the Returns or Empties Day Book or Journal and credited to customers' accounts, the total of the Day Book or Journal column being debited periodically to Containers Trading Account. Containers Stock Account will be debited with (a) opening stock, (b) purchases and will be credited with closing stock. Adjusting entries will be required, by crediting Containers Stock Account and debiting Containers Trading Account, for:

1. Containers retained by customers (the charge having already been credited to Containers Trading Account through the Sales Day Book or Journal as described above).

2. Depreciation of Stock and Stock destroyed, scrapped, etc.

At the end of the financial period, a certain number of containers will be still in customers' hands; customers have been charged for them and therefore Sundry Debtors will include this charge, the credit being in Containers Trading Account. Since these containers are returnable at a fixed price, a provision must be created to cover the liability to customers in respect thereof. This is done by debiting Containers Trading Account 'above the line,' the balance brought down being deducted from Sundry Debtors in the Balance Sheet. The Containers Trading Account may now be balanced off and the resultant profit or loss transferred to Profit and Loss Account.

Illustration 1

R Ltd. deliver goods to customers in cases (which are valued in the books at £0·15) charging them out at £0·30 each and crediting them if returned within a stipulated time limit at £0·20 each.

On 1st January 19.., there were 2,000 cases in stock and 4,200 cases in the hands of customers (all returnable). During the year to 31st December 19.., 3,000 cases were purchased at £0·25, 6,400 were sent out to customers, 4,600 were returned by customers, 60 were destroyed in an accident in the warehouse and 100 were sold as scrap for £5.

On 31st December 19.., 3,800 cases were in the hands of customers (all returnable).

Show the Ledger entries required in respect of the above transactions.

CASES STOCK

19..	Particulars	Price £p	Quantity	£
Jan. 1	Stock:			
	In hand	0·15	2,000	300
	With Customers	0·15	4,200	630
Dec. 31	Purchases	0·25	3,000	750
			9,200	£1,680
19..				
Jan. 1	Stock b/d:			
	In hand—old	0·15	40	6
	new	0·25	3,000	750
	With Customers	0·15	3,800	570

19..	Particulars	Price £p	Quantity	£
Dec. 31	Cases Trading Account—			
	Cases retained by Customers	0·15	2,200	330
	Cases destroyed		60[4]	5
	Cases Sold for Scrap		100	19[4]
	Cases Trading Account—			
	Loss on Cases destroyed and scrapped			
	Stock c/d—			
	In hand—old	0·15	40[5]	6
	new	0·25	3,000[5]	750
	With Customers	0·15	3,800[5]	570
			9,200	£1,680

CASES TRADING ACCOUNT

19..	Particulars	Price £p	Quantity	£
Dec. 31	Customers—			
	Cases returned	0·20	4,600	920
	Cases Stock—			
	Cases retained by Customers	0·15	2,200	330
	Cases Stock—			
	Loss on Cases destroyed and scrapped			19
	Profit and Loss Account—			
	Profit on Hire			420[2]
	Profit on Sale			330[3]
	Provision c/d—			
	Cases in hands of Customers	0·20	3,800	760[7]
			10,600	£2,779

19..	Particulars	Price £p	Quantity	£
Jan. 1	Provision b/d—			
	Cases in hands of Customers	0·20	4,200	840[6]
Dec. 31	Customers—			
	Cases charged out	0·30	6,400	1,920
	Profit and Loss Account—			
	Loss on Cases destroyed and scrapped			19
			10,600	£2,779
19..				
Jan. 1	Provision b/d—			
	Cases in hands of Customers	0·20	3,800	760[7]

(For footnotes see p. 0905.)

Alternatively, one account only may be employed by means of an additional column showing the cost price of all the cases sent out and returned, and the provision for cases still out.

CASES TRADING ACCOUNT

Dr.

	Price £p	Quantity	£	Price £p	£
19.. Dec. 31					
Customers— Cases returned	0·15	4,600	690	0·05	230
Cases Stock— Cases retained by Customers	0·15	2,200	330		
Cases Stock— Loss on Cases destroyed and scrapped					19
Profit and Loss Account— Profit on Hire					420
Profit on Sale					330
Provision c/d— Cases in hands of Customers	0·15	3,800	570	0·05	190
		10,600	£1,590		£1,189

Cr.

	Price £p	Quantity	£	Price £p	£
19.. Jan. 1 Provision b/d— Cases in hands of Customers	0·15	4,200	630	0·05	210
Dec. 31 Customers charged out: Hire	0·15	4,200	630	0·15	630
Sales	0·15	2,200	330	0·15	330
" Profit and Loss Account— Loss on cases destroyed and scrapped					19
		10,600	£1,590		£1,189
19.. Jan. 1 Provision b/d— Cases in hands of Customers	0·15	3,800	570	0·05	190

The cases charged out have been subdivided for the purpose of the illustration, showing clearly the profit on the cases 'sold,' i.e. retained by customers, at £330.

The profit on hire is 4,200 at £0·10 = £420 (charged out at £0·30, credited on return at £0·20).

As an alternative, the 'loaded' columns could be put in a separate account and the first columns written up as part of the Cases Stock Account (in which case no transfer from one account to another would be required).

(The 'loaded' columns are shown in italics.)

If the new stock is written down to £0·15, the closing stock credited would be £1,026 instead of £1,326, and therefore an entry for depreciation (£300) would be made on the credit side of Cases Stock Account and debited to Cases Trading Account. This would be followed by a credit of £300 to the latter account and a debit to Profit and Loss Account; or, more properly, a decrease of £300 in the transfer of profit to Profit and Loss Account, since depreciation should be taken into account before the profit on Cases Trading can be ascertained.

[1] Cases sent out during the year			6,400
Add already out on 1st January			4,200
			10,600
Less returned	4,600		
returnable	3,800		
			8,400
∴ Balance _sold_ to customers			2,200
[2] Cases sent out during the year			6,400
Less cases sold to customers (as above)			2,200
∴ Cases out _on hire_ during the year			4,200
Profit on Hire, 4,200 at £0·10 (£0·30 less £0·20)			£420
[3] Profit on Sale, 2,200 at £0·15 (£0·30 less £0·15)			£330
[4] Loss on cases destroyed, 60 at £0·15		£9	
Loss on cases scrapped, 100 at £0·10		£10	
(The sale price of scrap £0·05 as against cost £0·15)			
		£19	

It is assumed that the new £0·25 cases are intact and that no claim exists for loss of cases by the accident in the warehouse.

[5] Stock of Old Cases on 1st January			6,200
Less Sales to customers	2,200		
Destroyed	60		
Scrapped	100		
			2,360
			3,840

[6] The opening figure of £840 (4,200 at £0·20) is provided in respect of the company's liability to customers for cases not yet returned which have been charged up at £0·30 in the previous year.

[7] Similarly, a provision must be created at the end of the year for the same purpose. Sundry Debtors will include the charge for 3,800 cases at £0·30, so that the Provision of £760 will be deducted therefrom in the Balance Sheet to show the true Sundry Debtors' figure.

Alternatively, the two accounts may be consolidated into one, but generally this method is not recommended.

(ii) **Containers Reserve Account.** In this alternative method of writing up Containers Accounts, a Containers Stock Account and a Containers Reserve Account are used, the former containing all entries relating to the stock of containers, the latter being confined to the actual stock movements to and from customers. The entries in Sales Day Books or Journals,

Returns Books or Journals and customers' accounts will be similar to those described in the previous method.

The Containers Stock Account will be debited with opening stock and purchases and will be credited with closing stock and stock destroyed and scrapped. The Reserve Account will be credited with opening provision for returnable containers and with containers charged out to customers, and will be debited with containers returned and closing provision for returnable containers. When containers are retained by (i.e. sold to) customers, they must be eliminated from Stock by crediting Stock Account, the corresponding debit being to Reserve Account (as an offset to the credits to that account for containers charged out). When containers are returnable at a smaller price than that at which they are charged out, there will be a balance on Reserve Account representing profit on hire which must be transferred to Profit and Loss Account by debiting Reserve Account; the corresponding credit may be direct to Profit and Loss or to Stock Account whence it will be transferred to Profit and Loss along with the balance of that account, which will show the profit or loss on containers sold to customers, scrapped and destroyed.

It should be emphasized that the entries mentioned above for profit on hire are confined to the money columns as the quantity of stock is not affected, whereas those for sales of containers must include both quantities and money.

Illustration 2

Using the same data as in the preceding illustration write up Cases Stock and Cases Reserve Accounts.

As will be seen by reference to the previous illustration, most of the entries in the Cases Stock Account and Cases Reserve Account are the same as in the Cases Stock Account and Cases Trading Account respectively. In addition, there are the two cross transfers (*Dr.* Cases Reserve, *Cr.* Cases Stock) for Profit on Hire (money only) and for Sales to customers (quantities and money). [For the guidance of the student, these transfers are shown in heavy type. See p. 0907.]

Illustration 3

On 1st January 19.. Stock of Containers in hand was £800 (valued in the books at cost less 25 per cent), and £120 in the hands of customers at invoice price, which is cost plus 50 per cent.

For the year ended 31st December 19.. containers were charged out at cost plus 50 per cent and full credit was given in respect of those returned in good condition.

Containers sent out during the year were £1,600 (invoice price) and Returns (all in good condition) £1,000. Customers retained (and were charged up) Containers at an invoice price of £30. Closing Stock of Containers in hand *at cost* £666·67.

Write up Containers Stock and Reserve Accounts.

CASES STOCK

Date	Particulars	Price £p	Quantity	£	Date	Particulars	Price £p	Quantity	£
19.. Jan. 1	Stock—				19.. Dec. 31	Cases destroyed		60	5
	In hand	0·15	2,000	300		Cases Sold for Scrap		100	
	With Customers	0·15	4,200	630		Cases Reserve:			
Dec. 31	Purchases	0·25	3,000	750		**Cases retained by Customers**	**0·30**	**2,200**	**660**
	Profit and Loss Account—					**Profit on Hire**			**420**
	Profit on Hire			420		Profit and Loss Account—			
	Profit on Sale			330		Loss on Cases destroyed and scrapped			19
						Stock c/d—			
						In hand—old	0·15	40	6
						new	0·25	3,000	750
						With Customers	0·15	3,800	570
			9,200	£2,430				9,200	£2,430
19.. Jan. 1	Stock b/d—								
	In hand—old	0·15	40	6					
	new	0·25	3,000	750					
	With Customers	0·15	3,800	570					

CASES RESERVE

Date	Particulars	Price £p	Quantity	£	Date	Particulars	Price £p	Quantity	£
19.. Dec. 31	Customers—				19.. Jan. 1	Provision b/d—	0·20	4,200	840
	Cases returned	0·20	4,600	920	Dec. 31	Customers—			
	Cases Stock:					Cases charged out	0·30	6,400	1,920
	Cases retained by Customers	**0·30**	**2,200**	**660**					
	Profit on Hire			420					
	Provision c/d—								
	Cases in hands of Customers	0·20	3,800	760					
			10,600	£2,760				10,600	£2,760
					19.. Jan. 1	Provision b/d—			
						Cases in hands of Customers	0·20	3,800	760

As in the preceding illustration, if the stock of new cases is taken at £0·15, the profit becomes £450 (instead of £750) less loss £19—£431. Alternatively, the loss may not be separately shown, the Cases Stock Account being closed by a transfer of £731 (or £431 if new stock valued

CONTAINERS STOCK

19..		£	19..		£
Jan. 1	Opening Stock—		Dec. 31	Containers Reserve—	
	In own hands . .	800		Containers retained .	30
	With Customers . .	60[1]		Closing Stock—	
Dec. 31	Profit and Loss Account .	15[4]		In own hands .	500[3]
				With Customers .	345[2]
		£875			£875
19..					
Jan. 1	Stock b/d—				
	In own hands .	500			
	With Customers .	345			

CONTAINERS RESERVE

19..		£	19..		£
Dec. 31	Containers Stock . .	30	Jan. 1	Opening Provision b/d . .	120
	Customers—		Dec. 31	Customers—	
	Containers returned .	1,000		Containers charged out .	1,600
	Closing Provision c/d .	690			
		£1,720			£1,720
			9..		
			Jan. 1	Provision b/d . . .	690[5]

[1] The opening stock 'out' must be the reduced value of £120 (opening provision), viz. $66\frac{2}{3}\%$ of £120 (seeing that the loaded price is 50% of Cost), i.e. £80 less £20 (25% of Cost) = £60.

[2] The closing stock 'out' will be $66\frac{2}{3}\%$ of £690, i.e. £460 less £115 (25% Cost) = £345.

[3] The closing stock in own hands is £666·67 less £166·67 (25% of cost) = £500.

[4] Profit on Sale is £30 less £15 (Stock value is $66\frac{2}{3}\%$ of £30 = £20, less 25% = £15), which is £15, less any provision for repairs and maintenance required.

[5] Deducted from Sundry Debtors in the Balance Sheet.

	£p	£p	
Proof of Stock Transfers at Cost:			
Opening Stock per account .	60·00		
Add $33\frac{1}{3}\%$ to bring up to Cost .	20·00	80·00	[£80 − £20 (25%) = £60]
Amounts charged out .	1,600·00		
Less $33\frac{1}{3}\%$ to reduce to Cost .	533·33	1,066·67	[£1,066·67 + £533·33 (50%) = £1,600]
		1,146·67	
Deduct: Returns .	1,000·00		
Less $33\frac{1}{3}\%$ to reduce to Cost .	333·33	666·67	[£666·67 + £333·33 (50%) = £1,000]
		480·00	
Sales . .	30·00		
Less $33\frac{1}{3}\%$ to reduce to Cost .	10·00	20·00	[£20 + £10 (50%) = £30]
		460·00	
Balance at Cost . .		115·00	
Less 25% Reduction .			
Balance per Accounts .		£345·00	

GOODS OUT ON APPROVAL OR SALE OR RETURN

The property in goods out on approval, or on sale or return, does not pass to the buyer until he signifies his acceptance of them to the seller or, without giving notice of rejection, retains the goods beyond an agreed or reasonable time. Such transactions therefore require special treatment in the books; this will depend upon the circumstances in each particular concern, but the following three methods are the usual ones:

1. **When such Transactions are Rare.** Although theoretically incorrect, goods out on approval may be treated as sales: the entries should, however, be marked in some way so that provision may be made at the end of the financial period to eliminate any outstanding items from Sales and to reduce such items to say, the lower of cost and net realizable value, for inclusion in stock. This may be done by:

(a) Debiting Sales Account 'above the line' and crediting it 'below the line' with the amount of such outstanding items included in Sales and deducting the balance brought down from the Sundry Debtors figure in the Balance Sheet, and

(b) Entering the value—at the lower of cost and net realizable value— of the outstanding items in the Trading Account and Balance Sheet as 'Stock in hands of customers.'

2. **Where such Transactions are very Frequent or of Considerable Value.** It will be necessary to open up a special set of books, which, though compiled on Double Entry lines, will be outside the ordinary double entry book-keeping, that is to say, memorandum. These will consist of:

(a) Goods sent on Approval (Sale or Return) Day Book or Journal.

(b) Goods on Approval Sold and Returned Day Book or Journal—this book will be provided with columns to record separately Sales and Returns.

(c) Goods on Approval (Sale or Return) Ledger.

The procedure will be as follows:

(a) When goods are sent out, they are entered in the Goods sent on Approval Day Book or Journal and posted to the debit of the customer's account in the Goods on Approval Ledger. The Day Book or Journal total will be posted periodically to the credit of a Goods on Approval Total Account.

(b) When goods are returned, they are entered in the Returns column in the Sold and Returned Day Book or Journal and posted to the credit of the customer's account in the Goods on Approval Ledger. The Returns column total will be posted periodically to the debit of Goods on Approval Total Account.

(c) When goods are retained, they are entered in the Sales column in the Sold and Returned Day Book or Journal. This column is provided with two folio columns, one for the posting to the credit of the customer's account in the Goods on Approval Ledger and the other for the posting of the same amount to the debit of his account in the ordinary Sales Ledger. The Sales column total will be posted to the Debit of Goods on Approval Total Account *and* to the credit of ordinary Sales Account.

When accounts are prepared, NO goods on approval figures will appear herein, since the total of the balances of customers' accounts in the Goods on Approval Ledger should equal the balance of the Goods on Approval Total Account. The value of goods on approval in the hands of customers *at selling price* can be ascertained either in detail from the Ledger or in total from the Total Account. This value, reduced to say, the lower of cost and net realizable value will be included in the Trading Account and Balance Sheet as before.

3. **Where such Transactions are not sufficiently Rare to Deal with as in (1) and not Sufficiently Frequent to Deal with as in (2),** to employ a Goods on Approval Journal.

The procedure is:

(*a*) To enter the amount of goods delivered into a memorandum column.

(*b*) If the goods are returned, to enter the amount of goods returned into a memorandum column on the same line as the original entry for the goods delivered.

(*c*) If the goods are sold, to enter the amount of goods sold into the Sales column on the same line as the original entry for the goods delivered.

All the above entries will be at selling price.

At any time the total shown in the first column, less the total of the second and third columns, will equal the goods out on approval at selling price. This balance, when accounts are to be prepared, will be brought into the accounts at say, the lower of cost and net realizable value.

The third column is a 'Double Entry' column and performs the same functions as an ordinary Sales Day Book or Journal.

Illustration 4

X sends goods out on appro. as follows:

19..		£	19..
Jan. 15	Y	31	Jan. 17 returned £25, retained £6.
18	R	18	21 all retained.
21	Q	9	23 all retained.
30	Y	40	No intimation received as to sale and goods not yet returned.
31	L	17	do.

Show how these transactions will be dealt with under Methods (2) and (3) above.

Method 2.

GOODS SENT ON APPROVAL DAY BOOK OR JOURNAL

	Particulars				Folio		£
19..							
Jan. 15	Y .	.	.	.	G.o.A.L.	1	31
18	R .	.	.	.		2	18
21	Q .	.	.	.		3	9
30	Y .	.	.	.		1	40
31	L .	.	.	.		4	17
							£115

GOODS ON APPROVAL SOLD AND RETURNED DAY BOOK OR JOURNAL

	Particulars	G.o.A.L. Fol.	Returned	G.o.A.L. Fol.	S.L. Fol.	Sold
19..			£			£
Jan. 17	Y	1	25	1	?[1]	6
21	R			2	?[1]	18
23	Q			3	?[1]	9
			———			———
			£25			£33[2]

GOODS ON APPROVAL TOTAL ACCOUNT

19..			£	19..			£
Jan. 31	Returns		25	Jan. 31	Goods sent out on Approval		115
	Sales		33				
	Balance	c/d	57				
			———				———
			£115				£115
				Feb. 1	Balance	b/d	57[3]

GOODS ON APPROVAL LEDGER

Y

19..			£	19..			£
Jan. 15	Goods		31	Jan. 17	Returns		25
30	Goods		40		Sales		6
				31	Balance	c/d	40
			———				———
			£71				£71
Feb. 1	Balance	b/d	40[2]				

R

19..			£	19..			£
Jan. 18	Goods		18	Jan. 21	Sales		18

Q

19..			£	19..			£
Jan. 21	Goods		9	Jan. 23	Sales		9

L

19..			£				
Jan. 31	Goods		17[3]				

[1] Posted to the customer's account in the ordinary Sales Ledger.

[2] Posted to the credit of the ordinary Sales Account, as well as to the debit of Goods on Approval Total Account.

[3] The credit balance of £57 on Goods on Approval Total Account equals the debit balances in the Goods on Approval Ledger on the accounts of Y (£40) and L (£17). No balance on the special Goods on Approval books will appear in the ordinary Trial Balance on 31st January 19... These books are outside the ordinary double entry book-keeping.

GOODS ON APPROVAL JOURNAL

Deliveries			Returns			Sales				Remarks
Date	Particulars	Amount	Date	Particulars	Amount	Date	Particulars	Fol.	Amount	
19..		£	19..		£	19..			£	
Jan. 15	Y	31	Jan. 17		25	Jan. 17		?[1]	6	
18	R	18				21		?[1]	18	
21	Q	9				23		?[1]	9	
30	Y	40	31	Balance c/d . .	40					
31	L	17		Balance c/d . .	17					
		£115			£82				£33[2]	
Feb. 1	Balance Y b/d .	40[3]								
	Balance L b/d .	17[3]								

[1] Posted to the debit of the customer's account in the ordinary Sales Ledger.

[2] Posted to the credit of Sales Account.

[3] The Deliveries and Returns columns are memorandum only, no postings being made therefrom. The total of the Returns (£25) and Sales (£33) columns deducted from the Deliveries column (£115) gives the value (at selling price) of the goods on approval still outstanding = £57.

In order to avoid the work entailed in carrying down a considerable number of balances when the books are balanced and closed off, the Goods on Approval Journal may be provided with extra columns so that the uncleared entries of one period may be cleared in the next period on the same line as the original entry. This form of Journal will be as follows:

Period ending .... Period ending ....

GOODS ON APPROVAL JOURNAL

Deliveries	Returns	Sales	Balance	Returns			Sales		
				Date	Particulars	Amount	Date	Particulars	Amount
as in the illustration on p. 0912			.............[1]						

[1] Closing date of first period. The total of this column gives the amount of goods outstanding at the balancing date.

It is unlikely that any items would remain open at the end of the second period. If there were any, the balances would be carried down as in the previous illustration.

C.O.D.

The Cash on Delivery system plays a large part in the transactions of business in many concerns. By this system the Post Office, against delivery to the consignee, collects the cash for the goods and remits it to the sender.

A special adhesive address label, supplied free by the Post Office, is used on the parcel, which is then handed in at the Post Office together with a duly completed Trade Charge Form.

1. A C.O.D. Day Book or Journal should be kept with columns to accommodate the following:
- (a) Date of despatch,
- (b) Name and address of consignee,
- (c) Description of goods,
- (d) Price of goods per invoice,
- (e) Postage,
- (f) C.O.D. fees,
- (g) Total amount due from consignee per Trade Charge Form,
- (h) Trade Charge Form serial number,
- (i) Date cash received,
- (j) Goods returned,
- (k) Postage and fees on returns (where included in the charge),
- (l) Remarks,

and columns for reference to invoices, folios, etc., as may be found necessary.

2. Receipts from Trade Charge Money Orders should be entered in a C.O.D. Cash Received Book, the total of which is entered periodically in the Main Cash Book.

3. A C.O.D. Total Account should be kept.

4. Postings will be as follows:
- (i) Day Book or Journal
  - Column (d) (1) Dr. C.O.D. Total Account   Cr. Sales
  - (e) (1) if charged to customer—
    - Dr. C.O.D. Total Account   Cr. Cash
    - (2) if not so charged—
    - Dr. Postages   Cr. Cash
  - (f) as for column (e)
  - (j) Dr. Sales   Cr. C.O.D. Total Account
  - (k) Dr. Postages   Cr. C.O.D. Total Account
- (ii) Cash Received Book
  - Dr. Cash   Cr. C.O.D. Total Account

5. The balance on C.O.D. Total Account will show the amount of Trade Charges outstanding. Suitable provision should be made, when accounts are prepared, for damages in transit (unless covered by insurance) and goods refused.

C.O.D. DAY BOOK OR JOURNAL

Date	Name, etc.	Description of Goods	Invoice Price	Postage	C.O.D. Fees	Total per TCF	TCF Serial No.	Date Cash Received	Goods Re-turned	Postage & Fees on Returns	Remarks
			£	£p	£p	£p			£	£p	
19.. Jan. 2	X . .		5	0·30	0·11	5·41					
9	Y . .		4	0·20	0·11	4·31		Jan. 6		£p	
11	P . .		10	0·50	0·12	10·62		15			
20	Q . .		3	0·26	0·11	3·37		27	10	0·62	
30	Z . .		8	0·15	0·12	8·27					
			£30	£1·41	£0·57	£31·98			£10	£0·62	c/d
Feb. 1	Z .	b/d[1]	8	0·15	0·12	8·27					

CASH RECEIVED BOOK

		£p
Jan. 6. X .	. . .	5·41
15. Y .	. . .	4·31
27. Q .	. . .	3·37
		£13·09

[1] The balance brought down against Z has already been debited to C.O.D. Total Account in the January total. It is, therefore, ruled off in order to prevent its being included in the February total as well. Alternatively, the Day Book or Journal could be provided with extra columns for dealing with outstanding items, as shown previously in relation to Goods on Approval.

Illustration 5

A sends out the following goods C.O.D. during the month of January:

	Price	Postage	C.O.D. Fees	Cash Received	Goods Returned
	£	£p	£p		
Jan. 2 X	5	0·30	0·11	Jan. 6	
9 Y	4	0·20	0·11	15	
11 P	10	0·50	0·12		Jan. 18
20 Q	3	0·26	0·11	27	
30 Z	8	0·15	0·12	Outstanding	

A charges both postage and C.O.D. fees to his customers.
Show how these transactions would be dealt with in A's books. (See p. 0915.)

C.O.D. Purchases

These will be dealt with in the same way as ordinary purchases through the Petty Cash Book or through a C.O.D. Payments Book. A strict system of internal check is imperative in order to avoid fraud, but this consideration is outside the scope of this book.

C.O.D. TOTAL ACCOUNT

19..			£p	19..			£p
Jan. 31	Sales	.	30·00	Jan. 31	Cash	. .	13·09
	Cash (Postages)	.	1·41		Returns	. .	10·00
	Cash (C.O.D. Fees)	.	0·57		Postages	.	0·62
					Balance c/d	.	8·27
			£31·98				£31·98
Feb. 1	Balance b/d	.	8·27				

VOYAGE ACCOUNTS

It is a practice among shipowners to ascertain the results of *each* voyage of a chartered ship separately. To do this a Voyage Account is prepared, which is merely a Profit and Loss Account covering the period of the particular voyage. For this purpose the 'voyage' is taken as the outward and return journeys of the vessel.

The preparation of the Voyage Account should present no difficulty as it is essentially a Profit and Loss Account. The following points, however, which are peculiar to Voyage Accounts, should be noticed.

1. *Brokerage and Commission.* In addition to the Port charges, duties, harbour wages, and other expenses on the voyage a brokerage to the

charterers' agent is usually paid, and frequently an 'address' commission is payable to the charterers themselves, both these commissions being computed on the freights *earned*. Frequently the managers may be entitled to a commission on freights earned.

2. *Insurance.* The charges against the voyage must be exactly applicable to the particular voyage, e.g. a ship may be insured for a whole year, but the amount chargeable against the voyage must be such portion as is applicable to the duration thereof.

3. *Stores.* Similarly, a stock of stores may be bought for use during the voyage, and on ship's return the stores on hand must be brought into account.

4. *Depreciation.* Such items as depreciation on ship and tackle, repairs, renewals and replacements thereof, must be charged in order to ascertain the true results of each voyage.

5. *Passengers.* The freights earned may be supplemented by passage moneys in respect of passengers carried.

6. *Shares of Ships.* Every British ship is divided into 64 shares and each of these shares may be owned by not more than five persons.

Illustration 6

The steamship *Travancore* was chartered on 29th September 19.., to carry tin from Southampton to Lisbon at £3 per ton, and on the return journey to carry wine from Lisbon to Liverpool at £4 per dozen casks. The vessel was insured on 25th March 19.., for a year in advance, the premium being £4,800. From the following particulars you are required to prepare the Voyage Account, the vessel arriving in Liverpool on 31st October 19...

Freight carried, 1,200 tons of tin to Lisbon and 800 dozen casks of wine from Lisbon.

Sundry disbursements for voyage (including port charges, harbour wages, fuel, captain's expenses, etc.), £2,839. Stores purchased £1,620, there being opening stores on hand £420 and closing stores on hand £640. (*N.B.* Stock in hand 29th September, £52; 31st October, £64.)

Address commission 2 per cent on freight earned on outward journey, plus brokerage of 5 per cent, of which one-third is repayable to the vessel; 2 per cent on freight earned on inward journey.

Brokerage of one-third of 5 per cent to charterers on freight earnings for inward voyage. Managers to receive 5 per cent commission on net profits after charging such commission.

Passage money from passengers amounted to £112 on the outward journey and £122 on the inward.

The written-down value of the ship and tackle is £50,400. Depreciation is to be provided at the rate of 10 per cent per annum (calculate in months).

Before distributing the profit, £860 to be provided in respect of Repairs and Renewals.

Calculate to nearest £.

S.S. 'TRAVANCORE'

Voyage No. ——. 29th September 19.., to 31st October 19..

		£				£
Stores Account			Freights earned—			
(£1,620+£420−£640)		1,400	1,200 tons of tin at £3 a ton to LISBON			3,600
Sundry Disbursements (detailed)		2,839	800 doz. casks of wine at £4 a doz. casks			
Address Commission—			to LIVERPOOL			3,200
2% of £3,600	72		Brokerage refund—			
2% of £3,200	64		one-third of £180.			60
		136	Passage Money—			
Brokerage—			Outward		£112	
5% of £3,600	£180		Inward		122	
one-third of 5% of £3,200	53					234
		233				
Insurance (1 month)		400				
Depreciation (1 month)		420				
Provision for Repairs and Renewals		860				
Balance c/d		806				
		£7,094				£7,094
Managers' Commission—			Balance b/d			806
5% of £768		38				
Net Profit (divisible as to £12 per share)		768				
		£806				£806

VALUE ADDED TAX

A full explanation of the working of Value Added Tax would be out of
place in this book, but the following summary is given in order that the
book-keeping entries which are entailed may be better understood.

1. The Finance Act 1972 introduced in the United Kingdom, as from
1st April 1973, VAT which replaces Purchase Tax and Selective Employment Tax. It is administered by the Commissioners of Customs and
Excise. All persons trading in the U.K., including non-residents, must
register with the Commissioners of Customs and Excise unless specifically
excluded by statute. In particular, traders whose turnover does not exceed
£10,000[1] are excepted.

2. VAT is, theoretically, a tax paid by a trader in respect of the value
which he adds to goods or services during his stage of the production or
the distribution of those goods or services. However, in effect, VAT is a
tax on the amount expended by the final consumer of goods or services.

3. VAT is collected whenever goods or services are transferred for
value during the production—wholesale—retail process. When a trader
purchases goods or services liable to VAT he must pay the supplier a price
which includes the appropriate rate[2] of VAT on the taxable purchase
prices. In turn, the trader when selling goods or services to his customers
must charge them a price which includes the appropriate rate of VAT on
the taxable sales price.

4. VAT is chargeable at the appropriate rate[2] on the supply of all goods

[1] From 12th April 1978 the VAT registration limit was raised to £10,000.

[2] There are two positive rates, viz., the standard rate, currently 8%, and the higher rate,
currently $12\frac{1}{2}$%.

and services in the U.K. in the course of a business and on all imports of goods, except where specifically excluded. Exceptions to tax at the standard rate take the form of either, exemption or zero rating. In respect of goods or services which are exempt the trader does not charge his customer with any 'output tax'. Exemption, however, does not mean that VAT will not fall on exempt goods or services. What it means is that the purchaser does not pay tax directly on the goods or services purchased. The consequences of this are twofold, viz. (i) the supplier is not able to set off any 'input tax', in respect of the exempted goods or services, against 'output tax', (ii) the supplier in these circumstances, is a final consumer and the tax ends there; however, to recover the tax he has paid he will doubtless increase the selling price of his goods or services. When goods or services are zero-rated it means that such goods or services are taxable but that the tax charged is nil. The zero-rated trader can sell his goods or services VAT-free because he can reclaim any 'input tax' which he paid to his suppliers.

5. The registered trader is liable for tax on chargeable goods transferred to a separate retail branch or section of his business or which have been appropriated to other purposes, e.g. private use.

6. Returns are required by the Commissioners in respect of each quarter's trading.[1] Such returns must be made—and the tax paid—within one month of the end of each quarter. The amount of tax due is calculated by deducting from the VAT collectible on goods or services sold (output tax) the VAT payable on goods or services purchased (input tax). If, however, the amount of VAT exceeds that collected, a refund for the excess may be claimed.

7. In the event of the bankruptcy or liquidation of a registered person, VAT is a preferential debt if due up to twelve months prior to the Receiving Order (in Bankruptcy) or the commencement of the liquidation which will be the date of the resolution in Voluntary Liquidation or the date of the Court order or appointment of provisional liquidator in Compulsory Liquidation; or where there is a Receiver for Debenture Holders by way of floating charge, the date of appointment of the Receiver, or where the Debenture Holders take possession the date of their taking possession.

Accounting Entries

All registered persons are required to keep such records of their dealings in chargeable goods and services as will enable them to compute the proper tax chargeable and to pay such tax to the Commissioners of Customs and Excise at the due time. The actual records must vary with and be adapted to suit the requirements of each particular concern. The records and procedures for purchases and sales accounting and invoicing must be adequate to:

(a) calculate tax due or refundable;

---

[1] Tax quarters are generally staggered according to trade classification but may be fitted in with a business' financial year.

(b) complete the quarterly returns;

(c) facilitate verification by Customs and Excise officials. Vouchers must be preserved for at least three years. Where there are internal transfers of goods during manufacture or as mentioned in (5) above, special records will be required.

Periodic or yearly accounts may be either VAT inclusive or VAT exclusive depending upon the circumstances. Accounts of non-taxable traders must, of course, be prepared on the VAT inclusive basis, i.e. purchases and expenses (sales are not affected) will include VAT where charged. Accounts of wholly taxable traders may be VAT inclusive or VAT exclusive—either method is acceptable to H.M. Customs & Excise and to the Inland Revenue—but the VAT-exclusive method is recommended. Accounts of partially exempt traders may be either VAT inclusive or VAT exclusive in respect of taxable transactions—but the VAT-exclusive method is recommended—and the VAT-inclusive method will apply to exempt transactions.

In regard to ordinary tax-inclusive sales and purchases, the following procedure is recommended:

1. Purchases

(a) Separate columns should be provided for VAT in the Purchases Journal and in the Returns Inwards Journal.

(b) A VAT Account should be opened in the Nominal Ledger.

(c) The Supplier's accounts will be credited with the tax-inclusive prices and the total of the VAT columns in the Purchases Journal and Returns Inwards Journal will be posted periodically (e.g. monthly, but certainly at the end of each calendar quarter so that the necessary returns may be prepared) to the debit and credit respectively of the VAT Account; the Purchases (or Expense) Account will be debited with the total VAT-exclusive values for the period.

(d) Payments to suppliers will be entered in the Cash Book and posted to the debit of the respective accounts in the Creditors Ledger in the usual way.

2. Sales

(a) Separate columns should be provided for VAT in the Sales Journal and the Returns Inwards Journal.

(b) The ordinary sale price will be dealt with throughout in the usual way. The VAT on each sale will be entered in the special column in the Sales Journal, the amount agreeing with the tax shown on the invoice, and the tax-inclusive price will be posted to the debit side of the customers account. Credits for returns, etc., will, *mutatis mutandis*, be dealt with similarly.

(c) The total of the VAT columns in the Sales Journal and Returns Journal will be posted periodically (e.g. monthly, but certainly at the end of each calendar quarter so that the necessary returns may be prepared) to the credit and debit respectively of the VAT Account. The Sales Account will be credited with the total VAT-exclusive value of sales for the period.

The VAT Account will be debited, and Bank (or Cash) credited, when payment is made to the Commissioners.

(d) Receipts from customers will be entered in the Cash Book and posted to the credit of the respective accounts in the Sales Ledger in the usual way.

Illustration 7

Write up the VAT Account from the following transactions of a registered trader:

	Value (Excluding VAT) £
Purchases	12,000
Credit for Returns to Suppliers	250
Sales—Home	15,000
—Overseas	8,000
Wages	6,000
Heating, Lighting and Cleaning	560
Telephone	45
New dictating machines	120
Postal Charges	15
Debt Collection fees	54

Heating, Lighting and Cleaning includes £120 for fuel oil and £65 for cleaning materials. Assume VAT at 10 per cent.

VAT ACCOUNT

INPUT TAX	£	£p	OUTPUT TAX	£p
Capital Goods			Sales (Home)	1,500·00
(10% of £120)		12·00	Returns to Suppliers	25·00
Other Goods and Services				
Purchases	12,000			
Cleaning Materials	65			
Telephone	45			
Debt Collection	54			
	£12,164			
10% thereof		1,216·40		
Balance c/d—Net tax payable		296·60		
		£1,525·00		£1,525·00
			Balance b/d	296·60

Notes. (a) Goods or services exported are zero-rated.

(b) All fuel and power is zero-rated.

(c) Certain postal services are exempt. The carrying of letters, parcels, etc. is exempt. But the exemption does not extend to telegrams which are deemed not to be postal packages. Also telephone charges are chargeable to tax.

Statement of Standard Accounting Practice. Statement of Standard Accounting Practice 1/5 concerns Accounting for Value Added Tax the main aspects of which follow:

1. VAT is a tax on the supply of goods and service which is eventually borne by the final consumer but collected at each stage of the production and distribution chain. As a general principle, therefore, the treatment of VAT in the accounts of a trader should reflect his role as a collector of the tax and VAT should not be included in income or in expenditure whether of a capital or of a revenue nature. There will however be circumstances, as noted below, in which a trader will himself bear VAT and in such circumstances the accounting treatment should reflect that fact.

2. Persons not accountable for VAT will suffer VAT on inputs. For them VAT will increase the cost of all goods and services to which it applies and should be included in such costs. In particular, the VAT on fixed assets should be added to the cost of the fixed assets concerned.

3. In the case of persons who also carry on exempted activities there will be a residue of VAT, which will fall directly on the trader and which will normally be arrived at by division of his activities as between taxable outputs (including zero-rated) and those which are exempt. In such cases, the principle that such VAT will increase the costs to which it applies and should be included in such costs will be equally applicable. Hence the appropriate portion of the VAT allocable to fixed assets should, if irrecoverable, be added to the cost of the fixed assets concerned and the proportion allocable to other items should, if practicable and material, be included in such other items. In some cases, e.g. where financial and VAT accounting periods do not coincide, an estimate may be necessary.

4. All traders will bear tax in so far as it relates to non-deductible inputs (e.g. motor cars other than for resale and certain business entertaining expenses). Such tax should therefore be included as part of the cost of those items.

5. The net amount due to or from the Revenue Authorities in respect of VAT should be included as part of debtors or creditors and will not normally require separate disclosure.

6. The estimated amount of capital commitments should include the appropriate amount, if any, of irrecoverable VAT.

7. Turnover shown in the profit and loss account should exclude VAT on taxable outputs. If it is desired to show also the gross turnover, the VAT relevant to that turnover should be shown as a deduction in arriving at the turnover exclusive of VAT.

8. Irrecoverable VAT allocable to fixed assets and to other items disclosed separately in published accounts should be included in their cost where practicable and material.

P.A.Y.E.

The system of collecting Income Tax from employees known as Pay As You Earn or P.A.Y.E. has been in force since the beginning of the year

1944/45.[1] The amount of tax which the employer must deduct on any pay-day depends on (a) the employee's total gross pay since the beginning of the Income Tax year; (b) his Income Tax allowances and reliefs (or 'free pay') for the same period, determined by his code number; and (c) the total tax deducted on previous pay-days. By the end of the year, the total tax payable for the year from 6th April to 5th April following will have been deducted.

For each pay-day the employer ascertains the pay due to the employee, and adds to that pay the total of all previous payments made to the employee from 6th April up to date. In the Free Pay Table (Table A) he finds, from the employee's code number, the proportion of the employee's allowances and reliefs from 6th April up to date, and subtracts this figure from the total gross pay to date in the Taxable Pay Tables (Tables B to D), which shows the total tax due on any amount of taxable pay. From the total tax shown in Tables B to D the employer subtracts the total tax already deducted; the remainder is the amount to be deducted from the employee's gross pay on the pay-day in question. Sometimes—for example, if the employee has worked a short week—the total tax shown by the Tax Tables is less than the tax already deducted; the employer must then refund the difference to the employee instead of making a deduction.

The total of tax deducted on previous pay-days represents the total tax due to the date of the payment last made, and is obtained from the Deduction Card, or its equivalent. Weekly and monthly Tax Tables are issued.

Accounting Entries. There is no set method of accounting for P.A.Y.E. provided that the wages and the tax deductions (less refunds, if any) are clearly shown and that the latter are fully accounted for and agree with the sums shown on the Tax Deduction cards. The basic entries are:

Debit Wages with the gross amount.
Credit Cash with the net wages paid.
Credit P.A.Y.E. (or C.I.R.) with the tax deducted.

When the tax deducted is handed over to the Inland Revenue, the entries will be:

Debit P.A.Y.E. (or C.I.R.).
Credit Cash.

The exact manner of carrying out these entries will depend upon the circumstances in each case; there are many methods in use, two of which are:

1. On the credit side of the Cash Book are entered net wages paid and, in a special column, tax deducted. The two entries are together posted to the debit of Wages and/or Salaries. The monthly total of the Tax deducted column is posted to the credit of P.A.Y.E. Account.

[1] The detailed operation of P.A.Y.E. is governed by the Income Tax (Employments) Regulations made by the Board of Inland Revenue under S.204 of Income and Corporation Taxes Act 1970. Copies of the Regulations can be obtained from H.M. Stationery Office or through most booksellers.

2. The gross wages are debited to Wages and/or Salaries and credited to Cash. Tax deducted is debited to Cash and credited to P.A.Y.E. Account as before.

The Wages Book (in addition to the usual columns for N.I. and other deductions) will be ruled with two columns, one for tax deductions, the other for tax refunds. The wages and tax figures will either be summarized in a separate book or carried forward cumulatively, week by week, up to the last pay day before the 6th of April of each year. These summarized or cumulative figures should agree with the tax deduction/refund figures on the employees' cards, subject to adjustment for employees who have left during the year, and, in the case of new employees during the year, subject to the amounts introduced on to the cards (in respect of the previous employment) in accordance with the notification by the Inland Revenue.

The employee's code number is fixed by the Income Tax Inspector from the information supplied by the employee on his Income Tax Return. The Inspector notifies the code number to the employer and sends a Notice of Coding to the employee, giving the employee a statement of how the number has been computed. This Notice of Coding gives the amount of the Income Tax allowances and reliefs to which the employee is entitled and which are to be set against his pay for the succeeding year. As they are fixed at the beginning of the Income Tax year, they are based on the circumstances existing at the time of coding and are therefore provisional.

On receipt of the Notice the taxpayer (the employee) should check it and inform the Inspector of Taxes of any errors therein. If any change in the circumstances affecting allowances and reliefs takes place, e.g. marriage, birth of a child, death of a wife or child, the taxpayer should at once notify the Inspector so that he may alter the code number and notify the new number to the employer.

The employer receives in respect of each employee a Deduction Card. On this he must enter particulars of the wages paid and Income Tax deducted. Each month he pays over to the Collector of Taxes the tax deducted in the preceding month; at the end of the Income Tax year he sends the card back to the Collector so that the whole tax may be checked, and gives to the employee a certificate showing the amount of total tax (less refunds) deducted during the year.

It may be that from time to time, owing to a decrease in wages or absence without pay from work, the employee is entitled to a repayment of tax. This arises where, owing to decreased earnings for any cause, the Income Tax which has already been deducted from the employee is greater than the total tax payable up to date as shown by the Tax Tables. In this event, the employer either repays the amount at the pay-day or adds it to the payment of wages made after resumption of work. If a taxpayer becomes unemployed, any repayment to which he is entitled is arranged by the Inspector of Taxes.

After the end of the fiscal year, the Inspector may issue to the taxpayer a Notice of Assessment showing the total tax due and the amount of tax which has been paid by deduction from wages or salaries. If too much tax has been deducted, a repayment will be made either by direct remittance or by alteration of the code number for the next year so as to give repayment by decreasing future tax deductions. If too little tax has been deducted, future tax deductions will be increased so as to collect the tax still owing by spreading it over the succeeding year.

No formal Schedule E Assessment is made unless:

(a) Within five years after the fiscal year the taxpayer requires it;

(b) The emoluments paid during the fiscal year are not the same in amount as in the remuneration assessable for that year;

(c) Deductions have not been made in accordance with the Tax Tables;

(d) There has been a change in the circumstances not known throughout the year.

CHAPTER 10

SELF-BALANCING LEDGERS AND SECTIONAL BALANCING

WHERE numerous Ledgers are utilized by a concern, it will naturally follow that it may be of the utmost difficulty to trace book-keeping errors which disturb the agreement of the Trial Balance and consequently impede the construction of the Final Accounts. In order to reduce to a minimum the trouble of, or the time involved in, the localization of errors, the system of Self-balancing Ledgers, or Sectional Balancing, is employed.

The two terms are often employed synonymously, but strictly the former applies to one method only (see footnote p. 1004).

The advantages of Sectional Balancing are:

1. It provides a proof of the total arithmetical accuracy of the book-keeping entries in any Ledger. It must be appreciated, however, that the proof of a Ledger by means of sectional balancing provides only such proof of its accuracy as does the Trial Balance of the accuracy of the complete set of books. Thus, compensating errors, posting to the correct side of the Ledger but to wrong accounts, and errors in the books of original entry continued through the Ledgers, will not be disclosed.

2. In conjunction with other precautionary measures employed in a system of internal check, it may serve as a check on the honesty of the Ledger-keepers.

3. It is of material assistance in the location of errors which, causing the books to be out of balance, may impede the preparation of the Final Accounts and may take a considerable amount of time to discover, particularly where there are many Ledgers in use, as the Ledger in which the error is located may not be checked until all the others have been scrutinized.

4. The preparation of draft annual or periodical accounts pending the extraction of the schedules of debtors and creditors may be proceeded with.

The Construction of Total or Adjustment Accounts. The systems designated by these titles are extremely simple in principle, though it must be admitted that care and patience are demanded where there are numerous Ledgers in use.

A total account is a replica in summarized form of all the detailed entries in the Ledger to which it refers. The balance of such Account should be similar to the total of the detailed balances of the Ledger. Should the balance of the Total Account not agree with the total of the individual balances in the Ledger, it will be known that a mistake has been made in the compilation of the Total Account or that errors have been made in the casting of books of original entry or in the posting of the individual items to the Ledger.

The practice of Sectional Balancing is generally confined to the Purchases and Sales Ledgers although theoretically the principle may be extended to all the Ledgers.

Analysis of Subsidiary Books or Journals. It is essential, where it is desired to construct Total Accounts, that every entry in the Ledger shall have a complementary entry in some book or journal of original entry which is capable of analysis. The way in which the subsidiary books or journals are analysed will depend upon the number of Ledgers in use and the number of entries to be posted to each Ledger in each particular concern. Obviously, the system must be adapted to fit particular needs.

In cases where there are few Ledgers in use, each subsidiary book or journal will have columns for the different Ledgers so that an amount posted to a particular Ledger will be inserted in the appropriate column. As a result, the total of the postings to a particular Ledger will be shown in total form in the column used for that purpose in each subsidiary book or journal.

However, where the items posted to the Ledgers are few in number it may be considered unnecessary to have the subsidiary books or journals specially ruled with analysis columns. Bold index letters may be written beside the folio number against each item, if necessary in different coloured inks for different Ledgers, and at the end of suitable periods all the individual items posted to different Ledgers may be summarized into their respective groups.

On the other hand, where the items to be posted are very numerous it may be advisable to employ completely *separate* books or journals for each Ledger, thus dispensing with the analysis columns.

In the case of mechanized accounting, analysis is simplified by the fact that the required totals can be produced by the machine as the postings are made.

The individual subsidiary books will now be considered.

(a) **Cash Book.** Besides the usual three columns for Discount, Cash and Bank, it will be necessary to provide columns for the different Ledgers for which it is desired to prepare Total Accounts. The total amount of Cash plus Discount, or of Bank plus Discount, posted to individual accounts will be extended into the analysis columns.

Illustration 1

Cash has been received from the following customers:

I	£ 24,	discount £1.	Sales Ledger	A–L
E	£140,	" £3.	"	"	A–L
R	£ 45,	" £2.	"	"	M–Z
B	£ 71,	" £2.	"	"	A–L
S	£220,	" £6.	"	"	M–Z

There are two Sales Ledgers, A–L and M–Z.

The debit side of the Cash Book will be as follows:

	Discount	Cash	Bank	Ledgers	
				A-L	M-Z
	£	£	£	£	
I	1	24		25	
E	3	140		143	
R	2	45			47
B	2	71		73	
S	6	220			226
	£14	£500		£241	£273

The total of the discount column will be dealt with in the ordinary manner, and the Cash will be balanced off as usual. The totals of the 'A–L' Ledger column and of the 'M–Z' Ledger column will be carried to the credit of the Adjustment (or Total) Accounts maintained for those Ledgers, in addition to the posting of the items to the credit of the individual personal accounts. Where it is not possible to have sufficient columns in the Cash Book itself, subsidiary Cash Received Books will be used, the totals of which will be entered periodically in the Main Cash Book and posted to the relative Total Accounts.

(b) **Day Books or Journals.** The Day Books or Journals (Purchases and Sales, Purchases Returns and Sales Returns, Allowances, etc.) will be analysed in a manner similar in principle to the Cash Book, viz. by the use of an extra column for each Ledger employed, or by the use of separate books or journals for each Ledger or group of Ledgers.

(c) **General Journal.** Items of an extraordinary nature which are recorded in none of the other books or journals of original entry must be recorded in the General Journal, which must be analysed just as the other books or journals for the purpose of the preparation of Total Accounts. Items such as Bad Debts written off, Interest charged on accounts, and transfers from one Ledger to another must all be recorded in some book or journal of original entry, and since they are not to be found in any other book or journal will be entered in the General Journal. The General Journal is usually referred to simply as the Journal.

Where transfers are of frequent occurrence, it is sometimes found that a special Transfer Journal is employed to record them, as great confusion is likely to arise where transfers are improperly recorded.

The Journal may be ruled with analysis columns, or may be analysed by the medium of index letters, etc.

Illustration 2

Robertson keeps three Sales and two Purchases Ledgers. Johnson both buys from and sells to Robertson, and it is agreed to set off a debt of £30 due by Johnson to Robertson against an amount owing by the latter to Johnson. Johnson's debit appears in Sales Ledger 3 and his credit in Purchases Ledger 2. Furthermore, an amount of £40 has been credited to Williams in Sales Ledger 3 instead of to Williamson in Sales Ledger 2.

Show the Transfer Journal in Robertson's books in respect of these matters.

Robertson's Books:

TRANSFER JOURNAL

| | | | Debits | | | | | Credits | | | | |
| | | | Sales Ledger | | | Purchases Ledger | | Sales Ledger | | | Purchases Ledger | |
Date	Details	Fol.	1	2	3	1	2	1	2	3	1	2	Fol.
	Johnson—Set-off Williamson— Correcting entry posted to Williams in error		£	£	£ 30	£	£ 40	£	£	£ 30	£	£ 40	

When the books are closed off the balances of the Total Accounts will be equal to the sum of the balances in the Ledgers to which they relate, provided that:

(a) Whatever entry is made in a Ledger finds its way to the correct side in the Total Account;

(b) Whatever entry is made in the Total Account of a Ledger has been correctly recorded in the Ledger itself.

Balancing Methods. There are three methods of dealing with Sectional Balancing:

1. To prepare a Total Account for each Sales and Purchases Ledger by way of Memorandum only, serving to prove in total the separate balances in each Ledger. The Total Account includes the component items on the SAME side as in the Ledger to which it relates. Such a Total Account does not appear as an item in the Trial Balance.

2. To prepare Total Accounts as an integral part of the Double Entry system, such accounts displacing in the Trial Balance the individual personal balances of the Ledgers to which they relate. The Total Account being the epitome of the Ledger to which it refers will include the component items on the SAME side as that on which the separate items appear in the Ledger.

3. In order to incorporate in the Double Entry system both the balances of the Ledgers and the balances of the Total Accounts, two Total Accounts are prepared, the component items being exactly opposite.[1]

---

[1] The term 'Self-balancing Ledgers' is particularly applied to this method.

The Total Accounts will appear:

(a) At the back of each Ledger, the items being written up on the OPPOSITE side to the detailed entries in the personal accounts in the Ledger; and

(b) In the Nominal Ledger, the items being written up conversely to (a), i.e. on the SAME side as the detailed entries in the personal accounts in the Ledger.

Illustration 3

Assuming that sundry balances are: Debits, £1,200; Credits, £1,930; excepting Sales Ledger balances amounting to £730, the Trial Balance will be:

	METHODS.	1.		2.		3.	
		Dr.	Cr.	Dr.	Cr.	Dr.	Cr.
		£	£	£	£	£	£
Sundry Debits		1,200		1,200		1,200	
Sundry Credits			1,930		1,930		1,930
Sundry Debtors (per Sales Ledger)		730		Not in Trial Balance		730 (a)	
Total Account in Nominal Ledger		MEMO not in Trial Balance		730		730	
Total Account in Sales Ledger							730 (b)
		£1,930	£1,930	£1,930	£1,930	£2,660	£2,660

In method (3) the Sales Ledger is 'Self-balancing' in that the credit of the Total Account (b) balances the total of the individual Ledger balances in that Ledger (a).

The headings employed are:

(a) Sales Ledger.
  (i) At the back thereof. 'Nominal Ledger Adjustment Account' (Balance Credit).
  (ii) In the Nominal Ledger. 'Sales Ledger Adjustment Account' (Balance Debit).
(b) Purchases Ledger.
  (i) At the back thereof. 'Nominal Ledger Adjustment Account' (Balance Debit).
  (ii) In the Nominal Ledger. 'Purchases Ledger Adjustment Account' (Balance Credit).

It will be seen that the totals extracted from the subsidiary books will in each method be posted to the same side of the Total Account as if posted to the individual Ledger Account—and to the reverse side also if Method (3) be adopted, e.g. assuming that receipts from Debtors are £1,420, the postings of that Total (from the analysis column in the Cash Book) will be:

1. To 'Sales Ledger Adjustment Account' in Nominal Ledger (CREDIT side).

2. To 'Nominal Ledger Adjustment Account' in Sales Ledger (DEBIT side).

In the absence of errors, the balance as shown by the Total or Adjustment Account should equal the sum of the individual balances of the Ledger in question, but occasionally debit balances are found in the Purchases Ledger as well as credit balances; and credit balances in the Sales Ledger in addition to debit balances. The balance of the Total Account will then only equal the net balance of the Ledger. The usual practice is to bring down on the Total Account the totals of the debit balances and of the credit balances on the ledger to which it relates, but if the Trial Balance is prepared before the detailed balances of the Sales Ledgers are known, it is possible to bring down only the net balances of the Total Account. (The use of the reflective Total Accounts is extremely rare, and in fact the duplication of the Total Account in reverse is unnecessary.)

Illustration 4

Total Accounts are employed in the business of X in relation to the Sales Ledgers A and B. The following are the material details:

	A.	B.
	£	£
Opening Balances Dr.	1,250	3,100
Cr.	30	
Sales as per Sales Day Book	3,120	4,310
Returns as per Returns Day Book	317	205
Cash received as per Cash Book	2,005	5,120
Discounts allowed as per Cash Book	130	270
Bad Debts written off as per Journal	371	425
Provision for Bad Debts as per Journal	500	600
Bad Debts, previously written off, now received as per Cash Book	30	
Allowances as per Allowances Book	42	37
Bills Receivable as per Bill Book	130	
Bills dishonoured as per Cash Book	50	
Closing Credit Balances	72	21

The Transfer Journal contains a correcting entry in respect of £120 Sales which had been entered in error in the A Ledger analysis column in the Sales Day Book instead of in the B Ledger analysis column, although the item had been posted to the correct Ledger Account in B Ledger.

Prepare Total Accounts.

1. In the Nominal Ledger.

SALES LEDGER ADJUSTMENT ACCOUNTS

		A.£	B.£			A.£	B.£
Balances.	b/d	1,250	3,100	Balances	b/d	30	
Sales		3,120	4,310	Returns		317	205
Bills Receivable dishonoured .		50		Cash and Discount		2,135	5,390
				Bad Debts		371	425
Transfers			120	Allowances		42	37
Balances.	c/d	72	21	Bills Receivable		130	
				Transfers		120	
				Balances .	c/d	1,347	1,494
		£4,492	£7,551			£4,492	£7,551
Balances.	b/d	1,347	1,494	Balances .	b/d	72	21

2. At the back of the respective Sales Ledgers the above items will all be repeated on the reverse sides, e.g. in A Sales Ledger the balances on the Nominal Ledger Adjustment Account will be: Debit £72, Credit £1,347.

Notes. 1. The Bad Debts Provision does not concern the individual Ledger balances and the respective Total Accounts.

2. The receipt of Bad Debts written off is usually debited to Cash and credited direct to Bad Debts Received Account so that it does not affect the Total Account. Where, however, the receipt of such a Bad Debt written off is posted to a personal account the entries will be:

(*a*) *Dr.* Cash: *Cr.* Personal Account.
(*b*) *Dr.* Personal Account: *Cr.* Bad Debts.

There will then appear in the Total Account the Personal Account items, i.e. the same amount on both sides: (*a*) from the analysis column in the Cash Book; (*b*) from the Transfer Journal.

An illustration of a Purchases Ledger Adjustment Account will now be shown.

Illustration 5

	£		£
Opening Balances *Cr.*		.	6,000
Dr.		.	150
Purchases as per Purchases Day Book		.	9,000
Returns as per Returns Day Book		.	200
Cash paid as per Cash Book		.	8,700
Cash received as per Cash Book		.	50
Discounts received as per Cash Book		.	400
Allowances as per Allowances Book		.	130
Bills Payable as per Bills Payable Book		.	250
Closing Debit Balances		.	100
Transfers of Purchases to another Ledger		.	20

Prepare Total Accounts.

1. In the Nominal Ledger.

PURCHASES LEDGER ADJUSTMENT ACCOUNT

		£				£
Balances	b/d	150	Balances		b/d	6,000
Cash and Discount		9,100	Purchases			9,000
Returns		200	Cash			50
Allowances		130	Balances		c/d	100
Bills Payable		250				
Transfers		20				
Balances	c/d	5,300				
		£15,150				£15,150
Balances	b/d	100	Balances		b/d	5,300

2. At the back of the Purchases Ledger this account would appear in reverse form.

NOMINAL LEDGER ADJUSTMENT ACCOUNT

		£				£
Balances	b/d	6,000	Balances		b/d	150
Purchases		9,000	Cash and Discount			9,100
Cash		50	Returns			200
Balances	c/d	100	Allowances			130
			Bills Payable			250
			Transfers			20
			Balances		c/d	5,300
		£15,150				£15,150
Balances	b/d	5,300	Balances		b/d	100

Although method (3) is theoretically the most correct as far as making the Ledgers self-balancing is concerned, one of the total accounts is obviously superfluous since it is merely a duplication of the other. This method is therefore rarely employed in practice. The most effective practical method is for a responsible official to keep a separate book, containing a Total Account for each Ledger, which is not accessible to the various ledger clerks. The Total Accounts will then serve as a good check on the work of the clerks.

Other Uses of Total Accounts. The use of Total Accounts is not confined to Debtors and Creditors Accounts but is found in many other branches of accounting.

Examples are: Share Capital Accounts; Dividend Accounts; Hire Purchase Accounts; Double Entry Cost Accounts; Goods on Sale or Return; Solicitors' Accounts. In all these cases there is (or may be) a Total Account prepared on the principles already outlined.

Secret Accounts. It is a frequent practice to keep certain accounts secret from all but a few responsible higher officials—such accounts being Capital, Fixed Assets, Reserves, Profit and Loss, Taxation, Directors' Fees, Commissions, Dividends, and so on. This can be done by segregating the relevant accounts in the Private Ledger which is kept by one of the higher officials. It is obvious that, in order to maintain the secrecy, a separate or No. 2 Bank Account must be used and that a separate Cash

Book must be written up and the relevant vouchers kept away from the normal business ones. All these must be kept secret from the general staff.

In order that a Trial Balance may be extracted by the general staff without revealing the detailed balances in the Private Ledger and Cash Book, the latter will be represented in the Nominal Ledger (in which the general accounts are kept) by a Total Account, called the Private Ledger Adjustment Account, a corresponding Nominal Ledger Adjustment Account being kept in the Private Ledger. Provided that the two Adjustment Account balances agree (as they should do), the detailed Private Ledger balances may be substituted by one of the higher officials for the Private Ledger Adjustment Account balance appearing in the Trial Balance taken out by the general staff. Needless to say, a Trial Balance should first be extracted from the Private Ledger to ensure that the balances of the accounts therein equal the balance of the Adjustment Account.

When the system is first started, the asset and other debit balance accounts will be transferred to the Private Ledger by crediting the individual accounts in the Nominal Ledger and debiting Private Ledger Adjustment Account, then crediting Nominal Ledger Adjustment Account and debiting the various accounts in the Private Ledger, and *vice versa* in respect of Capital, Reserves and other credit balance accounts. When it is desired to transfer cash from the General to the Private Bank Account, the entries will be Dr. Private Ledger Adjustment Account, Cr. General Bank Account, Dr. Private Bank Account, Cr. Nominal Ledger Adjustment Account. Directors' Fees, Dividends, etc., will be paid by debiting the respective accounts in the Private Ledger and crediting Private Bank Account.

When accounts are prepared, the general accounts in the Nominal Ledger will be closed off to the Private Ledger Adjustment Account, the entries appearing on reverse sides in the Nominal Ledger Adjustment Account in the Private Ledger, whence they will be transferred, along with the balances of the Private Ledger Accounts to the Profit and Loss Account.

The system is sometimes operated with one bank account only, two or more Cash Books being used, one for secret entries and one or more for general transactions, the totals of the latter being periodically entered in the 'secret' Cash Book. The disadvantage of this method is that it is obviously necessary to keep the Bank Statements away from the general staff, since otherwise the private receipts and payments will no longer be secret, and therefore the checking of the Bank Statements must be done by one of the higher officials.

CHAPTER 11

SINGLE ENTRY

SINGLE entry book-keeping is a term which is in many cases very loosely employed without any real regard to the exact nature of the book-keeping system in question. Single entry is discussed in this chapter under two headings:

1. Pure single entry.
2. Single entry in the popular sense.

Pure Single Entry

Under this system the twofold aspect of each transaction as considered in the double entry system is ignored. The essential characteristic of this system is the keeping of Personal Accounts only; that is, no Real or Nominal Accounts find a place in the books of account. Such a book-keeping method is incomplete and unsatisfactory and it is clear that accurate information of the operations of the business is entirely lacking.

When the pure single entry system is in use the profit or loss for a period is ascertained by comparing the capital at the end of the period with that at the beginning, adjustments being effected in respect of withdrawals or introductions of capital during the period. If the closing capital exceeds the opening capital, such excess is considered to be profit for the period, and if the opening capital exceeds the closing capital, such excess is considered to be a loss for the period, subject to the adjustments mentioned above. Capital is, of course, the excess of assets over liabilities when considered for this purpose.

Illustration 1

	£
Capital at 1st January 19..	1,000
Capital at 31st December 19..	1,500

The profit for the year ended 31st December 19.., is therefore £500, i.e. £1,500–£1,000.

	£
Capital at 1st January 19..	800
Capital at 31st December 19...	600

The loss for the year ended 31st December 19.., is therefore £200 (i.e. £800–£600).

Two very important points requiring adjustment in ascertaining the profits under pure single entry are additions to, and withdrawals of, capital. As explained above, any increase of capital during the period is considered as profit, and any decrease as loss; but capital introduced from outside sources cannot be considered in the light of profit, and must consequently be added to losses or deducted from profits when ascertained as above, and withdrawals similarly cannot be considered as losses but must be either added to profits or deducted from losses.

The rule in regard to the adjustment for withdrawals of capital may be shortly stated thus—In order to ascertain profit or loss withdrawals must be (a) *added* to the increase of capital or (b) *deducted* from the decrease of capital.

Introductions of capital must be adjusted in exactly the converse manner, e.g. in order to ascertain profit or loss, introductions of capital must be (a) *deducted* from the increase of capital, or (b) *added* to the decrease of capital,

The following example illustrates the principles enunciated:

Illustration 2

Business	A	B	C	D
	£	£	£	£
Opening Capital	1,000	2,200	1,600	1,000
Closing Capital	2,000	2,000	1,500	1,200
Drawings	400	400	—	400
Introduction of Capital	600	—	200	700

The results of the businesses as regards profit or loss are as follows:

Business A: £2,000−£1,000 = £1,000+£400−£600 = £800 Profit
"   B: £2,000−£2,200 = −£200+£400   = £200 "
"   C: £1,500−£1,600 = −£100−£200   = £300 Loss
"   D: £1,200−£1,000 = £200+£400−£700 = £100 "

Preparation of Statement of Profit. In practice, the following method is adopted—(1) The opening and closing statements of affairs are compiled and from them the opening and closing capitals are obtained. As no records of Real Accounts are kept in the books, such statements will have to be prepared from information supplied by the proprietor himself, and from such other data as may be available. (2) Totals are made of withdrawals and introductions of capital during the period. (3) The particulars so obtained are present in double entry form by opening two accounts called 'Statement of Profit' and 'Capital Account', and such are compiled by applying the principles already outlined which may be summarized as follows:

(a) Debit Statement of Profit and credit Capital Account for the opening capital; *vice versa* for deficiency, i.e. where liabilities exceed assets.

(b) Debit Statement of Profit and credit Capital Account for capital introduced during the period.

(c) Debit Capital Account and credit Statement of Profit for withdrawals of capital during the period.

(d) Credit the Statement of Profit with the closing capital, as disclosed by the closing Statement of Affairs, and bring this figure down as a debit balance on this account.

(e) Transfer the balance of the Statement of Profit to the debit (or credit) of Capital Account according as a loss (or profit) has resulted.

In subsequent years, the same procedure as regards (b), (c), (d), and (e) only will be followed, as the credit balance of Capital at the commencement of each year will equal the debit balance on Statement of Profit brought down from the preceding year.

The credit balance on the Capital Account will now be similar to the debit balance brought down on the Statement of Profit.

The capital figure represents the excess of assets over liabilities, or *vice versa*, and the accounts may be presented in Balance Sheet form under the heading of 'Statement of Affairs'. It is usual also to prepare a Statement of Affairs as at the beginning of the period to determine the amount of the opening capital.

If it is desired to record Depreciation, Provision for Bad Debts, and similar provisions in the Statement of Profit, it is necessary to bring down the closing capital intact, i.e. at the full figure, to debit separately the depreciation or other provision to the Statement of Profit, bringing such provision down separately as a credit balance, and finally to offset these balances and bring down the net balance on the Statement of Profit which will correspond with the balance shown by the Capital Account.

Illustration 3

X keeps his books on the single-entry principle. The following information is disclosed:

Assets and Liabilities	1st Jan. 19..	31st Dec. 19..
	£	£
Fixtures and Fittings	2,000	2,000
Stock	1,000	1,250
Debtors	2,100	3,400
Cash	150	200
Creditors	1,750	1,900
Bills Payable	Nil	300
Loan by Y	Nil	500
Investments at 31st December 19..	Nil	1,000

X has drawn £500 on account of his profits. Fixtures and Fittings are to be written down to £1,800 and the proprietor wishes to create a Bad Debts Provision of 10 per cent on debtors.

A Statement of Affairs is drawn up at 1st January 19.., from which the opening capital is ascertained. The closing capital (before providing for depreciation and bad debts) will be obtained by deducting the liabilities from the assets, since the Capital Account is not overdrawn, and from the information thus obtained a Statement of Profit will be drawn up and finally a detailed Statement of Affairs at 31st December 19...

STATEMENT OF AFFAIRS AS AT 1ST JANUARY 19 . .

	£		£
Sundry Creditors .	1,750	Fixtures and Fittings .	2,000
Balance, being Capital at this date .	3,500	Stock . . .	1,000
		Sundry Debtors .	2,100
		Cash . .	150
	£5,250		£5,250

The capital at the close of the period is ascertained thus:

					£
ASSETS:					
Fixtures and Fittings	.	.	.		2,000
Stock .	.	.	.	.	1,250
Debtors	.	.	.	.	3,400
Cash .	.	.	.	.	200
Investments .	.	.	.		1,000
					7,850
LIABILITIES:			£		
Creditors	.	.	1,900		
Bills Payable	.	.	300		
Loan by Y .	.	.	500		
					2,700
Capital at 31st December 19 .[1]					£5,150

The Statement of Profit will be as follows:

STATEMENT OF PROFIT FOR THE YEAR ENDED
31ST DEMBER 19 . .

19 . .				£	19 . .			£
Jan. 1	Opening Capital .		b/d	3,500	Dec. 31	Drawings . . .		500
Dec. 31	Depreciation £200					Closing Capital .	c/d	5,150
	Bad Debts Provision 340							
			c/d	.540				
	Balance—Net Profit transferred to Capital Account .			1,610				
				£5,650				£5,650
	Closing Capital .		b/d	5,150		Depreciation and Bad Debts Provision .	b/d	540
						Balance . . .	c/d	4,610
				£5,150				£5,150
19 . .								
Jan. 1	Balance . .		b/d	4,610				

CAPITAL

19.. Dec. 31	Drawings Balance		c/d	£ 500 4,610	19.. Jan. 1 Dec. 31	Balance Statement of Profit— Net Profit	b/d	£ 3,500 1,610
				£5,110				£5,110
					19..² Jan. 1	Balance	b/d	4,610

¹ Before providing for depreciation and bad debts.
² Following year.

STATEMENT OF AFFAIRS AS AT 31ST DECEMBER 19..

		£			£
Sundry Creditors		1,900	Fixtures and Fittings £2,000 *Less* Depreciation 200		
Loan		500			1,800
Bills Payable		300	Stock		1,250
Capital at 1st Jan.			Sundry Debtors £3,400		
19..	£3,500		*Less* Provision 340		
Less Drawings	500				3,060
	3,000		Investments		1,000
Add Net Profit	1,610		Cash		200
		4,610			
		£7,310			£7,310

Students should be very careful to avoid stating that one of the methods of ascertaining profits and losses under *pure* single entry is by conversion to double entry, as this cannot be done when pure single entry is in force. Should, however, adequate records be available, then the results obtainable arise from double entry and not single entry.

Single Entry in the Popular Sense

Single entry in the popular sense or quasi single entry are terms covering numerous systems of book-keeping which, though differing one from the other in detail, are all characterized by one common feature, viz. the lack of completeness of the double entry.

It may be that a Cash Book is kept, but no Day Books or Journals, even though the business is not entirely on a cash basis; or it may be that no Personal Accounts are kept, or that full Personal Accounts are written up on double entry lines, but no Nominal Accounts kept. In short, whenever the system employed is such that a Trial Balance cannot ensue from the books, it cannot be accurately described as a double entry system. From this, however, it should not be inferred that because the formal Day Books or Journals are not kept that the full double entry results cannot be achieved, for many 'short cut' methods are employed as a means to complete the double entry.

Therefore, whenever a system is in force which goes beyond the keeping of Personal Accounts yet falls short of a complete system of double entry, it may be designated quasi single entry. It will usually be possible in the above circumstances to build up the double entry, i.e. to convert the partial double entry to a complete double entry. There are, then, two methods of ascertaining profits and losses under a single-entry system in its comprehensive sense:

1. **Pure Single Entry.** By means of the Statement of Profit method as previously mentioned. Such a method will be adopted when the information is sufficient to enable one to find opening and closing assets and liabilities, drawings, and introduction of capital.

2. **Conversion to Double Entry.** The number of entries necessary to complete the true double entry will vary according to the degree of completeness already existing in the books. A typical set of books kept under a quasi single entry system comprises: Purchases, Purchases Returns, Sales, and Sales Returns Books or Journals, the items from which are posted in detail to the relevant personal accounts, no posting being made of the periodical Day Book or Journal totals as no nominal accounts are kept; a cash book ruled in the familiar three-column style in which all receipts and payments are entered as made, together with all discounts either received or allowed. The cash (and discount) received from debtors, and paid to creditors, are posted to the respective personal accounts, the items in respect of personal accounts alone being posted. To put such a set of books on a true double entry basis for an accounting period, the following procedure will be necessary. A Statement of Affairs at the beginning of the period must be prepared and all the items therein (except Debtors and Creditors, and Cash and Bank, which are already in the books) must be debited or credited to the appropriate accounts in the Nominal Ledger. All assets will be on the debit and all liabilities on the credit side of the books. The balancing item will be Capital Account, which may be a debit or a credit. Now, so far as relates to the entries at the commencement of the period in question, the books are in balance. The double entry in respect of all the transactions of the period must now be completed.

The totals of the subsidiary books or journals will be posted to the appropriate side of the respective nominal accounts, and the totals of the discount columns in the Cash Book transferred to the Discount Accounts. The Cash Book will now be scrutinized for unposted items, all of which will now be posted to the appropriate accounts which will generally be Nominal or Real Accounts, e.g. Rates paid, Additions to Plant, Dividends and Rents received. Occasionally, it will be found that withdrawals of cash by the proprietor have not been posted or even entered in the Cash Book.

The degree of incompleteness of the double entry and the data available for bridging the gap must necessarily vary in every business, so that an attempt to lay down a detailed formula would be most misleading and futile. As a rule, however, it is first essential to *obtain the opening figures* (through the Statement of Affairs) and to open the necessary accounts to record them, including Capital Account, with the exception of the Cash and Bank items, and Debtors and Creditors, which are already recorded in the books; secondly, each book or journal of original entry must be dealt with separately, the double entry being completed by posting the necessary figures. If any of these books or journals are not completely written up it will be necessary to enter the missing items.

Before dismissing the matter an instance may be taken where the full double entry exists except that the Bought Ledger is compiled direct from the invoices and credit notes, and from the Cash Book in the usual way. It will readily be perceived that the Purchases and Returns figures must be extracted from the Bought Ledger. The Purchases Account will be debited with the ascertained total, and the Purchases Returns Account will be similarly credited. This may be illustrated by a simple example, as there is no difference in *principle* whatever between such an example and one which embraces a considerable number of detailed Ledger Accounts.

Illustration 4

The following are accounts extracted from a Bought Ledger compiled as described above:

B

		£				£
Cash and Discount		120		Goods		200
Returns		20				50
Balance	c/d	110				
		£250				£250
				Balance	b/d	110

C

						£
				Goods		100

D

		£				£
Cash and Discount	c/d	100		Balance	b/d	130
Balance		340		Goods		310
		£440				£440
				Balance	b/d	340

E

		£				£
Cash and Discount		46		Balance	b/d	50
Returns		4				
		£50				£50

F

		£				£
Cash		40		Balance	b/d	10
				Goods		30
		£40				£40

The Bought Ledger will be analysed:

Personal Account	Closing Balances	Cash and Discount	Returns	Total	Pur- chases	Opening Balances
	£	£	£	£	£	£
B	110	120	20	250	250	
C	100			100	100	
D	340	100		440	310	130
E		46	4	50		50
F		40		40	30	10
	£550	£306	£24	£880	£690	£190

From the above analysis the total of Purchases Returns, i.e. £24, will be posted to the credit of Purchases (Returns) Account, and the total of Purchases, i.e. £690, will be posted to the debit of Purchases Account. The items of cash and discount entered on the debit side of the Ledger Accounts have their credit entries in the Cash Book.

Usually a certain number of abnormal items will appear in the Ledger Accounts, a special column being provided in the analysis for the record of such items, the total of which column will have to be sub-analysed and posted to the different ledger accounts in question: e.g., if F had been sent a bill of exchange for £40 instead of cash, the £40 would be inserted in a special column, and (together with any other bills payable) would be posted to the credit of Bills Payable Account. Very probably, in this case the payment of the bill through the Cash Book would not have been posted, and the double entry in respect of the Cash Book entry would be effected by debiting the amount to Bills Payable Account.

Once the Trial Balance has been compiled, the Final Accounts are prepared in the normal manner, dealing with the usual accruals, prepayments, and other provisions.

When books are kept on a pure single entry system and it is desired to convert them to the double entry system in respect of future periods, a Statement of Affairs must be prepared from all available information, and all the items therein, including the balancing item of capital (except the Debtors and Creditors, Cash and Bank figures, which are already in the books), entered in the various ledgers on the debit and credit side according to whether the item in question is an asset or a liability. The books are now in balance and subsidiary books or journals must be opened to record the transactions, the ordinary double entry system being fully carried out.

It is possible, as a matter both of practice and for examination purposes, if the beginning capital (with details of assets and liabilities) is available together with analyses of the Sales and Purchases Ledgers, and the Cash Book, to convert the system of quasi single entry in force for the preceding period into a full double entry structure. This matter is important in as much as the more advanced problems almost invariably resolve themselves into performing three distinct operations:

1. Preparation of a Statement of Affairs.
2. Analysis of Sales and Purchases Ledgers.
3. Analysis of Cash Book.

The problem presented may disclose part only of the above information from which the required conversion is to proceed, and it is generally found that insufficient attention is paid to the Statement of Affairs (with the inclusion of capital) and the working of the double entry from the items appearing therein.

In examination work, there is usually no time to open *all* the Ledger Accounts, but they must be treated as though they had been opened. In the following example the Ledger Accounts will be opened in full, and it will be noted that the opening Debtors and Creditors, and Cash and Bank figures are ALREADY in the appropriate accounts.

It will be seen that a quicker way of dealing with most of the items (save Debtors and Creditors and Cash and Bank) is to place them directly in the Trial Balance, because even if such accounts are opened the items will remain undisturbed, and therefore the direct entry to the Trial Balance effects a very valuable economy in time. This device applies equally well to the postings of the nominal items from the Cash Book.

Illustration 5

M. Scipio wishes to have his books converted to double entry in order that he may keep them on this basis in future years, and also to have a Trading and Profit and Loss Account and Balance Sheet drawn up in respect of the year to 31st December 19... His expenses are kept in a rough Cash Book and his Bank transactions are found from the bank statements. An analysis of the various accounts will be made on the following lines.

The opening Statement of Affairs discloses the following position:

STATEMENT OF AFFAIRS AS AT 1ST JANUARY 19..

	£			£
Sundry Creditors	450	Cash in Hand £50		
Balance, being Capital at		Cash at Bank . 100		
this date . .	950			150
		Sundry Debtors . .		600
		Stock . .		400
		Plant and Machinery .		250
	£1,400			£1,400

The following are the analyses:

ANALYSIS OF THE SALES LEDGER ACCOUNTS

		£			£
Balances at 1st Jan. 19...	b/d	600	Cash . . .		3,470
Sales	T.B.	4,000	Discounts Allowed .	T.B.	120
			Returns. . .	T.B.	240
			Contras (Purchases Ledger)	C.	70
			Balances at 31st Dec.		
			19... . c/d	T.B.	700
		£4,600			£4,600
Balances . . .	b/d	700			

Analysis of the Purchases Ledger Accounts

		£			£
Cash and Cheques . .		2,170	Balances at 1st Jan. 19 . .	b/d	450
Discounts Received	T.B.	50	Purchases . . .	T.B.	2,500
Returns	T.B.	160			
Contras (Sales Ledger)	C.	70			
Balances at 31st Dec.					
19... . . . c/d	T.B.	500			
		£2,950			£2,950
			Balances . . .	b/d	500

Note. 'T.B.' in the folio column signifies that the item appears in the Trial Balance.

These items will be posted to their respective accounts and as a consequence every item in either the Sales or the Purchases Ledger will have an opposite entry elsewhere, the double entry being thus completed.

Cash Book Summary

		Cash	Bank				Cash	Bank
		£	£				£	£
Balances . .	b/d	50	100	Cash to				
Cash from Deb-				Creditors	P.L.		170	2,000
tors . .	S.L.	3,470		Expenses				
				(detailed)	T.B.		940	
Capital intro-				Drawings .	T.B.		260	
duced .	L	1,000		Bank: Contra.	C.		3,000	
Cash: Contra .	C		3,000	Balances	c/d		150	1,100
		£4,520	£3,100				£4,520	£3,100
Balances . .	b/d	150	1,100					

The Capital Account is in credit as below:

		£
Balance . .	b/d	950
Cash (C.B.) . . .		1,000
		£1,950

All the expenses will be posted to their respective accounts. Cash introduced will be credited to Capital Account; Drawings may be posted to the debit of a Drawings Account and thence transferred to Capital Account, or alternatively posted direct to the debit of Capital Account.

Complete double entry will now have been effected, and accordingly a Trial Balance at 31st December 19.., may be extracted, and a Trading and Profit and Loss Account and a Balance Sheet prepared therefrom. Closing Stock is £480.

M. SCIPIO

TRIAL BALANCE AS AT 31ST DECEMBER 19 . .

		Dr.	Cr.
		£	£
Capital	L.		1,950
Sales	S.L.		4,000
Sales Returns	S.L.	240	
Purchases	P.L.	2,500	
Purchases Returns	P.L.		160
Discounts Allowed	S.L.	120	
Discounts Received	P.L.		50
Drawings	C.B.	260	
Expenses (detailed)	C.B.	940	
Sundry Debtors	S.L.	700	
Sundry Creditors	P.L.		500
Stock	S.A.	400	
Plant and Machinery	S.A.	250	
Cash	C.B.	150	
Bank	C.B.	1,100	
		£6,660	£6,660

TRADING AND PROFIT AND LOSS ACCOUNT FOR THE YEAR
ENDED 31ST DEMBER 19 . .

		£			£
Stock		400	Sales . . .	£4,000	
Purchases . . .	£2,500		*Less* Returns . .	240	
Less Returns . .	160				3,760
		2,340	Stock		480
Gross Profit . . . c/d		1,500			
		£4,240			£4,240
Expenses (detailed) . .		940	Gross Profit . . b/d		1,500
Discounts Allowed . .		120	Discounts Received . .		50
Net Profit . . .		490			
		£1,550			£1,550

BALANCE SHEET AS AT 31ST DECEMBER 19 . .

		£			£
Sundry Creditors		500	Cash in Hand . .	£150	
Capital at 1st Jan. 19. .	£950		Cash at Bank . .	1,100	
Less Drawings .	260				1,250
	690		Sundry Debtors . . .		700
Add Net Profit .	490		Stock		480
Cash introduced .	1,000		Plant and Machinery . .		250
		2,180			
		£2,680			£2,680

Note. In this instance the traditional two-sided form of Final Accounts is shown.

Questions are very often set on single entry systems, it being required to convert them to double entry, and to prepare a Trading and Profit and Loss Account therefrom. To do this, it is necessary to 'build up' various accounts from the information given in the question. The following illustration is of such a type and should be checked up by the student, item by item.

Illustration 6

A client submits to you the following figures relating to his business in respect of the year to 31st December 19... You are required to prepare in vertical form a Trading and Profit and Loss Account for the year ended, and a Balance Sheet as at 31st December 19... Any difference in the Cash balance is assumed to be drawings.

	£
Cash paid into Bank	8,690
Private Dividends paid into the Business (Cash)	200
Private Payments out of Bank	750
Business Payments out of Bank	7,750
Cash and Cheques from Debtors	11,700
Payment for Goods by Cash and Cheques	7,950
Wages	1,500
Delivery Expenses	600
Rent and Rates	135
Lighting and Heating	90
General Expenses	250
Commission Received (credited direct through bank)	110

The Assets and Liabilities are as follows:

Assets and Liabilities	1st Jan. 19..	31st Dec. 19..
	£	£
Stock	600	750
Bank Balances	800	1,000
Cash in Hand	30	20
Trade Debtors	750	1,050
Trade Creditors	1,200	1,400
Investments	3,000	3,000

Any goods drawn out by the trader have been paid for by cash.

As in the previous examples, the first requisite is to prepare an opening Statement of Affairs to find the opening capital, after which the balances of debtors and creditors, cash and bank will be opened in their respective accounts, the remaining items being taken direct to the Profit and Loss Account and Balance Sheet (instead of opening the actual accounts). The double entry will be compiled through the medium of these accounts, expenses from the Cash Book being transferred direct to Profit and Loss Account (again, to save time, the Trial Balance being dispensed with).

The Cash Book will be written up and the balances therein should correspond with those shown in the opening Statement of Affairs. The receipts from customers will be posted to the credit of Sundry Debtors

Account. The closing balances of Debtors in total will be credited to the Sundry Debtors Account and brought down as an item to be shown in the Balance Sheet. The balancing figure on the account will be 'Sales' which will be debited to Sundry Debtors Account and credited to Trading Account.

The item of investments remains at £3,000 and will be merely carried forward from Balance Sheet to Balance Sheet.

A Sundry Creditors Account will be written up on the same principle as the Sundry Debtors Account, and from it the 'Purchases' figure will be obtained.

It will be seen that all the items given have been covered save the closing stock. This will be dealt with in the usual way, i.e. debit Stock Account and credit Trading Account (or in this example, where time-saving methods are adopted, the stock figure will be taken direct to the Balance Sheet, no Stock Account being written up).

As the trader lives on his business premises, one-third of the lighting and heating, and of the rent and rates, has been treated as a personal expense and thus charged as drawings. The proportion to be so dealt with cannot usually be ascertained with meticulous accuracy, but as the income tax practice is, generally, to allow two-thirds of such mixed expenditure as legitimate charges against profits, it is reasonable to consider that one-third is a fair proportion of such expenses to be attributed to private living.

TOTAL CREDITORS

19.. Dec. 31	Cash and Cheques Balances	. . c/d	£ 7,950 1,400	19.. Jan. 1 Dec. 31	Balances Purchases	. .	. .	b/d	£ 1,200 8,150
			£9,350						£9,350
				19.. Jan. 1	Balances	.	.	b/d	1,400

TOTAL DEBTORS

19.. Jan. 1 Dec. 31	Balances Sales	. .	. .	b/d	£ 750 12,000	19.. Dec. 31	Cash Balances	. .	. .	c/d	£ 11,700 1,050
					£12,750						£12,750
19.. Jan. 1	Balances	.	.	b/d	1,050						

CASH BOOK

19..			£	£	19..			£	£
Jan. 1	Balances	b/d	30	800	Dec. 31	Bank: *Contra*		8,690	
Dec. 31	Cash: *Contra*			8,690		Wages		1,500	
	Sales		11,700			Delivery Expenses		600	
	Dividends		200			Rent and Rates		135	
	Commission			110		Lighting and Heating		90	
						General Expenses		250	
						Drawings	(a)	**445**	750
						Purchases	(b)	200	7,750
						Balances	c/d	20	1,100
			£11,930	£9,600				£11,930	£9,600
19..									
Jan. 1	Balances	b/d	20	1,100					

Note. (a) The Cash Drawings item is a balancing figure.

(b) It will be observed that the payment for goods, £7,950, is made up of £7,750 bank payments (as per question) and £200 cash payments.

This is easily found, as the item required to balance the Bank column is £7,750.

Items in heavy type are balancing figures.

TRADING AND PROFIT AND LOSS ACCOUNT FOR THE YEAR
ENDED 31ST DECEMBER 19 . .

		£
Sales		12,000
Cost of Goods Sold:		
Purchases	£8,150	
Less increase in value of Stock	150	
		8,000
Trading Profit		£4,000
Add Commission received		110
		£4,110
Less Wages	£1,500	
Delivery Expenses	600	
Rent and Rates	90	
Lighting and Heating	60	
General Expenses	250	
		2,500
Net Profit transferred to Capital		£1,610

BALANCE SHEET AS AT 31ST DECEMBER 19 . .

CAPITAL		£
At 1st Jan...	. . .	3,980
Add Dividends	. . .	200
Net Profit	. . .	1,610
		£5,790
Less Drawings	£1,195	
One-third Rent, etc.	75	
		1,270
		£4,520

EMPLOYMENT OF CAPITAL

Current Assets:		
Investments		£3,000
Stock	. . .	750
Debtors	.	1,050
Cash in Hand	£20	
Cash at Bank	1,100	
		1,120
		£5,920
Current Liabilities:		
Creditors	. . .	£1,400
Working Capital	. . .	4,520
		£4,520

Note. The question states 'private dividends,' so that the amount is a credit to capital, but it should be noted that as there is an item of investments in the Balance Sheet, it may be that some or all of the dividends mentioned may arise from the business assets, in which case they would be credited to Profit and Loss Account.

Questions involving the principle of conversion of single entry into double entry may be presented in an infinite variety of ways, but all will demand, in common, the method of first preparing the opening Statement of Affairs (or such part as may be immediately prepared) and obtaining the opening figures therefrom, followed by the opening of the vital accounts, viz. Cash and/or Bank, Debtors and Creditors. It will then generally be necessary to place in such accounts the information given, by the utilization of which a double entry system may be constructed and any 'missing' items determined.

As an example, information may be given as to a trader's assets and liabilities as at the beginning date, with the exception that the figure for opening debtors is missing, so that without further data it is impossible to ascertain the capital at that date. Nevertheless, the Statement of Affairs should be written up, leaving blanks for the items—'Capital' and 'Debtors'. The three or four vital accounts should be opened and, as the writing up of the accounts proceeds, it usually will be possible to obtain the figure for opening debtors, as the sales will generally be disclosed by the question and also the closing debtors figure. It will still be necessary to find the cash received from debtors, but if this item is not given, it will be necessary perhaps to turn to the Cash Book to see whether the receipts from debtors can be deduced therefrom. If the Cash Book information is complete in all respects save this figure (as on the above hypothesis it has not been given in the question) the balancing item will be, *prima facie*, 'Receipts from Debtors'. Once this figure is ascertained, it is credited to 'Sundry Debtors Account', which account is now complete save for the opening debtors figure which will be a balancing item. The opening Statement of Affairs may now be completed by inserting the debtors figure, and consequently, the opening capital ascertained.

Illustration 7

The following information is supplied, from which you are required to prepare in two-sided form Trading and Profit and Loss Account for the year ended, and Balance Sheet as on 31st December, . . .

Assets and Liabilities	1st Jan. 19..	31st Dec. 19..
	£	£
Creditors	1,577	1,240
General Expenses Owing	60	33
Sundry Assets	1,161	1,204
Stock	804	1,112
Cash in Hand and at Bank	696	808
Debtors	?	1,787

Details relative to the year's transactions are:

	£
Cash and *Discount* credited to Debtors (a) See item (b)	6,400
Returns from Debtors	145
Bad Debts	42
Sales—Cash and Credit	7,181
Discount Allowed by Creditors	70
Returns to Creditors	40
Capital Introduced (paid into Bank)	850
Receipts from Debtors (paid into Bank) (b) See item (a)	6,250
Cash Purchases	103
Expenses paid by Cash	957
Purchase of Machinery by Cheque	43
Drawings by Cheque	318
Cash Payments into Bank	500
Withdrawn from Bank into Cash	924
Cash in Hand at end	120
Payments to Creditors by Cheque	6,027

The accounts are as follows:

ANALYSIS OF CASH BOOK, 19 . .

			Cash	Bank				Cash	Bank
			£	£	19 . .			£	£
19 . .					Dec. 31	Cash Purchases		103	
Jan. 1	Balances	b/d	296	400		Expenses		957	
Dec. 31	Cash Sales (see Note 4)		460			Plant and Machinery (purchased)			43
	Capital introduced			850		Drawings			318
	Debtors			6,250		Creditors			6,027
	Bank: Contra		924			Cash: Contra			924
	Cash: Contra			500		Bank: Contra		500	
						Balances	c/d	120	688
			£1,680	£8,000				£1,680	£8,000
19 . .									
Jan. 1	Balances	b/d	120	688					

The connecting links are arrived at in the following sequence:

1. Deduct from the Cash and Bank Balance at 31st December 19 . . (£808), the cash balance at that date (£120) to give the closing bank balance.

2. The resultant balance (£688) will enable the opening bank balance to be arrived at (£400).

3. The opening cash balance can now be reckoned, viz. £696 less £400 = £296.

4. This figure, in ture, will enable the figure of cash sales to be calculated, i.e. £460, being the balancing item in the Cash Column.

5. The sales in the Debtors Account are now found by deducting the cash sales from the figure of cash and credit sales supplied by the question, i.e. £7,181 less £460 = credit sales £6,721.

6. Discount allowed to customers is £6,400 less £6,250 = £150.

It will now be possible to prepare Total Debtors and Total Creditors Accounts to disclose the missing items, viz. opening Debtors and Capital at 1st January 19 . ., and Purchases (on credit) and a Balance Sheet at 1st January 19 . . :

TOTAL DEBTORS

			£					£
Balances		b/d	1,653	Cash				6,250
Sales (see Note 5 above)			6,721	Discount				150
				Returns				145
				Bad Debts				42
				Balances			c/d	1,787
			£8,374					£8,374
Balances		b/d	1,787					

TOTAL CREDITORS

		£			£
Cheques		6,027	Balances . . . b/d		1,577
Discount		70	Purchases		5,800
Returns		40			
Balances . . c/d		1,240			
		£7,377			£7,377
			Balances . . . b/d		1,240

BALANCE SHEET AS AT 1ST JANUARY 19 . .

		£			£
Capital .		2,677	Sundry Assets		1,161
Sundry Creditors . £1,577			Stock		804
General Expenses accrued . 60			Sundry Debtors		1,653
			Cash in Hand	£296	
			Cash at Bank	400	
					696
		£4,314			£4,314

TRADING AND PROFIT AND LOSS ACCOUNT FOR THE YEAR
ENDED 31ST DECEMBER 19 . .

		£			£
Stock (Opening)		804	Sales . . £7,181		
Purchases £5,903			Less Returns . 145		
Less Returns . 40					7,036
		5,863	Stock (Closing)		1,112
Gross Profit . c/d		1,481			
		£8,148			£8,148
Discount		80	Gross Profit . . b/d		1,481
Bad Debts		42			
General Expenses [957 + 33 − 60]		930			
Net Profit, transferred to Capital Account		429			
		£1,481			£1,481

BALANCE SHEET AS AT 31ST DECEMBER 19 . .

	£			£
Capital Account—		Sundry Assets	£1,161	
Balance, 1st Jan., 19 . . £2,677		Add Addition	43	
Amount introduced . 850				1,204
Net Profit per Profit and Loss Account . 429		Stock .		1,112
		Sundry Debtors		1,787
3,956		Cash in Hand .	120	
Less Drawings . 318		Cash at Bank .	688	
	3,638			808
Sundry Creditors . 1,240				
General Expenses accrued . 33				
	1,273			
	£4,911			£4,911

The opening figures are shown in heavy type.

Disadvantages of Single Entry. 1. Impossibility of obtaining accurate information as to results of trading operations.

2. Unreliability of the information relative to assets and liabilities.

3. As nominal accounts are not kept or, if kept, are generally of an incomplete character, interim accounts, or comparative or other statistical information cannot be obtained.

4. Arising from above, difficulties will be likely to accrue to the proprietor should he desire to sell the business, ascertain goodwill for the purposes of sale, appeal against excessive income tax assessments, or obtain assistance in financing the business.

5. The psychological effect is that the lack of double entry will engender lax accounting methods, thus opening the door to fraud and other evils.

6. The check on arithmetical accuracy of postings and the elasticity and adaptability of the double entry system are lacking in the single entry system.

Capital Statements. Where the affairs of a person are in such a state of confusion, arising particularly from the mixing of private affairs with business, rendering compilation of accounts impossible, it is usual to estimate business profits by constructing a capital statement. The fluctuations of capital, subject to living expenses and private income, are taken to indicate the profit of loss for each period.

Illustration 8

The following figures summarize the position of X:

Assets and Liabilities	1st Jan. 19.1	31st Dec. 19.1	31st Dec. 19.2
	£	£	£
Net Business Assets	4,000	3,800	3,700
Investments	1,700	2,100	2,750
Bank (overdrawn)	250	200	(in hand) 150
Car		100	100

	Year Ended 31st Dec. 19.1	Year Ended 31st Dec. 19.2
	£	£
Income from Investments	118	125
Bank Interest	18	
	(Paid)	
Drawings	450	500

It is required to ascertain the business profits for the years ended 31st December, 19.1 and 19.2.

First, it is necessary to find the total capital at the three dates: 1st January 19.1, 31st December 19.1 and 19.2. Secondly, from these figures will be found the increase of capital in the two years ended 31st December 19.1 and 19.2. Thirdly, the drawings will be added to this figure; and, finally, as the results obtained include profits, income and expenditure not arising from the business dealings, such must be deleted in order to arrive at the business profits.

The estimated business profits are obtained thus:

	1st Jan. 19.1	31st Dec. 19.1	31st Dec. 19.2
	£	£	£
(a) Total Capitals—			
Net Business Assets .	4,000	3,800	3,700
Investments .	1,700	2,100	2,750
Car .		100	100
Bank .			150
	5,700	6,000	6,700
Less Bank (overdrawn) .	250	200	
	£5,450	5,800	6,700
Less Capital at commencement of year		5,450	5,800
(b) Increase of Capital .		350	900
(c) Add Drawings .		450	500
		800	1,400
(d) Less—			
Income from Investments .		118	125
		682	1,275
Add Bank Interest Paid .		18	
Business Profits .		£700	£1,275

Proof:

		£
Total Income—		
Capital at 31st December 19.2 .		6,700
Capital at 1st January 19.1 .		5,450
Increase of Capital .		1,250
Add Drawings .		950
Total Income .		£2,200
Private Income—		£
Income from Investments .		243
Less—		
Bank Interest paid .		18
		£225
Business Profits—		£
Total Income .		2,200
Less Private Income .		225
		£1,975

SUMMARY OF POSITION

		£
Capital at 1st January 19.1	. . . . . .	5,450
Add Private Income	. . . . .	225
Business Profits	. . . . .	1,975
		7,650
Less Drawings	. . . . . .	950
∴ Capital at 31st December 19.2	.	£6,700

ABRIDGED DOUBLE ENTRY

Though it is desirable that a full system of double entry book-keeping should be in operation in all businesses, be they large or small, intricate or simple, the exigencies of time and expense may frequently call for some system which, though falling short of the conventional completeness, can be constructed on double entry lines. Such a system is well adapted to the requirements of many businesses, particularly to those of small traders. The method of book-keeping described below is distinguishable from single entry in that it is an abridged form of double entry book-keeping; the personal accounts which normally form an integral part of the complete double entry system are not eliminated, but employed for reference purposes, and, as such, as 'memorandum' only.

The characteristic feature of the system is that the double entry is completed from the Cash Book, i.e. receipts from debtors are considered as sales, and payments to creditors as purchases. At the end of the accounting period adjustments will be made in respect of debtors and creditors outstanding, as well as for discounts, bad debts, allowances, and the like.

It will be seen, therefore, that such a system does not dispense with the necessity for Personal Accounts; but it avoids the necessity of employing the Day Books or Journals and Returns Books or Journals as a formal part of the double entry system, or the completion thereof through the Ledger analysis. Frequently, the latter books or journals are employed to record sales, purchases and returns, postings being made therefrom to the Ledgers (or postings made direct from the invoices themselves if no such books or journals are kept), but in such instances the Ledger is kept purely for record and is outside the double entry system entirely. Obviously, as the cash is received or paid, it will be entered in the Memorandum Personal Accounts (i.e. posted in the usual way), but this is no part of the double entry, as such receipts and payments are posted to complete the double entry to Sales and Purchases Accounts respectively. It is to this point that the student should fix his attention, viz. that whatever is entered and wheresoever the original entries arise (except the entries in the Cash Book) they form no part of the double entry; the latter, as seen above, arises from the postings from the Cash Book to the Sales and Purchases Accounts.

At the end of the period, the Personal Ledger balances will have to be extracted as if the orthodox system were employed, but only to provide the necessary data for preparing final accounts. These figures will be brought into the accounts and, as such, are of no more consequence to the double entry than is the end stock before its incorporation in the final accounts. In addition, there will usually be several adjustments required, e.g. for Discounts.

The rules may be outlined as follows:

1. When cash is received from customers who have bought on credit the Cash Book is debited in the usual manner and the double entry is completed by a posting to the credit of Sales Account, precisely as if the transaction were a cash sale. A 'posting' is made of such receipt in the Memorandum Personal Account in order that such account may show the true state of the customer's balance. Upon cash (or cheque) being paid to a creditor, Cash (or Bank) is credited in the usual manner, and the double entry is completed by a posting to the debit of Purchases Account, precisely as if the transaction were a cash purchase. A 'posting' is made in the Memorandum Personal Account of the creditor in order that his account may record the true balance due to him.

2. Expenses are treated on a cash basis; that is, no record is made until they are finally paid, when a debit is made direct to the requisite Nominal Account.

3. At the end of the accounting period the Sales and Purchases Accounts will have been built up, not from Day Books or Journals (which, if kept, are purely memoranda), but from the Cash Book. In other words, they will record the cash received from debtors and paid to creditors.

4. The closing balances of debtors are brought down in the Sales Account as a debit balance; closing balances of creditors being brought down in the Purchases Account as a credit balance. The balances are respectively shown in the Balance Sheet as an Asset and a Liability.

5. Discounts allowed will be debited to Discount Allowed Account and credited to Sales Account. Converse entries in respect of Discounts received will be made. The same rules apply to Returns and Allowances.

6. If the closing balances of debtors are the *good* debts only, Bad Debts Account will be debited and Sales Account credited in respect of bad debts, but if such balances are the book balances, the entries required are:

Debit Bad Debts Account with bad debts.
Debit Sales Account (below the line) with good debtors.
Credit Sales Account (above the line) with book value of debtors.

7. The Bad Debts Provision in no way affects the Sales Account.

Illustration 9

A starts business on 1st January 19.1 The following facts relate to his business for the two years ended 31st December 19.2.

Cash received from debtors, 19.1, £1,000; ditto, 19.2, £1,200. Debtors 31st December 19.1 (per Ledger) £100; ditto, 31st December 19.2 (per Ledger), £130. Discounts allowed, 19.2, £10. Bad Debts, 19.2, £25.

Show accounts assuming the trader keeps his Sales Ledger purely as a memorandum book.

SALES

19.1 Dec. 31	Trading Account		£ 1,100	19.1 Dec. 31	Cash		£ 1,000
					Sundry Debtors	c/d	100
			£1,100				£1,100
19.2 Jan. 1	Balance	b/d	100	19.2 Dec. 31	Cash		1,200
Dec. 31	Trading Account		1,240		Discount Allowed		10
					Bad Debts		25
					Sundry Debtors	c/d	105
			£1,340				£1,340
19.3 Jan. 1	Balance	b/d	105				

Alternatively:

SALES

19.1 Dec. 31	Trading Account		£ 1,100	19.1 Dec. 31	Cash		£ 1,000
					Sundry Debtors	c/d	100
			£1,100				£1,100
19.2 Jan. 1	Balance (a)	b/d	100	19.2 Dec. 31	Cash		1,200
Dec. 31	Trading Account		1,240		Discounts Allowed		10
					Sundry Debtors:		
					Balance	c/d	105
					Bad Debts		25
			£1,340				£1,340
19.3 Jan. 1	Balance (b)	b/d	105				

(a) This item will appear as an asset on the Balance Sheet at 31st December 19.1.

(b) This item will appear as an asset on the Balance Sheet at 31st December 19.2; in addition £25 will appear as a debit in Bad Debts Account.

The Purchases Account would be treated conversely if credit purchases took place.

CHAPTER 12

RECEIPTS AND PAYMENTS, AND INCOME AND EXPENDITURE ACCOUNTS

These accounts should present no difficulties whatsoever to students once the function of each account is clearly understood.

Receipts and Payments Account. This is nothing more than a summary of the Cash Book (i.e. of cash and bank transactions), over a certain period. It is the form of account most commonly adopted by the treasurers of societies, clubs, associations, etc., when presenting the result of the year's working. All the receipts of each type (whether cash or cheque) are entered on the debit side, that is the same side as that on which they appear in the Cash Book; and all the payments (whether cash or cheque) are entered on the credit side. The opening and closing balances of cash and bank are shown in the usual way, unless (as is generally found) the cash and bank items are combined, when there will not be separate balances for cash *and* bank. The main features of the Receipts and Payments Account may be summarized thus:

1. It is an abbreviated copy of the Cash Book, usually merging cash and bank items, *Contras* between Cash and Bank thus being eliminated.

2. Hence, the items are entered on the same side as that on which they appear in the Cash Book, i.e. receipts on the debit side, and payments on the credit.

3. Just as the Cash Book itself may be part of the double entry book-keeping so may the Receipts and Payments Account. Accounts presented in this form however, almost invariably suggest an absence of double entry.

4. *All* receipts and payments, whether of revenue or capital nature are included.

5. The balance of Receipts and Payments Account must be debit, being Cash on hand and at Bank, unless there is a Bank overdraft; but that of Income and Expenditure Account may be debit or credit, being loss or profit, usually transferred, except in the case of a limited company, to the Capital Account.

6. There is no disclosure of gain or losses, as the account does not—indeed cannot—deal with:

   (*a*) Stock Increases or Decreases.
   (*b*) Depreciation or Appreciation of assets.
   (*c*) Provisions and Accruals or Prepayments.

Whilst on the other hand it includes:

   (*d*) Capital Receipts and Payments.
   (*e*) Appropriations of Profits, including Drawings.

No difficulty should arise if the NATURE rather than the name of the account is recognized, particularly as many Receipts and Payments Accounts are often misdescribed, e.g. as an Income and Expenditure Account, or even as a Balance Sheet.

Illustration 1

A club which was inaugurated on 1st January 19.., had the following receipts and payments during the year ended 31st December 19..:—
Receipts: Subscriptions, £330; Donations, £26. Payments: Investments, £100; Rent and Hire of Room, £40; General Expenses, £21; Postages and Stationary, £7; and Sundries, £3.

Cash in hand at 31st December—£2.

Cash at Bank at 31st December—£183.

Show the Receipts and Payments Account for the year ended 31st December 19...

RECEIPTS AND PAYMENTS ACCOUNT FOR THE YEAR ENDED 31ST DECEMBER 19..

Receipts		£	Payments			£
Subscriptions	. . . .	330	Investments. . . .			100
Donations .	. . . .	26	Rent and Hire of Room	. .		40
			General Expenses.	.		21
			Postages and Stationery	. .		7
			Sundries .	. .		3
			Cash in Hand	. . . .	c/d	2
			Cash at Bank	. . . .	c/d	183
		£356				£356
Cash in Hand	. . . .	b/d	2			
Cash at Bank	. . . .	b/d	183			

From a study of the above account it will be apparent at once that the amount of £185 cannot be the year's profit, as:

(i) The first item on the credit side records the purchase of an ASSET.

(ii) No account has been taken of subscriptions in arrear or in advance; nor of expenses accrued, accruing, or paid in advance.

This is obvious, the account being one dealing solely with receipts and payments through the medium of either Cash or Bank. In order to remedy the defective results thereby disclosed, it is necessary to prepare an Income and Expenditure Account usually by the construction of the double entry, in which case it will be supported by a Balance Sheet drawn up at the date of the close of the period in question.

Income and Expenditure Account. This may be described as the equivalent of the Profit and Loss Account drawn up for a non-trading concern; it performs the same functions, and is compiled and constructed on precisely the same principles. It is a normal account recording losses and expenses on the debit, and gains on the credit, normally postulating the existence of a double entry system.

It may be noted that the balance of the Receipts and Payments Account is brought down below the line and shown in the Balance Sheet as an asset if a debit balance, or liability if a credit balance. The balance of the Income and Expenditure Account will be transferred to the debit or credit of the Capital Account (or its equivalent) according to whether a loss or gain has resulted.

The excess of assets over liabilities will, as in the case of clubs, societies, and other organizations not having a formal Capital Account, be represented by a Capital Fund Account, or Accumulation Fund to which the net gains or losses are transferred in the usual way, the revised figure of which will be shown in the Balance Sheet on the liabilities side. The adjustments of a general nature and those peculiar to the organization itself, the chief of which will be accruals, prepayments, provisions, depreciation, and the adjustment in Expenses of opening and closing stocks (e.g. Stationery), will be made in the normal manner.

Illustration 2

The following is an abridged Receipts and Payments Account:

Receipts			£	*Payments*		£
Balance	. . .	b/d	200	Expenses		317
Subscriptions	. . .		520			

The outstandings are:

	Subscriptions	Expenses
	£	£
Beginning	40	120
End	37	39

Prepare Income and Expenditure Account.

SUBSCRIPTIONS

		£				£
Balance, outstandings (beginning).	b/d	40	Cash			520
			Outstandings (end) . .	c/d	37
Income and Expenditure Account		517			
		£557				£557
Balance, outstandings .	b/d	37			

EXPENSES

		£				£
Cash		317	Balance, outstandings (beginning)	b/d	120
Outstandings (end) .	c/d	39			
			Income and Expenditure Account		236
		£356				£356
			Balance, outstandings . .	b/d	39

INCOME AND EXPENDITURE ACCOUNT

	£			£
Expenses	236	Subscriptions	. . .	517
Surplus transferred to Capital Fund	281			
	£517			£517

In examination work, in order to avoid opening the Ledger Accounts, the Income and Expenditure Account may be prepared thus:

INCOME AND EXPENDITURE ACCOUNT

	£	£	£		£	£	£
Expenses Paid .	317			Subscriptions Received .	520		
Add Outstandings at end .	39			Add Outstandings at end .	37		
		356				557	
Less Outstandings at beginning . .		120		Less Outstandings at beginning . . .		40	
			236				517
Surplus transferred to Capital Fund. .			281				
			£517				£517

The items may be presented in a manner more abbreviated (which is recommended in simple adjustments), thus:

	£		£
Expenses (317+39−120) . .	236	Subscriptions (520+37−40) .	517

It must be remembered that the beginning outstandings are part of the OPENING balances; those at the end part of the END balances (and therefore in the Balance Sheet prepared in conjunction with the Income and Expenditure Account for the period under review): hence, in the above case £37 is an asset: £39 a liability.

Many examination problems involve the compilation of an Income and Expenditure Account and a Balance Sheet from a summarized Receipts and Payments Account. Students, when confronted by this type of problem, should always build up the opening Balance Sheet or Statement of Affairs, particulars of the assets and liabilities of which are usually given. The opening cash balance will be found from the Receipts and Payments Account, whilst the creditors may appear in total under the heading of creditors, or the expense creditors may appear separately, being found on the credit of the respective expense accounts which represent the service supplied. Particulars of the adjustments necessary will be given at the foot of the Receipts and Payments Account, and these (*mutatis mutandis*) are made in the same way as the usual Trading and Profit and Loss Account and Balance Sheet adjustments.

Illustration 3

The following is the Receipts and Payments Account of the Y. G. Club in respect of the year to 31st December 19.2:

RECEIPTS AND PAYMENTS FOR THE YEAR ENDED 31ST DECEMBER 19.2

			£			£
Balance .	.	b/d	205	Salaries		416
Subscriptions—				Stationery . . .		80
19.1 .	. .	£8		Rates		120
19.2 .	. .	422		Telephone . . .		20
19.3 .	. .	16		Investment in £250 4%		
			446	Stock (6th Dec.) at par		250
Sports Meeting Profit	.		310	Sundry Expenses . .		185
Dividends on Investments	.		200	Balance		90
			£1,161			£1,161
Balance .	.	b/d	90			

In addition to information contained in the above account the following additional facts are ascertained:

1. There are 450 members each paying an annual subscription of £1, £9 being in arrears for 19.1 at the beginning of 19.2.
2. Stock of Stationery at 31st December 19.1, was £10; at 31st December 19.2, £18.
3. At 31st December 19.2, the rates were prepaid to the following 31st March, the yearly charge being £120. A quarter's charge for telephone is outstanding, the amount accrued being £7. Expenses accruing at 31st December 19.1, £14.
4. At 31st December 19.1, the Buildings stood in the books at £2,000 and it is required to write off depreciation at 5 per cent per annum. Investments at 31st December 19.1, were £4,000.

It is required to prepare an Income and Expenditure Account in respect of the year ended 31st December 19.2, and a Balance Sheet as at that date.

Y. G. CLUB

INCOME AND EXPENDITURE ACCOUNT FOR THE YEAR ENDED 31ST DECEMBER 19.2

	£		£
Salaries	416	Subscriptions . . .	450
Stationery . . .	72	Profits on Sports Meetings	310
Rates . . .	120	Dividends received . .	200
Telephone . .	27		
Sundry Expenses [£185−£14]	171		
Depreciation of Buildings .	100		
Surplus for year transferred			
to Capital Fund . .	54		
	£960		£960

BALANCE SHEET AS AT 31ST DECEMBER 19.2

	£	£		£	£
Capital Fund as at 1st Jan. 19.2	6,240		Buildings as at 1st Jan. 19.2 .	2,000	
Add Surplus of Income over Expenditure for the year ended 31st December 19.2.	54		*Less* Depreciation . .	100	1,900
		6,294	Investments as at 1st Jan. 19.2	4,000	
Subscriptions Paid in Advance		16	*Add* Additions . .	250	4,250
Telephone accrued . . .		7	Stock of Stationery . .		18
			Rates Prepaid . . .		30
			Subscriptions in arrear .		29
			Cash at Bank and in Hand .		90
		£6,317			£6,317

The opening balance of the Capital Fund is:

	£
Buildings	2,000
Investments	4,000
Cash	205
Subscriptions	9
Stationery Stock	10
Rates Prepaid	30
	£6,254
Less Expenses Accruing . . .	14
Capital Fund	£6,240

The Subscriptions Account will be as follows:

SUBSCRIPTIONS

19.2			£	19.2				£
Jan. 1	Balance . . .	b/d	9	Dec. 31	Cash—			
Dec. 31	Income and Expenditure Account . .		450		19.1(a) . . .			8
	Balance (c) . .	c/d	16		19.2(b) . . .			422
					19.3(c) . . .			16
					Balance . . .	c/d		29
			£475					£475
19.3				19.3				
Jan. 1	Balance . . .	b/d	29	Jan. 1	Balance . . .	b/d		16

(a) There must be £9−£8 still owing 1
(b) There must be £450−£422 still owing 28
(c) All in advance being in respect of 19.3

£29

To economize time, the adjustments of beginning and end outstandings may be inserted in parentheses by the side of the amount in the Income and Expenditure Account, thus: Stationery (10+80−18) = 72; thus avoiding the opening of the account, which would appear:

STATIONERY

19.2			£	19.2			£
Jan. 1	Balance (Stock) . . .	b/d	10	Dec. 31	Income and Expenditure		
Dec. 31	Purchases . . .		80		Account . . .		72
					Stock in hand . .	c/d	18
			£90				£90
19.3							
Jan. 1	Balance (Stock) . .	b/d	18				

Preparation of Receipts and Payments Account from Income and Expenditure Account. Where the reverse is required, i.e. to obtain a Receipts and Payments Account from an Income and Expenditure Account, the problem will necessitate the opening of a Ledger Account to find the balancing figure of cash: e.g. if the charge from Expenses Account is £40—£5 being owing at the beginning of the period and £7 at the end of the period—the Expenses Account will appear as follows:

EXPENSES

19..			£	19..			£
Dec. 31	Cash		38	Jan. 1	Balance . . .	b/d	5
	Balance	c/d	7	Dec. 31	Income and Expenditure		
					Account . .		40
			£45				£45
				19..			
				Jan. 1	Balance . . .	b/d	7

Cash paid, therefore, is £38.

Illustration 4

The Income and Expenditure Account of the 'Homely' Club is as follows:

INCOME AND EXPENDITURE ACCOUNT FOR THE YEAR ENDED
31ST DECEMBER 19.2

	£		£
Salaries	175	Subscriptions . . .	200
General Expenses . .	50	Donations . . .	105
Depreciation . . .	30		
Surplus for Year . .	50		
	£305		£305

Adjustments were made in respect of the following:

Subscriptions for 19.1 unpaid at 1st January 19.2, £20; £18 of which were received in 19.2.
Subscriptions paid in advance at 1st January 19.2, £5.
Subscriptions paid in advance at 31st December 19.2, £4.
Subscriptions for 19.2 unpaid at 31st December 19.2, £7.
Sundry Assets at beginning of period, £260. Sundry Assets, after depreciation, £270 at end of period.
Cash balance at 1st January 19.2, £16.

Prepare Receipts and Payments Account.

'HOMELY' CLUB

RECEIPTS AND PAYMENTS ACCOUNT FOR THE YEAR ENDED 31ST DECEMBER 19.2

		£			£
Opening Balance	b/d	16	Salaries		175
Donations . . .		105	General Expenses . .		50
Subscriptions . . .		**210**	Sundry Assets purchased .		40
			Closing Balance	c/d	66
		£331			£331
Balance	b/d	66			

The cash received on account of subscriptions is found from the Subscriptions Accounts, which is as follows:

SUBSCRIPTIONS

19.2				£	19.2				£
Jan. 1	Balance . . .	b/d		20	Jan. 1	Balance	b/d		5
Dec. 31	Balance, 19.3, Paid in				Dec. 31	Balance (19.1, Unpaid) .	c/d		2
	Advance . .	c/d		4		Balance (19.2, Unpaid) .	c/d		7
	Income and Expenditure					**Cash Received** . .			**210**
	Account . . .			200					
				£224					£224
19.3					19.3				
Jan. 1	Balance (19.1) . .	b/d		2	Jan. 1	Balance (19.3) . .	b/d		4
	Balance (19.2) . .	b/d		7					

The procedure, as already indicated, is reverse to the ordinary way; that is, the Subscriptions Account is built up from the figures available, but instead of posting *from* Cash thereto, and hence finding the balance to transfer to Income and Expenditure Account, the latter figure is given so that one 'posts' from the credit of Income and Expenditure Account back to the debit of Subscriptions Account, the resulting balance being the cash received, which is then credited to Subscriptions Account and 'posted' back to the Cash Account, thus completing one of the Cash Book entries.

General Illustration 5

The following is a copy of the accounts of a Students Union. Prepare therefrom: (*a*) Income and Expenditure Account, and (*b*) Balance Sheet.

BALANCE SHEET FOR THE YEAR ENDING 31ST DECEMBER 19. .

	£		£
Cash in Treasurer's Hands . .	35	General Purposes . . .	2,335
Property at 1st Jan. 19., .	1,632	Affiliation Fees . . .	33
Cash at Bank at 1st Jan. 19.. .	8,675	Administration Expenses . .	241
Contributions and Fees—		Miscellaneous Expenses . .	69
Branch No. 3 . . .	2,431	Remitted to Branch No. 2 .	9
Branch No. 1 . . .	122	Legal Expenses on Purchase of	
Dividends Received . . .	289	Property	90
Rents Received . . .	85	Investments Purchased . .	9,000
Bank Overdraft . . .	800	Property to Date . . .	2,264
		Cash in Treasurer's Hands .	28
	£14,069		£14,069

The funds in the hands of Branch Secretaries—not included in the above statement:

	No. 1	No. 2
	£	£
1st January 19..	11	3
31st December 19..	18	11

In accordance with the principles explained, it is essential to construct the opening Statement of Affairs, i.e. assets and liabilities. The Balance Sheet produced is merely a summary of Cash and Bank transactions.

The Assets are:	£	£
Cash in Treasurer's Hands		35
Property.		1,632
Bank		8,675
Branch: No. 1: Cash	11	
No. 2: Cash	3	
	—	14
		10,356
The Liabilities		Nil
Accumulated Fund at 1st January 19..		£10,356

The accounts will therefore appear as below, the items in heavy print being opening entries. The Cash Book will be written up and posted (direct to Final Accounts, where possible, in order to save time).

CASH AND BANK ACCOUNT

		£			£
Balance—			General Purposes	I. & E.	2,335
Cash . . b/d	S.A.	**35**	Affiliation Fees	I. & E.	33
Bank . . b/d	S.A.	**8,675**	Administration Exes.	I. & E.	241
Contributions and			Miscellaneous Exes.	I. & E.	69
Fees—			Branch No. 2 .	L.	9
Branch No. 3	I. & E.	2,431	Legal Exes. (Pro-		
Branch No. 1	L.	122	perty)	L. or B.S.	90
Dividends received	I. & E.	289	Investments	L. or B.S.	9,000
Rents	I.& E.	85	Property Purchased	L. or B.S.	632
Balance: Bank Over-			Balance: Cash c/d	B.S.	28
draft c/d	B.S.	800			
		£12,437			£12,437
Balance: Cash b/d		28	Balance: Bank b/d		800

It will be advisable to show accounts for the branches—if pressed for time in examination work, merely rough working accounts will suffice.

BRANCHES

		No. 1	No. 2			No. 1	No. 2
		£	£			£	£
Balances b/d	S.A.	11	3	Cash . . . C.B.		122	
Cash . . .	C.B.		9	Income and Expenditure			
Income and Expenditure				Account . I. & E.			1
Account .	I. & E.	129		Balances c/d	B.S.	18	11
		£140	£12			£140	£12
Balances b/d		18	11				

The other accounts may be worked through to the Balance Sheet direct, but will be given for completeness.

PROPERTY

		£			£
Balance b/d	S.A.	1,632	Balance c/d B.S.		2,354
Purchase .	C.B.	632			
Legal Expenses .	C.B.	90			
		£2,354			£2,354
Balance b/d		2,354			

ACCUMULATED FUND

		£			£
Balance c/d	B.S.	10,611	Balance b/d	S.A.	10,356
			Income and Expenditure		
			Account .	I. & E.	255
		£10,611			£10,611
			Balance b/d		10,611

The abbreviations against each item indicate how the item has been dealt with and will serve to assist the student in building up the Final Accounts without using Ledger accounts, save perhaps a rough working account of the branches.

S.A. = Statement of Affairs.
L = Ledger Account.
B.S. = Balance Sheet.
I. & E. = Income and Expenditure Account.
C.B. = Cash Book.

The Income and Expenditure Account and Balance Sheet will now be:

INCOME AND EXPENDITURE ACCOUNT FOR THE YEAR ENDED
31ST DECEMBER 19..

Expenditure	£		Income	£	£
General Purposes . . .	2,335		Contributions		
Affiliation Fees . . .	33		and Fees—		
Administration			No. 1 Branch . . .	129	
Expenses . . .	241		No. 3 Branch . . .	2,431	
				2,560	
Miscellaneous Expenses . .	69				
Balance, being Surplus of Income			Less No. 2 Branch . .	1	
over Expenditure transferred to					2,559
Accumulated Fund . .	255		Dividends Received . .		289
			Rents		85
	£2,933				£2,933

BALANCE SHEET AS AT DECEMBER 19..

	£	£		£	£
Accumulated Fund at 1st			Property: Balance at 1st		
Jan. 19.. .		10,356	Jan. 19.. . .	1,632	
Add Surplus of Income			Add Purchase[1] .	722	
over Expenditure for the					2,354
year ended 31st Dec.			Investments, at Cost (Market		
19.. . . .	255		Value £..) . .		9,000
		10,611	Cash on Hand . .	28	
Bank Overdraft . .		800	Cash at Branches—		
			No. 1 . . £18		
			No. 2 . . 11		
			—	29	
					57
		£11,411			£11,411

[1] In examination work, having accounted for the opening entries, the student will save time by using the so-called Balance Sheet of the Treasurer, which is merely a combined Cash and Bank Account, together with the beginning and closing Property figures; the difference between the beginning Property (£1,632) and the closing Property (£2,264) is merely the cost of the Property acquired during the year. Hence the opening Property may be inset immediately in the 31st December 19.., Balance Sheet, and the cost of the Property acquired added thereto. This is ascertained by eliminating the Property figures from the Cash and Bank Account and substituting on the credit side thereof the difference, i.e. £2,264−£1,632 = £632. The sum of £90 for Legal Expenses in connection with such purchase is added to the Property Account; thus, £772 is the sum of £632 plus £90.

It is assumed that there are no expenses accrued or accruing either at 1st January 19.., or at 31st December 19...

More detail would be required as to investments, e.g. date of purchase, dividend rate, etc.

Receipts and Expenditure Account. An account of this nature confines the income earned to the cash received and at the same time includes *all* expenses, whether paid or not. This method is usually adopted in preparing the accounts of a business of a professional nature (e.g. doctors and solicitors) on the ground that the debtors are of a very uncertain nature, so that a fee may not be considered as earned until the cash is received. Nevertheless, the proprietor desires to ascertain what are the fees *earned* in the business so as to obtain the true profits for each period. Hence the rule is that the fees are incorporated into the accounts in the usual way just as if there were no likelihood of any of the outstandings proving bad. A 100 per cent Debtors Provision (or Reserve) is made, which reduces fees 'earned' to a 'cash received' basis. Alternatively, a proportion of profit equalling Debtors and the completed work may be carried forward at the end of each year.

Similar treatment may be accorded to uncompleted work of a professional man.

The adjustment of the Provision is made through the Appropriation section of the Receipts and Expenditure Account so that both true profits and the fees received profits are disclosed, as circumstances may arise, necessitating the use of the true profits (e.g. on sale of the business, introduction of a partner, and the like).

In the Balance Sheet will be shown the debtors and uncompleted work, from which will be deducted the Debtors Provision covering the full amounts thereof.

Bad Debts written off are treated in the usual way.

The rules may be summarized thus:

1. Where there are no initial debtors create a 100 per cent Debtors Provision at the end by debiting Receipts and Expenditure Appropriation section and crediting Debtors Provision; and in future years:

2. Debit previous year's Provision and credit Receipts and Expenditure Appropriation section; and debit the latter and credit new Debtors Provision with 100 per cent on current debtors outstanding.

Alternatively, the adjustment may be made through the Provision Account or through the Fees Account.

It may be observed that uncompleted work may be that performed in its very early stages, or on the other hand, work almost complete, so that a very careful estimate is required in order that the true position may be shown.

In addition, work may be COMPLETE in respect of which no bill may yet have been rendered. In these circumstances the amount of such a bill, if not already entered through the books, must be treated like Debtors, whilst occasionally work may be paid for by the client in advance.

The double-entry aspect is precisely the same as that relating to debtors, so that the adjustment may be made on the same lines, through (a) the Receipts and Expenditure Appropriation section, or (b) the Provision, or (c) Fees Account.

Illustration 6

The following is the Trial Balance of a professional man at the end of the first year of his business:

TRIAL BALANCE

	£	£
Fixtures	3,000	
Capital		15,000
Bank	4,300	
Fees		12,000
Drawings	7,300	
Debtors	7,000	
Expenses	5,400	
	£27,000	£27,000

Uncompleted work is £1,500 completed work not yet entered, £3,200 payments in advance by clients, £700.

Prepare accounts on the usual professional lines.

RECEIPTS AND EXPENDITURE ACCOUNT FOR THE YEAR ENDED . . .

Expenditure		£	Receipts		£	£
Expenses	. . .	5,400	Fees Earned—			
'Earned Profit'	c/d	10,600	Cash Received and Debtors	12,000		
			Add Completed Work	3,200		
			Uncompleted Work	1,500		
					16,700	
			Less Cash Received in Advance	.	700	
						16,000
		16,000				16,000
Provision for Debtors' Completed Work	. .	10,200	'Earned' Profit b/d			10,600
Provision for Uncompleted Work	.	1,500	'Cash' Loss transferred to Capital Account	.		1,100
		£11,700				£11,700

BALANCE SHEET AS AT. . . . .

		£	£		£	£
Clients' Payments in Advance	.		700[1]	Fixtures . .		3,000
Capital Account	. . .	15,000 .	.	Debtors (as per Ledger)	7,000	
Less Drawings	. . .	7,300		Add Completed .Work.	3,200	
		7,700			10,200	
Less 'Cash' Loss as per Receipts and Expenditure Account	.	1,100		Less Debtors Provision	10,200	nil
			6,600	Uncompleted Work	1,500	
				Less Provision . .	1,500	nil
				Bank . . .		4,300
			£7,300			£7,300

[1] Part of this might be absorbed in work done, and would be deducted from the total debtors, the provision being accordingly reduced; further, if the amount so received will under no circumstances be returnable, the whole £700 may be deducted from debtors and the provision reduced to £9,500 as the £700 portion of the debtors cannot become 'bad.' Depreciation ignored.

Illustration 7

The following is the Trial Balance of X:

	£	£
Debtors Provision, 19.1		3,200
Uncompleted Work	3,070	
Expenses	5,950	
Uncompleted Work Provision, 19.1 . . .		3,070
Work done and Charged		21,200
Capital		20,000
Sundry Assets (including Bank) . . .	33,350	
Debtors	5,100	
	£47,470	£47,470

Uncompleted Work, 19.2	.	.	.	£4,900
Fees Received during 19.2	.	.	.	£19,300
Bad Debts to be written off during 19.2	.	£1,200

RECEIPTS AND EXPENDITURE ACCOUNT FOR YEAR ENDED 31ST DECEMBER 19.2

		£			£
Uncompleted Work . . .		3,070	Fees Earned . . .		21,200
Expenses		5,950	Uncompleted Work . . .		4,900
Bad Debts . . .		1,200			
'Earned' Profit . . .	c/d	15,880			
		£26,100			£26,100

		£			£
19.2 Provision—			'Earned' Profit . . .	b/d	15,880
Debtors		3,900*	19.1 Provision—		
Uncompleted Work . . .		4,900	Debtors . . .		3,200*
'Cash' Profit transferred to Capital			Uncompleted Work . . .		3,070
Account . . .		13,350			
		£22,150			£22,150

* See below

BALANCE SHEET AS AT 31ST DECEMBER 19.2

		&	£			£	£
Capital . . .		20,000		Sundry Assets . .			33,350
Add 'Cash' Profit . .		13,350		Debtors . .		3,900	
			33,350	Less Provision . .		3,900	nil
				Uncompleted Work . .		4,900	
				Less Provision . .		4,900	nil
			£33,350				£33,350

* Alternatively the net difference may be inserted thus:

DEBTORS PROVISION

		£			£
19.2 Balance . . .	c/d	3,900	19.1 Balance . . .	b/d	3,200
			Income and Expenditure		
			Account . .		700
		£3,900			£3,900
			19.2 Balance . . .	b/d	3,900

The Debtors Accounts are (totalled):

DEBTORS

		£			£
Balances . . .	b/d	3,200	Cash		19,300
Fees Charged . . .		21,120	Balances . . .	c/d	5,100
		£24,400			£24,400
Balances . . .	b/d	5,100	Bad Debts written off .		1,200
			Balances . . .	c/d	3,900
		£5,100			£5,100
Balances . . .	b/d	3,900			

A similar procedure may be adopted in respect of the Uncompleted Work Provision.

If the uncompleted work had been incorporated in Fees Account and Receipt and Expenditure Account would be:

RECEIPTS AND EXPENDITURE ACCOUNT

Expenditure	£	*Receipts*	£
Expenses	5,950	Fees	23,030
Bad Debts	1,200		
'Earned' Profit[1]	15,880		
	£23,030		£23,030

[1] Corresponding with earned profit brought down on p. 1214.

The Fees Account would be:

FEES ACCOUNT (19.2)

		£				£
Uncompleted Work	b/d	3,070	Fees Charged		c/d	21,200
Receipts and Expenditure Account		23,030	Uncompleted Work			4,900
		£26,100				£26,100
Uncompleted Work	b/d	4,900				

It should be noticed that the method adopted here is the 'full' double entry, thus making the personal accounts an integral part of the double entry system, whereas in the example given on p. 1212 the method adopted was the 'abridged' double entry; but neither method affects the '100 per cent Provision' system because the true position is properly disclosed both in the full and abridged method.

It is unusual to reduce Expenses to a cash basis by a 100 per cent Provision, but if this procedure is adopted the same principles apply, all the entries being reverse to those already outlined.

It should be clearly borne in mind that the full double entry system may be used or the abridged method, from which the true profits are ascertained, after which the necessary adjustments for Debtors and Uncompleted Work will be made.

If the full double entry is in use the Fees Accounts and Debtors will appear in the Trial Balance in the ordinary way; but in the abridged method the Cash received only will appear, the Fees and Debtors being memoranda only, so that the procedure outlined in Chapter 11 must FIRST be followed prior to the creation of the 100 per cent provision.

The same principle may be adopted when the parties desire that only a proportion of Debtors be taken in as good, e.g. 50 per cent; in fact it may be repeated that once the significance of the provision is grasped, viz. that the principles applicable to ordinary Bad Debts Provisions are applicable, except that a very large rate (100 per cent or less as desired) is taken, no difficulty should be encountered.

CHAPTER 13

TABULAR BOOK-KEEPING

THE student will have observed during the course of his practical work that, where feasible, much labour may be avoided by the judicious use of the columnar and tabular system. Wherever transactions are of a regular type and frequent in number, the system can be profitably employed; and, without being conscious of it, students meet with the method almost every day: the discounts column of the Cash Book, the analysis of the Petty Cash Book, the departmental columns in the Sales Day Book or Journal, and the analysis columns in the Expenses Day Book or Journal are common examples of the employment of this system.

In all cases the principle is the same; that is, the insertion of the record of the transaction in its appropriate column and the completion of the double entry by means of the posting of the total thereof. As a rule, the student tends to become confused only when the system departs in any way from that usually met with as a matter of daily routine.

The most familiar examples of the use of the tabular system are found in the accounts of:

1. Estate Companies for tenants' accounts.
2. Gas, Water, and Electricity Undertakings for customers' accounts.
3. Hotels for visitors' accounts.
4. Insurance Companies for premiums.

In almost every business use is made of the tabular principle in order to avoid unnecessary repetition of detail, the most obvious example being the Columnar Cash book.

In accounts relating to a regular and permanent service, such as Rents, Gas, Water, Electricity, and the like, instead of separate pages being employed for each individual customer, one or more pages are used for each period and the appropriate records made by taking one line for each CUSTOMER. The ledger will be suitably ruled in the light of the circumstances obtaining, as for instance in Rental Ledgers the customers' names will be entered in the sequence of the numbers of their residences, thus facilitating the making of the entries, e.g. Nos. 1, 3, 5, etc., Queen's Drive. The first accounting column will contain the carry-forward from the preceding account, and will in total equal the outstanding debtors. Such a total will have appeared in the Balance Sheet in the ordinary way and differs only from the normal in that the balances on the individual accounts do not appear on separate pages. The next column on the debit side will contain the entries for charges, the total of which will be posted to the credit of Rent, Sales of Gas, etc., or whatever the particular service comprises. The next column will be the cross total of the two debit columns. On the credit side will be columns recording cash received, allowances, and other credits, according to circumstances, the last two columns being for the carry forward of balances and for the cross totals of the credit items on each line.

1301

The principle may be illustrated by reference to a very simple example; so simple, in fact, that the employment of the tabular method would not be considered worth while.

Illustration 1

Estate & Co. own four houses, Nos. 1, 3, 5, and 7 Lord Street, Northport; the tenants are respectively A, B, C, and D; the quarterly rents being £150, £230, £250, and £180 respectively. A, at the beginning of the quarter ended 29th September 19.., owes £30. The receipts from tenants are: A, £180, B, £210 (allowance for repairs, £20); and C on account, £200. D left by arrangement on 1st September, the rent for the period of occupation being £120.

Write up the Rental Ledger and show how the double entry is effected. (See p. 1303.)

The double entry will be effected thus:

1. £30 is the amount brought forward and will be part of the balances at the opening date.
2. Total Rents will be posted to credit of Rents, £810.
3. Totals on each side cancel each other.
4. The debits for the Cash received will appear in the Cash Book. (A separate column may be employed in the Cash Book, the total of which should correspond with the total of the column in the Ledger.)
5. The total will be posted to the debit of the allowance in question, and if warranted, would be further analysed; in this case the £20 will be posted to the debit of Repairs Account.
6. The total will be posted to the debit of Rent Account.
7. This is a balance forward to the next quarter, and will appear on the debit side on the No. 5 Lord Street line as £50.
8. See (3) above.

Thus the 'Trial Balance' of the above items is:

	£	£
(1) Opening Balance		30
(2) Rents		810
(6) Rents	60	
(4) Cash	710	
(5) Repairs	20	
(7) End Balance	50	
	£840	£840

RENTAL LEDGER (See p. 1304)

No of Property	Name of Tenant	Arrears Brought Forward	Quarterly Rent	Total Debits	Date of Receipt	Receipt No.	C.B. Fol.	Cash Received	Allowances	Empties	(Other Cols. as Required)	Arrears Carried Forward	Total Credits	Observations
1 Lord St.	A .	£ 30	£ 150	£ 180				£ 180	£	£	£	£	£ 180	
3 ,,	B .		230	230				210	20				230	
5 ,,	C .		250	250				200		60		50	250	
7 ,,	D .		180	180				120					180	Left Sept. 1
		£30	£810	£840				£710	£20	£60		£50	£840	
		(1)	(2)	(3)				(4)	(5)	(6)		(7)	(8)	

GAS CONSUMPTION LEDGER (See p. 1304)

Number and Street	Particulars	Meter Reading Cub. Ft.	Meter Reading Therms	Arrears Brought Forward	¹Charges	Total Debits	Date Received	No. of Receipt	Cash Received	Allowance	Irrecoverable	Arrears Carried Forward	Total Credits	Observations
				£	£	£			£	£	£	£	£	

¹ The Charges column will, where required, be subdivided, e.g. Maintenance, Stove Hire, Meter Hire, etc.

If presented in the form of a 'Total' account this would be:

TOTAL DEBTORS

		£			£
Balance	b/d	30	Cash (*Dr.* Cash)		710
Rents (*Cr.* Rent)		810	Repairs (*Cr.* Repairs)		20
			Empties (*Dr.* Rent)		60
			Balance	c/d	50
		£840			£840
Balance	b/d	50			

Illustration 2

The following simple ruling (eliminating the detail columns) illustrates the principle of columnar book-keeping applied to the Cash Book.

CASH BOOK

Cash Sales	Allow-ances	Dis-count	Cash	Bank	Draw-ings	Com-mission	Rent, Rates	Dis-count	Cash	Bank

The receipts from Cash Sales will be entered in the cash column in the ordinary way, and inserted in the Cash Sales column, the total of which will be posted to the *credit* of Cash Sales. The allowances column (where they are settled as accounts are paid) is treated exactly like the discount column; that is, the total will be transferred to the DEBIT of allowances (the credits having been made to the customers' accounts). The other columns on the debit side require no comment.

The credit-side columns of the Cash Book will, as regards Drawings, Commission, Rent, and Rates (and any other additional column), have entered in them the appropriate payment as shown in either the Cash or Bank column, and their totals will be posted to the DEBIT of the respective accounts.

Illustration 3

The ruling of a Gas Consumption Ledger will be as shown on p. 1303.

In the case of a Water Rental Ledger, the rulings will be somewhat similar, exept that normally as the charge is based on Rateable Value, a column for this figure will be inserted next to the charge column, but obviously none will be required for Meter Readings, except where special arrangements exist (as in the case of works, breweries, laundries, etc.), owing to the abnormally large consumption of water.

Visitors' Ledger. The method employed by hotels is to rule the ledger—called the Visitors' Ledger—so that from left to right are rulings for each room, the appropriate charges for which are entered on the line against the item printed on the extreme left. Instead of the debit side being shown in the usual manner, the top portion of the folio contains the charges above-mentioned and the bottom portion the credit items, e.g. cash paid, allowances, etc. The top portion columns added vertically will therefore show the total debits for each room, which should, allowing for carrying forward of balances, equal the vertical additions of the bottom portion. The horizontal totals will represent the total charges to the rooms detailed on the folio, and will be posted to the credit of the particular account to which they refer, e.g. apartments, either directly or through the medium of an Abstract Book or Journal.

One folio is employed for each day, any balances being carried forward to the next folio.

Occasionally, as in the case of a permanent resident, it will be necessary to transfer the total at the end of each week to an ordinary Ledger Account, so that the bottom portion of the Visitors' Ledger (representing the credit side of the Ledger) will have a line for transfers.

Where necessary, e.g. owing to the large number of rooms in use, there will be several Ledgers, usually subdivided on the 'storey' basis, e.g. first floor, second floor, etc.

Although not strictly material to the explanation of the tabular system of book-keeping, the following matters relating to hotel accounting should be noted:

1. Separate accounts may and certainly ought to be kept for receipts in respect of Wines, Beer, Spirits, Rooms, etc., the appropriate expenses being debited against them and the resulting balance transferred to Profit and Loss Account.

2. Appropriate entries are necessary in respect of accommodation, Meals, Laundry, and the like, of the staff, and of the Proprietor and his family, so that the true results of each section may be correctly ascertained. The transfer will be debit to Drawings (in the case of proprietor) or Wages (in the case of staff) and a credit to the account in question, e.g. Meals Account. Apart from these, there are frequently transfers between the various sections of the hotel, e.g. in respect of kitchen staff, who will have their overalls laundered in the hotel.

3. Each section should be charged with a fair proportion of rent and rates, and in cases where the hotel premises are owned by the management, a charge, correctly apportioned, should be made to cover rent, and Profit and Loss Account credited.

Illustration 4

VISITORS' LEDGER

Date...............Aug. 1......19..

	Room No. 1	Room No. 2	Room No. 3	Etc.	Total	
Dr.	£p	£p	£p	£p	£p	
Brought forward		5·55			5·55	Brought forward Posted to credit
Apartments	4·00	3·50	2·00		9·50	Apartments
Board	3·75	0·50	1·50		5·75	Board
Wine			0·75		0·75	Wine
Laundry	0·75	0·25	0·25		1·25	Laundry
Minerals	0·25				0·25	Minerals
	£8·75	£9·80	£4·50		£23·05	
Cr.						
Cash		9·80	4·00		13·80	Posted from debit of Cash Book
Allowances			0·50		0·50	Posted to debit of Allowances
Transfers						
Carried forward	8·75				8·75[1]	Carried forward
	£8·75	£9·80	£4·50		£23·05	

[1] If the amount of £8·75 is to be transferred to the ordinary ledger it would be inserted in the line above and posted to the debit of the Personal Account. The totals at the right hand of the folio (top section) might alternatively be entered in an abstract book or journal and the total thereof posted to the credit of the relevant accounts. The Abstract Book or Journal would be ruled thus:

ABSTRACT BOOK (OR JOURNAL)

Date	Folio	Apartments	Board	Wine	Laundry	Minerals	Total
19..		£p	£p	£p	£p	£p	£p
Aug. 1	£p	9·50	5·75	0·75	1·25	0·25	17·50
2							
3							
Etc..							
Etc..							

If the above entries were shown in ordinary Ledger form, the result would be:

VISITORS' LEDGER (TOTAL ACCOUNT)

		£p			£p
Balance	Brought forward	5·55	Cash	Debit Cash Book	13·80
Apartments, etc. (as detailed)	Credit Apartments, etc., Accounts	17·50	Allowances Balance	Debit Allowances Carried forward	0·50 8·75
		£23·05			£23·05
Balance	Brought forward	8·75			

The subsidiary books or journals (e.g. the Cash Book, Invoice Book or Journal, etc.) would be analysed on the following lines:

INVOICE BOOK (OR JOURNAL)

Date	Name	Led. Fol.	Total	Provisions	Beer, Wines, and Minerals	Cutlery, Glass, and Plate	Etc.	Etc.
			£	£	£	£	£	£

The Cash Book is shown on p. 1308 (No. 1).

In order to give a clearer conception of the principle, a simple system of tabular book-keeping applicable to a medical practitioner is outlined, but it should be remembered that the working of it would require adaptation to fit in with any peculiar features of the practice in question.

The main book is the Cash Book, which is supported by total accounts in respect of each Ledger.

Illustration 5

The accounts are constructed as shown on p. 1308 (No. 2).

Debit Side. Each total is posted to the respective account; the collectors' column, being a 'Total' column, will therefore be posted to the credit of Collectors' Nos. 1 and 2 Total Accounts respectively; the details making up these totals will be posted from the Collectors' Cash Received books to the credit of the patients' accounts. The 'Private Patients' column is dealt with on the same lines.

Credit Side. The total cash paid will be the sum of columns (a) and (d), i.e. £6·18+£336·03 = £342·21 (thus balancing the cash received). The total payments for expenses will be the total of (a) and (c), i.e. £6·18+ £218·86 = £225·04, the analysis of which will be:

	£p
Drugs and Bottles . .	24·50
Sundries . . .	29·96
Drawings . .	164·40
Collectors' Commission .	6·18
	£225·04

These items will be posted to the appropriate accounts.

Total (c) and (d) are the Bank items and, apart from the beginning balance, (d) less (c) equals the increase of the Bank Balance: these totals usually being debited to a separate Bank account, thus:

BANK

	£p			£p
Receipts . . .	336·03	Payments . . .		218·86

If desired, the above totals may be carried into an Abstract book and one posting effected at the end of the accounting period.

No. 1

CASH BOOK

Date	Particulars	Led. Fol.	Ledger Account	Visitors' Payments	Bar and Billiards Receipts	Total
			£	£	£	£

CASH BOOK

Date	Particulars	Led. Fol.	Provisions	Beer, Wines, and Minerals	Cutlery, Glass, and Plate	Etc.	Total
			£	£	£	£	£

No. 2

CASH BOOK

Date	From Whom Received	Fol.	Total Cash	Collectors 1	Collectors 2	Private	National Health Service	Box
			£p 342·21	£p 333·45	£p 20·25	£p 9·55	£p 268·92	£p 10·04

CASH BOOK

Date	To Whom Paid	Fol.	Paid by Cash	Paid by Cheque	Paid into Bank	Drugs and Bottles	Sundries	Drawings	Collectors' Commission
			£p 6·18	£p 218·86	£p 336·03	£p 24·50	£p 29·96	£p 164·40	£p 6·18
			(a)	(c)	(d)				

The Trial Balance, therefore, will be:

	£p	£p	£p
Expenses (detailed) . .	225·04		
Cash Service (Box) . .		10·04	
National Health Service .		268·92	
Private Ledger . . .		9·55	
Collectors' Total Accounts (1)		33·45	
" " " (2)		20·25	
Bank Lodgments . . .	336·03		
Less Payments . . .	218·86		
		117·17	
		£342·21	£342·21

Day Books or Journals. The Day Books or Journals will be analysed into various Ledgers: (1), (2), and 'Private'; and the totals will be posted to the debit of the appropriate Total Account, the individual postings being made to the debit of each patient and the total of the Day Book or Journal to the credit of Fees Account. If the services performed for a period were: Ledger (1) £48, Ledger (2) £120, 'Private' Patients Ledger £60, the debits would be (1) in the Total Account, (2) in detail to the patients in the appropriate Ledger, and the credit to Fees Account in one figure.

Transfers. Transfers from one account to another, which may arise not only through errors, but by patients changing their residence, will be put through a Transfer Journal, the totals of which will be posted to the Total Account of the Ledger concerned and the detailed entries to the appropriate individual accounts, thus:

TRANSFER JOURNAL

Date		Fol.	No. 1	No. 2	Private		Fol.	No. 1	No. 2	Private
	W. Jones Dixon Robinson		£ 2	£	£ 3 7	R. Jones Walters Robertson		£ 3	£ 2	£ 7
			£2		£10			£2	£2	£7
			Debit of Total Accounts					Credit of Total Accounts		

By way of illustration on the above information, No. 1 Total Account would be:

No. 1 LEDGER TOTAL ACCOUNT

	Fol.	£p		Fol.	£p
Fees (per Day Book) .		48·00	Cash (per Cash book) .		33·45
Transfer (per Transfer Journal) . .		2·00	Transfer (per Transfer Journal) . . .		3·00
			Balance . . .	c/d	13·55
		£50·00			£50·00
Balance . .	b/d	13·55			

The individual ledger balances in No. 1 Ledger should therefore equal £13·55.

The use of the tabular system in the books of an accountant is shown by the following:

Illustration 6

From the following tabular entries prepare a Trial Balance. (The letters in parentheses are for the guidance of the student.)

CASH BOOK

	Professional[1]	Tuition	Rent[2]	Rates[2]	Bank
Total *Dr.* side . . .	£ 1,735 (a)	£ 420 (a)	£ 60 (b)	£ 45 (b)	£ 2,260 (e)

	Drawings	Expenses	Rent	Rates	Bank
Total *Cr.* side . . .	£ 530 (c)	£ 230 (d)	£ 100 (b)	£ 75 (b)	£ 935 (e)

[1] Divided as required, e.g. Auditing, Taxation, etc.
[2] The receipts in respect of Rent and Rates indicate that part of the offices was sublet.

TRIAL BALANCE

		£	£
(a)	Fees received		2,155
(b)	Rent net paid	40	
(b)	Rates net paid	30	
(c)	Drawings	530	
(d)	Expenses	230	
(e)	Excess of Bank lodgments over withdrawals	1,325	
		£2,155	£2,155

Combined Day Book or Journal and Ledger. Where practicable, the employment of a combined Purchases Day Book or Journal and Ledger will save a considerable amount of time and labour.

The book or journal is ruled in ledger form, the credit side being used for purchases and the debit for returns and payments. At a suitable date the total of the purchases will be posted to the debit of Purchases Account and the total of the returns to the credit of Returns Outwards, or of Purchases, Account. Cash and Discounts will be posted to the debit side of the book or journal from the credit of the Cash Book in the usual way. If the settlement is by Bill, the credit will be to Bills Payable Account.

COMBINED PURCHASES DAY BOOK (OR JOURNAL) AND LEDGER

Debits

Date	Settled by	Fol.	Cash and Discount	Bill	Returns	Transfers	Total
			£p	£p	£p	£p	£p
19.. June 10	Returns				1·45		
July 1	Cash and Disct.		23·83				25·28
2	Cash and Disct.		37·25				37.25
	Bill			100·00			100·00
						25·00	25·00
31	Forward						
			£61·08	£100·00	£1·45	£25·00	£187·53

Credits

Date	Name	Details		Total
		£p		£p
19.. June 2	H. Laycock	17·15		
9	H. Laycock	8·13		25·28
12	E. Cosslet			37·25
17	H. Andrews			100·00
29	A. Easton			25·00
				£187·53

The invoices may be entered in strict date order or as they are received, but it will probably be found more convenient to file them in alphabetical or some other order until the end of each, say, month, when all the invoices relating to each supplier will be entered together in date order in a details column and the monthly total for each supplier carried out into the main column.

Returns may be dealt with either:

1. in a separate column on the debit side, or
2. as a deduction in the details column before the total is carried out, or
3. as deductions on the invoices to which they apply, the latter being entered net in the details column.

Items which are not paid at the usual date may either be transferred into a Creditors Account in a Ledger, or preferably, by means of a special column, into the succeeding period, thus enabling both sides of the book or journal to be totalled and agreed. If transactions are numerous, the book or journal should be cleared at least once a month, but leaving one month open where it is the practice to settle in the month following the purchase.

Illustration 7 (See p. 1311.)

Where the settlement is always by Cash (with or without discount), the work can be further curtailed by dispensing with the debit side and having a date-paid column and folio column, returns being dealt with on the credit side by method (2) or (3) above.

Illustration 8

COMBINED PURCHASES DAY BOOK (OR JOURNAL) AND LEDGER

Date	Name	Details	Total	Date Paid	Fol.
19..		£p	£p	19..	
June 2	H. Laycock . .	17·15			
9	H. Laycock . .	8·13			
		25·28			
10	Returns . .	1·45			
			23·83	July 1	
12	E. Cosslett . .		37·25	2	
17	H. Andrews . .		100·00	2	
29	A. Easton . .		25·00	Transfer[1]	
			£186·08		

[1] Transferred to a Creditors Account or carried forward into a special column in the succeeding period.

At the end of the financial period, it is desirable to transfer ALL unpaid items to a Creditors Account in a Ledger and to debit them, when paid, in that account.

A combined Day Book or Journal and Ledger can be utilized on similar lines for Sales, but, unless the receipts are reasonably regular and full (apart from the fact that there may be a far greater number of sales than purchases), the method is not worth while, although it has been found that frequently it is perfectly satisfactory, particularly if:

(a) a Total Account is prepared, say, monthly and

(b) unpaid items are transferred to a Debtors Account in a Ledger not later than the end of the following month, thus leaving no more that two months open, e.g. April Sales will be entered up and April and May allowed for entering the receipts. At the end of May, any unpaid items will be transferred into the Ledger.

CHAPTER 14

CORRECTION OF ERRORS

ERRORS calling for correction arise by reason of:

> Errors in the amount posted.
> Posting to the wrong side of an account.
> Errors of additions and carry forwards.
> Posting to the incorrect account.
> Omissions in the books of original entry.

The student, particularly in the intermediate examinations of the professional accountancy bodies, is very frequently called upon to give the entries for correcting errors.

The methods vary somewhat in detail, and no rigid rule can be formulated: but the procedure outlined below is simple and effective.

1. Deal with the amount of discrepancy of the Trial Balance by raising on the 'short' side a Suspense Account.

2. Correct the *arithmetical* error, ignoring any omission in the books or journals of original entry and the incorrectness of the account; this will be done by entering the necessary figure on the opposite side of the Suspense Account (thus eliminating it) and a reverse entry to the account to which the original posting was made. The result is to dispose completely of the 'out of balance'.

3. If necessary, next deal with the figure—now correct in *amount* but in the wrong *account*—by an ordinary transfer through the journal. This will result in giving the correct amount in the proper account.

4. If necessary, next deal with the omission in the books or journals of original entry by entering the omitted amount in the journal and posting in the ordinary way.

An error in addition will be dealt with in the same manner as an incorrect posting.

Some of the corrections of errors will merely affect assets and liabilities, whilst others will cause a modification of the Profit and Loss Account.

The four processes may be consolidated into one entry, but in cases of extreme complication the separate processes should be worked and either entered separately or attached to the consolidated entry by way of explanation.

Illustration 1

An item of £40 has been posted as £4 from the debit of the Cash Book to the credit of a customer's account. Taken alone, the obvious amount of discrepancy is £36 'short' credit.

The correction, therefore, is (using Ledger Accounts for clarity):

SUSPENSE

		£				£
Ledger Account (Name of customer)		36		Error . .		36

CUSTOMER

							£ 36
					Suspense Account		

The above is a simple example and illustrates the position where there is merely *one* error of arithmetic, that is where no error has arisen either in the books or journals of original entry or in the correctness of the account. As will be seen from rule 2, the necessary figure is *debited* to Suspense Account in order to eliminate it and credited to the account to which the original posting was made. No further adjustment is required, the correction merely affecting assets and not the Profit and Loss Account. The rules applied are 1 and 2.

The following illustrates the position where there is a double error—one of arithmetic and one of posting to an incorrect account.

Illustration 2

A sale of £30 was made to X and entered correctly in the Sales Journal, but posted to the debit of Y as £3.

The position, dealing with the arithmetical error, is that sales includes a sum of £30, but the debit therefor is £3 only, thus disclosing a 'short' debit (or 'over' credit) of £27, this being the amount for the *debit* to Suspense Account (Rule 1). The next entry is to debit Y with £27 and credit the same amount to Suspense Account (Rule 2). The effect is to correct the arithmetic, but it still leaves the corrected amount in the wrong account; hence a Journal transfer is required by which X is debited and Y credited with £30 (Rule 3). The above correction, again, does not affect the Profit and Loss Account.

Where, however, the original entry is incorrect it is necessary, in addition, to apply Rule 4.

Illustration 3

If the amount of sale to Y (using similar circumstances to those in the preceding example) had been £50 and entered as £30 only, the same procedure would be employed; and, in addition, a Journal entry would be finally made to correct the omission in the book of original entry, viz., debit Y £20; credit sales £20. This applies Rule 4 and augments the sales and, therefore, profits by £20.

Having obtained a grasp of these principles, the student will be in a position to apply them to all questions dealing with correction of errors which are usually considerably more involved than those outlined above, as they may require the correction of numerous errors.

The following are illustrations of typical questions:

Illustration 4

The Returns Inwards Journal includes an item of £7·30, which has been posted to the debit of a customer. Correct the error.

The Returns Inwards (debit) includes £7·30, but the posting should have been made to the *credit* of the person returning the goods (credit supplier), hence there are, in effect, two debits and no credits, totalling

£14·60. Suspense Account will, therefore, be credited with £14·60. The Suspense Account must then be debited and the Personal Account credited with £14·60, thus correcting the error.

SUSPENSE

		£p				£p
Customer (Correction of error)		14·60		Error		14·60

CUSTOMER

		£p				£p
Returns Inwards		7·30		Suspense Account		14·60

Thus, the customer is in *credit* for £7·30, represented by the debit of £7·30 in Returns Inward (or Sales) Account.

Illustration 5

An item of Purchases of £150 is entered in the Purchases Day Book as £15 and posted to the debit of the supplier's accounts as £51. (Perhaps an exaggerated and preposterous supposition, but many of the examination problems postulate errors even more unlikely and fanciful.) Correct the error.

As the working is likely to cause a student embarrassment, each step may be taken separately. The more advanced student will proceed to make the corrections without the subjoined detailed processes.

Rule 1. The Suspense Account, which merely deals, as has been noticed already, with arithmetical errors arising in the double entry book-keeping, is found by visualizing the actual posting, viz. Purchases £15 debit, and Supplier's Account £51 debit, this being the book-keeper's attempt at double entry. Hence, there is £66 debit and no credit, so that the Suspense Account must be created in credit for £66.

Rule 2. The Suspense Account must be eliminated by debiting it (to cancel the credit raised) with £66 and crediting Supplier's Account. The effect now obtained is that the error in balancing has been corrected and the supplier's account is in credit for £15, which is correct so far as the double-entry books show.

Rule 4. As the original entry should have been £150, it is necessary to book a further £135 through the Journal and post it in the usual way.

SUSPENSE

		£				£
Supplier Correction of Error		66		Error		66

SUPPLIER

		£				£
Purchases		51		Suspense Account Purchases[1]		66 135

[1] This item will be posted to the debit of Purchases Account from the Journal.

The Supplier's Account is now in credit for £150.

Illustration 6

A trader effects a sale of furniture, realizing £33·80. The amount is entered to the debit of Cash as £23·08 and posted to the debit of Repairs Account as £32·08. Correct the error, employing Ledger Accounts.

SUSPENSE

	£p			£p
Repairs Account Correction of Error	55·16	Error . . .		55·16

REPAIRS

	£p			£p
Cash . . Transfer to Furniture Account .	32·08 23·08	Suspense Account .		55·16
	£55·16			£55·16

FURNITURE

	£p		£p
Profit on Realization[2]	?	Transfer from Repairs Account[1] Cash . . . Depreciation . . Loss on Realization[2]	23·08 10·72 ? ?

CASH BOOK (*includes*)

	£p	
Sale of Furniture . „ „	23·08 10·72	

[1] Alternatively, the Suspense Account could be cleared by debiting it with £55·16, crediting Repairs with £32·08 and furniture £23·08, thus avoiding the transfer from Repairs to Furniture.

[2] The *book* value is not given and the above entries formally correct the error, yet it is necessary to note the probable loss or possible profit on Realization, as well as Depreciation. This may be described as a consequential entry, which is of vital importance, notwithstanding that no mention of it is made in the question itself.

Examples will now be given illustrative of the treatment of several errors contained in a Trial Balance.

Illustration 7

The following errors are discovered in the books of a trader, the Trial Balance containing a Difference in Balance Account:

1. Discount allowed to customers was correctly posted to the personal

accounts, but the discount column in the Cash Book was over-added by
£15.

2. The Purchases Book additions for December were added and posted
as £22,176, but should have been £22,426.

3. Goods returned (£10·42) by J. Jones had not been posted to his
account from the Returns Journal and the credit side of his Ledger
Account had been over-added by £5·50.

4. A cheque (£21) received from XY in settlement of his account had
been returned dishonoured, and posted to the debit of Allowances Account.

Give the amount of discrepancy in the Difference in Balance Account
and state how you would rectify the above errors.

The difference will be made up as follows:

	£p	£p
(1) Excess debit of . . .	15·00	
(2) Short debit (or excess credit) . .		250·00
(3) Short credit (or excess debit) .	10·42	
Short debit (or excess credit)		5·50
(4) No arithmetical error . . .		
	25·42	255·50
∴ Amount to be inserted in Difference in Balance account to make Trial Balance agree . . .	230·08	
	£255·50	£255·50

DIFFERENCE IN BALANCE (OR SUSPENSE)

			£p				£p
Balance . . .			230·08	Purchases . .		(c)	250·00
Discounts Allowed .	(a)		15·00	J. Jones . . .		(d)	5·50
J. Jones . . .	(b)		10·42				
			£255·50				£255·50

As to (4), XY's account will be debited with £21 and Allowances
Account credited by Journal entry.

Notes. (a) Discount Allowed Account will be credited to cancel the excessive *debit*.

(b) Jones's account will be credited with the Returns previously omitted from being posted to
his credit.

(c) Purchases Account will be debited as the original posting to the debit of Purchases should
have been £250 more.

(d) Jones's account will be debited with £5·50 for the over-credit.

The Profit and Loss Account will benefit by (1) £15, and (4) £21, but
will suffer by (2) £250.

It may eventually be necessary to write off the whole or part of XY's
account, and this possibility should be noted in the answer to the question.

After a student has gained proficiency in this type of question he will be
able to perform the correcting entries first from which he can ascertain the

original difference; that is, in reference to the above illustration, entries (a), (b), (c) and (d) would be made, the balancing item of £230·08 (debit) in Difference in Balance Account being ascertained at sight.

Illustration 8

The book-keeper of a firm having been unable to agree the Trial Balance, raised a Suspense Account in which he entered the amount by which he was out of balance. The following errors were discovered:

(a) The addition of the analysis column in the tabular Purchases Journal posted to Goods Purchased for Resale Account was found to be £15 short, though the addition of the total column was correct.

(b) Goods bought from a supplier amounting to £1·77 had been posted to the credit of his account as £177.

(c) A dishonoured Bill of Exchange receivable for £160 returned to the firm's bank had been credited to the Bank Account and debited to Bills Receivable Account. A cheque was received later from the customer for £160 and duly paid.

(d) An item of £8 entered in the Sales Returns Book had been posted to the debit of the customer who returned the goods.

(e) Sundry items of plant sold, amounting to £300, had been entered in the Sales Day Book, the total of which book had been posted to the credit of Sales Account.

(f) An amount of £80, owing by a customer, had been omitted from the list of Sundry Debtors.

(g) Discount amounting to £3, allowed to a customer, had been duly entered in his account, but not posted to the Discount Account.

(h) An amount of £10, being rates treated as paid in advance in the previous year, had not been brought forward as a balance on the Rates Account.

(i) Show the Suspense Account as raised by the book-keeper, with the adjusting entries you would find it necessary to make therein, and

(ii) Explain what effect any of the corrections would have on the profit shown in the unrectified accounts.

SUSPENSE

	£p		£p
Difference in Trial Balance	267·23	(a) Goods purchased for Resale Account .	15·00
(d) Customer's Account	16·00	(b) Supplier's Account .	175·23
		(f) Debtor's Account .	80·00
		(g) Discount Allowed Account .	3·00
		(h) Rates Account .	10·00
	£283·23		£283·23

Subject to (e) in respect of which Depreciation and Profit or Loss on Sale would be written off the book value of the plant sold, the above corrections reduce the profit by £328, made up as follows:

					£
(a)	.	.	.	.	15
(e)	.	.	.	.	300
(g)	.	.	.	.	3
(h)	.	.	.	.	10
					£328

As to (c), a Journal transfer will be required to debit the defaulting Acceptor's Account and credit Bills Receivable.

As to (e), a transfer will be required to debit Sales Account and credit Plant—together with any adjustment, as above indicated.

As to (f), there will be no actual posting as the omitted balance will be incorporated in the list of debtor balances.

In preceding examples the Ledger Accounts have been constructed for the purpose of clarity, from which the Journal entries may be easily written up. The following examples are appended showing the rectifying entries in Journal form.

Illustration 9

You are presented with a Trial Balance showing a difference which has been carried to Suspense Account, and the following errors are revealed:

1. £35 paid in cash for a typewriter was charged to Office Expenses Account.

2. Goods amounting to £66 sold to White were correctly entered in the Sales Journal but posted to White's account as £76. The total sales for the month were overcast by £10.

3. A cash sale of £15 to Brown, correctly entered in the Cash Book, was posted to the credit of Brown's personal account in the Sales Ledger.

4. Goods £13, returned by Green, were entered in the Sales Journal and posted therefrom to the credit of Green's personal account.

5. Goods invoiced at £124, and debited on 20th December to Black, were returned by him on the 23rd and taken into stock on 31st December, no entries being made in the books.

6. Sales Returns Journal was overcast by £100, and the total of a folio in the same journal, £1,730, carried forward as £1,703.

7. Goods £200, purchased from Robertson on 28th December, had been entered in the Purchases Journal and credited to him, but were not delivered till 5th January; stock being taken by the purchaser on 31st December.

8. Bill Receivable from H. Jones £160, posted to the credit of Bills Payable Account and credited to H. Jones.

Journalize the necessary corrections.

JOURNAL

		£	£
1.	Office Furniture	35	
	Office Expenses		35
	Being cost of typewriter incorrectly debited to Office Expenses.		
2.	*Assuming the posting made to the* **correct side** *of White's Account:*		
	(a) Sales	10	
	Suspense		10
	Being correction of £10 over addition in Sales Journal.		
	(b) Suspense	10	
	White		10
	Being correction of posting of £66 as £76 to debit of White's Account		
3.	Brown	15	
	Sales		15
	Being correction of entry of Cash Sale posted to credit of Brown's Account.		
4.	Sales	13	
	Sales Returns	13	
	Suspense		26
	Being correction of Returns by Green entered as Sales inadvertently for Sales Returns.		
5.	Sales Returns	124	
	Black		124
	Being goods returned by Black unentered and included in Stock.		
6.	Suspense	73	
	Sales Returns		73
	Being correction of errors in Sales Returns Journal, viz.:		
	(a) Excessive addition £100		
	(b) *Less* short carry forward 27		
	£73		
7.	(a) *If the title in the goods has passed at the end of the financial year:*		
	Stock in Transit	200	
	Trading Account		200
	Being goods purchased in the hands of Robertson.		
	(b) *If the title in the Goods has* **not** *passed:*		
	Robertson	200	
	Purchases		200
	Being cancellation of purchase of goods entry in respect of goods purchased on 5th January 19.. (following year).		
8.	Bills Payable	160	
	Bills Receivable	160	
	Suspense		320
	Being correction of bill entered in Bills Payable Account instead of Bills Receivable Account.		

Where sectional balancing is in operation it will be necessary to make adjustments in the total accounts so that there will be no disturbance of the agreement of the totals with the sum of the individual Ledger balances.

Illustration 10

1. A Bill Receivable was accepted by Johnson for £350 and entered in the account of Johnson as £305.

2. Goods sold to Williamson for £100 were posted to Williams's

JOURNAL

	£	£
(1) Suspense	45	
Johnson		45
Being correction of posting to the credit of his account as £305 instead of £350		
(2) Williamson	100	
Suspense . . —	35	
Williams		135
Being correction of error of goods sold to Williamson for £100 entered against Williams as £135.		

JOURNAL

	£	£
(1) No correcting entry is required in the Total Accounts, since the only error is the incorrect figure on the credit side of Johnson's account. The original entries, from which the Total Accounts are prepared, are apparently correct.		
(2) Nominal Ledger Adjustment Account . . . . [in No. 2 Ledger]	100	
No. 2 Sales Ledger Adjustment Account . . . [in Nominal Ledger]		100
Being adjustment of Total Accounts in respect of cancellation of debit incorrectly made to Williams's Account.		
No. 1 Sales Ledger Adjustment Account . . . . [in Nominal Ledger]	100	
Nominal Ledger Adjustment Account . . . [in No. 1 Sales Ledger]		100
Being adjustment of Total Accounts in respect of sales of £100 to Williamson not debited to him.		
Note: As in (1), no correcting entry is required in the Total Accounts for the £35 error, since the original entry in the Sales Journal from which the Total Accounts are compiled showed the correct figure of £100. The Total Accounts are however, affected by the inter-Ledger transfer, since the original entry was carried out into the wrong analysis column in the Sales Journal. Had the original entry been carried out into No. 1 Ledger (i.e. Williamson's Ledger) analysis column, none of the above Journal entries affecting the Adjustment Accounts would be required.		

Account as £135, the £100 in the Sales Journal having been carried out into the No. 2 Ledger analysis column.

Total Ledger Accounts were employed, Johnson and Williamson Ledger Accounts being in No. 1 Ledger and Williams in No. 2 Ledger.

Assuming that both Nominal Ledger and Sales Ledger Adjustment Accounts are employed, the Journal entries for the adjustment of the Personal Accounts and the Total Accounts are as shown on p. 1409.

The entries are simple if it is remembered that the amounts entered *in* the Sales Ledger Adjustment Account (in the Nominal Ledger) will correspond to the side in which the individual entry is made in the Sales Ledger, the entry *in* the Nominal Ledger Adjustment Account (in the Sales Ledger) being reverse, e.g. taking the entry to Williamson: as his account in the above adjustment is debited with £100, so must the No. 1 Sales Ledger Adjustment Account *in* the Nominal Ledger and the reverse entry be made to Nominal Ledger Adjustment Account *in* No. 1 Sales Ledger.

In all probability the total accounts may contain the correct TOTALS, so that the 'total' entries above are not required, the personal account adjustments—apart from the errors—effecting the agreement with the amount disclosed in the Total Accounts.

Entry (2) has been consolidated in substitution for the longer process, viz.:

JOURNAL

		£	£
Suspense		35	
Williams			35
Williamson		100	
Williams			100

Illustration 11

X keeps two Sales Ledgers, employing an Adjustment Account for each Ledger. *The Double Entry is built up from the totals of each journal of Prime Entry.* You discover that:

1. The balance due by Jones, £20, has been transferred, owing to removal, direct from Ledger 1 to Ledger 2.
2. £15 Cash received from Williamson (Ledger 1) not posted to his Personal Account.
3. Sales Returns (Ledger 2) under-added, £10.
4. A Bill Receivable £100 from Ronald & Co. (Ledger 2) entered as cash from debtors and posted to the credit of Bills Receivable.

Show what differences will be found in the Sales Ledger Adjustment Accounts and Trial Balance, and how the errors would be corrected.

1. The transfer will affect the ADJUSTMENT accounts (assuming the items appear on the *same* sides as in Ledgers 1 and 2 respectively) as follows:

The amount of £20 must be credited to No. 1 Sales Ledger Adjustment Account and debited to No. 2 Sales Ledger Adjustment Account. This being merely a transfer from one Ledger to another, the Trial Balance will not have been influenced as regards total agreement because in fact the TOTAL balances will be correct, but there will be a disagreement between the Schedule of Debtors of each Ledger and the total shown by each of the Sales Ledger Adjustment Accounts.

2. This sum will have been duly included in the total posted to the credit of Sales Ledger Adjustment Account so that the Trial Balance agreement is again undisturbed; but there will be a discrepancy between the Schedule of Debtors and the balance of No. 1 Sales Ledger Adjustment Account, the former being £15 in excess of the latter.

As the Ledger Accounts are here treated as 'Memoranda' (the Adjustment Accounts showing the true position), no Suspense Account will be opened, the adjustment being made by posting the unposted item.

3. The total to the debit of Sales Returns will be the same as that posted to the credit of the Sales Ledger Adjustment Account so that the effect is to create a discrepancy between the Schedule of Debtors and the total, this having no effect on the agreement of the Trial Balance; but as the total is incorrect, it will become necessary to adjust as follows:

Debit Sales Returns, £10   Credit No. 2 Ledger Adjustment Account, £10

4. The amount of £100 being entered amongst Receipts from Debtors, will have been included in the postings to the credit of No. 2 Sales Ledger Adjustment Account as well as to the credit of Bills Receivable, and thus there are two credits: (1) in No. 2 Sales Ledger Adjustment Account, and (2) in Bills Receivable, whilst at the same time the Schedule of Debtors will not agree with the total because the debtor has not been credited with the bill £100.

The adjusting entries would be:

| Debit Bills Receivable | £100 | | Credit Suspense Account | £100 |
| „   „   „ | £100 | | Credit cash. | £100 |

Having corrected the out-of-balance and cancelled thereby the erroneous credit, it is necessary to post £100 to the credit of Ronald & Co. (the amount already having been included in the credits to No. 2 Sales Ledger Adjustment Account).

The above Adjustment Accounts will appear in the Nominal Ledger.

If an Adjustment Account were raised *in* each Sales Ledger, there would be entries therein reverse to those appearing in the Adjustment Accounts in the Nominal Ledger.

CHAPTER 15

ROYALTY ACCOUNTS

ROYALTY is the remuneration payable to a person in respect of the use of an asset, whether hired or purchased from such person, calculated by reference to and varying with quantities produced or sold as a result of the use of such asset. The expression used in a broad sense has a more extended meaning as it is frequently employed in connection with hiring of machines where the charge, instead of being upon a fixed base, say £5 per machine, is calculated on the number of revolutions, or in textile machinery, the number of stitches.

The chief forms of royalty are Mining Royalties,[1] Patent Royalties, and Copyright Royalties, based respectively upon ore raised, product sold, and books sold. There are many other varieties, but the examination candidate's attention may be confined to those above mentioned.

In the case of Mining and similar Royalties, a considerable time must elapse before production can commence on a commercial scale, whilst similarly in the other instances considerable time must pass before sales can take place, e.g. when a lengthy advertising campaign is undertaken. In order to afford some reward during this intervening period to the lessor, inventor, or author, whilst avoiding hardship to the producer, an arrangement is usually entered into whereby the former is guaranteed a MINIMUM sum—designated Minimum Rent—usually accompanied by a proviso that if the sum due, calculated at so much per unit (e.g. ton of ore raised) does not reach the minimum, such deficiency may be carried forward, and deducted from future royalties. Such deduction may not be made indiscriminately because it is so limited that the recipient of the royalty at least receives the minimum rent. Such an arrangement is known as a **right to recoup short workings.** Where no such rights exists on the part of the user, the deduction is not allowed.

In certain circumstances a minimum rent is not payable, but merely the royalty, so that the question of short workings does not arise, the payment made being calculated on quantities, e.g. tons of ore raised and charged-up each year against production, whilst the recipient takes his chance as to the amount he will receive without being guaranteed any minimum periodic sum.

Another question arises in connection with the minimum rent. Even if the right to recoup short workings exists it may be either unlimited or limited as to time; in the latter instance, the time for recoupment may be calculated from the commencement of the AGREEMENT or from the year (or other period) during which the deficiency arose.

The above-mentioned alternatives may be stated thus:

The royalty owner may receive:

1. Royalty without any minimum rent.

---

[1] Acquisition of Coal Mining Royalties by the State and nationalization of the coal mines has rendered obsolete *Coal* Mining Royalties so far as the United Kingdom is concerned, but other mining royalties still exist, e.g. tin mines in Cornwall.

2. Royalty with a minimum rent.
(a) *With* the right of the other party to recoup short workings
    (i) recoupable without any limitation of time;
    (ii) recoupable, but within a limited time,
          either (α) to a certain period commencing with the agreement;
          or (β) to a certain period from the year of deficiency.
(b) *Without* the right of the other party to recoup short workings.

Illustration 1

A landlord granted a lease to a mining company whereby he is to receive
£0.05 per ton of ore raised.

1st Year	.	.	.	10,000 tons	3rd Year .	24,000 tons
2nd ,,	.	.	.	20,000 ,,		

In case 1, the landlord will receive in the first year £500, the second
year £1,000, and the third year £1,200; total, £2,700.

In case 2 (a) (i) (assuming a minimum of £800), the landlord will receive
£800 in the first year, but as this is £300 more than he would otherwise
receive, the latter is recoupable in future years. He will receive in the
second year £1,000, less £200, i.e. £800. The reason why the whole sum
of £300 cannot be deducted is that the landlord must receive *at least*
£800. This leaves the sum of £100 to be carried forward. The landlord in
the third year will receive £1,200, less £100, i.e. £1,100. Students, in a case
of this sort, must be careful to avoid the error of deducting from the
£1,200 the sum of £400 to leave the landlord with £800, because the
landlord is not restricted to £800—it is a **minimum,** not a maximum—after
the short workings have been absorbed. It will be perceived that in the
future years when output has fully developed, there is every probability
that the temporary overpayments (i.e. short workings) will be eliminated,
leaving in the long run the same amount of royalties as if no minimum had
been bargained for. Thus, the landlord receives (comparing the two
methods so far illustrated):

				1	2(a) (i)
				£	£
1st Year	.	.	.	500	800
2nd ,,	.	.	.	1,000	800
3rd ,,	.	.	.	1,200	1,100
				£2,700	£2,700

2 (a) (ii) (α). If the limitation is for two years from the commencement
of the lease, the short workings at the end of the second year, i.e. £100,
will be no longer recoupable and must be written off, so that in the third
year the landlord suffers no deduction and therefore receives £1,200.

2 (a) (ii) (β). If the limitation is for one year after the deficiency arises,
the amount short in the first year will be recoupable only in the second
year, that of the second year in the third year, that of the third year in the
fourth year, and so on. Thus, the £300 short in the first year is available
for the second year, but only £200 can be utilized therein (because the

landlord must receive his minimum of £800), so that the sum of £100 is now irrecoverable, the landlord receiving £1,200 in the third year. Whatever the royalties in the fourth year, the landlord will suffer no deduction because in the third year there is no shortage, and it is only the third-year shortage that is available for the fourth year.

2 (b). In this case, the landlord receives in any one year the amount of royalties or his minimum rent, whichever be the LARGER. The landlord thus receives, 1st Year, £800 (Minimum); 2nd Year, £1,000 (Royalty); 3rd Year, £1,200 (Royalty).

Income Tax. It is the duty of the payer in the case of Patent Royalties, Mining Royalties, and in certain circumstances Copyright Royalties, to deduct income tax, and account for such deduction to the Inland Revenue authorities.

Such a deduction obviously in no way affects the amount of charge for royalties, as the amount of tax is merely accounted for to the Inland Revenue instead of being paid to the royalty owner. (See Chapter 21.)

Book-keeping Entries. 1. Where no minimum rent exists:

For Royalty:
    Debit Royalty   Credit Landlord[1] (or Royalty owner)
For Payment:
    Debit Landlord   Credit Cash[2]
                 Income Tax (at current rate)

2 (a). Where a minimum rent exists *with* right to recoup short workings. (This applies in *all* the sub-headings of (2) as the distinctions explained under this head do not affect the type of entry required.)

(i) Where the royalty is *less* than the minimum rent:

Debit Royalty (for Royalty) . . } Credit Landlord with Minimum
  ,,   Short Workings (for Deficiency) }   Rent

The amount of royalties is transferred to Production Account whilst the short workings is carried forward and shown in the Balance Sheet as an asset.

(ii) Where royalty *exceeds* the minimum rent.

Debit Royalty (for Royalty)   Credit Landlord (for Royalty)

with the following consequential entry IF there is ALREADY a balance on short workings.

Debit Landlord to the extent of   Credit Short Workings
short workings, but limited if
necessary so as to leave the
Landlord's balance in credit
for his minimum rent

[It will be clear that no such consequential entry can arise in the first year, unless the agreement provides therefor, as there is no balance on short workings.]

---

[1] The word Landlord will be used in the remainder of the entries outlined.
[2] As this is an ordinary book-keeping entry, it is not repeated in the remainder of the entries outlined.

The latter entry may or may not be available, according as to whether the time limit (if any) has expired. When the right to recoup has expired the amount should be written off thus:

Debit Short Workings Irrecoverable | Credit Short Workings

As before, Royalty Account is subsequently transferred to the debit of Production Account, but the Short Workings Irrecoverable Account is transferred to the debit of Profit and Loss Account.

It may be noted that in two instances it may be desirable to write off at least a portion of the short workings even before they prove irrecoverable, viz.:

(a) When production in the future is not likely to be of sufficient magnitude to absorb the Short Workings Account, and

(b) When the lease is nearing expiry, because there will not be the opportunity to recoup in the future, as production will cease with the expiry of the lease.

2 (*b*). Where there is a minimum rent but *without* right to recoup short workings.

Where the Royalty *exceeds* the Minimum Rent:
  Debit Royalty (for Royalty) Credit Landlord (for Royalty)
Where the Royalty *is less than* the Minimum Rent:
  Debit Royalty (for Royalty) Credit Landlord (for Minimum
  „ [1] Short Workings Irrecoverable Rent)
    (for Deficiency)

It will be seen, therefore, that there is no difference between 2 (*a*) and 2 (*b*) except that in the latter case there is no transfer against the landlord for recoupment of short workings and the short workings are immediately written off, whilst in (1) the question of short workings does not arise, so that all the principles may be elucidated by explanatory examples of entries arising in 2 (*a*).

Illustration 2

The Everbrite Tin Co. obtains a lease of land from Lord X, the terms being a royalty of £0.10 a ton raised with a minimum rent of £200; with a right to recoup short workings.

In the first year 1,600 tons were raised. Show Accounts in the Lessee's books. Assume Income Tax at 45 per cent.

The Ledger Accounts will be:

ROYALTY

		£			£
Lord X		160	Production Account . .		160

SHORT WORKINGS

		£			£
Lord X		40			

[1] This account would have been carried forward had the right to recoup existed.

LORD X (LANDLORD)

	£			£
Cash	110	Royalty[3]		160
Income Tax[2] . . .	90	Short Workings[3] . .		40
	£200			£200

[2] 45% on £200.
[3] Making up the minimum rent of £200.

Illustration 3

The same terms as in the preceding illustration, the tons raised in the succeeding years being:

	Tons			Tons
Year 1 . .	950	Year 4 . .		3,800
Year 3 .	1,100	Year 5 .		2,600

Show Accounts in the Lessee's books.
The entries (shown in tabular form) will be:

	Royalty		Landlord		Short Workings	
	Dr.	Cr.	Dr.	Cr.	Dr.	Cr.
	£	£	£	£	£	£
Year 1 (repeated for sake of clarity) . . .	160			200	40	
„ 2.	95			200	105	
„ 3.	110			200	90	
„ 4.	380		(a) 180	380		(a) 180
„ 5.	260		(b) 55	260		(b) 55
	[Total £1,005]		Total net credit [£1,005]			
	4		5		6	

[4] Transferred to Production Account.
[5] Discharged in Cash and Tax.
[6] Shown in Balance Sheet as an asset so long as available for recoupment.

Notes. (a) The most that can be transferred is £180, because if the whole of the Short Workings Account were transferred it would reduce the landlord's sum to less than £200.

(b) There is a balance only of £55 on short workings at the end of the fourth year, so that in the fifth year it can be wholly absorbed (still leaving the landlord with £205). Care must be taken to avoid transferring £60, as the landlord is always entitled to at least £200; and where the royalty exceeds that sum he is entitled to the excess when the short workings are exhausted, as in the fifth year.

It will be seen that total royalties are £1,005, whilst the landlord receives in all the same amount.

Illustration 4

The same facts as in the preceding illustration, except that the right to recoup short workings endures for four years, commencing with the date of the lease—or more properly for three years after the expiry of the first year of the working (i.e. all short workings must be written off unless recouped by the end of the fourth year), and that the output in the sixth year is 1,800 tons.

In this case the entries in respect of the first three years will be identical with those shown above.

The remaining entries will be:

Year	Royalty Dr.	Royalty Cr.	Landlord Dr.	Landlord Cr.	Short Workings Dr.	Short Workings Cr.	Short Workings Irrecoverable Dr.	Short Workings Irrecoverable Cr.
	£	£	£	£	£	£	£	£
4 . . .	380		(a) 180	380	235[1]	(a) 180	(b) 55	2
						(b) 55		
5 . . .	260			260				
6 . . .	180			200			20	2

[1] This is the balance of Short Workings Account from the third year.
[2] Written off to Profit and Loss Account.

Illustration 5

Assuming that the lease permitted short workings to be recouped within two years from the year of the DEFICIENCY the entries, in tabular form, will be:

Year	Royalty Dr.	Royalty Cr.	Landlord Dr.	Landlord Cr.	Short Workings Dr.	Short Workings Cr.	Short Workings Irrecoverable Dr.	Short Workings Irrecoverable Cr.	Notes
	Dr.	Cr.	Dr.	Cr.	Dr.	Cr.	Dr.	Cr.	
	£	£	£	£	£	£	£	£	
1	160			200	40				
2	95			200	105				
3	110			200	90	40	40		Year 1 Deficiency now irrecoverable
4	380		180	380		180			Year 2 Deficiency completely recouped plus £75 of year 3
	260		15	260		15			Year 3 Balance recouped
	[Total £1,005]		[Total Net Credit £1,045]				[Total £40]		

As a variation from those already treated, the following example applies the same principles to the case of royalties based on stitches made by a machine employed under a hiring agreement.

Illustration 6

A. S. Lacker, on 1st January 19.., leases a machine to H. Ardy on terms that the charge for royalty be £0·01 per 1,000 stitches with a minimum monthly payment of £10, with right to recoup 'short workings' over the three months immediately succeeding the month of the shortage.

From the special counters employed, the numbers of stitches for each month are:

19.		Stitches	19..		Stitches
Jan.	. . .	500,000	May	. . .	1,300,000
Feb.	. . .	800,000	June	. . .	1,000,000
Mar.	. . .	1,000,000	July	. . .	1,500,000
Apr.	. . .	1,200,000			

Show the entries required in the books of H. Ardy.
The entries, in tabular form, will be:

Date	Royalty		A. S. Lacker		Short Workings		Short Workings Irrecoverable		Notes
19..	Dr. £	Cr. £	Dr. £	Cr. £	Dr. £	Cr. £	Dr. £	Cr. £	
Jan. 31	5			10	5				Short Workings recoverable until 30th April
Feb. 28	8			10	2				
Mar. 31	10			10					
Apr. 30	12		2	12		2	3		£2 of the January Short Workings recouped. The balance is now irrecoverable. February Short Workings recouped in May
May 31	13		2	13		2			
June 30	10			10					
July 31	15			15					
	[Total £73]		[Total net credit £76]				[Total £3]		

The full accounts will present no difficulty, but for sake of clarity the April accounts are shown below:

ROYALTY

19.. Apr. 30	Lacker . . .	£ 12	19..	(Total of Account transferred to Production Account)		£

A. S. LACKER

19..			£	19..			£
Apr. 30	Short Workings		2	Apr. 30	Royalty . . .		12
	Cash . . .		10				
			£12				£12

Short Workings

19..			£	19..			£
Apr. 1	Balance . . .	b/d	7	Apr. 30	Lacker–Short Workings recouped .		2
					Profit and Loss Account:		
					Short Workings irrecoverable .		3
					Balance . . .	c/d	2
			£7				£7
May 1	Balance . . .	b/d	2				

It will no doubt have been observed that where the right to recoup short workings exists for a specified period from the *commencement* of the agreement, the question really resolves itself into two parts: (1) The right of recoupment of short workings extending in the ordinary way, taking the last year in which the recoupment is possible as the equivalent of the last year of a lease, and after the expiry of the specified period (2) without right of recoupment existing at all. In other words, there are two distinct arrangements just as if the early years where recoupment is possible were covered by one lease and superseded by a new one containing no such right.

Therefore, at the expiry of the first 'break' it will be necessary to write off the short workings irrecoverable (if any).

Illustration 7

Royalty is £0.05 per ton; the right of recoupment of short workings to extend for four years only from the commencement of the lease (i.e. three years from the end of the first year). Minimum rent, £70 per annum. Yearly output as shown in column 2 below. Show, in columnar form, the accounts in the books of the Lessee.

(1) Year	(2) Tons	Royalty		Landlord		Short Workings		Short Workings Irrecoverable	
		Dr.	Cr.	Dr.	Cr.	Dr.	Cr.	Dr.	Cr.
		£	£	£	£	£	£	£	£
1.	1,000	50			70	20			
2.	1,500	75		5	75		5		
3.	2,000	100		15	100		15		
4.	1,200	60 [expiry of the 'recoupment' period]			70			10 [expiry of the 'recoupment' period]	
5.	1,000	50			70			20	
6.	800	40			70			30	
7.	1,500	75			75				
8.	2,100	105			105				

In the fourth year the whole of the balance of short workings unrecouped must be written off. In the fifth year (and subsequently) the short workings are written off *at once* because they are not recoupable.

It will therefore be clear that from the *fourth* year the landlord obtains the royalty or minimum rent, whichever is the greater.

Taxation and Royalties Receivable. On and after 6 April 1970 mineral royalties (i.e. so much of any rents, tolls, royalty or periodical payments relating to the winning and working of minerals) receivable by a person resident or ordinarily resident in the U.K. under a lease, licence, etc. are reduced by 50% for purposes of any years of assessment for income tax or corporation tax on profits other than chargeable gains. Management expenses deductible are similarly reduced by 50%.

Summary of General Principles. Before sub-royalties are dealt with, the general principles already dealt with are summarized below:

1. There may be no right at all to recoup short workings.
2. Where the right to recoup short workings exists, it may be subject to a limitation as to the period within which the right may be exercised, e.g.:

(a) A certain number of years from the commencement of the lease or agreement.

(b) A certain number of years from the end of the year in which the deficiency occurs.

Therefore particular attention should be given to the *dates and the terms of the Lease.*

3. Unless some covenant to the contrary is contained in the lease, the balance of short workings, inclusive of the amount arising in the last year of the lease, is irrecoverable.

4. The landlord, in circumstances (1), will always be entitled to the amount of royalty or minimum rent, whichever is the *greater*.

5. Once the short workings balance is eliminated, the landlord will receive in one year (until another deficient year arises) the full royalty, subject to the deduction of income tax where necessary.

6. Where the time limit for recouping short workings has expired, the treatment of royalties for subsequent years is exactly as if no right to recoup existed, and the irrecoverable short workings are at once written off.

7. The Short Workings Account must never have a CREDIT balance unless there is some exceptional agreement, e.g. to anticipate short workings in future years.

8. (*a*) If the royalty is LESS than the minimum rent, the landlord is credited with the higher figure (i.e. minimum rent) and the Short Workings Account debited with the difference.

(*b*) If the royalty EXCEEDS the minimum rent the landlord is first credited with the higher figure (i.e. royalty), and, secondly, his account is debited and Short Workings Account credited with the recoupable short workings, if any, the latter transfer being restricted where necessary, to leave the landlord in credit for his minimum rent.

Sub-Royalties. It frequently happens that a concern obtains a lease of land on which to work a mine or quarry, the terms being the usual royalty, merging in a minimum rent with a right of recoupment of short workings, coupled with the right to sublet part of the land to a sub-lessee.

The entries in the lessee's books in respect of royalty receivable are reverse to those relating to royalty payable. Should the sub-letting be at a higher rate than that payable by the lessee to the landlord, such excess is a profit to be credited to Profit and Loss Account; otherwise the amount receivable from the sub-lessee is credited to the Production Account against the royalty payable by the lessee, since the latter accounts to his landlord for the royalty upon the WHOLE output. Usually separate accounts for the royalty receivable and payable are opened, although one account only may be employed; but in both instances the net royalty payable will be transferred to the debit of Production Account.

Illustration 8

P. Quick obtains a lease from R. Rich to work a mine, the terms being a royalty of £0·05 per ton merging into a minimum rent of £100 per annum, there being granted to the lessee the right to recoup short workings over the whole period of the lease. P. Quick sublets part of the property to V. Poor, the terms being a royalty of £0·5 per ton merging in a minimum rent of £48 per annum, recoupment being available over the whole period of the sub-lease. The amount of ore extracted is as follows:

Year	P. Quick	V. Poor	Total Production
	(Tons)	(Tons)	(Tons)
1 . .	1,100	400	1.500
2 . .	1,160	540	1,700
3 . .	1,300	700	2,000
4 . .	1,400	900	2,300
5 . .	1,800	1,200	3,000
6 . .	800	1,200	2,000

The entries in the books of the lessee, in abbreviated tabular form, will be:

Year	Royalty Payable	Landlord		Short Workings		Sub-lessee		Royalty Receivable	Royalty Suspense		[Yearly Balance of Royalty Suspense]
	Dr.	Dr.	Cr.	Dr.	Cr.	Dr.	Cr.	Cr.	Dr.	Cr.	Cr.
	£	£	£	£	£	£	£	£	£	£	£
1 .	75		100	25		48		20		28	28
2 .	85		100	15		48		27		21	49
3 .	100		100			48		35		13	62
4 .	115	15	115		15	48		45		3	65
5 .	150	25	150		25	60	12	60			53
6 .	100		100			60	12	60	12		41
	[Total £625	[Total net credit, £625]				[Total net debit, £288]		[Total £247]	12		[Carry fwd. as liability £41]

It will be observed that the lessee, having no more short workings, has paid over the period the precise sum due based on output.

As regards the sub-lessee (who will make entries in his books on the principles outlined), he may be regarded as in a similar position in respect of the lessee as the latter is to the landlord, so that the entries in the books of the lessee, so far as the royalty he obtains from the sub-lessee is concerned, are, as mentioned, the reverse to those already explained. So long as it is perceived that for the purposes of book-keeping, Quick is Poor's landlord, the entries are identical with those of a landlord in the strict legal sense, and are reverse to those made in Poor's books.

The suspense is obviously the equivalent, viewed from the opposite angle, of short workings, and just as the lessee carries forward as an asset his short workings, so a landlord carries forward the suspense to cover diminutions of royalty receivable arising from recoupments of short workings.

The student will readily observe that in the books of Poor the figures will (with the altered headings of accounts) be found on the opposite sides to the above, e.g. year 1:

	Royalty Payable	'Landlord' (i.e. Quick)	Short Workings
	Dr. £	Cr. £	Dr. £
Year 1 . .	20	48	28

It should be noted that Quick so far will have received £288 against royalty of £247, leaving £41 in suspense; but if the sixth year were the final year, Quick would lose nothing (he has no short workings) but Poor would lose £41 short workings now irrecoverable. Quick would therefore debit the suspense and credit his Profit and Loss Account with £41.

The Ledger Accounts are shown for the first and second years:

ROYALTY RECEIVABLE

			£					£
Year 1	Royalty Payable . .		20	Year 1	V. Poor . .			20
,, 2	,, ,, . .		27	,, 2	,, . . .			27

ROYALTY SUSPENSE

			£					£
Year 1	Balance . .	c/d	28	Year 1	V. Poor . .			28
,, 2	. .	c/d	49	,, 2	Balance . . . V. Poor	b/d	28 21
			49					49
				,, 3	Balance . .	b/d		49

V. POOR

			£					£
Year. 1	Sundries		48	Year 1.	Cash (and Tax)			48
,, 2	,,		48	,, 2	,, ,,			48

ROYALTY PAYABLE

			£				£
Year 1	R. Rich . .		75	Year 1	Royalty Receivable . Production Account .		20 55
			£75				£75
,, 2	,, . .		85	,, 2	Royalty Receivable . Production Account .		27 58
			£85				£85

SHORT WORKINGS

			£					£
Year 1	R. Rich . . .		25	Year 1	Balance . . .	c/d		25
„ 2	Balance . . .	b/d	25	„ 2	„ . . .	c/d		40
	R. Rich . . .		15					
			£40					£40
„ 3	Balance . . .	b/d	40					

R. RICH

			£				£
Year 1	Cash (and Tax) . .		100	Year 1	Sundries		100
„ 2	„ „ . .		100	„ 2	„		100

ACCOUNTS IN QUICK'S BOOKS (see p. 1515)

Year	Royalty Payable Dr. £	Royalty Payable Cr. £	Landlord (Rich) Dr. £	Landlord (Rich) Cr. £	Short Workings Dr. £	Short Workings Cr. £	Short Workings Irrecoverable Dr. £	Short Workings Irrecoverable Cr. £	Royalty Receivable Dr. £	Royalty Receivable Cr. £	Sub-Lessee (Poor) Dr. £	Sub-Lessee (Poor) Cr. £	Royalty Suspense Dr. £	Royalty Suspense Cr. £	Profit and Loss Dr. £	Profit and Loss Cr. £	Yearly Balance of Royalty Suspense Dr. £	Yearly Balance of Royalty Suspense Cr. £
1	75			100	25					20	48			28				28
2	85			100	15					27	48			21				49
3	100			100						35	48		(a) 28	13		(a) 28		34
4	115		15	115		15	25			45	48		(b) 21	3		(b) 21		16
5	150	—				25				60	60	(c) 12	(c) 12					nil
5													(d) 4			(d) 4		
	£525		[Net credit £5 50]		£40	£40	£25			£187	[Net debit £2 40]		£65	£65		£53		

Notes:

(a) In year 3 there is a commencing balance of £49, of which £28 must be recouped, if at all, in that year; but it is not possible, as another deficiency has arisen, so that £28 becomes profit to Quick (and loss to Poor). This reduces the Suspense to £21, but a further addition of £13 arises, thus making the carry forward £34.

(b) In year 4 the short workings recoupable from year 2 are not utilizable by Poor, as another shortage has occurred, hence this is treated as profit to Quick, thus reducing the balance of Suspense from £34 to £13, to which, however, must be added £3 (the current year shortage), making a carry forward of £16. (It must be remembered that the £3 can only be recovered by Poor in year 5, as this is the FINAL year of the lease.)

(c) In year 5 the maximum amount of short workings recoverable by Poor is £12, as Quick must at least receive £48. The balance of £16 less £12 recoupable leaves a net balance of £4 to be taken to the Profit and Loss Account of Quick.

(d) The £4 is made up of the balance of year 3 [£13 less £12 recouped] £1, plus year 4, £3.

The position, when there is a limitation to the time of recoupment, is now shown.

Illustration 9

Using the same data as in the foregoing illustration save that there is a clause whereby Quick is to have a right of recoupment over the first four years of the lease, whilst Poor has the right of recoupment as against Quick for the two years following the short workings, and that the lease and sub-lease are for five years only (so that the sixth-year figures are eliminated), show Accounts in Quick's books (see p. 1514).

It will be seen that the total royalties are £525 [10,500 tons at £0·05] but the landlord has received £550, reflected in the former figure and short workings irrecoverable.

The Royalty receivable is £187 [3,740 tons at £0·05] but the lessee has received £240, reflected in the former figure and the short workings irrecoverable by the sub-lessee.

If the lessee sublets at a profit, e.g. he pays a royalty of £0·05 per ton on the whole output, but charges £0·08 per ton on the output of the sub-lesse, he has, subject to short workings adjustments, a profit of £0·03 per ton on the sub-lessee's output, which will be credited to Profit and Loss Account.

Illustration 10

Assume that short workings are recoverable during the period of a lease of three years, and the output is as follows:

Year	Output in Tons [Total]	Lessee's Output in Tons	Sub-lessee's Output in Tons
1	1,400	400	937·5
2	2,300	1,700	562·5
3	3,000	2,280	675
	[at £0·05 per ton]		[at £0·08 per ton]

Minimum Rent—Landlord to Lessee, £100.
　　　　　　　,,　　　Lessee to Sub-lessee, £60.

Show entries in Lessee's books.
The entries, in summary form in the books of the Lessee, will be:

Year	Royalty Payable	Landlord		Short Workings		Royalty Receivable	Sub-lessee	Royalty Suspense
	Dr.	Dr.	Cr.	Dr.	Cr.	Cr.	Dr.	Cr.
	£	£	£	£	£	£	£	£
1	70		100	30		75	75	
2	115	15	115		15	45	60	15
3	150	15	150		15	54	60	6
	(a) £335	[Total net credit £335]		£30	£30	(b) £174	£195	(c) £21

(a) 6,700 tons at £0·05.
(b) 2,175 tons at £0·08.
(c) Transferred to credit of Profit and Loss Account.

CHAPTER 16

JOINT VENTURE ACCOUNTS

The most usual ventures met with in practice are those relating to the dealings in a consignment of merchandise (e.g. the purchase and sale of a bankrupt firm's stock) or to dealings in stocks and shares.

If the venture is of sufficient magnitude to warrant a distinct set of books being kept, no special book-keeping treatment is necessary; but where the books of each party record *only* such transactions as directly concern him, special treatment is necessary.

In cases of this type, each party opens one account only; that is, the account relating to the venture. This account is treated as a personal account, being debited with all payments made by, and credited with all receipts of, the person in whose books it is opened. The account is headed 'Joint Venture with ——' and forms part of the double entry of the party making the entries.

Illustration 1

A and B enter into a joint venture. The neccessary accounts are, therefore:

In A's books:
Joint Venture with B

In B's books:
Joint Venture with A

In addition to the personal accounts, a Memorandum Joint Venture Account will be written up in order to ascertain the total profit or loss on the adventure. When the profit or loss has been ascertained, it will be divided between the parties in their agreed ratio, or if none is agreed, equally. If a profit has been made, each party will debit the Personal Account of his co-venturer in his books with his *own* share and credit 'Profit and Loss on Joint Venture Account'. There will be converse entries for a loss. This is the entry that causes most difficulty in Joint Venture Accounts, and particular note should be made of the correct treatment. The ordinary rule for nominal accounts applies, namely, DEBIT LOSSES, CREDIT GAINS.

Rules for Joint Venture Accounts. The rules for Joint Venture Accounts may be summarized as follows:

1. Each party will open a Personal Account, Joint Venture with... Account, and will make the following entries therein:

DEBIT Joint Venture with... Account with the contributions and expenses incurred by him on behalf of the Joint Venture.
CREDIT Cash or Creditors.
DEBIT Cash or Debtors.
CREDIT Joint Venture with... Account with all Sales made by him appertaining to the Joint Venture.
2. The Memorandum Joint Venture Account will be drawn up in the same manner as a Profit and Loss Account, i.e. DEBIT losses, CREDIT

gains. This Memorandum Account represents a complete account of all the transactions affecting the venture, i.e. the details contained in the Personal Accounts of both parties are entered in full in the Memorandum Account on the same side as in the Personal Accounts (*contra* items, such as cash and bills of exchange passing between the parties, being eliminated). The balance of this account will represent the profit or loss on the venture.

3. Each party will, in his own books:

(*a*) **Debit** the Personal Account of the other party with his *own* share of profit (**credit** Profit and Loss on Joint Venture Account).

(*b*) Credit the Personal Account of the other party with his *own* share of loss (**debit** Profit and Loss on Joint Venture Account).

4. The Personal Accounts of each party will now be found to show the same balance; such balances, however, will appear on the opposite sides in the respective books. For example, if A's books show a credit balance of £100 in favour of B, B's books will show a debit balance against A for the same amount.

Illustration 2

A and B enter into a joint venture in timber. A pays for timber £100, and expenses £10. B sells all the timber for £200 and pays expenses £40. They share profits and losses, three-fifths to A and two-fifths to B. Show Accounts (see p. 1603).

The balances on the accounts, which agree, will be settled by B giving A a cheque for £140.

It should be noted, therefore, that the Memorandum Joint Account is merely a combination of the two Personal Accounts. The vital object of this account is to find the Profit or Loss, from which each party will enter in his own books his share of profit by DEBITING his co-venturer (and crediting Profit and Loss on Joint Venture Account); and conversely for losses. As the two separate Personal Accounts contain, on the SAME sides, the contents of the Memorandum Joint Venture Account they must as between themselves be reflective, provided the balancing figure of the Memorandum Joint Venture Account is shown on the *same* side in the Personal Accounts and in the Memorandum Joint Venture Account.

Stock. Where the goods relating to the adventure are provided by one of the parties out of his ordinary business goods, that party will DEBIT the Personal Account of the other and CREDIT Purchases[1] Account with the

---

[1] If the goods are valued above or below cost, Purchases Account should be credited with the cost of the goods and the balance credited or debited to Profit and Loss on Joint Venture Account.

A's Books:

JOINT VENTURE WITH B

		£			£
Cash (or Creditors):			Balance . c/d		140
Cost of Timber .		100			
Expenses . .		10			
Share of Profit ($\frac{3}{5}$) .		30			
		£140			£140
Balance . b/d		140			

B's Books:

JOINT VENTURE WITH A

		£			£
Cash (or Creditors):			Cash (or Debtors):		
Expenses . .		40	Sale of Timber .		200
Share of Profit ($\frac{2}{5}$) .		20			
Balance . c/d		140			
		£200			£200
			Balance . b/d		140

Memorandum JOINT VENTURE

		£			£
Cost of Timber .		100	Proceeds of Sale of		
Expenses—			Timber . .		200
A . . .		10			
B . . .		40			
Profit—					
A, $\frac{3}{5}$ . . £30					
B, $\frac{2}{5}$ . . 20					
		50			
		£200			£200

figure at which it is agreed the goods shall be valued. This figure will, of course, be entered in the Memorandum Joint Venture Account on the debit (i.e. 'SAME' side).

If, at the close of the venture, there are goods on hand, and one of the parties takes them over at an agreed figure, he will **credit** the Personal Account of the other party (and debit Purchases Account with that amount). The same amount will be entered on the CREDIT side of the Memorandum Joint Venture Account (i.e. 'SAME' side).

Where an intermediate settlement is desired prior to the completion of the venture, and there is a certain amount of stock in the hands of either or both parties, special treatment is necessary. The total value of the stocks is brought down on the debit side of the Memorandum Joint Venture Account as a balance, and each party will bring down in the Personal Account in his books the amount of stock that he has on hand; this representing his share of assets still employed in the venture.

Illustration 3

A and B enter into a joint venture to sell a consignment of timber on 1st January 19.., sharing profits and losses equally. A provides the timber from stock at a mutually agreed value of £500. He pays expenses amounting to £25 during January. During the month B incurs expenses £65, and receives cash for sales £300. He also takes over goods to the value of £100 for use in his own business. At 31st January the stock in A's hands is valued at £110. The remaining stock of £110 was taken over by A for £120 on 2nd February 19...

The accounts for January and February will be as follows:

A's Books:

JOINT VENTURE WITH B

19..			£	19..			£
Jan. 1	Purchases Account .		500	Jan. 31	Share of Loss . .		40
31	Cash: Expenses .		25		Stock . . . c/d		110
					Balance . . c/d		375
			£525				£525
Feb. 1	Stock . . . b/d		110	Feb. 2	Purchases Account .		120
	Balance . . b/d		375		Balance . . c/d		370
2	*Share of Profit*		5				
			£490				£490
3	*Balance* . . b/d		370				

B's Books:

JOINT VENTURE WITH A

19..			£	19..			£
Jan. 31	Cash: Expenses .		65	Jan. 31	Cash: Sales . .		300
	Balance . . c/d		375		Purchase Account .		100
					Share of Loss .		40
			£440				£440
Feb. 2	*Share of Profit* .		5	Feb. 1	Balance . . b/d		375
	Balance . . c/d		370				
			£375				£375
				Feb. 3	*Balance* . . b/d		370

Memorandum JOINT VENTURE

19..			£	19..			£
Jan. 1	Cost of Timber		500	Jan. 31	Sales		300
	Expenses:				B: Stock taken over		100
31	A . . £25				Stock . . c/d		110
	B . . 65				Loss—		
			90		A, ½ . £40		
					B, ½ . 40		
							80
			£590				£590
Feb. 1	Stock . . b/d		110	Feb. 2	A: Stock taken over		120
2	Profit:—						
	A, ½ . . £5						
	B, ½ . . 5						
			10				
			£120				£120

NOTE. *February entries are in italics.*

An alternative method of bringing down the stock is to divide it up between the two parties in their profit-sharing ratios, and for each party to bring into the account in his books his share of the stock. In the account, this balance should be brought down separately and not merged in with the other items.

In the above illustration the balances brought down in the respective accounts would be as follows:

A's Books:

JOINT VENTURE WITH B

19..			£	19..			£
Jan. 1	Purchases Account .		500	Jan. 31	Share of Loss . .		40
31	Cash: Expenses .		25		Stock . . c/d		55
					Balance . . c/d		430
			£525				£525
Feb. 1	Stock . . b/d		55	Feb. 2	*Purchases Account .*		*120*
	Balance . . b/d		430		*Balance . . c/d*		*370*
2	*Share of Profit*		*5*				
			£490				£490
3	*Balance . . b/d*		*370*				

B's Books:

JOINT VENTURE WITH A

19.. Jan. 31			£	19.. Jan. 31			£
Jan. 31	Cash:			Jan. 31	Cash: Sales		300
	Expenses		65		Purchases Account		100
	Balance	c/d	430		Share of Loss		40
					Stock	c/d	55
			£495				£495
Feb. 1	Stock	b/d	55	Feb. 1	Balance	b/d	430
2	*Share of Profit*		5				
	Balance	c/d	370				
			£430				£430
				Feb. 3	Balance	b/d	370

This method has the advantage of showing:

1. the reflective nature of the balances in each person's books;
2. the respective interests in the stock.

If, in the above method, the whole of the stock is lost and written off, each party will write off £55, thus leaving a reciprocal balance of £430 to be settled by a cash payment in the ordinary way.

Stock in hand at the balancing date may usually be valued on the basis of cost plus a due proportion of the expenses attributable thereto (e.g. purchasing expenses, carriage inwards, etc., but not selling or distribution costs) or at net realizable value, if lower. Where other assets are held and depreciation is to be taken into account, the assets may be brought into the account at the balancing date at their written-down value, the depreciation charge being thus automatically included in the Profit or Loss figure. This can, of course, only be done where the assets have been previously debited to the Joint Venture Accounts. Otherwise, the agreed depreciation charges will be debited to the respective Joint Venture Accounts and credited to the respective Depreciation Accounts (or Asset Accounts).

Interest. Where the parties agree to the charging of interest on the various debits and credits to the date of completion of balancing, the Joint Venture Accounts are treated as Accounts Current.

In the *Memorandum* Joint Venture Account care must be taken to insert the interest figure **before** ascertaining the profit or loss on the venture. In the books of the respective parties the double entry for the amount of interest charged or allowed in the Joint Venture Accounts occurs in the INTEREST ACCOUNT, the balance of which is transferred to Profit and Loss Account. The interest on the cash transactions between the parties will not appear in the Memorandum Joint Venture Account as this is a charge affecting the parties themselves and distinct from the venture expenses.

A's Books (see p. 1609): (see p. 1609)

JOINT VENTURE WITH B

Dr.

Date		Fol.	Months	Interest	Principal
19..				£p	£p
Jan. 1	Cash: Goods		6	10·00	400·00
Feb. 1	" Expenses		5	0·63	30·00
Apr. 1	" "		3	0·38	30·00
June 30	Interest on Bill Contra		2	2·08	
	Share of Profit				36·88
	Interest				13·08
				£13·09	£509·96

Cr.

Date		Fol.	Months	Interest	Principal
19..				£p	£p
Jan. 1	Cheque				150·00
June 1	Bill due 1st Sept.		6	3·75	250·00
30	Interest				3·75
	Cheque from B				106·21
				£3·75	£509·96

B's Books:

JOINT VENTURE WITH A

Dr.

Date		Fol.	Months	Interest	Principal
19..				£p	£p
Jan. 1	Cheque		6	3·75	150·00
Mar. 1	Cash: Expenses		4	0·67	40·00
May 31	" "		1	0·58	140·00
June 1	Bill due 1st Sept.				250·00
	Share of Profit				36·87
30	Interest				5·00
	Cheque to A				106·21
				£5·00	£728·08

Cr.

Date		Fol.	Months	Interest	Principal
19..				£p	£p
Apr. 1	Cash: Sales		3	6·00	480·00
June 30	Interest on Bill Contra				240·00
	Interest		2	2·08	8·08
				£8·08	£728·08

Memorandum Joint Venture

Date		Months	Interest £p	Principal £p			Principal £p	Interest £p	Months	Date	
19..						19..					
Jan. 1	Goods	6	10·00	400·00		Apr. 1	480·00	6·00	3	Apr. 1	Sales
Feb. 1	Expenses—A	5	0·63	30·00			240·00		—		
Mar. 1	„ B	4	0·67	40·00			6·00			June 30	Interest
Apr. 1	„ A	3	0·38	30·00							
May 31	„ B	1	0·58	140·00							
June 30	Interest			12·25							
	Profit— A, ½ . 36·88										
	B, ½ . 36·87			73·75							
			£12·26	£726·00			£726·00	£6·00			

Note. No interest on Cash passing between the partners is included in the Memorandum Joint Venture Account. Except for the items in italics, the entries in the Personal Accounts are virtually duplicates of those on the SAME side as those in the Memorandum Joint Venture Account. The *net* interest in debit in the latter account is £6·25, i.e. £12·25 *less* £6.

In the Personal Accounts the interest items are shown:

		£p	
(1) B's Account in A's books	.	Dr.	9·33 [i.e. *Dr.* £13·08: *Cr.* £3·75]
(2) A's Account in B's books	.	Cr.	3·08 [i.e. *Cr.* £8·08: *Dr.* £5·00]
Net Interest, as above	.	Dr.	£6·25

In examinations, the details of interest need not be repeated in the memorandum Joint Venture Account, but merely the *net balance* of interest as per the personal accounts of the ventures (i.e. £6·25 debit).

Illustration 4

A and B enter into a joint venture in timber. On 1st January 19.., A buys timber, costing £400, and on the same day he receives a cheque from B for £150. A and B pay expenses as follows:

	A		B
1st Feb. . . . £30		1st Mar . . . . £ 40	
1st Apr. . . . £30		31st May £140	

B sells the timber in two amounts, namely, 1st April £480 and 30th June £240. They share profits and losses equally, and interest is to be allowed at 5 per cent per annum. On 1st June B gives A a three months' bill for £250, and on 30th June the venture is completed by a cheque between the parties. Calculate interest in months. Show accounts (see pp. 1607 and 1608).

Complete Double Entry Books. It has already been mentioned that, where the circumstances warrant the inauguration of a complete set of double entry books for the venture, no peculiarity of treatment usually arises in respect of the transactions. At the same time, it must be pointed out that in the separate books of each venturer cognizance must be taken of the amounts invested in, and the final result of, the venture. These entries in the latter books will be very similar to those arising where no separate double entry system of accounts exists for the venture. In other words, whatever the mode of procedure adopted for the ascertainment of the profit or loss on the venture may be, the entries made by each venturer in his own books will remain unaffected by the completeness or incompleteness of the records of the joint venture transactions themselves. The entries in the venturer's own books are:

1. The Assets brought into the joint venture are debited to the Personal Account of the co-venturer. (Cash, Bank, Purchases or Asset Account credited.)

2. Any receipt of bills of exchange or cash from the joint venture is credited to the Personal Account of the co-venturer. (Cash or Bills Receivable Account debited.)

3. Any taking over of goods or other assets: the Personal Account of the co-venturer is credited. (Purchases or Asset Account debited.)

4. Profit on the venture is **debited** to the Personal Account of the co-venturer and credited to Profit and Loss Account; and loss being **credited** to the Personal Account and debited to Profit and Loss Account.

In the Double Entry Joint Venture books there will appear a Personal Account for each venturer, who will be in credit for his contributions plus profits and less losses and drawings (if any). The balance of such Personal Account, if in credit, must correspond to the **debit** balance standing on the Joint Venture or Co-venturer's Account in the books of the venturer to whom the Personal Account relates.

The important point that requires emphasis is that if the parties are, say, A and B, the debit balance in A's books of account against B will be identical with the credit balance in the joint venture books in favour of A in respect of the latter's contributions, expenses, and share of profit, less any amounts received in respect of sales, withdrawals of cash or goods, and share of losses, because from each point of view it represents an amount owing to A and B. In the joint-venture books A is a creditor; in A's own books, therefore, B is a debtor. Similarly, in B's books, A will be in debit for B's contributions, expenses, and share of profit, less any amounts received in respect of sales, withdrawals of cash or goods, and share of losses, and this amount will be reflective of the amount of the credit balance standing in favour of B in the books of account of the joint venture. Thus in B's books A is a debtor and in the joint venture books B is a creditor. If the co-venturers have overdrawn the amount of their original capital contributions the position will be reversed, the debit balances appearing in the joint venture books, being the credit balances on the accounts of the respective venturers in each other's books.

The principle is illustrated below. The facts are made simple in order that the student may concentrate his attention solely on the principle involved above.

Illustration 5

A and B enter into a joint venture, contributing £1,000 and £800 respectively and sharing profits and losses 3:4. The purchases are £1,600 and the sales £2,000. The remaining stock is taken over by B for £100. Expenses paid are £60, and expenses outstanding unpaid, £20. Complete double entry records are kept. All transactions are for cash. A drew out £400.

Show the accounts:

1. In the separate joint venture books.
2. In each of the co-venturers' books as regards the Personal Accounts only.

JOINT VENTURE BOOKS
JOINT VENTURE TRADING ACCOUNT

			£				£
Purchases	.	.	1,600	Sales	.	.	2,000
Cash: Expenses			60	B: Goods taken			
Expenses	.	c/d	20	over	.	.	100
Profits—							
A, $\frac{3}{7}$.	. £180						
B, $\frac{4}{7}$.	. 240						
			——				
			420				
			£2,100				£2,100
				Expenses	.	b/d	20

A

			£				£
Cash	.	.	400		Cash	.	.	1,000
Balance	.	c/d	780		Share of Profits	.	180
			£1,180				£1,180
					Balance	.	b/d	780

B

			£				£
Joint Venture Trad-ing Account: Goods taken over	.	.	100		Cash	.	.	800
Balance	.	c/d	940		Share of Profits	.	240
			£1,040				£1,040
					Balance	.	b/d	940

CASH

			£				£
A	.	.	1,000		Joint Venture Trad-ing Account: Purchases	.	1,600
B	.	.	800				
Sales	.	.	2,000		Joint Venture Trad-ing Account: Expenses	.	60
					A	.	.	400
					Balance	.	c/d	1,740
			£3,800				£3,800
Balance	.	b/d	1,740				

It will be observed that the cash balance in hand is now sufficient to pay off the expense creditor (or creditors) for £20, and to pay out the venturers' balances.

The personal accounts of B and A in the books of A and B respectively are:

A's Books:

JOINT VENTURE WITH B .

		£				£
Cash . . .		1,000		Cash . . .		400
Share of Profits .		180		Balance . . c/d		780
		£1,180				£1.180
Balance . . b/d		780				

B's Books:

JOINT VENTURE WITH A

		£				£
Cash . . .		800		Goods taken over .		100
Share of Profits :		240		Balance . . c/d		940
		£1,040				£1,040
Balance . . b/d		940				

On settlement of the final balance the usual entries will be made:

In the Joint Venture books: debit A, £780; debit B, £940; debit Joint Venture Trading Account, £20: credit cash, £1,740.

In A's books: debit cash, £780; credit Joint Venture with B Account, £780.

In B's Books: debit cash, £940; credit Joint Venture with A Account, £940.

The following illustration should be carefully worked through, as it is considerably involved in detail.

General Illustration 6

Andrews and Bailey enter into a joint venture for the holding, purchase, and sale of investments, profits and losses to be shared in the ratio 3:2.

On 30th September 19.1, are purchased the following shares:

200 in A, Ltd., for £384
200 in B, Ltd., for £757
40 in R, Ltd., for £733

These are paid for on 1st October: Andrews provides £1,174 and Bailey pays the balance direct to the broker. The following are the dividends received and the transactions entered into:

Dividends Received:

		£
19.1		
Nov. 30.	Interim Dividend, A, Ltd	36
Dec. 30.	Dividend, X, Ltd.	7
19.2		
Jan. 1.	Dividend B, Ltd.	58
	Bonus of one Share for every two held, A, Ltd.	

Dealings:

		£
19.1		
Nov. 8.	Sale of 30 shares in R, Ltd.	405
Dec. 6.	100 Shares in B, Ltd., taken over by Andrews	280
19.2		
Jan. 15.	Sale of 10 Shares in R, Ltd.	120
Feb. 21.	Sale of 250 Shares in A, Ltd.	455

On 8th November 19.1, £81 is remitted to Bailey by the broker out of the proceeds of sale of 30 shares in R, Ltd.

On 1st December 19.1 were purchased 100 shares in X, Ltd., the broker, Roberts, agreeing to lend the £200 necessary for their purchase with interest at 5 per cent per annum, the sum to be repaid not later than 31st January 19.2. The shares are registered in the name of Roberts, and the dividend of £7 received on 30th December is applied in part repayment of the loan. The money received from the sale of ten shares in R, Ltd., on 15th January 19.2 is similarly applied in part repayment of the loan. On 31st January 19.2, the balance of the loan is completely repaid by cash.

The values of the holdings at 28th February 19.2 are:

100 Shares in B, Ltd., £450
100 Shares in X, Ltd., £80

The value of the holding in A, Ltd., is to be based on the fact that the purchase price at 30th September 19.1, included provision for four months' dividend, the half-year's dividend of £36 being paid on 30th November 19.1. The true cost value at 28th February 19.2 (taking bonus shares into account), is to be the basis of valuation of this investment. Subject to this proviso, all other dividends are to be considered as income.

The accounts recording these transactions in the Joint Venture books are required.

JOINT VENTURE BANK

19.1				£p	19.1				£p
Sept. 30	Andrews			1,174·00	Oct. 1	Broker			1,174·00
Nov. 8	Broker			324·00	19.2				
30	Dividend:				Jan. 31	,,			74·39
	A, Ltd			36·00	Feb. 28	Balance		c/d	798·61
19.2									
Jan. 1	Dividend:								
	B, Ltd.			58·00					
Feb. 21	Broker			455·00					
				£2,047·00					£2,047·00
19.2									
Mar. 1	Balance		b/d	798·61					

Joint Venture Books:

JOINT VENTURE

Date	Particulars		Nominal £	Principal £p
19.1				
Sept. 30	Broker— Purchase of Shares:			
	A, Ltd.		200	384·00
	B, Ltd.		200	757·00
	R, Ltd.		40	733·00
Dec. 1	Broker—Purchase of Shares: X, Ltd.		100	200·00
19.2				
Jan. 1	Bonus Dividend—A, Ltd.		100	
31	Broker's Interest			1·39
			£640	£2,075·39
19.2				
Mar. 1	Balance	b/d	250	590·00

Date	Particulars		Nominal £	Principal £p
19.1				
Nov. 8	Broker— Sale of Shares: R. Ltd.		30	405·00
30	Cash— Dividend, A, Ltd.			36·00
Dec. 6	Andrews: Investment taken over —Shares B, Ltd.		100	280·00
30	Broker— Dividend: X, Ltd.			7·00
19.2				
Jan. 1	Cash— Dividend, B, Ltd.			58·00
15	Broker—Sale of Shares: R, Ltd.		10	120·00
Feb. 21	Broker—Sale of Shares: A, Ltd.		250	455·00
28	Balance— Shares, A, Ltd.	c/d	50	60·00
	" B, Ltd.	c/d	100	450·00
	" X, Ltd.	c/d	100	80·00
	Loss— Andrews £74·63			
	Bailey 49·76			124·39
			£640	£2,075·39

BAILEY

		£p				£p
19.1				19.1		
Nov. 8	Broker	81·00		Oct. 1	Broker	700·00
19.2		49·76				
Feb. 28	Loss from Joint Venture Account	569·24				
	Balance c/d					
		£700·00				£700·00
				19.2		
				Mar. 1	Balance b/d	569·24

ANDREWS

		£p				£p
19.1				19.1		
Dec. 6	Joint Venture Account— 100 Shares in B, Ltd.	280·00		Oct. 1	Cash	1,174·00
19.2		74·63				
Feb. 28	Loss from Joint Venture Account	819·37				
	Balance c/d					
		£1,174·00				£1,174·00
				19.2		
				Mar. 1	Balance b/d	819·37

In order to show the credit balances of Bailey and Andrews more analytically, they might be subdivided into two parts, attributable to realized and unrealized capital invested respectively, i.e.:

	Bailey	Andrews
	£p	£p
Realized	215·24	583·37
Unrealized	354·00	236·00
	£569·24	£819·37

The realized capital invested represent the 'safe' and the unrealized the speculative balances: the latter would, or should, be held back pending the disposal of the remaining shares valued in the books at £590, which, if wholly lost, would be debited to Bailey and Andrews in the ratio of 3 : 2, i.e. £354 and £236.

LOAN (BROKER)

Debit

Date	Particulars	Months	Interest £p	Principal £p
19.1 Dec. 30	Dividend—X, Ltd.	1	0·03	7·00
19.2 Jan. 15	Sale of Shares in R, Ltd.	½	0·25	120·00
Jan. 31	Cheque			74·39
	Interest to contra		1·39	
			£1·67	£201·39

Credit

Date	Particulars	Months	Interest £p	Principal £p
19.1 Dec. 1	Joint Venture Account—Purchase of 100 Shares in X, Ltd.	2	1·67	200·00
19.2 Jan. 31	Interest from contra			1·39
			£1·67	£201·39

BROKER

Debit

Date	Particulars	Principal £
19.1 Oct. 1	Bailey—Cash	700
	Cheque	1,174
		£1,874
Nov. 8	Joint Venture Account—Sale of 30 Shares in R, Ltd.	405
19.2 Feb. 21	Joint Venture Account—Sale of 250 Shares in A, Ltd.	455

Credit

Date	Particulars	Principal £
19.1 Sept. 30	Joint Venture Account—200 Shares: A, Ltd.	384
	200 Shares: B, Ltd.	757
	40 Shares: R, Ltd.	733
		£1,874
Nov. 8	Bailey	81
	Cash	324
19.2 Feb. 21	Cash	455

TRIAL BALANCE
28th Feb. 19.2

	£p	£p
Bank	798·61	
Shares per Joint Venture Account	590·00	
Andrews		819·37
Bailey		569·24
	£1,388·61	£1,388·61

As regards the valuation of the holding in A, Ltd., after the issue of the bonus, 300 shares are held for a cost of £360; 50 shares, i.e. one-sixth, remain at 28th February 19.2, and are valued at

$$\tfrac{1}{6} \times £360 = £60$$

It should be noted that the opening payment by Bailey is transferred direct from Bailey's account to that of Roberts, the broker. In theory, such a transfer requires a Journal entry to record it.

The actual results, profit or loss, of the dealings in each investment can be shown (apart from dividends received, which may be recorded in a separate Dividend Account) by opening a separate account for each investment.

SHARES IN A, LTD.

			Nom £	£				Nom £	£
19.1 Sept. 30	Broker . .		200	384	19.1 Nov. 30	Dividend .			24
19.2 Jan. 1	Bonus. .		100		19.2 Feb. 21	Broker: Sale		250	455
Feb. 28	Profit . .			155	28	Balance .	c/d	50	60
			£300	£539				£300	£539
19.2 Mar. 1	Balance .	b/d	50	60					

SHARES IN B, LTD.

			Nom £	£				Nom £	£
19.1 Sept. 30	Broker . .		200	757	19.1 Dec. 6	Andrews . .		100	280
					19.2 Feb. 28	Balance	c/d	100	450
						Loss .			27
			£200	£757				£200	£757
19.2 Mar. 1	Balance .	b/d	100	450					

SHARES IN R, LTD.

19.1 Sept. 30	Broker		Nom £ 40	£ 733	19.1 Nov. 8 19.2 Jan. 15 Feb. 28	Broker: Sale. Broker: Sale Loss .		Nom £ 30 10	£ 405 120 208
			£40	£733				£40	£733

SHARES IN X, LTD.

19.1 Dec. 1	Broker: Loan	.	Nom £ 100	£ 200	19.2 Feb. 28	Balance Loss .	c/d	Nom £ 100	£ 80 120
			£100	£200				£100	£200
19.2 Mar. 1	Balance	b/d	100	80					

The foregoing accounts, if opened, will displace the detailed Joint Venture Account so far as shares are concerned, the profit or loss thereon being transferred to the Joint Venture Account which will then be:

JOINT VENTURE

			£p				£p
Loss on Shares— B, Ltd. R, Ltd. X, Ltd.	. . .	. . .	27·00 208·00 120·00	Profit on Shares— A, Ltd. Loss	. .	c/d	155·00 200·00
			£355·00				£355·00
Loss Broker's Interest	. .	b/d	200·00 1·39	Dividends— A, Ltd. £36 (less £24 credited to Assets) . £12 X, Ltd. . . 7 B, Ltd. . . 58			
				Loss	. .		77·00 124·39
			£201·39				£201·39

The balances on the separate Shares Accounts must be equal to that appearing in the Joint Venture Account constructed by the first method.

CHAPTER 17

CONSIGNMENT ACCOUNTS

IT is a common practice of exporters to dispatch goods to representatives abroad for the purpose of sale. The knowledge possessed by the agent of local conditions, the availability of the goods for the foreign customer by reason of the present possession of stock in the foreign agent's warehouse, and many other reasons, form a strong inducement to the exporter to enter into an arrangement with a reliable local trader whereby the latter will receive goods for sale on behalf of the exporter.

Goods forwarded by an exporter to his agent for the purpose of warehousing and ultimate sale are described as a consignment, the sender of the goods being called the consignor and the recipient the consignee. Alternatively, the parties concerned are often respectively designated principal and agent.

Such a dispatch of goods, from the point of view of the consignor, is called a Consignment Outwards; from that of the consignee, a Consignment Inwards.

At periodical intervals, the consignee renders to his consignor a statement showing the goods received, sales, expenses incurred, commission charged, and remittances made, with the resultant balance due by him. This is called an Account Sales.

Illustration 1

H. Andrews, of Manchester, consigned 40 cases of goods to his agent, H. Butler, of Sydney, per S.S. *San Pedro*, invoiced at £15 per case, and drew a bill at 90 days for £400. An Account Sales was received in due course from the consignee showing gross proceeds of sale £900 made up of 30 cases at £20 each and 10 at £30 each. He deducted the following items: Dock dues, £15; Marine Insurance, £7; Storage, £18; Import duty, £30; Commission, 5 per cent and 1 per cent *del credere* on sales. Show the Account Sales submitted to H. Andrews by H. Butler in respect of the above consignment. (See p. 1702.)

It is of considerable importance to observe that a consignment is not in the nature of a SALE by the consignor, nor of a PURCHASE by the consignee. It is clear that mere removal of goods from one department to another does not make a sale, and whether the removal is a matter of yards or miles it does not alter the significance of the transaction. It is usual to send to the consignee a memorandum, called a *pro forma* invoice, but this merely serves as a guide to the consignee unless, indeed, it is an actual instruction to sell at the price indicated in the invoice. For similar reasons, a consignment does not come under the heading of 'Goods on Sale or Return', 'Hire Purchase', or 'Forward Sale'. It is, then, merely a transfer of goods from one place to another with a view to the sale by the recipient on behalf of the sender.

ACCOUNT SALES of 40 cases of Goods ex S.S. *San Pedro*, sold for account of H. ANDREWS,
Manchester, by

H. BUTLER
10 OLD BAILEY STREET,
SYDNEY.

Marks and Number		£	£	£
	10 Cases at £20 per case			600
	10 ,, at £30 ,,			300
				900
	Less—			
	Dock Dues	15		
	Import Duty	30		
	Marine Insurance	7		
	Storage	18		
		—	70	
	Commission—			
	5% of £880	44		
	Del Credere—			
	1% of £900	9		
		—	53	
			—	123
				777
	Less Draft accepted against Consignment			400
	Balance due to H. Andrews			£377

E. & O.E.
Sydney.   (Signed) ...... *H. Butler* ....
Date ....

The consignee is entitled to be reimbursed for his legitimate expenditure, and to be paid his remuneration, it being clear that the consignee is neither a buyer nor a seller on his own account: consequently, the remuneration is his reward for services rendered to his consignor. The remuneration, which is termed commission, is usually calculated upon the total value of goods sold by the consignee. An additional commission, called *del credere* commission, is paid where the consignee agrees to meet any loss which the consignor may suffer by reason of bad debts. It must be noted that arrangements are frequently made whereby the consignee is paid on a percentage of profits.

Consignor's Books

The object of the book entries relating to Consignments Outwards is to ascertain the NET profit or NET loss on each separate consignment, and to transfer this figure to a Profit and Loss on Consignment Account.

A special account is opened to ascertain the profit or loss on each consignment, headed Consignment to — Account; thus if the consignment is sent to B, Bombay, the account will be headed Consignment to B, Bombay.

The Consignment Account is not a *personal* Account but a *nominal* account; it is, in fact, a special Trading and Profit and Loss Account. It is important that the nature of this account be clearly grasped, because the principles applied to Trading and Profit and Loss Accounts are applicable to Consignment Accounts. The consignee is not the consignor's *debtor* for the goods (either at sale or cost price), the relationship of the parties being respectively Agent and Principal as distinct from Purchaser and Vendor.

Usually the Consignment Account is debited with the goods at cost[1] price and a Goods on Consignment Account credited; the balance of the latter account at the end of the accounting period being transferred in total to the credit of Purchases Account, or, alternatively, direct to the Trading Account.

All the expenses incurred by the consignor in respect of the consignment are debited to the Consignment Account and credited to cash or creditors, according to whether the expense is a cash or credit transaction. If the consignment expenses have been posted to the different expenses accounts, they will be transferred therefrom to the debit of the Consignment Account.

Upon receipt of the Account Sales from the consignee, a Personal Account is opened for him. The consignee owes to the consignor the proceeds of the sale, less any expenses (including commission) that he has properly incurred in respect of the particular consignment. Accordingly, the GROSS proceeds of the sale are debited to the Personal Account of the consignee and credited to the Consignment Account, or the net figure (i.e. the gross proceeds, less expenses) may be debited to the account of the consignee and credited to the Consignment Account. The latter method, however, is emphatically not recommended, because the true sales and expenses are not disclosed. Where the consignee remits a bill or draft in final settlement of the balance due, his Personal Account will be credited, and Bills Receivable or Bank debited. It must not be inferred that the consignee always remits in full the balance due to his consignor, and it may happen at any particular date that the consignee's Personal Account is not 'in balance', but as it is an ordinary Personal Account the student is not likely to be confronted with any difficulty in his treatment of it. If the consignee has not remitted the balance due by him in FULL, but only in PART, he will be a *debtor*, whereas if he has remitted MORE than the balance due by him he will be a *creditor*. In practice, considerable difficulties arise by reason of the failure of the parties to 'clear' each consignment as and when closed, particularly when the consignee remits round sums from time to time.

The Consignment Account will now contain on the debit side: (a) the cost[1] price of the goods, and (b) all the expenses relevant to the consignment, and on the credit (a) the Total Sales and (b) the Stock on Hand, if any, which will either be brought down as a balance on the debit of the Consignment Account for the succeeding period or be transferred to the debit of Consignment Stock Account (the second procedure being analogous to that pursued in the case of the Trading Account). the balance now standing on the account represents the profit or loss on the consignment. If a profit has resulted, it will be entered on the debit side, and transferred to the credit of Profit and Loss on Consignment Account; if a loss has ensued, it will be entered on the credit side and transferred to the debit of

---

[1] The consignor may, however, have charged the goods to the Consignment Account at SELLING PRICE. The treatment arising therefrom is shown on p. 1711.

Profit and Loss on Consignment Account. The balance of the latter will be transferred to the General Profit and Loss Account at the end of the accounting period.

Finally, it must be noted that where transactions with the consignee are numerous, it is usually advisable to open separate accounts duly referenced for each consignment so as to avoid the confusion which is likely to arise by consolidating all the consignments in one account.

Cost Price Method

Summary of Entries. Before proceeding with an example, it is proposed to give a summary of the entries appropriate to Consignment Accounts, namely:

1. Debit Consignment Account with the cost price of the goods and credit Goods on Consignment Account.

2. Debit Consignment Account with all expenses paid by the consignor in respect of the consignment and credit cash, creditors or expenses accounts.

3. When the Account Sales is received from the consignee, two entries are made, viz.:

(a) Debit consignee, credit Consignment Account with TOTAL SALES.

(b) Debit Consignment Account, credit consignee with all expenses incurred by the consignee and with his commission.

4. Credit consignment Account with Stock on Hand, and

(a) bring down as a balance *or*
(b) debit Consignment Stock Account.

5. Transfer the balance of the Consignment Account to Profit and Loss on Consignment Account and the balance of that account to General Profit and Loss Account.

6. Debit the balance of Goods on Consignment Account and credit

(a) Purchases Account *or*
(b) Trading Account.

7. Credit consignee, debit Cash or Bills Receivable with remittances received from the consignee.

Illustration 2

C. Cotton, of Manchester, on 3rd January consigns goods, costing £1,000, to R. Rajah, his foreign agent. C. Cotton pays the following expenses on the same date, viz.: Marine Insurance, £20; Carriage and Freight, £70. R. Rajah is entitled to a 5 per cent selling commission and a $1\frac{1}{4}$ per cent *del credere* commission. In due course R. Rajah sends his Account Sales, which shows that he has sold goods for £1,600 and paid expenses amounting to £120; the expenses were paid on 4th February and the sale effected on 12th February. stock in consignee's hands on 28th February, £30.

With the Account Sales, R. Rajah encloses a sight draft for the net amount due to C. Cotton. Show accounts of the consignment at 28th February in the books of the consignor.

GOODS ON CONSIGNMENT

				19..		£
				Jan. 3	Consignment to R. Rajah . . .	1,000[1]

[1] Subsequently transferred to the credit of Purchases or Trading Account.

CONSIGNMENT TO R. RAJAH

19..			£	19..			£
Jan. 3	Goods on Consignment . . .		1,000	Feb. 12	R. Rajah—Sales—per Account Sales . . .		1,600
	Cash—Insurance .		20	28	Stock . . . c/d		30
	Carriage and Freight		70				
Feb. 4	R. Rajah—Expenses .		120				
12	Commissions . .		100				
28	Profit and Loss on Consignment Account		320				
			£1,630				£1,630
19..							
Mar. 1	Stock . . . b/d		30				

PROFIT AND LOSS ON CONSIGNMENT

				19..		£
				Feb. 28	Consignment to R. Rajah . . .	320[2]

[2] Subsequently transferred to the credit of General Profit and Loss Account.

R. RAJAH

19..			£	19..		£
Feb. 12	Consignment to R. Rajah—Sales . . .		1,600	Feb. 4	Expenses . .	120
				12	Commissions . .	100
				28	Draft . .	1,380
			£1,600			£1,600

It should now be clear that the Consignment Account is a Profit and Loss Account, whilst the Consignee's Account is a personal Account to which the ordinary principles of book-keeping apply.

Should there be a large number of consignments, the consignor will almost invariably employ a special Day Book or Journal and Ledger. In the Day Book or Journal (called the Consignments Day Book or Journal) will be entered the cost price of the goods sent on consignment (and, if necessary, a memorandum column therein will show the *pro forma* invoice price). From the Day Book or Journal the cost price of the Consignment will be debited to the consignment Account in question. The total of such Day Book or Journal will be periodically posted to the credit of goods on Consignment Account. The memorandum column may also be totalled, but it forms no part of the double entry.

Valuation of Unsold Stock

Where all the goods have not been sold it is necessary to value the unsold stock when preparing the Balance Sheet of the consignor. The valuation will be at the lower of cost price or local net realizable value, and to the *former* figure must be added the non-recurring expenses, such as freight, insurance, duties, etc., the total of these expenses being apportioned between stock on hand and goods sold. It should be emphasized, however, that if the cost price (with the addition mentioned) exceeds the local net realizable value, the latter must be taken as the basis of valuation.

Regarding the choice of cost or net realizable value reference to the dates and prices of recent sales will afford some guide; whilst other factors might materially alter valuations, e.g. devaluation of currency.

If the goods have a poor market at the local establishment it may be advisable to transfer them to another establishment offering better prospects, thus involving cost of transport, further duties, and possibly deterioration through climatic or other causes, so that the values may have to be adjusted accordingly, regard being had to local selling price (if lower than the adjusted value).

If goods are in transit or in 'risk' areas they should be taken into account at a value not exceeding the insured value.

Illustration 3

G. Britain consigns 1,000 units of goods to H. Kong, the cost price of which is £800. G. Britain pays expenses:

1.	Carriage	£200
2.	Marine Insurance	80
3.	Freight	90

and H. Kong has incurred expenses to date of:

4.	Carriage from Docks to Consignee's Warehouse	£15
5.	Import Duty	45
6.	Carriage to the Buyer's Warehouse	50
7.	Commission	8
8.	Expenses on goods sold	5

At a date when 600 units of the stock have been sold, it is required to balance off the Consignment Account, and accordingly the stock remaining must be carried down, being valued as shown on p. 1707.

Only the items (1) to (5) may be described as being attachable to the whole of the goods, and accordingly four-tenths (i.e. the ratio of the unsold stock to the total stock consigned) of these expenses are carried down with the stock in one figure.

The amount to be carried down is £492 arrived at as follows:

$$\frac{4}{10} \times (£800 + 430) = £492, \text{ i.e. 400 units at £0·80 per unit (£320) plus } \frac{4}{10} \text{ of £430 (£172).}$$

Another way of stating the rule is this: that the stock on hand at the end of the accounting period of the consignor must be evaluated at the lower of current local net realizable value or cost, as understood in a special sense, viz., by the inclusion of a proportionate part of all expenses incurred in respect of the *whole* consignment and not being of a RECUR-RING nature, such as Selling expenses. Therefore, in order to arrive at true cost, one must add to cost such proportion of the 'all in' expenses that the UNSOLD stock bears to the WHOLE stock; or what amounts to the same thing, the valuation of the stock is the remaining stock divided by original stock multiplied by the *whole* cost of the consignment.

Illustration 4

100 units are consigned at £1 each. Expenses paid by the consignor are £20; by the consignee (applicable to the whole consignment) £30; 75 units of the goods are sold by the agent for £250, his commission being 6 per cent on sales.

Show the Consignment Account as it appears in the consignor's books.

CONSIGNMENT ACCOUNT

		Units	£p				Units	£p
Goods on Consignment Account		100	100·00		Consignee: Sales per Account Sales		75	250·00
Expenses			20·00		Stock[1]	c/d	25	37·50
,,			30·00					
Commission 6% on £250			15·00					
Profit and Loss on Consignment Account			122·50					
		100	£287·50				100	£287·50
Stock	b/d	25	37·50					

[1] i.e. $\frac{25}{100} \times £100 = £25$ (£1 per unit) plus $\frac{25}{100} \times £50 = £12·50$ Total, £37·50 *or* $\frac{25}{100} \times £150 = £37·50$. The "all in" cost per unit is £1·50 $\left[\text{i.e. } \frac{150}{100} \text{ of £1}\right]$ hence the value of Stock at cost is 25 units at £1·50 each = £37·50.

If the current net realizable value is less than £37·50, the former valuation would be substituted for that shown above.

Loss of Stock. Where some of the goods are lost or damaged, the entries to adjust the position in the books will depend upon whether the loss has been insured against or not. If the goods have been insured against loss or damage, the loss (without taking into account any anticipated profit) will be credited to Consignment Account and debited to Insurance or Underwriter's Account. In cases of this type, care must be taken in arriving at the value of the stock carried down, as the expenses relating thereto must be added to the cost in the proper proportion.

The valuation of the remaining goods in case of goods lost will be made up of two parts as follows:

1. Proportion of the cost of the goods, plus expenses incurred on all goods.

2. Proportion of the expenses incurred subsequent to loss.

As to (1), this proportion will be the remaining goods divided by the total goods consigned.

As to (2), this proportion will be the remaining goods divided by the total goods saved.

Illustration 5

100 bales of goods are consigned (value £500) and 5 bales are damaged by fire and rendered worthless, a claim being made therefor against the insurance company.

The expenses may be summarized as follows:

Prior to Loss	Subsequent to Loss	
Non-recurring £ 80	Non-recurring £ 190	Selling £ 300

Up to the end of the accounting period 55 bales had been sold for £700. Show Consignment Account in the books of the consignor.

CONSIGNMENT ACCOUNT

19..		Bales	£	19..		Bales	£
	Cost of Goods	100	500		Sales	55	700
	Expenses prior to Loss		80		Insurance Claim Account	5	29
	Expenses subsequent to Loss		190		Stock c/d	40	312
	Selling Expenses		300		Transfer to Profit and Loss on Consignment Account: Loss		29
		100	£1,070			100	£1,070
	Stock b/d	40	312				

The claim against the insurer for £29 is made up:

$$\text{Cost of Goods} = \tfrac{5}{100} \times £500 \qquad £25$$
$$\text{Expenses prior to Loss} = \tfrac{5}{100} \times £80 = \qquad 4$$
$$\overline{£29}$$

The Stock value of £312 is arrived at:

		£	£
Cost of Goods	$\tfrac{40}{100} \times £500 = 200$		
Expenses prior to Loss	$\tfrac{40}{100} \times £80 = 32$		
		232	(per rule 1)
Expenses subsequent to Loss	$\tfrac{40}{95} \times £190 =$	80	(per rule 2)
		£312	

The result may be more clearly explained by opening two separate accounts as follows:

(*a*) Consignment Account (I) showing goods lost.
(*b*) Consignment Account (II) showing saleable goods.

CONSIGNMENT ACCOUNT (I)

19..		Bales	£	19..			Bales	£
	Cost of Goods	5	25		Insurance Claim			
	Expenses prior to Loss[1]		4		Account	.	5	29
		5	£29				5	£29

[1] $\frac{5}{100} \times £80$.

CONSIGNMENT ACCOUNT (II)

19..		Bales	£	19..			Bales	£
	Cost of Goods	95	475		Sales . .		55	700
	Expenses prior to Loss		76		Stock[2] . . c/d		40	312
	Expenses subsequent to Loss		190		Transfer to Profit and Loss on Consignment Account:			
	Selling Expenses		300		Loss . .			29
		95	£1,041				95	£1,041
	Stock . . b/d	40	312					

[2] i.e. $\frac{40}{95} \times £741$, as ALL these expenses have reference to the 95 bales.

Where the loss is not insured against, it must not be left to adjust itself in the Consignment Account by merely inserting the stock as reduced by the loss, but, as the consignor is bearing his own insurance, the loss should be dealt with by crediting Consignment Account as if the stock actually existed, and debiting Uninsured Loss Account. This method has the additional advantage of permitting comparison of the results of several consignments as shown by the Consignment Accounts (as the abnormal loss has been eliminated). The entries necessary to adjust such a loss in the above circumstances are the same as where the loss has been insured against, except that the amount of loss is carried to the debit of Uninsured Loss Account instead of to the Insurance Claim Account.

Loss Due to Natural Causes. Where the loss is due to natural causes, e.g. evaporation, the amount of stock to be carried down is the proportion of the total cost that the number of units on hand bears to the total number of units diminished by the loss.

Illustration 6

100 tons consigned, costing £200,000; 5 tons loss due to weighing, carting, etc.; 38 tons in hand. The stock in hand is therefore valued $\frac{38}{95} \times £200,000 = £80,000$.

Deficiency of Stock. Where there is a deficiency of stock at stocktaking, and the consignee is under a liability to account for the value of the missing stock, the following entry will be made in the consignor's books:

Dr. Consignee.   Cr. Consignment Account.

If, on the other hand, he is not liable, then the stock will be brought in at the gross figure (the amount it **ought** to be) and the deficiency debited to consignment account, only the actual stock figure being brought down. Alternatively, the closing stock will be brought in at the reduced figure automatically giving effect to the deficiency, e.g. if the stock ought to be £400, and there is a shortage of £50, the credit to Consignment Account will be £350 only, thus reducing the profit (or augmenting the loss) automatically by £50. This latter method is not recommended.

The entries are:

(1)   CONSIGNMENT ACCOUNT[1]

		£			£
Goods		—	Proceeds . . .		
Expenses		—	Stock . . .		400
Loss in Stock . . .		50			
Stock	b/d	350			

or

(2)   CONSIGNMENT ACCOUNT

		£			£
			Stock	c/d	350
Stock . . .	b/d	350			

[1] The figures are confined to the point under discussion.

On no account must the deficiency of Stock be debited to Consignment Account, unless it is included in the closing stock on the credit side.

Where an allowance is given, say, for damage (the goods still being saleable) the expenses to be added to the remaining stock may be apportioned as shown in the following illustration.

Illustration 7

Goods worth £1,000 are sent to Y on consignment; expenses, other than Selling Expenses of 5 per cent on sales, being £100. £500 of the goods are received in a damaged condition, the consignor making an allowance of £300. Sales by the consignee are £400 (cost £250), and the damaged goods are disposed of for £210. Show the treatment of the end stock.

The value of the closing stock will be the cost price plus a proportion of expenses. Expenses may be apportioned:

1. In the ratio that unsold stock bears to the revised value of goods consigned: $\frac{250}{700} \times £100 = £35·71$.

2. In the ratio that undamaged stock unsold bears to the total undamaged goods consigned: $\frac{250}{500} \times £100 = £50$.

Method (1) is probably preferable, for the expenses are incurred in respect of the total consignment, and damaged goods must bear their proportion as well as undamaged goods.

If no *damaged* goods are sold, the proportion to be added to cost will be computed as follows:

Original value of Goods sent	£1,000
Less Allowance	300
∴ Revised value of Goods sent	£700
The damaged goods remaining $= £500 - 300 =$	£200
The undamaged goods remaining $= £500 - 250 =$	250
(i.e. £250 have been sold) TOTAL	$= £450$
Proof—	
Revised value of Goods	£700
Less Sales	250
Goods remaining	£450

The addition for Expenses will be (under method (1))—
$\frac{450}{700} \times £100$ (Expenses) . . £64·29

If the goods are considered in units rather than in bulk, each unit should bear its due proportion of expenses and the closing stock will be valued in accordance with the rules enunciated earlier in this chapter.

Invoice Price Method

It is sometimes found that the goods sent on consignment are entered up in the books at the *pro forma* price; that is, they may be entered, either at the minimum price at which the consignee is entitled to sell the goods, or at the price which is considered by the consignee to represent a satisfactory profit on the goods. The actual price realized is not known by the consignor until the consignee renders the Account Sales.

Summary of Entries—Invoice Price Method. Where goods are invoiced at selling price, the entries in the consignor's books are:

1. Debit Consignment Stock Account and credit Goods on Consignment Account with consignment at SELLING PRICE.

2. At the end of the accounting period:

Debit Goods on Consignment Account and credit Purchases Account with the *true* cost of the goods;

Debit Goods on Consignment Account and credit Consignment Stock

Adjustment Account with the amount added to cost or, as it is termed, 'Loading'.

3. The sales by the consignee will be debited to the consignee and credited to the Consignment Stock Account.

4. The balance of stock on consignment will be credited at the SELLING price and brought down to the opposite side (like any other balance) on Consignment Stock Account.

5. The 'all in' expenses must be shown in a SEPARATE expenses account and apportioned in the ratio of the unsold stock to the stock sold; the amount apportionable to unsold stock must be carried forward and the balance transferred to Consignment Trading Account. The expenses may be debited direct to Consignment Trading Account and the amount apportionable to unsold stock brought down as a balance thereon.

6. Debit the Stock Adjustment Account and credit the Consignment Trading Account with the REALIZED profit representing the excess of selling price over cost.

7. Bring down the balance on Consignment Stock Adjustment Account (debit above the line: credit below the line) being the loading on REMAINING stock. This balance will, in the Balance Sheet, be deducted from stock at selling price shown in (4), plus (5). If the current net realizable value is less than the cost, as shown by the excess of (4) and (5) over (7), a provision must be created by debiting Profit and Loss on Consignment Account and crediting Stock Provision, representing the depreciation of stock value.

8. The balance of Profit and Loss on Consignment Account is transferred to the General Profit and Loss Account.

Illustration 8

A, of London, consigned 100 cases of goods (cost £750) to B, of Singapore, on 1st January 19.., charging them up at a *pro forma* invoice price to show a profit of 25 per cent on sales. A paid at the same date £60 in respect of freight and insurance. On 22nd January, B paid expenses, £20, and on 29th January sold 80 cases of the consignment for £800. B is entitled to a commission on sales of 5 per cent, which he duly charged up.

The following are the accounts recording the transaction in the books of A, the consignor, the books being balanced on 30th January 19...

GOODS ON CONSIGNMENT

			£	19..			£
Jan. 30	Purchases (or Trading) Account . . Consignment Stock Adjustment Account .		750 250	Jan. 1	Consignment Stock Account . .		1,000
			£1,000				£1,000

CONSIGNMENT STOCK

19..		Cases	£	19..			Cases	£
Jan. 1	Goods on Consignment Account	100	1,000	Jan. 29	B—(Consignee) Sales		80	800
				30	Stock . c/d		20	200
		100	£1,000				100	£1,000
19..								
Jan. 31	Stock . b/d	20	200					

CONSIGNMENT TRADING ACCOUNT

19..				£	19..				£
Jan. 1	Cash—Freight and Insurance			60	Jan. 29	Consignment Stock Adjustment Account			200
22	B—(Consignee) Expenses			20	30	Expenses $\frac{20}{100}[£60 + £20]$ c/d			16
29	Commission			40					
30	Profit and Loss on Consignment Account			96					
				£216					£216
19..									
Jan. 31	Expenses b/d			16					

B (CONSIGNEE)

19..				£	19..				£
Jan. 29	Consignment Stock Account—Sales			800	Jan. 22	Consignment Trading Account—Expenses			20
					29	Commission			40
					30	Balance . c/d			740
				£800					£800
19..									
Jan. 31	Balance . b/d			740					

CONSIGNMENT STOCK ADJUSTMENT ACCOUNT

19..			Cases	£	19..			Cases	£
Jan. 29	Consignment Trading Account[1]		80	200	Jan. 30	Goods on Consignment Account		100	250
30	Balance . c/d		20	50					
			100	£250				100	£250
					19..				
					Jan. 31	Balance . b/d		20	50

PROFIT AND LOSS ON CONSIGNMENT ACCOUNT

				19..			£
				Jan. 30	Consignment Trading Account		96

[1] i.e. 80 cases at £2·50 each.

The stock brought down will be shown in the Balance Sheet as follows:

	£
Consignment Stock	200
Trading Account (Expenses b/d) . .	16
	216
Less Stock Adjustment Account . .	50
	£166

Memorandum Column Method

It is important to note that, wherever practicable, and most certainly in examinations where no other method is specifically called for, the memorandum column method should be employed.

Illustration 9

With particulars identical to those set out in the preceding illustration, the accounts under this method appear as follows:

CONSIGNMENT STOCK

			Cases	Memo. £	£				Cases	Memo. £	£
19.. Jan. 1	Goods on Consignment Account	.	100	1,000	750	19.. Jan. 29 30	B (Consignee) . Stock . .	c/d	80 20	800 200	800 150
30	Consignment Trading Account	.			200						
			100	£1,000	£950				100	£1,000	£950
Jan. 31	Stock .	b/d	20	200	150						

CONSIGNMENT TRADING ACCOUNT

				£				£
19.. Jan. 1	Cash— Freight and Insurance			60	19.. Jan. 30	Consignment Stock Account Expenses ⅘ (60+£20)	c/d	200 16
22	B: (Consignee)— Expenses . .			20				
29	B: Commission			40				
30	Profit and Loss on Consignment Account			96				
				£216				£216
Jan. 31	Expenses . . .	b/d		16				

B (Consignee)

			£					£
19.. Jan. 29	Consignment Stock Account— Sales		800	19.. Jan. 22	Consignment Trading Account— Expenses			20
				29	Commission			40
				30	Balance		c/d	740
			£800					£800
Jan. 31	Balance	b/d	740					

Goods on Consignment

		Cases	Memo. £	£			Cases	Memo. £	£
19.. Jan. 30	Purchases or Trading Account	100	£1,000	£750	19.. Jan. 1	Consignment Stock Account	100	£1,000	£750

The Consignment Account would appear (if charged up at cost) as follows:

Consignment Account (abbreviated)

		Cases	£			Cases	£
Goods, etc.		100	750 ⎫	Sales		80	800
Expenses			60 ⎬	Stock	c/d	20	166
,,			20 ⎭	[$\frac{20}{100} \times £830$]			
Selling Commission			40				
Profit and Loss on Consignment Account			96				
		100	£966			100	£966
Stock	b/d	20	166				

Illustration 10

On 5th March 19 . ., X consigns 200 record players to Y, costing £15 each. The *pro forma* invoice is made out to him at a figure to show a *gross* profit of 20 per cent on sales, below which figure the consignee Y is not permitted to sell. On 25th March the consignee sells half the consignment at a profit of 25 per cent on sales. The expenses were as follows:

Mar. 5.	Freight and Insurance	£50 (paid by consignor)
20.	Landing Charges, including Import Duties	£50 (paid by consignee)

The consignee is entitled to a commission of 5 per cent on sales and to one-sixth of the profits after charging up both commission and share of profits. On 31st March 19 . ., Y remits a sight draft—the balance on his account having been agreed—to settle his account.

Show the entries in the books of X, the consignor.

Y (CONSIGNEE)

19..			£	19..			£
Mar. 25	Consignment to Y Account—			Mar. 20	Consignment to Y Account—		
	Sales		2,000		Landing Charges, etc.		50
				25	Commission		100
				31	Share of Profits		50
					Sight Draft		1,800
			£2,000				£2,000

Goods on Consignment

			Units	Memo	
				£	£
19.. Mar. 5	Consignment to Y Account		200	3,750	3,000

Consignment to Y

Dr. side

		Units	Memo		
			£	£	
19.. Mar. 5	Goods on Consignment Account	200	3,750	3,000	
	Bank—Freight and Insurance			50	
20	Y (Consignee)—Landing Charges, etc.			50	
25	Commission			100	
31	Share of Profit			50	
	Profit and Loss on Consignment Account			300	
		200	£3,750	£3,550	
Apr. 1	Stock b/d	100	1,875	1,550	

Cr. side

		Units	Memo		
			£	£	
19.. Mar. 25	Y (Consignee)—Sales	100	1,875	2,000	
31	Stock c/d i.e. $\frac{1}{2} \times £[3,000 + 50 + 50]$	100	1,875	1,550	
		200	£3,750	£3,550	

BANK

19..			£	19..			£
Mar. 31	Y (Sight Draft)		1,800	Mar. 5	Consignment to Y Account— Freight and Insurance .		50

PROFIT AND LOSS ON CONSIGNMENT ACCOUNT

				19..			£
				Mar. 31	Consignment to Y Account . . .		300

Note. Y, the consignee, is entitled to 5 per cent on sales, i.e. 5 per cent on £2,000 = £100; and one-sixth of £300 [i.e. one-seventh of £350].

Consignor's Books—Alternative Entries. The following procedure may be adopted in dealing with the closing stock in the consignor's books:

1. The closing stock is credited to the Consignment Account and brought down in the usual way.

2. The closing stock is debited to Goods on Consignment Account and brought down as a credit balance.

3. The effect, therefore, is to eliminate the stock balance on the Consignment Account and to reduce the credit to Purchases Account, i.e. the General Purchases Account of the business only shows a reduction to the extent of the Goods on Consignment actually **sold**; consequently, the General Trading Account must include the **cost price** of the unsold Stock on Consignment.

4. The loading for carried-forward expenses is brought down as a debit balance on Goods on Consignment Account.

In short, the unsold Stock on Consignment is considered as general stock, since the reduced credit to Purchases from Goods on Consignment Account, as it were, brings back into the General Trading Account such unsold stock, and hence it must be included in the stock figure in the General Trading Account.

Illustration 11

A consigns to B 100 units of goods (costing £1,000) and pays expenses, £50. B sells 60 units for £700, landing expenses being £20. B is entitled to a selling commission of 5 per cent.

Show the treatment of end stock in the books of the consignor.

CONSIGNMENT TO B

	Units	£			Units	£
Goods on Consignment Account	100	1,000	B—Sales . . .		60	700
Cash—Expenses .		50	Stock . . . c/d		40	428
B—Expenses		20				
B—Commission		35				
Profit and Loss on Consignment Account . .		23				
	100	£1,128			100	£1,128
Stock . . b/d	40	428				

GOODS ON CONSIGNMENT

		£				£
Stock . . c/d		428	Consignment to B Account . .			1,000
Purchases (or Trading) Account		600	Expenses prepaid . . c/d			28
		£1,028				£1,028
Expenses prepaid . b/d		28	Stock . . . b/d			428

STOCK ON CONSIGNMENT

	£		
Trading Account .	400		

The Trading Account will have been credited with £600 only, and therefore stock of £400 will have to be credited to Trading Account and debited to Stock on Consignment Account.

This item, 'Stock on Consignment', will be shown as an asset on the Balance Sheet of the consignor, as also will be the item of 'Expenses prepaid' in respect of this stock. If, when the Consignor's Accounts are being drawn up, it is found that a considerable loss has resulted on the consignment to date, it may be necessary to create a provision against a similar loss resulting on the remaining portion of the goods unless the realized loss is due to some abnormal cause. Further, if the net realizable value is less than the cost price plus the expenses, it will be necessary to introduce such lower figure into the books.

Where goods are invoiced at selling price, it by no means follows that the consignee's sales will exactly produce such a price. As, however, the Consignment Stock Account is built up on the basis of precise selling price, any difference between the 'charge up' price to the consignee and the actual realization must be transferred to Consignment Trading Account, which will increase the profit in the event of an 'excess' realized price, and conversely for a 'deficient' realized price. There will, therefore, be three separate elements in the Consignment Trading Account, as listed on p. 1720.

1. Profit on the stock realized, representing the excess of the 'charge up' price over the cost.

2. Profit or loss, representing excess or deficiency between realized price and 'charge up' price.

3. Expenses.

Illustration 12

A buys 100 cases costing £1 each and consigns them to his agent at $33\frac{1}{3}$ per cent on selling price. The agent sells 60 cases at a profit of 5 per cent on the cost to him. A pays expenses amounting to £100; and the agent's commission amounts to £9.

Show the Ledger Accounts in the books of the consignor.

Invoice Price Method

CONSIGNMENT STOCK

		Cases	£p			Cases	£p
Goods on Consignment Account		100	150·00	Sales[1]		60	94·50
Consignment Trading Account[1]			4·50	Stock	c/d	40	60·00
		100	£154·50			100	£154·50
Stock	b/d	40	60·00				

GOODS ON CONSIGNMENT

	£p		£p
Purchases (or Trading) Account	100·00	Consignment Stock Account	150·00
Consignment Stock Adjustment Account	50·00		
	£150·00		£150·00

CONSIGNMENT TRADING ACCOUNT

	£p		£p
Expenses[2]	100·00	Consignment Stock Account—	
Consignee's Commission[2]	9·00	Profit on Consignment Stock[1]	4·50
		Consignment Stock Adjustment Account—	
		Profit on "charge up" price[3]	30·00
		Proportion of Expenses[2] c/d	40·00
		Profit and Loss on Consignment Account	34·50
	£109·00		£109·00
Expenses b/d	40·00		

CONSIGNMENT STOCK ADJUSTMENT ACCOUNT

		£p				£p
Provision on Unsold Stock	c/d	20·00		Goods on Consignment Account		50·00
Consignment Trading Account						
Profit on Stock realized		30·00				
		£50·00				£50·00
				Provision	b/d	20·00

CONSIGNEE

		£p				£p
Consignment Stock— Sales		94·50		Consignment Trading Account:		
				Commission		9·00
				Balance	c/d	85·50
		£94·50				£94·50
Balance	b/d	85·50				

The Balance Sheet will show Consignment Stock £80, made up as follows:

	£
Consignment Stock	60
Consignment Expenses	40
	100
Less Consignment Stock Adjustment Account	20
	£80

If the ordinary procedure be adopted the Consignment Account and Goods sent on Consignment Account would in abbreviated form be as below (no difference arising in the case of the Consignee's Account).

---

[1] If the goods were sold at the precise loaded price, this would be 60 at £1·50, i.e. £90. They were sold at £90 plus 5 per cent thereon, realizing £94·50, therefore £4·50 is the 'excess' profit, transferred to Consignment Trading Account.

[2] These items could be shown on a separate Expenses Account, and the balance of £69 only transferred.

[3] 50% of £60, or $33\frac{1}{3}$% of £90.

Cost Price Method

CONSIGNMENT ACCOUNT

		Cases	£p			Cases	£p
Goods		100	100·00	Sales . .		60	94·50
Expenses			100·00	Stock . . c/d		40	80·00
Commission .			9·00	Profit and Loss on Consignment Account .			
							34·50
		100	£209·00			100	£209·00
Stock[1] .	b/d	40	80·00				

[1] i.e. $\frac{40}{100}$ of £200.

GOODS ON CONSIGNMENT

		£p			£p
Purchases (or Trading) Account . .		100·00	Consignment Account .		100·00

ALTERNATIVE ENTRIES

CONSIGNMENT STOCK

		Cases	£p			Cases	£p
Goods on Consignment Account		100	100·00	Sales . .		60	94·50
Consignment Trading Account[2] .			34·50	Stock . . c/d		40	40·00
		100	£134·50			100	£134·50
Stock . .	b/d	40	40·00				

[2] See note[1] on p. 1723.

GOODS ON CONSIGNMENT

		£			£
Purchases (or Trading) Account . .		60	Consignment Stock Account . .		100
Stock . . c/d		40			
		£100			£100
			Stock. . . b/d		40

CONSIGNMENT EXPENSES

		£				£
Expenses		100	Proportion of Expenses			
Commission		9	Forward	c/d	40	
			Consignment Trading Account[1]		69	
		£109			£109	
Expenses[2]	b/d	40				

[1] The Consignment Trading Account will show a final loss of £69 − £34·50 = £34·50. This is the identical result as shown on p. 1724.
[2] i.e. $\frac{40}{100} \times £100$.

In this alternative method, the credit balance on Goods on Consignment cancels the debit on Consignment Stock Account and therefore, as £60 (instead of £100) has been transferred to the credit of purchases, the amount of stock MUST be brought into the General Trading and Profit and Loss Account as £40 or at net realizable value if less.

The Balance Sheet will show consignment Stock, £80, made up as follows:

	£
Consignment Stock Account	40
Consignment Expenses	40
	£80

It will be observed that the expenses per unit of stock are the same as the cost price per unit; hence the 'carry-forward' will be the same.

Memorandum Column Method. Where the simple method of recording the selling price of the goods in a Memorandum column and of debiting the Consignment Account at cost price is employed, the accounts will in abbreviated form be as shown on p. 1724.

Correction of Errors

Many questions in examinations involve the correction of errors in connection with Consignment Accounts. They usually take the form of adjusting the position when goods sent on consignment have been (wrongly) debited against the *Personal* Account of the consignee, the cash being credited thereto either with or without a transfer being made to Profit and Loss Account.

CONSIGNMENT STOCK

	Cases	Nominal Selling Price	Cost Price		Cases	Nominal Selling Price	Actual Selling Price
		£	£p			£	£p
Goods	100	150	100·00	Sales	60	90	94·50
Consignment Trading Account			34·50	Stock	40	60	40·00
				c/d			
	100	£150	£134·50		100	£150	£134·50
Stock b/d	40	60	40·00				

CONSIGNMENT TRADING ACCOUNT

	£p			£p
Expenses	100·00	Profit on Consignment		34·50
Commission	9·00	Proportion of Expenses forward on Consignment	c/d	40·00
		Profit and Loss on Consignment Account		
	£109·00			£109·00
Expenses b/d	40·00			

The adjusting entries are:

   (1) If goods have been debited at COST PRICE:
      Debit Sales Account.[1]
      Credit Consignee for cost price of goods sent.
   (2) If goods have been debited AT SELLING PRICE:
      Debit Sales Account.[1]
      Credit Consignee for selling price of goods sent.
   (3) If goods have been debited AT COST PRICE and the consignee has been charged with PROFIT:
      Debit Sales Account with the Cost.[1]
      Debit Profit and Loss Account with the 'Loading.'
      Credit Consignee for invoice price of goods sent.

In all the above instances the incorrect entries have been adjusted.

These adjustments having been made, there remains in the Consignee's Account merely his original balance, if any, and the credit for the cash paid by him. The usual entries will then be made.

Illustration 13

The following Ledger Account is shown in the books of a consignor. Make the necessary adjustments.

CONSIGNEE

			£					£
Goods . . . (1)			1,200		Cash . . . (x)			600
Profit and Loss					Balance . . (y)	c/d		850
Account . . (2)			250					
			£1,450					£1,450
Balance . . (y)	b/d		850					

Adjusting entries, assuming the credit has been made to Goods on Consignment Account, will be:

   (1) Debit Consignment Account, £1,200   Credit Consignee, £1,200
   (2) Debit Profit and Loss Account, £250   Credit Consignee, £250

No entries are required in respect of x and y. As a result, the account of the consignee is:

CONSIGNEE

		£				£
Balance (as above) . .	b/d	850	Consignment Account			1,200
Balance . .	c/d	600	Profit and Loss			
			Account . .			250
		£1,450				£1,450
			Balance . .	b/d		600

The Consignment Account will now be in debit for £1,200, whilst the previous credit to Profit and Loss Account will be eliminated. The subsequent entries in the Consignment Account will be made in the usual way.

  [1] If the original credit was to Goods on Consignment Account, Consignment Account must be substituted for Sales Account.

Illustration 14

A consigns goods to his agent at cost price £3,400. The agent's account in A's books is as follows:

AGENT

		£				£
Goods		3,400	Cash			2,800
Profit and Loss Account		430	Balance . . .	c/d		1,030
		£3,830				£3,830
Balance . . .	b/d	1,030				

The agent sells the goods for £3,960, which exceeds by £850 the invoice prices. The agent collects £3,400. Discount allowed, £20; Bad Debts, £110; Expenses, £120. The agent is entitled to 5 per cent commission on cash collected. End stock to be valued at invoice price. Show the correcting entries in the consignor's books in ledger form.

The entries in the consignor's books are:

AGENT

		£			£
Balance (as above) .	b/d	1,030	*Consignment Account* .		3,400
Balance . . .	c/d	2,800	*Profit and Losts Account* .		430
		£3,830			£3,830
Consignment Account:			Balance . . .	b/d	2,800
Sales		3,960	Consignment Account		
			Discount . . .		20
			Bad Debts . . .		110
			Expenses . . .		120
			Commission . . .		170
			Balance . . .	c/d	740
		£3,960			£3,960
Balance . . .	b/d	740			

CONSIGNMENT ACCOUNT

		£			Invoice Value £	£
Agent:			Sales . . .		3,110	3,960
Goods on Consignment		3,400	Stock . . .	c/d	290	290
Discount . .		20				
Bad Debts . .		110				
Expenses . .		120				
Commission . .		170				
(5% on £3,400)						
Profit and Loss						
Account .		430				
		£4,250			£3,400	£4,250
Stock . . .	b/d	290				

PROFIT AND LOSS ACCOUNT

		£				£
Agent[1]		*430*	Balance . . .	b/d		430
			Consignment Account .			430

[1] Alternatively the transfer may be made by debiting Consignment Account and crediting agent.

Note. Items in italics are reversing entries.

The two balances £(740 + 290) equal the original balance £1,030. The profit can be checked as follows:

	£	£
Gross Profit [£3,960 *less* £3,110] .		850
Less Discount . . .	20	
Bad Debts . .	110	
Expenses . .	120	
Commission . .	170	420
Net Profit . . .		£430

Where a Consignment Debtors' Account is employed the entries will be as below, the other accounts remaining the same.

AGENT

		£				£
Consignment Debtors .		**3,400**	Balance (as before) .	b/d		2,800
			Expenses . .			120
			Commission . .			170
			Balance . .	c/d		310
		£3,400				£3,400
Balance . . .	b/d	310				

CONSIGNMENT DEBTORS

		£				£
Consignment Account .		3,960	**Agent** .			**3,400**
			Discount . .			20
			Bad Debts . .			110
			Balances . .	c/d		430
		£3,960				£3,960
Balance . . .	b/d	430				

These two accounts equal the amount shown against the agent on p. 1726, the only difference in entries being those shown in heavy type for receipts from debtors.

Profits and Losses on Exchange

In most cases where the consignee remits in foreign currency the problem of foreign exchange will enter into the accounts. The usual method is to adopt an arbitrary rate, and at the end of the consignment to deal separately with any profit or loss on exchange in order that the true result of the consignment may be ascertained. Accounts should be ruled with two columns, one for sterling as part of the double entry, and the other for foreign currency by way of memorandum.

The rules for treatment may be summarized thus:

1. Where the consignee remits immediately at the close of the account, the profit or loss on exchange will be posted to Profit and Loss on Exchange Account and thence to Profit and Loss on Consignment Account, or *direct* to the latter account; or treated as a general Profit and Loss item.

2. Where the consignee does not remit immediately at the close of the account, the profit or loss on exchange, being the difference between the arbitrary rate taken and the ruling rate, will be transferred to Profit and Loss on Exchange Account. Any profit or loss on exchange when the amount is actually remitted will similarly be transferred to Profit and Loss on Exchange Account, the final balance being transferred to Profit and Loss on Consignment Account.

3. Under (2), where there is a profit on exchange at the close of the consignment, it is more prudent to credit the amount to an Exchange Reserve Account, to which account any subsequent profit or loss on exchange arising on the actual remittance will be posted, the final balance being transferred to Profit and Loss on Consignment Account.

4. If the consignment is not completely disposed of at the date of the close of the consignor's accounting period, valuations of the balance of the Consignee's Account and of Stock will be required, the exchange position being dealt with as indicated in the foregoing paragraphs.

Illustration 15

D consigns goods to M, in Xland. The cost of the goods is £200, D paying expenses £30 and M 18,000 fcs. The latter sells all the goods for 112,500 fcs. and settles with a sight draft of 94,500 fcs., the rate of exchange being 480 fcs. to the £1. For the purposes of the accounts the other items are converted at an arbitrary rate of 450 to the £. Ignore commission. Show the accounts in D's books.

The important accounts will be as follows:

CONSIGNMENT TO M

	Fcs.	£		Fcs.	£
Goods on Consignment Account .	90,000	200	M (Consignee): Sales . . .	112,500	250
Cash—Expenses	13,500	30	Profit and Loss on Consignment A/c .	9,000	20
M (Consignee)— Expenses .	18,000	40			
	121,500	£270		121,500	£270

M (CONSIGNEE)

	Fcs.	£p			Fcs.	£p
Consignment to M—Sales	112,500	250·00		Consignment to M—Expenses	18,000	40·00
				Draft	94,500	196·88
				Loss on Exch'ge transferred to Profit and Loss on Exchange Account[1]		13·12
	112,500	£250·00			112,500	£250·00

[1] The balance of this Account will be transferred to the debit of Profit and Loss on Consignment Account, leaving a final loss of £33·12 (£20+£13·12).

It will be observed that the English exporter expended £230 and finally received £196·88, therefore losing £33·12 in all.

Illustration 16

At the date of the completion of the consignment the rate was 440 fcs. to the £. M, however, withholds payment, and the rate depreciates to 500 to the £ before he remits. Show the accounts in D's books. (Calculate to the nearest £.)

M (CONSIGNEE)

		Fcs.	£				Fcs.	£
Consignment to M—Sales		112,500	250		Consignment to M—Expenses		18,000	40
Profit on Exchange transferred to Profit and Loss on Exchange A/c[1]			5		Balance	c/d	94,500	215
		112,500	£255				112,500	£255
Balance	b/d	94,500	215		Draft		94,500	189
					Loss on Exchange transferred to Profit and Loss on Exchange A/c[1]			26
		94,500	£215				94,500	£215

CONSIGNMENT TO M

	Fcs.	£			Fcs.	£
Goods on Consignment Account	90,000	200		M (Consignee)—Sales	112,500	250
Cash—Expenses	13,500	30		Profit and Loss on Consignment A/c	9,000	20
M (Consignee)—Expenses	18,000	40				
	121,500	£270			121,500	£270

[1] See footnote on p. 1730.

PROFIT AND LOSS ON CONSIGNMENT ACCOUNT

		£			£
Loss on Consignment .		20	Profit on Exchange[1] .	.	5
„ „ Exchange[1]	.	26	General Profit and Loss Account	.	41
		£46			£46

[1] In order to save opening a Profit and Loss on Exchange Account, and transferring the balance to Profit and Loss on Consignment Account, the items marked thus have been posted direct to the latter account.

It will be observed that the English exporter expended £230 and finally received £189, thus losing £41 in all.

Illustration 17

Assuming, in the above illustration, that the rate at the date of the completion of the consignment was 500 fcs. to the £ and 440 fcs. to the £ at the date of the remittance, show the Consignment Account and the Account of the Consignee in the books of the Consignor in abbreviated form. (Calculate to nearest £.)

CONSIGNMENT ACCOUNT (*abbreviated*)

		£				£
Goods .		200	Sales .	.	.	250
Expenses .		30	Loss			20
„		40				
		£270				£270

M (CONSIGNEE) (*abbreviated*)

	Fcs.	£			Fcs.	£
Sales .	112,500	250	Expenses— .		18,000	40
			Profit and Loss on Exchange Account .			21
			Balance . . c/d		94,500	189
	112,500	£250			112,500	£250
Balance . b/d	94,500	189	Draft .		94,500	215
Profit and Loss on Exchange Account .		26				
	94,500	£215			94,500	£215

It will be observed that the English exporter expended £230 and finally received £215, thus losing £15 in all.

Consignee's Books

Entries in Consignee's Books. There are two recognized methods of dealing with Consignments Inwards, the first of which is the one more generally in use and is outlined below.

First Method. On receipt of the goods, the consignee will only make entries in respect thereof in his Stock Books. He will make no entries at all in the books of account, because the receipt is clearly not a purchase, as the goods are not the property of, but merely in the custody of, the consignee. If the consignee incurs any expenses in respect of the consignment, e.g. landing charges, import duties, warehousing and storing, etc., he will make the following entry:

> Debit Consignor's Personal Account
> Credit Cash (or Creditors or Expenses).

As the goods are sold a memorandum entry will be made in the Stock Books. When a sale is effected the entry is:

> Debit Cash (or Debtors).
> Credit Consignor's Personal Account.

The entries made will be exactly the same as those made for the ordinary sales of the business, except that the total of consignment sales will be credited to the personal account of the consignor, and not to Sales Account. For the amount of commission due to the consignee for sales effected by him, the entry is:

> Debit Consignor's Personal Account.
> Credit Commission Account.

The Consignor's Account may now be closed off in the usual manner, the settlement being effected by means of a draft or bill. If, at the end of the consignee's financial year, the consignor has not been paid in full, the balance due to or by consignor will appear in the Balance Sheet as a creditor or debtor, as the case may be. *Del credere* commission should be credited to a special account, and any Bad Debts incurred in respect of the particular consignment debited thereto. At the end of the accounting period, so much of the balance of the Commission Account as may be said to refer to completed transactions may be written off to Profit and Loss Account as a separate item.

Illustration 18

Taking the facts of the illustration on p. 1704 and assuming that the sales of the consignee, R. Rajah, were made in three items:

19..		£
Feb. 12.	Cash	400
	M. Madras (on credit) .	700
	G. Ganges (on credit) .	500

Show the accounts in the books of R. Rajah.

M. MADRAS

19.. Feb. 12	C. Cotton—Sales	.	£ 700					

G. GANGES

19.. Feb. 12	Cotton—Sales	.	£ 500					

BANK

19.. Feb. 12	C. Cotton—Sales	.	£ 400	19.. Feb. 4	C. Cotton—Expenses	.		£ 120

C. COTTON (CONSIGNOR)

19..
Feb. 4
12
12
24
	Bank—Expenses .
	Selling Commission
	Del Cred. Commission
	Bills Payable
		.
		
		.
			£
			120
			80
			20
			1,380
			————
			£1,600
				19..
				Feb. 12
					Sales—
					  M. Madras .£700
					  G. Ganges . 500
					  Cash . 400
							£
							
							1,600
							————
							£1,600

COMMISSION

				19.. Feb. 12	C. Cotton	.	.	£ 80

'DEL CREDERE' COMMISSION

				19.. Feb. 12	C. Cotton	.	.	£ 20

BILLS PAYABLE

				19.. Feb. 24	C. Cotton	.	.	£ 1,380

Assuming that G. GANGES defaulted, paying only 75 naye paise in the rupee[1] £125 would be credited to his account and debited to *Del Credere* Commission Account. The balance on this account (namely £105, debit balance) being a loss will be transferred to Profit and Loss Account, unless the consignee has in the past credited any balance in *Del Credere* Commission Account (after writing off Bad Debts) to a Reserve Account, in which case the £105 would be debited to that account.

[1] There are 100 naye paise to the rupee.

Discounts and Allowances. Unless the terms of the contract specify otherwise, any accounts and allowances to debtors will be borne by the consignor, the consignee making the entry as follows:

Debit Consignor's Personal Account.
Credit Debtors.

Closing stock. As the goods have not been purchased by the consignee, the Stock at the end must *not* be included in his final accounts, whether the first or the second method (explained below) be employed.

Second Method. The second method of dealing with consignments ·in the books of the consignee may be briefly tabulated as follows:

(*a*) Open a Consignment Inward Account, debiting that account with the invoice price of the goods; and crediting the Consignor's Personal Account.

(*b*) Debit the expenses paid by the consignee in respect of the consignment to Consignment Inward Account and credit cash or creditors.

(*c*) Debit commission and *Del Credere* Commission on Sales to Consignment Inward Account and credit Commission Account and *Del Credere* Commission Account respectively.

(*d*) Debit Cash or Debtors and credit Consignment Inward Account for Sales.

(*e*) The balance of Consignment Inward Account will be transferred to the Consignor's Personal Account.

(*f*) The payment to the consignor will be debited to his account and Bank (or Bills Payable) credited.

If the whole of the goods have not been sold by the consignee, the closing Stock will be entered in the books as follows:

(i) Credit Consignment Inward Account and bring down as a balance on the debit side.

(ii) Debit Consignor's Personal Account and bring down as a balance on the credit side.

This method is rarely used.

Illustration 19

The entries (in respect of the transactions on pp. 1731–1732) under this method will be:

CONSIGNMENT INWARD

19..			£	19..			£
Feb. 4	Consignor—Goods		1,600	Feb. 12	Sales (Cash or Debtors)		1,600
	Bank—Expenses		120	24	Balance—Stock c/d		220
12	Commission Account		80				
	Del Credere (Commission Account		20				
			£1,820				£1,820
Feb. 25	Balance b/d		220				

C. Cotton (Consignor)

19.. Feb. 24	Bills Payable Account Balance . . .	c/d	£ 1,380 220	19.. Feb. 4	Consignment Inward Account . . .		£ 1,600
			£1,600				£1,600
				Feb. 25	Balance . . .	b/d	220

Commission

				19.. Feb. 12	Consignment Inward Account . .		£ 80

'Del Credere' Commission

				19.. Feb. 12	Consignment Inward Account . .		£ 20

Advanced Problem. The following example is illustrative of the advanced type of problem. The working is explained fully where required, but it should be borne in mind that the principles to be applied are those already outlined.

Illustration 20

A, in London, consigns goods to B, in Belfast, for sale at invoice price or over. B is entitled to a commission of 5 per cent on invoice price and 25 per cent of any surplus price realized. A draws on B at 90 days' sight for 80 per cent of the invoice price, and, upon sale, B remits the balance of proceeds, after deducting his commission, by sight draft.

Goods consigned by A to B in the year 19.., cost A £10,450, including freight, and were invoiced at £14,200. Sales made by B were £13,380, and goods in his hands, unsold at 31st December 19.., represented an invoice value of £3,460 (original cost £2,370, plus freight £240). Sight drafts actually received by A from B up to 31st December 19.. were £3,140; others were in transit.

Prepare accounts in A's books of these transactions and show (by Ledger accounts) the manner in which the books would be closed at 31st December 19...

Solution

CONSIGNMENT TO B

19.. Dec. 31		Memo. £	£	19.. Dec. 31		Memo. £	£
	Goods (including Freight)	14,200	10,450		Sales[1]	10,740	13,380
	B: Commission—				Stock (including Freight)		
	5% on £10,740		537		c/d	3,460	2,610
	25% on £2,640		660				
	Profit and Loss Account		4,343				
19..		£14,200	£15,990			£14,200	£15,990
Jan. 1	Stock. etc. b/d	3,460	2,610				

[1] This figure is the balancing item of the memorandum column.

B (CONSIGNEE)

19.. Dec. 31			£	19.. Dec. 31		£
	Consignment to B Account—				Bills[1]	11,360
	Sales		13,380		Commission	1,197
	Balance[2] c/d		2,768		Bills[1]	3,140
					Bills in Transit	451
			£16,148			£16,148
				19.. Jan. 1	Balance b/d	2,768

[1] Posted to the debit of Bills Receivable Account.
[2] The Bills in transit may be calculated by writing up B's account and inserting the amount owing *to* him, viz., £2,768, which is 80% of the remaining stock of £3,460. The balance of the account represents Bills in transit.

BILLS IN TRANSIT

19.. Dec. 31	B (Consignee)		£ 451				

GOODS ON CONSIGNMENT

19.. Dec. 31		£	£	19.. Dec. 31		Invoice Price £	£
	Purchases (or Trading) Account	?			Consignment to B	14,200	10,450
	Freight	?	10,450				

PROOF OF B's ACCOUNT. B, according to the agreement, is to account to A for the profit on the goods he sells, less commission.
The profit is:

		£	£
(1)	Sales		13,380
(2)	*Less* Invoice price of Goods consigned	14,200	
	Less Invoice price of Goods on hand	3,460	
			10,740
	∴ Profit		2,640

The commission thereon:

	£	£
5% of £10,740 (Invoice price) .	537	
25% of £2,640 (profit, as above)	660	
		1,197
Hence B owes for the difference		£1,443

When the goods were sent to B he paid A for four-fifths of the value of the WHOLE consignment of £14,200, his acceptance therefore being

$$\tfrac{4}{5} \times £14,200 = £11,360$$

Of the whole consignment, £10,740 has been sold by B so that, subject to his commission, he must account to A for the remaining one-fifth of the invoice price of the goods sold. It is clear that he has paid for four-fifths of the goods still unsold, but this is ignored for the present.

Consequently, B must account to A for $\tfrac{1}{5} \times £10,740$, which is £2,148 added to the *net* profit of £1,443 as shown in the *above* statement. B is thus indebted to A for:

	£	£
(a) Net Profit	1,443	
(b) Balance of Invoice price of the Goods sold . . .	2,148	
		3,591
Against which he has already remitted		3,140
Therefore Drafts in transit to clear are		£451

When B has received credit for his remittances and his commission, his account is clear so far as the Goods SOLD are concerned, but he has paid not only for the goods sold, but for four-fifths of the goods unsold, as he accepted a bill at the outset for four-fifths of the invoice price of the WHOLE consignment. Such unsold goods are:

	£
Invoice price of WHOLE Consignment . . .	14,200
Less Invoice price of Goods sold . . .	10,740
Remaining Goods	£3,460
B has paid for $\tfrac{4}{5}$ thereof =	£2,768

The latter figure is the amount standing to the credit of B's account.

The proof becomes simple if the student will imagine that two separate consignments were made, the first representing the goods sold, the second representing goods unsold.

Consignments	Invoice Price	Paid for by B	Unpaid for by B
	£	£	£
1st Consignment	10,740	8,592(a)	2,148(b)
2nd Consignment	3,460	2,768(c)	692(d)
Total . .	£14,200	£11,360	£2,840

The Ledger Account in A's books will be:

B

	1st Con-signment	2nd Con-signment		1st Con-signment	2nd Con-signment
	£	£		£	£
Sales . . .	13,380	nil	Bill . . .	8,592	2,768
Balance . c/d		2,768	Commission .	1,197	
			Bill . .	3,140	
			Bill in transit .	451	
	£13,380	£2,768		£13,380	£2,768
			Balance . b/d		2,768

It can readily be understood that the first consignment is now completely disposed of, the proof of which is:

1st Consignment—B owes for Sales		13,380
Less Amount paid by B when goods consigned (See a)		8,592
		£4,788

or

	£	£
Profit on Sales = Sales . . .	13,380	
Less Invoice Price of Goods sold .	10,740	
	2,640	
Plus Proportion of Cost still unpaid [$\frac{1}{5} \times$ £10,740] (See b) . . .	2,148	
		£4,788

This is discharged by—

(1) Commission due to B . . .	1,197	
(2) Remittances	3,591	
		£4,788

In order to make the problem complete, the second consignment will be dealt with; and for this purpose it is assumed that the remaining goods are sold for £4,460, the commission terms as before.

The account of B as to the second Consignment is continued from the balance brought down of £2,768.

B (SECOND CONSIGNMENT)

	£			£
Sales	4,460	Balance . . . b/d		2,768
		Commission . .		423
		Bills, etc. . .		1,269
	£4,460			£4,460

		£	£
Proof—			
2nd Consignment—Sales			4,460
Less Amount paid by B when Goods were consigned . . .			2,768
[$\frac{4}{5} \times$ £3,460] (See *c*) . . .			
			£1,692

or

	£	£
Profit on Sale = Sales	4,460	
Less Invoice Price of Goods sold .	3,460	
	1,000	
Plus Proportion of Cost still unpaid [$\frac{1}{5} \times$ £3,460] (See *d*) . .	692	
		£1,692

	£
This is discharged by—	
(1) Commission[1]	423
(2) Remittances	1,269
	£1,692

	£
[1] The Commission is calculated thus—	
5% on £3,460	173
25% on £4,460 − 3,460, i.e. on £1,000 .	250
	£423

The Consignment Account in A's books will be:

CONSIGNMENT TO B

		Invoice price			Invoice price	
		£	£		£	£
Balance[1]	b/d	3,460	2,610	Sales (per Account Sales)	3,460	4,460
Commission—						
5% on £3,460			173			
25% on £1,000			250			
Profit and Loss Account			1,427			
		£3,460	£4,460		£3,460	£4,460

[1] See Consignment Account on p. 1735.

The total profit will be:

	1st Consignment		2nd Consignment		Total	
	£	£	£	£	£	£
Sales		13,380		4,460		17,840
Less Cost	7,840		2,610		10,450	
Commission	1,197		423		1,620	
		9,037		3,033		12,070
Profit and Loss Account per Consignment Account		£4,343		£1,427		£5,770

The following illustration is appended to demonstrate a joint venture completed on full double entry lines involving the principles applicable to Joint Venture and Consignment Accounts.

Illustration 21

A and B enter into a joint venture. A contributes £100 and B £150. They purchase for cash 20 transistors at £6 each, and consign 17 to their agent in Xland invoiced at $30 each. A pays freight of £10·20. The agent pays landing charges of $189 on 15 only; the remaining 2, being irreparably damaged by water, are destroyed, a claim being preferred against the underwriters. The agent incurs selling costs of $89 and is entitled to 5 per cent commission on sales and a further 10 per cent commission on net profits *after* charging up *both* commissions.

The sales of the Xland agent are 5 at $58 each.

As to the remaining 10, 5 have been sent from Xland to Yland, and the Yland agent reports that he has sold them for $660 net, and remits to Xland a draft therefor.

Of the 3 remaining in England, 2 are sold for cash for £8 each. In the meantime A and B have withdrawn respectively £40 and £60 from the Joint Cash Account. They share profits 1 : 2.

The Xland agent remits a draft for $250.

Rates of Exchange may be taken as:

Xland .   .   .   . $ 5 to £
Yland .   .   .   . $10 to £

The accounts in the joint venture books are shown below:

JOINT VENTURE BOOKS

A

		£p			£p
Cash		40·00	Cash		100·00
Balance . . .	c/d	74·20	Consignment to Xland Account		
			—Expenses . .		10·20
			⅓ Profit . . .		4·00
		£114·20			£114·20
			Balance . . .	b/d	74·20

B

		£			£
Cash		60	Cash		150
Balance . . .	c/d	98	⅔ Profit . . .		8
		£158			£158
			Balance . . .	b/d	98

CASH

		£			£
A and B . . .		250	Joint Venture Account		120
Xland Agent[1] . .		50	A		40
Sales . . .		16	B		60
			Balance . . .	c/d	96
		£316			£316
Balance . . .	b/d	96			

[1] Paid into cash for convenience.

UNDERWRITERS

		£p			
Consignment to Xland Account .		13·20			

GOODS ON CONSIGNMENT

	Units	$	£		Units	$	£
Joint Venture Account	17	510	102	Consignment to Xland Account	17	510	102

CONSIGNMENT TO XLAND

	Units	$	£p			Units	$	£p
Goods on Consignment	17	510	102·00	Underwriters		2	66	13·20
A—Freight		51	10·20	Sales		10	620	124·00
Xland Agent—				Stock²	c/d	5	228	45·60
Landing Charges		189	37·80					
Selling Expenses		89	17·80					
5% Sales Commission		31	6·20					
Profit—								
Xland Agent¹ 1/10		4	0·80					
Joint Venture Account 9/10		40	8·00					
	17	$914	£182·80			17	$914	£182·80
Stock	5	228	45·60					

¹ i.e. 1/11 of £8·80.
² i.e. 5/15 of £136·80 made up as follows—

	£p	$
Cost of 17 units	112·20	561
Less 2 covered by Insurance	13·20	66
Cost of 15 units	99·00	495
Add Landing Charges	37·80	189
	£136·80	$684

Alternatively, this may be calculated as follows: 5/17 of £112·20 plus 5/15 of £37·80.

	$	£p			$	£p
Sales	290	58·00	Consignment to Xland Account—			
"	330	66·00	Landing Expenses	189	37·80
			Selling Expenses	89	17·80
			Commission 5% of $620	31	6·20
			$\frac{1}{10}$ Profits	4	0·80
			Draft	250	50·00
			Balance c/d	57	11·40
	$620	£124·00		$620	£124·00
Balance b/d	57	11·40				

JOINT VENTURE ACCOUNT

	Units	£			Units	£
Cash Purchase	20	120	Goods on Consignment Account	17	102
Profit—			Cash Sales	2	16
A, $\frac{1}{3}$ 4.			Consignment to Xland Account—		
B, $\frac{2}{3}$ 8.			Profit		8
— 12	20	12	Stock c/d	1	6
	20	£132		20	£132
Stock b/d	1	6				

1 660 Yland dollars equal 330 Xland dollars.

TRIAL BALANCE

	£p	£p
A		74·20
B		98·00
Cash	96·00	
Underwriters	13·20	
Consignment to Xland	45·60	
Xland Agent	11·40	
Joint Venture Account (Stock)	6·00	
	£172·20	£172·20

Note. The gross sales of the Yland Agent (if given) would be credited to Consignment Account and the expenses debited to the same account—NOT the *net* realized Value AFTER expenses, unless the Yland Agent is the Agent of the Xland Agent, in which case the net proceeds will be credited to the latter and his commission based thereon. The entries are made in the Xland Consignment Account, as for practical purposes it is part of the latter consignment.

B's Books:

A

		£			£
Cash		150	Cash		60
⅔ Profit		8	Balance c/d		98
		£158			£158
Balance b/d		98			

Note. This account corresponds to B's Account in the Joint Venture books.

A's Books:

B

		£p			£p
Cash		100·00	Cash		40·00
Consignment Expenses		10·20	Balance c/d		74·20
⅓ Profit		4·00			
		£114·20			£114·20
Balance b/d		74·20			

Note. This account corresponds to A's Account in the Joint Venture books.

CHAPTER 18

DEPARTMENTAL ACCOUNTS

ONE of the most important aims of accounting is the segregation and recording of activities, whether of buying or selling; of production, administration, or distribution. Departmental accounting aims at segregating the severable activities of a business in order to:

(i) Compare results.
(ii) Assist the proprietor in formulating policy.
(iii) Reward the departmental managers on results shown.

Departments may be classified according to functions, e.g. Buying, Selling, Production or Manufacturing, Subsidiary service, e.g. Transport, Packing, Repairs, and the like.

In most large businesses departmental accounts are employed, e.g. in the large general stores, whilst insurance companies are compelled by law to prepare separate accounts for Life, Marine, and Industrial branches. An Accountant may have Audit, Tax, Bankruptcy Departments, and so on.

It is usually not a matter of difficulty to ascertain the gross profit of each department, as the transactions may be easily analysed by means of columnar day books or journals, of either the bound or the loose-leaf variety. So far as purchases are concerned there is, as a rule, one Ledger only to contain the accounts of the creditors, but if the departments *buy* from distinct and separate sources, a separate set of ledgers and day books or journals may be employed. As regards sales, if customers buy from several departments it will be necessary to employ one Ledger (subdivided into areas or alphabetically, rather than departmentally), so that the whole of the transactions of the customer are contained under the one heading. The sales day books or journals, bound or loose-leaf, will be columnarized or, where necessary, a separate sales day-book or journal for each department employed. Returns Inwards and Outwards will be dealt with on the lines of Sales and Purchases, conversely treated.

Stock records will be employed where practicable, and at the end of each accounting period the stock will be ascertained for each department and compared with details disclosed by the stock records.

Where a concern occupies a warehouse, the whole of the purchases will first be passed through as purchases of the warehouse and charged out to departments, an amount usually being added to the cost to cover expenses of handling. Any stock not sent to the departments will be considered as warehouse stock.

Where other items are included in the Trading Account they are normally of such a nature as to lend themselves to simple analysis, e.g. Wages and Carriage Inwards.

The general expenses chargeable against the gross profit will require allocation between the departments according to the actual circumstances; and even if a certain amount of latitude is allowed, in the absence of some rigid method of precise allocation, an attempt should be made to spread the expenses, because a department cannot be said to have earned a net profit until all the legitimate expenses of administration, selling, and distribution have been charged against its gross profit.

Allocation of Expenses. The methods of allocating expenses may be dealt with as follows:

1. Expenses incurred *specifically* for the department will be charged direct thereto, e.g. Repairs to Motors in a Transport Department.

2. Expenses for the benefit of *all* the departments and capable of precise allocation will be debited accordingly, e.g. lighting, according to separate meterage.

3. Expenses for the benefit of *all* departments *not* capable of precise allocation will be treated as follows:

(i) *Selling Expenses.* These will be charged on a sales basis, either (*a*) value or (*b*) units or quantities sold, e.g. Discounts allowed, Bad Debts, Selling Commissions, although occasionally some of these expenses may come under one of the other headings as in the case of bad debts, where separate sales Ledgers are used for each department.

(ii) *Administration Charges.* Many charges, like Rent and Rates, may be apportioned to give approximately true results on the basis of (*a*) area, (*b*) windows used, (*c*) cubic content, (*d*) average stock held or sold. With regard to the apportionment of Rent and Rates, it is usual to charge a basic rate for each floor, the higher the storey the lower the proportion, and subdivide the amount into departments on the above lines, unless the department occupies one whole storey. For example, if three floors are used the ratios might be:

> 1st floor . . 3   2nd floor . . 2   3rd floor . . 1

Heating and Lighting (in absence of separate meters) may be apportioned on the basis of points wired, lamps used, areas, or inversely to the number of windows.

Power, where not separately metered, is best apportioned on the basis of probable usage as determined by numbers and types of machines, adjusted where necessary according to running hours.

Many expenses may be apportioned exactly or approximately by examining the precise nature and function of the expenditure, e.g. advertising, insurance. Advertising may produce enormous sales to one department and not to another, but that is no valid reason for allocating the cost on the basis of results produced—as is done in the case of selling commission—because the advertising expenditure will have been incurred even if no sales are effected, and may, in respect of a particular department, have proved abortive because of the relative inefficiency of that department. Although apportionment of the advertising expenses is usually made on the basis of sales, an approximation based upon advertising space occupied may be preferable. An electric sign advertisement will probably benefit all departments (unless one department is particularly singled out) and the cost should be apportioned equally to all departments for whose benefit the sign is utilized.

Insurance premiums may relate to stock, premises, loss of profits, or workmen's compensation, and should be apportioned on the basis of stocks carried, proportion of premises occupied, profits earned in the preceding year, and wages respectively, unless some abnormal feature exists, e.g. extraordinary risk by reason of the nature of the goods—oil; or in the case of workmen's compensation, an abnormal degree of risk of accident to workmen and employees of one department as contrasted with another.

Depreciation will usually be allocable on the basis of assets employed in each department. (Depreciation of boilers will normally be included in the heating charge, depreciation of lorries in the transport charge, etc.)

4. Where expenses are incurred for which *no basis of apportionment is practicable*, it is usual to bring down the departmental balance of profits and apportion these expenses equally against it so that the management will not be misled by the arbitrary nature of the apportionments, and at the same time will be able to ascertain the approximate net profit of each department.

In some concerns an apportionment of these expenses is made according to one of the following cases: (*a*) units sold, (*b*) floor space occupied, (*c*) assessment of valuation of space occupied, (*d*) average value of stock held by the particular department, (*e*) wages paid. Where bonuses and further remuneration are dependent upon net departmental results, some apportionment is required, but it is submitted that where no real basis exists, it is preferable to make such apportionments on an equal basis.

Where the concern is in receipt of non-departmental profits, e.g. dividends, the income should be added to the net profit of the departments **equally**, following the same principle.

Alternatively, the balance of departmental profits subject to any non-allocable expenses may be brought down in one total, and such expenses be debited and non-departmental profits credited without any attempt at apportionment.

5. A charge (which does not represent an actual item of expenditure) is often made for *Interest* based upon the estimated amount of average capital employed by each department. This entry does not affect the total net profit, since it is an internal adjustment only, viz. a debit to each department and a total credit to Profit and Loss Account. Similarly, a 'notional' rent charge is often made to departments which occupy premises owned by the firm.

Inter-departmental Transfers. Where goods, or the employment of staff or performance of services are exchanged as between departments, they should be separately recorded and shown as separate items in the departmental columns of the Trading and Profit and Loss Account. The transfers will be either at cost or at loaded price, care being taken in the latter case to eliminate from the total results the unrealized profit. Such profit is not realized by the concern as a WHOLE until the goods have been disposed of to outside purchasers. (The treatment of unrealized profit in departments is considered in Chapter 30.)

Illustration 1

A. Ltd., Hotel Proprietors, have incurred, *inter alia*, expenditure as follows:

				Rooms £	Meals £	
Chambermaids	.	.	.	4,730	2,110	(= £6,840)
Kitchen Staff	.	.	.	5,210	3,170	(= £8,380)
				£9,940	£5,280	

Show how these items are dealt with in the Departmental Profit and
Loss Account.

				£	£
Apartments	.	.	Dr.	6,840	
Restaurant	.	.	Dr.	8,380	
To Apartments	.	.	.		9,940
„ Restaurant	.	.	.		5,280
				£15,220	£15,220

Illustration 2

Code & Dray Ltd. are in business as coal retailers and carriers. They
transport the coal they purchase from the railway siding and deliver it in
their own vehicles.

For a certain period, the wages of their transport staff, debited to
Transport Department, are £16,950, of which £1,730 are attributable to
transport of coal to their depot, £4,080 to delivery of coal to customers
and staff, and £11,140 to transport work for customers.

The depot consumes coal estimated at £350, depot expenses being
apportionable 3/7 to coal and 4/7 to transport. The staff are supplied with
coal free, estimated at £1,200 and wages connected therewith £240. The
quantities of coal delivered to the staff are roughly in proportion to their
respective wages, exclusive of those incurred in delivery to the staff.

Show how the above would appear in the Departmental Profit and Loss
Account, assuming that no outside transport expenses are incurred.

DEPARTMENTAL PROFIT AND LOSS ACCOUNT (includes)

	Coal	Transport		Coal	Transport
	£	£ (b) 16,950		£	
Wages . . .					
Transfers—			Transfer . . .		(b) 1,730
Wages in Transport of Coal to Depot .	(a) 1,730		Transfer (£4,080−240)		(b) 3,840
Wages re Delivery to Customers .	(a) 3,840		Transfer . . .	350	
Coal Consumed at Depot .	150	200	Transfer (£4,080−3840)	1,200	(b) 240
Coal Supplied to Staff .	(x) 400	(x) 800			
Wages re Staff Coal .	(x) 80	(x) 160			

(x) Wages in (a) Coal £1,730 + £3,840   = £5,570.
    (b) Transport £16,950 − £1,730 − £3,840 − £240 = £11,140.
∴ Proportion is 1:2.

The following examples are typical, and illustrative of the principles explained.

Illustration 3

From the following Trial Balance prepare, in two-sided form, Departmental Trading and Profit and Loss Account for the year ended 31st December 19.., and Balance Sheet at that date.

TRIAL BALANCE
AS AT 31ST DECEMBER 19..

	£	£
Stock at 1st January 19. .—A Dept.	1,700	
B ,,	1,450	
Purchases— A ,,	3,540	
B ,,	3,020	
Sales— A ,,		9,080
B ,,		8,125
Wages— A ,,	1,820	
B ,,	1,270	
Rent, Rates, Ground Burdens, and Insurance	939	
Sundry Expenses	360	
Salaries	3,300	
Lighting and Heating	210	
Discounts Allowed	222	
Discounts Received		65
Advertising	368	
Carriage Inwards	234	
Furniture and Fittings	300	
Plant and Machinery	2,100	
Sundry Debtors	606	
Sundry Creditors		1,860
VAT		86
A—Capital		4,766
A—Drawings	1,450	
Cash at Bank	1,076	
Cash in hand	17	
	£23,982	£23,982

The following information is also provided:

1. Internal transfer of goods from A Department to B Department, £42.

2. The items: Rent, Rates, Ground Burdens, and Insurance; Sundry Expenses; Lighting and Heating; Salaries; and Carriage Inwards to be apportioned—$\frac{2}{3}$ A Dept., $\frac{1}{3}$ B Dept.

3. Advertising to be apportioned equally.

4. Discounts allowed and received are apportioned on the basis of Departmental Sales and Purchases (excluding transfers).

5. Depreciation at 10 per cent per annum on Furniture and Fittings and on Plant and Machinery to be charged $\frac{3}{4}$ to A Dept., $\frac{1}{4}$ to B Dept.

6. Services rendered by B Dept to A Dept. included in Wages, £50.

7. The Stock at 31st December 19..: A Dept., £1,674; B Dept., £1,205.

8. There have been no additions to or Sales of Plant or Furniture.

DEPARTMENTAL TRADING AND PROFIT AND LOSS ACCOUNT
FOR THE YEAR ENDED 31ST DECEMBER 19..

	A Dept.	B Dept.	Total		A Dept.	B Dept.	Total
	£	£	£		£	£	£
Stock	1,700	1,450	3,150	Sales	9,080	8,125	17,205
Purchases	3,540	3,020	6,560	Departmental			
Carriage				Transfers	42	50	
Inwards	156	78	234	Stock	1,674	1,205	2,879
Wages	1,820	1,270	3,090				
Goods		42					
Wages	50						
Gross Profit							
c/d	3,530	3,520	7,050				
	£10,796	£9,380	£20,084		£10,796	£9,380	£20,084
Salaries	2,200	1,100	3,300	Gross Profit b/d	3,530	3,520	7,050
Rent, Rates,				Discounts			
Ground				Received (b)	35	30	65
Burdens, and				Loss	122		
Insurance	626	313	939				
Lighting and							
Heating	140	70	210				
Sundry							
Expenses	240	120	360				
Advertising	184	184	368				
Discounts							
Allowed (a)	117	105	222				
Depreciation	180	60	240				
Profit[1]		1,598	1,476				
	£3,687	£3,550	£7,115		£3,687	£3,550	£7,115

(a) Ratio of Sales, 9,080:8,125; (b) ratio of Purchases, 3,540:3,020.

[1] The total net profit of £1,476 is arrived at thus:

		£
B Dept	Net Profit	1,598
A Dept.	Net Loss	122
	Balance	£1,476

BALANCE SHEET AS AT 31ST DECEMBER 19..

	£	£		£	£
Capital at 1st Jan. 19..	4,766		Fixed Assets—		
Add Profit for year	1,476		Plant and Machinery		
			at 1st Jan. 19..	2,100	
	6,242		*Less* Depreciation at		
Less Drawings	1,450		10% per annum	210	
		4,792			1,890
Current Liabilities—			Furniture and Fittings		
Sundry Creditors		1,946[1]	at 1st Jan. 19..	300	
			Less Depreciation at		
			10% per annum	30	
					270
					2,160
			Current Assets—		
			Stock	2,879	
			Sundry Debtors	606	
			Cash at Bank	1,076	
			Cash in hand	17	
					4,578
		£6,738			£6,738

[1] Includes VAT £86.

Illustration 4

Carr was the proprietor of a garage, the following Trial Balance being extracted from his book on 31st December 19...

TRIAL BALANCE
AS AT 31ST DECEMBER 19..

	£	£
Capital		3,300
Drawings	2,400	
Opening Stocks—		
Tools	150	
Petrol and Oil	556	
Spare Parts and Tyres	495	
Private Cars (including Repair Van £210)	4,770	
Purchases—		
Tools	176	
Spare Parts and Tyres	812	
Petrol and Oil	6,625	
Advertising	104	
Rent, Rates and Lighting	680	
Insurance—		
Hire Cars	340	
Fire, Burglary, etc.	120	
Carried forward	£17,228	£3,300

TRIAL BALANCE AS AT 31ST DECEMBER 19. .—(Contd.)

	£	£
Brought Forward .	17,228	3,300
Wages—		
Chauffeurs	2,650	
Repair Department	2,706	
Office	1,250	
Garage	450	
Sales—		
Petrol and Oil		8,532
Spare Parts and Tyres		1,146
Receipts—		
Hiring		7,326
Repairs		5,542
Garaging		950
Licence for Hire Cars	250	
Office Expenses	296	
Sundry Debtors	95	
Sundry Creditors		164
Commission on Cars Sold		840
Cash at Bank	2,875	
	£27,800	£27,800

The following additional information was extracted:

(a) The stocks on hand, 31st December 19. ., were valued at:

Tools .	£106
Petrol and Oil	842
Spare Parts and Tyres	464

(b) Petrol valued £840 and oil £162 were used by the Hire Department during the year; petrol, valued at £58 and oil at £24 were used by the Repairs Department; private consumption amounted to £86.

(c) Repairs Department performed work on hire cars valued at £434. In addition, £40 work was performed on the proprietor's own car.

(d) Spare parts used by Repairs Department during the year were valued at £322.

(e) Depreciation of Private Hire Cars and Repair Van at 20 per cent per annum.

(f) Rent, Rates and Lighting to be apportioned as follows—

Repairs Dept.	$\frac{1}{4}$	Garage	$\frac{1}{2}$
Hire Dept..	$\frac{1}{8}$	Office	$\frac{1}{8}$

(g) The licence £25 and insurance £40, for the proprietor's own car are included in the insurance and licences paid by the business.

You are required to prepare Departmental Trading Account and Profit and Loss Account in two-sided form for the year ended 31st December 19. ., and a Balance Sheet at that date.

PROFIT AND LOSS ACCOUNT FOR THE YEAR ENDED
31ST DECEMBER 19..

	£			£	£
Wages (Office) . . .	1,250	Balance, being Gross			
Rent, Rates and Lighting .	85	Profit— . . b/d			
Advertising	104	Petrol and Oil . . .	4,123		
Office Expenses . . .	296	Spare Parts and Tyres .	625		
Insurance	120	Repairs	1,464		
Net Profit transferred to Capital		Hire	1,968		
Account	7,325	Garage	160		
					8,340
		Commission on Cars . .			840
	£9,180				£9,180

DEPARTMENTAL TRADING ACCOUNT
for the Year ended 31st December 19..

Debit

	Petrol and Oil	Spare Parts, etc.	Repair Dept.	Hire Dept.	Garage
	£	£	£	£	£
Stock	556	495	150	—	
Purchases[1]	6,625	812	176		
Wages			2,706	2,650	450
Licences[2]				250[1]	340
Rent, Rates and Lighting			170	85	
Depreciation on Private Cars				912	
Depreciation on Repair Van			42		
Insurance on Cars[2]				340[1]	
Spare Parts and Tyres (b)			322	1,002	
Petrol and Oil (a)			842	434	
Repairs (c)					
Balance, being Gross Profit c/d	4,123	625	1,714	1,718	160
	£11,304	£1,932	£6,122	£7,391	£950

Credit

	Petrol and Oil	Spare Parts, etc.	Repair Dept.	Hire Dept.	Garage
	£	£	£	£	£
Sales	8,532	1,146	5,542		950
Receipts				7,326	
Department Transfers	(a)1,844	(b)322	(c)434		
Stock	842	464	106		
Drawings— Licence[1] £25 Insurance[1] £40					
Repairs				65	
Petrol and Oil[1]	86		40		
	£11,304	£1,932	£6,122	£7,391	£950

[1] The transfers for Drawings are shown separately for sake of clarity. Actually they would be credited to the respective accounts, leaving a net charge to the Trading Account, e.g. Licences in Hire Department would be £225 net; Insurance, £300 net; Petrol and Oil Purchases, £6,539 net.

[2] No amounts are given for insurance and licence on Repair Van.

BALANCE SHEET AS AT 31ST DECEMBER 19..

	£	£		£	£
Capital—			Fixed Assets—		
Balance 1st Jan. 19..	3,300		Private Hire Cars	4,560	
Add Profit for Year	7,325		Less Depreciation	912	
					3,648
	10,625		Repair Van	210	
Less Drawings[1]	2,591		Less Depreciation	42	
		8,034			168
			Current Assets—		
			Stock—		
			Petrol and Oil	842	
			Spare Parts and		
Current Liabilities—			Tyres	464	
Sundry Creditors		164	Tools	106	
					1,412
			Sundry Debtors		95
			Cash		2,875
		£8,198			£8,198

[1] The proprietor's Drawings Account is made up as follows:

	£
Cash	2,400
Petrol and Oil	86
Repairs	40
Insurance	40
Licence	25
	£2,591

Illustration 5

Jones Bros., wholesale stores, purchase goods as follows:

A Dept.	500 articles	
B Dept.	1,000 articles	Total cost £10,000
C Dept.	1,200 articles	

Commencing stocks were:

A Dept. 60 articles   B Dept. 40 articles   C Dept. 76 articles

Their sales were:

A Dept.	510 articles at £4·00 each
B Dept.	960 articles at £4·50 each
C Dept.	1,248 articles at £5·00 each

Assuming the percentage rate of gross profit is the same in the case of all three articles, prepare Departmental Trading Account showing the gross profit on trading to be carried to the firm's Profit and Loss Account. Stocks to be valued on the same basis as purchases.

As the rates of gross profit are the same for each type of article, the cost price of the goods sold must be in the ratio 8:9:10, so that the total cost £10,000 must be divided thus:

$$500 \times 8 = 4,000 = \tfrac{4}{25} \times £10,000 = £1,600 = £3 \cdot 20 \text{ per article}$$
$$1,000 \times 9 = 9,000 = \tfrac{9}{25} \times £10,000 = £3,600 = £3 \cdot 60 \text{ per article}$$
$$1,200 \times 10 = 12,000 = \tfrac{12}{25} \times £10,000 = £4,800 = £4 \cdot 00 \text{ per article}$$

25,000

Profit per article:

	Sale price £p		Cost price £p
A Dept.	4·00	less	3·20 = 0·80
B Dept.	4·50	,,	3·60 = 0·90
C Dept.	5·00	,,	4·00 = 1·00

The numbers of different articles sold are:

	A	B	C
Opening Stock . . .	60	40	76
Purchases . . .	500	1,000	1,200
	560	1,040	1,276
Closing Stock . . .	50	80	28
Sales	510	960	1,248

The profit must therefore be:

A Dept.	510 × £0·80 =	408
B Dept.	960 × £0·90 =	864
C Dept.	1,248 × £1·00 =	1,248
	[as below]	£2,520

The Departmental Trading Account may now be prepared:

DEPARTMENTAL TRADING ACCOUNT FOR THE YEAR ENDED................

	A £	B £	C £	Total £		A £	B £	C £	Total £
Stock[1] .	192	144	304	640	Sales[2] .	2,040	4,320	6,240	12,600
Purchases .	1,600	3,600	4,800	10,000	Stock	160	288	112	560
Gross Profit	408	864	1,248	2,520					
	£2,200	£4,608	£6,352	£13,160		£2,200	£4,608	£6,352	£13,160

[1] Columns may be inserted for quantities.
[2] A Dept. Sales are 510 articles at £4 each = £2,040.

The opening and closing stocks are valued on the same basis as purchases, e.g.:

$$\text{Opening Stock of A Dept.} \quad 60 \times \pounds 3 \cdot 20 = \pounds 192$$
$$\text{Closing} \quad ,, \quad ,, \quad 50 \times \pounds 3 \cdot 20 = \pounds 160$$

Alternatively, the cost price and gross profit per article may be calculated:
Total Sale price of articles purchased:

						£
A	.	.	.	$500 \times \pounds 4 \cdot 00$	.	2,000
B	.	.	.	$1,000 \times \pounds 4 \cdot 50$	.	4,500
C	.	.	.	$1,200 \times \pounds 5 \cdot 00$	.	6,000
						12,500
Total Cost price	.	.	.	.	.	10,000
Gross Profit	.	.	.	.	.	£2,500

This shows a rate of gross profit of 20% on Sales, therefore:

$$\text{Cost price of A} \quad \pounds 4 \cdot 00 - \pounds 0 \cdot 80 = \pounds 3 \cdot 20$$
$$\text{B} \quad \pounds 4 \cdot 50 - \pounds 0 \cdot 90 = \pounds 3 \cdot 60$$
$$\text{C} \quad \pounds 5 \cdot 00 - \pounds 1 \cdot 00 = \pounds 4 \cdot 00$$

Illustration 6

A commenced business on 1st January 19.., with:

Stock—				£
A Dept. .	.	.	.	300
B Dept. .	.	.	.	500
Fixtures	.	.	.	400
Cash .	.	.	.	600

The transactions are:

					£
Purchases—A Dept. .	.	.	.	.	3,100
B Dept. .	.	.	.	.	2,900
Receipts from Debtors	.	.	.	.	5,200
Discounts Allowed to Debtors	.	.	.	.	200
Payments to Creditors	.	.	.	.	4,720
Cash Sales—A Dept..	.	.	.	.	380
B Dept.	.	.	.	.	920
Credit Sales—A Dept.	.	.	.	.	3,700
B Dept.	.	.	.	.	2,900
General Expenses—A Dept.	.	.	.	.	300
B Dept.	.	.	.	.	420
Unallocated expenses	.	.	.	.	480
Drawings	.	.	.	.	400
Cash in hand	.	.	.	.	580
Selling Expenses	.	.	.	.	200
Cartons, etc., purchased	.	.	.	.	320
Creditors outstanding	.	.	.	.	1,600
Stock on hand at 31st December 19. .—A Dept.			.	.	420
B Dept.				.	580
Cartons on hand at 31st December 19...	.	.	.	110

Unallocated general expenses are to be apportioned on the basis of floor space occupied, which is in the ratio of 5:3.

Selling expenses are to be apportioned on the basis of cartons sold, viz., A 60,000, B 45,000.

Prepare: (1) Trial balance.
    (2) Departmental Trading and Profit and Loss Account.
    (3) Balance Sheet as at 31st December 19…

It will be necessary to open and write up the following accounts before preparing the Trial Balance and accounts:

CASH

19..		£	19..			£
Jan. 1	Sundries	600	Dec. 31	Creditors—		
Dec. 31	Cash Sales—			Cash Paid		4,720
	A Dept.	380		Expenses—		
	B Dept.	920		A Dept.		300
	Debtors—			B Dept.		420
	Cash Received	5,200		Unallocated		480
				Selling Expenses		200
				Drawings		400
				Balance	c/d	580
		£7,100				£7,100
19..						
Jan. 1	Balance	b/d 580				

FIXTURES

19..		£				
Jan. 1	Sundries	400				

SUNDRY CREDITORS

19..			£	19..		£
Dec. 31	Cash		4,720	Dec. 31	Purchases[1]—	
	Balances	c/d	1,600		A Dept.	3,100
					B Dept.	2,900
					Cartons	320
			£6,320			£6,320
				19..		
				Jan.	Balances	b/d 1,600

[1] Direct to Trial Balance.

STOCK

19..		A £	B £			
Jan. 1	Sundries	300	500			

GENERAL EXPENSES

19..		A £	B £			
Dec. 31	Cash	300	420			

CAPITAL

				19.. Jan. 1	Sundries			£ **1,800**

GENERAL EXPENSES (*unallocated*)

19.. Dec. 31	Cash			£ 400				

SUNDRY DEBTORS

19.. Dec. 31	Sales—A Dept. ,, B Dept.			£ 3,700 2,900	19.. Dec. 31	Cash Discounts Balances	c/d	£ 5,200 200 1,200
				£6,600				£6,600
19.. Jan. 1	Balances	b/d		1,200				

DISCOUNTS ALLOWED

19.. Dec. 31	Debtors			£ 200				

SALES

				19.. Dec. 31	Cash Debtors		A £ 380 3,700	B £ 920 2,900

Heavy type denotes opening entries, posted from the Journal.

TRIAL BALANCE AS AT 31ST DECEMBER 19..

	Dr.	Cr.
	£	£
Cash in hand	580	
Capital		1,800
[1] Drawings	400	
Creditors		1,600
[2] Purchases—Goods: A Dept.	3,100	
B Dept.	2,900	
Cartons	320	
Sales—A Dept.		4,080
B Dept.		3,820
Debtors	1,200	
Discount	200	
[1] Selling Expenses	200	
General Expenses—A Dept.	300	
B Dept.	420	
Unallocated	480	
Fixtures	400	
Stock—1st January 19..: A Dept.	300	
B Dept.	500	
	£11,300	£11,300

[1] Direct from Cash Book.

[2] Direct from Ledger Account (Creditors).

DEPARTMENTAL TRADING AND PROFIT AND LOSS ACCOUNT
FOR THE YEAR ENDED 31ST DECEMBER 19. .

	A Dept.	B Dept.	Total		A Dept.	B Dept.	Total
	£	£	£		£	£	£
Stock	300	500	800	Sales	4,080	3,820	7,900
Purchases—Goods	3,100	2,900	6,000	Stock	420	580	1,000
Cartons(1)	120	90	210				
Gross Profit c/d	980	910	1,890				
	£4,500	£4,400	£8,900		£4,500	£4,400	£8,900
General Expenses (2)	600	600	1,200	Gross Profit b/d	980	910	1,890
Selling Expenses (3)	115	85	200				
Discounts Allowed (4)	114	86	200				
Net Profit transferred to Capital Account	151	139	290				
	£980	£910	£1,890		£980	£910	£1,890

BALANCE SHEET AS AT 31ST DECEMBER 19. .

	£	£		£	£
Capital—			Fixed Assets—		400
Balance 1st Jan. 19. .	1,800		Fixtures		
Add Profit for year to			Current Assets—		
date	290		Stock—Goods	1,000	
			Cartons	110	
	2,090		Sundry Debtors	1,200	
Less Drawings	400		Cash	580	
		1,690			2,890
Current Liabilities—					
Sundry Creditors		1,600			
		£3,290			£3,290

(1) Cartons are apportioned in the ratio of 60,000:45,000, or as 4:3.

	£
Cartons as per Trial Balance	320
Less Stock as per Balance Sheet	110
	£210

(2) General Expenses apportionment:

	A Dept.	B Dept.
	£	£
(a) As per Trial Balance	300	420
(b) Unallocated General Expenses (Ratio 5:3)	300	180
	£600	£600

(3) and (4). Selling Expenses and Discounts are apportioned in the same ratio as the cartons, viz. 4:3.

Illustration 7

From the following details, prepare vertical Trading and Profit and Loss Account, showing (i) percentage of gross profit to sales; (ii) percentage of net profit to sales; (iii) expenses per £ of sales:

Departments	A	B	C
	£	£	£
Stocks (opening)	2,000	1,300	1,000
Purchases	7,000	4,200	3,630
Sales	8,127	5,418	4,515
Stocks (closing)	3,073	1,332	1,165

Expenses:	£
Rent, Rates, and Insurance . . .	2,100
General	840

Apportion rent, rates, and insurance equally to departments.
Apportion general expenses in relation to sales of each department.

TRADING AND PROFIT AND LOSS ACCOUNT FOR THE.................

	Dept. A £	Dept. B £	Dept. C £	Total £
Sales	8,127	5,418	4,515	18,060
Cost of Sales—				
Opening Stock	2,000	1,300	1,000	4,300
Purchases	7,000	4,200	3,630	14,830
	9,000	5,500	4,630	19,130
Less Closing Stock	3,073	1,332	1,165	5,570
	5,927	4,168	3,465	13,560
Gross Profit	2,200	1,250	1,050	4,500
	£8,127	£5,418	£4,515	£18,060
Percentage of Gross Profit to Sales	27·07%	23·07%	23·26%	24·92%
Administrative Expenses—				
Rent, Rates and Insurance	700	700	700	2,100
General	378	252	210	840
	1,078	952	910	2,940
Net Profit	1,122	298	140	1,560
	£2,200	£1,250	£1,050	£4,500
Percentage of Net Profit to Sales	13·80%	5·50%	3·10%	8·64%
Expenses per £ of Sales	£0·13	£0·18	£0·20	£0·16

Illustration 8

The Directors of Dockets Ltd. wish to ascertain approximately the separate net profits of three particular departments, viz. A, B, and C, for the three months ended 31st March 19...

It is not practicable to take stock on that date, but the accounting system is adequate and the rates of gross profit (calculated without reference to direct expenses) are stable at 40 per cent, 30 per cent, and 15 per cent on Sales of the three departments respectively.

Indirect expenses are to be charged in proportion to departmental sales, except as to one-sixth, which is to be divided equally.

The following figures are extracted from the books:

		A £	B £	C £
Stock, 1st January, 19..		3,000	2,800	4,100
Sales	for the three	14,000	12,000	20,000
Purchases	months ended	9,000	7,200	16,400
Direct Expenses	31st March 19..	1,830	2,840	2,300

Indirect Expenses covering all five departments were £3,600. The Sales of the other departments were £14,000.

Prepare a statement showing estimated net profits of the three departments for the three months to 31st March 19.., making a Stock Reserve for each department (due to special temporary conditions) of 5 per cent on the estimated value at 31st March 19...

DOCKETS LIMITED

STATEMENT OF ESTIMATED PROFIT FOR THE THREE MONTHS
ENDED 31ST MARCH 19..

		Departments				
		A		B		C
£	£	£	£	£	£	
Stock, 1st January 19..		3,000		2,800		4,100
Purchases		9,000		7,200		16,400
		12,000		10,000		20,500
Less Sales	14,000		12,000		20,000	
Less Gross Profit	(40%) 5,600	8,400	(30%) 3,600	8,400	(15%) 3,000	17,000
Estimated Stock, 31/3/19..		£3,600		£1,600		£3,500
Estimated Gross Profit		5,600		3,600		3,000
Less Stock Reserve (5%)	180		80		175	
Direct Expenses	1,830		2,840		2,300	
Indirect Expenses:						
On Sales	700		600		1,000	
Equally	120		120		120	
		2,830		3,640		3,595
Profit		£2,770	Loss	£40	Loss	£595

Notes: (1) It is assumed that there is no Stock Reserve at the beginning of the period.
(2) Indirect Expenses are calculated as follows:

			Sales Proportion £		Equally £
Indirect Expenses—Total £3,600		$\frac{5}{6}$	3,000	$\frac{1}{6}$	600
Less attributable to other departments	$\frac{14,000}{60,000} \times £3,000$		700 $\frac{2}{3} \times £600$		240
			£2,300		£360
Proportion: A	$\frac{14}{60} \times £3,000$		700 $\frac{1}{3} \times 600$		120
B	$\frac{12}{60} \times £3,000$		600 ,,		120
C	$\frac{20}{60} \times £3,000$		1,000 ,,		120
			£2,300		£360

Alternatively, as the expenses to be apportioned on a sales basis are £3,000 and the total sales are £60,000, the percentage is 5 per cent of the respective sales, e.g. A, 5 per cent of £14,000 = £700, etc.

(3) The total Trading Account of the three departments is:

	£		£
Stock	9,900	Sales	46,000
Purchases	32,600	Stock (estimated)	8,700
Gross Profit c/d	12,200		
	£54,700		£54,700
Stock Reserve	435	Gross Profit b/d	12,200
Direct Expenses	6,970		
Indirect Expenses	2,660		
Net Profit	2,135[1]		
	£12,200		£12,200

[1] A, Profit £2,770, *less* B and C, Losses £40 and £595.

CHAPTER 19

BRANCH ACCOUNTS

BRANCH Accounts have for their purpose the recording of the transactions of branches, whether they relate to dealings with the head office, with outsiders, or to dealings between different branches of the same concern. No hard-and-fast rule can be laid down as defining the distinction between a branch and a department; in fact, in many instances a system of accounting suitable for dealing with departmental activities will be entirely adequate for branches. As a general statement, it may be said that where a section of a business is segregated physically from the main section it is a branch; in other words, if the location of activities is separated from the main place of operation, there may be said to be a head office and a branch.

In spite of this statement, it should be borne in mind that in circumstances where complete control is exercised over the activities of a subsidiary section, the management may, and often does, consider it in the light of a mere department.

The methods of accounting applicable to dealings and transactions of and with branches are legion, so that what is the most practical and efficient method applicable to any particular case can only be determined in the light of the particular circumstances of the concern. The branch may be a small retail shop run by a single employee, selling only goods sent by the head office; or, taking the other extreme, it may be a foreign branch situate thousands of miles from the head office, buying its own materials, and manufacturing and distributing the products in its own area—whose activities can only be controlled in a very small degree by the head office.

Thus location, the degree of control exercised by the head office, the nature of the activities and the goods dealt in, the character and status of the personnel, and the number of the branches will all be determining factors in considering what system of accounting is to be adopted.

In many instances mere academic theory must be sacrificed for the sake of expediency and practical results, but whatever treatment is adopted, it should, so far as possible, furnish the head office readily and reliably with the means of arriving at the financial results (in such detail as may be required) and with a check on the efficiency and integrity of the staff of each branch, as well as details as to the comparative efficiency of each branch.

Main Divisions. The main divisions of branch accounting are consequential upon the question of whether full accounting records are, or are not, kept at the branch.

The two main divisions are:

1. Where the accounting of the branch is performed at the head office.
2. Where the branch performs the accounting functions for itself.

It will be necessary to outline the different systems briefly, and each will then be duly considered and illustrated.

1901

As to (1), the system adopted may be:

(a) *Departmental Method.* (See Chapter 18.)

(b) *Debtors Systems*, where all the goods are supplied and the expenses paid by the head office. This merely involves debiting the branch with opening debtors (if any), goods, and expenses, and crediting it with its sales, returns to head office, closing stock, and the closing debtors (if any). Where the assets of the branch are to be recorded distinct from the head office assets, separate Branch Asset Accounts will be opened in the head office books.

If small local purchases are made by the branch, and petty cash disbursements permitted, the same principle will apply, except that the branch must furnish details of these purchases; or, if they are paid for out of receipts, furnish, in addition, a detailed summary of its Cash Account. As to petty cash payments, a detailed summary will have to be furnished to head office. These payments, both as to local purchases and as to petty cash, may be financed on the Imprest System, but this merely obviates any incursion into actual receipts, as the latter will be banked intact locally, daily or at suitable intervals, as required.

(c) *The 'Stock and Debtors' System.* By this method a Branch Stock Account, and (where credit sales are made) a Branch Debtors Account, are kept for the branch quite distinct from the Branch Expenses Account. The Branch Stock Account will be debited with the goods received, credited with returns to head office, sales and the closing stock brought down in the ordinary way. The treatment of the Stock Account will vary according to the method employed of charging the goods out to the branch. The three most common methods are:

(i) At cost price.

(ii) At selling price.

(iii) At cost price to which a certain percentage (loading) is added. This system involves the keeping at the head office of two, or (if credit sales are made) three accounts in respect of the Branch, i.e. (1) Branch Stock Account, (2) Branch Expenses Account, and (3) Branch Debtors Account. If local purchases and petty cash disbursements are permitted, similar treatment to that in (b) will be accorded thereto, except that goods purchased locally must be recorded separately from goods obtained from head office. As a rule, the selling price and cost price plus loading methods are not adopted where considerable local purchases are permitted, because such methods are employed for the purpose of enabling a simple check to be kept on stock, and the presence of locally bought goods will tend to render such a check more complicated.

2. Where the branch performs its own book-keeping, the characteristic features are that in the first place in the head office books the branch is debited with the initial outlay, and with goods sent (if any) and credited with remittances and returns; at the same time, the branch will maintain in its books a Head Office Account which will be reciprocal to the Branch Account in the head office books. Secondly, the branch profit or loss will be ascertained from the branch results compiled from the double entry book-keeping at the branch, and the Branch Account in the head office books will be adjusted (as will be shown) from such results. Thus, in

branches of type (1) the profit or loss is ascertained from the Branch Accounts in the head office books, whereas as regards those of type (2) the profit or loss is obtained from the accounts kept by the branch, and the result subsequently incorporated in the head office books.

No difference in principle exists as regards foreign branches, but its application is complicated by the necessity for converting inter-branch transactions, remittances, and the Branch Profit and Loss Account and Balance Sheet compiled in foreign currency into sterling.

Miscellaneous Points. Before proceeding to illustrate the methods outlined it will be convenient here to deal with a few general matters with reference to Branch Accounts.

1. The head office may be purely a 'clearing house', i.e. it may be responsible for the buying on behalf of ALL the branches, and its function may extend no further. On the other hand, side by side with such a function, it may carry on its own business and sell goods in the ordinary way.

2. Where the branches are dispersed over a wide area, the head office may perform functions as in (1), except that it delegates to special branches the work of intensive distribution, i.e. of distributing goods within certain circumscribed areas, e.g. a multiple concern with branches in every large town might have its head office and chief distributing centre in London with distributing branches (*a*) in Manchester for Lancashire, Yorkshire, Derbyshire, etc.; (*b*) in Bristol for the West Country, and (*c*) in Birmingham for the Midlands. A special feature (affecting detail but not principle) arises here in that the costs of distributing and handling the goods is a cost, the burden of which should be allocated equitably as between all the branches.

3. Sales may be expressed (in the absence of abnormal features) not as *sales,* but as *cash received plus discounts plus closing debtors, less opening debtors,* and this roundabout presentation in place of an ordinary straightforward statement tends to create difficulties for students. In dealing with Branch Accounts this matter is important, particularly as the item 'cash received' is sometimes split into (*a*) 'cash sales' and (*b*) 'cash received from debtors'. If, however, it is perceived that in both cases the receipt simply relates to *cash,* and that other elements mentioned above are given (or are ascertainable), no difficulty should be encountered in determining the amount of **sales** by the process of building up the Branch Debtors Account.

4. Although no precise dividing line can be laid down, it is most usual for wholesale branches (or head office where all orders are executed by it) to be treated departmentally and for retail branches to be treated in one or other of the methods of branch accounting, more often, perhaps, with the main records at the head office.

This procedure will be adopted where the branch merely acts as agent, the actual execution of transactions being performed by the head office, the only difference being that there will be no goods physically supplied to the branch, but a transfer will have to be made to the debit of Branch Profit and Loss Account for the cost of such goods as if they had actually been sent to the branch instead of being consigned elsewhere on its behalf.

Any profit or loss will be transferred from the Branch Profit and Loss Account to the Head Office Profit and Loss Account. In *all* cases, provision should be made for bringing stock on hand down, if necessary, to, say, net realizable value; but where there are loaded values (see p. 1913) the adjustment should be made by means of Stock Reserve or Provision, leaving the loaded price and cost price undisturbed.

The principles will now be illustrated.

DEBTORS SYSTEM

Illustration 1

Entries in head office books:

X BRANCH

19.. Jan. 1 Dec. 31			£	19.. Dec. 31				£
Jan. 1	Sundry Assets	(a)	100	Dec. 31	Cash		(d)	200
Dec. 31	Goods from H.O.	(b)	580		Returns		(e)	22
	Expenses (paid by Branch)	(c)	30		Stock . . £50			
	Expenses (paid by H.O.)		7		Debtors . . 500			
	Profit and Loss Account		155		Sundry-Assets . 100			
						——	c/d	650
			£872					£872
19.. Jan. 1	Balances	b/d	650					

As regards the items on the debit side, the double entry will be completed by credits as follows: (*a*) to Cash, Creditors or Sundry Assets Accounts, (*b*) to Purchases Account, and (*c*) to Cash representing the reimbursement to the branch by the Head Office in respect of petty cash expenses: the double entry for the items on the credit side will be completed by debits as follows: (*d*) to Cash Account, (*e*) to Purchases Account.

The two deficiencies of the above method are that no checks are provided on stock and debtors. These deficiencies may be counteracted by an efficient system of control of stock and debtors, the latter being usually capable of more accurate check than the former.

In this illustration a *pro forma* Debtors Account by way of *memorandum* may be built up as follows:

SUNDRY DEBTORS

			£					£
Opening Balances		b/d	Nil		Cash		c/d	200
Sales			700		Closing Balances			500
			£700					£700
Balances		b/d	500					

It can be seen that, assuming that moneys received by the branch are banked without retention of any part at all, the actual sales figure is the total of the cash received and closing debtors (there being no opening debtors).

It should further be noted that the branch may not pay into the bank intact all moneys received from debtors, or in respect of cash sales; or, even if it does, there may be a lapse of a few days in so doing. In the latter case, it will be necessary to take such lapse of time into account in arriving at the sales figure.

Not infrequently the branch assets are segregated and shown in separate accounts, in which case the sundry assets items of £100 will not appear in this account at all, but in the Branch Assets Account.

The Debtors System, as will be seen, may be supplemented by a memorandum Trading Account. The information is furnished by the branch in its weekly or other periodic returns. Where there are numerous branches a total account may be compiled by means of summary sheets.

It is not unusual for examiners to present summarized data as supplied from the branches (in fact, a copy of the information as it appears in the branch books), from which the head office accounts are to be compiled.

The principles may be best explained by means of a simple example.

Illustration 2[1]

The following is a summary of the accounts as supplied by the branches:

(M) Branches Cash

		£				£
Balance	b/d	100	Head Office		c/d	2,350
Cash Sales	(A)	400	Balance			70
Receipts from Debtors	(B)	1,920				
		£2,420				£2,420
Balance	b/d	70				

(M) Branches Debtors

		£				£
Balances	b/d	300	Cash	(B)		1,920
Sales	(C)	1,960	Discounts	(D)		50
			Returns	(E)		60
			Balances	c/d		230
		£2,260				£2,260
Balances	b/d	230				

The following is the account of the branches in the head office books:

Branches

			£				£
Balance—				Cash			2,350
Cash	£100			Balance—			
Debtors	300			Cash	£70		
Stock	200		600	Debtors	230		
Goods		b/d	2,000	Stock	240	c/d	540
Profit to Profit and Loss Account			290				
			£2,890				£2,890
Balance		b/d	540				

[1] Elementary students of Branch Accounts should defer the study of this with the succeeding illustration until the whole chapter has been read.

Prepare Memorandum Branches Final Accounts.

The first two accounts marked (M) are merely memorandum serving to supply details necessary to analyse the amount of profit.

It will be seen from the Branches Account that they are accountable for the opening balance of £600 plus goods received £2,000, less cash remitted £2,350. This amounts to £250, but as the assets at the end are £540 there must be a profit of £290.

The amount of £290 is now to be proved.

This figure may be proved by building up the 'Double Entry', on the assumption that the information contained in the Memorandum Accounts is to be converted into full double entry:

Memorandum

BRANCHES TRADING AND PROFIT AND LOSS ACCOUNT

		£					£
Stock		200	Cash Sales (A)	£400			
Purchases		2,000	Credit Sales (C)	1,960			2,360
Discounts (D)		50				B.S.	240
Sales Returns (E)		60	Stock				
Net Profit		290					
		£2,600					£2,600

BRANCHES BALANCE SHEET

	£			£
Head Office (Ledger)	540	Cash (Ledger)		70
		Debtors (Ledger)		230
		Stock (Profit and Loss)		240
	£540			£540

The branch books would, if built up on double-entry lines, contain the following accounts:

HEAD OFFICE[1]

		£				£
Cash	(g)	2,350	Balance	b/d		600
Balance	c/d	540	[i.e. Stock (o) £200			
			Cash (o) 100			
			Debtors (o) 300]			
			Goods	(c)		2,000
			Profit and Loss Account	(f)		290
		£2,890				£2,890
			Balance	b/d		540

[1] This account is exactly reverse to the Branches Account in the head office books, and consequently in preparing the accounts the vital account is the Head Office Account as it would appear in the books of the Branches. This account, together with the above information, would supply the usual Double Entry, but as the Branches Account as it appears in the head office books is given instead of the Head Office Account as it would appear in the books of the Branches, the compilation must be adjusted accordingly.

CASH

			£				£
Balance	b/d	(o)	100	Cash remitted to H.O.	(g)	2,350
Cash Sales		(a)	400	Balance	c/d	70
Debtors			1,920			
			£2,420				£2,420
Balance	b/d		70			

DEBTORS

			£				£
Balances	b/d	(o)	300	Cash			1,920
Sales		(b)	1,960	Discounts	(d)	50
				Returns	(e)	60
				Balances	c/d	230
			£2,260				£2,260
Balances	b/d		230			

The following rules should be carried out:

1. All the items on the debit and credit sides of the Branch Accounts must be accounted for on the SAME side in the Memorandum Accounts.

2. All the remaining items in the Memorandum Accounts must contain double entry amongst themselves.

The items in the Branch Accounts will now be considered in detail:

		£	MEMO. figures
(1)	Balances Debit Cash	100	DEBIT of Cash Account
	Debtors	300	Debtors
	Stock	200	Trading Account
(2)	Goods Debit	2,000	DEBIT of Trading Account
(3)	Profit Debit	290	DEBIT of Profit and Loss Account
(4)	Cash Credit	2,350	CREDIT of Cash Account
(5)	Balances Credit Cash	70	CREDIT of Cash Account
	Debtors	230	Debtors
	Stock	240	Trading Account

All these are in heavy type in the preceding example.

It will now be seen that the remaining items in the Memorandum Accounts have double entry, viz.:

(A) Cash Sales	Debit Cash	Credit Trading Account
(B) Receipts from Debtors	,, ,,	,, Debtors
(C) (Credit) Sales	,, Debtors	,, Trading Account
(D) Discounts	,, Profit and Loss Account	,, Debtors
(E) Returns	,, Trading Account	,, ,,

It may be observed that if a Head Office Account in the books of the branches were opened it would be the same on the *reverse side* as the Branches Account in the head office books; so that if the Branches Account in the head office books be viewed as if it were the reciprocal account in the branch books, the double entry aspect is simple enough.

Lest any confusion arises it must be stated that the only double entry that appears in the head office books is comprised of the postings to and from Branches Account; **the Memorandum Accounts being merely supplementary information to that shown in the Branches Account in the head office books.**

Illustration 3

The head office supplies its branches with goods at cost price, and pays all expenses other than petty cash of the branches. Weekly returns are furnished to the head office, the summaries of which are as follows:

BRANCHES CASH

Balances . . b/d	(1)	200	Petty Cash . . .	(c)	270
Receipts from Debtors .	(a)	15,000	Bank . . .	(2)	19,730
Cash Sales . . .	(b)	5,000	Balances . . c/d	(8)	200
		£20,200			£20,200
Balances . . b/d	(8)	200			

BRANCHES DEBTORS

			£				£
Balances . . b/d	(3)	1,200	Cash . . .	(a)	15,000
Sales	(e)	18,600	Discounts . .	(f)	420
			Bad Debts . .		580
			Balances . . c/d	(8)	3,800
		£19,800			£19,800
Balances . . b/d	(8)	3,800			

HEAD OFFICE books:

BRANCHES

				£					£
Balance—					Expenses . . b/d	(6)	350
Cash (1)	£200				Bank . . .	(2)	19,730
Debtors (3)	1,200				Balance . . c/d	(h)	2,920
Sundry							
Assets (9)	2,000						
Stock (4)	3,000		b/d	6,400			
Goods . . .			(5)	16,000			
Expenses . .			(6)	500			
Sundry Assets purchased			(10)	100			
				£23,000			£23,000
Balance . . b/d		(h)	2,920		Balance—		
Expenses . . c/d		(11)	150		Cash . £200	(6)	
Profit and Loss Account		(12)	5,080		Debtors . 3,800		
					Sundry		
					Assets . 2,050		
					Stock . 2,100	c/d	8,150
				£8,150			£8,150
Balance . . b/d		(8)	8,150		Expenses . . b/d	(11)	150

Closing stock, £2,100. Expenses outstanding, £150. Write off £50 depreciation on sundry assets.

Prepare Memorandum Trading and Profit and Loss Account.

Memorandum TRADING AND PROFIT AND LOSS

			£					£
Stock	. . .	(4)	3,000	Sales—				
Purchases	. .	(5)	16,000	Cash	.	£5,000	(b)	
Gross Profit	. c/d	(d)	6,700	Credit	.	18,000	(e)	
						———		23,600
				Stock	. . .		(8)	2,100
			£25,700					£25,700
Sundry Expenses .	.	(j)	300	Gross Profit	. b/d		(d)	6,700
Petty Cash	. .	(c)	270					
Discounts	. .	(f)	{ 420					
Bad Debts			{ 580					
Depreciation	.	(i)	50					
Net Profit	. .	(12)	5,080					
			£6,700					£6,700

Memorandum SUNDRY ASSETS

			£				£
Balance	. b/d	(9)	2,000	Profit and Loss Account	(i)	50
Cash Purchase	. .	(10)	100	Balances . . c/d	(8)	2,050
			£2,100			£2,100
Balances	. b/d	(8)	2,050			

Memorandum SUNDRY EXPENSES

			£				£
Cash .	. .	(6)	500	Expenses o/s . b/d	(6)	350
Expenses o/s	. c/d	(10)	150	Profit and Loss Account	(j)	300
			£650			£650
				Expenses o/s . b/d	(11)	150

Items numbered are 'same side' items.

Items lettered are 'double entry' items.

As has been indicated, if the Branches Account in the head office books were written up in the Branch Accounts on the reverse side, the four accounts, viz.:

1. Branches Cash;
2. Branches Debtors;
3. Head Office Account;
4. Trading and Profit and Loss Account,

would provide the complete double entry; therefore, in compiling the Memorandum Trading and Profit and Loss Account, the items in Branches Account in the head office books are to be accounted for on the SAME side.

If account (3) were actually in the branches, it would appear as follows:

HEAD OFFICE

			£				£
Balance . . .	c/d		8,000	Balance . . .	b/d		2,920
				Profit and Loss Account			5,080
			£8,000				£8,000
				Balance . . .	b/d		8,000

This account is reverse to the Branches Account in the head office books.

The Branch Balance Sheet would be:

BRANCH BALANCE SHEET

	£			£	£
Expenses Outstanding . .	150	Cash			200
Head Office . . .	8,000	Debtors			3,800
		Sundry Assets . . .		2,100	
		Less Depreciation . .		50	
					2,050
		Stock			2,100
	£8,150				£8,150

'STOCK AND DEBTORS' SYSTEM

(i) Where the Goods are Invoiced at Cost

Illustration 4

From the facts contained in the illustration on p. 1904, the following accounts will appear in the head office books.

BRANCH STOCK

19..			£	19..			£
Dec. 31	Goods (Purchases Account)		580	Dec. 31	Sales		700
	Gross Profit to Branch				Returns (Purchases Account)		22
	Profit and Loss Account .		192		Balance	c/d	50
			£772				£772
19..							
Jan. 1	Balance	b/d	50				

BRANCH DEBTORS

19..			£	19..			£
Dec. 31	Sales		700	Dec. 31	Cash		200
					Balances . . .	c/d	500
			£700				£700
19..							
Jan. 1	Balances	b/d	500				

BRANCH EXPENSES

19.. Dec. 31	Head Office Cash " " "		£ 30 7 £37	19.. Dec. 31	Branch Profit and Loss Account		£ 37 £37

SUNDRY ASSETS

19.. Jan. 1	Balances .	b/d	£ 100				

BRANCH PROFIT AND LOSS ACCOUNT

19.. Dec. 31	Expenses . Net Profit to General Profit and Loss Account .		£ 37 155 £192	19.. Dec. 31	Gross Profit from Branch Stock Account		£ 192 £192

It has been assumed that there are no discounts allowed to debtors or bad debts, and that all receipts from debtors are immediately banked.

In the Stock and Debtors System, Discounts and Allowances will be dealt with in the usual way, i.e. debit Discounts Allowed and Allowances, credit Branch Debtors.

Illustration 5

The following are the details of a new branch.

	£
Goods sent to Branch at Cost	500
Goods returned from Branch at Cost . .	30
Expenses Paid by Head Office	100
Remittances from Branch	420
Receipts from Debtors not paid in by Branch . .	30
Cash Sales	25
Credit Sales	520
Branch Stock—closing	170
Branch Debtors—closing	77
Discounts Allowed to Customers by Branch . .	18

Show accounts both under the Debtors System and under the Stock and Debtors System.

1. In the Debtors System, the following account will appear in the head office books:

BRANCH

Goods from H.O.		£ 500		Returns			£ 30
Expenses		100		Remittances to H.O.			420
Profit to General Profit and				Cash		£30	
Loss Account		127		Stock		170	
				Debtors		77	
						——	c/d 277
		£727					£727
Balance	b/d	277					

Proof of Debtors:

Memorandum DEBTORS

Sales		£ 520		Cash			£ 425
				Discounts			18
				Balance		c/d	77
		£520					£520
Balance	b/d	77					

The cash received must be:

		£
Cash Sales		25
Receipts from Debtors		425
		£450
Accounted for by:		
Remittances	£420	
Balance in hand	30	
	——	£450

The sales are made up as follows:

		£
Cash received from Debtors		425
Discounts		18
Closing Debtors		77
		520
Less Opening Debtors		nil
		£520

2. In the Stock and Debtors System the accounts in the books of the head office would be:

BRANCH STOCK

	£			£
Goods	500	Returns . . .		30
Gross Profit to Branch		Cash Sales . .		25
Profit and Loss Account	245	Credit Sales . .		520
		Balance . . .	c/d	170
	£745			£745
Balance . . .	b/d 170			

BRANCH EXPENSES

	£		£
Expenses	100	Branch Profit and Loss	
Discounts . . .	18	Account . . .	118
	£118		£118

BRANCH DEBTORS

	£			£
Sales	520	Cash		425
		Discounts .		18
		Balance . . .	c/d	77
	£520			£520
Balance . . .	b/d 77			

BRANCH CASH

	£			£
Branch Debtors . .	425	Remittances to H.O. .		420
Cash Sales . .	25	Balance . . .	c/d	30
	£450			£450
Balance . . .	b/d 30			

BRANCH PROFIT AND LOSS ACCOUNT

	£		£
Expenses (detailed) . .	118	Gross Profit from Branch	
Net Profit to General Profit		Stock Account . .	245
and Loss Account . .	127		
	£245		£245

(ii) **Where Goods are Invoiced at Selling or Loaded Price.** The second manner of dealing with the Stock and Debtors method is to invoice goods to the branch at loaded prices, either at selling price, or at a price which represents cost plus a percentage.

Where the goods sent from head office are invoiced to the branch at selling price, the cash remitted and retained, plus the closing stock, should equal the total of the opening stock and the goods invoiced, less returns. An efficient check may thus be kept on the branch manager.

The suitability of this method must depend on circumstances, the chief of which are:

1. Type and size of the business;
2. Stability of prices, buying and selling, quantities and qualities, particular regard being paid to storage facilities;
3. The number of different classes of goods handled;
4. The degree of variability in gross profit rates, particularly where goods purchased cannot be returned, e.g. newspapers;
5. Whether price reductions are required or usual through end-of-season sales, change in fashions, perishable goods, etc.

The advantages of the method are:

(a) Efficient check on stock and receipts from sales, especially where goods are sold at absolutely fixed prices;

(b) Even where many lines are dealt in, the method will be helpful as a check, although not so close as in (a);

(c) As the stock (at selling price) is known at any time, interim accounts can be prepared without the need for approximating stock;

(d) The Branch Manager need not be informed of the cost price.

The disadvantages are:

(i) The need for pricing out all the lines at both cost and selling price, although many large firms do not attempt a strictly accurate result and price out by sampling only;

(ii) The method is useless where goods are perishable or deteriorate quickly, or where selling prices are not fixed or wide discretion as to prices is given to Branch Managers.

The selling-price method is adopted where the goods are sold at certain fixed prices, e.g. proprietary articles, whereas the 'percentage on cost' method is adopted where the selling price cannot be rigidly determined beforehand, or where the goods are of a mixed type, e.g. costumiers, greengrocers, and butchers. Where the loaded price method is adopted, the books kept by the branch will be memorandum, the essential double entry book-keeping being done by the head office. Three accounts will be kept in the head office books:

1. Branch Stock Account.
2. Goods sent to Branches Account.
3. Branch Adjustment Account.

The Branch Stock Account deals with all goods received, returned, and sold by the branch, whereas the Branch Adjustment Account is in effect a Branch Trading Account. These accounts seem to cause students a considerable amount of difficulty, but if their functions are thoroughly understood no difficulties should arise.

When goods are sent to the branch, Branch Stock Account is debited with the full invoice price of the goods, the cost price being credited to a Goods Sent to Branches Account and the loading (i.e. the difference between the cost price and the invoice price) credited to the Branch Adjustment Account, it being in effect the anticipated profit that will be made by the branch on the sale of these goods. The converse entries will be made for returns by the branch to the head office. Alternatively, the goods may be credited at the invoice price to the Goods Sent to Branches Account and returns from the branch to head office debited thereto at full invoice price, the net loading being transferred in one sum to the Branch Adjustment Account at periodic intervals.

Illustration 6

A, Ltd., sends to its Oxford branch goods costing £150. They are invoiced at selling price, £200, being $33\frac{1}{3}$ per cent on *cost*. Goods £40 are returned to head office. The entries showing the record of these transactions in the head office books are:

			£	£
Oxford Branch stock	. . . . .	Dr.	200	
Goods sent to Branches	. . . . .	Cr.		150
Oxford Branch adjustment	. . . . .	Cr.		50
Goods sent to Branches	. . . . .	Dr.	30	
Oxford Branch Adjustment	. . . . .	Dr.	10	
Oxford Branch stock	. . . . .	Cr.		40

or alternatively:

			£	£
Oxford Branch Stock	. . . . .	Dr.	200	
Goods sent to Branches	. . . . .	Cr.		200
Goods sent to Branches	. . . . .	Dr.	40	
Oxford Branch Stock	. . . . .	Cr.		40
Goods sent to Branches	. . . . .	Dr.	40	
Oxford Branch adjustment	. . . . .	Cr.		40

It will be seen that in each case the credit balances are £120 on Goods Sent to Branches Account and £40 on Oxford Branch Adjustment Account, being cost price of goods sent (less returns), £120 and loading of £40. The latter is $33\frac{1}{3}$ per cent of £120, or 25 per cent of £160.

At the end of the accounting period, Goods Sent to Branches Account will be closed off by a transfer to Purchases Account in order that the Head Office Trading Account may show the true figure in respect of head office purchases.

The branch will periodically send details of sales effected to the head office accompanied by the cash in respect of such sales. From the information supplied, the head office will debit cash for cash received in respect of sales, debit Branch Debtors Account in respect of credit sales (if any), and credit Branch Stock Account with the total sales.

At the end of the accounting period, the balance of Branch Stock Account will be brought down to the debit of that account. This figure represents the amount of stock at *loaded* price held by the branch. This figure must be reduced to cost for the purposes of determining the profit, and this result is achieved by debiting the Branch Adjustment Account above the line and crediting it below the line with the amount of the loading on the closing stock, this being the *unrealized* profit on the stock. In the Balance Sheet the balances on the Branch Stock Account and of the Branch Adjustment Account will be offset, the result being shown as

Stock at Branches at cost. The balance on the Branch Adjustment Account will now represent the gross profit made by the branch during the period, and be transferred to Branch Profit and Loss Account.

Illustration 6

B, Ltd., has a branch at Bristol. The firm deals in one standard article, the gross profit on which is 25 per cent on cost price. All goods are invoiced to the branch at selling price. All sales are for cash. The branch transactions for the year to 31st December 19.., are:

	£
Goods from Head Office at Invoiced Price	6,000
Goods returned to Head Office at Invoiced Price	100
Cash Sales	4,900
Stock on hand at 31st Dec. 19.., at Invoiced Price	1,000

All cash is remitted to the head office weekly. The Bristol Branch Stock Account, the Bristol Branch Adjustment Account, and the Goods Sent to Branch Account will appear in the head office books as follows:

BRISTOL BRANCH STOCK

19..			£	19..			£
Dec. 31	Goods		6,000	Dec. 31	Returns		100
					Sales—Cash		4,900
					Balance	c/d	1,000
			£6,000				£6,000
19..							
Jan. 1	Balance	b/d	1,000				

BRISTOL BRANCH ADJUSTMENT ACCOUNT

19..			£	19..			£
Dec. 31	Branch Stock Account 20% on £100		20	Dec. 31	Branch Stock Account— 20% on £6,000		1,200
	Gross Profit transferred to Branch Profit and Loss Account		980				
	Balance— 20% on £1,000	c/d	200				
			£1,200				£1,200
				19..			
				Jan. 1	Balance	b/d	200

GOODS SENT TO BRANCH

19..			£	19..			£
Dec. 31	Branch Stock Account —Returns		80	Dec. 31	Bristol Branch Stock		4,800
	Transfer to Head Office Purchases Account		4,720				
			£4,800				£4,800

In the Balance Sheet, the stock at branch will be shown at cost, i.e. £1,000 − £200 = £800. It must be remembered that if goods are loaded at 25 per cent on cost price, it is necessary to deduct 20 per cent from the loaded figure, i.e. selling price, to find the cost price. In questions of this type, students must exercise great care in the conversion to cost or selling price. If the question states the loading in terms of the cost price, it can easily be converted into a percentage on selling price, as in the above illustration. In loading-up from cost to selling price (i.e. to find the amount to charge-up to the branch) the increase must be in terms of *cost* price, whereas in 'loading down' (i.e. to obtain the internal profit to transfer to Branch Adjustment Account) the decrease must be in terms of *selling* price.

In the above illustration the gross profit shown on the Branch Adjustment Account can be proved from the fact that the sales of the branch are £4,900. The rate of gross profit on sales is 20 per cent; therefore, the gross profit is £980.

Branch Expenses. It will usually be found in cases of this type that the branch will be allowed to make certain small payments on its own account. These may be dealt with in two ways:

1. On the imprest system, cash being sent each week to the branch in respect of the past week's expenses.
2. By allowing the branch to deduct the expenses from the cash received. In such cases, it will be necessary to open a Branch Cash Account, to which all cash sales will be debited, the credit for which will appear in the Branch Stock Account. All expenses paid by the branch must be credited to this account and debited to a Branch Expenses Account. Finally, the cash remitted will be credited to the Branch Cash Account. If no money is retained, the Branch Cash Account will balance; should any cash be retained, it will be equal to the debit balance on the account.

Illustration 7

Cash sales by branch are £2,000, of which £200 has been utilized in payment of expenses and £1,780 remitted. The Branch Cash Account will appear in the Head Office books as follows:

BRANCH CASH

			£					£
Sales—					Expenses—			
Branch Stock Account			2,000		Branch Expenses Account			200
					Head Office Account			1,780
					Balance		c/d	20
			£2,000					£2,000
Balance		b/d	20					

Where the branch makes, in addition to cash sales, a number of credit sales, the branch will usually keep Memorandum Sales Ledgers. In the head office books, the total of the credit sales will be credited to Branch Stock Account and debited to Branch Debtors Account. Converse entries are required for returns tc Branch by its customers. The cash received from each branch must be split into two portions, that relating to cash sales being posted to the credit of Branch Stock Account and that relating to credit sales to the credit of Branch Debtors Account. Thus, the balance on the Branch Debtors Account should always equal the total of the individual balances shown on the accounts in the Memorandum Ledger kept at the branch, subject to adjustment for bad debts, discounts, and allowances.

Illustration 8

A opens a new branch at Brighton to which all goods are invoiced at selling price, the gross profit being 25 per cent on Sales. For the year to 31st December 19.., the branch has the following transactions:-

	£
Goods from Head Office (cost price)	6,300
Goods returned to Head Office (invoice price)	800
Cash Sales	4,000
Credit Sales	2,000
Cash received from Debtors	1,600
Cash remitted to Head Office by Branch	5,300
Expenses paid by Branch	300

The accounts in the head office books will be as follows:

BRIGHTON BRANCH STOCK

19.. Dec. 31			£	19.. Dec. 31			£
	Goods sent to Branches Account[1]		8,400		Returns		800
					Cash Sales		4,000
					Credit Sales		2,000
					Balance	c/d	1,600
			£8,400				£8,400
19.. Jan. 1	Balance	b/d	1,600				

BRIGHTON BRANCH ADJUSTMENT ACCOUNT

19.. Dec. 31			£	19.. Dec. 31		£
	Transfer to Branch Profit and Loss Account— Gross Profit[2]		1,500		Goods sent to Branches Account	1,900
	Balance— 25% on £1,600	c/d	400			
			£1,900			£1,900
				19.. Jan. 1	Balance b/d	400

[1] i.e. 25 per cent on selling price = 33⅓ per cent on cost price; i.e. £6,300+£2,100 = £8,400.
[2] i.e. 25 per cent on Sales, £6,000.

BRIGHTON BRANCH DEBTORS

19..			£	19..			£
Dec. 31	Brighton Branch Stock Account— Sales		2,000	Dec. 31	Cash Balances	c/d	1,600 400
			£2,000				£2,000
19.. Jan. 1	Balances	b/d	400				

GOODS SENT TO BRANCHES

19..		£	19..		£
Dec. 31	Brighton Branch Stock Account	800	Dec. 31	Brighton Branch Stock Account	8,400
	Brighton Branch Adjustment Account— 25% on £7,600	1,900			
	Head Office Purchases Account— 75% on £7,600	5,700			
		£8,400			£8,400

BRIGHTON BRANCH EXPENSES

19..		£			
Dec. 31	Brighton Branch Cash Account	300			

BRIGHTON BRANCH CASH

19..		£	19..		£
Dec. 31	Brighton Branch Stock Account: Cash Sales Brighton Branch Debtors	4,000 1,600	Dec. 31	Brighton Branch Expenses Account Head Office	300 5,300
		£5,600			£5,600

Note. If £50 cash had been retained by the branch to meet current expenditure, there would be a balance (debit) of £50 on the Branch Cash Account, the amount of cash remitted to the Head Office being reduced to £5,250.

The cost plus percentage method will be treated in exactly the same manner so far as the accounts are concerned, but there will almost inevitably be a discrepancy between the balancing figure on the Branch Stock Account and the actual stock in hand. The treatment of these and other differences will now be dealt with, it being similar whether the cost plus percentage or the selling price system is in force.

Goods in Transit. Where goods are lost in transit the head office accounts will, where the loss arises in the transit to the branch, be adjusted by debiting the *cost* price of the goods to a special account, called Goods Lost in Transit Account, and the *loading* to Branch Adjustment Account, the total loaded price being credited to Branch Stock Account. At the same time the transfer from Goods Sent to Branches Account in respect of the cost price of the goods sent (and lost) should be credited to Head Office Purchases Account. If the loss is covered by insurance, the amount in Goods Lost in Transit Account will be transferred to the debit of the Insurance Company, otherwise the loss will be debited to the Branch Profit and Loss Account or the Head Office Profit and Loss Account, according to whether the branch or the head office is at fault.

Illustration 9

Goods costing £1,600 are sent to branch, loading being 20 per cent of selling price (or 25 per cent of cost). During transit the whole consignment is lost. Show Ledger entries in the head office books.

Head Office books:

BRANCH STOCK

	£		£
Goods	2,000	*Branch Adjustment Account*	400
		Goods Lost in Transit Account .	1,600
	£2,000		£2,000

GOODS SENT TO BRANCHES

	£		£
Branch Adjustment Account	400	Branch Stock Account .	2,000
Head Office Purchases Account .	1,600		
	£2,000		£2,000

BRANCH ADJUSTMENT ACCOUNT

	£		£
Branch Stock Account—re Goods lost in transit	400	Goods sent to Branches Account . .	400

GOODS LOST IN TRANSIT

	£		
[1] *Branch Stock Account—re Goods lost in transit*	1,600		

[1] If fully insured, this amount will be transferred to the debit of the Insurance Company; otherwise to the debit of Branch Profit and Loss Account or Head Office Profit and Loss Account.

The adjusting entries are shown in italics.

Where the goods are lost in transit from the branch to the head office, the entries will be made as for returns from branch (as if they had actually reached the head office), and the loss recorded by debiting Goods Lost in

Transit Account and crediting Trading Account with the cost price of the goods under the heading of Stock. A transfer from Goods Lost in Transit Account will be made to the Insurance Company if the loss is covered by insurance, otherwise the loss will be debited to the Branch Profit and Loss Account or the Head Office Profit and Loss Account.

Illustration 10

Goods costing £1,600 are sent to a branch, loading being 20 per cent of selling price. The whole of the goods are returned to head office, and during reconveyance are lost. Show Ledger entries in the head office books.

Head Office books:

BRANCH STOCK

	£			
Goods sent to Branches . .	2,000	Returns . . .		£ 2,000

GOODS SENT TO BRANCHES

Branch Stock Account— Goods returned . .	2,000	Branch Stock Account— Goods sent . . .	2,000

GOODS LOST IN TRANSIT

	£		
Trading Account . .	1,600		

TRADING ACCOUNT (includes)

				£
			Stock lost in transit . .	1,600

Handling Charges. Where the head office charges out goods to the branch loaded with a nominal percentage to cover cost of handling, the same principles, as already outlined, are applicable.

Illustration 11

A limited company has its head office in London and a branch in Birmingham. The head office supplies the branch with all its goods, which are charged out at cost, plus 10 per cent to cover the cost of handling.

The branch sales are for cash, and no provision is made in the system of book-keeping for credit sales at the branch, but in actual practice limited credit is given in a few selected cases. All takings are paid into the bank for credit of head office.

Show how the following items relating to the branch would appear in the Head Office Ledger, and close off the accounts concerned:

	£
Stock—1st January 19.. (at cost to Branch)	2,200
Cash received from Debtors during the year	20,000
Debtors—1st January 19..	80
Goods sent to Branch during the year (at Cost to Head Office)	14,000
Debtors—31st December 19..	100
Stock—31st December 19.. (at Cost to Branch)	1,980

Head Office books:

BIRMINGHAM BRANCH STOCK

19.. Jan. 1 Dec. 31	Stock Goods sent to Branch (Birmingham) Account Gross Profit	b/d (a)	£ 2,200 15,400 4,400 —— £22,000	19.. Dec. 31	Sales Balance	 c/d	£ 20,020 1,980 —— £22,000
19.. Jan. 1	Balance	b/d	1,980				

BIRMINGHAM BRANCH DEBTORS

19.. Jan. 1 Dec. 31	Balances Sales	b/d	£ 80 20,020 —— £20,100	19.. Dec. 31	Cash Balances	 c/d	£ 20,000 100 —— £20,100
19.. Jan. 1	Balances	b/d	100				

GOODS SENT TO BRANCH (BIRMINGHAM)

19.. Dec. 31	Purchases Account Birmingham Branch Adjustment Account		£ 14,000 1,400 —— £15,400	19.. Dec. 31	Birmingham Branch Stock Account		£ 15,400 —— £15,400

BIRMINGHAM BRANCH ADJUSTMENT ACCOUNT

19.. Dec. 31	Trading Account— 10% on cost of Goods sold Balance being 10% of £1,800	 (b) c/d	£ 1,420 180 —— £1,600	19.. Jan. 1 Dec. 31	Balance Goods sent to Branch (Birmingham) Account	b/d	£ 200 1,400 —— £1,600
				19.. Jan. 1	Balance	b/d	180

Note. Items in italics are opening balances.

Reconciliation of Profit:

£

Cost of the goods sold:

				£
Beginning Stock	.	.	.	2,000
Plus Transfers				14,000
				16,000
Less Closing Stock	.		.	1,800
Cost	.		.	£14,200
Sales	.	.	.	20,020
Cost	.	.	.	14,200
Profit [see (*a*) and (*b*)]	.	.		£5,820

The profit is made up of items marked (*a*) and (*b*) above.

The item of £1,420 will be credited to the appropriate account recording the handling charges.

It should be remembered, in dealing with the accounts of subsequent periods, that the balance on Branch Adjustment Account at the end of the preceding year must be duly taken into account.

Illustration 12

Goods are *invoiced* in the first year to a new branch at £2,400, being cost price plus 20 per cent on cost. The sales by branch are: cash, £210; credit, £1,800. The stock on hand at loaded price is £390. Bad debts written off are £200, and discounts allowed to debtors, £50; £1,300 is received from debtors, and all proceeds are remitted to head office intact.

In the second year goods *costing* £1,440 are sent to the branch, while total sales are £1,980 (£100 cash sales). The stock on hand at loaded price is £108. Discounts allowed to debtors are £100. £50 cash received has not yet been remitted by the branch. Closing debtors, £130. There is a discrepancy between the balance on the Branch Stock Account and the actual value (at selling price) of the stock in hand, the Branch Stock Account recording £30 in excess.

Show Ledger Accounts in the head office books.

Head Office books:

BRANCH STOCK

			£				£
Year 1	Goods sent to Branches Account . . .		2,400	Year 1	Sales—		
					Branch Cash Account		210
					Branch Debtors .		1,800
					Balance. . . .	c/d	390
			£2,400				£2,400
Year 2	Balance. . .	b/d	390	Year 2	Sales—		
	Goods sent to Branches Account .		1,728		Branch Cash Account		100
					Branch Debtors .		1,880
					Branch Stock Shortage Account . .		*30*
					Balance. . . .	c/d	108
			£2,118				£2,118
Year 3	Balance. . . .	b/d	108				

GOODS SENT TO BRANCHES

			£				£
Year 1	Branch Adjustment Account.		400	Year 1	Branch Stock Account .		2,400
	Purchases (or Trading) Account . .		2,000				
			£2,400				£2,400
Year 2	Branch Adjustment Account.		288	Year 2	Branch Stock Account .		1,728
	Purchases (or Trading) Account . .		1,440				
			£1,728				£1,728

BRANCH ADJUSTMENT ACCOUNT

			£				£
Year 1	Branch Profit and Loss Account . . .	(a)	335	Year 1	Goods sent to Branches Account . .		400
	Balance. . .	c/d	65				
			£400				£400
Year 2	Branch Stock Shortage Account		5	Year 2	Balance. . .	b/d	65
	Branch Profit and Loss Account . .	(b)	330		Goods sent to Branches Account . .		288
	Balance. . .	c/d	18				
			£353				£353
				Year 3	Balance. . . .	b/d	18

BRANCH DEBTORS

			£				£
Year 1	Branch Stock Account .		1,800	Year 1	Branch Cash Account .		1,300
					Bad Debts . .		200
					Discounts . .		50
					Balances . .	c/d	250
			£1,800				£1,800
Year 2	Balances . .	b/d	250	Year 2	Branch Cash Account .		1,900
	Branch Stock Account .		1,880		Discounts . .		100
					Balances . .	c/d	130
			£2,130				£2,130
Year 3	Balances . . .	b/d	130				

BRANCH CASH

			£				£
Year 1	Branch Debtors .		1,300	Year 1	Head Office . . .		1,510
	Branch Stock Account .		210				
			£1,510				£1,510
Year 2	Branch Debtors .		1,900	Year 2	Head Office . . .		1,950
	Branch Stock Account .		100		Balance. . .	c/d	50
			£2,000				£2,000
Year 3	Balance. . .	b/d	50				

BRANCH STOCK SHORTAGE ACCOUNT

			£			£
Year 2	Branch Stock Account	.	30	Year 2	Branch Adjustment Account Branch Profit and Loss Account . . .	5 25
			£30			£30

The gross profit = 20% of cost or 16⅔% of selling price.
  (a) 1st year: ⅙ × £2,101 = £335.
  (b) 2nd year: ⅙ × £1,980 = £330.

Double-column Method. Instead of maintaining separate Branch Stock Accounts and Branch Adjustment Accounts, it is possible to open one account ruled with double columns, one to record the goods at the loaded or selling price (which is merely memorandum, the entries therein not being part of the double entry system), and the other to record the double entry detail, including the purchases and stock figures at cost price and the sales at selling price in the ordinary way.

Illustration 13

The Bristol branch of A, Ltd., to which goods are invoiced at 25 per cent above cost, has the following transactions for the year to 31st December 19..:

	£
Stock on hand at 1st January 19.. . . .	1,000 (invoice price)
Stock on hand at 31st December 19.. . . .	4,600 (,,)
Goods from Head Office during year . . .	20,000 (,,)
Sales for year	16,400
Discounts allowed	400
Cash remitted to Head Office during year . .	16,000

The double-column Branch Account will then be as follows:

BRISTOL BRANCH

			Invoice Price					Invoice Price	
19.. Jan. 1 Dec. 31	Balance . Goods sent to Branches Account . Gross Profit transferred to Branch Profit and Loss Account .	b/d	£ 1,000 20,000	£ 800 16,000 3,280	19.. Dec. 31	Sales— Branch Debtors . Balance: Stock	c/d	£ 16,400 4,600	£ 16,400 3,680
			£21,000	£20,080				£21,000	£20,080
19.. Jan. 1	Balance . .	b/d	4,600	3,680					

The other accounts require no special comment.

The employment of the Branch Adjustment Account method will produce an identical result, thus:

BRANCH ADJUSTMENT ACCOUNT

19.. Dec. 31	Branch Profit and Loss Account [10% on £16,400] Balance. [20% on £4,600]	c/d	£ 3,280 920	19.. Jan. 1 Dec. 31	Balance. Goods sent to Branches Account	b/d	£ 200 4,000
			£4,200				£4,200
				Jan. 1	Balance[1]	b/d	920

[1] This item (if the loaded price were charged to Branch) would be offset against the Stock of £4,600, leaving a net figure of £3,680.

Any difference in the stock arising during the year would be inserted in the invoice column at its nominal selling value, the actual amount when discovered being inserted in the main column and from there transferred to a special loss account or to Profit and Loss Account unless covered by insurance, when the transfer would be made to the debit of the insurance company. (See p. 1934.)

X carried on a retail business with branches B and C, the accounting being performed at head office.

From the following information, write up the Branch Stock Accounts with columns for selling-price figures.

1. Goods are invoiced to branches at a selling price of cost plus 25 per cent.

2. When stock was taken at the end of the year, B showed a deficiency of actual stock in relation to book value of £30, C a surplus of £60 (both at selling price).

3. During the year, B sent goods to C, goods at invoiced price of £300.

4. On investigation it was found that B had been debited inadvertently with £40 goods sent to C, and goods sent to B of £120 had been charged out at £140.

	B £	C £
Opening Stocks at selling price	7,000	5,700
Goods sent to Branches at selling price	31,000	33,000
Sales	33,350	36,250
Closing Stock at selling price	4,360	2,850

B BRANCH STOCK

	Selling Price	Cost Price		Selling Price	Cost Price other than Sales
	£	£		£	£
Balance b/d . . .	7,000	5,600	Sales	33,250	33,250
Goods . . .	31,000	24,800	Transfer to C, goods sent .	300	240
Gross Profit . .		6,650	Transfer to C, goods sent .	40	32
			Goods—correction of invoice		
			(£140 − £120) . .	20	16
			Deficiency . . .	30	24
			Balance c/d . . .	4,360	3,488
	£38,000	£37,050		£38,000	£37,050
Balance b/d . . .	4,360	3,488			

C BRANCH STOCK

	Selling Price	Cost Price		Selling Price	Cost Price other than Sales
	£	£		£	£
Balance b/d . . .	5,700	4,560	Sales	36,250	36,250
Goods . . .	33,000	26,400	Balance c/d . . .	2,850	2,280
Transfer from B . . .	300	240			
Transfer from B . . .	40	32			
Surplus . . .	60	48			
Gross Profit . .		7,250			
	£39,100	£38,530		£39,100	£38,530
Balance b/d . . .	2,850	2,280			

The surplus and deficiency will be shown separately in the Branch Profit and Loss Accounts.

Alternatively, the cost price figures in the above accounts may be omitted, giving the Gross Profit on the basis of the actual stock and dispensing with the transfers to the Branch Profit and Loss Accounts for surplus and deficiency, in which case the Gross Profits are:

B	£6,626	and C	£7,298	as against:
B	£6,650	and C	£7,250	in Stock Accounts
Deficiency	24	Surplus	48	in Profit and Loss Accounts
	£6,626		£7,298	

Alternative Method

Where the gross profit of a branch is not required to be ascertained separately, although the selling price is uniform, the procedure is to employ a Branch Stock Account and a Goods Sent to Branches Account. No Branch Adjustment Account is possible, if the cost price of the goods sent to branches is not recorded. The method is as follows:

1. Debit Branch Stock at selling price
   Credit Goods sent to Branches } for Goods sent to Branches
2. Reverse of (1)   for returns *from* Branch
3. Debit Cash or Debtors
   Credit Branch Stock } for Branch Sales
4. Debit Branch Stock
   Credit Debtors } for returns *to* Branch
5. Balance off Branch Stock at selling price } for closing Stock at selling price
6. Debit Goods sent to Branches
   Credit Branch Trading Account } for Branch net Sales
7. Balance off Goods sent to Branches at selling price } for closing Stock at selling price
8. The effect of the entries under (5) and (7) is to eliminate closing Stock from the accounts, so that closing Stock at cost will be introduced into the Trading Account in the ordinary way.
9. Any shortage of stock at the branch will be debited to Goods sent to Branches and credited to Branch Stock at selling price; such loss being shown by debiting Branch Profit and Loss Account and crediting Branch Trading Account at cost.

The employment of the two accounts mentioned above results in a check on stock. The two accounts are reciprocal except that the credit for Sales in the Branch Stock Account is reflected in a debit to branch debtors or cash, and the debit for sales in the Goods sent to Branches Account is reflected in the credit to Branch Trading Account. In other words, the net result is that the branch debtors or cash will be debited and the Branch Sales Account credited. The opening and closing branch stock at cost (or net realizable value, if lower) will be brought into the Branch Trading Account in the usual way and the general Purchases Account will remain undisturbed, if the transfer figure is not disclosed in the question (see p. 1933). Otherwise, Branch Purchases Account will be debited and general Purchases Account credited.

Illustration 14

Goods are sent to branch loaded with $33\frac{1}{3}$ per cent on *cost*, invoiced at £2,000 Branch Returns to head office, £200; Sales by Branch, £1,870; Returns to branch, £470. Stock (at price charged to branch), £400. Show accounts in the head office books.

Head office books (the numbers in brackets refer to the foregoing rules):

BRANCH STOCK

			£					£
Goods .	.	(1)	2,000	Returns .	.	(2)		200
Returns.	.	(4)	470	Sales .	.	(3)		1,870
				Balance .	.	(5)	c/d	400
			£2,470					£2,470
Balance.	.	b/d	400					

BRANCH TRADING ACCOUNT

		£			£		£
Purchases[1] . . .		1,350		Sales . .	1,870		
Gross Profit . . .		350		Less Returns .	470		
						(6)	1,400
				Stock . . .			300
		£1,700					£1,700

GOODS SENT TO BRANCHES

		£			£
Returns. . . (2)		200	Branch Stock . . (1)		2,000
Branch Trading and Profit and Loss Account (6)		1,400			
Balance—Stock . (7) c/d		400			
		£2,000			£2,000
			Balance. . . . b/d		400

[1] Goods sent less returns, at selling price—£1,800, less £450.

As the Branch Stock Account and Goods sent to Branches Account are self-effacing, the ordinary entries are necessary for the preparation of the Branch Trading Account.

Notes.

1. Expenses ignored.
2. Percentage to be deducted from selling price is 25 per cent [i.e. $\frac{1}{3}$ of cost price $= \frac{1}{4}$ of selling price]: therefore Stock is £400 less £100 = £300.

If compiled in the usual way, the accounts would be:

BRANCH STOCK

		£			£
Goods		2,000	Returns. . . .		200
Returns. . .		470	Sales		1,870
			Balance. . . c/d		400
		£2,470			£2,470
Balance. . . b/d		400			

GOODS SENT TO BRANCHES

	£		£
Branch Stock Account Returns	200	Branch Stock Account .	2,000
Purchases (or Trading) Account	1,350		
Branch Adjustment Account. . .	450		
	£2,000		£2,000

BRANCH ADJUSTMENT ACCOUNT

		£			£
Branch Profit and Loss Account		350	Goods sent to Branches Account		450
Balance. . . .	c/d	100			
		£450			£450
			Balance. . . .	b/d	100

PURCHASES

				£
		Goods sent to Branches Account . .		1,350

BRANCH PROFIT AND LOSS ACCOUNT

				£
		Branch Adjustment Account. . .		350

Illustration 15

Head office invoiced to their Birmingham Branch during the year goods at selling price amounting to £7,400. The credit sales of the branch were £3,100 and cash sales £1,700. The branch returned £200 stock at selling price, and had returned from customers £100. The discounts allowed to customers by the branch amounted to £120. The branch remitted to head office £3,860, being the amount of cash sales and receipts from customers. The beginning and closing stocks of the branch were £1,500 (cost £1,120) and £3,900 (cost £3,270). The branch had debtors at £1,200 at the beginning and £1,920 at the end. Loss through pilferage was ascertained to be £100. (Cost £80.)

The head office had beginning and ending stock of £13,000 and £17,000. The purchases (*less* returns) and sales (*less* returns) during the year were £31,300 and £37,200.

Write up the necessary accounts to record the above in the head office books by the foregoing method, and show the gross profit of the business for the year.

Head Office books:

BRANCH STOCK

		£			£
Balance . . .	b/d	1,500	Cash Sales . . .		1,700
Goods from Head Office		7,400	Credit Sales . . .		3,100
Returns from Customers		100	Loss through Pilferage[1] .		100
			Returns to Head Office		200
			Balance. . . .	c/d	3,900
		£9,000			£9,000
Balance . . .	b/d	3,900			

[1] See rule 9, p. 1928.

GOODS SENT TO BRANCHES

		£			£
Returns . .		200	Balance. . . .	b/d	1,500
Transfer to Trading Account . .		4,700	Branch Stock Account .		7.400
Loss through Pilferage .		100			
Balance—Stock . .	c/d	3,900			
		£8,900			£8,900
			Balance . . .	b/d	3,900

BRANCH DEBTORS

		£			£
Balance . . .	b/d	1,200	Cash		2,160
Credit Sales. . .		3,100	Discounts . . .		120
			Returns. . . .		100
			Balances . . .	c/d	1,920
		£4,300			£4,300
Balances . . .	b/d	1,920			

TRADING ACCOUNT

	£	£		£	£
Opening Stock—			Sales (net)—		
Head Office .	13,000		Head Office .	37,200	
Branch . .	1,120		Branch . .	4,700	
		14,120			41,900
Purchases (net) .		31,300	Closing Stock—		
Gross Profit to Profit and Loss Account			Head Office .	17,000	
			Branch . .	3,270	
		16,830			20,270
			Loss of Stock by Pilferage[1] . .		80
		£62,250			£62,250

[1] This item will be debited to the Profit and Loss Account.

A modification of this method is to use only the Branch Account (in place of Branch Stock, Branch Cash, and Branch Debtors Account) and Goods sent to Branch Account. Although it is preferable to use the full accounts, the net result will be the same.

The entries will be:

1. Debit Branch at selling price
   Credit Goods sent to Branch } for transfers of Goods to Branch.
2. Reverse of (1)   for returns from Branch.
3. Debit Cash
   Credit Branch } for remittances by Branch to Head Office.
4. Debit branch expenses (including Bad Debts)
   Credit Branch } for expenses paid by Branch.
5. Bring down as balances on Branch Account closing cash at Branch, Debtors, and Stock at selling price.

6. Debit Goods sent to Branch   } for Branch Sales.
   Credit Branch Trading Account
7. Debit Branch Expenses   } for expenses paid by Head Office for
   Credit Head Office Cash   }   Branch.
8. Bring down the balance of Goods sent to
   Branch Account which will offset Stock
   Brought down in (5).
9. Closing stock (having been eliminated as shown
   in (8)) will appear in the final accounts at
   cost, subject to any provision for lower value,
   in the usual way.
10. Debit Branch Profit and Loss Account } for amounts in debit in (4) and (7).
    Credit Branch expenses

Illustration 16

During the year a Branch was opened and the following particulars are ascertained

		£
1. Goods sent to Branch at selling price		2,300
2. Goods returned by Branch at selling price		100
3. Closing Debtors, after deducting Bad Debts £50		200
4. Expenses paid by Branch		40
5. Expenses paid by Head Office for Branch		170
6. Petty Cash on hand		10
7. Closing stock at selling price		440

Show Branch Account and Goods sent to Branch Account in the head office books.

BRANCH

	£			£
Goods[1]	2,300	Returns to H.O.		100
		Remittance to H.O.		1,460
		Bad Debts		50
		Expenses		40
		Balances c/d—		
		Goods[1]	£440	
		Cash	10	
		Debtors	200	
			——	650
	£2,300			£2,300
Balances b/d—				
Goods[1]	£440			
Cash	10			
Debtors	200			
	—— 650			

[1] At selling price.

Goods Sent to Branch

	£		£
Branch (Returns) . .	100	Branch (Transfer) . . .	2,300
Sales Trading Account:			
Branch . . .	1,760		
Branch Stock[1] c/d . .	440		
	£2,300		£2,300
		Branch Stock[1] b/d . . .	440

[1] At selling price.

The item £170 will not appear in the above accounts and the items of £440 cancel each other and stock at cost (or net realizable value if less) will be debited to Branch Stock Account and credited to Branch Trading Account.

The debit to Branch Account for goods at selling price will, or should, equal the sum of the remittances and returns by Branch to Head Office, Bad Debts, Expenses paid, and the increase (or decrease) in the closing stock, cash and debtors.

If there is an excess of debits over credits in the Branch Account, it will represent a deficiency (or a surplus in the converse case).

If the accounts were written up in the ordinary way, they would be as follows (abbreviated in form):

Branch Stock

	£		£
Goods (S.P.)	2,300	Returns	100
		Credit Sales . . .	1,760[1]
		Stock (S.P.) . . .	440

[1] Even if some of these sales were for cash instead of credit, the result would be the same.

Debtors

	£		£
Branch Stock	1,760	Cash	1,510
		Bad Debts . . .	50
		Balance	200

Branch Cash

	£		£
Debtors	1,510	H.O.	1,460
		Expenses . . .	40
		Balance	10

	£		
Branch Cash	40		
H.O.	170		

Differences in Balance of Stock. It will often be found in practice that there is a difference between the actual stock held by the branch and the balance shown by the Branch Stock Account, and the cause of such discrepancy must be ascertained before the difference can be treated in the books. It may arise from many different reasons, some of which are:

1. Error in the percentage of loading.
2. The sale of the goods below or above the estimated selling price.
3. Omission of returns and allowances.
4. Loss of stock (rain, fire, etc.), or theft.
5. Errors in stocktaking.

Assuming that the balance brought down on the Branch Stock Account is £100 in excess of the physical stock held by the branch, and that the goods are loaded by 25 per cent on cost when invoiced to the branch, the discrepancy being due to theft, the real loss to the firm will only be £80, as 20 per cent of the invoiced price is loading. To bring this into account: (a) the Branch Stock Account must be credited with £100, as must be done in all cases because the stock has 'gone out', and as this stock is not in hand there must be no debit balance brought down in respect of it; (b) Branch Stock Shortage Account must be debited with £80 (the actual loss); and (c) Branch Adjustment Account must be debited with the £20 loading (as this represents cancellation of anticipated profit which cannot materialize).

The adjusting entries would be as follows:

		£	£
Branch Stock Shortage	Dr.	80	
Branch Adjustment	Dr.	20	
Branch Stock	Cr.		100

Alternatively, £100 may be transferred to the debit of Branch Stock Shortage Account and £20 transferred therefrom to the debit of Branch Adjustment Account.

The claim (if any) against an insurance company in respect of the loss would be set off against the Branch Stock Shortage Account, and the balance of this account would be written off to the debit of Branch Profit and Loss Account.

If the loss has arisen from a theft of cash, the actual loss is £100, and accordingly the entries are:

1. Where the cash has been entered:

		£	£
Branch Cash Shortage	Dr.	100	
Branch Cash	Cr.		100

2. Where no cash entry has been made:

Branch Cash Shortage	Dr.	100	
Branch Stock (cash sales)			Cr. 100
or			
Branch Debtors (credit sales)			Cr. 100

If the loss has arisen from bad debts or discounts allowed to customers, the actual loss is £100, and the entries are:

1. Where no Debtors Accounts are kept, although credit sales are made:

		£	£
Branch Profit and Loss Account	Dr.	100	
Branch Stock			Cr. 100

2. Where Debtors Accounts are kept:

Branch Profit and Loss Account	Dr.	100	
Branch Debtors			Cr. 100

If the loss has arisen from allowances made to customers, the actual loss is £100, and the entries are:

		£	£
Branch Adjustment	Dr.	100	
Branch Stock			Cr. 100

It may be that the balance shown by the Branch Stock Account is less than the value of the actual stock (at selling price) held by the branch. In the absence of any special reason, this will generally be due to the fact that the loading is insufficient to cover the full difference between cost and selling price, and accordingly the estimated profit in the Branch Adjustment Account is *understated*. The correcting entry is to debit the full amount of the difference to Branch Stock Account and to credit it to Branch Adjustment Account.

In examinations, unless additional facts are given (*vide infra*), or the question specially deals with such differences, any profit or loss should always be transferred to the Branch Adjustment Account in the head office books, with a note as to alternative treatments.

Where from information in a question the inference is that the branch may perform a certain amount of work on the goods received in respect of some of the sales, and there is more stock in hand (at selling price) than is shown by the balance of the Branch Stock Account, a probable cause of the discrepancy is that the branch has charged customers for the proportion of the wages bill attributable to such work.

Depreciation. Depreciation, where the Branch accounts are kept at the head office, will be recorded by debiting Branch Profit and Loss Account and crediting the particular Branch Asset.

Illustration 17

Goods are invoiced to a newly-opened branch by head office at £4,600, representing cost plus 25 per cent. Returns to head office are £50; Branch

Sales (cash), £4,230, all of which is remitted to head office except the sum of £400 for current trading expenses. Stock at end at selling price, £300. The head office has furnished cash for purchase of Fixtures, etc., £900. Expenses paid by head office on behalf of the branch, £100. Write £65 off fixtures and show accounts in the head office books.

BRANCH STOCK

		£			£
Goods		4,600	Returns.		50
			Sales		4.230
			Branch Adjustment (or		
			Stock Shortage) Account		20
			Balance.	c/d	300
		£4,600			£4,600
Balance.	b/d	300			

GOODS SENT TO BRANCHES

	£		£
Branch Stock Account:		Branch Stock Account	4,600
Returns	50		
Branch Adjustment Account.	910		
Purchases (or Trading)			
Account	3,640		
	£4,600		£4,600

BRANCH ADJUSTMENT ACCOUNT

		£			£
Branch Stock Account:			Goods sent to Branches		
Shortage		20	Account		910
Gross Profit to Branch			Shortage of Stock (at *Cost*)		
Profit and Loss Account		846	to Branch Profit and		
Balance.	c/d	60	Loss Account[1]		16
		£926			£926
			Balance[2]	b/d	60

BRANCH CASH

	£		£
Sales	4,230	Expenses[3]	400
		Remittances	3,830
	£4,230		£4,230

[1] True shortage is £20, less loading of 20% of £20 = £16.
[2] 20% of £300.
[3] Actually a detailed Expenses Account would be opened.

BRANCH PROFIT AND LOSS ACCOUNT

	£			£
Cash—		Gross Profit . . .		846
Expenses (detailed) .	100			
Branch Expenses . .	400			
Stock Shortage . .	16			
Depreciation of Fixtures .	65			
Net Profit to General				
Profit and Loss Account	265			
	£846			£846

BRANCH FIXTURES

		£			£
Cash		900	Branch Profit and Loss		
			Account . . .		65
			Balance. . . . c/d		835
		£900			£900
Balance. . . . b/d		835			

Sundry Adjustments. Where, as often happens, goods are consigned to a particular branch by error, and are consigned therefrom to the branch to which they should originally have been dispatched, the transfer must be dealt with in the accounts of both branches. The goods should be considered as having been returned from the first branch to head office and re-consigned to the second branch.

Illustration 18

£1,000 goods are inadvertently sent to Branch A instead of to Branch B. Upon instructions from head office they are sent direct from Branch A to Branch B. The entries therefore are in Journal form:

Goods sent to Branch A	.	.	.	.	.	Dr.	£1,000
Branch A Stock	.	.	.	.	.		£1,000
Branch B Stock	.	.	.	.	.	Dr.	£1,000
Goods sent to Branch B	.	.	.	.			£1,000

In certain circumstances (e.g. owing to locality) goods may be loaded up to different branches at different rates, e.g. the cost price may be loaded to Branch A at 10 per cent and to Branch B at 20 per cent. Where such a procedure operates, particular care is needed in dealing with transfers from one branch to another because the goods are evaluated at different prices for each branch, necessitating a recalculation of the cost price and invoice price according to the loading required for the branch in question.

If goods are sent to Branch A, loaded and charged to it at a figure which is correct for Branch B (the branch to which the goods should originally have been dispatched), a simple transfer is made as already illustrated, because Branch B is by the transfer correctly debited, while the incorrect debit to Branch A is exactly eliminated. If, however, goods are sent to Branch A (instead of to B) and loaded with the percentage applicable to A, the transfer to B upon the goods being re-directed to B will be effected as follows: (1) the incorrect debit to A will be credited to A (eliminating the original entries); but (2) the debit to B must be at the loaded figure applicable to B. In other words, in the first case the entries required call for no adjustment in price, as the price was already correct as regards B; but in the second case the price must be adjusted, as it was incorrect as regards B.

Illustration 19

There are two branches, A and B. Goods are consigned to them at loaded figures of 20 per cent and 25 per cent on cost respectively. The invoices to the branches are £1,200 and £2,000 respectively. Included in the item £1,200 are invoices for goods costing £300, invoiced to Branch A at £360, which should have been invoiced to B. Sales are all for cash, being A, £720; B, £1,500.

Show the appropriate ledger entries in the head office books. It may be assumed that the closing stocks are correct.

BRANCH STOCK

		A	B				A	B
		£	£				£	£
Goods sent to Branches Accounts .		1,200	2,000		Goods sent to Branches Accounts.		360	
do. do. .	(a)		375		Sales. .		720	1,500
					Balances .	c/d	120	875
		£1,200	£2,375				£1,200	£2,375
Balances . .	b/d	120	875					

GOODS SENT TO BRANCHES

		A	B				A	B
		£	£				£	£
Branch Stock Account . .		360			Branch Stock Accounts .		1,200	2,000
Branch Adjustment Accounts .		140	475		do. do.			375
Purchases (or Trading) Account . .		700	1,900					
		£1,200	£2,375				£1,200	£2,375

BRANCH ADJUSTMENT ACCOUNTS

			A	B				A	B
			£	£				£	£
Branch Profit and Loss Accounts	(b)		120	300	Goods sent to Branches Accounts			140	475
Branches	c/d		20	175					
			£140	£475				£140	£475
					Balances	b/d		20	175

Notes. (*a*) The goods costing £300 will be charged up to A at £300 + $\frac{1}{5}$ = £360, and to B at £300 + $\frac{1}{4}$ = £375. The transfers from Goods sent to Branches Accounts to Branch Adjustment Accounts are made in total as follows: For A, $\frac{1}{6}$ (£1,200 − £360) = £140; for B, $\frac{1}{5}$ (£2,000 + £375) = £475 [$\frac{1}{5}$ of cost price = $\frac{1}{6}$ of selling price and $\frac{1}{4}$ of cost price = $\frac{1}{5}$ of selling price]. The balances carried down in the Branch Adjustment Accounts on the stocks outstanding are calculated similarly: A, $\frac{1}{6}$; B, $\frac{1}{5}$. The figures in the Branch Accounts are at SELLING price, therefore the 'loading down' fractions are respectively $\frac{1}{6}$ and $\frac{1}{5}$ of selling price.

(*b*) The gross profits are: (i) $\frac{1}{6}$ of £720 = £120; (ii) $\frac{1}{5}$ of £1,500 = £300.

Adjustments in Respect of Price Changes. As has been seen, the stocks at branches are shown at loaded prices, whether at selling price or at cost price plus a percentage, and consequently if there is to be an increase or a decrease in the selling price an adjustment must be passed through the books in respect thereof.

The adjustments for price change may best be explained by the use of illustrations.

Illustration 20

The balance of Branch Stock Account at 1st January 19.., is £2,200 (to represent a profit of 10 per cent on cost price). As and from 1st January 19.., the price is to be increased so that there is to be earned a profit of $12\frac{1}{2}$ per cent on cost price. Make the required adjustments.

BRANCH STOCK

			£			
Balance	b/d		2,200			
Branch Adjustment Account *re* Selling Price Adjustment			50			

BRANCH ADJUSTMENT ACCOUNT

							£
				Balance		b/d	200
				Branch Stock			50

The *old* provision was:

		£	£
$\frac{1}{11} \times$ selling price of	. .	2,200	= 200
or			
$\frac{1}{10} \times$ cost price of .	. .	2,000	= 200

The *new* provision is—

		£	£
$\frac{1}{9} \times$ revised selling price of	. .	2,250	= 250
or			
$\frac{1}{8} \times$ cost price of .	. .	2,000	= 250

The revised selling price is arrived at thus:

			£
Cost of Goods	. .	. .	2,000
Loading of 12½% thereof	. .	.	250
Revised Selling Price	. .	.	£2,250

Where the selling price is to be reduced reverse entries will be required, the Branch Adjustment Account being debited and the Branch Stock Account credited with the appropriate reduction of the provision on unsold stock.

Illustration 21

Assuming the same facts as in the foregoing question, except that the new selling price is to be such as to give a profit of 5 per cent on cost price, show the necessary adjustments.

BRANCH STOCK

			£				£
Balance	b/d		2,200		Branch Adjustment Account *re* Selling Price Adjustment . . .		100

BRANCH ADJUSTMENT ACCOUNT

		£				£
Branch Stock . . .		100		Balance	b/d	200

The *old* provision was:

		£	£
$\frac{1}{11} \times$ selling price of	. .	2,200	= 200
or			
$\frac{1}{10} \times$ cost price of .	. .	2,000	= 200

The *new* provision is:

		£	£
$\frac{1}{21} \times$ revised selling price of	. .	2,100	= 100
or			
$\frac{1}{20} \times$ cost price of .	. .	2,000	= 100

The revised selling price is arrived at thus:

		£
Cost of Goods		2,000
Loading of 5% thereof		100
Revised Selling Price		£2,100

Hence, the Branch Stock Account must be reduced by £100 as must the Branch Adjustment Account.

As the cost is nowise affected, the above transfer will not alter the amount shown in the Balance Sheet, as before the transfer was made the stock would be shown as £2,200 less Branch Adjustment Account £200 = £2,000. After the adjustment it will appear as £2,100, less Branch Adjustment Account £100 = £2,000.

Where there is an alteration in the cost price, it may be that the branch is to earn the same *rate* of gross profit, or an *altered* rate (corresponding with the increased or decreased cost price), or the same AMOUNT of profit per quantity sold.

The same principles will apply whether the alteration is an increase or decrease. The problem lies in the ascertainment of the AMOUNT that is to be transferred, as the book-keeping is simple, i.e. a transfer from Branch Stock Account to Branch Adjustment Account.

A decrease in price will now be illustrated.

Illustration 22

The following are the balances of the branch in the head office books at 1st July:

BRANCH STOCK

			£					
Balance . . .	b/d		2,000					

BRANCH ADJUSTMENT ACCOUNT

					Balance . . .	b/d	£ 400

As on 1st July cost prices have fallen by 20 per cent and selling prices are to be adjusted accordingly. Show accounts in the head office books.

BRANCH STOCK

		(a) £	(b) £	(c) £			(a) £	(b) £	(c) £
Balance . .	b/d	2,000	2,000	2,000	Trading Account .		320	320	320
Branch Adjustment Account . .			320		Branch Adjustment. Account .	c/d	80		
					Balance .		1,600	2,000	1,680
		£2,000	£2,320	£2,000			£2,000	£2,320	£2,000
Balance . .	b/d	1,600	2,000	1,680					

BRANCH ADJUSTMENT ACCOUNT

			(a) £	(b) £	(c) £			(a) £	(b) £	(c) £
Branch Stock .		c/d	80	720	400	Balance .	b/d	400	400	400
Balance . .			320			Branch Stock .			320	
			£400	£720	£400			£400	£720	£400
						Balance . .	b/d	320	720	400

(a) **If the selling price is to be** *reduced* **by 20 per cent and the** RATE **of gross profit to remain the same.**

The cost is obviously £1,600, therefore the revised 'cost' figure is £1,600, less 20 per cent of £1,600, i.e. £1,600−£320 = £1,280. Hence, the revised selling price is £1,280 plus 25 per cent of £1,280 = £1,600. The amount of 25 per cent is added to cost because it is the equivalent of 20 per cent of selling price. Therefore the new loading will be 20 per cent of £1,600, or 25 per cent of £1,280, viz. £320. The transfer consequently will be:

Debit Trading Account, £320   } Credit Branch Stock, £400
Debit Branch Adjustment Account, £80

This will leave the branch stock at selling price at £1,600, and the Branch Adjustment Account at £320.

In the Balance Sheet the branch stock will be carried out at £1,280. Future loading will be 25 per cent of cost.

(b) **If the selling price is to be** *maintained* **at original.**

As the figure of £2,000 is the selling price, no alteration will be entailed in the Branch Stock Account, but as the revised 'cost' figure is, as has been seen, £1,280, the Branch Adjustment Account will be increased by £320, as the loading is now correspondingly higher. As the 'cost' figure is reduced, the adjustment must be considered as a loss.

The transfers consequently will be:

Debit Trading Account, £320:   Credit Branch Stock, £320,
Debit Branch Stock, £320:   Credit Branch Adjustment Account, £320.

The above entries may be curtailed by making the transfer without the intervention of the Branch Stock Account, thus:

Debit Trading Account, £320:   Credit Branch Adjustment Account, £320.

In the Balance Sheet the branch stock will be carried out at £1,280, i.e. £2,000 (Branch Stock Account) less £720 (Branch Adjustment Account). Future loading will be $\frac{72}{128}$ of cost, i.e. $\frac{9}{16}$.

(c) **Where the same** *amount* **of profit is to be earned on quantity sold.**

As the revised cost is £1,280 and the same amount of profit on sales is to be earned, the selling price must be £1,680. Hence, the balance on

Branch Adjustment Account remains undisturbed and the balance on the Branch Stock Account will be reduced from £2,000 to £1,680.

The transfer consequently will be:

Debit Trading Account, £320:　　　　　Credit Branch Stock, £320.

In the balance sheet the branch stock will be shown at £1,280.

Future loading will be $\frac{40}{128}$ of cost, i.e. $\frac{5}{16}$.

The three results may be shown in summary form as on pp. 1941 and 1942.

In each case, a book loss is entailed by virtue of the reduction in the value of the stock.

The difference between the two accounts is, in each case, £1,280, representing the revised cost figure of £1,600 *less* 20 per cent thereof.

The result in each case is shown as follows:

(*a*) The Selling Price is reduced by 20 per cent (i.e. from £2,000 to £1,600), and the Branch Adjustment Account is £320, being the loading of 20 per cent on £1,600.

(*b*) The Selling Price is maintained at the old figure, £2,000.

(*c*) The old loading figure of £400 is retained in the Branch Adjustment Account.

Illustration 23

Barn & Sons are wholesale grocers with a head office (which is the warehouse as well as a selling department) and one branch. The control of buying and the accounting therefore are at head office. The branch sends weekly returns to head office from which the branch accounting is performed, and pays its own sundry expenses (including wages), for which it is recouped weekly.

The general expenses at head office are apportioned between the warehouse and the head office selling department in the proportion 2:1. The warehouse charges out goods at 25 per cent on cost price. The handling charges incurred by warehouse are to be debited to the head office and branch at a 'load' of 20 per cent of cost price of the goods sent to them. The transport costs are separately booked and charged to the head office selling department at a profit of 10 per cent on cost, and to branch at competitive rates.

The following are the details of the Head Office Bank Account:

	£		£
Balance	1,000	Payments—	
Receipts from—		General Expenses . .	2,700
H.O. Selling Dept. . .	10,400	Transport Creditors . .	700
Branch	4,300	Trade Creditors .	8,000
		Sundry Expenses . .	1,680
		Warehouse . . .	420

The following details are revealed from the Branch Returns and other books:

	Head Office £	Branch £
Petty Cash Balance at commencement	140	60
Sundry Expenses	1,210	470
Sales—Credit	9,000	4,800
Cash	1,900	600
Receipts from Debtors	8,500	3,700

	£
General Purchases	11,200
Goods charged at selling price from—	
Warehouse to Head Office	9,000
Warehouse to Branch	5,000
Transport costs to—	
Head Office	440
Branch	253
Closing Stock on hand—	
Head Office (Selling Price)	100
Branch (Selling Price)	480
Warehouse (Cost Price)	3,000
Sundry Creditors (re Transport) at end	120

The period relates to the year ended 31st December ...

The balances at commencement of the year were:

	£	£
Sundry Assets—		
Warehouse	1,500	
Head Office	3,500	
Branch	1,000	
Stock—		
Warehouse (Cost Price)	3,000	
Head Office (Selling Price)	2,000	
Branch (Selling Price)	1,000	
Bank	1,000	
Stock Adjustment Accounts—		
Head Office		400
Branch		200
Petty Cash	200	
Sundry Creditors (including £200 re Transport)		5,400
Sundry Debtors—		
Head Office	2,300	
Branch	500	
Capital		10,000
	£16,000	£16,000

From the foregoing information prepare accounts, ignoring any question of drawings and depreciation.

DEBTORS

		H.O.	Branch				H.O.	Branch
		£	£				£	£
Balances	b/d	*2,300*	*500*	Cash			8,500	3,700
Sales		9,000	4,800	Balances	c/d		2,800	1,600
		£11,300	£5,300				£11,300	£5,300
Balances	b/d	2,800	1,600					

CAPITAL

		£				£
Net Loss from Profit and Loss Account		2,256	*Balance*		b/d	*10,000*
Balance	c/d	7,744				
		£10,000				£10,000
			Balance		b/d	7,744

BANK

		£			
Balance	b/d	*1,000*	General Expenses:		
H.O. Cash Sales		1,900	Warehouse		2,700
H.O. Debtors		8,500	Transport		700
Branch Cash Sales		600	Creditors		8,000
Branch Debtors		3,700	Sundry Expenses		1,680
			Warehouse		420
			Balance	c/d	2,200
		£15,700			£15,700
Balance	b/d	2,200			

SUNDRY ASSETS

		W.	H.O.	Branch				
		£	£	£				
Balances	b/d	*1,500*	*3,500*	*1,000*				

GOODS SENT TO BRANCHES

	H.O.	Branch			H.O.	Branch
	£	£			£	£
Warehouse Stock Account	7,200	4,000	Stock Account		9,000	5,000
Stock Adjustment Account	1,800	1,000				
	£9,000	£5,000			£9,000	£5,000

[Opening balances are in italics.]

GENERAL EXPENSES

	W.	H.O.		W.	H.O.
	£	£		£	£
Bank	1,800	900	H.O. Expenses Account	1,440	
	420		Branch Expenses Account	800	
Profit and Loss Account	20		Profit and Loss Account		900
	£2,240	£900		£2,240	£900

TRANSPORT TRADING

	£		£
Cost per Creditors Account	620	Head Office Expenses	440
Profit and Loss Account: Transport Profit	73	Branch Expenses	253
	£693		£693

WAREHOUSE STOCK

		£			£
Balance	b/d	3,000	Goods sent to Branches Account—		
Purchases		11,200	Head Office		7,200
			Branch		4,000
			Balance	c/d	3,000
		£14,200			£14,200
Balance	b/d	3,000			

STOCK

		H.O.	Branch			H.O.	Branch
		£	£			£	£
Balances	b/d	2,000	1,000	Sales—			
Goods sent to Branches Account		9,000	5,000	Cash		1,900	600
				Credit		9,000	4,800
				Stock Shortage Account			120
				Stock	c/d	100	480
		£11,000	£6,000			£11,000	£6,000
Stock	b/d	100	480				

[Opening balances are in italics.]

STOCK ADJUSTMENT ACCOUNTS

		H.O.	Branch			H.O.	Branch
		£	£			£	£
Profit and Loss Account		2,180	1,080	*Balances* b/d		*400*	*200*
Stock Shortage Account			24	Goods sent to Branches Account		1,800	1,000
Balances	c/d	20	96				
		£2,200	£1,200			£2,200	£1,200
				Balances	b/d	20	96

CREDITORS (TRADE)

		£			£
Bank		8,000	*Balances* b/d		*5,200*
Balances	c/d	8,400	Purchases		11,200
		£16,400			£16,400
			Balances	b/d	8,400

CREDITORS (TRANSPORT)

		£			£
Bank		700	*Balances* b/d		*200*
Balances	c/d	120	Transport Trading Account		620
		£820			£820
			Balances	b/d	120

PETTY CASH

		H.O.	Branch				
		£	£				
Balances	b/d	*140*	*60*				

[Opening balances are in italics.]

SUNDRY EXPENSES

		H.O.	Branch			H.O.	Branch
		£	£			£	£
Cash		1,210	470	Profit and Loss Account		3,090	1,523
Transport[1]		440	253				
Warehouse[1]		1,440	800				
		£3,090	£1,523			£3,090	£1,523

[Expenses grouped under one head for convenience.]   [1] See notes on p. 1949.

STOCK SHORTAGE ACCOUNT

	£		£
Branch Stock Account .	120	Profit and Loss Account .	96
		Stock Adjustment Account .	24
	£120		£120

PROFIT AND LOSS ACCOUNT
FOR THE YEAR ENDED 31ST DECEMBER 19. .

		H.O.	Branch			H.O.	Branch
		£	£			£	£
Sundry Expenses .		3,090	1,523	Gross Profit .		2,180	1,080
General Expenses .		900		Loss . . . c/d		1,810	539
Stock Shortage .			96				
		£3,990	£1,619			£3,990	£1,619
Loss—	b/d			Profit on Transport[1] .			73
H.O. . .		1,810		Over-allocation of Handling Charges[1]			20
Branch . .		539	2,349	Balance—			
				Net Loss to Capital Account			2,256
			£2,349				£2,349

[1] See notes on p. 1949.

The above gross profit may be shown in Memorandum Trading Account form as follows.

Memorandum TRADING ACCOUNT
FOR THE YEAR ENDED 31ST DECEMBER 19. .

	H.O.	Branch		H.O.	Branch
	£	£		£	£
Stock . .	1,600	800	Sales . . .	10,900	5,400
Purchases .	7,200	4,000	Stock . .	80	384
Gross Profit .	2,180	1,080	Stock Shortage .		96
	£10,980	£5,880		£10,980	£5,880

BALANCE SHEET AS AT 31ST DECEMBER 19..

	£	£		£	£
Capital—			Fixed Assets—		
Balance—1st January 19..	10,000		Sundry—Warehouse	1,500	
Less net Loss	2,256		Head Office	3,500	
		7,744	Branch	1,000	
Current Liabilities—					6,000
Creditors—			Current Assets—		
Trade	8,400		Stock—Warehouse	3,000	
Transport	120		Head Office	80	
		8,520	Branch	384	
					3,464
			Debtors—Head Office	2,800	
			Branch	1,600	
					4,400
			Bank		2,200
			Petty Cash—Head Office	140	
			Branch	60	
					200
		£16,264			£16,264

Notes:

1. The Stock in the Balance Sheet is shown at cost, and will be the difference between the Stock at selling price and the Stock Adjustment Account, i.e.:

	H.O.	Branch
	£	£
Stock	100	480
Less Stock Adjustment Account	20	96
	£80	£384

2. The handling charges are £2,220 as shown in General Expenses, but the 'load' to Head Office and Branch is 20 per cent of the cost price of the goods, i.e.:

	£
20% of £7,200 to Head Office	1,440
20% of £4,000 to Branch	800
	£2,240

There is, therefore, an over-allocation of £20.

3. The profit on transport is made up of:

	£
(a) 10% of £400 [i.e. $\frac{1}{11} \times £440$] charged to Head Office	40
(b) Profit on £220 charged to Branch [i.e. £253 − £220]	33
(c) i.e. cost of £620 charged out at £693	£73

4. The true loss on stock shortage is $\frac{100}{125}$ of £120 = £96.

WHERE THE BRANCH HAS FULL SYSTEM OF DOUBLE ENTRY

Each branch will maintain a separate set of double entry books, the connection between the branches and the head office book-keeping system being maintained by means of:

1. A Branch Account in the head office books.
2. A Head Office Account in the branch books.

The Head Office Account in the branch books will be analogous to the Capital Account of an ordinary business, the balance usually being on the credit side.

The branch is considered as a definite accounting unit, the results of whose operations will be disclosed by a Branch Profit and Loss Account and Balance Sheet drawn up on ordinary principles.

The first entries made in the branch books will usually be the purchase of certain fixed assets, e.g. shop counters and shelves, with money supplied by the head office. Upon receipt of the cash from the head office, cash will be debited and Head Office Account credited, and when the assets are purchased the Asset Accounts will be debited and cash (or creditors) credited. In the head office books the entries will be a debit to Branch Account and a credit to cash for the money remitted, no cognizance being taken of how such cash is expended by the branch.

Upon the dispatch of goods by the head office to the branch (the goods usually being invoiced at cost price plus a small charge for handling, etc.), in the head office books Goods Sent to Branches Account will be credited and the Branch Account debited with the invoiced price of the goods. In the branch books, Purchases Account will be debited and Head Office Account credited. Returns of goods will be treated in exactly the reverse way, viz.: in the head office books the Goods Sent to Branches Account will be debited and Branch Account credited; and in the branch books the Head Office Account will be debited and purchases or Purchases Returns Account credited. In the head office books the Goods Sent to Branches Account will be closed off at the end of the accounting period by a transfer to the credit or Purchases or Trading Account; though strictly the small loading in respect of handling should be credited to the account recording the handling expenses and the balance only transferred to Purchases Account. Remittances by the branch to the head office in the books of the latter will be debited to the Cash Account and credited to the Branch Account; in the books of the branch, such remittances will be debited to the Head Office Account and credited to the Cash Account.

The reverse procedure is necessary for remittances to the branch by the head office.

All the purchases and sales of the branch from, and to, outside persons will be dealt with in the ordinary way in the books of the branch. At the end of the accounting period, the branch will prepare its own Profit and Loss Account and Balance Sheet, and if a profit is made it will be transferred to the credit of Head Office Account, and if a loss to the debit of Head Office Account. A copy of the Branch Trial Balance, Profit and Loss Account and Balance Sheet, if such are prepared at the branch, will be sent to the head office. In the head office books, if a profit has been made, Branch Account will be debited and Branch Profit and Loss Account credited. If a loss has been made, Branch Account will be credited and Branch Profit and Loss Account debited. When the trading results of all the branches have been obtained, the balance on Branch Profit and Loss Account will be transferred to the ordinary Profit and Loss Account. It can now be seen that the Branch Account in the head office books and the Head Office Account in the branch books will normally be in contraposition, i.e. they will show the same balance but on opposite sides, the balance on the Head Office Account in the branch books representing the net amount of assets that the branch possesses. Accordingly, when the head office prepares its Balance Sheet, the branch will appear often as a single account, as either a debtor or a creditor. But instead of showing the balance of the Branch Account as *one* item in the Head Office Balance Sheet, the detailed assets and liabilities of the branch comprising such balance may be substituted therefor.

The following illustration incorporates all the above features.

Illustration 24

A, a London merchant, has a branch in Manchester which trades on its own account. The following is a condensed summary of the transactions of the branch for the year to 31st December 19...

	£
Purchases from Head Office	16,000
Purchases from outsiders—Credit	13,500
Cash	4,500
Sales—Credit	33,000
Cash	27,000
Cash received from Debtors	28,000
Cash paid to Creditors	9,500
Expenses paid by Branch	10,000
,, ,, ,, Head Office for Branch	3,000
Assets purchased at commencement of year	1,000
Cash received from Head Office	2,000
Cash remitted to Head Office	28,000

The branch prepares its own final accounts. Write off depreciation at 10 per cent per annum. Stock on hand at 31st December 19.., £6,000. Show Ledger Accounts in the Branch books.

The Ledger accounts of the branch are:

HEAD OFFICE

			£				£
Cash			28,000	Cash			2,000
Balance		c/d	11,900	Goods			16,000
				Cash for expenses			3,000
				Net Profit for Year			18,900
			£39,900				£39,900
				Balance		b/d	11,900

PURCHASES

		£			£
Head Office		16,000	Trading Account		34,000
Sundry Creditors		13,500			
Cash		4,500			
		£34,000			£34,000

SALES

		£			£
Trading Account . .		60,000	Sundry Debtors . .		33,000
			Cash		27,000
		£60,000			£60,000

SUNDRY CREDITORS

		£			£
Cash		9,500	Purchases . . .		13,500
Balances . . .	c/d	4,000			
		£13,500			£13,500
			Balances . . .	b/d	4,000

SUNDRY DEBTORS

		£			£
Sales		33,000	Cash		28,000
			Balances . . .	c/d	5,000
		£33,000			£33,000
Balances . . .	b/d	5,000			

EXPENSES

		£			£
Cash		10,000	Profit and Loss Account .		13,000
Head Office . .		3,000			
		£13,000			£13,000

SUNDRY ASSETS

		£			£
Cash		1,000	Profit and Loss Account:		
			Depreciation .		100
			Balances . .	c/d	900
		£1,000			£1,000
Balances . .	b/d	900			

CASH

		£			£
Head Office . .		2,000	Sundry Assets . .		1,000
Sundry Debtors . .		28,000	Head Office . .		28,000
Sales . . .		27,000	Expenses . .		10,000
			Sundry Creditors .		9,500
			Purchases . .		4,500
			Balance . .	c/d	4,000
		£57,000			£57,000
Balance . . .	b/d	4,000			

STOCK

		£				
Trading Account . .		6,000				.

BRANCH TRADING AND PROFIT AND LOSS ACCOUNT
for the YEAR ENDED 31ST DECEMBER 19..

		£				£
Purchases . . .		34,000	Sales			60,000
Gross Profit . . .	c/d	32,000	Stock . . .			6,000
		£66,000				£66,000
Expenses . . .		13,000	Gross Profit . . .	b/d		32,000
Depreciation . . .		100				
Net Profit to Head Office						
Account . .		18,900				
		£32,000				£32,000

BRANCH BALANCE SHEET, AS AT 31ST DECEMBER 19..

	£			£
Head Office	11,900	Sundry Assets . £1,000		
Sundry Creditors . . .	4,000	Less Depreciation 100		900
		Stock		6,000
		Sundry Debtors . . .		5,000
		Cash		4,000
	£15,900			£15,900

Notes. The branch having no opening stock appears to be a new one, in which event the head office will have probably remitted an initial sum to set it going.

The detailed accounts would actually be opened in the usual way, e.g. Debtors, Expenses.

The Profit and Loss Account and Balance Sheet will be supplied to the head office, or the ordinary Trial Balance with details of stock and adjustments. In the latter case, the head office prepares the final accounts of the branch. The final accounts must be closed off in the books of the *branch*, the usual entries being made, except that the balance of profit or loss of the branch is (in the branch books) transferred to HEAD OFFICE ACCOUNT, being the equivalent of a Capital Account for book-keeping purposes.

From the above information, the head office incorporates the **results** only of the branch operations through the instrumentality of the Branch Account in the head office books. The branch accounts themselves are *not* incorporated in the head office books, as they belong to an entirely self-contained separate system of accounting. This point is important because students are apt to think because combined presentation of the Profit and Loss Account and Balance Sheet is possible, that these details appear in the head office books as part of the double entry. This is not so.

The combination above-mentioned is simple and will be noticed presently, but the real connecting link is the reconciliation of the Branch Account in the head office books with the Head Office Account in the branch books. Hence, mistakes and abnormal circumstances apart, the entries in the head office books are such as to incorporate the results of the branch operations through the medium of the Branch Account. In the head office books, the closing entries are, normally, those relating to profit and loss of the branch. These are:

1. Debit Branch Account (with branch profit).	Credit Profit and Loss Account.
2. Debit Profit and Loss Account.	Credit Branch Account (with branch loss).

These entries (whether a profit or a loss) are opposite to those which the branch makes in its books under the heading of Head Office Account, to which, as has been seen, it transfers its profit or loss. The result is that the two accounts will agree (on *opposite* sides), that is, if the Head Office Account in the branch books is in debit, the Branch Account in the head office books will be in credit; and conversely.

So far as the head office books are concerned, the balance of the Branch Account (as adjusted) will appear as a DEBTOR or a CREDITOR, and that completes the entries.

If the combined accounts are shown they are the results of *two* (or more) distinct and separate sets of books, but as there will be in each set a reciprocal account (Head Office Account in branch; Branch Account in head office), the amounts thereof will connect and consequently be eliminated from the combined figures. But it must be remembered that when two (or more) separate Balance Sheets are combined, the details of the Branch Balance Sheet do not appear in the head office books, the latter recording only the Branch Account as outlined above. This will receive consideration shortly, the matter being referred to at this stage to impress the fact upon the student's mind that the book-keeping entries in the head office are simple, merely involving one transfer, leaving the branch a debtor or creditor.

The entries may now be made in the head office books. These will be, being a branch profit:

Debit Branch Account, £18,900. Credit Profit and Loss Account, £18,900.

The account of the Branch in the head office books will thus be:

BRANCH

		£			£
Cash		2,000	Cash		28,000
Goods		16,000	Balance	c/d	11,900
Cash for Expenses		3,000			
Profit and Loss Account: Branch Net Profit for Year		18,900[1]			
		£39,900			£39,900
Balance	b/d	11,900[2]			

[1] Ascertained from the figures sent by branch (and as shown in branch books).
[2] This account agrees with that of the Head Office Account in the branch (see p. 1951), and will appear in the Head Office Balance Sheet as an asset.

After these entries have been made the head office will normally proceed to prepare its own final accounts.

It is usual to have, in the head office books, two separate accounts for each branch, viz. (1) Branch Capital Account, to record the capital invested in the branch; and (2) Branch Current Account, to record the transfers of goods, ordinary remittances to and from the branch, and profit and loss of the branch.

Obviously, in the branch books there will be two separate accounts for the head office: (1) Head Office Capital Account and (2) Head Office Current Account.

On the same principle, remittances may be recorded in a separate account.

Inter-Branch Transfers. The entries required for transfers between branches are: Debit receiving branch, credit Purchases or Sales Account in the sending branch books; and in the receiving branch books, debit Purchases and credit sending branch at either cost or selling price, as the case may be. Alternatively, the entries may be made through the medium of the head office, thus:

Debit Head Office	Credit Purchases or Sales Account (in the sending branch books)
Debit Purchases	Credit Head Office (in the receiving branch books)
Debit Receiving Branch	Credit Sending Branch (in the head office books)

It must be understood thoroughly that inter-branch transfers at selling price, whilst showing a profit to the sending branch, cannot be a true profit of the organization as a whole until a sale by the receiving branch has been made, so that a provision for profit on unsold stock must be created at the time when accounts are prepared. This principle is dealt with on p. 1961 *et seq.* (See also Chapter 22.)

Illustration 25

'A' Branch transfers goods to 'B' Branch at selling price of £200, all transfers being effected through the head office.

The entries are:

'A' Branch books—				
Debit Head Office .	. £200	Credit Sales .	.	. £200
'B' Branch books—				
Debit Purchases .	. £200	Credit Head Office .		. £200
Head Office books—				
Debit 'B' Branch .	. £200	Credit 'A' Branch .		. £200

A very common procedure, as has been seen, is to open for current transactions a separate account, designated Current Account, so that the above-mentioned transfers would be posted to the accounts named under the heading of Current Account, e.g. in 'A' branch books, debit Head Office Current Account, credit Sales.

Adjustments and Reconciliation of Branch and Head Office Accounts. When occasion requires, e.g. preparation of final accounts (or even interim accounts), any difference in the reflective accounts must be ascertained and either adjusted or corrected.

It is not very difficult to see that the disagreement on any one date between the two accounts may arise from ordinary and normal causes, e.g. cash in transit; goods in transit; receipt of debt due to branch, notification of which has not reached the branch; bill drawn by branch on head office not yet to hand, and so on.

The general principle is, to reconcile the *incomplete* account to the *complete* account, and as has been seen, the accounts being reciprocal, the necessary entry must appear on the opposite side in the Head Office Account in the branch books to that in the Branch Account in the head office books, and vice versa.

Illustration 26

At 31st December 19.., the head office books contain the following account:

BRANCH

19..				£	19..			£
Jan. 1	Balance .	. .	b/d	1,500	Dec. 31	Remittances . . .		800
Dec. 31	Goods .	. .		1,100		Returns . . .		94
						Bills Receivable Account .		200
						Balance . . .	c/d	1,506
				£2,600				£2,600
19..	Balance .	. .	b/d	1,506				

The account of the head office in the branch books is:

HEAD OFFICE

19..				£	19..			£
Dec. 31	Remittances .	. .		830	Jan. 1	Balance . . .	b/d	1,500
	Returns .	. .		120	Dec. 31	Goods . . .		1,060
	Balance .	. .	c/d	1,610				
				£2,560				£2,560
					19..			
					Jan. 1	Balance . . .	b/d	1,610

It is ascertained that a remittance of £30 and returns of £26 *from* branch to head office are in transit; whilst an amount of £40 goods *from* head office to branch is in transit. A Bill of Exchange of £200 drawn by the head office on the branch had not reached the branch on 31st December.

Proceeding on the rule to reconcile the *incomplete* to the *complete*, the items of £30 and £26 dealt with by branch but not by head office, must be brought into the latter's books. Thus:

Debit Cash in transit   . £30   Credit Branch (*a*) . £30 } in Head
Debit Stock in Transit . £26   Credit Branch (*b*) . £26 } Office books

Following the same rule, the items of £40 and £200 must be introduced into the branch books.

Debit Head Office (*c*) . £200   Credit Bills Payable   . £200 } in Branch
Debit Stock in transit . £40   Credit Head Office (*d*) . £40 } books

The accounts will now be:

(1)   BRANCH ACCOUNT (IN HEAD OFFICE BOOKS)

		£			£
Balance (as above) . .	b/d	1,506	Cash in Transit . .	(a)	30
			Stock in Transit . .	(b)	26
			Balance . . .	c/d	1,450
		£1,506			£1,506
Balance	b/d	1,450			

(2)   HEAD OFFICE ACCOUNT (IN BRANCH BOOKS)

		£			£
Bill Payable . . .	(c)	200	Balance (as above) . .	b/d	1,610
Balance	c/d	1,450	Stock in Transit .	(d)	40
		£1,650			£1,650
			Balance . . .	b/d	1,450

The other items will be posted to the respective accounts.

Alternatively, it may be more convenient to treat as correct the Head Office Account in the branch (save for the transfer required in respect of profit or loss of branch and charges incurred by one for another), in which case the adjustments necessary will be made in the head office books to arrive at the branch figure of £1,610, thus:

Debit Cash in transit . £30⎫
     Stock in Transit . £26 ⎬ Credit Branch . . . £96
     Stock in Transit . £40⎭
Debit Branch . . £200 Credit Bills Receivable . £200

The Branch Account in the head office will now be:

BRANCH

		£			£
Balance . . .	b/d	1,506	Sundries (as above) . .		96
Bills Receivable . .		200	Balance . . .	c/d	1,610
		£1,706			£1,706
Balance . . .	b/d	1,610			

The first method reflects the true position; the second does not, as it cancels entries omitted in one set of books, instead of introducing them into the books which ought to have included them. (It will be remembered that in Bank Reconciliation Accounts the same point arises, viz. first to correct omissions in the Cash Book and then work from the Bank Statement balance to the Cash Book balance.)

In the succeeding period, using the second method, the items adjusted above would be re-transferred, e.g. in the head office books the Bill

Receivable would be re-debited and credited to the Branch Account, whilst in due course the branch on acceptance of the bill would debit head office and credit Bills Payable.

In the first method these entries in the head office books would not be necessary, as the bill already appears in the proper account. When the cash (which at the date of the Balance Sheet is in transit) is received from the branch, it must be credited to cash in transit, and not to branch, as the latter account has already been credited. The same principle applies to stock in transit.

Illustration 27

The following account is in the head office books:

BRANCH

			£				
Balance	b/d		2,400				

In the branch books:

HEAD OFFICE

							£
				Balance	b/d		2,300

The difference arises by reason of a remittance of £100 by the branch, not yet to hand.

Using the first method, the entries required in the head office books are: debit Cash in Transit Account, £100; credit Branch Account, £100. This reconciles the account with the balance of £2,300 in the branch. When (normally in the course of a few days) the cash is received, the entries will be: debit Cash, £100: credit Cash in Transit account, £100.[1]

It may be noted that where there are numerous adjustments the whole of them may be brought down into one account, e.g. Suspense Account, instead of in separate accounts, e.g. Cash in Transit, Stock in Transit, etc., in which case the postings in the new period will be made to the one account.

Illustration 28

Head office makes its accounts up to 31st December. Branch Account is in debit for £4,000. The amounts as rendered by the branch show the head office to be in credit for £3,600, the difference being accounted for by the following entries, which appear in the branch books only.

		£
Dec. 26. (1) Goods returned to Head Office . .	.	200
30. (2) Cash sent to Head Office . .	.	450
31. (3) Proceeds of Bill collected for Head Office		250

---

[1] Alternatively the first entries may be reversed in the new period, bringing the account back to £2,400, in which case £100 is credited to Branch Account upon receipt of cash.

The Branch Account in the head office books will be:

BRANCH

		£			£
Balance . . .	b/d	4,000	Suspense Account—		
Suspense Account—			Goods in Transit .		200
Cash Collected . .		250	Cash in Transit .		450
			Balance . . .	c/d	3,600
		£4,250			£4,250
Balance . . .	b/d	3,600			

SUSPENSE

		£			£
Branch Account—			Branch Account—		
Goods in Transit .		200	Cash Collected[1] .		250
Cash in Transit . .		450	Balance . . .	c/d	400
		£650			£650
Balance . . .	b/d	400			

[1] Alternatively this may be credited to the account which is in debit, e.g. Bills Receivable or debtor.

Illustration 29

The following balances appeared in the books of Manchester (Head Office) and Stockport (Branch) at 31st December 19.2:

	Manchester		Stockport	
	Dr.	Cr.	Dr.	Cr.
	£	£	£	£
Current Account Manchester . . .				8,500
Current Account Stockport . . .	11,470			
Plant and Fixtures at cost . . .	1,900		420	
Depreciation Provision . . .		620		130
Unrealized Profit Reserve, 19.1 . . .		730		

Goods are charged out to Branch at cost plus 25 per cent.
The Branch deals solely with Head Office goods.

The following were the movements at the end of the year, but entries have been made only in *one set of books:*

Goods sent by Head Office to Branch £800, of which £300 were lost and not covered by insurance.

Expenses (£170) incurred by Head Office on account of Branch have not been entered by Branch. Plant costing £500 is in transit to Branch from Head Office. This plant was estimated to have an eight-year life, the residual value being taken at £100. It has been in use for three years to the end of 19.1, and depreciation accordingly provided for three years, but no provision has yet been made on plant for 19.2.

Goods (returns) and cash are in transit at 31st December from Branch to Head Office, £100 and £1,400 respectively.

(All the references to goods above are at internal invoice price.)

The Closing stocks on hand are:

	£
Head Office	4,200
Branch (at internal invoice price) . .	2,600

Make the entries in both sets of books giving effect to the above.

(The usual entries will be required for the year's provision for depreciation in both sets of books and incorporation of Branch results in Head Office books, but are not dealt with in this illustration, attention being confined to consideration of the entries appropriate to the foregoing details.)

Head Office:

STOCKPORT CURRENT ACCOUNT

			£				£
19.. Dec. 31	Balance (per T.B.) . .		11,470	19.2 Dec. 31	Cash in Transit . .		1,400
					Goods in Transit . .		100
					Goods in Transit . .		500
					Stock lost . . .		300
					Depreciation provision .		150
					Balance . . .	c/d	9,020
			£11,470				£11,470
19.3 Jan. 1	Balance . . .	b/d	9,020				

CASH IN TRANSIT

			£				
19.2 Dec. 31	Branch		1,400				

GOODS IN TRANSIT

			£				
19.2 Dec. 31	Branch		100				
	Branch		500				
			£600				

DEPRECIATION PROVISION

			£				£
19.2 Dec. 31	Transfer to Branch, re Plant £600 transferred .		150	19.2 Dec. 31	Balance . . .		620

UNREALIZED PROFIT RESERVE

				£					£
19.2 Dec. 31	Reserve for 19.2 .	c/d		640	19.2 Jan. 1	Balance . . .	b/d		730
	Profit and Loss Account .			90					
				£730					£730
					19.3 Jan. 1	Balance . . .	b/d		640

The item of £300 will be debited back to Goods sent to Branch at £300, and as the goods so lost will not come into Closing Stock the loss is automatically effective.

This loss is $\frac{4}{5}$ of £300, i.e. Cost £240. Alternatively, this may be credited to Head Office Trading Account and debited to its Profit and Loss Account.

Branch Books:

MANCHESTER CURRENT ACCOUNT

19.2 Dec. 31				£	19.2 Dec. 31				£
	Depreciation Provision	. .	b/d	150		Balance	. .	b/d	8,500
	Balance	. .	b/d	9,020		Plant	.		500
						Expenses	. .		170
				£9,170					£9,170
					19.3 Jan. 1	Balance	. .	b/d	9,020

The depreciation provision brought into Stockport books is:

	£
Cost	500
Less Residual Value . . .	100
Eight year life, i.e. £50 per annum . .	£400
£50 × 3 = ...	£150

Provision for depreciation will be required in both books for 19.2, amended in consequence of the transfer of Plant £600.

	£
Provision for unrealized profit—	
Goods on hand—Stockport . .	2,600
Goods in transit . . .	600[1]
	£3,200
20 per cent thereof = . .	£640

Illustration 30

The Universal Providers Co. have one branch which draws its supplies chiefly from its head office and partly from outside suppliers. The goods sent from head office are invoiced at cost plus 25 per cent.

The Head Office trial Balance is:

[1] It should be borne in mind that this stock is not 'on hand' and profit has been taken in Head Office books, because the £600 item has not yet been charged back to Goods sent to Branch and thus includes the profit on £600.

Trial Balance, 31st December 19..

	£	£
Capital		20,000
Sundry Fixed Assets	10,600	
Stock	9,000	
Debtors	10,400	
Creditors		9,000
Cash at Bank	1,350	
Purchases	80,000	
Sales		92,000
Sundry Expenses	10,000	
Goods invoiced to Branch at Selling Price		8,000
Goods returned from Branch at Selling Price	450	
Branch Capital Account	6,000	
Branch Current Account	1,200	
	£129,000	£129,000

Closing Stock—
   £7,500, Head Office.
   £1,900, Branch [Head Office Goods, £650], exclusive of Stock of £350 in
      transit from Head Office to branch.

From the above and the following figures prepare in two-sided form a combined Trading and Profit and Loss account for the year ended 31st December 19.., and Balance Sheet at that date. Make the adjustments for 'transit' items in the head office books.

	£
Branch details—	
Debtors	900
Creditors	1,100
Sales	13,650
Purchases (from outsiders)	4,500
Stock ('outside' Goods)	1,250
Sundry Fixed Assets	5,400
Sundry Expenses	1,500
Cash at Bank (after deduction of £100 Cash in transit from	
Branch to Head Office)	750
Depreciation—	
Head Office Fixed Assets	310
Branch Fixed Assets	165

Before proceeding with the illustration, the student should at once observe that as the branch keeps separate accounts, balances of the latter must be completed by the introduction of the stock received from and returned to the head office, and that the question involves the treatment of cash, stock in transit, and the elimination of profit on unsold stock.

Trial-Balances, 31st December 19. .

	Head Office		Branch	
	Dr. £	Cr. £	Dr. £	Cr. £
Capital		20,000		
Sundry Fixed Assets	10,600		5,400	
Stock	9,000		1,250	
Debtors	10,400		900	
Creditors		9,000		1,100
Cash at Bank	1,350		750	
Purchases	80,000		4,500	
Sales.		92,000		13,650
Sundry Expenses.	10,000		1,500	
Internal Transfers of Goods . . .		8,000	7,650	
Internal Transfers of Goods (Returns) .	450			450
Branch Capital	6,000			6,000
Branch Current Account . . .	750			750
Cash in Transit	100			
Goods in Transit	350			
	£129,000	£129,000	£21,950	£21,950

Depreciation of fixed assets: Head Office, £310; Branch, £165.

COMBINED TRADING AND PROFIT AND LOSS ACCOUNT FOR THE YEAR ENDED 31ST DECEMBER 19..

	Branch £	Head Office £	Total £		Branch £	Head Office £	Total £
Stock	1,250	9,000	10,250	Sales	13,650	92,000	105,650
Purchases	4,500	80,000	84,500	Transfers (at cost) contra	360	6,120	
Transfers (at cost) contra	6,120	360		Stock in Transit (at cost)		280	280
Gross Profit c/d	3,910	16,540	20,450	Stock (at cost)	1,770	7,500	9,270
	£15,780	£105,900	£115,200		£15,780	£105,900	£115,200
Sundry Expenses	1,500	10,000	11,500	Gross Profit b/d	3,910	16,540	20,450
Depreciation	165	310	475				
Net Profit	2,245	6,230	8,475				
	£3,910	£16,540	£20,450		£3,910	£16,540	£20,450

In the books, the accounts of the branch will be closed off in the usual way, the balance of profit or loss being transferred to head office. The books of the latter will be closed off in the usual way after incorporating the branch results, and reconciling the Branch Account and eliminating profit on unsold stock.

The question, however, does not require the ACTUAL entries in the books, so the student must be prepared to proceed directly to the ultimate results without recording entries in the books.

The Trial Balance of the branch will be placed side by side with that of the head office, after which the inflated price of goods transferred will be reduced in both books (on opposite sides), which will still preserve the agreement of the collective balances.

The items in italics are omitted in the question. The £100 represents cash in transit, and this will probably have been debited to head office, reducing the balance on credit of Head Office Current Account; but it is shown separately, as it must be featured separately. The reconciliation is made in head office books, but it is immaterial for the purpose of obtaining the final accounts in which set of books the reconciliation is made.

As to stock in transit, this has been entered in the head office books only, so that there will be a separate account for stock in transit of £350, the amount thereof having been included in the goods sent to branches.

COMBINED BALANCE SHEET AS AT 31ST DECEMBER 19..

	£	£		£	£
Capital		20,000	Fixed Assets—		
Profit and Loss Account . .		8,475	Sundry (less Depreciation)—		
			Head Office . . .	10,290	
		28,475	Branch . . .	5,235	
					15,525
Current Liabilities—			Current Assets—		
Creditors—			Stock—		
Head Office . .	9,000		Head Office . . 7,500		
Branch . . .	1,100		Branch . . 1,770		
		10,100	Transit . . 280		
				9,550	
			Debtors—		
			Head Office . 10,400		
			Branch . . 900		
				11,300	
			Cash at Bank—		
			Head Office . . 1,350		
			Branch . . . 750		
			Transit . . . 100		
				2,200	
					23,050
		£38,575			£38,575

Notes.

1. Goods £7,650, being at selling price, must be reduced by 20%, i.e. £1,530, leaving the figures per Trading Account at £6,120.

2. Similarly, the returns of £450 must be reduced by 20%, leaving £360.

3. The Stock of Head Office goods at selling price is £650 as given in question, at cost is £650 less 20%, i.e. £130 = £520: to this must be added the remainder of the goods (i.e. outside purchases) of £1,250, the total, therefore, being £1,770.

4. The goods in transit must be brought in at cost [viz. £350 less 20%, i.e. £70 = £280].

The adjusted items may now be brought down to cost, and as the reduction will be equally effective on opposite sides of each Trial Balance, it will not disturb the total agreement. The final accounts may now be prepared. (The Combined Trading and Profit and Loss Account appears on p. 1964.)

FOREIGN BRANCHES

There are no special book-keeping methods employed in recording the transactions of foreign branches, the only distinctive feature being the treatment of the foreign exchange. If foreign branches are considered to be in the nature of a foreign investment, no difficulty will be encountered. The head office, if in a sterling country, will keep its accounts in sterling, and the branch will keep its accounts in foreign currency. The branch will open a Head Office Account in its books to record all transactions with the head office; the head office recording these transactions in a Branch Account. There are three methods of converting branch transactions in foreign currency into sterling, and *vice versa*:

1. To convert all transactions at a certain fixed rate (e.g. the official rate at a certain date or at the beginning of the accounting period). Where the exchange is comparatively stable there will be a small difference to transfer to a Profit and Loss on Exchange Account at the end of each accounting period.

2. Where the exchange fluctuates widely, an artificial parity is sometimes assumed as in (1), with periodic adjustments in the books.

3. Where the exchange fluctuates within comparatively narrow limits, the usual procedure is to allow the head office and branch books to be kept independently, and at the end of the accounting period each item in the Trial Balance or Balance Sheet forwarded by the branch will be converted at certain rates relative to the nature of each item.

The various methods will now be dealt with in detail:

1. and 2. Stable Exchanges and Violently Fluctuating Exchanges. The method adopted is to enter in each set of books the actual receipts or payments incurred, which will be converted at the fixed rate. At the end of the accounting period the head office will value its 'investment' in foreign currency at the fixed rate, and the difference between such value and the balance of the account in foreign currency will be transferred to Exchange Reserve Account. This balance will equal the figures as to both foreign currency and sterling in the branch books. The reserve merely serves to maintain the figures at the fixed rate of exchange, and does not bring the valuation of the foreign currency to the TRUE rate of exchange unless special provision is made separately therefor.

Illustration 31

A concern in London has a foreign branch. Transactions are recorded as between the head office and the branch at $5 to £. During the year to 31st December, the following transactions arise between the head office and the branch:

Sterling bought by Branch and remitted to London, £2,004 cost $10,000.
Sterling bought by Branch and remitted to London, £2,000 cost $9,840.
Dollars bought in London and remitted to Branch, $5,000 cost £970.
Dollars bought in London and remitted to Branch, $1,040 cost £200.

Write up the Branch and London books.

BRANCH BOOKS:

HEAD OFFICE

		£	$				£	$
Cash		2,000	10,000	Cash			1,000	5,000
,,		1,968	9,840	,,			208	1,040
				Balance	c/d		2,760	13,800
		£3,968	$19,840				£3,968	$19,840
Balance	b/d	2,760	13,800					

LONDON BOOKS:

BRANCH

		$	£				$	£
Cash		4,850	970	Cash			10,020	2,004
,,		1,000	200	,,			10,000	2,000
Exchange Reserve		370	74					
Balance	c/d	13,800	2,760					
		$20,020	£4,004				$20,020	£4,004
				Balance	b/d		13,800	2,760

EXCHANGE RESERVE

							$	£
				Branch			370	74

Stores Accounts. When branches are situated in countries having a violently fluctuating rate of exchange, it is customary to transfer all capital expenditure to head office as and when it is incurred in order that a permanent record of the asset shall be kept in a non-fluctuating exchange. In order that the results shown by the books concerned should be reflective of the true position, it is equally important that a sound basis be used to eliminate the exchange fluctuations from Stores Account (which appears in the branch books).

Illustration 32

During January 19.., a head office consigns stores to its foreign branch of a sterling equivalent of £1,000, the rate of exchange being $10 = £1. Fluctuations in this example are ignored. The entries in the branch books will be:

HEAD OFFICE

				19.. Jan. 31	Stores		$ 10,000	£ 1,000

STORES

19.. Jan. 31	Head Office	$ 10,000						

It is now assumed that half of these stores are used on Capital Account during the month of February 19.., when the rate of exchange is $8 = £1, and that the other half are used on account of revenue during the month of March, when the rate of exchange is $11 = £1.

The entries in journal form will be as follows:

JOURNAL

19.. Feb. 28	Capital Expenditure		$ 5,000	$
	Stores			5,000
Mar. 31	Revenue		5,000	
	Stores			5,000

The capital expenditure will be transferred to Head Office Account at an average rate of $8 = £1, that is £625, and the Revenue items will be transferred at $11 = £1, that is £455 (approx.). Thus, stores costing £1,000 have all been used and charged out at £1,080, which is very unsatisfactory.

In order to obviate this, the following method is adopted. The Stores Account is ruled with double columns, one to record the transactions at a *nominal* rate of exchange, and the other to record them at the *actual* rate at which they take place.

When stores are transferred from head office, Head Office Account is credited and Stores Account debited, and at the same time an entry is made in the memorandum column on the basis of the rate adopted therein. The transactions in the above example (that is, half the stores are utilized for capital purposes and half for revenue purposes) will first be entered on the credit side in the memorandum column in terms of the nominal standard rate adopted. Using this as a basis, they are then inserted in the other column at the actual rate then ruling.

Illustration 33

Assume the same facts as in the previous illustration, and that the nominal standard rate adopted is $20 = £1. the entries will be as follows:

STORES

		Nom- inal	Real Value			Nom- inal	Real Value
19.. Jan. 31	Head Office .	$ 20,000	$ 10,000	19.. Feb. 28 Mar. 31	Capital . Revenue . H.O. Account: Diff. in Ex- change .	$ 10,000 10,000	$ 4,000 5,500 500
		$20,000	$10,000			$20,000	$10,000

HEAD OFFICE

19..		$	£	19..		$	£
Feb. 28	Capital Expenditure Account	4,000	500	Jan. 31	Stores	10,000	1,000
Mar. 31	Revenue Account	5,500	500				
	Difference in Exchange	500					
		$10,000	£1,000			$10,000	£1,000

REVENUE ACCOUNT

19..			$	19..			$
Mar. 31	Stores		5,500	Mar. 31	Head Office		5,500

CAPITAL EXPENDITURE ACCOUNT

19..			$	19..			$
Feb. 28	Stores		4,000	Feb. 28	Head Office		4,000

It will be seen from the above that each item now bears its appropriate sterling equivalent of the total stores consumed. The Stores Account is closed off by transferring the difference on exchange to the Head Office Account, inserting the figure in the dollar column only.

If, at the end of the accounting period, there are certain stores on hand, the procedure in bringing down the balance is briefly described as follows:

The amount of stores in terms of foreign currency at the nominal or *standard* rate is inserted in the nominal column; its equivalent is then entered in the real column, having regard to the current rate of exchange. Any difference is transferred to the Head Office Account (foreign currency column only).

The following example illustrates all the principles involved.

Illustration 34

A foreign branch, situated in a country having a fluctuating dollar currency has the following transactions with the London head office during July 19...

Stores received from London ($15 = £1)	£3,000
Stores purchased locally	$10,000
Stores used on Capital (standard rate)	$5,000
Stores used on Revenue (standard rate)	$30,000
Sales (all cash)	$60,000
Wages (Capital)	$5,000
Wages (Revenue)	$12,000

During the month $20,000 were remitted to head office at an **actual** rate of $12·50 = £1; **standard** rate $20 = £1.

Average rate for the month, $10 = £1. Rate on the 31st July, $8 = £1.

Show entries in branch books.

STORES

	Rate	Nominal Value	Real Value			Rate	Nominal Value	Real Value
		$	$				$	$
19.. July 31 Head Office	15	60,000	45,000	19.. July 31	Capital Expenditure (2)	10	5,000	2,500
Cash (1)	10	20,000	10,000		Revenue Account	10	30,000	15,000
					Head Office—Difference in Exchange			19,500
					Balance (3) c/d	8	45,000	18,000
		$80,000	$55,000				$80,000	$55,000
Aug. 1 Balance b/d	8	45,000	18,000					

HEAD OFFICE

	Rate	$	£			Rate	$	£
19.. July 31 Cash	12·50	20,000	1,600	19.. July 31	Stores	15	45,000	3,000
Capital	10·00	7,500	750		Profit	10	33,000	3,300
Stores—Difference in Exchange		19,500						
Balance c/d		31,000	3,950					
		$78,000	£6,300				$78,000	£6,300
				Aug. 1	Balance b/d		31,000	3,950

REVENUE ACCOUNT

		$			$
19.. July 31	Stores	15,000	19.. July 31	Sales	60,000
	Wages	12,000			
	Head Office Account Profit	33,000			
		$60,000			$60,000

CAPITAL EXPENDITURE

	Rate	$	£			Rate	$	£
19.. July 31 Stores Account	10	2,500	250	19.. July 31	Head Office Transfer	10	7,500	750
Wages	10	5,000	500					
		$7,500	£750				$7,500	£750

CASH

		$			$
19.. July 31	Sales	60,000	19.. July 31	Stores	10,000
				Head Office	20,000
				Wages	17,000
				Balance c/d	13,000
		$60,000			$60,000
Aug. 1	Balance b/d	13,000			

BRANCH TRIAL BALANCE, 31ST JULY 19..

	Rate	Dr.	Cr.	Dr.	Cr.
		£	£	$	$
Stores	8	2,250		18,000	
Head Office (per ledger) . . .			3,950		31,000
Cash at Bank	8	1,625		13,000	
Difference in Exchange . . .		75			
		£3,950	£3,950	$31,000	$31,000

The sterling columns are those used for inclusion in the head office books. It should be noted that as a matter of good financial policy, if the rate is expected to return to, say, $10 = £1 it will be beneficial to the concern to send all cash from the branch when the rate is at $8 = £1.

Nominal Value and its relation to Real Value. In the foregoing Stores Account, the following points should be noted:

1. To cash (i.e. Local Purchases) (Nominal Value) $20,000, (Real Value) $10,000

    Sterling equivalent of **$10,000** = £1,000 $\left[\dfrac{10,000}{10}\right]$

    Nominal Value of £1,000 = £1,000 × 20 = **$20,000**

2. By Capital Expenditure (Nominal Value) $5,000, (Real Value) $2,500

    Sterling equivalent of **$2,500** = £250 $\left[\dfrac{2,500}{10}\right]$

    Nominal Value of £250 = £250 × 20 = **$5,000**

3. By Balance (Nominal Value) $45,000, (Real Value) $18,000

    Sterling equivalent of **$45,000** = £2,250 $\left[\dfrac{45,000}{20}\right]$

    Real Value of £2,250 = £2,250 × 8 = **$18,000**

The rule may be formulated as follows:

$$\text{Nominal Value} = \text{Real Value} \times \frac{\text{Standard Rate of Conversion}}{\text{Real Rate of Conversion}}$$

e.g. (1) $20,000 = $10,000 × $\dfrac{20}{10}$

and conversely–

$$\text{Real Value} = \text{Nominal Value} \times \frac{\text{Real Rate of Conversion}}{\text{Standard Rate of Conversion}}$$

3. **Moderately Fluctuating Exchange.** Where the rate of exchange fluctuates moderately, the rates of conversion used vary according to circumstances, but the generally accepted rules will be those outlined on pp. 1975 and 1976.

The principles broadly follow those already outlined, the only modification being that the rate of conversion of the branch balance is not uniform; nevertheless, as has been shown, the vital account is the Branch Account in the head office books, which must agree with the Head Office Account in the branch books: but as the one account is in sterling and the other in currency, it is necessary to employ in the Branch Account of the head office an extra column on each side of the Ledger, but not as part of the double entry. By this means the balances of the reciprocal accounts will agree in currency, from which the double entry will be compiled.

Before formally enunciating the rules, a very simple set of circumstances may be imagined from which the whole idea may be assimilated. It will be remembered that the foreign branch will keep its accounts in its native currency, and, as a rule, has no sterling entries contained in its financial books, whether or not the rate of exchange is a stable or erratic one.

Illustration 35

Let it be assumed that a head office starts a branch in Bulganaland and for that purpose remits £1,000, which produces, at 50 to £, 50,000 bulgans. During the year, the foreign branch makes a profit of 10,000 bulgans. No further remittances are made either way. Now it should be quite apparent that in the foreign branch books the final Balance Sheet will be:

BALANCE SHEET

		Bulgans			Bulgans
Head Office	50,000		Sundry Assets		60,000
Plus Profit	10,000		(Less Liabilities) . . .		
		60,000			

The head office has, so speak, invested £1,000 in a foreign venture so that the entry will be:

Debit Bulganaland Branch, £1,000   Credit Cash, £1,000

As, however, the sum has been converted into another form of currency, it is necessary to have a memorandum column showing the quantity of foreign currency representing the original investment, just as in the instance of an investor who will show that number of shares or quantity of stock bought; but this, it must be remembered, is NO PART of the DOUBLE ENTRY.

The account of the foreign branch will, at the initial stage, appear thus:

BULGANALAND BRANCH

	Bulgans	Stg.				
Cash . . .	50,000	£ 1,000				

The account will (in this instance, no further transactions with the branch having taken place) remain dormant until the receipt of necessary details from the branch. It is the next step that causes confusion to students, so that particular attention should be paid thereto.

The memorandum columns should be completed from the entries appearing in the Head Office Account of the branch—on, obviously, the opposite side to those in the branch. No double entry whatever as yet comes into these entries. Continuing the account, it will now appear:

BULGANALAND BRANCH

	Bulgans	Stg.			Bulgans	Stg.
Cash . . .	50,000	1,000	Balance . . c/d	60,000	(2)
Profit and Loss Account .	10,000	(1)			
	60,000			60,000	
Balance . . b/d	60,000				

It will be seen that there is agreement as regards CURRENCY between the two reflective accounts.

The next step is merely to fill up the sterling equivalents and obtain the DOUBLE ENTRY therefrom; that is, gaps represented by (1) and (2) must be filled, and in case of (1) a credit to Profit and Loss Account, and (2) the balance brought down. The general rules for conversion will be fully stated on pp. 1986 and 1987, but it may be stated that usually the profit and loss item is converted at the average rate of exchange obtaining over the year. The closing balance will be valued according to the type of assets and liabilities contained in the Branch Balance Sheet, and in this particular problem the current rate of exchange ruling at the date of taking out the final accounts will be used. These will be assumed (1) average rate at 28 to £; (2) current rate at 31 to £.

The figures arising therefrom (to nearest £) are:

$$(1)\ 10,000\ @\ 28 = \tfrac{10000}{28} = £357$$
$$(2)\ 60,000\ @\ 31 = \tfrac{60000}{31} = £1,936$$

As each set of figures is based upon different rates of exchange, the balance of sterling will be inserted to make the account balance and to transfer to Profit or Loss on Exchange Account. No entry will be made in the memorandum columns as these exactly agree with the Head Office Account in the branch. The accounts will finally appear:

BULGANALAND BRANCH

	Bulgans	Stg.			Bulgans	Stg.
		£				£
Cash	50,000	1,000	Balance . . c/d	60,000	1,936
Profit and Loss Account	10,000	357			
Profit and Loss on Exchange Account		579			
	60,000	£1,936		60,000	£1,936
Balance	60,000	1,936			

The position is that the original investment was £1,000, augmented by £357, equalling £1,357 (on rates of exchange given), and represented by 60,000 bulgans. At the date of the final accounts these bulgans are more valuable as the rate of exchange has APPRECIATED from 50 to £ to 31 to £, thus giving a very high exchange profit of £579—far higher in fact than the trading profits. It is therefore a simple matter to obtain the double entry once the sterling values have been calculated.

Before proceeding further it may be as well to point out the other side of the picture. Assuming that the 'investment' at the date of the final accounts, viz. 60,000, is worth 100 to £, it will be apparent that the value is £600 only, thus bringing about not only a complete cancellation of the profits, but a loss on the capital invested. The account will be (eliminating currency, which will remain constant, whatever may be the rate of exchange):

BULGANALAND BRANCH

		£			£
Cash		1,000	Balance . c/d		600
Profit and Loss Account		357	[i.e. 60,000 @ 100 to £1		
			Loss on Exchange .		757
		£1,357			£1,357
Balance . b/d		600			

The average rate of 28 in view of the end rate of 100 to £ is unlikely unless, indeed, some catastrophic event has occurred towards the end of the financial year in question, but this does not affect the principle. Although the method under review postulates reasonable stability of exchange, extremes have been taken to make the illustrations clear.

To discuss this aspect fully would lead to a protracted and lengthy incursion into economic science, but it may be dismissed by mentioning that with the adverse rate of Bulganaland earnings would tend to rise and so offset a portion of the loss on exchange.

Rules for Conversion of Foreign Currency. The rules for conversion of foreign currency may be stated thus:

Item	Rate employed for conversion
1. Fixed Assets	At the rate ruling either: (a) At the date of contract. (b) At the date of delivery. (c) At the date or dates of payment. (d) At the date of remittance or dates of remittances therefor.

The *same* rate will be used in future years in respect of the fixed assets actually acquired at the commencement of the period, e.g. if fixed assets were acquired in 19.2, say 12,000 francs at 120 to £, the amount shown in 19.2 and subsequent years, in sterling, will (apart from Depreciation and Sales) be £100.

Item	Rate employed for conversion
2. Fixed Liabilities	At the rate ruling: (a) At the date of contract. (b) At the date incurred.

It must be realized, however, that a liability which is 'fixed', that is a *long-term* liability, will usually sooner or later become a current liability, so that as the date for repayment approaches, it should, particularly if the rate of exchange has moved adversely, be viewed as a *current* liability.[1] If the liability is undertaken in terms of payment in STERLING, then the commitment is, whatever the rate of exchange, only the same amount of sterling that has been shown in the books throughout the period of the loan, e.g. if 12,000 francs at 120 to £ had been borrowed to be repaid in twenty years' time in STERLING, the liability to be discharged is £100 only; but if the loan had been in terms of francs and the rate had appreciated to 60 to £, the cost of acquiring 12,000 francs would be £200.

Items	Rate employed for conversion
3. Current Assets and Liabilities	At the rate ruling: At the date of the end of the accounting period.
4. Remittances	The cost of the foreign currency where remittances made *to* branch. The amount produced in sterling where remittance made *from* branch.
5. Transfer of Goods	At the rate ruling: (a) At the date of dispatch. (b) At the date of receipt. (c) At the date the customer would be debited.

---

[1] When long-term liabilities are repayable in foreign currency, they are often converted at the year-end rate of exchange so that any probable loss on repayment is shown in each Balance Sheet.

Items	*Rate employed for conversion*
6. Profit and Loss items . . .	At the average rate ruling over the whole period except for:

    (a) Depreciation of fixed assets, which will be taken at the rate ruling at acquisition.

    (b) Opening stock which will have been valued at the end of the preceding accounting period as a current asset. (Rule 3.)

    (c) Closing stock which will be valued as a current asset at the date of the end of the accounting period. (Rule 3.)[1]

[1] It may be objected that by adopting rule 6 (c) a valuation at higher than cost would result if the average rate of exchange (used for the purchases and expenses) were lower than the closing rate. The effect would be to inflate the profit of the Branch by an appreciation in exchange which may quite probably be only temporary; on the other hand, use of the conventional conversion rates is arbitrary, and the conversion into sterling is merely symbolic and does not produce a true sterling result at all.

If, however, the Stock can be identified as that sent out to the Branch on a particular date, the rate of exchange on that date would be equally correct as the basis of conversion; separate identification with varying rates is not, however, usually practicable or possible.

It may even be that some of the closing stock is part of the stock at the commencement of the accounting period, suggesting the probability that it is not readily saleable.

The principles to follow should therefore be:

1. Stock held at the commencement of the period and still unsold at the end should be converted at the rate taken at the former date.

2. Stock which is easily identifiable, at the rate of exchange at the date of purchase or transfer.

3. Otherwise, at the average rate for the accounting period or at the rate ruling at the close of the accounting period.

In all cases the foreign currency equivalent should, if necessary, be reduced to net realizable value before conversion.

The exchange fluctuation element is a factor in every year, and provided (a) that due regard is paid to any depreciated values (without reference to conversion rates), (b) that a uniform method is adopted, and (c) that exchange fluctuations are effected through an Exchange Suspense or Reserve, then the exact method is not material in normal circumstances.

The rule of average rate is one of convenience, but where it is practicable a rate more closely conforming to facts may be employed.

(i) Where the branch opens up new premises during the accounting period, the rent may be taken at the average rate for the period elapsing between the occupation of the premises and the end of the accounting period.

(ii) Where there are cross supplies of goods between head office and the branch, the rates ruling at the dates of consignment or arrival may be employed. (see Rule 5.)

(iii) Where expenses and sales and purchases are not spread fairly evenly over the accounting period a WEIGHTED average may be employed.

It will be clear that no conversion rate appears for the commencing balances of the reciprocal accounts of Branch Account in the head office and Head Office Account in the branch, as at the commencement of the period the amount shown in *sterling* for or against the branch in the head office books *is* the valuation of the branch; whilst the balances between the head office and branch in *currency* are equal.

Alternative methods of conversion are:

(i) To convert only the balance of and not the individual items in the Trading and Profit and Loss Account. Those who employ this method argue that the true profit (or loss) is represented by the increase (or decrease) of net assets during the year, assuming no receipts or expenditure of Capital. Where such receipts or expenditure do take place, the Profit or Loss on Exchange should be brought into account either at the time of the transaction or at the end of the year.

(ii) To convert the balance of the Trading and Profit and Loss Account as the balancing item of the Branch Current Account. The resulting sterling value of the Trading and Profit and Loss Account figure, containing as it does the Profit and Loss on Exchange, will be different from that obtained by converting the individual items, but the Balance Sheet will be the same in either method.

Profit and Loss on Exchange. The orthodox treatment is:

1. If a profit, carry forward against future losses;
2. If a loss, utilize the reserve of (1), otherwise write off.

If, however, the accounts have been properly drawn up, it can quite reasonably be accepted that a profit (or loss) has actually been earned (or lost), reflected in the Profit and Loss on Exchange balance for the year, particularly as it is not necessary to have turned a profit on paper into cash to be able to consider it as true profit (if it were so, such items as Debtors would have to be turned into cash as a necessary preliminary to obtaining the profit figure).

On the other hand, if it is reasonably certain that a loss on exchange will arise in the next period, proper provision should be made.

If a profit or loss on exchange is attachable to any capital receipt or expenditure, it should be transferred thereto from the Profit and Loss on Exchange Account.

In examinations the candidate is often called upon to prepare draft final accounts direct from the Trial Balance figures without making the actual entries in the books of the concern.

The procedure is:

1. Prepare the Branch Profit and Loss Account (in currency), unless this has already been done by the branch.
2. The balance of (1) is shown as a separate item in currency.
3. The assets and liabilities, placed in debit and credit columns, along with balance of (2), are *converted* into sterling, but as the rates of conversion differ, there will be a difference in the two columns. This figure is merely inserted as a balance which will, if inserted on the debit, be loss on exchange and, if credit, will be a profit.
4. Remittance Account will be transferred to the Head Office Account which will agree with the Branch Account in the head office books, ignoring 'transit' items.

5. The assets and liabilities of both the head office and the branch may be combined (eliminating the reciprocal account).

A number of illustrations are now appended dealing with the principles outlined.

Illustration 36

The Branch Trial Balance is:

	$	$
Furniture	4,046	
Debtors	11,281	
Creditors		500
Cash at Bank	14,560	
Profit and Loss Account—Profit for year . . .		3,413
Head Office (£6,862) . . .		32,067
Stock	6,093	
	$35,980	$35,980

The Head Office Trial Balance is:

	£	£
Branch	6,862	
Capital		7,500
Cash at Bank	826	
Profit and Loss Account . .		188
	£7,688	£7,688

Rate of Exchange at close of accounting period . . . . 4·67
Average Exchange over period . . . . . . 4·65
Rate of Exchange at date of purchase of Furniture . . . . 4·88

Prepare Balance Sheet.

The question will be worked (1) as usually required for examination purposes; and (2) as required in practice.

BRANCH TRIAL BALANCE | HEAD OFFICE TRIAL BALANCE

	Rate of Exchange	$	$	£p	£p	£	£
		Dr	Cr.	Dr.	Cr.	Dr.	Cr.
Furniture	4·88	4,046		829·10			
Debtors	4·67	11,281		2,415·63			
Creditors	4·67		500		107·07		
Cash at Bank	4·67	14,560		3,117·78		826	
Profit and Loss Account	4·65		3,413		733·98		188
Head Office and Branch	—		32,067		6,862·00	6,862	
Stock	4·67	6,093		1,304·71			
DIFFERENCE IN EXCHANGE				35·83			
Capital							7,500
		$35,980	$35,980	£7,703·05	£7,703·05	£7,688	£7,688

BALANCE SHEET

	£p	£p			£p	£p
Capital		7,500·00	Fixed Assets—			
Profit and Loss Account:			Furniture—Branch			829·10
Balance	188·00		Current Assets—			
Add Branch Profit	733·98		Stock—Branch		1,304·71	
	921·98		Debtors—Branch		2,415·63	
Less Loss on Exchange	35·83		Cash at Bank—			
		886·15	Head Office		826·00	
		8,386·15	Branch		3,117·78	7,664·12
Current Liabilities—						
Creditors		107·07				
		£8,493·22				£8,493·22

2. Actual entries in Head Office books:

BRANCH

		$	£p			$	£p
Bank		32,067	6,862·00	Balance	c/d	35,480	7,560·15
Profit and Loss Account		3,413	733·98	Loss on Exchange			35·83
		$35,480	£7,595·98			$35,480	£7,595·98
Balance	b/d (a)	35,480	7,560·15				

PROFIT AND LOSS ACCOUNT

		£p			£p
Branch Account—			Balance	b/d	188·00
Loss on exchange	c/d	35·83	Branch Account—		
Balance		886·15	**Branch Profit**		733·98
		£921·98			£921·98
			Balance	b/d	886·15

BALANCE SHEET

	£p		£p
Capital	7,500·00	Cash at Bank . . .	826·00
Profit and Loss Account . .	886·15	Branch Account (b) . .	7,560·15
	£8,386·15		£8,386·15

(a) The value of $35,480 is made up of:

	£p
Furniture . . .	829·10
Debtors . . .	2,415·63
Cash at Bank . .	3,117·78
Stock	1,304·71
	7,667·22
Less Creditors . .	107·07
	£7,560·15

(b) The combined Balance Sheet will now be prepared by substituting for the amount of £7,560·15 the detailed assets and liabilities as shown in (a).

Note. The Capital Account is shown separate from the Profit and Loss Account for the sake of clarity.

It will now be clear that although in examination work the results may be quickly arrived at by placing the currency and sterling columns in juxtaposition, the accounting entries actually take place in the head office through the Branch Account. Nevertheless, it is possible, as has been shown, to proceed in columnar form with the combined Balance Sheet. In the same way, the Profit and Loss Account of the branch may be shown side by side with that of the head office, although this is somewhat unusual and generally impracticable.

Illustration 37

Transactions between the London and branch offices of a concern are converted in the books at £5·55 per 100 rupees.

Assume the average rate for the period was £5·53, the rate at date of Trial Balance was £5·52, and that the fixed assets were originally acquired at £5·55 per 100 rupees.

(a) Prepare Balance Sheet at, and Profit and Loss Account for period to 31st December 19...

(b) Show Branch Current Account.

(c) Workings to nearest £.

(Before proceeding to the draft accounts a rough Trial Balance should be prepared in respect of both Head Office and Branch, with a double set of columns for the latter, showing Rupees and the Sterling equivalents according to the rules already laid down.)

The final balances are:

	London	Branch
	£	Rupees
Branch Office (debit balance)	11,156	
Buildings		60,000
Capital	13,500	
Cash at Bank	10,104	12,600
Creditors	5,010	3,000
Debtors		15,000
Directors' Fees	500	19,000
General Expenses	850	
London Office (credit balance)		201,000
Machinery		120,000
Rent and Rates	400	12,500
Rent Receivable		75,000
Provision for Depreciation	2,000	
Salaries	500	87,000
Stock-in-Trade (at date)		90,000
Trading Profit for six months to date . . .	3,000	137,000

BRANCH CURRENT ACCOUNT

	Rupees	£		Rupees	£
Balance . . b/d	201,000	11,156	Loss on Exchange .		16
Branch Profit . .	**93,600**	5,176	Balance . . c/d	294,600	16,316
	294,600	£16,332		294,600	£16,332
Balance . . b/d	294,600	16,316			

PROFIT AND LOSS ACCOUNTS
FOR THE SIX MONTHS ENDED 31ST DECEMBER 19..

	Branch	London		Branch	London
	Rupees	£		Rupees	£
Directors' Fees . .	19,000	500	Trading Profit . .	137,100	3,000
General Expenses .		850	Rents Receivable .	75,000	
Rent and Rates . .	12,500	400			
Salaries . . .	87,000	500			
Net Profit . . c/d	93,600	750			
	212,100	£3,000		212,100	£3,000
		£			£
Loss on Exchange .		16	Balances— b/d		
Balance . . c/d		5,910	Net Profit:		
			London . .		750
			Branch . .		5,176
			[93,600 Rs @		
		£5,926	£5·53 per 100 rupees]		£5,926
			Balance . . b/d		5,910

COMBINED BALANCE SHEET AS AT 31ST DECEMBER 19..

	£	£		£	£
Capital . . .		13,500	Fixed Assets—		
Profit and Loss Account .		5,910	Buildings—Branch . .		3,330
		19,410	Machinery—Branch .	6,660	
			Less Provision for Deprecia-		
Current Liabilities—			tion—London . .	2,000	
Creditors—					4,660
London . . .	5,010				7,990
Branch . . .	166				
		5,176	Current Assets—		
			Stock-in-Trade—Branch .	4,968	
			Debtors—Branch . .	828	
			Cash at Bank—		
			London . . .	1,104	
			Branch . . .	696	
					16,596
		£24,586			£24,586

The closing balance on the Branch Current Account in the London books is made up as follows:

	Rupees	Rate per 100 r'ps	£
		£	
Buildings	60,000	5·55	3,330
Machinery	120,000	5·55	6,660
Stock	90,000	5·52	4,968
Debtors	15,000	5·52	828
Cash	12,600	5·52	696
	297,600		16,482
Less Creditors . . .	3,000	5·52	166
	294,000		£16,316

Note. This balance would appear to the credit of Head Office in the branch books and agrees with the Memorandum column of the Branch Account of the Head Office.

In recent years it has become more frequent to ignore this somewhat artificial appraisement of the sterling equivalent of currency trading operations and to ignore, as a result, any formal rate of conversion of the operations of a foreign branch.

Instead of attempting to evaluate independently the profit or loss sterling equivalent, with a consequent balance treated as profit or loss on exchange, the growing practice is to take the sterling value of the closing assets and liabilities and automatically the balancing item in the sterling column of the Branch Account in the Head Office books as the profit or loss. This predicates that remittances to and from the branch have been brought into account.[1]

If this procedure is adopted in the above illustration the balance of profit as shown in the Branch Current Account will be £5,160 with no loss on exchange, the profit being the excess of closing balances in sterling £16,316 over the opening balances in sterling £11,156.

Examination Problem

The following is a Trial Balance sent from the foreign branch of a London Company. In the London books the branch balance on 1st January 19.., was £5,218; and on 30th June 19.., the Remittance Account balance was £2,641. There was no cash in transit.

The Rates of Exchange were as follows:

1st January, 86½; 30th June, 91½. At the time of purchase of the Fixtures the rate was 124.

Prepare a Converted Trial Balance in columnar form, so as to disclose results of the operations of the six months.

How would you deal with the above details in order to show the Branch results of trading and incorporate them in the London books?

(*Adapted from Institute of Chartered Accountants, Inter.*)

---

[1] Examination questions have been known requiring this method to be used so that no difference on exchange appeared in the Head Office accounts, but with the Branch profit converted in accordance with the usual formula. In such a case it is obvious that a difference on exchange must arise and, if it is not to appear in the Head Office accounts, it *must* be put in the memorandum currency columns.

TRIAL BALANCE, 30TH JUNE 19..

	Ptas.	Ptas.
Head Office Account, 1st January 19..		451,373
Remittances to Head Office	236,062	
Fixtures and Fittings	26,040	
Sundry Debtors	171,288	
Stock, 1st January 19..	87,365	
Sundry Creditors		57,828
Purchases	186,989	
Sales		270,738
General Expenses	68,352	
Cash in hand	3,843	
[Stock, 30th June, 19.., Ptas. 91,683]		
	779,939	779,939

Solution

CONVERTED TRIAL BALANCE, 30TH JUNE 19..

	Ptas.	Rate	Profit and Loss Account		Balance Sheet	
			£	£	£	£
Head Office Account	451,373	—				5,218
Remittances	236,062	—			2,641	
Fixtures and Fittings	26,040	124			210	
Sundry Debtors	171,288	91½			1,872	
Stock, 1st January	87,365	86½	1,010			
Sundry Creditors	57,828	91½				632
Purchases	186,989	[1]89	2,101			
Sales	270,738	89		3,042		
General Expenses	68,352	89	768			
Cash in hand	3,843	91½			42	
Stock, 30th June	91,683	91½		1,002	1,002	
			(b) 3,879	(a) 4,044	5,767	5,850
Difference in Exchange			248			
Net Loss (after allowing for difference in Exchange)				83	83	
[1] i.e. $\dfrac{86\frac{1}{2} + 91\frac{1}{2}}{2}$			£4,127	£4,127	£5,850	£5,850

It will be observed that the question requires the Trial Balance to be drawn up so as to show results of the operations of the six months, hence a Profit and Loss and Balance Sheet column. After conversion of items into sterling as above, Journal entries will be made as follows:

JOURNAL

	£	£
Branch	[1]165	
Profit and Loss Account		165
Being Profit for six months.		
Difference on Exchange	248	
Branch		248
Being Difference in Exchange.		

[1] Surplus of (a) over (b) in Converted Trial Balance above.

The Branch Account will then show a debit balance of £2,494, made up as follows:

		£
Opening Balance	Dr.	5,218
Less Remittances		2,641
		2,577
Less Journal transfers		83
Closing Balance	Dr.	£2,494

Recording Assets and Liabilities in the Head Office Books. Although it is usual to keep entirely separate accounts for foreign branches, there is no reason why the assets and liabilities of the branch should not be recorded in the head office books. In this method the Branch Current Account is nothing more than a simple Cash Account, but as the actual Branch Cash Account in the foreign country will be in foreign currency, it will be necessary to employ an additional column for currency in the head office books so as to account for the cash received, paid, and the balance. The branch double entry will be compiled from the *sterling* column. In short, the currency column is purely memorandum.

Illustration 38

TRIAL BALANCE AT 1ST JANUARY

	£	£
Fixed Assets	2,500	
Stock	1,000	
Cash in Hand[1]	200	
Remittance	400	
Sundry Assets	2,400	
Sundry Liabilities		700
Profit and Loss Account		800
Capital		5,000
	£6,500	£6,500

[1] Sterling equivalent of 2,000 pesos.

Accounts from the foreign branch, exchange taken at 10 pesos to £, were as follows for the year ended 31st December:

	Pesos	Pesos
Balance	2,000	
Sales	7,500	
Fixed Assets Purchased and Sold	500	5,660
General Expenses		3,500
Remittance Account	4,160	
Investment in Foreign Subsidiary		4,500
Balance		500
	14,160	14,160

Closing stock is valued at 7,800 pesos. The fixed assets sold were in the books at 800 pesos.

The procedure is simply to convert the above to sterling, to consider it (in a separate account) merely as a Cash Account and to complete the double entry. The opening balance is 2,000 pesos at 10 to £, which is the £200 appearing in the head office Trial Balance.

FOREIGN BRANCH CURRENT ACCOUNT

	Pesos	£		Pesos	£
Balance b/d	2,000	200	General Expenses	3,500	350
Sales	7,500	750	Fixed Assets purchases	5,660	566
Fixed Assets sold	500	50	Investment in Foreign		
Remittances	4,160	400	Subsidiary	4,500	450
Profit on Exchange		16	Balance c/d	500	50
	14,160	£1,416		14,160	£1,416
Balance b/d	500	50			

PROFIT AND LOSS ACCOUNT
FOR THE YEAR ENDED 31ST DECEMBER

	£		£
Stock	1,000	Sales	750
General Expenses	350	Stock	780
Loss on Sale of Fixed Assets	30	Profit on Exchange	16
Profit	166		
	£1,546		£1,546

The Balance Sheet extracted by the head office will now be as follows:

BALANCE SHEET AS AT 31ST DECEMBER

		£		£
Capital		5,000	Fixed Assets[1]	2,986
Profit and Loss Account	£800		Stock	780
Add Profit for year	166		Sundry Assets	2,400
		966	Investments	450
Sundry Liabilities		700	Cash in Hand	50
		£6,666		£6,666

[1] i.e. £2,500 + £566 − £50 − £30.

Capital Expenditure and its Recording. (1) Where the head office incurs large expenses of a capital nature in connection with a foreign branch, it will debit the branch in currency (memo.) and in sterling; and the branch will debit the asset and credit head office. The practice is to ignore fluctuations of exchange and upon incorporating the results of the branch activities in the head office books to bring into the valuation of the worth of the branch the asset, if of a fixed nature, at the rate of exchange ruling as at the date of its acquisition, subject to depreciation, which will be converted, not at the average rate of exchange of the period, but at the same rate as at the date of acquisition.

2. If desired, the head office may show the branch asset as a separate account in its own books, in which case the cost in sterling will be debited, not to branch but to Branch Asset Account, so that no conversion from foreign currency into sterling is required. No entry will be made in the branch books. In other words, the entry in no way affects the reflective Head Office and Branch Accounts, the book-keeping entry being precisely the same as that of acquiring a 'home' asset. If desired, a memorandum column may be employed to show the amount of currency involved in the expenditure.

It will, however, be advisable to write off depreciation, whichever method of recording the fixed assets be adopted.

If the first method is used the amount of depreciation will automatically appear in the branch books, and its conversion in head office books will be made at the rate ruling as at the date of acquiring the asset.

If the second method is used the depreciation will be recorded in the ordinary way in the head office books, except that it will be debited against the Branch Profit and Loss Account.

3. Where capital expenditure is incurred by the branch, the entry will be to the debit of the asset and to the credit of cash (or supplier), unless it is intended to have the record of the asset in the head office books, in which case the head office will be debited and cash or supplier credited. It will then be necessary for the head office to debit the branch asset in sterling with the currency equivalent in the memorandum column and credit the branch.

BRANCH CONTROL

The question of branch control is an important one, and is such that no hard-and-fast rules can be laid down, as much depends on the existing circumstances, e.g. the number of branches, the type of operations, commodities, or services, the degree to which the branches are self-contained, location, special local conditions, and the like.

The chief aims of branch control are:

1. To supervise stock, making the branch accountable to the head office; thus, where possible, there will be required from the branch returns showing the receipts, returns, and sales of goods, the goods being charged to branch at either selling price or at cost plus a percentage. Supplementing this may be an inspection staff whose duty it is to make surprise visits to branches in order to inspect and check the branch records. So far as possible, it will be advisable to have all goods supplied by head office.

2. To avoid losses by reason of bad debts, and to this end the branch may be required to furnish details as to the amount and age of its debts, so that as required these accounts may be handed over to the head office for collection. Usually strict limitations are placed upon the branch in regard to credit allowed to customers.

3. To prevent—especially where the branch is staffed by one person—the branch from exercising fraudulent manipulations (e.g. the staff selling its *own* goods) by comparing percentages of profit, comparisons of results of various branches, fixation of a minimum amount of goods that should normally be sold within a period, close watch on periodical variations in sales and the like.

4. To avoid extravagance in expenses by requiring the branch to account for its expenditure, and making comparisons of comparative efficiencies of the branches, e.g. sales, gross and net profit per £ of sales, or per person employed, or per £100 of capital sunk in the branch.

5. To prevent pilfering of cash by requiring a weekly cash statement and daily bankings. The branch, if retail, will be required to employ cash registers, counter books, tear-off checks (as in restaurants) so that either the cash is not handled by any person other than the cashier or, if it is necessary for all the staff to receive it, they will be required to complete the forms used at the back of the counter books—a duplicate invoice receipt being given to the customer.

Occasionally, where there are 'regular' customers, an invoice receipt may be given to the customer, which, upon his having collected a stipulated number, may be presented to the shop for exchange into an article, thus facilitating comparison with the entries at the back of the counter books and encouraging custom.

It is obviously advisable to charge up goods to branch at selling price if practicable, but where prices are highly fluctuating on either the buying or the selling side, or branch labour is to be expended, or where many purchases are made locally, it will be usually found unreliable, so that the method of charging-up at cost plus percentage expected to be earned may better serve the aim in view, although under this method it may be extremely difficult to fix with reasonable accuracy the required percentage. In the case of a branch with many lines, the management usually are content to fix an approximate percentage by 'sampling' that is, by taking at random a proportion only of the goods transferred and by comparing cost and selling price and basing the required percentage on those comparisons for each period, say, monthly. It is quite clear that academically this is not accurate, particularly as SEVERAL different percentages may obtain during the period, but experience, trial and error usually enable the percentage to be forecast with sufficient accuracy to answer all reasonable requirements.

To keep the percentage figures as accurate as possible, 'loading' is usually confined to the bare cost of the goods, ignoring indirect expenses.

In the head office an Abstract Book or Journal will be kept containing the above information, so that at any time it will be possible to ascertain:

Total sales and returns—divided into cash and credit [with quantities, where possible].

Weekly average of sales.

Total (and separate) expenses.

Weekly average of expenses.

Stock records.

Weekly amounts and values of stocks retained in branches.

Debtors separately showing those transferred to Head Office for collection.

Approximate gross and net profit (after allowing for DEPRECIATION, INTEREST, and, if necessary, a share of the head office expenses).

Obviously, the precise form of the branch control will be based on the particular circumstances, as will the reliability of the inferences deducible from the returns, e.g. stock may be such that an accurate percentage of profit can be always gauged, as where certain articles are packed goods sold at a fixed price. On the other hand, where there is intense local competition, or the goods are both perishable and/or subject to rapid price fluctuations, no rigid percentage can be fixed. The branch manager may be 'tuned up' to earn a certain percentage on sales, but a certain reasonable allowance must be given. Again, a branch may be a manufacturing or productive one, whilst in any case circumstances may dictate a departure from the ordinary routine. In the case of many concerns, e.g. as in the large stores in London and the provinces, the post season sale will vitiate normal percentages.

Account must be taken of and adjustments made accordingly for price alterations, wholesale or retail, whilst full cognizance must be taken of price differentiation as where prices are reduced for purchases of large quantities. Even where prices are fixed, careful stock recording is needed if there are several different sizes of commodity, each having a proportionately different price as, for instance, patent medicines, as very frequently 'treble size' bottles or tins are sold at the price of two 'single' sizes.

Many points of detail will arise in addition, such as the proper system of stock and store preserving, e.g. suitable warehousing, storing, shelving, internal transport, protection from weather changes and from destruction by vermin.

With retail branches, a weekly or other periodical return is usual, on the following lines, modified to meet the circumstances.

Branch No........

Town........
Week ended..............

BRANCH RETURN

Day	RECEIPTS			Receipts from Debtors per Receipt Books	Total	PAID INTO BANK	
		Cash Sales					
	Dept.	Dept.	Dept.			Date	Amount
Monday	£	£	£	Receipt No.	£		£
Tuesday							
Wednesday							
Thursday							
Friday							
Saturday							

The columns are ruled on the receipts side to accommodate the various departments.

DEBITS TO DEBTORS (CREDIT SALES)

	Dept.	Dept.	Dept.	Total
	£	£	£	£
Monday				
Tuesday				
Wednesday				
Thursday				
Friday				
Saturday				
Total				
Commencing Debtors				
Total				[1]£

CREDITS TO DEBTORS

£

Cash received from Debtors . . . .

    Returns from Debtors . . . . . .

    Bad Debts ⎱

    Discounts ⎰ (per List) . . . . . .

    Allowances ⎰

    Transfers to Head Office (per List) . . . .

    Closing Debtors . . . .

    Total . . . . [1]£

[1] These totals should agree.

[The details are shown below in Ledger form for sake of clarity.]

Dr.		Cr.
	£	£
Commencing Debtors	Cash received from Debtors . .	
Sales	Returns from Debtors . .	
	Bad Debts	
	Discounts	
	Allowances . . .	
	Transfers to Head Office . .	
	Closing Debtors . . .	
£	£	

EXPENDITURE

Details	Voucher No.	Amount
		£
Wages .		
Cleaning		
Etc..		
Etc.		
Sundry Local Purchases per list		
Total		
Add Petty Cash on hand		
Imprest Total		£

STOCKS

		£
Commencing Stock .		
Receipts from Head Office		
Sundry Local Purchases .		
Less Net Sales (at cost).		
Returns to Head Office .		
Closing Stocks		£

[Signed and dated]

Observations, e.g. as to holidays, staff changes, local conditions, opening up or closing down of local competitive shop, results of advertising campaigns, etc.

In brief summary form the following may be cited as the main headings of branch control:

1. Accounting at head office.
2. Systematic stock control.
3. Adherence to the terms of sale, e.g. prices, credit (if any), transfer of debts of doubtful nature to head office.
4. Local purchases forbidden, or within prescribed limits.
5. Periodic detailed returns.
6. Daily bankings, imprest for petty cash.
7. Surveillance of overheads.
8. Establishment of a MINIMUM sale period (per convenient unit).
9. Surprise inspections as to stock, store conditions, CIVILITY of staff, cash recording, debtor balances, allowances and discounts, AGE of debts, internal audit staff, etc.

10. Quantitative control where possible, e.g. stereograms, motor-cars, heavy furniture, jewellery, antiques, packed goods, etc.

11. Statistical data, comparisons, index figures, graphs, and their interpretation in the light of general economic conditions, conditions affecting the class of trade (e.g. changes in fashions, eclipse of radiograms by stereograms, revival of demand for pianos), and those applicable solely to local conditions (e.g. competition by co-operative societies, closing down of works upon which a large proportion of the local customers depends).

CHAPTER 20

HIRE PURCHASE ACCOUNTS

By hire purchase is meant the system under which property or a chattel is acquired by payments made in instalments, during the period of which the title in the property remains with the hire vendor. The payments prior to the final one are regarded as being purely in respect of hire, and the title in the property does not pass to the hire purchaser until such final payment or some other consideration provided for in the contract has been fulfilled. The hire vendor is bound to sell, but the hire purchaser has the *option* to buy.

The owner parts with the *possession* of his property (but not with the *ownership*) to the other party on condition that the latter fulfils his obligation to pay his instalments, on completion of which or the fulfilment of the other consideration, if any, the ownership is transferred to the hire purchaser. In the meantime the hire purchaser cannot sell, destroy, damage, exchange, or pledge such goods.

The agreement usually contains a clause providing that the owner may recover his property in the event of default of the buyer in paying any one of his instalments.

As the instalments payable are really intended to be made on account of the purchase price, they are much greater than for ordinary hire. It would often entail a hardship to the hire purchaser if, having paid most of his instalments, he became unable to complete the payments of the remainder, consequently being deprived of the property in his possession whilst remaining liable for the outstanding instalments. To mitigate such a misfortune, the hire purchase agreement usually contains a proviso under which the hire purchaser is permitted to return the property during the currency of the agreement on condition that payment of all accrued instalments is made, thus converting the agreement into one of hire. Alternatively, under certain conditions the hire purchaser may be allowed to retain a certain part of the property, or the hire vendor may make an allowance for the property returned to him by the hire purchaser.

Hire purchase transactions must be clearly distinguished from actual sales, the payments for which are made in instalments (i.e. the Credit sale method), for in the latter case the title in the property has actually been transferred—not merely the possession, but the full legal ownership subject to the right of an unpaid seller to sue the buyer where the title to the goods has passed to the buyer on the fulfilment of a condition other than full payment. In spite of the fact that the book-keeping entries are often treated alike, the fundamental difference should be constantly kept in mind. In hire purchase the hire vendor still retains ownership, so that the question of valuation and insurance of the property is a material one for him to bear in mind.

On the other hand, if a *sale* has been made, *payment* of the price being made by the buyer in instalments, the asset has changed not only its **location** but its **legal form**, inasmuch as the money value of the property is now represented in the vendor's books by a debtor. In other words, under hire purchase the property is still the hire vendor's, the hire purchaser being a debtor only for accrued instalments, while under the credit sale plan the buyer is a debtor for the purchase price of the property, less the instalments paid.

The contrasts may be summarized as follows:

Hire:
    Property *must* be returned to owner.
Sale:
    Property *cannot* be returned to sender.
Hire-Purchase:
    Property may be either *returned or retained* by the hire purchaser, *at his own option.*

It will be clear that the vendor, or the hire vendor, as the case may be, will make a charge not only for what is described as the 'cash price' but also for interest and the risk involved, for even in hire purchase the hire vendor may incur loss due to the return of badly damaged property as well as costs of transport and storage.

Hire Purchase Act 1965[1]

The legal relationship between the Hire Purchaser and the Hire Vendor is affected by the Hire Purchase Act 1965. The main provisions of the Act are:

1. The Act embraces ALL contracts of Hire Purchase and Credit Sales where the *total* price exceeds £30 but does not exceed £2,000.

2. The Act does not afford protection to a hirer or buyer who is a body corporate.

3. Where the value of the goods exceeds the relative limit, the hirer is deprived of the protection of the Act, the parties being free to make their own conditions.

4. The full terms of the agreement must be made and signed by the hirer or buyer and by or on behalf of all other parties to the agreement and if such agreement is signed by or on behalf of all other parties at the same time as the hirer or buyer signs, a copy of the agreement must be given to him immediately. If the agreement is sent to him for his signature it must be accompanied by a copy in the form in which it then is.

5. Anyone signing an agreement—under which the total purchase price exceeds £30—at any place other than the appropriate trade premises shall have an opportunity of cancelling the agreement at any time before the end of the period of four days beginning with the day on which he received his copy of the agreement.

Persons cancelling the agreement will also be entitled to a return of any deposit paid.

[1] Consumer Credit Act 1974. Some parts of this Act came into force at the date of passing, viz. 31 July 1974, but most provisions will become operative in stages by Statutory Orders made by the Secretary of State. When fully operative the Act will wholly repeal: the Hire Purchase Act 1965, the Hire Purchase (Scotland) Act 1965, the Advertisements (Hire Purchase) Act 1967, the Moneylenders Acts 1900–1927 and the Pawnbrokers Acts 1872–1960.

6. Where an agreement is effectively cancelled and goods already have been taken by the dealer in part exchange, he must return the goods within ten days of the date of service of the notice of cancellation, in a condition substantially the same as when he received them, otherwise he will be liable to pay a sum equal to the part exchange allowance.

7. The Board of Trade[1] has made regulations, as to minimum size of type, disposition of lettering, etc., so as to secure that documents issued in connection with a transaction are easily legible. For example, the height of the smallest letter shall be not less than ·056 of an inch and the width of any column in a document shall not exceed $4\frac{1}{2}$ inches. Every document requiring a signature shall have an outlined space for the signature. The outlining and any printed words in the space (calling for special attention) shall be in red.

Where the right of cancellation as set out in (5) above, applies—the statement relating to this right shall be printed in red and the space on which this print appears outlined in red.

8. For the protection of persons who purchase motor vehicles from others who hold cars under a hire purchase agreement, without knowledge of the hiring agreement and who therefore cannot get a better title than the fraudulent seller had, the following provision is made:

A purchaser in good faith under the above conditions gets a good title or as good a title as the finance company which let the car to the fraudulent seller had. This provision only applies to a private person and motor-dealers and finance houses are excluded from the protection of the provision.

9. Certain conditions and stipulations which are often included in Hire Purchase agreements (which operate unfairly to Hire Purchasers) are declared void.

10. A Hirer or buyer is entitled to require the Hire Vendor, at any time before the final payment has been made and on tending the sum of $12\frac{1}{2}$p, to supply him within four days with a copy of any note or memorandum of the agreement and various details as to the amount already paid, the amounts due but unpaid and the future payments to be made.

11. A Hire Purchaser must keep the goods under his possession and control and, if requested by the Hire Vendor, inform him where the goods are.

12. Several conditions and warranties are implied in every Hire Purchase agreement, notwithstanding *any* provision or agreement to the contrary, e.g. right of quiet possession.

13. If a Hire Purchaser has two (or more) agreements running, he has the right of appropriation where an amount paid is less than the total of the amounts then due. Otherwise the appropriation is proportionate to the amounts that are outstanding on all the agreements.

14. When the total amount paid (or tendered) under a Hire Purchase agreement *equals* or *exceeds* one-third of the Hire Purchase price, the Hire Vendor is not permitted to obtain repossession except with the consent of the County Court, and on the commencement of any such

---

[1] Now known as the Department of Trade.

action the Vendor cannot enforce payment of any sum, except by claim in the action. In such an action, the Court may order:

(a) redelivery unconditionally,
(b) redelivery under certain conditions, or
(c) redelivery of part of the goods.

15. Advertisements relating to such transactions are regulated by the Advertisements (Hire Purchase) Act 1957.[1] This Act has been amended to the extent that where an advertisement contains details of payments in respect of goods for hire-purchase, additional information must be given regarding the rate of interest or the rate of charge to be borne by the hirer or purchaser and the sum stated as the hire-purchase price or total purchase price of the goods; i.e. the amount (directly expressed) of the aggregate of the amount of the deposit (if any) and all the instalments payable.

Methods of Financing Hire Purchase and Credit Sale Transactions. A dealer, that is a trader supplying goods by way of hire purchase or credit sale agreements, may either finance the transactions himself whereby he remains a principal party to the transactions, of if he is unable or does not wish to provide the necessary finance himself may obtain it from specialist companies called hire purchase finance companies or simply finance companies.

Treatment and Description in Dealer's Final Accounts. Where a dealer finances his own hire purchase and credit sale transactions his profit thereon is derived from the aggregate of his normal trading profit from the cash sale price of the goods and the finance charges imposed, less his normal selling and administrative expenses and the additional cost incurred in financing and administering the agreements. Where agreements extend over more than the accounting period of the dealer there must be ascertained an appropriate method of computing the amount to be carried forward at the end of each accounting period in respect of trading profit and finance charges not yet earned. The methods of computation adopted in practice vary according to the nature of the business concerned and the form of agreement utilized. The following is adapted from the Recommendations of the Institute of Chartered Accountants on Hire Purchase, Credit Sale and Rental Transactions:

In a dealer's balance sheet there should be shown, where he finances his own hire purchase and credit sale transactions and where material, the total amounts outstanding after providing for bad debts in respect of hire purchase and credit sale agreements and in each case there should be deducted the total carried forward in respect of trading profit, collection and finance charges relating to future periods.

For hire purchase transactions with customers there should be carried forward in the dealer's final accounts an amount, computed on a

[1] This Act was superseded by the Advertisements (Hire Purchase) Act 1967 but see preceding page footnote.

consistent basis and appropriate to the nature of his business, in respect of trading profit and finance charges not yet earned. The amount for trading profit not yet earned should consist of the proportion of trading profit estimated to relate to instalments receivable in future accounting periods and should be not less than the percentage of net trading profit or more than the percentage of gross trading profit appropriate to the goods involved. The amount for finance charges not yet earned should be the proportion of the charges relating to instalments receivable in future accounting periods computed on a basis which enable the final accounts to show a true and fair view. The total amount carried forward for trading profit and finance charges not yet earned should be not less than the greater of:

(a) the estimated cost of free maintenance, finance and collection charges relating to future periods, or

(b) any rebates which would be allowed if all agreements were discharged and all obligations settled on the day immediately following the balance sheet date.

For credit sale agreements with customers credit may be taken immediately for the trading profit on the cash price of the goods sold provided that adequate provision is made for future free maintenance and finance and collection costs relating to balances not yet due.

Specific provision should be made for all accounts considered bad or doubtful at the balance sheet date and an adequate general provision against further bad debts should be made in respect of the amount carried forward as income yet to mature.

Where a dealer's sales on hire purchase are financed by a finance company, the finance company purchases the goods from the dealer and hires out the goods, with the option to purchase, to customers. The dealer may introduce customers to the finance company or the customer may approach the finance company direct. It is important to notice that in either of the aforementioned cases the parties to the contract of sale are the finance company, who now own the goods, and the customer; the dealer is not a party to the contract unless he enters into an agreement whereby he repurchases the goods from the finance company in the event of default by the customer.

Accounting Methods. Many systems of accounting are in vogue, some scientific, others crude, but the principle involved in *all* is that the profit is not earned until the final instalment has been paid; hence, some provision must be made to avoid showing inflated profits. It can readily be perceived that no rigid rule of accounting can be laid down owing to the large number of varying circumstances in different businesses, e.g. nature of the property, the number and regularity or otherwise of the 'Sales,' the length of the instalment period (long, medium, or short); the ratio of defaulters to sound customers, financial policy, size and capacity of accounting staff, and the proportion of this class of business to others.

It will be convenient to treat hire purchase transactions under the following heads:

HIRE VENDOR'S BOOKS

(A) Sales Method

1. **Including Interest.** Each transaction, *including* interest, is treated as a sale, the usual entries being made, no separate account appearing for interest.

2. **Excluding Interest.** Each transaction, *excluding* interest, is treated as a sale and interest is charged to the hire purchaser and recorded separately.

The entries are:

(a) Upon delivery of goods or property:

    Debit Hire Purchaser   [1]Credit Hire Purchase Sales

(b) Upon interest becoming due periodically:

    Debit Hire Purchaser   Credit Interest

Alternatively, the hire vendor may credit Trading Account for the sale in two parts: (a) proportion representing hire, and (b) proportion representing sale. (This method is purely academic as the enormous detailed calculations involved render it impracticable.)

Illustration 1

A sells machinery on hire purchase to B, the cash price being £1,000. The hire purchaser agrees to pay in two instalments each half year with interest at 5 per cent per annum, the interest to be paid each half year in addition to the amount due on the machinery. Show B's account in A's books.

It is important to observe in all cases whether the first payment is to be made at the time of delivery (i.e. 'cash down') or at the end of the first period.

The agreement might provide for the instalments to be EQUAL, as distinct from equal proportions of the cash price. The payment of each instalment is of a composite nature as it includes both principal (or cash price) and interest, each subsequent payment discharging an increasingly greater proportion of the principal than the one preceding it.

HIRE VENDOR'S BOOKS:

B

		£p				£p
Machinery . . (a)		1,000·00	Cash			525·00
Half-year's Interest on £1,000 at 5% per annum . . (b)		25·00	Balance . . .	c/d		500·00
		£1,025·00				£1,025·00
Balance . . .	b/d	500·00	Cash			512·50
Half-year's Interest on £500 at 5% per annum . .		12·50				
		£512·50				£512·50

(a) Credit Hire Purchase Sales Account (through the Sales Journal).
(b) Credit Interest Account (through the Interest Journal).

[1] Alternatively the term 'Hire Sales' is employed.

Illustration 2

Assume that the facts are as in the foregoing illustration, except that the two payments are to be EQUAL. The instalment required to the nearest penny is £518·83. Show B's account in A's books.

HIRE VENDOR'S BOOKS:

B

		£p				£p
Machinery . . .		1,000·00	Cash			518·83
Interest . . .		25·00	Balance . . .	c/d		506·17
		£1,025·00				£1,025·00
Balance . . .	b/d	506·17	Cash . . .	1		518·83
Interest . . .		12·66				
		£518·83				£518·83

1 Calculated to the nearest new penny

The hire vendor will show in his Balance Sheet the amount due (as if an actual sale had taken place) from the hire purchaser, but as in the case of the latter, some designating expression should be employed to indicate that the subject matter is that of hire purchase. Whether it is described as a debtor for hire purchase (from a meticulous point of view inaccurate), or goods out on hire purchase, is not of material importance so long as a clear reference is made to the nature of the asset. As regards the hire purchaser's books, which will be dealt with later in this chapter, a phrase, termed EQUITY, is occasionally used in juxtaposition to the asset described, and if, despite this phrase, it is clearly understood that the title to the property is not in the hire purchaser, it is quite acceptable; but from a purist's point of view, the term is not entirely unchallengeable as the hire purchaser's position, though analogous to, is not that of having a full equitable interest.

No depreciation will be dealt with (as the asset is considered as a sale) but provision should be made in respect of loss likely to be entailed if the property is returned in a damaged condition.

A variation of the above method is to debit the hire purchaser with the whole sum—cash price and interest, crediting respectively hire purchase sales and Interest Suspense Account: at the end of each year the proportionate amount of interest arising during the year is debited to Interest Suspense Account and credited to Interest Account, and thence to Hire Purchase Trading Account. In the meantime, the balance in credit is shown as a deduction from hire purchase debtors.

Illustration 3

A delivers machinery on the hire purchase system for £2,500 to be paid as follows: on delivery, £400; at the end of the first year, £600; second year, £400; third year, £1,100; interest, included in the £2,500, being charged on the cash value at 10 per cent per annum. Show entries in the books of the hire vendor.

Hire Vendor's Books:

HIRE PURCHASER

		£			£
Year 1	Hire Purchase Sales[1] .	2,500	Year 1	Cash Deposit . . .	400
				Cash (1st inst.) . .	600
				Balance. . . c/d	1,500
		£2,500			£2,500
Year 2	Balance . . b/d .	1,500	Year 2	Cash (2nd inst.) . .	400
				Balance. . . c/d	1,100
		£1,500			£1,500
Year 3	Balance. . . b/d	£1,100	Year 3	Cash (3rd and last instalment). . .	£1,100

[1] £2,102·48 to Credit of Hire Purchase Sales and £397·52 to Interest Suspense Account.

INTEREST SUSPENSE

			£p			£p
Year 1	Interest Account . .		170·25	Year 1	Hire Purchaser . .	397·52
	Balance. . . c/d		227·27			
			£397·52			£397·52
Year 2	Interest Account . .		127·27	Year 2	Balance. . . b/d	227·27
	Balance. . . c/d		100·00			
			£227·27			£227·27
Year 3	Interest Account . .		£100·00	Year 3	Balance. . . b/d	100·00

The interest is calculated as follows:

$$
\begin{array}{llll}
& & £p & £p & £p \\
\text{3rd year} & . & \frac{1}{11} \times 1,100\!\cdot\!00 = 100\!\cdot\!00 = \frac{1}{10} \times 1,000\!\cdot\!00 \\
\text{2nd year} & . & \frac{1}{11} \times 1,400\!\cdot\!00 = 127\!\cdot\!27 = \frac{1}{10} \times 1,272\!\cdot\!73 \\
\text{1st year} & . & \frac{1}{11} \times 1,872\!\cdot\!73 = 170\!\cdot\!25 = \frac{1}{10} \times 1,702\!\cdot\!48^{1}
\end{array}
$$

3. **Interest Suspense Method.** The third method is adopted by concerns having a large number of transactions, with the instalments extending over fixed periods, and is known as the Interest Suspense Method. It aims at crediting the period in which the sale is made with the gross profit thereon, separating the interest appertaining to each transaction, and allocating it over the years during which the instalments are paid. Separate sales journals must be kept to record the sales of each different duration, e.g. 'twelve-monthly instalments.'

The amount chargeable to the hire purchaser is divided into hire purchase sales and interest, the double entry being:

Debit Hire Purchase.
Credit Hire Purchase Sales Account.
Credit Interest Suspense Account.

---

[1] £2,500, *less* deposit £400, *less* interest £397·52.

The latter is allocated to Trading Account proportionately over the length of the instalment period by debiting such proportion to Interest Suspense Account and crediting Trading Account.

Illustration 4

If the instalments are paid quarterly and are spread over thirty-six months and interest at 10 per cent per annum is charged, it will be found that the interest credited to Interest Suspense Account should be allocated as follows:

1st Year	52·4%	of the total interest
2nd ,,	33·9%	,, ,,
3rd ,,	13·7%	,, ,,
	100·0%	

The above result is obtained as under:

Assume the hire purchase price of a stereogram is £106·60, to be paid for in thirteen quarterly instalments of £8·20, the first instalment to be paid when the 'sale' is effected and interest at 10 per cent per annum to be charged.

The cash price of the stereogram is £84·11 plus the deposit of £8·20 = £92·31.

	Balance		Interest[1]	Total	Instalment	Balance
	£p		£p	£p	£p	£p
	92·31			92·31	8·20	84·11
	84·11	$\frac{1}{41}\times$ £86·22	2·11	86·22	8·20	78·02
Year 1	78·02	$\frac{1}{41}\times$ £79·97	1·95	79·97	8·20	71·77
	71·77	$\frac{1}{41}\times$ £73·56	1·79	73·56	8·20	65·36
	65·36	$\frac{1}{41}\times$ £66·99	1·63	66·99	8·20	58·79
			£7·48			
	58·79	$\frac{1}{41}\times$ £60·26	1·47	60·26	8·20	52·06
Year 2	52·06	$\frac{1}{41}\times$ £53·36	1·30	53·36	8·20	45·16
	45·16	$\frac{1}{41}\times$ £46·29	1·13	46·29	8·20	38·09
	38·09	$\frac{1}{41}\times$ £39·05	0·95	39·04	8·20	30·84
			£4·85			
	30·84	$\frac{1}{41}\times$ £31·62	0·77	31·61	8·20	23·41
Year 3	23·41	$\frac{1}{41}\times$ £24·00	0·59	24·00	8·20	15·80
	15·80	$\frac{1}{41}\times$ £16.20	0·40	16·20	8·20	8·00
	8·00	$\frac{1}{41}\times$ £8.20	0·20	8·20	8·20	nil
			£1·96			

[1] The entry in this column is $2\frac{1}{2}$ per cent [i.e. 10 per cent per annum on balance], e.g. $2\frac{1}{2}$ per cent on £84·11 = £2·11.

The 'spread' of the interest of £14·29 is as follows:

$$\text{1st year} \quad \frac{£7·48}{£14·29} \times 100\% = 52·4\%$$

$$\text{2nd year} \quad \frac{£4·85}{£14·29} \times 100\% = 33·9\%$$

$$\text{3rd year} \quad \frac{£1·96}{£14·29} \times 100\% = 13·7\%$$

The table can be easily proved by working back from the end. The last payment of £8·20 discharges the balance owing in the penultimate quarter plus interest thereon at $2\frac{1}{2}$ per cent. Such interest is $\frac{2\frac{1}{2}}{102\frac{1}{2}}$ or $\frac{1}{41} \times £8·20 =$ £0·20; thus the balance at the beginning of the last quarter is £8. The interest for the penultimate period is $\frac{1}{41} \times £16·20 = £0·40$, and so on.[1]

It is obvious that as the instalments are spread over three years, unless the sale is made on the 1st January in any year (assuming the accounting period to end 31st December) the instalments will be received during four accounting periods, and accordingly the interest for the three years **must** be divided amongst the four accounting periods in which the instalments are received. It is quite impracticable to do this accurately by taking every sale and making a mathematical calculation in respect thereof; accordingly an average basis is taken. One method is to assume that all the sales are made halfway through the financial period and to assume that the interest is spread over each year evenly. With the above figures the interest would be spread over as follows:

1st accounting period—$\frac{1}{2} \times 52·4\%$	= 26·2%
2nd accounting period—$\frac{1}{2} \times 52·4\% + \frac{1}{2} \times 33·9\%$	= 43·1%
3rd accounting period—$\frac{1}{2} \times 33·9\% + \frac{1}{2} \times 13·7\%$	= 23·8%
4th accounting period—$\frac{1}{2} \times 13·7\%$	= 6·9%
Total	100·0%

If the first accounting period half year is taken as the basis of the calculation, the second accounting period being made up of the second half of the first year plus the first half of the second year and so on, the

---

[1] If the student finds the computation difficult, the above schedule should be built up in Ledger form, for example:

First Quarter of Year 2:

HIRE PURCHASER

			£p				£p
Balance	b/d		58·79	Cash			8·20
Interest			1·47	Balance	c/d		52·06
			£60·26				£60·26
Balance	b/d		52·06				

percentages will be more accurately:

1st Accounting period—

1st half, 1st year

$$\frac{£4 \cdot 06}{£14 \cdot 29} \times 100\%$$
$$= 28 \cdot 3\%$$

2nd Accounting period—

2nd half, 1st year $\qquad \frac{£3 \cdot 42}{£14 \cdot 29} \times 100\%$

1st half, 2nd year $\qquad \frac{£2 \cdot 77}{£14 \cdot 29} \times 100\%$

$$\left. \right\} = \frac{£6 \cdot 19}{£14 \cdot 29} \times 100\%$$
$$= 43 \cdot 4\%$$

3rd Accounting period—

2nd half, 2nd year $\qquad \frac{£2 \cdot 08}{£14 \cdot 29} \times 100\%$

1st half, 3rd year $\qquad \frac{£1 \cdot 36}{£14 \cdot 29} \times 100\%$

$$\left. \right\} = \frac{£3 \cdot 44}{£14 \cdot 29} \times 100\%$$
$$= 24 \cdot 1\%$$

4th Accounting period—

2nd half, 3rd year

$$\frac{£0 \cdot 60}{£14 \cdot 29} \times 100\%$$
$$= 4 \cdot 2\%$$

An alternative method is to find the average due date of the sales, having regard to the seasonal fluctuations of the business. It might then be found that each of the three full years' interest is split, say, eight months to the first year, eight months and four months to the second year, etc.

Dealing with the first two periods, the 'spread' would be as shown below:

1st period $\qquad$. $\frac{2}{3} \times 52 \cdot 4\%$
2nd period $\qquad$. $\frac{1}{3} \times 52 \cdot 4\% + \frac{2}{3} \times 33 \cdot 9\%$

Separate calculations will obviously be made in respect of each type of sale, each having its own Interest Suspense Account. Thus if the sales of three types are spread over three years, there will always be twelve Suspense Accounts open at any one time, that is, four for each type.

Illustration 5

Assuming that the interest is allocated as on p. 2010, (first method) show the entries necessary to record the foregoing transactions in the Hire Vendor's books, taking 19.1 as the first year:

HIRE PURCHASE INTEREST SUSPENSE—19.1 SALES

			£p				£p
19.1 Dec. 31	Transfer: Profit and Loss Account	(a)	3·74	19.1 Dec. 31	Interest per Hire Purchase Sales Journal		14·29
	Balance	c/d	10·55				
			£14·29				£14·29
19.2 Dec. 31	Transfer: Profit and Loss Account	(b)	6·16	19.2 Jan. 1	Balance	b/d	10·55
	Balance	c/d	4·39				
			£10·55				£10·55
19.3 Dec. 31	Transfer: Profit and Loss Account	(c)	3·40	19.3 Jan. 1	Balance	b/d	4·39
	Balance	c/d	0·99				
			£4·39				£4·39
19.4 Dec. 31	Transfer: Profit and Loss Account	(d)	0·99	19.4 Jan. 1	Balance	b/d	0·99

(a) 26·2% × £14·29   (c) 23·8% × £14·29
(b) 43·1% × £14·29   (d) 6·9% × £14·29

HIRE PURCHASE DEBTORS

			£p				£p
19.1 Dec. 31	Hire Purchase Sales per Sales Journal	1	106·60	19.1 Dec. 31	Cash: Instalments received during year		41·00
					Balance	c/d	65·60
			£106·60				£106·60
19.2 Jan. 1	Balance	b/d	65·60				

[1] The double entry will be effected by passing the transaction through the Hire Purchase Sales Journal, thus:

Date	Details	Fo.	Total	Hire Purchase Sales	Interest Suspense
			£p 106·60	£p 92·31	£p 14·29

For the purpose of illustration it is assumed that there was one transaction only.

The example illustrates the principle involved following through the Interest Suspense Account method during the period of instalments, but it deals with one year's sales only. Normally, there would be further sales in subsequent years, if the spread of interest is over four years there will be four Suspense Accounts in respect of each type of sale when the business has been established four years, and henceforward one will drop out as another is added. This may be shown by the following example:

Illustration 6

A Hire Purchase business is started and certain Hire Purchase sales are:

1st Year	£1,000,	of which £200 is interest
2nd Year	£1,200,	„ £250 „
3rd Year	£3,000,	„ £580 „
4th Year	£2,800,	„ £520 „
5th Year	£5,000,	£950 „

Assume that the interest is allocated as follows (all the sales spreading over four years):

1st Year	25%
2nd Year	50%
3rd Year	15%
4th Year	10%
	100%

Show Interest Suspense Accounts.

INTEREST SUSPENSE (*Year* 1)

Year 1				£	Year 1			£
	Profit and Loss Account	25%		50		Sundry Debtors		200
2	„ „	50%		100				
3	„ „	15%		30				
4	„ „	10%		20				
				£200				£200

INTEREST SUSPENSE (*Year* 2)

Year 2				£p	Year 2			£p
	Profit and Loss Account	25%		62·50		Sundry Debtors		250·00
3	„ „	50%		125·00				
4	„ „	15%		37·50				
5	„ „	10%		25·00				
				£250·00				£250·00

INTEREST SUSPENSE (*Year* 3)

Year 3				£	Year 3			£
	Profit and Loss Account	25%		145		Sundry Debtors		580
4	„ „	50%		290				
5	„ „	15%		87				
6	„ „	10%		58				
				£580				£580

INTEREST SUSPENSE (*Year 4*)

				£				£
Year 4	Profit and Loss Account	25%		130	Year 4	Sundry Debtors		520
5	,, ,,	50%		260				
6	,, ,,	15%		78				
7	,, ,,	10%		52				
				£520				£520

INTEREST SUSPENSE (*Year 5*)

				£p				£p
Year 5	Profit and Loss Account	25%		237·50	Year 5	Sundry Debtors		950·00
6	,, ,,	50%		475·00				
7	,, ,,	15%		142·50				
8	,, ,,	10%		95·00				
				£950·00				£950·00

PROFIT AND LOSS (*Year 1*)

			£				£
				Year 1	Interest Suspense Account (1)		50

PROFIT AND LOSS (*Year 2*)

			£				£p
				2 Year	Interest Suspense Account (1)		100·00
					,, ,, (2)		62.50

PROFIT AND LOSS (*Year 3*)

			£				£p
				Year 3	Interest Suspense Account (1)		30·00
					,, ,, (2)		125·00
					,, ,, (3)		145·00

PROFIT AND LOSS (*Year 4*)

			£				£p
				Year 4	Interest Suspense Account (1)		20·00
					,, ,, (2)		37·50
					,, ,, (3)		290·00
					,, ,, (4)		130·00

PROFIT AND LOSS (*Year 5*)

			£				£
				Year 5	Interest Suspense Account (2)		25·00
					,, ,, (3)		87·00
					,, ,, (4)		260·00
					,, ,, (5)		237·50

The Interest Suspense Account (year 1), it will be observed, is exhausted after four allocations to Profit and Loss Account at the end of the fourth period, as is Interest Suspense Account (year 2) at the end of the fifth period. In the next year, an Interest Suspense Account (year 6) would come into being, there being always four such accounts in the books in respect of each type of hire purchase sale, extending over four periods. Similarly, there would always be three in the books in respect of a type extending over three accounting periods.

The problem, it is evident, merely involves writing off from the Suspense Accounts the proportion of interest allocable to particular years to Profit and Loss Account (or to the Hire Purchase Trading Account in the first place). The balances on the Suspense Accounts will be shown on the Balance Sheet as deductions from Hire Purchase debtors.

Where the necessary *percentages* are given, the amount to be written off in any year is easily arrived at, e.g. taking Suspense Account (year 1) which, as has been demonstrated, has been credited to Profit and Loss Account in four instalments in the proportions: year 1, 25 per cent; year 2, 50 per cent; year 3, 15 per cent; year 4, 10 per cent. Sometimes a question appears in which the original suspense figure is not given, but a balance after one or more years have been written off, e.g. in reference to the above illustration, the balance of Suspense Account (Year 1) as at the beginning of the third year, i.e. £50. As 75 per cent has been written off, therefore 25 per cent remains, of which 15 per cent and 10 per cent of the original are to be cleared in years 3 and 4. The amounts to be written off in these years may be found, thus:

$$
\begin{array}{llll}
 & & & \pounds \quad \pounds \\
\text{Year 3} & . & . & \frac{15}{25} \times 50 = 30 \\
\text{Year 4} & . & . & \frac{10}{25} \times 50 = 20 \\
\end{array}
$$

There is no necessity to work the account back to the commencing figure in ordinary circumstances, but where necessary, the computation can be easily made as follows:

$$
\begin{array}{l}
\pounds \\
50 = 25\% \text{ of the original} \\
\therefore \frac{100}{25} \times 50 = \pounds 200 = \text{the original}
\end{array}
$$

Illustration 7

The Suspense Account at the end of the second year (i.e. after two instalments had been credited to Profit and Loss Account), was £240; the proportions to be written off were:

Year 1, 15%.   Year 2, 25%.   Year 3, 40%.   Year 4, 15%.   Year 5, 5%.

As 40 per cent has been written off there remains 60 per cent in three parts (40% + 15% + 5%) to be disposed of. The amounts to be credited to Profit and Loss Account in the three subsequent years therefore are:

$$
\begin{array}{llll}
 & & & \pounds \\
\text{Year 3} & & . & \frac{40}{60} \times \pounds 240 = 160 \\
\text{Year 4} & . & . & \frac{15}{60} \times \pounds 240 = 60 \\
\text{Year 5} & . & . & \frac{5}{60} \times \pounds 240 = 20 \\
\hline
 & & & \pounds 240 \\
\end{array}
$$

The original sum must have been $\dfrac{100}{60} \times £240 = £400$.

The amounts written off in years 1 and 2 were:

$$
\begin{array}{lll}
\text{Year 1} & \tfrac{15}{100} \times £400 = £\ 60, \text{ leaving } £340 \\
\text{Year 2} & \tfrac{25}{100} \times £400 = £100, \text{ leaving } £240 \\
& \text{or } (\tfrac{25}{85} \times £340)
\end{array}
$$

The Interest Suspense Account may alternatively be written off according to a 'progression' method, e.g. in inverse proportion to the years elapsing from the commencement of the instalment period. For instance, if the period is five years, the Interest Suspense Account will be disposed of as follows:

$$
\begin{array}{llll}
\text{Year 1} & . & . & 5 \text{ i.e. } \tfrac{5}{15} \\
\text{Year 2} & . & . & 4 \text{ ,, } \tfrac{4}{15} \\
\text{Year 3} & . & . & 3 \text{ ,, } \tfrac{3}{15} \\
\text{Year 4} & . & . & 2 \text{ ,, } \tfrac{2}{15} \\
\text{Year 5} & . & . & 1 \text{ ,, } \tfrac{1}{15} \\
\end{array}
$$

$$[\textit{See note at foot }(a)]\quad \overline{\underline{15}}$$

Illustration 8

Assuming the Interest Account was £150 show the transfers to Profit and Loss Account in the foregoing proportions:

$$
\begin{array}{lllll}
& & & & £ \\
\text{Year 1} & . & . & \tfrac{5}{15} \times £150 = & 50 \\
\text{Year 2} & . & . & \tfrac{4}{15} \times £150 = & 40 \\
\text{Year 3} & . & . & \tfrac{3}{15} \times £150 = & 30 \\
\text{Year 4} & . & . & \tfrac{2}{15} \times £150 = & 20 \\
\text{Year 5} & . & . & \tfrac{1}{15} \times £150 = & 10 \\
\end{array}
$$

$$\overline{\underline{£150}}$$

If the first payment was made 'cash down' at the time of sale, and the duration of the instalment period was consequently reduced to four years, the proportionate amounts of interest to be written off in the four years would be:

$$
\begin{array}{llllll}
& & & & & £ \\
\text{Year 1} & . & . & 4 \text{ i.e. } \tfrac{4}{10} \times £150 = & 60 \\
\text{Year 2} & . & . & 3 \text{ ,, } \tfrac{3}{10} \times £150 = & 45 \\
\text{Year 3} & . & . & 2 \text{ ,, } \tfrac{2}{10} \times £150 = & 30 \\
\text{Year 4} & . & . & 1 \text{ ,, } \tfrac{1}{10} \times £150 = & 15 \\
\end{array}
$$

$$(b)\quad \overline{\underline{10}} \qquad\qquad \overline{\underline{£150}}$$

Note: If the sales are taken at an average date of half-way through the accounting period, the proportions will be computed as shown on p. 2010, thus:

(a) $2\tfrac{1}{2} : 4\tfrac{1}{2} : 3\tfrac{1}{2} : 2\tfrac{1}{2} : 1\tfrac{1}{2} : \tfrac{1}{2}$, involving six periods.
(b) $2 : 3\tfrac{1}{2} : 2\tfrac{1}{2} : 1\tfrac{1}{2} : \tfrac{1}{2}$, involving five periods.

The advantages and disadvantages of the Interest Suspense method are shortly:

Advantages. (*a*) Provided that suitable provision is made, the true profit is shown in the period of delivery (the transaction being regarded for practical purposes as a sale).

(*b*) Interest is taken into account and is properly spread over the relevant period.

(*c*) It is more acceptable for taxation purposes.

Disadvantages. (*a*) Complicated.

(*b*) Not suitable for transactions of small amounts or covering a short period or where agreements differ in rate of interest.

(*c*) Not suitable for agreements of varying periods.

(*d*) Provision must be made for Bad Debts and for losses on unfulfilled agreements.

(*e*) Not suitable for Hire Purchase transactions where an option to settle for cash on reduced terms is exercised with any degree of frequency.

Sales with Hire Purchase Reserve. Small traders often adopt the simple device of making a reserve representing profit on the hire purchase transactions.

Illustration 9

A, who has a mixed business of the above type, has hire purchase debtors outstanding as follows: 1st January 19.., £2,000; 31st December 19.., £3,500. He treats all hire purchase transactions as sales and creates a 20 per cent hire purchase reserve.

HIRE PURCHASE RESERVE

19..			£	19..			£
Dec. 31	Balance . . . [20% on £3,500]	c/d	700	Jan. 1	Balance . . . [20% on £2,000]	b/d	400
				Dec. 31	Transfer to Hire Purchase Sales Account . .		300
			£700				£700
				19..			
				Jan. 1	Balance	b/d	700

The Balance Sheet would include, on the Assets side:

		£
Balances under Hire Purchase Agreement . . .		3,500
Less Hire Purchase Reserve		700
		2,800

(B) Goods Out or Stock system

Method 1—At Cost. The cardinal feature of this system is to consider all the goods out on hire as stock. In order to keep a full record of goods out on hire purchase, it is necessary to have Ledger Accounts of the customers showing the same detail therein as if the goods had actually been sold, but these accounts are not part of the ordinary double entry system; and although the principle of double entry may be employed in balancing the accounts, they are purely MEMORANDA. They supply important information showing what each customer owes, but they form no part of the double entry.

The procedure may be outlined as follows:

1. Debit Hire Purchase Trading Account and credit Purchases Account with COST PRICE of goods sent to customers on hire purchase. At the same time each Customer's (MEMORANDUM) Account will be debited with the SALE PRICE of such goods.

2. Returns from customers. (See p. 2032 *et seq.*)

3. The instalments paid will be debited to cash and credited to Hire Purchase Trading Account. At the same time, the Customer's (MEMORANDUM) Account will be credited.

4. The instalments due and unpaid will be debited to Instalments Due Account and credited to Hire Purchase Trading Account.

5. The stock 'out.'

Where the rate of Gross Profit is uniform the cost of the goods in the hands of customers may be computed in three ways:

(i) $\dfrac{\text{Unpaid instalments}}{\text{Total instalments, including deposit (i.e. Sale Price)}} \times \text{Cost Price}$

(ii) Unpaid instalments
    Less Gross Profit thereon.

(iii) Where the deposit and instalments are all of equal amount—

$\dfrac{\text{Number of unpaid instalments}}{\text{Number of instalments including deposit}} \times \text{Cost}$

In the illustrations on pp. 2019 and 2021–2022 method (iii) is used and on p. 2023 are shown methods (i) and (ii).

Where the rate of gross profit is not uniform, separate calculations will be required for each class of goods according to their appropriate percentages.

6. The MEMORANDA accounts will show the balances against the customers, but not being part of the double entry are not brought into the Trial Balance. Thus, the customers' accounts are 'reference' accounts only. A transfer may be made similar to that in (4).

The gross profit is the excess of the sum of instalments due and paid, plus stock out on hire purchase at the end of the period over the stock out on hire purchase at the beginning, plus goods sent to customers during the period, less returns, at cost.

Shown in account form:

HIRE PURCHASE TRADING ACCOUNT

		£				£
Stock at Cost . . .	b/d			Instalments Paid . .		
Goods sent to Customers at Cost				,, Due		
Gross Profit . .				Stock at Cost . . .	c/d	
Stock at Cost[1] . .	b/d					

[1] Or transferred to and from a separate Stock Account.

Before illustrating the working of the above a simple example is given to show the computation of the value of the stock out on hire purchase.

Illustration 10

Goods costing £10 are sent to B on hire purchase, the price being £20, payable in twenty instalments of equal intervals. At the end of the accounting period of the Hire Vendor, five instalments are yet unpaid (fifteen having been paid at due dates).

The stock in the hands of the customer is valued as follows:

$$\tfrac{5}{20} \times £10 = £2 \cdot 50$$

Assuming, further, that (for sake of simplicity) it is the only transaction of the period, the Hire Purchase Trading Account would appear as follows:

HIRE PURCHASE TRADING

	£p			£p
Goods at Cost . . .	10·00	Instalments Paid . .		15·00
Gross Profit . . .	7·50	Stock . . .		2·50
	£17·50			£17·50

HIRE PURCHASE STOCK

	£p		£p
Hire Purchase Trading Account . .	2·50		

In the *Memorandum* Hire Purchase Ledger:

B

		£			£
Goods		20	Cash . . .		15
			(detailed as each payment is made)		
			Balance . . .	c/d	5
		£20			£20
Balance . . .	b/d	5			

It should be now quite clear that the balances on the customer's accounts do not appear as part of double entry accounting and hence do not form a part of the Trial Balance. *Practically*, these MEMORANDA Accounts are vital, but from a *double entry* point of view entirely unnecessary, as the Hire Purchase Trading Account gives the necessary results and forms an integral part of the double entry. This point is stressed because of the confusion in the minds of students as to the function of the Memoranda Accounts. Important as the Memoranda Accounts are for reference, they can be ignored in completing the double entry.

The books employed will be the Journals, the Cash Book, and supplementary to the double entry, the MEMORANDUM Ledger.

The Journals, as to sales and returns inwards, will usually contain supplementary columns in order to fulfil the functions of the double entry *and* to furnish the necessary data from which may be compiled the MEMORANDA accounts, i.e. there will be a column for the purpose of the double entry and others recording the detail necessary for the complication of the MEMORANDA Accounts. Columns in the Sales Journal, apart from data and folio columns, are usually necessary to record:

1. Cost price of the goods sold.
2. Sale price of the goods sold.
3. Number and amounts of instalments.
4. Periodicity of instalments.
5. Any other information that circumstances require.

There will be no difficulty if it is remembered that the first column is for the double entry, the others being for 'MEMORANDUM' purposes only, forming no part of the double entry; but column (2) provides the data for entering up the MEMORANDA Accounts. The total of column (1) will be debited to the Hire Purchase Trading Account and credited to Purchase Account, and so far as this side of the transaction is concerned, this is the only double entry. The individal items in column (2) will be posted to the debit of the customers' accounts in the MEMORANDUM Ledger, and these postings are of no account so far as the double entry is concerned. It is usual, however, to total column (2) and post this total to a MEMORANDUM Ledger Adjustment Account, the entries being made in total to the credit, i.e. the opposite side to that to which the individual item are posted.

Returns Inwards (at cost) will be dealt with conversely, i.e. column (1) is totalled and such total is posted to the debit of Purchases Account and to the credit of Hire Purchase Trading Account as part of the ordinary double entry, while the details of returns (at selling price) will be posted from column (2) to the credit of the respective customers' accounts in the MEMORANDUM Ledger, and if a MEMORANDUM Ledger Adjustment Account is employed, the total of column (2) will be posted to the debit of this account.

The other columns call for no special mention as they are self-explanatory. It may here be mentioned that if the accounts of customers are very numerous, a Card Ledger system is frequently employed.

With regard to cash received, the entries will be made in the Cash Book in the usual way, but such entries fulfil a twofold function: (1) for the double entry, (2) for writing up the MEMORANDA Accounts. The total of cash received from hire purchase customers is posted (as part of the double entry) to the credit of Hire Purchase Trading Account, whilst the individual receipts are posted to the credit of the customers' accounts in the MEMORANDUM Ledger. If a MEMORANDUM Ledger Adjustment Account is employed the total of such receipts will be posted to the debit thereof.

The MEMORANDUM Ledger Adjustment Account, when totalled, will have the balance on the opposite side to the detailed balances in the MEMORANDUM Ledger. Thus the system is to adapt the double entry idea in the verification of the MEMORANDUM Ledger total by means of the Adjustment Account, but still it is quite independent of the normal double entry accounting.

Lastly, any instalments actually due and unpaid will be ascertained from the MEMORANDUM Ledger, and these will be credited to the Hire Purchase Trading Account and debited to a separate account called Instalments Due Account. Frequently the latter are ignored for the purpose of the Hire Purchase Trading Account, in which case the cost equivalent of the unpaid instalments will be included in stock.

The balance of the Hire Purchase Trading Account will be transferred to the Trading Account, subject to suitable provision for losses, depreciation, and the like.

Illustration 11

Easy Payments, Ltd., forwards a stereogram to A on the hire purchase system, the cost being £144 and the selling price £192, payable in twenty-four monthly instalments of £8 each, commencing on 31st August. The sale takes place on 31st August 19..; the instalments are regularly paid. Accounts are drawn up to 31st December 19...

On 1st October 19.., a similar sale is made to B, the cost price being £78, the sale price £104 payable in weekly instalments of £2, commencing on 1st October; the instalments are paid regularly. Show the various entries necessary in the books of the Hire Vendor.

HIRE VENDOR'S BOOKS:

HIRE PURCHASE SALES JOURNAL

Date	Particulars	No. of Instalments	Period of Instalments	Amount of Instalment	Cost Price	Fol.	Selling Price
				£	£		£
19..							
Aug. 31	A	24	monthly	8	144	1	192
Oct. 1	B	52	weekly	2	78	2	104
					£222		£296

The total of the cost price column (as part of the double entry) is posted to the debit of the Hire Purchase Trading Account. If such an account is to be drawn up to 31st December 19.., the cash received and the value of the stock in the hands of customers will be found as follows:

1. Cash received from:

A—£40, i.e. 5 payments of £8.   B—£28, i.e. 14 payments of £2.

2. Stock 'out':

$$\text{Instalments outstanding} \times \text{Cost}$$

$$
\begin{array}{ll}
 & \qquad\qquad \pounds \\
A = \frac{19}{24} \times \pounds 144 = & 114 \\
B = \frac{38}{52} \times \pounds\ 78 = & 57 \\
\hline
 & 171 \\
\hline
\end{array}
$$

Ordinarily, *in practice*, a schedule will be prepared for the purpose of arriving at the valuation of the hire purchase stock out, thus:

HIRE PURCHASE STOCK SCHEDULE

Contract No.	Name	No. of Instalments	No. of Instalments:		Cost Price	Proportion of Cost Price
			Paid	Unpaid		
					£	£
1	A	24	5	19	144	114
2	B	52	14	38	78	57
					£222	£171[1]

[1] The end column shows the hire purchase stock 'out', the total of which is incorporated into the Double Entry Accounts, as below:

HIRE PURCHASE TRADING ACCOUNT

		£			£
Goods at Cost (Cr. *Purchases*) .		222	Instalments Paid (*Dr. Cash*)		68
Gross Profit transferred to Trading Account . .		17	Stock (as above)[2] . . . c/d		171
		£239			£239
Balance—Stock . . b/d		171			

[2] Or transferred to Hire Purchase Stock Account.

The separate instalments of cash, detailed above, will be entered in the Cash Book (in practice a separate subsidiary Cash Book will be employed). The debit entry will thus occur in the Cash Book, the totals (daily, weekly, monthly, as required) of which will be credited to the Hire Purchase Trading Account. In this case £68 is the sum to be so treated.

The above entries complete the formal double entry, but entries are also made in respect of cash received in the MEMORANDUM Books. The individual items in the Selling price column of the Hire Purchase Sales Journal will be debited to the Personal Accounts in the MEMORANDUM Ledger and the total will be posted to the credit of the MEMORANDUM Ledger Adjustment Account, if one be employed.

The cash received will be posted in individual items, as recorded in the Cash Book, to the crédit of the individual accounts in the MEMORANDUM Ledger, and in total to the debit of the MEMORANDUM Ledger Adjustment Account.

No. 1   MEMORANDUM HIRE PURCHASE LEDGER
A

19..			£	19..			£
Aug. 31	Goods		192	Dec. 31	Cash		40
					Balance	c/d	152
			£192				£192
19..							
Jan. 1	Balance	b/d	152				

No. 2
B

19..			£	19..			£
Oct. 1	Goods		104	Dec. 31	Cash		28
					Balance	c/d	76
			£104				£104
19..							
Jan. 1	Balance	b/d	76				

It is again emphasized that the Cash Book fulfils the dual function (a) of supplying the double entry, and (b) of supplementing the MEMORANDA Accounts, which are completely outside the double entry.

As already stated, where the rate of Gross Profit is uniform on all the transactions there is no necessity to calculate each balance separately, as the cost equivalent of the total will be in the same proportion as for each individual item. This can be seen from the following illustration.

Illustration 12

	Cost £	Price £	Number of Instalments	Number of Instalments paid	Cash received £	Stock 'out' at cost	£
A	200	300	10 (of £30)	7	210	$\frac{3}{10} \times £200$	60
B	90	135	5 (of £27)	3	81	$\frac{2}{5} \times £90$	36
C	220	330	22 (of £15)	2	30	$\frac{20}{22} \times £220$	200
	£510	£765			£321		£296

The stock out at cost may be calculated (without the details shown in italics) thus:

$$\frac{\text{Cost}}{\text{'Sales'}} \times \text{outstanding instalments}$$

The outstandings are £444, i.e. £765 − £321.
Therefore, stock 'out' is:

$$\tfrac{510}{765} \times £444 = \tfrac{2}{3} \times £444 = £296$$

Alternatively, the instalments outstanding may be brought down to the cost equivalent by deducting therefrom the profit based thereon, i.e.:

	£
Outstanding instalments . . .	444
Less 33⅓ per cent thereon . .	148
	£296

Reference to the illustration on p. 2022 will show that where the rate of gross profit is uniform, the cost price of the goods 'out' can be computed by the other (and quicker) methods; the uniform percentage is taken in that illustration to show that it in no way conflicts with the other methods, e.g.:

	£
Goods sent out at Selling Price	296
Less instalments paid	68
Goods 'out' at Selling Price (i.e. outstanding instalments) . . .	228
Less 25 per cent thereon	57
	£171

Method 2—At Selling Price.

An alternative method to that already outlined is to debit the goods out on hire at selling prices. If the method of dealing with goods sent to branches at selling price is thoroughly understood, no difficulty arises. The goods out with customers are treated, as far as the double entry books are concerned, exactly like goods sent to branches; thus it is merely necessary to use the correct heading, i.e. Hire Purchase Stock Account instead of Branch Stock Account. An advantage accruing to this method is that the sundry debtors (in total) will be in agreement with the actual debtor balances, thus enabling the individual accounts to be linked up with the double entry.

Illustration 13

A, Ltd, which sells a patent product on hire purchase terms, has the following transactions for the year to 31st December 19... The gross profit is 25 per cent on selling price:

19..		£
Jan. 1	Stock out on Hire at Hire Purchase price . .	400,000
	Stock on hand (in the shop)	50,000
	Instalments due (customers still paying) . .	30,000
Dec. 31.	Stock out on Hire at Hire Purchase price . .	460,000
	Stock on hand (in the shop)	70,000
	Instalments due	50,000
	Cash received in Instalments during the year . .	800,000

To prepare the Trading Account for the year to 31st December 19.., the following accounts are necessary:

SUNDRY DEBTORS

19..			£	19..				£
Jan. 1	Balances	b/d	30,000	Dec. 31	Cash			800,000
Dec. 31	Sales		820,000		Balances		c/d	50,000
			£850,000					£850,000
19..								
Jan. 1	Balances	b/d	50,000					

HIRE PURCHASE STOCK

19..			£	19..				£
Jan. 1	Balance[1]	b/d	400,000	Dec. 31	Sales for Year			820,000
Dec. 31	Goods on Hire				Stock		c/d	460,000
	Purchase Account		880,000					
			£1,280,000					£1,280,000
19..								
Jan. 1	Balance	b/d	460,000					

[1] Opening stock at cost is, therefore, £300,000.

SHOP STOCK

19..			£	19..				£
Jan. 1	Balance	b/d	50,000	Dec. 31	Goods on Hire			
Dec. 31	Purchases		680,000		Purchase Account			
					(at cost)			660,000
					Balance		c/d	70,000
			£730,000					£730,000
19..								
Jan. 1	Balance	b/d	70,000					

GOODS ON HIRE PURCHASE

19..		£	19..		£
Dec. 31	Shop Stock Account	660,000	Dec. 31	Hire Purchase Stock	
	Hire Purchase Ad-			Account	880,000
	justment Account				
	(loading)	220,000			
		£880,000			£880,000

HIRE PURCHASE ADJUSTMENT ACCOUNT

19..			£	19..			£
Dec. 31	Gross Profit to Profit			Jan. 1	Balance[1]	b/d	100,000
	and Loss Account		205,000		[25% on £400,000]		
	Provision [25% on			Dec. 31	Goods on Hire		
	£460,000]	c/d	115,000		Purchase Account		220,000
			£320,000				£320,000
				19..			
				Jan. 1	Provision	b/d	115,000

[1] Opening stock at cost is, therefore, £300,000.

The Sales are found after writing up the Sundry Debtors Account.

The balances on the Memoranda Accounts will equal in total the balance brought down on the Sundry Debtors Account.

. In the Balance sheet the items will appear as follows at 31st December 19..:

		£	£
Stock out on Hire Purchase	. .	460,000	
Less Provision .	. :	115,000	
			345,000
Stock on hand	. . .		70,000

If memorandum columns (Double Column Method, see p. 1927) are used, the two following accounts will appear instead of the corresponding accounts on p. 2025, the Stock being brought down at cost, thus dispensing with the Hire Purchase Adjustment Account.

HIRE PURCHASE STOCK

19..			Memo. £	£	19..		Memo. £	£
Jan. 1	Balance	b/d	400,000	300,000	Dec. 31	Sales for Year Stock .	820,000	820,000
Dec. 31	Goods on Hire Purchase Gross Profit		880,000	660,000 205,000			460,000	345,000
			£1,280,000	£1,165,000			£1,280,000	£1,165,000
19.. Jan. 1	Balance	b/d	460,000	345,000				

GOODS ON HIRE PURCHASE

19..				£	19..			£
Dec. 31	Shop Stock	.	. .	660,000	Dec. 31	Hire Purchase Stock	.	660,000

If it is practicable to adopt these methods (e.g. where there is a uniformity of rate of gross profit) the accounts will be, *mutatis mutandis*, on the same lines as Branch Accounts; and the result will be similar to the preceding method. This will now be illustrated, and a comparison between the Selling price and Cost price methods will be shown.

Illustration 14

X, Ltd., sells goods to A for £150 and to B for £100; the gross profit being 20 per cent on selling price (i.e. 25 per cent on cost price). A is to pay six instalments of £25 each and B ten instalments of £10 each. At the end of the accounting period A has paid two and B five instalments. B is in arrear for one instalment.

(*a*) The 'Branch' method at *selling price:*

HIRE PURCHASE STOCK

		£				£
Sundries per Journal . .		250	Cash . . .			100
			Instalments Due Account .			10
			Balance . . .	c/d		140
		£250				£250
Balance	b/d	140				

STOCK

					£
			Goods on Hire Purchase Account. . .		200

HIRE PURCHASE ADJUSTMENT ACCOUNT

		£			£
Gross Profit to Profit and Loss Account. .		22	Goods on Hire Purchase Account . .		50
Provision . . .	c/d	28			
		£50			£50
			Provision . . .	b/d	28

INSTALMENTS DUE

		£			
Hire Purchase Stock . .		10			

The Personal Accounts in the MEMORANDUM Hire Purchase Ledger, which should agree with the balance of Hire Purchase Stock Account, are as follows:

A

		£			£
Goods		150	Cash		50
			Balance	c/d	100
		£150			£150
Balance	b/d	100			

B

		£			£
Goods		100	Cash		50
			Transfer to Instalments Due Account . .		10
			Balance	c/d	40
		£100			£100
Balance	b/d	40			

The stock at selling price must be reduced to cost price by means of a provision in the Hire Purchase Adjustment Account, i.e. $\frac{1}{5} \times £140 = £28$, leaving the amount of stock to be shown in the Balance Sheet as $£140 - 28 = £112$.

The latter figure is proved by employing the rule of proportion shown on p. 2019 i.e.:

$$
\begin{array}{lr}
& £ \\
A—\frac{4}{6} \times £120 \text{ (cost price of £150)} = & 80 \\
B—\frac{4}{10} \times £ \ 80 \text{ (cost price of £100)} = & 32 \\
\hline
& £112 \\
\end{array}
$$

(*b*) The 'Branch' method at *cost price*:

If this method be employed, the MEMORANDA Accounts will be altered, and the Hire Purchase Trading Account will appear:

HIRE PURCHASE TRADING ACCOUNT

	£			£
Goods	200	Instalments Paid		100
Goods Profit to Profit and Loss Account	22	Instalments Due Account		10
		Stock c/d		112
	£222			£222
Stock b/d	112			

If the Double Column method is used, the Trading Account will be:

HIRE PURCHASE TRADING ACCOUNT

		Memo. Selling Price				Memo. Selling Price
	£	£			£	£
Goods	200	250		Cash	100	100
Gross Profit to Profit and Loss Account	22			Debtors	10	10
				Stock (at cost) c/d	112	
				„ (at selling) c/d		140
	£222	£250			£222	£250
Stock b/d	112	140				

In this case the selling price columns are purely MEMORANDA, the full double entry being effected from the inner columns. The advantages and disadvantages of the Goods Out or Stock system are shortly:

Advantages. 1. Simplicity.

2. Convenience in regard to transactions which are small or varying in amount or period.

3. Profit is taken as earned only when instalments are paid or become due, thus providing for further losses on unfulfilled agreements.

4. The balance of goods for which payment is not yet due can easily be reduced to net realizable value if lower than cost.

5. Where profit is taken only when instalments have been paid no provision for Bad Debts is required.

Disadvantages. 1. Difficulties with taxation assessment.

2. Over-cautious and not reflective of the true yearly profit.

3. Interest is not taken into account.

Summary of Hire Vendor's accounts

No particular difficulty is encountered in dealing with the books of the hire purchaser. On the other hand, students generally experience considerable trouble in writing up the books of the hire vendor. It will therefore be advisable to summarize the methods dealt with in reference to the hire vendor.

The methods are:

1. Sales Methods

(*a*) Ordinary sale (inclusive of interest).

(*b*) Ordinary sale (exclusive of interest) and charging interest separately either (i) as it arises or (ii) by crediting a Suspense for the full amount and writing off a proportionate amount yearly to the credit of Profit and Loss Account.

(*c*) Ordinary sale (exclusive of interest) and raising an Interest Suspense Account.

(*d*) Ordinary sale (inclusive of interest) and creating a Hire Purchase Reserve for unearned profit.

(*e*) Ordinary sale but apportioning profit as well as interest.

2. Goods Out or Stock Methods

(*a*) *At cost.*

(*b*) *At selling price.*

The two methods of paramount importance which must be known thoroughly are:

(i) Sale method whereby the profit is taken in the year of the transaction, with the employment of an Interest Suspense Account whereby interest is spread over the period of the agreement. (Method 1c.)

(ii) Goods out or Stock method whereby profit is taken in relation to instalments actually received, interest generally being ignored. (Method 2a.)

The remaining methods are usually adopted only in abnormal circumstances.

Illustration 15

Below are given five different methods of dealing with Hire Purchase transactions in the books of the seller:

1. The buyer is debited with the *cash* price when the agreement is made. The hire charge is periodically debited to him, so that at the end of each year the amount so charged corresponds with the number of instalments paid (excluding deposits), and credited to Interest Account.

2. The buyer is debited with the Hire Purchase price, the excess of which over the cash price is credited to Interest Suspense Account and cleared to Profit and Loss Account only when the transaction is completed.

3. A Hire Purchase Trading Account is debited with the cost price of the goods delivered on Hire Purchase and credited with the total of deposits and instalments received during the period. The Hire Purchase Trading Account is credited, at the end of each year, with the proportion of the cost price of the goods sent out on Hire Purchase, which the amount of instalments outstanding bears to the total amount of instalments (and deposits) arising on each transaction.[1] The balance on the account is considered profit on Hire Purchase Trading.

4. A Hire Purchase Trading Account is dealt with as in (3), except that at the end of the year the account is credited with the instalments still outstanding reduced to cost.

5. The same method is employed as in (4), except that the closing credit is computed on the basis of the full amounts outstanding on Hire Purchase transactions, less a general provision of 25 per cent.

Show how, in the seller's books, the profit for the year 19.. arising out of the undermentioned transactions would differ in each of the above methods, assuming that

(a) instalments are regularly paid,
(b) sales all took place on 1st January 19.., and that
(c) instalments are payable monthly, commencing 31st January 19...

Hire Purchaser	A	B	C	Total
	£	£	£	£
Cost Price	80	100	30	210
Hire-purchase Price . .	110	130	59	299
Cash Price	100	120	45	265
Deposit	10	20	5	
Number of Instalments . .	10	22	18	
Amount of each Instalment . .	10	5	3	

1.

	Profit on Cash Price		Interest	Total Profit 19..
	£		£p	£p
A . . .	20		10·00	30·00
B . . .	20	$12/22 \times £10$	5·46	25·46
C . . .	15	$12/18 \times £14$	9·33	24·33
	£55		£24·79	£79·79

---

[1] There is no need to separate each transaction where the rate of gross profit is uniform on all transactions. (See pp. 2022–2023.)

The profit on the whole completed transactions would be £299 less £210 = £89. This is reconciled with the profit shown above as follows:

			£p	£p
Total Profit on the whole transactions	.			89·00
Less Credit not taken for Interest:				
B	.	.	$\frac{10}{22} \times £10$	4·54
C	.	.	$\frac{6}{18} \times £14$	4·67
				9·21
				79·79

2.

	Profit on Cash Price	Interest	Total Profit 19..
	£	£	£
A	20	10	30
B	20		20
C	15		15
	£55	£10	£65

None of the interest for B and C (£24) is credited, thus accounting for the difference between the profit on the whole completed transactions (£89) and the £65 shown above.

3.

			£p
Deposits received	.	.	35·00
Instalments received:			
A	.	.	$10 \times £10 = £100$
B	.	.	$12 \times £5 = 60$
C	.	.	$12 \times £3 = 36$
			196·00
			231·00

Add Hire-purchase goods reduced to cost:

£p

$$B \quad \frac{10 \times 5}{20 + (22 \times 5)} = \frac{50}{130} \times £100 = \quad 38·46$$

$$C \quad \frac{6 \times 3}{5 + (18 \times 3)} = \frac{18}{59} \times £30 = \quad 9·15$$

		47·61
		278·61
Less Cost Price of goods	.	210·00
Total Profit 19..	.	£68·61

Reconciliation with total profit on completed transactions of £89 is:

			£p	£p
Profit as above				68·61
Add instalments outstanding:				
B	.	.	50·00	
C	.	.	18·00	
			68·00	
Less credited above as stock at cost	.	.	47·61	
				20·39
				£89·00

4. As (3)

Methods (3) and (4) are identical because the denominator, used in the calculation in (3) to reduce the outstanding goods to cost, of 'Total instalments and deposits' is the same as that used in (4) of 'Hire-purchase Price,' as the latter must equal 'Total instalments and deposits.'

		£	£
5.	Deposits and instalments received as in (3) above		231
	Add amounts outstanding—		
	B	50	
	C	18	
		68	
	Less 25% Provision	17	
			51
			282
	Less Cost Price of goods		210
	Total Profit 19..		£72

Profit as shown £72, plus the provision of £17, equals the profit on the whole completed transactions of £89.

Illustration 16

The balance due by hire purchaser at the date of default is £1,000. The goods are seized by the hire vendor, who allows the purchaser to pay £200 to close the account. The goods are revalued at £450. Expenses are incurred thereon totalling £75 and the goods sold for cash £617. Show accounts in the hire vendor's books, using the ordinary sale method. Ignore interest.

HIRE VENDOR'S BOOKS:

HIRE PURCHASER

		£			£
Balance	b/d	1,000	Cash		200
			Hire Purchase Returns Account		800

HIRE PURCHASE RETURNS

	£			£
Hire Purchaser	800	Returned Hire Purchase Trading Account		450
		Loss on Returned Hire Purchase Goods Account		350

CASH (includes)

	£			£
Hire Purchaser	200	Expenses on Returned Hire Purchased Goods		75
Sale of Returned Hire Purchase Goods	617			

RETURNED HIRE PURCHASE TRADING ACCOUNT

	£		Sales (Cash) . . .	£ 617
Hire Purchase Returns Account . . .	450			
Expenses . . .	75			
Profit and Loss on Sale of Returned Hire Purchase Goods Account .	92			
	£617			£617

LOSS ON RETURNED HIRE PURCHASE GOODS

	£			
Hire Purchase Returns Account. . . .	350			

PROFIT AND LOSS ON SALE OF
RETURNED HIRE PURCHASE GOODS

			Returned Hire Purchase Trading Account . .	£ 92

Ignoring interest, the vendor would in due course have received £1,000. His receipts are, however, £817, less £75 = £742, thus disclosing a net loss of £258, which is explained by:

		£
1. Loss on Returned Goods . . .		350
2. *Less* Profit on Resale . . .		92
Net Loss		£258

Illustration 17

On 1st January 19.., A agrees to acquire furnishings on the hire purchase system, agreeing to pay four half-yearly instalments of £400 each, commencing on 30th June 19... Interest at 5 per cent per annum on cash price of £1,505.

On 30th September 19.., A defaulted and the hire vendor seized the property. It is agreed that A should pay the due proportion of his half-yearly instalment, £200, and £180 for depreciation of the furnishings. The returned goods are revalued at £600.

The furnishings were resold on 15th November 19.., for £920 after renovating expenses had been paid of £150 on 31st October.

Show the accounts in the hire vendor's books, assuming that he passes hire purchase transactions through the books as sales.

The student should realize that the problem is one that is divisible into four main parts, viz.:

1. The hire purchase transaction and payments.

2. The return of the goods and adjustment of the balance of the Hire Purchaser's Account.

3. Loss arising from revaluation of the returned goods.

4. The subsequent sale of the goods after any necessary expenditure has been incurred.

HIRE VENDOR'S BOOKS:

A (HIRE PURCHASER)

19..		£p	19..		£p
Jan. 1	Furnishings	1,505·00	June 30	Cash	400·00
June 30	Interest at 5% p.a. on		Sept. 30	„	200·00
	£1,505 for ½ year	37·63		„ re Depreciation	180·00
Sept. 30	Interest at 5% p.a. on			Hire Purchase Returns	
	£1,142·63 for 3 months	14·28		Account	776·91
		£1,556·91			£1,556·91

¹ i.e. £1,505 plus £37·63, less 400.

HIRE PURCHASE RETURNS

19..		£p	19..		£p
Sept. 30	A	776·91	Sept. 30	Hire Purchase Returns	
				Trading Account	600·00
				Loss on Returned Hire	
				Purchase Goods	
				Account	176·91
		£776·91			£776·91

HIRE PURCHASE SALES

		£p	19..		£
			Jan. 1	A	1,505

HIRE PURCHASE INTEREST

		£p	19..		£p
			June 30	A	37·63
			Sept. 30	„	14·28

CASH (includes)

19..		£	19..		£
June 30	A	400	Oct. 31	Expenses on Returned	
Sept. 30	„	200		Hire Purchase	
		180		Goods	150
Nov. 15	Sale of Hire Purchase				
	Returns	920			

HIRE PURCHASE RETURNS TRADING ACCOUNT

19..		£	19..		£
Sept. 30	Hire Purchase Returns		Nov. 15	Cash	920
	Account	600			
Oct. 31	Expenses	150			
Nov. 15	Profit on Resale	170			
		£920			£920

LOSS ON RETURNED HIRE PURCHASE GOODS

19.. Sept. 30	Hire Purchase Returns Account . . .		£p 176·91				

PROFIT AND LOSS ON SALE OF RETURNED HIRE PURCHASE GOODS

		£	19.. Nov. 15	Hire Purchase Returns Trading Account .		£ 170

The whole position may be summarized, showing the profit on the transaction, and for this purpose the goods will be taken as costing the hire vendor £1,000.

		£p
Goods Cost	£1,000	
Profit on Hire Purchase Sale		505·00
Loss on Return		176·91
		328·09
Profit on Resale		170·00
		498·09
Hire Purchase Interest		51·91
Net Profit		£550·00

	£
Net Cash received per Cash Book . . .	1,550
Less Cost of Goods Sold . . .	1,000
Net Profit [as above]	£550

Returns and Repossessions. The treatment of returns will largely depend on circumstances, particularly the extent to which returns arise as compared with sales made, and also upon the desired information required by the proprietor.

The method that gives the maximum information is that whereby the repossessed goods are credited to the customer as ordinary returns corresponding with the balance still outstanding, the figures being charged to a Hire Purchase Returns Account: this in turn is closed by transferring the returns to a Returned Hire Purchase Trading Account at the revalued price of the goods returned and the Returns Account closed off as a profit or (as is usual) a loss.

The Returned Hire Purchase Trading Account will be debited with the necessary expenses incurred in the repossession and credited with the sale of the returned goods, the balance being closed off as a profit or loss.

A modification of this method is to ignore the 'intermediate' figure, i.e.

the value of the returned goods at the date of the repossession and treat the returns in the ordinary way, so that at the end of the year the Hire Purchase Trading Account will be included on the credit side the item of returned goods sold or in stock, valued in the usual way.

Alternatively, the returned goods may be taken back into General Stock and include in the ordinary Trading Account.

Where, however, the Hire Purchase Trading Account takes account only of instalments paid (or instalments paid and payable) the eliminating entry will be the 'Cost equivalent' of the Hire Purchase instalments still unpaid.

The transfer will be to the debit of Returned Hire Purchase Trading Account at such 'Cost equivalent'; the account will be debited with the appropriate expenses and the credit side of the returned Hire Purchase Trading Account will be made up of the Sales of the Returned Goods or brought in as stock in the usual way.

If the detail of profit or loss on Returned Goods is not required, the 'Cost equivalent' will be taken out of the Hire Purchase Trading Account and charged back to the general purchases, and dealt with in the ordinary trading account as a purchase; and the credit to Trading Account will be made up of the sales of such returned goods or brought in as stock in the ordinary way.

(In the Memorandum Ledger Accounts the balance standing to the debit of the defaulting customer will be credited to close the account.)

Where the returns are unimportant they can be dealt with within the Hire Purchase Trading Account itself without opening other accounts; otherwise, the goods taken back and their subsequent disposal should be dealt with as a separate accounting element.

Where the 'stock out' method is adopted the treatment of repossessed goods may be dealt with as follows:

1. By retaining in the Hire Purchase Trading Account the amount paid by the hire purchaser and crediting in the same account the repossessed goods at saleable value. A memorandum column will be used to show the amount of cash received from the hire purchaser and also the unpaid instalments (the two together representing the total hire purchase price). In the double-entry column will be credited such repossessed goods at valuation and repossessed hire purchase goods debited. As a result, the balance of the Account will represent the profit on the hire purchase transactions plus (or minus) the profit (or loss) arising from the hire purchase transactions which have been cancelled, that is, the excess of the cash paid by the hire purchaser plus the goods repossessed at valuation.

2. By eliminating the whole of the hire purchase transactions cancelled. This will be effected by leaving undisturbed the cash paid (as in (1)) and crediting (as in (1)) the memorandum column with the instalments unpaid, but (instead of bringing in the balance at revaluation of the repossessed goods) crediting the Hire Purchase Trading Account with the cost equivalent of the goods repossessed and debiting repossessed hire purchase goods.

The profit on the hire purchase transaction completed will be debited to Hire Purchase Trading Account and credited to Hire Purchase Repossessed Goods Suspense Account; the balance of the Hire Purchase Repossessed Goods Account will be closed off to the Suspense Account.

The combined result as shown in the two accounts will equal that shown by Method 1.

It will be noted that the balance representing the 'Cost equivalent' of the repossessed goods is credited to the Hire Purchase Trading Account just as if, in fact, there has been no repossession, but (instead of being brought down as stock in hand of customers in the ordinary way) it is **debited** to Hire Purchase Repossessed Goods Account.

Illustration 18

Goods are delivered (first year) on hire purchase, amounting to £10,560 cash retail price, showing gross profit of 25 per cent of that price, to which 10 per cent is added for the Hire Purchase Price.[1] Goods costing £600 were returned by the hire purchaser, who had paid nothing, and the goods returned were brought into account at their cost (and are still on hand).

The instalments received amounted to £1,936.

The profit to be taken into account is such proportion of the profit as instalments received bear to the total goods out on hire purchase. Show Hire Purchase Trading Account.

In addition to the Hire Purchase Trading Account there must be kept the Memorandum Ledger Accounts, and these are shown below, for convenience in italics and in total form.

HIRE PURCHASE TRADING ACCOUNT

	£	£		£	£
Goods sent on Hire Purchase (Cost)	*10,560*	7,200	Instalments Received . .	*1,936*	1,936
Gross Profit		616	Goods Returned (Cost) .	*880*	600
			Balance, Goods in hands of Customers (Cost) .	*7,744*	5,280
	£10,560	£7,816		*£10,560*	£7,816

The hire purchase price is loaded by $\frac{7}{15}$ of Cost thus:

	£
Cost price, say, ...	150
Percentage increase $33\frac{1}{3}$ per cent . . .	50
Retail Selling Price	200
Percentage increase 10 per cent of £200	20
Hire Purchase Selling price . . .	£220

Profit: $\frac{7}{15}$ of Cost or $\frac{7}{22}$ of Hire Purchase Sale Price.
$= \frac{7}{22} \times £1,936$ (profit being taken on instalments received)
The goods 'out' at Selling price $= £7,744$
The goods 'out' at Cost $= \frac{15}{22} \times £7,744 = \frac{15}{2} \times £704 = £5,280$
The goods which cost £600 carry a hire purchase price of £880 (i.e. $\frac{22}{15} \times £600$)

---

[1] It should be noted carefully the way the loading for Hire Purchase price is worded. The above is $\frac{1}{10}$ 'up.'

The goods returned will be debited to the purchase account of the General Trading Account and no difficulty arises as the goods are brought back at cost (and assumed to be worth cost).

Where (as is likely) the goods returned are worth less than cost and a deposit paid by the purchaser who has had the goods taken back for non-fulfilment of the hire purchase contract, the two factors may be dealt with as separate from the remaining transactions or as part of the Hire Purchase Trading Account.

Illustration 19

The transactions are as in the previous illustration except that (a) the customer has paid instalments of £110 (instalments received £2,046) and (b) the goods were brought back into general Stock at a valuation of £500.

Show Hire Purchase Trading Account.

HIRE PURCHASE TRADING ACCOUNT (Method 1)

	£	£		£	£
Goods sent on Hire Purchase (Cost)	10,560	7,200	Instalments received	1,936	1,936 [2]
Gross Profit[1]		626	Instalments received	110	110
			Unpaid Instalments	770	
			Goods returned (valuation)		500
			Balance, Goods in hands of Customers, at Cost	7,744	5,280
	£10,560	£7,826		£10,560	£7,826

[1] On Hire Purchase £616. On goods returned £10.   [2] £2,046 separated for clarity.

The difference in profit between the above and the preceding illustration is £10 (£626 − £616). This difference is explained thus:

Instalments £100—Loss on goods £100 (Cost Price £600—Valuation £500)

In regard to the item of £110, it is profit, because the goods have been returned, so that (subject to any loss in valuation—in this instance £100) the hire vendor gets his goods back again with £110 'thrown-in.'

If, however, it is desired to keep the returned goods transactions separate, the above account would be as below (the memorandum columns being omitted, as these will be unaffected).

HIRE PURCHASE TRADING ACCOUNT (Method 2)

	£		£
Goods sent on Hire Purchase (Cost)	7,200	Instalments received	2,046
Transfer to Hire Purchase Goods Repossessed Suspense Account, instalments received on goods returned	110	Goods returned at cost	600
Gross Profit	616	Balance, Goods in hands of customers, at cost	5,280
	£7,926		£7,926

HIRE PURCHASE REPOSSESSED GOODS ACCOUNT

		£			£
Hire Purchase Trading Account		600	Stock at valuation . . . Deficiency—transfer to Hire Purchase Repossessed Suspense Account .	c/d	500 100
		£600			£600
Stock	b/d	500			

HIRE PURCHASE REPOSSESSED GOODS SUSPENSE ACCOUNT

		£			£
Hire Purchase Repossessed Goods Account . .		100	Hire Purchase Trading Account		110

[Alternatively, these two accounts could be combined.]

The above account separately features the extra £10 profit previously indicated and would probably be held in the account.

The accounts above, as previously suggested, would only be used where goods taken back were a normal feature.

Change in Accounting Method. Where it is decided to change from the ordinary method of having the debtors as part of the double entry and treating (modified according to circumstances) deliveries as sales, taking into account only cash received by the use of the Hire Purchase Trading Account, and treating debtors as memoranda, it will be necessary to make suitable adjustments.

1. If the amendment is made at the *commencement* of an accounting period the adjusting entries are:

Debit Hire Purchase Trading Account (stock out at cost).
Debit Profit and Loss Adjustment Account (unearned profit).
Credit Hire Purchase Debtors Total Account (balances representing unpaid instalments).

The individual accounts will not be disturbed, but they become 'memoranda' only.

2. If the amendment is made at the end of the accounting period, the adjusting entries are:

(a) Debit Hire Purchase Trading Account: (Stock out at commencement)   Credit Hire Purchase Debtors Total

(b) Debit sales cancelled: Credit Hire Purchase Debtors Total

(c) Credit Hire Purchase Trading Account: Cash received from customers)   Debit Hire Purchase Debtors Total

After the above entries have been made, the Hire Purchase Trading Account is as it would have been if the entries had originally been dealt through that account, subject to the transfer thereto of the goods sent out on hire purchase—i.e. Debit Hire Purchase Trading Account and Credit General Purchases in respect of the goods sent out to hire purchasers, at cost.

Repossessed goods and the closing stock out with hire purchasers, at cost, will be dealt with on the lines already indicated. If, however, such stock had been brought into the General Trading Account, the amounts would have to be eliminated therefrom (Debit Trading Account and Credit Stock) as this will have to be dealt with, as mentioned, through the Hire Purchase Trading Account.

Illustration 20

(The eliminating entries are shown in italics.)

HIRE PURCHASE DEBTORS TOTAL ACCOUNT

	£		£
Opening Balances	10,000	Cash	17,000
Sales	20,000	Balances	13,000
	£30,000		£30,000
Balances	13,000	*Hire Purchase Trading Account*	*10,000*
Hire Purchase Trading Account	*17,000*	*Sales Account*	*20,000*
	£30,000		£30,000

Illustration 21

Sputnik, Ltd., sells goods retail for cash and hire purchase. The rate of gross profit for hire purchase sales is 32 per cent on cost, and cash sales are made at the hire purchase price as reduced by $\frac{1}{11}$.

The Trading Account is constructed on the basis that full credit is taken on hire purchase deliveries as well as on the Cash Sales.

The hire purchase trading did not commence till 1st February 19...

TRADING ACCOUNT FOR THE YEAR ENDED 31ST DECEMBER 19..

		£		£
Stock 1st January 19..		4,200	Sales, Hire Purchase	26,400
Purchases		21,500	Sales, Cash	3,600
Gross Profit—			Stock, 31st December 19..	2,700
Hire Purchase	£6,400			
Cash	600			
		7,000		
		£32,700		£32,700

The instalments that had been received during the year amounted to £15,840.

The company requires the above account amending, as it wishes to take credit for such proportion of profit as the instalments bear to the total amounts receivable under the hire purchase agreements and to adopt the 'Stock' method of dealing with the hire purchase transactions. Set out the adjusting entries in Journal form.

The first step is to obtain the various rates of gross profit, thus—

If the Hire Purchase Gross Profit is 32 per cent of *Cost*, then if the sales are £132, the cost is £100, whilst the Cash Sales must be $\frac{10}{11} \times £132$, viz. £120.

Therefore the 'table' can be shown thus:

	£
Cost	100
Gross Profit on Cash Sales	20
Cash Sale Price	120
Gross Profit addition on Hire Purchase transactions . .	12
	£132

It is essential to remember that the Hire Purchase Sales and Outstanding Debtors cancelled out (the latter accounts being made Memoranda only) whilst all the goods 'out' are taken as Stock at cost and the instalments paid considered as Sales.

If the net realizable value is less than the cost, a separate provision should be made to cover the deficiency.

Adjusting entries:

JOURNAL

	£	£
Hire Purchase Sales (Trading Account)		
(To cancel Hire Purchase Sales item) .	26,400	
Debtors (To cancel balance on Debtors) .		10,560
(£26,400—Cash paid £15,840)		
Hire Purchase Trading Account		
(For instalments received) . . .		15,840

	£	£
Hire Purchase Trading (Cost price of Goods 'out') . . .	20,000	
Purchases (Trading Account) (To cancel hire purchase goods no longer to remain in General Purchases) . .		20,000

The cost price of hire purchase sales is $\frac{100}{132} \times £26,000 = £20,000$

Hire Purchase selling price . . .	£26,400
Less $\frac{1}{11}$ to reduce to cash selling price	2,400
	24,000
Less $\frac{1}{6} \times £24,000$ (or $\frac{1}{5} \times £20,000$) .	4,000
	£20,000

	£	£
Hire Purchase Stock (stock at cost with hire purchase customers) .	8,000	
Hire Purchase Trading Account		8,000

This may be calculated—

(1) Cost equivalent of £10,560 (unpaid instalments)
$= \frac{100}{132} \times £10,560$ or $\frac{120}{132} \times \frac{5}{6} \times £10,560$

(2) Total goods 'out' at cost		£20,000
Less goods paid for at cost—		
Hire purchase price . .	£15,840	
Less profit $\frac{32}{132} \times £15,840$	3,840	
		12,000
		£8,000

The deduction of £3,840 in (2) is the profit.

Amended Accounts:

GENERAL TRADING ACCOUNT

		£			£
Stock		4,200	Sales, Cash . .		3,600
Purchases	£21,500		Sales, Hire Purchase	£26,400	
Less Goods sent on Hire Purchase at Cost . .	20,000		Less Hire Purchase Sales cancelled .	26,400	—
		1,500	Stock . . .		2,700
Gross Profit[1] . .		600			
		£6,300			£6,300

[1] 20 per cent of Cost of £3,000 (£4,200 + £1,500 − £2,700) = 20 per cent of £3,000; or $\frac{1}{6}$ of £3,600.

HIRE PURCHASE TRADING ACCOUNT

	£		£
Goods sent on Hire Purchase (Cost) . . . . . :	20,000	*Instalments received* . . .	15,840
Gross Profit[1]	3,840	*Balance Goods in hands of customers, at Cost* . . .	8,000
	£23,840		£23,840

[1] 32 per cent of Cost (£20,000 − £8,000) = 32 per cent of £12,000; or $\frac{32}{132}$ of 'Sales' (i.e. instalments received) £15,840.

For clarity, the items in italics are from the Journal entries (*supra*).

Note. It will be observed that the gross profit on hire purchase transactions in the original Trading Account and in the Hire Purchase Trading Account as newly constructed are £6,400 and £3,840 respectively, thus showing a reduction of £2,560. This is accounted for by the fact that in the original account profit was taken on £26,400 as against the amended figure of £15,840; hence the profit reduction $\frac{32}{132}$ of £10,560 ($\frac{8}{33} \times$ £10,560 or $\frac{8}{3} \times$ £960 or 8 × £320) equals £2,560.

POST-SALES SERVICES

Where the transaction carries an obligation on the part of the vendor or hire vendor to perform services subsequent to the transfer of the goods, e.g. to repair and maintain, it is obvious that the cost of such services will be 'loaded' on to the price, so that the excess of the price of the goods carrying such an obligation over an ordinary transaction represents the advance payment by the consumer in respect of those future services. Experience must guide the vendor in estimating such loading, always bearing in mind competitive prices; but whatever be the loading, its apportionment is required, depending upon the duration of the service obligation. Where the duration is lengthy, a Suspense Account will be opened to cover all the separate years, against which will be debited the annual cost of effecting the agreed services. There are many services that may be fairly accurately computed, e.g. replacement of faulty parts in television sets, items of machinery and the like, but generally the cost will tend to increase each period, so that the Suspense Account should have allocated to it a smaller percentage in the early periods than in the later.

The expenses actually incurred in performing the service will be debited (in the period in which they occur) to the appropriate Suspense Account.

Except in fortuitous circumstances, such suspense accounts will never balance, that is, the allocation of the loading included in sale or hire purchase price will not be exactly equal to the service cost. Hence, there will either be a debit or a credit balance, representing respectively a deficiency or a surplus on the loading. In other words, in the instance of a debit balance the service cost exceeds the amount credited to Suspense (included in sale price), whilst a credit balance shows that the service cost has been less than the amount credited to Suspense.

Although it is prudent to write off the debit balance, yet if there have been credit balances arising in previous years and not credited to Profit and Loss Account, a debit balance may be set off against the credit balance in question, and, therefore, so long as a credit balance exists on the Suspense Accounts, any subsequent debit balance thereon may be written off against it; any unabsorbed debit balance of Suspense Account being transferred to Trading or Profit and Loss Account.

Where there is a debit balance on Suspense Account it theoretically results from an incorrect estimate of service cost so that future prices may have to be adjusted accordingly (if competition will permit!). On the other hand the discrepancy may be purely accidental and/or temporary. If, for instance, the general price level has increased, the service costs will be incurred in terms of such enhanced level, so that a loss will be likely to arise as the sales would normally have been based on the lower price levels ruling at the date of the Hire Purchase transaction.

Again, such 'deficiency' may be deliberate, and therefore may be considered as a selling expense—advertising, in fact—just in the same way as several chain stores run cafés (charging comparatively low prices) at a loss; but such a policy attracts customers who probably look round the stores and make purchases.

Illustration 22

Wireless, Ltd., manufactures a transistor radio for £22 and sells both outright and on hire purchase. The respective prices are £30 outright and £37 hire purchase—under the latter an initial payment of £10 and four equal half-yearly instalments of £6·75, the first being payable at the end of the half-year after sale. The company agrees to maintain *all* sets delivered for a period of two years free of charge. From experience the cost of maintenance per set is estimated at £4 (£1·50 incurred in the first year). Show entries, assuming:

1. The 'pure' sales of sets are 120 per annum.
2. The hire purchase sales of sets are 300 per annum.
3. The actual cost of maintence in the first year was £215.
4. The sales are uniformly maintained.

The double entry involved is[1]:

1. Debit Cash £30. Credit Sales £30.
2. Debit Hire Purchase Debtors £37.
   Credit Sales (for sale price) £30.
   Credit Interest Suspense £7.
3. Debit Sales £4. Credit Maintenance Suspense £4.
4. Debit Maintenance Suspense. Credit Cash (for actual cost).

[1] The figures show the appropriate amounts for the sale of one set.

5. The balance on the Maintenance Suspense Account will be written off:

(a) If Debit:
> Debit Trading Account (or Reserve if a surplus arising in past years has been carried forward).
> Credit Maintenance Suspense Account.

(b) If Credit:
> Debit Maintenance Suspense Account.
> Credit Reserve.

Computations. It is necessary first to compute two loadings, viz. maintenance and interest.

The loading for maintenance is contained in ALL sales, Cash or Hire Purchase, and is $\frac{4}{30} \times 100\% = 13\frac{1}{3}\%$; this must now be apportioned over the two separate years in the light of experience, which in the question is:

$$\text{1st year} \qquad \text{£1·50} \quad \text{i.e.} \quad \frac{1\frac{1}{2}}{30} \times 100\% = 5\%$$

$$\text{2nd year} \qquad \text{£2·50} \quad \text{i.e.} \quad \frac{2\frac{1}{2}}{30} \times 100\% = 8\frac{1}{3}\%$$

But as sales may be taken as being made at an average date of half-way through the financial year, the maintenance will accordingly be split and affect three financial periods, thus:

	%	%
1st year	$\frac{1}{2} \times 5\ \%$	$2\frac{1}{2}$
2nd year	$\frac{1}{2} \times 5\ \% = 2\frac{1}{2}$	
3rd year	$\frac{1}{2} \times 8\frac{1}{3}\% = 4\frac{1}{6}$	$6\frac{2}{3}$
	$\frac{1}{2} \times 8\frac{1}{3}\% = 4\frac{1}{6}$	$4\frac{1}{6}$
		$13\frac{1}{3}\%$

This percentage applies to ALL the transactions based upon the 'pure' sales figures, viz:

	Sets	£	£
Pure Sales	$120 \times 30 =$		3,600
Hire Purchase Sales	$300 \times 30 =$		9,000
			£12,600

The loading for maintenance is therefore:

	£	£
$2\frac{1}{2}\% \times 12,600 =$		315
$6\frac{2}{3}\% \times 12,600 =$		840
$4\frac{1}{6}\% \times 12,600 =$		525
$13\frac{1}{3}\% \times 12,600 =$		£1,680

Alternatively, the loading may be computed thus:

	£	£	£		£
1st year maintenance per set	$\frac{1}{2}\times 1\cdot50$			$0\cdot75\times420=$	315
2nd year ,, ,,	$\frac{1}{2}\times 1\cdot50$	0·75			
	$+\frac{1}{2}\times 2\cdot50$	1·25	2·00×420 =	840
3rd year " "	$\frac{1}{2}\times 2\cdot50$			$1\cdot25\times420=$	525
					£1,680

[See p. 2048]

These figures now form the basis of the entry to the credit of Maintenance Suspense Account, leaving the Hire Purchase Interest Suspense on hire purchase sales to be dealt with.

In both instances the loading for maintenance being segregated, attention must now be given to the loading of £7 for interest on the hire purchase transactions. The net selling price for cash *without* maintenance is £26 per set, but the interest should be calculated upon the amount of £20, not £16, because the initial payment of £10 must first be deducted and the maintenance charge of £4 added as compared with the cash purchasers who pay the £4 *at once* for maintenance the hire purchasers are paying in instalments, hence the £4 must be regarded in the light of a loan. The vendors are obviously deprived of the immediate sum of £4 per set when they permit it to be paid over in instalments.

Therefore the sum of £37 is paid in instalments as against £30 at once, so that the interest is £7 per set.

Assuming the sales (on hire purchase) to take place at the commencement of the year, the interest would be:

			£p	£p
Year 1	. (approx.)	$\frac{1}{2}$ yr.	2·64	
		$\frac{1}{2}$ yr.	2·10	
				4·74
Year 2	. (approx.)	$\frac{1}{2}$ yr.	1·48	
		$\frac{1}{2}$ yr.	0·78	
				2·26
	Total			£7·00

Averaging these on the basis of sales at an average date of halfway through the period, the interest is:

		£p	£p	£p
Year 1.	$\frac{1}{2}\times 4\cdot74$			2·37
Year 2.	$\frac{1}{2}\times 4\cdot74$	2·37		
	$\frac{1}{2}\times 2\cdot26$	1·13		
				3·50
Year 3.	$\frac{1}{2}\times 2\cdot26$			1·13
	Total			£7·00

Total interest, therefore, is $300 \times £7 = £2,100$, apportioned as follows:

$$\text{Year 1.} \quad £\frac{2 \cdot 37}{7} \times 2,100 = \quad 711$$

$$\text{Year 2.} \quad £\frac{3 \cdot 50}{7} \times 2,100 = \quad 1,050$$

$$\text{Year 3.} \quad £\frac{1 \cdot 13}{7} \times 2,100 = \quad 339$$

$$£2,100$$

[See p. 2048]

Alternatively, calculated in terms of sets delivered under hire purchase agreements:

	£p	£
Year 1.	$300 \times 2 \cdot 37 =$	711
Year 2.	$300 \times 3 \cdot 50 =$	1,050
Year 3.	$300 \times 1 \cdot 13 =$	339
		£2,100

Calculation:

	Balance		Interest	Total	Instalment	Balance
	£p		£p	£p	£p	£p
Year 1—½ year	20·00		2·64	22·64	6·75	15·89
½ year	15·89		2·10	17·99	6·75	11·24
Year 2—½ year	11·24		1·48	12·72	6·75	5·97
½ year	5·97		0·78	6·75	6·75	
			£7·00			

Alternative calculation:

Where the calculation is based upon £16 (instead of £20), the proportions are as below. (The difference between this and the preceding method is negligible.)

	Balance		Interest	Total	Instalment	Balance
	£p		£p	£p	£p	£p
Year 1—½ year	16·00		2·62	18·62	5·75	12·87
½ year	12·87		2·09	14·96	5·75	9·21
Year 2—½ year	9·21		1·49	10·70	5·75	4·95
½ year	4·95		0·80	5·75	5·75	
			£7·00			

The full entries may now be shown:

JOURNAL

	£	£
Cash	3,600	
Sales		3,600
Being sales outright of 120 transistor radios.		
Hire Purchase Debtors . . .	11,100	
Sales		9,000
Interest Suspense—		
Year 1		711
,, 2		1,050
,, 3		339
Being deliveries under hire purchase agreements and interest allocations, in respect of 300 transistor radios.		
Sales	1,680	
Maintenance Suspense—		
Year 1		315
,, 2		840
,, 3		525
Being proportion of estimated maintenance chargeable in the relevant years.		

The cost of maintenance in the first year of £215 will be debited against the item of £315, leaving a balance of £100, which will be credited to Reserve.

HIRE PURCHASER'S BOOKS

The various methods of recording hire purchase transactions in the books of the hire vendor having been separately explained in the earlier pages of this chapter, the methods of recording such transactions in the books of the hire purchaser will now be dealt with.

Separation has been effected in order to preclude any possibility of confusion arising in the mind of the student, and so that the comparatively simple entries required in the books of the hire purchaser may be readily grasped.

There are, of course, more methods of record than it is found expedient to set out here, and of them three of the more important are explained on pp. 2049 and 2051.

1. (a) Debit the asset with the cash value and credit the Hire Vendor (as if it were an outright purchase).

(b) Debit Interest and Credit Hire Vendor for Interest at due dates.

(c) Debit Hire Vendor and credit Cash with each payment.

2. Similarly as (1), except the Hire Vendor is credited with the *total of instalments*, i.e. cash price and interest, in which case the amount representing interest will be debited to Interest Suspense Account. No further credits will be then given to Hire Vendor as he has already been credited

with the inclusive figure. The Interest Suspense Account will be credited with the proportion of interest allocable to the year in question, this being debited to Interest Account; the cash payment to the Hire Vendor is debited to his account and credited to Cash in the ordinary way, as 1(c) above.

3. No entry is made until payment to the Hire Vendor is made, whereupon such sum is allocated between the cost of the asset and interest, the respective proportions being respectively debited to Asset and Interest, the Hire Vendor being credited with the amount of instalment due.

The question of Depreciation will be dealt with on p. 2051.

Illustration 23

B buys Machinery on the hire purchase system from A—cash price, £1,000—agreeing to pay for it in two half-yearly instalments with interest at 5 per cent per annum (the interest to be paid each half-year in addition to the amount due on the machinery).

Method 1. The entries in the Hire Purchaser's books for the above illustration will be:

A

Half Year 1	Cash Balance		c/d	£p 525·00 500·00	Half Year 1	Machinery Half year's Interest on £1,000 at 5% per annum			£p 1,000·00 25·00
				£1,025·00					£1,025·00
Half Year 2	Cash			512·50	Half Year 2	Balance Half year's Interest on £500 at 5% per annum	b/d		500·00 12·50
				£512·50					£512·50

MACHINERY

Half Year 1	A			£ 1,000				£

Where the Hire Purchaser pays equal instalments to cover principal and interest, the account of the Hire Vendor, in the Hire Purchaser's books, will be reverse of that appearing in the books of the former.

Illustration 24

Assuming the facts used in Illustration 2 on p. 2007, the entries in the books of the Hire Purchaser relative to the Hire Vendor will be:

A

			£p				£p
Half Year 1	Cash		518·83	Half Year 1	Machinery		1,000·00
	Balance	c/d	506·17		Half year's Interest on £1,000 at 5% per annum		25·00
			£1,025·00				£1,025·00
Half Year 2	Cash		518·83	Half Year 2	Balance	b/d	506·17
					Half year's Interest on £506·17 at 5% per annum		12·66
			£518·83				£518·83

See also p. 2007 for entries in Hire Vendor's Books.

Method 2:

MACHINERY

			£				£
Half Year 1	Hire Vendor		1,000				

INTEREST SUSPENSE

			£p				£p
Half Year 1	Hire Vendor		37·50	Half Year 1	Profit and Loss Account		25·00
					Balance	c/d	12·50
			£37·50				37·50
Half Year 2	Balance	b/d	12·50	Half Year 2	Profit and Loss Account		12·50

HIRE VENDOR

			£p				£p
Half Year 1	Cash		525·00	Half Year 1	Sundries		1,037·50
	Balance	c/d	512·50				
			£1,037·50				£1,037·50
Half Year 2	Cash		512·50	Half Year 2	Balance	b/d	512·50

Method 3:

MACHINERY

			£				£
Half Year 1	Hire Vendor		500	Half Year 1	Balance	c/d	500
Half Year 2	Balance	b/d	500	Half Year 2	Balance	c/d	1,000
	Hire vendor		500				
			£1,000				£1,000
Half Year 3	Balance	b/d	1,000				

INTEREST

Half Year 1	Vendor . . .	£p 25·00	Half Year 1	Profit and Loss Account . . .			£p 25·00
Half Year 2	Vendor . . .	12·50	Half Year 2	Profit and Loss Account . . .			12·50

HIRE VENDOR

Half Year 1	Cash . . .	£p 525·00	Half Year 1	Machinery . . . Interest . . .			£p 500·00 25·00
		£525·00					£525·00
Half Year 2	Cash . . .	512·50	Half Year 2	Machinery . . . Interest . . .			500·00 12·50
		£512·50					£512·50

The above would appear in the Balance Sheet:

ASSETS	£p	£p	£p
Method 1—			
Half Year 1. Machinery		1,000·00	
Less H.P. Creditor		500·00	
			500·00
Half Year 2. Machinery			1,000·00
Method 2—			
Half Year 1. Machinery		1,000·00	
Less H.P. Creditor . . .	512·50		
Less Interest unaccrued . . .	12·50		
		500·00	
			500·00
Half Year 2. Machinery			1,000·00
Method 3—			
Half Year 1. Machinery			500·00
Half Year 2. Machinery			1,000·00

Depreciation. The depreciation to be written off must be calculated on the cash value of the asset, that is to say, its full value, but the student must bear in mind that the cash value in method 3 is not arrived at until the end of the period. The entries recording the depreciation are the usual ones, viz.:

Debit Depreciation   Credit Asset

In method 3, however, it is advisable to keep a Depreciation Account quite separate from the Asset Account. Further, it must be noted that neither the Interest Account nor the Hire Vendor's Account will be affected by the depreciation entries.

Illustration 25

In the above illustration the rate of depreciation is to be taken at 10 per cent on the decreasing balance each half year.

Methods (1) and (2):

MACHINERY

			£					£
Half Year 1	Hire Vendor . . .		1,000	Half Year 1	Depreciation . . . Balance . . .	c/d		100 900
			£1,000					£1,000
Half Year 2	Balance . . .	b/d	900	Half Year 2	Depreciation . . . Balance . . .	c/d		90 810
			£900					£900
Half Year 3	Balance . . .	b/d	810					

Method (3):

MACHINERY

			£					£
Half Year 1	Hire Vendor . . .		500	Half Year 1	Depreciation . . . Balance . . .	c/d		100 400
			£500					£500
Half Year 2	Balance . . . Hire Vendor . . .	b/d	400 500	Half Year 2	Depreciation . . . Balance . . .	c/d		90 810
			£900					£900
Half Year 3	Balance . . .	b/d	810					

Alternatively

MACHINERY

			£					£
Half Year 1	Hire Vendor . . .		500	Half Year 1	Balance . . .	c/d		500
Half Year 2	Balance . . . Hire Vendor . . .	b/d	500 500	Half Year 2	Balance . . .	c/d		1,000
			£1,000					£1,000
Half Year 3	Balance . . .	b/d	1,000					

DEPRECIATION

				£					£
Half Year 1	Balance	c/d	100	Half Year 1	Profit and Loss Account .			100
Half Year 2	Balance	c/d	190	Half Year 2	Balance . . .	b/d	100
					Profit and Loss Account		90
			£190					£190
				Half Year 3	Balance	b/d	190

The alternative merely shows depreciation as a separate Provision instead of by way of deduction from the asset.

The Balance Sheet would appear as shown in the previous illustration, with the additional deduction of depreciation, e.g.

Method (3):

Assets	£	£
Half Year 1. Machinery	500	
Less Depreciation	100	
		400
Half Year 2. Machinery	900	
Less Depreciation	90	
		810

Illustration 26

A delivers machinery on the hire purchase system for £2,500 to be paid as follows: on delivery, £400; at the end of the first year, £600; second year, £400; third year £1,100; interest, included in the £2,500, being charged on the cash value at 10 per cent per annum. Show entries in the books of the hire purchaser, the latter writing off Depreciation at the rate of 5 per cent per annum on the diminishing balance system.

HIRE PURCHASER'S BOOKS:

MACHINERY

			£p					£p
Year 1	Hire Vendor . .		2,102·48	Year 1	Depreciation . .		105·13
					Balance . .	c/d	1,997·35
			£2,102·48				£2,102·48
Year 2	Balance . .	b/d	1,997·35	Year 2	Depreciation . .		99·87
					Balance . .	c/d	1,897·48
			£1,997·35				£1,997·35
Year 3	Balance . .	b/d	1,887·48	Year 3	Depreciation . .		94·87
					Balance . .	c/d	1,802·61
			£1,897·48				£1,897·48
Year 4	Balance . .	b/d	1,802·61				

HIRE VENDOR

Year 1			£p	Year 1			£p
	Cash (beginning) .		400·00		Machinery . . .		2,102·48
	Cash (end) . .		600·00		Interest		170·25
	Balance . . .	c/d	1,272·73		(10% on £1,702·48)[1]		
			£2,272·73				£2,272·73
Year 2	Cash . . .		400·00	Year 2	Balance . . .	b/d	1,272·73
	Balance . . .	c/d	1,000·00		Interest		127·27
					(10% on £1,272·73)[1]		
			£1,400·00				£1,400·00
Year 3	Cash . . .		1,100	Year 3		b/d	1,000
					Interest		100
					(10% on £1,000)[1]		
			£1,100				£1,100

[1] The interest is calculated as follows:

		£p	£p
3rd year .	.	$\frac{1}{11} \times 1,100·00 =$	100·00
2nd year .	.	$\frac{1}{11} \times 1,400·00 =$	127·27
1st year .	.	$\frac{1}{11} \times 1,872·73 =$	170·25

The hire purchaser will show the asset in the Balance Sheet (as if he had actually bought it), less depreciation, less the amount still owing to the hire vendor on hire purchase, e.g. in the second year:

	£p	£p
Machinery on Hire Purchase—		
Balance . . .	1,997·35	
Less Depreciation at 5% p.a. .	99·87	
	1,897·48	
Less Hire Vendor .	1,000·00	
		897·48

Method 3. The entries are shown in journal form, as the examiners usually ask for Journal entries in this particular type of problem. Narratives are ignored.

JOURNAL

		£p	£p
Year 1 (commencement)	Machinery . . . . Hire Vendor	*400·00	400·00
Year 1 (end)	Machinery . . . . Interest . . . . Hire Vendor	*429·75 170·25	600·00
Year 1 (end)	Profit and Loss Account . . . . . Machinery—Depreciation . . .	105·13	105·13
Year 2 (end)	Machinery . . . . Interest . . . . Hire Vendor	*272·73 127·27	400·00
Year 2 (end)	Profit and Loss Account . . . . . Machinery—Depreciation . . .	99·87	99·87
Year 3 (end)	Machinery . . . . Interest . . . . Hire Vendor	*1,000·00 100·00	1,100·00
Year 3 (end)	Profit and Loss Account . . . . . Machinery—Depreciation . . .	94·87	94·87

Notes:

1. The Hire Vendor's Account will be debited in the usual way with the cash paid.

2. If the entries are to be made as 'Cash' entries, i.e. without the employment of the personal account of the Hire Vendor, the word Cash will take the place of Hire Vendor.

3. The depreciation may be written off the account each year, or credited to a Depreciation Account, and at the end of the third year transferred to Machinery Account.

4.* The total of the debits to Machinery Account is £2,102·48, as shown in the account on p. 2053.

General Illustration 27

On 1st January 19.1, A acquires on hire purchase from B, machinery valued at £12,000 payable in three yearly instalments of £4,000, plus interest at 6 per cent per annum. Only one instalment was paid, and B arranged immediately the second instalment had become due to take back machinery, which cost £8,000, allowing £4,500 therefor, providing that A paid all the interest due to that date on the full amount owing.

A had written off depreciation at 10 per cent per annum on the diminishing balance. Show the Machinery Account and B's Account in the books of A.

MACHINERY

Date	Particulars		£	Date	Particulars		£
19.1 Jan. 1	B		12,000	19.1 Dec. 31	Depreciation		1,200
					Balance	c/d	10,800
			£12,000				£12,000
19.2 Jan. 1	Balance	b/d	10,800	19.2 Dec. 31	Depreciation[1]		1,080
					B		4,500
					Profit and Loss Account— Loss		1,980
					Balance	c/d	3,240
			£10,800				£10,800
19.3 Jan. 1	Balance	b/d	3,240				

[1] Diminishing balance method employed.

B

Date	Particulars		£	Date	Particulars		£
19.1 Dec. 31	Balance	c/d	12,720	19.1 Jan. 1	Machinery		12,000
				Dec. 31	Interest at 6% per annum on £12,000 for Year		720
			£12,720				£12,720
19.2 Jan. 1	Cash		4,720	19.2 Jan. 1	Balance	b/d	12,720
Dec. 31	Balance	c/d	8,480	Dec. 31	Interest at 6% per annum on £8,000 for Year		480
			£13,200				£13,200
	Cash (Interest)		480		Balance	b/d	8,480
	Machinery		4,500				
	Balance	c/d	3,500				
			£8,480				£8,480
				19.3 Jan. 1	Balance	b/d	3,500

The amount to be written off from the Machinery Account may be found as follows:

	Machinery Retained	Machinery Returned	Total
	£	£	£
Cost Price	4,000	8,000	12,000
Less 1st year's Depreciation—10%	400	800	1,200
	3,600	7,200	10,800
Less 2nd year's Depreciation—10%	360	720	1,080
	£3,240	6,480	£9,720
Less Allowance		4,500	
Balance = Loss		£1,980	

The cost of the machinery retained has been paid for together with the interest to date, and so if the machinery were taken back at the original price of £8,000, the account would be clear; but only £4,500 is allowed on its return by the vendor B, and thus his account stands in credit for the sum of £3,500.

As the machinery retained is paid for, and there is still £3,500 due to B, it is necessary to reconcile this with the loss of £1,980 on the returned machinery written off from the Machinery Account. The £3,500 is made up thus:

	£
Depreciation—1st year	800
2nd year	720
Loss on Machinery returned	1,980
	£3,500

Thus, apart from the machinery retained, the Hire Purchaser owes B £3,500, of which £1,520 represents normal depreciation and £1,980 loss. The latter sum is equal to £6,480, less £4,500 allowed by B, as shown above.

Examination Problem

Renters, Ltd., entered into a hire purchase agreement with Owners, Ltd., for the purchase of 100 surfboards over a period of three years from 1st January 19.1, by half-yearly instalments of £738·39, payable on the 30th June, and 31st December each year, the cash price being £40 per surfboard and the rate of interest at 6 per cent per annum with half-yearly rests.

On 1st January 19.2, after paying two instalments, Renters, Ltd., transferred their rights in the agreement to Assignees, Ltd., for a consideration of £1,000. Assignees, Ltd., paid this sum to Renters, Ltd., on 1st January 19.2, and the next instalment to Owners, Ltd., on the due date.

Show in the form of Journal Entries how the transaction should appear in the books of Assignees, Ltd., up to 30th June 19.2, when their financial year ended, writing off depreciation at the rate of 10 per cent per annum.

(Adapted from Institute of Chartered Accountants Final.)

Solution

JOURNAL

19.2		£p	£p
Jan. 1	Surfboards	3,744·67	
	Renters, Ltd.		1,000·00
	Owners, Ltd.		2,744·67
	Being the taking over of 100 Surfboards on hire purchase as per agreement.		
June 30	Interest	82·34	
	Owners, Ltd.		82·34
	Being Interest on £2,744·67 at 6 per cent per annum for six months to date, under hire purchase agreement.		
	Owners, Ltd.	738·39	
	Cash		738·39
	Being payment of instalment per agreement.		
	Depreciation	187·23	
	Surfboards		187·23
	Being Depreciation at 10 per cent per annum on £3,744·67 for six months to date.		

The Balance due to Owners, Ltd., on 1st January 19.2, is computed as follows:

	£p
Cash Value of Surfboards, 1st January 19.1	4,000·00
Interest, six months to 30th June 19.1 . . .	120·00
	4,120·00
Less Instalment paid	738·39
	3,381·61
Interest, six months to 31st December 19.1 . . .	101·45
	3,483·06
Less Instalment paid	738·39
Balance, 31st December 19.1	£2,744·67

SALE FOR DEFERRED PAYMENT BY INSTALMENTS

Hire Purchase and Purchase by instalments, although outwardly similar transactions as they both involve periodical payments to the vendor, are fundamentally different, the former being a transaction of hire with ultimate sale, the latter of immediate sale in which the price, instead of being paid in one sum, is spread over a period, interest being charged. In a deferred payment sale the vendor has no legal right to reclaim the goods upon default, his only remedy being to sue for the unpaid balance. It is therefore of great importance to make adequate provision against bad debts.

Summary of Difference between Hire Purchase and Purchase by Instalments

	H.P.	P.I.
Nature of Contract	Agreement of Hiring.	Agreement of Sale.
Governing Acts.	Hire Purchase Act 1965.[1]	None.
Passing of Title.	As agreed, usually on last payment or final nominal consideration.	When parties agree as with usual sale.
Rights of Deliveree	As laid down in Hire Purchase Act 1965;[1] briefly, may return goods without further payment, except for accrued instalments.	Unless seller defaults, goods not returnable and deliveree liable for price agreed, or reasonable price if not agreed.
Rights of Seller.	May recover goods if hirer is in default.	Can sue for price if buyer in default.
Rights of disposal	Hirer cannot hire out, sell, pledge nor assign entitling transferee to retain as against Hire Seller.	May dispose, and give good title to bona fide purchaser.
Advertising Goods.	Advertisements (Hire-purchase) Act 1967	As H.P.

Entries in the Vendor's Books

Subject to the different legal position, the entries are similar to those for ordinary sales; the cash value of the goods is credited to Sales Account and debited to the Personal Account of the purchaser. Interest at the agreed amount is credited to Interest Account and debited to the account of the purchaser as each instalment is paid; alternatively, as in the case of hire purchase transactions, a composite sum representing interest plus cash value may be debited to the account of the purchaser, who agrees to pay in equal instalments. In the Balance Sheet the balance of the Purchaser's Account is shown as a debtor for the amount owing. The entries are thus similar to those effected where hire purchase transactions are recorded as sales and interest charged; the entries in the books of the purchaser are also similar.

Note. In regard to rates of interest on hire purchase transactions the nominal rate is liable to mislead as the real rate is much in excess of the nominal rate, particularly where the payments are weekly or monthly.

The interest will be payable on the balance outstanding after the deposit has been paid, and the balance diminishes with each instalment paid.

The true rate (assuming equal instalments) is:

$$\frac{\text{Nominal rate} \times 2 \times \text{number of instalments}}{\text{number of instalments} + 1}$$

Assuming a 10 per cent interest rate for a purchase with 24 monthly (equal) instalments the true rate is:

$$\frac{10 \times 2 \times 24}{24 + 1} = \frac{480}{25} = 19 \cdot 2 \text{ per cent per annum.}$$

[1]These Acts will be superseded by the Consumer Credit Act 1974. See footnote, p. 2002.

CHAPTER 21

INCOME TAX IN RELATION TO ACCOUNTS

TAXATION is a branch of accounting work which is of such importance and scope that it is not possible in a work of accountancy to deal with it on adequate lines. It is, however, of importance to the student to understand the book-keeping entries relating to Income Tax and Corporation Tax[1]—many examination candidates have great difficulty in dealing with the purely accounting entries, even where the computed liability is given in the question. For intricate and detailed tax problems reference should be made to one of the many excellent works on taxation, but in order to assist in the understanding of the subject, a very broad and general outline of the main principles of Income Tax is given below.

INCOME TAX

Income Tax is an annual tax levied on the statutory income for the tax year (6th April to 5th April following). Statutory income is very rarely the actual income for the year, but is the income computed under the various Income Tax rules. The tax is levied (a) by *assessment* on income and profits according to classification under the Schedules listed below, and (b) by *deduction* from certain payments, e.g. annuities, the person making the deduction having to account for the tax to the Inland Revenue.

The Schedules

Schedule	Tax on	Levied on the
A[2]	Annual profits or gains from rents, ground annuals, feu-duties etc. relating to Land-lord property in U.K.	Landlord
B	Profits from woodlands in U.K. managed on a commercial basis and with a view to realisation of profits	Occupier
C	Certain income arising from public funds	Paying agent

---

[1] Corporation Tax relates to limited companies and is dealt with on p. 2353.

[2] Schedule A formerly applied to income from ownership of property in the U.K. but was repealed by the Finance Act 1963, for 1964–65 onwards. The Finance Act 1969, however, reintroduced Schedule A in place of Schedule D Case VIII, with the same rules applying to Schedule A as applied to Schedule D Case VIII, for Income Tax years of assessment and Corporation Tax accounting periods ending on and after 6th April 1970.

Schedule		Tax on	Levied on the
D		Annual profits or gains of	
	Case I	(a) Trade or business in U.K.	Persons making the profits or receiving the income, if resident in U.K. wherever the income arises; if non-resident, on income arising in U.K.
	II	(b) Profession or vocation in U.K.	
	III	Untaxed dividends and interest	
	IV / V	Certain foreign income	
	VI	Income not classified elsewhere	
	VII[1]	Short-term gains arising from the acquisition and disposal of certain assets	Individual, resident and ordinarily resident in U.K., making the capital gain
E		Income from employments, pensions, and offices	Recipient (through the system of P.A.Y.E.)
F		Amount of distributions plus amount of tax credits received from a limited company on and after 6th April 1973	Persons receiving dividends and certain other distributions from U.K. companies.

Basis of Assessment and Due Date of Payment.

The normal basis of assessment and due date of payment in respect of each of the current six Schedules is as follows:

Schedule		Normal basis of Assessment	Due date of Payment
A		Current year's profits or gains	One instalment on 1st January of year of assessment[2]
B		Current year's profit	Two instalments—1st on or before 1st January of year of assessment; 2nd on or before the following 1st July
C		Current year's income	Paying Agent deducts tax at time of payment and is required to remit tax to Inland Revenue through the Bank of England
D	Cases I–V	Preceding year's profits or gains	Cases I and II two instalments—1st on or before 1st January of year of assessment; 2nd on or before the following 1st July. Cases III to V one instalment on or before 1st January of year of assessment
	VI	Current year's income	One instalment on 1st January of year of assessment[3]
	VII	Current year's gains	One instalment on 1st January of year of assessment[3]

---

[1] Schedule D Case VII was abolished as from 6th April 1971 by the Finance Act 1971.

[2] A provisional assessment based on the preceding year's income is raised and this is payable on 1st January of the year of assessment. Any adjustment is made after the 5th April following.

[3] Payment is strictly due on 1st January of the actual year of assessment but as the actual income can only be ascertained after the end of the relevant fiscal year the amount, in practice, is payable immediately the liability is ascertained.

Schedule	Normal basis of Assessment	Due date of Payment
E	Current year's income	Collected under P.A.Y.E. system. Employer required to pay amount of tax deducted monthly to Collector of Taxes
F	Amounts of dividends or value of other distributions received for current year plus tax credits	Individual's tax liability is reduced by tax credits and thus, if individual is liable to basic rate of tax only, there is no further liability.

Payment of Tax. When Income tax is paid, the book-keeping entries are:

Debit Income Tax   Credit Bank

If it is preferred to enter the tax liability immediately on its ascertainment, the entries are:

Debit Income Tax   Credit Commissioners of Inland Revenue

and, on subsequent payment:

Debit Commissioners of Inland Revenue   Credit Bank

In the problem of ordinary accounting (excluding those questions comprising purely taxation matters), a knowledge of taxation is required in dealing with (1) annuities, mortgage interest, patent royalties, etc; (2) Loan interest; (3) dividends and interest received; (4) taxation in the accounts of limited companies,[1] and (5) partnerships.[2]

1. **Annuities, etc.** The Inland Revenue authorities, in order to facilitate the collection of tax, cause the payer of annuities (but not loan interest) and the like to deduct tax and account for it direct. This is simply part of the machinery of tax collection, the payer having to pay an increased assessment caused by the adding back to the profits of the particular payment, so that the true burden of the payer is unaffected.

Illustration 1

X has a gross profit of £2,000 from which he deducts general expenses £250, and an annuity of £100 which he has paid less tax of £40. Show how these items would be dealt with in the books of X, ignoring personal reliefs.

The book-keeping entries are:

1. Debit Annuity Account with the gross amount of annuity (Credit Annuitant).
2. Debit Annuitant with income tax (Credit Income Tax Account).
3. Debit Annuitant with cash (Credit Cash Account).

The Accounts would be thus:

ANNUITY

	£		£
Annuitant .	100	Profit and Loss Account	100

[1] This is dealt with on p. 2356.
[2] This is dealt with on p. 2226.

ANNUITANT

	£		£
Income Tax . . .	40	Annuity	100
Cash	60		
	£100		£100

INCOME TAX

	£		£
Commissioners of Inland		Annuitant . . .	40
Revenue . . .	700	Capital Account . .	660
	£700		£700

PROFIT AND LOSS ACCOUNT

	£		£
General Expenses . .	250	Gross Profit . . .	2,000
Annuity . . .	100		
Profit . . .	1,650		
	£2,000		£2,000

The adjusted profits for Income Tax purposes will be £1,650 + £100 = £1,750, making a tax liability at 40 per cent of £700. But, when paying the Annuity X deducted tax of £40 making the true burden of tax £700 − £40 = £660 (as shown by the Income Tax Account), which is 40 per cent of his net profit of £1,650.

If at the end of the accounting period the annuity remained unpaid, entry (3) would be postponed until the subsequent period when payment was made.

The personal account of the Annuitant may be dispensed with, the entries being made direct to Annuity Account as follows:

Debit Annuity (Gross)	Credit Income Tax
	Credit Cash
or Debit Annuity (Net Payment)	Credit Cash
Debit Annuity (Income Tax)	Credit Income Tax

If this is done, the following will take the place of the first three accounts in the above illustration:

ANNUITY

	£		£
Cash	60	Profit and Loss Account .	100
Income Tax . . .	40		
	£100		£100

INCOME TAX (includes)

					Annuity		£ 40

If at the end of the accounting period the annuity was unpaid, the item of £60 shown as Cash paid in the Annuity Account would not appear, and £60 would be brought down as an accrual (by debiting the account 'above the line' and crediting 'below the line') and shown as a liability in the Balance Sheet.

It happens frequently in examination papers that provision has to be made for a half year's liability for an annuity. This often causes confusion in the mind of the candidate. If the personal account is being used, the double entry will be:

Debit Annuity (Gross: ½ year)

Credit Income Tax (for Tax)
Credit Personal Account (for net liability, which will be shown in the Balance Sheet).

If there is no personal account, the accrual should be brought down in the Annuity Account, as described in the preceding paragraph.

The important points to remember are:

1. The *liability* must be shown either in the personal account or as an accrual in the Annuity Account, and

2. There will be a credit to Income Tax Account in respect of the income tax deductible (apart from exceptional circumstances), because the assessment (causing the debit to Income Tax Account) is based upon the adjusted profits after adding back the annuity, the tax deductible from such annuity being in effect a reduction of the inflated liability.

At the end of the year the Annuity Account will be closed off to Profit and Loss Account and will represent the *gross*, not net Annuity.

Illustration 2

In the accounts of L appears £120 net Annuity for the half year to 30th June 19.1, paid on that date. L's accounting period ends on 31st December 19.1, and provision is to be made for the half year's accrual of Annuity. Show Ledger Accounts, assuming no personal accounts opened and taking income tax at 40 per cent.

ANNUITY

19.1			£	19.1			£
June 30	Cash . . .		120	Dec. 31	Profit and Loss A/c .		400
	Income Tax . .		80				
Dec. 31	Annuity Accrued .	c/d	120				
	Income Tax . .		80				
			£400				£400
				19.2			
				Jan. 1	Balance	b/d	120

				19.1				£
				June 30	Annuity .			80
				Dec. 31	Annuity .			80

2. **Interest Payments.**[1] Interest paid on and after 6th April 1970 is generally paid gross, i.e. without deduction of Income Tax and is assessable on the recipient under Schedule D, Case III. Where, however, interest is paid by companies or local authorities or to a person ordinarily resident abroad the amount is payable net, i.e. under deduction of Income Tax at the basic rate ruling at the date of payment.

Interest payments concerning a business are generally deductible in arriving at profits assessable under Schedule D, Case I or II. Included as deductible are interest payments on a fixed debt whatever the purpose of borrowing. Interest charged to capital in the accounts of the payer is not deductible and interest payable to non-residents is deductible only where the rate of interest is at a reasonable commercial rate.

Interest payments on private borrowings have been considerably affected by the Finance Act 1974. Disregarding certain transitional provisions tax relief for interest paid on and after 27 March 1974 on private borrowings will be granted on loans related to the following:

1. Purchase or improvement of a property, caravan or house-boat occupied as the only or main residence of—

    (i) the borrower, or

    (ii) a divorced or separated spouse, whether the residence is owned solely by the borrower or jointly,

    (iii) the borrower's widowed, divorced or separated mother or mother-in-law, or any other relative incapacitated by old age or infirmity, who occupies the residence rent free and without any other consideration.

    (*Note.* Interest on option mortgages, bank overdrafts and credit cards is not deductible.)

2. Purchase of machinery or plant for use in a partnership business of which the borrower is an active member.

3. Purchase of machinery or plant (by the holder of an office or employment) for use in performing the duties of that office or employment.

4. Purchase of ordinary shares in or loan to a close company for use in its business provided that the borrower owns more than 5 per cent of the ordinary share capital of the relevant company and devotes the greater part of his time in the management of the relevant company's business.

5. Purchase of an interest in or loan to a partnership for use in its

---

[1] Legislation on allowable interest is fairly detailed and complex and is subject to frequent change. Coverage here is superficial and consequently for practical purposes reference should be made to either the enactments concerned or to an up-to-date authoritative taxation manual or text book.

business provided that the borrower is an active (and not a sleeping) member of the partnership.

6. Purchase of a life annuity where the borrower is 65 years or over and the loan is secured on the borrower's only or main residence.

7. Payment of British or Northern Irish capital transfer tax on the personal property of a deceased person which passes to the personal representatives who in fact borrowed the money to pay capital transfer tax on delivery of the Inland Revenue affidavit in order to obtain a grant or representation.

Where loans, privately borrowed, are used only partly for the purpose intended, relief is allowed only on a proportion of the interest corresponding to the proportion of the money borrowed which was so spent.

3. **Dividends[1] and Annuities[2] Received net**, i.e. after deduction of Tax at source. Where an annuity is paid it has been seen that the payer must account to the Inland Revenue for the Tax deducted by him from the payment. This is so even if the borrower is not liable for Income Tax. On the other hand, a dividend and an annuity will be received 'net', that is, after the deduction of Tax by the payer, so that such income must be deleted from the profits of a business for taxation purposes, as Tax has already been suffered. The amount to be deleted is that actually appearing in the accounts analogous to the adding back of an annuity paid (as was seen on p. 2104). If the income has been 'grossed up' there will be a corresponding debit for Tax on the Profit and Loss Account which will have to be added back, so that the gross dividend will be deleted and the Tax on it added back, giving the same result as if the amount had been entered in the accounts at the net figure. In the case of an individual, owing to personal reliefs, the recipient of the net dividend and annuity may obtain total repayment of relief according to circumstances; but this does not affect the treatment of the dividend and annuity in the accounts for the purposes of taxation computation on the business profits.

The book-keeping entries are:

Debit Cash (with net amount received ⎫
Debit Taxation (with Tax deducted) ⎬ Credit Dividends Received (gross)
                                    ⎭

Alternatively:

Debit Cash (with net amount received) Credit Dividends Received (net)

Debit Taxation (with Tax deducted) Credit Dividends Received (net)

[1] Under the imputation system of Corporation Tax in addition to receiving the cash amount of dividend a U.K. taxpayer receives a 'tax credit' (related to ACT paid by the distributing limited company) and the total of the actual dividend received plus the tax credit is assessable on the taxpayer; however, his tax liability is reduced by the tax credit. Consequently where a taxpayer is liable to basic rate tax only the tax credit meets that liability and there is no further liability on that dividend income. See p. 2357 for further details.

[2] Annuities could also include interest payments received from a limited company or local authority which are still paid net, i.e. after deduction of Income Tax.

The entries for Annuity received after deduction of Tax will be similar to the above. Where personal accounts are used, the entries will be reverse to those given on p. 2103.

It should be noted that (as with payments made after deduction of Tax) the correct figure to bring into the accounts is the *gross* amount of the dividend or annuity and not the net amount actually received.

Illustration 3

A has a gross profit of £2,000 from which is deducted £250 general expenses, and to which is added £60 dividend with a tax credit of £40. Show how these items would be dealt with in A's books, ignoring personal reliefs.

TAXATION

	£			£
Commissioners of Inland Revenue	700	Capital Account		740
Tax credit on dividend	40			
	£740			£740

DIVIDENDS RECEIVED

	£			£
Profit and Loss Account	100	Cash		60
		Tax credit		40
	£100			£100

COMMISSIONERS OF INLAND REVENUE

				£
		Taxation		740

PROFIT and LOSS ACCOUNT

	£			£
General Expenses	250	Gross Profit		2,000
Net Profit	1,850	Dividend		100
	£2,100			£2,100

The adjusted profits for taxation purposes will be £1,850 less £100 = £1,750, making an Income Tax liability at 40 per cent of £700. A has, however, already suffered Tax of £40 deducted from his dividends, so that his true Tax burden is £740 (as shown by the Taxation Account) which is equal to 40 per cent his net profit of £1,850.

(3a) **Dividends and Interest Received Gross (Case III, Schedule D).** Dividends are receivable gross in the following cases:

1. On certain Government securities, e.g. $3\frac{1}{2}$ per cent War Loan.

2. On all Government securities on the National Savings Stock Register.

3. On Government securities on the Bank of England Register, provided that the annual interest does not exceed £5.

4. Bank interest.

5. Interest paid by Hire Purchase Finance Houses.

The matter is simply adjusted by deletion from the adjusted profits of the business and Income Tax paid on the basis of the income up to the 5th April preceding the year of assessment; so that, where the accounting period is not coincident with the Income Tax year, the figure deleted from the accounts may not correspond with the amount assessed, as in the first case the deletion may be in respect of interest for the year to (say) 31st October, whilst the assessment will be based upon the income to the 5th April, but over a period the same total assessment will generally result. The book-keeping entries are:

Debit Cash   Credit Dividends or Interest Received (with amount received)

Since there will be an assessment under Sch. D, Case III in respect of the income, the necessary provision should be made by debiting Income Tax Account and crediting Commissioners of Inland Revenue, or by debiting Income Tax Account, 'above the line' and crediting 'below the line'. When the Income Tax is paid, Income Tax (or Commissioners) will be debited and Cash credited.

It may here be noted that a 'tax free' or 'free of tax' dividend is not the same as a dividend received gross. It is merely an alternative although misleading expression for a dividend after allowing for Advance Corporation Tax. Thus, a dividend of £120 'free of tax' is the same, taking ACT at 40 per cent, as a gross dividend of £200 with a tax credit of £80. Such dividends must, therefore, be grossed up and treated in the manner described in section (3).

Illustration 4

Write up the undermentioned transactions of A:

Jan. 3. Payment of 1st instalment of Income Tax Schedule D Case I, liability for 19.1–19.2 is £480.
    5. Received interest on $2\frac{1}{2}$ per cent Consols (National Savings Stock Register) of £20.
Mar. 1. Paid Annuity of £100 less tax.
   10. Received year's Dividend of £42.
Apr. 5. Received Interest on $2\frac{1}{2}$ per cent Consols of £20.
     Provide for Income Tax as on 5th April, assuming liability of taxpayer at 40 per cent. Work to the nearest £.

CASH BOOK

19.2		£	19.2		£
Jan. 5	Annuity, Interest and Dividend Account: one quarter's interest on $2\frac{1}{2}$ per cent Consols (Gross)	20	Jan. 3	Commissioners of Inland Revenue Income Tax Sch. D Case I 19.1–19.2 1st instalment $\frac{1}{2} \times £480$	240
Mar. 10	Annuity, Interest and dividend Account: dividend on shares . £70 Less tax credit . 28	42	Mar. 1	Annuity . . . £100 Less tax . . 40	60
Apr. 5	Annuity, Interest and Dividend Account: one quarter's interest on $2\frac{1}{2}$ per cent Consols (Gross)	20			

ANNUITY, INTEREST AND DIVIDEND

19.2		£	19.2		£
Mar. 1	Cash: Annuity to date £100 Less tax . 40	60	Jan. 5	Cash: $2\frac{1}{2}$ per cent Consols quarter's Interest .	20
	Income Tax Account	40	Mar. 10	Cash: Dividend on shares . . £70 Less tax credit 28	42
	Profit and Loss Account .	10		Income Tax Account .	28
			Apr. 5	Cash: $2\frac{1}{2}$ per cent Consols quarter's interest .	20
		£110			£110

INCOME TAX

19.2			£	19.2			£
Jan. 3	Cash—Sch. D. Case I, 19.1–19.2 1st instalment . . .		240	Mar. 1	Annuity		40
Mar. 10	Dividend on shares .		28		Drawings Account . .		484
Apr. 5	Balance: 2nd Instalment of Sch. D Case I 19.1–19.2 . . .	c/d	240				
	[1]Balance: Sch. D Case III 19.1–19.2 . .	c/d	16				
			£524				£524
				Apr. 6	Balance: Sch. D. Case I .	b/d	240
					Balance: Sch. D. Case III .	b/d	16

[1] Assumed that the income on the $2\frac{1}{2}$ per cent Consols was first received on 5th January, 19.2, Income Tax thereon being £40 at 40% = £16).

CHAPTER 22

PARTNERSHIP ACCOUNTS

Section A. General Principles and Division of Profits

It is not within the scope of this work to attempt a complete analysis of Partnership Law, but to consider it only in so far as it relates to Accounting. Partnership Accounts call for a knowledge of law as laid down in the Partnership Act 1890, and in decided Cases, but the principles of accounting are basically similar to those applying to a sole trader.

The following legal points relating to partnership have a direct bearing upon accounting and are of extreme importance:

1. The definition of Partnership as laid down in the Act is: *'Partnership is the relation which subsists between persons carrying on a business in common with a view of profit.'*[1]

2. No statutory books are required, nor is any creditor or other outside person entitled to inspect the partnership accounts, except by the consent of the partners, nor are accounts required to be filed with any Government department, nor are any formal returns necessary, except:

(*a*) a Limited Partnership must be registered;

(*b*) a firm name which does not consist of the true surnames of all the partners without any addition except the Christian names or the initials or recognized abbreviation, must be registered under the Registration of Business Names Act 1916;[2]

(*c*) returns required by and right of inspection of accounts given to officials of:

(i) Customs and Excise in respect of Value Added Tax.

(ii) the Inland Revenue under the system of P.A.Y.E.

In practice accounts will have to be submitted to the Inland Revenue in support of the partners' Income Tax Returns.

3. The partners may make such arrangements as they wish for the purpose of regulating the rights, duties, and powers as between themselves.

4. The arrangements may be formulated in a deed; or in a written document signed by the partners; or even orally. In addition there may be an implied variation of the original agreement ascertainable by a course of dealing.

---

[1] By Sect. 434 of the Companies Act 1948, no more than twenty persons are permitted to be associated in partnership. Sect. 119 of the Companies Act 1967, permits banking partnerships to have a maximum of twenty members instead of ten as previously. Sect. 120 of the 1967 Act allows unlimited membership to partnerships of Solicitors, Accountants (recognized or authorized by the Department of Trade and Industry), members of a recognized stock exchange or to other bodies which may be specified by the Department of Trade and Industry provided that each member of such partnership is a member of a relevant professional body or has been approved by the Department of Trade and Industry.

[2] The Act applies similarly to an individual carrying on a business.

It should be noted that if any matter is not dealt with in the agreement, the relevant provisions of the Partnership Act 1890 will apply. It is quite possible, though in most cases not advisable, for a partnership to exist without any agreement (except merely that the parties have agreed to work in partnership, and to be bound only by the provisions of the Act). Variation of an agreement, by a course of dealing is frequently met with, e.g. if the partnership agreement provides that a partner shall be permitted to withdraw £8,000 yearly, and with consent of the other partner he withdraws £10,000, the original agreement to this extent is altered by a course of dealing.

The accounting provisions of the Act, which must be applied in working all partnership problems, unless information to the contrary is given, are:

Sect. 19. The mutual rights and duties of partners, whether ascertained by agreement or defined by this Act, may be varied by the consent of all partners, and such consent may be either express or inferred from a course of dealing.

Sect. 24. The interests of the partners in the partnership property and their rights and duties in relation to the partnership shall be determined, *subject to any agreement express or implied*, between the partners, by the following rules:

1. All the partners are entitled to share equally in the capital and profits of the business, and must contribute equally towards the losses, whether of capital or otherwise, sustained by the firm.

2. The firm must indemnify every partner in respect of payments made and personal liabilities incurred by him:

   (a) In the ordinary and proper conduct of the business of the firm; or
   (b) In or about anything necessarily done for the preservation of the business or property of the firm.

3. A partner making, for the purpose of the partnership, any actual payment or advance beyond the amount of capital which he has agreed to subscribe, is entitled to interest at the rate of 5 per cent per annum from the date of the payment or advance.

4. A partner is not entitled, before the ascertainment of profits, to interest on the capital subscribed by him; even if interest on capital is agreed upon, it ceases on dissolution (*Watney* v. *Wells*).

5. Every partner may take part in the management of the partnership business.

6. No partner shall be entitled to remuneration for acting in the partnership business.

7. No person may be introduced as a partner without the consent of all existing partners.

8. All differences arising as to ordinary matters connected with the partnership business may be decided by a majority of the partners, but no change may be made in the nature of the partnership business without consent of all existing partners.

9. The partnership books are to be kept at the place of business of the partnership (or the principal place, if there is more than one), and every partner may, when he thinks fit, have access to and inspect and copy any of them.

As far as the accounts are concerned, the most important clauses of the above are (1), (3), (4), and (6), and all students must obtain a thorough grasp of them.

In reference to (3), no interest (unless agreed upon) is chargeable to a partner for loans or advances by the firm to him.

Sect. 42. This section deals with the right of a retiring partner to receive interest or share in the profits made after the dissolution of the partnership:

1. Where any member of a firm has died or otherwise ceased to be a partner, and the surviving or continuing partners carry on the business of the firm with its capital or assets without any final settlement of accounts as between the firm and the outgoing partner or his estate, then, in the absence of any agreement to the contrary, the outgoing partner or his estate is entitled at the option of himself or his representatives to such share of the profits made since the dissolution as the **Court** may find to be attributable to the use of his share of the partnership ASSETS, *or* to interest at the rate of 5 per cent per annum on the amount of his share of the partnership ASSETS.

2. Provided that where, by the partnership contract, an option is given to surviving or continuing partners to purchase the interest of a deceased or outgoing partner, and the option is duly exercised, the estate of the deceased partner, or outgoing partner or his estate, as the case may be, is not entitled to any further or other share of profits; but, if any partner assuming to act in exercise of the option does not in all material respects comply with the terms thereof, he is liable to account under the foregoing provisions of this section.

Where an account of the profits is ordered, the Court may make an allowance to the continuing partner for carrying on the business.

Even if the partnership agreement provides that the share of an outgoing partner should be ascertained by reference to the next annual account, the assets of the firm, in the absence of evidence or any uniform usage to the contrary, must be taken at their **fair value** at the date of the account, and not at the value appearing in the books (*Cruikshank* v. *Sutherland*). This includes the asset goodwill, and may involve a complete revaluation (up or down) of assets and liabilities. In other words, the book values of assets and liabilities are ignored, and their fair values substituted. This does not necessarily involve permanent alterations of values in the books, as will be shown later; but the revised figures form the basis of computing the share of the outgoing partner.

Sect. 43. *Subject to any agreement between the partners*, the amount due from surviving or continuing partners to an outgoing partner, or the representatives of a deceased partner in respect of the outgoing or deceased partner's share, is a debt accruing at the date of the dissolution or death. Thus, the liability of the surviving or continuing partners will depend on the partnership agreement, but otherwise the amount due to the retiring partner is a debt accruing at the date of dissolution (or death), and such is the relevant date for the purpose of the Law Reform (Limitation of Actions, etc.) Act 1954.

Sect. 44 of the Act deals with the rules for the distribution of the assets on dissolution, both when there is a surplus and when there is a deficiency:

(a) Losses, including losses and deficiencies of capital, shall be paid first out of profits, next out of capital, and lastly, if necessary, by the partners individually in the proportion in which they were entitled to share profits.

(b) The assets of the firm including the sums, if any, contributed by the partners to make up losses or deficiencies of capital, shall be applied in the following manner and order:

(i) In paying the debts and liabilities of the firm to persons who are not partners therein.

(ii) In paying to each partner rateably what is due from the firm to him for *advances* as distinguished from capital.

(iii) In paying to each partner rateably what is due from the firm to him in respect of capital.

(iv) The ultimate residue, if any, shall be divided among the partners in the proportion in which profits are divisible.

It should be observed that an advance by the firm to the partner is a debt which the latter must either discharge in cash, or which (if no question of deficiency of assets arises) may be set off against the capital and profits due to such partner. In a dissolution, **costs of dissolution** must be met before moneys are available for partners.

Although the partnership agreement may provide an alternative method of distribution between the partners themselves, it cannot take away the rights of third parties to be paid in due priority.

Where, after a dissolution one of the partners has, after the final realization of assets and part settlement of liabilities, a deficiency of capital which he is unable wholly to make good, such deficiency is a loss which must be borne by the partners as laid down in *Garner* v. *Murray*, a decision which has received much adverse criticism. It was laid down in this case that such loss must be borne by the solvent partners, not as they share ordinary profits and losses, but in proportion to their **last agreed capitals.** The interpretation of 'last agreed capitals' often causes difficulty. The matter is dealt with in detail in Section H. (pp. 22158 *et seq.*)

The Limited Partnership Act 1907. There are no provisions in this Act relating to the actual book entries, the most important point being, for the purpose of this book, the definition of a limited partner.

This is defined by Sect. 4 (2) of the Limited Partnership Act 1907, as:

A limited partnership shall not consist, in the case of a partnership carrying on the business of banking, of more than ten persons, and in the case of any other partnership, of more than twenty persons, and must consist of one or more persons called general partners, who shall be liable for all debts and obligations of the firm, and one or more persons to be called limited partners, who shall at the time of entering into such partnership contribute thereto a sum or sums as capital or property valued at a stated amount, and who shall not be liable for the debts or obligations of the firm beyond the amount so contributed.

Sect. 121 of the Companies Act 1967, has modified Sect. 4 (2) by permitting unlimited membership to partnerships of solicitors, accountants and stockbrokers.

Sect. 4 (3) A limited partner shall not during the continuance of the partnership, either directly or indirectly, draw out or receive back any part of his contribution, and if he does so draw out or receive back any such part, shall be liable for the debts and obligations of the firm up to the amount so drawn out or received back.

(4) A body corporate may be a limited partner.

The essential differences between a general partnership and a limited partnership should be learnt from a legal textbook, and particular attention should be paid to the following matters:

(i) Registration of the limited partnership (no limited partnership exists UNTIL REGISTRATION).

(ii) Registration of the changes in personnel.

(iii) Effect of lunacy or death of limited partner.

(iv) Effect of assignment by limited partner.

(v) Right of inspection of books by limited partner.

(vi) Right of the limited partner to ADVISE, but not to participate in the MANAGEMENT.

Summary. Summarized, the chief legal points appropriate to partnership accounting may be stated thus:

1. Partners are entitled to share profits equally, and must likewise bear losses equally irrespective of the amount of their respective Capital Accounts, unless otherwise agreed.

2. Partners are entitled neither to interest on capital nor to salaries, unless otherwise agreed.

3. Partners who advance money (or other assets) beyond the amount of their capitals *are* entitled to charge interest thereon, at the rate of 5 per cent per annum, unless otherwise agreed.

4. No interest is charged to partners in respect of their drawings (or advances by the firm), unless otherwise agreed.

5. Any increase or decrease in the value of an asset or liability is, as the case may be, a profit or loss, and all partners participate in the profit or bear the loss equally in the absence of agreement, or otherwise as the agreement provides.

6. A partnership agreement may be constituted (a) by deed, (b) by writing, (c) by word of mouth. It may be varied by a COURSE of DEALING.

7. Generally, an outgoing partner is entitled to have his proper share of the **net** assets (i.e. assets less liabilities), including GOODWILL, as they exist at the date of his retirement, quite apart from the values placed on them in the books. This may involve a revaluation and readjustment of accounts.

8. Although in proper cases a partner is entitled to be indemnified for expenses properly incurred, it must be remembered that he will inevitably bear a proportion of such expenses, so that consequently such indemnity is in reality only partial.

9. Finally, the student should thoroughly assimilate Sects. 19, 24, 42, and 44 of the Partnership Act 1890.

Partnership Agreement

In the majority of instances partners will have drawn up a written agreement, the exact terms of which will depend upon circumstances, but, generally speaking, provision will be made to cover the undermentioned points:

1. The firm name and the business to be carried on under that name.
2. Business address or addresses.
3. Commencement and duration of the partnership.
4. Whether, and in what circumstances, notice of retirement can be given by a partner.
5. The Capital (whether fixed or otherwise) and the contribution of each partner.
6. Provision for further capital and loans by partners to the firm.
7. Partners' Drawings.
8. Interest on Capital, loans, drawings and Current Accounts.
9. Partners' Salaries, commissions and other remuneration.
10. Division of profits and losses.
11. The keeping of proper books of account, inspection and audit. Bank Accounts.
12. The date to which accounts are to be drawn up and the period of accounts. Signatures of partners to Balance Sheets.
13. Conduct, powers and duties of partners.
14. Income Tax.
15. Provision that death or retirement of a partner shall not, as regards the remaining partners, dissolve the partnership.
16. Dissolution and Winding Up provisions with special regard to the valuation of goodwill. Manner and date of payment of the share due to a deceased or retired partner, and manner in which such moneys may be provided for during the partnership, e.g. Assurance policies.
17. Nomination by partners of successors and the introduction of sons and other near relatives.
18. Formulae for valuation of assets (and liabilities), including goodwill, on the death or retirement of a partner; whether, if a partner retires, as distinct from his decease, he is entitled to *any* goodwill.
19. Provision in exceptional and serious circumstances for partners to expel an offending partner.

20. Provision for the position arising through absence on account of ill-health or other justifiable cause.

21. Provision for the position arising on the sale of the business to a limited company.

22. The settlement of disputes, e.g. arbitration.

Partnership Accounts

Upon commencement of the study of partnership accounts a student usually approaches it under the impression that a departure from the ordinary principles of book-keeping is entailed. Such is not the case; for, allowing for different circumstances that must necessarily arise in partnership accounts as compared with sole traders' accounts, a student will follow in the ordinary way the elementary principles he has already acquired, e.g. the closing of the Profit and Loss Account involves a debit to that account and a credit to Capital. As, however, there will be more than one participant in the profits and more than one Capital Account, it is necessary to know in what ratio the profits are shared, so that each partner's Capital Account may be credited with the appropriate share.

In order that the partners may know what is the amount of their respective interest in the firm, it is clearly of the greatest importance that a proper system of accounting should be in force.

It will be apparent that most of the problems peculiar to partnership accounts have some connection with the ascertainment of the amount of each partner's share in the profits and in the assets, both during the continuance of the partnership and upon death or dissolution. As the student proceeds in his study he will realize that most of the problems have some relation to these points. In the elucidation of such problems— some of which are rather involved in their detail—there will be involved the application of partnership law, the principles of ordinary arithmetic, and the practice of business men.

The following decided cases which have a bearing on the accounts should be noted:

1. Persons who share net profits and losses are *prima facie* partners (*Walker* v. *Hirsch*).

2. Although interest on Capitals has been agreed upon, it ceases on dissolution (*Watney* v. *Wells*).

3. Unless the Partnership agreement forbids, a partner may carry on a non-competing business so long as he does not represent it to be that of the firm, notwithstanding that the knowledge he possesses as a partner may, and his connection with the firm will, be of material use in his other business (*Aas* v. *Benham*). Further it may even be a *similar* business provided that it is non-competitive (*Trimble and Bennett* v. *Goldberg*).

4. An assignee of a partner's share in a partnership will be bound by any *bona fide* agreement between the partners and would not be able to object to the remaining partners taking a salary on account of the extra work falling upon them. (*Garwood* v. *Poynter*).

5. Goodwill, although omitted from a Balance Sheet, must be taken into account on dissolution and every partner is entitled to have it sold for the benefit of *all* the partners. (*Turner* v. *Major*.)

6. The omission of goodwill from the books is not to be regarded as a 'course of dealing' so as to prevent its being dealt with as a partnership asset for the common benefit of all the partners. (*Barrow* v. *Barrow*.) If, however, the Partnership Articles provide that the last annual account shall be the *final* account on dissolution, this will bind, in the absence of fraud, all the partners. (*Stewart* v. *Gladstone*.)

7. Where, under Section 42, the option to take profits is exercised, the Court will usually grant reasonable remuneration to the continuing partners (*Brown* v. *de Tastet*), unless they themselves are the personal representatives of the deceased partner. (*Stocken* v. *Dawson*.)

8. Where a partner's estate is entitled to goodwill on *death* but a partner is not so entitled on terminating the partnership by *notice*, and death occurs *after* notice has been given but *before* it reaches the firm, the dissolution is deemed to arise by *death* and not by notice, so that goodwill is payable. (*McLeod* v. *Dowling*.)

9. Partnership, except where agreed otherwise, to be dissolved as respects all partners by the death or bankruptcy of *any* partner (Sect. 33).

Partners' Accounts

The normal 'proprietorship' accounts in a partnership will be (*a*) Capital, (*b*) Current, (*c*) Drawings accounts for EACH partner; whilst in addition, circumstances may call for (*d*) Interest accounts, and (*e*) Loan accounts for one or more partners.

Each account will be dealt with separately.

(*a*) **Capital Account.** The amounts contributed by each partner, whether in cash or in other assets, will be credited to his Capital Account, and unless partners agree otherwise, this account remains intact during the continuance of the partnership, as the presumption in partnership law is that the Capital Account of each partner is **fixed**, thus involving the burden on each partner to restore his capital to its original level where his drawings exceed his share of profits, or where losses occur or losses are accompanied by drawings. This restoration is rarely made, as a separate account—described as a Current Account—is opened in respect of each partner to record the position of each partner *vis-à-vis* the firm otherwise than in relation to his capital. Yet, if partners are agreed, profits, losses and drawings may be entered in the Capital Accounts without the utilization of the Current Accounts. It is, however, important to remember that if a partner makes an advance to the firm, whether by way of money or otherwise, the amount should be credited to that partner's Loan Account, as such advance attracts interest at the rate of 5 per cent per annum, unless the partners otherwise agree.

Should the partners decide upon the employment of a Capital Account only for each partner it will usually contain items as illustrated below:

A. JOHNSON CAPITAL

19..			£	19..			£
June 30	Cash (Drawings) .		400	Jan. 1	Balance	b/d	2,000
	(Cr. Cash)			Dec. 31	Interest on Capital .		100
	Cash (Drawings) .		300		(Dr. Profit and Loss)[1]		
	(Cr. Cash)				Profit and Loss Account:		
Dec. 31	Interest on Drawings[2]		15		½ share of Profits . .		750
	(Cr. Profit and Loss)[1]				(Dr. Profit and Loss)[1]		
	Balance	c/d	2,135				
			£2,850				£2,850
			·	19..			
				Jan. 1	Balance	b/d	2,135

[1] Strictly Profit and Loss Appropriation Account.
[2] See note 1, p. 2210.

The above illustration assumes that partners are entitled to interest at 5 per cent per annum on their capitals as at the beginning of the year, and are charged at the same rate of interest on drawings from the date of the withdrawal to the end of the accounting period. If the items are numerous, interest will be computed by means of an additional column on the lines of an account current.

In the following year, interest on capital will be calculated on the 'merged' balance £2,135.

(b) **Current Account.** In order to preserve the original capital intact, subject to further agreed contributions and special withdrawals of capital, a separate account may be employed. This is termed a Current Account, and will contain on the debit side drawings and interest on drawings (if any), and on the credit side interest on capital (if any), and the two items below:

1. Opening and closing balance which may be debit or credit.
2. Transfers from Profit and Loss Account which will be (a) debit for loss, and (b) credit for profit.

Interest may also be debited or credited on the balance of the Current Account itself.

Illustration 1

Using the same facts as shown in the preceding illustration, the position of A. Johnson, assuming £500 appears as the balance of his Current Account, will be recorded as follows:

A. JOHNSON CAPITAL

				19..			£
				Jan. 1	Balance	b/d	1,500

A. Johnson Current Account

19..				£	19..				b/d	£
June 30	Drawings		.	400	Jan. 1	Balance . . .	.	.	b/d	500
Aug. 31	,,		.	300	Dec. 31	Interest on Capital	.			75[2]
Dec. 31	Interest on Drawings		.	15[1]		Interest on Current				
	Balance .	.	c/d	635		Account	.	.		25[3]
						Profit and Loss Account:				
						½ share of Profits .		.		750
				£1,350						£1,350
					19..					
					Jan. 1	Balance .	.	.	b/d	635

		£
[1] £400 at 5% per annum for 6 months (1st July to 31st Dec.) . . .		£10
£300 at 5% per annum for 4 months (1st Sept. to 31st Dec.) . .		5
		15
[2] £1,500 at 5% per annum for 12 months (1st Jan. to 31st Dec.) . .		75
[3] £500 at 5% per annum for 12 months (1st Jan. to 31st Dec.) . . .		25

The combined balances are £2,135, as in the preceding illustration. This must be so because the interest allowed is upon the Capital (£1,500) and the Current Account (£500). It must be noted that there would be no interest on either account unless the partners so agreed.

(c) **Drawings Account.** This account will be almost self-explanatory inasmuch as partners may regularly withdraw sums from the business, and as a result, the Current Account would become congested with a large number of entries. By opening a Drawings Account (with an interest calculation column if necessary) all the detailed withdrawals may be recorded in this account, the total thereof being transferred to the debit of the Current Account in the one sum at the end of the accounting period; whilst the interest thereon (if any) will be debited (i) to Current Account and credited to Profit and Loss Account, or (ii) to Drawings Account and transferred in one figure with the drawings to the debit of the Current Account, or (iii) debited to the partner's Interest Account.

(d) **Interest Account.** Where it is desired to have separately recorded the interest charged and credited to each partner an Interest Account is opened in the name of each partner. The entries for interest due to the partner are: debit Profit and Loss Account, and credit the partner's Interest Account; whilst the opposite entries are made for interest due by the partner. The balance of the account will be transferred to the partner's Current Account.

Again, the student is reminded that there is no interest to or against a partner except (i) in respect of advances by a partner, or (ii) by AGREEMENT.

Illustration 2

In reference to the preceding example, Johnson's accounts will, utilizing Interest and Drawings Accounts, appear thus:

A. Johnson Capital

				19..			£
				Jan. 1	Balance	b/d	1,500

A. Johnson Current Account

19..				£	19..			£
Dec. 31	Drawings . . .	c/d	700	Jan. 1	Balance . . .		500
	Balance		635	Dec. 31	Interest Account . .		85
					Profit and Loss Account:		
					½ share of Profits .		750
			£1,335				£1,335
				19..			
				Jan. 1	Balance	b/d	635

A. Johnson Interest

19..			£	19..			£
Dec. 31	Interest on Drawings		15	Dec. 31	Interest on Capital		
	Current Account .		85		Account . .		75
					Interest on Current		
					Account . .		25
			£100				£100

A. Johnson Drawings

			Mos.	Interest	Principal				Mos.	Interest	Principal
19..				£	£	19..				£	£
June 30	Cash . .		6	10	400	Dec. 31	Current				
Aug. 31	,, . .		4	5	300		Account				700
							Interest, per				
							contra			15	
				£15	£700					£15	£700

It should be remembered that the interest column in the Drawings Account is purely for calculation purposes, and the double entry must be completed by crediting Profit and Loss Account direct, or by crediting Interest on Drawings Account, and subsequently transferring the balance of this account to the credit of Profit and Loss Account.

(e) **Loan Account.** This account calls for no special comment, except that the interest thereon is treated usually like interest on capital and on drawings by the appropriate entries into the Current Account or Interest Account of the partner making the advance.

Withdrawal of Goods. It should be noted that where a partner withdraws goods, his Current Account or Capital Account, as the case may be, will be debited and Purchases Account credited, as it is usual to permit the withdrawal at cost price.[1]

Two other matters require treatment at this stage, viz. (a) Partners' Salaries, and (b) Interest on Capital.

(a) **Partners' Salaries.** Circumstances frequently arise in partnership affairs necessitating the allowance to a partner of an extra share in the profits of the firm because of extraordinary circumstances, e.g. absence of another partner. This is often effected by giving the partner upon whom the additional burden has fallen a salary. This may be dealt with in any of the following ways:

1. If the salary is paid in cash the double entry is similar to that for any salary, i.e. debit partner's Salary Account and credit cash, the balance on the former account being transferred to the Profit and Loss Appropriation Account at the end of the year.

2. Where the partner withdraws amounts at irregular intervals, the total salary should be debited to Profit and Loss Appropriation Account and credited to the partner's Salary Account, and on withdrawal of the whole or part, the partner's Salary Account should be debited and cash credited.

In the latter instance, interest may or may not be allowed on the balance standing to the credit of partners' Salary Accounts. Any balance standing on a partner's Salary Account at the end of the year should be transferred to either his Current or his Drawings Account.

(b) **Interest on Capital.** Save by certain statutes and certain exceptional rules of equity, a debt does not carry interest, so that in partnership no partner is entitled to, nor is *prima facie* bound to be charged with, interest unless there is an advance by the partner, or an agreement permitting interest. But in order to give a partner a 'return' for his investment an agreement is usually made to allow interest on capital, the justice of which is apparent if the capital contributions are highly disproportionate, e.g. where there are two partners, one of whom contributes capital to the extent of £10,000, and another of only £500. This adjustment is, however, an APPROPRIATION of profits—it represents such share of the profits as is attributable to the use of capital, and, in fact, forms a SPECIAL division of profits. Thus, even assuming profits and losses are shared equally, if capitals are UNEQUAL and interest on capital is provided for, the partners in reality do not share all the profits and losses equally because the first 'share' thereof depends on capitals and must be divided in capital ratios, and only the **residue** can properly be considered available for division in

---

[1] For tax purposes, however, the decision laid down in *Sharkey* v. *Wernher* requires the adding back to profit of goods withdrawn at *retail* price. It is worth noting that in a later case, *Mason* v. *Innes*, which concerned the gift of the copyright from a novel, it was decided that professional men do not, in fact, have stock in trade and consequently the principle upheld in *Sharkey* v. *Wernher* did not apply thereto. It was contended, as an example, that if an artist painted a picture and either gifted it to someone or destroyed it, it was absurd to tax the artist on a notional profit. Note also, however, that an asset gifted or destroyed constitutes a disposal for Capital Gains Tax purposes and therefore the asset involved requires to be valued to ascertain any taxable gain arising.

equal shares: the smaller this residue, the more does the true profit-sharing ratio depart from an equal-sharing basis.

If interest on capital is not charged, the real division of the profit of the partnership will not be affected if both the capital and profit-sharing ratios are equal, or the ratios of both capital and profit-sharing are the same; for example, if A and B share profits equally and their capitals are equal; or they share profits in the ratio of, say, 3:2 and their capitals are in the ratio of 3:2 the division of the profit is the same whether interest on capital is charged or not.

If, however, such a situation does not exist, the omission of the charge for interest on capital will have the following effect:

Capitals	Profits	Effect
Equal	Unequal	Partner with *smaller* share of profit loses.
Unequal	Equal	Partner with *larger* capital loses.
Unequal	Unequal	Depends on proportion in which the partners share profits and the amount of capitals of each partner [e.g. if the inequality is proportionably the same (say profit-sharing 2:1 and capitals in like ratio, say £6,000 and £3,000). No effect adverse or beneficial to a partner].

Illustration 3

A and B are partners with capitals of £5,000 and £600 respectively. The partnership agreement provides for 5 per cent interest on capital, and for the balance of profits to be shared equally. The trading profits are £5,000 for the year.

Show the distribution of profits as between the partners, both in the ordinary form of account to be headed Profit and Loss Appropriation Account, and in statement form.

The distribution will be:

	£	£
Interest on Capital:		
A—5% on £5,000	250	
B—5% on £600	30	
		280
Balance of Profits:		
A—½ of £4,720	2,360	
B—½ of £4,720	2,360	
		4,720
Total		£5,000

PROFIT AND LOSS APPROPRIATION ACCOUNT

	£	£			£
Interest on Capital			Balance . b/d		5,000
A	250				
B	30				
		280			
Balance of Profits					
A—½	2,360				
B—½	2,360	4,720			
		£5,000			£5,000

Where there are not sufficient profits to cover interest on capital, the general opinion is that in the absence of a clear agreement to the contrary, the partners are entitled only to such interest as will just absorb the profits. Otherwise, provision for the full interest would involve the firm in a loss.

Illustration 4

A and B are partners with capitals of £3,000 and £1,000. They agree to allow interest on capital at the rate of 5 per cent per annum, and to share profits and losses equally. The profits for the year before charging their interest are £160. Show the Profit and Loss Appropriation Account.

PROFIT AND LOSS APPROPRIATION ACCOUNT

	£			£
Interest on Capital—		Balance . . b/d		160
A . . £120				
B . . 40				
	160			
	£160			£160

Otherwise,

PROFIT AND LOSS APPROPRIATION ACCOUNT

	£			£
Interest on Capital—			b/d	160
A . . £150		Loss—		
B . . 50		A—½ . £20		
	200	B—½ 20		
				40
	£200			£200

The following illustration embodies the principles outlined so far.

Illustration 5

J. Caesar and M. Antony are in partnership sharing profits and losses equally. J. Caesar's capital is £5,000; M. Antony's, £1,000. M. Antony is entitled to be *paid* a partnership salary of £1,300 per annum; J. Caesar, in addition to the above, made a loan to the firm of £2,000 (before 1st January 19..) on which interest is to be allowed at 5 per cent per annum. Profits for the year to 31st December 19.., were £4,000, *after* charging up salary, interest on loans and interest on drawings. Interest at 10 per cent per annum is to be charged on drawings, which were as follows:

	J. Caesar	M. Antony
19..	£	£
Mar. 31	340	220
June 30	460	310
Sept. 30	340	320
Dec. 31	340	560

Show the partners' Capital Accounts, Loan Accounts, Current Accounts, and Drawings Accounts.

CAPITAL

		J. Caesar	M. Antony				J. Caesar	M. Antony
				19.. Jan. 1	Balances	b/d	£ 5,000	£ 1,000

J. CAESAR—LOAN

				19.. Jan. 1	Balance	b/d		£ 2,000

(See also following pages.)

The average due date method of computing interest might be employed:

J. Caesar—Interest on Drawings

$$\begin{array}{ccc} \pounds & \text{Mos.} & \pounds \\ 340\times9= & & 3,060 \\ 460\times6= & & 2,760 \\ 340\times3= & & 1,020 \\ \hline \pounds1,140 & & \pounds6,840 \end{array}$$

∴ Average date of drawings $\dfrac{6,840}{1,140}$ = 6 months from 31st Dec. = 30th June.

Interest on £1,140 for 6 months at 10% per annum = £57.

The calculation for M. Antony will be made similarly.

J. CAESAR—DRAWINGS

19..		Mos.	Int. £	£	19..				£
Mar. 31	Cash.	9	25·50	340	Dec. 31	Transfer to			
June 30	,,	6	23·00	460		Current			
Sept. 30	,,	3	8·50	340		Account .			1,537
Dec. 31	,,			340					
	Interest Account .			57					
				£1,537					£1,537

M. ANTONY—DRAWINGS

19..		Mos.	Int. £	£	19..				£
Mar. 31	Cash.	9	16·50	220	Dec. 31	Transfer to			
June 30	,,	6	15·50	310		Current			
Sept. 30	,,	3	8·00	320		Account .			1,450
Dec. 31	,,			560					
	Interest Account .			40					
				£1,450					£1,450

CURRENT ACCOUNTS

			J. Caesar	M. Antony				J. Caesar	M. Antony
			£	£	19..			£	£
19.. Dec. 31	Drawings Balances	c/d	1,537 563	1,450 550	Dec. 31	Interest on Loan Profit and Loss Appropria- tion Account		100 2,000	 2,000
			£2,100	£2,000				£2,100	£2,000
					19.. Jan. 1	Balances	b/d	563	550

PROFIT AND LOSS APPROPRIATION ACCOUNT

	£	£			£
J. Caesar— Loan Interest		100	Balance . b/d		5,303
M. Antony— Salary		1,300	Interest on Drawings .		97
Net Profit J. Caesar: one-half	2,000				
M. Antony: one-half	2,000				
		4,000			
		£5,400			£5,400

Notes. 1. There is no interest allowed on Capitals.

2. If M. Antony's salary was to be *credited* to him instead of being *paid* throughout the year, his Current Account would have been credited with £1,300 and debited as he made drawings against it.

3. Interest on Drawings will be credited to a separate Interest Account (thence transferred to Profit and Loss Appropriation Account) as shown below.

INTEREST

	£		£
Profit and Loss Appropriation Account	97	J. Caesar—Drawings Account . M. Antony—Drawings Account	57 40
	£97		£97

Illustration 6

A, B and C are partners with capitals at 1st July 19.1, of £5,000, £4,000, and £1,000 respectively.

The partnership agreement provides:

(*a*) C shall be *credited* with a management salary of £1,500.

(*b*) After providing for (*a*), extra remuneration as provided in this paragraph (*b*), and 5 per cent interest on capital, C shall be entitled to 10 per cent of all the profits in excess of £2,000 per annum.

(*c*) B is to have one-third of the profits, after charging all provisions in (*a*), (*b*), and (*c*).

(*d*) The balance to be divided between A and C in the ratio of 4:1.

The profits for the year to 30th June 19.2 (*before* making ANY provision for the above) were £5,320.

PROFIT AND LOSS APPROPRIATION ACCOUNT
FOR THE YEAR ENDED 30TH JUNE 19.2

		£			£
Salary—C		1,500	Balance	. b/d	5,320
Interest on Capital—					
A	. £250				
B	. 200				
C	. 50				
		500			
Balance¹	. c/d	3,320			
		£5,320			£5,320
C $\frac{1}{10}$ of £1,200 (i)	.	120	Balance	. b/d	3,320
B $\frac{1}{3}$ of £2,400 (ii)	.	800			
Balance—					
A $\frac{4}{5}$	. £1,920				
C $\frac{1}{5}$	. 480				
		2,400			
		£3,320			£3,320

¹ The balance of £3,320 is struck to make the subsequent division clear.

Computations:
   (i) C obtains $\frac{1}{11}$ of (£3,320−£2,000)   (ii) B obtains $\frac{1}{4}$ of £3,200
   B is entitled to one-third of the profits after charging his remuneration *and* his one-third, i.e. $\frac{1}{3}\times[£3,320-£120-£800]$.

Interest as Proportion of Profits. It will be a question of construction of the partnership agreement as to the precise significance of such an agreement, e.g. as to whether the interest is or is not to be treated as a *charge*; if, for instance, A is to have one-fifth of the profits (as interest), whether he is to receive (or be credited with) one-fifth or one-sixth, the former being treated as an appropriation of the profits and the latter as a charge.

Agreements may vary considerably in detail; a frequent method being to allow interest on capital at a flat rate in the ordinary way, but to treat advances on a 'profit' basis, the proportion of the advances to the total capital of, and advances to, the firm being the basis of the calculations, consideration being given to the date of the advance. The loan or advance will be converted, if necessary, to an annual basis, and a simple proportion calculation made, e.g. if the advance of £1,000 is made half way through the financial year it is equivalent to £500 for the year, and further supposing that the combined capitals of the firm are £3,500, then the 'interest' on the advance, if deemed to be an **appropriation** of profits, will be $\frac{500}{3,500+500}=\frac{500}{4,000}\times$ profits, or if the interest on advance is to be deemed a **charge**, $\frac{500}{4,500}\times$ profits; in other words, one-eighth or one-ninth of the profits as the case may be. Again, each alternative may be based upon the profits either *before* or *after* interest on CAPITAL.

Illustration 7

A and B are partners sharing profits equally. Their capitals, upon which interest at 5 per cent per annum is payable, are £3,000 and £2,000 respectively. Any advance over and above capital made by a partner is to be remunerated on a profit basis, in the proportion that the advances bear to the total capital and advances.

During the year, A advanced £200 on 31st March and £1,000 on 30th September; B advanced £1,200 on 30th June.

The profits for the year ended 31st December 19.., before charging interest on capital, were £750. The 'advance' remuneration is to be taken as an appropriation of profits (AFTER charging interest on capitals). Show Profit and Loss Appropriation Account.

AVERAGE DATE OF ADVANCES

A	B
$200 \times 9 = 1,800$	$1,200 \times 6 = 7,200$
$1,000 \times 3 = 3,000$	
1,200	4,800

$$\frac{4,800}{1,200} = 4 \text{ months} \qquad \frac{7,200}{1,200} = 6 \text{ months}$$

The Advances are equivalent to—
    A—£1,200 for 4 months = £400
    B—£1,200 for 6 months = £600

$$\text{A's ratio of profits} = \frac{400}{5,000 + 400 + 600} = \frac{400}{6,000} = \frac{1}{15}$$

$$\text{B's} \quad \text{,,} \qquad \text{,,} = \frac{600}{5,000 + 400 + 600} = \frac{600}{6,000} = \frac{1}{10}$$

In this particular illustration the calculation can be done mentally, e.g. in the case of A:

			£	
(1) £200 for 9 months	.	.	150 per annum	
(2) £1,000 for 3 months	.	.	250 ,, ,,	Total £400

PROFIT AND LOSS APPROPRIATION ACCOUNT
FOR THE YEAR ENDED 31ST DECEMBER 19 . .

	£p	£p			£p
Interest on Capital—			Balance .	. b/d	750·00
A . . .	150·00				
B . . .	100·00				
		250·00			
Profits[1] attributable to Advances—					
A—$\frac{1}{15}$×£500	33·34				
B—$\frac{1}{10}$×£500	50·00				
		83·34			
Balance—					
A—$\frac{1}{2}$.	. 208·33				
B—$\frac{1}{2}$.	. 208·33				
		416·66			
		£750·00			£750·00

If the proportion were based on profits AFTER charging up interest on capital and profits on advances, the calculations would be:

Let
$$a = \text{A's commission}$$
$$b = \text{B's commission}$$
then
$$a = \tfrac{1}{16}(500-b) \quad \text{and} \quad b = \tfrac{1}{11}(500-a)$$
$$16a = 500-b$$
$$11b = 500-a$$
∴
$$a = \tfrac{200}{7}$$
$$= £28·57$$
and
$$b = £42·86$$

Alternatively, as A and B jointly are entitled to one-sixth[2] 'Advance' profits after charging them to Profit and Loss Account, the equivalent sum is *one-seventh* of £500 (divided between them in the ratio 2:3). viz. £71·43.

There is no need to make a separate calculation for B, for inasmuch as he receives one-tenth of the net divisible profits as against A's one-fifteenth, he must receive half as much again as A; and if A receive £28·57, then B must receive £28·57 plus 50 per cent of £28·57, i.e. £42·86.

[1] If the proportion were based upon profits BEFORE charging Interest, the figures would be:

	£
A: $\frac{1}{15}$×£750	50
B: $\frac{1}{10}$×£750	75
Total £125	

Divisible profits would be £375 (i.e. £500−£125).

[2] $\frac{1}{15} + \frac{1}{10}$

The Profit and Loss Appropriation Account will now be:

PROFIT AND LOSS APPROPRIATION ACCOUNT

	£p	£p			£p
Interest on Capital—			Balance . . b/d		750·00
A . . .	150·00				
B . . .	100·00				
		250·00			
Profits[1] attributable to Advances—					
A:					
$\frac{1}{15} \times £428·57$	28·57				
B:					
$\frac{1}{10} \times £428·57$	42·86				
		71·43			
Balance . . c/d		428·57			
		£750·00			£750·00
Balance—			Balance . . b/d		428·57
A—$\frac{1}{2}$ . .	214·29				
B—$\frac{1}{2}$ . .	214·28				
		428·57			

Examination Problem

A and B were in partnership sharing profits equally after crediting interest at 5 per cent per annum on their capitals. No interest was to be charged or allowed on Current Account balances.

On 31st December 19.1, their capitals in the business were £60,000 and £30,000 respectively. On the same date B owed A £3,000 being the balance of an amount which B had agreed to pay A for an interest in the goodwill of the business. This debt carried no interest, and was to be discharged out of any surplus arising on B's Current Account at the end of each year, but was to be kept in the business as additional capital of A.

Balance Sheets had not been prepared regularly, and the partners had not been credited with interest or their share of profits, but investigation disclosed that A had drawn £5,000 per annum on account of profits and B £4,000 per annum, and that the surplus of assets over liabilities, as shown by the books, was as follows:

31st December 19.2	.	.	.	£92,500
19.3	.	.	.	£94,500
19.4	.	.	.	£97,000
19.5	.	.	.	£101,000

You are required to show the relative positions of the partners on 31st December 19.5 (*Adapted from Institute of Chartered Accountants Inter.*)

Solution

It is necessary to compute *each* year's profit so as to ascertain what amount is available for transfer from B's Current Account to A's *Capital*

---

[1] It will be observed that these figures are respectively $\frac{1}{15}$th and $\frac{1}{10}$th of the final total DIVISIBLE profits. Similar calculations would be made on £750 if the 'profits' on advances were to be AFTER charging such 'profits,' but BEFORE charging interest on Capital.

Account. No interest is allowed on Current Accounts, and B's capital remains unchanged, so that the only alteration in interest arises on A's increased capital.

STATEMENT OF PARTNERS' POSITIONS AS AT 31ST DECEMBER 19.5

Profits:	£
Closing Net Assets . . .	101,000
Less Opening Net Assets . .	90,000
Increase of Net Assets . .	11,000
Add Drawings, £9,000×4 . .	36,000
Total Profits . . .	£47,000

Division	Total	A	B
	£p	£p	£p
Current Accounts—			
Interest on Capital	18,000·00	12,000·00	6,000·00
Interest increase for A	270·20	270·20	
Divisible Profits	28,729·80	14,364·90	14,364·90
[See p. 2224]	[1]47,000·00	26,635·10	20,364·90
Less Drawings	36,000·00	20,000·00	16,000·00
Increase of Net Assets	11,000·00	6,635·10	4364·90
Transfer re Goodwill	−3,000·00		−3,000·00
	8,000·00	6,635·10	1,364·90
Capital Accounts—	90,000·00	60,000·00	30,000·00
Transfer re Goodwill	[2]+3,000·00	[2]+3,000·00	
	£93,000·00	£63,000·00	£30,000·00

[1] As there is an increase of £270·20 to A, the divisible profits are reduced by the same figure. A will suffer half of such reduced profits, hence there is a net gain to A of £135·10, so that the above might have been shown as in the summary at the top of the next page.

[2] It will be seen that there are the following transfers from B's Current Account to A's Capital Account.

	£p
19.2	1,000·00
19.3	725·00
19.4	956·90
19.5	318·10
	£3,000·00

This will increase the interest on capital to A:

	£p
19.3—5% on £1,000 . . .	50·00
19.4—5% on £1,725 . . .	86·20
19.5—5% on £2,681·90 . . .	134·00
	£270·20

CURRENT ACCOUNTS

Dr.

Date	Particulars		A £p	B £p
19.2	Drawings		5,000·00	4,000·00
	Surplus, Transferred to A's Capital Account			1,000·00
	Balance	c/d	1,500·00	
			£6,500·00	£5,000·00
19.3	Drawings		5,000·00	4,000·00
	Surplus, Transferred to A's Capital Account			725·00
	Balance	c/d	2,775·00	
			£7,775·00	£4,725·00
19.4	Drawings		5,000·00	4,000·00
	Surplus, Transferred to A's Capital Account			956·90
	Balance	c/d	4,318·10	
			£9,318·10	£4,956·90
19.5	Drawings		5,000·00	4,000·00
	Surplus, Transferred to A's Capital Account			318·10
	Balances	c/d	6,635·10	1,364·90
			£11,635·10	£5,683·00

Cr.

Date	Particulars		A £p	B £p
19.2	Interest on Capital		3,000·00	1,500·00
	Profits		3,500·00	3,500·00
			£6,500·00	£5,000·00
19.3	Balance	b/d	1,500·00	1,500·00
	Interest on Capital		3,050·00	
	Profits		3,225·00	3,225·00
			£7,775·00	£4,725·00
19.4	Balance	b/d	2,775·00	1,500·00
	Interest on Capital		3,086·20	
	Profits		3,456·90	3,456·90
			£9,318·10	£4,956·90
19.5	Balance	b/d	4,318·10	1,500·00
	Interest on Capital		3,134·00	
	Profits		4,183·00	4,183·00
			£11,635·10	£5,683·00
19.6	Balances	b/d	6,635·10	1,364·90

Profit and Loss Appropriation Accounts

	19.2 £	19.3 £p	19.4 £p	19.5 £p		Profit¹ b/d	19.2 £	19.3 £	19.4 £	19.5 £
Interest on Capital							11,500	11,000	11,500	13,000
A £3,000		3,050·00	3,086·20	3,134·00						
B 1,500		1,500·00	1,500·00	1,500·00						
	4,500	4,550	4,586·20	4,634·00						
Balance—										
A £3,500		3,225·00	3,456·90	4,183·00						
B 3,500		3,225·00	3,456·90	4,183·00						
	7,000	6,450	6,913·80	8,366·00						
	£11,500	£11,000	£11,500·00	£13,000·00			£11,500	£11,000	£11,500	£13,000

Capital

			A £p	B £
19.2 Jan. 1	Balances	b/d	60,000·00	30,000
Dec. 31	B's Current Account		1,000·00	
			61,000·00	30,000
19.3 Dec. 31	B's Current Account		725·00	
			61,725·00	30,000
19.4 Dec. 31	B's Current Account		956·90	
			62,681·90	30,000
19.5 Dec. 31	B's Current Account		318·10	
			63,000·00	30,000
19.6 Jan. 1	Balances	b/d	63,000·00	30,000

¹ Profits are computed by subtracting the opening surplus of assets over liabilities from the closing surplus, and adding the Drawings [e.g. profit for 19.4 = £97,000 − £94,500 + £9,000 = £11,500].

	£	£p	£p
Interest on Capital	18,000	12,000·00	6,000·00
Divisible Profits (before adjustment) . .	29,000	14,500·00	14,500·00
	47,000	26,500·00	20,500·00
Adjustment		+135·10	−135·10
	£47,000	£26,635·10	£20,364·90
[See p. 222]			

[See p. 222]

SUMMARY

	Total	A	B
	£	£p	£p
Current Accounts	8,000	6,635·10	1,364·90
Capital Accounts	93,000	63,000·00	30,000·00
	£101,000	£69,635·10	£31,364·90

Illustration 8

A, B and C are in partnership, the Head Office being in London, with branches at Bristol and Cardiff, managed by A, B, and C respectively.

B is entitled to a salary of £1,500 per annum and to 25 per cent of the net profit of his Branch *after* charging (i) such salary and (ii) interest at 10 per cent per annum on the *average* net assets, excluding Cash, of the Branch. Similar arrangements exist for C in respect of his share of the Cardiff Branch profit.

No interest is to be charged on drawings, but allowed on Capitals at 5 per cent per annum.

The balance of profits is divisible as to one-half to A, three-tenths to B, and one-fifth to C.

The balances in the books at 31st December 19.. are:

	Dr.	Cr.
	£	£
Drawings and Capitals:		
A	2,000	10,000
B	1,700	9,000
C	1,200	7,000
Assets (except Cash) and Liabilities:		
London	14,300	2,200
Bristol	9,200	2,100
Cardiff	6,500	1,800
Cash	5,210	
Profits for year ended 31st December 19.. (before foregoing adjustments)—		
London		3,100
Bristol		2,800
Cardiff		2,110
	£40,110	£40,110

The net assets (as compared with the beginning of the year) have increased by £600 and £400 at Bristol and Cardiff respectively.

Prepare *Statement* to show the division of the profits of £6,010 (items above). Take to nearest £.

A, B, AND C

STATEMENT OF DIVISION OF PROFITS FOR THE YEAR ENDED
31ST DECEMBER 19 . .

			A	B	C	Total
			£	£	£	£
Salaries				1,500	1,500	3,000
Interest on Capitals			500	500	400	1,400
Branches' Remuneration—	*Bristol*	*Cardiff*				
	£	£				
Profit	2,800	2,110				
Less Salary	1,500	1,500				
	1,300	610				
Less 10% on Average Net Assets	680	450				
25% £620[1]	25%	£160		155	40	195
Balance of Profits—		£				
Bristol [£2,800−£1,500−£155]		1,145				
Cardiff [£2,110−£1,500−£40]		570				
London		3,100				
		4,815				
Less Interest on Capitals		1,400				
		£3,415	(½) 1,708	(3/10) 1,024	(⅕) 683	3,415
			£2,208	£3,179	£2,623	£8,010

[1]See Note iii on p. 2226.

The Balance Sheet is not called for, but is given below to show completion:

BALANCE SHEET (SUMMARIZED) AT 31ST DECEMBER 19 . .

Liabilities				£ 6,100	Sundry Assets			£ 30,000
Capitals:	A	B	C		Cash			5,210
	£	£	£					
At 1st January 19..	10,000	9,000	7,000					
Profits, etc.	2,208	3,179	2,623					
	12,208	12,179	9,623					
Drawings	2,000	1,700	1,200					
	£10,208	£10,479	£8,423	29,110				
				£35,210				£35,210

Notes. (i) As the profits are all brought into the Head Office books, the division will be made according to the amounts attributable to each partner as per statement.

(ii) No actual debit will be made to the Branch in respect of the 10 per cent interest chargeable, as this is necessary merely for the calculation of the percentage due to B and C in respect of their Branch profits. If it were, it would merely *decrease* the remaining Branch profits and increase the residue of the profits, so cancelling out each other.

(iii) The average net assets of Branches are:

		Bristol £		Cardiff £
Closing [£9,200 − £2,100]	. .	7,100	[£6,500 − £1,800]	4,700
Opening	. .	6,500		4,300
		2)13,600		2)9,000
		£6,800		£4,500

The opening net assets must have been £600 and £400 respectively *less* than the closing net assets.

INCOME TAX

Partnership Accounts. Owing to the existence of private income, abatements and personal reliefs, there will usually be no uniformity of incidence of liability of partners to Income Tax, so that the firm's liability to Schedule D Case I or Case II (see p. 2102) must be apportioned between the partners (from which will be deducted the appropriate personal reliefs), and the final amount due from each partner charged to his Current or Drawings Account. Hence, although partners may be 'equal' the incidence of Income Tax will normally be unequal.

The allocation of liability between partners is dealt with in the following manner:

1. The firm's profits are adjusted in the usual way (adding back **partners' salaries and interest on capitals,** and eliminating **interest on drawings,** taxed dividends and income assessable elsewhere (e.g. Case III, Schedule D)). From the adjusted profits will be deducted the capital allowances (if any).

2. Having arrived at the final figure, it is necessary to apportion it as between the partners in the ratio in which profits are shared in the **Current Fiscal** Year, it being quite immaterial what the constitution of the partnership was when the profits (as adjusted) brought into the assessment were earned. The assessment is the liability not for the last year, but the current year.[1] The PRESENT partners must bear the PRESENT burden, however it is computed.

3. Personal reliefs are deducted from each partner's share of assessment as determined in (2).

Thus, the two important rules are:

(*a*) Ascertain the adjusted profits of the firm, ignoring the question of the *personnel* of the firm.
(*b*) Apportion adjusted profits as above ascertained in the manner in which profits and losses are shared in the *current* fiscal year.

It may be noted that a change in the constitution of the partnership will be treated for taxation purposes as a discontinuance of the old, and a

---

[1] Although in normal circumstances (early and closing years are exceptions) based on the profits of the preceding year.

commencement of a new business except where there is a continuing partner and all the old and new partners (or their legal representatives) apply within twelve months of the change for assessment in the ordinary way as a continuing business. The former will entail an adjustment of the old firm's profits down to the change as a closed business, involving a readjustment of the two years of assessment before the year of discontinuance, i.e. the antepenultimate and penultimate years' assessments, should the aggregate of the actual profits of these years of assessment exceed the aggregate of the assessments already made for these years on the preceding year basis. The alternative methods, however, do not affect the rule as to the *apportionment* of the liability.

Where assessment as a continuing business is applied for, i.e. on the profits of the preceding year, the adjusted profits will be split if the change has occurred at any date other than the 6th April of the year of assessment, the two parts being respectively the old and the new firm liability. For instance, if a change took place on the 5th October 1982, the proportion of the adjusted profits brought into liability for the years 1982–83 (based on the preceding year's accounts) will be one-half, that is, from 6th April 1982, to 5th October 1982, to the old firm and the remaining half, that is, from 6th October 1982, to the 5th April 1983, to the new firm, each part being allocated in the manner of sharing profits (including interest on capital and partnership salaries) in the respective periods.

The above rule applies to all income of the firm, including taxed income. Although the latter will be excluded from the computation for assessment, the gross amount of the shares of dividends and interest must be included in the income tax returns of the partners for the purposes of ascertaining their statutory incomes.

Provisions for Partners' Income Tax. At the end of the accounting period, provision should be made for the estimated liability for tax by debiting each Partner's Current Account with his share of liability and crediting Income Tax Account, the latter being debited and cash credited upon payment. Any difference between the amount provided for and actually paid in respect of each partner should be transferred back to each Partner's Current Account.

In many cases no provision is made at all for the partners' Income Tax, so that the appropriate entries will be made only upon payment by debiting each Partner's Current or Drawings Account and crediting cash. In any case, no provision is required as regards income which has already suffered Income Tax.

Readjustment of Profit Sharing Ratios over Past Years.

Illustration 9

C and D had been in partnership for three years, sharing profits and losses in proportion to their capitals, which had not changed during the period, and were £10,000 and £5,000 respectively. At the end of the third year (31st December 19.3) they agree to admit their Manager E into partnership as from the beginning of the partnership. E had been in receipt of a salary of £2,350 per annum during the period, and had had £3,000 on loan to the firm since its inception, upon which he had received 6 per cent per annum interest.

The Profit and Loss Accounts of the firm had shown the following results *after* charging partners' interest upon capitals at 5 per cent per annum C's salary £3,000, D's salary £2,650 and E's salary and the interest upon his loan:

							£p
19.1	Profit	.	.	.	.	.	2,562·35
19.2	Loss	.	.	.	.	.	418·75
19.3	Profit	.	.	.	.	.	1,762·70

The terms upon which E was to be admitted a partner were that he should have a salary of £2,250 per annum and a sixth interest in the business as from 1st January 19.1, and that his loan should be treated as his capital, upon which he should receive, from the commencement of the partnership, the same rate of interest as C and D instead of the 6 per cent already paid to him, C and D's ratio as between themselves to remain unaltered.

You are required to adjust the results of each of the three years, and to show how they should be divided in accordance with the new arrangement.

Under the new arrangement the divisions are as follows:

First year, 19.1
  Profit £2,562·35 + Interest £30 and Salary £100 = Profit £2,692·35

					£p
C—$\frac{10}{18}$	.	.	.	.	1,495·75
D—$\frac{5}{18}$	.	.	.	.	747·87
E—$\frac{3}{18}$	.	.	.	.	448·73
					£2,692·35

Second year, 19.2—
  Loss £418·75 − Interest £30 and Salary £100 = Loss £288·75

					£p
C—$\frac{10}{18}$	.	.	.	.	160·42
D—$\frac{5}{18}$	.	.	.	.	80·20
E—$\frac{3}{18}$	.	.	.	.	48·13
					£288·75

Third year, 19.3—
Profit £1,762·70 + Interest £30 and Salary £100 = Profit £1,892·70

		£p
C—$\frac{10}{18}$	. . . . .	1,051·50
D—$\frac{5}{18}$	. . . .	525·75
E—$\frac{3}{18}$	. . . .	315·45
		£1,892·70

By the above arrangement E receives the following:

	£	£p
19.1		448·73
19.3		315·45
		764·18
Less 19.2 Loss . .	48·13	
Reduction of £130 for 3 years = £30 interest (1% on £3,000) and £100 salary .	390·00	
		438·13
∴ Credit to E . . .		£326·05
Debit to C—$\frac{2}{3}$ of £326·05 .		217·37
Debit to D—$\frac{1}{3}$ of £326·05 .		108·68
		£326·05

Alternative Method. A much shorter method may be adopted in examinations by taking the three years together, thus:

	£p
Profits for the three years—	
Profit, 31st Dec., 19.1.	2,562·35
Profit, 31st Dec., 19.3.	1,762·70
	4,325·05
Loss, 31st Dec., 19.2	418·75
	3,906·30
Add Augmented Profit in respect of E— £130 per annum × 3	390·00
	£4,296·30
∴ E's share = $\frac{3}{18}$	716·05
Less Diminished Interest and Salary— £130 × 3	390·00
∴ Credit to E	£326·05
which must be borne by—	
Debit to C—$\frac{2}{3}$ of £326·05 . .	217·37
Debit to D—$\frac{1}{3}$ of £326·05 . .	108·68
	£326·05

It is assumed that (1) interest on capital is to be charged whether there are profits or losses.

(2) Interest based upon FIXED capitals and not upon Current Accounts, otherwise the amount for each year would have to be separately computed.

'Cash' Profits. It is usual in many professional business partnerships to take profits on the basis of RECEIPTS less PAYMENTS, that is to say, all outstandings, whether in favour or against the firm, are ignored. On the other hand, profits may be taken on a 'receipts' basis, but outstandings against the firm taken into account. Both methods are unsatisfactory as full account should be taken of the following:

1. Debtors including prepayments.
2. Uncompleted work.
3. Creditors, including:
   (a) Payments by clients in advance.
   (b) Accrued and accruing expenses.
4. Depreciation.
5. Stocks. (Although stocks are likely to be fairly constant in a non-trading business, nevertheless the value of stock should be brought into the accounts.)
6. Bad debts. (As receipts only are recorded, the accounts do not disclose the amount of bad debts.)

Where the partners decide to bring the accounts on to an 'earned' basis, the items introduced into the books, whether assets or liabilities, must be credited or debited to the partners either (a) directly to the partners who introduced them (less depreciation borne in profit and loss ratios), or otherwise (b) in the profit or loss ratios. No difficulty arises where no change has occurred in the CONSTITUTION of the partnership; but the true position as at each change (if any) must be established (unless this has already been done) upon such change, whether by way of admission or retirement of a partner, or upon the alteration of ratios of profit and loss sharing.

It is of importance to distinguish carefully between the assets specifically brought in by partners, and those created during the tenure of the partnership, as the former will be credited to the partners according to their respective contributions, and the latter in profit and loss ratio.

The rules may be thus formulated:

1. Ascertain the undisclosed assets and liabilities at the commencing date, and credit in case of assets, and debit in case of liabilities, the partners, either in profit and loss ratios or rateably to contributions, for such amounts; depreciation being charged in profit and loss ratios.
2. Ascertain the increase or decrease in assets and liabilities treating them as ordinary partnership profits or losses; computing *each* year separately (if necessary, e.g. on changes in constitution of the firm), or treating the *whole* of the intervening years together.
3. Prepare the above information in schedule form, analysed into columns for each partner.
4. Debit assets ascertained by the total of (1) and (2), credit liabilities similarly obtained.
5. Credit or debit the partners as shown in the schedule according to the result obtained by (4), i.e. if increase of assets exceeds increase of liabilities a credit will ensue to the partners; the converse will apply on a decrease of assets.

Illustration 10

A and B are in partnership, drawing up accounts on a cash basis. Up to 31st December 19.1, they shared profits in the ratio 3:2, and at that date the debtors were £100, creditors £75; from that date till 31st December 19.4, profits were shared equally.

No Interest on Capital was allowed. The debtors and creditors were:

Year ended	Debtors	Creditors	'Net' Assets Undisclosed
£	£	£	£
31 December 19.2	250	90	160
,, 19.3	120	40	80
,, 19.4	300	119	181

It was agreed on 31st December 19.4, that the last three year's accounts should be computed on an 'earned' basis, with Double Entry Accounts for debtors, etc. Ignore all other considerations.

The schedule will be constructed thus:

	Dr. (Debtors)	Cr. (Creditors)	A Dr.	A Cr.	B Dr.	B Cr.
	£	£	£	£	£	£
'Net' Undisclosed Assets at 31st December, 19.1.	100	75	$\frac{3}{5}$ 45	$\frac{3}{5}$ 60	$\frac{2}{5}$ 30	$\frac{2}{5}$ 40
Increase to 31st December, 19.4						
Debtors £300−£100	200			$\frac{1}{2}$100		$\frac{1}{2}$100
Creditors £119− £75		44	$\frac{1}{2}$ 22		$\frac{1}{2}$ 22	
	300	119	67	160	52	140
Balance		181	93		88	
	£300	£300	£160	£160	£140	£140

Alternatively:

	Total	A	B
	£	£	£
Opening 'Net' Undisclosed Assets	25	$\frac{3}{5}$ 15	$\frac{2}{5}$ 10
Increase in 'Net' Assets from 31st Dec. 19.1, to 31st Dec. 19.4 [£181 less £25]	156	$\frac{1}{2}$ 78	$\frac{1}{2}$ 78
	£181	£93	£88

The adjusting Journal entry will be:

JOURNAL

19.4				£	£
Dec. 31	Debtors (detailed)[1]	Dr.		300	
	Creditors (detailed)				119
	A Current Account				93
	B Current Account				88
	Being introduction of assets and liabilities at this date.			£300	£300

[1] If the practice had been to write back the debtors (cf. Receipt and Expenditure method), the adjustment would be to the debit of a Debtors' Reserve Account.

If the net assets at 31st December 19.1, of £25 represented *original* assets, the Journal entry (ignoring narrative) at 31st December 19.4, would be:

JOURNAL

19.4				£	£
Dec. 31	Debtors			300	
	Creditors				119
	A Current Account				78
	B Current Account				78
	Capital Adjustment Account . . .				25

The amount of £25 would be transferred to the credit of the partners' Capital Accounts according to their original contribution, e.g. entirely to B if at the commencement of the partnership all the assets *less* liabilities were contributed by B.

Adjustment of 'Cash Profits'—'Cash' Basis to 'Earned' Basis. Where a firm has been carrying on business on a 'cash' basis, an occasion may arise which necessitates the precise ascertainment of profits, such as require-ments of income tax authorities or the dissolution of partnership. It is both inexpedient and undesirable to interfere with the partners' capital or other accounts already in the books, so that a Statement or Memorandum Account is prepared showing the excess or diminished profits ascertained on a cash basis, the differences being allocated to each partner. Where no questions arise which demand the ascertainment of true profit or loss for *each* year the matter is extremely simple, as all that requires to be done is to have two columns, one for increase of profit and the other for decrease, for each year, the difference being the increased or decreased profit or loss which is then allocated in total between the partners. It is clear that any difference in profit or loss must be reflected by an increase or decrease in asset or liability, and this forms the reciprocal entry to that debited or credited to the partners' accounts.

Illustration 11

A and B have shared profits and losses equally, but only on a 'cash' basis. It is now desired to adjust the profits and losses over the past years, and no occasion arises for obtaining each separate year's results. No interest on capital is chargeable. It has always·been the practice to pay all the expenses and creditors at the end of each year, but stock, debtors, and depreciation on machinery have never been brought into the accounts.

The following are the figures for the above assets on:

	Debtors	Stock	Machinery	'Cash' Profits and Loss
	£	£	£	£
1st January 19.1 . . .	1,000	500	800	
31st December 19.1 . . .	900	750	900	+600
,, 19.2 . . .	1,300	900	900	−100
,, 19.3 . . .	1,200	500	900	+800

Depreciation of machinery may be taken at 10 per cent (diminishing balance) each year from 1st January 19.1, to be calculated on the balances at 31st December of each current year.

Prepare Memorandum Adjustment Statement.

Memorandum ADJUSTMENT STATEMENT

		Increase of 'Net' Assets	Decrease of 'Net' Assets
31st December 19.1	£	£	£
Debtors	−100		
Stock	+250		
Machinery[1]	+ 10		
		160	
31st December 19.2			
Debtors	+400		
Stock	+150		
Machinery[1]	− 81		
		469	
31st December 19.3			
Debtors	−100		
Stock	−400		
Machinery[1]	− 73		
			573
Balance—Increase of 'Net' Assets . .			56
		£629	£629

[1] See p. 2234.

In addition the assets, which *ex hypothesi* are not in the books at the commencement of the adjustment period, are:

		£
Debtors	. . . . .	1,000
Stock	. . . . .	500
Machinery	. . . .	800
		£2,300

The figures must be incorporated in the books, and the introduction of assets into the books will show an increase of capital, thus:

Assets at 31st December 19.3—

	£		
Debtors	1,200		
Stock .	500		
Machinery[1] .	656		
			£
£2,356 made up of:	Additional Profit for three years . .	56
	Undisclosed Assets at commencement .	2,300
		£2,356

JOURNAL

19.3			£	£
Dec. 31	Debtors	Dr.	1,200	
	Stock	Dr.	500	
	Machinery[1]	Dr.	656	
	A Capital			1,150
	B ,, ...			1,150
	A Current Account			28
	B ,, ...			28
	Being assets and adjustments of profits introduced for the three years to date as per Memorandum Adjustment Statement.			
			£2,356	£2,356

[1] Machinery Account is as follows:

			£
1st Jan., 19.1.	Balance	. . . .	800
31st Dec., 19.1.	Additions	. . . .	100
			900
	Depreciation	. . .	90
31st Dec., 19.2.	Balance	. . .	810
	Depreciation	. .	81
31st Dec., 19.3.	Balance	. . .	729
	Depreciation	. . .	73
	Balance	. .	£656

The amount of £2,300 represents assets undisclosed at the commence-ment of 19.1, and if it represents accumulated earnings to that date it will be divided in the partnership ratio; if, on the other hand, it represents *initial* capital, it must be credited to A and B according to their respective contributions.

The net profit for the three years on a cash basis is £600+£800−£100 = £1,300, already credited in the accounts, to which will be added £56, totalling £1,356, i.e. A, £678; B, £678. There is no need to add to or deduct from the 'cash' profits or losses, but if desired (or required) the adjustment in detail will be as shown below.

Where the information may be required in respect of *each* year, e.g. (1) for income tax purposes, or (2) by reason of alteration in profit-sharing ratios, or (3) where profit-sharing fluctuates according to amount of profits, each year's result **must** be *separately* ascertained.

MEMORANDUM ADJUSTMENT STATEMENT

	Total		A		B	
	£	£	£	£	£	£
Profits for the Year ended 31st Dec. 19.1	+600		+300		+300	
Add Increase of 'Net' Assets	+160	+760	+80	+380	+80	+380
Increase of 'Net' Assets to 31st Dec. 19.2	+469		+235		+234	
Less Loss for Year ended 31st Dec. 19.2	−100	+369	−50	+185	−50	+184
Profits for the Year ended 31st Dec. 19.3	+800		+400		+400	
Less Decrease of 'Net' Assets to 31st Dec. 19.3	−573	+227	−287	+113	−286	+114
Revised profits		1,356		678		678
Less already credited		1,300		650		650
Remaining amount to be credited in respect of profits		£56		£28		£28

Illustration 12

Assume the same figures as in the preceding example, but that the partners share profits and losses equally to 1st January 19.1, after which the division is to be as follows:

> First £300 to A
> Next £200 to A and B in the ratio of 3:2
> Next £200 to A and B in the ratio of 3:1
> Remainder to A entirely.

You are required to adjust the positions.

The adjustment will be as shown already so far as it relates to adjusted profit or loss, but the allocation will require careful working owing to the fluctuating rates of profit.

It is therefore necessary to take each year and compute the effect of the adjustment upon the total profits, as any increase as shown in the adjustment must be allocated according to what is necessary to give effect to the partnership agreement.

1. The first year's increase of £160. The 'cash' profits have been divided as follows:

	Total	A	B
	£	£	£
First £300	300	300	—
Next £200	200	$\frac{3}{5}$ 120	$\frac{2}{5}$ 80
Balance (part of next £200) .	100	$\frac{3}{4}$ 75	$\frac{1}{4}$ 25
	£600	£495	£105

The increase of £160 is dealt with thus:

	Total	A	B
	£	£	£
Balance of £200 . . .	100	$\frac{3}{4}$ 75	$\frac{1}{4}$ 25
Remainder	60	60	
	£160	£135	£25

2. The second year's increase of £469. On a 'cash' basis a loss has been shown and charged to A. The increase of £469 will be dealt with thus:

	£
Increase of capital	469
Less cancellation of loss previously debited to A .	100
Balance divisible . .	£369

The increase of £469 is dealt with thus:

	Total	A	B
	£	£	£
First £300	300	300	
Balance	69	$\frac{3}{5}$ 41	$\frac{2}{5}$ 28
	369	341	28
Cancellation of Loss . .	100	100	—
	£469	£441	£28

3. The third year's decrease of £573. The 'cash' profits of £800 have been allocated thus:

	Total	A	B
	£	£	£
1st stage . .	300	300	
2nd stage . .	200	120	80
3rd stage . .	200	150	50
4th stage . .	100	100	
	£800	£670	£130

The decrease in profits must be allocated in order that the division between the partners of true profits shall conform to the partnership agreement, hence the allocation of the decreases must be resolved by the reverse process, for after each stage of profits increase is exhausted the next stage is taken so that the decreases will first affect the final stage.

The decreases then will be dealt thus:

	Total	A	B
	£	£	£
4th stage . .	100	100	
3rd stage . .	200	150	50
2nd stage . .	200	120	80
1st stage . .	73	73	
	£573	£443	£130

It is clear from inspection that the figures within the quadrilaterals eliminate each other, thus leaving A with his original profits of £300 less decrease of £73, i.e. finally with £227; or, taken from the total figures, the true profits are £800 less £573, giving £227, all of which must belong to A, he having the exclusive right to the first £300 of profits.

Alternatively this may be shown thus:

	Total	A	B
	£	£	£
'Cash' profits	800	670	130
Less decrease	573	443	130
Revised profits . . .	£227	£227	Nil

The figures for adjustment are now:

Memorandum ADJUSTMENT STATEMENT

Year	Total		A		B	
	£	£	£	£	£	£
19.1	+ 160		+ 135		+ 25	
19.2	+ 469		+ 441		+ 28	
19.3		− 573		− 443		− 130
Leaving revised profits . .	+£629 − £573		+£576 − £443		+£53 − £130	
	+£56		+£133		−£77	

The original undisclosed assets will be dealt with as before, as they must belong to the partners as at 1st January 19.1, and assuming that they represent undisclosed profits the division of the increase of assets at this date will be made on the old basis, £1,150 each for A and B. It will be seen that the only difference between the consequential entries in this illustration as compared with those in the preceding illustration lies in the *allocation* of the £56 item.

JOURNAL

19.3 Dec. 31		£	£
	Debtors	1,200	
	Stock	500	
	Machinery	656	
	A Capital		1,150
	B ,, ...		1,150
	Capital Adjustment Account		56
	Being assets at 1st January 19.1, entered into the books.		
	Capital Adjustment Account . . .	56	
	B Current Account	77	
	A Current Account		133
	Being adjustment of profits as shown by Memorandum Adjustment Statement as per agreement.		

The Capital Accounts, ignoring other assets or liabilities, and assuming that Capital and Current Accounts are to be merged, will be as follows:

CAPITAL ACCOUNTS

					£
A—£1,150+£133	.	.	.	.	1,283
B—£1,150−£77	.	.	.	.	1,073
Total Increase (as above)	.	.	.	.	£2,356

Alternative Proposals as to Profit Sharing

Illustration 13

B is offered a partnership with A, and is given the following alternatives:

1. A salary of £2,450 per annum plus a fifth share in profits *after* charging up his salary, or
2. A quarter share of profits, without salary, but carrying a guarantee by A of a minimum of £2,400 a year.
Show which alternative is preferable.

There are several preliminary factors which must be considered before B is in a position to decide:

1. The nature of the business, e.g. whether highly fluctuating profits.
2. The reasonable probability of the maintenance of profits in the light of all circumstances, e.g. the business may be almost entirely 'personal,' and consequently, the death or incapacity of A might cause a collapse or decline of the business.
3. The profit curve in conjunction with capital employed.
4. The valuation of assets including goodwill.
5. Precise meaning of profits.
6. The price required for goodwill.
7. The treatment of goodwill in the books which will materially affect disposable profits, where interest on capital is to be charged.

Assuming, however, that due allowance has been made for the foregoing points, it will be seen that where the profits are on a big scale there will be no need to invoke the aid of the guaranteed minimum, but if upon a small scale the guaranteed minimum may be a valuable right, although an intending partner will naturally exercise considerable caution if the permanent profit level is so meagre that it is likely to call for the continued assistance of the guaranteed minimum. Taking an extreme case, if the profit is, say, nil, the intending partner will normally employ business sense, and avoid being a partner in a concern unable to earn profits.

Subject to the above, the advantages of one alternative over the other may be ascertained as follows:

(a) Where the profit level is *low*, so that the comparison is between salary plus profits as contrasted with the GUARANTEED MINIMUM, i.e.

Let P = profits, then

$$2,450 + \frac{P - 2,450}{5} = 2,400$$

$$12,250 + P - 2,450 = 12,000$$
$$\therefore P = £2,200$$

If the profits are exactly £2,200, this amount will be divided as follows:

PROFIT AND LOSS APPROPRIATION ACCOUNT

	£				£
Salary	2,450	Balance	. . .	b/d	2,200
		A—$\frac{4}{5}$ of £250. £200			
		B—$\frac{1}{5}$ of £250. 50			250
	£2,450				£2,450

B obtains a salary of £2,450 less share of loss of £50 = £2,400.

This exactly equals the Guaranteed Minimum.

Hence if the profits, before salary, are under £2,200, the guaranteed **minimum** is preferable.

(b) Where the profit level is *high*, so that the comparison is between salary plus profits as contrasted with the quarter share of profits without salary:

Let P = profits, then

$$\frac{P}{4} = 2,450 + \frac{P - 2,450}{5} \qquad P = £39,200$$

If profits are exactly £39,200, this amount will be divided as follows:

First alternative.

PROFIT AND LOSS APPROPRIATION ACCOUNT

	£				£
Salary (B)	2,450	Balance	. . .	b/d	39,200
A—$\frac{4}{5}$ of Profit £36,750	29,400				
B—$\frac{1}{5}$ of £36,750	7,350				
	£39,200				£39,200

B thus obtains £9,800.

Second alternative.

PROFIT AND LOSS APPROPRIATION ACCOUNT

	£				£
A $\frac{3}{4}$	29,400	Balance	. . .	b/d	39,200
B $\frac{1}{4}$	9,800				
	£39,200				£39,200

If the profits are exactly £39,200, both methods produce the same amount of gain to B. Hence, if the profits are less than £2,200 or greater than £39,200, the second choice, i.e. one-quarter of profits with guaranteed minimum of £2,400, is preferable, because if the profits are low, B enjoys the protection of the guaranteed minimum; if high, he resorts to the quarter share of profits; if the profits fall between £2,200 and £39,200, the first alternative is better, i.e. 'salary plus profits.'

Guarantee of Profits to a Partner. Upon the admission of a new partner into a firm, the old partners may give a guarantee that he shall receive a certain minimum should the normal share to which he is entitled fall short of a stipulated amount. Such an inducement may be necessary, particularly where the new partner, in order to enter the firm, is sacrificing some other source of income, e.g. by resigning his post as a secretary to a limited company. Generally speaking, the old firm, i.e. the old partners, undertake this obligation, although in certain circumstances one only of such partners may himself assume responsibility.

The problems on this point may accordingly be divided into two sections: (1) where the guaranteed minimum is borne by *all* the remaining partners; (2) where the guaranteed minimum is borne by *one* partner only.

The 'shortage' made up to the new partner is treated as a loss between the guaranteeing partners, and may be adjusted in the Profit and Loss Appropriation Account, or by means of a Journal entry to the respective Capital or Current Accounts in profit ratios. An important matter to be settled—apart from the *duration* of the guarantee—is as to whether the principle of *short workings* applies, so that in a profitable year, subsequent to that in which the benefit of the guarantee was applicable, the guaranteed partner must recredit the guaranteeing partners for the amount made up by them. In other words, the question at issue is whether the amount made up to the guaranteed partner should be carried forward against him, provided that he always receives his minimum, or whether each year is to be self-contained, and once the guarantee has been applied the amount paid thereunder is to be ignored in future years.

The principle applicable is similar to that of short-workings.

It is therefore extremely important that the partnership agreement shall deal clearly and unambiguously with this point, as well as that relating to the period during which the guarantee is to continue in force.

Illustration 14

Q and S share profits and losses in the ratio of $3:2$, and as from 1st January 19 . . they admit O, who is to have a tenth share of the profits, with a guaranteed minimum of £1,500, Q and S continuing to share profits, as between themselves, as before. The profits of the firm in respect of the year are £10,000. Prepare Profit and Loss Appropriation Account.

PROFIT AND LOSS APPROPRIATION ACCOUNT

	£	£				£
Q($\frac{27}{50}$)	5,400		Balance	. . .	b/d	10,000
Less Transfer to O						
$\frac{3}{5} \times £500$	300					
		5,100				
S($\frac{18}{50}$)	3,600					
Less Transfer to O						
$\frac{2}{5} \times £500$	200					
		3,400				
O($\frac{5}{50}$)	1,000					
Add Transfer from Q	300					
Add Transfer from S	200					
		1,500				
		£10,000				£10,000

Alternatively:

PROFIT AND LOSS APPROPRIATION ACCOUNT

	£				£
Q	5,400	Balance	. . .	b/d	10,000
S	3,600				
O	1,000				
	£10,000				£10,000
O—Transfer for Guaranteed Minimum[1]	500	Q: $\frac{3}{5} \times £500$[1]	. .		300
		S: $\frac{2}{5} \times £500$[1]	. .		200
	£500				£500

Where there are partnership salaries and interest on capital to be charged which MUST be allowed irrespective of whether there is a profit or loss, the entries, should there be either a loss or insufficient profit to provide fully for partnership salaries and interest on capital, are more involved, although the principle remains the same.

Junior Partners' Shares of Profit and Salaries. Junior partners' shares of profit and salaries are frequently borne personally by one of the senior partners, particularly where the senior partner in question is a relative of the junior.

There are various alternative methods of dealing with this type of problem, which are best explained by means of illustrations.

Illustration 15

Q and S are in partnership, sharing profits 2 : 1. Q desires to admit his son M as and from 1st January 19 . . . It is agreed that M shall have a twelfth share of the firm's profits, such share to be borne by his father.

The profits for the year ended 31st December 19 . ., are £7,200. Show Profit and Loss Appropriation Account.

PROFIT AND LOSS APPROPRIATION ACCOUNT
FOR THE YEAR ENDED 31ST DECEMBER 19 . . .

	£	£			£	£
Q $\frac{2}{3}$ of £7,200	4,800		Balance	. b/d		7,200
Less Transfer to M	600					
		4,200				
S $\frac{1}{3}$ of £7,200		2,400				
M $\frac{1}{12}$ of £7,200		600				
		£7,200				£7,200

[1] Or entered through the Journal.

Illustration 16

Q and S, partners sharing profits equally, agree as from 1st January 19.., to admit M as a partner. He is to have a tenth share of the profits, after being credited with a salary of £800. Q, in consequence of his partial retirement, agrees to bear one-quarter of the profits, and ALL the salary, of M. The profits (after charging salary) for the year to 31st December 19.., were £8,000.

Show division of profits by means of a profit and Loss Appropriation Account.

PROFIT AND LOSS APPROPRIATION ACCOUNT
FOR THE YEAR ENDED 31ST DECEMBER 19..

		£			£
M—$\frac{1}{10}$ of £8,000		800	Balance . . . b/d		8,000
Balance . . . . . c/d		7,200			
		£8,000			£8,000
Q—$\frac{1}{2}$ of £8,200*		4,100	Balance . . . b/d		7,200
S—$\frac{1}{2}$ of £8,200*		4,100	Q—		
			M: Salary. . £800		
			$\frac{1}{4}$ of Profit . . 200		1,000
		£8,200			£8,200

*Alternatively

	£	£			£
Q—$\frac{1}{2}$ of £8,200 .	4,100		Balance . . . b/d		7,200
Less M	1,000				
		3,100			
S—$\frac{1}{2}$ of £8,200		4,100			
		£7,200			£7,200

In dealing with the guaranteed minimum the length of the accounting period is important. Many instances arise in which the guaranteed partner will be entitled to a proportion only of the annual guarantee, as in the first and last years of a partnership. If, for example, A is the guaranteed partner and he enters into the firm on 1st September, and the accounting period runs to 31st December, he will, unless otherwise agreed, be entitled to the guarantee to the extent of four months, that is, if the accounting period is for one year, to four-twelfths of the annual guarantee.

Various Junior Partner's Agreements. Agreements similar to the above may take varying forms according to the particular circumstances, but the underlying principle in all cases is the same, viz., to find (1) what portion of the profits accruing to the junior partner is to be considered as a charge to the FIRM, and to see that this is properly debited before the normal shares of the other partners are ascertained; and (2) what portion of the profits accruing to the junior partner is to be considered as a *personal adjustment* between him and another partner, that is, constituting a charge to be borne *personally* by the latter.

An arrangement frequently adopted is to give to the junior partner a CHOICE between 'Salary plus Profits' or 'flat rate of Profit without Salary,' whichever be greater, the excess of the latter over the former to be considered as a *personal debit* to one or other of the partners. The whole problem is that of finding (1) the 'normal' profit and (2) the 'alternative' profit, after which the amount of the difference between (2) and (1) will be adjusted against one of the partners personally. Should the 'alternative' profit NOT be greater than the 'normal' profit there is no amount to adjust.

Illustration 17

Henty senior, Wrey, and Henty junior are partners sharing profits as to Henty senior three-quarters, and as to Wrey one-quarter. Henty junior is entitled to RECEIVE a salary of £1,400 per annum plus 10 per cent of the profits *after* charging up *both* salary and such 10 per cent share of the profits, *or* one-fifth share of the profits, whichever is the greater; should the latter exceed the former, the excess is to be borne by Henty senior alone.

The profits for the year ended 31st December 19.., *after* charging the salary were £12,100. Ignore interest on capital. The salary has been paid. Show accounts.

It will first be necessary to discover which is the preferable alternative so far as Henty junior is concerned.

As the profits divisible are '*after* charging salary,' the latter must be added for the purpose of ascertaining the flat share due to Henty junior, thus:

	£
Profits	12,100
Plus Salary	1,400
Profits before Salary	£13,500

Henty Jnr.'s share $= \frac{1}{5} \times £13,500 = £2,700$

Under the ordinary arrangement he would be entitled to one-tenth of the profits after charging (1) salary and (2) such one-tenth share of profits, thus:

	£
Salary	1,400
Plus share of Profits: $\frac{1}{11} \times £12,100$	1,100
	£2,500

It follows, therefore, that the 'excess' profit share for Henty junior is £200 (2,700 less £2,500). This excess, under the partnership agreement, is to be borne PERSONALLY by Henty senior.

The division is as follows:

PROFIT AND LOSS APPROPRIATION ACCOUNT

	£			£
Henty Jnr.—$\frac{1}{5} \times £13,500$	2,700	Balance	b/d	12,100
Henty Senr.—$\frac{3}{4} \times £11,000$	8,250	Salary added back		1,400
Less Excess Profit due to Henty, Jnr.	200			
	8,050			
Wrey—$\frac{1}{4} \times £11,000$	2,750			
	£13,500			£13,500

HENTY JNR. CURRENT ACCOUNT

	£		£
Salary added back	1,400	Profit and Loss Appropriation	
Balance . . . . c/d	1,300	Account	2,700
	£2,700		£2,700
		Balance . . . . b/d	£1,300

Henty, Junr., will thus obtain from the firm £1,300 PLUS the salary £1,400 already PAID to him.

The Profit and Loss Appropriation Account may alternatively be drawn up thus:

PROFIT AND LOSS APPROPRIATION ACCOUNT

	£		£
Henty Jnr.—$\frac{1}{12} \times$£12,100 . . .	1,100	Balance . . . . b/d	12,100
Balance. . . . . c/d	11,000		
	£12,100		£12,100
Henty Jnr.—Further Share of Profits .	200	Balance . . . . b/d	11,000
Henty Senr.—$\frac{3}{4} \times$£11,000 . £8,250			
Less Share above due to Henty Jnr. 200			
	8,050		
Wrey—$\frac{1}{4} \times$£11,000	2,750		
	£11,000		£11,000

With the necessary changes, the same principle is applied if a loss ensues.

Another alternative is the 'hotchpot' method thus:

1. Profit divisible as if no special arrangement existed.
2. Add amount to be charged personally to partner(s).
3. Divide the total of 1 and 2 in profit ratios.
4. Deduct (2) from the share of partner(s) to be charged.

Illustration 18

Working of previous illustration

	Total	Henty, senr.	Wrey
	£	£	£
1. Profit . . .	10,800		
2. 'Charge' . . .	200		
3. Division . . .	11,000 $\frac{3}{4}$	8,250 $\frac{1}{4}$	2,750
4. Deduction . . .	200	200	—
	£10,800	£8,050	£2,750

Illustration 19

X and Y share profits in the following way:

(a) Salaries £1,500 and £1,250 respectively. (b) Balance equally.

X, wishing to take a less active part in the affairs of the firm, agrees with Y that the latter shall in future receive £1,500 and X £1,250, the ratio of interest in the firm remaining as before, subject to Z being introduced as a partner at a salary of £1,750 and one-seventh share in the profits and losses of the firm (after charging interest on capital and all salaries), all of which was to be charged to X with the exception of £1,500, the amount of salary Z had formerly received as manager. X and Y each had £5,000 capital in the firm, upon which they were entitled to 5 per cent interest, and Z was admitted a partner without capital on 1st January 19 . . . The profit for the year ended 31st December 19 . . , BEFORE charging interest on capital or partners' salaries, was £4,370.

Prepare Profit and Loss Appropriation Account of the firm.

PROFIT AND LOSS APPROPRIATION ACCOUNT
FOR THE YEAR ENDED 31ST DECEMBER 19 . .

		£			£	£
Interest on Capital		500	Balance . . . b/d			4,370
Salaries[1]		4,250	Loss for the purpose of computing Y's Share . c/d			380
		£4,750				£4,750
Balance . . . b/d		380	Loss for the purpose of computing Z's Share . c/d			630
Salary Z (£1,750 − £1,500)		250				
		£630				£630
Balance . . . b/d		630	Y: ½ × £380 . . .			190
			Z: ⅐ × £630 . . .			90
			X: ½ × £380 . . .		190	
			[2] Add Z's extra Share of Profits . .		160	
						350
		£630				£630

The above adjustments may be entered through the Journal and posted therefrom to the current accounts of the partners.

Alternatively, this may be worked as follows:

PROFIT AND LOSS APPROPRIATION ACCOUNT
FOR THE YEAR ENDED 31ST DECEMBER 19 . .

		£			£	£
Balance (as above) . . b/d		380	Y: ½ × £380 . . .			190
Z's extra Share of Profits borne by X (as below) . . .		160	X: ½ × £380 . . .		190	
			Add Z's extra Share of Profits		160	
						350
		£540				£540

[1] Per question.
[2] £250 less £90 (see p. 2247).

Computation of Z's extra share:

		£	£
Salary			250
Loss after charging—			
Interest on Capital and Normal			
Salaries		380	
Z's Extra salary . . .		250	
Total Loss . .		£630	
Less ½ thereof . . .			90
Extra share due to Z.			£160

Illustration 20

Alfred Stone, George Rock and his son, Arthur Rock, were partners in the firm of Stone & Rock, solicitors. Alfred Stone had a son, Eric, who was not a partner and who was paid a salary of £5,000 per annum.

On 1st January 19.1, Henry Flint, the managing clerk, was admitted as a partner, the new profit-sharing ratios being:

Alfred Stone 45 per cent, George Rock 25 per cent, Arthur Rock 20 per cent and a salary of £4,000, Henry Flint 10 per cent.

Flint had previously been paid, as managing clerk, a salary of £10,000 per annum and a commission of two per cent of the profits after charging his salary and commission and all bonuses and salaries other than those payable to partners. It was agreed that, should his share of profits for the first year exceed the amount he would have received as managing clerk, the amount of the excess should be charged against Alfred Stone's share of profits.

On considering the draft accounts at the end of the year, the partners agreed that for special services on partnership work, performed for their respective fathers, Eric Stone should be paid a bonus of £2,000 chargeable against his father's share of profits and George Rock should give a similar sum out of his share to his son, Arthur.

The profits of the partnership for the year ended 31st December 19.1, after providing for Eric Stone's bonus, but before charging Arthur Rock's salary, amounted to £255,000.

You are required to prepare a statement showing the division of the profit of £255,000 between the partners.

STATEMENT OF DISTRIBUTION OF PROFIT FOR THE YEAR ENDED
31ST DECEMBER 19.1

		Alfred Stone 45 per cent	George Rock 25 per cent	Arthur Rock 20 per cent	Henry Flint 10 per cent
	£	£	£	£	£
Profit subject to special adjustments	257,000				
Less Bonus—Eric Stone	2,000				
Profit (as given in question)	255,000				
Less Salary—Arthur Rock	4,000				
	251,000				
Add back Bonus—Eric Stone (not a charge in reducing divisible profit, i.e. personal charge against Alfred Stone)	2,000				
	253,000	113,850	63,250	50,600	25,300
Less Bonus—					
Eric Stone, chargeable to Alfred Stone	2,000	2,000			
Arthur Rock, chargeable to George Rock [1]			−2,000	+2,000	
	251,000	111,850	61,250	52,600	25,300
Add Salary—Arthur Rock	4,000			4,000	
	255,000	111,850	61,250	56,600	25,300

Adjustment re Flint— Previous Share of Profit		£
Profit	[2] £255,000	
Less Salary	10,000	10,000
	£245,000	
Commission $\frac{2}{102}$ thereof		4,800
		14,800
Excess of present share of profit £25,300 chargeable to Alfred Stone		10,500
		£25,300

		Alfred Stone	George Rock	Arthur Rock	Henry Flint
		−10,500	+5,830 $(\frac{25}{45})$	+4,670 $(\frac{20}{45})$	
	£255,000	£101,350	£67,080	£61,270	£25,300

[1] Unlike the bonus to Eric Stone, this item had not been charged in the Profit and Loss Account, so it does not alter the 'divisible' profit.
[2] Profit £257,000, less bonus to Eric Stone, £2,000.

Recoupment of Minimum in Subsequent Years. It has been seen that if the profits are insufficient to give the guaranteed partner his normal share of profits, the shortage is made up by the guaranteeing partners. If it is agreed that the amount necessary to give the guaranteed partner his minimum shall be recoupable in succeeding years, such carry forward may be shown as a Suspense Account rather than as a debit against the guaranteeing partners' Capital Accounts; and in the subsequent years surplus profits will be credited back thereto. When the recoupment takes place, the guaranteed partner's account will be debited and the Suspense

Account credited. Summarized, the entries are:

(A) (1) For the 'shortage' year:
    Debit Capital or Current Accounts of guaranteeing partners in profit and loss ratios.
    Credit Capital or Current Account of guaranteed partner.
  (2) In the year of recoupment the entries will be the reverse of (1).

or

(B) (1) Debit Suspense Account.
    Credit Capital or Current Account of guaranteed partner.
  (2) Reverse of (1).

If the opportunity to recoup has gone by, owing to effluxion of time or from any other cause, the balance in (B) on Suspense Account must be debited to the Capital or Current Accounts of the guaranteeing partners in their profit and loss ratios; and if such ratios have changed during the period in which the guarantee is operative, the amount of shortage must be debited in the proportions applicable to the years in which the constituent shortages making up the balance *arose.*

It will be seen that the latter method may be extremely troublesome should profit-sharing ratios change during such a period, and consequently in such cases method (A) is preferable.

Where a LOSS is incurred, the guaranteeing partners, in addition to bearing their normal share of loss, incur a further liability by paying the guaranteed minimum, so that the two figures, i.e. loss and guaranteed minimum, must be added together in dealing with the problem involved.

Illustration 21

A and B share profits in the ratio of 3:1. C is admitted on the basis of one-fifth of the profits, the balance between the old partners remaining in the old ratio. Under the partnership agreement C is to have a guaranteed minimum for *four* years to the extent of £1,500, A and B to have the right of recoupment out of C's share of profits for *five* years only, that is, any balance to be available for recoupment until, but no longer than, the end of the year subsequent to the expiry of the 'guarantee' period.

The results were:

	£			£
Year 1—Profit	6,800	Year 4—Profit	.	4,600
Year 2—Profit	7,100	Year 5—Profit	.	4,000
Year 3—Profit	8,000			

The effect of the above may be best shown in statement form, the double entry being elementary once the figures are ascertained.

	Profit		A	B	C	Recoupable	
		Ratios =	3	1	1		
	£		£	£	·£	£	£
Year 1 . .	6,800		4,080	1,360	1,360		
		Guarantee	−105	−35	+140	140	
Total .	£6,800		£3,975	£1,325	£1,500		
Year 2 . .	7,100		4,260	1,420	1,420		
		Guarantee	−60	−20	+80	80	
Total .	£7,100		£4,200	£1,400	£1,500		
Year 3 .	8,000	Guarantee	4,800	1,600	1,600		
		Recoupment	+75	+25	−100		100
Total .	£8,000		£4,875	£1,625	£1,500		
Year 4 . .	4,600		2,760	920	920		
		Guarantee	−435	−145	+580	580	
Total .	£4,600		£2,325	£775	£1,500	£800	£100
						Balance—£700 (See year 5)	

In Year 5 the guarantee ceases and the sum of £700 is recoupable from C, but only out of his *profits*; that is, if his share of profits is less than £700, only such share of profits is available for appropriation against the carry forward, the balance being a loss against A and B in the ratio of 3 : 1.

	Profit			A	B	C
		Ratios . . .		3	1	1
	£			£	£	£
Year 5 . .	4,000	Guarantee . . .		2,400	800	800
		Recoupment . . .		+525	+175	−700
Total .	£4,000			£2,925	£975	£100

In the above illustration the guarantee has been dealt with each year against the partners' Accounts, and the end column inserted as a note to show the amount capable of being recouped.

As there is a sufficiency of profits in favour of C to enable A and B to recoup their guarantee payments, the total of the profits to each partner will be precisely the same as if no guarantee had existed.

If the Suspense method had been used, the partners and Suspense Accounts would be as shown on p. 2251 (eliminating details).

If the profits for Year 5 had been, say, £2,000, C's share thereof would be £400 only; hence of £700 unrecouped, £400 only would be available, and A and B would be involved in a final loss on guarantee to the extent of £300, divided as to £225 and £75 to A and B respectively, being their ratio (as between themselves) of losses.

	Suspense Account		A		B		C	
	Dr. £	Cr. £	Dr. £	Cr. £	Dr. £	Cr. £	Dr. £	Cr. £
Year 1	140[1]			4,080		1,360		1,360 140[1]
„ 2	80[1]			4,260		1,420		1,420 80[1]
„ 3		100[1]		4,800		1,600	100[1]	1,600
„ 4	580[1]			2,760		920		920[1]
„ 5		700[1]		2,400		800	700[1]	800
	£800	£800		18,300		6,100	800	6,900
	(as on p. 2250)		18,300		6,100		6,100	
			£18,300	£18,300	£6,100	£6,100	£6,900	£6,900

[1] These items show the creation and elimination of the Suspense Account.

If interest on merged Capital and Current Accounts is to be credited to partners, or where profit and loss ratios are constantly changing, the first method is preferable.

It is impossible entirely to cover the infinite range of problems that arise on (1) guaranteed shares of profits, (2) guaranteed profits from the particular portion of the business brought in by one partner, and (3) shares of profits and losses and salaries paid to junior partners which are borne entirely by one of the senior partners.

Further illustrations are given below and on p. 2252, not so much with a view to exhaust the whole scope of different variations that are encountered, but rather to provide a firm basis of principle which will serve to establish a technique for the solution of all problems of this nature.

Illustration 22

A, B and C, each carrying on business as accountants, decided to amalgamate; the sharing of profits and losses to be 4, 3, and 1, provided:

(a) That C is to have a guaranteed minimum of £24,000.
(b) That the gross fees earned by B on the average of the last three years are to be guaranteed to the firm by B.

The profits of the first year of the new partnership were £171,200 before any adjustments had been made.

The gross fees earned by B in the three years prior to the amalgamation were:

Year 1, £52,000. Year 2, £53,000. Year 3, £51,000.

The gross fees attributable to B's connection in the first year of the partnership were £48,000.

Show Profit and Loss Appropriation and Current Accounts.

PROFIT AND LOSS APPROPRIATION ACCOUNT

	£			£
Capital Accounts—		Balance . . . b/d		171,200
A: $\frac{4}{8}$.	87,600	Fees guaranteed by B .		4,000
B: $\frac{3}{8}$.	65,700	[£52,000−£48,000]		
C: $\frac{1}{8}$.	21,900			
	£175,200			£175,200

CURRENT ACCOUNTS

		A	B	C			A	B	C
		£	£	£			£	£	£
C for Guaranteed Minimum .		$\frac{4}{7}$ 1,200	$\frac{3}{7}$ 900		Profit and Loss Appropriation Account .		87,600	65,700	21,900
Profit and Loss Appropriation Account: Fees Guaranteed .			4,000		A and B for Guaranteed Minimum per contra .				2,100
Balances . . .	c/d	86,400	60,800	24,000					
		£87,600	£65,700	£24,000			£87,600	£65,700	£24,000
					Balances .	b/d	86,400	60,800	24,000

Illustration 23

A and B are equal partners. On 31st March 19.1, the following balances stood to the credit of the partners:

A—Capital Account . £300,000   B—Capital Account . £126,000
A—Current Account . £20,800   B—Current Account . £8,600

The partners agree that A junior (A's son) shall be admitted into the firm as and from 1st April 19.1, it being provided that:

(a) Partnership salaries to be CREDITED: B £7,500 and A junior £6,000.

(b) A junior to have a tenth share of the profits, such share being borne by A.

(c) Interest on Capital and Current Accounts at 5 per cent per annum.

(d) Interest to be charged on drawings of A and B.

On 1st April 19.1, B transferred his rights in a patent to the firm, and it was agreed that £30,000 should be credited to his Capital Account therefor.

On 1st October 19.1, A paid £50,000 into the firm by way of additional capital.

The partners' drawings were: A £26,000 (interest £650), B £18,000 (interest £400), A junior £5,000.

In addition to the accounts necessary to give effect to the above, the following balances were extracted from the books of the firm as on 31st March 19.2.

	£
Factory	205,660
Sundry Creditors	40,810
General Expenses	147,370
Stock, 31st March 19.2	102,240
Provision for Bad Debts, 31st March 19.1	4,000
Sundry Debtors	128,600
Furniture, Plant, and Machinery	215,060
Cash in Bank	40,480
Shares in 'X', Ltd. (20,000 of £1 each fully paid)	20,000
Gross Profit	358,200

After making the adjustments as required below, prepare Profit and Loss Account for the year ended, and Balance Sheet as at, 31st March 19.2.

(a) The furniture, plant, and machinery were revalued at £173,880; shares at £15,000.

(b) Expenses outstanding at 31st March 19.2, £2,260; prepayments £6,580.

(c) Provision for Bad Debts to be increased to £7,000.

The second portion of the account on p. 2254 is the appropriation section of the Profit and Loss Account, as every item contained therein is an 'internal' matter and, as such, affects not the dimension of the profits, but their allocation as between the partners. Unless otherwise stated, profits should always be split **before any 'internal' adjustments,** e.g. Interest on Capital, are made, the latter being as clearly appropriation items as those comprising the formal division of profits.

TRIAL BALANCE AS AT 31ST MARCH 19.2

	£	£
Capitals—		
A		350,000
B		156,000
Current Accounts—		
A		20,800
B		8,600
Drawings—		
A	26,000	
B	18,000	
A Jnr.	5,000	
Sundry Creditors		40,810
Factory	205,660	
Patent	30,000	
Furniture, Plant, and Machinery	215,060	
Stock	102,240	
Shares in 'X', Ltd.	20,000	
Sundry Debtors	128,600	
Bad Debts Provision		4,000
Bank	40,480	
Gross Profit		358,200
General Expenses	147,370	
	£938,410	£938,410

PROFIT AND LOSS ACCOUNT FOR THE
YEAR ENDED 31ST MARCH 19.2

		£	£			£	£
General Expenses			143,050	Gross Profit	b/d		358,200
Depreciation			41,180				
Bad Debts			3,000				
Loss on Investment			5,000				
Balance	c/d		159,970				
			£358,200				£358,200
Salaries—				Balance	b/d		165,970
A Jnr.		6,000		Interest on Drawings—			
B		7,500		A.		650	
			13,500	B		400	
							1,050
Interest on Capitals—							
A¹		16,250					
B¹		7,800					
			24,050				
Interest on Current Accounts—							
A		1,040					
B		430					
			1,470				
Balance: Profit divided—							
A							
½ × £128,000	£64,000						
Less A Jnr.	12,800						
		51,200					
B							
½ × £128,000		64,000					
A Jnr.							
1/10 × £128,000		12,800					
			128,000				
			£167,020				£167,020

[The Balance Sheet is shown on p. 2255]

Receipts and Expenditure Accounts. Reference has already been made to this method of drawing up accounts, so that no difficulty should be encountered in the case of professional partnerships.

Illustration 24

A and B share profits in the ratio of 3:2, on the basis of fees received. The first year's Trial Balance dated 30th September 19.. is as follows:

TRIAL BALANCE

	£	£
Capitals (after adjustment of Drawings)—		
A		4,000
B		3,400
General Expenses	13,000	
Furniture and Equipment	2,500	
Bank	39,200	
Debtors	12,300	
Fees Account (per Bills Delivered Book)		59,600
	£67,000	£67,000

	£	£
¹ Interest on Capitals—		
A: £300,000 at 5% per annum for one year	15,000	
£50,000 at 5% per annum for six months	1,250	
		16,250
B: £156,000 at 5% per annum for one year		7,800

BALANCE SHEET as at 31st March 19.2

Liabilities

	£	£
Capitals—		
Current Accounts	40,810	
Current Liabilities	2,260	43,070
Capitals—		
A: Balance, 1st April 19.1	300,000	
Add Cash brought in	50,000	350,000
B: Balance, 1st April 19.1	126,000	
Add Patent introduced	30,000	156,000
Current Accounts		146,370
		£695,440

Assets

	£	£	£
Fixed Assets—			
Patent			30,000
Factory			205,660
Furniture, Plant, and Machinery		215,060	
Less Depreciation		41,180	173,880
Investment—			
Shares in 'X' Ltd.		20,000	
Less Provision for Loss in Value		5,000	15,000
Current Assets—			
Stock			102,240
Sundry Debtors	£128,600		
Less Bad Debts Provision	7,000		
	121,600		
Add Prepayments	6,580	128,180	
Cash at Bank		40,480	270,900
			£695,440

CURRENT ACCOUNTS

	A £	A £	B £	B £	A Jr. £	A Jr. £
Balance, 1st April 19.1	20,800		8,600			
Add Interest on Capital	16,250		7,800			
" Interest on Current Account	1,040		430			
" Profits	51,200		64,000		12,800	
" Salary			7,500		6,000	
		89,290		88,330		18,800
Less Drawings	26,000		18,000		5,000	
" Interest thereon	650	26,650	400	18,400		5,000
		£62,640		£69,930		£13,800

Show Profit and Loss Account and Balance Sheet.

PROFIT AND LOSS ACCOUNT FOR THE
YEAR ENDED 30TH SEPTEMBER 19 . .

	£	£		£	£
General Expenses.		13,000	Fees .		47,300*
Profit to Capital Accounts—					
A $\frac{3}{5}$	20,580				
B $\frac{2}{5}$	13,720				
		34,300			
		£47,300			£47,300

* This account may be shown thus:

FEES

	£		£
Debtors Reserve .	12,300	Sundries	59,600
Profit and Loss Account	47,300		
	£59,600		£59,600

To save time in examination work, the details may be inserted in the Profit and Loss Account itself as an inset column, e.g.:

Fees £59,600, *less* Debtors Reserve £12,300, equals £47,300.

BALANCE SHEET AS AT 30TH SEPTEMBER 19 . .

	£	£		£	£
Capital Accounts—			Bank .		39,200
A: Balance .	4,000		Debtors .	12,300	
Plus Profit	20,580		Less Debtors Reserve .	12,300	
		24,580			nil
B: Balance .	3,400		Furniture and Equipment		2,500
Plus Profit	13,720				
		17,120			
		£41,700			£41,700

Preparation of Partnership Accounts by Single Entry. If accounts are prepared on the single entry system, the methods already explained apply, except that separate capital and current accounts will be kept.

Illustration 25

A and B are partners keeping their books on the single entry system.
  The assets, less liabilities at 1st January 19 . ., were £80,000.
  The assets, less liabilities at 30th June 19 . ., were £68,000.
  Drawings, A £10,000, B £8,200.
  B has used £1,000 firm goods for private purposes.
  The charge for interest on capital is A £1,250, B £750, being at the rate of 5 per cent per annum.
  They share profits equally. No interest is charged on drawings.

Provide £3,000 depreciation. Show Statement of Profits and Statement of Affairs at 30th June 19..

STATEMENT OF PROFITS FOR THE HALF-YEAR
ENDED 30TH JUNE 19..

	£	£		£	£
Commencing Capitals—			Closing Capitals . . .		68,000
A	50,000		Drawings—		
B	30,000		A: Cash . . .	10,000	
		80,000	B: Cash . £8,200		
Depreciation . . .		3,000	Goods . 1,000	9,200	
Balance . . . c/d		4,200			19,200
		£87,200			£87,200
Interest on Capitals— . .			Balance . . . b/d		4,200
A	1,250				
B	750				
		2,000			
Net Profit—					
A ½ . . .	1,100				
B ½ . . .	1,100				
		2,200			
		£4,200			£4,200

STATEMENT OF AFFAIRS, AS AT 30TH JUNE 19..

		£		£	£	£
Capital Accounts—			Sundry Assets (less Liabilities) . . .		68,000	
A	50,000		Less Depreciation .		3,000	
B	30,000					65,000
		80,000	Current Accounts—			
			A: Drawings . .	10,000		
			Less Profit £1,100			
			,, Interest on			
			Capital . 1,250			
				2,350		
					7,650	
			B: Drawings . .	9,200		
			Less Profit £1,100			
			,, Interest on			
			Capital . 750			
				1,850		
					7,350	15,000
		£80,000				£80,000

Note. Detailed assets and liabilities eliminated. Interest for *half-year* is 2½ per cent.

∴ The capitals are: A $\frac{100}{2\frac{1}{2}}$ × £1,250 = £50,000; B $\frac{100}{2\frac{1}{2}}$ × £750 = £30,000.

Division of Profits. The methods of division of profits are unlimited, but the principles involved are usually simple, depending upon the method of computing the particular figure. As an illustration, the following may be considered as typical.

Illustration 26

A and B are partners sharing profits 3:2. Their capitals are £30,600 and £10,000. On 1st November 19.., C enters the partnership, the terms being that he shall pay £5,000 for his share of the goodwill (which sum will be paid out to the other partners in their profit-sharing ratio) and introduce £5,000 capital, and that the profit and loss-sharing ratio be so adjusted that between A and B the former ratio is maintained, while between B and C there shall be the same ratio as between A and B.

The capitals are to be adjusted in cash (without disturbing the new total capital) so as to correspond with the new ratio; and interest on capital is to be taken at the rate of 5 per cent per annum throughout the period. The profits for the year before adjusting interest are £19,000, the proportion due to the period before and after the admission of C being found on the basis that profits are in uniform ratio to sales, the average monthly sales for the first eight months being twice as high as for the latter four months (i.e. 1st September to 31st December).

Show the partners' accounts and the Profit and Loss Appropriation Account for the year ended 31st December 19 . . . Entries are to be made to nearest £. Ignore Drawings.

CAPITAL ACCOUNTS

			A	B	C				A	B	C
19..			£	£	£	19..			£	£	£
Nov. 1	Cash		9,000			Jan. 1	Balances		30,600	10,000	
Dec. 31	Balances	c/d	21,600	14,400	9,600	Nov. 1	Cash				5,000
							,,			4,440	4,600
			£30,600	£14,400	£9,600				£30,600	£14,440	£9,600
						19..					
						Jan. 1	Balances	b/d	21,600	14,400	9,600

CURRENT ACCOUNTS

			A	B	C				A	B	C
19..			£	£	£	19..			£	£	£
Dec. 31	Balances	c/d	11,420	7,180	400	Dec. 31	Interest on Capital		1,455	537	80
							Profits—				
							(10 months)		9,245	6,163	
							(2 months)		720	480	320
			£11,420	£7,180	£400				£11,420	7,180	400
						19..					
						Jan. 1	By Balances	b/d	11,420	7,180	400

PROFIT AND LOSS APPROPRIATION ACCOUNT
FOR THE YEAR ENDED 31ST DECEMBER 19..

	£	£	£				£
Interest on Capitals				Balance	b/d		19,000
A (10 months)	1,275						
(2 ,,)	180						
		1,455					
B (10 ,,)	417						
(2 ,,)	120						
		537					
C (2 ,,)		80					
			2,072				
Profits (10 months)							
A: $\frac{3}{5}$	9,245						
B: $\frac{2}{5}$	6,163						
		[1]15,408					
Profits (2 months)							
A: $\frac{9}{19}$	720						
B: $\frac{6}{19}$	480						
C: $\frac{4}{19}$	320						
		[2]1,520					
		£19,000					£19,000

The interest is calculated as follows (to the nearest £):

	£	£
5% per annum on—		
A—£30,600 for 10 months	1,275	
B—£10,000 ,,	417	
		1,692
A—£21,600 for 2 months	180	
B—£14,400 ,,	120	
C—£ 9,600 ,,	80	
		380
		£2,072

The profits are split up:
(a) As regards partners—

For the first ten months: A, $\frac{3}{5}$; B, $\frac{2}{5}$.

For the latter period this ratio must be maintained, and a similar one put into force between B and C. Thus:

A:B:C = 9:6:4
∴ For the last two months: A, $\frac{9}{19}$; B, $\frac{6}{19}$; C, $\frac{4}{19}$

(b) As regards time—

In the first eight months, the average monthly sales are twice as heavy as in the last four. Therefore, as the gross profits vary directly with sales, the profits will be apportioned thus:

$$8 \times 2 = 16: \quad 4 \times 1 = 4 \quad \text{Total, 20}$$

---

[1] £17,100 less Interest on Capital £1,692 = £15,408. (See this page and p. 2260.)
[2] £1,900 less Interest on Capital £380 = £1,520. (See this page and p. 2260.)

In the first period of ten months $\frac{16}{20}+\frac{2}{20}=\frac{18}{20}$ of the profits have been earned, i.e. $£19,000 \times \frac{18}{20} = £171,000$, and in the latter period of two months $\frac{2}{20}$, i.e. $£19,000 \times \frac{2}{20} = £1,900$.

These amounts are split amongst the partners in the ratios shown above, less interest on capital for the appropriate period.

SECTION B. ADMISSION OF A PARTNER

The most important adjustments necessitated by the admission of a partner are those involved by the revaluation of the assets and liabilities at true values in place of book values.

Revaluation of Assets and Liabilities on an Admission

1. **Values to be Altered in Books.** It has been seen that upon the admission of a partner it is necessary to make a revaluation of all the assets and liabilities so that the true position of the partners at the date of such admission may be ascertained.

Method 1. The entries are as follows:

(a) The assets at book values are debited to a Revaluation Account, corresponding credits being made in the Assets Accounts.

(b) The assets at **REVISED** values are debited to the Assets Accounts and credited to the Revaluation Account.

(c) The liabilities at book values are debited to the Liabilities Accounts and credited to the Revaluation Account.

(d) The liabilities at **REVISED** values are debited to the Revaluation Account and credited to the Liabilities Accounts.

(e) Depreciation in such assets as debtors, investments, and stock is treated by creating an appropriate provision, that is, the book values remain constant and are not passed through the Revaluation Account, or, if desired, may be shown on both sides at the same value. The amount of provision required, either new or to the extent of an increase, if any, is debited to Revaluation Account and credited to PROVISION Account, e.g. Investment Provision. If the provision is to be reduced or eliminated, the entries will be the reverse.

(f) The balance of Revaluation Account is treated precisely like a Profit and Loss Account balance, viz.:

(i) If there is an excess of debits over credits, the Revaluation Account is credited to balance off and the partners' Capital (or Capital Adjustment) Accounts are debited.

(ii) If there is an excess of credits over debits the Revaluation Account is debited to balance off, and the partners' Capital (or Capital Adjustment) Accounts are credited.

Illustration 27

A and B are partners sharing profits equally. They decide to admit C as a partner. It is necessary to adjust the values of assets and liabilities in the books before C's admission.

BALANCE SHEET, AS AT 31ST DECEMBER 19 . .

	£	£		£	£
Creditors		1,000	Cash in Bank		600
Capitals—			Debtors		1,500
A	1,700		Stock		1,400
B	1,200		Fixtures		400
		2,900			
		£3,900			£3,900

At this date (when C is to be admitted) it is found that the estimated value of the debtors is £1,200 and fixtures £250, whilst an investment not recorded in the books previously taken over in part payment of a debt is worth £400.

You are required to prepare (1) Journal entries; (2) Revaluation Account; and (3) Balance Sheet after giving effect to the above. For the purpose of this illustration, goodwill may be ignored.

JOURNAL

19 . .		£	£
Dec. 31	Revaluation Account	700	
	Fixtures		400
	Bad Debts Provision		300
	Being transfers to Revaluation Account at date of C's admission.		
	Investments	400	
	Fixtures	250	
	Revaluation Account		650
	Being items revalued at date of C's admission.		
	A Capital	25	
	B ,,	25	
	Revaluation Account		50
	Being loss on revaluation transferred to Capital Account		

REVALUATION ACCOUNT

19 . .		£	19 . .			£
Dec. 31	Fixtures	400	Dec. 31	Fixtures		250
	Bad Debts Provision	300		Investments		400
				A Capital	£25	
				B ,,	25	
						50
		£700				£700

BALANCE SHEET (*after* giving effect to the above)

	£	£		£	£
Creditors . . .		1,000	Cash in Bank. , .		600
A Capital . . .	1,700		Debtors . . .	1,500	
Less Loss on Revaluation . .	25		Less Bad Debts Provision . .	300	
		1,675			1,200
B Capital . . .	1,200		Stock		1,400
Less Loss on Revaluation . .	25		Investments . .		400
		1,175	Fixtures . . .		250
		£3,850			£3,850

Alternatively the entries may be made as below:

Method 2.
Debit Revaluation Account with:

(*a*) Increased Liabilities (credit Liabilities).
(*b*) Decreased Assets   (credit Assets).[1]

Credit Revaluation Account with:

(*a*) Decreased Liabilities (debit Liabilities).
(*b*) Increased Assets   (debit Assets).

The balance will be treated as profit or loss exactly as (*f*) in the previous set of entries. The entries for the foregoing revaluations will be:

JOURNAL

		£	£
19 . .			
Dec. 31	Investments	400	
	A Capital	25	
	B ,, ...	25	
	Fixtures		150
	Bad Debts Provision		300
	Being adjustments of values of assets and liabilities at date of C's admission.		
		£450	£450

The resultant Balance Sheet will be identical with that shown above.

2. **Values to Remain Unaltered in Books.** Where the new firm desire to keep the old values of assets and liabilities unchanged in the books, the following procedure is adopted:

[1] In the case of Investments, Debtors, and Stock the old book value will be undisturbed and the credit will be to a Provision, e.g. Investments Provision.

(a) The OLD firm credits the increase in value of assets (and/or decrease in amount of liabilities) to a *Memorandum* Adjustment or Revaluation Account and, instead of being posted to the Ledger Accounts, the items are **brought down on the opposite side,** in the manner of balancing an account. The credit in the top portion is closed by a transfer to the credit of the *old* partners' Capital or Current Accounts in the old profit ratio; whilst the debit below the line is treated as a **LOSS** to the NEW firm and closed by a transfer to the debit of Capital or Current Accounts of the *new* partners, just as if the increase in worth to the old firm has been actually lost at the very inception of the new firm.

(b) The converse procedure is followed in the case of a decrease in value of assets (and/or increase in amount of liabilities).

From the above figures the appropriate Journal entries are made and posted to the Ledger.

Illustration 28

If the altered values in the example below were not to be permanently recorded in the books (and assuming new profit-sharing ratio to be: A $\frac{2}{5}$, B $\frac{2}{5}$, and C $\frac{1}{5}$) the adjustment would be:

Memorandum REVALUATION ACCOUNT

			£				£
19.. Dec. 31	Decrease in Value of Assets: Fixtures . . £150 Debtors . . 300 ———	c/d	450	19.. Dec. 31	Increase in Value of Assets: Investments . . . Capital Accounts: A: $\frac{1}{2}$ . . . £25 B: $\frac{1}{2}$ . . . 25	c/d	400
							50
			£450				£450
19.. Jan. 1	Reversal of Entry . . Capital Accounts: A: $\frac{2}{5}$ . . . £20 B: $\frac{2}{5}$ . . . 20 C: $\frac{1}{5}$ . . . 10 ———	b/d	400 50	19.. Jan. 1	Reversal of Entries . .	b/d	450
			£450				£450

CAPITAL ACCOUNTS

		A	B	C			A	B	C
		£	£	£			£	£	£
Loss on Revaluation . Balances . . .	c/d	25 1,695	25 1,195	10	Balances . b/d Loss on Revaluation written back . .	b/d	1,700 20	1,200 20	10
		£1,720	£1,220	£10			£1,720	£1,720	£10
					Balances . .	b/d	1,695	1,195	10

Goodwill. Goodwill is an intangible asset; as has been judicially said—'It is easy to describe but difficult to define.'

It represents the value to a business attaching to all the factors, internal and external, which enable it to earn a differential return of profit on the capital employed; that is, a better return than that which arises in other comparable businesses, having regard to the nature, size, location and risk inherent in such a business, and which is capable of being enjoyed by a successor.

There are many businesses which possess this 'differential,' but arising only or mainly from the personal attributes of an owner and thus not normally capable of being enjoyed by (and so transferred to) a new owner.

There exist numerous definitions of Goodwill, some of which are given below:

'The goodwill of a business is the advantage, whatever it may be, which a person gets by continuing to carry on, and being entitled to represent to the outside world that he is carrying on a business, which has been carried on for some time previously' (*Hill* v. *Fearis*).

'The attractive force which brings in custom.'

'The benefit of a good name, reputation and connection of a business.'

'The one thing which distinguishes an old-established business from a new business at its first start.'

'The monetary measurement of the benefits attaching to the ownership of a successful business.'

'The capitalized value attaching to the differential profit capacity of a business.'

'The whole advantage, whatever it may be, of the reputation and connection of the firm which may have been built up by years of honest work or gained by lavish expenditure of money' (*Trego* v. *Hunt*).

Goodwill is an intangible, but not necessarily a fictitious, asset representing the value—however difficult its appraisement may be—to its owner of benefits arising from the business in question, such as the sole right to enjoy the profits of the business, and, where goodwill has been *acquired*, the sole right of succession to the advantages of the business which have been built up in the past. Goodwill arises mainly (a) by personal reputation of the owners, (b) by reputation of the goods dealt in, (c) by site monopoly or advantage, (d) by access to sources of supply, e.g. large quotas, (e) for patent and trademark protection, (f) effectiveness of publicity, (g) reputation of the firm's goods and methods, (h) relationship between firm and personnel, and (i) growth element.

The purchaser of goodwill acquires the trade marks, patents, copyrights, etc., of the business as well as the benefits of contracts and all the benefits accruing from the location, reputation, connection, organization and other exceptional features of the business. The purchaser will seek to express the sum payable in terms of the compounded or capitalized value of an annuity of future differential or 'super' profits, that is those profits in excess of the marginal return normally arising.

No formula can be laid down for the accurate measurement of the value of goodwill, and in practice a purchaser will be prepared to pay a sum representing a number of years' purchase of recent annual average profits, e.g. three years' purchase, according to the estimated worth to the buyer of the FUTURE earning capacity of the business, the risk of the discontinuance or diminution in such future profits being duly considered. Obviously, if the nature of the business is such that the profits are likely to decline, or that there is an abnormal risk of a discontinuance of reasonable earnings, the buyer will naturally reduce his buying price accordingly. Such circumstances as the business being largely successful owing to (1) the personality of the past proprietor, (2) the particular situation of the premises held on a short lease, (3) monopoly conditions which are not likely to continue, or (4) a temporary fashion or craze will also influence the goodwill estimate.

In the same way as a prospective purchaser is prepared to make a payment for goodwill in acquiring a business, so is a prospective partner prepared to lay out a sum for a *share* in a business. The principle is the same in both cases; in the first payment is for the *whole*, in the second for a *share* of the business. In both instances the owner, or owners, will require compensation for loss of benefits.

Following this rule, a retiring partner will naturally expect to receive compensation for the surrender of his rights in the partnership, whether a new partner be admitted or not.

The books of account may or may not record a figure for goodwill; in fact, unless arising by purchase, goodwill does not usually appear in the books, it being regarded as contrary to good accounting practice to write up a *created* goodwill.

Even if the record be made it may not represent the true value because of the inherent difficulties of valuation, particularly as from time to time the asset is susceptible to extreme fluctuations. Hence it is always necessary to find the true (or nearest possible approximation) value of goodwill, and for that matter of ANY OTHER ASSET and LIABILITY upon *any* change in the constitution of the firm—whether in respect of PERSONNEL or of PROFIT PROPORTIONS. Nor is the valuation less essential merely because at the time of change no record appears in the books of account.

The circumstances usually calling for the ascertainment of the true value of goodwill are:

1. The admission of a new partner.
2. The death or retirement of a partner.
3. A combination of (1) and (2), i.e. where a new partner is substituted for an old partner.
4. A dissolution of partnership, which includes the sale of the business to any other individual, firm, or company.
5. A change in the ratio of sharing profits and losses by whatever name such shares are designated.
6. A change in the mode of ascertaining profits and losses.

Calculation of Value. For the purpose of a sale, goodwill is generally valued on the basis of a number of years' purchase of the annual net profits calculated by reference to recent years and having regard to the probable maintenance of such profits in the future. No fixed number of years is used, but it will generally be from three to five, depending upon all the circumstances. When this method is used, the purchase-price will be either:

(a) the figure arising from the multiplication of the average profit by the number of years chosen, without modification, or

(b) that figure less deductions for:

(i) reasonable remuneration of management;
(ii) interest on capital, divided between (a) 'pure' interest and (b) 'risk' interest, or

(c) that figure used as the basis of a return from an investment, less the net assets other than goodwill.

Illustration 29

Goodwill is to be valued at two years' purchase of the average profits of the last five years, viz:

£1,200; £1,800; £3,000; £800; £2,400; Total £9,200.

(1) Average profits $= \dfrac{9,200}{5} = £1,840$

(2) Two years' purchase $= £1,840 \times 2 = £3,680$

Illustration 30

The net assets of a business belonging to S are £6,000, exclusive of goodwill, and the profits are £3,200 per annum before charging any proprietorship salary, or interest on capital.

Assuming that these profits may reasonably be expected to continue and that the owner expects a minimum return of $6\frac{1}{2}$ per cent for 'pure' interest—equivalent to that obtainable on a British Government Stock—and $8\frac{1}{2}$ per cent for risk, together with a remuneration for service of £2,000, the super-profits will be:

Profits of business			£3,200
Less (1) 'Pure' Interest on £6,000 at $6\frac{1}{2}$% p.a.		£390	
(2) 'Risk' Return on £6,000 at $8\frac{1}{2}$% p.a.		510	
(3) Remuneration		2,000	
			2,900
Super profits			£300

As the proprietor expects a minimum return of 15 per cent per annum on his capital invested in the business, the maximum valuation of goodwill is the sum invested at this rate that will produce a yearly return of £300, i.e. $\frac{100}{15} \times £300 = £2,000$, although the valuation is often made by taking a certain number of years purchase of the super profits.

Looking upon the business as the equivalent of an investment, the value of the business (having regard to risk involved and the return expected of businesses of a similar nature), taking a minimum return of 15 per cent, will be the sum invested at 15 per cent per annum that will produce a yearly return of £1,000 [i.e. net profits of £3,200 less remuneration of management £2,000]. Such a sum equals $\frac{100}{15} \times £1,200 = £8,000$. As the net assets of the business, excluding goodwill, are £6,000, the value of goodwill is £2,000.

Thus, a purchaser of the above business would, given normal circumstances, be prepared to invest £8,000 therein, in order to derive an annual income of £3,200, the purchase price being comprised of two parts, viz. for net tangible assets, £6,000; and for goodwill, £2,000.

In respect of professional businesses where the earning capacity is largely based upon the individuality and personality of the proprietor, the saleable goodwill is normally less than that of a non-professional business, and usually based on a number of years purchase of the gross annual recurring fees.

In all cases, ruling rates of interest will exert a strong influence on the question of the number of years to be taken for the calculation, the lower the ruling rate, the greater the number of years.

It is sometimes suggested that, when there are available profits, goodwill should be written down, but it will be seen that the higher the profits of a business, the higher is the goodwill value and if the profit trend is upwards so will be the goodwill value, and vice versa. Thus it is in adverse times that goodwill should really be written down.

Goodwill on Admission of a New Partner

Goodwill is dealt with on the introduction of a new partner as follows:

1. **Where Goodwill is to be brought into the Books at the Revised Value.** Goodwill Account is created or adjusted to represent the value of the whole asset, the necessary credit being made to the Capital Accounts of the old partners in their old profit-sharing ratio. *The* TOTAL *sum paid by the incoming partner,* INCLUDING *that paid for his share of goodwill, is credited to his own Capital Account.*[1]

2. **Where Goodwill is not to be brought into the Books.**

(*a*) MEMORANDUM REVALUATION METHOD. The created or adjusted goodwill is credited to the old partners in their old profit-sharing ratio and debited to the new partners in their new profit-sharing ratio. The total sum paid by the incoming partner, including that paid for his share of goodwill, is credited to his own Capital Account.

(*b*) PURCHASE AND SALE METHOD. The fractions of goodwill bought and sold by the partners are found, and adjustments are made between the partners for the sums represented by these fractions of the total goodwill. The total sum paid by the incoming partner, including that paid for his share of goodwill, is credited to his own Capital Account.

(*c*) PREMIUM METHOD. (i) The sum paid by the incoming partner for his share of the total goodwill, being the same proportion of the whole goodwill of the firm as is his share of the total profits, is divided between the old partners in their old profit-sharing ratio.

[1] This simple rule is frequently broken by students. There is *no* further entry required to record the above, and it is incorrect (in this method) to credit the old partners with the incoming partner's premium (i.e. share of goodwill acquired) paid in.

This receipt may be dealt with:

(α) As a private transaction—no entries being made in the firm's books.

(β) As a firm transaction, the cash being immediately withdrawn.

(γ) As a firm transaction, the cash being retained in the business.

(ii) Where there is an *alteration* in the profit-sharing ratio between the old partners, a further adjustment is called for in respect of the share of goodwill passing from one old partner to another.

The premium method is convenient only when the profit-sharing ratio of the old partners *remains undisturbed*, because it entails a further adjustment. [See p. 2270 (c) (ii).]

It should be noted that whichever method is adopted the total contribution of an incoming partner, i.e. the amount of capital contribution **and** the premium for share of goodwill, is credited to his Capital Account, the difference being that under method (a) no adjusting entries are required whereas in (b) and (c) adjustments are required.

Illustration 31

A and B were partners sharing profits in the ratio of 3:2. They agree to admit C as a partner, the new ratio of profit sharing to be 4:1:1. For the purpose of the change, goodwill is valued at £2,400. No figure for goodwill appears in the books. Make the necessary entries in Journal form.

METHODS OF RECORD. (1) *Where Goodwill is to be brought into the Books.*

JOURNAL

	£	£
Goodwill	2,400	
A—Capital: $\frac{3}{5}$		1,440
B— ,, $\frac{2}{5}$		960
Being Goodwill at the date of C's admission.		

(2) (a) *Memorandum Revaluation Method.* The whole goodwill is brought in at the old ratio and written out in the new ratio.

JOURNAL

	£	£
Goodwill	2,400	
A—Capital: $\frac{3}{5}$		1,440
B— ,, $\frac{2}{5}$		960
Being Goodwill at the date of C's admission.		
A—Capital: $\frac{2}{3}$	1,600	
B— ,, $\frac{1}{6}$	400	
C— ,, $\frac{1}{6}$	400	
Goodwill Account		2,400
Being the elimination of Goodwill from the books at the date of C's admission.		

	£	£
Net result is A in debit for . .	160	
C in debit for . .	400	
B in credit for . .		560

(*b*) *Purchase and Sale Method.* A schedule must be drawn up to ascertain the fractions of goodwill purchased or sold by each partner, from which are obtained the requisite amounts for the appropriate Journal entries.

SCHEDULE OF SHARES OF GOODWILL
[Goodwill = £2,400]

	A	B	C
Old Shares Sold	$\frac{3}{5}$	$\frac{2}{5}$	—
New Shares Purchased	$\frac{4}{6}$	$\frac{1}{6}$	$\frac{1}{6}$
Differences	Buy $\frac{2}{30}$	Sell $\frac{7}{30}$	Buy $\frac{5}{30}$
	£160	£560	£400
	Dr.	Cr.	Dr.

JOURNAL

		£	£
A—Capital	.	160	
C— ,,	.	400	
B—Capital	.		560
Being adjustments in respect of purchase and sale of Goodwill on C's admission.			

(*c*) *Premium Method.* C will pay a premium of £400 on admission as a partner to take one-sixth share of the profits. This will be credited to A and B in their old profit-sharing ratio. As goodwill is not to be brought into the books, it is necessary further to adjust between A and B for the transfer of one-fifth of the *remaining* five-sixths goodwill belonging to A and B (after the sale of one-sixth to C), the ratio of sharing such five-sixths being altered from A$\frac{3}{5}$:B$\frac{2}{5}$ to A$\frac{4}{5}$:B$\frac{1}{5}$. The remaining goodwill is £2,000.

(i)   JOURNAL

		£	£
C—Capital Account[1]	.	400	
A—Capital: $\frac{3}{5}$	.		240
B— ,, $\frac{2}{5}$	.		160
Being premium of £400 charged to C on his admission.			

[1] This debit might be made direct to Cash or C's Loan Account.

	£ 400	£
A—Capital	400	
B—Capital		400
Transfer of $\frac{1}{6}$ of the total Goodwill, being $\frac{1}{5}$ of A and B's *combined share* of such total from B to A on the alteration of the ratio in which they share their combined proportion of total profits from A $\frac{3}{5}$: B $\frac{2}{5}$ to A $\frac{4}{5}$: B $\frac{1}{5}$.[1]		

[1] [i.e. $\frac{1}{5} \times £2,000$].

The combined result of the above entries is the same as that previously obtained.

Old Goodwill Figure to be Undisturbed. Problems frequently arise where the old goodwill figure is recorded in the books, and although the revised amount of goodwill must be utilized as the basis for the premium of a new partner, the old figure is to remain unaltered in the books.

The *undisclosed* goodwill must be treated just as if it were the true goodwill, methods (2) (a), (b) and (c) shown on pp. 2268 and 2269 being applicable thereto. If the bare goodwill is *less* than that disclosed, converse entries should be made.

Illustration 32

A and B are partners sharing profits in the ratio of 3 : 2. Goodwill appears in the books at £4,000. C is admitted a partner for one-fifth share, paying therefor a premium of £1,000. Show the Journal entry in respect of the above, utilizing the 'premium' method, assuming that the ratio of profit sharing as between A and B remains unchanged.

	£	£
C—Capital[1]	200	
A—Capital		120
B— ,, ...		80
Being premium charged to C for one-fifth share of the undisclosed Goodwill.		
Cash	1,000	
C—Capital		1,000
Being payment by C of the premium for one-fifth share of Goodwill.		

[1] As C is acquiring one-fifth share of the Goodwill for £1,000, the whole Goodwill is £5,000, of which £4,000 already appears in the books of the firm. Hence the value of the *undisclosed* Goodwill is £1,000, C's share thereof being £200. As a result of being debited with £200 and credited with £1,000, C's Capital Account is credited with £800. If Goodwill realized £5,000, C would receive the £800 aforesaid, plus his one-fifth share of the profit on book value, such profit being £1,000.

Illustration 33

Q and S sharing profits and losses in the ratio of 3:2 have been in partnership for several years.

O is to be admitted a partner to pay in cash for capital £600, and to have a one-tenth share in profits and losses. The premium for acquiring such share is £200, but he is unable to bring in cash.

Show how the position may be dealt with.

It is clear that the WHOLE goodwill is £2,000, i.e. £200 × 10, which belongs exclusively to Q and S. Accordingly, a Goodwill Account will be opened therefor and credited to the old partners' Capital Accounts in their *old* ratios. The Goodwill Account will either remain in the books or be written back by the reversal process.

Alternatively, the premium may be charged to O by way of loan—with or without interest—to be reduced out of profits. If the old partners change, as between themselves, their profit-sharing ratios, an adjustment of their Capital Accounts is necessary, as shown under Method (c) (ii) on p. 2270.

Distinction Between Contribution and Purchase of Share. A point of importance must now be considered, viz. the distinction between an actual contribution to the firm's assets and the purchase of a partner's share, and in both instances the question of goodwill arises. In the former case the firm's assets will be augmented by the amount paid in, whilst in the latter the only alterations will be in the shares of the partners *inter se*, the combined capitals as a *whole* remaining unchanged.

Illustration 34

A and B share profit equally and have equal capitals. Their Balance Sheet on C's admission (who is to pay in sufficient to give him a third share in the partnership) is:

A AND B BALANCE SHEET

	£		£
A Capital	3,000	Sundry Assets	6,000
B ,,	3,000		
	£6,000		£6,000

C would contribute the sum of £3,000, the resulting Balance Sheet being:

A, B, AND C BALANCE SHEET

	£		£
A Capital	3,000	Sundry Assets	6,000
B ,,	3,000	Cash	3,000
C ,,	3,000		
	£9,000		£9,000

Where he is to purchase his third SHARE from a partner (say B), the asset side (where goodwill is ignored) will remain unchanged, thus:

A, B, AND C BALANCE SHEET

	£		£
A Capital	3,000	Sundry Assets . . .	6,000
B ,, ...	1,000		
C ,, ...	2,000		
	£6,000		£6,000

Illustration 35

Taking the same facts as in Illustration 34 with the addition of goodwill, assuming that C, on his admission, is to pay into the firm £5,000 for a third share in the partnership, the obvious inference is that A and B's combined share in the partnership must be twice that of C, and hence the total assets are £10,000. Goodwill, therefore, is £4,000 divided between A and B equally. The resultant Balance Sheet is:

A, B, AND C BALANCE SHEET

	£	£		£
A Capital . . .	3,000		Sundry Assets . .	6,000
Add Goodwill . .	2,000		Goodwill . . .	4,000
		5,000	Cash . . .	5,000
B Capital . . .	3,000			
Add Goodwill . .	2,000			
		5,000		
C Capital . . .		5,000		
		£15,000		£15,000

If C is to purchase a portion of a partner's share for £5,000—in this case, a third share in the partnership from B—the inference is that the combined worth of the assets of A and B is three times £5,000, viz. £15,000. Hence the goodwill is £9,000, which will be divided equally between A and B.

A, B, AND C BALANCE SHEET

	£	£		£	£
A Capital . . .	3,000		Sundry Assets . .		6,000
Add Goodwill . .	4,500		Goodwill . . .		9,000
		7,500			
B Capital . . .	3,000				
Add Goodwill . .	4,500				
	7,500				
Less Sale to C .	5,000				
		2,500			
C Capital . . .		5,000			
		£15,000			£15,000

The same principle occurs on the *formation* of a partnership as distinct from the *admission* of a partner.

Illustration 36

A and B commence partnership as equal partners, A bringing in cash £2,000, and B sundry assets £3,000.

The assets would be debited in the ordinary way, A and B respectively being credited with £2,000 and £3,000, but if they are to have an *equal share in the partnership* the entries will be:

$$\begin{array}{llll} & £ & & £ \\ \text{Debit Cash} & . \quad . \quad 2,000 & \text{Credit A} & . \quad 3,000 \\ \text{Goodwill} & . \quad 1,000 & \text{B} & . \quad 3,000 \\ \text{Sundry Assets} & . \quad 3,000 & & \end{array}$$

If goodwill be ignored, the entries will be:

$$\begin{array}{lllll} & & £ & & £ \\ \text{either } (a) & \text{Debit Cash} & . \quad . \quad 2,000 & \text{Credit A} & . \quad 2,500 \\ & \text{Sundry Assets} & . \quad 3,000 & \text{B} & . \quad 2,500 \\ \text{or} \quad (b) & \text{Debit Cash} & . \quad . \quad 2,000 & \text{Credit A} & . \quad 2,000 \\ & \text{Sundry Assets} & . \quad 2,000 & \text{B} & . \quad 2,000 \end{array}$$

If the respective interests were 2 : 1, A is to be assumed to bring in an equivalent of twice the assets of B, viz. £6,000, of which cash is £2,000, and, therefore, goodwill £4,000. The entries will be:

$$\begin{array}{llll} & £ & & £ \\ \text{Debit Cash} & . \quad . \quad 2,000 & \text{Credit A} & . \quad 6,000 \\ \text{Goodwill} & . \quad 4,000 & \text{B} & . \quad 3,000 \\ \text{Sundry Assets} & . \quad 3,000 & & \end{array}$$

If goodwill be ignored, the entries will be:

$$\begin{array}{lllll} & & £ & & £ \\ \text{either } (a) & \text{Debit Cash} & . \quad . \quad 2,000 & \text{Credit A} & . \quad 3,333 \text{ to nearest £} \\ & \text{Sundry Assets} & . \quad 3,000 & \text{B} & . \quad 1,667 \\ \text{or} \quad (b) & \text{Debit Cash} & . \quad . \quad 2,000 & \text{Credit A} & . \quad 2,000 \\ & \text{Sundry Assets} & . \quad 1,000 & \text{B} & . \quad 1,000 \end{array}$$

Adjustment of New Partner's Capital Account

An incoming partner may be required to contribute capital in the same proportion as his proposed profit sharing ratio; for instance, if he is to have one-quarter share of profits he must contribute one-quarter of the capital. This question is one largely of arithmetic, and students are apt to become confused in examination work because of neglect of obtaining proficiency in dealing with questions of this type so frequently presented to the examinee in an ambiguous manner. Leaving aside all other considerations, the various phases of this problem will now be considered.

1. Incoming Partner to Contribute his Due Proportion of Capital, and the ORIGINAL Total Capital is to Remain Unchanged.

The rule in this case is that the incoming partner's capital contribution must be his profit proportion based upon the total capital existing at the date of his admission.

Illustration 37

A's and B's capitals are £3,000 and £2,000; they share profits in the same proportion. C is to have one-fifth share of the profits; A and B continuing to share as between themselves as before. C's capital to be proportionate to his profit-sharing ratio. The capital of the new firm is to remain at £5,000. Show Capital Accounts.

As C is to have one-fifth of the capital and the combined capital of the new firm is to remain at £5,000, he must contribute the sum of £1,000, and this sum will be taken out by A and B proportionately, thus:

	A	B	C	Total
	£	£	£	£
Original Capitals	3,000	2,000	nil	5,000
Revised Capitals[1]	2,400	1,600	1,000	5,000
	Receive	Receive	Pay	
Cash Adjustments	[2]£600	£400	£1,000	

2. Where the Contribution by the Incoming Partner is to Remain in the Business.

The proportionate contribution will be arrived at by taking the profit proportion and deducting from the denominator the amount of the numerator, e.g. one-fifth proportion becomes one-quarter, one-seventh becomes one-sixth, two-sevenths becomes two-fifths, and so on.

Illustration 38

Same facts as in the preceding illustration, except that the amount of C's contribution is to remain in the business, i.e. the new combined capital is to be increased by C's contribution.

The amount of capital C must introduce is $\dfrac{1}{5-1}$, i.e. $\frac{1}{4} \times £5,000$, viz. £1,250.

---

[1] C thus has one-fifth of the combined capital.
[2] Withdrawals are "proportionate" if the original capitals are "proportionate."

The capitals, after C has contributed the £1,250, will appear:

A	B	C	Total
£	£	£	£
3,000	2,000	1,250	6,250

C thus has one-fifth of the combined capital.

A's share of profits is now $\frac{3}{5} \times \frac{4}{5} = \frac{12}{25}$.

B's share of profits is now $\frac{2}{5} \times \frac{4}{5} = \frac{8}{25}$.

As the original capitals of A and B were proportionate to their profit ratios, they should so remain after the above introduction of capital by C.

Thus A's capital is $\frac{12}{25} \times £6,250 = £3,000$.

Thus B's capital is $\frac{8}{25} \times £6,250 = £2,000$.

In problems of this nature the fact that the other partners' capital ratios are not equal to their profit ratios must be ignored, unless the question requires adjustment of *all* the capitals; in any case, in determining the amount of the incoming partner's capital the disproportionate ratios of capitals of the old partners may be ignored. Reverting to the preceding illustration, C must bring in either £1,000 or £1,250, as the case may be, quite irrespective of the composition of the old capital of £5,000.

If the capitals of A and B were disproportionate as between themselves, it would be advisable to adjust the position, e.g. if A's capital was £2,350 and B's capital was £2,650, A would pay and B would receive £650.

Restriction of Drawings until Capital Subscribed. On the admission of a new partner it is frequently stipulated that his drawings shall be restricted to a certain amount until his capital has been augmented to an agreed figure.

The important feature is that the balance of the new partner's Current Account or Drawings Account is transferred at the end of each year to his Capital Account in pursuance of the agreement to bring it to the required amount.

Illustration 39

A admits his two teenage sons B and C as partners. He placed to the credit of their Capital Accounts the sum of £32,000 and £8,000 respectively, representing a profit on revaluation of assets. The capital of A is £70,000. The partnership agreement provides:

1. Interest on capital at 5 per cent per annum.
2. Profits and losses to be shared in the ratio of 3:2:1.
3. Drawings of B and C to be limited to £5,000 and £3,500 respectively, until their capitals become proportionate to their profit-sharing ratio.

The net profit of the first year *after* interest on capital was £54,000. The drawings were A £2,500, B £400, and C £250 per month.

Prepare Appropriation Account, Capital and Current Accounts of the partners.

Profit and Loss Appropriation Account

	£	£			£	£
Interest on Capitals—			Balance . . . b/d			59,500
A . . .	3,500					
B . . .	1,600					
C . . .	400					
		5,500				
Balance—						
A: $\frac{1}{2}$ . . .	27,000					
B: $\frac{1}{3}$ . . .	18,000					
C: $\frac{1}{6}$ . . .	9,000					
		54,000				
		£59,500				£59,500

Partners' Current Accounts

		A	B	C			A	B	C
		£	£	£			£	£	£
Drawings . .		30,000	4,800	3,000	Interest on Capitals		3,500	1,600	400
Transfer to Capital					Profit . .		27,000	18,000	9,000
Accounts . .			14,667	6,400					
Balances . .	c/d	500	133						
		£30,500	£19,600	£9,400			£30,500	£19,600	£9,400
					Balances . .	b/d	500	133	

Capital Accounts

		A	B	C			A	B	C
		£	£	£			£	£	£
Balances . .	c/d	70,000	46,667	14,400	Balance . .	b/d	70,000		
					Revaluation				
					Account . .			32,000	8,000
					Current Accounts			14,667	6,400
		£70,000	£46,667	£14,400			£70,000	£46,667	£14,400
					Balances . .	b/d	70,000	46,667	14,400

The capitals to be proportionate to profit-sharing ratios should be, taking A's to be the basic capital, A £70,000, B £46,667, C £23,333. B, having reached his capital quota, will be free from the original restriction on drawings, but C is short of the required quota by £8,933, i.e. (£23,333 − £14,400).

Illustration 40

A and B are partners sharing profits and losses equally. On 1st September 19 . ., they admit C as a partner. The new profit ratios are 2 : 2 : 1. The profits for the year ended 31st December 19 . ., are £30,000.

Interest on capital is 5 per cent per annum as and from 1st September 19 . ., the capitals being: A, £18,000; B, £12,000; and C, £12,000.

A reserve is to be created of £1,000 at 31st December 19 . . .

C is to have a guaranteed minimum of £5,100 per annum, excluding interest on capital.

The profits are to be apportioned on a time basis. Goodwill is to be ignored. Show Profit and Loss Appropriation Account.

PROFIT AND LOSS APPROPRIATION ACCOUNT
FOR THE YEAR ENDED 31ST DECEMBER 19..

		A and B	A, B and C				A and B	A, B and C
		£					£	£
Interest on Capitals:				Balance	. . . b/d		20,000	10,000
A .			300					
B .			200					
C .			200					
Reserve			1,000					
Balance, Net Profit:								
A .	(½)	10,000	(⅖) 3,320					
B .	(½)	10,000	(⅖) 3,320					
C .			(⅕) 1,660					
		£20,000	£10,000				£20,000	£10,000

It is assumed that the reserve represents undistributed profits and is debited against the **new** firm, because, if and when it is restored, it will be credited to all the partners in the ratio of 2:2:1, assuming no further change in the constitution of the partnership.

C is entitled to a guaranteed minimum of £1,700 for the four months ended 31st December 19..; but as his proportion of reserve is £200, his *real* share of profits is £1,860,[1] so that no adjustment is necessary. If, on the other hand, the partners agree to increase C's share of the profits as shown by the Profit and Loss Appropriation Account to £1,700, there will be a transfer of £40 to the credit of C and £20 each to the debit of A and B; but in this event, when the reserve is recredited to the partners, a reversing adjustment of £40 will be required.

The position may be shown by assuming that the reserve is to be eliminated on the 1st January following.

	(1) Where no Reserve was created	(2) Where Reserve created and C credited with £1,660 and Reserve cancelled		Total	(3) Where Reserve created and C credited with £1,700 and Reserve cancelled			Total
	£	£	£	£	£	£	£	£
A—⅖ . .	3,720	3,320+	400	= 3,720	3,300+	400+20		= 3,720
B—⅖ . .	3,720	3,320+	400	= 3,720	3,300+	400+20		= 3,720
C—⅕ . .	1,860	1,660+	200	= 1,860	1,700+	200−40		= 1,860
Total .	[2]£9,300	£8,300+£1,000		£9,300	£8,300+£1,000			£9,300

[1] i.e. £1,660+£200.
[2] i.e. £10,000−£700.

If the reserve is in respect of a *liability*,[1] it will be charged according to the time or period when the necessity arose; or apportioned between the old and the new firm on a time basis, i.e. £666·67 and £333·33. In the latter case the balance of profits would be £8,966·67, of which C's share is £1,793·33, which exceeds his guaranteed minimum.

If the reserve was in respect of a *liability* **existing on 1st September,** the old partners might have dealt with it by debiting their accounts equally and crediting reserve. Further, they might have decided to reverse the above entry and charge it as a new firm (i.e. 2:2:1) loss, in which case the debit to Profit and Loss Appropriation Account would be against the **new** firm. C would thus have been credited with one-fifth reserve at 1st September and £1,660 at 31st December, i.e. £1,860 being one-fifth of the profit of £9,300, no adjustment being required for the guaranteed minimum. This has the same effect as if the reserve at 1st September had not been brought in till 31st December, and charged in the Profit and Loss Appropriation Account entirely against the old firm.

If the reserve is in respect of a *liability* **arising since the 1st September,** the Profit and Loss Appropriation Account gives the true profit necessitating an adjustment of £40 for the guaranteed minimum, that is, to bring C's share of profit up from £1,660 to £1,700.

Illustration 41

Denholme and Wilsden were partners sharing profits 3 : 1, there being no interest on Capital, partnership salaries, etc. On 1st January 19.2, Cullingworth was admitted a partner. Goodwill was valued at £4,800, not to be brought into the books. The new basis of profit sharing was Denholme one-quarter, Wilsden one-half, Cullingworth one-quarter. No interest on Capital nor salaries are to be charged, except that Wilsden is to receive £2,200 per annum as from 1st April 19.2.

Wilsden and Cullingworth paid Denholme their share of goodwill, the money being left in the business as additional capital of Denholme at 4 per cent per annum as from 1st January 19.2. Cullingworth paid in cash capital of £3,000.

The last Balance Sheet of the old firm as at 30th June 19.1 was:

BALANCE SHEET AT 30TH JUNE 19.1

	£	£		£
Creditors		4,171	Fixtures, etc.	2,160
Accruals		187	Motor Vehicles	1,750
Capitals—			Debtors	6,230
Denholme	8,359		Stock	4,167
Wilsden	4,713		Bank	3,123
		13,072		
		£17,430		£17,430

[1] i.e. provision.

The following information is disclosed by the books:

	To 31st Dec. 19.1	To 30th June 19.2
	£	£
Cash received from Debtors.	7,432	10,622
Cash paid: Expenses	1,848	2,290
Creditors	3,269	7,567
Drawings: Denholme	1,520	1,330
Wilsden	1,400	1,700
Cullingworth	—	960
Sales	8,310	12,800
Purchases	4,230	8,180
Bad Debts	270	nil

Expenses outstanding at 31st December 19.1 and 30th June 19.2 were £173 and £123 respectively. Stock at 30th June, 19.2, was £3,200. No Stock was taken at 31st December 19.1, but it was agreed that it should be estimated at a figure consistent with the total rate of gross profit earned for the whole year. Depreciation is to be provided on the Motor Vehicles at 20 per cent per annum.

Prepare Trading and Profit and Loss Account for the year ended 30th June 19.2 and Balance Sheet at that date.

TRADING AND PROFIT AND LOSS ACCOUNT FOR THE YEAR ENDED
30TH JUNE 19.2

	To 31st Dec. 19.1	To 30th June 19.2	Total		To 31st Dec. 19.1	To 30th June 19.2	Total
	£	£	£		£	£	£
Stock	4,167	3,131	4,167	Sales	8,310	12,800	21,110
Purchases	4,230	8,180	12,410	Stock	3,131	3,200	3,200
Gross Profit c/d	3,044[1]	4,689	7,733				
	£11,441	£16,000	£24,310		£11,441	£16,000	£24,310
Expenses[2]	1,834	2,240	4,074	Gross Profit b/d	3,044	4,689	7,733
Bad Debts	270	—	270				
Depreciation	175	175	350				
Balance c/d	765	2,274	3,039				
	£3,044	£4,689	£7,733		£3,044	£4,689	£7,733
Salary	—	550	550	Balance b/d	765	2,274	3,039
Interest on Capital	—	48[3]	48				
Profit—							
Denholme	574	419	993				
Wilsden	191	838	1,029				
Cullingworth	—	419	419				
	£765	£2,274	£3,039		£765	£2,274	£3,039

For notes [1] and [2] and [3] see next page.

BALANCE SHEET AS AT 30TH JUNE 19.2

	D £	W £	C £	£	£			£	£
Creditors—						Fixtures, etc.			2,160
Goods			5,745[4]			Motor Vehicles		1,750	
Expenses			123			Less Depreciation		350	
				5,868					1,400
Capitals—						Stock			3,200
Balance, 1st July						Debtors			9,016[7]
19.1	8,359	4,713				Bank			4,693[6]
Cash intro-duced			3,000						
Goodwill	2,400[5]								
Interest on Capital	48								
Salary		550							
Profit	993	1,029	419						
	11,800	6,292	3,419						
Drawings	2,850	3,100	960						
	£8,950	£3,192	£2,459	14,601					
				£20,469					£20,469

Notes:

(1) $\dfrac{8,310}{21,110} \times £7,733 = £3,044$

∴ Stock at 31st December 19.1 automatically £3,131.

(2) EXPENSES

	£		£
Cash	1,848	Balance b/d	187
Balance c/d	173	Profit and Loss Account	1,834
	£2,021		£2,021
Cash	2,290	Balance b/d	173
Balance c/d	123	Profit and Loss Account	2,240
	£2,413		£2,413
		Balance b/d	123

(3) 4 per cent p.a. for 6 mos. on £2,400 (see Note 5 below).

(4) CREDITORS

	£		£
Cash (1)	3,269	Balance b/d	4,171
Cash (2)	7,567	Purchases (1)	4,230
Balance c/d	5,745	Purchases (2)	8,180
	£16,581		£16,581
		Balance b/d	5,745

Notes:—(contd.)

(5) GOODWILL

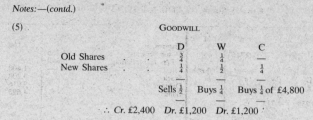

		D	W	C
Old Shares	. .	$\frac{3}{4}$	$\frac{1}{4}$	—
New Shares	. .	$\frac{1}{4}$	$\frac{1}{2}$	$\frac{1}{4}$
		Sells $\frac{1}{2}$	Buys $\frac{1}{4}$	Buys $\frac{1}{4}$ of £4,800
	∴ Cr. £2,400		Dr. £1,200	Dr. £1,200

[For explanation of method used in adjustment of goodwill, see pp. 2269 (2b) and 2270.]

(6) BANK

	£		£
Balance b/d	3,123	Expenses (1)	1,848
Debtors (1)	7,432	Expenses (2)	2,290
Debtors (2)	10,622	Creditors (1)	3,269
Goodwill	2,400	Creditors (2)	7,567
Cullingworth	3,000	Drawings (1)	2,920
		Drawings (2)	3,990
		Balance c/d	4,693
	£26,577		£26,577
Balance b/d	4,693		

(7) DEBTORS

	£		£
Balance b/d	6,230	Cash (1)	7,432
Sales (1)	8,310	Cash (2)	10,622
Sales (2)	12,800	Bad Debts	270
		Balance c/d	9,016
	£27,340		£27,340
Balance b/d	9,016		

SECTION C. AMALGAMATIONS AND ACQUISITIONS OF BUSINESSES

Amalgamation

Where a new partner brings into the firm assets with or without liabilities, it is usually in consequence of an amalgamation of two businesses, and the question of valuation of the assets and liabilities of both businesses will require settlement before the introduction of the new partner into the firm, so that the true capitals are shown at the date of such amalgamation.

The entries are similar to those occasioned by a purchase of a business, viz.:

Debit Assets acquired.
Credit Liabilities assumed.
Credit Vendor (i.e. new partner's capital).
The entries in Journal form therefore are:

JOURNAL

Date	Sundry Assets (detailed)		
	Sundry Liabilities (detailed) . . .		
	New Partner's Capital		
	Being assets and liabilities introduced by . . . . . at this date as per agreement dated		

Illustration 42

A and B are partners sharing profits equally.

BALANCE SHEET AS AT 1ST JANUARY 19 . .

	£	£			£
Capital—			Cash . . .		300
A	1,500		Debtors. . . .		1,200
B	1,000		Stock . . .		1,500
		2,500			
Creditors . .		500			
		£3,000			£3,000

C is to be admitted as partner to have one-quarter share in profits and losses; and to contribute the assets less liabilities of his own business, which for this purpose are valued at £800, goodwill to be ignored. The assets and liabilities of C as revalued are Stock £450, Debtors (Book Value £692) £550, Cash £100; Creditors £300.

Show Journal entries and resulting Balance Sheet of new firm.

A, B, AND C JOURNAL

19 . .		£	£
Jan. 1	Stock	450	
	Debtors	692	
	Cash	100	
	Creditors		300
	BAD DEBTS PROVISION		142
	C Capital		800
	Being assets and liabilities introduced by C at this date as per agreement dated	£1,242	£1,242

BALANCE SHEET AS AT 1ST JANUARY 19. .

	£	£		£	£
Capital—			Cash . . .		400
A	1,500		Debtors. . .	1,892	
B	1,000		*Less* Bad Debts		
C	800		Provision . .	142	
		3,300			1,750
Creditors . . .		800	Stock . . .		1,950
		£4,100			£4,100

Illustration 43

A and B with a London office share profits 3 : 2, and amalgamate with C
with a Manchester office, on the following terms:

	A	B	C
Profits of London	$\frac{1}{2}$	$\frac{1}{4}$	$\frac{1}{4}$
Profits of Manchester . . .	$\frac{3}{10}$	$\frac{1}{5}$	$\frac{1}{2}$

The Goodwill of A and B is £4,000 and C £1,600 and an adjustment is
required in respect of the goodwill attributable to each but the asset is not
to appear in the books. Show the necessary entries.

REVALUATION ACCOUNT—A AND B

	£		£	£
A—$\frac{3}{5}$	2,400			
B—$\frac{2}{5}$	1,600	Goodwill introduced c/d .		£4,000
Goodwill cancelled b/d .	£4,000	A—$\frac{1}{2}$	2,000	
		B—$\frac{1}{4}$	1,000	
		C—$\frac{1}{4}$	1,000	
				£4,000

REVALUATION ACCOUNT—C

	£		£	£
C	1,600	Goodwill introduced c/d .		£1,600
Goodwill cancelled b/d .	£1,600	A.	480	
		B.	320	
		C.	800	
				£1,600

Admission of Partner or Amalgamation during a Financial Period

Where a partner is admitted or an amalgamation takes place *during* the financial year, it is necessary to agree upon some mutually acceptable basis of arriving at profits prior to, and subsequent to, the date of admission, e.g. on a turnover or time basis, or other reliable data. Care should be exercised in the division as interest on capital (being an appropriation of profits) must not be charged *before* the ascertainment of the profits; whilst should a guarantee be given to the incoming partner the amount in the first accounts (as with interest on capital) will be proportionate to the period in which the new partner has been a partner.

Illustration 44

A and B, who made up their accounts yearly to 31st December, decided to amalgamate with C and D, who made up their accounts to the 30th June of each year. The amalgamation was to take place as from 1st July 19.1, and the first accounts of the new firm A, B, C, and D were to be drawn up to 30th June 19.2. As stock had not been taken at the date of merger, it was agreed that A and B should have 10 per cent of their net sales for that period in lieu of their actual profits.

Profits were shared as follows:

A and B: A, $\frac{3}{5}$; B, $\frac{2}{5}$.
C and D: C, $\frac{1}{2}$; D, $\frac{1}{2}$.

and in the new firm it was agreed that as between A and B, and C and D the same ratios were to continue. A and B taking half of the profits and C and D half.

The Trial Balance of the new firm at 30th June 19.2, is as follows:

TRIAL BALANCE

	£	£
Capital—		
A		6,000
B		4,000
C		3,000
D		3,000
Sundry Assets	20,000	
Sales—		
A and B: ½ yr. to 30th June 19.1		5,000
A, B, C, and D: year to 30th June 19.2		24,000
Purchases	18,000	
Stock—		
A and B: 1st January 19.1	5,000	
C and D: 1st July 19.1	3,000	
Selling and Administration Expenses	6,000	
Creditors		7,000
	£52,000	£52,000

Assuming the closing stock to be £10,000, show the Trading and Profit and Loss Account of A, B, C, and D for the period to 30th June 19.2, and the Balance Sheet at that date. Show the division of the profit in a separate section.

TRADING AND PROFIT AND LOSS ACCOUNT
FOR THE PERIOD ENDED 30TH JUNE 19.2

		£			£
Stock—			Sales	. . . .	29,000
A and B	. . . .	5,000	Stock	. . . .	10,000
C and D	. . . .	3,000			
Purchases	. . . .	18,000			
Gross Profit	. . . . c/d	13,000			
		£39,000			£39,000
Selling and Administration Expenses	.	6,000	Gross Profit	. . . b/d	13,000
Balance	. . . . c/d	7,000			
		£13,000			£13,000

A and B: 10% of £5,000—			Balance	. . . b/d	7,000
A. $\frac{3}{5}$	. . . £300				
B. $\frac{2}{5}$	. . . 200				
		500			
A and B: $\frac{1}{2}$ of £6,500—					
A. $\frac{3}{5}$	. . . £1,950				
B. $\frac{2}{5}$	. . . 1,300				
		3,250			
C and D: $\frac{1}{2}$ of £6,500—					
C. $\frac{1}{2}$	. . . £1,625				
D. $\frac{1}{2}$	. . . 1,625				
		3,250			
		£7,000			£7,000

A, B, C, AND D BALANCE SHEET AS AT 30TH JUNE 19.2

	£	£		£
Capital—			Sundry Assets . .	20,000
A . . .	6,000		Stock . . .	10,000
B . . .	4,000			
C . . :	3,000			
D . . .	3,000			
		16,000		
Current Accounts—				
A . . .	2,250			
B . . .	1,500			
C . . .	1,625			
D . . .	1,625			
		7,000		
Sundry Creditors .		7,000		
		£30,000		£30,000

Illustration 45

A and C decided to amalgamate their businesses on 1st January 19 . . . Their Balance Sheets were:

BALANCE SHEETS AS AT 1ST JANUARY 19. .

	A	C		A	C
	£	£		£	£
Creditors . . .	2,500	1,700	Sundry Assets . .	5,000	2,000
Capitals . . .	3,780	1,380	Stock . . .	480	680
			Debtors . . .	800	400
	£6,280	£3,080		£6,280	£3,080

Assets are to be taken over on the basis that sundry assets and stock are worth book values, debtors of A worth £620, of C £320. C to bring in cash £2,000. Goodwill to be valued, A £500 and C £300, and to be brought into the books at the combined value. Profits to be shared 3:2. Show opening entries in Journal form and combined Balance Sheet of the new firm.

JOURNAL

		£	£
19 . . Jan. 1	Sundry Assets	5,000	
	Stock	480	
	Debtors	800	
	Goodwill	500	
	Bad Debts Provision		180
	Creditors		2,500
	A Capital		4,100
	Being assets and liabilities introduced by A into the partnership on this date, as per agreement dated	£6,780	£6,780
19 . . Jan. 1	Sundry Assets	2,000	
	Stock	680	
	Debtors	400	
	Goodwill	300	
	Bad Debts Provision		80
	Creditors		1,700
	C Capital		1,600
	Being assets and liabilities introduced by C into the partnership on this date, as per agreement dated	£3,380	£3,380
	Cash	2,000	
	C Capital		2,000
	Being cash introduced on this date as per agreement.		

A AND C COMBINED BALANCE SHEET AS AT 1ST JANUARY 19..

	£	£		£	£
Creditors . . .		4,200	Sundry Assets . .		7,000
Capital—			Goodwill . .		800
A	4,100		Stock . . .		1,160
C	3,600		Debtors . . .	1,200	
		7,700	*Less* Bad Debts Provision . .	260	
					940
			Cash		2,000
		£11,900			£11,900

If goodwill is not to be retained in the books, it is necessary for a transfer of £20 to be made to the credit of A and to the debit of C, as A sells two-fifths of his goodwill to C, and buys three-fifths of C's goodwill, viz.:

	£
Sale: $\frac{2}{5} \times$ £500 . . .	200
Purchase: $\frac{3}{5} \times$ £300 . .	180
Net Sale by A . .	£20

This can be seen by the fact that if the goodwill was ignored in the opening entries of the partnership (the respective capitals being proportionately less than shown in the foregoing entries) and subsequently introduced into the books, there would be a book profit of £800, shared as follows:

	£
A: $\frac{3}{5} =$ £480 as against true share . .	500
C: $\frac{2}{5} =$ £320 as against true share . .	300

Assets and Liabilities Not Taken Over. Where a business is acquired it not infrequently happens that certain assets and liabilities are not taken over by the purchaser, e.g. an insurance policy. If a Balance Sheet is prepared at the date of acquisition from which entries are made in the new books, the non-acquired items do not appear amongst the opening entries, so the exclusion is automatic; but where the same set of books is continued it is necessary to make eliminating entries through the Vendor's Account or Purchase of Business Account, and for this purpose it will be necessary to prepare a Balance Sheet or a statement of assets and liabilities as at the date of acquisition, so as to ascertain the amount due to the vendor.

The adjustments required for eliminating the non-acquired items are best explained by the employment of an illustration followed by the formal rules.

Illustration 46

The following is the position at 1st May 19.., of A, who sells his business to X and Y on this date.

A BALANCE SHEET AS AT 1ST MAY 19..

		£				£
Creditors	T	1,500	Sundry Assets	. . .	T	1,400
Bill Payable	R	240	Debtors	. . .	T	1,350
Capital	R	1,500	Car .	. . .	R	420
			Loan.	. . .	R	70
		£3,240				£3,240

X and Y take over at book values, ignoring goodwill. Items marked T are taken over, and items marked R are retained by vendor. X and Y equally contribute the sum of £2,000. Show the necessary entries.

1. If new books are opened the Journal entries are:

JOURNAL

19..			£	£
May 1	Sundry Assets .	. . . . . .	1,400	
	Debtors .	. . . . . .	1,350	
	Creditors .	. . . . . .		1,500
	Vendor .	. . . . . .		1,250
	Cash	. . . . . .	2,000	
	X Capital	. . . . . .		1,000
	Y ,,	. . . . . .		1,000
	Vendor.	. . . . . .	1,250	
	Cash	. . . . . .		1,250

Cash has been journalized in order to present the whole transactions together, and narrations have been excluded. The Balance Sheet will be:

X AND Y BALANCE SHEET AS AT 1ST MAY 19..

	£	£			£
Creditors . .		1,500	Sundry Assets . .		1,400
Capital—			Debtors. . .		1,350
X . . .	1,000		Cash . . .		750
Y . . .	1,000				
		2,000			
		£3,500			£3,500

2. If the old books are continued the accounts are:

PURCHASE OF BUSINESS ACCOUNT

	£		£
Vendor[1]	1,250	Bill Payable . . .	240
Car	420	Capital	1,500
Loan	70		
	£1,740		£1,740

[1] Alternatively, the Purchase of Business Account may be disposed with, in which case all the items contained in such account and Vendor will appear in one account under the heading of Vendor, except the transfer between the two accounts (e.g. the transfer of £1,250 from Purchase of Business Account to Vendor); the transactions would be recorded thus:

VENDOR

	£		£
Car	420	Bill Payable	240
Loan	70	Capital	1,500
Balance c/d	1,250		
	£1,740		£1,740
Bank	£1,250	Balance b/d	£1,250

VENDOR

	£		£
Cash	1,250	Purchase of Business Account	1,250

CASH

	£			£
X	1,000	Vendor		1,250
Y	1,000	Balance	c/d	750
	£2,000			£2,000
Balance . . . . b/d	750			

The Balance Sheet may now be drawn up in respect of the items remaining which will be precisely the same as in (1).

It is obvious that if every item in the Balance Sheet at the date of acquisition of the business is in the books, then those not acquired must be eliminated as T = R, i.e.:

'T' items	£	'R' items		£
Sundry Assets . . .	1,400	Bill Payable . . .		240
Debtors . . .	1,350	Capital		1,500
	2,750			1,740
Less Creditors . .	1,500	Less Car . £420		
		,, Loan . 70		
				490
Net DEBITS . .	£1,250 =	Net CREDITS .		£1,250

The italicized items are eliminated through the Purchase of Business Account.

Where the precise position is ascertained and dealt with as outlined, the profits or losses up to the date of acquisition are automatically reflected in the statement drawn up at such a date, otherwise it will be necessary to apportion the profits or losses of the business to and from the date of the sale thereof through the Purchase of Business Account. In practice, moreover, goodwill will usually have to be dealt with and this, again, will be adjusted through the Purchase of Business Account. Reverting to the preceding illustration, if the purchase price had been £1,350 (i.e. £100 for goodwill), the Purchase of Business Account would have been debited with £1,350, leaving a debit balance of £100 after making the entries as shown in that account. Hence, an entry to the debit of Goodwill Account (£100) and a credit to Purchase of Business Account (£100) are required.

The entries required for disposing of items *not* taken over in the case of the whole assets, liabilities, and capital appearing in the books at the date of acquisition, that is, where the old books are continued, may now be summarized:

1. Debit Purchase of Business Account (*abbreviated below to P.B.*), and credit vendor with the **purchase consideration** of the business acquired.
2. Debit P.B. with **assets not taken over** (i.e. retained by vendor) and credit Asset Accounts.
3. Debit **liabilities not acquired** (i.e. to be discharged by the vendor) and credit P.B.
4. Debit Profit and Loss Account with **profit to date of acquisition,** and credit P.B.; or debit P.B. with **loss to date of acquisition,** and credit Profit and Loss Account.
5. Debit goodwill and credit P.B. for **goodwill.**
6. Debit P.B. and credit assets or provision (or reserve) in respect of reductions in book value of assets, and conversely for increase in book value of assets.
7. Reverse entries to (6) in respect of alterations in amounts of liabilities.
8. Debit Vendor's Capital Account and credit P.B. to eliminate **Vendor's Capital Account.**[1]
9. Debit vendor and credit cash upon payment of purchase consideration.

The principles involved in dealing with such circumstances will now be illustrated.

Illustration 47

On p. 2291 is the Balance Sheet of A and B on 31st December 19.1.

On 30th April 19.2, X acquires the business, taking over debtors £1,800, fittings £300, stock £700, less creditors £1,300, i.e. net assets of £1;500, and agrees to pay therefor the sum of £1,800.

[1] Alternatively, the Vendor's original Capital Account can be utilized instead of Vendor Account, so that this transfer will not arise.

BALANCE SHEET AS AT 31ST DECEMBER 19.1

	£	£			£
Creditors . . .		1,250	Debtors . . .		1,500
Bank Loan . . .		450	Stock . . .		550
Capital—			Fittings . . .		300
A . . .	1,000		Investments. . .		650
B . . .	700		Insurance Policy . .		400
		1,700			
		£3,400			£3,400

On 31st December 19.2, the Trial Balance is:

		£	£
Stock		550	
Fittings		300	
Investments	(a)	650	
Insurance Policy	(b)	400	
Purchase of Business Account		1,800	
Bank Loan	(c)		450
Capitals: A			1,000
B	(e)		700
X			2,300
Bank		890	
Debtors		1,830	
Creditors			1,230
Purchases		7,200	
Sales			8,180
Expenses		240	
		£13,860	£13,860
Closing Stock £480.			

Between 1st January 19.2, and 30th April 19.2, there have been no alterations to the amounts shown in the books in respect of the items which are not to be acquired by X from A and B.

Prepare final accounts showing in detail the Purchase of Business Account.

The Trial Balance, it will be observed, includes the *whole* of the assets and liabilities; consequently, eliminating entries are required in order to exclude assets and liabilities RETAINED by the vendor, applying the rules outlined on the previous page. These will be:

PURCHASE OF BUSINESS ACCOUNT

		£			£
Balance	b/d	1,800	Loan . . . . (c)		450
Investments	(a)	650	Capital A . . . (d)		1,000
Insurance Policy.	(b)	400	Capital B . . . (e)		700
			Goodwill[1]		300
			Profit and Loss Account		400
		£2,850			£2,850

[1] Goodwill Account will be opened in the usual way.

PROFIT AND LOSS ACCOUNT
FOR THE YEAR ENDED 31ST DECEMBER 19.2

		£			£
Stock .		550	Sales		8,180
Purchases		7,200	Stock		480
Gross Profit .	c/d	910			
		£8,660			£8,660
Expenses .		240	Gross Profit . . .	b/d	910
Profit—					
X . . . £270					
A and B[1] . . 400					
		670			
		£910			£910

X. BALANCE SHEET AS AT 31ST DECEMBER 19.2

	£	£			£
Creditors . .		1,230	Bank . . .		890
X Capital . .	2,300		Debtors . .		1,830
Add Profit per Profit			Stock . . .		480
and Loss Account .	270		Fittings . .		300
		2,570	Goodwill . .		300
		£3,800			£3,800

The profits arising prior to the sale of the business may be confirmed by showing a Statement of Affairs on 30th April 19.2, viz.:

STATEMENT OF AFFAIRS AS AT 30TH APRIL 19.2

	£		£
Creditors . . .	1,300	Debtors . . .	1,800
Bank Loan . . .	450	Stock . . .	700
Capital at 31st December 19.1	1,700	Fittings . . .	300
Profit . . .	400	Investments . .	650
		Insurance Policy . .	400
	£3,850		£3,850

[1] Credited to Purchase of Business Account.

SECTION D. RETIREMENT OF PARTNER

Retirement or Death of Partner. Upon the retirement or death of a partner, the balance due to him or his estate is the first matter that claims attention. Just as it has been seen that prior to the introduction of a new partner, the old partners will usually adjust their Capital Accounts by revaluation, so in the case of retirement or death of a partner a revaluation—subject always to the provisions of the partnership agreement—will take place in order to arrive at the true balance due to the ex-partner.

Where no adjusting entries are required, a simple transfer will be made by debiting Capital Account and crediting Loan Account of the retired or deceased partner; in addition, if other accounts relating to the latter exist, e.g. Drawings Account and Current Account, they must be transferred to the Loan Account.

In the event of the accounts being drawn up to the date of death or retirement, no departure from the normal procedure arises, but it will be necessary to see that every revaluation required by the terms of the partnership agreement is made. It has been laid down judicially that, in the absence of contrary agreement, all assets and liabilities must be taken at a 'fair value,' not merely a 'book value' basis, thus involving recording entries for both appreciation and depreciation of assets and liabilities. This rule is applicable, notwithstanding the omission of a particular item from the books, e.g. investments, goodwill (*Cruikshank* v. *Sutherland*). Obviously, the net effect of the revaluation will be a profit or loss divisible in the agreed profit- or loss-sharing ratios.

Goodwill will be payable to the outgoing partner, always subject to the terms of the partnership agreement, e.g. in *McLeod* v. *Dowling* (see p. 2205 *et seq.*).

Just as upon the admission of a new partner, so in the present circumstances the revaluations made for the purposes of dissolution may be written back, but clearly such procedure cannot affect the amount due to the retired or deceased partner. It will be recollected that the rule of procedure is to take the result of the revaluation as a profit (or loss) to the old firm, and the reversal as a loss (or profit) to the new firm, so that if A, B, and C are partners sharing profits in the ratio of 3 : 1 : 1 and C retires, any profit on revaluation will be divided in that ratio, and, if reversed, debited against A and B either as to 3 : 1 or in some other ratio, if upon C's retirement a change of profit sharing is agreed upon.

Illustration 48

Q, S and O are in partnership sharing profits and losses in the ratio of 3 : 3 : 1.

Q, S AND O BALANCE SHEET AS AT 31ST DECEMBER 19..

	£	£			£
Capital—			Cash		22,000
Q . . .	10,000				
S . . .	8,000				
O . . .	4,000				
		22,000			
		£22,000			£22,000

At this date Q decided to retire, and goodwill is valued in accordance with the partnership agreement at £8,000. In addition, the firm holds $3\frac{1}{2}$ per cent Conversion Loan to the cash equivalent of £2,500.

S and O decide to carry on the business, sharing profits equally. You are required to show the amount due to Q and to give the necessary Journal entries to record the above transactions, and to show the new Balance Sheet of S and O.

JOURNAL

	£	£
19..		
Dec. 31 Goodwill	8,000	
$3\frac{1}{2}$% Conversion Loan	2,500	
Q Loan		4,500
S Capital		4,500
O ,, ...		1,500
Being the insertion in the books of unrecorded assets at this date.		
Q Capital	10,000	
Q Loan		10,000
Being transfer of Capital Account to Loan Account.		
Q[1] Loan	14,500	
Cash		14,500
Being the discharge of liability to Q.		

[1] Actually this entry would not be journalized, but posted direct from the Cash Book.

S AND O BALANCE SHEET AS AT 1ST JANUARY 19..

	£		£
Capitals—		Cash	7,500
S (£8,000+£4,500) .	12,500	$3\frac{1}{2}$% Conversion Loan .	2,500
O (£4,000+£1,500) .	5,500	Goodwill	8,000
	£18,000		£18,000

Illustration 49

A, B, and C are partners sharing profits in the ratio of 3:2:1. At 31st December 19.., B retires.

It is agreed that all the assets and liabilities shall be revalued.

The following are the material facts:

	Revised Values £			£
Goodwill	20,000	in the books at		Nil
Reserve	5,000	,,	,,	5,000
Containers with Customers—deposits refundable	1,900	,,	,,	4,200
Debtors	10,000	,,	,,	12,500
Creditors	9,000	,,	,,	8,000
Joint Life Policy	3,000	,,	,,	4,000
Hire Purchase Machinery . . .	3,000	,,	,,	Nil
(All paid for, except £500 agreed to be brought in as a liability and paid on the day after B's retirement)				
Investments	15,000	,,	,,	30,000
(Investments Provision stands at £4,000)				
Accrued Income on Investments . .	1,000	,,	,,	Nil

A and C are to continue the business with profit-sharing ratio of 3:2—the book values to remain unchanged. Prepare Memorandum Revaluation Account.

Memorandum REVALUATION ACCOUNT

19..			£	19..			£
Dec. 31	Bad Debts Provision	c/d	2,500	Dec. 31	Goodwill Introduced c/d		20,000
	Creditors (or Provision) .	,,	1,000		Reserve . . . ,,		5,000
	Life Policy . .	,,	1,000		Containers with Customers. . . ,,		2,300
	Creditors (re H.P.). :	,,	500		Machinery[1] . . ,,		3,000
	Investments Provision .	,,	11,000		Dividends accrued . ,,		1,000
	A Capital Account: ½ £7,650						
	B Loan Account: ⅓ 5,100						
	C Capital Account: ⅙ 2,550		15,300				
			£31,300				£31,300
19..				19..			
Jan. 1	Reversal of Items . .	b/d	31,300	Jan. 1	Reversal of Items . b/d		16,000
					A Capital Account: ⅗ £9,180		
					C Capital Account: ⅖ 6,120		15,300
			£31,300				£31,300

[1] The true value will be considerably less than £3,000 owing to depreciation, but seeing that no information is given as to date of purchase and rate of depreciation, the amount of £3,000 will be inserted and a suitable footnote made. If the depreciation has been, say, £400, the figure of £2,600 would be substituted for £3,000.

It should be remembered that whilst the reserve is not altered, if the item indicates, not a liability, but undistributed profits, it belongs to the partners. In other words, in the Balance Sheet the reserve will have appeared on the liabilities side, but as in reality it is not a liability it must be brought to the credit of revaluation account, so that the retiring partner duly obtains his share thereof.

Further provision for depreciation of investments is £11,000, as there already exists a provision of £4,000.

The effect of the above is that it provides the basis for the Journal entries, either showing the adjustment of the profit in one set and the adjustment of the reversal in another set, or consolidated into one set of entries only.

The same principles apply where some of the revaluations are brought into the books permanently and the others written back.

Illustration 50

A and B are partners sharing profits equally. B retires, and it is agreed to bring into account for dissolution purposes:

(a) Capital expenditure on fixtures £3,000 (depreciation £400).
(b) Pension Fund liability, £10,000.
(c) Bad Debts provision of £2,000.

A writes back the Pension Fund and the Fixtures.
Show Memorandum Revaluation Account.

Memorandum REVALUATION ACCOUNT

		£				£
Bad Debts Provision[1]		2,000	Fixtures		c/d	2,600
Pension Fund	c/d	10,000	Balance—			
			A. ½	£4,700		
			B. ½	4,700		
						9,400
		£12,000				£12,000
Reversal of Item	b/d	2,600	Reversal of Item		b/d	10,000
Balance—A		7,400				
		£10,000				£10,000

[1] This item will be posted to the credit of Bad Debts Provision.

Last Balance Sheet Basis of Determining Partner's Share

Share of Profit of Outgoing Partner. It frequently happens that a partner retires during the course of a normal accounting period. He will be entitled in the ordinary way to his share of profit, including interest on capital, if any, to the date of retirement. This will be ascertained by:

1. drawing up accounts to the actual date of retirement, or
2. drawing up accounts for the full normal accounting period and splitting them into the (a) pre- and (b) post-retirement period.

The former method is the more satisfactory, but circumstances may prevent this being carried out. In regard to the second method, the procedure is:

1. Prepare the Profit and Loss Account for the whole period excluding

those items, whether debit or credit, which are not apportionable on a normal time basis.

2. Apportion the balance of the account in (1) on a time basis into:

(*a*) pre- and (*b*) post-retirement.

3. Debit or credit, as the case may be, any of the remaining items which refer to one specific period.

4. Debit or credit, as the case may be, any of the remaining items which, though related to the whole year, are not apportionable on a time basis.

5. Where assets are revalued, depreciation should be apportioned between the two periods and any profit or loss on revaluation dealt with through the partners' accounts in the usual way.

6. Bring down the balance into the Appropriation section, divided between the two periods.

7. Debit the Appropriation section with the usual appropriations, viz. partners' salaries, interest on capital and share of profit apportioned on a time basis, and similarly with the usual credits, subject to:

(*a*) No entries being made in respect of the retired partner *after* the date of retirement, i.e. in the second period column.

(*b*) If one partner alone remains there will be no point in entering up interest on capital, etc., in the second period.

(*c*) An amount representing interest on the amount due to the retired partner will be debited in the post-retirement column.

In regard to (1), an alternative method of arriving at the same result is to prepare the accounts for the whole period, and then to add back debits and deduct credits which have been included but which are not apportionable on a time basis.

Illustration 51

The profits of A, B, and C, equal partners, for the year ended 31st December are £4,800. C retires on 30th September, it being agreed that C shall have his proportionate share of profits to date of retirement calculated on a 'time' basis. Interest on capital is chargeable at the rate of 5 per cent per annum. The capitals are £6,000, £2,000, £1,200. Show Profit and Loss Appropriation Account, assuming that A and B continue to share profits and losses equally.

PROFIT AND LOSS APPROPRIATION ACCOUNT

	9 mos. to 30 Sept. 19..		3 mos. to 31 Dec. 19..		9 mos. to 30 Sept. 19..	3 mos. to 31 Dec. 19..
	£	£	£	Net Profit b/d	£ (¾) 3,600	£ (¼) 1,200
Interest on Capital:						
A . £225		75				
B . 75		25				
C . 45		Nil				
	345		100			
Balance:						
A: ⅓ £1,085		½ 550				
B: ⅓ 1,085		½ 550				
C: ⅓ 1,085		Nil				
	3,255		1,100			
	£3,600		£1,200		£3,600	£1,200

Illustration 52

A and B were partners sharing profits and losses:

1. Interest on capital 5 per cent per annum of £42,000 and £12,000 respectively. No interest on drawings.

2. Balance in the ratio of 3:2.

On 31st October 19.., B died, and according to the partnership agreement his executors were entitled to:

(a) Capital at the last Balance Sheet subject to normal provisions for losses.

(b) Goodwill on the basis of profit-sharing ratio of the average *trading* profits of the last two completed years, and the last year or part thereof prior to death.

(c) Bad debts arising within one year from death on debts existing on the date of a partner's death to be considered as bad on the date of death.

Drawings of B to 31st December 19.., were £5,000, of which £1,500 were since death, and drawn by his executor.

The profit for the year ended 31st December 19.., was £9,400, *after* charging interest on capital and making all provision for known or likely losses.

The profits for the two years to 31st December prior to B's death were £12,000 and £6,000 respectively.

During the following year £3,000 balances in respect of debtors in the books at 31st October 19.., were written off as irrecoverable, against which £350 previously written off was received.

Show the necessary accounts.

Ignore interest on the balance due to B's estate at date of death.

B CAPITAL

19..			£	19..			b/d	£
Oct. 31	Cash—Drawings . . .		3,500	Jan. 1	Balance . . .		b/d	12,000
	Balance, transferred to			Oct. 31	Interest on Capital.			500
	Exors. of B Loan				Share of Profits .			3,100
	Account . .		16,053		,, ,, Goodwill .			3,953
			£19,553					£19,553

EXECUTORS OF B LOAN

19..				£	19..			£
Dec. 31	Cash			1,500	Oct. 31	Transfer from B's Capital		16,053
	Balance . . .	c/d		14,553		Account . . .		
				£16,053				£16,053
					19..			
					Jan. 1	Balance . . .	b/d	14,553

PROFIT AND LOSS APPROPRIATION ACCOUNT

19..			£	19..			b/d	£
Oct. 31	Interest on Capital—			Dec. 31	Balance . . .		b/d	12,000
	A: 5% on £42,000							
	for 10 mos. £1,750							
	B: 5% on £12,000							
	for 10 mos. 500							
			2,250					
	Balance—							
	A: ⅗ . . £4,650							
	B: ⅖ . . 3,100							
			7,750					
	Balance . . .	c/d	2,000					
			£12,000					£12,000
Dec. 31	Interest on Capital—			Dec. 31	Balance . . .		b/d	2,000
	A: 5% on £42,000 for							
	2 mos. . .		350					
	Balance to A . .		1,650					
			£2,000					£2,000

Alternatively, this division may be ascertained in tabular form, and the Profit and Loss Appropriation Account presented in the ordinary way, thus:

	£	Proportion prior to B's death, i.e. 10 months	Proportion subsequent to B's death, i.e. 2 months	Total
Net Profit for Year	9,400			
Add Interest on Capitals on— £42,000 at 5% for one year £2,100 £12,000 at 5% for 10 months 500	2,600			
Profit prior to Charging Interest	£12,000	($\frac{10}{12}$) 10,000	($\frac{2}{12}$) 2,000	12,000
Less Interest on Capital— £42,000 at 5% for 10 months (a) do. for 2 months (b) £12,000 at 5% for 10 months (c)		(a) £1,750 (c) 500 ——— 2,250	(b) 350	A £2,100 B 500 ——— 2,600
		7,750	1,650	9,400
Division of Net Profit		A $\frac{3}{5}$ £4,650 B $\frac{2}{5}$ 3,100 ——— £7,750	A £1,650 B — ——— £1,650	A £6,300 B 3,100 ——— £9,400

PROFIT AND LOSS APPROPRIATION ACCOUNT
FOR THE YEAR ENDED 31ST DECEMBER 19 . .

	£			£
Interest on Capitals— A £2,100 B 500	2,600	Balance . . . b/d		12,000
Profit— A £6,300 B 3,100	9,400			
	£12,000			£12,000

Total profit for Goodwill purposes is £28,000, i.e. £12,000 plus £6,000 plus $\frac{10}{12}$ of £12,000. B's share of Goodwill = £28,000 × $\frac{12}{34}$ × $\frac{2}{5}$ = £3,953 [to nearest £].

Adjustments in Respect of Bad Debts. 1. It is a question of construction whether the bad debts recovered should be set off against the bad debts written off. It is purely a legal question, which is for the legal adviser to answer, but where the question is ambiguous it is advisable to take the fair view (that is, what appears to the student as such), adding a footnote that where EXPEDIENT legal opinion would be sought, and at the same time observing whether persons of ordinary intelligence and mind would, having regard to the amount at stake, incur such an expense; whilst reference might be made to ARBITRATION (again if the occasion warrants it). It is assumed here that the £350 is to be set off against the £3,000 written off, leaving bad debts referable to ten months ended 31st October 19 . ., of £2,650; although the executors would doubtless require some evidence that the debts were in fact bad.

2. The ten months' profits are, therefore, diminished by £2,650, of which B's share is two-fifths, that is, £1,060.

3. As a result, the profits for the 34 months to 31st October 19 . ., being diminished by £2,650, B's share of goodwill is reduced by £2,650 × $\frac{12}{34}$ × $\frac{2}{5}$ = £374 (to nearest £); hence B's executors will be debited with

£1,060 and £374 and A's account credited, thus reducing the credit to the account of B's executors of £14,553 by £1,434 = £13,119. This may be shown by the following statement.

STATEMENT OF ACCOUNT OF EXECUTORS OF B WITH A

19..			£	£
Jan. 1	Credit balance of Capital Account			12,000
Oct. 31	Interest on Capital			500
·	Profits (to 31st October 19..)	£10,000		
	Less Bad Debts (net)	2,650		
			7,350	
	„ Interest on Capitals of A and B		2,250	
	Divisible profits [i.e. £7,750 less £2,650]		£5,100	
	⅖ thereof			2,040
	Goodwill:			
	Profits last two completed years prior to B's death		12,000	
	„		6,000	
	„ 19.. (10 months, as above)		7,350	
			£25,350	
	Average = 12/34		£8,947	
	⅖ thereof			3,579
				18,119
	Less Cash (£3,500 plus £1,500)		·	5,000
	Credit balance of Executors of B Loan Account			13,119

Illustration 53

The following is the Trial Balance of X, Y and Z for the year ended 31st December 19..

	£	£
Sundry Assets (excluding Stock) and Liabilities	12,000	5,000
Capital and Drawings—		
X	600	3,000
Y	840	6,000
Z	960	4,000
General Expenses	1,160	
Gross Profit		3,200
Repairs	430	
Bad Debts	360	
Stock (closing valuation)	4,850	
	£21,200	£21,200

Profits were shared in the ratio of 2:1:1, after providing for interest on capital at 5 per cent per annum, annual salaries of £500 each to Y and Z, and interest on drawings at 6 per cent per annum.

Drawings were made monthly as follows: X £50, Y £70, and Z £80.

Z retired on the 30th September 19 . . and his drawings continued with the consent of X and Y to 31st December 19 . .

You find that:

1. Sundry assets at 30th September were worth £10,600 and depreciation is to be provided at £400 for the year.

2. There was an opening Bad Debts Provision of £200; Bad Debts at 30th September were estimated at £150 and at 31st December nil. Bad Debts actually written off to 30th September were £490.

3. Repairs were incurred of £370 prior to 30th September.

4. Interest on Z's balance after 30th September, less drawings on account, to be at the rate of 4 per cent per annum till 31st December when settlement was to be made.

5. X and Y continue to share profits as between themselves in the old ratio and Y's salary continues unchanged.

6. Goodwill, not in the books, is to be valued at 30th September at £4,000.

Show—(i) Profit and Loss Account for the year to 31st December 19 . . ; (i) Balance Sheet at that date; and (iii) Z's account showing the final balance due to him. Work to the nearest £.

PROFIT AND LOSS ACCOUNT FOR THE YEAR ENDED
31ST DECEMBER 19 . .

	£	£		£	£
General Expenses[1] . . .		1,160	Gross Profit b/d . . .		3,200
Balance c/d . . .		2,040			
		£3,200			£3,200
	(1) (9 mos.)	(2) (3 mos.)		(1) (9 mos.)	(2) (3 mos.)
Repairs . . .	370	60	Balance b/d . .	1,530	510
Bad Debts . . .	440		Bad Debts recovered .		80
Depreciation . .	300	100			
Loan Interest . .		42			
Net Profit c/d . .	420	388			
	£1,530	£590		£1,530	£590
Interest on Capitals—			Net Profit b/d . .	420	388
X . . .	113	22	Interest on Drawings—		
Y . . .	225	67	X . . .	10	1
Z . . .	150		Y . . .	14	2
Salaries—			Z . . .	16	
Y . . .	375	125	Balance—		
Z . . .	375		X . . .	389	
Balance—			Y . . .	194	
X . . .		118	Z . . .	195	
Y . . .		59			
	£1,238	£391		£1,238	£391

[1] Alternatively, instead of apportioning the balance after taking into account all the items which are apportionable on a time basis, the whole account may be shown in two columns, starting with the individual items in the Trading Account. If this method is adopted, the Profit and Loss Account will begin thus—

	(1)	(2)		(1)	(2)
	£	£		£	£
General Expenses, etc..	870	290	Gross Profit, etc. . . .	2,400	800

BALANCE SHEET AS AT 31ST DECEMBER 19 . .

	£		£	£
Sundry Liabilities	5,000	Sundry Assets . . .	12,000	
Loan—Z	4,121	Less Depreciation (9 mos.) .	300	
Capitals—				
X	1,783		11,700	
Y	5,392	Loss on Revaluation .	1,100	
			10,600	
		Less Depreciation (3 mos.) .	100	
				10,500
		Stock		4,850
		Current Accounts—		
		X	747	
		Y	199	
				946
	£16,296			£16,296

Z LOAN

	£		£
Current Account	406	Capital Account . . .	4,725
Balance c/d	4,319		
	£4,725		£4,725
Drawings	240	Balance b/d	4,319
Interest thereon	1	Interest thereon . . .	43
Balance c/d	4,121		
	£4,362		£4,362
		Balance b/d	4,121

Notes. (1) Interest on Drawings (in the absence of exact dates of withdrawals) are taken at an average due date of $4\frac{1}{2}$ and $1\frac{1}{2}$ months respectively.

(2) Assumed that X and Y calculate interest on capital on the revised capitals after the retirement of Z, and not for the whole year on the capitals at 1st January, 19 . . .

(3)

BAD DEBTS

	£		£
Bad Debts written off	490	Opening Provision b/d	200
Provision, 30th September . .	150	P. and L. Account (9 mos. to 30th September)	440
	£640		£640
Bad Debts written off	70	Provision b/d	150
P. and L. Account (3 mos. to 31st Dec.) .	80		
	£150		£150

CAPITALS

	X	Y	Z		X	Y	Z
	£	£	£		£	£	£
Loss on Sundry Assets	550	275	275	Balance b/d	3,000	6,000	4,000
Goodwill (2:1)	667	333	—	Goodwill ($\frac{1}{4}$)	—	—	1,000
Transfer to Loan	—	—	4,725				
Balances c/d	1,783	5,392	—				
	£3,000	£6,000	£5,000		£3,000	£6,000	£5,000
				Balances b/d	1,783	5,392	—

CURRENT ACCOUNTS

	X	Y	Z		X	Y	Z
	£	£	£		£	£	£
Drawings (9 mos.)	450	630	720	Salaries	—	375	375
Interest thereon	10	14	16	Interest on Capital	113	225	150
Loss (to 30th Sept.)	389	194	195	Transfer to Loan Account	—	—	406
				Balances c/d	736	238	—
	£849	£838	£931		£849	£838	£931
Balances b/d	736	238	—	Salary	—	125	—
Drawings (3 mos.)	150	210	—	Interest on Capital	22	67	—
Interest thereon	1	2	—	Profit (to 31st Dec.)	118	59	—
				Balances c/d	747	199	—
	£887	£450			£887	£450	
Balances b/d	747	199					

Retired Partner's Balance as Loan. Upon the retirement or death of a partner, arrangements are frequently concluded whereby the final amount due to the ex-partner shall be paid by instalments, or even retained in the business in the form of a permanent loan. In either case, the agreement usually provides for interest to be paid either at a flat rate per cent, e.g. 6 per cent; or at a rate of interest varying with profits, e.g. 8 per cent of the net profits, or a rateable proportion of profits calculated by taking the ratio of the loan to the capitals and loans of all the partners; or both methods may be employed. However ascertained, the amount of loan interest is debited, without deduction of income tax, to the Profit and Loss Account of the firm and credited to the account of the ex-partner. (See p. 2106.)

It is necessary in order to ascertain the amount due to the ex-partner to transfer to his Loan Account ALL his interest in the firm, so that the account will contain all or some of the following items according to the particular circumstances, e.g.

Y LOAN

| 19..
Dec. 31 | Drawings . . .
Interest on Drawings .

Balance . . . | | £ | 19..
Dec. 31 | Balance of Capital . .
Share of Goodwill . .
Profit[1] on Revaluation of
Assets and Liabilities
Profits[1] to date of Retire-
ment
Advance Account
Current[2] Account . .
Salary[2] Account
Interest on Capital . .
Interest on Advance .
Interest[2] on Current Ac-
count . . .
Reserves written back . | | £ |

[1] If losses these entries will be debits.
[2] Debits if overdrawn.

Illustration 54

On 1st January 19.1, X retires from a firm, and the remaining partners agree to give him 5 per cent interest on the balance due to him, and to discharge the debt and interest in three equal instalments. The amount due on 1st January 19.1, is £720.

X LOAN

19.1 Dec. 31	Cash . . . . Balance . . .	 c/d	£p 264·39 491·61	19.1 Jan. 1 Dec. 31	Transfer from Capital Account . . . Interest at 5% per annum		£p 720·00 36·00
			£756·00				£756·00
19.2 Dec. 31	Cash . . . . Balance . . .	 c/d	264·39 251·80	19.2 Jan. 1 Dec. 31	Balance . . . Interest at 5% per annum	b/d	491·61 24·58
			£516·19				£516·19
19.3 Dec. 31	Cash		264·39	19.3 Jan. 1 Dec. 31	Balance . . Interest at 5% per annum	b/d	251·80 12·59
			£264·39				£264·39

Payment to Retired Partner Based Upon Profits. After agreeing the amount due to the retired partner, the terms of repayment must be agreed upon, having regard to the financial position of all the parties. In many cases the precise amount of repayment is made to depend upon the ability to pay as measured by the profits in succeeding periods, e.g. the repayment in the first year may be 20 per cent of the profits, in the second 25 per cent, and so on, always remembering that such a payment is not a SHARE OF PROFITS, but merely an instalment of a debt, such instalment being dependent upon the relative prosperity of the firm; moreover, it should be remembered that the retired partner can at the most receive the amount of his debt with interest (except in the case where he applies and gets leave of the Court to have a share of profits in lieu of interest).

Illustration 55

Upon dissolution, the final adjusted balance due to X is £2,000. It is agreed that the *total* payment to him for the first year after dissolution shall be 20 per cent of the profits before adjusting interest on capital at 5 per cent per annum. The remaining partners, Y and Z, share profits equally, their capitals being £5,000 and £2,500 respectively. Drawings for the year: Y £1,600, Z £1,400.

Interest is payable to the retired partner at 6 per cent per annum.

Show Appropriation Account, Capital Accounts, and X's Loan Account.

The profits for the year after dissolution prior to charging interest on loan or interest on capital were £3,295.

PROFIT AND LOSS APPROPRIATION ACCOUNT

		£				£
X—Interest on Loan		120	Balance	. . . .	b/d	3,295
Interest on Capital—						
Y	£250					
Z	125					
		375				
Balance—						
Y ½	£1,400					
Z ½	1,400					
		2,800				
		£3,295				£3,295

CAPITALS

		Y	Z				Y	Z
		£	£				£	£
Drawings		1,600	1,400		Balance	b/d	5,000	2,500
Balances	c/d	5,050	2,625		Interest on Capital		250	125
					Profits .		1,400	1,400
		£6,650	£4,025				£6,650	£4,025
					Balances	b/d	5,050	2,625

X LOAN

			£				£
Cash			635	Balance . . .	b/d		2,000
Balance	c/d		1,485	Interest thereon for one year at 6% per annum . .			120
			£2,120				£2,120
				Balance . . .	b/d		1,485

Note 1. When the figure of instalment has been computed the ordinary entry is made; debit X, credit cash. The amount of £635 is *not* a share of profits due to X, and therefore must not be credited to him.

Note 2. The item of £120 is not an appropriation; it is interest on a debit and a charge against profits. The profits of the firm are thus £3,295 *less* £120 equals £3,175; 20 per cent of this figure merely measures the quantum of the cash to be applied in reduction of debt and interest due to X at the end of the year. The question definitely states 20 per cent of the profits before adjusting *Interests on Capital*. Had it stated 20 per cent of the profits before adjusting INTEREST, the figure would be 20 per cent of £3,295.

Illustration 56

A, B, and C are partners sharing profits and losses equally, and having £2,000 each as capital. Their accounts are always prepared on a cash basis.

A retires on 31st December 19.2, and is to receive 5 per cent per annum on the outstanding balance on his Loan Account. It is provided, *inter alia*, in the agreement of dissolution that A's share of goodwill is to be computed at[1] one-half of the cash profits of the last two years. A is to have the sum of £500 immediately; £500 plus interest at the rate of 5 per cent per annum on the outstanding balance due to him, together with a sum representing 35 per cent of the net profits of the business calculated on an *earned basis* at the end of 19.3. The profits computed on a cash basis were: 19.1, £1,500, 19.2 £2,100. Fees received 19.3, £4,500. Fees outstanding at 31st December 19.2, were £1,500; those at 31st December 19.3, £465. Ignore the matter of uncompleted work. Expenses for the year ended 31st December 19.3, were £1,300. There were no expenses outstanding at either 31st December 19.2, or at 31st December 19.3.

Show Profit and Loss Account for the year ended, and A's account as at 31st December 19.3.

PROFIT AND LOSS ACCOUNT FOR THE YEAR
ENDED 31ST DECEMBER 19.2

		£			£
Expenses		1,300	Fees Received		4,500
Interest on Loan: A—5% on £3,300 .		165			
Balance—					
B ½ .	£1,517·50				
C ½ .	£1,517·50				
		3,035			
		£4,500			£4,500

A LOAN

19.3			£	19.3			£
Jan. 1	Cash		500	Jan. 1	Transfer from Capital		
Dec. 31	,, (See note (2) over) .		1,365		Account		3,800
	Balance .	c/d	2,100	Dec. 31	Interest .		165
			£3,965				£3,965
				19.4			
				Jan. 1	Balance .	b/d	2,100

A CAPITAL

19.3		£	19.2			£
Jan. 1	Transfer to Loan Account	3,800	Dec. 31	Balance .		2,000
				½ Share of Goodwill		1,800
				(see note (1) over)		
		£3,800				£3,800

[1] [*Observe that the question does NOT state 'average of the last two years'.*]

(1) Computation of Goodwill:

$\frac{1}{3} \times (£1,500 + £2,100) = £1,800$

Total Goodwill is therefore £5,400, hence it is correct to describe the credit to A as $\frac{1}{3}$ share of Goodwill.

(2) Computation of Cash payable:

£500 + £165 + 35% of 'EARNED' profits £2,000 (See note (3)).

= £665 + £700

= £1,365

(3) Computation of 'Earned' Profits:

	£	£
Fees Received	4,500	
Less Fees Outstanding at 31st Dec. 19.2	1,500	
		3,000
Add Fees Outstanding at 31st Dec. 19.3		465
		3,465
Total 'Earned' Fees		
Less Expenses	1,300	
Interest on Loan	165	
		1,465
Net 'Earned' Profit		£2,000

It is assumed that (*a*) there is no interest on capital, (*b*) B and C continue to share profits equally on a cash basis, (*c*) all the payments ARE made on the due dates.

It is noted that (*a*) no account is taken of depreciation or stocks (e.g. stationery, books, etc.), (*b*) no provision is mentioned for the payment to B in the second year, this probably being included in the term '*inter alia.*'

No mention is made of the existence of Current and/or Drawings Accounts which would, especially considering the equal capitals in a round sum, be in the books; nor of any share of the profits to date of dissolution, which further strengthens the assumption as to the existence of Current and/or Drawings Accounts.

The statement in the question 'such sum representing 35 per cent of the net profits' merely indicates that B's Loan Account will be reduced by a PAYMENT of such a sum. The amount of the payment depends upon the success or otherwise of the business in 19.3, but the statement does *not* mean that A is entitled to 35 per cent of the PROFITS. Had the words 'such a sum representing' been omitted the question might be capable of this interpretation, although hardly likely, since A retired obtains a greater share than if he were a partner, as well as interest, quite apart from the fact that he has been credited with his share of goodwill.

Share of Profits in Lieu of Goodwill. As an alternative to a payment for goodwill, a retiring partner may elect to receive a proportion of profits. It is a matter of agreement between the parties as to what constitutes profits, whether, for instance, salaries and interest on capital should be charged in the Profit and Loss Account before ascertainment of profit. In the absence of agreement it would appear that as between the remaining partners on the one hand, and the retired partner on the other, the proportion of profits due to the latter is a CHARGE and, consequently, it should be chargeable BEFORE the ascertainment of such figure.

Illustration 57

A is to have one-ninth of the profits of the firm for one year after his retirement, and the profits before A's share is ascertained are £1,800. Show the proportion due to A.

The proportion due to A is:

(1) $\frac{1}{9} \times £1,800 = £200$, *or*

(2) $\frac{1}{10} \times £1,800 = £180$ [i.e. $\frac{1}{9}$ of the remaining profits, £1,620]

Illustration 58

A partnership consisting of four partners A, B, C, and D is dissolved, A retiring, the others continuing; the profit-sharing ratio was: $1:3:3:1$. After A's retirement B, C, and D continue to share profits in the same ratio as before. The trading profits for the first year after dissolution are £1,200. Show the manner of dealing with the trading profits, assuming that in lieu of goodwill A is to receive one-fifth share of profits.

The following are the divisions (to nearest £):

If A's share is to be considered as a *charge*, the following is the division between B, C, D.

	£	£
Profits	1,200	
Less A, $\frac{1}{6}$	200	
Balance divisible		1,000
B, $\frac{3}{7}$	429	
C, $\frac{3}{7}$	428	
D, $\frac{1}{7}$	143	
		1,000

If A's share is to be considered as an *appropriation*, i.e. one-fifth of £1,200, the following is the division between B, C, D.

	£	£
Profits	1,200	
Less A, $\frac{1}{5}$	240	
Balance divisible		960
B, $\frac{3}{7}$	412	
C, $\frac{3}{7}$	411	
D, $\frac{1}{7}$	137	
		960

Elliott *v.* **Elliott.** In normal circumstances the amount due to a retired partner is a debt payable by the firm. Where, however, as in *Elliott* v. *Elliott*, the remaining partners have agreed personally to buy the retired partner's share, the amount is no longer a *firm* debt, but one due individually by the remaining partners in the agreed ratio. Failing agreement on this latter point, the liability should be divided in profit and loss sharing ratio. Thus, after the *total* amount due to the deceased or retired partner has been credited to his account, it should be transferred to the Capital Accounts of the remaining partners in their profit and loss sharing or other agreed ratio, and if cash is paid to the ex-partner out of firm's money, it will be debited to the Current Account or Drawings Account of the partner on whose behalf the money is paid. The principle behind this is that the 'buying out' partners are personally liable to the retired partner, and therefore the *firm* is absolved from liability, and so the amount due to the retiring partner must be **eliminated** from the firm's books. The retired partner's or deceased partner's representative must look for payment, not to the *firm*, but to the **individual** partners in their *private* capacity.[1]

Illustration 59

Q, S, and O are in partnership, sharing profits and losses 3:2:1, and Q retires as from 31st December 19.., when their Balance Sheet is as follows:

Q, S, AND O BALANCE SHEET AS AT 31ST DECEMBER 19:.

	£	£		£	£
Capitals—			Sundry Assets . .		15,000
Q . . .	8,000				
S . . .	5,000				
O . . .	2,000				
		15,000			
		£15,000			£15,000

Show entries applying the rule in *Elliott* v. *Elliott*, assuming that S and O share profits in the ratio of 2:1. In addition, the goodwill (not in the books) is worth £12,000.

The entries in accordance with *Elliott* v. *Elliott* are as under:

JOURNAL

19..			£	
Dec. 31	Goodwill		12,000	
	Q Capital			6,000
	S ,, ...			4,000
	O ,, ...			2,000
	Being division of Goodwill in profit-sharing ratio.			
	Q Capital		14,000	
	S Capital*			9,333
	O ,, *			4,667
	Being transfer of Q's balance on his retirement.			

* To nearest £.

[1] The provisions of Sect. 42, Partnership Act 1890, will not apply.

Q CAPITAL

19.. Dec. 31		£	19.. Dec. 31			£
	Transfers—			Balance	b/d	8,000
	S Capital	9,333		Share of Goodwill .		6,000
	O ,, . . .	4,667				
		£14,000				£14,000

S AND O BALANCE SHEET AS AT 1ST JANUARY 19 . .

		£			£
Capitals—			Sundry Assets		15,000
S	. . . . .	18,333	Goodwill		12,000
O	. . . . .	8,667			
		£27,000			£27,000

If the goodwill is to be written out again, it will be treated as a loss to the new firm, and cannot alter the amount due to the retiring or deceased partner, so that the transfer required in *Elliott* v. *Elliott* is unaffected. The entries required will be:

JOURNAL

19.. Jan. 1		£	£
	S Capital $\frac{2}{3}$	8,000	
	O ,, $\frac{1}{3}$	4,000	
	Goodwill		12,000
	Being Goodwill written out of the books.		

S AND O BALANCE SHEET AS AT 1ST JANUARY 19..

		£			£
Capitals—			Sundry Assets		15,000
S	. . . . .	10,333			
O	. . . . .	4,667			
		£15,000			£15,000

Provision for Payment to a Retiring Partner. Where a firm wishes to be in a position to make prompt payment of the amount due to a retiring partner, or in the event of death to his estate, an amount of money is set aside and invested in Stock Exchange securities, or in the form of an assurance policy.

The investments will be made and entered in the manner of acquiring any other asset, whilst the dividends will usually be reinvested; and when the need for the cash arises the investments will be realized, any profit or loss thereon being credited or debited to Profit and Loss Account.

With regard to the policy, there are two methods used.

1. To consider the premium as an ordinary business expense, that is, by debiting Profit and Loss Account or Drawings or Current Accounts in profit and loss ratio, and crediting cash, so that NO ASSET appears in the books of the partnership; when the policy becomes payable, normally by the decease of one of the partners, the amount due from the insurance company is treated as a profit. The division of such 'profit' must be made in profit sharing ratio (always subject to a contrary agreement). Where there have been CHANGES in the CONSTITUTION, the method employed is to prepare a schedule showing the 'build up' of the amount during each period measured by the changes, whether of profit sharing or of personnel. In the last period there will very probably be a substantial surplus over the estimated value at the date of the last change because of the maturity of the policy. It is, moreover, a frequent practice to agree and pay to an outgoing partner the estimated value of the policy at the date of retirement, whilst if the partner retiring is BOUGHT out the settlement will almost invariably include the estimated value of the policy. In these circumstances the continuing partners who bore the charge—seeing that no asset appears in the books—will be credited, when the policy matures, with the amount in due proportion previously credited to the retiring partner and debited back to them.

2. To treat the payment of the premium upon the policy as an INVESTMENT, either with or without an annual revaluation.

It should be realized that the policy is an ASSET of the **Firm.** Usually there is a policy on the life of EACH partner, unless a joint or survivorship policy is taken out in respect of the joint lives of the partners.

Illustration 60

Q, S, and O are in partnership as and from the 1st January 19.1, sharing profits and losses 3:2:1. They took out a survivorship assurance policy for £6,000, upon which the annual premium is £300 payable 1st February yearly. S dies on 31st December 19.3 the insurance company in due course paying the amount due. The firm closes its books on 31st December of each year. Show Journal entries.

Method 1.

JOURNAL

		£	£
19.1 Feb. 1	Profit and Loss Account[1] . . . . . . Cash . . . . Being annual premium on survivorship policy.	300	300
19.2 Feb. 1	Profit and Loss Account[1] . . . . . Cash . . . . Being annual premium on survivorship policy.	300	300
19.3 Feb. 1	Profit and Loss Account[1] . . . . . Cash . . . . Being annual premium on survivorship policy.	300	300

Dec. 31	*(Upon the receipt of the policy money)*
	Cash . . . .
	
	   Q . . . .
	   S . . . .
	   O . . . .
	Being receipt of policy money on the death of S apportioned
	amongst the partners as per partnership agreement.
		6,000	3,000
			2,000
			1,000

[1] Or Drawings Account in the ratio 3:2:1.

Method 2.

Assume that the surrender values of the policy dealt with in the foregoing example were:

		£
31st December 19.1	. . .	Nil
31st December 19.2	. .	200

Show Policy Account.

The Policy Account for the three years will be as below:

POLICY

						£			£
19.1 Feb. 1	Cash: Premium .			300	19.1 Dec. 31	Surrender Value Profit and Loss Account .			Nil 300
19.2 Feb. 1	Cash: Premium .			300	19.2 Dec. 31	Surrender Value . . c/d Profit and Loss Account			200 100
				£300					£300
19.3 Jan. 1 Feb. 1 Dec. 31	Surrender Value . b/d Cash: Premium Capital—			200 300	19.3 Dec. 31	Cash: Policy Money .			6,000
	Q . £2,750[1] S . 1,833 O . 917			5,500					
				£6,000					£6,000

[1] To nearest £.

Assignment of Life Policies. Although not confined to Partnership Accounts, it will be convenient to deal here with the assignment of a life policy in discharge of a debt, in order that the broad outlines of the treatment of life policy may be dealt with under one heading.

It frequently happens that a debtor assigns his life policy to a creditor in satisfaction of his liability, in which case the assignee must pay the premiums. In taking over the policy the creditor will credit the debtor only with its surrender value, as that is the value which is available on surrender, the assignee being in no better position than the assignor.

If there remains a debit balance on the debtor's account after the credit given for the surrender value of the policy, it will be written off to Bad Debts Account.

In the creditor's book there are alternative treatments in respect of the policy and the premiums, viz.:

> Upon receipt of policy:
> 1. (*a*) Debit Policy Account with surrender value.
>   Credit Debtor with surrender value.
>   (*b*) Debit Bad Debts Account with loss.
>   Credit Debtor.
> 2. Debit Policy Account with investment value.
>   Credit Debtor with surrender value, and write off balance as in (1) (*b*) above.
>   Credit (*a*) Policy Reserve Account with the excess of investment over surrender value, or
>   (*b*) Bad Debts Account.
> 3. See (*d*) below.

Treatment of Premiums. The premiums paid may be dealt with as shown below.

> (*a*) Debit Profit and Loss Account. Credit Cash.
> (*b*) Debit Capital, Drawings, Current or Reserve Account in profit and loss ratios. Credit Cash.
> (*c*) Debit Life Policy Account. Credit Cash.
> (*d*) Debit Life Policy Account with the *nominal* amount of the policy and credit Life Policy Reserve Account (on taking out or receiving the policy); debit the Life Policy Reserve Account and credit Cash upon the payment of premiums.
> (*e*) As in (*c*) or (*d*), and debit the Life Policy Account (*c*) or Life Policy Reserve Account (*d*) with loading for interest, and credit Profit and Loss Account.
> (*f*) Each year bring down the balance (representing the investment or surrender value) either in the Life Policy Account or by adjustment of the Reserve, writing off the difference as in (*a*) or (*b*).
> (*g*) Debit premiums to the Life Policy Account and revise the value thereof through the Life Policy Reserve Account, the value in question being investment or surrender value.[1]

If the policy is to be maintained at investment value, interest may be debited thereto and credited to Profit and Loss Account; but if it is to be maintained at surrender value, the latter value will be credited in the Policy Account and brought down, the difference being transferred to the debit of Profit and Loss Account, as the increase in surrender value will be *less* than the premium paid. (See Illustration p. 22113.)

---

[1] Companies exist which deal with policies by way of purchase and sale. Their price will be generally higher than surrender and lower than investment value.

Upon receipt of policy money:

Debit Cash. Credit Policy Account.
Debit Policy Account. Credit Profit and Loss Account.

Illustration 61

Fraser, owing Jones £1,000, agrees to assign his life policy to him in complete discharge of the debt. The assignment is made on 1st July 19.1, the policy being for £1,750. The premium is £60, payable yearly on 1st September.

On 15th January 19.3, Fraser dies, the policy money being paid to Jones on 31st January, 19.3.

The surrender values are (1) at the date of assignment, £320; (2) at 31st October 19.1, £358; and (3) at 31st October 19.2, £398.

Jones prepares his accounts annually at 31st October.

Assuming that Jones desires to keep the policy at its surrender value, show the necessary Ledger Accounts in his books.

FRASER

19.1 July 1	Balance . . .	b/d	£ 1,000	19.1 July 1	Life Policy Account re Fraser— Policy taken over in discharge, Surrender Value . . . Bad Debts Account .		£ 320 680
			£1,000				£1,000

LIFE POLICY ACCOUNT No. ......
re FRASER

19.1 July 1	Fraser—Policy taken over, Surrender Value . .		£ 320	19.1 Oct. 31	Profit and Loss Account		£ 22
Sept. 1	Cash—Yearly Premium .		60		Balance	c/d	358
			£380				£380
Nov. 1 19.2	Balance	b/d	358	19.2 Oct. 31	Profit and Loss Account .		20
Sept. 1	Cash—Yearly Premium .		60		Balance	c/d	398
			£418				£418
Nov. 1 19.3	Balance	b/d	398	19.3 Jan. 31	Cash	—	1,750
Jan. 15	Profit and Loss Account .		1,352				
			£1,750				£1,750

[Alternatively, the same result may be arrived at by showing the Policy at its *nominal* value and opening a Policy Reserve Account thus (dealing only with the first year)]:

LIFE POLICY ACCOUNT
re FRASER

| 19.1 July 1 | Fraser—Policy taken over, Surrender Value Life Policy Reserve . | | £ 320 1,430 | | | | |
| | | | 1,750 | | | | |

LIFE POLICY RESERVE
re FRASER

19.1 Sept. 1 Oct. 31	Cash—Yearly Premium Balance[1] . . .	c/d	£ 60 1,392	19.1 July 1 Oct. 31	Life Policy Account—*re* Fraser Profit and Loss Account .		£ 1,430 22
			£1,452				£1,452
				19.1 Nov. 1	Balance	b/d	1,392

[1] Nominal value of policy, £1,750, less surrender value of policy, £358

Ignoring interest, there is a profit of £630 to Jones, arrived at as follows:

	£	£
Profit on Life Policy		1,352
Less amounts written off—		
Year ended 31st October 19.1	22	
„ „ 19.2	20	
	—	42
Balance		1,310
Less Bad Debt written off		680
Profit		£630

This may be reconciled with the cash receipts as follows:

	£	£
Cash received on 31st January 19.3 . . .		1,750
Less Premium paid on 1st September 19.1 . .	60	
„ „ „ 19.2 . .	60	
	—	120
Net Cash received		1,630
Less Debt due by Fraser		1,000
Profit		£630

Illustration 62

On 1st July 19.8, the total surrender value of the life policies of £3,500 of the partnership is £1,500. The annual premiums of £100 paid to date are

£2,000. Show in columnar form the accounts, assuming that the premiums are paid on 1st November 19.2, and that the surrender value on 30th June 19.9, is £1,575, using Methods (d) and (g), and adjusting as required by paragraph (f). The accounts appear on p. 22118.

If the partners have taken out a joint policy, the account will be closed upon the maturity of the policy, any profit being credited to Profit and Loss Account, or Capital Accounts in profit ratios.

Where *separate* policies exist, the one which has matured will be similarly dealt with and, in addition, a revaluation of the other policies will be necessitated.

Capitals of Remaining Partners to be Adjusted to New Profit-sharing Ratio. The treatment of accounts where a partner is required to bring in cash so that capitals are in profit-sharing ratios has been dealt with on p. 2274 *et seq.*, and the same principle applies on a retirement or death of a partner.

Illustration 63

The following is the Balance Sheet of A, B, and C, sharing profits and losses in the ratio of 2:2:1.

A, B, AND C BALANCE SHEET

	£	£		£	£
Capitals—			Sundry Assets (including		
A	2,000		Goodwill)		5,500
B	3,000		Cash		500
C	1,000				
		6,000			
		£6,000			£6,000

A retires and is to be paid in cash, B and C agreeing to provide the necessary funds, and at the same time to increase the cash balance to £800, the contributions to be such as to leave their capitals in their profit-sharing ratio which is to be unchanged.

METHOD (d)

DEBIT SIDE
LIFE POLICY

			£
19.8 July 1	Balance	b/d	3,500
	(a)		

DEBIT SIDE
LIFE POLICY RESERVE

			£
19.8 Nov. 1	Cash: Premium		100
19.9 June 30	Balance	c/d	1,925
			£2,025

CREDIT SIDE
LIFE POLICY RESERVE

			£
19.8 July 1	Balance	b/d	2,000
19.9 June 30	Profit and Loss Account		25
			£2,025
July 1	Balance (b)	b/d	1,925

[a − b = £1,575.]

METHOD (g)

DEBIT SIDE
LIFE POLICY

			£
19.8 July 1	Balance	b/d	2,000
Nov. 1	Cash: Premium		100
	(c)		£2,100

CREDIT SIDE
LIFE POLICY RESERVE

			£
19.8 July 1	Balance	b/d	500
19.9 June 30	Profit and Loss Account		25
	(d)		£525

[c − d = £1,575.]

The amount of cash required is:	£	£
Due to A 2,000		
Plus increase of cash balance 300		
		2,300
to which will be added the combined capitals of B and C . .		4,000
gives the total resultant capitals of B and C		£6,300

STATEMENT OF CAPITAL; (B AND C)

	Total	B	C
	£	£	£
New Capitals	6,300	4,200	2,100
Old Capitals	4,000	3,000	1,000
Contributions	£2,300	£1,200	£1,100

BALANCE SHEET (after completing aforesaid arrangements)

	£	£		£	£
Capitals—			Sundry Assets . .		5,500
A Balance:			Cash		800
£2,000−Cash £2,000	nil				
B Balance:					
£3,000+Cash £1,200	4,200				
C Balance:					
£1,000+Cash £1,100	2,100				
		6,300			
		£6,300			£6,300

Interest from Last Balance Sheet in Lieu of Profits. In order to avoid splitting of profits, the partnership agreement may provide that interest be paid in lieu of profits from the date of the last Balance Sheet to the date of death or retirement. The agreement should be carefully worded so that any dispute as to the amount on which the interest is to be paid (e.g. on Capital Account alone or Capital plus Current Account, etc.) will be avoided.

Illustration 64

A, B, and C are in partnership sharing profits 3:2:1. The partnership agreement provided that, on the death or retirement of a partner, the partner or his estate shall be entitled to 10 per cent per annum on his share of partnership assets from the date of the last Balance Sheet to the date of death, in lieu of profits. On 31st December 19.1, the date of the last Balance Sheet, the Capital Accounts stood as follows: A £6,000, B £5,000, C £3,000, and the Current Accounts as follows: A £1,000, B £1,200, C £600. B died on 30th June 19.2, and his share of goodwill, which was not included in the books, was valued at £2,000. The amount payable to the executors of B would appear in his Loan Account as follows:

EXORS. OF B LOAN

19.2 June 30	Balance .	.	.	.	c/d	£ 8,610	19.2 Jan. 1 June 30	Balance of Capital Account ¹Transfer from Current Account . . . Share of Goodwill . . Interest		†	£ 5,000 1,200 2,000 410
						£8,610					£8,610
							19.2 July 1	Balance	b/d		8,610

† £8,200 at 10% per annum for 6 months.
¹ In the event of any changes having taken place in the Current Account balance during the period between the last Balance Sheet and the date of death, the interest will have to be calculated in the form of an Account Current.

SECTION E. RETIREMENT AND ADMISSION

The positions arising upon a partner's retirement and admission have been dealt with separately. It now remains to deal with the combined change: the retirement *and* admission taking place at the same time. It very frequently happens that when one partner retires another is admitted, the capital introduced by the new partner being utilized wholly or partly in discharge of the liability of the old firm to the retiring partner.

No departure from the principles enumerated is entailed, the question being more one of detail caused by the two 'sets' of transactions.

Illustration 65

Q, S, and O, partners, share profits and losses in the ratio of 3 : 2 : 1. S retires on 31st December 19 . ., and D is admitted a partner on the same date, the new ratio to be 4 : 4 : 3. The latter is required to bring into the firm so much capital as will make his share one-third of the total assets as revalued.

The following is the Balance Sheet of Q, S, and O:

BALANCE SHEET AS AT 31ST DECEMBER 19 . .

	£	£		£	£
Capitals—			Stock . . .		10,000
Q . . .	7,000		Debtors . . .	4,000	
S . . .	5,000		*Less* Bad Debts Provision . . .	400	
O . . .	3,000		vision . . .		3,600
		15,000			2,800
Reserve . . .		1,400	Cash . . .		
		£16,400			£16,400

The partnership agreement gives certain directions as to the value of the assets to be taken for the purpose of dissolution, these being: stock, £9,600; sundry debtors, £3,800; and goodwill, £5,400. D agrees to his admission being based upon these valuations.

CAPITALS

Dr.

19..			Q £	S £	O £	D £
Dec. 31	Cash¹			7,200		
	Balances	c/d	10,300		4,100	
			£10,300	£7,200	£4,100	
19..						
Jan. 1	Memorandum Revaluation Account		2,400		2,400	1,800
	Balances	c/d	7,900		1,700	5,400
			£10,300		£4,100	£7,200

Cr.

19..			Q £	S £	O £	D £
Dec. 31	Balances	b/d	7,000	5,000	3,000	
	Memorandum Revaluation Account		3,300	2,200	1,100	
			£10,300	£7,200	£4,100	
19..						
Jan. 1	Balances	b/d	10,300			
	Cash				4,100	7,200
			£10,300		£4,100	£7,200
	Balances	b/d	7,900		1,700	5,400

¹The balance of capital is usually transferred to Partner's Loan Account and cash debited thereto.

Memorandum REVALUATION ACCOUNT

19..			£	£
Dec. 31	Decrease in Asset—Stock	c/d		400
	Profit on Revaluation—			
	Q: $\frac{1}{2}$		3,300	
	S: $\frac{1}{3}$		2,200	
	O: $\frac{1}{6}$		1,100	6,600
				£7,000
19..				
Jan. 1	Reversal of Items	b/d		7,000
				£7,000

19..			£	£
Dec. 31	Increase in Assets—			
	Debtors (Bad Debts Provision)	c/d	200	5,600
	Goodwill	c/d	5,400	1,400
	Decrease in Liability—Reserve	c/d		
				£7,000
19..				
Jan. 1	Reversal of Item	b/d		400
	Balance—			
	O: $\frac{4}{11}$		2,400	
	O: $\frac{4}{11}$		2,400	
	D: $\frac{3}{11}$		1,800	6,600
				£7,000

Show the Capital Accounts of the partners, the revised Balance Sheet, and a Memorandum Revaluation Account.

If the adjustments are **not to be shown permanently** in the books, the above question naturally falls into two main parts, viz.:

1. The adjustment of asset values upon the retirement of S.
2. The admission of D and the book readjustment of asset values.

BALANCE SHEET AS AT 1ST JANUARY 19..

	£	£		£	£
Capitals—			Stock . . .		10,000
Q . . .	7,900		Debtors . .	4,000	
O . . .	1,700		*Less* Bad Debts Pro-		
D . . .	5,400		vision . .	400	
		15,000	Cash [£2,800 + £7,200		3,600
Reserve . . .		.1,400	− £7,200] .		2,800
		£16,400			£16,400

It will be seen that the capital to be introduced by D is based upon the combined capitals of Q and O before the elimination of the adjustments from the books, i.e. $\frac{1}{2} \times (£10,300 + £4,100) = £7,200$.

If it were decided, *after* the reversal has been made, to bring the adjustments permanently into the books, there would be a book profit of £6,600 which would be credited to Q £2,400: O £2,400 and D £1,800, thus eliminating the reversing entries of 1st January 19.., and restoring the true position.

The TRUE position at 1st January 19.., is:

	£	£
Capital Accounts as per books		15,000
Add Net Undisclosed Assets, i.e.—		
Debtors, Goodwill and Reserve . . .	7,000	
Less Stock Depreciation . . .	400	
		6,600
		£21,600

The Capital Accounts would be revised on entering the undisclosed figures, and the table given at top of p. 22124 shows the position.

This is the precise result that would have been obtained by a 'straight' entry of the net assets and a credit to the old partners.

CAPITALS

		Q	O	D
		£	£	£
Balances per Balance Sheet . .		7,900	1,700	5,400
Add—'Profit' £6,600		$\frac{4}{11}$ 2,400	$\frac{4}{11}$ 2,400	$\frac{3}{11}$ 1,800
True Capitals . .		£10,300	£4,100	[1] £7,200

[1] $\frac{1}{3}$ of total Capital.

Illustration 66

A, B, and C are partners with capitals of £2,000, £2,500, and £1,800 respectively. On the retirement of A and the introduction of D, goodwill (which is not in the books) is valued at £750, other undisclosed assets at £600. The profits were shared in the proportion of 2 : 2 : 1, the new firm to divide profits equally. D is to introduce cash £1,000. The book values of the assets are to remain unchanged. Show Capital Accounts. See p. 22125.

Illustration 67

At 31st December 19.1, when C was admitted a partner on a one-sixth basis the undisclosed assets not brought into account were an insurance policy £400, and investments £600. A and B had previously been equal partners. On 31st December 19.2, D was admitted as a partner, the new ratios being 10 : 10 : 4 : 3. On 31st December 19.3, A died and the policy fell in for £700 and the investments were sold for £690. Goodwill is to be adjusted outside the business. The estimated values of insurance policy and investments as at 31st December 19.2, were £600 and £520—the insurance premiums being charged and the dividends credited to Profit and Loss Account in the ordinary way. Show the division of the proceeds.

	Insur-ance Policy	Increase	Invest-ments	Increase or Decrease	Net Increase or Decrease	A	B	C	D
	£	£	£	£	£	£	£	£	£
31st Dec. 19.1	400		600		1,000	500	500		
19.2	600	+200	520	[2] − 80	120	50	50	20	
19.3	700	+100	690	+170	270	100	100	40	30
					£1,390	£650	£650	£60	£30

When entered into the books cash will be debited with £1,390, and the Capital Accounts credited in the above proportions.

[2] Assumed A and B continue to share profits equally as between themselves in 19.2.

If A had *retired* on 31st December 19.3, the values of the undisclosed assets would be dealt with on the lines already explained. Further, if A's share is purchased there will be a transfer from A's account (after having given him credit on the revaluation) by debiting his account and crediting the continuing partners, the latter being personally liable to A.

CAPITALS

Credit side

		A £	B £	C £	D £
Balances	b/d	2,000	2,500	1,800	
Revaluation of Assets	c/d	240	240	120	
Goodwill	c/d	300	300	150	
		£2,540	£3,040	£2,070	
Balances [see note]	b/d	[2]2,540	[2]3,040	[2]2,070	
Cash					[1]1,000
		£2,540	£3,040	£2,070	£1,000
Balances	b/d		2,590	1,620	550

Debit side

		A £	B £	C £	D £
Balances	c/d	2,540	3,040	2,070	
		£2,540	£3,040	£2,070	
Revaluation of Assets	b/d		200	200	200
Goodwill	b/d		250	250	250
Balances	b/d		[2]2,590	[2]1,620	[2]550
Loan Account	c/d	2,540			
		£2,540	£3,040	£2,070	£1,000

[1] True Capitals.

[2] 'Book' Capitals.

Note.—If the partners decided to adjust their capitals to profit sharing ratios D would bring in a further £1,036·67, B and C respectively withdrawing £1,003·33 and £33·33, leaving all the partners with £2,036·67 each.

Illustration 68

A, B, and C are partners. The business is divided into £30 shares owned as follows: A, 60; B, 15; C, 25. The goodwill value of a share is £100, but no amount for goodwill stands in the books. The capital accounts are: A, £1,800; B, £450; and C, £750.

On 1st January 19.., D is admitted as a partner on terms that

   (i) A is to sell 10 shares to B.
  (ii) A is to sell 10 shares to D.
 (iii) C is to sell 5 shares to D.

The total capital is to remain undisturbed and individual capitals are to be adjusted according to these shares. D is permitted to pay half of the amount due immediately, the balance due to be treated as a loan bearing interest at 10 per cent per annum, such amount being transferred proportionately to the credit of the selling partners. There is to be no other selling adjustment. Any surplus on D's Current Account at the end of a year is to be applied in payment of the loans by A and C.

Drawings are to be £5 per share per month. The profit for the year to 31st December 19.., is £8,000. Sundry assets of £500 at the commencement of the business remain unchanged. There are no other assets save cash and no liabilities.

At 31st December 19.. (one year after D's admittance) B retires. The other partners purchase his share in the business, including the balance on his current account. The goodwill value of a share is to be taken at £80.

Prepare Partners' Capital, Current, and Loan Accounts, and extract Balance Sheets at 31st December 19.., (a) before and (b) after retirement of B. Workings to nearest £.

The opening accounts are:

	£	£
Cash	2,500	
Sundry Assets	500	
Capitals	——	3,000

The cash at the end will be—

	£	£
Balance at commencement	2,500	
Plus Profit	8,000	
	——	10,500
Less Drawings per—		
Current Account	6,000	
Loan Account	203	
	——	6,203
		£4,297

The cash paid in by B and D is not retained in the business, but taken out by A and C.

D pays in £975, B £1,300.   Total £2,275.⎫
A receives £1,950, C, £325.   Total £2,275.⎬ See p. 22130.
                                           ⎭

The problem is not nearly so complex as at first appears. It is clear that the capitals are to be in ratio to the profit-sharing proportions so that the end capitals must be in the ratio of $40:25:20:15$, and seeing that the cash introduced by B and D is to be withdrawn, the end capitals will still be £3,000, and the amount to be brought in by D will be $\frac{15}{100} \times £3,000 = £450$. Actually only one-half of this amount is brought in at present in cash, the balance being on loan, but the effect is just the same so far as the capital is concerned. If the total capital is £3,000, each hundredth must be equal to £30.

The total goodwill must be $£100 \times 100 = £10,000$, and as A sells a $\frac{1}{5}$ proportion (i.e. $\frac{60}{100}$ less $\frac{40}{100}$) he must be credited with £2,000 which is the total amount credited to his account, viz. £500 plus £500 plus £1,000.

Likewise C sells a $\frac{1}{20}$ proportion (i.e. $\frac{25}{100}$ less $\frac{20}{100}$) and so must be credited with £500 ($\frac{1}{20} \times £10,000$), which is the total credited to his account, viz. £250 plus £250.

Once the significance of the phraseology is grasped, the problem of goodwill and capital can be dealt with on the lines already outlined on previous pages, e.g. if the goodwill account were created it would be debited with £10,000, and credits would be:

A £6,000, B £1,500, C £2,500, Total: £10,000.

If reversed, the goodwill would be eliminated and the debits would be:

A £4,000, B £2,500, C £2,000, D £1,500, Total: £10,000.

Combined, the results would be:

	Dr.	Cr.
	£	£
A . . .		2,000
B . . .	1,000	
C . . .		500
D . . .	1,500	
	£2,500	£2,500

In the accounts outlined, A and C are duly credited with these figures, whilst B is credited with £300 and D £450, which are the total contributions of B (£1,300 less debit as above £1,000), and D (£1,950 less debit as above £1,500). As has been shown, if the *whole* goodwill is put through the books, the contributions for *both* goodwill and capital must be credited to the contributing partners, and on reversal the 'pure' capital contributions will remain in the books.

In regard to the retiring partner B, he is selling his twenty-five shares of the capital and goodwill to the other partners.

The whole goodwill now being valued at £8,000, i.e. 100 shares of £80 each, will be shown as follows:

GOODWILL ADJUSTMENTS STATEMENT

	A		B		C		D	
		£		£		£		£
Old Shares	40%	3,200	25%	2,000	20%	1,600	15%	1,200
New Shares	53⅓%	4,267	Nil	Nil	26⅔%	2,133	20%	1,600
Differences	−13⅓%	Dr. £1,067	+25%	Cr. £2,000	−6⅔%	Dr. £533	−5%	Dr. £400

The Journal entry is:

JOURNAL

		£	£
A Capital	(b)	1,067	
C „	(d)	533	
D „	(f)	400	
B Capital			2,000
Being shares of Goodwill taken over from B by continuing partners.			

At this stage, therefore, B is in credit for £2,750, being his capital of £750 plus his share of goodwill, as above, £2,000. In addition, his Current Account is in credit for £500.

The acquisition of B's Capital balance of £2,750 will be recorded in the Journal thus:

JOURNAL

	£		£
B Capital	2,750		
A Capital		(a)	1,467[1]
C „		(c)	733[1]
D „		(e)	550[1]
Being shares of Capital and Goodwill purchased from B by continuing partners as agreed.			

[1] Ratios of 53⅓% : 26⅔% : 20% of £2,750.

The Capital Accounts (as a result of the above entries) are now:

	A	C	D
	£	£	£
Balances per previous Balance Sheet	1,200	600	450
Adjustments	400	200	150
	$(a-b)$	$(c-d)$	$(e-f)$
Total (see p. 22133)	£1,600	£800	£600

CAPITALS

Debit side

Date	Particulars	A £	B £	C £	D £
19.. Jan. 1	Cash—Shares sold to D, payment of ½ thereof	650		325	
	Cash—Shares sold to B	1,300			
	Loan Accounts—½ value of Shares sold to D	650		325	
	Balances c/d	1,200	750	600	450
		£3,800	£750	£1,250	£450
Dec. 31	Goodwill — Transfer to A, C, D, per agreement	1,067		533	400
	Balances c/d	1,600	2,750	800	600
		£2,667	£2,750	£1,333	£1,000

Credit side

Date	Particulars	A £	B £	C £	D £
19.. Jan. 1	Balances b/d	1,800	450	750	225
	(a) Cash—½ payment for 15 Shares at £30 each	500		250	
	(b) Cash—½ payment for 15 Shares at £100 each in respect of Goodwill purchased by D				
	(a) D Loan Account—Balance for 15 Shares at £30 each transferred	500		250	
	(b) D Loan Account Balance for 15 Shares at £100 each for Goodwill transferred				
	(a) Cash—payment for 10 Shares purchased from A at £30		300		225
	(b) Cash—payment for 10 Shares in respect of Goodwill at £100 each	1,000			
	See footnote				
		£3,800	£750	£1,250	£450
Jan. 1 / Dec. 31	Balances b/d	1,200	750	600	450
	Goodwill		2,000		
	Transfer from B, Shares purchased	1,467		733	550
		£2,667	£2,750	£1,333	£1,000
19.. Jan. 1	Balances b/d	1,600		800	600

(a) Payment for Capital.

i.e. Shares in Capital:

					@ 30	
A	60 less sold	20	10 = 40	@ 30 =	1,200
B	15 add bought	5	10 = 25	@ 30 =	750
C	25 less sold		15 = 20	@ 30 =	600
D	Nil add bought		15 = 15	@ 30 =	450
	100	25	25 = 100	@ 30 =	£3,000

(b) Payment for Goodwill.

	£	£
		1,200
		750
		600
		450
		£3,000

CURRENT ACCOUNTS

Dr.

	A £	B £	C £	D £
19.. Dec. 31				
Cash Drawings	2,400	1,500	1,200	900
Interest on Loan				97
Transfer to Loan Account				203
Balances c/d	865	500	433	
	£3,265	£2,000	£1,633	£1,200
Transfer to A, C, and D per agreement		500		
Balances c/d	1,132		566	100
	£1,132	£500	£566	£100

Cr.

	A £	B £	C £	D £
19.. Dec. 31				
Interest on Loan	65		33	
Profit	3,200	2,000	1,600	1,200
	£3,265	£2,000	£1,633	£1,200
Balances b/d	865	500	433	
Transfer from B to A, C, and D	267		133	100
	£1,132	£500	£566	£100
19.. Jan. 1 Balances b/d	1,132		566	100

LOANS

Dr.

	A £	B £	C £	D £
19.. Jan. 1 Transfer from Capital Account	135		68	
Dec. 31 Cash	515		257	975
	£650		£325	£975
19.. Jan. 1 Balance b/d				772

Cr.

	A £	B £	C £	D £
19.. Jan. 1 Transfer from Capital Accounts	650		325	203
Dec. 31 Transfer from Current Account				772
	£650		£325	£975
19.. Jan. 1 Balances b/d	515		257	

Note. The adjustments on B's retirement are shown in separate sections of the Capital and Current Accounts.

BALANCE SHEET AS AT 31ST DECEMBER 19.. (*before* THE RETIREMENT OF B)

	£	£		£	£
Capitals—			Cash		4,298
A	1,200		Sundry Assets		500
B	750		Loan—D[1]		772
C	600				
D	450	3,000			
Current Accounts—					
A	865				
B	500				
C	433	1,798			
Loans—					
A	515				
C	257	772			
		£5,570			£5,570

[1] As D, by transferring £203 (the balance of his Current Account) to the credit of his Loan Account has in effect drawn out that sum, A and C will draw a like amount in proportion, thus leaving the amount owing to the partners A and C in respect of the loan equal to that owed by D. If the Loan Accounts are to be considered purely personal matters, they will not appear in the books of the firm, and D will withdraw the sum of £203 and pay over to A and C £135 and £68 respectively, giving the identical result as regards the partnership, as the Loan Accounts cancel each other.

BALANCE SHEET AS AT 31ST DECEMBER 19.. (*after* RETIREMENT OF B)

	£	£		£	£
Capitals (a)—			Cash		4,298
A . . .	1,600		Sundry Assets . .		500
C . . .	800		D—Loan . . .		772
D . . .	600	3,000			
Current Accounts (b)—					
A . . .	1,132				
C . . .	566				
D . . .	100	1,798			
Loans—					
A . . .	515				
C . . .	257	772			
		£5,570			£5,570

(a) These are respectively 53⅓ per cent, 26⅔ per cent, and 20 per cent of 100 shares of £30 each.
(b) If the Current Accounts are to be in 'ratio,' there will be a cash adjustment between the partners.

The Current Accounts transfers will be journalized thus:

JOURNAL

	£	£
B Current Account	500	
A Current Account		267
C ,, ,, ...		133
D ,, ,, ...		100
Being B's Current Account taken over by the continuing partners.		

CURRENT ACCOUNTS

	A	B	C	D
	£	£	£	£
Balances, from last Balance Sheet . . .	865	500	433	Nil
Adjustments, as above . .	+267	−500	+133	+100
Balances (see p. 22133) . .	£1,132	Nil	£566	£100

Illustration 69

A and B are in partnership as equal partners. A, by agreement, retires and his son S joins the firm on a basis of one-third share of profits.

The balances on the books were:

	Dr. £	Cr. £
Goodwill.	1,200	
Bank	800	
Other Assets	5,900	
Creditors		400
Capital Accounts: A		3,800
B		3,700
	£7,900	£7,900

Goodwill is agreed at £3,000 and written up accordingly. Sufficient money is to be introduced so as to enable A to be paid off and leave £500 cash in bank; B and S are to provide such sum as will make their capitals proportionate to their shares of profit. A agrees to contribute from his Capital half of the amount S has to provide.

Assuming the arrangement was carried out show the journal entries required.

JOURNAL

	£	£
Goodwill	1,800	
Capital—A		900
Capital—B		900
Increase in value of Goodwill on dissolution.		
Capital—A	1,500	
Capital—S		1,500
Half amount required from S contributed by A, as follows—		
Capital A revalued £4,700		
Capital B revalued 4,600		

	9,300
Less Cash available [£800 − £500] . . .	300
Proposed amended Capital	£9,000
of which—	
S is to pay one-third	£3,000
Half thereof	£1,500

	£	£
Cash	2,900	
B		1,400
S		1,500
Cash required—		
B—two-thirds £6,000		
Less existing revalued Capital 4,600		

	£1,400
S—Half of £3,000	£1,500

	£	£
Capital—A	3,200[1]	
Cash		3,200
Balance due £4,700		
Less Gift to S 1,500		

	£3,200

[1] This is equal to the following

	£
(1) Cash at Bank available for A [£800—£500] . . .	300
(2) Amount paid in by B	1,400
(3) Amount paid in by S	1,500
	£3,200

The revised Balances would be:

	Dr.	Cr.
	£	£
Goodwill [£1,200 + £1,800] . . .	3,000	
Cash at Bank [£800 + £1,400 + £1,500 − £3,200] . .	500	
Other Assets	5,900	
Creditors		400
A [£3,800 + £900 − £1,500 − £3,200] . .	—	
B [£3,700 + £900 + £1,400] . .		6,000
S [£1,500 (from father) + £1,500 (Cash)] . .		3,000
	£9,400	£9,400

Illustration 70

A, B and C shared profits equally, without interest on capital.

On 31st December 19.4, C retired, and it was agreed that he should receive for his share of the partnership goodwill twice his average annual share of the profits for the last three years.

On 31st December 19.6, D was admitted a partner on the basis of acquiring a one-fifth share of the partnership goodwill (in addition to £8,000 as capital), as to one-quarter thereof from A and three-quarters from B, the price therefor being agreed at one-tenth of the total profits of the firm for the five years ended 31st December 19.6.

The profits of the last five years were:

			£
31st December 19.2	. . .		3,000
,, 19.3	. . .		9,000
,, 19.4	. . .		18,000
,, 19.5	. . .		10,000
,, 19.6	. . .		15,000

Goodwill has not been shown as an asset in the books and this policy is to continue.

Prepare statements showing the adjustments to be made arising from the above.

1. On C's retirement:

		£	£
A.	Dr.	3,334	
B.	Dr.	3,333	
To C			6,667

$$[\tfrac{2}{3}(\tfrac{30,000}{3})]$$

2. On D's admission:

D's share of goodwill:

Total profits of the five preceding years	. . .	£55,000	
D's share of Goodwill $\frac{55,000}{10}$ . . .		= £5,500	

The position now is that by the agreed formula D is purchasing for £5,500 a one-fifth share of goodwill, hence the total goodwill is £27,500, of which A and B are selling a one-fifth share to D.

		A	B	D
		$\frac{1}{4} \times \frac{1}{5}$	$\frac{3}{4} \times \frac{1}{5}$	
Sellers		$(= \frac{1}{20})$	$(= \frac{3}{20})$	
Buyer . . .				
		Cr. £1,375	Cr. £4,125	Dr. £5,500

		£	£
D	Dr.	5,500	
To A			1,375
,, B			4,125

If the goodwill is brought into the books after the preceding entries have been made, the entries would be:

		£	£
Goodwill	. . .	Dr. 27,500	
A $\frac{9}{20}$			12,375
B $\frac{7}{20}$			9,625
D $\frac{4}{20}$			5,500

If the goodwill is brought into the books immediately on D's admission, the entries would be:

		£	£
Goodwill	. . .	Dr. 27,500	
A $\frac{1}{2}$ (See note *infra*)			13,750
B $\frac{1}{2}$ (See note *infra*)			13,750

Note. It will be seen that the effect of immediately bringing the goodwill into the books as compared with making the adjustments *without* the introduction of goodwill into the books, followed by its being brought in, is the same, i.e.:

	First adjustment	Second adjustment	Total
	£	£	£
A	Cr. 1,375	Cr. 12,375	13,750
B	Cr. 4,125	Cr. 9,625	13,750
D	Dr. 5,500	Cr. 5,500	—

SECTION F. CONTINUANCE OF PERSONNEL WITH REVISED PROFIT-SHARING RATIO

Where the same partners continue in business but decide upon a change in PROFIT-SHARING ratios, the position may be regarded as if there had been a change in personnel, that is an old firm and a new one for the purpose of adjusting assets (including goodwill) and liabilities.

The procedure will follow the usual lines as on a change in personnel, the revaluation being necessary so that profits or losses may be dealt with in favour of or against the partners in their proper proportions.

Illustration 71

The following are the Capital Accounts of A, B, and C sharing profits 2:2:1.

		£
A	. . . .	2,000
B	. . . .	1,400
C	. . . .	1,000
		£4,400

No goodwill appears in the books. It is decided that they shall share profits in future in the proportions 4:3:1. For this purpose the assets are to be written down by £100 and the goodwill to be taken as worth £900. Capitals are then to be adjusted (by cash payments) to the same proportions as the new profit-sharing ratios and no alterations are to be made to book values.

Show Ledger entries. (See p. 22138.)

Memorandum REVALUATION ACCOUNT

Dr	£			Cr	£
Depreciation of Assets		c/d	Appreciation of Asset—Goodwill . .	c/d	900
Profit on Revaluation—	100				
A: £320					
B: 320					
C: 160	800				
	£900				£900
Reversal of Item	900	b/d	Reversal of Item	b/d	100
			A: £400		
			B: 300		
			C: 100		800
	£900				£900

CAPITALS

	A	B	C			A	B	C
	£	£	£			£	£	£
Profit on Revaluation written back	(x) 400	(y) 300	(z) 100		Balances b/d	2,000	1,400	1,000
Cash			510		Profit on Revaluation	(x) 320	(y) 320	(z) 160
Balances—(a) c/d	(4/9) 2,200	(3/9) 1,650	(2/9) 550		Cash	280	230	
	£2,600	£1,950	£1,160			£2,600	£1,950	£1,160
					Balances b/d	2,200	1,650	550

(a) Based upon 'book value' capital, i.e. £4,400. The cash paid in by A and B equals the amount received by C.

Interest on Capital

If the partnership agreement provides for interest on capital it has the effect of giving a certain portion of trading profits in the capital ratio, i.e. by way of interest on capital, so that the 'net' influence of the changed ratio is not synonymous with the 'gross'. For instance, two partners may previously have shared profits equally, and agree to revise the ratio to 3 : 1. The difference as between each is nominally from 1 : 1 to 3 : 1, but if interest on capital is allowed a certain proportion of the profits will be thus absorbed.

Illustration 72

A and B are partners sharing profits equally, after allowing 5 per cent interest on their capitals of £8,000 and £7,000. Assets, including goodwill, are to be reduced by £10,000 and thereafter profits are to be shared as to 4 : 1 after providing interest on capital at 5 per cent per annum on their revised capitals. The profit before taking into account interest on capital is £1,250.

Show the division of profit in both the old and the new manner.

	A	B	Total
	£	£	£
(1) *Old Division—*			
Interest on Capital	400	350	750
Profits equally	250	250	500
	£650	£600	£1,250
(2) *New Division—*			
Interest on Capital	150	100	250
Profits 4 : 1	800	200	1,000
	£950	£300	£1,250

It will be seen that, in the new division, the first £250 is absorbed in interest on capital leaving an extra £500 divisible profit. The partners lose on interest on capital £500 [i.e. £750−£250] equally, as can be seen above. This must be so because the interest is at the same rate as before but upon a lower capital and the capitals have been reduced EQUALLY by the loss on revaluation, which the partners bear equally. Thus, the difference between the profits to A and B in the new and old ratios is explained:

£
250 Interest. A takes £50 more than B in both instances
500 'Released' Interest, now as divisible profit
500 other profit
£1,000 new divisible profit, as above.

This may be further explained in the following table:

$$\text{A gains } \overset{New}{\tfrac{4}{5}} - \overset{Old}{\tfrac{1}{2}} = \tfrac{3}{10} \times £1,000 = £300, \text{ i.e. } \overset{Old}{£650} \quad \overset{New}{£950}$$

$$\text{B loses } \overset{Old}{\tfrac{1}{2}} - \overset{New}{\tfrac{1}{5}} = \tfrac{3}{10} \times £1,000 = £300, \text{ i.e. } £600 \quad £300$$

It must further be remembered that A will gain on any capital profit, e.g. assuming that the assets fetch the old book values, A will gain £3,000 [i.e. $\tfrac{3}{10} \times £10,000$] as he was previously debited with his *half* share of the capital loss, i.e. £5,000, and will now be credited with *four-fifths* of the capital gain, i.e. £8,000.

Subsequent Receipts of Debts Written Off, etc. Where assets, e.g. debtors, are written off wholly or in part, it is a question of importance to determine upon a change in profit-sharing ratios whether it represents a revaluation or not.

1. If the former, any subsequent appreciation or profit upon the revised book value, e.g. receipt of a debt written off as bad, must be credited to the new partners in the *new* ratio.

2. If the writing off was merely a precautionary measure, then any appreciation subsequent to the change in constitution will be credited to the old partners in the *old* ratio.

Where the Memorandum Revaluation method is employed it will be obvious that the assets still remain undisturbed in the books, and the entries will be as in either (3) or (4).

3. Where a true revaluation is made and the amount considered bad at the date of the change:

> *Dr.* Old partners in the old ratio.
> *Cr.* New partners in the new ratio.

(*a*) The amount subsequently received will be credited to the DEBTORS accounts (debts not having been actually written off as in the Memorandum Revaluation system, the book values of assets remain unchanged). The partners' accounts will, therefore, not be credited as they would in the case of an ordinary writing-off as in (1) and (2), the partners already having obtained the benefit in the new ratio by entry in the Memorandum Revaluation Account.

(*b*) If the asset proves to be finally bad, the loss will be written off in the new ratio.

4. Where there is merely a 'precautionary' adjustment, at the date of the change:

> *Dr.* Old partners in the old ratio.
> *Cr.* New partners in the old ratio.

(*a*) The amount subsequently received will be credited to the DEBTORS accounts (debts not having been actually written off, as in the Memorandum Revaluation system the book values of assets remain unchanged). The partners' accounts will, therefore, not be credited as they would in the case of an ordinary writing-off as in (1) and (2), the partners having obtained the benefit in the old ratio by the entry in the Memorandum Revaluation Account.

(b) If the asset proves to be bad, the loss may be considered to have taken place in the course of the new partnership, and will be debited to the partners in the *new* ratio.

Illustration 73

A and B were partners sharing profits and losses equally. On 31st December 19.., they decided to share profits and losses in future in the ratio of 3 : 2. Bad Debts were written off amounting to £100 on the date of the change, and in the following year the amount written off was received in full. Show entries relating to the above.

Entries at Date of Change			*Entries on Receipt of Cash*		
(1) Debit A £50	Credit Debtors	£100	Debit Cash £100	Credit Debtors	£100
,, B £50			Debit Debtors £100	Credit A	£60
				,, B	£40
				(through the Profit and Loss Account)	
(2) Debit A £50	Credit Debtors	£100	Debit Cash £100	Credit Debtors	£100
,, B £50			Debit Debtors £100	Credit A	£50
				,, B	£50
				(through the Profit and Loss Account)	
(3a) Debit A £50	Credit Memoran-		Debit Cash £100	Credit Debtors	£100
,, B £50	dum Revaluation				
	Account	£100			
Debit Mem-	Credit A	£60			
orandum	,, B	£40			
Revaluation					
Account £100					
(4a) Debit A £50	Credit Memoran-		Debit Cash £100	Credit Debtors	£100
,, B £50	dum Revaluation				
	Account	£100			
Debit Mem-	Credit A	£50			
orandum	,, B	£50			
Revaluation					
Account £100					

Illustration 74

In reference to the preceding illustration, if no amount is received in respect of the Bad Debts the entries already made at the date of change will remain undisturbed and no receipts at all will appear in the right hand column above.

As no actual writing off has taken place in (3a) and (4a) the entry for actual writing off the debts will be:

(3b) Debit A £60   Credit Debtors £100
    ,, B £40
(4b) Debit A £60   Credit Debtors £100
    ,, B £40
    (through the Profit
    and Loss Account
    in each case)

The position of (1) and (2) is clear, but in regard to (3) the effect of the entries representing a true revaluation may be seen in reference to the non-receipt of the cash. The partners were debited equally (3a) and *credited* in the ratio of 3:2 (3a), and when the debt proved to be bad the partners were *debited* in the ratio to 3:2 (3b), thus leaving the partners in debit equally—the true allocation of loss as the debts were considered bad at the date of the change, thus being a loss of the 'old' firm.

In regard to (4) the debts were not considered bad, so that when the adjustment takes place the loss must be taken as appertaining to the 'new' firm. This may be seen by the combined effect of entries in (4a) and (4b). In the former A and B were debited and credited equally, and in the latter (4b) were debited in the ratio of 3:2. As the entries in (4a) cancel each other the 'new' firm is debited with the loss in the ratio of 3:2 by the entry in (4b).

Alternatively, the entries in (4) at the date of change need not be made, and subsequently the new partners' Capital Accounts will be debited in the new ratio (if the debts prove bad), or cash debited and Debtors Accounts credited (if the debts are received).

Illustration 75

A and B are in partnership sharing profits as follows: 8 per cent interest on capital, one-quarter of the remaining profits to B in salary, the residue between A and B as to 3:2. They hold as a partnership asset shares which cost £4,000: A considers them to be worth £6,500 and proposes that they shall be written up to that value, and that henceforth the profit-sharing ratio between A and B shall be 8:7, B's salary arrangement being as before. Interest on capitals is to continue at 8 per cent. What is B's position (1) on the old basis, (2) on the new basis?

1. *Old Basis.* As the capitals of A and B will be augmented by the credit in respect of the written-up value of the shares, there will accordingly be an increase of INTEREST on capital to the extent of 8 per cent on the increased capital of £2,500, i.e. £200, allocated as follows:

A, $\frac{3}{5}$ = £120. B, $\frac{2}{5}$ = £80. Total, £200.

(the capital increase being credited to the partners in the old profit-sharing ratios, viz. 3:2). This will reduce the remaining profits by £200.

	A	B	Total
Interest on Capital	+£120	+ £80	+£200
Divisible profits will be reduced by £200 and borne in the ratio 45:55 (*see below*). .	− £90	−£110	−£200
Net result	+ £30	− £30	

Under the first method of sharing profits the division was:

	A	B	Total
Salary		25%	25%
Remainder	45%	30%	75%
Total	45%	55%	100%

If the old profit sharing ratio continues, B loses £30 of profits annually by the writing up of the asset.

Assume profits, after providing interest on original Capital, are £1,000.

1*a*. Division *before* the writing up of asset:

PROFIT AND LOSS APPROPRIATION ACCOUNT

	£		£
Salary: B	250	Balance . . . . . b/d	1,000
Balance—			
A: ⅗ £450			
B: ⅖ 300			
	750		
	£1,000		£1,000

1*b*. Division *after* writing up of asset:

PROFIT AND LOSS APPROPRIATION ACCOUNT

	£		£
Interest on Capital—		Balance . . . . . b/d	1,000
A £120			
B 80			
	200		
Balance . . . . . c/d	800		
	£1,000		£1,000
Salary: B. . . . 25%	200	Balance . . . . . b/d	800
Balance—			
A: ⅗ £360			
B: ⅖ 240			
	600		
	£800		£800

Alternatively (1*b*) may be shown as follows:

PROFIT AND LOSS APPROPRIATION ACCOUNT

	£		£
Interest on Capital—		Balance . . . . . b/d	1,000
A £120			
B 80			
	200		
Balance—			
A: 45% £360			
B: 55% 440			
	800		
	£1,000		£1,000

It will be observed that the partners receive the same by both alternative methods of (1b), i.e. A, £480: B, £520, as compared with the amounts receivable before the writing up of the asset, i.e. A, £450: B, £550.

Thus, if the profit sharing basis after providing for interest on capital remains unchanged, B loses £30 of profits annually.

2. *New Basis.* Under the proposed method of sharing profits the division will be:

	A	B	Total
Salary		25%	25%
Remainder	40%	35%	75%
Total	40%	60%	100%

The remaining profits will, as before, be reduced by £200, giving the result as follows:

	A	B	Total
Interest on Capital	+£120	+ £80	+£200
Divisible profits will be reduced by £200 and borne in the ratio of 40:60* . .	− £80	−£120	−£200
Net result	+£40	− £40	

* See Table *supra.*

B thus loses by the writing up of the asset, but gains 5 per cent increase in remaining profits: 60 per cent less 55 per cent (per old division).

Therefore, the proposed scheme will be advantageous to B if the profits after interest on *original* capital exceed $\frac{100}{5} \times £40 = £800$, and will be detrimental if the profits are less than £800; or where the remaining profits *after* interest on the *revised* capital exceed $\frac{75}{5} \times £40 = £600$, the scheme will be advantageous to B and *vice versa.* Alternatively, as mentioned, if the profits remain unchanged B loses £30, and as he gains 5 per cent of profits after charging interest the increased profits to cover his loss must be £600.

The position as regards capital losses and profits must also be considered.

(a) As regards losses, B will now bear any capital loss in the new ratio 8:7 instead of in the old ratio 3:2. He will thus have to bear a further $\frac{1}{15}$ of any capital loss, i.e. $\frac{7}{15} - \frac{6}{15} = \frac{1}{15}$.

(b) As regards profits, B will now receive any trading profit in the new ratio 40:60 instead of in the old ratio 45:55, and thus he gains a further 5 per cent on any trading profit under the new arrangement.

On the other hand, capital profits, not being *trading* profits, will not be taken into account for the purpose of calculating B's salary, hence they would be shared in the ratio $8:7$ instead of in the old ratio $3:2$, and thus B would gain a further $\frac{1}{15}$ under the proposed new arrangement.[1]

Note. The *original* capitals of the partners are of no consequence, as the partners will receive the same amounts of interest on capital under both the new and old arrangements as regards such original portion of their capitals.

The contrast between the old and the new divisions may now be shown.

Illustration 76

Assume that the profits *after* providing interest on original capital are £800.

1. *Old Basis.*

PROFIT AND LOSS APPROPRIATION ACCOUNT

	£		£
Salary: B 25%	200	Balance . . . . . . b/d	800
Balance—			
A: $\frac{3}{5}$ £360			
B: $\frac{2}{5}$ 240			
	600		
	£800		£800

2. *New Basis.*

PROFIT AND LOSS APPROPRIATION ACCOUNT

	£		£
Interest on Capital—		Balance . . . . b/d	800
A £120			
B 80			
	200		
Balance . . . . c/d	600		
	£800		£800
Salary: B 25%	150	Balance . . . . b/d	600
Balance—			
A: $\frac{8}{15}$ . . . £240			
B: $\frac{7}{15}$ . . . 210	450		
	£600		£600

Alternatively (2) may be shown as follows:

PROFIT AND LOSS APPROPRIATION ACCOUNT

	£		£
Interest on Capital—		Balance . . . . b/d	800
A £120			
B 80			
	200		
Balance—			
A: 40% £240			
B: 60% 360			
	600		
	£800		£800

[1] (The original capital profit of £2,500 was treated in this manner and divided in the ratio $3:2$, and not in the trading profits ratio $45:55$.)

It will be observed that the partners receive the same in both (1) and (2), i.e. A £360, B £440.

Where the profits after providing interest on original capital exceed £800 the proposition is advantageous to B, e.g. if the trading profits were £2,000 B would (in all) receive £1,100 under the old arrangement, and £1,160 under the proposed new arrangement.

The trading profits at the 'margin' are thus £800 plus interest on *original* capital. If their original capitals were, say, A £5,000, B £4,000, the 'margin' profits before charging any interest on capital would be £1,520, thus:

	£	£
Original Profits		1,520
Less Interest on *original* Capital: 8 per cent on £9,000 .		720
Balance after charging Interest on *original* Capital . .		800
Less Interest on *increased* Capitals—		
A	120	
B	80	
	——	
		200
Balance after charging Interest on *revised* Capital . .		600
Less B—Salary	150	
Balance of Profits—		
A: $\frac{8}{15}$	240	
B: $\frac{7}{15}$	210	
	——	
	450	
		——
		600

In practice, the interest on capital would be shown in the accounts debited in one total and would not be split up into two portions.

Alternatively, the required minimum figure to compensate B may be found by simple algebra.

Let $\quad P$ = profits *after* interest on original capital

then $\quad \frac{55}{100}P = 80 + \frac{60}{100}(P - 200)$

$\qquad 55P = 8,000 + 60P - 12,000$

$\qquad 5P = 4,000$

$\therefore \qquad P = £800$

B receives the same amount of the profits (*after* providing for interest on *original* capital) when they are £800 under both the old and the new basis.

SECTION G. ANNUITIES

The question of annuities is treated separately, although its place is essentially amongst the problems arising upon the retirement of a partner. This separation has been made because the old partners may bring in a new partner, and there may be subsequent changes in personnel and/or profit-sharing ratios; and the treatment under all these circumstances may be best shown under one heading rather than by separate working under each particular section.

Annuity to Retiring Partner and its Treatment in Partnership Changes. It may be convenient for all parties to agree to pay a retired partner or in the case of the death of partner to pay the widow and/or children by means of an annuity, that is, a yearly payment either for life or terminable at the end of a certain number of years; or an agreement may be reached to pay a certain amount of the indebtedness of the firm to the retired partner at once and to discharge the balance in the above-mentioned manner. The problem does not affect the principles of ascertaining the balance due, but its *discharge*.

There are many ways of dealing with the annuity and space will not permit of full treatment of each, so that the alternative methods will be shown below, and the more important aspects illustrated. The annuity payments may be treated thus:

1. Debit Capital or Current Accounts in Profit and Loss ratios.
     Credit Cash.[1]
2. Debit Drawings Accounts similarly.
     Credit Cash.[1]
3. Debit Profit and Loss Account.
     Credit Cash.[1]
4. Debit Reserve Account.
     Credit Cash.[1]

In the above instances the balance due to the retired partner after making the usual adjustments for revaluation of liabilities and assets, including goodwill, will on his retirement be credited to the Capital or Current Accounts of the continuing partners in Profit and Loss ratios and debited to the retired partner.

5. Debit Capital or Loan Account of retired partner.
     Credit Cash [just as if they had discharged the debt by ordinary payment] if and when the continuing partners actually PUR-CHASE the required Annuity from an Insurance Company.
6. Debit Capital or Loan Account of retired partner.
     Credit Annuity Suspense Account at the date of retirement and the yearly payments will be then treated thus—
     Debit Annuity Suspense Account,
     Credit Cash.[2]
7. Debit Capital or Loan Account of retired partner.
     Credit the continuing partners, the latter paying in their shares of the Annuity payments due, no further entries being made in the partnership books.

The death of the retired partner or expiry of time will not cause further entries in the partnership books except in (6), where the balance will be transferred to the Capital or Current Accounts of the continuing partners.

---

[1] Actually the credit will be made to the retired Partner's Annuity Account, and the latter account debited with Cash.

[2] Occasionally, the continuing partners agree to become personally liable for the payments of the annuity in the profit and loss ratios, thus involving no further entries in the partnership books. Interest may be brought into account by crediting the Annuity Suspense Account and debiting Profit and Loss Account for such Interest, the annuity liability being taken as analogous to a loan by the firm repayable in instalments.

It is quite possible that there may be a combination of the above methods where the continuing partners decide to buy part of the annuity and discharge the balance themselves, treating their own yearly payments either by methods (1) to (4) on the one hand, or by method (6) on the other.

Where an Annuity to the retired partner (or widow and child) is paid for his share of the unrecorded Goodwill, a method sometimes adopted is to debit the annual payments for such share to Goodwill Account. Strictly, when the total payments reach the share of goodwill the continuing payments are losses of capital by reason of the continuing partners having to pay more than the share of the goodwill attributable to the retired partner, and these further payments ought to be debited to the continuing partners' drawings accounts. They could be continued to be charged to the Goodwill Account until the value of the Goodwill at the time of retirement had been reached and subsequent payments charged to drawings accounts in profit ratios. On a dissolution the net effect would be the same whichever alternative in this paragraph were adopted because, if the payments are debited to drawings instead of Goodwill, there would be a corresponding larger sum debited to Goodwill and credited to the partners to bring the Goodwill up to its current value.

This method is very undesirable inasmuch as if the charges to Goodwill cease after reaching the outgoing partner's share, the amount in the books representing Goodwill is merely the premium on the outgoing partner's share and in any case the true value of the Goodwill as at the date of retirement is not shown till such time as the continued payments to the outgoing partner have reached that figure. Furthermore in case of change in profit ratios and/or personnel, the adjustments become complicated.

The above principles postulate a continuity of *the constitution of the partnership*. When a change in constitution occurs important considerations arise necessitating the application of the rules previously indicated, viz. that upon a change REVALUATIONS are required. Both positions will now be illustrated.

1. Continuity

Illustration 77

A, B, and C sharing profits in the ratio of 1:4:1 agree to dissolve as on 31st December 19.1. Their respective capitals after all adjustments have been considered, agreed and dealt with, are £6,000, £9,000, and £2,000. B agrees to have a life annuity of £450 in full discharge of his interest in the firm. A and C are to continue and divide profits and losses in the ratio of 3:1.

The first annuity is paid on 31st December 19.2. Write up Ledger Accounts. [The accounts appear on p. 22150.]

Methods 1–4.

The example on page 22150 illustrates points 1, 2, 3, and 4, and although there are various alternatives as regards the particular account to be debited, the effects are (*a*) to consider the liability to the old partner as a gain to the new partnership, and (*b*) to consider each annuity payment as a partnership loss for the year in question.

CAPITALS

	A £	B £	C £			A £	B £	C £
19.1				**19.1**				
Dec. 31 Transfer to A¹		6,750		Dec. 31 Balances	b/d	6,000	9,000	2,000
" C¹		2,250		Transfer from B		6,750		2,250
Balances c/d	12,750		4,250			£12,750	£9,000	£4,250
	£12,750	£9,000	£4,250	**19.2**				
				Jan. 1 Balances	b/d	12,750		4,250

¹ i.e. 3:1.

On Payment of Annuity (First Year)
B ANNUITY

	£			£
19.2		**19.2**		
Dec. 31 Cash	450	Dec. 31 Profit and Loss Account	450
	£450		£450

¹ Alternatively, the posting may be made to Current, Drawings (divided in Profit and Loss ratios, i.e. 3:1), or to Reserve Account.

Method 5.

Where the annuity is PURCHASED the cost of the annuity may be considered as the equivalent of payment to the partner, and as no payments of the annuity will be made by the continuing partners but by the Insurance Office the matter ends with the payment of the purchase price of the annuity to the Insurance Company, unless the latter hands the required sum to the partners for them to make the actual payment, and in such circumstances the Cash Book will have a contra entry, viz., the receipt of the annuity from the company and the payment to the annuitant.

Illustration 78

If A and C decided to purchase the annuity the entry would be (assuming that the cost exactly equals the amount due to B): Debit B capital, £9,000; Credit cash, £9,000.

If, say, half the annuity was purchased, the entries would be:

(1) Debit B, £4,500.   Credit Cash, £4,500.
    ”   ”   £4,500.   Credit Capitals A £3,375. C £1,125.
(2) Annuity payment borne by firm £225 (instead of £450).

Method 6—see p. 22152.

Death of Annuitant. No entries will be involved in respect of methods 1–5, but under method 6 the balance of the Annuity Suspense Account will be closed off to the benefit of partners in one of the ways previously outlined.

Illustration 79

Assuming that B died on 12th January 19.3, the Annuity Suspense Account having been revalued as follows: 31st December 19.1, £8,500; 31st December 19.2, £7,980, show Ledger Accounts.

CAPITAL ACCOUNTS (CREDIT SIDE)

		A	C
Balances	b/d	£6,000	£2,000

Illustration 80

Method 6.

The same facts as before.

CAPITALS

		A £	B £	C £				A £	B £	C £
19.1 Dec. 31	Balances . . . c/d	6,000		2,000	19.1 Dec. 31	Balances . . . b/d	6,000	9,000	2,000
	Transfer Annuity Suspense Account .		9,000						
		£6,000	£9,000	£2,000			£6,000	£9,000	£2,000
					19.2 Jan. 1	Balances . . . b/d	6,000		2,000

ANNUITY SUSPENSE

		£			£
19.2 Dec. 31	Annuity Account[1] . . .	450	19.2 Jan. 1	Transfer—B Capital Account	9,000
	Balance[2] . . . c/d	8,550			
		£9,000			£9,000
			19.3 Jan. 1	Balance . . . b/d	8,550

[1] Dealt with as in the preceding illustration.

[2] The actuarial liability may be recomputed each year, (although this is somewhat exceptional in practice), and the difference between the book liability and the actuarial liability written off to Profit and Loss, Capital, Current or Reserve Account, e.g. if the actuarial value, say, at the end of the first year were £8,500, instead of bringing down £8,550, the former amount would be brought down, the remaining £50 being transferred to the benefit of partners just indicated. (See p. 22153.)

ANNUITY SUSPENSE

			£				£
19.1 Dec. 31	Annuity Account		450	19.1 Jan. 1	Transfer—B Capital Account		9,000
	Profit and Loss (or Capital, etc.) Account		50				
	Balance	c/d	8,500				
			£9,000				£9,000
19.2 Dec. 31	Annuity Account		450	19.2 Jan. 1	Balance	b/d	8,500
	Profit and Loss (or Capital, etc.) Account		70				
	Balance	c/d	7,980				
			£8,500				£8,500
19.3 Jan. 12	Profit and Loss (or Capital, etc.) Account[1]		7,980	19.3 Jan. 1	Balance	b/d	7,980
			£7,980				£7,980

[1] If transferred to Capital Accounts the above Capitals would be credited thus:
A $\frac{3}{4} \times £7,980 = £5,985$ C $\frac{1}{4} \times £7,980 = £1,995$

2. Where a Change in the Constitution of the Partnership takes place

(a) **Introduction of New Partner.** 1. The old partners may continue to deal with the payments (unless the annuity has been purchased) as between themselves, in which case the entries will be precisely as before, except that the new partner cannot be expected to bear part of the cost of the annuity which is but an instalment payment of a liability existing before he was admitted into the business; hence Profit and Loss must **not** be debited, otherwise the new partner bears a share of the annuity cost, unless at the commencement of the new partnership the new partner was *credited* and the other partners *debited* with the proportion (rateable to profit shares) of the estimated amount of the annuity liability. Such an adjusting entry will, without injustice to the new partner, enable the partnership henceforth to treat the payments as a firm charge.

Illustration 81

In reference to the preceding illustration, on 1st January 19.3, D is admitted a partner with a fifth share, A and C continuing to share as between themselves 3:1. Show Accounts.

On 1st January 19.3, the estimated liability of the annuity being £8,500, it will be necessary either (i) to compel A and C to bear (through their Capital, Drawings, or Current Accounts) the annual payment; or (ii) to debit A and C and credit D (as below) if the charge is to be made a firm charge, that is, debited to the Profit and Loss Account or to Capital, etc., Accounts of ALL partners in the profit and loss ratio of the firm as newly constituted.

The debit and credit adjustments for this purpose are:

	£	£
Debit A, $\frac{3}{4} \times \frac{1}{5} \times £8,500$	1,275	
„ C, $\frac{1}{4} \times \frac{1}{5} \times £8,500$	425	
Credit D, $\frac{1}{5} \times £8,500$		1,700

The adjustments may be made on lines similar to those discussed in reference to goodwill (entries being opposite).

ANNUITY LIABILITY ADJUSTMENT SCHEDULE
(Liability £8,500)

	A	C	D
Old Share	$\frac{3}{4}$	$\frac{1}{4}$	
New Share	$\frac{3}{5}$	$\frac{1}{5}$	$\frac{1}{5}$
Differences	$-\frac{3}{20}$	$-\frac{1}{20}$	$+\frac{4}{20}$
Liability	£1,275 Dr.	£425 Dr.	£1,700 Cr.

2. If the Annuity Suspense Account is employed, the liability will be shown thus:

ANNUITY SUSPENSE

19.3 Dec. 31	Annuity Account			£ 450	19.3 Jan. 1	Balance			b/d	£ 8,500
	Profit and Loss Account			70						
	Balance		c/d	7,980						
				£8,500						£8,500
19.4 Jan. 12	Profit and Loss Account			7,980	19.4 Jan. 1	Balance			b/d	7,980
				£7,980						£7,980

As the liability appears in the books at 1st January 19.3 the whole of the profits belong to the three partners in their profit and loss ratios, thus:

	Total	A	B	C
	£p	£p	£p	£p
Profit in 2nd year	70·00			
„ „ 3rd „	7,480·00			
	8,050·00	$\frac{3}{5}$ 4,830·00	$\frac{1}{5}$ 1,610·00	$\frac{1}{5}$ 1,610·00
Profit in 1st year[1]	50·00	$\frac{3}{4}$ 37·50	$\frac{1}{4}$ 12·50	
	£8,100·00	£4,867·50	£1,622·50	£1,610·00

[1] See p. 22153

(b) **Retirement, and Retirement and Admission.** Similar principles apply as laid down in preceding paragraphs.

Illustration 82

In reference to the preceding illustrations: (i) If on 1st January 19.3, A retired, C continuing alone, it would be necessary to debit A with $\frac{3}{4} \times £8,500$ and C $\frac{1}{4} \times £8,500$, credit C with £8,500, or *debit* A and *credit* C with $\frac{3}{4} \times £8,500 = £6,375$, so that C in future bears the onus of discharging the liability.

(ii) If on 1st January 19.3, A retired and upon the same date D was admitted to a fifth share, it would be necessary to *debit* A with $\frac{3}{4} \times £8,500$ and C $\frac{1}{4} \times £8,500$; *credit* C with $\frac{4}{5} \times £8,500$ and D $\frac{1}{5} \times £8,500$, i.e.:

Debit A £6,375   Credit C £6,800
„   C £2,125   „   D £1,700

or, more shortly:

Debit A £6,375   Credit C £4,675
„   D £1,700

(c) **Change in Profit-sharing Ratios.** The same principle applies, viz. that the charge may be considered as referring to the old firm and the new firm, thus debiting the liability existing at the date of the change to the old partners and crediting it to the new. The fact that the *personnel* is unchanged is immaterial.

Illustration 83

If on 1st January 19.3, A and C partners agreed to share profits and losses equally the adjustments would be:

Debit A $\frac{3}{4} \times 8,500$ £6,375   Credit A $\frac{1}{2} \times £8,500$ £4,250
„   C $\frac{1}{4} \times 8,500$ £2,125   „   C $\frac{1}{2} \times £8,500$ £4,250

or, more shortly:

Debit A   £2,125   Credit C   £2,125

As already mentioned, the principle dealt with under the heading of undisclosed assets is equally applicable to the treatment of annuities where the **liability** is not shown in the books, the entries being converse.

Illustration 84

The foregoing adjustments would be dealt with, if the Revaluation method was adopted, thus:

REVALUATION ACCOUNT

			£				£
Annuity Revaluation	. .	c/d	8,500	A $\frac{3}{4}$			6,375
				C $\frac{1}{4}$			2,125
			£8,500				£8,500
A $\frac{1}{2}$			4,250	Annuity Revaluation	.	b/d	8,500
C $\frac{1}{2}$			4,250				
			£8,500				£8,500

Having adjusted the position at date of the change, admission, and/or retirement, the payments are debited to Profit and Loss Account, Drawings, Current or Reserve Account, and when the annuitant dies there will be no further entry.

The above adjustments predicate the use of methods 1–4.

Where the Annuity Suspense Account is employed, normally there will be no adjusting entries in respect of any change as the liability for the annuity is recorded. If the balance of the above account be *incorrect* it will be adjusted as a gain or loss as the case may be.

Purchase of an Annuity.[1] It has been assumed that in purchasing an annuity the cost will be precisely equal to the balance of the retired partner's capital; actually, this is by no means necessarily the position; the cost may be either more or less. Ordinarily, such difference in cost is dealt with by means of an adjustment for or against the remaining partners (unless the retired partner by agreement adjusts the difference by the payment or withdrawal of cash).

There is an alternative interpretation which is of importance in examination work, viz. (illustrating the position in reference to a retired partner receiving an annuity) where the capitalized value of the annuity is LESS than the balance due to him. In such a case the diminution in value may be reflective of his share of a total diminution of capital necessitating, not a debit to the retired partner and a credit to the remaining partners, but a debit to the retired partner, and ALSO a debit to the remaining partners, and a credit to the assets and/or liabilities. The converse position would arise where the capitalized value of the annuity was in EXCESS of the balance due to the retired partner, and might be interpreted as measuring the share of goodwill payable to him.

Illustration 85

A, B, and C were partners sharing profits and losses in the ratio of 3 : 4 : 1. On 1st January 19.3, B retired and agreed to be paid an annuity of £500 which is capitalized at £10,200. Capitals as per book values including profits less drawings to date were A £6,000, B £9,000, and C £2,000. B is to have as his share of goodwill three-fifths of the average profits of the last three years. The profits were £1,500, £3,500, and £2,500; no amount for goodwill exists in the books.

An Annuity Suspense Account is to be created.

You are required to show the Capital Accounts of the partners, together with the computation for the ascertainment of goodwill.

Note (1). The goodwill calculation is as follows:

$$\text{B's share} = \tfrac{3}{5} \times \left[\frac{1,500 + 3,500 + 2,500}{3} \right]$$

$$= \tfrac{3}{5} \times \frac{7,500}{3} = £1,500$$

Therefore the WHOLE goodwill $= \tfrac{8}{4} \times £1,500 = £3,000$.

[1] There is generally no point in purchasing an annuity, as if this is done there will be a depletion of so much of the firm's assets equal to or approximating to the liability to the outgoing (for the estate of the deceased) partner.

The calculation of goodwill of the firm must not be $\frac{2}{3} \times £1,500$ because once having found B's *share*, the basis of arriving at such share may be now ignored. As B is entitled to $\frac{4}{8}$ of the goodwill, such proportion being valued at £1,500, the whole goodwill must be double the latter sum, i.e. £3,000. Therefore, Goodwill Account is debited with £3,000 and the partners credited with their due proportions.◦

(2) As B's annuity is capitalized at £300 less than the balance of his account which difference is not to be given to him in cash, his loss is £300, which may be a 'personal' affair whereby B is debited with £300 and A credited with $\frac{3}{4} \times £300 = £225$, and B $\frac{1}{4} \times £300 = £75$: or it may be presumed in absence of guidance in the question to represent B's share of loss on revaluation; therefore the whole loss is £600 [i.e. $\frac{2}{3} \times £300$] which is debited to the partners and credited to a Depreciation Account or specifically to assets.

The balance of Capitals is now £9,200 made up of:

		£
Capitals at 1st Jan. 19.3, per books .		17,000
Add Goodwill		3,000
		20,000
Less Loss on Revaluation . .	£600	
,, Annuity Suspense . .	10,200	10,800
Revised Capitals		£9,200

If the continuing partners (i.e. A and C) desire to delete from the books the items of Goodwill and Annuity Suspense, the consequent entries will be:

Debit Annuity Suspense	£10,200	Credit Goodwill	£3,000
		,, A $\frac{3}{4} \times £7,200$	£5,400
		,, C $\frac{1}{4} \times £7,200$	£1,800

CAPITALS

			A	B	C				A	B	C
19.3 Jan. 1	Annuity Suspense Account Loss on Revaluation of Assets (2) Balances	c/d	£ 225 6,900	£ 10,200 300	£ 75 2,300	19.3 Jan. 1	Balances Goodwill (1)	b/d	£ 6,000 1,125	£ 9,000 1,500	£ 2,000 375
			£7,125	£10,500	£2,375				£7,125	£10,500	£2,375
						19.3 Jan. 2	Balances	b/d	6,900		2,300

If on 2nd January 19.3, a new partner X was introduced, to have a quarter share (A and C ratios to remain unchanged as between themselves), the necessary entries will be:

1. If the undisclosed items are to be permanently shown in the books (to cancel the previous elimination):

Debit Goodwill	£3,000	Credit Annuity Suspense £10,200
,, A $\frac{3}{4} \times £7,200$	£5,400	
,, C $\frac{1}{4} \times £7,200$	£1,800	

2. If the undisclosed items are not to be permanently shown in the books:

(a) As (1) above

(b) Debit Annuity Suspense £10,200	Credit Goodwill	£3,000
	„ A $\frac{9}{16} \times$ £7,200	£4,050
	„ C $\frac{3}{16} \times$ £1,200	£1,350
	„ X $\frac{4}{16} \times$ £7,200	£1,800

SECTION H. DISSOLUTION

When a partnership ceases to exist it is said to be dissolved. It may be so occasioned by the retirement or death of a partner notwithstanding a new agreement for the remaining partners to continue the business, but the term is usually employed to signify (1) that the partnership business has come to an end, resulting in the assets being sold separately, or taken over as a whole: or (2) that the partners are henceforth to carry on business separately, one or more taking over certain assets and liabilities. The position arising when one partner takes over the business may be dealt with on the lines applicable to the retirement of one partner, or as a sale, as laid down in this chapter. On dissolution the following book-keeping procedure is usually followed:

A. 1. Assets (other than cash and bank) are transferred to a Realization Account, by debiting the latter account and crediting the assets.[1]

2. Expenses of realization are debited to Realization Account and credited to cash or bank; and conversely for gains.

3. Credit balances not being creditors or debts due to partners, e.g. Bad Debts Provision. Debit the particular credit balance and credit Realization Account.

4. On sale of the business or individual assets. Debit cash (or particular asset received, e.g. shares) or purchaser and credit Realization Account. If the purchaser is a partner his account will be debited.

5. The balance of Realization Account is closed in the same manner as the ordinary Profit and Loss Account, that is:

(a) If a profit, debit Realization Account and credit Partners' Capital Accounts.

(b) If a loss, debit Partners' Capital Accounts and credit Realization Account.

6. If the creditors of the firm are paid off by the firm, debit creditors, credit cash or bank; but if taken over they will be credited to the Realization Account.

7. The partners are next paid in respect of advances, the entry being: debit Partner's Advance Account, credit cash, unless his Capital and/or Current Accounts are in debit when a transfer will be made to clear it (them) if the credit or advance account is sufficient. The remaining balance on advance account (if any) will then be paid.

8. The various Partners' Accounts, e.g. Current and Capital Accounts,

---

[1] Debtors will be debited 'gross' (i.e. per Sales Ledger) and not 'net'. Where a Bad Debt Provision exists, it is transferred to the credit of Realization Account.

are merged and the balance of the combined or merged account inclusive of the transfer made under heading (5) will equal the remaining cash (or shares).

9. The cash (or shares) are paid in discharge of the final balances due to partners by debiting Partners' Accounts and crediting cash (or shares).

10. If one of the partners as a result of realization is in debit, he will either bring in cash or his account will, to the extent that he cannot bring in cash, be written off against the other solvent partners in their *capital* ratios. (*Garner* v. *Murray*, see p. 22171.)

B. Alternatively to (1). Each asset may be taken as a separate Sub-realization Account, that is, the amount realized is credited to such asset, the profit or loss being transferred, as the case may be, to the credit or debit of Realization Account; e.g. if the asset were fixtures in the books at £120, and realized £100, the latter would be debited to cash and credited to the Fixtures Account, and the remaining balance of £20 transferred by debiting Realization Account and crediting Fixtures Account.

Illustration 86

The following is the Balance Sheet of A and B who share profits and losses in the ratio 3:2.

BALANCE SHEET

		£			£
Creditors		400	Cash		100
Loan—A		50	Debtors		1,800
Capitals—			Stock		150
A	. £900				
B	. 700				
		1,600			
		£2,050			£2,050

They decide to go out of business; the debtors realize £1,430 and stock £180. Expenses of realization £20. Show closing accounts.

Method A.

REALIZATION ACCOUNT

		£			£
Debtors		1,800	Cash—		
Stock		150	Debtors		1,430
Expenses of Realization		20	Stock		180
			Balance: Loss—		
			A: $\frac{3}{5}$	. £216	
			B: $\frac{2}{5}$	. 144	
					360
		£1,970			£1,970

CASH

		£			£
Balance	b/d	100	Expenses of Realization		20
Debtors		1,430	Creditors		400
Stock		180	A Loan		50
			Balance —		
			A £684		
			B 556		
					1,240
		£1,710			£1,710

DEBTORS

		£			£
Balances	b/d	1,800	Realization Account		1,800

STOCK

		£			£
Balance	b/d	150	Realization Account		150

CAPITALS

		A	B			A	B
		£	£			£	£
Realization Account—				Balances	b/d	900	700
Loss		216	144				
Cash		684	556				
		£900	£700			£900	£700

CREDITORS

		£			£
Cash		400	Balances	b/d	400

A LOAN

		£			£
Cash		50	Balance	b/d	50

REALIZATION ACCOUNT

	£		£
Debtors: Loss on Realization	370	Stock: Profit on Realization	30
Expenses of Realization	20	Balance: Loss—	
		A $\frac{3}{5}$ . . . £216	
		B $\frac{2}{5}$ . . . 144	
			360
	£390		£390

CASH

		£			£
Balance	b/d	100	Expenses of Realization		20
Debtors		1,430	Creditors		400
Stock		180	A Loan Account		50
			Balance—		
			A . . . £684		
			B . . . 556		
					1,240
		£1,710			£1,710

DEBTORS

		£		£
Balances	b/d	1,800	Cash	1,430
			Balance to Realization Account	370
		£1,800		£1,800

STOCK

		£		£
Balance	b/d	150	Cash	180
Realization Account		30		
		£180		£180

CAPITALS

		A	B			A	B
		£	£			£	£
Realization Account—				Balances	b/d	900	700
Loss		216	144				
Cash		684	556				
		£900	£700			£900	£700

CREDITORS

		£			£
Cash		400	Balances	b/d	400

A LOAN

		£			£
Cash		50	Balance	b/d	50

Illustration 87

The assets of A, B and C sharing profits and losses 3:1:1, are £1,400, liabilities £500, and capitals A £500, B £300 and C £100.

The assets realize £400. Ignoring expenses, show accounts assuming all partners are insolvent, owning no private assets.

REALIZATION ACCOUNT

	£		£
Sundry Assets	1,400	Cash	400
		Loss transferred to Capital Adjustment Account	1,000
	£1,400		£1,400

CREDITORS

	£			£
Cash	400	Balances	b/d	500
Balance transferred to Capital Adjustment Account	100			
	£500			£500

CASH

	£		£
Realization Account	400	Creditors, Payment of £0·80	400
	£400		£400

CAPITAL ADJUSTMENT ACCOUNT

	£			£
Loss on Realization	1,000	Creditors		100
		Loss transferred—		
		A. £540		
		B. 180		
		C. 180		900
	£1,000			£1,000

CAPITALS

	A	B	C			A	B	C
	£	£	£			£	£	£
Loss	540	180	180	Balances	b/d	500	300	100
Balance transferred from A and C		120		Balance transferred to B		40		80
	£540	£300	£180			£540	£300	£180

Note. As the Capital Accounts of A and C are both overdrawn the whole of the loss must be borne by B.

It should be clearly appreciated that the mere fact that a partner is insolvent does not necessarily justify an inference that he can contribute nothing at all.

As the creditors are still entitled to a further £0·20 in the £ those partners (if any) who are able to contribute any sum will be required to do so in profit and loss ratio, and even then whatever amounts still remain unpaid can be claimed from *any* individual partner.

Illustration 88

Q, S, and O, partners, share profits and losses as to 2:2:1. Their Balance Sheet at 31st December 19.., is as follows:

Q, S, AND O BALANCE SHEETS AS AT 31ST DECEMBER 19..

	£	£		£	£
Creditors . . .		2,000	Cash		2,000
Capitals—			Sundry Debtors	1,300	
Q . . .	5,000		*Less* Bad Debts		
S . . .	2,000		Provision .	300	
O . . .	1,000				1,000
		8,000	Stock . .		2,000
			Fixtures and other		
			Assets .		5,000
		£10,000			£10,000

The following are the amounts realized:

	£
Fixtures and other Assets	4,500
Stock	2,260
Debtors	900

	£
Creditors paid in complete discharge . .	1,900
Expenses of Realization	60

Show Accounts (using Method A).

CASH

		£				£
Balance . . . b/d		2,000	Realization Account—			
Realization Account—			Expenses of Realization[1]			60
Assets realized:			Creditors . . .			1,900
Stock . . .		2,260	Capital Accounts—			
Debtors . .		900	Q . .	£4,880		
Fixtures and other			S . .	1,880		
Assets . .		4,500	O . .	940		
						7,700
		£9,660				£9,660

[1] The entries should be made in this order; repayments of advances by partners (if any) would be shown after creditors and before repayments of Capital Accounts.

DEBTORS

Balances	b/d	£ 1,300	Realization Account		£ 1,300

STOCK

Balance	b/d	£ 2,000	Realization Account		£ 2,000

FIXTURES (AND OTHER ASSETS)

Balances	b/d	£ 5,000	Realization Account		£ 5,000

BAD DEBTS PROVISION

Realization Account		£ 300	Balance	b/d	£ 300

CREDITORS

Cash		£ 1,900	Balances	b/d	£ 2,000
Realization Account		100			
		£2,000			£2,000

CAPITALS

	Q	S	O			Q	S	O
	£	£	£		b/d	£	£	£
Loss on Realization	120	120	60	Balances		5,000	2,000	1,000
Cash—Balance of Capitals	4,880	1,880	940					
	£5,000	£2,000	£1,000			£5,000	£2,000	£1,000

REALIZATION ACCOUNT

	£				£
Debtors	1,300	Bad Debts Provision . .			300
Stock	2,000	Cash: Assets realized—			
Fixtures (and other Assets) .	5,000	Stock . .	£2,260		
Expenses of Realization .	60	Debtors . .	900		
		Fixtures (and other			
		Assets .	4,500		
					7,660
		Discounts Received . .			100
		Loss on Realization—			
		O:: $\frac{2}{5}$ . . .	£120		
		S: $\frac{2}{5}$ . . .	120		
		O: $\frac{1}{5}$ . . .	60		
					300
	£8,360				£8,360

Note. The actual transfers would (except for the purely cash transactions) be journalized, e.g. the transfers to Realization Account would be:

JOURNAL

	£	£
Realization Account	8,300	
Debtors		1,300
Stock		2,000
Fixtures (and other Assets) . . .		5,000
Being Assets transferred to Realization Account.		
	£8,300	£8,300

Partners Taking Over Assets and Liabilities on Dissolution.

Where a partner takes over assets and/or liabilities upon dissolution the entries are:

1. On taking over Assets:
   Debit Partner's Capital Account   Credit Realization (or Dissolution) Account

2. On taking over liabilities:
   Debit Realization (or Dissolution)   Credit Partner's Capital Account
   Account

In the ordinary course of events no cash will be received or paid in respect of the foregoing transactions as they will merely decrease or increase the final amount due to the partner in question.

The term 'dissolution' is usually employed in reference to profits and losses upon the dissolution of a partnership where no actual realizations take place.

It will readily be observed that the partnership as a whole will reap a profit (or suffer a loss) by reason of the difference in the book value and the amount debited to the purchasing partner in respect of an asset the latter acquires, such partner being credited (or debited) with his due proportion of such profit (or loss).

Assets sold will be dealt with in the normal way so that the final balance in the bank, that is the balance (unless taken over by a partner) at the date of the dissolution, together with cash realizations less expenses, will be equal to the final balance of the partners' Capital Accounts.

Illustration 89

A, B, and C sharing profits 3:1:1 agree upon dissolution. They each decide to take over certain assets and liabilities and continue business separately.

BALANCE SHEET AS AT 31ST DECEMBER 19.. (DATE OF DISSOLUTION)

	£	£		£	£
Creditors		600	Cash		320
Loan		150	Sundry Assets		1,700
Capitals—			Debtors	2,420	
A	2,750		Less Bad Debts Provision	120	
B	1,000				2,300
C	700	4,450	Stock		780
			Fixtures		100
		£5,200			£5,200

It is agreed as follows:

1. Goodwill is to be ignored.

2. A is to take over all the fixtures at £80; debtors amounting to £2,000 at £1,720. The creditors of £600 to be assumed by A at that figure.

3. B is to take over all the stock at £700 and certain of the sundry assets at £720 (being book values, less 10 per cent).

4. C is to take over the remaining sundry assets at 90 per cent of book values less £10 allowances and assume responsibility for the discharge of the loan, together with accruing interest of £3 which has not been recorded in the books of the firm.

5. The expenses of dissolution were £27. The remaining debtors were sold to a debt collecting agency for 50 per cent of book values.

Prepare accounts.

DISSOLUTION ACCOUNT

	£	£			£	£
Assets (except Cash)		5,000	Bad Debt Provision			120
Expenses of Dissolution		27	Assets taken over—			
Loan Interest		3	A: Fixtures £80			
			Debtors 1,720		1,800	
			B: Stock £700			
			Sundry Assets 720		1,420	
			C: Sundry Assets		800	4,020
			Cash: Sale of Debtors			210
			Loss on Dissolution:			
			A: $\frac{3}{5}$		408	
			B: $\frac{1}{5}$		136	
			C: $\frac{1}{5}$		136	680
		£5,030				£5,030

CAPITALS

		A	B	C			A	B	C
		£	£	£			£	£	£
Assets taken over (per Dissolution Account)		1,800	1,420	800	Balances	b/d	2,750	1,000	700
					Liabilities taken over		600		
					Loan taken over				153
Loss on Dissolution		408	136	136	Balances	c/d		556	83
Balance	c/d	1,142							
		£3,350	£1,556	£936			£3,350	£1,556	£936
Balances	b/d		556	83	Balance	b/d	1,142		
Cash		1,142			Cash			556	83

CASH

		£			£
Balance	b/d	320	Expenses of Dissolution		27
Sale of Debtors		210	Balance	c/d	503
		£530			£530
Balance	b/d	503	A		1,142
B		556			
C		83			
		£1,142			£1,142

LOAN

	£			£
Transfer to C	153	Balance	b/d	150
		Dissolution Account: Loan Interest		3
	£153			£153

CREDITORS

	£			£
Transfer to A	600	Balances	b/d	600

Notes. It is assumed that the usual novation contracts have been made.

The loan interest is not, strictly, a loss on dissolution and should be adjusted direct to the Capital Accounts, but so long as the matter is noted at the foot of the answer the treatment above is in order, particularly so as the division of £3 into fifths (and similarly with the item of £27) would involve introducing decimals of a £.

The items in italics comprise the final settlement. The Creditors' Account is shown, but this account need not be opened, the £600 being placed DIRECT to the credit of A.

The loss on dissolution may be proved as follows:

	£	£
Loss on Fixtures	20	
" " Stock	80	
" " Sundry Assets . . .	180	
" " Debtors[1]	370	
	——	650
Expenses of Dissolution . . .	27	
Loan Interest	3	
	——	30
		£680

[1] As the book value of debtors is £2,420 there is a loss of £280 upon the transfer to A as he takes over £2,000 debtors for £1,720. The remaining debtors are, therefore, £420 [£2,420 – £2,000] which are sold for £210, being 50 per cent of their book values; hence, the loss in this connection is £490 made up of £280 and £210. Against this sum there exists a provision of £120, leaving a final loss of £370.

Examination Problem

Old, Middle, and Young, are in partnership as accountants carrying on practices at Brighton and Eastbourne, and sharing profits in the proportion of 7, 6, and 5 respectively. Interest at the rate of 5 per cent per annum is allowed on Capital Accounts. They decide to dissolve.

The terms of dissolution were as follows:

(a) Old to retire from business, his share of goodwill being valued at £33,000 to be paid by Middle and Young in the ratio in which they had been sharing profits.

(b) Middle to carry on business at Brighton, taking over at book values furniture and debtors in Brighton, and all liabilities; he also has to pay £6,000 for the lease of the Brighton office which he kept on.

(c) Young to take over the furniture and debtors at Eastbourne.

(d) Middle and Young each to be credited with 2 per cent of the amount of the book debts taken over by them respectively by way of an allowance to cover the cost of collection.

(e) Each partner to take over a third of the cash balance and to pay his own costs in connection with the dissolution.

The following Trial Balance was extracted from the firm's books as on 30th June 19.., on which date the partnership was dissolved by agreement:

TRIAL BALANCE

	£	£
Capitals as at 1st July 19..—		
Old		40,000
Middle		40,000
Young		30,000
Drawings—		
Old	15,730	
Middle	12,920	
Young	8,160	
Goodwill	24,000	
Sundry Creditors		780
Cash	3,180	
Profit and Loss Account for the year to 30th June,		
19.. (before charging interest)		57,160
Sundry Debtors—		
Brighton	67,500	
Eastbourne	31,500	
Furniture—		
Brighton	3,200	
Eastbourne	1,750	
	£167,940	£167,940

You are required to close the books of the firm, assuming that Middle and Young each settled his liability by paying a cheque to Old on 30th September. Interest after 30th June to be ignored.

(Adapted from *Institute of Chartered Accountants Final*.)

Solution

DISSOLUTION ACCOUNT

19..		£	19..			£
June 30	Goodwill* . . .	24,000	June 30	Middle—		
	Debtors . . .	99,000		Lease . . .		6,000
	Furniture . . .	4,950		Debtors . . .		67,500
	Allowance on			Furniture . . .		3,200
	Debtors—			Young—		
	Middle . .	1,350		Debtors . . .		31,500
	Young . .	630		Furniture . .		1,750
				Loss transferred—		
				Old: $\frac{7}{18}$.	£7,770	
				Middle: $\frac{6}{18}$.	6,660	
				Young: $\frac{5}{18}$.	5,550	
						19,980
		£129,930				£129,930

* A further alternative is to increase the goodwill from £24,000 to £84,850 (i.e. not to write the £24,000 off to Dissolution Account) and to credit the partners with their due proportion of the resultant increase, and to debit Middle and Young with the whole of the goodwill as revalued. See p. 22170.)

CAPITALS

Dr.

Date	Particulars	Old £	Middle £	Young £
19.. June 30	Drawings	15,730	12,920	8,160
	Debtors		67,500	31,500
	Furniture		3,200	1,750
	Lease		6,000	
	Goodwill—Old[1]		18,000	15,000
	Dissolution Account	7,770	6,660	5,550
	Cash	1,060	1,060	1,060
Sept. 30	Cash from Middle and Young	(a)70,530		
		£95,090	£115,340	£63,020

Cr.

Date	Particulars	Old £	Middle £	Young £
19.. July 1	Balances b/d	40,000	40,000	30,000
19.. June 30	Interest on Capital	2,000	2,000	1,500
	Profit	20,090	17,220	14,350
	Allowance on Debtors		1,350	630
	Goodwill—Middle and Young	33,000		
	Liabilities taken over[1]		780	
Sept. 30	Cash to Old		(a)53,990	(a)16,540
		£95,090	£115,340	£63,020

[1] See statement at top of p. 22171. Alternatively, the whole Goodwill could be raised to the full after writing out the old book value, viz. $\frac{18}{7} \times £33{,}000 = £84{,}850$ dealt with as follows:

GOODWILL STATEMENT

	Old		Middle		Young		Total	
		£		£		£	£	
Credited	7/18	33,000	6/18	28,280	5/18	23,570	84,850	(Dr. Goodwill)
Upon Reversal, debited			6/11	46,280	5/11	38,570	84,850	(Cr. Goodwill)
	+	£33,000	−	£18,000	−	£15,000	−	

(a) These items are the only cash items, seeing that the cash balance at the date of dissolution is taken out by the partners in equal proportions.

GOODWILL STATEMENT

	Old	Middle	Young	Total
	£	£	£	£
Increase in value of Goodwill (7:6:5) . .	23,660	20,280	16,910	60,850
Goodwill written back (6:5) . .		46,280	38,570	84,850
Net Adjustment[1]	+ 23,660	− 26,000	− 21,660	− 24,000
Goodwill £24,000 already in books (7:6:5) .	+ 9,340	+ 8,000	+ 6,660	+ 24,000
Net + or − per p. 22170 . . .	+ £33,000	− £18,000	− £15,000	—

[1] The above transfers eliminate the asset Goodwill, £24,000.

Garner v. Murray. The principle laid down in *Garner* v. *Murray* is that where, upon dissolution, a partner's Capital Account is in debit and the partner is unable to contribute the full deficiency, the loss must be divided amongst the solvent partners in the ratio of their *last agreed* capitals. The correctness of this decision has been the subject of much criticism, and it is now customary expressly to exclude the rule in partnership agreements.

The Procedure. When *Garner* v. *Murray* has to be applied the Realization Account is dealt with in the usual way and the profit or loss on realization divided amongst the partners in their ordinary profit or loss sharing ratio. If, after this division, there is a debit balance on one of the partner's capital accounts, the partner must pay in as much of this as he is able, and the balance, if any, which is a loss, must, unless otherwise agreed, be divided amongst the other remaining partners in the ratio of their *last agreed* capitals. It will be observed that the operation of *Garner* v. *Murray* will not be dealt till *after* the profit or loss on realization has been recorded in the normal manner. Theoretically, the solvent partners should pay cash into the firm to the extent of any loss on Realization Account, but as this would merely increase their capitals and the amount be automatically repaid in the final settlement, the cash contribution in respect of the loss is not usually made, but merely brought into account.

As the liability of the solvent partners is based upon their last *agreed* capitals, it is important to remember that such agreed capitals may have arisen through a 'course of dealing', and the basis of allocation must be on the capital *before* any loss on realization, whether or not the solvent partners have contributed cash in respect of their share of the loss on realization.

Illustration 90

A, B, and C are in partnership, sharing profits and losses equally. Their capital accounts are A, *Cr.* £6,000; B, *Cr.* £4,000; and C, *Dr.* £300.

They dissolve partnership and a loss of £900 is incurred on realization, and C is insolvent, being unable to contribute anything towards his deficiency.

Show the partners' Capital Accounts.

CAPITALS

		A	B	C			A	B	C
		£	£	£			£	£	£
Balance	b/d			300	Balances	b/d	6,000	4,000	
Loss on Realization		300	300	300	Transfer—				
Transfer C¹		360	240		A $\frac{6}{10}\times$ £600¹				360
Balances	c/d	5,340	3,460		B $\frac{4}{10}\times$ £600¹				240
		£6,000	£4,000	£600			£6,000	£4,000	£600
					Balances	b/d	5,340	3,460	

¹ Per *Garner* v. *Murray*.

The problem is not involved; it merely requires that C's deficiency is to be debited to A and B in the ratio of 3 : 2 instead of equally, and obviously the question of the DIVISION of the loss between A and B does not affect C's account at all; whether the loss is charged to A and B equally, or in any other ratio has no bearing on the fact that C's account must be credited with £600. The loss to A and B, but for *Garner* v. *Murray*, would have been £300 each, so that as a result of the decision B gains £60 at A's expense.

Illustration 91

Q, S, and O are in partnership sharing profits and losses 4 : 3 : 1. They decide to dissolve partnership. During the dissolution O is adjudicated bankrupt and can pay only £0·50 in the £. The original capitals were Q, £4,000; S, £3,000; and O, £1,000; but by agreement amongst the partners the drawings had been merged in the capital accounts and the balances at the date of dissolution were as shown in the following Balance Sheet.

Q, S, AND O, BALANCE SHEET AS AT . . .

	£	£		£
Capitals—			Land and Buildings	4,000
Q	£6,000		Plant and Machinery	2,500
S	1,500		Stock	800
		7,500	Debtors	1,400
Sundry Creditors		2,500	Cash	300
			O, Capital overdrawn	1,000
		£10,000		£10,000

The assets are realized as follows:

	£
Land and Buildings	3,000
Plant and Machinery	2,000
Stock	900
Sundry Debtors	1,350

Five per cent discount is allowed by creditors and a contingent liability of £165 matures. The expenses of realization are £110.

Show accounts, assuming that the loss or profit on realization of each asset is separately transferred from the Asset Accounts.

REALIZATION ACCOUNT

	£		£
Losses—		Profits—	
Land and Buildings .	1,000	Stock . .	100
Plant and Machinery .	500	Discount Received . .	125
Debtors . .	50	Loss on Realization:	
Contingent Liability matured	165	Q: $\frac{1}{2}$ . . . £800	
Expenses . . .	110	S: $\frac{3}{8}$ . . . 600	
		O: $\frac{1}{8}$ . . . 200	
			1,600
	£1,825		£1,825

CASH

		£		£
Balance . . .	b/d	300	Expenses of Realization . .	110
Land and Buildings . .	(a)	3,000	Creditors . . .	2,375
Plant and Machinery . .	(a)	2,000	Contingent Liability paid .	165
Stock . . .	(a)	900	Capitals—	
Debtors . . .	(a)	1,350	Q	4,720
Dividend: O . . .		600	S	780
		£8,150		£8,150

(*a*) In examination work the four items may be entered in one figure thus: Assets realized per question, £7,250.

CAPITALS

		Q	S	O			Q	S	O
		£	£	£			£	£	£
Balance .	b/d			1,000	Balances	b/d	6,000	1,500	
Loss on Re-					Dividend of				
alization		800	600	200	£0·50 in £.				600
Transfer:					Transfer to				
Loss on O					Q:				
deficiency					[$\frac{6\frac{2}{3}}{73} \times$ £600]				480
per *Garner*					S:				
v. *Murray*		480	120		[$\frac{1\frac{2}{3}}{73} \times$ £600]				120
Cash .		4,720	780						
		£6,000	£1,500	£1,200			£6,000	£1,500	£1,200

The Ledger Accounts need not be given unless specifically required, but it is advisable to submit a 'sample' thus:

LAND AND BUILDINGS

	£		£
Balance	4,000	Cash	3,000
		Realization Account:	
		Loss . . .	1,000
	£4,000		£4,000

That the decision in *Garner* v. *Murray* may harshly affect a partner may be demonstrated by the following example.

Illustration 92

A, B, and C are partners; the partnership is dissolved; C is insolvent and unable to contribute anything in payment of his debt to the firm; B has ample private means. At the date of dissolution the following is the position:

A, B, AND C BALANCE SHEET AS AT ...

	£		£
Capital—A	2,000	Cash	600
		Capitals—	
		B	200
		C	1,200
	£2,000		£2,000

Show the partners' Capital Accounts.

Applying the rule in *Garner* v. *Murray*, the deficiency of C is to be borne by A and B in the ratio of their last agreed capitals, but A being the only person with capital in the firm will have to bear the WHOLE of such deficiency: so that notwithstanding B's comparative affluence—and quite conceivably he is much more wealthy than A—the latter must bear the entire burden merely because it so happens that B's share at the date of dissolution is overdrawn. The decision does not mean in this problem that B is able to avoid bringing cash into the firm in respect of his own debt.

CAPITALS

		A	B	C			A	B	C
		£	£	£			£	£	£
Balances	b/d		200	1,200	Balance	b/d	2,000		
Transfer from					Transfer to A				1,200
C		1,200			Cash . .			200	
Cash . .		800							
		£2,000	£200	£1,200			£2,000	£200	£1,200

CASH

		£		£
Balance	b/d	600	A Capital . . .	800
B Capital . . .		200		
		£800		£800

Piecemeal Payments

Not infrequently does it happen in dissolution that considerable difficulty is encountered in the realization of assets with the natural result that the final distribution to the partners is delayed; but circumstances may render it imperative that the partners be paid sums on account as and when received, particularly if the dissolution process is protracted. It is necessary to avoid, so far as possible, the unpleasant consequences of a partner's account at the later stages of realization being overdrawn, as it might be, if he had a small capital with a comparatively high ratio of profit sharing and loss bearing, and were paid out on a capital basis followed by subsequent heavy losses in realization.

The principle which underlies the payments on account, always subject to any other AGREEMENT between the partners themselves, is to assume that at each stage the remaining Unrealized assets are WORTHLESS and the Capital Accounts adjusted accordingly, applying where compatible with the circumstances the *Garner* v. *Murray* rule; the balance of the adjusted Capital Accounts will then be the same as the amount of cash, such balance being withdrawn by partners, reducing the Capital accordingly: this process is repeated at each stage and for the purpose of distribution the remaining assets are considered worthless. It is obvious that before this state of affairs is reached current realization expenses, creditors, and advances by partners, must FIRST be paid.

Illustration 93

The following is the Balance Sheet of A, B, and C, sharing profits and losses 1:2:1.

BALANCE SHEET AS AT........

		£			£
Creditors		1,000	Sundry Assets	.	6,000
Capitals—					
A	£2,500				
B	1,800				
C	700				
		5,000			
		£6,000			£6,000

The assets are realized piecemeal and distributions are made on account as and when realized.

The realizations are, ignoring expenses:

Reali-zation No.	Book Value	Cash Realized	Available for	
			Creditors	Partners
	£	£	£	£
(1)	500	500[1]	500	
(2)	2,200	2,000[1] (∴ Loss £200)	500	1,500
(3)	600	600		600
(4)	1,600	1,600		1,600
(5)	1,100	1,300 (∴ Gain £200)		1,300
	£6,000	£6,000	£1,000	£5,000

[1] Creditors will take the first £500 and £500 of the second realization leaving £1,500 for the partners.

Show distributions.

It will be necessary to construct a statement of Capital Accounts (preferably in tabular form), so that the resultant balances after each set of realizations are disclosed. This statement will show the basis of repayment of capital to each partner at each stage.

STATEMENT OF CAPITAL ACCOUNTS

	Total	A	B	C
	£	£	£	£
Balances	5,000	2,500	1,800	700
Less Loss on Realization	200	50	100	50
	4,800	2,450	1,700	650
Less possible Loss in respect of remaining Assets of £3,300 being worthless	3,300	825	1,650	825
	1,500	+1,625	+50	−175
Deficiency of C's Capital written off in ratio of 25:18 per *Garner* v. *Murray*		−102	−73	+175
	1,500	+1,523	−23	
Deficiency of B's Capital written off against A		−23	+23	
Repay	£1,500	£1,500		

SATEMENT OF CAPITAL ACCOUNTS (contd.)

	Total	A	B	C
Balances of Capital Accounts after Loss on Realization . .	4,800	2,450	1,700	650
Less Cash (as above) . .	1,500	1,500		
	3,300	950	1,700	650
As £600 is realized without loss, there is now a possibility of the remaining Assets of £2,700 being worth nil	2,700	675	1,350	675
	600	+275	+350	−25
Deficiency of C's Capital written off in ratio of 25:18 per Garner v. Murray		−15	−10	+25
Repay .	£600	£260	£340	
Balances of Capital Accounts after payment of £1,500 . . .	3,300	950	1,700	650
Less Cash (as above) . . .	600	260	340	
	2,700	690	1,360	650
As £1,600 is realized without loss there is now a possibility of the remaining Assets of £1,100 being worth nil	1,100	275	550	275
Repay .	£1,600	£415	£810	£375
Balances of Capital Accounts after payment of £600 . . .	2,700	690	1,360	650
Less Cash (as above) . . .	1,600	415	810	375
Balances of Capital Accounts after payment of £1,600 . . .	1,100	275	550	275
Add Profit on Realization .	200	50	100	50
Repay .	£1,300	£325	£650	£325
Balances of Capital Account after payment of £1,300 . . .	nil	nil	nil	nil

Summary of distributions:

	Total	A	B	C
	£	£	£	£
First	1,500	1,500		
Second	600	260	340	
Third	1,600	415	810	375
Fourth	1,300	325	650	325
	£5,000	£2,500	£1,800	£700

This gives precisely the same result as if the assets had been realized in one sum.

Thus, the total cash paid equals their capitals because the only loss on realization (No. 2) of £200 is counterbalanced by the profit on realization (No. 5) of £200.

Alternative Method of Piecemeal Payments. Alternatively, a less severe method may be adopted by applying the same principles without the adoption of the assumption that unrealized assets are worthless. The method is to pay off first partners who have the highest RELATIVE capitals; that is, whose capitals are greatest in proportion to their profit and loss sharing ratios.

The object is to find the largest possible capitals the partners could have had if their capitals had been proportionate to profit sharing, working from the worst placed partner's *actual* capital.

The procedure is to divide each partner's capital by his profit ratio figure; the lowest capital after this division constitutes the basic capital from which the remaining hypothetical capitals are calculated.

Illustration 94

Using the figures in the Balance Sheet on p. 22175

A, B, and C profit ratio is 1:2:1
A, B, and C capitals are £2,500, £1,800, and £700.

Applying the rule above:

$$A = £2,500 \div 1 \qquad B = £1,800 \div 2 \qquad C = £700 \div 1$$
$$= £2,500 \qquad\quad\ = £900 \qquad\qquad = £700$$

C is thus the basic capital and the hypothetical capitals relative to profit sharing (working from C's actual capital) are £700, £1,400, and £700.

Illustration 95

The distributions would, using the same facts, except *ignoring* losses and profits on realization as in the preceding example, be thus:

CAPITALS

	A	B	C
Profit and Loss Ratio	1	2	1
	£	£	£
Actual Capitals	2,500	1,800	700
Capitals if in ratio	700 (1)	1,400 (2)	700 (1)
Capitals in Excess . . .	1,800	400	
Capitals of A and B if in ratio as between themselves	200 (1)	400 (2)	
A's Final Excess Capital . . .	£1,600		

Thus the first   £1,600 (1) will be given to A
      next   £600 (2) will be given to A and B in the ratio of 1:2
      balance £2,800 (3) will be given to A, B, and C in the ratio of 1:2:1

The distribution would thus be (after paying £1,000 to creditors out of the first realization of £500 and £500 from the second realization of £2,200):

Realization No.	Cash Available	Payment No.	Total		A	B	C
	£		£	£	£	£	£
(2)	1,700	(1)	1,600	1,600	1,600		
		(2)	100 ⎱		33	67	
				600			
(3)	600	(2)	500 ⎰		167	333	
		(3)	100 ⎱		25	50	25
(4)	1,600	(3)	1,600 ⎱	2,800	400	800	400
(5)	1,100	(3)	1,100 ⎰		275	550	275
	£5,000		£5,000	£5,000	£2,500	£1,800	£700

Illustration 96

If the losses and profits are considered, the distribution would be:

Realization No.	Cash Available	Payment No.	Total		A		B		C
	£		£	£	£	£	£	£	£
(2)	1,500	1	1,500 ⎱	1,600		1,500			
			100 ⎰		100				
(3)	600	2 ⎰							333
		⎱	500 ⎱		167				
				600	———	267			
			100 ⎰		33		67		
(4)	1,600	3 ⎰							
		⎱	1,500 ⎱		375		750		375
				2,800		408		817	
(5)	1,300	4	1,300 ⎰		325		650		325
	£5,000		£5,000	£5,000	£2,500		£1,800		£700

Sale of Business to a Limited Company. Where the partnership business is sold to a Limited Company the sale price, termed the purchase consideration, may be received partly in cash and partly in shares. Usually such a consideration includes payment for goodwill with an enhanced value possibly for the other assets, thus showing a profit to the partnership over and above book values. In addition, the acquiring company may take over the liabilities if the creditors also agree. So far as the book entries are concerned the virtual cancellation of liabilities of the partnership is a profit, so that REALIZATION ACCOUNT in lieu of CASH will be credited (and liabilities debited) when this arrangement takes place. The 'profit' is more apparent than real because the purchasing company will make its purchase consideration less by an amount equal to the liabilities assumed, and hence the Realization Account will be credited with a smaller figure than it otherwise would have been had the partnership *paid* its liabilities.

When all the entries relevant to the sale have been completed, the final balances will be: (1) Partners' Capital Accounts, (2) Cash, and (3) Shares. As to the division of the assets it is for the partners themselves to decide, but in the absence of agreement the fairest way is to divide the shares out first in the *same ratio as profits and losses are shared*, so as to give the partners the same right to the benefit of appreciation, and the same liability to loss by way of depreciation, in the value of the shares, or in respect of liability to calls,[1] just as if they had still remained as partnership assets; after which the cash is paid off to BALANCE the Capital Accounts. Only ONE asset out of the two (i.e. shares and cash) is capable of being dealt with in profit and loss ratio, unless the balances of Capital Accounts before any transfer of shares or payment of cash are ALSO in profit and loss ratio. This topic is dealt with in more detail in Chapter 23.

If an indivisible asset (e.g. Property) remains unrealized and it is agreed to close off the partnership, the value thereof may be debited to the partners in the profit ratios; or the value counted as nil (and the partners debited with the book loss in the profit ratios) and when the asset is sold proceeds paid to the partners in the profit ratios, whether the sum realized involves a gain or loss on the book value before writing it down to nil. The payments so made will not involve any entries in the old partnership books (if still existing) except by way of memorandum.

Unless otherwise agreed, the current market valuation of the shares will be taken as the basis of division.

If it so happens that a partner's balance of capital is small but his profit and loss ratio is large, he must be content with a sufficient number of shares to clear his account (and will receive no cash) of if he is desirous of having his 'quota' of shares corresponding with his profit and loss ratio he must contribute to the firm sufficient cash to make up the difference.

Illustration 97

Q, S, and O, partners, share profits and losses in the ratio of $3:2:1$. Their Balance Sheet at 31st December 19.., is:

---

[1] Strictly, the contribution for calls if the shares were still partnership assets would not be in profit ratios, but out of the firm's cash; but any loss or profit arising on sale would be rateable to the profit ratios.

Q, S, AND O BALANCE SHEET AS AT 31ST DECEMBER 19..

	£	£		£	£
Capitals—			Sundry Assets . .		21,300
Q . . .	11,000		Debtors . . .	6,000	
S . . .	6,000		*Less* Bad Debts Provision . . .	600	
O . . .	4,000				
		21,000			5,400
Creditors . . .		6,300	Cash		600
		£27,300			£27,300

They agree to sell their business for £27,000, payable £3,000 in cash; balance in shares worth £1 each; creditors are taken over by the purchasing company. Date of sale is 1st January 19...

Show Accounts, ignoring expenses of realization.

The accounts are (proceeding direct to Realization Account):

REALIZATION ACCOUNT

19.. Jan. 1		£	19.. Jan. 1		£
	Sundry Assets .	21,300		Creditors . .	6,300
	Debtors. . .	6,000		Bad Debts Provision .	600
	Cash[1]	600		Purchasing Company:	
	Profit on Realization—			Purchase Consideration	27,000
	Q: $\frac{3}{6}$ . . £3,000				
	S: $\frac{2}{6}$ . . 2,000				
	O: $\frac{1}{6}$ . . 1,000				
		6,000			
		£33,900			£33,900

PURCHASING COMPANY

19.. Jan. 1		£	19.. Jan. 1			£
	Realization Account Purchase Consideration	27,000		Shares . . .	(a)	24,000
				Cash . . .	(b)	3,000
		£27,000				£27,000

CAPITALS

			Q	S	O				Q	S	O
19.. Jan. 1			£	£	£	19.. Jan. 1			£	£	£
	Shares .	(a)[2]	12,000	8,000	4,000		Balances	b/d	11,000	6,000	4,000
	Cash .	(b)[3]	2,000		1,000		Profit on Realization .		3,000	2,000	1,000
			£14,000	£8,000	£5,000				£14,000	£8,000	£5,000

[1] As *all* assets are taken over the cash must be handed over—it would have amounted to the same thing if the purchasing company had permitted the partners to retain the cash and reduced the cash payable from £3,000 to £2,400.

[2] Division of £24,000 worth of shares in ratio of profits 3:2:1.

[3] Cash paid to clear the accounts.

(a) and (b). The shares and cash received would be posted to the debit of the respective accounts and when transferred and paid to the partners the amounts would be credited, thus balancing both accounts.

It is important to note that the *number* of shares will not necessarily be 24,000 because the nominal value may be an amount other than £1, e.g. £0·50.

Illustration 98

X and Y trading in partnership share profits and losses equally. On 30th September 19.., they sold their business to P, Ltd.

Their Balance Sheet at this date was:

BALANCE SHEET AS AT 30TH SEPTEMBER 19..

		£		£
Creditors. . . .		4,900	Sundry Assets. . . .	16,350
Capitals—			Cash	470
X . . . £5,280			Current Account X . . .	500
Y . . . 4,560				
		9,840		
Loan X		2,100		
Current Account Y . . .		480		
		£17,320		£17,320

The purchasers agreed as follows:

(a) To pay deposit of £5,000 immediately so that the firm could discharge its liabilities.

(b) To give £3,000 for goodwill and £15,920 in cash for the remaining assets (excluding cash which is not taken over).

(c) To pay interest on the balance of purchase price at 5 per cent per annum, full completion to be made on 31st December 19...

X and Y are to be allowed interest on their capitals at 5 per cent per annum, and X to be allowed interest on his loan at 4 per cent per annum till settlement.

Show accounts in the books of the vendors.

REALIZATION ACCOUNT

19..			£	19..		£
Sept. 30	Assets. . . .		16,350	Sept. 30	P. Ltd.—	18,920
	Expenses . . .		?		Purchase Consideration	
	Profit—					
	X . . £1,285					
	Y . . 1,285					
			2,570			
			£18,920			£18,920

CASH

19..			£	19..			£
Sept. 30	Balance	b/d	470	Sept. 30	Expenses of Realization		?
Oct. 1	P., Ltd.		5,000	Oct. 1	Creditors		4,900
Dec. 31	,, ,, : Balance		14,094	Dec. 31	Loan Account		2,121
					Capital Accounts—		
					X		6.146
					Y		6,397
			£19,564				£19,564

P., LTD.

19..		£	19..		£
Sept. 30	Realization Account— Purchase Consideration	18,920	Oct. 1	Cash: (Deposit)	5,000
Dec. 31	Interest on Balance— £13,920 at 5% per annum for 3 months	174	Dec. 31	Cash: Balance	14,094
		£19,094			£19,094

CAPITALS

19..			X £	Y £	19..			X £	Y £
Dec. 31	Cash		6,146	6,397	Sept. 30	Balances	b/d	5,280	4,560
						Current Accounts		785	1,765
					Dec. 31	Interest on Capital		66	57
						Interest Account Balance		15	15
			£6,146	£6,397				£6,146	£6,397

CURRENT ACCOUNTS

19..			X £	Y £	19..			X £	Y £
Sept. 30	Balance	b/d	500		Sept. 30	Balance	b/d		480
	Capital Accounts		785	1,765		Profit on Realization		1,285	1,285
			£1,285	£1,765				£1,285	£1,765

X LOAN

19..			£	19..			£
Dec. 31	Cash		2,121	Sept. 30	Balance	b/d	2,100
				Dec. 31	Interest on Loan		21
			£2,121				£2,121

INTEREST

19.. Dec. 31			£	19.. Dec. 31	P. Ltd. . . . . —	£ 174
	Interest on Capital—					
	X . . .	£66				
	Y . . .	57				
			123			
	Interest on Loan X . .		21			
	Balance: Capital					
	Accounts:					
	X: ½ . .	£15				
	Y: ½ . .	15				
			30			
			£174			£174

Note 1. The order of payment should be carefully observed. If the balance of Current Account of X had still remained in debit after balancing Realization Account it would have been set off against his Loan Account.

2. The items in italics (disposing of the Balance Sheet items) should FIRST be interested so as to commence 'in balance'.

In a dissolution it occasionally happens that there are assets which are unrealizable or not easily realizable. The method of dealing with such assets must first depend upon the agreement between the partners; otherwise, unless the final dissolution is to be unduly delayed, such assets should where capable of division be divided in *profit* ratios, so that theoretically any profit or loss on ultimate disposal will be in profit ratios, thus putting the partners in the same position as if the firm had kept them and ultimately sold them. In fact, each ex-partner will be able to decide for himself when to sell, and his profit or loss might be much greater or less than if the firm sold them piecemeal or *in toto*. The equity of the procedure is clear because from the moment of distribution it is a matter for each ex-partner to exercise his own discretion as a personal matter.

No difficulty will generally arise with regard to shares in a Limited Company but the firm might have other unsaleable assets which in fact cannot be divided, e.g. a building, in which case there can be no 'distribution': usually, if there are non-divisible and unrealizable assets, the partners come to some arrangement as to taking them over personally at an agreed valuation. Often shares which are unsaleable will be partly paid and the division in profit ratios throws a potential liability fairly as between the parties.

Illustration 99

A and B who shared profits 3 : 2, are partners and the position, after realization, is:

BALANCE SHEET

		£		£
A	.	1,900	Cash	2,700
B	.	1,700	Shares at cost . . .	500
			Other Assets . . .	400
		£3,600		£3,600

It is agreed that 'other assets' shall be taken over by A for £300; the Shares divided out equitably and settlement of balance in Cash. Show A's and B's accounts dealing with the above, ignoring transfer costs.

CAPITALS

	A	B		A	B
	£	£		£	£
Other Assets . .	300		Balances . . .	1,900	1,700
Loss on Book Value of					
Other Assets .	60	40			
Shares[1] . . .	300	200			
Cash . . .	1,240	1,460			
	£1,900	£1,700		£1,900	£1,700

[1] Alternatively, the shares may be written down to, say, *nil*, the loss being debited to A and B (in lieu of item shares: A, £300; and B, £200; but the net result is unaltered).

Illustration 100

Barlick and Earby are partners sharing profits 3:2.

On the 30th June 19.., they admit Colne as a partner, and the new profit ratio is 2:2:1. Colne brought in Fixtures £3,000 and Cash £10,000, the Goodwill being (*a*) Barlick and Earby £20,000 and (*b*) Colne £10,000, but neither figure is to be brought into the books.

On the 31st December 19.., the partnership is dissolved, Barlick retiring and the other two partners forming a Limited Company with equal capitals, taking over all remaining assets and liabilities, Goodwill being agreed at £40,000 and brought into the books of the Limited Company. Barlick agrees to take over the business car at £3,700. Plant was sold for £3,000, being in excess of requirements. The profits of the two preceding years were £17,200 and £19,000 respectively and it was agreed that for the half-year ended 30th June 19.., the net profit was to be taken as equal to the average of the two preceding years and the current year.

No entries had been made when Colne entered, except for Cash.

From the following Trial Balance and the information given above, show the Ledger entries in the books of the firm and the limited company, no new books being opened by the latter. There is no interest on drawings or capital. Ignore depreciation, Tax and expenses connected with the dissolution of the firm and formation of the new company. Barlick agreed to leave £50,000 on loan to the Company, secured by 6 per cent Debentures.

TRIAL BALANCE, 31ST DECEMBER 19..

	£	£
Barlick—Drawings and Capital	6,000	35,000
Earby— ,, ,, ...	5,000	20,000
Colne— ,, ,, ...	2,800	10,000
Debtors	31,000	
Creditors		12,000
Plant [book value of Plant sold, £4,000] . . .	23,000	
Fixtures	7,000	
Motor Car	2,700	
Stock at 31st December 19..	13,000	
Cash at Bank	16,300	
Profit and Loss Account for year		29,800
	£106,800	£106,800

MOTOR CAR

19..			£	19..			£
Jan. 1	Balance . . .	b/d	2,700	Dec. 31	Barlick		3,700
Dec. 31	Profit on Realization .		1,000				
			£3,700				£3,700

PLANT

19..			£	19..			£
Jan. 1	Balance . . .	b/d	23,000	Dec. 31	Cash		3,000
					Loss on Realization .		1,000
					Balance . . .	c/d	19,000
			£23,000				£23,000
19..							
Jan. 1	Balance . . .	b/d	19,000				

FIXTURES

19..			£	19..			£
Jan. 1	Balance . . .	b/d	7,000	Dec. 31	Balance . . .	c/d	10,000
June 30	Colne . . .		3,000				
			£10,000				£10,000
19..							
Jan. 1	Balance . . .	b/d	10,000				

PROFIT AND LOSS ON REALIZATION

19..		£	19..		£
Dec. 31	Loss on Sale of Plant .	1,000	Dec. 31	Profit on Sale of Car .	1,000

GOODWILL ADJUSTMENT

Date	Particulars	Barlick £	Earby £	Colne £
19.. June 30	Contra	(⅖) 8,000	(⅖) 8,000	(⅕) 4,000
June 30	Contra	(⅖) 4,000	(⅖) 4,000	(⅕) 2,000
Dec. 31	Capitals	16,000	12,000	12,000
		£28,000	£24,000	£18,000

Date	Particulars	Barlick £	Earby £	Colne £
19.. June 30	Contra	(⅗) 12,000	(⅖) 8,000	(⅕) 10,000
Dec. 31	Goodwill	(⅖) 16,000	(⅖) 16,000	(⅕) 8,000
		£28,000	£24,000	£18,000

CAPITALS

Date	Particulars	Barlick £	Earby £	Colne £
19.. Dec. 31	Cash (Drawings)	6,000	5,000	2,800
	Car	3,700		
	Debentures	50,000		
	Cash	7,620	7,580	
	Share Capital		31,340	31,340
		£67,320	£43,920	£34,140

Date	Particulars	Barlick £	Earby £	Colne £
19.. Jan. 1	Balances b/d	35,000	20,000	10,000
June 30	Cash[1]			3,000
	Fixtures			
	Profit	13,200	8,800	1,560
Dec. 31	Profit	3,120	3,120	
	Goodwill Adjustment	16,000	12,000	12,000
	Cash			7,580
		£67,320	£43,920	£34,140

[1] This item is already in the books and the debit therefor merged in the Bank balance at 31st December 19...

GOODWILL

19..			£				
Dec. 31	Goodwill Adjustment Account		40,000				

PROFIT AND LOSS [APPROPRIATION] ACCOUNT

19..			£	£	19..			£
June 30	Barlick—$\frac{3}{5}$ [See Note 1]		13,200		Dec. 31	Balance, Net Profit	b/d	29,800
	Earby—$\frac{2}{5}$ [See Note 1]		8,800	22,000				
Dec. 31	Barlick—$\frac{2}{5}$		3,120					
	Earby—$\frac{2}{5}$		3,120					
	Colne—$\frac{1}{5}$		1,560	7,800				
				£29,800				£29,800

CASH

19..			£	19..			£
Dec. 31	Balance	b/d	16,300	Dec. 31	Barlick		7,620
	Sale of Plant		3,000		Earby (to adjust Share Capital)		7,580
	Colne (to adjust Share Capital)		7,580		Balance	c/d	11,680
			£26,880				£26,880
19..							
Jan. 1	Balance	b/d	11,680				

SIX PER CENT DEBENTURES

				19..			£
				Dec. 31	Barlick		50,000

SHARE CAPITAL

19..			£	19..			£
Dec. 31	Balance	c/d	62,680	Dec. 31	Earby		31,340
					Colne		31,340
			£62,680				£62,680
				19..			
				Jan. 1	Balance	b/d	62,680

TRIAL BALANCE

	£	£
Debtors	31,000	
Creditors		12,000
Fixtures	10,000	
Plant	19,000	
Goodwill	40,000	
Cash at Bank	11,680	
Stock	13,000	
Share Capital		62,680
6% Debentures		50,000
	£124,680	£124,680

Note 1. Profit for preceding years: £17,200 + £19,000 = £36,200
Profit for current year: 29,800

3) 66,000

£22,000

2. The profit for the half year to 30th June, 19.., is *equal* to the above average and not at the annual *rate* of such profits, in which case the amount would be £11,000 only.

SECTION I. LIMITED PARTNERSHIP

Limited Partnership.[1] Under the Limited Partnership Act 1907, so long as there is at least one general partner who is personally liable for the obligations and liabilities of the firm, a person may become a partner in a limited sense. He is personally liable only for liabilities to the extent of his *agreed contribution, including* any withdrawal of such contribution, but beyond that is not personally liable for obligations and liabilities, however disastrously the firm's course may run. He cannot be made in any way liable to repay anything to the firm or to its creditors for such losses (unless he has withdrawn the whole or part of his contribution, in which case he is liable to that extent). Hence, the debit balance of his account for losses is nothing more than a contingent asset, something akin to Short Workings Account (dealt with in Royalties) because of the right of the firm to withhold payment of any future profits until his share thereof has been sufficient to eliminate his debit balance.

After the limited partner has withdrawn the share of profits to which he is legitimately entitled, the limited partnership has no control over such share, nor can it be taken into account in dealing with any subsequent events of the firm. Hence, if the limited partner decides to pay back (or probably merely transfer from Profit and Loss Account or his Current Account) his profits as a loan, he is entitled, after the other creditors, to claim for repayment when the term of the loan has expired, or on

[1] In general accounting problems dealing with partnerships, it usually will be clear as to whether or not the reference is to a general or limited partnership, but problems involving general points of law and accounting may merely refer to a 'partnership', and this should be construed as a reference both to general *and* limited partnerships.

dissolution, whichever be the earlier, notwithstanding the fact that subsequent losses are such that his share thereof exceeds the amount of his loan. The loan is a debt due to him by the firm, just as if he had lent the money to an entirely independent concern; on the other hand, his share of subsequent losses is merely a 'Debit Balance'.

The vital point is that the Limited Partner is liable to refund sums withdrawn on account of *future* profits.

It will be clear that it is essential to have the following accounts relating to the limited partner quite separately recorded:

1. Capital Account to be maintained at 'contribution' amount.
2. Loan Account (if any).
3. Current Account, in which will be recorded profits and losses, interest and drawings. If a debit balance arises by reason of excessive withdrawals, it represents to the extent that it is due thereto a definite debt (as it is deemed to be a withdrawal of his contribution); but if the debit balance arises because of losses it is merely a debit balance, a mere contingent asset, which can be effective only in the event of future profits being of sufficient magnitude to enable the general partners to recoup the balance out of the limited partner's share of profits.

The main differences between a Limited and General Partnership are as follows:

	General	Limited
1. Registration	Not necessary, except in certain cases, e.g. under Business Names Act 1916.[1]	With Registrar of Companies under Limited Partnership Act 1907, otherwise deemed to be general Partnership. Alteration of contribution of limited partner must be registered.
2. Inspection of books	Partner may inspect, personally or by agent, books, documents, accounts, and take copies.	A limited partner may inspect, personally or by agent, books, documents, accounts, and take copies.
3. Management.	Partner may take part, in absence of agreement.	Limited partners may only *advise*, not allowed to intermeddle: penalty—liable for firm's debts as a general partner while he so acts.
4. Assignment	Partner cannot assign his position without consent, may assign his *share*, but assignee entitled during partnership to: (a) Receive Accounts. (b) Inspect the books. (c) But cannot interfere with management.	A limited partner may assign with consent and assignee entitled to: (a) Advise. (b) Receive Accounts. (c) Inspect the books; but notice of assignment to be gazetted.
5. Death, Bankruptcy and Lunacy	Partnership dissolved. In case of Lunacy, other partners may apply to Court for dissolution.	Not dissolved, unless his share cannot be otherwise ascertained.
6. Charges	Partner may charge his share, but other partners may dissolve at their option.	Limited partner may charge his share, but this gives no right to other partners to dissolve.

[1] See footnote 1 on p. 2306.

	General	Limited
7. Winding up .	All partners liable for the firm's debts to the full extent of debts.	Limited partner liable only to the amount of his agreed capital, or drawings in excess of share of profits.
8. Stamp Duty .	None.	£0·50 per £100 or part of £100 on capital contributed by limited partner (also £2 on registration).

Illustration 101

G, P and L are equal partners in a limited partnership, L being a limited partner. Their Balance Sheet at dissolution was:

	£		£
Capitals—		Sundry Assets (including Cash	
G	3,500	of £80)	13,580
P	5,500	Current Accounts—	
L	2,000	G	2,000
Creditors	6,380	P	1,000
		L	800
	£17,380		£17,380

Of the balance of £800 standing to the debit of L, £250 represents drawings and £550 represents his share of trading losses.

The Sundry Assets, excluding the cash, realized 60 per cent of book values.

Close off the partnership accounts (ignore Realization Expenses).

REALIZATION ACCOUNT

	£			£
Sundry Assets . . .	13,500	Cash		8,100
		Loss on Realization—		
		G . .	£1,800	
		P . .	1,800	
		L . .	1,800	
				5,400
	£13,500			£13,500

CAPITALS

	G.	P.	L.		G.	P.	L.
	£	£	£		£	£	£
Current Accounts	2,000	1,000	800	Balances b/d	3,500	5,500	2,000
Loss on Realization	1,800	1,800	1,800	Balances c/d	300		600
Balance c/d		2,700					
	£3,800	£5,500	£2,600		£3,800	£5,500	£2,600
Balance b/d	300		600	Balance b/d		2,700	
Transfer from L	175	175		Transfer of unrealizable			
Cash		2,525		Balance			
				G			175
				P			175
				Cash	475		250
	£475	£2,700	£600		£475	£2,700	£600

CASH

		£			£
Balance	b/d	80	Creditors		6,380
Realization Account		8,100	P		2,525
G		475			
L		250			
		£8,905			£8,905

It is important in the case of a limited partner that withdrawals of capital against future profits should be shown in a separate account from his share of the firm's losses so that his position on a dissolution can be readily seen.

Illustration 102

Heaton and Moor are partners sharing profits 3:2, Moor being a limited partner. The Capitals are Heaton £7,000 and Moor £6,000.

The first year resulted in a loss of £4,500.

The Sundry Assets and Creditors at the end of the first year were £8,800 and £3,000 respectively.

Drawings were Heaton £1,500 and Moor £1,200.

1. Show Balance Sheet of firm.

2. Assuming the profits of the second year are £5,500 how will they be dealt with as regards Moor?

(1)   BALANCE SHEET

		£			£
Capitals—			Sundry Assets . . .		8,800
Heaton . . .	£7,000		Current Accounts—		
			Heaton—		
Moor . . .	6,000		⅗ Loss . .	£2,700	
		13,000	Drawings .	1,500	
Creditors		3,000			4,200
			Moor—		
			⅖ Loss . . .		1,800
			Drawings . .		1,200
		£16,000			£16,000

(2) Moor is entitled to £2,200, which must be first placed against the balance of his Current Account of £1,800 and £400 against his Drawings Account, leaving the latter at £800.

Illustration 103

Assuming that in reference to the preceding illustration, in the third year the firm incurred a loss of £13,500, Sundry Assets being £16,500 and Creditors £18,700, show the Balance Sheet of the firm.

There were no drawings in the second and third years.

BALANCE SHEET

		£			£
Capitals—			Sundry Assets		16,500
Heaton	£7,000		Current Accounts— . . .		
Moor	6,000		Heaton:		
		13,000	Balance 1st year .	£4,200	
Creditors		18,700	⅗ Profit 2nd year .	3,300	
				900	
			⅗ Loss 3rd year .	8,100	
					9,000
			Moor:		
			Balance 1st year .	1,800	
			⅖ Profit (part) 2nd year .	1,800	
			⅖ Loss 3rd year .		5,400
			Drawings:		
			Balance 1st year .	1,200	
			⅖ Profit (part) 2nd year .	400	
					800
		£31,700			£31,700

If dissolution takes place Moor is liable in full for £800, notwithstanding that he is in credit for £600 (Capital £6,000 less Current Account £5,400) which cannot be withdrawn unless the Creditors of the firm are fully discharged, inasmuch as he is a deferred Creditor; if Heaton is solvent and pays into the firm his deficiency of £2,000 (Current Account £9,000 less Capital £7,000) and assets realize book values and creditors are paid off as far as possible the position will be:

	£		£
Heaton (£7,000−£9,000+£2,000) .	—	Cash (£16,500+£2,000−£18,500) . .	—
Moor (£6,000−£5,400) . .	600	Moor (Drawings) . . .	800
Creditors (£18,700−£18,500) .	200		

Moor will be required to bring in £200 to be used in paying off the Creditors. This will reduce the debit of Moor's drawings to £600 which will be written off against his credit of £600 (Capital £6,000—Current Account £5,400).

Illustration 104

F, R, and S are in partnership under the Limited Partnership Act 1907, F and R being general partners with capitals of £40,000 and £30,000 respectively, and S, a limited partner with £15,000, his agreed contribution. At 1st January 19.1, all profits had been distributed. The ratio of profit and loss sharing is $3:2:1$.

From the following details prepare partners' accounts:

	Profits	Drawings		
		F	R	S
	£	£	£	£
Year ended 31st Dec. 19.1	18,000	5,000	3,500	3,700
,, ,, ,, ,, 19.2	30,000	17,000	8,900	2,500
,, ,, ,, ,, 19.3 Loss . . .	12,000	4,000	4,000	1,800
,, ,, ,, ,, 19.4	10,500	5,000	4,000	1,200
,, ,, ,, ,, 19.5	24,000	6,000	6,000	1,300

On 31st December 19.2, S lent £1,000 to the firm (out of profits) free of interest.

CAPITALS OF GENERAL PARTNERS

								F	R
								£	£
					19.1 Jan. 1	Balances . .	b/d	40,000	30,000

S LOAN

							R
							£
				19.2 Dec. 31	Current Account . . .		1,000

[The remaining accounts appear on pp. 22195–22199]

As has been seen, the debit balance on Capital Account of a limited partner will be dealt with according to whether the balance has arisen through excessive drawings or share of losses. If the balance arises by reason of excessive *drawings*, and the limited partner is unable to contribute by reason of his insolvency (unless the rule in *Garner* v. *Murray* is

CURRENT ACCOUNTS OF GENERAL PARTNERS

Date		F	R		Date		F	R
		£	£				£	£
19.1					19.1			
Dec. 31	Drawings	5,000	3,500		Dec. 31	Profit and Loss Account—		
	Balances c/d	4,000	2,500			F. $\frac{3}{5} \times$ £18,000	9,000	
						R. $\frac{2}{5} \times$ £18,000		6,000
		£9,000	£6000				£9,000	£6,000
19.2					19.2			
Dec. 31	Drawings	17,000	8,900		Jan. 1	Balances b/d	4,000	2,500
	Balances c/d	2,000	3,600		Dec. 31	Profit and Loss Account—		
						F. $\frac{3}{5} \times$ £30,000	15,000	
						R. $\frac{2}{5} \times$ £30,000		10,000
		£19,000	£12,500				£19,000	£12,500
19.3					19.3			
Dec. 31	Profit and Loss Account—				Jan. 1	Balances b/d	2,000	3,600
	F. $\frac{3}{5} \times$ £12,000	6,000			Dec. 31	Balances c/d	8,000	4,400
	R. $\frac{2}{5} \times$ £12,000		4,000					
	Drawings	4,000	4,000					
		£10,000	£8,000				£10,000	£8,000

CURRENT ACCOUNTS OF GENERAL PARTNERS

Date	Particulars				Date	Particulars		
19.4 Jan. 1	Balances	b/d	8,000	4,400	19.4 Dec. 31	Profit and Loss Account—		
Dec. 31	Drawings		5,000	4,000		F. $\frac{3}{6} \times$ £10,500		5,250	3,500
						R. $\frac{2}{6} \times$ £10,500		
						Balances	c/d	7,750	4,900
			£13,000	£8,400				£13,000	£8,400
19.5 Jan. 1	Balances	b/d	7,750	4,900	19.5 Dec. 31	Profit and Loss Account—		
Dec. 31	Drawings		6,000	6,000		F. $\frac{3}{6} \times$ £24,000		12,000	8,000
						R. $\frac{2}{6} \times$ £24,000		
						Balances	c/d	1,750	2,900
			£13,750	£10,900				£13,750	£10,900
19.6 Jan. 1	Balances	b/d	1,750	2,900				

CAPITAL OF LIMITED PARTNER S

Date	Particulars		£		Date	Particulars		£
19.1 Dec. 31	Transfer from Current Account		700		19.1 Jan. 1	Balance	b/d	15,000
	Balance	c/d	14,300					
			£15,000					£15,000
19.2 Dec. 31	Balance	c/d	15,000		19.2 Jan. 1	Balance	b/d	14,300
					Dec. 31	Transfer from Current Account		700
			£15,000					£15,000
19.3 Dec. 31	Transfer from Current Account		1,000		19.3 Jan. 1	Balance	b/d	15,000
	Balance	c/d	14,000					
			£15,000					£15,000
19.4 Dec. 31	Balance	c/d	14,550		19.4 Jan. 1	Balance	b/d	14,000
					Dec. 31	Transfer from Current Account		550
			£14,550					£14,550
19.5 Dec. 31	Balance	c/d	15,000		19.5 Jan. 1	Balance	b/d	14,550
					Dec. 31	Transfer from Current Account		450
			£15,000					£15,000
					19.6 Jan. 1	Balance	b/d	15,000

CURRENT ACCOUNT OF LIMITED PARTNER S

Date	Particulars		£		Date	Particulars		£
19.1 Dec. 31	Drawings		3,700		19.1 Dec. 31	Profit and Loss Account ½×£18,000		3,000
						Transfer to Capital Account		700
			£3,700					£3,700
19.2 Dec. 31	Drawings		2,500		19.2 Dec. 31	Profit and Loss Account ½×£30,000		5,000
	Transfer to Capital Account		700					
	„ Loan Account		1,000					
	Balance	c/d	800					
			£5,000					£5,000
19.3 Dec. 31	Profit and Loss Account ½×£12,000		2,000		19.3 Jan. 1	Balance	b/d	800
	Drawings		1,800		Dec. 31	Transfer to Capital Account £1,800−£800		1,000
						Balance	c/d	2,000
			£3,800					£3,800
19.4 Jan. 1	Balance	b/d	2,000		19.4 Dec. 31	Profit and Loss Account ½×£10,500		1,750
Dec. 31	Drawings		1,200			Balance	c/d	2,000
	Transfer to Capital Account		550					
			£3,750					£3,750
19.5 Jan. 1	Balance	b/d	2,000		19.5 Dec. 31	Profit and Loss Account ½×£24,000		4,000
Dec. 31	Drawings		1,300					
	Transfer to Capital Account		450					
	Balance	b/d	250					
			£4,000					£4,000
					19.6 Jan. 1	Balance	b/d	250

CAPITALS

Section 1

Date	Particulars	Ref	A £p	B £p	L £	M £	Ref	A £p	B £p	L £	M £	Particulars	Date
19.. Dec. 31	Drawings		2,000	1,500	500	800	b/d	10,600	7,000	1,000	2,400	Balances	19.. Jan. 1
	Loss on Realization		3,000	3,000	1,500	1,500	c/d			1,000		Balance	Dec. 31
	Balances	c/d	5,600	2,500		100							
			£10,600	£7,000	£2,000	£2,400		£10,600	£7,000	£2,000	£2,400		

Section 2

Particulars	Ref	A £p	B £p	L £	M £	Ref	A £p	B £p	L £	M £	Particulars
Balance	b/d					b/d	5,600	2,500		100	Balances A., B. and M. per contra
Loss not brought in by L, £1,000:						c/d			1,000	60	Balance
£500 per Garner v. Murray[1]	(a)	265	175		60						
£500 in Profit and Loss Ratios	(b)	200	200		100						
Balances	c/d	5,135	2,125	1,000							
		£5,600	£2,500	£1,000	£160		£5,600	£2,500	£1,000	£160	

Section 3

Particulars	Ref	A £p	B £p	L £	M £	Ref	A £p	B £p	L £	M £	Particulars	Date
Balance	b/d					b/d	5,135	2,125			Balances A. and B. per contra	
Loss not brought in by M per Garner v. Murray[2]	(c)	36·10	23·90		60	c/d				60	Balances	
Balances	c/d	5,098·90	2,101·10									
		£5,135·00	£2,125·00		£60		£5,135·00	£2,125·00		£60		
						c/d	5,098·90	2,101·10		60	Balances	19.. Jan. 1

(a) This amount being a debt due by L for drawings must be dealt with as above.

(b) This amount not being a debt, must be dealt with as above.

(c) This amount being a debt due by M for drawings must be dealt with as above.

[It is assumed that the withdrawals of L and M are made, not from profits but out of Capital, otherwise their balances are mere 'debit balances' and not debts.]

[1] In ratio of 106:70:24.   [2] In ratio of 106:70.

[1] In ratio of 106:70.

barred), such loss must be borne by the continuing solvent partners in capital ratios; on the other hand, that part of the balance arising through a limited partner's share of *loss* must be borne in profit and loss ratios. By excessive drawings is meant withdrawals in excess of the limited partner's share of profits.

It may be mentioned that in the absence of judicial ruling other views are held in the profession. It is argued for instance that *Garner* v. *Murray* can never apply in a Limited Partnership. Others equally ardently maintain that whether the debit against the limited partner is—to employ the language used in this book—a mere debit balance or an actual debt, the *Garner* v. *Murray* rule is applicable where the limited partner will not or cannot pay the amount in question to the firm, but it seems clear that unless the debit represents a *debt* due by the Limited Partner *and* the deficiency arises through his insolvency the rule in *Garner* v. *Murray* is not applicable; and in any case the general partner(s) admit him on the footing that he is not liable in respect of any sum that merely represents the excess of losses over profits. The Limited Partner before participating in profits earned in the future would be required to bring into account such excess, but this does not constitute a DEBT.

Illustration 105

A, B, L, M are in partnership, sharing profits and losses in the ratio of 2:2:1:1. Their capitals on 1st January were £10,600, £7,000, £1,000, and £2,400 respectively. A and B are general partners, L and M being limited partners. The drawings for the year were A, £2,000; B, £1,500; L, £500; and M, £800. It was decided on 31st December that the partnership should be dissolved, the loss on realization being £9,000. Show the accounts of the partners, assuming that the limited partners cannot subscribe towards their deficiency. (See p. 22199.)

SECTION J. MISCELLANEOUS

Reconstruction. Where a firm is in financial difficulties, the creditors may decide to give assistance so that the necessity for bankruptcy proceedings may be avoided. Such assistance may take the form of granting to the firm a moratorium, that is, an agreement to forbear for a defined period of time from suing or taking such other remedies for the payment of debts as the law permits. This forbearance is usually accompanied by an agreement for a cancellation of a portion of the firm's liability to the creditors.

In addition, a person, whether a creditor or not, may advance money to the firm for purposes of paying creditors and for working capital. In the latter circumstances the lender may stipulate for an agreed rate of interest, varying with profits or at a definite rate. In consideration of their forbearance, the creditors may stipulate for a share in the profits to cover the discount granted to the firm and reasonable interest.

Where a loanholder agrees to become a partner, the usual entries consequent upon the admission of a new partner will be made, except that the balance of loan will be credited to the Capital Account of the loanholder; but in any case it is usual to open a Reconstruction Account to give effect to the terms of the arrangements entered into with the creditors where they agree to a reduction of their claims.

The Reconstruction Account will be debited with losses on revaluation of assets and the expenses of reconstruction, assets and cash being respectively credited. In accordance with the principles previously stated, a revaluation of debtors will take the form of the creation of, or increase in, a Bad Debts Provision, Reconstruction Account being debited and the Bad Debts Provision credited.

Increases in the value of assets and the profit arising from the reduction in the amount of liabilities to the creditors will be debited respectively to the assets and creditors and the Reconstruction Account credited.

The balance of Reconstruction Account will be transferred to the Capital Accounts of the old partners in exactly the same manner as the balance of an ordinary Profit and Loss Account.

Any subsequent profit or loss as compared with the revised book values will accrue to the new firm, so that if a lender has become a partner he will share such profit and bear such loss in the agreed ratio in the usual way. Where the creditors stipulate for a certain proportion of profit in consideration of the assistance rendered to the firm, their accounts will be credited (usually in the form of a total account) and Profit and Loss Appropriation Account debited with the amount to which they are entitled. Upon payment the creditors (or the total account) will be debited and cash credited.

Illustration 106

The following is the Balance Sheet of Ryland at 31st December 19..

BALANCE SHEET AS AT 31ST DECEMBER 19..

	£		£
Creditors	5,000	Sundry Assets	1,500
Bank	1,400	Debtors	3,500
Fletcher—Loan	1,000	Stock	2,100
		Ryland—Capital	300
	£7,400		£7,400

On 1st January following, a meeting of creditors was summoned owing to the serious financial position of Ryland, at which the creditors, other than the bank, agreed to accept £0·75 in the £ in full settlement. Fletcher agrees to make a further advance of £4,500, and to be credited with £5,500 as a partner. Stock is to be revalued at £1,840, and the debtors at £2,300.

In due course the debtors realized £2,480.

Show accounts, assuming that the profit-sharing ratios are to be Ryland 3: Fletcher 2.

RECONSTRUCTION (OR CAPITAL ADJUSTMENT) ACCOUNT

19..			£	19..			£
Jan. 1	Bad Debts Provision		1,200	Jan. 1	Creditors— Allowance £0·25 in £ on £5,000		1,250
	Stock Provision		260		Loss transferred to Ryland Capital Account		210
			£1,460				£1,460

CAPITALS

			Ryland	Fletcher				Ryland	Fletcher
19..			£	£	19..			£	£
Jan. 1	Balance	b/d	300		Jan. 1	Cash			4,500
	Loss on Recon- struction		210			Transfer from Loan Ac- count			1,000
?	Balance	c/d		5,572	?	Bad Debts Pro- vision writ- ten back[1]		108	72
						Balance	c/d	402	
			£510	£5,572				£510	£5,572
?	Balance	b/d	402		?	Balance	b/d		5,572

CASH

19..			£	19..				£
Jan. 1	Fletcher—Capital Account		4,500	Jan. ?	Bank			1,400
	Debtors		2,480	?	Creditors			3,750
				?	Balance		c/d	1,830
			£6,980					£6,980
?	Balance	b/d	1,830					

BALANCE SHEET AS AT ?[2]

		£				£
Fletcher—Capital		5,572	Sundry Assets			1,500
			Stock	£2,100		
			Less Provision	260		
						1,840
			Cash			1,830
			Ryland—Capital			402
		£5,572				£5,572

[1] The profit on realization of Debtors is a partnership profit, and is arrived at as follows: Debtors' valuation is £3,500 less Provision £1,200. As the debts realize £2,480 there will be a transfer from Debtors Accounts to the Bad Debts Provision of the loss on book values, viz. £1,020 (£3,500 less £2,480), leaving a credit balance to Bad Debts Provision of £180, which is written back to Capitals in the ratio of 3:2.

[2] After realization of debtors and payment of creditors.

Partnership Branch Accounts. Where a partnership is carried on at several distinct places it is often arranged to have one partner at each place or group of places, and for such partner in charge to have a profit ratio higher than the others.

The accounting arrangements will vary according to circumstances; for instance, the whole series of separate establishments may be regarded and dealt with as departments with all the assets, liabilities and capitals incorporated in the books of the chief place of business, or the establishments may be regarded as branches and treated accordingly. As will have been seen in Chapter 19 the particular form of branch accounting will vary considerably according to circumstances. Where the establishments are regarded as separate accounting units, the procedure will follow substantially the general pattern of 'self-contained' Branches and the incorporation of the separate establishment profits or losses will call for attention.

The entries for the profit of *each* establishment are:

1. Profit of Local establishment:
   Debit Profit and Loss (Appropriation) Account of the establishment.
   Credit Resident Partner with his share.
       Current Account of each of the other establishments according to the ratio attributable to the resident partner there.
2. Profit of other establishments:
   Debit Current Account of each respective establishment.
   Credit Local partner's Capital Account for the share attributable to him from the other establishments.
   (The treatment of losses will be the reverse.)

Illustration 107

A, B and C are partners, managing establishments at Andover, Bournemouth, and Canterbury respectively, each place being self-contained. Each partner takes one-half of the profit of his local establishment, the remainder going equally to the non-resident partners. Assuming that the profits are Andover £30,000, Bournemouth £20,000, and Canterbury £8,000, show in abridged form the entries required for dealing therewith.

A's BOOKS

PROFIT AND LOSS ACCOUNT

	£		£
A—$\frac{1}{2}$	15,000	Balance	30,000
B—$\frac{1}{4}$	7,500		
C—$\frac{1}{4}$	7,500		
	£30,000		£30,000

A

						£
			Profit—½ (A) . . .			15,000
			Profit—¼ (B) . . .			5,000
			Profit—¼ (C) . . .			2,000
						22,000

BOURNEMOUTH CURRENT ACCOUNT

		£				£
A—¼	c/d	5,000	Profit—¼			7,500
Balance		2,500				
		£7,500				£7,500
			Balance	b/d		2,500

CANTERBURY CURRENT ACCOUNT

		£				£
C—¼	c/d	2,000	Profit—¼			7,500
Balance		5,500				
		£7,500				£7,500
			Balance	b/d		5,500

B's BOOKS
PROFIT AND LOSS ACCOUNT

		£				£
B—½		10,000	Balance			20,000
A—¼		5,000				
C—¼		5,000				
		£20,000				£20,000

B

						£
			Profit—½ . . .			10,000
			Profit—¼ (A) . .			7,500
			Profit—¼ (C) . .			2,000
						19,500

ANDOVER CURRENT ACCOUNT

		£				£
A—¼		7,500	Profit—¼			5,000
			Balance	c/d		2,500
		£7,500				£7,500
Balance . . .	b/d	2,500				

CANTERBURY CURRENT ACCOUNT

		£				£
C—¼		2,000	Profit—¼			5,000
Balance	c/d	3,000				
		£5,000				£5,000
			Balance . . .	b/d		3,000

C's BOOKS
PROFIT AND LOSS ACCOUNT

		£			£
C—½		4,000	Balance . . .		8,000
A—¼		2,000			
B—¼		2,000			
		£8,000			£8,000

C

				£
	Profit—½ . . .			4,000
	Profit—¼ . . .			7,500
	Profit—¼ . . .			5,000
				16,500

ANDOVER CURRENT ACCOUNT

		£				£
A—¼		7,500	Profit—¼			2,000
			Balance	c/d		5,500
		£7,500				£7,500
Balance . . .	b/d	5,500				

BOURNEMOUTH CURRENT ACCOUNT

		£				£
C—$\frac{1}{4}$		*5,000*	Profit—$\frac{1}{4}$. . . .			*2,000*
			Balance	c/d		3,000
		£5,000				£5,000
Balance	b/d	3,000				

The current accounts in each set of books agree, e.g. the credit (in Andover books) in favour of Canterbury is £5,500, which agrees with the debit (in Canterbury books) against Andover.

These balances will appear in the separate Balance Sheets of the three establishments and will disappear in the combined Balance Sheet of the firm (similar to Head Office Current and Branch Current Accounts in Branch Accounts where the Branches are self-contained accounting units).

[The figures in ordinary type illustrate rule (1); those in italics rule (2) (see p. 22203).]

Foreign Exchange

Illustration 108

J. Bull and U. Samson are in partnership as cotton merchants and brokers, Bull managing the Manchester Office and Samson the New York Office. The profit sharing ratios are:

Manchester	New York
J. Bull—three quarters	J. Bull—one half.
U. Samson—one quarter	U. Samson—one half.

The profits for the year to 31st December 19 . . , are (1) Manchester, £2,000; and (2) New York, $3,200, a rate of $2 to £ to be taken. Show accounts.

The profits will be split thus:

	J. Bull			U. Samson		
	$	£		$	£	
Manchester	3,000	1,500 *(a)*	1,000	500 *(b)*	$a+b = £2,000$
New York	1,600 *(c)*	800	1,600 *(d)*	800	$c+d = \$3,200$
(see p. 22207)		£2,300	$2,600		

Entries in the New York books:

1. Debit Profit and Loss Appropriation Account with J. Bull's share of the American profits.
   Credit J. Bull's Current Account with his share of the American profits.
2. Debit J. Bull's Current Account with the dollar equivalent of U. Samson's share of English profits.
   Credit Profit and Loss Appropriation Account with the dollar equivalent of U. Samson's share of English profits.

Entries in the Manchester books:

1. Debit Profit and Loss Appropriation Account with U. Samson's share of the English profits.
   Credit U. Samson's Current Account with his share of the English profits.
2. Debit U. Samson's Current Account with the sterling equivalent of J. Bull's share of the American profits.
   Credit Profit and Loss Appropriation Account with the sterling equivalent of J. Bull's share of the American profits.
   Converse entries would be made for losses.

NEW YORK BOOKS

J. BULL CURRENT ACCOUNT

	$		$
Profit and Loss Appropriation Account:		Profit and Loss Appropriation Account:	
¼ Share of £2,000 at $2 to £ .	1,000	½ Share of $3,200 . .	1,600

PROFIT AND LOSS APPROPRIATION ACCOUNT

	$		$
J. Bull Current Account:		Profit	3,200
½ share	1,600	Manchester Profit . .	1,000
Balance—U. Samson . . .	2,600		
	$4,200		$4,200

MANCHESTER BOOKS

U. SAMSON CURRENT ACCOUNT

	£		£
Profit and Loss Appropriation Account:		Profit and Loss Appropriation Account:	
½ share of $3,200 at $2 to £	800	¼ share of £2,000 .	500

PROFIT AND LOSS APPROPRIATION ACCOUNT

	£		£
U. Samson Current Account: .		Profit	2,000
¼ share	500	New York Profit . . .	800
Balance—J. Bull	2,300		
	£2,800		£2,800

Dissolution. On dissolution it will be necessary to adjust any profit or loss on exchange, such being treated as a profit or loss on realization. It is usual to treat the latter equally between the partners as it cannot strictly be said to arise in the course of trading operations of either of the businesses, but from a settlement of capital balances.

Illustration 109

The following are the Balance Sheets of the partners in the foregoing illustration.

MANCHESTER BALANCE SHEET

	£		£
J. Bull—Capital	5,000	Sundry Assets	4,000
		U. Samson—Current Account	1,000
	£5,000		£5,000

NEW YORK BALANCE SHEET

Assets [1]	$	Liabilities [1]	$
Sundry Assets	52,400	U. Samson—Capital	50,000
		J. Bull—Current Account	2,400
	$52,400		$52,400

[1] In accordance with American practice.

On that date the partnership is dissolved and the assets realize: Manchester, £5,000; New York, $50,000. All the entries relative to the dissolution are to be put through the books at the rate of $2.40 to £. When the final remittance is made the rate is $2.20 to £. Show accounts.

MANCHESTER BOOKS

REALIZATION ACCOUNT

		£		£
Sundry Assets		4,000	Cash	5,000
Expenses		?		
Profit on Realization—				
J. Bull ¾ £750				
U. Samson ¼ 250		1,000		
		£5,000		£5,000

J. BULL CAPITAL

		£			£
Loss on Realization—			Balance b/d		5,000
New York $1,200 at			Profit on Realization—Man-		
$2.40 to £		500	chester		750
Balance c/d		5,250			
		£5,750			£5,750
			Balance b/d		5,250

U. Samson Current Account

		£			£
Balance	b/d	1,000	Profit on Realization—Manchester .		250
			Loss on Realization—New York $1,200 at $2.40 to £ .		500
			Balance . . .	c/d	250
		£1,000			£1,000
Balance	b/d	250			

Cash

		£			
Realization Account . .		5,000			

It will be seen that the total of the Cash and U. Samson Current Account equals the balance due to J. Bull as shown in his Capital Account.

New York Books

Realization Account

	$		$
Sundry Assets . . .	52,400	Cash	50,000
Expenses . . .	?	Loss of Realization—	
		U. Samson ½ 1,200	
		J. Bull ½ 1,200	2,400
	$52,400		$52,400

U. Samson—Capital

		$			$
Loss on Realization—New York . . .		1,200	Balance . . .	b/d	50,000
Balance . . .	c/d	49,400	Profit on Realization—Manchester £250 at $2.40 to £		600
		$50,600			$50,600
			Balance . . .	b/d	49,400

J. BULL —CURRENT ACCOUNT

		$			$
Profit on Realization—Manchester £250 at $2.40 to £		600	Balance . . . . b/d		2,400
Loss on Realization—New York		1,200			
Balance . . . . c/d		600			
		$2,400			$2,400
			Balance . . . . b/d		600

CASH

		$			
Realization Account . .		50,000			

As the rate of exchange at the date of the final remittance is $2.20 to the £ the dollar price of £250 is $550, hence a profit of $50; as this profit is shared equally, U. Samson will retain $25 of the $600 remitting $575 due to J. Bull, i.e. $550 plus his share of profit on exchange of $25. The remittance of $575 at $2.20 to £ (ignoring expenses) will produce £261·36.

The final entries will be:

MANCHESTER BOOKS

J. BULL—CAPITAL

		£p			£p
Balance . . . c/d		5,261·36	Balance . . . b/d		5,250·00
			Profit on remittance—$25 at $2.20 to £ . .		11·36
		£5,261·36			£5,261·36
			Balance . . . b/d		5,261·36

U. SAMSON—CURRENT ACCOUNT

		£p			£p
Balance. . . b/d		250·00	Draft . . .		261·36
Profit on remittance—$25 at $2.20 to £ . .		11·36			
		£261·36			£261·36

CASH

		£p				£p
Balance. . . .	b/d	5,000·00	Balance . . .	c/d	5,261·36
Remittance—						
U. Samson Current Account—£575 at $2.20 to £ .		261·36				
		£5,261·36				£5,261·36
Balance. . . .	b/d	5,261·36				

NEW YORK BOOKS

U. SAMSON—CAPITAL

		$				$
Balance . . .	c/d	49,425	*Balance* . . .	b/d	49,400
			Profit on remittance—£11·36 at $2.20 to £ .		25
		$49,425				$49,425
			Balance . . .	b/d	49,425

J. BULL—CURRENT ACCOUNT

	$				$
Draft—		*Balance* . . .	b/d	600
£261·36 at $2·20 to £ .	575			
Profit on remittance at $2.20 to £ . .	25			
	$600			$600

CASH

		$				$
Balance. . . .	b/d	50,000	Remittance—		
			J. Bull Current Account—£261·36 at $2.20 to £		575
			Balance . . .	c/d	49,425
		$50,000				$50,000
Balance. . .	b/d	49,425				

The cash in hand in each country is now sufficient to pay out the Capital Accounts of J. Bull and U. Samson.

Examination Problem

A, B, and C were in partnership, sharing profits in the proportions of 5, 4, and 3, and accounts were prepared annually as on 31st December. Interest at 5 per cent per annum was allowed on capital accounts, but no interest was charged on drawings.

The partnership agreement provided that in the event of the death of a partner during any year no special accounts should be prepared until the end of the year, when the amount due to the deceased partner's estate was to be calculated as follows:

(a) *Profits* (before charging partnership interest) were to be apportioned *on a time basis* in months up to the end of the calendar month in which the partner died, the profits accruing up to such date to be divided as though the partner had lived to the end of the month.

(b) Goodwill was to be calculated on the basis of *two years' purchase* of the average *profits* (*after deducting partners' interest*) for the three years immediately preceding the end of the month in which the partner died, a year's profits to be apportioned (in months) if necessary.

(c) The deceased partner's capital and current accounts, share of profits under (a) above and of goodwill under (b) above to be added together, and the total so found to carry interest at the rate of 5 per cent per annum from the first day of the month following his death until paid.

The surviving partners, failing any other agreement, were to continue sharing subsequent profits in the same ratio as had previously applied as between themselves.

A died on 20th June 19.4.

On 1st October 19.4, D was admitted as a partner, and the profit sharing ratio from that date as between B, C, and D was 5, 4, and 2; the profits of the year in which D became a partner were agreed to be apportioned on a time basis.

Profits *before* charging any interest, were as follows

Year to 31st December 19.1	.	.	.	£5,142
,,	,,	,,	19.2	.	.	£4,192
,,	,,	,,	19.3	.	.	£3,627
,,	,,	,,	19.4	.	.	£3,976

At no time previous to 19.4 did the Balance Sheet include any Goodwill Account. A's Capital Account stood at £10,000 throughout the whole period up to his death, and B's at £6,000. C had £4,000 up to 1st August 19.4 when he brought in a further £1,200. On 1st October 19.4, D brought in £3,200, of which £2,000 was credited to his Capital Account, while the balance, agreed as representing his share of goodwill, was credited to the Capital Accounts of B and C in their old profit sharing ratios. These several sums were paid over to A's executors immediately they were received, and, in addition, £1,000 was paid over on 1st December 19.4 out of cash in hand.

As on 31st December 19.3, A's Current Account was in credit to the extent of £805, and during 19.3 he had drawn £100 at the commencement of each month.

You are required to calculate the balance due to A's estate and the division of profits between the other partners as on 31st December 19.4. (Calculations to the nearest £.)

(*Adapted from Institute of Chartered Accountants Final.*)

Relevant accounts appear on p. 22214.

Solution

The division of the Interest on the amount due to A's executors is as follows:

		£	£
Interest @ 5% per annum for 1 month on £13,680 .	.	57	
,, ,, ,, ,, 2 months on £12,480 .	.	104	
		—	161
,, ,, ,, ,, 2 months on £9,280 .	.	77	
,, ,, ,, ,, 1 month on £8,280 .	.	35	
		—	112
			£273

Notes (i) Computation of Goodwill:

	£
One-half of profits to 31st December 19.1 . . .	2,571
Profits to 31st December 19.2 . . .	4,192
,, ,, ,, 19.3 . . .	3,627
One-half of profits to 31st December 19.4 . . .	1,988
	12,378
Less Interest on Capital (£1,000 annually) . . .	3,000
	3)9,378
Average	£3,126
2 years' purchase.	£6,252
A's *share* thereof $\frac{5}{12} \times £6,252$. . . .	£2,605

(ii) Statement of Capital Accounts of B and C:

		B £		C £
19.4				
Jan. 1. Balances		6,000		4,000
June 30. *Less* Share of Goodwill credited to A	$\frac{4}{7}$	1,489	$\frac{3}{7}$	1,116
Balances at *30th June* . .		4,511		2,884
Aug. 1. Cash brought in		—		1,200
Balances at *1st August* . .		4,511		4,084
Oct. 1. Share of Goodwill purchased by D .		686	$\frac{3}{7}$	514
		5,197		4,598
Adjustment between B and C *re* purchase of share of goodwill consequent upon change of profit-sharing ratios (per Statement iii). +		86		86
Balances at *1st October* . .		£5,283		£4,512

(iii) Statement of Goodwill Adjustment:

Goodwill (£6,600)

		B £		C £
Old ratio of $\frac{9}{11}$ of Goodwill [i.e. £5,400] . .	$\frac{4}{7}$	3,086	$\frac{3}{7}$	2,314
New ratio of $\frac{9}{11}$ of Goodwill . . .	$\frac{5}{9}$	3,000	$\frac{4}{9}$	2,400
	Cr.	£86	Dr.	£86

The amount of £6,600 is $\frac{11}{2} \times £1,200$—D paying £1,200 for $\frac{2}{11}$ share.

PROFIT AND LOSS APPROPRIATION ACCOUNT FOR THE YEAR ENDED 31ST DECEMBER 19.4

	6 months to 30th June £	3 months to 30th Sept. £	3 months to 31st Dec. £		6 months to 30th June £	3 months to 30th Sept. £	3 months to 31st Dec. £
Interest on Capital				Balance . . . b/d	1,988	994	994
A.	250	57	66				
B.	150	46	56				
C.	100		25				
D.			25				
		161	112				
Interest on Loan (A)—							
Balance							
A.	5/12 620	4/11 417	5/11 334				
B.	4/12 496	4/11 313	4/11 267				
C.	3/12 372		2/11 134				
D.							
	£1,988	£994	£994		£1,988	£994	£994

EXECUTORS OF A (LOAN)

		Months	Interest £	Principal £			Months	Interest £	Principal £
19.4					19.4				
Aug. 1	Cash	5	25	1,200	June 20	Transfer from Capital Account			10,000
Oct. 1	„	3	40	3,200		Transfer from Current Account			205
Dec. 1	„	1	4	1,000		Interest on Capital (to 30th June 19.4)			250
Dec. 31	Balance of Interest to Contra		273			Share of Profits (to 30th June 19.4)			620
	Balance . . . c/d			8,553		B and C—Transfer re Share of Goodwill			2,605
					Dec. 31	Interest on £13,680	6	342	13,680
						Balance of Interest from Contra			273
			£342	£13,953				£342	£13,953
					19.5				
					Jan. 1	Balance . . . b/d			8,553

As B previously had $\frac{4}{7}$ as against $\frac{3}{7}$ to C and is now to have $\frac{5}{9}$ he is a seller of $\frac{1}{63}$ $\left[\dfrac{36-35}{63}\right]$. Such proportion of $\frac{9}{11}$ of £6,600 equals £86.

Treating the Goodwill on the 'Share sold' method the computation is—

(Goodwill £6,600)

	B	C	D
Old ratio . .	$\frac{4}{7}$	$\frac{3}{7}$	—
New ratio . .	$\frac{5}{11}$	$\frac{4}{11}$	$\frac{2}{11}$
	Cr. $\frac{9}{77}$ = £772	Cr. $\frac{5}{77}$ = £428	Dr. $\frac{2}{11}$ = £1,200

Thus D having paid the £1,200, the adjustment as between B and C is:

	B £	C £
Share of Goodwill due . . .	772	428
Credited in accounts . . .	686	514
Adjustment	Cr. £86	Dr. £86

(iv) Statement of Interest on Capital

Dates	M'ths	A Interest	A Capital	B Interest	B Capital¹	C Interest	C Capital¹	D Interest	D Capital
19.4		£	£	£	£	£	£	£	£
Jan. 1 to June 30 .	6	250	10,000	150	6,000	100	4,000		
July 1 to July 31 .	1			57	4,511	12	2,884		
Aug. 1 to Sept. 30.	2			66	4,511	34	4,084		
				— 57		— 46			
Oct. 1 to Dec. 31 .	3			66	5,283	56	4,512	25	2,000
		£250		£273		£202		£25	

(v) *The balances of the Current Accounts of B and C assumed to be kept separately from the Capital Accounts.*

¹ Per Capital Statement (see note ii).

CHAPTER 23

LIMITED COMPANY ACCOUNTS

SECTION A: INTRODUCTION

General Principles

THE subject-matter comprised under this head is probably the most important of all for the examination student, special papers being set in almost all the examinations of the professional bodies on the subject of Limited Company Accounts.

Before proceeding to the accounts proper, it is essential to outline briefly certain important general principles.

These may be summarized as follows:

1. A limited company is a body corporate, that is, an aggregation of persons and individuals, arising by Statute or Royal Charter, having the status of a separate 'being' or person, the liability of whose members is limited according to circumstances.

The type of limited company which most concerns the accountancy profession is that formed under the Companies Acts 1948 to 1976.[1] The company may have a share capital with the liability of the shareholders limited to the amount remaining unpaid on the shares for which they have subscribed; or it may have no share capital, the liability being limited to the amount members agree in the form of a guarantee. It must always be considered as a separate 'being', irrespective of the individuals who have subscribed the necessary capital. As such, it is able to sue or be sued, hold land, carry on business, and, subject to the obvious fact that it must exercise these activities through the medium of animate persons, is generally capable of exercising the functions of an individual, with certain penalties for transgression. Penalties of a monetary nature can be enforced against the company; in addition, companies, like individuals, are liable to have their property seized, e.g. by distress; but clearly, many penalties of a more 'physical' nature must be visited upon the individuals in control. Although it is beyond the scope of this work to deal with legal topics, it may be stated that a limited liability company is incapable of committing a felony; the law of slander has a limited application thereto; whilst the criminal code is but partly applicable to companies. The company begins its legal life by being incorporated, which is evidenced by a certificate of incorporation, and closes it when it is dissolved through the legal process known as 'liquidation'.

2. Share Capital must ALWAYS be kept quite distinct from the balance of profit and loss. In partnership, the proprietors transfer their proportions of profit or loss either to their respective Capital Accounts or to their Current (or Drawings) Accounts. In limited companies, however, no member is entitled to receive a share of the profits until there has been a

---

[1] And older companies incorporated under previous Companies Acts.

declaration of a dividend by the directors, approved by the members. In addition, it will be remembered that partners (subject to contrary agreement) share profits or losses equally, but members of a company share on a CAPITAL basis whenever a distribution of profits is made.

3. There are frequently distinct grades or classes of share capital, distinguished generally by one class having a privilege not possessed by another, e.g. a prior right to the payment of dividends or the first right to capital repayment as against another class of share capital if the company goes into liquidation.

4. A person who LENDS money to a limited liability company usually receives an acknowledgement under seal (which, when witnessed by authorized persons, is the evidence of an act done by a limited liability company). Such lender is termed a Debenture-holder. A loan may or may not be accompanied by a charge on some of the assets of the company; but the existence of a charge is not a necessary LEGAL element, however desirable from a business point of view. It is therefore of the greatest importance to note the contrast between the position of a member and a debenture holder. Where one person holds *both* share *and* debentures, then his right as a member are distinct from those as a debenture holder.

The main distinctions between debentures (and debenture-holders) and shares (and members) are summarized thus:

(*a*) A member is a part owner, i.e. a co-proprietor, whilst a debenture-holder is a CREDITOR, so that:

(*b*) In a liquidation the latter claims payment as a creditor, whilst the member together with his co-members may receive repayment wholly, or in part, only after the costs of liquidation and the liability to creditors, including debenture-holders, have been met.

(*c*) The right to INTEREST on a debenture is not dependent upon profits. It is a right, varying according to the terms of the debenture, which may be enforceable against the company—even if during the period in which the interest is accruing the company has sustained a loss; it therefore constitutes a definite CHARGE against profits; in other words, profits cannot be said to have been earned unless and until full provision has been made in the accounts for debenture interest. Furthermore, the right to payment is not dependent upon any declaration as in the case of a dividend. On the other hand, the member obtains a dividend only when:

(i) there have been profits earned; followed by
(ii) declaration of dividend; which will rarely be such as to divide the whole of the profits earned.

Therefore, such a payment of dividend is a DISPOSITION, DISTRIBUTION, or APPROPRIATION of profits and in no way charge against them. In short, it may be stated: 'no profits and declaration, no dividend'.

(*d*) A debenture may be issued as par, at premium or at a discount, whilst a share (i.e. a portion of the capital) may be issued at par or at a premium; but ONLY SUBJECT TO IMPORTANT RESTRICTIONS laid down in the Companies Acts 1948 and 1967, may it be issued at a discount.

Further, capital (with one exception) is not ordinarily repayable to the members other than in liquidation. Debentures, however, may be either redeemable or permanent.

On the other hand, a common feature is that upon payment, income tax at the standard rate must be deducted from the gross sum payable by way of INTEREST on debentures. In the case of dividends on shares, advance corporation tax (ACT) must be paid to the collector. Such ACT will normally be regarded as a payment on account of the Corporation Tax due on the profits of the year for which the dividend is paid.[1]

5. A limited liability company can only exercise such functions as come within the scope of its powers as laid down by the objects clause of the Memorandum of Association—one of the documents that must be filed with the Registrar of Companies, before incorporation; whilst the directors are endowed with certain powers as laid down in the Articles of Association (which must be filed along with the Memorandum). The Memorandum is the vital document because no confirmation of an act improperly done in contravention of the Memorandum can give validity to the act; being in sharp contrast to the Articles which, as it were, form the by-laws of the company, for an act done beyond the powers defined in the Articles may be confirmed or ratified by the members of the company.

6. The Companies Act 1948 to 1976, require the registration of many acts and transactions. In addition, the company is compelled to furnish details of members and their holdings and many other particulars in a document called the Annual Return; whilst certain books, called statutory Books, must be kept, and subject to certain limitation, some of them, e.g. register of members, are open for inspection by the public.

7. The Companies Act 1948 to 1976, contain provisions as to keeping accounts, furnishing accounts to members and debenture-holders, the holding of meetings, the voting rights of the members, and the contents of the Profit and Loss Account and Balance Sheet.

8. In certain exceptional cases, subject to the sanction of the Court, the share capital of the company may be reduced, modified, or re-arranged.

Alphabetical Summary. In order to assist the student to observe the essential differences between non-limited company and limited company matters the following alphabetical summary is given:

A = Articles; authority of directors; agency of directors and their strict accountability to members; auditor necessary.

B = Borrowing powers; no Bill of Sale can be given as security nor can there be bankruptcy of a limited company; books of account.

C = Capital; control; importance of case law *re* limited companies; corporation tax position.

D = Direction by directors; debentures only in limited company; no drawings in limited companies; dividends; disclosure of certain details, e.g. directors' names, etc.; distringas notice; death of

---

[1] See p. 2356 for further details.

       member does not dissolve the company; disclosure of required
       details.

E = Enlargement of scope of company activities limited by statute;
       legal entity of a limited company.

F = Forfeiture of share in limited companies; foreign holders of shares
       do not affect domicile of company; regulations regarding com-
       panies registered in foreign countries; fiduciary position of direc-
       tors; filing documents.

G = Governing Acts—Companies Acts 1948 to 1976; [Partnership Act
       1890; Limited Partnership Act 1907; Business Names Act 1916,
       the latter applying equally to sole traders, partnership, and
       Limited Companies].

H = Home or domicile.

 I = Taxation position; invalidity of certain acts beyond the scope of the
       company: Interest on Construction Capital: Investigation regula-
       tions.

J = (Usually) joint and several liability of holders of shares to pay the
       amount necessary on the shares.

K = Keeping open certain Statutory Books in the case of a limited
       company.

L = Liability of members limited; lien of company on shares; lunacy or
       insanity of member of company does not give any right to
       dissolve; liquidation.

M = Meetings; memorandum; management; minutes.

N = Notices of meetings; name of company; numbers of members and
       directors, minimum and maximum.

O = Office (registered); objects clause; officers.

P = Prospectus; profits; preliminary expenses; priorities of classes of
       members to dividends and capital; proxies; polls; public and
       private companies.

Q = Qualification share of directors; quorum.

R = Reserves; Reduction of Capital; Reports of Directors and Au-
       ditors; Requisitionist meetings; Registered office.

S = Stamp duties; seal of company; Stock Exchange quotation; secret-
       ary; Stock Transfer Act 1963 and Stock Exchange (Completion
       of Bargains) Act 1976.

T = Transfer of shares; termination of company, time limits for regis-
       tering documents, notices, etc., Table A; Tax.

U = Underwriting.

V = Voting power.

W = Winding-up provisions.

The above alphabetical indicator, it must be understood, does no more
than point out to the student the dominant legal topics connected with the
affiairs of limited companies.

Before proceeding with the treatment of the accounts a brief summary is appended showing the chief differences between a partnership and a limited company; and private and public companies.

Points	Partnership	Limited Company
1. Regulating Act(s)	Partnership Act 1890. Limited Partnership Act 1907. Business Names Act 1916.[1]	Companies Acts 1948 to 1976. Business Names Act 1916.[1]
2. Members	Unlimited in respect of Solicitors, Accountants and Stockbrokers provided that in all such partnerships each partner is qualified. Limited to 20 generally (including banking partnerships).	Private company—minimum of 2 and maximum of 50 (exclusive of certain individuals). Public company—minimum of 7 and no maximum (except there can be no more members than shares).
3. Entity	Not a legal entity, except in Scotland	Is a legal entity.
4. Liability	Unlimited, except in a limited partnership as regards the limited partner.	Limited. [Directors' Liability may be made unlimited.]
5. Capital	As partners agree. Alterations as partners agree. Withdrawals as partners agree.	Maximum issued share capital must not exceed authorized capital. A duty of £1% is payable on issued capital. Alterations in rights must conform to certain formalities; capital cannot usually be withdrawn.
6. Profits	As partners agree, otherwise equally. May be added to capitals.	Distribution of profits depends upon declaration based upon type and numbers of shares held. Cannot be added to capital unless by way of bonus shares.
7. Management	All entitled to take part (excepting a limited partner); inspect books and take copies.	Management vested in a number of individuals, usually but not necessarily shareholders, called directors. Members cannot inspect account books, but must be sent Balance Sheets and Profit and Loss Accounts.[2]
8. Tax	Profits liable to Income Tax. Profits not liable to Corporation Tax. *All* income receivable by a partner from the firm is included in the partnership assessments for Income Tax. No tax deduction on distribution. Upon a change of partners the business may be assessed as a continuing or a new business. Loan interest is paid *gross*, i.e. without deduction of Income Tax.	Profits not liable to Income Tax. Profits liable to Corporation Tax. Remuneration of directors is a proper charge against company profits. When a distribution is made to shareholders an advance payment of Corporation Tax (ACT) must be made to the Inland Revenue. ACT can normally be set off against total Corporation Tax liability. Upon partners converting the business into a limited company, the taxation rules relating to a discontinued business (*re* partners) and to a new business (*re* limited company) must be observed. Capital allowances unused by partnership will be lost, but losses unused may be set off against the income of the partners who are shareholders in the new company. Loan interest is paid net, i.e. after deduction of Income Tax.
9. Audit	Not compulsory.	Compulsory.
10. Winding-up	Carried out under bankruptcy rules if bankrupt.	Carried out in alternative ways under the Companies Acts.

Points	Partnership	Limited Company
11. Books	No legal necessity to keep books of account but, in practice, books of account are necessary and open to inspection of all partners.	Proper books of account must be kept. Not accessible to members (unless regulations so provide).
12. Powers, including rights	Can carry on such trade or business agreed upon; and variation by agreement.	Limited to what is prescribed in the Memorandum of Association. [In practice, very wide powers are prescribed in the memorandum.] Further powers can be acquired within certain stated limits. Powers of *Directors* can by special resolution be curtailed or varied.
13. Control	Equal, subject to contrary agreement.	Immediate control by Directors. Ultimate control by the members, but in both cases voting power is *deciding* factor. As shares can be issued carrying no voting power real control might be exercised by Directors without holding more than a very small amount of the capital.
14. Devolution and Transfer	Share transferable only if remaining partners agree. Death dissolves firm (unless partnership agreement provides otherwise) and deceased's share *must* be paid as agreed.	Shares (subject to restrictions or conditions in Articles) are transferable without consent of other members; thus on death of member share is more readily renderable. Death of member does not dissolve the company. Shares are not repayable: personal representative must either (a) hold, (b) sell, or (c) transfer to a legatee where empowered to do so.
15. Capital Transfer Tax on death	Payable always on value of partner's share based on 'asset values' [including goodwill].	Payable on market value of shares held by deceased member, based on asset values in certain cases under the Finance Acts (notably S.55 F.A. 1940).
16. Statutory Requirements	No special stamp duties. No publicity or returns. (Except in Limited Partnership.)	Special stamp duties on formation. Publicity of the information required on registration: on creating charges or through annual return to Registrar of Companies.
17. Death of member	Disturbance of business dissolves partnership.	No disturbance; legal entity continues.

[1] The Registrar can refuse to register names he considers undesirable, both in the case of partnerships and sole traders and also companies. The control of business names is now contained in Companies Act 1981 Secs. 28 to 30.

[2] In addition, it is possible to give an interest in the business to members of a family by a parent Director without disturbance of control or involving the donees in the risk of personal liability; similarly, an interest in the business can be given to responsible and deserving employees.

Private Companies. A private company is defined by the Companies Act 1948, Sect. 28, as follows:

A company which *by its articles*:

(*a*) restricts the right to transfer its shares;

(*b*) limits the number of its members to fifty, not including persons who are in the employment of the company and persons who, having been formerly in the employment of the company, were while in that employment, and have continued after the determination of that employment to be, members of the company; and

(c) prohibits any invitation to the public to subscribe for any shares or debentures of the company.[1]

Joint-holders of share are counted for this purpose as one person.

The differences between private and public companies may be tabulated as under:

Points	Private	Public
1. Minimum number of members	Two.	Seven.
2. Maximum number of members	Fifty (cf. above).	Unlimited (cf. above).
3. Transfer of shares	Restricted.	Unrestricted.
4. Invitations to the public to subscribe	Not allowed.	Allowed.
5. Statutory report and meeting	Not necessary.	Necessary.
6. Minimum number of directors	One.	Two.
7. Restrictions on appointment of directors	Not applicable.	Applicable.
8. Filing of statement in lieu of prospectus	Not required.	Required.
9. Restrictions as to minimum subscription and allotment	Not applicable.	Applicable.
10. Restrictions as to commencement of business	Not applicable.	Applicable.
11. Annual Return—inclusion therein of the last Profit and Loss Account and Balance Sheet and Auditor's Report and other documents	Must be sent to Registrar of Companies.	Must be sent to Registrar of Companies.
12. Share warrants	Cannot issue.	May issue.
13. Proxy holders	May speak at meetings.	May not speak at meetings.
14. Age limit	None.	Normally 70 years of age.
15. Resolution for appointment of Directors	Not applicable.	Separate for each.

[1] Including an offer or invitation made to any section of the public, whether selected as members or debenture-holders of the company concerned, or as clients of the person issuing the prospectus or in any other manner. But the offer or invitation will not be so treated if in all the circumstances it can properly be regarded as not being calculated to result, directly or indirectly, in the shares or debentures becoming available for subscription or purchase by persons other than those receiving the offer or invitation, or otherwise as being a domestic concern of the persons making and receiving it, so that a provision in a company's articles prohibiting invitations to the public to subscribe for shares or debentures shall not be taken as prohibiting an invitation to members or debenture-holders which can properly be regarded as conforming to the above conditions (vide Companies Act 1948, Sect. 55).

SUMMARY OF DIFFERENT TYPES OF COMPANIES

Point of Difference	Statutory Company	Joint Stock Company	Chartered Company
Constitution Powers	Special Act of Parliament Laid down by Act; and alterable thereunder	Companies Acts Laid down by Memorandum of Association; with right to amend within certain stated limits	Royal Charter Laid down by Royal Charter and unalterable (except by new Charter)
Liability	Limited	Usually limited; may be unlimited if laid down by Memorandum of Association	Limited
Numbers	Limited by number of shares	Limited by number of shares in a public company. Limited to 50 (excluding past or present employees) in a private company. Minimum numbers, public 7; private 2	Limited by shares; or may be unlimited according to the terms of the Charter
Control Accounts	Directors Compulsory (each Act lays down particular requirements)	Directors Compulsory	Directors (or Governors) As laid down by Charter—usually compulsory
Audit	Do.	Do.	Do.

LIMITED COMPANY ACCOUNTS

The general principles of accounting apply to the accounts of limited companies, modified in detail to fit the special peculiarities of such companies and in certain instances to comply with legal requirements. In addition, certain books are required to be kept, and certain information furnished to the Registrar of Companies.

It will readily be perceived that some measure of protection must be afforded to the members of the company, who, unlike partners, cannot usually personally direct the business of the company and (in the case of a large company) will not be acquainted with each other. The Companies Act 1929, modified in the light of the experience gained from the operation of previous Companies Acts, permitted the exercise of reasonable powers by the persons in control of the company free from unwarranted interference from the body of members, whilst at the same time it made numerous provisions for the safeguarding of the interests of the members.

The Companies Act 1947 (substantially enacting the recommendations of the Cohen Committee's Report, made after a very exhaustive inquiry into the deficiencies, ambiguities and weakness of the Companies Act 1929) considerably stabilized this relationship between directors and members.

In order to obtain a thorough mastery of company accounting, the essential requirements of the Companies Acts 1948 to 1976 so far as they have bearing on the accountancy aspect, must be assimilated. Below are enumerated the vital matters, full treatment of which cannot be contemplated here as much of the explanation lies within the scope of a legal treatise.

1. The definition of a joint-stock company.
2. The classification of incorporated bodies.
3. The method of formation of an incorporated body.
4. The distinction between private and public companies.
5. The contents and significance of the Memorandum of Association, particularly in relation to objects.
6. The contents and significance of the Articles of Association.
7. The contents and significance of Table 'A'.
8. Prospectus; minimum subscription.
9. Statement in lieu of prospectus.
10. Certificate of incorporation and certificate entitling company to commence business.
11. The meaning of the company terms: vendor, promoter, etc.
12. Common and offical seal.
13. Officers of the company.
14. Share certificates and share warrants.
15. Types of meetings: procedure, quorum, polls, proxies, and resolutions.
16. Stamp duties.
17. Preliminary expenses.
18. The law relating to transfers, particularly blank transfers, and certified transfers.

In addition, the following matters relating to the accounting side will be specifically dealt with as under—

(I) In Chapter 23, Section B.

19. Profit and Loss Account and Balance Sheet; the keeping of accounts; the furnishing of accounts to members; Auditors' and Directors' Reports.
20. Statutory Books; Annual Return.
21. Statistical Books.
22. (II) In Chapter 23 Section C. Registration and filing of resolutions and documents.
23. Company Taxation comprising: Corporation Tax; Advance Corporation Tax; Treatment of Taxation in Limited Company Accounts; Close Companies.

(III) In the following sub-chapters limited company accounting will be dealt with in detail.

24. Share capital: issue, alteration, reduction, consolidation and sub-division, reorganization, forfeiture and reissue of shares. (Chapter 23, Section D. and Section F.)
25. Debentures: issue, interest, and redemption. (Chapter 23, Section E.)
26. Openings and 'acquisition' entries of a company; underwriting commission. (Chapter 23, Section G.)
27. Profits: divisible, capital, prior to incorporation (and losses; Final Accounts and Illustration of Published Final Accounts with annexed Report of the Auditors and Report of the Directors. (Chapter 23, Sections H and G.)

28. Dividends, including arrears of cumulative preference dividends; forfeiture; scrip dividends and bonus shares. (Chapter 23, Section I.)

30. Reconstructions, amalgamations, and absorptions. (Chapter 23, Section J.)

NOTE. IN SECTIONS B TO J WHICH FOLLOW, REFERENCES IN BRACKETS ARE TO THE COMPANIES ACT 1948, UNLESS OTHERWISE STATED. IN SECTION B, HOWEVER, REFERENCES IN BRACKETS TO SCHEDULE 2 RELATE TO THE COMPANIES ACT 1967.

SECTION B. ACCOUNTING PERIOD, ACCOUNTING RECORDS, DUTIES OF DIRECTORS ETC.

The Companies Act 1976, introduced two new expressions:

(a) *The Accounting Reference Period* is the period which the Directors are required to prepare a profit and loss account and balance sheet in terms of S.1 of the C.A. 1976.

(b) *The Accounting Reference Date* is the last date of the Accounting Reference Period.

S.2 C.A. 1976 details the method of determining the Accounting Reference Period, which in brief permits a company to notify the Registrar the date to which the annual accounts will be prepared; in the case of an established company the notice requires to be given before the S.1 C.A. 1976 operational date (which was 1st October 1977), and in the case of a new company within 6 months of the date of incorporation. If no such notice is given, the Accounting Reference Date will usually be 31st March. However the Registrar within 2 years from 1st October 1977 may agree with the company an alternative date (S.2(3) C.A. 1976).

In terms of S.2(4) C.A. 1976 the first Accounting Reference Period shall be more than 6 months and not more than 18 months from either the date of the accounts prepared before 1st October 1977 or in the case of a new company from the date of incorporation. Thereafter accounts will be prepared for 12 monthly periods ending on successive accounting reference dates. The Directors may in terms of S.1(2) and (3) C.A. 1976 in fact prepare the accounts to a date not more than seven days on either side of the Accounting Reference Date.

S.3 C.A. 1976 gives the company an option in prescribed circumstances to subsequently amend the Accounting Reference Date. In terms of S.1(1) C.A. 1976 each Accounting Reference Period is a 'Financial Year' whether it is a 12-month period or not.

Accounting Records

Under S.12 C.A. 1976, every company must keep adequate accounting records in order to:

(a) disclose with reasonable accuracy, at any time, the financial position of the company at that time: and

(b) enable the directors to ensure that any balance sheet and profit and loss account published give a true and fair view of the company's state of affairs and profit or loss.

(c) provide details of all sums of money received and expended;

(d) record the assets and liabilities of the company;

(e) maintain stocktaking records at the end of the financial year;

(f) maintain, except for retail sales, sufficient detail to enable the goods and the buyers and sellers to be identified.

The accounting records must be kept at the registered office of the company or at such other place as the directors of the company think fit and shall at all times be open to inspection by the officers of the company.

The accountancy records must be kept, in the case of a private company for three years and in any other case for six years.

When accounting records are kept outside Great Britain, such accounts and returns with respect thereto as will disclose with reasonable accuracy the financial position, at intervals not exceeding six months, must be:

(i) sent to, and

(ii) kept at a place in Great Britain.

They must be open to inspection at all times by the officers of the company and be such as will enable the company's Balance Sheet and Profit and Loss Account to be prepared.

Reasonable steps must be taken to comply with the accounting provisions of the Act, but an officer of the company will not be liable if he can show that he acted honestly and in the circumstances in which the business was carried on the default was excusable (S.12(10) C.A. 1976).

Accounting records other than bound books are permitted provided adequate precautions are taken against falsification (S. 436).

Duties of Directors to Lay and Deliver Accounts

The Directors must lay before the company in general meeting accounts for each financial year. The accounts comprise (a) Profit and Loss Account (or in the case of a non trading company an Income and Expenditure Account) and Balance Sheet which must comply with the requirements of Schedule 2 to the Companies Act 1967.[1] (b) Auditors' Report (c) Directors' Report. In the case of companies with subsidiaries, group accounts must be prepared (S.8(1) C.A. 1976). Copies of accounts must be delivered to the Registrar of Companies (S.7 C.A. 1976).

The time limit for laying the accounts before the company in general meeting and delivery to the Registrar are (a) for a private company not later than 10 months and (b) for a company other than a private company not later than 7 months after the end of the financial year (S.6(2) C.A. 1976). Exceptional circumstances where these limits may be varied are detailed in S.6(2) C.A. 1976. Severe penalties for non-compliance are contained in S.4 and 5 C.A. 1976.

Miscellaneous Provisions of the Companies Act 1976

S.21 Provides inter alia that a formal notification must accompany any memorandum registered under S.12 of the C.A. 1948 of the names, addresses and other particulars of the first directors and secretaries.

S.22 Deals with notification to the Registrar of subsequent changes to

[1] A comprehensive illustration appears in p. 23236.

directors and secretaries.

S.23 All companies are now required to have a registered office as from the date of incorporation.

S.24 Directors must notify their own (or their spouses' or infant children's) interests in the shares of the company or its group companies within 5 days of acquisition or any change (formerly 14 days S.31(2) C.A. 1967).

S.25 A new obligation is placed on a company to notify directors share and debenture-holdings to a Stock Exchange which lists the shares and debentures of that company.

S.26 Any person who acquires 5% of the voting share capital must notify the company accordingly within 5 days.

S.27 An important power is given to companies to establish the beneficial interests in its share capital.

S.31 The Secretary of State may serve a notice on an oversea company trading in Great Britain that the corporate name is undesirable for use in this country.

S.42 Inter alia replaces the expression 'books of account' throughout the 1948 and 1967 Acts by 'accounting records'.

Disclosure Requirements in Respect of Directors' Reports

The current law concerning the matters required to be disclosed in Directors' Reports is contained in the following sections of the Companies Act 1948 to 1976.

Companies Act 1948 (as amended by Companies Act 1976)

SECTION 157 (1). There shall be attached to every balance sheet prepared under S.1 of the Companies Act 1976 (or under that section taken with S.150 of this Act) a report by the directors with respect to the state of the company's affairs, the amount, if any, which they recommend should be paid by way of dividend, and the amount, if any, which they propose to carry to reserves.

Companies Act 1967

SECTION 16 (1). The Directors' Report shall state the names of the persons who, at any time during the financial year, were directors of the company and the principal activities of the company and of its subsidiaries in the course of that year and any significant change in those activities in that year, and shall also:

(a) if significant changes in the fixed assets of the company or of any of its subsidiaries have occurred in that year, contain particulars of the changes, and, if, in the case of such of those assets as consist in interests in land, the market value thereof (as at the end of that year) differs substantially from the amount at which they are included in the balance sheet and the difference is, in the opinion of the directors, of such significance as to require that the attention of members of the company or of holders of debentures thereof should be drawn thereto, indicate the difference with such degree of precision as is practicable;

[Note. Paragraph (a) does not apply to a banking, discount, insurance or shipping company.]

(b) if, in that year, the company has issued any shares, state the reason for making the issue, the classes of shares issued and, as respects each class of shares, the number issued and the consideration received by the company for the issue, and if, in that year, it has issued any debentures, state the reason for making the issue, the classes of debentures issued and, as respects each class of debentures, the amount issued and the consideration received by the company for the issue;

(c) if, at the end of that year, there subsists a contract with the company in which a director of the company has, or at any time in that year had, in any way, whether directly or indirectly, an interest, or there has, at any time in that year, subsisted a contract with the company in which a director of the company had, at any time in that year, in any way, whether directly or indirectly, an interest (being, in either case, in the opinion of the directors, a contract of significance in relation to the company's business and in which the director's interest is or was material), contain:

   (i) a statement of the fact of the contract's subsisting or, as the case may be, having subsisted;

   (ii) the names of the parties to the contract (other than the company);

   (iii) the name of the director (if not a party to the contract);

   (iv) an indication of the nature of the contract; and

   (v) an indication of the nature of the director's interest in the contract;

Note. The references in paragraph (c) to a contract do not include references to a director's contract of service or to a contract between the company and another body corporate, being a contract in which a director of the company has or had an interest by virtue only of his being a director of that other body.

(d) if, at the end of that year, there subsist arrangements to which the company is a party, being arrangements whose objects are, or one of whose objects is, to enable directors of the company to acquire benefits by means of the acquisition of shares in, or debentures of, the company or any other body corporate, or there have, at any time in that year, subsisted such arrangements as aforesaid to which the company was a party, contain a statement explaining the effect of the arrangements and giving the names of the persons who at any time in that year were directors of the company and held, or whose nominees held, shares or debentures acquired in pursuance of the arrangements;

(e) *Note.* This sub-section is exceptionally long and complex, and it is considered that merely to reproduce it would confuse students. Consequently the FOLLOWING PARAPHRASE is considered to be sufficient for present purposes:

   State the interests of directors[1] in shares or debentures of the company or any other company in the group at the beginning and the end of the financial year or the date of first appointment as a director if later.

(f) contain particulars of any matters (other than those required to be dealt with by paragraphs (a) to (d) above in the circumstances therein mentioned, that required to be dealt with by paragraph (e) above or those required to be dealt with by the following provisions of this Part of this Act) so far as they are material for the appreciation of the state of the company's affairs by its members, being matters the disclosures or which will not, in the opinion of the directors, be harmful to the business of the company or any of its subsidiaries.

Note. The matters contained in Sections 17–20 and 22 which follow, concerning the content of the Directors' Report, are the AUTHOR'S INTERPRETATION of these Sections of the Act.

SECTION 17. If the company or group has carried on two or more classes of business, other than banking or discounting or a class exempted by the Department of Trade, that in the opinion of the directors differ substantially[2] from each other the Directors' Report must state the proportions in which the turnover and the profit or loss before taxation is attributable to each class. However a company which is neither a holding company nor a subsidiary is exempted from the requirement to disclose in its Directors' Report the turnover and profit and loss before taxation where classes of business carried on differ substantially provided that the total turnover does not exceed £250,000[3].

---

[1] Interests of directors include the interests of directors' spouses and infant children who are not themselves directors of the company, C.A. 1967, S.31 as amended by S.24 C.A. 1976.

[2] Many accountants are of the opinion that classes of business differ substantially mainly in circumstances of vertically integrated businesses. For example where machine tools and furniture are manufactured separate statements in respect of each class should be shown.

[3] Irrespective of the different classes of business carried on exemption from disclosure is provided by C.A. 1967 Schedule 2 (13A) where the turnover does not exceed £250,000 [Companies (Accounts) Regulations 1971].

SECTION 18. The Directors' Report must contain a statement of the average number[1] of persons employed by the company and any subsidiaries in each week of the financial year concerned and the aggregate gross remuneration (including bonuses) paid or payable in respect of that financial year to the persons by reference to whom the number employed is ascertained. This requirement does not apply to companies with less than 100 employees or to companies which are wholly owned subsidiaries of a company incorporated in Great Britain.

SECTION 19. The Directors' Report must contain a statement of the amount of money given during the financial year in excess of £50 for political and/or charitable purposes showing the total amounts respectively. In respect of political contributions in excess of £50 the name of each recipient and the identity of the political parties must be disclosed. A wholly owned subsidiary of a company incorporated in Great Britain is relieved of these requirements. For a group, however, the report concerning the parent company must disclose the appropriate information relating to the group as a whole.

SECTION 20.[2] In respect of a company without subsidiaries whose business involves the supplying of goods and whose turnover exceeds £250,000 the director's report must contain a statement showing the value of goods exported from the United Kingdom during the financial year. If no goods have been exported from the United Kingdom that fact must be stated. Disclosures of the exports must be given in group accounts where the total turnover of the group exceeds £50,000.

SECTION 22. Where an item is shown in the directors' report instead of in the accounts the corresponding amount for the immediately preceding year of that item must normally be shown in the report.

The Balance Sheet must be signed by two of the directors or the sole director (Sect. 155) and the Directors' Report (Sect. 157), Profit and Loss Account and Auditors' Report (Sect. 156) must be attached.

A copy of the Balance Sheet and Profit and Loss Account (with group accounts if applicable) together with all documents required by law to be annexed thereto, must be sent to all the members and debenture-holders not less than twenty-one days before the meeting takes place (Sect. 158). If sent less than twenty-one days before the meeting, it will be deemed to have been duly circulated if all members entitled to attend and vote so agree (Sect. 158 (1) (c)). The above requirements apply equally to private as well as public companies.

Where a company has subsidiaries, group accounts must be circulated to members and laid before the company in Annual General Meeting, subject to certain exceptions, e.g. where the company is itself a wholly-owned subsidiary of a body corporate in Great Britain.

Auditors. Sect. 14 of the Companies Act 1967 provides:

1. The auditors of a company shall make a report to the members on the accounts examined by them, and on every Balance Sheet, every Profit and Loss Account, and all group accounts laid before the company in general meeting during their tenure of office.

2. The auditors' report shall be read before the company in general meeting and shall be opened to inspection by any member.

3. The report shall:

(a) except in the case of a company that is entitled to avail itself, and has availed itself, of the benefit of any of the provisions of Part III of Schedule 8 to the principal Act, state whether in the auditors' opinion the company's balance sheet and profit and loss account and (if it is a holding company submitting group accounts) the group accounts have been properly

---

[1] The average number is ascertained by aggregating the number of employees, under contracts of service, employed full time or part time for each week (or part thereof) of the financial year, and dividing by the number of weeks in the financial year.

[2] As amended by Companies (Accounts) Regulations 1971.

prepared in accordance with the provisions of the principal Act and this Act and whether in their opinion a true and fair view is given:

(i) in the case of the balance sheet, of the state of the company's affairs as at the end of its financial year;

(ii) in the case of the profit and loss account (if it be not framed as a consolidated profit and loss account), of the company's profit or loss for its financial year;

(iii) in the case of group accounts submitted by a holding company, of the state of affairs and profit or loss of the company and its subsidiaries dealt with thereby, so far as concerns members of the company;

(b) in the said excepted case, state whether in the auditor's opinion the company's balance sheet and profit and loss account and (if it is a holding company submitting group accounts) the group accounts have been properly prepared in accordance with the provisions of the principal Act and this Act.

4. It shall be the duty of the auditors of a company, in preparing their report under this section, to carry out such investigations as will enable them to form an opinion as to the following matters, that is to say:

(a) whether proper books of account have been kept by the company and proper returns adequate for their audit have been received from branches not visited by them; and

(b) whether the company's balance sheet and (unless it is framed as a consolidated profit and loss account) profit and loss account are in agreement with the books of account and returns;

and if the auditors are of opinion that proper books of account have not been kept by the company or that proper returns adequate for their audit have not been received from branches not visited by them, or if the balance sheet and (unless it is framed as a consolidated profit and loss account) profit and loss account are not in agreement with the books of account and returns, the auditors shall state that fact in their report.

5. Every auditor of a company shall have a right of access at all times to the books and accounts and vouchers of the company, and shall be entitled to require from the officers of the company such information and explanation as he thinks necessary for the performance of the duties of the auditors.

6. If the auditors fail to obtain all the information and explanations which, to the best of their knowledge and belief, are necessary for the purposes of their audit, they shall state that fact in their report.

7. The auditors of a company shall be entitled to attend any general meeting of the company and to receive all notices of, and other communications relating to, any general meeting which any member of the company is entitled to receive, and to be heard at any general meeting which they attend on any part of the business of the meeting which concerns them as auditors.

Furthermore, there is a provision in each of:

(a) Sect. 196 of the 1948 Act which requires disclosure of the amounts of directors' emoluments, pensions, etc. (see pp 2342–2344).

(b) Sect. 6 of the 1967 Act which requires further particulars of directors' emoluments (see pp. 2344–2345).

(c) Sect. 8 of the 1967 Act which requires particulars of employees whose emoluments are £10,000 or more (see p. 2345), that:

If in the case of any accounts the requirements of these sections are not complied with, it shall be the duty of the auditors of the company by whom the accounts are examined to include in their report thereon, so far as they are reasonably able to do so, a statement giving the required particulars.

Reserve Liability. This term (which is to be seen on the liabilities side of the Balance Sheet of some limited companies) is given to that part of the subscribed capital of a limited company that can only be called up in the event of, and for the purpose of, liquidation. Under Sect. 60,

Companies Act 1948, a company may, by special resolution, take power to determine that a specified part of each share shall remain uncalled, except for the above-mentioned purpose.

A considerable reserve liability is maintained by most of the large banks for the protection of depositors.

The Statutory Report and Meeting. Every *public* company which has a share capital, whether limited by shares or guarantee, must hold a general meeting of the company not less than one and not more than three months from the date at which the company is entitled to commence business. (Sect. 130 (1).)

At least FOURTEEN DAYS before this meeting the directors must forward to every member of the company a copy of the statutory report.

The statutory report must be certified by NOT less than TWO directors of the company, or where there are less than two directors, by the sole director and manager. It must contain the following:

(i) The total number of shares allotted, distinguishing shares allotted as fully or partly paid up otherwise than in cash, and stating in the case of shares partly paid up to the extent to which they are paid up, and in either case the consideration for which they were allotted.

(ii) The total amount of cash received by the company in respect of all the shares allotted, distinguished as in (i) above.

(iii) An abstract of the receipts and payments of the company made up to a date within SEVEN DAYS of the DATE OF THE REPORT, showing under separate headings the receipts in respect of shares and *debentures* and *other* sources, and the payments thereout, and the particulars of the balance in hand.

(iv) An account or estimate of the preliminary expenses of the company.

(v) The names, addresses, and description of the directors, auditors (if any), managers (if any), and secretary of the company.

(vi) The particulars of any contract, the modification of which is to be submitted to the meeting for its approval, together with the particulars of the modification or proposed modification.

The statutory report shall, so far as it relates to the shares allotted by the company, and to the cash received in respect of such shares, and to the receipts and payments of the company on capital account, be certified as correct by the auditors, if any of the company. The above provisions do NOT apply to a **private** company.

Illustration 1

On 1st January a company was formed under the name of Stationers Co., Ltd., to take over the business of A. Page, wholesale stationer. On 15th January a prospectus was issued by the company inviting applications for 90,000 shares of £1 each payable £0·25 on application, £0·25 on allotment, and £0·25 three months after allotment, and £0·25 six months after allotment; the vendor was to receive 10,000 fully-paid shares as part discharge of the purchase consideration of £40,000. The offer was fully subscribed, and the vendor duly paid.

The trading receipts to 3rd March amounted to £10,500 and trading payments to the same date £1,800; the date to which the Cash Account is drawn is 3rd March.

The preliminary expenses amounted to £4,500, and it was estimated that they would eventually reach £7,000.

A further £16,000 was expended on 1st March on the purchase of additional plant.

The company received the certificate entitling it to commence business on 26th January, the statutory meeting being held on 21st March, and the report dated 6th March.

THE COMPANIES ACT 1948

No. of Company...............

REPORT pursuant to Sect. 130 of the Companies Act 1948, of...

......................*Stationers Company*,......................*Limited.*

(*a*) The total number of shares allotted is..........*100,000*.......... of which.........*10,000* ....are allotted.........*as fully paid up in consideration of part of the purchase price of sundry assets acquired by the company*.........and upon each of the remaining shares the sum of..........*£0·50*..........has been paid in cash.

(*b*) The total amount of cash received by the Company in respect of the shares issued wholly for cash is..........*£45,000*..........and on the shares issued partly for cash is £..........*nil*.......... .

(*c*) The Receipts and Payments of the Company to the Third day of March are as follows:

Particulars of Receipts	£	Particulars of Payments	£
Amount Received on Application and Allotment of 90,000 shares	45,000	*Preliminary Expenses*	4,500
Trading Receipts .	10,500	*Purchase of Plant* . . .	16,000
		Vendor	30,000
		Trading Payments . . .	1,800
		Balance Deposit and Current Accounts at the Central Bank, Ltd. . .	3,200
	£55,500		£55,500

The following is an account (estimate) of the Preliminary Expenses of the Company:

Contract Stamps, Solicitors' Fees, etc..	£7,000

(*d*) Names, Addresses, and Descriptions of the Directors, auditors (if any), managers (if any), and Secretary of the Company:

Surname	Christian Name	Address	Description

(*e*) Particulars of any Contract the modification of which is to be submitted to the Meeting for its approval, together with particulars of the modification or proposed modification:

....

....

We hereby certify this Report,

....

.... } Directors.

We hereby certify that so much of this Report as relates to the shares allotted by the Company and to the Cash received in respect of such shares and to the receipts and payments of the Company on Capital Account is correct.

....

Auditors.

Dated this.......*Sixth*.......day of......*March*.......19...

Statutory Books. The Statutory books are:

(*a*) Register of members. (*b*) Annual return. (*c*) Minute book.

(*d*) Register of directors and their interests in the company or group as the case may be.

(*e*) Register of charges.

(*f*) A copy of every instrument creating a CHARGE, although this is not strictly a book; but if a debenture is issued without conferring upon the lender any charge (which includes mortgage) there is no compulsion to keep a debenture register.[1]

Register of Members. A person acquiring shares becomes a member of the company on the date of the entry into the register, except for the signatories to the memorandum who become members from the date of incorporation of the company.

A member ceases to be such upon the date of the entry of cessation in the register.

A person may become (or cease to be) a member by transfer or

---

[1] Whether the debenture is secured or not, there is no legal necessity to keep a register of debenture-holders, although this will usually be essential in practice. If one is kept, Sections 86 and 87 of the 1948 Act apply.

transmission; become a member by allotment; and cease to be a member by surrender, forfeiture, rescission, repudiation, expropriation, enforcement by the company of its lien, and by the winding-up of the company.

The Register which contains the details required by the Companies Act 1948, must be kept open at the prescribed office for inspection by members (gratis) and other persons (upon payment).

The office above mentioned is (a) the Registered Office of the company, (b) that where the work of making up the register is done, or (c), where the work of making it up is done by an agent, e.g. Registrar employed by the company, at that agent's office.

The Register must be kept in England by an English Company and in Scotland by a Scottish Company. The Registrar of Companies must be notified of the place where the Register of members is kept and of any change in that place unless it has always been and is still kept at the Registered office (Sect. 110).

Annual Return.[2] The return must be made within forty-two days after the annual general meeting (whether or not that meeting is the first or only ordinary general meeting, or the first or only general meeting of that year) and forwarded to the Registrar of Companies *forthwith* (Sect. 126).

If a company has a share capital, it must in every year make a return of all persons who, on the fourteenth day after the annual general meeting of the company for the year, are members of the company and of all persons who ceased to be members since the date of the last return.

The company need not make up an annual return in the year of its incorporation, or, if it is not required to hold an annual general meeting during the following year, in *that* year (Sect. 124).

The return is required from **all** companies—public and private—and, except for assurance companies which have submitted a copy of their accounts when depositing copies with the Department of Trade, may include:

(a) A written and certified true copy of every Balance Sheet laid before the company in general meeting **during the period** to which the return relates, and

(b) A copy of the Directors' Report accompanying any such Balance Sheet (and prescribed annexable documents) certified in the same way as the Balance Sheet.

The Annual Return, the certificate as to any Balance Sheet included therein, and any certificate as to the annual return of a private company must be signed by *both* a director and the secretary of the company S.128.

Minute Book. The Companies Act 1948 (Sects. 145 and 146), requires the keeping and availability for inspection by members of a book containing the minutes of every general meeting of the COMPANY; in addition, there must be a Minute Book of the directors—not available for general inspection. It should be observed that where a company adopts Table A it must keep a DIRECTORS' ATTENDANCE BOOK.

[2] A registration fee, currently £20, is due on an Annual Return.

An auditor is entitled to inspect the minute books at any time.

Register of Directors. This book contains the prescribed details of directors and secretary, and may be kept at a place other than the REGISTERED OFFICE of the company (Sect. 200).

Register of Director's Interests. Every director of a company must notify the company in writing of all interests in shares and debentures of the company or group as the case may be, stating the number or amount, and class, of shares and debentures involved. In addition, all changes of interests must be notified within five days after any change and where a contract has been entered into for the purchase or sale of shares or debentures the date of the transaction and the price or consideration therefor must be stated. Details of options to subscribe for shares or debentures must also be notified.

Every company must keep a properly indexed register made up in chronological order from notifications received from directors. Entries in the register must be made within three days after receipt of notifications. Any rights granted by the company to directors to subscribe for the company's shares or debentures must be recorded in detail whenever granted. If so required by a director, the nature and extent of an interest must be recorded. Where the register is not kept at the registered office the Registrar of Companies must be notified of the place where the register is kept and of any changes of that place. Any person may obtain a copy of the register on payment of a small fee. The register must be made available to anyone attending the annual general meeting. (C.A. 67, Sects. 27 to 29.)

Register of Charges. A charge created by the company for or in respect of the following purposes or matters must be entered in the register, and the prescribed details thereof filed with the Registrar of Companies within twenty-one days of creation of the charge:

(a) For the purpose of securing any issue of debentures.

(b) A charge on uncalled share capital of the company.

(c) A charge created or evidenced by an instrument which, if executed by an individual, needs registration as a bill of sale.

(d) A charge on land, wherever situate, or any interest therein (except for a charge for any rent or other periodical sum issuing out of land).

(e) A charge on book debts of the company.

(f) A floating charge on the undertaking or property of the company.

(g) A charge on calls made but not paid.

(h) A charge on a ship or share in a ship.

(i) A charge on goodwill, a patent or licence under a patent, trade-mark, copyright, or licence under copyright (Sect. 95).

Briefly, the failure to file invalidates the *security*, but not the *debt*, with the result that the creditor is on the same 'level' as unsecured creditors of the company.

Statistical Books. The statistical books of a company will vary according to circumstances, e.g. nature of the business, frequency of meetings, and the number of members. The following list, whilst not exhaustive, contains the chief statistical books. There is no legal compulsion to keep books under this heading.

Register of debenture-holders (compulsory if Table A is adopted) or debenture stockholders.

Interest on debenture register.

Registered and documents relating to issue of shares, e.g.:

Application sheets.	Certification.
Allotment sheets.	Notices in lieu of distringas.
Share certificates.	Probate.
Calls.	Power of Attorney.
Transfers.	Sealed documents.
Transfer fees.	Dividends Register.
Register of transfers.	Register of share warrants.
Directors' Attendance Book (optional unless Table A adopted).	Agenda Book.

The chief documents to be filed with the Register of Companies are:

1. Those required on incorporation. (See Chapter 23, Section G.)

2. Prospectus or statement in lieu of prospectus. (Public Companies.)

3. Return of particulars of directors and secretaries (S.21 C.A. 1976)

4. Return of changes in the list of directors and secretaries (within fourteen days of such change).

5. A return of details of the allotment of shares WITHIN ONE MONTH. If the shares are issued otherwise than for cash, particulars of the consideration therefore must be stated, and in addition:

6. The contract evidencing the allotment, or if not already embodied in writing, the prescribed particulars of the contract.

7. In respect of charges:

(a) Certain details WITHIN TWENTY-ONE DAYS of creation of charge. (b) Memorandum of satisfaction of charge together with declaration of verification.

8. In respect of capital changes:

(a) Notice of consolidation, subdivision, conversion of share into stock or stock into shares. (b) Notice of increase.[1] (c) Copy of Court Order authorizing reorganization or reduction.

9. Statutory Report.

10. Copy of every extraordinary or special resolution within FIFTEEN DAYS of its being passed.[2]

11. The Annual Return.[2]

---

[1] Under the 1948 Act printed copies of resolutions or agreements were required to be submitted to the Registrar. By Sect. 51 of the 1967 Act such copies need no longer be printed but can be reproduced in some other form approved by the Registrar.

[2] The Annual Return with the various documents which may be annexed thereto must now be made by all limited companies, both public and private. A registration fee, currently £20, must be paid.

12. The prescribed form, signed by a director or the secretary, in respect of re-registration of either: (a) a limited company as unlimited, or (b) an unlimited company as limited.

Specimen Rulings and Forms

Specimens are now shown of the rulings of the more important books, etc., referred to in this chapter.

PITCH BLACK, LTD.

(Incorporated under the Companies Acts 1948 to 1976)

ISSUE OF 30,000 ORDINARY SHARES OF £1 EACH

No. .....25.....

ALLOTMENT LETTER

56 BARKER'S LANE,

........*C. Light, Esq.,* ....   MANCHESTER.

........*10 Dark Lane,* ....   *28th April 19. . 1*

........*Heaton.* ....

SIR (MADAM),

In reference to your application, I am pleased to inform you that........*2,000*........Ordinary Shares of £1 each in the Capital of the above Company have been allotted to you by the directors.

	£
The amount payable on application and allotment, viz.	
£0·50........ per share on........2,000.......shares is	1,000
You have already paid on application	500
Making the amount due from you upon allotment	£500

This amount is now due from you, and should be paid forthwith to the Company's Bankers, the Central Bank, Ltd., Hatton Street, Manchester. Due notice will be given when the share certificates are ready, and they will then only be delivered in exchange for this letter, accompanied by the receipts from the Bankers for the amounts paid on application and allotment.

BY ORDER OF THE BOARD,

....

Secretary.

....(*Perforation*)...

BANKERS' RECEIPT FOR ALLOTMENT MONEY

PITCH BLACK, LTD.

RECEIVED this........*Fifth*..........day of..........*May*..........19......., the sum of..........*£500*..........., due in respect of allotment No.....*25*........

Cashier.

....(*Perforation*)...

PITCH BLACK, LTD.

(This slip to be detached and retained by Bankers)

No. ....*25*............   Amount............*£500*...........

............*Fifth*................day of............*May*............19.......

REGISTER OF MEMBERS AND SHARE LEDGER

Name.. 19....

Address ....

Date of Entry as a Member.. 19....

Date of Ceasing to be a Member..

Dr. SHARES ACQUIRED							Dr. CASH PAYABLE ON SHARES					CASH PAID ON SHARES Cr.				SHARES TRANSFERRED Cr.				
No. of Allotment	No. of Transfer	Date of Allotment or Entry of Transfer	No. of Shares Alloted or Transferred	Distinctive Numbers (inclusive) From	To	Transferor's Folio	Total Value of Shares Held	Date when Called	Description of Payment of Call	No. of Call	Amount per Share	Total Amount	Date when Due	Date of Payment	Cash Book Folio	Amount	Date of Entry of Transfer	No. of Shares Transferred	Distinctive Numbers (inclusive) From	To	Transferee's Folio	Total of Shares Transferred
							£				£	£				£						£

TRANSFER REGISTER

Date when Lodged	Number of Transfer	Number of Old Certificate	Folio in Register of Members	TRANSFEROR'S Name	Address	TRANSFEREE'S Name	Address	Folio in Register of Members	Number of Shares Transferred	Number of New Certificate	Distinctive Numbers of Shares Transferred	Folio in Register of Members	Transfer Value

REGISTER OF CHARGES

No. of Charge	Date Charge	Brief Description of the Property Charged	Rate of Interest	Amount of the Charge	Persons Entitled to Charge		Date Filed with Registrar	Date of Memorandum of Satisfaction
					Name	Address		
				£				

REGISTER OF SHARE WARRANTS

Date of Application	No. of Warrant	To Whom Issued	Particulars of Shares, etc., Exchanged						Warrants Surrendered				
			Folio of Share Register	Shares Exchanged			Stock Exchanged		Nos. of Warrants		By Whom Surrendered	Ledger Folio	Date of Surrender
				No. of Shares	Distinctive Numbers		Folio of Stock Ledger	Amount	From	To			
					From	To							
								£					

TRANSFER FORM

I,

in * consideration of the sum of

paid by

hereinafter called the Transferee,

Do hereby bargain, sell, assign and transfer, to the said Transferee,

of and in the undertaking called

TO HOLD unto the said Transferee,   Executors, Administrators and Assignees, subject to the several conditions on which   held the same immediately before the execution hereof, and the said Transferee do hereby agree to accept and take the said subject to the conditions aforesaid.

AS WITNESS our Hands and Seals this   day of in the year of our Lord, One thousand nine hundred

SIGNED, sealed, and delivered by the above-named
in the presence of

Witness's †
{ Signature
  Address
  Occupation

Seal

SIGNED, sealed, and delivered by the above-named
in the presence of

Witness's †
{ Signature
  Address
  Occupation

Seal

SIGNED, sealed, and delivered by the above-named
in the presence of

Witness's †
{ Signature
  Address
  Occupation

Seal

SIGNED, sealed, and delivered by the above-named
in the presence of

Witness's †
{ Signature
  Address
  Occupation

Seal

SIGNED, sealed, and delivered by the above-named
in the presence of

Witness's †
{ Signature
  Address
  Occupation

Seal

---

* The Consideration-money set forth in a Transfer may differ from that which the first seller will receive, owing to sub-sales by the original Buyer; the Stamp Act requires that in such cases the consideration-money paid by the Sub-purchaser shall be the one inserted in the Deed, as regulating the *ad valorem* Duty; the following is the *Clause* in question—

"Where a person, having contracted for the purchase of any Property, but not having obtained a Conveyance thereof, contracts to sell the same to any other person, and the Property is in consequence conveyed immediately to the Sub-purchaser, the Conveyance is to be charged with *ad valorem* Duty in respect of the consideration moving from the Sub-purchaser.'—(54 & 55, Vic., cap. 39, sec. 58, sub-sec. 4.)

Instructions for executing Transfers

† *When a Transfer is executed out of Great Britain it is recommended that the signatures be attested by H.M. Consul or Vice-Consul, a Clergyman, Magistrate, Notary Public, or by some other Person holding a public position—as most Companies refuse to recognize Signatures not so attested. When a Witness is a Female she must state whether she is a Spinster, Wife, or Widow; and if a Wife she must give her husband's Name, Address and Quality, Profession or Occupation. The Date must be inserted in Words and not in Figures.*

Where the Transfer is made for a nominal consideration and is required to be stamped with the fixed duty of £0·50 the following Certificate must be filled up and signed.

By (1) *both transferor and transferee, or* (2) *a Solicitor or a member of a Stock Exchange acting for one or other of the parties, or* (3) *an accredited representative of a Bank. In the case of* (3) *the certificate may, where the Bank or its official nominee is a party to the transfer, to be the effect that 'the transfer is excepted from Section 74 of the Finance (1909/10) Act 1910'.*

I HEREBY CERTIFY that this Transfer is made on the occasion of:

(*a*) On the appointment of a new trustee of a pre-existing trust, or on the retirement of a trustee.

(*b*) A transfer as for a nominal consideration to a mere nominee of the transferor where no beneficial interest in the property passes.

(*c*) A security for a loan; or a re-transfer to the original transferor on payment of a loan.

(*d*) A transfer to a residuary legatee of stock, etc., which forms part of the residue divisible under a Will.

(*e*) A transfer to a beneficiary under a Will of a *specific* legacy of Stock, etc.

(*f*) A transfer of Stock, etc., being the property of a person dying intestate to the party or parties entitled to it.

(*g*) A transfer to a beneficiary under a settlement, on distribution of the trust funds, of Stock, etc., forming the share, or part of the share, of those funds to which the beneficiary is entitled in accordance with the terms of the settlement.

Strike out all those clauses not applicable.

Dated this   day of   19.

Signed

Address

[Various declarations and certificates under the Exchange Control Act 1947, must also be annexed.]

Stock Transfer Act 1963.

As will be seen from the foregoing Transfer Form, both the transferor and the transferee are required to execute the deed, and the signatures of each are required to be witnessed. It should be noted, however that a formal deed of transfer is not needed unless required by the Articles of the company. Now, as a result of the Stock Transfer Act 1963,[1] where the Articles require a formal deed of transfer the transfer of FULLY PAID Shares need only be signed by the transferor, and an attestation is not required irrespective of any clause to the contrary in the Articles of the company. The following are specimens of a Stock Transfer Form and a Brokers Transfer form:

[1] As amended by the Stock Transfer (Amendment of Forms) Order 1974.

STOCK TRANSFER FORM

(Above this line for Registrars only)

Certificate lodged with the Registrar

Consideration Money £ ....   **(For completion by the Registrar/Stock Exchange)**

Name of Undertaking		
Description of Security.		
Number or amount of Shares, Stock or other security and, in figures column only, number and denomination of units, if any.	Words	Figures (units of)
Name(s) of registered holder(s) should be given in full; the address should be given where there is only one holder. **If the transfer is not made by the registered holder(s) insert also the name(s) and capacity (e.g., Executor(s)) of the person(s) making the transfer.**	In the name(s) of	

I/We hereby transfer the above security out of the name(s) aforesaid to the person(s) named below *or to the several persons named in Parts 2 of Brokers Transfer Forms relating to the above security:*

Stamp of Selling Broker(s) or, for transactions which are not stock exchange transactions, of Agent(s), if any, acting for the Transferor(s).

Delete words in italics except for stock exchange transactions.
Signature(s) of transferor(s)

1. ....
2. ....
3. ....
4. ....

Bodies corporate should execute under their common seal.

Date ....

Full name(s) and full postal address(es) (including County or, if applicable, Postal District number) of the person(s) to whom the security is transferred.

Please state title, if any, or whether Mr., Mrs. or Miss.

Please complete in type-writing or in Block Capitals.

I/we request that such entries be made in the register as are necessary to give effect to this transfer.

Stamp of Buying Broker(s) if any	**Stamp or name and address of person lodging this form (if other than the Buying Broker(s))**

The security represented by the transfer overleaf has been sold as follows:

.... Shares/Stock .... Shares/Stock

.... Shares/Stock .... Shares/Stock

.... Shares/Stock .... Shares/Stock

.... Shares/Stock .... Shares/Stock

.... Shares/Stock .... Shares/Stock

.... Shares/Stock .... Shares/Stock

.... Shares/Stock .... Shares/Stock

.... Shares/Stock .... Shares/Stock

.... Shares/Stock Shares/Stock

.... Shares/Stock .... Shares/Stock

.... Shares/Stock .... Shares/Stock

.... Shares/Stock .... Shares/Stock

Balance (if any) due to Selling Broker(s)

Amount of Certificate(s)

Brokers Transfer Forms for above amounts certified
  Stamp of certifying Stock Exchange   *Stamp of Selling Broker(s)*

FORM OF CERTIFICATE REQUIRED WHERE TRANSFER IS NOT LIABLE TO
AD VALOREM STAMP DUTY

Instruments of transfer are liable to a fixed duty of £0·50 when the transaction falls within one of the following categories:

(a) Transfer vesting the property in new trustees on the appointment of a new trustee of a pre-existing trust, or on the retirement of a trustee.

*(b) Transfer by way of security for a loan or re-transfer to the original transferor on repayment of a loan.

(c) Transfer to a beneficiary under a will of a specific legacy of stock, etc. (NOTE—Transfers by executors in discharge or partial discharge of a pecuniary legacy are chargeable with *ad valorem* duty on the amount of the legacy so discharged unless the will confers on the executors power so to discharge the pecuniary legacy without the consent of the legatee.)

(d) A Transfer of Stock, etc., being the property of a person dying intestate, to the party or parties entitled to it, not being a transfer to the surviving spouse in satisfaction or part satisfaction of the sum of £5,000 to which he or she is entitled under the intestacy, where the total net value of the heritable and moveable estate exceeds £5,000.

(e) Transfer to a residuary legatee of stock, etc., forming part of the residue divisible under a will.

(f) Transfer to a beneficiary under a settlement, on distribution of the trust funds, of stock, etc., forming the share or part of the share of those funds to which the beneficiary is entitled in accordance with the terms of the settlement.

　　(NOTE—Categories (e) and (f) so not include a transfer to a beneficiary under a will or settlement who takes not only by reason of being entitled under the will or settlement but also

　　(i) following a purchase by him of some other interest in the trust property, e.g., a life interest or the interest of some other beneficiary; in such a case *ad valorem* transfer on sale duty is payable; or

　　(ii) where there is an element of gift *inter vivos* in the transaction in consequence of which a beneficiary under a will or settlement takes a share greater in value than his share under the will or settlement; in such a case *ad valorem* voluntary disposition duty is payable.)

(g) Transfer on and in consideration of marriage of stocks, etc., to either party to marriage or to trustees to be held on the terms of a duty stamped settlement made in consideration of the marriage. (NOTE—A transfer made to the husband or wife after the date of the marriage is not within this category unless it is made pursuant to an ante-nuptial contract.)

(h) Transfer by the liquidator of a company of stocks, etc., forming part of the assets of the company to the persons who were shareholders, in satisfaction of their rights on a winding-up.

*(j) Transfer, not on sale and not arising under any contract of sale and where no beneficial interest in the property passes: (i) to a person who is a mere nominee of, and is nominated only by, the transferor; (ii) from a mere nominee who has at all times held the property on behalf of the transferee; (iii) from one nominee to another nominee of the same beneficial owner where the first nominee has at all times held the property on behalf of that beneficial owner. (NOTE—This category does not include a transfer made in any of the following circumstances: (i) by a holder of stock, etc., following the grant of an option to purchase the stock, to the person entitled to the option or his nominee; (ii) to a nominee in contemplation of a contract for the sale of the stock, etc., then about to be entered into; (iii) from the nominee of a vendor, who has instructed the nominee orally or by some unstamped writing to hold stock, etc., in trust for a purchaser, to such purchaser.)

(1) 'I' or 'We'.

(2) Insert '(a)', '(b)' or appropriate category.

(3) Here set out concisely the facts explaining the transaction in cases falling within (b) and (j) or in any case which does not clearly fall within any of the categories (a) to (j). Adjudication may be required.

(1) .... hereby certify that the transaction in respect of which this transfer is made is one which falls within the category(2) .... above.

(3) ....

....

....

....

* Signature ....

Date ....19....

Description ....

Transfers {
....
....
....
....
}

Transfers {
....
....
....
....
}

N.B.—A transfer by way of a gift *inter vivos* is chargeable with *ad valorem* stamp duty and must be adjudicated.

　*NOTE—The above certificate should be signed in the case of (b) or (j) either by all the transferors and transferees, or a member of a Stock Exchange or a Solicitor acting for one or other of the parties, or an accredited representative of a Bank; where the bank or its official nominee is a party to the transfer, the certificate may be to the effect that 'the transfer is excepted from Section 74 of the Finance (1909–10) Act 1910'. In other cases the certificate should be signed by a Solicitor or other person (e.g., a Bank acting as trustee or executor) having a full knowledge of the facts.

BROKERS TRANSFER FORM

(Above this line for Registrars only)

	Certificate lodged with the Registrar
Consideration Money £	**(For completion by the Registrar/Stock Exchange)**

Part 1 **Name of Undertaking.**	
Description of Security.	
Number or amount of shares, Stock or other security and, in figures column only, number and denomination of units, if any.	Words Figures **(units of)**
Name(s) of registered holder(s) should be given in full; the address should be given where there is only one holder. **If the transfer is not made by the registered holder(s) insert also the name(s) and capacity (e.g., Executor(s)) of the person(s)) making the transfer.**	In the name(s) of

I/We confirm that the Stock Transfer Form relating to the security set out above has been lodged with the Registrar, and that the said security has been sold by me/us by a stock exchange transaction within the meaning of the Stock Transfer Act 1963.

Date and Stamp of Selling Broker(s)

Part 2 **Full name(s) and full postal address(es) (including County or, if applicable Postal District number) of the person(s) to whom the security is transferred.** **Please state title, if any, or whether Mr., Mrs. or Miss.** **Please complete in type-writing or in Block Capitals.**	

I/We confirm that the security set out in Part 1 above has been purchased by a stock exchange transaction within the meaning of the Stock Transfer Act 1963, and I/We request that such entries be made in the register as are necessary to give effect to this transfer.

Stamp of Buying Broker(s)	**Stamp of Lodging Agent (if other than the Buying Broker(s))**

CONTENTS OF THE BALANCE SHEET AND ACCOUNTS[1]

The Companies Act 1929, introduced for the first time in the history of Company Law numerous provisions concerning disclosure of information in the published accounts of limited companies.

Subsequent events have shown that those provisions were not sufficiently comprehensive to give that amount of information which, particularly having regard to the continued growth of holding companies, is regarded as necessary to serve the public need.

The constant endeavours of the Professional Accountants' organizations to set a standard of good accounting practice and the recommendations of the Cohen Committee bore fruit in the passing of the Companies Act 1947, which embodied in the main the recommendations and suggestions so made.

The laws relating to companies was consolidated in the Companies Act 1948. The Companies Act 1967, whilst amending and augmenting certain parts of the 1948 Act is, in effect, an extension of that Act. Consequently, the laws relating to companies are now contained in the Companies Acts 1948 and 1967. The status of the 'exempt' private company which was introduced by the 1948 Act has been abolished by the 1967 Act. An 'exempt' private company enjoyed the following privileges:

1. It did not require to file a copy of its final accounts with the Registrar of Companies.

2. The auditor did not need to possess professional qualifications or be authorized by the Department of Trade.

3. A partner or employee or an officer or servent of the company was not disqualified from appointment as auditor.

4. Copies of such resolutions and agreements as are required to be filed with the Registrar of Companies did not need to be filed provided that a copy was forwarded in a form approved by the Registrar (typed copies were usually accepted).

5. Loans could be made by the company to its directors.

The Companies Act 1967, withdrew all of the aforementioned privileges as from 27th January 1968.

Before the Companies Act 1967 was passed, the rules relating to the contents of published Profit and Loss Accounts and Balance Sheets (called final Accounts) were contained mainly in Schedule 8 to the Companies Act 1948. Schedule 1 to the 1967 Act, however, amends Schedule 8 to the 1948 Act. Schedule 1 contains the amendments only, and Schedule 2 to the 1967 Act contains the form of Schedule 8 to the 1948 Act as amended by Schedule 1 to the 1967 Act. In effect, therefore, the rules relating to the contents of final accounts are now largely contained in Schedule 2 to the Companies Act 1967.

The laws relating to companies as contained in the Companies Acts 1948 and 1967, so far as they are of an accounting nature, are given in the succeeding pages. It is important to observe that:

[1] The Companies Act 1976 does not affect the contents of the Balance Sheet and Accounts.

(a) the accounting provisions generally concern the accounts of all limited companies, and

(b) In addition, certain provisions concern the accounts of holding companies and subsidiaries. These are dealt with in detail in the next chapter.

Note. In the data which follow, Section references appertain to the Companies Act 1948, unless otherwise indicated. All Schedule 2 references concern Schedule 2 to the Companies Act 1967. Obsolete terms have been removed or updated as appropriate.

General

(A) Every Balance Sheet of a company shall give a true and fair view of the state of affairs of the company as at the end of its financial year, and every Profit and Loss Account of a company shall give a true and fair view of the profit or loss of the company for the financial year. (Sect. 149.(1).)[1]

A company's Balance Sheet and Profit and Loss Account shall comply with the requirements of Schedule 8 to this Act (as amended by the Companies Act 1967), so far as applicable thereto. (Sect. 149 (2).)

The Department of Trade may, on the application or with the consent of a company's directors, modify in relation to that company any of the requirements of this Act as to the matters to be stated in a company's Balance Sheet or Profit and Loss Account (except the requirements of subsection (1) of this section) for the purpose of adapting them to the circumstances of the company. (Sect. 149 (4).)

Subsections (1) and (2) of this section shall not apply to a company's Profit and Loss Account, if:

(a) The company has subsidiaries; and

(b) The Profit and Loss Account is framed as a consolidated Profit and Loss Account dealing with all or any of the company's subsidiaries as well as the company, and:

(i) complies with the requirements of this Act relating to consolidated Profit and Loss Accounts; and

(ii) show how much of the consolidated profit or loss for the financial year is dealt with in the accounts of the company. (Sect. 149 (5).)

(B) The Profit and Loss Account and, so far as not incorporated in the Balance Sheet or Profit and Loss Account, any group accounts laid before a company in general meeting shall be annexed to the Balance Sheet and approved by the board of directors before the Balance Sheet is signed on their behalf. The auditors' report shall be attached thereto. (Sect. 156 (1) and (2).)

Every Balance Sheet of a company shall be signed on behalf of the board by two of the directors of the company, or, if there is only one director, by that director.

In the case of a banking company registered after the fifteenth day of August, eighteen hundred and seventy-nine, the Balance Sheet must be signed by the secretary or manager, if any; and where there are more than three directors of the company by at least three of those directors, and where there are not more than three directors by all the directors. (Sect. 155 (1) and (2).)

(C) The authorized capital, liabilities and assets shall be summarized, with such particulars as are necessary to disclose the general nature of the assets and liabilities, and there shall be specified:

(a) Any part of the issued capital that consists of redeemable preference shares the earliest and latest dates on which the company has power to redeem those shares, whether those shares must be redeemed in any event or are liable to be redeemed at the option of the company and whether (and, if so, what) premium is payable on redemption.

(b) So far as the information is not given in the Profit and loss Account, any share capital on which interest has been paid out of capital during the financial year, and the rate at which interest has been so paid.

(c) the amount of the Share Premium Account.

(d) Particulars of any redeemed debentures which the company has power to reissue. (Para. 2, Part I, Sch. 2.)

[1] See p. 23355 for SSAP 1/17 Accounting for Post Balance Sheet Events.

(D) The reserves, provisions, liabilities and assets shall be classified under headings appropriate to the company's business:

Provided that:

(a) Where the amount of any class is not material, it may be included under the same heading as some other class; and

(b) Where any assets of one class are not separable from assets of another class, those assets may be included under the same heading. (Para. 4 (1), Part I, Sch. 2.)

(E) (1) For the purposes of this Schedule, unless the context otherwise requires:

(a) The expression 'provision' shall, subject to sub-paragraph (2) of this paragraph, mean any amount written off or retained by way of providing for depreciation, renewals or diminution in value of assets or retained by way of providing for any known liability of which the amount cannot be determined with substantial accuracy;

(b) The expression 'reserve' shall not, subject as aforesaid, include any amount written off or retained by way of providing for depreciation, renewals or diminution in value of assets or retained by way of providing for any known liability or any sum set aside for the purpose of its being used to prevent undue fluctuations in charges for taxation;

and in this paragraph the expression 'liability' shall include all liabilities in respect of expenditure contracted for and all disputed or contingent liabilities.

(2) Where:

(a) Any amount written off or retained by way of providing for depreciation, renewals or diminution in value of assets, not being an amount written off in relation to fixed assets before the commencement of this Act;[1] or

(b) Any amount retained by way of providing for any known liability:

is in excess of that which in the opinion of the directors is reasonably necessary for the purpose, the excess shall be treated for the purposes of this Schedule as a reserve and not a provision. (Para. 27, Part IV, Sch. 2.)

Share Capital

(A) (1) Where a company issues shares at a premium, whether for cash or otherwise, a sum equal to the aggregate amount or value of the premiums on those shares shall be transferred to an account, to be called 'the Share Premium Account' and the provisions of this Act relating to the reduction of the share capital of a company shall, except as provided in this section, apply as if the Share Premium Account were paid up share capital of the company.

(2) The Share Premium Account may, notwithstanding anything in the foregoing subsection, be applied by the company in paying up unissued shares of the company to be issued to members of the company as fully-paid bonus shares, in writing off:

(a) The preliminary expenses of the company; or

(b) The expenses of, or the commission paid or discount allowed on, any issue of shares or debentures of the company;

or in providing for the premium payable on redemption of any redeemable preference shares or of any debentures of the company.

(3) Where a company has before the commencement of this Act[1] issued any shares at a premium, this section shall apply as if the shares had been issued after the commencement of this Act:

Provided that any part of the premiums which has been so applied that it does not at the commencement of this Act[1] form an identifiable part of the company's reserves within the meaning of the Eighth Schedule to this Act (as amended) shall be disregarded in determining the sum to be included in the share premium account. (Sect. 56.)

(B) Redeemable Preference shares—see p. 23147.

(C) Interest on construction Capital—see p. 23222.

---

[1] Ist July 1948.

Assets

(A) (1) Fixed assets, current assets and assets that are neither fixed nor current shall be separately identified.

(2) The method or methods used to arrive at the amount of the fixed assets under each heading shall be stated. (Para. 4 (2) and (3), Part I, Sch. 2.)

(B) (1) The method of arriving at the amount of any fixed asset shall, subject to the next following sub-paragraph, be to take the difference between:

(a) Its cost or, if it stands in the company's books at a valuation, the amount of the valuation; and

(b) The aggregate amount provided or written off since the date of acquisition or valuation, as the case may be, for depreciation or diminution in value;

and for the purposes of this paragraph the net amount at which any assets stand in the company's books at the commencement of this Act[1] (after deduction of the amounts previously provided or written off for depreciation or diminution in value) shall, if the figures relating to the period before the commencement of this Act cannot be obtained without unreasonable expense or delay, be treated as if it were the amount of a valuation of those assets made at that date and, where any of those assets are sold, the said net amount less the amount of the sales shall be treated as if it were the amount of a valuation so made of the remaining assets.

(2) The foregoing sub-paragraph shall not apply:

(a) To assets for which the figures relating to the period beginning with the commencement of this Act[1] cannot be obtained without unreasonable expense or delay; or

(b) To assets, the replacement of which is provided for wholly or partly by making provision for renewals and charging the cost of replacement against the provision so made; or by charging the cost of replacement direct to revenue; or

(c) To any quoted investments or to any unquoted investments of which the value as estimated by the directors is shown either as the amount of the investments or by way of note; or

(d) To goodwill, patents or trade marks.

(3) For the assets under each heading whose amount is arrived at in accordance with sub-paragraph (1) of this paragraph, there shall be shown—

(a) The aggregate of the amounts referred to in paragraph (a) of that sub-paragraph; and

(b) The aggregate of the amounts referred to in paragraph (b) thereof.

(4) As respects the assets under each heading whose amount is not arrived at in accordance with the said sub-paragraph (1) because their replacement is provided for as mentioned in sub-paragraph (2) (b) of this paragraph, there shall be stated—

(a) The means by which their replacement is provided for; and

(b) The aggregate amount of the provision (if any) made for renewals and not used. (Para. 5, Part I, Sch. 2.)

Investments[2]

In the case of unquoted investments consisting in equity share capital (as defined by subsection (5) of Section 154 of this Act) of other bodies corporate (other than any whose values as estimated by the directors are separately shown, either individually or collectively or as to some individually and as to the rest collectively, and are so shown either as the amount thereof, or by way of note), the matter referred to in the following heads shall, if not otherwise shown, be stated by way of note or in a statement or report annexed—

(a) the amount of the company's income for the financial year that is ascribable to the investments;

(b) the amount of the company's share before taxation, and the amount of that share after taxation, of the net aggregate amount of the profits of the bodies in which the investments are held, being profits for the several periods to which accounts sent by them during the financial year to the company related, after deducting those bodies' losses for those periods (or vice versa);

---

[1] 1st July 1948.
[2] See p. 2649 for SSAP 1/19 Accounting for Investment Properties.

(c) the amount of the company's share of the net aggregate amount of the undistributed profits accumulated by the bodies in which the investments are held since the time when the investments were acquired, after deducting the losses accumulated by them since that time (or vice versa);

(d) the manner in which any losses incurred by the said bodies have been dealt with in the company's accounts. (Para. 5A, Part 1, sch. 2.)

There shall be shown under separate headings the aggregate amounts respectively of the company's quoted investments and unquoted investments. (Para. 8 (1) (a), Part I, Sch. 2.)

The heading showing the amount of the quoted investments shall be subdivided, where necessary, to distinguish the investments as respects which there has, and those as respects which there has not, been granted a quotation or permission to deal on a recognized stock exchange. (Para. 8 (3), Part I, Sch. 2.)

For the purposes aforesaid, the expression 'quoted investment' means an investment as respects which there has been granted a quotation or permission to deal on a recognized stock exchange, or on any stock exchange of repute outside Great Britain, and the expression 'unquoted investment' shall be construed accordingly. (Para. 28, Part IV, Sch. 2)

Goodwill, Patents and Trade-marks

(A) There shall be shown under a separate heading . . . if the amount of the goodwill and of any patents and trade-marks or part of that amount is shown as a separate item in or is otherwise ascertainable from the books of the company, or from any contract for the sale or purchase of any property to be acquired by the company, or from any documents in the possession of the company relating to the stamp duty payable in respect of any such contract or the conveyance of any such property, the said amount so shown or ascertained so far as not written off, or, as the case may be, said amount so far as it is shown or ascertainable and as so shown or ascertained, as the case may be. (Para. 8 (1) (b), Part I, Sch. 2.)

(B) Nothing in the foregoing sub-paragraph shall be taken as requiring the amount of the goodwill, patents and trade-marks to be stated otherwise than as a single item. (Para. 8 (2), Part I, Sch. 2.)

Liabilities

(A) Where any liability of the company is secured otherwise than by *operation of law* on any assets of the company, the Balance Sheet shall include a statement that that liability is so secured, but it shall not not be necessary to specify in the Balance Sheet the assets on which the liability is secured. (Para. 9, Part I, Sch. 2.)

[Operation of Law—where a creditor in addition to being able to sue for the debt has also the right to some type of security given to him under statute or by the general body of law, e.g. (1) lien of an unpaid vendor; (2) charge on a house or land by a local authority in respect of road-making charges.]

(B) Where a company has power to re-issue debentures which have been redeemed, particulars with respect to the debentures which can be so reissued shall be included in every Balance Sheet of the company. (*Vide* Para. 2 (d), Part I, Sch. 2.)

(C) Where any of the company's debentures are held by a nominee of or trustee for the company, the nominal amount of the debentures and the amount at which they are stated in the books of the company shall be stated (Para. 10, Part I, Sch. 2.)

(D) There shall be shown under a separate heading the aggregate amount of bank loans and overdrafts and the aggregate amount of loans made to the Company which—

(i) are repayable otherwise than by instalments and fall due for repayment after the expiration of the period of five years begining with the day next following the expiration of the financial year; or

(ii) are repayable by instalments any of which fall due for payment after the expiration of that period; not being in either case, bank loans or overdrafts. (Para. 8 (1) (d), Part I, Sch. 2.)

Reserves and Provisions[1]

(A) The aggregate amounts respectively of reserves and provisions (other than provisions for depreciation, renewals or diminution in value of assets) shall be stated under separate headings—
Provided that:

(a) This paragraph shall not require a separate statement of either of the said amounts which is not material; and

(b) The Department of Trade may direct that it shall not require a separate statement of the amount of provisions where they are satisfied that that is not required in the public interest and would predjudice the company, but subject to the condition that any heading stating an amount arrived at after taking into account a provision (other than as aforesaid) shall be so framed or marked as to indicate that fact. (Para. 6, Part I, Sch. 2.)

(B) (1) There shall also be shown (unless it is shown in the Profit and Loss Account or a statement or report annexed thereto, or the amount involved is not material)—

(a) Where the amount of the reserves or of the provisions (other than provisions for depreciation, renewals of diminution in value of assets) shows an increase as compared with the amount at the end of the immediately preceding financial year, the source from which the amount of the increase has been derived; and

(b) Where the amount of the reserves shows a decrease as compared with the amount at the end of the immediately preceding financial year; or the amount at the end of the immediately preceding financial year of the provisions (other than provisions for depreciation, renewals or diminution in value of assets) exceeded the aggregate of the sums since applied and amounts still retained for the purposes thereof; the application of the amounts derived from the difference.

(2) Where the heading showing the reserves or any of the provisions aforesaid is divided into sub-headings, this paragraph shall apply to each of the separate amounts shown in the sub-headings instead of applying to the aggregate amount thereof. (Para. 7, Part I, Sch. 2.)

(C) If an amount is set aside for the purpose of its being used to prevent undue fluctuations in charges for taxation, it shall be stated (Para. 7A, Part I, Sch. 2.)

Preliminary and Issue Expenses

There shall be stated under separate headings, so far as they are not written off—
(a) The preliminary expenses.
(b) Any expense incurred in connection with any issue of share capital or debentures.
(c) Any sums paid by way of commission in respect of any shares or debentures.
(d) Any sums allowed by way of discount in respect of any debentures; and
(e) The amount of the discount allowed on any issue of shares at a discount. (Para. 3, Part I, Sch. 2.)

Proposed dividend

There shall be shown under a separate heading in the Balance Sheet the aggregate amount which is recommended for distribution by way of dividend. (Para. 8 (1) (e), Part I, Sch. 2.)

Subsidiary Companies

Where any of the assets of a company consist of shares in, or amounts owing (whether on account of a loan or otherwise) from a subsidiary company or subsidiary companies, the aggregate amount of those assets, distinguishing shares from indebtedness, shall be set out in the Balance Sheet of the first-mentioned company separately from all its other assets, and where a company is indebted, whether on account of a loan or otherwise, to a subsidiary company or subsidiary companies, the aggregate amount of that indebtedness shall be set out in the Balance

---

[1] See p. 2334 for definitions.

Sheet of that company separately from all its other liabilities. (Para. 15 (2), Part II, Sch. 2.)

See also next chapter for detailed requirements, group accounts, etc.

Balance Sheet Notes

1. The matters referred to in the following sub-paragraphs shall be stated by way of note, or in a statement or report annexed, if not otherwise shown.

2. The number, description, and amount of any shares in the company which any person has an option to subscribe for, together with the following particulars of the option, that is to say:

(a) the period during which it is exercisable.

(b) The price to be paid for shares subscribed for under it.

3. The amount of any arrears of fixed cumulative dividends on the company's shares and the period for which the dividends or, if there is more than one class, each class of them are in arrear. The amount of the Advance Corporation Tax which will become payable should also be shown.

4. Particulars of any charge on the assets of the company to secure the liabilities of any other person, including, where practicable, the amount secured.

5. The general nature of any other contingent liabilities not provided for and, where practicable, the aggregate amount or estimated amount of those liabilities, if it is material.[1]

6. Where practicable, the aggregate amount or estimated amount, if it is material, of contracts for capital expenditure, so far as not provided for and, where practicable, the aggregate amount or estimated amount, if it is material, of capital expenditure authorized by the directors which has not been contracted for.

6A. In the case of fixed assets under any heading whose amount is required to be arrived at in accordance with paragraph 5(1) of this Schedule (other than unquoted investments) and is so arrived at by reference to a valuation, the years (so far as they are known to the directors) in which the assets were severally valued and the several values, and, in the case of assets that have been valued during the financial year, the names of the persons who valued them or particulars of their qualifications for doing so and (whichever is stated) the bases of valuation used by them.

6B. If there are included amongst fixed assets under any heading (other than investments) assets that have been acquired during the financial year, the aggregate amount of the assets acquired as determined for the purpose of making up the Balance Sheet, and if during that year any fixed assets included under a heading in the balance sheet made up with respect to the immediately preceding financial year (other than investments) have been disposed of or destroyed, the aggregate amount thereof as determined for the purpose of making up that balance sheet.

6C. Of the amount of fixed assets consisting of land, how much is ascribable to land of freehold tenure and how much to land of leasehold tenure, and, of the latter, how much is ascribable to land held on long lease and how much to land held on short lease.

7. If in the opinion of the directors any of the current assets have not a value, on realization in the ordinary course of the company's business, at least equal to the amount at which they are stated, the fact that the directors are of that opinion.

8. The aggregate market value of the company's quoted investments where it differs from the amount of the investments as stated, and the Stock Exchange value of any investments of which the market value is shown (whether separately or not) and is taken as being higher than their Stock Exchange value.

9. The basis on which foreign currencies have been converted into sterling, where the amount of the assets or liabilities affected is material.

10. The basis on which the amount, if any, set aside for United Kingdom tax is computed.

11. Except in the case of the first Balance Sheet laid before the company after the coming into force of this Act,[2] the corresponding amounts at the end of the immediately preceding financial year for all items shown in the Balance Sheet. (Para. 11, Part I, Sch. 2.)

---

[1] See p. 23359 for SSAP 1/18 Accounting for Contingencies.

[2] 1st July 1948.

Loans to Employees for Purchase of Shares in the Company

Subject as provided in this section, it shall not be lawful for a company to give, whether directly or indirectly, and whether by means of a loan, guarantee, the provision of security or otherwise, any financial assistance for the purpose of or in connection with a purchase or subscription made or to be made by any person of any shares in the company; or where the company is a subsidiary company, in its holding company.

Provised that nothing in this section shall be taken to prohibit:

(a) Where the lending of money is part of the ordinary business of a company, the lending of money in the ordinary course of its business.

(b) The provision by a company, in accordance with any scheme for the time being in force, of money for the purchase by trustees of fully-paid shares in the company to be held by or for the benefit of employees of the company, including any director holding salaried employment or office in the company.

(c) The making by a company of loans to persons, other than directors, *bona fide* in the employment of the company with a view to enabling those persons to purchase fully-paid shares in the company to be held by themselves by way of beneficial ownership. (Sect. 54 (1).)

The aggregate amount of any outstanding loans under the authority of provisos (b) and (c) to sub-section (1) of Section 54 of this Act shall be shown as a separate item in every Balance Sheet of the company. (Para. 8 (1) (c), Part I, Sch. 2.)

Items to be Shown in the Profit and Loss Account

1. There shall be shown:

(a) The amount charged to revenue by way of provision for depreciation, renewals or diminution in value of fixed assets.

(b) the amount of the interest on loans of the following kinds made to the company (whether on the security of debentures or not), namely bank loans, overdrafts and loans which, not being bank loans or overdrafts—

   (i) are repayable otherwise than by instalments and fall due for repayment before the expiration of the period of five years beginning with the day next following the expiration of the financial year; or

   (ii) are repayable by instalments the last of which falls due for payment before the expiration of that period;

and the amount of the interest on loans of other kinds so made (whether on the security of debentures or not).

(c) the amount of the charge to revenue for United Kingdom Corporation Tax and, if that amount would have been greater but for relief from double taxation, the amount which it would have been but for such relief, and the amount of the charge for taxation imposed outside the United Kingdom of profits, income and (so far as charged to revenue) capital gains;

(d) The amounts respectively provided for redemption of share capital and for redemption of loans.

(e) The amount, if material, set aside or proposed to be set aside to, or withdrawn from, reserves.

(f) subject to sub-paragraph (2) of this paragraph, the amount, if material, set aside to provisions other than provisions for depreciation, renewals or diminution in value of assets or, as the case may be, the amount, if material, withdrawn from such provisions and not applied for the purposes thereof.

(g) The amounts respectively of income from quoted investments and income from unquoted investments.

   (i) If a substantial part of the company's revenue for the financial year consists of rents from land, the amount thereof (after deduction of ground-rents, rates and other outgoings).

   (ii) The amount, if material, charged to revenue in respect of sums payable in respect of the hire of plant and machinery.

(h) The aggregate amount of the dividends paid and proposed.

2. The Department of Trade may direct that a company shall not be obliged to show an amount set aside to provisions in accordance with sub-paragraph (1) (f) of this paragraph, if the Department is satisfied that that is not required in the public interest and would prejudice the

company, but subject to the condition that any heading stating an amount arrived at after taking into account the amount set aside as aforesaid shall be so framed or marked as to indicate that fact. (Para. 12, Part I, Sch. 2.)

Profit and Loss Account Notes

1. The matters referred to in the following sub-paragraphs shall be stated by way of note, if not otherwise shown.

2. If depreciation or replacement of fixed assets is provided for by some method other than a depreciation charge or provision for renewals, or is not provided for, the method by which it is provided for or the fact that it is not provided for, as the case may be.

3. The basis on which the charge for United Kingdom corporation tax is computed.

3A. Any special circumstances which affect liability in respect of taxation of profits, income or capital gains for the financial year or liability in respect of taxation of profits, income or capital gains for succeeding financial years.

4. Except in the case of the first Profit and Loss Account laid before the company after the commencement of this Act,[1] the corresponding amounts for the immediately preceding financial year for all items shown in the Profit and Loss Account.

5. Any material respects in which any items shown in the Profit and Loss Account are affected:

   (a) By transactions of a sort not usually undertaken by the company or otherwise by circumstances of an exceptional or non-recurrent nature; or

   (b) By any change in the basis of accounting. (Para. 14, Part I, Sch. 2.)

Auditor's Remuneration

The amount of the remuneration of the auditors shall be shown under a separate heading, and for the purpose of this subsection, any sums paid by the company in respect of the auditors' expenses shall be deemed to be included in the expression 'remuneration.' (Para. 13, Part I, Sch. 2.)

Exceptions for Certain Classes of Company

Such banking and discount companies as the Department of Trade may designate are exempted from complying with certain of the foregoing requirements, but where in the Balance Sheet of such a company reserves or provisions (other than provisions for depreciation, renewals of diminution in the value of assets) are not stated separately, any heading stating an amount arrived at after taking into account a reserve or such provision shall be so framed or marked as to indicate that fact. (Para. 23, Part III, Sch. 2.)

Assurance companies are also exempted from compliance with certain of the foregoing requirements. (Vide Para. 24, Part III, Sch. 2.)

Loans to Directors and Officers of the Company

(A) Prohibition of loans to directors:

1. It shall not be lawful for a company to make a loan to any person who is its director or a director of its holding company, or to enter into any guarantee or provide any security in connection with a loan made to such a person as aforesaid by any other person:

Provided that nothing in this section shall apply:

   (a) To anything done by a subsidiary, where the director is its holding company; or

   (b) Subject to the next following subsection, to anything done to provide any such person as aforesaid with funds to meet expenditure incurred or to be incurred by him for the purposes of the company or for the purpose of enabling him properly to perform his duties as an officer of the company; or

---

[1] 1st July, 1948.

(c) In the case of a company whose ordinary business includes the lending of moneys or the giving of guarantees in connection with loans made by other persons, to anything done by the company in the ordinary course of that business.

2. Proviso (b) to the foregoing subsection shall not authorize the making of any loan, or the entering into any guarantee, or the provision of any security, except either:

(a) With the prior approval of the company given at a general meeting at which the purposes of the expenditure and the amount of the loan or the extent of the guarantee or security, as the case may be, are disclosed; or

(b) On condition that, if the approval of the company is not given as aforesaid at or before the next following annual general meeting, the loan shall be repaid or the liability under the guarantee or security shall be discharged, as the case may be, within six months from the conclusion of that meeting.

3. Where the approval of the company is not given as required by any such condition, the directors authorizing the making of the loan, or the entering into the guarantee, or the provision of the security, shall be jointly and severally liable to indemnity the company against any loss arising therefrom. (Sect. 190).

(B) Disclosure in accounts:

1. The accounts which, in pursuance of this Act, are to be laid before every company in general meeting shall, subject to the provisions of this section, contain particulars showing—

(a) The amount of any loans made during the company's financial year to:

(i) Any officer of the company; or

(ii) Any person who, after the making of the loan, became during that year an officer of the company;

by the company or a sudsidiary thereof or by any other person under a guarantee from or on a security provided by the company or a subsidiary thereof (including any such loans which were repaid during that year); and

(b) The amount of any loans made in manner aforesaid to any such officer or person as aforesaid at any time before the company's financial year and outstanding at the expiration thereof.

2. The foregoing subsection shall not require the inclusion in accounts of particulars of:

(a) A loan made in the ordinary course of its business by the company or a subsidiary thereof, where the ordinary business of the company or, as the case may be, the subsidiary, includes the lending of money; or

(b) A loan made by the company or a subsidiary thereof to an employee of the company or subsidiary, as the case may be, if the loan does not exceed two thousand pounds and is certified by the directors of the company or subsidiary, as the case may be, to have been made in accordance with any practice adopted or about to be adopted by the company or subsidiary with respect to loans to its employees;

not being, in either case, a loan made by the company under a guarantee from or on a security provided by a subsidiary thereof or a loan made by a subsidiary of the company under a guarantee from or on a security provided by the company or any other subsidiary thereof.

3. If in the case of any such accounts as aforesaid the requirements of this section are not complied with, it shall be the duty of the auditors of the company by whom the accounts are examined to include in their report on the Balance Sheet of the company, so far as they are reasonably able to do so, a statement giving the required particulars.

4. References in this section to a subsidiary shall be taken as referring to a subsidiary at the end of the company's financial year whether or not a subsidiary at the date of the loan). (Sect. 197).

Payments to Directors and Officers of the Company

Detailed provisions are contained in the 1948 Act for the disclosure in the accounts of the aggregate amount of Directors' emoluments, including those of the managing director and all directors' salaried remuneration and other benefits, including past and present directors' pensions and compensation for loss of office. Moreover, the Act prohibits the making of 'tax free' payments to directors, except for those arising under a contract in force on 18th July 1945. There are also exceptions for remuneration due or in respect of a period before the Act comes into force.[1] The relevant sections of the 1948 Act are:

(A) Prohibition of tax-free payments (Sect. 189):

1. It shall not be lawful for a company to pay a director remuneration (whether as director or otherwise) free of income tax, or otherwise calculated by reference to or varying with the amount of his income tax or to or with the rate or standard rate of income tax, except under a contract which was in force on the eighteenth day of July, nineteen hundred and forty-five, and provides expressly, and not by reference to the Articles, for payment of remuneration as aforesaid.

2. Any provision contained in a company's Articles, or in any contract other than such a contract as aforesaid, or in any resolution of a company or a company's directors, for payment to a director of remuneration as aforesaid shall have effect as if it provided for payment, as a gross sum subject to income tax, of the net sum for which it actually provides.

(B) Payments for loss of office or on retirement (Sect. 191):

It shall not be lawful for a company to make to any director of the company any payment by way of compensation for loss of office, or as consideration for or in connection with his retirement from office, without particulars with respect to the proposed payment (including the amount thereof) being disclosed to the members of the company and the proposal being approved by the company.

The next two sections (192 and 193) deal with payments involving the transfer of a company's property to a director for loss of office, etc., the approval of the company being again necessary.

(C) Particulars in accounts of directors' salaries, etc. (Sect. 196):

1. In any accounts of a company laid before it in general meeting, or in a statement annexed thereto, there shall, subject to and in accordance with the provisions of this section, be shown so far as the information is contained in the company's books and papers or the company has the right to obtain it from the persons concerned:

(a) The aggregate amount of the directors' emoluments;
(b) The aggregate amount of directors' or past directors' pensions; and
(c) The aggregate amount of any compensation to directors or past directors in respect of loss of office.

2. The amount to be shown under paragraph (a) of subsection (1) of this section:

(a) Shall include any emoluments paid to or receivable by any person in respect of his services as director of the company or in respect of his services, while director of the company, as director of any subsidiary thereof or otherwise in connection with the management of the affairs of the company or any subsidiary thereof; and
(b) Shall distinguish between emoluments in respect of services as director, whether of the company or its subsidiary, and other emoluments;

and for the purposes of this section the expression 'emoluments', in relation to a director, includes fees and percentages, any sums paid by way of expenses allowance in so far as those sums are charged to United Kingdom income tax, and contribution paid in respect of him under any pension scheme and the estimated money value of any other benefits received by him otherwise than in cash.

---

[1] 1st July 1948.

3. The amount to be shown under paragraph (b) of the said subsection (1):

(a) Shall not include any pension paid or receivable under a pension scheme if the scheme is such that the contributions thereunder are substantially adequate for the maintenance of the scheme, but save as aforesaid shall include any pension paid or receivable in respect of any such services of a director or past director of the company as are mentioned in the last foregoing subsection, whether to or by him or, on his nomination or by virtue of dependence on or other connection with him, to or by any other person; and

(b) Shall distinguish between pensions in respect of services as director, whether of the company or its subsidiary, and other pensions;

and for the purposes of this section the expression 'pension' includes any superannuation allowance, superannuation gratuity or similar payment, and the expression 'pension scheme' means a scheme for the provision of pensions in respect of services as director or otherwise which is maintained in whole or in part by means of contributions and the expression 'contribution' in relation to a pension scheme means any payment (including an insurance premium) paid for the purposes of the scheme by or in respect of persons rendering services in respect of which pensions will or may become payable under the scheme, except that it does not include any payment in respect of two or more persons if the amount paid in respect of each of them is not ascertainable.

4. The amount to be shown under paragraph (c) of the said subsection (1):

(a) Shall include any sums paid to or receivable by a director or past director by way of compensation for loss of office as director of the company or for the loss, while director of the company or on or in connection with his ceasing to be a director of the company, of any other office in connection with the management of the company's affairs or of any office as director or otherwise in connection with the management of the affairs of any subsidiary thereof; and

(b) Shall distinguish between compensation in respect of the office of director, whether of the company or its subsidiary, and compensation in respect of other offices;

and for the purposes of this section references to compensation for loss of office shall include sums paid as consideration for or in connection with a person's retirement from office.

5. The amounts to be shown under each paragraph of the said subsection (1):

(a) Shall include all relevant sums paid by or receivable from the company, and the company's subsidiaries, and any other person; except sums to be *accounted for to the company or any of its subsidiaries* or, by virtue of section one hundred and ninty-three of this Act, to past and present members of the company or any of its subsidiaries or any class of those members; and

(b) Shall distinguish, in the case of the amount to be shown under paragraph (c) of the said subsection (1), between the sums respectively paid by or receivable from the company, the company's subsidiaries and persons other than the company and its subsidiaries.

6. The amounts to be shown under this section for any financial year shall be the sums receivable in respect of that year, whenever paid, or, in the case of sums not receivable in respect of a period, the sums paid during that year, so, however, that where:

(a) Any sums are not shown in the accounts for the relevant financial year on the ground that the person receiving them is liable to account therefor as mentioned in paragraph (a) of the last foregoing subsection, but the liability is thereafter wholly or partly released or is not enforced within a period of two years; or

(b) Any sums paid by way of expenses allowance are charged to United Kingdom income tax after the end of the relevant financial year;

those sums shall to the extent to which the liability is released or not enforced or they are charged as aforesaid, as the case may be, be shown in the first accounts in which it is practicable to show them or in a statement annexed thereto and shall be distinguished from the amounts to be shown therein apart from this provision.

7. Where it is necessary so to do for the purpose of making any distinction required by this section in any amount to be shown thereunder, the directors may apportion any payments between the matters in respect of which they have been paid or are receivable in such a manner as they think appropriate.

8. If in the case of any accounts the requirements of this section are not complied with, it shall be the duty of the auditors of the company by whom the accounts are examined to include in their report thereon, so far as they are reasonably able to do so, a statement giving the required particulars.

9. In this section any reference to a company's subsidiary:

(a) In relation to a person who is or was, while a director of the company, a director also, by virtue of the company's nomination, direct or indirect, of any other body corporate, shall, subject to the following paragraph, include that body corporate, whether or not it is or was in fact the company's subsidiary; and

(b) Shall for the purposes of subsections (2) and (3) be taken as referring to a subsidiary at the time the services were rendered, and for the purposes of subsection (4) be taken as referring to a subsidiary immediately before the loss of office as director of the company.

The Companies Act 1967, in addition to the requirements of Sect. 196 of the 1948 Act to show particulars of directors' salaries, pensions, etc., requires to be shown the emoluments of the chairman and of the highest-paid director where his emoluments exceed those of the chairman. There must also be shown the number of directors in bands of emoluments of £2,500 and the number who have waived rights to receive emoluments and the aggregate amount of the emoluments waived. The relevant sections of the 1967 Act are:

(A) Particulars in accounts of directors' emoluments (C.A., 1967, Sect. 6):

1. In any accounts of a company laid before it in general meeting, or in a statement annexed thereto, there shall, so far as the information is contained in the company's books and papers or the company has the right to obtain it from the persons concerned:

(a) if one person has been chairman throughout the financial year, be shown his emoluments (unless his duties as chairman were wholly or mainly discharged outside the United Kingdom), and if not, be shown with respect to each person who has been chairman during the year, his emoluments so far as attributable to the period during which he was chairman (unless his duties as chairman were wholly or mainly so discharged);

(b) with respect to all the directors (other than any who discharged their duties as such wholly or mainly outside the United Kingdom), be shown the number (if any) who had no emoluments or whose several emoluments amounted to not more than £2,500 and by reference to each pair of adjacent points on a scale whereon the lowest point is £2,500 and the succeeding ones are successive integral multiples of £2,500, the number (if any) whose several emoluments exceeded the lower point but did not exceed the higher.

2. If, of the directors of a company (other than any who discharge their duties as such wholly or mainly outside the United Kingdom), the emoluments of one only (so far as ascertainable from information contained in the company's books and papers or obtainable by right by the company from him) exceed the relevant amount, his emoluments (so far as so ascertainable) shall also be shown in the said accounts or in a statement annexed thereto; and if, of the directors of a company (other than any who discharged their duties as such wholly or mainly outside the United Kingdom), the emoluments (so far as so ascertainable) of each of two or more exceed the relevant amount, the emoluments (so far as so ascertainable) of him (or them, in the case of equality) who had the greater or, as the case may be, the greatest shall also be shown in the said accounts or in a statement annexed thereto.

3. For the purposes of this section there shall be brought into account as emoluments of any person all such amounts (other than contributions paid in respect of him under any pension scheme) as in his case are, by virtue of section 196 of the principal Act (disclosure of aggregates of directors' salaries, pensions, etc.), required to be included in the amount shown under subsection (1)(a) of that section.

4. If, in the case of any accounts, the requirements of this section are not complied with, it shall be the duty of the auditors of the company by whom the accounts are examined to include in their report thereon, so far as they are reasonably able to do so, a statement giving the required particulars.

5. In section 198 of the principal Act (general duty to make disclosure for the purposes of sections 195 to 197), the reference in subsection (1) to sections 195 and 196 of that Act and the reference in subsection (3) to the said section 196 shall each be construed as including a reference to this section.

6. A company which is neither a holding company nor a subsidiary of another body corporate shall not be subject to the requirements of this section as respects a financial year in the case of which the amount shown in its account under section 196(1)(a) of the principal Act does not exceed £7,500.

7. In this section:

(a) 'chairman', in relation to a company, means the person elected by the directors of the company to be chairman of their meetings and includes a person who, though not so elected, holds any office (however designated) which, in accordance with the constitution of the company, carries with it functions substantially similar to those discharged by a person so elected; and

(b) 'the relevant amount':

(i) if one person has been chairman throughout the year, means the amount of his emoluments;

(ii) if not, means an amount equal to the aggregate of the emoluments, so far as attributable to the period during which he was chairman, of each person who has been chairman during the year.

(B) Particulars in accounts of directors' emoluments the rights to receive which have been waived (C.A., 1967, Sect. 7):

1. In any accounts of a company laid before it in general meeting, or in a statement annexed thereto, there shall be shown, so far as the information is contained in the company's books and papers or the company has the right to obtain it from the persons concerned—

(a) the number of directors who have waived rights to receive emoluments which, but for the waiver, would have fallen to be included in the amount shown in those accounts under section 196(1)(a) of the principal Act;

(b) the aggregate amount of the said emoluments.

2. For the purposes of this section:

(a) it shall be assumed that a sum not receivable in respect of a period would have been paid at the time at which it was due to be paid;

(b) a sum not so receivable that was payable only on demand, being a sum the right to receive which has been waived, shall be deemed to have been due for payment at the time of the waiver.

3. Subsections (4), (5) and (6) of the last foregoing section shall, with the substitution, for references to that section, of references to this section, apply for the purposes of this section as they apply for the purposes of that section.

The Companies Act 1967 requires to be shown the number of employees, other than directors or those who were wholly or mainly employed outside the United Kingdom, whose emoluments are £10,000 or more per annum. The relevant section of the 1967 Act is:

(C) Particulars in accounts of salaries of employees receiving more than £10,000 a year. (C.A., 1967, Sect. 8):

1. In any accounts of a company laid before it in general meeting, or in a statement annexed thereto, there shall be shown by reference to each pair of adjacent points on a scale whereon the lowest point is £10,000 and the succeeding ones are successive integral multiples of £2,500 beginning with that in the case of which the multiplier is five, the number (if any) of persons in the company's employment whose several emoluments exceeded the lower point but did not exceed the higher, other than:

(a) directors of the company; and

(b) persons, other than directors of the company, being persons who:

(i) if employed by the company throughout the financial year to which the accounts relate, worked wholly or mainly during the year outside the United Kingdom; or

(ii) if employed by the company for part only of that year, worked wholly or mainly during that part outside the United Kingdom.

2. For the purposes of this section, a person's emoluments shall include any paid to or receivable by him from the company, the company's subsidiaries and any other person in respect of his services as a person in the employment of the company or a subsidiary thereof or as a director of a subsidiary thereof (except sums to be accounted for to the company or any of its subsidiaries) and 'emoluments', in relation to a person, includes fees and percentages, any sums paid by way of expenses allowance in so far as those sums are charged to United Kingdom income tax, and the estimated money value of any other benefits received by him otherwise than in cash.

3. The amounts to be brought into account for the purpose of complying with subsection (1) above as respects a financial year shall be the sums receivable in respect of that year, whenever paid, or, in the case of sums not receivable in respect of a period, the sums paid during that year, so, however, that where:

(a) any sums are not brought into account for the relevant financial year on the ground that the person receiving them is liable to account thereof as mentioned in the last foregoing subsection, but the liability is wholly or partly released or is not enforced within a period of two years; or

(b) any sums paid to a person by way of expenses allowance are charged to United Kingdom income tax after the end of the relevant financial year;

those sums shall, to the extent to which the liability is released or not enforced or they are charged as aforesaid, as the case may be, be brought into account for the purpose of complying with subsection (1) above on the first occasion on which it is practicable to do so.

4. If, in the case of any accounts, the requirements of this section are not complied with, it shall be the duty of the auditors of the company by whom the accounts are examined to include in their report thereon, so far as they are reasonably able to do so, a statement giving the required particulars.

5. References in subsection (2) above to a company's subsidiary:

(a) in relation to a person who is or was, while employed by the company a director, by virtue of the company's nomination, direct or indirect, of any other body corporate, shall, subject to the following paragraph, include that body corporate, whether or not it is or was in fact the company's subsidiary; and

(b) shall be taken as referring to a subsidiary at the time the services were rendered.

As will be seen in the next chapter, Sect. 196 and Sect. 197 of the Act, and Sects. 6 to 8 of the 1967 Act, do not apply for the purposes of consolidated accounts.[1] (Para. 19, Part II, Sch. 2.)

Statements or Documents Annexed to the Accounts

References in this Act to a document annexed or required to be annexed to a company's accounts or any of them shall not include the directors' report or the auditors' report:

Provided that any information which is required by this Act to be given in accounts and is thereby allowed to be given in a statement annexed may be given in the directors' report instead of the accounts and, if any such information is so given, the report shall be annexed to the accounts and this Act shall apply in relation thereto accordingly, except that the auditors shall report thereon only so far as it gives the said information. (Sect. 163.)[2]

General Observations

1. Minimum information is extended to the Profit and Loss Account.

2. Accounts, Auditors' Report and Directors' Report may be filed with the Annual Return.

---

[1] But Sect. 196 and Sects. 6 to 8 *do* apply to emoluments, etc., of the directors and executives of a parent company where the option is taken under Sect. 149 (5) of showing the parent company's Profit and Loss Account framed as a consolidated Profit and Loss Account.

[2] This section is referable to the 1948 Act and to the 1967 Act.

3. Alternative means are afforded in certain instances of giving information by way of note or statement or report annexed.

4. The Department of Trade have power to modify certain of the requirements (at the company's request).

5. The Department has power by regulations to alter the provisions dealing with accounts, but such alterations are not to make the requirements more onerous unless the draft is approved by both Houses of Parliament.

6. Four types of fixed assets are excepted from the rule for disclosure of such assets at cost (or valuation) less aggregate depreciation, etc., written off, e.g.:

(*a*) assets for which the necessary figures cannot be obtained without unnecessary cost or delay (relating to the period commencing with the operation of the Act);

(*b*) assets to be replaced by the renewal method wholly or in part (means of replacement and unused provision thereof must be shown in the Balance Sheet);

(*c*) to any quoted investments or to any unquoted investments of which the value as estimated by the directors is shown either as the amount of the investments or by way of note;

(*d*) goodwill, patents, and trademarks.

7. These extensive requirements for disclosure of amount and movement of reserves and provisions. The objects are to make a clear distinction between what are virtually liabilities (or diminished assets) and undistributed profits of a revenue or capital nature. No adjustments are necessary in respect of amounts *written* off (but not excess provisions for depreciation or diminished value) before 1st July 1948.

8. As will be seen in the next chapter, profit or loss of a subsidiary arising before purchase by a holding company is to be regarded as Capital.

9. Investments are to be divided into the following classes:

(*a*) In subsidiaries.
(*b*) Quoted.
(*c*) Unquoted.

The aggregate amount of quoted investments (including trade investments) must be shown, and also the aggregate market value where it differs from the book value. Where the market value of any investments is greater than the stock-exchange value, this fact must be stated.

The aggregate amount of unquoted investments must be shown, and the cost and aggregate amounts written-off must be shown. In respect of unquoted investments in equity share capital there must be shown the total income receivable therefrom for the year, the share of profits less losses (before and after taxation) in the companies in which the investments are held and from whom accounts have been received, the share in the total undistributed profits less losses since the investments were acquired, and the manner in which losses incurred have been dealt with in the company's own account.

It should be noted that the immediately aforementioned requirements concerning unquoted investments in equity share capital are avoided if a separate directors' valuation is shown of the investments whether individually or collectively.

10. Elaborate provisions are made for the disclosure of directors' emoluments (including 'expenses'), pensions and compensation for loss of office, and in each case a distinction is made between the payments in respect of services as directors and those in respect of services connected with the management of the company.

11. The Companies Act 1976 (S13/20) contains important provisions in respect of the auditor's qualifications, duties, powers, and position.

Statements of Source and Application of Funds

The object of the Statement of Standard Accounting Practice reproduced hereunder is to establish the practice of providing source and application of funds statements as a part of audited accounts and to lay down a minimum standard of disclosure in such statements. (SSAP 1/10).

I Explanatory note

1. The profit and loss account and the balance sheet of a company show, *inter alia*, the amount of profit made during the year and the disposition of the company's resources at the beginning and the end of that year. However, for a fuller understanding of a company's affairs it is necessary also to identify the movements in assets, liabilities and capital which have taken place during the year and the resultant effect of net liquid funds. This information is not specifically disclosed by a profit and loss account and balance sheet but can be made available in the form of a statement of source and application of funds (a "funds statement").

2. The funds statement is in no way a replacement for the profit and loss account and balance sheet although the information which it contains is a selection, reclassification and summarisation of information contained in those two statements. The objective of such a statement is to show the manner in which the operations of a company have been financed and in which its financial resources have been used and the format selected should be designed to achieve this objective. A funds statement does not purport to indicate the requirements of a business for capital nor the extent of seasonal peaks of stocks, debtors, etc.

3. A funds statement should show the sources from which funds have flowed into the company and the way in which they have been used. It should show clearly the funds generated or absorbed by the operations of the business and the manner in which any resulting surplus of liquid assets has been applied or any deficiency of such assets has been financed, distinguishing the long term from the short term. The statement should distinguish the use of funds for the purchase of new fixed assets from funds used in increasing the working capital of the company.

4. The funds statement will provide a link between the balance sheet at the beginning of the period, the profit and loss account for the period and

the balance sheet at the end of the period. A minimum of "netting off" should take place as this may tend to mask the significance of individually important figures; for example, the sale of one building and the purchase of another should generally be kept separate in a funds statement. The figures from which a funds statement is constructed should generally be identifiable in the profit and loss account, balance sheet and related notes. If adjustments to those published figures are necessary, details should be given to enable the related figures to be rapidly located.

5. Funds statements should, in the case of companies with subsidiaries, be based on the group accounts. They should reflect any purchases of disposals of subsidiary companies either (a) as separate items, or (b) by reflecting the effects on the separate assets and liabilities dealt with in the statement, so that the acquisition of a subsidiary company would be dealt with as an application of funds in acquiring the fixed assets (including goodwill) of that subsidiary and as a change in working capital. In either case, in the interests of clarity, it will generally also be necessary to summarise the effects of the acquisition or disposal by way of a footnote indicating, in the case of an acquisition, how much of the purchase price has been discharged in cash and how much by the issue of shares. Examples of the alternative treatments are shown in examples 2 and 3 in the Appendix.

6. A funds statement should form part of the audited accounts of a company.

7. Although this accounting standard is for application to all enterprises other than small enterprises with a turnover or gross income less than £25,000 per annum, consideration should nevertheless be given to the particular circumstances of such enterprises with a view to furnishing the funds statement wherever it is desirable.

II Definition of terms

8. *Net liquid funds:* cash at bank and in hand and cash equivalents (e.g. investments held as current assets) less bank overdrafts and other borrowings repayable within one year of the accounting date.

III Standard accounting practice

9. This accounting standard shall apply to all financial accounts intended to give a true and fair view of financial position and profit or loss other than those of enterprises with turnover or gross income of less than £25,000 per annum.

10. Audited financial accounts should, subject to paragraph 9 above, include a statement of source and application of funds both for the period under review and for the corresponding previous period.

11. The statement should show the profit or loss for the period together with the adjustments required for items which did not use (or provide) funds in the period. The following other sources and applications of funds

should, where material, also be shown:

   (a) dividends paid;

   (b) acquisitions and disposals of fixed and other non-current assets;

   (c) funds raised by increasing, or expended in repaying or redeeming medium or long-term loans or the issued capital of the company; and

   (d) increase or decrease in working capital subdivided into its components, and movements in net liquid funds.

12. Where the accounts are those of a group, the statement of source and application of funds should be so framed as to reflect the operations of the group.

Appendix

The Appendix is for general guidance and does not form part of the Statement of Standard Accounting Practice.

Appendix

This appendix does not form part of the Statement of Standard Accounting Practice. The methods of presentation used are illustrative only and in no way prescriptive and other methods of presentation may equally comply with the accounting standard. The format used should be selected with a view to demonstrating clearly the manner in which the operations of the company have been financed and in which its financial resources have been utilised.

Example 1

Company without Subsidiaries Ltd.

Statement of Source and Application of Funds

	This Year £'000		Last Year £'000	
Source of Funds				
Profit before tax		1,430		440
Adjustments for items not involving the movement of funds:				
Depreciation		380		325
Total generated from Operations		1,810		765
Funds from other Sources				
Issue of shares for cash		100		80
		1,910		845
Application of Funds				
Dividends paid	(400)		(400)	
Tax paid	(690)		(230)	
Purchase of fixed assets	(460)	(1,550)	(236)	(866)
		360		(21)

Increase/Decrease in Working Capital

Increase in stocks		80		114
Increase in debtors		120		22
(Increase) decrease in creditors (excluding taxation and proposed dividends)		115		(107)
Movement in net liquid funds: Increase (decrease) in:				
Cash balances	(5)		35	
Short-term investments	50		(85)	
	—	45	—	(50)
		360		(21)

Example 2

Groups Limited

Statement of Source and Application of Funds

(based on the accounts of the Group and showing the effects of acquiring a subsidiary on the separate assets and liabilities of the Group).

	This Year £'000	Last Year £'000
Source of Funds		
Profit before tax and extraordinary items, less minority interests	2,025	2,610
Extraordinary items	450	(170)
	2,475	2,440
Adjustments for items not involving the movement of funds:		
Minority interests in the retained profits of the year	25	30
Depreciation	345	295
Profits retained in associated companies	(40)	—
Total generated from Operations	2,805	2,765
Funds from other Sources		
Shares issued in part consideration of the acquisition of subsidiary*	290	—
Capital raised under executive option scheme	100	80
	3,195	2,845
Application of Funds		
Dividends paid	(650)	(650)
Tax paid	(770)	(970)
Purchase of fixed assets*	(660)	(736)
Purchase of goodwill on acquisition of subsidiary*	(30)	—
Debentures redeemed	(890)	—
	(3,000)	(2,356)
	195	489

Increase/Decrease in Working Capital

Increase in stocks*		120		166
Increase in debtors*		100		122
Decrease in creditors (excluding taxation and proposed dividends)*		75		17
Movement in net liquid funds:				
increase (decrease) in cash balance*	(35)		10	
increase (decrease) in short-term investments	(65)		174	
		(100)		184
		195		489

* *SUMMARY of the effects of the acquisition of Subsidiary Limited:*

Net assets acquired		Discharged by	
Fixed assets	290	Shares issued	290
Goodwill	30	Cash paid	60
Stocks	40		
Debtors	30		
Creditors	(40)		
	350		350

Example 3

Groups Limited

Statement of Source and Application of funds

(based on the accounts of the Group and showing the acquisition of a subsidiary as a separate item).

	This Year £'000	Last Year £'000
Source of Funds		
Profit before tax and extraordinary items, less minority interests	2,025	2,610
Extraordinary items	450	(170)
	2,475	2,440
Adjustments for items not involving the movement of funds:		
Minority interests in the retained profits of the year	25	30
Depreciation	345	295
Profits retained in associated companies	(40)	—
Total generated from Operations	2,805	2,765
Funds from other Sources		
Shares issued in part consideration of the acquisition of subsidiary*	290	—
Capital raised under executive option scheme	100	80
	3,195	2,845

Application of Funds

Dividends paid	(650)		(650)	
Tax paid	(770)		(970)	
Purchase of fixed assets	(370)		(736)	
Purchase of Subsidiary Ltd*	(350)		—	
Debentures redeemed	(890)		—	
		(3,030)		(2,356)
		165		489

Increase/Decrease in Working Capital

Increase in stocks		80		166	
Increase in debtors		70		122	
Decrease in creditors (excluding taxation and proposed dividends)		115		17	
Movement in net liquid funds: increase (decrease) in cash balance*	(35)		10		
increase (decrease) in short-term investments	(65)		174		
		(100)		184	
			165		489

* ANALYSIS *of the acquisition of Subsidiary Limited:*

Net assets acquired		Discharged by	
Fixed assets	290	Shares issued	290
Goodwill	30	Cash paid	60
Stocks	40		
Debtors	30		
Creditors	(40)		
	350		350

SECTION C. COMPANY TAXATION—CORPORATION TAX— ADVANCE CORPORATION TAX (ACT)—TREATMENT OF TAXATION IN LIMITED COMPANY ACCOUNTS, CLOSE COMPANIES

Corporation Tax

The finance Act 1965, introduced Corporation Tax, which is levied on the total chargeable profits of limited companies. Corporation Tax replaces Income Tax and Profit Tax to which the profits of limited companies were formerly liable. Corporation Tax is assessed on the profits of the accounting period, and the rate of tax imposed is at a specified rate for the 'financial year' as distinct from Income Tax in the case of individuals, sole traders and partnerships, which is imposed for a 'year of assessment'.

A financial year is any year commencing on 1st April and ending on 31st March following, and is identified by the calender year in which it begins. For example, the financial year 1980 is the year from 1st April 1980 to 31st March 1981.

A year of assessment (more commonly known as a fiscal year) for Income Tax purposes is any year commencing on the 6th April and ending on the 5th April of the succeeding year. For example, the fiscal year 1980/81 is the year from 6th April 1980 to 5th April 1981.

The rate of Corporation Tax is fixed in the annual Finance Act for the preceding financial year ended 31st March, and consequently when a change is made in the rate of Corporation Tax, part of the total chargeable profits may be taxed at one rate and part at another rate. For example, the total profits of an accounting year ended 31st December 1980 would be chargeable to Corporation Tax as follows:

$\frac{1}{4}$ (3 months ended 31st March 1980) at the 1979/80 rate;
$\frac{3}{4}$ (9 months ended 31st December 1980) at the 1980/81 rate.

From 6th April 1966 to 5th April 1973 inclusive Income Tax at the standard rate ruling at date of payment had to be deducted from all company dividend payments and other distributions. Income Tax so deducted had to be accounted for to the Inland Revenue under Income Tax Schedule F. On and after 6th April 1973 the rate of Corporation Tax was increased to 52% (for each of the three preceding financial years the rate was 40%) and a small companies rate of 42% was introduced to apply to companies whose yearly profit did not exceed £25,000 with tapering relief up to £40,000.[1] Commencing 6th April 1973 Income Tax Schedule F was abolished and consequently Income Tax no longer has to be deducted from dividend payments and other distributions and accounted for to the Inland Revenue. Instead, on and after 6th April 1973 when a U.K. resident company pays a dividend or makes other distributions an advance payment of Corporation Tax is payable calculated by reference to the rate in force for the financial year in which that distribution is made. Additionally capital gains, which are included in arriving at total profits for Corporation Tax purposes, are reduced; the reduction for the financial year 1973 was 11/26ths which thereby reduced the full rate of 52% to 30% thereon.[2]

Companies Chargeable. All companies resident in the United Kingdom and also those which, although not resident in the United Kingdom, carry on a trade in the United Kingdom through a branch or agency are liable to Corporation Tax. The country in which a company is resident is that country in which its real business and the management and control thereof exists. For the purpose of Corporation Tax, a company is defined as any body corporate or an unincorporated association but does not include a partnership, individuals, or local authorities.

[1] For the financial year 1980 (i.e. year ending 31st March 1981—(i) the Corporation Tax rate is 00%. (ii) the small companies rate is 40% and the profit threshold is £80,000 and the upper limit for marginal relief is £200,000.

[2] As from 1 April 1978 the fraction is also 11/26ths, the full rate of Corporation Tax is thus effectively reduced from 52% to 30%.

Computation of Profits. Corporation Tax is assessed for any accounting period on the total profits, meaning income and chargeable gains,[1] arising in the accounting period, computed in accordance with Income Tax principles applicable to each type of income, as if the accounting period was the year of assessment. The Income Tax law applied is that which is in force for the year of assessment in which the accounting period ends.

It cannot be over-emphasized that for full details of the intricacies of Corporation Tax reference must be made to a standard textbook dealing solely with this tax. For present purposes, however, it should be specially noted that:

1. In respect of the computation of adjusted trading profits (which normally form the major part of the total profits of a company) the profits are the ACTUAL profits of the accounting period concerned computed generally on the normal basis of Income Tax principles, except that:

(a) dividends and other distributions received from other companies resident in the United Kingdom which are liable to Corporation Tax are franked investment income and as such are not again subject to Corporation Tax in the hands of the recipient company. Franked investment income is thus excluded;

(b) capital allowances for the accounting period are deductible as if the allowances were a trading expense for that period;

(c) directors' remuneration is deductible in full;[2]

(d) yearly interest paid to a United Kingdom bank is deductible provided that it is a proper business expense.[3]

2. Regarding other types of income:

(a) Income assessable to Corporation Tax under Schedule D, Cases IV and V, is reduced by any unrelieved foreign Income Tax paid in the country where it arose;

(b) in computing a company's income for any accounting period, expenses of management or supervision of minerals are deductible from rents from letting rights to work them.

3. In computing income from any one source, payments of yearly interest, annuities or other annual payments are NOT deductible. such payments are deductible from the TOTAL PROFITS, as also are:

(a) bank interest which has not been charged against trading profits;

(b) interest paid to a stockbroker;

(c) interest paid to a discount house.

---

[1] As reduced by the appropriate fraction.

[2] The Finance Act 1969, removed in respect of close companies the limits on allowable directors' remunerations as respects accounting periods ending on and after 1st April 1969.

[3] The Finance Act 1969, introduced complex legislation regarding loan interest payments. However, interest payments to a U.K. bank are made gross, and provided the loan was received for business purposes the gross payments are allowed as a charge for taxation purposes.

Furthermore, payments of yearly interest, etc., will be allowed only if:

(a) they are charged to revenue and not capital by the company, and not ultimately borne by capital;

(b) they are borne by the company;

(c) valuable and sufficient consideration has been received except in the case of donations to charity, covenanted for a period which can exceed six years, which ARE ALLOWABLE.

Date of Payment. Prior to the introduction of Corporation Tax, limited companies were liable to pay: (i) Income Tax on 1st January falling within the relevant fiscal year, and (ii) Profits Tax one month from the date of assessment. Since the basis of an Income Tax Schedule D Case I or II assessment is the profit of the preceding year, the liability in respect of assessable profits is not due and payable until from nine to twenty months later, depending on the date of the Company's year end. Although Corporation Tax assessments are made for accounting periods and not fiscal years, the changeover from Income Tax Schedule D does not affect the interval between the accounting year end and the date of payment so far as companies operating before 1st April 1965 are concerned. In these circumstances, except in the case aftermentioned, Corporation Tax is payable on 1st January in the financial year following the financial year in which the accounting year ended. Where, however, the accounting year of a company operating before 1st April 1965, ends on a day falling between 31st March and 6th April, Corporation Tax is payable on 1st January following.

Where companies commenced trading on or after 1st April 1965, Corporation Tax is payable within nine months from the end of the accounting period for which it is assessed.

Advance Corporation Tax

The Finance Act 1972 introduced Advance Corporation Tax (ACT) which is payable by companies resident in the U.K. on all dividend payments and other distributions on and after 6th April 1973. As already mentioned Income Tax is no longer deducted from dividends payments, etc. and thus the percentage or per share dividend etc. declared is the actual amount which is due to be paid to shareholders. The rate of ACT is expressed as a fraction of the amount of the dividend etc. payable. For the financial year 1978 (1st April 1978 to 31st March 1979) the rate of ACT was 33/67ths or 33% of the dividend etc. plus ACT. Thus a dividend of £67 attracted a liability of £33 ACT.[1]

The amount of the dividend etc. plus the relevant ACT is known as a Franked Payment. In the immediately foregoing example the Franked Payment is £100. A U.K. recipient of a dividend etc. in respect of which ACT is payable is entitled to a tax credit which can be set off against his or her personal tax liability and in appropriate circumstances a repayment of the tax credit may be claimed.

[1] For the financial year 1981 (i.e. year ended 31st March 1980) the rate of ACT is 3/7ths or 30%.

When first introduced the rate of ACT was 3/7ths (30% of the dividend etc. plus VAT) and the Finance Act 1972 determined that preference shares issued before 6th April 1973 were to be reduced to 7/10ths of their former rate. This means, for example, that a former 10% preference share is reduced to 7% actual and this percentage is unalterable irrespective of changes in rates of ACT. The tax credit is, of course, variable with changes in the rates of ACT and as a consequence a former 10% preference share may in future yield more or less than 10% on nominal value.

Dividends include capital dividends, and other distributions briefly include:

(i) A distribution, other than a dividend, made in respect of shares, except a repayment of capital or a distribution in exchange for new consideration;

(ii) a bonus issue of securities or redeemable shares;

(iii) interest or other payments, such as premiums on redemption, in respect of certain securities granted by a company;

(iv) any net benefit, being the difference between the assets or liabilities transferred and their market value, received by a member of the company, arising out of transfer of assets or liabilities between the member and the company.

Dividends or Other Distributions Received. All Companies are liable to pay ACT on dividend payments or other distributions and the ACT paid is regarded as a tax credit from the recipient shareholder's viewpoint. Dividends or other distributions received by any company, whether resident or not, from a U.K. resident Company are not liable to Corporation Tax. Such dividends, etc. received are termed Franked Investment Income (FII). FII comprises the amount or value of the dividend etc. received plus the related tax credit. Thus a dividend received of £67 actual represents FII of £100 where the rate of ACT is 33/67ths. FII may be set off against Franked Payments in determining ACT liability.

Illustrations

In the two following illustrations the first shows how the set-off of ACT operates and the second shows how a surplus of ACT can arise. (In both cases Corporation Tax is taken at 55% and ACT as 3/7ths.)

1. In its year ended 31/3/19.2 a limited company has a Corporation Tax profit of £150,000 and pays £63,000 in dividends that year.

The taxation position is:

ACT	63,000 × 3/7		£27,000
Corporation Tax liability	£150,000 × 55%	£82,500	
Less ACT		27,000	
Mainstream Corporation Tax			55,500
Total Corporation Tax			£82,500

Note. The U.K. resident shareholders of the company receive cash dividend of £63,000. However, their income assessable to Income Tax is £90,000 i.e. cash dividend of £63,000 plus tax credit £27,000. The tax credit satisfies Income Tax liability at the basic rate or where liability does not arise can be reclaimed.

2. The same company in the following year ended 31st March 19.3 has a Corporation Tax profit of £77,000 and the dividend paid is £63,000 as before.

The taxation position is:

ACT	£63,000×3/7		£27,000
Corporation Tax			
liability	£77,000×55%	£42,350	
Less ACT (restricted)		22,100	
Mainstream Corporation Tax			20,250
Total Corporation Tax			£47,250

Notes. (i) As before, the U.K. resident shareholders receive cash of £63,000 plus tax credit of £27,000.

(ii) The ACT set-off is restricted to £22,100 being ACT at 3/7ths on £54,900 making a total of £77,000 that is the amount of the Corporation Tax profit.

(iii) The company is entitled to relief on the surplus ACT i.e. £27,000 less £22,100 = £4,900. The company can opt either to carry forward the £4,900 for set off in a subsequent accounting period or to have immediate repayment by set off against the previous accounting period. Option for the latter would result in a revised 19.2 computation as follows:

Corporation Tax			
liability	£150,000×55%		£82,500
Less ACT 19.2		£27,000	
ACT 19.3		4,900	
			31,900
Revised Mainstream Corporation Tax			50,600
Already paid			55,500
Repayable			£4,900

'Charges on Income' Paid. Charges on income such as annual interest (e.g. debenture interest), annuities, royalties and other annual payments[1] must be paid by a company after deduction of Income Tax at the standard rate ruling at date of payment. The Income Tax so deducted should be remitted to the Collector of Taxes within 14 days after the return period

[1] The rule, introduced by the Finance Act 1969, that payments of loan interest should now be made gross, i.e. without deduction of Income Tax, does NOT apply to limited companies. (See p. 2106.)

in which the charges on income were paid. For example, if debenture interest were paid on 5th September, then the relevant amount of Income Tax on the gross amount should be remitted by 14th October.

If charges on income are accrued at a company's year end Income Tax thereon should be deducted only if the charges are due and payable at date of accrual. The net amount of charges on income due and payable at a company's year end and the relevant amount of Income Tax on the gross amounts may both be seen separately in the Balance Sheet as Current Liabilities. In the case of published accounts, however, the Income Tax may be merged with Sundry Creditors. In the Profit and Loss Account the gross amount only need be shown.

If charges on income are accrued, but not actually due and payable at a company's year end, then no liability to Income Tax has yet arisen and consequently the gross amounts only should be shown, if material, in the Profit and Loss Account and Balance Sheet.

Annual Payments, etc., Received. Income Tax suffered by deduction on annual payments, etc., received is deductible from the Corporation Tax payable in respect of the accounting period in which the income is included. For the purpose of the quarterly accounting (see later) the Income Tax suffered may be set off against any Income Tax due on annual payments, etc., made, but where this is done the Income Tax originally suffered cannot be deducted from Corporation Tax payable.

Collection of Taxation—Return Period Accounting. The provisions of Schedule 14, Finance act 1972 require a return to the Collector of Taxes of dividend payments etc. and of franked investment income. The provisions of Schedule 20 of the same act require a return of annual payments etc. made and received. The returns required by Schedule 14 and Schedule 20 are made on Inland Revenue Form CT 61.

A return under Schedule 14 should be for each return period in which a dividend payment, etc. is made. Further, where a company has paid ACT for a return period within an accounting period and in a later return period in the same accounting period FII is received a return must be made for the later return period whether or not any dividends etc. were paid in that later return period.

Similarly, under Schedule 20 a return to the Collector should be made of annual payments, etc. made in any return period within an accounting period.

Returns should be made within 14 days after the end of a return period. Generally each calendar quarter is a return period; thus a company whose accounting period is the year ending 31 December is required, where appropriate, to submit returns within 14 days after 31 March, 30 June, 30 September and 31 December. However, where a company's accounting period does not commence immediately after or end with a calendar quarter return periods of less than three months will apply; thus a company whose year ends 31 October is required to submit returns within 14 days after 31 December, 31 March, 30 June, 30 September, 31 October, i.e. five return periods in the accounting year, of duration 2 months, three 3 months, and 1 month respectively.

The amount of tax due should be remitted with the return made. Interest is charged on overdue tax unless the interest would amount to £5 or less.

Treatment of Taxation in Limited Company Accounts

Statutory Requirements. Requirements concerning the minimum amount of information to be disclosed in the published accounts of limited companies are contained in Schedule 2 to the Companies Act 1967. The relevant requirements, obsolete terms having been removed or updated, are as follows:

1. Profit and Loss Account. There must be shown:

(i) The amount of the charge to revenue for United Kingdom Corporation Tax and, if that amount would have been greater but for relief from double taxation, the amount which it would have been but for such relief, the amount of the charge for United Kingdom Income Tax and the amount of the charge for taxation imposed outside the United Kingdom of profits, income and (so far as charged to revenue) capital gains (Para. 12 (1) (c)).

(ii) The aggregate amount of the dividends paid and proposed. (Para. 12 (1) (h)).

There must also be shown by way of note if not otherwise shown:

(i) The basis on which the charge for United Kingdom Corporation Tax and United Kingdom Income Tax is computed (Para. 14 (3)).

(ii) Any special circumstances which affect liability in respect of taxation or profits, income or capital gains for the financial year or liability in respect of taxation of profits, income or capital gains for succeeding financial years (Para. 14 (3A)).

2. Balance Sheet. There must be shown:

(i) Any amount set aside for the purpose of its being used to prevent undue fluctuations in charges for taxation (Para. 7A);

(ii) under a separate heading the aggregate amount which is recommended for distribution by way of dividend (Para. 8 (I) (e)).

There must also be shown by way of note or in a statement or report annexed if not otherwise shown:

(i) If a sum set aside for the purpose of its being used to prevent undue fluctuations in charges for taxation has been used during the financial year for another purpose, the amount thereof and the fact that it has been so used. (Para 11 (8A)).

(ii) The basis on which the amount, if any, set aside for United Kingdom Corporation Tax is computed (Para. 11 (10)).

Statement of Standard Accounting Practice. The imputation system of company taxation started in the UK in April 1973. The purpose of the statement is to establish a standard treatment of taxation in company accounts.

(*Note.* Assumed rates of taxation—Corporation Tax 50%, ACT 3/7ths) (Ref. SSAP No. 1/8).

I. Explanatory Note

Introduction

1. The principal feature of the imputation system of corporation tax are broadly as follows. Corporation tax is charged at a single rate on a company's income whether distributed or undistributed; in the absence of a dividend the whole of the tax is payable on a date which may be a year or more after the end of the relevant accounting period. When in an accounting period a company makes a distribution to shareholders, it does not withhold income tax from the payment, but is required to make an advance payment of corporation tax ("ACT"). This ACT will normally be set off against the company's total liability for corporation tax on its income (but not on its chargeable gains) of the same accounting period. The resultant net liability is known as the mainstream corporation tax. The charge for corporation tax therefore comprises the mainstream corporation tax and the ACT. From the paying company's point of view the concept of "gross" dividends and the deduction of income tax at source therefrom has disappeared. However, an individual shareholder receiving the dividend is chargable to tax on an amount of income equivalent to the dividend plus the imputed tax credit. This tax credit (generally equivalent to the ACT paid by the company) will discharge the basic rate liability to income tax of a United Kingdom resident or will in certain circumstances be recoverable. For corporate shareholders the concept of franked investment income continues.

2. The ACT set off against the final corporation tax bill is effectively restricted to 30% (assuming a 50% tax rate) of the company's taxable income. Any ACT thereby unrelieved (i.e. ACT on a distribution which together with the related ACT is in excess of taxable income) can be carried back for two years or forward without time limit (but cannot be set against corporation tax on income arising before April 1, 1973).

3. The main accounting problems arising from the imputation system are:

(*a*) the treatment in the profit and loss account of outgoing dividends and the related ACT;

(*b*) determing the recoverability of ACT;

(*c*) the treatment of irrecoverable ACT and of unrelieved overseas tax arising from the payment or proposed payment of dividends;

(*d*) the treatment in the balance sheet of taxation liabilities, recoverable ACT and dividends;

(*e*) the treatment of franked investment income.

Dividends and the related ACT

4. The treatment in the profit and loss account of outgoing dividends and the related ACT is concerned with whether ACT should be treated as part of the cost of the dividend or whether it should be treated as part of tax on the company's profits. The right of a company to deduct income tax from dividends no longer applies. Whatever percentage or pre-share dividend is declared, that is the amount which the company will pay to its members. The fact that the dividend will carry a tax credit is a matter affecting the recipient rather than the company's method of accounting for the dividend. Accordingly it is considered appropriate that dividends should be shown in the profit and loss account at the amount paid or payable to the shareholders and that neither the related ACT nor the imputed tax credit should be treated as part of the cost of the dividend. It follows that the charge for taxation in the profit and loss account should embrace the full amount of corporation tax, and not merely the mainstream liability.

Recoverability of ACT

5. ACT is primarily recovered by being set off against the corporation tax on the income of the year in which the related distribution is made. In the case of dividends paid during the year under review, the taxable income of that year and of the two previous years will normally be available to absorb the relief. Where a proposed dividend is to be paid in the following year, the related ACT falls to be set off against the corporation tax on the taxable income of the year of payment of the proposed dividend and, in default of that, against the taxable income of the year under review or of the year previous to that. In both cases ACT can be carried forward indefinitely if necessary. In each year there is an overriding restriction on the use of ACT for the set off, by reference to the taxable income of that year.

6. For accounting purposes it is necessary to decide whether recovery of the ACT is reasonably certain and foreseeable or whether it should be written off in the profit and loss account. If the taxable income of the year under review and the amounts available from the preceding year or years are insufficient to cover the ACT, then recoverability of ACT will depend on the extent to which income is earned in future periods in excess of dividends paid or on the existence of a deferred taxation account of adequate size (see paragraph 7). Although the relief remains available indefinitely it will be prudent to have regard only to the immediate and foreseeable future; how long this future period should be will depend upon the circumstances of each case, but it is suggested that where there is no deferred taxation account it should normally not extend beyond the next accounting period.

7. Where a deferred taxation account is maintained, the attitude to recoverability may be different. The balance on the deferred taxation account usually represents an amount which will be released to profit and loss account over the life of related fixed assets. Unrelieved ACT is

available to offset against future taxable profits for an indefinite period. There is thus a similarity between unrelieved ACT and the balance on the deferred taxation account and it is therefore reasonable to regard unrelieved ACT as being available for deduction from the amount at which the deferred taxation account is stated in the accounts. Only a proportion of the balance on the account (at the rates assumed 30% of the amount on which the credit balance of the account has been calculated) can be used for this purpose: this is the extent to which ACT can be set off against the corporation tax liability. It should be noted however that to the extent to which the deferred taxation account represents deferred chargeable gains, it is not available for this purpose.

Irrecoverable ACT

8. Any irrecoverable ACT (i.e. ACT the recoverability of which is not reasonably certain and foreseeable) should be written off in the profit and loss account in which the related dividend is shown.

9. There are two differing views on the presentation in the profit and loss account of irrecoverable ACT written off. One view is that irrecoverable ACT should be treated as part of the tax charge upon the company to be deducted in arriving at profits after tax; the other that the irrecoverable ACT, being a cost stemming from the payment of a dividend, should be treated as an appropriation like the dividend itself. Of the two methods the first is supported as the appropriate accounting treatment because unrelieved ACT constitutes tax upon the company or group, as opposed to tax on the share holders, and is not an appropriation of profits. It is appreciated however that some readers or analysts of accounts may wish for their purposes to regard irrecoverable ACT in some other manner. The amount of irrecoverable ACT should therefore be separately disclosed if material.

10. The question remains whether irrecoverable ACT could appropriately be treated as an "extraordinary item" as defined in SSAP 6.[1] The test laid down in that document needs to be applied to each individual case, but it is unlikely that a cost arising from the payment of a normal dividend would be derived from "transactions outside the ordinary activities of the business", and accordingly irrecoverable ACT will normally constitute part of the ordinary tax charge.

Unrelieved overseas tax

11. Although for tax purposes unrelieved overseas tax cannot be carried forward, the accounting treatment of unrelieved overseas tax arising from the payment of a dividend is similar to that of irrecoverable ACT.

Franked Investment income

12. The concept of franked investment income established under earlier tax systems is continued under the imputation system. Franked investment

[1] SSAP 6. Extraordinary items and prior year adjustments.

income comprises the amount of a qualifying distribution received from another UK resident company with the addition of the related tax credit. The net amount can be redistributed to shareholders of the recipient company without payment of ACT and the related tax credit remains attached from the viewpoint of the shareholder.

13. There are several possible methods of dealing with franked investment income in accounts. The two main possibilities are:

(a) to bring into the Profit & Loss Account the cash amount received or receivable (i.e. excluding the tax credit); or

(b) to bring in the amount of the franked investment income (i.e. including the tax credit, an equivalent amount then being treated as part of the charge for taxation).

The first method would involve treating the income either as an item of profit before taxation, or as an addition to the profit after taxation—both alternatives are open to objection. The second method would allow recognition of the income both at the pre-tax and at the after-tax stage in a way which is consistent with other elements of profit, and is therefore adopted as the standard accounting practice.

Mainstream corporation tax

14. Apart from ACT the dates of payments of corporation tax under the new system remain as before. Depending on the date to which a company makes up its accounts, the balance sheet should contain either (a) one liability for mainstream corporation tax, being that on the profit of the year, or (b) two liabilities. In the latter case they will be the mainstream corporation tax on the profits of the previous year payable within nine months of the balance sheet date, and mainstream corporation tax for the year under review payable twelve months later than the above liability. These liabilities should be separately disclosed, under current liabilities or otherwise as appropriate. If they are not shown under current liabilities, the due date of payment should be stated.

ACT

15. ACT on dividends paid will either have been paid by the balance sheet date or will be due for payment shortly afterwards. Where the ACT is regarded as recoverable, then it will normally be deducted from the full corporation tax charge based on the profit of the period in arriving at the mainstream corporation tax liability shown in the balance sheet.

16. In the case of dividends proposed but not paid at the balance sheet date, the related ACT will become due for payment within about three months of the dividend itself, and should be shown as a current liability. The right of set-off, however, (assuming the ACT is regarded as recoverable) will not arise for at least 21 months from the balance sheet date. This right is, therefore, in the nature of a deferred asset, and should be shown

as such on the balance sheet, unless there is a deferred tax account from the balance of which the amount may be deducted.

17. If ACT on dividends paid or proposed is treated as irrecoverable (see paragraph 8 to 10) there is no corresponding asset to be dealt with in the balance sheet.

Preference shares

18. Any dividend right established before April 6, 1973 at a gross rate or a gross amount was reduced by the Finance Act 1972, Schedule 23 para. 18[1] to seven-tenths of its former rate or amount. Steps should therefore be taken to distinguish, for example, a 10% preference share issued before April 6, 1973 on which the dividend is now 7%, from such a preference share issued after that date. A change in the basic rate of income tax and a corresponding change in the rate of ACT would not affect this once-for-all "netting down". Thus a former 10% preference share may in the future yield, with related tax credit, either more or less than 10% on nominal value. The new rate of dividend on preference shares[2] should therefore be incorporated in the description of the shares in the balance sheet, e.g.

		Authorised	*Issued*
100,000	10% (now 7% + Tax Credit) Preference Shares of £1.	£100,000	£100,000

2. Definition of Terms

Recoverable ACT

19. That amount of the ACT paid or payable on outgoing dividends paid and proposed which can be:

(a) set off against a corporation tax liability on the profits of the period under review or of previous periods; or

(b) properly set off against a credit balance on deferred tax account; or

(c) expected to be recoverable taking into account expected profits and dividends—normally those of the next accounting period only.

Irrecoverable ACT

20. ACT paid or payable on outgoing dividends paid and proposed other than recoverable ACT.

[1] Subsequent changes in the rate of ACT have varied the rate of tax credit but not the amount of the cash dividend payable to shareholders.

[2] Including participating preference and preferred ordinary shares where the former rate of dividend forms part of the title.

3. Standard Accounting Practice

Profit and loss account

21. The following items should be included in the taxation charge in the profit and loss account and, where material, should be separately disclosed:

(*a*) the amount of the United Kingdom corporation tax specifying:

(i)   the charge for corporation tax on the income of the year (where such corporation tax includes transfers between the deferred taxation account and the profit and loss account these also should be separately disclosed where material);
(ii) tax attributable to franked investment income;
(iii) irrecoverable ACT;
(iv) the relief for overseas taxation;

(*b*) the total overseas taxation, relieved and unrelieved, specifying that part of the unrelieved overseas taxation which arises from the payment or proposed payment or proposed payment of dividends.

22. If the rate of corporation tax is not known for the whole or part of the period covered by the accounts, the latest known rate should be used and disclosed.

23. Outgoing dividends should not include either the related ACT or the attributable tax credit.

24. Incoming dividends from United Kingdom resident companies should be included at the amount of cash received or receivable plus the tax credit.

Balance sheet

25. Dividends proposed (or declared and not yet payable) should be included in current liabilities, without the addition of the related ACT. The ACT on proposed dividends (whether recoverable or irrecoverable) should be included as a current tax liability.

· 26. If the ACT on proposed dividends is regarded as recoverable, it should be deducted from the deferred tax account if such an account is available for this purpose. In the absence of a deferred taxation account ACT recoverable should be shown as a deferred asset.

27. Where the title of a class of preference shares (or participating or preferred ordinary shares issued before April 6, 1973 includes a fixed rate of dividend, the new rate of dividend should be incorporated in the description of the shares in the balance sheet.

Appendix

Note: *This appendix is for general guidance and does not form part of the Statement of Standard Accounting Practice.*

This example indicates one method of showing (by way of note) the taxation items required to be disclosed under the Companies Act 1967 and Part III of this Statement. In simple cases taxation may be dealt with entirely within the profit and loss account.

	£'000
Corporation tax on income at x% (including £b transferred to/from deferred taxation account)	a
Less relief for overseas taxation	c
	d
Overseas taxation*	e
Tax credit on UK dividends received	f
Irrecoverable Advance Corporation Tax	g
	H

Accounting for Deferred Taxation. Statement of Standard Accounting Practice 1/15 concerns accounting for deferred taxation and is fairly fully reproduced hereunder:

1. Explanatory Note

Background

1. The amount of taxation payable on the profits of a particular period often bears little relationship to the amount of income and expenditure appearing in the profit and loss account. This results from the different basis on which profits are arrived at for the purpose of computing taxation as opposed to the basis on which profits are stated in financial statements.

2. This different basis of arriving at profits for taxation purposes derives from two main sources. Firstly, the fact that certain types of income may be tax-free or that certain expenditure is disallowable, giving rise to "permanent differences" between taxable and accounting profits. Secondly, the existence of items which are included in the financial statements of a period different from that in which they are dealt with for taxation, giving rise to "timing differences"; stock appreciation relief, to the extent to which it is subject to withdrawal, comes into this category.

3. The effect of timing differences on taxation liabilities in relation to reported profits would be of little significance if taxation was not regarded as relevant to the performance of the business for the period, and the only accepted indicator was the profit before taxation. The view is widely held, however, that the profit after taxation is an important indicator of performance being the fund of earnings which supports (or perhaps does not support) the distribution of profit by way of dividend.

4. So far as the balance sheet is concerned, the relationship between funds provided by shareholders and other sources of finance may be distorted if provision is made for deferred taxation which can be demonstrated with reasonable probability not to be needed.

Timing differences

5. There is wide agreement on the need to identify timing differences and to disclose in financial statements the amounts by which the taxation assessed on a company has been affected by those differences. Paragraph 7A Schedule 2 of the UK Companies Act 1967 requires disclosure of amounts set aside to prevent undue fluctuations in charges for taxation and Paragraph 14 (3A) Schedule 2 of the Act requires disclosure of special circumstances which affect liability in respect of taxation in the current or succeeding financial years.

6. Timing differences arise under five main categories:

(*a*) short-term timing differences from the use of the receipts and payments basis for taxation purposes and the accruals basis in financial statements: these differences normally reverse in the next accounting period;

(*b*) availability of capital allowances in taxation computations which are in excess of the related depreciation charges in financial statements;

(*c*) availability of stock appreciation relief in taxation computations for which there is no equivalent charge in financial statements;

(*d*) revaluation surpluses on fixed assets for which a taxation charge does not arise until the gain is realised on disposal;

(*e*) surpluses on disposals of fixed assets which are subject to rollover relief.

7. In determining whether a deferred taxation provision is required the elements which give rise to timing differences should be calculated separately, although any charge or credit would be based on the net position taking into account all differences.

Short-term timing differences

8. It is generally accepted that deferred taxation should be fully provided for on short-term timing differences.

Accelerated capital allowances

9. In many businesses timing differences arising from accelerated capital allowances are of a recurring nature, and reversing differences are themselves offset, wholly or partially, or are exceeded, by new originating differences, thereby giving rise to continuing tax reductions or the indefinite postponement of any liability attributable to the tax benefits received. An example of a recurring timing difference is that arising when a company having a relatively stable or growing investment in depreciable assets takes tax relief year by year on capital expenditure of an amount which equals or exceeds the additional taxation which would otherwise have been payable in consequence of the reversal of the original timing difference. There may on the contrary be cases where timing differences are not recurring, e.g., because of a spasmodic, declining or highly irregular pattern of capital expenditure, which may indicate that a liability in subsequent years should be provided for in full.

10. It is therefore appropriate that in the case of accelerated capital allowances, provision be made for deferred taxation except in so far as the tax benefit can be expected with reasonable probability to be retained in the future in consequence of recurring timing differences of the same type. The assessment of reasonable probability of the current intentions of the directors and of the company's expectations and plans for the future viewed in relation to the historical pattern of capital expenditure.

Stock appreciation relief

11. Stock appreciation relief arises from both volume and price increases in stocks and work in progress between two balance sheet dates. Full provision for deferred taxation should be made in respect of stock appreciation relief except to the extent that it can be demonstrated with reasonable probability that stock values will not be reduced in the future by reason of lower volumes or prices or that the relief is unlikely to be reclaimed by the Government by reason of any time limits for recovery which may be introduced. The risk of a fall in stock values is of particular importance in the case of stocks which are seasonal in production or subject to sharp fluctuations in price.

Revaluations and disposals of fixed assets

12. A charge for taxation does not arise when a fixed asset is revalued. Normally a taxation charge only arises when an asset is disposed of at a price in excess of its original cost or tax written down value and no rollover or similar relief is available. Provision for taxation payable on the disposal of a fixed asset which has been revalued should be made out of the revaluation surplus as soon as a liability is foreseen based on the volume at which the fixed asset is carried in the balance sheet. A liability would usually be foreseen (in the absence of rollover relief) at the time a company decides in principle to dispose of the assets.

Debit balances arising from timing differences

13. Debit balances on deferred taxation account arising from timing differences should be carried forward only if there is reasonable certainty of their recovery in future periods.

Trading losses

14. While trading losses give rise to timing differences, prudence dictates that they should not be recognised through the deferred taxation account, since there can be no certainty that future profits will be earned of sufficient amount to absorb them.

15. Credit for the tax effects of a trading loss should only be taken when the loss is utilised for tax purposes, unless there is a credit balance on deferred taxation account at the time when the loss carry-forward arises.

16. In such circumstances credit balances on deferred taxation account should be released to profit and loss account to the extent of the notional tax relief attributable to the loss, but not exceeding that part of the deferred taxation account which represents tax on income which can properly be offset against the loss for tax purposes. When trading profits are subsequently earned a deferred taxation account balance may require to be reinstated to the extent of the tax relief resulting from the loss, but not exceeding tax on the equivalent amount of timing differences previously released when the losses were carried forward.

Advance corporation tax ("ACT")

17. The minimum tax charge in the profit and loss account in any accounting period should normally be the amount payable as ACT (net of any recovery) plus any amounts charged in respect of overseas taxation. As noted in paragraph 7 of Statement of Standard Accounting Practice No 8 "The Treatment of Taxation under the Imputation System in the Accounts of Companies", ACT which cannot be recovered out of the corporation tax liability on the income of the year, but which is carried forward to be recovered out of the corporation tax liability on the income of future periods, may be deducted from the balance on the deferred taxation account subject to certain limitations set out in SSAP 8. Where in an accounting period ACT is payable in respect of a dividend, but there is no mainstream corporation tax payable, the ACT if deemed irrecoverable is required by SSAP 8 to be included in the tax charge for the year.

Transitional Arrangements

18. Companies which have heretofore taken account of timing differences in a deferred taxation account should, at the time when they change over to this standard, release to reserve any part of the deferred tax balance which is not required. Such changes would be dealt with as a prior year adjustment (change of accounting policy) under Statement of Standard Accounting Practice No 6 "Extraordinary Items and Prior Year Adjustments". Thereafter, any transfers to or from the deferred taxation account, other than those relating to revaluation surpluses, should be passed through the profit and loss account as part of the tax charge for the year or, to the extent that they relate to extraordinary items, as part of the extraordinary items.

2. Definition of Terms

19. *Timing differences* are differences between profits as computed for taxation purposes and profits as stated in financial statements which result from the inclusion of items of income and expenditure in taxation computations in periods different from those in which they are included in financial statements. Timing differences originate in one period and are capable of reversal in one or more subsequent periods. Stock appreciation relief, to the extent to which it is subject to withdrawal, comes into this category. The revaluation of an asset is regarded as creating a timing

difference when it is incorporated in financial statements.

20. *Originating timing differences* are timing differences which arise in an accounting period when a transaction or event is treated differently in financial statements from the treatment according to the same transaction or event for taxation purposes.

21. *Short-term timing differences* are originating timing differences which arise from the use of the receipts and payments basis for tax purposes and the accruals basis in financial statements. They can be identified with specific transactions and normally reverse in the next accounting period.

22. *Deferred taxation* is the taxation attributable to timing differences.

23. *Financial statements* are balance sheets, profit and loss accounts, statements of source and application of funds, notes and other statements, which collectively are intended to give a true and fair view of financial position and profit or loss.

24. *Company* includes any enterprise which comes within the scope of statements of standard accounting practice.

25. *Directors* include the corresponding officers of organisations which do not have directors.

3. Standard Accounting Practice

26. Deferred taxation should be accounted for on all short-term differences.

27. Deferred taxation should be accounted for in respect of the tax effects arising from all other originating timing differences of material amount other than any tax effects which, based on the criteria set out in paragraphs 28 to 30, can be demonstrated with reasonable probability to continue in the future. This may be by reason of recurring or continuing timing differences or, in the case of revalued assets, by the continuing use of the assets or the postponement of liability on their sale.

28. It will be reasonable to assume that timing differences will not reverse and tax liabilities will therefore not crystallise if, but only if, the company is a going concern and:

(a) the directors are able to foresee on reasonable evidence that no liability is likely to arise as a result of reversal of timing differences for some considerable period (at least three years) ahead; and

(b) there is no indication that after this period the situation is likely to change so as to crystallise the liabilities.

29. Where the criteria in paragraph 28 are satisfied it will be reasonable to assume that the period which can be foreseen sets the pattern for the indefinite future, and accordingly the deferred tax provision relating to such timing differences can be eliminated. The position should be reviewed each year and regard should be had to the past pattern of capital expenditure and stock levels and whether forecasts made in the past have proved to be reliable.

30. Where the criteria in paragraph 28 are not fully satisfied it may be appropriate to provide only part of the full potential deferred taxation. The partial amount not provided should be based on substantiated calculations and assumptions which are explained in the financial statements.

31. Where the criteria in paragraph 28 are not satisfied the directors will have no basis for assuming that timing differences will not reverse and accordingly deferred taxation should be provided.

32. Notwithstanding the provisions of paragraphs 26 and 27 debit balances on deferred taxation account arising from either timing differences or the payment of ACT should be carried forward only if there is reasonable certainty of their recovery in future periods.

33. The potential amount of deferred tax for all timing differences should be disclosed by way of note, distinguishing between the various principal categories of deferred tax and showing for each category the amount that has been provided within the accounts.

Profit and loss account

34. Deferred taxation dealt with in the profit and loss account should be shown separately as a component of the total tax charge or credit in the profit and loss account or by way of note to the financial statements.

35. The profit and loss account or a note to the financial statements should indicate the extent to which the taxation charge for the period has been reduced by accelerated capital allowances, stock appreciation relief and other timing differences.

36. Adjustments to the deferred taxation account resulting from a change in the rate of taxation should be separately disclosed as part of the taxation charge for the period, unless the change in the rate is associated with a fundamental change in the basis of taxation, in which case the adjustment should be treated as an extraordinary item. Deferred taxation charges or credits which relate to extraordinary items should themselves be shown separately as part of such items.

Balance sheet

37. Deferred taxation account balances should be shown separately in the balance sheet and described as "deferred taxation". They should not be shown as part of shareholders' funds. A note in the financial statements should indicate the nature and amount of the major elements of which the net balance is composed and a description of the method of calculation adopted.

38. Where amounts of deferred taxation arise which relate to movements on reserves (e.g. resulting from a revaluation of assets) the amounts transferred to or from deferred taxation account should be shown separately as part of such movements.

39. Where the value of an asset is shown by way of note on the face of or annexed to the financial statements and that value differs from the book value of the asset, the note should also show, if material, the tax implications which would result from the realisation of the asset at the balance sheet date at the stated value.

Transitional arrangements

40. On the introduction of this standard the opening balance on deferred taxation account should be calculated or recalculated on the basis set

out in this standard and the necessary provision set up or the existing provision adjusted accordingly, as a prior year adjustment.

Surplus of Franked Investment Income. A surplus of Franked Investment Income arises where the DIVIDENDS OR OTHER DISTRIBUTIONS RECEIVED by a company resident in the United Kingdom from any other Company resident in the United Kingdom (that is, the Franked Investment Income) EXCEEDS THE DIVIDENDS OR OTHER DISTRIBUTIONS PAID OR MADE by that company. The tax credit attaching to the surplus of Franked Investment Income may be repaid to the extent of any charges on income, management expenses of investment companies, or trading losses, for the same accounting period. The remaining excess may be carried forward and treated as Franked Investment Income of a later accounting period.

Illustration 2

Assume T. Easer Ltd.'s profit for year 19.9 before taxation £200,000, Franked Investment Income £30,000 received 30/4/19.9, Corporation Tax at 45 per cent £90,000, interim dividend of 10 per cent paid 31/7/19.9 £10,000 and final dividend of 15 per cent proposed £15,000. Assume Tax at 40 per cent.

Method of Presentation (i)

T. EASER LTD.

		£
Profit for year before taxation		200,000
Franked Investment Income—quoted Investments		30,000
		230,000
Deduct Taxation based on the profits for the year—		
Corporation Tax at 45% . .	£90,000	
Tax attributable to Franked Investment Income . .	12,000	
		102,000
Profit for year after taxation . . .		£128,000
Dividends paid and proposed—		
Paid—Interim of 10% . . .	£10,000	
Proposed—Final of 15% . .	15,000	
		25,000
Balance Carried Forward		£103,000

Note. ACT will not have been paid on the interim dividend because the ACT thereon of £6,666$\frac{1}{6}$ (i.e. 40/60ths of £10,000) will have been wholly set off by FII tax suffered of £12,000. The surplus of FII tax of £3,333$\frac{2}{6}$ will be carried forward and set against ACT of £10,000 on the final dividend.

The Balance Sheet entries in respect of the foregoing are as follows—

CORPORATION TAX   45% due 1/19.1   £90,000

Current liabilities
Final dividend	£15,000	
ACT	6,666$\frac{1}{6}$	*Deferred asset*
		Recoverable ACT £6,666$\frac{1}{6}$

Close Companies

Definitions. A CLOSE COMPANY is a Limited Company which is resident in the United Kingdom and is under the control of five or fewer participators, or of participators who are directors.

A PARTICIPATOR, briefly, is a person having a share or interest in the capital or income of the company or having the right of securing that present or future income or assets of the company will be applied for his benefit.

In determining the shares, interests and rights of a participator, the shares, interests and right of his associates are regarded as those of the participator. For this purpose an ASSOCIATE is a participator's husband or wife, lineal ancestor or descendant, brother or sister, or business partner.

It should be noted that a company is not regarded as a close company where shares carrying not less than 35 per cent of the voting power in the company are held by the public.[1]

Special Matters. Certain matters relating to close companies require special treatment. The principal matters for present purposes are as follows:

1. *Directors' Remuneration.* Whilst there never was any ACCOUNTING restriction on the amount of remuneration which could be paid to directors or close companies, the amount allowable for CORPORATION TAX PURPOSES up until the passing of the Finance Act 1969, was determined by the number of directors involved and the category of each. Complications arose in determining for taxation purposes first, who was considered to be a director and then, of the directors, who was a Whole Time Service Director (W.T.S.D.) and who was a Working Proprietor. A W.T.S.D. is a director who devotes substantially his whole time to the company in a managerial or technical capacity and does not (by himself or with associates) own or control more than 5 per cent of the ordinary share capital. WORKING PROPRIETOR (W.P.) is not a term used in tax legislation, but is useful to describe a director who devotes substantially the whole of his time to the company in a managerial or technical capacity but who does not qualify as a whole-time service director because by himself or with associates he controls more than 5 per cent of the ordinary share capital.

For Corporation Tax purposes the remuneration charged in respect of whole-time service directors was ALLOWED IN FULL. The remuneration of part-time directors was generally DISALLOWED. However, fees paid to non-W.T.S.D.s for professional services rendered (e.g. Accountants and Solicitors) were generally ALLOWED. The allowable deduction in respect of the remuneration of W.P.s was subject to certain limitations and restrictions. It should be mentioned again that limits were not imposed on the amounts which could be paid for directors' remuneration but any amount in excess of the prescribed limits were not allowed as a deduction for

[1] For full information concerning various conditions which apply to his exemption reference should be made to Sect 283 of the Income and Corporation Taxes Act 1970.

Corporation Tax purposes. However, the Finance Act 1969, lifted the restriction on the deductible amounts for the remuneration of directors of close companies, and the actual remuneration paid to all directors is allowed in full in respect of accounting periods ending on and after 1st April 1969. Where, however, the accounting period of a close company commenced before the end of March 1969, that proportion of the full amount of directors' remuneration which the part of the accounting period falling before the end of March 1969 bears to the whole accounting period is DISALLOWED.

2. In addition to the distributions mentioned on p. 2357, the following are regarded as distributions in the case of close companies:

(a) Excess interest paid to a director of a close company or his associate (or of any close company which controls, or is controlled by it) if he has a material interest in the company or in any company that controls it. The prescribed limit is 12% on the lesser of the loan or the nominal value of the issued share capital.

(b) any annuity or other annual payment (other than interest) paid by the company to a participator or his associate;[1]

(c) any rent or royalty paid by the company to a participator or his associate for the use of intangible property (other than literary, dramatic, musical or artistic copyright);[1]

(d) benefits in kind provided by the company for a participator or his associate (other than those which are refunded, or are taxable under Schedule E, or are made for death or retirement benefits for directors or employees and their dependants).

SECTION D. SHARE CAPITAL

Shares. Shares are units of ownership of a limited company. Before a company can begin its operations, it must raise the necessary capital either by subscription amongst the friends of the promoters or by means of a public offer.[2] In either case, the shares may be issued at par or at a premium; moreover, they may be payable in instalments, or the whole sum at once, provided that the sum payable on application amounts at least to 5 per cent of the nominal amount, e.g. if the shares are to be £1 each the minimum amount payable on application is £0·05 per share.

---

[1] Applicable up to 5th April 1973 only.

[2] Where an allotment is made by a company issuing a prospectus stating that an application has been (or will be) made for permission for the shares or debentures offered therein to be listed on any Stock Exchange, the allotment is void if permission has not been applied for before the third day after the first issue of the prospectus; or if permission is refused before the expiration of three weeks from the closing of the subscription lists, or such longer period not exceeding six weeks as may within the said three weeks have been notified to the applicant by the Stock Exchange.

Where there is no application as mentioned above, or it has been refused, the company must repay moneys to the applicants forthwith, and in the meantime the application moneys must have been kept in a separate banking account. (*Vide* Sect. 51, Companies Act 1948.)

Issue of Shares of One Class at Par, Payable in One Sum. This procedure is the simplest. The entries are:

Debit Sundry Members.   Credit Share Capital.
Debit Cash.   Credit Sundry Members.

Issue of Shares in Instalments. The entries are (for each allotment class, if more than one):

(a) Upon receipt of money from applicants for shares:

1. Debit Cash.   Credit Application Account.
2. Debit Application Account.   Credit Share Capital.

(b) Upon shares being allotted to the applicant and cash received therefore:

1. Debit Allotment Account.   Credit Share Capital.
2. Debit Cash.   Credit Allotment Account.

It should be carefully observed that in (b) the Allotment Account should first be debited so that the cash receipt entry is the second and not the first in the set; but both (a) and (b) result in the same thing, viz. a debit of cash and a credit to Share Capital Account.

Notification of all shares allotted must be made to the Registrar of Companies within one month of allotment.

(c) Upon the occasion of each call and cash received therefor:

1. Debit Call Account.   Credit Share Capital.
2. Debit Cash.   Credit Call Account.

(See p. 2368.)

Draft Journal entries to record the following transactions:

1. Freehold properties (cost £1,000,000, accumulated depreciation £200,000) have been revalued at £3,500,000.

2. Revenue reserves have been applied in paying up in full, at par, two ordinary shares for every three £1 units of stock. (The issued share capital was £1,500,000 ordinary stock.)

3. Provisional allotment letters were posted to stockholders offering, by way of rights, one new ordinary share of £1 for every five £1 units of stock, at the price of £2·25 each, payable as to £1·25 (£0·25 premium) within three weeks, and the balance one month later. These rights were taken up to the extent of 95 per cent, and applications included 25,000 shares on which the full issue price was received.

4. Applications were received from members for 100,000 shares in excess of those provisionally allotted to them. These were accompanied by separate cheques, including the full issue price on 10,000 shares.

5. The excess shares were suitably allotted and cheques issued for unsuccessful applications, which included 9,000 shares for which the full issue price had been received.

6. The balance payable on the shares was duly received.

JOURNAL

	£	£
Freehold Properties	2,500,000	
Capital Reserve		2,500,000
Being surplus on revaluation of freehold properties.		
Provision for Depreciation of Freehold Properties	200,000	
Revenue Reserve		200,000
Being the writing-back of Provision for Depreciation no longer required.		
Revenue Reserves	1,000,000	
Ordinary Share Capital		1,000,000
Being application of revenue reserves in paying up in full, at par, two ordinary shares of £1 each for every three £1 units of ordinary stock in issue.		
Rights Issue Acceptance Account	356,250	
Ordinary Share Capital		285,000
Share Premium Account		71,250
Being acceptance of provisional allotment, by way of rights, by 95 per cent of the ordinary stockholders, of one new ordinary share of £1 for every five £1 ordinary stock units, at £2·25 per share, of which £1·25 per share (including £0·25 premium) is payable on acceptance, as per minute dated ....*vide* Minute Book, p.		
Cash	381,250	
Rights Issue Acceptance Account		356,250
Call Account		25,000
Being cash received with acceptance as above, including cash for 25,000 shares which have been paid in full.		
Cash	135,000	
Application and Allotment Account		125,000
Call Account		10,000
Being cash received for 100,000 shares of £1 each in excess of those provisionally allotted, including the full issue price on 10,000 shares.		
Application and Allotment Account	18,750	
Ordinary Share Capital		15,000
Share Premium Account		3,750
Being allotment of 15,000 £1 Ordinary shares, not taken up under rights issue, to applicants for excess shares as above, as per minute dated .... *vide* Minute Book, p.		

JOURNAL—(contd.)

	£	£
Application and Allotment Account . . .	106,250	
Cash Account.	9,000	
Call		115,250
Being surplus application money to unsuccessful applicants, including those who paid the full issue price for 9,000 shares, as per minute dated .... vide Minute Book, p.		
Call Account	300,000	
Share Premium Account . . .		300,000
Being balance of £1 per share (balance of share premium of £1·25 per share) payable one month after allotment.		
Cash	274,000	
Call Account		274,000
Being balance of cash received in respect of call now due, as per minute dated .... vide Minute Book, p.		

Illustration 3

On 1st January 19. . ., X Ltd. makes an issue of 10,000 ordinary shares of £1 each and 10,000 6 per cent preference shares of £1 each, both at par, payable as below:

	Ordinary Shares	Preference Shares
	£p	£p
On Application	0·10	0·25
On Allotment	0·15	0·35
On First Call	0·50	0·40
On Second Call	0·25	

Journalize and post, assuming that the precise numbers are applied for and all payments are made at due dates.

For the purpose of giving a clear view of the transactions the cash entries are journalized, although, in practice, these would be made in the Cash Book and posted direct to the Ledger.

JOURNAL

	£	£
Cash	1,000	
Application (Ordinary Shares) . .		1,000
Being £0·10 per share application money on 10,000 ordinary shares.		
Cash	2,500	
Application (Preference Shares) . .		2,500
Being £0·25 per share application money on 10,000 preference shares.		
Application (Ordinary Shares) . . .	1,000	
Share Capital (Ordinary) . .		1,000
Being £0·10 per share on 10,000 shares as per minute dated .... *vide* Minute Book, p.		
Application (Preference Shares) . . .	2,500	
Share Capital (Preference) . .		2,500
Being £0·25 per share on 10,000 shares as per minute dated .... *vide* Minute Book, p.		
Allotment (Ordinary Shares) . . .	1,500	
Share Capital (Ordinary) . .		1,500
Being £0·15 per share on 10,000 shares as per minute dated .... *vide* Minute Book, p.		
Allotment (Preference Shares) . . .	3,500	
Share Capital (Preference) . .		3,500
Being £0·35 per share on 10,000 shares as per minute dated .... *vide* Minute book, p.		
Cash	1,500	
Allotment (Ordinary Shares) . .		1,500
Being £0·15 per share allotment money on 10,000 ordinary shares.		
Cash	3,500	
Allotment (Preference Shares) . .		3,500
Being £0·35 per share allotment money on 10,000 preference shares.		
First Call (Ordinary Shares) . . .	5,000	
Share Capital (Ordinary) . .		5,000
Being £0·50 per share on 10,000 shares as per minute dated .... *vide* Minute Book, p.		
First Call (Preference Shares) . . .	3,500	
Share Capital (Preference) . .		3,500
Being £0·35 per share on 10,000 shares as per minute dated .... *vide* Minute Book, p.		
Cash	5,000	
First Call (Ordinary Shares) . .		5,000
Being first call money of £0·50 per share on 10,000 ordinary shares.		

JOURNAL—(contd.)

	£	£
Cash	4,000	
First Call (Preference Shares) . .		4,000
Being first call money on £0·40 per share on 10,000 preference shares.		
Second Call (Ordinary Shares) . . .	2,500	
Share Capital (Ordinary) . . .		2,500
Being second call of £0·25 per share on 10,000 shares as per minute dated .... *vide* Minute Book, p.		
Cash	2,500	
Second Call (Ordinary Shares) . .		2,500
Being second call money on £0·25 per share on 10,000 ordinary shares.		

Note. In practice cash entries will be made direct into the Cash Book.

SHARE CAPITAL (ORDINARY)

			£
	Application Moneys. .		1,000
	Allotment Moneys . .		1,500
	First Call . . .		5,000
	Second Call . .		2,500
			£10,000

CASH (ORDINARY SHARES)

	£		
Application Moneys . .	1,000		
Allotment Moneys . .	1,500		
First Call . .	5,000		
Second Call . .	2,500		
	£10,000		

APPLICATION (ORDINARY SHARES)

	£		£
Share Capital . .	1,000	Cash	1,000

ALLOTMENT (ORDINARY SHARES)

	£		£
Share Capital . .	1,500	Cash	1,500

FIRST CALL (ORDINARY SHARES)

	£		£
Share Capital . .	5,000	Cash	5,000

SECOND CALL (ORDINARY SHARES)

	£		£
Share Capital . . .	2,500	Cash	2,500

SHARE CAPITAL (PREFERENCE)

			£
		Application Moneys. .	2,500
		Allotment Moneys . .	3,500
		First Call . .	4,000
			£10,000

CASH (PREFERENCE SHARES)

	£		
Application Moneys. .	2,500		
Allotment Moneys . .	3,500		
First Call . . .	4,000		
	£10,000		

APPLICATION (PREFERENCE SHARES)

	£		£
Share Capital . .	2,500	Cash	2,500

ALLOTMENT (PREFERENCE SHARES)

	£		£
Share Capital . . .	3,500	Cash	3,500

FIRST CALL (PREFERENCE SHARES)

	£		£
Share Capital . . .	4,000		4,000

Note. The Cash Accounts have been shown separately, although in practice one combined account would normally be employed.

It is, however, more usual to combine the Application and Allotment Accounts, in which case the Journal entries will appear (illustrating merely the ordinary shares):

JOURNAL

	£	£
Cash	1,000	
Application and Allotment (Ordinary Shares)		1,000
Being £0·10 per share application money on 10,000 ordinary shares.		
Application and Allotment (Ordinary Shares) .	2,500	
Share Capital (Ordinary) . . .		2,500
Being £0·25 per share (£0·10 on application and £0·15 on allotment) on 10,000 ordinary shares of £1 each allotted as per minute dated .... vide Minute Book, p. ...		
Cash	1,500	
Application and Allotment (Ordinary Shares) .		1,500
Being £0·15 per share allotment money on 10,000 ordinary shares.		

In examination work, it is permissible to combine in one Journal entry the above entries with other classes of shares, e.g. the first entry would be (reverting to the above illustration), ignoring narrative:

JOURNAL

	£	£
Cash	3,500	
Application and Allotment—		
Ordinary. Shares . . .		1,000
Preference Shares		2,500

Calls. Calls are the instalments due by members of a company otherwise than by way of allotment in respect of shares allotted, and are specified in the prospectus, if any; otherwise, the directors may make the calls at discretion or according to the company's regulations. Where Table A is adopted members are entitled to 14 days' notice of the call, which must not exceed—exclusive of premium—more than one-fourth of the nominal amount of each share (e.g. £0·25 on a £1 share) and the call must not be payable at less than one month from the last call.

Most companies take power to accept payment of calls before their due dates and allow interest on the sums so prepaid. Where Table A is adopted the company may pay interest at a rate not exceeding 5 per cent per annum, unless the company otherwise directs by resolution at a general meeting; but so long as calls in advance are bearing interest, the holder in question is entitled to a dividend only upon the called-up portion. In other words, he does not receive both interest *and* dividend on the prepaid call.

A call in advance is a debt against the company, and the interest (if any), unlike a dividend, is a definite charge against the company's profits.

The call in advance is credited to Calls in Advance Account and upon appropriation when the call is due for payment is transferred to the Call Account.

Illustration 4

X, Ltd., has made an issue of 10,000 shares of £1 each, £0·50 of which has been received by way of application and allotment. The first call of £0·25 is made and all members pay, including several members holding 400 shares, who pay for the balance due in full. Later, the final call is made and fully met.

Show Journal entries relating to the calls, ignoring narratives.

JOURNAL

	£	£
First Call	2,500	
Share Capital		2,500
Cash	2,600	
First Call		2,500
Calls in Advance		100
Final Call	2,500	
Share Capital		2,500
Cash	2,400	
Calls in Advance	100	
Final Call		2,500

Calls in Arrear. The treatment here is to transfer the amount of the arrears to the debit of Calls in Arrear Account, or to bring the balance down on the Call Account. Upon payment cash will be debited, and the Calls in Arrear Account or the Call Account credited. A failure to pay a call at due date may imperil the holding of the member where the company has power to forfeit shares. This will be dealt with on p. 2392 *et seq.*

Illustration 5

The facts are the same as in the preceding example, except that members holding 400 shares fail to pay the first call, but owing to special reason the directors permit the members to postpone payment until the final call is made. The defaulting members pay up in full on the final call.

Show Journal entries relative to the calls (ignoring narratives).

JOURNAL

	£	£
First Call	2,500	
Share Capital		2,500
Cash	2,400	
Calls in Arrear	100	
First Call		2,500
Final Call	2,500	
Share Capital		2,500
Cash	2,600	
Final Call		2,500
Calls in Arrear		100
Alternatively:		
Cash	2,400	
First Call		2,400
[This leaves automatically a debit of £100 on First Call.]		
Cash	2,600	
Final Call		2,500
First Call[1]		100

[1] This clears the balance on First Call Account.

If Table A is adopted the company may charge interest at a rate not exceeding 5 per cent per annum upon calls in arrear, although the practice of public companies at all events is to fix a rate (often as high as 10 per cent) in the articles.

Further, Table A provides for dividends only upon the amount PAID up on shares, although, again, articles may provide for some other mode, e.g. upon the nominal amount.

Interest on Calls in Advance and in Arrear. The book-keeping entries are:

(a) Calls in Advance:

(1) Debit Interest on Calls in Advance } for interest.
    Credit Sundry Members

(2) Debit Sundry Members }
    Credit Cash   } for payment of Interest.
    Credit Income Tax Account[1] }

(3) Debit Profit and Loss Account   } for transfer of Interest
    Credit Interest on Calls in Advance } charged to Profit and
                                         } Loss Account.

(b) Calls in arrear:

The entries are converse to the above, the name of the Interest Account being Interest on Calls in Arrear Account.

The company may deem it a matter of prudence to carry forward the interest on calls in arrear instead of crediting it to Profit and Loss Account except to the extent of cash actually received for interest; but the *charge* for interest on calls in advance **must** be transferred to the debit of Profit and Loss Account. A company may, unless its Articles state otherwise, set

[1] This sum will be accounted for to the Inland Revenue Authorities. [See Chapter 21.]

off interest on calls in arrear against a dividend payable to the member whose calls are in arrear.

Illustration 6

Holders of 400 shares pay their call of £0·25 in advance. The due date of the call is 1st July, the date of payment in advance being 1st June. The interest allowed is 6 per cent per annum. Show Ledger Accounts.

SUNDRY MEMBERS

19..			£p	19..			£p
July 1	Cash		0·30	July 1	By Interest on Calls in Advance Account[1] [Interest on £100 for one month at 6 per cent per annum.] .		
	Income Tax [£0·40 in £] .		0·20				0·50
			£0·50				£0·50

[1] Transferred to the debit of Profit and Loss Account.

Converse entries will be made for interest on calls in arrear if the payments therefor be received by the company in the usual way. If, however, a member holding 200 shares (400 being in arrear) pays his interest, the Ledger would be:

SUNDRY MEMBERS

19..			£p	19..				£p
July 1	Interest on Calls in Arrear .		0·50	July 1	Cash			0·15
					Income Tax [£0·40 in £] .			0·10
					Balance . . .	c/d		0·25
			£0·50					£0·50
July 2	Balance . . .	b/d	0·25					

INTEREST ON CALLS IN ARREAR

19..			£p	19..				£p
?	Profit and Loss Account .		0·25	July 1	Sundry Members . .			0·50
?	Balance		0·25					
			£0·50					£0·50
				19..				
				?	Balance . . .	b/d		0·25

[2] That is, £0·25 only is credited to Profit and Loss Account, the balance being brought down. This has the effect of creating a full provision in respect of the debt due by members.

The Balance Sheet of a company usually shows the calls in arrear—a debit balance—as a *deduction* from the issued share capital, whilst the calls in advance, a credit balance, is added thereto, but as a separate item, the former appearing before the latter.

Interest outstanding on the above accounts is shown separately, respectively in assets and liabilities; a provision may be created in respect of the former.

The following shows the presentation indicated:

LIABILITIES SIDE OF BALANCE SHEET

		£	£
Authorized Capital (details)	. . . .		
Issued Share Capital—			
5,000 Shares of £1 each, £0·75 called	.	3,750	
Less Calls in Arrear.	. . . .	250	
			3,500
Add Calls in Advance	. . . .	350	
			3,850
Interest on Calls in Advance (in Creditors)	.		10

ASSETS SIDE OF BALANCE SHEET

		£	£
Interest on Calls in Arrear (in Debtors)	. .	7	
Less Provision	. . . . .	3	
		–	4

Over-subscription. It very rarely happens, in practice, that the *exact* amount required by the company is applied for. If *less*, the entries will be made on the basis of the number of shares applied for if the company goes to allotment; if *greater*, some applications may be totally rejected and the application money returned; others may receive a smaller allotment than that applied for, and the excess application money returned or held on account of amounts due on allotment and calls.

It will be necessary to prepare application and allotment lists and this usually entails a considerable amount of detail work. The book-keeping entries are (other than the normal entries):

1. Debit Application and Allotment Account, credit cash (in respect of amounts returned).

2. Debit Application and Allotment Account, credit Calls Account (in respect of amounts held on account of calls).

Illustration 7

The following list shows the details of application moneys, allotments, and cash retained and returned in an over-subscribed issue of shares.

ISSUE OF 1,000 SHARES OF £1 EACH

Applicant	Shares Applied for	Shares Allotted	Amounts Paid on Application (£0·25) £	Amount Due on Application and Allotment (£0·75) £	Balance Due £	Amounts Transferred to Calls in Advance Account £	Amounts Returned £
A	300	100	75	75			
B	200	120	50	90	40		
C	1,820	400	455	300		100	55
D	800	300	200	225	25		
E	200	30	50	$22\frac{1}{2}$		$7\frac{1}{2}$	20
F	100	Nil	25				25
G	160	50	40	$37\frac{1}{2}$		$2\frac{1}{2}$	
	3,580	1,000	£895 (a)	£750 (b)	£65 (c)	£100 (d)	£100 (e)
	(1)	(2)	(3)	(4)	(5)	(6)	(7)

Note. Column 3 = £0·25 in £ being application money, i.e. $\frac{1}{4}$ of column 1.
 Column 4 = £0·75 in £ being application and allotment money, i.e. $\frac{3}{4}$ of column 2.
 Columns 4 + 6 + 7 = columns 3 + 5.

Show entries in Ledger form.

APPLICATION AND ALLOTMENT

			£				£
Share Capital	(b)	750		Cash (Application)	(a)	895
Calls in Advance	(d)	110		„ (Allottment)	(c)	65
Cash returned	(e)	100				
		£960				£960

CALLS IN ADVANCE

					£
			Application and Allotment Account	(d)	110

CASH

		£			£
Application and Allotment Account—			Application and Allotment Account	(e)	100
(Applications)	(a)	895	Balance.	c/d	860
(Balances on Allotment)	(c)	65			
		£960			£960
Balance	b/d	860			

SHARE CAPITAL

					£
			Application and Allotment Account	(b)	750

Upon the making of future calls, the proportion of calls in advance absorbed by the calls made will be debited to Calls in Advance Account and credited to Call Account.

Illustration 8

Assuming for simplicity that the balance of £0·25 per share is called up in one sum there will be received £140, which with the transfer from Calls in Advance Account will make up the requisite credit to Call Account of 1,000 shares at £0·25. In summary form the entries are:

JOURNAL

	£	£
Cash	140	
Calls in Advance	110	
Call		250

The amounts receivable are:

Applicant	Shares Allotted	Call—£0·25 £	Amount Brought Forward (Calls in Advance) £	Balance Due £
A	100	25		25
B	120	30		30
C	400	100	100	Nil
D	300	75		75
E	30	$7\frac{1}{2}$	$7\frac{1}{2}$	Nil
F	Nil			Nil
G	50	$12\frac{1}{2}$	$2\frac{1}{2}$	10
	1,000	£250	£110	£140

If separate Application and Allotment Accounts were used, they would be as follows:

APPLICATION

	£			£
Share Capital . . .	250		Cash	895
Allotment Account	435			
Calls in Advance . . .	110			
Cash returned . . .	100			
	£895			£895

ALLOTMENT

	£			£
Share Capital . . .	500		*Application Account* .	435
			Cash	65
	£500			£500

It will be observed that the combination of the two accounts gives the same result as is shown by the Application and Allotment Account, the italicized items cancelling themselves out.

The amount of £435 is arrived at by taking the cash received £895 less transferable to calls and cash returnable £210, leaving £685 net as against application money allocable against the amount due in respect of shares allotted, £250.

The components of the items of £435 are:

Appli-cant	Effective Applications		Paid	'Over' (i.e. transferable to Allotment Account	Transferred to Calls or Repayable (per previous List— Columns 6 and 7)
	£	£	£	£	£
A	100 at 0·25	25	75	50	
B	120 at 0·25	30	50	20	
C	400 at 0·25	100	455	200	155
D	300 at 0·25	75	200	125	
E	30 at 0·25	7½	50	15	27½
F	nil	nil	25		25
G	50 at 0·25	12½	40	25	2½
		£250	£895	£435	£210
		(1)	(2)	(3)	(4)

Note. Columns 1 + 3 + 4 = 2.

Issue of Shares at a Premium. A company may, owing to the attractiveness of its shares, be able to make an issue of shares at a premium by which it will receive an amount per share exceeding the nominal amount or the paid-up amount, e.g. a £1 share, fully paid, issued at £1·13; or a £0·10 share, fully paid at £0·12; or a £1 share, £0·50 paid, at £0·56. The premiums are £0·13, £0·02, and £0·06 respectively.

Many successful companies are, by reason of continuous development and expansion, constantly requiring further capital, which they raise by an issue of shares to the public, or by offering to the members the right to take up a certain number at a stipulated price which usually is lower than the quoted market price. The member thus may obtain a valuable saleable right.

Where shares are issued at a premium, whether for cash or otherwise, the premium receivable is credited to a separate account called Share Premium Account, the class of share (where necessary) being described. The amount must be regarded as capital, but it may be used wholly or in part towards paying the premium on the redemption of redeemable preferences shares, writing off preliminary expenses, commissions and discounts on issue of shares or debentures.

Illustration 9

X, Ltd., issues 10,000 shares of £1 at £1·15 payable £0·25 on application, £0·40 on allotment (including the premium of £0·15), £0·50 call. All the shares are subscribed, allotted, and paid for at due dates. Show Journal entries, opening a combined Application and Allotment Account, entering the cash entries in the Cash Book and posting to Ledger.

JOURNAL

	£	£
Application and Allotment	6,500	
Share Capital		5,000
Share Premium[1]		1,500
Being £0·25 per share on application and £0·40 per share on allotment inclusive of premium of £0·15 on 10,000 shares of £1 allotted as per directors' resolution dated .... *vide* Minute Book, p.		
Call	5,000	
Share Capital		5,000
Being £0·50 per share on 10,000 shares of £1 each for the first and final call made in accordance with terms of issue as per directors' resolution dated .... *vide* Minute Book, p.		

[1] See p. 23214.

The following is the Cash Account, which, as already stated, may be journalized in examination work, where the posting to the Ledger is not called for:

CASH

Application and Allotment Account—			
Sundry Applicants, Receipt of Application Moneys, £0·25 per Share on 10,000 Shares of £1 each	2,500		
Receipt of Allotment Moneys £0·40 per Share on 10,000 Shares of £1 each, viz. £0·25 Allotment, 0·14 Premium	4,000		
Call Account—			
Receipt of Call Moneys, £0·50 per Share on 10,000 Shares of £1 each	5,000		

SHARE CAPITAL

					£
			Application and Allotment Account . . .	J.	5,000
			Call Account . .	J.	5,000

SHARE PREMIUM

					£
			Application and Allotment Account . .	J.	1,500

APPLICATION AND ALLOTMENT

			£				£
Share Capital	. . .	J.	5,000		Cash: Application Moneys	C.B.	2,500
Share Premium	. . .	J.	1,500		,, Allotment Moneys (including Premium) .	C.B.	4,000
			£6,500				£6,500

CALL

			£				£
Share Capital	. . .	J.	5,000		Cash	C.B.	5,000

Note. J Signifies posting from Journal.

It is clear that without further transactions, the Balance Sheet will be

BALANCE SHEET

	£		£
Authorized Capital . . .	?	Cash	11,500
Issued Share Capital:			
10,000 Shares of £1 each fully paid	10,000		
Share Premium Account . .	1,500		
	£11,500		£11,500

Issue of Shares at a Discount. Until the passing of the Companies Act 1929, it was illegal to issue shares at a discount. The severity of this rule has been modified by permitting an issue of shares at a discount, provided that the company conforms to Sect. 57 of the Companies Act 1948.

The material requirements of this section are:

1. The shares are of a class *already* issued.

2. More than one year has elapsed at the date of the issue since the date on which the company was entitled to commence business.

3. The issue must be authorized by an *ordinary* resolution passed in general meeting, such resolution to specify the maximum rate of discount. (This resolution is not effective unless filed with the Registrar of Companies within 15 days.)

4. Sanction of the Court must be obtained (the issue must be made within either one month from the date of the sanction or such extended time as the Court may allow). The Court may give sanction on such terms and conditions as it thinks fit.

It is essential that every prospectus relating to the issue of shares and every subsequent Balance Sheet issued by the company shall contain particulars of such discount as has not been written off at the date of the issue of the prospectus or Balance Sheet in question.

Illustration 10

A company finds itself in need of further capital and the directors decide to make a further issue of £1 ordinary shares, which are at present quoted at £0·75. It is decided to apply to the Court for an order under Sect. 57 sanctioning the new issue to be made at a discount of 25 per cent. The necessary formalities are carried out and 50,000 shares are issued, the whole number being applied for and allotted (£0·25 on application, £0·50 on allotment).

Show Journal entries.

JOURNAL

	£	£
Cash	37,500	
Application and Allotment . . .		37,500
Being application and allotment moneys of £0·25 per share on application, £0·50 per share on allotment issued in accordance with ordinary resolution dated .... *vide* Minute Book, p.		
Application and Allotment	37,500	
Discount on Shares	12,500	
Ordinary Share Capital		50,000
Being 50,000 ordinary shares issued at a discount of 25% in accordance with ordinary resolution dated .... and sanction of the Court dated .... *vide* Minute Book, p.		

Forfeiture of Shares. As a matter of practice almost every company takes power, either by the adoption of Table A or by an express provision in its articles, to forfeit the shares of members who have failed to pay the due calls; otherwise no right of forfeiture of shares exists. Table A provides that notice must be given by the company to the defaulting member of the intention to forfeit; such notice must state the amount due, with interest, if any, and intimate that if payment is not made within fourteen days (or such longer time as the directors may decide) from the date of the notice the shares will be forfeited. If the notice is not properly complied with by the member, the directors may pass a resolution of forfeiture. Under Table A, the person whose shares have been forfeited remains liable to the company for all calls owing as at the date of forfeiture until the company has received payment in full—it matters not from whom.

After forfeiture the company is entitled, subject to any contrary provision in the articles, to reissue the shares at ANY price whatsoever so long as the amount received on reissue, added to the amount received on the shares reissued from the original holder, is at least equal to the called-up values in the case of shares not fully paid or to the nominal value in the case of fully-paid shares.

Upon reissue of the forfeited shares and the payment by the new holder of unpaid balance on the shares, the original holder, notwithstanding any proviso in the company's articles, is *pro tanto* absolved, and can never be called upon to pay more than the net balance remaining, i.e. the balance unpaid as the date of forfeiture, less the amount paid by the new holder.

The entries in the books of account are:

1. Debit Share Capital Account with the NUMBER of shares forfeited at the CALLED-UP value.
   Credit forfeited Shares Account.
2. Debit Forfeited shares Account.
   Credit Call Account

in respect of the unpaid call of the defaulting member.

Two very frequent mistakes common to most students may be mentioned.

1. The debit to share capital must be proportionate to the amount in terms of money standing to the credit of this account. Many students debit the account with the number of shares forfeited at the *nominal* value, e.g. £1.

The debit must be based, as mentioned, upon the CALLED-UP value and may be alternatively stated thus: the amount to be debited to share capital is the amount produced by the number of shares forfeited, divided by the whole number of shares of that class issued, multiplied by the amount standing to the credit of share capital of that class. Expressed briefly the formula is:

$$\frac{\text{number of shares forfeited}}{\text{number of shares issued}} \times \text{credit balance of Share Capital Account.}$$

2. The balance of unpaid calls must not be transferred to the debit of share capital, but to the debit of Forfeited Share Account.

Illustration 11

Ten thousand shares of £1 each have been issued upon which £0·75 has been called. Owing to failure to pay the call of £0·10 a member's shares numbering 1,000 are forfeited.

The requisite debit to share capital is 1,000 times £0·75, i.e. £750, or, computed in the alternative way:

$$\frac{\text{number of shares forfeited}}{\text{number of shares issued}} \times \text{credit balance of Share Capital Account,}$$

i.e. $\dfrac{1,000}{10,000} \times {}^{1}7,500 = £750.$

The balance of Forfeited Shares Account may always be proved because it represents the excess of amounts called on the defaulting member over those unpaid by him, i.e. the amount actually paid, which is the member's loss and the company's gain. In the above illustration, the amount called is £0·75, and the amount unpaid £0·10; hence there is a profit of £0·65 per share on 1,000 shares, as shown below. (Narratives ignored.)

[1] It will be recollected that the Share Capital Account is credited on the occasion of each call and is, in the normal course of events, reflected in Cash or Debtors (Call Account).

JOURNAL

		£	£
Share Capital		750	
Forfeited Shares			750
Forfeited Shares		100	
Call			100

In examination work, it is permissible to combine the two entries thus:

JOURNAL

		£	£
Share Capital		750	
Call			100
Forfeited Shares			650[1]

[1] i.e. £0·65 on 1,000 shares = £650.

Illustration 12

Prosperity, Ltd., made an issue of 50,000 ordinary shares of £1 each. The £0·50 payable on application, allotment, and first call has been paid in full. A second call of £0·25 a share is made, and V. Jones a holder of 100 shares fails to meet the call. After due notice the directors passed a resolution effecting the forfeiture of his shares. Show Journal entries relative to the second call and the forfeiture and Share Capital Account.

		£	£
Ordinary Share Capital		75	
Forfeited Shares			75
Being 100 ordinary shares, £0·75 called up forfeited in accordance with resolution of directors dated .... *vide* Minute Book, p.			
Forfeited Shares		25	
Second Call			25
Being transfer of amount unpaid by Jones on second call on 100 ordinary shares forfeited as above.			

ORDINARY SHARE CAPITAL

		No. of Shares	£			No. of Shares	£
Forfeited Shares Account .		100	75	Balance . . b/d		50,000	25,000
Balance . .	c/d	49,900	37,425	Second Call Account			12,500
		50,000	£37,500			50,000	£37,500
				Balance . . b/d		49,900	37,425

SECOND CALL

	£		£
Ordinary Share Capital Account . .	12,500	Cash . . . Forfeited Shares Account	12,475 25
	£12,500		£12,500

FORFEITED SHARES

		£		£
Second Call Account . Balance . . c/d		25 50	Ordinary Share Capital Account . .	75[1]
		£75		£75
			Balance . . . b/d	50

[1] i.e. 100 at the called-up value of £0·75, or $\dfrac{100}{50,000} \times £37,500 = £75$.

Alternatively, the credit of £75 may be made to the second Call Account, leaving £50 to be transferred to Forfeited Shares Account, thus:

SECOND CALL

	£		£
Ordinary Share Capital Account . . . Forfeited Shares Account .	12,500 50	Cash . . . Share Capital . . .	12,475 75
	£12,550		£12,550

The credit balance on forfeited shares is the total calls on 100 shares at £0·75, less £0·25 per share unpaid, leaving a profit to the company of £50, that is, the amount actually paid by Jones.

The profit on forfeiture is legally available for dividend, subject to any contrary provisions in the articles of the company, but until the shares have been reissued and fully paid no profit can arise.

The Balance Sheet, after giving effect to the above entries, will contain the following items on the liabilities side:

	£
Issued Share Capital—	
49,900 Ordinary Shares of £1 each, £0·75 paid	37,425
Forfeited Shares	50

This will equal the bank balance of £37,475 shown as an asset in the ordinary way.

Reissue of Forfeited Shares. It has been seen that the company may *reissue* shares at a discount, provided that it receives (in all) at least the amount per share with which the member is credited after the reissue, e.g. if a share is credited with £0·75 at least this sum must have been received by the company in respect of such share; if it is a £1 share credited as fully paid the sum received must be at least £1.

Entries on reissue are:

(i) Debit Sundry Members} for the amount payable by
    Credit Share Capital } new member.
(ii) Debit Forfeited shares} for discount on reissue.
    Credit share Capital }
(iii) Debit Cash } for receipt of amount payable by
    Credit Sundry Members} new member.

Or more shortly:

(i) Debit Sundry Members.
        Forfeited Shares.
    Credit Share Capital.
(ii) Debit Cash
    Credit Sundry Members.

Illustration 13

X, Ltd., has received from a member, on 100 shares of £1 each the sum of £0·75, but the subsequent call of £0·15 thereon being unpaid the shares are forfeited. As there is a profit of £0·75 on each share, the company may pass on this gain to the person who takes up the reissued shares, and if they are to be credited as fully paid the applicant must pay on each share at least £0·25, so that in all the company has received £1 on each share credited as fully paid. If the company's price for reissue of the shares as fully paid is £0·40, it has still a profit of £0·15 for it has received £0·75 plus £0·40 for a £1 share; in other words, the discount on reissue is £0·60, i.e. £1 less £0·40, but the previous profit was £0·75, still leaving a gain of £0·15 for the company.

If the company reissues the shares at a premium, this is in the nature of further profit.

Some accountants prefer to open a new account called Forfeited Shares Reissued Account, in which case the entries are:

(i) Debit Forfeited Shares Reissued { for the mumber of shares
    Credit share Capital { at the price at which the
                          { shares are to be credited.

(ii) Debit Sundry Members { for amount due payable
                          { by new members.

    Forfeited Shares   for discount on reissue.
                            { for the number of shares
    Credit Forfeited shares Reissued { at the price at which the
                            { shares are to be credited.

(iii) Debit Cash { for amount paid by new
    Credit Sundry Members { members.

If the shares are reissued at a premium, the amount thereof will be credited to Share Premium Account or Premium on Shares Reissued Account. (See p. 23214.)

Illustration 14

Assume that, in the illustration on p. 2394, 100 shares are reissued to G. Smith at £0·70 a share to be credited as fully paid, the Ledger entries (entering only the last set of entries) are:

ORDINARY SHARE CAPITAL

							No. of Shares	£
					Balance . . b/d		49,900	37,425

ORDINARY SHARE CAPITAL[1]

						No. of Shares	£
					Forfeited Shares Reissued Account .	100	100

[1] Until the other shares are fully paid it is preferable to open a separate account of those reissued as fully paid.

FORFEITED SHARES REISSUED

	£			£
Ordinary Share Capital Account	100	Smith[2]		70
		Forfeited Shares Account[2] .		30
	£100			£100

[2] Shown separately for clarity.

FORFEITED SHARES

Forfeited Shares Reissued Account	(a) c/d	30	Balance . . . b/d	50
Balance		20		
		£50		£50
			Balance . . . b/d	20

(a) Unless there are other shares which may be reissued, the balance of this account may be transferred to a Share Premium Account or used to write off Preliminary Expenses; or even to Profit and Loss Account, although the latter procedure violates the principles of sound financial policy. It must be observed that the second or final call will be on 49,900 and not 50,000 shares, and when disposed of, the two Share Capital Accounts may be merged.

G. Smith

		£				£
Forfeited Shares Account	.	70	Cash .	.	.	70

Cash

			£			
Balance.	.	*b/d*	37,475			
Smith	.	.	70			

Note. Items in italics are the balances as shown on pp. 2394 and 2395.

The final profit on the 100 shares is proved by taking the total cash received in respect of the 100 shares, and deducting from it the amount at which the shares are credited, viz. cash received £0·50 (from first holder) plus £0·70 (from the second holder), in all £1·20 a share credited as fully paid; hence, a profit on 100 shares at £0·20 per share, viz. £20.

Treatment of Balance of Forfeited Shares Account. It will be clear that until the shares are fully paid the credit balance on forfeited shares cannot be considered as a final profit, because the company may, on reissue, allow a discount to the purchaser of the shares forfeited to the full extent of the amount in credit therefor in Forfeited Shares Account. Thus, if there were 100 shares previously forfeited upon which there was a credit balance on Forfeited Shares Account of £0·40 per share the company might reissue then as fully paid for £0·60 per share. When, therefore, part of the shares forfeited are reissued, only such portion of the amount in credit in Forfeited Shares Account may be taken as final profit representing profit on the shares reissued as fully paid. Thus, if of the foregoing 100 shares upon which there is a credit on forfeited shares of £40 (£0·40 a share) sixty are reissued for £0·75 per share to be credited as fully paid, the final profit will be $60 \times (£0·40 + £0·75 - £1)$ £0·15 = £9. The company has finally credited share capital with £60, but it has received in all £1·15 per share, against which £1 per share stands to the credit of share capital. The balance of Forfeited Shares Account will be brought down, pending the result of the further reissue in respect of the forty shares.

The Ledger entries would be:

Forfeited Shares

			£				£
Loss on Reissue of Shares Credited as fully paid [60 at £0·25]	.		15	Balance	.	*b/d*	40
Profit on Shares Reissued Account	.		9				
Balance	.	*c/d*	16				
			£40				£40
				Balance[1]	.	*b/d*	16

[1] The balance represents amounts paid in respect of 40 shares forfeited and not yet reissued, i.e. 40 at £0·40.

CASH

		£			
Share Capital Account [60 at £0·75] . . .		45			

PROFIT ON SHARES REISSUED

			Forfeited Shares Account[2]	£ 9

[2] The balance represents the sum of the payments on 60 shares (1) by the original allottee of £0·40, and (2) by the subsequent holder of £0·75, amounting to £1·15 less the amount credited in respect thereof, i.e. £1. This gives a profit of £0·15 on 60 shares.

SHARE CAPITAL

				£
		Cash		45
		Forfeited Shares Account .		15
				60

The Forfeited Shares Account can be the more readily understood by splitting the account as follows:

FORFEITED SHARES

		40 Shares	60 Shares			40 Shares	60 Shares
		£	£	Balance . .	b/d	£ 16	£ 24
Loss, etc. . .			15				
Profit, etc. . .			9				
Balance . .	c/d	16					
		£16	£24			£16	£24
				Balance . .	b/d	16	

Reissue of Forfeited Shares Previously Issued at a Premium and Forfeited. Where shares have been issued at a premium, it has already been seen that the premium must be credited to Share Premium Account which can only be reduced in the special ways permitted by Sect. 56. Companies Act 1948. If, therefore, shares are forfeited in respect of which a premium has already been received, the premium cannot be transferred to the credit of Forfeited Shares Account. The Share Premium Account will accordingly be no longer proportionate to the balance on Share Capital Account.

Illustration 15

A, Ltd., whose authorized share capital is £10,000 in £1 shares, issued the whole of its capital to the public at a premium of £0·10 per share, payable as follows: On application and allotment £0·60 per share (including premium), first call of £0·10 per share.

The application and allotment moneys were received in full, but members holding 1,000 shares failed to pay the call of £0·10, and in consequence the shares were forfeited. At a later date and before further calls were made, 500 of these shares were reissued as fully paid for a consideration of £0·80 per share. Write up Ledger Accounts.

SHARE CAPITAL

		Shares	£			Shares	£
Forfeited Shares Account . .		1,000	600	Application and Allotment Account .		10,000	5,000
Balance . .	c/d	9,000	5,400	First Call Account			1,000
		10,000	£6,000			10,000	£6,000
				Balance . .	b/d	9,000	5,400

SHARE CAPITAL (FULLY PAID)

		Shares	£			Shares	£
Balance . .	c/d	500	500	Cash. . .		500	400
				Forfeited Shares Account . .			100
		500	£500			500	£500
				Balance . .	b/d	500	500

As soon as the amount owing on the balance of 9,000 shares has been fully paid, the two accounts will be merged and made into one account.

SHARE PREMIUM

		Shares	£			Shares	£
				Cash. . .		10,000	1,000[1]

[1] The premium received on the subsequently forfeited shares must remain in this account, £0·50 per share being transferred from Share Capital Account to Forfeited Shares Account.

FIRST CALL

		Shares	£			Shares	£
Share Capital Account . .		10,000	1,000	Cash. . .		9,000	900
				Forfeited Shares Account . .		1,000	100
		10,000	£1,000			10,000	£1,000

FORFEITED SHARES

		£				£
First Call Account		100		Share Capital Account		600
Balance	c/d	500				
		£600				£600
Share Capital Account		100		Balance	b/d	500
Profit on Shares Reissued						
Account		150				
Balance	c/d	250				
		£500				£500
				Balance	b/d	250

PROFIT ON SHARES REISSUED

					£
				Forfeited Shares Account	150

Notes. 1. The accuracy of the book-keeping in respect of the 500 shares reissued may be verified as follows:

	£
Cash received from original allottee (excluding premium), 500 at £0·50	250
Cash received from new holder, 500 at £0·80	400
Total cash received	£650

Since the Share Capital Account is credited with £500, there is a profit on the reissue of £150. The profit is thus 500 × £0·30.

2. The balance on Forfeited Shares Account represents the temporary profit on the shares forfeited and not yet reissued, i.e. 500 shares at £0·50 = £250. The balance of the account shows the maximum amount the company may lose on the reissued shares to keep within the law [i.e. 500 at £0·50 = £250]. If therefore the company reissues the 500 shares as fully paid for £0·50 it will have received in all £1·10, viz. £0·50 plus £0·10 premium from original allottee and £0·50 from the new holder.

3. The student must bear in mind that the Share Capital Account will be debited and Forfeited Shares Account credited with the full amount called up, and not the amount which has been paid up on the shares to the date of the forfeiture.

Reissue of Forfeited Shares Issued at a Discount. Where shares issued at a discount are forfeited, a proportionate part of the discount should be written off to Forfeited Shares Account. On reissue, discount proportionate to the shares reissued may be reinstated in the books, so that the discount on shares will always remain in proportion to the shares actually issued. This treatment differs from that in respect of premiums, outlined in the preceding paragraph.

The Discount on Shares Account will be opened *on allotment* when the company becomes liable to allow the discount.

Illustration 16

A, Ltd., makes an issue of 10,000 £1 ordinary shares at a discount of £0·10 per share, payable as follows:

On Application and Allotment	£0·40
On First Call	£0·25
On Second Call	£0·25

Members holding 400 shares do not pay the second call and the shares are duly forfeited, 200 of which are reissued as fully paid at £0·50 per share.

Show Ledger Accounts.

ORDINARY SHARE CAPITAL

		£			£
Forfeited Shares Account	c/d	400	Application and Allotment Account		4,000
Balance		9,800	Discount on Shares Account		1,000
			First Call Account		2,500
			Second Call Account		2,500
			Forfeited Shares Account		200
		£10,200			£10,200
			Balance	b/d	9,800

DISCOUNT ON SHARES

		£			£
Ordinary Share Capital Account		1,000	Forfeited Shares Account		40
Forfeited shares Account		20	Balance	c/d	980
		£1,020			£1,020
Balance	b/d	980			

SECOND CALL

		£			£
Share Capital Account		2,500	Cash		2,400
			Forfeited Shares Account		100
		£2,500			£2,500

FORFEITED SHARES

		£			£
Discount on Shares Account		40	Share Capital Account		400
Second Call Account		100	Cash		100
Share Capital Account		200	Discount on Shares Account		20
Profit on Shares Reissued Account[1]		50			
Balance[2]	c/d	130			
		£520			£520
			Balance	b/d	130

[1,2] See footnotes opposite.

Surrender of Shares. Without the sanction of the Court, shares can only be surrendered as a short cut to forfeiture, and, generally speaking, surrender takes place where the purchase consideration satisfied in shares has turned out to be excessive.

Illustration 17

Spes, Ltd., purchased from Trader his business as a going concern, the consideration being the allotment to him of 10,000 shares of £1 each, credited as fully paid. Owing to over-valuation of certain assets at the date of sale, it was agreed that Trader should surrender 2,000 of his shares. The Court sanctioned the agreement.

Show Journal entries in the book of the company.

JOURNAL

	£	£
Share Capital	2,000	
Assets (as specified)		2,000
Being the surrender of 2,000 shares of £1 each fully paid in respect of adjustment of purchase consideration by reason of over-valuation of assets as per agreement dated .... per directors' resolution and sanctioned by the Court *vide* Minute Book, p.		

The issued share capital, obviously, is now £8,000.

Illustration 18

Anti-Grab, Ltd., make an issue of 10,000 shares of £1 each at £1·125 per share, as follows:

	Amount	Date
	£p	
Payable on Application	0·125	1st August
Payable on Allotment (including Premium) . . .	0·25	10th August
First Call	0·50	30th September
Second Call	0·15	31st October
Third Call	0·10	30th November

[1] This is a final profit on 200 shares as the combined net sum received is £1·15 [i.e. £0·65 and £0·50] to which must be added £0·10 discount (this loss being shown in Discount on Shares Account), showing £1·25 as against £1 per share credited to share capital, this giving a profit of £0·25 on 200 shares = £50.

It would be advisable to write-off the above-mentioned £0·10 discount on the 200 shares by debiting Profit on Reissued Shares Account and crediting Discount on Shares Account.

[2] The balance represents 200 shares forfeited and not yet reissued upon which £0·65 has been received per share. The account has been debited with the discount of £40 less £20 (which will be written back when the remaining shares are reissued as fully paid), so that the balance brought down is the net receipt and not the £0·75 per share.

The Discount on Shares Account shows a net debit of £980, which is £0·10 in £ on the issued share capital of £9,800.

The application and allotment moneys are duly received and, in addition, holders of 5,000 shares pay in full on allotment, interest being credited to them at 6 per cent per annum.[1] Holders of 200 shares fail to pay the first call, and after due notice their shares are forfeited. The amounts payable on the second call (made after the forfeiture) are paid in full, except that a holder of 100 shares fails to pay. On the 15th November, 150 of the 200 shares forfeited are reissued, credited with £0·90 paid for £0·65 per share. The new holder pays for these shares in full, the balance of £0·10 per share being counted as a call in advance. The final call is met in full, including the arrears of the second call, on which has been charged interest at 5 per cent per annum.

Show Journal entries including cash (ignoring narratives), assuming that cash has not been received or paid in respect of interest on calls in arrear and in advance. Income tax to be ignored.

JOURNAL

19..		£p	£p
Aug. 1	Cash	7,500·00	
	Application and Allotment . . .		2,500·00
	Calls in Advance . . .		3,750·00
	Share Premium		1,250·00
10	Application and Allotment . . .	2,500·00	
	Share Capital		2,500·00
Sept. 30	First Call	5,000·00	
	Share Capital		5,000·00
	Calls in Advance	2,500·00	
	Calls in Arrear	100·00	
	Cash	2,400·00	
	First Call		5,000·00
	Interest on Calls in Advance . . .	31·44	
	(£3,750 at 6% p.a. for 51 days, i.e. 10th Aug. to 30th Sept.)		
	Sundry Members		31·44
	Share Capital	150·00	
	Calls in Arrear		100·00
	Forfeited Shares		50·00
Oct. 31	Second Call	1,470·00	
	Share Capital		1,470·00
	Calls in Advance	750·00	
	Calls in Arrear	15·00	
	Cash	705·00	
	Second Call		1,470·00

[1] Five per cent per annum only is allowed by Table A (C.A., 1948), unless the company in general meeting directs otherwise.

JOURNAL (*contd.*)

19..		£p	£p
	Interest on Calls in Advance	6·37	
	(£1,250 at 6% p.a. for 31 days, i.e. 1st Oct, to 31st Oct.)		
	Sundry Members		6·37
Nov. 15	Cash	112·50	
	Forfeited Shares	37·50	
	Share Capital		135·00
	Calls in Advance		15·00
30	Final Call	995·00	
	Share Capital		995·00
	Calls in Advance	515·00	
	Cash	495·00	
	Calls in Arrear		15·00
	Final Call		995·00
	Interest on Calls in Advance . . .	2·50	
	(£500 at 6% p.a. for 30 days and £15 at 6% p.a. for 15 days, i.e. 1st Nov. to 30th Nov., and 15th Nov. to 30th Nov. respectively.)		
	Sundry Members		2·50
	Sundry Members	0·06	
	Interest on Calls in Arrear		0·06
	(£15 at 5% p.a. for 30 days, i.e. 1st Nov. to 30th Nov.)		

The Ledger Accounts will be written up in the ordinary way from the above Journal entries.

When the postings have been completed the balances will appear as follows:

TRIAL BALANCE

	£p	£p
Cash	11,212·50	
Share Capital		9,950·00
(*a*) Share Premium		1,250·00
(*b*) Forfeited Shares		12·50
Interest—		
Calls in Arrear		0·06
Calls in Advance	40·31	
Sundry Members for Interest—		
Calls in Arrear	0·06	
Calls in Advance		40·31
	£11,252·87	£11,252·87

Notes. (*a*) £0·125 per share received in respect of 10,000 shares.

(*b*) The amount paid on 50 shares forfeited, but not reissued, i.e. 50 at £0·375 less premium of £0·125.

There is no final profit on the 150 shares reissued as the total amount received for shares credited as £0·90 paid is £0·125 (i.e. original holder £0·375, new holder £0·75), but of this £0·125 is in respect of premium, whilst £0·10 is in respect of call in advance, thus leaving a net receipt of £0·90. Alternatively, as the new holder pays £0·75, of which £0·10 represents a call in advance, the company by crediting share capital with £0·90 as against a receipt for it of £0·65 incurs a loss of £0·25, which is exactly covered by the amount paid by the original allottee, excluding premium. Further, as the reissued shares are fully paid at the date of the above Trial Balance, it can be seen that the company has received in all £1·125 (i.e. original holder £0·375, new holder £0·75), but £0·125 thereof has been credited to Premium Account, leaving the sum of £1 per share credited to Share Capital.

Balancing the Share Register. In large companies, prior to the preparation of the dividend warrants from the dividend sheets it is essential to strike a balance on the Share Register the total of which must agree with the issued capital of the company.

Usually, as a matter of practical necessity, the Register is subdivided, as with Ledgers in the sectional balancing principle, so that it is necessary to employ a Transfers Posting Journal, rules for the number of separate Registers in use, thus:

Date	Details	Shares Transferred	TRANSFEREES' REGISTERS			TRANSFERORS' REGISTERS		
			1	2	3	1	2	3
		100	100					100
		400		400			400	
		50			50	50		
		200	200				200	
		750	300	400	50	50	600	100

At the date of closing the Register, the totals will be incorporated into an adjustments summary, the total of the individual balances in each Register agreeing therewith.

[If not the error(s) will have to be located.]

Illustration 19

Assuming the transfers for the year are as above and the opening balances of the Registers are as below, show Share Adjustment Summary.

					Shares
No. 1	.	.	.	.	35,000
No. 2	.	.	.	.	47,000
No. 3	.	.	.	.	18,000
					100,000

SHARES ADJUSTMENT SUMMARY

					Registers			Totals
					1	2	3	
Balances, opening					35,000	47,000	18,000	100,000
Add Transferees					300	400	50	750
					35,300	47,400	18,050	100,750
Less Transferors					50	600	100	750
Balances, closing					35,250	46,800	17,950	100,000

Stock Units. In recent years large numbers of companies have introduced Stock units in order to save the enormous trouble involved in handling transfers of Shares because of the necessity to register their distinctive numbers.

Stock (as distinct from Shares) involves no registered numbers and therefore facilitates transfers, but is not a popular form of investment, so that the Stock unit has been devised, allowing the share equivalent to be negotiated in the ordinary way; e.g. Kotes Ltd. has shares of £0·50 each fully paid, so that if it desires to take advantage of the use of stock units, it will convert its Shares into the form of Stock divided into units of £0·50 each. This form satisfies both needs (a) to avoid dealing with distinctive numbers and (b) permitting transactions in 'Share' form.

Illustration 20

X, Ltd., has a share capital of 1,000,000 shares of £0·25 each fully paid. This is converted into £250,000 stock divided into 1,000,000 £0·25 units. As far as a member of the company is concerned, he is in just the same position after the conversion as before. If he wishes to sell part of his holding, the only difference is that he sells so many stock units instead of share of the same nominal amount.

It will, no doubt, be remembered that of necessity the Stock must be *fully paid.*

The need for this procedure is to a great extent obviated by Secf. 74 of the Companies Act 1948, which provides that if *all* the issued share in a company (or *all* the issued shares of any class) are *fully paid* and rank *pari passu* for all purposes, such shares need not have distinguishing numbers.

SECTION E. DEBENTURES

Debentures. A debenture is a document acknowledging a loan to a company and is generally executed under the seal of the company, usually (but not necessarily) containing provisions as to payment of interest and the payment of the principal and giving a charge on the assets of such company, and may give security for the payment over some or all of the assets and undertaking of the company (*Lemon* v. *Austin Friars Investment Trust*). A debenture may be classified thus:

1. As to **security.** Containing a charge either:

(*a*) Specific, which constitutes a mortgage to trustees with a deed of trust, in respect of specified and definite assets.

(*b*) Floating, which constitutes a charge on the undertaking as a whole (subject to any specific charge).[1]

The former precludes the company from dealing with the subject-matter comprised in the charge, but the latter does not prevent the company from changing the assets from time to time.

(*c*) Naked debenture which confers on the holder no security of any kind.

2. As to **priority**—First debenture. Second debenture.

3. As to **permanence**—Redeemable debenture. Irredeemable debenture.

4. As to **form**-Bearer or Registered; stock[2] or separate units.

Debentures may be issued at par, at a premium or at a discount; either in a series or in the form of stock.

Issue of Debentures. A company must have borrowing powers so as to give validity to debentures, such powers being implied in the case of a trading company unless expressly prohibited in the Memorandum of Association; whilst non-trading companies have no such implied power and so must obtain in the Memorandum of Association express power to borrow; but even where borrowing powers exist, the Articles may limit the amount and manner of borrowing.

Upon the issue of **registered** debentures, stamp duty is payable on the amount secured (including premium on redemption).

Mutatis mutandis, the entries are similar to those for shares.

Illustration 21

X, Ltd., issues ten £100 debentures at 105, payable £20 on application and £85 on allotment. Show Journal entries (ignoring narratives).

---

[1] If created by an insolvent company for a past debt within twelve months of the commencement of liquidation, the charge is void, but the loan is valid and carries interest at 5 per cent per annum. The Treasury may by order alter the rate. (Sect. 322.)

[2] Debenture stock may *ab initio* be issued (contrast this with stock (share capital) which must, in the first instance, be in the form of shares and cannot be so converted till fully paid as mentioned above).

JOURNAL

	£	£
Cash	200	
Application and Allotment (Debentures) .		200 (a)
Application and Allotment (Debentures) . .	1,050 (a)	
Debentures		1,000
Debentures Premium[1]		50
Cash	850	
Application and Allotment (Debentures) .		850 (a)

Items marked (a) cancel themselves out in the Ledger.

Illustration 22

X, Ltd., issues ten £100 debentures at 95 per cent, payable £20 on application and £50 on allotment: £25 call. Show Journal entries (ignoring narratives).

JOURNAL

	£	£
Cash	200	
Application and Allotment (Debentures) .		200 (a)
Application and Allotment (Debentures) . .	700 (a)	
Debentures Discount[1]	50	
Debentures		750
Cash	500	
Application and Allotment (Debentures) .		500 (a)
Call Account (Debentures) . . .	250 (b)	
Debentures		250
Cash	250	
Call Account (Debentures) . .		250 (b)

Items marked (a) and (b) cancel themselves out in the Ledger.

[1] Note that the discount and premium entries are entered with those made on *allotment*.

A premium on debentures, except in a company operating under the Double Account System, is legally available for distribution as dividend unless the Articles forbid, although such application is contrary to sound financial practice.

The law requires that the discount on debentures be separately shown in the Balance Sheet till written off, and in consequence this entails the disclosure of the debenture liability at the nominal value, **i.e. gross.** In the above illustration, the Balance Sheet will show the debentures at £1,000 as a liability and the discount of £50 on the assets side (unless written off). The amount of discount must be disclosed in the Annual Return.

In all cases, a debenture containing a charge must be registered with the Registrar of Companies within twenty-one days of the creation of the charge.

The Companies Act 1967, provides that the following items (appropriate to the matters under discussion) shall be shown separately in the Balance Sheet till written off:

1. Discount on debentures.
2. Discount on shares.
3. Commission on shares and debentures.
4. Expenses of issue of shares *and* debentures.

It will be observed that whilst commission on both shares and debentures may be merged (similarly with expenses) the discounts must be shown separately.

Issue of Shares and Debentures to Vendor. The opening entries will be dealt with in Chapter 23, Section G, but it is necessary, to complete the explanation of entries for shares and debentures, to refer very briefly to the discharge of the debt to the vendor of a business acquired by the company.

A student will have no difficulty in understanding that the vendor will be a credit in respect of the purchase consideration which with goodwill, if necessary, will be exactly equal to the *net* assets acquired. If the vendor receives his debt in cash there will be required a credit entry in the Cash Book for the payment, the vendor being debited. If, however, shares and/or debentures are alloted, an entry in Share Capital Account and/or Debentures Account takes the place of the entry in the Cash Book. So far as relates to the vendor's shares and/or debentures there will be no need for Application and Allotment and Call Accounts.

Illustration 23

The purchase consideration payable to the vendor is £2,000, to be discharged by the issue of 1,100 shares of £1, credited as fully paid, and £1,000 7 per cent debentures at a discount of 10 per cent.

Show the Journal entries in the books of the company.

JOURNAL

	£	£
Vendor . . . . Share Capital[1] . . . . . . Being the issue of 1,100 shares of £1 each fully paid in part discharge of purchase consideration per directors' resolution dated .... *vide* Minute Book, p.	1,100	1,100
Vendor . . . . Discount on Debentures . . . . . 7% Debentures . . . . . . Being the issue of £1,000 debentures at 90% in final discharge of purchase consideration per directors' resolution dated .... *vide* Minute Book, p.	900 100 (a)	1,000 (b)

[1] See footnote opposite.

Assuming that the vendor sold to the company sundry assets worth £1,850, excluding goodwill, for £2,000, the initial entry would be:

JOURNAL

		£	£
Goodwill		150	
Sundry Assets		1,850	
Vendor[2]			2,000
Being assets taken over from Vendor as per purchase agreement dated			

[2] Upon the issue of shares and debentures the debits from the Journal will eliminate the above credit.

The Balance Sheet will be:

BALANCE SHEET AS AT ....

	£		£
Authorized Capital . . .		Sundry Assets	1,850
Issued Share Capital—		Goodwill	150
1,100 Shares of £1 each fully		Discount on Debentures . .	100
paid	1,100		
7% Debentures	1,000		
	£2,100		£2,100

The company, in practice, would probably issue further shares and this would be essential if the vendor is to receive part or all of the purchase consideration in cash, the entries for which will be made according to the principles already outlined.

Issue of Debentures as Collateral Security for a Loan. A company may issue its own debentures as collateral security for a loan or for a bank overdraft by way of total or partial security therefor.

A collateral security is one which can be realized by the party in possession in the event of the original loan not being repaid at the due date or in the event of other breach of agreement between the parties. On repayment of the loan the collateral security is at once released.

Thus, in the case of debentures issued by a company as collateral, these debentures will normally be withdrawn if the loan is repaid at the due date.

---

[1] Particulars of the allotment stating the consideration therefor must be notified to the Registrar of Companies within one month of allotment.

(a) Shown as 'asset' till written off.

(b) Shown as liability for £1,000.

In examination work the two Journal entries may be combined, although (unless pressed for time) it is preferable that the student write them up separately.

Sect. 90 (3) of the Companies Act 1948, however, provides that debentures deposited as security for advances from time to time on current account or otherwise shall not be considered to have been redeemed *by reason only* of the account of the company having ceased to be in debit whilst the debentures still remain deposited.

There are two ways of dealing with these debentures in the accounts of the company.

1. No entry whatsoever is made in the financial books of the company in respect of such debentures, their existence being recorded simply by a note on the Balance Sheet under the liability secured.

Illustration 24

Aldine, Ltd., obtains an overdraft from its bankers of £20,000, giving as collateral security £25,000 debentures. The Balance Sheet of Aldine, Ltd., will appear as follows:

BALANCE SHEET AS AT ....

Liabilities Side	£
Bank Overdraft . . .	20,000
(Collaterally secured by an issue of £25,000 debentures.)	

2. By recording the transaction in the financial books of the company. The debentures issued will be debited to Debentures Suspense Account and credited to Debentures Account. The Debentures Suspense Account will appear as an asset on the Balance Sheet. Upon repayment on the loan the entries will be reversed, Debentures Account being debited and Debentures Suspense Account credited.

Illustration 25

Taking the same details as in the above illustrations, the entries on issue are:

JOURNAL

	£	£
Debentures Suspense	25,000	
Debentures		25,000
Being debentures issued collaterally to X Bank to secure an overdraft of £20,000 as per directors' resolution dated .... *vide* Minute Book, p.		

No question of interest on DEBENTURES arises in such a case: the interest on Bank Overdraft is dealt with in the normal manner.

Debenture Interest. Debenture interest is the interest payable by the borrowing company in return for money lent in debenture; it constitutes a charge against profits whether profits are earned or not. Upon payment of debenture interest, the company is bound to deduct Income Tax at the standard rate from the interest, and account for the tax deducted to the Inland Revenue. (See Chapter 21.)

Book-keeping Entries. 1. Debit the Debenture Interest Account with the GROSS amount of the interest.

2. Credit the net amount to Debenture-holders.

3. Credit the Income Tax on the interest to Income Tax Account.

The Debenture-holders Account will be debited upon the payment by the company, and the Income Tax should be remitted to the Collector of Taxes within 14 days after the assessable month (ending on 5th day) in which the debenture interest is paid. At the end of the accounting period, the Debenture Interest Account will be transferred to the debit of Profit and Loss Account.

Illustration 26

Borrowers, Ltd., has 500 7 per cent debentures of £100 each outstanding, the interest being payable half-yearly on 5th April and 5th October. The company's year ends on 5th April, and the liability for Corporation Tax, based on the profits, after deducting debenture interest, gross, is £2,500. Show Journal entries in the company's books. Take Income Tax at 40 per cent.

In addition, write up the necessary ledger accounts.

JOURNAL

19..		£	£
Oct. 5	Debenture Interest	1,750	
	Debenture-holders		1,050
	Income Tax		700
	Being half-year's debenture interest and income tax thereon at 40%		
19..			
April 5	Debenture Interest	1,750	
	Debenture-holders		1,050
	Income Tax		700
	Being half-year's debenture interest and income tax thereon at 40%		

DEBENTURE INTEREST

19..		£	19..		£
Oct. 5	Half-year's Interest[1] . .	1,750	April 5	Profit and Loss Account .	3,500
19..					
April 5	,, ,, [1] . .	1,750			

[1] The net and tax may be entered separately.

INCOME TAX

19..		£	19..		£
Oct. 19	Cash—remittance to Collector of Taxes . .	700	Oct. 5	Debenture Interest Account	700
19..			19..		
April 5	Balance—due to Collector of Taxes on 19/4/19.. .	700	April 5	,, ,,	700
		£1,400			£1,400
			19..		
			April 6	Balance—due to Collector of Taxes on 19/4/19.. .	700[2]

[2] The amount due to the Collector of Taxes does not require to appear as a separate item in published accounts, and may be included with ordinary creditors in the balance sheet.

DEBENTURE-HOLDERS

19..		£	19..		£
Oct. 5	Cash	1,050	Oct. 5	Debenture Interest Account . .	1,050
19..			19..		
April 5	,, ...	1,050	April. 5	,, . .	1,050
		£2,100			£2,100

CORPORATION TAX

			19..		£
			April 5	Profit and Loss Account .	2,500

Redemption of Debentures. Where a company has redeemed any debentures it has power to reissue, either by way of reissue of the *same* or *other* debentures in their place, unless:

(a) Contrary provisions, express or implied, are in the Articles or the terms of issue; or

(b) Intention is shown by resolution or by some other act that the debentures are to be *cancelled*. (Sect. 90, Companies Act 1948.)

The Balance Sheet must show particulars in respect of such debentures which, having been redeemed, are available for reissue.

Reissued debentures retain the same priorities as the *original* debentures, but must bear stamp duty is if they were an original issue. Where debentures are redeemable the method usually adopted to safeguard the interests of the debenture-holders is to require a Sinking Fund to be created out of profits and a sum equivalent thereto invested in outside securities or in an insurance policy. This usually takes place where the debentures are redeemable at a *fixed* date.

Instead of requiring a fixed appropriation to a Sinking Fund, provision is sometimes made whereby the company is precluded from paying dividends over and above a certain fixed rate. This proviso will not of itself ensure the reasonable certainty that the CASH will be forthcoming, so that a further provision is advisable to compel the setting aside of moneys, e.g. by an insurance policy, so that cash may be available when required for debenture redemption.

The three ways of discharging a debenture debt are:

1. By payment to the holder, either at par or at a premium, at the *expiry* of a specified period or at the company's option at a date *within* a specified period.

2. By purchase of the debentures in the open market, usually permitted only if the market price falls to, or below, a specified figure, e.g. in the case of £100 debenture stock if the market price falls to, or below, say 97.

3. By payment year by year of a certain portion, say one-tenth, of the total debenture debt by 'drawings', that is, by withdrawal from a sealed drum of slips, each representing a number of debentures to be repaid.

Payment of Debentures at Maturity. The practice is to set aside annually an equal sum which, with compound interest at a rate decided upon, will amount to the sum required to pay off the debentures at the date fixed for redemption. Simultaneously with the above appropriation, a like sum of money is invested in first-class fixed-income securities together with the interest received therefrom year by year, so that in each Balance Sheet of the company until the debentures are redeemed, will appear the debentures and the Sinking Fund as liabilities and the Sinking Fund Investment as an asset.

It is necessary to distinguish carefully between the two items; the first is merely a certain amount of undistributed profit kept on one side and not available for immediate distribution to the members, but nevertheless, still *profits of the company*; whilst the investment of the same amount is merely an asset of the company invested 'outside' so it becomes an available cash asset when required.

In making calculations for the amount to set on one side, the actual figure is obtainable from Tables. Consideration must be given to the cost of purchase, income tax on the interest (the rate of which obviously cannot be accurately prognosticated), possible depreciation of the investment at the date when it is necessary to realize it for the purpose of providing cash to repay the debenture-holders. For these reasons many companies provide the cash by taking out an insurance policy, the yearly premiums being the equivalent of the yearly investment in securities; others prefer to take a security which has a redemption date coinciding with that of the date on which the repayment of the debentures falls due.

The book-keeping entries are at the date of the creation of fund:

1. Debit Profit and Loss Appropriation Account[1] } with the yearly sum
   Credit Sinking Fund Account   } to be set aside.
2. Debit Sinking Fund Investment Account   } with the yearly sum
   Credit Cash   } invested.

This process will be repeated each year.
In addition, the annual interest will have to be dealt with thus:

1. Debit Cash   } on receipt of
   Credit Sinking Fund Account   } Interest.
2. Debit Sinking Fund Investment Account   } on reinvestment of
   Credit Cash   } Interest.

[1] The amount in question is *NOT a charge* against profits.

Upon realization and redemption the entries are:

1. Debit cash.
   Credit Sinking Fund Investment Account. } on sale of investments.
2. Debit Debentures Account. } on redemption of
   Credit Cash.   debentures
3. Debit Sinking Fund Account. } with part of Sinking Fund
   Credit Reserve   no longer required.

Where debentures are redeemed at a *premium*, the additional entries necessitated are as follows:

1. Debit Premium on Redemption of Debentures Account.
   Credit Debentures Account.
2. Debit Sinking Fund Account.
   Credit Premium on Redemption of Debentures Account.

The converse applies in the case of a redemption at a *discount.*

Alternatively, the balance of Debentures Account may be transferred to the credit of Debenture-holders Account, and upon redemption cash debited thereto.

Illustration 27

Ushant, Ltd., has made an issue of £10,000 7 per cent debentures at par on 1st January 19.1, the terms of which include that the company must provide a Sinking Fund for redemption on 31st December, three years later. It is ascertained from Tables that the annual sum to be set on one side for three years at 5 per cent (rate chosen) compound interest to accumulate to £1 is £0·317209. The first investment to be made on 31st December following issue.

Show Journal entries for the first two years and Ledger Accounts for the three years, ignoring tax and expenses.

[It should first be mentioned that so short a life is unlikely, the period being thus chosen so as to show all the transaction. Secondly, the fund will not come into being until the end of the year and no interest will arise till the end of the second year, i.e. on the first investment.]

The amount to be set side is:

10,000 times 317,209 = £3,172·09.

JOURNAL

19.1			£p	£p
Dec. 31	Profit and Loss Appropriation		3,172·09	
	Sinking Fund			3,172·09
	Being annual sum set aside out of profits.			
	Sinking Fund Investment		3,172·09	
	Cash			3,172·09
	Being annual sum invested at 5% p.a.			
19.2				
Dec. 31	Cash		158·60	
	Sinking Fund			158·60
	Being interest received on £3,172·09 at 5% per annum			
	Sinking Fund Investment		158·60	
	Cash			158·60
	Being investment of interest received.			
	[this date entries will in addition, be made similar to those in 19.1]			

7% DEBENTURES

19.3 Dec. 31	Cash: Debentures re-deemed .	£ 10,000	19.1 Jan. 1	Cash: £10,000 Debentures issued at par .		£ 10,000

SINKING FUND INVESTMENT

19.1 Dec. 31	Cash . . .		£p 3,172·09	19.1 Dec. 31	Balance . . .	c/d	£p 3,172·09
19.2 Jan. 1 Dec. 31	Balance . . . Cash . . . Interest at 5% p.a. on £3,172·09 for one year .	b/d	3,172·09 3,172·09 158·60	19.2 Dec. 31	Balance . . .	c/d	6,502·78
			£6,502·78				£6,502·78
19.3 Jan. 1 Dec. 31	Balance . . . Cash[1] . . . Interest at 5% p.a. on £6,502·78 for one year[1]	b/d	6,502·78 3,172·09 [2]325·13	19.3 Dec. 31	Cash . . .		10,000·00
			£10,000·00				£10,000·00

[1] As redemption takes place the same day, these items would obviously not be actually invested.

[2] The calculation of interest is strictly £325·139, as the tables used are given to six decimal places only.

SINKING FUND

		£p				£p
			19.1 Dec. 31	Profit and Loss Appropriation Account . .		3,172·09
			19.2 Dec. 31	Profit and Loss Appropriation Account . .		3,172·09
				Cash: Interest . .		158·60
19.3 Dec. 31	Transfer to General Reserve . .	10,000·00	19.3 Dec. 31	Profit and Loss Appropriation Account . .		3,172·09
				Cash: Interest . .		325·13
		£10,000·00				£10,000·00

BALANCE SHEET
(as relates to Debentures immediately *prior* to their redemption)

	£		£
£10,000 7% Debentures redeemable on 31st December 19.3 .	10,000	Cash	10,000
Sinking Fund	10,000		

It may be here noted that frequently the term 'Debenture Redemption Account (or Fund)' is employed instead of 'Sinking Fund'.

Although it is not usual to redeem debentures until the completion of the build up of the Sinking Fund, problems occur frequently in examinations which require the entries for redemption when part of the debentures are paid off out of the Redemption Fund Investments.

It will be clear that in connection with debenture redemption there will normally arise two distinct profits or losses, viz.:

1. Profit or loss on the *realization* of the Sinking Fund Investments.
2. Profit or loss on the *redemption* of the debentures.

Unless the question indicates to the contrary, both the above results should be transferred to the Sinking Fund (or Debenture Redemption Account). After this is done the balance of the Fund will be made up of:

1. The amount representing the nominal amount of debentures redeemed.

2. The amount representing the book value of the remaining Debenture Redemption Fund Investments (including any cash balance where the investments sold have produced more than the sum required for redemption).

Item (1) will be transferred to General Reserve (or as the question indicates), leaving item (2) as the final balance.

Illustration 28

The Debenture Redemption Account of X, Ltd., stood at £8,000 represented by £10,000 (nominal) investments. The debentures stood at

£30,000 and the company sold £6,000 (nominal) investments at 84 for the purpose of redeeming £5,000 debentures at 100½. Show Ledger Accounts, ignoring interest and brokerage.

DEBENTURES

		£			£
Cash		5,025	Balance . . . . b/d		30,000
Balance . . . . c/d		25,000	Debenture Redemption Account, Premium on Redemption . .		25
		£30,025			£30,025
			Balance . . . . b/d		25,000

DEBENTURE REDEMPTION

		£			£
Premium on Redemption of £5,000 Debentures . .		25	Balance . . . b/d		8,000
General Reserve (1) .		5,000	Profit on Realization of Investments .		240
Balance . . . . c/d		3,215			
		£8,240			£8,240
			Balance (2) . . . b/d		3,215

DEBENTURE REDEMPTION FUND INVESTMENT

		Nominal	Price			Nominal	Price
		£	£			£	£
Balance . b/d		10,000	80	8,000	Cash . . c/d	6,000	84	5,040
Debenture Redemption Account—Profit on Realization				240	Balance . c/d	4,000	80	3,200
		£10,000		£8,240		£10,000		£8,240
Balance (2) . b/d		4,000	80	3,200				

GENERAL RESERVE

					£
			Debenture Redemption Account		5,000

CASH

		£			£
Debenture Redemption Fund Investment Account . .		5,040	Debentures Account . .		5,025
			Balance . . . c/d		15
		£5,040			£5,040
Balance (2) . . . b/d		15			

Note 1. The transfer to General Reserve equals the nominal amount of debentures redeemed.

Note 2. The balance on Debenture Redemption Account equals the book value of investments, viz. investments £3,200, PLUS cash £15. The latter is merely the balance remaining by reason of the sale of investments providing slightly more cash than is required for redemption.

Insurance Policy Method. The principle outlined above applies to this method, except that no interest is receivable during the period. Accordingly, the instalments (i.e. the premiums payable) will be less than the total sum of the policy divided by the number of premiums, e.g. if the amount to be provided is £5,000 in five years, the premium will be considerably less than £1,000 seeing that no interest as such is receivable; on the other hand it will be higher than the sum set aside by the investment method, because the latter will presuppose a rate of interest of, say, 5 per cent to $5\frac{1}{2}$ per cent, whereas the yearly premiums will be based at a rate approximating to $4\frac{1}{2}$ to 5 per cent.

Again, the investment into securities can be realized at any time, subject to any depreciation or appreciation in value, whereas if the policy is surrendered there will be a very serious loss entailed. This, however, may be avoided by obtaining a loan on the security of the policy.

The premium must be paid at the commencement of the first year, as one year must elapse after the last premium is paid before the policy moneys fall due.

The entries upon the yearly appropriation and payment of premium will be as follows:

1. Debit Profit and Loss Appropriation Account.
   Credit Debenture Redemption Account.
2. Debit Debenture Redemption Policy Account.
   Credit cash.

Upon realization and redemption:

1. Debit cash.
   Credit Debenture Redemption Policy Account.
2. Debit Debentures Account.
   Credit cash.
3. Debit Debenture Redemption Account.
   Credit Reserve Account.

Where debentures are redeemed at a *premium*, the entries necessitated are as follows:

1. Debit Premium on Redemption of Debentures Account.
   Credit Debentures Account.
2. Debit Debenture Redemption Account
   Credit Premium on Redemption of Debentures Account.

The converse applies in the case of a redemption at a *discount*.

As the amount receivable will be in excess of the sum of the premiums, there will be a profit at the end of the period on the policy, unless a transfer is made yearly on the basis of an estimated rate of interest earned, in which case the yearly transfer would be:

Debit Debenture Redemption Policy Account.
Credit Debenture Redemption Account.

Illustration 29

Ushant, Ltd., has made an issue of £10,000 7 per cent debentures on 1st January 19.., the terms of which include that the company must provide a Sinking Fund for redemption on 31st December 19.. (three years later). The directors decide to take out an insurance policy to provide the necessary cash, the annual premium being £3,021·034,[1] on which the return is 5 per cent per annum compound interest.

Show Ledger Accounts.

7% DEBENTURES

Year 3 (end)	Cash	£ 10,000	Year 1 (commencement)	Cash	£ 10,000

DEBENTURE[2] REDEMPTION

			Year 1 (end)	Profit and Loss Appropriation Account	3,021·034
				Debenture Redemption Policy Account— Interest at 5% p.a. on £3,021·034 for one year	151·052
					3,172·086
			2 (end)	Profit and Loss Appropriation Account	3,021·034
				Debenture Redemption Policy Account— Interest at 5% p.a. on £6,193·120 for one year	309·656
Year 3 (end)	General Reserve	10,000·000	3 (end)	Profit and Loss Appropriation Account	6,502·776 3,021·034
				Debenture Redemption Policy Account— Interest at 5% p.a. on £9,523·810 for one year	476·190
		£10,000·000			£10,000·000

[1] The annual premium of £3,021·034 is obtained from Annuity Tables using the formula:

$$\frac{£10,000}{S\frac{5\%}{4}-1}$$

[2] These accounts will be balanced off yearly in the usual way.

DEBENTURE[1] REDEMPTION POLICY

			£p			£p
Year 1 (commencement) (end)	Cash— Premium		3,021·034			
	Debenture Redemption Account— Interest		151·052			
			3,172·086			
Year 2 (commencement) (end)	Cash— Premium		3,021·034			
	Debenture Redemption Account— Interest		309·656			
			6,502·776	Year 3 (end)	Cash	10,000·000
Year 3 (commencement) (end)	Cash— Premium		3,021·034			
	Debenture Redemption Account— Interest		476·190			
			£10,000·000			£10,000·000

[1] These accounts will be balanced off yearly in the usual way.

CASH (re REDEMPTION)

		£			£
Year 3 (end)	Debenture Redemption Policy Account	10,000	Year 3 (end)	7% Debentures Account	10,000

It will be observed that the principles enumerated are precisely those discussed in Chapter 7, so far as they relate to the construction of the accounts for the amortization of an asset. The balance of the Debenture Redemption Account upon the repayment of debentures becomes a free reserve, whereas the Asset Amortization Account must be used to write down an asset. (See p. 0706 *et seq.*)

Redemption by Annual Drawings. The repayments taking place annually preclude the building up of a Sinking Fund and investments to accumulate to the required sum due on a fixed date, so that it is usual to restrict the rate of dividends on ordinary shares to a certain percentage until the final repayment or to permit the rate of dividend to increase as the debenture debt diminishes. The entries required are: debit debentures credit cash with the yearly drawings.

Debenture Discount. Where debentures have been issued at a discount the prudent company will write off to Profit and Loss Appropriation Account the whole amount or a proportion of it year by year, although it is not legally necessary unless the company's own provisions require it.

The two methods usually employed are (1) to write off an amount yearly, proportionate to the life of the debentures, e.g. if the maturity of the debentures is ten years after issue, one-tenth of the debenture discount will be written off; or (2) to write off discount proportionate to the debenture debt outstanding at the commencement of each year, less repayments, if any, during that year.

Illustration 30

A. Ltd., issues £10,000 debentures on 1st January 19.., at a discount of 5 per cent repayable in annual drawings of £2,000, commencing 31st December following. The company's year ends on 31st December. Show the amounts to be written off in five years, assuming that the company decides to write off Debenture Discount Account during the life of the debentures.

METHOD 1.

One-fifth of £500 = £100 per annum.

METHOD 2.

Amount of debentures outstanding at the commencement of each year, viz.:

Year	Proportion	Amount
	£	£p
1	$10,000 = \frac{10}{30} \times 500 =$	166·67
2	$8,000 = \frac{8}{30} \times 500 =$	133·33
3	$6,000 = \frac{6}{30} \times 500 =$	100·00
4	$4,000 = \frac{4}{30} \times 500 =$	66·67
5	$2,000 = \frac{2}{30} \times 500 =$	33·33
	30,000	£500·00

The Ledger Account for Debenture discount as dealt with by Method 2 is as follows:

DEBENTURE DISCOUNT

Year				£p	Year				£p
1	Debentures . . .			500·00	1	Profit and Loss Appropriation Account . Balance . .		c/d	166·67 333·33
				£500·00					£500·00
2	Balance . . .	b/d		333·33	2	Profit and Loss Appropriation Account . Balance . .		c/d	133·33 200·00
				£333·33					£333·33
3	Balance . . .	b/d		200·00	3	Profit and Loss Appropriation Account . Balance . .		c/d	100·00 100·00
				£200·00					£200·00
4	Balance . . .	b/d		100·00	4	Profit and Loss Appropriation Account . Balance . .		c/d	66·67 33·33
				£100·00					£100·00
5	Balance . . .	b/d		£33·33	5	Profit and Loss Appropriation Account .			£33·33

Illustration 31

Debenture discount is £120 in respect of £6,000 debentures issued on 1st April 19.1, repayable by three equal drawings of £2,000 each. The company makes its account up to 31st December. The calculation for the amount of discount to be written off is as follows:

Year ended			Amount written off	
£			£	£
31st Dec 19.1	6,000 × ¾ [i.e. 1st April to 31st Dec.]		$4,500 \frac{45}{120} \times 120 =$	45
19.2	6,000 × ¼ [i.e. 1st Jan. to 31st Mar.]	1,500		
	4,000 × ¾ [i.e. 1st April to 31st Dec.]	3,000		
		——	$4,500 \frac{45}{120} \times 120 =$	45
19.3	4,000 × ¼ [as in 19.2]	1,000		
	2,000 × ¾ [as in 19.2]	1,500		
		——	$2,500 \frac{25}{120} \times 120 =$	25
19.4	2,000 × ¼ [i.e. 1st Jan. to 31st Mar.]		$500 \frac{5}{120} \times 120 =$	5
		£12,000		£120

It is assumed that the first repayment takes place on 1st April 19..

The writing-off in the above illustration involves four accounting periods, the first and last being respectively for nine months (of 19.1) and three months (of 19.4), during which time debentures are outstanding. After the first full year operates (i.e. 19.2) the ratios decrease by £2,000.[1]

The position in regard to an issue of debentures at a premium or at a discount demands further attention. The principles involved are similar, so that the question of an issue at a premium will also be considered. Where debentures are issued at a premium it is usually because the interest payable thereon is higher than that reasonably obtained on a security of that kind, after making due allowance for business risk. Therefore, the real burden to the company should be that arising from a payment of interest at the normal rate so that the premium on issue is not a true profit at all. If the debentures are redeemable at a fixed date, the premium charged should be the PRESENT WORTH of the DIFFERENTIAL interest, so that the difference between the ACTUAL and NORMAL rate of interest will exhaust the amount of the premium by the expiry of the term of the debentures.

For instance, if a company issues £1,000 debentures (ruling rate of interest being 4 per cent) they may be issued at a premium with a higher rate of interest than 4 per cent or at a discount with a lower rate of interest than 4 per cent having regard to date of maturity.

Illustration 32

Assuming that the £1,000 debentures are redeemable at the expiry of five years the issue price would be (on a 4 per cent yield basis, but a 6 per cent interest payment basis) at a premium of £89·03 to the nearest second place of decimals or in practice £89.

The above figure may be obtained from an Annuity Table. The book-keeping entry will be:

				£	£
Debit Cash	.	.	.	1,089·03	
Credit Debentures	.	.	.		1,000
,, Premium	.	.	.		89·03

---

[1] If method (1) is used, the amounts written off will be £30, £40, £40, and £10 respectively.

As the interest on £1,089·03 at 4 per cent per annum is really £43·56 annually, debenture interest should be debited therewith; the difference between such amount and the 6 per cent on £1,000 = £60 is virtually a part repayment of the premium, so that at the beginning of the second year the amount of premium has been returned to the extent of £16·44, leaving premium outstanding at £72·59 (i.e. £89·03 less £16·44). Hence, in the second year the return of premium will be the difference between the £60 and 4 per cent interest on £1072·59 (£42·90), viz £17·10, thus continuing the process until the end of the fifth year, when £1,000 remains for payments.

The book-keeping entries for each of the five years will be:

	Dr. Debenture Interest [per next column]	4% on	Dr. Premium	Cr. Cash	Balances	
					Cr. Debentures	Cr. Premium
	£	£	£	£	£	£
Commencement of 1st year					1,000	89·03
End of 1st year	43·56	(1,089·03)	(b) 16·44	60	1,000	(a) 72·59
2nd	42·90	(1,072·59)	(d) 17·10	60	1,000	(c) 55·49
3rd	42·22	(1,055·49)	(f) 17·78	60	1,000	(e) 37·71
4th	41·51	(1,037·71)	(h) 18·49	60	1,000	(g) 19·22
5th	[1]40·78	(1,019·22)	(j) 19·22	60	1,000	(i) nil
			£89·03			

[1] Actually 40·77 [·01 error arises by taking two places of decimals only].

$$
\begin{array}{llllll}
& £ & & & £ & £ \\
(a) & 89·03 & less \text{ repayment of} & (b) & 16·44 & = 72·59 \\
(c) & 72·59 & ,, & ,, & (d) & 17·10 & = 55·49 \\
(e) & 55·49 & ,, & ,, & (f) & 17·78 & = 37·71 \\
(g) & 37·71 & ,, & ,, & (h) & 18·49 & = 19·22 \\
(i) & 19·22 & ,, & ,, & (j) & 19·22 & = nil \\
\end{array}
$$

The results may now be compared thus:

(a) By the above method.

Debenture Interest	
	£
Year 1	43·56
,, 2	42·90
,, 3	42·22
,, 4	41·51
5	40·78
Total (Debit)	£210·97

(b) By taking the premium as profit.

Debenture Interest	Premium
£	£
60	89·03
60	
60	
60	
60	
(Debit) £300 [net Debit £210·97] (Credit)	£89·03

There is no LEGAL necessity for treatment on strict theoretical lines, but the method is scientifically sound and in examination work the principle should be mentioned and (time permitting) illustrated. No provision exists in the Companies Acts laying down any particular treatment of PREMIUMS on debentures, but only as regards DISCOUNTS.

Illustration 33

The same principle applies in treating debentures at a discount. The company, in offering debentures at a discount, would have to compute on a 4 per cent basis with interest at 2 per cent to permit of the same figures being employed. Just as, in the previous illustration, the 2 per cent extra interest was merged in the premium, so the 2 per cent less interest will be merged in the discount. Hence, as the premium for the differential 2 per cent was 89·03 per £1,000, so the discount will be the same figure; therefore, the debentures will be issued on that basis, the entry on receipt being:

		£	£
Debit Cash	. . . . .	910·97	
,, Discount on Debentures	. . .	89·03	
Credit Debentures	. . . .		1,000

The law, it will be remembered, insists on the discount on debentures being shown in the Balance Sheet as a separate item (and the debentures as a consequence at the gross figure). The reverse process now applies, viz. the true rate of interest is £20 [2 per cent on £1,000] plus £16·44 to make up 4 per cent on £910·97 [£36·44], so that the sum of £36·44 will be debited to Profit and Loss Account, Cash and Debenture Discount being respectively credited with £20 and £16·44. Although the law does not require an ACTUAL writing-off of the debenture discount, it must be shown in the Balance Sheet TILL written off.

The entry, therefore, for the first year will be:

		£	£
Debit Debenture Interest	. . .	36·44	
Credit Cash	. . . . .		20·00
,, Debenture Discount	. . .		16·44

This process will be continued until the date for repayment of debentures.

The entries year by year will therefore be:

	Dr. Debenture Interest [per next column]	4% on	Cr. Debenture Discount	Cr. Cash	Balances	
					Cr. Debentures	Dr. Debenture Discount
	£	£	£	£	£	£
Commencement of 1st year					1,000	89·03
End of 1st year	36·44	(a) (910·97)	16·44	20	1,000	72·59
2nd	37·10	(b) (927·41)	17·10	20	1,000	55·49
3rd	37·78	(c) (944·51)	17·78	20	1,000	37·71
4th	48·49	(d) (962·29)	18·49	20	1,000	19·22
5th	¹39·22	(e) (980·78)	19·22	20	1,000	nil
			£89·03			

¹ Actually 39·23 [·01 error arises by taking two places of decimals only].

		£				£	£
(a)	Balance	1,000	*less* Debenture Discount			89·03 =	910·97
(b)	,,	1,000	,,	,,	,,	72·59 =	927·41
(c)	,,	1,000	,,	,,	,,	55·49 =	944·51
(d)	,,	1,000	,,	,,	,,	37·71 =	962·29
(e)	,,	1,000	,,	,,	,,	19·22 =	980·78

The results may now be compared, thus:

(a) By the above method.
(b) By taking the discount as loss.

Debenture Interest		Discount Dr.	Cr.		Debenture Interest		Discount
	£	£	£			£	£
Year 1	36·44	89·03	16·44			20	
,, 2	37·10		17·10			20	
,, 3	37·78		17·78			20	
,, 4	38·49		18·49			20	
,, 5	39·22		19·22			20	89·03
Total (Debit)	£189·03	£89·03	£89·03		(Debit) £100 [Total Debit (Debit) £189·03]		£89·03

[The premium (and conversely for discount) is the present worth of the differential annuity of 2 per cent for five years, taking 4 per cent as the basic rate:

$$\text{Present worth} = 2 \times \frac{\left(1 - \dfrac{1}{(1 \cdot 04)^5}\right)}{\cdot 04}$$

$$= 50 \left(1 - \frac{1}{1 \cdot 21665}\right)$$

$$= £8 \cdot 903$$

The present worth of an annuity of £2 at 4 per cent for 5 years is £8·903, or £89·03 for an annuity of £20. The investor is, theoretically, prepared to pay £89·03 premium to receive, over and above 4 per cent on £1,000, five annual payments of £20 each (i.e. 2 per cent on £1,000).

Conversely, the investor would, in consideration of losing five annual payments of £20, require a rebate on the purchase price of £1,000 debentures on which he wants a 4 per cent yield, to the extent of £89·03.]

Purchase of Debentures in Open Market. This is the method adopted when it is desired to keep the debentures alive with a view to future reissue. They may be purchased as the investment on the Sinking Fund or a certain amount may be spent each year out of the liquid capital of the business, even where there is no specific obligation to redeem. If the purchase is made immediately after the interest has been paid the question of accrued interest will not, of course, enter into the calculations. In practice, however, the purchase will be made at a time when the market is most favourable, that is, when the market price is low. Where the debentures so purchased represent investments on the Sinking Fund, it is advisable to write-off any premium or discount involved in the purchase price to the Sinking Fund, so that at the date of redemption the balance of Debenture Investment Account will equal the balance of the Debentures Account. If, however, the debentures are merely held as an investment in the ordinary course of the company's business, a Debentures Investment Account will be opened and treated as an Investment Account in the ordinary way.

It may be noted that, where there is a Sinking Fund in existence, debentures purchased in the open market are often utilized as the Sinking Fund Investment.

Treatment of Interest on Own Debentures. 1. *Where no Sinking Fund exists*, the interest will be credited either as a separate item to Profit and Loss Account or to Debenture Interest Account,[1] the net balance of the latter being transferred to the debit of Profit and Loss Account in the ordinary way.

2. *Where a Sinking Fund is being built up*, if the debentures have been acquired either out of the proceeds of sale of Sinking Fund Investments or out of profit to the Sinking Fund, then inasmuch as such debentures will form part of the Sinking Fund Investments, the interest will be credited to the Fund, precisely as if the investments were outside investments. Obviously, the *debit* for such interest will be to Profit and Loss Account, as the latter account should include the interest on the *whole* of the debentures, i.e. those held by outsiders and those held by the company itself.

Profits and losses on Sinking Fund Investments will be dealt with on the same principle.

3. *Where no Sinking Fund exists*, if the debentures are purchased for cancellation or redeemed by drawings, it is a common practice to transfer an amount equal to the debentures purchased for cancellation from Profit and Loss Account to General Reserve—ignoring interest—having the same effect as if a fund had been built up annually and upon redemption of the debentures transferred to General Reserve.

Should the purchase be made within the interest period, the price will be inclusive of accruing interest if bought "cum interest"; but if purchased "ex interest", the forthcoming interest is retained by the seller. In order to adjust the matter, the accrued interest at the date of purchase will be debited in the interest column of the Investment Account and the interest for the whole period credited in the interest column. Thus a credit is left covering the proportion of interest arising since the date of purchase of the debentures.

Illustration 34

X, Ltd., purchases on 1st April 19.., £200 nominal of its own 6 per cent debentures at $98\frac{1}{2}$, brokerage and expenses being £1. A further purchase of £600 nominal was made on 31st October at $101\frac{1}{2}$, brokerage and expenses being £2. Debenture interest is payable on 30th June and 31st December. Ignore income tax. Show Ledger Accounts.

(*a*) Included in the price is 3 months' interest at 6 per cent per annum on £200 = £3, so that of the £6 received £3 is 'pure' interest.

(*b*) Included in the price is 4 months' interest (1st July to 31st October) at 6 per cent per annum on £600 = £12, so that out of the £24 received on 31st December there remains £12 'pure' interest, made up of:

	£
6 months' Interest at 6 per cent per annum on £200 . . .	6
2 months' Interest at 6 per cent per annum on £600 . . .	6
As per Investment Account	£12

---

[1] Either credited to Debenture Interest Received Account and transferred to Debenture Interest Paid Account, or credited direct to the latter account.

Own Debentures Investment

Date	Particulars	Nominal	Interest	Capital	Date	Particulars	Nominal	Interest	Capital
19.. April 1	Cash—Purchase £200 at 98½ = £197 / Plus Expenses = 1 / £198	£200	(a) £3	£195	19.. June 30	Cash—half-year's Interest on £200 at 6% per annum	£	(a) 6	£
Oct. 31	Cash—Purchase £600 at 101½ = £609 / Plus Expenses = 2 / £611	600	(b) 12	599	Dec. 31	Cash—half-year's Interest on £800 at 6% per annum		(b) 24	
Dec. 31	Debenture Interest Received Account		15		Dec. 31	Balance c/d	800		794
		£800	£30	£794			£800	£30	£794
19.. Jan. 1	Balance b/d	800		794					

(a) and (b). See notes at bottom of p. 23128.

If on 1st January 19.., the £800 debentures are cancelled, the Investment Account will be debited with £6 and Profit and Loss on Cancellation of Debentures Account credited with £6, followed by a debit of £800 to Debentures and a credit of £800 to the above Investment Account.

This results as follows:

OWN DEBENTURES INVESTMENT

			Nominal £	£				Nominal £	£
19.. Jan. 1	Balance Profit and Loss on Cancellation of Debentures Account	b/d	800	794 6	19.. Jan. 1	Debentures Account		800	800
			£800	£800				£800	£800

DEBENTURES

			£				£
19.. Jan. 1	Debentures purchased and cancelled		800	19.. Jan. 1	Balance	b/d	?

PROFIT AND LOSS ON CANCELLATION OF DEBENTURES

							£
				19.. Jan. 1	Profit on purchase and cancellation of £800 Debentures[1]		6

[1] This account should be left as a Reserve to cover possible subsequent losses until all the Debentures have been discharged. The balance of profit, if any, is usually utilized to eliminate expenses of issue and discount on Debentures if this has not already been done during the life of the Debentures.

Where debentures are purchased on the open market for immediate cancellation, the purchase price, if 'cum interest', includes the accruing interest, and the portion of the price that relates to interest must be transferred to Debenture Interest Account. When the interest date is approaching, the price paid above par may be less than the amount represented by the accruing interest, so that what appears to be a premium on purchase may really be a discount.

Where the debentures are acquired 'ex interest', the converse applies, and the debenture interest will have to be paid at the end of the period, but as, at the date of acquisition, the FULL period interest was deducted from the 'cum interest' price, an adjustment in relief of interest against capital is required. This is necessary because the debenture interest on the debentures bought and cancelled does not cover the whole period, but the capital cost has been relieved to the extent of the interest for the full period by reason of the deduction of the interest for the full period from the price when the latter is quoted 'ex interest'.

Illustration 35

On 1st January, X, Ltd., has £12,000 6 per cent debentures. In accordance with the powers under the deed, the directors acquire in the open market for immediate cancellation debentures, as follows:

Mar. 1. £2,000 at 98
Aug. 1. £4,000 at $100\frac{1}{4}$
Dec. 15. £1,000 at $98\frac{1}{2}$ ex interest

Debenture interest is payable half-yearly, 30th June and 31st December. Show Ledger accounts of Debentures, Debenture Interest, Profit and Loss on Cancellation. Strike a balance half-yearly. (Take Income Tax at 40 per cent.)

1st Half-year

DEBENTURES

19..				£	19..			£
Mar. 1	Debentures purchased £1,960 Profit and Loss on Cancellation of Debentures Account 40	(a)		2,000	Jan. 1	Balance . . . b/d		12,000
June 30	Balance . .	c/d		10,000				
				£12,000				£12,000
					July 1	Balance . . . b/d		10,000

PROFIT AND LOSS ON CANCELLATION OF DEBENTURES

19..		£	19..			£
June 30	Reserve. . . .	60	Mar. 1	Debentures Account . (b) Debenture Interest Account		40 20
		£60				£60

DEBENTURE INTEREST

19..		£	19..		£
Mar. 1	Profit and Loss on Cancellation of Debentures Account . .	20	June 30	Profit and Loss Account	320
June 30	Debenture-holders (Interest) Account . Income Tax Account (at 40%). . .	180 120			
		£320			£320

DEBENTURE-HOLDERS (INTEREST)

19..		£	19..		£
June 30	Cash	180	June 30	Debenture Interest Account . . . [£10,000 at 6% per annum for six months less tax]	180
		£180			£180

INCOME TAX

19.. June 30	Balance	.	.	c/d	£ 120	19.. June 30	Debenture Interest Account	.	.		£ 120
						19.. July 1st	Balance			b/d	120

NOTES.

1. $a - b = £2,000 - £40 = £1,960$. £2,000 Debentures at 98 . . $= £1,960$

2. The true Debenture Interest on £2,000 from 1st Jan. to 28th February
    at 6 per cent per annum . . . . $=$ £ 20
    The true Debenture Interest on £10,000 for $\frac{1}{2}$ year to June 30th at 6 per
    cent per annum . . . . $=$ 300

    Charged to Profit and Loss Account, as above £320

3. The par value of each £100 of Debentures plus accruing interest at 6 per cent per annum
for 2 months (i.e. 1st Jan. to 28th February) = £101. The Debentures were bought back at £98
only, leaving a profit on the £2,000 at 3 per cent = £60.

2nd Half-year

DEBENTURES

19.. Aug. 1 Dec. 15	Debentures purchased . Debentures pur- chased £985 Profit and Loss on Cancellation of Debentures Account . 15		£ 4,010	19.. July 1 Aug. 1	Balance . . . Profit and Loss on Can- cellation of Debentures Account . . .	b/d	£ 10,000 10
31	Balance . . .	c/d	1,000 5,000				
			£10,010				£10,010
				19.. Jan. 1	Balance . . .	b/d	5,000

PROFIT AND LOSS ON CANCELLATION OF DEBENTURES

19.. Aug. 1	Debentures Account Balance. . .	. c/d	£p 10·00 ·10·00	19.. Aug. 1	Debenture Interest Account . .	.	£p 20·00
			£20·00				£20·00
Dec. 31	Debenture Interest Account . . Balance. . .	. c/d	2·50 22·50	Aug. 1 Dec. 15	Balance. . . Debentures Account	b/d	10·00 15·00
			£25·00				£25·00
				19.. Jan. 1	Balance . .	b/d	22·50

DEBENTURE INTEREST

19.. Aug. 1	Profit and Loss on Cancellation of Debentures Account[1]		£p 20·00	19.. Dec. 31	Profit and Loss on Cancellation of Debentures Account Profit and Loss Account		£p 2·50 197·50
Dec. 31	Debenture-holders (Interest) Account		108·00				
	Income Tax Account at 40%		72·00				
			£200·00				£200·00

[1] One month's interest on £4,000 at 6 per cent per annum.

DEBENTURE-HOLDERS (INTEREST)

19.. Dec. 31	Cash		£ 108	19.. Dec. 31	Debenture Interest Account £6,000 at 6% per annum for six months [less tax]		£ 108
			£108				£108

INCOME TAX

19.. July 14	Cash Remittance to Collector of Taxes		£ 120	19.. July 1	Balance	b/d	£ 120
Dec. 31	Balance	c/d	72	Dec. 31	Debenture Interest Account		72
			£192				£192
				19.. Jan. 1	Balance[1]	b/d	72

[1] The Income Tax should be remitted to the Collector of Taxes on or before 14th January 19...

The respective profits on cancellation may be proved as follows:

1. 1st August cancellation. The price at *true* par, i.e. principal plus interest to date should be $100 + \frac{1}{2}$ per cent [i.e. 6 per cent per annum for 1 month] $= 100\frac{1}{2}$. This burden is discharged at $100\frac{1}{4}$, leaving a profit of $\frac{1}{4}$ per cent on £4,000 = £10, which is the balance shown in the account.

2. 15th December cancellation. The 'cum interest' price at this date should be:

$$100 + 5\tfrac{1}{2} \text{ months' interest at 6 per cent per annum} = 102\tfrac{3}{4}\%.$$

But seeing that the price is to be reckoned 'ex interest', 6 months interest must be deducted, viz. 3 per cent:

True 'par' value $[102\frac{3}{4}\% - 3\%]$.	.	.	.	.	.	$= 99\frac{3}{4}\%$
The purchse price .	.	.	.	.	.	$= 98\frac{1}{2}\%$
Leaving a profit of.	.	.	.	.	.	$= 1\frac{1}{4}\%$

Hence $\dfrac{1\frac{1}{4}}{100} \times £1,000 = £12 \cdot 50$ profit over par value is made by the company.

In order, therefore, to adjust capital and income, a debit to capital and a credit to interest of £2·50 is required, bringing the true cost of purchased debentures to $99\frac{3}{4}$. This reduces the redemption profit to £12·50. In other words, $99\frac{3}{4}$ 'ex interest' is the actual 'no profit no loss' price, but the actual price being $98\frac{1}{2}$ there is clearly a gain of $1\frac{1}{4}$ per cent on £1,000.

It must be noted that the interest on 31st December is upon £6,000, that is, the remaining debentures plus those redeemed 'ex interest' because the debenture-holders are on the register at the time of the sale 'ex interest', and are thus entitled to the interest.

The net charge to Profit and Loss for the half-year ended 31st December is computed as follows:

	£p
1 month's interest on £4,000 at 6% per annum . .	20·00
$5\frac{1}{2}$ months' interest on £1,000 at 6% per annum . .	27·50
6 months' interest on £5,000 at 6% per annum . .	150·00
[on debentures still outstanding]	
[See p. 23133]	£197·50

Illustration 36

A company raises a loan of £20,000 upon debenture stock at a discount of 10 per cent on 1st January 19.1. The loan is redeemable at par at the end of a period of years by a cumulative Sinking Fund, but the company has power to call upon the trustees to apply the Sinking Fund investments in the purchase of stock, *if below par*, at any time. The annual Sinking Fund contribution, exclusive of interest accumulated, is £2,000. This amount is promptly invested, together with income accumulations, on 1st January in each year; capital balances arising from realization of investments are reinvested at the same time. The Sinking Fund instalments are calculated on a 3 per cent basis, but are invested to give a higher yield.

Sinking Fund investments produce interest, less tax, as follows: 19.2, £86; 19·3, £139.

Realizations of Sinking Fund investments are as follows:

1st Oct., 19.2, £1,014;   original cost, £1,000.
1st July, 19.3, £373;   original cost, £400.

The proceeds of realizations are applied in redemption of stock as follows:

1st Oct., 19.2, £960;   in cancellation of £1,000 Stock.
1st July, 19.3, £383;   in cancellation of £400 Stock.

Ignore interest on debenture stock.

Prepare accounts in respect of the Sinking Fund transactions given for the years 19.1 to 19.3 inclusive, showing the manner in which the Sinking Fund would be compensated for the loss of interest resulting from the realization of investments. State also how you would deal with the accounts relating to discount on issue, profit on cancellation of stock, and profit and loss on realization of investments.

[For sake of completeness a Cash Account and Profit and Loss Appropriation Account in relation to the whole set of transactions is given, together with a 'Trial Balance'.]

CASH (*re* DEBENTURE STOCK)

19.1 Jan. 1	Debenture Stock Account .		£ 18,000	19.1 Dec. 31	Balance . . .	c/d	£ 18,000
19.2 Jan. 1 Oct. 1 Dec. 31	Balance . . . Sinking Fund Investments Account . . Sinking Fund Account— Interest . .	b/d	18,000 1,014 86	19.2 Jan. 1 Oct. 1 Dec. 31	Sinking Fund Investments Account . . . Debenture Stock Account Deposit Account . . Balance . . .	c/d	2,000 960 54 16,086
			£19,100				£19,100
19.3 Jan. 1 July 1 Dec. 31	Balance . . . Sinking Fund Investments Account . . Suspense Account . . Sinking Fund Account— Interest . .	b/d	16,086 373 10 139	19.3 Jan. 1 July 1 Dec. 31	Sinking Fund Investments Account . . . „ „ Debenture Stock Account Balance . . .	c/d	2,000 86 383 14,139
			£16,608				£16,608
19.4 Jan. 1	Balance . . .	b/d	14,139				

DEPOSIT ACCOUNT

19.2 Dec. 31	Cash		£ 54	19.3 Jan. 1	Sinking Fund Investments Account . . .		£ 54

PROFIT AND LOSS APPROPRIATION ACCOUNT

19.1 Dec. 31	Sinking Fund Account .		£ 2,000				
19.2 Dec. 31	Sinking Fund Account .		2,000				
19.3 Dec. 31	Sinking Fund Account .		2,000				

DEBENTURE STOCK

			£				£
19.2 Oct. 1	Cash		960	19.1 Jan. 1	Sundries		20,000
	Profit and Loss on Cancellation of Debenture Stock Account		40				
Dec. 31	Balance	c/d	19,000				
			£20,000				£20,000
19.3 July 1	Cash		383	19.3 Jan. 1	Balance	b/d	19,000
	Profit and Loss on Cancellation of Debenture Stock Account		17				
Dec. 31	Balance	c/d	18,600				
			£19,000				£19,000
				19.4 Jan. 1	Balance	b/d	18,600

SINKING FUND INVESTMENTS

			£				£
19.2 Jan. 1	Cash		2,000	19.2 Oct. 1	Cash		1,014
Oct. 1	Profit and Loss on realization of Investments Account		14	Dec. 31	Balance	c/d	1,000
			£2,014				£2,014
19.3 Jan. 1	Balance	b/d	1,000	19.3 July 1	Cash		373
	Cash invested— Amount annually set aside £2,000				Profit and Loss on realization of Investments Account		27
	Interest on Investments 86						
	Balance of sale of Investments 54		2,140	Dec. 31	Balance	c/d	2,740
			£3,140				£3,140
19.4 Jan. 1	Balance	b/d	2,740				

SUSPENSE (re CASH)

							£
				19.3 July 1	Cash		10

SINKING FUND

Date	Particulars		£	Date	Particulars		£
19.2 Dec. 31	General Reserve		1,000	19.1 Dec. 31	Profit and Loss Appropriation Account		2,000
	Balance	c/d	3,140	19.2 Oct. 1	Profit and Loss on Cancellation of Debenture Stock Account		40
					Profit and Loss on realization of Investments Account		14
				Dec. 31	Interest on Investments Account		86
					Profit and Loss Appropriation Account		2,000
			£4,140				£4,140
19.3 July 1	Profit and Loss on realization of Investments Account		27	19.3 Jan. 1	Balance	b/d	3,140
Dec. 31	General Reserve		400	July 1	Profit and Loss on Cancellation of Debenture Stock Account		17
	Balance	c/d	4,869	Dec. 31	Interest on Investments Account		139
					Profit and Loss Appropriation Account		2,000
			£5,296				£5,296
				19.4 Jan. 1	Balance	b/d	4,869

PROFIT AND LOSS ON CANCELLATION OF DEBENTURE STOCK

Date	Particulars	£	Date	Particulars	£
19.2 Oct. 1	Sinking Fund Account	40	19.2 Oct. 1	Debenture Stock Account	40
19.3 July 1	Sinking Fund Account	17	19.3 July 1	Debenture Stock Account	17

PROFIT AND LOSS ON REALIZATION OF INVESTMENTS

Date	Particulars	£	Date	Particulars	£
19.2 Oct. 1	Sinking Fund Account	14	19.2 Oct. 1	Sinking Fund Investments Account	14
19.3 July 1	Sinking Fund Investments Account	27	19.3 July 1	Sinking Fund Account	27

GENERAL RESERVE

Date	Particulars	£	Date	Particulars	£
19.2 Dec. 31	Discount on Debenture Stock Account	1,000	19.2 Dec. 31	Sinking Fund Account	1,000
19.3 Dec. 31	Discount on Debenture Stock Account	400	19.3 Dec. 31	Sinking Fund Account	400

DISCOUNT ON DEBENTURE STOCK

			£					£
19.2 Jan. 1	*Debenture Stock Account*	.	*2,000*	19.2 Dec. 31	General Reserve Balance	. .	c/d	1,000 1,000
			£2,000					£2,000
19.3 Jan. 1	Balance	b/d	1,000	19.3 Dec. 31	General Reserve Balance .	. .	c/d	400 600
			£1,000					£1,000
19.4 Jan. 1	Balance . . .	b/d	600					

Opening items are in italics.

TRIAL BALANCES

	31st Dec. 19.2			31st Dec. 19.3	
	Dr.	Cr.		Dr.	Cr.
	£	£		£	£
Debenture Stock		19,000			18,600
Sinking Fund		3,140			4,869
Sinking Fund Investments . .	(a) 1,000			(a) 2,740	
Cash: General (x) £16,000			(y) £14,000		
Interest (b) 86			(b) 139		
Deposit . (c) 54			———	14,139	
——— 16,140					
Suspense					(c)[1] 10
Discount on Debenture Stock .	1,000			600	
Profit and Loss Appropriation .	4,000			6,000	
	£22,140	£22,140		£23,479	£23,479

[1] This is shown in a separate account for clearness and signifies that £10 of General Cash has been used in redeeming the Debenture Stock. On reference to the Cash Account it will be seen that £373 was received from the sale of Investments and £383 used to repay the Debenture Stock.

NOTES on 31st December 19.2, Trial Balance.

(1) The sum of (a) (b) and (c) together with £2,000 to be invested on 1st Jan. 19.3, will equal the balance of Sinking Fund Account.

(x) This is £18,000 less £2,000 invested in Sinking Fund Investment Account.

NOTES on 31st December 19.3, Trial Balance.

(1) The sum of (a) and (b) less (c) together with £2,000 to be invested on 1st Jan., 19.4, will equal the balance of Sinking Fund Account.

(y) This is £16,000 less £2,000 invested in Sinking Fund Investment Account.

NOTES. (i) As the Sinking Fund is used to cancel the Debenture Stock a proportion of the former is now 'free', and, subject to the desirability of eliminating part of the Debenture Discount, becomes a general reserve.

(ii) Compensation to the Sinking Fund in respect of loss of interest on investments sold is unnecessary since debentures have been cancelled by the proceeds of sale of Investments and so the charge for Debenture Interest diminished, but the Sinking Fund should be reconstituted so as to provide for redemption of the remaining debentures at the expiry of the period of ten years from 1st January 19.1.

Conversion of Debentures into Shares. It will be remembered that debentures may be issued at a discount, whilst shares cannot, except as provided by Sect. 57 of the Companies Act 1948. The Courts will not permit the evasion of the latter restriction by the device of an issue of debentures at a discount and their conversion into the equivalent *number* of *fully* paid shares, but it is permissible to make the conversion as indicated if the debentures have become *bone fide* redeemable, there being no necessity for a formal repayment to the debenture-holders with an immediate return of the money by them to acquire shares.

It is quite legal, however, even when the debentures have not become repayable, to convert into the same number of shares (representing the nominal value of the debentures) if they are partly paid to the extent of the cash originally paid for the debentures, or even into fully paid shares on a basis that their number is in the same proportion that the cash paid on the original debentures bore to their nominal value.

Illustration 37

A company issued £10,000 debentures at 95. On what basis can they be converted into shares?

1. If they have become (*bona fide*) due for repayment, 10,000 shares of £1 each fully paid may be issued in exchange.

2. Otherwise, 9,500 shares of £1 each fully paid (i.e. 19 shares of £1 each fully paid for £20 debentures) or 10,000 shares of £1 each £0·95 paid (i.e. one share of £1 each, £0·95 paid for every £1 debenture) may be issued in exchange.

The same principles will apply where power is given to the debenture-holder to require his debenture to be converted into shares.

Any 'profit' on conversion of debentures into shares should be credited to Share Premium Account or utilized to write off the debenture discount outstanding.

Illustration 38

The terms of an issue of 100,000 5 per cent debentures of £1 each included the following:

1. Interest payable half-yearly, 31st March and 30th September.

2. Twenty-five per cent of the profits of any year are to be applied in redeeming debentures and, upon being redeemed, they are to be cancelled.

3. The company may purchase its debentures in the open market without limitation to the amount redeemable as above; those to be redeemed, if not obtainable by purchase, being drawn by lot and surrendered at £1·025.

4. Any debentures purchased in excess of the obligatory amount may, entirely at the option of the company, be cancelled or kept alive for reissue.

5. Upon giving three months' notice, the company can redeem the debentures outstanding at £1·10.

On 1st October 19.1:

1. £48,200 debentures had been redeemed and cancelled.
2. The profits for the year to date are £42,000.
3. The company held £28,200 of its live debentures (cost £25,380).

On the above date the debentures to be redeemed and cancelled were appropriated out of the company's holding, and three months' notice to redeem the ['outside'] debentures was given.

The redemption was duly completed on 1st January 19.2, and the interest for the three months duly paid.

On 31st March 19.2, following, it was resolved that the remaining debentures should be cancelled.

Show Ledger Accounts, ignoring taxation.

The student as a rule finds a difficulty in presenting a reasonably good answer to this type of question because the terms indicated are not clearly grasped. What the terms really amount to are that a certain *minimum* number must be redeemed and cancelled yearly. This mininum is to be equal to 25 per cent of the profits in any one year, but the company *may* purchase as many as it thinks fit; and similarly may use those debentures in part or whole discharge of its obligatory minimum. As for the remainder of the debentures so purchased, the company may keep them alive for reissue. If the company has not bought sufficient of its own debentures to pay off the minimum, then it must draw lots as to the balance and pay off these debentures at £1·025. Quite apart from the above, the company can always, if it so desired, give due notice to the debenture-holders and redeem with interest at £1·10.

DEBENTURES

		£				£
19.1 Oct. 1	Own Debentures Purchased Account . .	10,500	19.1 Oct. 1	Balance . . b/d		51,800
19.2 Jan. 1	Cash . . .	25,960	19.2 Jan. 1	Premium on Redemption of Debentures Account		2,360
April 1	Own Debentures Purchased Account .	17,700				
		£54,160				£54,160

DEBENTURE REDEMPTION FUND

		£			£
19.2 April 1	General Reserve . .	10,500	19.2 Oct. 1	Profit and Loss Appropriation Account[1] .	10,500

[1] i.e. 25 per cent of £42,000 = £10,500.

Own Debentures Purchased

			Nominal					Nominal	
			£	£				£	£
19.1 Oct. 1	Balance.	b/d	28,200	25,380	19.1 Oct. 1	Debentures Account		10,500	10,500
	Profit on Redemption of Debentures Account			1,050	19.2 Apr. 1	Do.		17,700	17,700
19.2 Apr. 1	Do.			1,770					
			£28,200	£28,200				£28,200	£28,200

Profit on Redemption of Debentures

		£			£
19.2 Jan. 1	Premium on Redemption of Debentures Account	2,360	19.1 Oct. 1	Own Debentures Purchased Account	1,050
April 1	General Reserve	460	19.2 April 1	Do.	1,770
		£2,820			£2,820

Debenture Interest

		£p			£p
19.2 Jan. 1	Debenture-holders Account	516·25	19.2 Jan. 1	Debenture-holders Account (own debentures)	221·25
April 1	Do.	221·25	April 1	Do. Do.	221·25
				Profit and Loss Account	295·00
		£737·50			£737·50

Premium on Redemption of Debenture

		£			£
19.2 Jan. 1	Debenture Account: Premium on Redemption	2,360	19.2 Jan. 1	Profit on Redemption of Debentures Account	2,360

General Reserve

			£			£
19.2 April 1	Balance	c/d	10,960	19.2 April 1	Debenture Redemption Fund Account	10,500
					Profit on Redemption of Debentures Account	460
			£10,960			£10,960
				19.2 April 2	Balance	b/d	10,960

The first transaction is the cancellation of debentures out of those purchased, which reduces the debentures to £41,300 and the investment to £17,000. The second transaction is the redemption by notice at £1·10 of all the debentures outstanding, viz. £23,600, made up as follows:

			£
Balance [as above]	. . .	.	41,300
Less Debentures in hands of the Company	. .	£28,200	
Less Cancelled .	. . . .	10,500	
		———	17,700
Balance still 'out'.	. . . .	.	£23,600

On 1st January 19.2, interest (after taking into account the debentures held by the company as an investment) is 5 per cent on £23,600 for a quarter year, viz. £295. The Debenture Interest Account should show both the interest payable and the interest receivable, but the cash *payments* can only be to the holders of £23,600—the 'outsiders'. The Journal form of entry would be:

						£p	£p
Debenture Interest (*a*)	.	.	.	.	Dr.	516·25	
To Debenture Interest (*b*)	.	.	.	.			221·25
Cash	.	.	.	.	.		295·00

(*a*) Interest at 5% per annum for quarter year on £41,300 = £516·25
(*b*) Interest at 5% per annum for quarter year on £17,700 = £221·25

On 1st Jan. 19.2, all the 'outside' debentures have been paid off and therefore the balance of debentures as a liability must be equalled by those held by the company as an investment, viz. £17,700 nominal; the interest receivable on which will cancel the interest payable, i.e. £221·25.

As the debentures were purchased at the price of £0·90 (£28,200 at £0·90 = £25,380) and as all the debentures purchased are used to extinguish the debentures as a liability at *par*, there must be a profit of £2,820 (£28,200 at £0·10) as shown by Profit on Redemption of Debentures Accounts. The ultimate profit, after debiting the loss on redemption, is £460, which is transferred, together with the balance of the redemption fund, to general reserve.

Although it is not called for in this case, students should note that the debentures held as an investment might be treated as the Redemption Fund investment, the interest on which will be debited to the former and credited to the Redemption Fund. Final profit is proved thus:

The cost to redeem £51,800 debentures is:

	Nominal	Cost	
	£	£	
(*a*)	28,200 at £0·90	25,380	(*ex* Debentures purchased)
(*b*)	23,600 at £1·10	25,960	(*ex* Cash)
	£51,800	51,340	
	leaving a profit of	460	
Total	£51,800	£51,800	

The entries for the redemption would be as shown in the Ledger, or as below:

JOURNAL

19.2		£	£
Jan. 1	Debentures	23,600	
	Premium on Redemption of Debentures . .	2,360	
	Cash		25,960
	Being redemption of £23,600 Debentures at £1·10 each by three months' notice, in accordance with the terms of the Debenture Deed as per Directors' resolution dated .... *vide* Minute Book, p.		

The proviso as to drawings by lot does not operate because there is an adequate 'supply' of debentures purchased, i.e. £28,200 to redeem £10,500; it is only in the event of this 'supply' being less than the latter figure that the above term in the debenture deed becomes applicable.

Illustration 39

Aldley & Co. has issued Share Capital of 100,000 ordinary shares of £1 each fully paid and 100,000 7 per cent preference shares of £1 each fully paid. The company has £140,000 6 per cent Debenture Stock, now redeemable at 25 per cent premium.

In order to provide funds for the redemption of the Debenture Stock, the company issued a further 100,000 ordinary shares and a further 100,000 7 per cent preference shares at a premium of £0·10 and £0·25 each respectively, all of which were paid up in full. No Sinking Fund existed.

Show the Balance Sheet, immediately after the completion of the above arrangements, in so far as the facts given permit.

BALANCE SHEET (includes)

	£		£
Share Capital: Issued and fully paid—		Cash	60,000
200,000 7% Preference Shares of £1 each	200,000		
200,000 Ordinary Shares of £1 each	200,000		
Share Premium Account—			
Ordinary Shares . . £10,000			
7% Preference Shares . 25,000			
	35,000		
Less Transfer to Debenture Stock . . . 35,000			
	—		
	400,000		
6 per cent Debenture Stock £140,000			
Add Premium . . 35,000			
	175,000		
Less Cash . . . 175,000			
	—		

[*Note.* The Cash received is (*a*) Ordinary Shares, £110,000; (*b*) Preference Shares, £125,000; Cash paid to redeem Debenture Stock, £175,000, giving a balance of £60,000.]

Mine Redemption Funds. In accounts of concerns such as mines holding wasting assets, provision may be made against the depletion of the assets by charging up so much per ton mined as depreciation. Provision may similarly be made for redeeming debentures.

It must be appreciated that while the first provision is a charge against profits in respect of depletion, the second is merely an appropriation of profits to funds for the repayment of a liability.

Illustration 40

The X Tin Mining Co., Ltd., with Debenture Stock £20,000, sets aside £0·05 per ton mined to cover depletion of assets and provision for redemption of debentures, the sum being apportioned in the ratio 3 : 1 to the respective objects.

The number of tons raised in the year ended 31st December 19.., was 200,000. Total sales, £220,000. Total expenses, £180,000. Show Profit and Loss Account for year ended 31st December 19...

PROFIT AND LOSS ACCOUNT FOR THE YEAR ENDED
31ST DEC. 19..

	£			£
Expenses	180,000	Sales		220,000
Depreciation—				
Depletion Account . .	7,500			
Balance, being net profit for year . c/d	32,500			
	£220,000			£220,000
Debenture Redemption Fund . .	2,500	Balance . . . . b/d		32,500
Balance . . . . c/d	30,000			
	£32,500			£32,500
		Balance . . . . b/d		30,000

SECTION F. ALTERATIONS OF SHARE CAPITAL

The alterations of share capital comprise the following:

1. Increase or decrease of authorized capital.
2. Conversion of fully-paid shares into stock and stock into shares.
3. Subdivision of shares.
4. Consolidation of shares.
5. Redemption of redeemable preference shares.
6. Reduction of shared capital.
7. Reorganization of share capital.
8. Bonus share issue.

1. **Increase or Decrease in Authorized Capital.**[1] A company may increase or decrease its authorized capital as it wishes, according to its Articles; but if Table A is adopted, the necessary authority is an ORDINARY Resolution. The student must not confuse a reduction of *authorized* capital with reduction of *issued* capital, which is dealt with on p. 23150.

2. **Conversion of Fully-paid Shares into Stock and Stock into Shares.** Stock is the consolidation of the share capital into one unit divisible into aliquot parts. Whilst it is impossible to transfer less than one share, any amount of stock may be transferred, although in practice companies may restrict the transfers of stock to multiples of say £10. The transfer of stock avoids dealing with the distinctive numbers required in share transfers, and thus saves considerable clerical work (see p. 23107).

In recent years a practice has been established whereby stock is transferable in £ units, e.g. £100 stock may be transferable in the form of 100 units, so that a buyer of 50 units is buying the equivalent of £50 of stock or 50 £1 shares fully paid.

A company must first issue fully-paid shares and then proceed to make the conversion, an *original* issue of stock not being permissible, subject to the proviso that it must follow its own articles regulating the resolution required; and if Table A is adopted, it is necessary to obtain the consent of the company in general meeting. Every copy of the Memorandum and Articles of Association must thereafter have such alterations incorporated therein.

The book-keeping entries merely record the transfer from Share Capital Account to Stock Account, but a Stock Register will be opened to contain the statutory details of members' holdings, and the Annual Return modified accordingly.

Illustration 41

Y, Ltd., after passing the necessary resolution, converts its 20,000 ordinary shares of £1 each fully paid into £20,000 ordinary stock. Show Journal entry.

JOURNAL

	£	£
Ordinary Share Capital	20,000	
Ordinary Stock		20,000
Being the conversion of 20,000 ordinary shares of £1 each fully-paid into £20,000 ordinary stock per resolution (described) dated .... *vide* Minute Book, p.		

[1] Duty is no longer payable on authorized Capital. A rate of £1 per £100 or part of £100 is payable on Issued Capital.

If the company's articles require the passing of a special resolution, a copy thereof must be filed with the Registrar of Companies within fifteen days.

Illustration 42

Y, Ltd., after passing the necessary resolution, converts its 20,000 ordinary shares of £1 each fully paid into £19,000 ordinary stock on the basis of £95 of stock for every 100 fully-paid shares of £1 each.[1] Show Journal entry.

JOURNAL

	£	£
Ordinary Share Capital	20,000	
Ordinary Stock :		19,000
Premium on Stock		1,000
Being the conversion of 20,000 fully-paid ordinary shares of £1 each into £19,000 stock at the rate of £95 per 100 shares per resolution (described) dated .... and sanction of the Court dated .... *vide* Minute Book, p.		

Illustration 43

Y, Ltd., after passing the necessary resolution, converts its 20,000 ordinary shares of £1 each fully paid into £21,000 ordinary stock on the basis of £105 of stock for every 100 fully-paid shares of £1 each.[1] Show Journal entry.

JOURNAL

	£	£
Ordinary Share Capital	20,000	
Discount on Stock	1,000	
Ordinary Stock		21,000
Being the conversion of 20,000 fully-paid ordinary shares of £1 each into £21,000 stock at the rate of £105 per 100 shares per resolution and sanction as above.		

Converse entries will be required for reconverting stock into shares.

3. **Subdivision of Shares.** A company may find that, owing to the high nominal value of its shares, dealing in the shares are impeded and, in consequence, desires to subdivide them into shares with a small nominal value.

The members are entitled to have a proportionately large number of shares of the smaller denomination in exchange for the shares of the higher, e.g. if a share is of a £10 denomination the holder is entitled to receive, say, 10 shares of £1 each, or 100 shares of £0·10 paid up proportionately. If the £10 share mentioned is fully paid, so must be the subdivided shares; if partly paid, the subdivided shares must be proportionately paid up, e.g. if the above shares are paid up to the extent of £8,

[1] Tantamount respectively to a reduction of capital and an issue at a discount, so the procedure required therefore must be followed. (See pp. 2391 and 23150.)

there will be £0·80 and £0·08 paid up on a £1 share and a £0·10 share respectively.

Subdivision must be authorized by the Articles, otherwise a special resolution will be necessary to *create* such power. When authority is obtained, an ORDINARY resolution suffices to *exercise* the power as it does if Table A is adopted.

The book-keeping entry involves merely a transfer from the original to the revised share capital account—the totals being unaltered.

Illustration 44

A company with a share capital of 20,000 ordinary shares of £1 each fully paid carries out by proper resolution a subdivision into shares of £0·25 each fully paid. Show Journal entry.

JOURNAL

	£	£
Ordinary Share Capital (£1)	20,000	
Ordinary Share Capital (£0·25) . .		20,000
Being the subdivision of 20,000 fully-paid ordinary shares of £1 each into 80,000 shares of £0·25 each fully paid per resolution (described) dated .... *vide* Minute Book, p.		

Each member will receive four fully-paid new shares for every one old share.

If the shares to be subdivided had been 40,000 shares of £1 each, £0·60 paid, the holders would receive 160,000 shares of £0·25 each, £0·15 paid, involving the same Journal entry so far as relates to the money column, the narrative being adjusted accordingly.

It will be necessary to prepare a subdivision list, so as to facilitate the work involved in making the exchange to each member.

The Annual Return, Register of Members, Register of Directors' Interests, and the description of the shares in the Balance Sheet will be altered accordingly.

4. **Consolidation of Shares.** The book-keeping entries are the reverse of those in the preceding paragraph. The authority required is an ordinary resolution, if Table A is adopted.

5. **Redemption of Preference Share Capital.** The following are the provisions relating to the issue and redemption of Redeemable Preference Shares contained in Sect. 58 of the Companies Act 1948.

(*a*) A company having share capital may issue redeemable preference shares, provided that no such shares shall be redeemed except out of *profits* of the company which would otherwise be available for dividend; or out of the *proceeds* of a fresh issue of shares made for the purposes of the redemption.

(*b*) No such shares shall be redeemed unless *fully* paid.

(*c*) The issue must be authorized by the Articles.

(*d*) Where any such shares are redeemed otherwise than out of the proceeds of a fresh issue, there shall be transferred out of profits which would otherwise have been available for dividend, to a reserve fund, to be called 'THE CAPITAL REDEMPTION RESERVE FUND', a sum equal to the nominal amount of the shares redeemed.

(e) The redemption is not to be regarded as a reduction of the authorized share capital of a company.

(f) The Capital Redemption Reserve may be used wholly or in part in paying up unissued shares of the company to be issued as Bonus Shares; but otherwise the provisions of the Act relating to reduction of share capital apply as if it were paid-up share capital of the company.

(g) Every Balance Sheet must include a statement specifying what part of the issued capital of the company consists of such shares and the earliest and latest dates on which the company can redeem the shares, whether the shares must be redeemed or at the company's option and the amount of any premium payable on redemption.

(h) The premium, if any, payable on redemption must have been provided out of the profits of the company or out of the company's share premium account before the shares are redeemed.

(i) Notice to Registrar (see (e) next paragraph).

Notice to Registrar. If a company having a share capital has:

(a) Consolidated and divided its share capital into shares of larger amount than its existing shares; or

(b) converted any of its shares into stock; or

(c) re-converted stock into shares; or

(d) subdivided its shares or any of them; or

(e) redeemed any redeemable preference shares. Where a company has redeemed, or is about to redeem, preference shares, it is entitled to issue other shares of any class, not exceeding the nominal amount of the shares redeemed, just as if such redeemed shares had never been issued.

There is no liability for stamp duty on the reissue:

(i) If such reissue is made before the old shares are redeemed; and

(ii) If the shares to be redeemed are in fact redeemed within *one month* of the reissue as in (i).

(f) cancelled any shares (otherwise than in connection with a reduction of capital),

it shall within *one month* after so doing give notice thereof to the Registrar of Companies, specifying, as the case may be, the shares consolidated, divided, converted, subdivided, redeemed, or cancelled, or the stock re-converted. (Sect. 62.)

Illustration 45

Ten thousand 6 per cent redeemable preference shares of £1 each fully paid in A, Ltd., are outstanding on 1st Jan. 19... This being the date of redemption, the shares are redeemed at £1·10 each 4,000 Ordinary Shares of £1 each are issued at £1·05 for cash for the purpose of redemption. Show Ledger entries, assuming that the balance of Profit and Loss Appropriation Account is £24,600.

6% REDEEMABLE PREFERENCE SHARES

19..			£	19..			£
Jan. 1	Sundry Members	.	10,000	Jan. 1	Balance . .	b/d	10,000

SUNDRY MEMBERS

19..			£	19..		£
Jan. 1	Cash		11,000	Jan. 1	6% Redeemable Preference Shares Account	10,000
					Premium on Redemption of Shares Account .	1,000
			£11,000			£11,000

PREMIUM ON REDEMPTION OF SHARES

19..			£	19..		£
Jan. 1	Sundry Members .	.	1,000	Jan. 1	Profit and Loss Appropriation Account	1,000

ORDINARY SHARE CAPITAL

				19..		£
				Jan. 1	Cash . .	4,000

SHARE PREMIUM

				19..		£
				Jan. 1	Cash[1]	200

[1] This may be used towards payment of the premium on redemption, in which case the debit to Profit and Loss Appropriation Account for that item will be £800 instead of £1,000.

PROFIT AND LOSS APPROPRIATION

19..			£	19..			£
Jan. 1	Premium on Redemption of Preference Shares .		1,000	Jan. 1	Balance . .	b/d	24,600
	Capital Redemption Reserve Fund . .		6,000				
	Balance . . .	c/d	17,600				
			£24,600				£24,600
				Jan. 2	Balance . .	b/d	17,600

CAPITAL REDEMPTION RESERVE FUND

				19..		£
				Jan. 1	Profit and Loss Appropriation Account .	6,000

6. **Reduction of Capital.** By Section 66 of the Companies Act 1948, a company may reduce its capital IN ANY WAY, provided it is authorized in its ARTICLES and in particular:

(*a*) Extinguish or reduce the LIABILITY on any of its shares in respect of capital not paid up, e.g. £1 share, £0·25 paid, may be changed into a £0·25, fully-paid share (*extinguishing* the liability entirely) or a £0·50 share, £0·25 paid (*reducing* the liability by £0·50).

(*b*) Cancel any paid-up capital which is LOST or unrepresented by available assets—either *with or without* extinguishing or reducing the liability on any of its shares.

(*c*) Pay-off any share capital in EXCESS of the requirements of the company either *with or without* extinguishing or reducing the liability on any of its shares, e.g. where a £1 share fully paid is repaid £0·40, leaving a £1 share £0·60 paid or a £0·60 share fully paid.

If the authority required under this section is not contained in the Articles (NOT Memorandum), the company must by special resolution supply such omission in the Articles; after which the scheme must be carried out, in any case, by a special resolution. Where necessary, the two resolutions may be validly passed at one meeting of members.

The proposed scheme must be submitted to the Court for its approval, failure to obtain which renders it ineffective.

The Court may require the addition of the words 'and reduced' after the company's name, but this formality is not required unless the Court so orders.

The resolution for the reduction of share capital will not take effect until there has been filed with the Registrar of Companies:

1. A copy of the order of the Court sanctioning the scheme.
2. A minute, approved by the Court, showing with respect to the share capital of the company as altered by the order, the amount of the share capital, the number of shares into which it is to be divided and the amount of each share, and the amount, if any, at the date of registration deemed to be paid up on each share.

The certificate of the Registrar that the order and minute have been registered is conclusive evidence that all the provisions of the Act have been complied with.

The entries in respect of extinguishing or reducing uncalled capital merely involve a transfer similar to subdivision, viz. from the 'old' to the 'new'. The Annual Return, Register of Members, Register of Directors' Interests, and Balance Sheet as affected by the reduction of share capital will require suitable amendment.

At the same meeting as the reduction resolution is passed a further resolution will usually be passed to increase the share capital to its authorized prereduction amount by the creation of unissued shares (which need not be classified) as otherwise capital stamp duty will be payable if later it is desired to issue further shares.

Illustration 46

The following is the Balance Sheet of X, Ltd.:

BALANCE SHEET

	£		£
Authorized Share Capital . .	200,000		
Issued Share Capital:			
50,000 Ordinary Shares . .	50,000		
100,000 6% First Preference		Fixed Assets	107,000
Shares	100,000	Current Assets . . .	68,000
50,000 8% Second Preference		Development Account . .	21,000
Shares	50,000	Profit and Loss Account . .	27,000
(All of £1 each fully paid)			
Sundry Creditors . . .	23,000		
	£223,000		£223,000

The scheme of a reduction of capital, duly passed, provides for a revaluation of the value of fixed assets at £60,000 and the writing-off of Development Account; the share capital to be adjusted by writing-off:

(a) 6 per cent Preference Shares   £30,000
(b) 8 per cent Preference Shares   £25,000
(c) Ordinary shares: such an amount per share so as to absorb the loss on the reduction of capital.

Show Journal entries and Balance Sheet arising out of the scheme.

JOURNAL

	£	£
Capital Reduction Account	95,000	
Fixed Assets		47,000
Development Account		21,000
Profit and Loss Account		27,000
Being losses written-off in accordance with scheme of reduction of capital sanctioned by order of the Court dated .... *vide* Minute Book, p.		
Ordinary Share Capital	40,000	
6% Preference Share Capital	30,000	
8% Preference Share Capital	25,000	
Capital Reduction Account		95,000
Being reduction of £0·30 per share on 100,000 6% Preference Shares; reduction of £0·50 per share on 50,000 8% Preference Shares; and £0·80 per share on 50,000 Ordinary Shares, in accordance with scheme of reduction of capital sanctioned by order of the Court dated .... *vide* Minute Book, p.		

BALANCE SHEET
(after reduction of capital)

	£		£	£
Authorized Share Capital	200,000			
		Fixed Assets	107,000	
Issued Share Capital:		Less written-off by		
50,000 Ordinary Shares of £1 each fully paid, reduced by order of the Court to £0·20 each fully paid	10,000	order of the Court	47,000	60,000
		Current Assets		68,000
100,000 6% First Preference Shares of £1 each fully paid, reduced by order of the Court to £0·70 each fully paid	70,000	Development Account	21,000	
		Less written-off by order of the Court	21,000	—
50,000 8% Second Preference Shares of £1 each fully paid, reduced by order of the Court to £0·50 each fully paid	25,000	Profit and Loss Account	27,000	
		Less written-off by order of the Court	27,000	—
Sundry Creditors	23,000			
	£128,000			£128,000

Notes.

1. It is assumed that a resolution to restore the pre-reduction amount of authorized share capital has been duly passed.

2. The preference shareholders would receive some compensation for higher dividend rate and/or some participating rate of dividend with the ordinary shareholders.

Illustration 47

X, Ltd., has an issued share capital of 10,000 shares of £1 each, £0·25 paid, and having complied with all legal formalities, proceeds to extinguish the uncalled liability on its shares. Show Journal entry.

JOURNAL

	£	£
Ordinary Share Capital (£1)	2,500	
Ordinary Share Capital (£0·25)		2,500
Being the extinguishing of the uncalled liability of £0·75 on shares per special resolution dated .... Court order dated .... *vide* Minute Book, p.		

Upon the ascertainment of the loss on the assets and/or the addition to liabilities, the method of adjusting the revised state of affairs is:

(i)   Debit Capital Reduction Account.
    Credit Assets (in detail), including fictitious assets, e.g. debit } for writings-off.
    balance of Profit and Loss Account
    Credit Liabilities (in detail).

(ii)   Debit Share Capital Account } for reduction of Share Capital.
    Credit Capital Reduction Account

(iii)[1] If there is a credit balance on Capital Reduction Account—
    Debit Capital Reduction Account (to close).
    Credit Capital Reserve Account.

As the student will have learned, revaluations of items like debtors, investments and stock will usually be made through the medium of a Reserve or Provision Account.

The accounting principles involved in reduction (including reorganization) of capital are of supreme importance and somewhat formidable to the student. Being, in addition, a very frequent question in the professional accountancy examinations, the subject is dealt with as exhaustively as space will permit in Section (I) of this chapter.

Reduction by Return of Cash to Members. Where owing to closing of departments, exhaustion of wasting assets (e.g. mines), or declining business, a company finds itself with a surplus of floating assets, it may decide to make a return of cash to members, thus reducing the share capital.

It is a frequent practice for companies to revise their assets and liabilities to current valuations at the same time as the cash representing excessive capital is repaid to members, such amendments being made through the Capital Reduction Account.

It may be noted that the latter account is often designated Reduction of Capital Account.

The book-keeping entries are:

(i) Debit Share Capital
    Credit Sundry Members } in respect of the amount to be repaid.
(ii) Debit Sundry Members
    Credit Cash } upon discharge of liability.

Alternatively,

(i) Debit Share Capital (old).
    Credit Sundry Members (amount to be repaid).
    Credit Share Capital (new, as reduced).
(ii) As above (ii).

Illustration 48

W, Ltd., with a share capital of 10,000 shares of £1 each fully paid, decides to repay members £0·40 in the £, the reduced share capital to be £0·60 fully paid. Show Journal entry.

---

[1] Reverse entries would be required if the balance was debit, but this is very unlikely to happen, as the Court would not sanction a scheme of reduction in such a case.

JOURNAL

	£	£
Share Capital (£1)	10,000	
Sundry Members		4,000
Share Capital (£0·60)		6,000
Being reduction of 10,000 shares of £1 each fully paid to 10,000 shares of £0·60 each fully paid to be discharged by a cash payment of £0·40 a share per special resolution dated .... and confirmed by Court Order, dated .... *vide* Minute Book, p.		

This may be shown in two Journal entries as follows:

JOURNAL

	£	£
Share Capital (Old)	4,000	
Sundry Members		4,000
Share Capital (Old)	6,000	
Share Capital Account (New)		6,000

The payment item will be posted from the Cash Book in the ordinary way, viz. debit sundry members, £4,000; and credit cash, £4,000.

The Statutory books, Annual Return and Balance Sheet will require amending accordingly.

If the shares are to remain as £1 credited as fully paid, but reduced in number, the Journal entry will be:

JOURNAL

	£	£
Share Capital	4,000	
Sundry Members		4,000
Being reduction from 10,000 shares of £1 each fully paid to 6,000 shares of £1 each fully paid, to be discharged by a cash payment of £0·40 per share per special resolution dated .... and confirmed by Court Order dated .... *vide* Minute Book, p.		

Where the 'security' to the creditors is likely to be impaired, e.g. by a repayment of cash, the creditors are entitled to oppose the application for Court confirmation of the proposed reduction.

Reduction of capital may, in addition, arise where:

(*a*) Shares are forfeited in respect of failure to pay calls, including premium (if any) on shares; the authority therefor being the Articles of Association or Table A.

(*b*) Redeemable preference shares have been redeemed; but the effectual capital position must be restored, because to the extent the redemption is not covered by a fresh issue of shares a transfer must be made to Capital Redemption Reserve Fund.

An attempt to reduce share capital by:

(i) Surrender (except by way of forfeiture duly made), or

(ii) A company purchasing its own shares,

is invalid.

7. **Reorganization of Share Capital.** Although a reorganization may include reduction of capital, many other matters will also be involved. It is an important feature of company accounting, and special attention is given thereto in Section J.

8. **Bonus Shares.** See Section I.

SECTION G. ACQUISITION ENTRIES

Before dealing with the acquisition entries, the following general matters should be noted.

Preliminary Expenses. The term 'Preliminary Expenses' embraces all expenses necessary to promote the company, of which the most important are:

(*a*) Costs attendant upon the issue of the prospectus.

(*b*) Legal, accounting, valuation, and other professional charges.

(*c*) Costs of printing the memorandum and articles, certificates, statutory books, letters of allotment and regret (usually available at law stationers in printed form) and books of account; company's seal.

(*d*) Stamp duties and resistration fees.

(*e*) Underwriting and other commissions; Brokerage on applications.

Such expenses must be shown separately in the Balance Sheet till written off. In the case of private companies, there are no expenses of issuing a prospectus.

Registration of a Company. To register a limited company, certain formalities must be complied with. Numerous documents must be filed and registration fee paid.

The documents to be filed with the Registrar of Companies are:

1. Memorandum and articles of association.
2. Statement of nominal capital.
3. Notice of situation of registered office.
4. List of directors and secretary.
5. Consent of directors to act.[1]
6. Contract of directors to take qualification shares in cases where they are not signatories to the memorandum.[1]

---

[1] Only necessary for a public company.

7. Statutory declaration that all requirements have been complied with.
8. Prospectus, or statement in lieu of prospectus.[1]
9. Particulars of contract of sale.

The memorandum of association must also be impressed with a standard registration fee stamp, presently £50, irrespective of the amount of the nominal capital.

Capital duty, currently at £1 per £100 or part of £100, is charged on the greater of the nominal value of the shares allotted and the actual value of the assets of any kind less any liabilities which have been taken over by the company in consideration of the contribution.

An *ad valorem* duty is payable on a conveyance or transfer of:

(a) Legal and equitable estates in any property.
(b) Patents, licences, trade-marks, and copyrights.
(c) Goodwill.
(d) Debt, including cash at bank.
(e) The benefit of contracts.
(f) Tenant's and trade fixtures and fittings which are not in a state of complete severance.

No stamp duty is payable where the property passes by mere delivery, e.g. stock-in-trade.

The stamp is in accordance with an *ad valorem* scale in terms of Finance Act 1974, Sch 11, as follows—

Up to £15,000	*nil*
£15,000 to £20,000	$\frac{1}{2}$%
£20,001 to £25,000	1%
£25,001 to £30,000	$1\frac{1}{2}$%
over £30,000	2%

The lower rates are applicable where an amount is certified as not forming part of a large transaction or series of transactions in respect of which the consideration does not exceed the ceiling value of the particular group determining the rate of duty.

This duty may be avoided or reduced by:

(i) An agreement whereby debtors are not taken over, but are collected by the purchasing company on behalf of the vendors.[2]

(ii) An agreement whereby land and buildings are to be held in trust for the company by the vendors, no conveyance therefore being required.

(iii) Where possible by having no written agreement of sale, the transfer of assets being effected for cash.

---

[1] Only necessary for a public company.
[2] Frequently the arrangement is that neither the debtors nor creditors are taken over, but the purchasing company, as agents for the vendor, collects the debts, out of which the creditors are paid and a settlement of the balance made with the vendor.

Underwriting Commission. Underwriting commission may be paid to any person in consideration of his subscribing or agreeing to subscribe for any share, or procuring or agreeing to procure subscriptions, whether absolute or conditional, for any shares in the company, provided that Sect. 53 of the Companies Act 1948, is complied with, viz. the payment must be authorized by the articles and in no case shall the rate exceed 10 per cent of the *price* at which the shares are issued or the *amount* or *rate* authorized by the articles, whichever is the less. The amount or rate of the commission and the number of shares agreed for a commission to be subscribed must be disclosed in the prospectus or statement in lieu of prospectus duly furnished to the Registrar of Companies. The total amount paid as underwriting commission must be *separately* shown in the Balance Sheet and in the Annual Return.

By entering into arrangements with REPUTABLE underwriters, the success of an issue of shares or debentures is at the outset fully assured.

The underwriters almost invariably distribute their risk amongst others by way of sub-underwriting, the sub-underwriters not being in any contractual relationship with the company (*Collins* v. *Greyhound Racing Association*). Thus the commission is paid to the underwriters, sub-underwriters looking to the underwriters for their commission.

A special commission is sometimes paid to underwriters (in addition to the underwriting commission) for placing blocks of the underwriting with their clients. Just as the underwriting commission is paid direct to the underwriters themselves, leaving them to make their own arrangements with the sub-underwriters, so is the special commission paid direct to the underwriters. This special commission is called OVERRIDING COMMISSION.

Purchase Consideration. When an existing business is acquired by a limited company, one of the most important matters to settle is the purchase consideration. Usually a revaluation of assets and liabilities will be required, as well as an agreement upon the value of goodwill. In practice, it is usual to fix the purchase consideration in terms of a round figure, so that the goodwill item—approximating to the agreed value—will merely be a balancing figure. Occasionally, the purchase consideration is accounted for by a writing-up of the assets taken over in place of the introduction of a Goodwill Account, e.g. if the net assets taken over are worth £1,000 and the purchase consideration is £1,250, the balancing figure is: Goodwill, £250, unless the net assets are themselves written-up to £1,250.

The principle underlying the opening entries is simple; if the purchasing company is prepared to give £100,000 for £80,000 of assets (exclusive of Goodwill) it is obvious that the Goodwill is £20,000; yet in examination-work candidates frequently become confused because of the form in which the particular question is set, the problem being one in *ascertaining* the purchase consideration.

Suppose that a company is acquiring a business comprising Stock £5,000; Debtors £6,300; and Fixtures £3,000; against which are liabilities £7,300. The company agrees to acquire the whole business for £15,000 to be discharged as to £10,000 in Cash and £5,000 in £1 Shares at par. This question can be framed in several ways, e.g.:

(a) By giving details of the purchase money discharge.

In this case the sum of £15,000 represents the cost of acquiring the whole business. In order to complete the goodwill, tangible assets, separately or in total, must be given as well as the liabilities, and it is vital to know if the latter are being taken over by the purchasing company. Therefore (i) if liabilities *are* taken over, it is clear that (assuming no amendments of valuations) assets are £14,300 and liabilities £7,300, net £7,000. Hence the Goodwill is £8,000, being purchase price of £15,000 less £7,000; (ii) if liabilities are *not* taken over, the Goodwill is £700, as the purchase price is £15,000 for assets of £14,300.

(b) By giving the gross purchase price of the assets (stating the goodwill or the means of computing it) and giving the liabilities taken over. [If the liabilities are not taken over there is no GROSS purchase price, the figure given *is* the purchase price.] Assuming that the liabilities are taken over and the figures given in the preceding paragraphs are used, the question will be set in the form that states that the gross purchase price of the various assets is £14,300, the liabilities taken over are £7,300 and the Goodwill (either supplied or to be computed) is £8,000. From the above, it is seen that the 'net' tangible assets are £7,000, which together with goodwill of £8,000, equals the purchase price of £15,000.

(c) By giving the 'net' Tangible Assets, purchase price and liabilities, the figures supplied would be £7,000, £15,000 and £7,300, from which goodwill would be deduced as £8,000. This form of presentment frequently bewilders the examination candidate, as except that it indicates what the gross tangible assets are, the item of £7,300 is superfluous, as the term 'net' tangible assets means tangible assets *less* liabilities. Therefore if the 'net' tangible assets of £7,000 are acquired for £15,000 the goodwill is £8,000. In order, however, to enter more fully the opening figures, the addition of the liabilities of £7,300, simply means that the tangible assets (Stock, Debtors and Fixtures) are £7,000 + £7,300, i.e. £14,300; and as the purchasing company is, in consideration for acquiring those assets of £14,300, willing to pay-off liabilities £7,300 *and* give the purchase price of £15,000, it commits itself for £22,300 as against tangible assets of £14,300, thus giving £8,000 for the goodwill.

The purchase price may in fact be *less* than the net tangible assets but the principle is the same, the balance being put to Capital Reserve, or the assets and/or liabilities revalued: or, if the purchase consideration is discharged by the issue of shares at par, to Share Premium Account.

Goodwill. On the acquisition of a business, goodwill is frequently based upon super profits, necessitating the ascertainment of net profits and the average capital employed in the business. When these have been computed, super profits are arrived at by taking: (1) Net profits, (2) less 'normal risk' profits, i.e. profits reasonably expected on a business of the same NATURE and CAPITAL.

This difference represents differential or super profits, and will be capitalized by taking a number of years' purchase, considering all the circumstances, e.g.:

1. Trend of profits in relation to CAPITAL REQUIREMENTS.
2. Prospects:

   (a) General all-round conditions.
   (b) General prospects in the particular trade.
   (c) Prospects of the particular business, especially having regard to the possibility of the company having reached 'saturation' point.

3. Status of the business.
4. Continuity of management.
5. Market value of shares of companies in similar occupations.
6. Possibility of legislative or political changes (e.g. Nationalization).
7. Valuation of assets and modernity of the equipment.
8. Existence of favourable or unfavourable contracts, long-term leases, etc.
9. Financial structure and financial and technical efficiency.
10. Adequacy of labour and raw materials; quota allocations, etc.

Illustration 49

A company's net profit is £20,000: the average capital employed is £200,000. Assuming that 8 per cent represents 'normal risk' return, show the super-profit of the company.

	£
Net Profit	20,000
Less 8% of £200,000 representing 'normal risk' return	16,000
Super-profit	£4,000

The capitalization is frequently graded into portions capitalized at a decreasing number of years, the first portion being capitalized at the highest as being more likely to be maintained than the next portion, each portion being less than its predecessor.

The profits brought into computation may require adjustment, e.g. the Profit and Loss Account of the vending company may have included exceptional items, e.g. a charge for rent in respect of premiums which are to be acquired by the purchasing company.

Illustration 50

Assuming that the super-profit of a company is £7,800, each portion being taken at £2,000, the first being taken at four years' purchase, each scale to be diminished by one year's purchase, goodwill is £19,800, computed as follows:

			£
(1) First	£2,000 × 4		8,000
(2) Second	£2,000 × 3		6,000
(3) Third	£2,000 × 2		4,000
(4) Balance	£1,800 × 1		1,800
Goodwill			£19,800

Computation of Goodwill. The usual ways of computing goodwill in connection with the acquisition of a business by a limited company are:

1. To take net profits and capitalize them for a certain number of years (varying with circumstances), and deduct therefrom the value of the net tangible assets.

2. To take net profits and deduct therefrom the amount of net profits required to cover risk (based upon a percentage on the net assets employed), capitalizing the balance at a certain number of years' purchase.

Illustration 51

Assuming that the net profit of a business is £20,000 and 10 per cent is considered to represent the normal risk, and the tangible assets are £90,000, show goodwill computed in accordance with the methods stated above.

	£
Method (1)	
Net Profit of £20,000 capitalized at 10 years' purchase	200,000
Less Tangible Assets	90,000
Goodwill	£110,000[1]
Method (2)	
Net Profit	20,000
Less 10% on £90,000	9,000
Super-profit	£11,000
Goodwill—10 years' purchase	£110,000[1]

Book-keeping Entries. Where one company acquires another, the general principles of accounting apply, but particular attention is required in dealing with the following matters:

1. The purchasing company may place values on the assets taken over quite different from those appearing in the books of the vendor. The former are important in order to arrive at the goodwill or capital reserve figure; but of no importance in the vendor's books, unless they are the only means of ascertaining the purchase consideration.

2. Losses and fictitious assets existing at the date of liquidation should be transferred out to the debit of Sundry Members; likewise profits—e.g. Share Premium Account, Debenture Redemption Fund—and capital credits—e.g. Capital Redemption Reserve Fund—to the credit of Sundry Members.

3. Profits and losses occurring in and arising out of the liquidation should be credited or debited, as the case may be, to the Realization Account, including debtors and creditors taken over in the liquidation, etc.

4. Where creditors are not taken over they will usually be formally paid out by the liquidator of the vendor company, e.g. if the purchase consider-

---

[1] The same result can be arrived at only if the number of years' purchase (Method (1)) multiplied by rate of interest on capital (Method (2)) equals 100, e.g. if the former is taken at 12½ years, the latter will be taken at 8 per cent.

ation is £50,000 plus the taking over of £10,000 liabilities, the purchasing company will have to enter £60,000 of liabilities, £50,000 to Vendor and £10,000 for liabilities. If, on the other hand, the liabilities are not taken over the purchase consideration will be £60,000 all due to the Vendor, so that, in fact, instead of the purchasing company paying the individual creditors, it will pay one cheque therefor to the liquidator of the vendor company.

The vendor company may either:

(*a*) transfer £60,000 to the credit of Realization Account (and therefore *not* transfer the £10,000 from liabilities). The item of £60,000 will be debited to the purchasing company which will be credited with £10,000 on receipt of the cheque which will be used for payment of the creditors. (The remaining £50,000 will be credited when discharged and debited to the various assets comprised in the settlement); or

(*b*) debit the purchasing company and credit Realization Account with the true purchase consideration of £50,000, followed by a similar double-entry of £10,000 in respect of the liabilities, with subsequent entries as in (*a*).

5. Items which are connected with those taken over should be transferred to Realization Account, e.g. Provisions for depreciation, bad debts and discounts, Leasehold Amortization Account.

6. Where some of the assets (apart from cash) are not taken over, they will be dealt with on the usual lines by transfer to a Realization Account (preferably kept separate from that relating to the main realization) which will be credited with sale, etc., proceeds, the profit or loss being transferred (as with the main Realization Account) to Sundry Members. Alternatively, each asset account may be kept open until the asset is realized, the profit or loss being then transferred to Realization Account from which the net profit or loss is finally transferred to Sundry Members.

7. Expenses of realization will be debited to Realization Account (or to the purchasing company if the latter agrees to pay them).

8. The question arises with some items as to whether they are profits (or losses) or assets (or liabilities) or partly both. Such items are Employees' Pension Funds, Accident Compensation Funds, Superannuation Funds, and Employees' Profit-sharing Funds. These items will be treated on the principles already outlined according to their nature.

9. Provision may be required to cover fractions (see p. 23288).

10. The distribution of the assets of the vendor company will depend upon the Memorandum and Articles of that company; otherwise according to the general principles of law (see p. 23281 *et seq.*).

From the book-keeping point of view the purchasing company is concerned only with the assets and liabilities taken over and not with the conventional items which go to complete the double entry in the books of the vendor company, such as the proprietorship element, however described, into which will be merged the profit-and-loss balance, debit or credit, and the fictitious assets. Care will be necessary with certain items as mentioned in (8) above.

Illustration 52

The following is the abridged Balance Sheet of X, Ltd., which is being taken over by Y, Ltd. Show the acquisition entries in the books of the latter, assuming that all assets and liabilities are taken over at their present valuation and ignoring the question of goodwill.

X, LTD.
BALANCE SHEET

	£		£
Share Capital	15,000	Fixed Assets	30,000
General Reserve	10,000	Current Assets	60,000
Leasehold Amortization Fund	15,000	Preliminary Expenses	2,000
Debenture Sinking Fund	10,000	Profit and Loss Account	8,000
Pension Fund	20,000		
Debentures	30,000		
	£100,000		£100,000

The estimated liability on Pension Fund is £14,000.
The Balance Sheet items may be classed as follows:

Real		Conventional	
	£		£
Fixed Assets	30,000	Share Capital	15,000
Current Assets	60,000	Reserve	10,000
		Debenture Sinking Fund	10,000
	90,000	Pension Fund	6,000
Less Debentures £30,000			41,000
„ Leasehold Amortization Fund 15,000		Less Profit and Loss Account	8,000
Pension Fund 14,000			33,000
	59,000	„ Preliminary Expenses	2,000
	£31,000	Net Proprietorship	£31,000

The entries in the books of Y, Ltd., will therefore be:

JOURNAL

	£	£
Fixed Assets (detailed)	30,000	
Current Assets (detailed)	60,000	
Debentures		30,000
Leasehold Amortization Fund		15,000
Pension Fund		14,000
X Ltd.		31,000

The 'conventional' items will not appear in the books of Y, Ltd.
The opening entries on the acquisition of a business by a company will

occasion no difficulty, as the assets *other than goodwill* will be debited and the liabilities taken over credited, as will be the amount due to the vendor. The excess of the purchase consideration over the net assets acquired (excluding goodwill) is debited to Goodwill Account; and in the converse case, the excess of net assets acquired after eliminating goodwill (if any) over the purchase consideration credited to capital reserve, assets, or provision for depreciation.

The liability to the vendor will be discharged by a payment of cash and/or allotment of fully-paid shares and/or debentures.

The entries will be a debit to the vendor and a credit to cash, share capital and/or debentures.

Where, in addition to the net tangible assets acquired, the purchasing company discharges the realization expenses of the vendor, the amount is debited to goodwill or preliminary expenses and the vendor credited, unless the amount is already included in the credit to the vendor for purchase consideration. The cash in the latter instance will be debited to the vendor.

There may be a revaluation of assets, in which case the revised figures will be introduced into the books of the purchasing company, goodwill or capital reserve being modified accordingly.

Where debtors and/or stock are revalued (if taken over), the method is to retain the *book value intact* and provide for the reduced value of the debtors and/or stock by way of a provision.

In many examinations, problems are set in which the values of the net tangible assets are not disclosed, but merely the details of liabilities taken over, together with the amount of purchase consideration. In these circumstances the amount of goodwill is not ascertainable unless given, or the necessary data for its computation provided.

Illustration 53

A, Ltd., acquires the business of L, Ltd., as a going concern, the purchase consideration being £3,700, to be discharged in 2,500 shares of £1 each fully paid at par, the balance in cash.

The assets and liabilities are taken over as follows:

	£	£
Debtors	3,250	
Stock	1,230	
Plant	1,000	
Creditors		720
Debentures		800
Rent owing		5

A, Ltd., agrees to pay out the debentures holders at 5% premium.

The debtors are revalued in the books of A, Ltd., at £2,500.

In addition, A, Ltd., is to discharge the realization expenses of L, Ltd., the amount thereof being £170.

Show the opening Journal entries in the books of A, Ltd.

JOURNAL

	£	£
Goodwill[1]	535	
Preliminary Expenses (or Goodwill) . . .	170	
Debtors	3,250	
Stock	1,230	
Plant	1,000	
Debenture Holders of L, Ltd. . . .		840
Debtors Provision		750
Creditors		720
Rent owing		5
Vendor		3,870
Being assets and liabilities taken over from L, Ltd., as per purchase agreement dated .... Opening assets and liabilities of A, Ltd.		
	£6,185	£6,185
Vendor	3,870	
Cash		1,370
Share Capital		2,500
Being satisfaction of purchase consideration.		

[1] Balancing entry.

Notes. 1. If the purchase consideration had been, say, £2,870, capital reserve would be £465 and the goodwill item eliminated.

2. The cash to meet the realization expenses will be paid to the liquidator of L, Ltd.

3. The amount due to vendor (L, Ltd.) is £3,870, viz. the purchase consideration £3,700 plus £170, as the question states that the latter amount is payable 'in addition'.

Alternatively, a Business Purchase Account may be opened as below:

JOURNAL

	£	£
Goodwill	535	
Preliminary Expenses	170	
Debtors	3,250	
Stock	1,230	
Plant	1,000	
Debenture Holders of L, Ltd. . . .		840
Debtors Provision		750
Creditors		720
Rent owing		5
Purchase of Business Account . . .		3,870
Being assets and liabilities taken over from L, Ltd., as per vending agreement dated .... Opening assets and liabilities of A, Ltd.	£6,185	£6,185
Purchase of Business Account	3,870	
Vendor		3,870
Being purchase consideration for business taken over from L, Ltd., as per vending agreement dated		

Illustration 54

X, Ltd., acquires the business of W, Ltd., the purchase consideration being: (1) cash payment of £1,200; (2) issue to the vendor of 2,000 shares of £1 each fully paid at par; (3) issue of £1,000 debentures at 95 per cent; (4) pay the realization expenses £130; and (5) assumption of liabilities £720.

Show the opening Journal entries, ignoring narratives.

JOURNAL

		£	£
Preliminary Expenses		130	
Sundry Assets[1]		4,870	
Liabilities			720
Vendor			4,280
Vendor		4,280	
Discount on Debentures		50	
Cash [i.e £1,200+£130]			1,330
Debentures			1,000
Share Capital			2,000

[1] Balancing item.

It should be noted that:

1. In both illustrations a separate entry might be made for the payment of realization expenses of the vendor.

2. If the liabilities were not disclosed, the 'net assets' would be taken as £4,150.

3. Goodwill is not known in the absence of the valuation of Sundry Assets.

Illustration 55

On 30th June 19.2., X, Ltd., was registered with a nominal capital of 6,000 ordinary shares of £1 each. The new company is to take over the old-established business of A. Vendor, the consideration being the allotment to him of 1,000 ordinary shares at par credited as fully paid. In addition, 1,500 ordinary shares are to be issued to him at par for cash.

On 6th July, the company offered to the public 3,500 ordinary shares of £1 each at a premium of £0·10 per share, the whole having been underwritten at the same price, the underwriting commission being 4 per cent. Only 2,000 of the shares were subscribed for by, and allotted to, the public, the balance being allotted to the underwriters.

£0·25 per share was payable on application and £0·30 per share on allotment, which included £0·10 premium, and a first call of £0·20 per share due on 30th September. The whole of the moneys due from the public were received and the company paid £84 on account of underwriting commission. At the date of allotment, the underwriter pays in £1,650 as discharge of his liability. Give the opening Journal entries and Balance Sheet. Ignore dates.

JOURNAL

	£	£
Sundry Net Assets	1,000	
A. Vendor		1,000
Being sundry assets taken over from A. Vendor as per agreement dated		
A. Vendor	1,000	
Ordinary Share Capital		1,000
Being discharge of consideration for assets taken over.		
Cash	1,500	
Ordinary Share Capital		1,500
Being shares purchased by A. Vendor.		
Cash	500	
Application and Allotment		500
Being £0·25 per share received on application for 2,000 shares.		
Application and Allotment	1,100	
Ordinary Share Capital		900
Share Premium		200
Being allotment of 2,000 shares at £1·10 per share, payable £0·25 per share on application and £0·30 per share on allotment (including £0·10 premium) as per directors' resolution, etc.		
Cash	600	
Application and Allotment		600
Being cash received on allotment.		
Underwriter	1,650	
Ordinary Share Capital		1,500
Share Premium		150
Being liability of underwriter on 1,500 shares of £1 each, at £1·10 per share unapplied for.		
Cash	1,650	
Underwriter		1,650
Being discharge of liability by underwriter.		
First Call	400	
Ordinary Share Capital		400
Being call of £0·20 per share on 2,000 shares.		
Cash	400	
First Call		400
Being cash received on 1st call being £0·20 per share on 2,000 shares.		
Underwriting Commission	154	
Underwriter		154
Being underwriting commission of 4% on 3,500 shares issued at £1·10 per share.		
Underwriter	84	
Cash		84
Being payment on account of underwriting commission.		

BALANCE SHEET AS AT ....

		£			£
Authorized Capital—			Cash		4,566
6,000 Ordinary Shares of £1 each		£6,000	Sundry Assets . . .		1,000
			Underwriting Commission .		154
Issued Capital—					
4,000 Ordinary Shares of £1 each fully paid		4,000			
2,000 Ordinary Shares of £1 each £0·65 per Share called and paid		1,300			
Share Premium Account . .		350			
Underwriter . . .		70			
		£5,720			£5,720

Illustration 56

The Balance Sheet of J. Halden was:

BALANCE SHEET AS AT 31ST DECEMBER 19.8

	£	£		£	£
Creditors . . .	3,100		Sundry Assets . .		10,500
Less Reserve . .	100		Debtors . .	6,720	
		3,000	*Less* Reserve	220	
Loans . . .		2,000			6,500
J. Halden . . .		12,000			
		£17,000			£17,000

On 15th April 19.9, J. Halden, Ltd., was incorporated, taking over all the assets (except debtors) and the liability for loans; interest at 6 per cent per annum on the purchase price to be allowed to the vendor from 1st January 19.9, to the date of completion. The credit balance of J. Halden's capital to be satisfied by the issue of ordinary shares in J. Halden, Ltd.

The loanholders accept 8 per cent preference shares in discharge of their debts.

The company, as agent for the vendor, agrees to collect the debts, which realize £6,300, out of which they pay, as agent for the vendor, the creditors at the net figure shown in the Balance Sheet. Of the balance, they paid on account to J. Halden, including interest, to be discharged in the form of £2,500 debentures at 96 and cash.

The new company is to be entitled to all the intervening profit (i.e. between 1st January 19.9, and 15th April 19.9).

Show the opening entries of J. Halden, Ltd., and the closing entries of J. Halden in respect of the above, assuming that the date of completion is 31st May 19.9. Take income tax at 45 per cent.

In the books of J. Halden, Ltd.

JOURNAL

19.9		£p	£p
April 15	Sundry Assets	10,500·00	
	Loans		2,000·00
	J. Halden [*See below*][1] . . .		8,500·00
	Being assets and liabilities taken over as on 31st December 19.8, in pursuance of purchase agreement dated		
May 31	Loans	2,000·00	
	8% Preference Share Capital . .		2,000·00
	Being issue of 2,000 8% preference shares of £1 each fully paid in settlement of loan holders' claims.		
	Interest[2]	212·50	
	J. Halden		116·88
	Income Tax		95·62
	Being interest on purchase price of £8,500 at 6% for five months to 31st May 19.9, and Income Tax at 45% thereon.		
	Cash	6,300·00	
	J. Halden		6,300·00
	Being debts collected.		
	J. Halden	1,000·00	
	Cash		1,000·00
	Being payment on account of amounts collected.		
	J. Halden	3,000·00	
	Cash		3,000·00
	Being payment of creditors.		
	J. Halden	10,916·88	
	Discount on Debentures . . .	100·00	
	Ordinary Share Capital . . .		8,500·00
	Debentures		2,500·00
	Cash		16·88
	Being discharge of liability to vendor by issue of 8,500 shares of £1 each fully paid, £2,500 debentures at 96%, and cash £16·88.		

[1] and [2] see p. 23169.

In J. Halden's books

JOURNAL

19.9		£p	£p
April 15	Realization Account	10,500·00	
	Sundry Assets		10,500·00
	Being assets transferred to J. Halden, Ltd., as on 31st December 19.8, in pursuance of purchase agreement dated		
	Loan	2,000·00	
	Realization Account		2,000·00
	Being liability assumed by J. Halden, Ltd., in pursuance agreement of purchase dated		
	J. Halden, Ltd.[1]	8,500·00	
	Realization Account		8,500·00
	Being purchase consideration as per purchase agreement dated		
May 31	J. Halden, Ltd., Interest[2]	116·88	
	J. Halden Capital		116·88
	Being interest at 6% per annum on £8,500 for 5 months—		

                                           £p

    1st Jan. 19.9, to 31st May 19.9   212·50
    Less Income Tax at 45%   ·95·62

                                    £116·88

		£p	£p
	J. Halden, Ltd. Collection Account . .	6,300·00	
	Bad Debts Provision	220·00	
	J. Halden Capital	200·00	
	Debtors		6,720·00
	Being final adjustment of debtors through the collection by J. Halden, Ltd.		
	Creditors	3,100·00	
	J. Halden, Ltd. Collection Account . .		3,000·00
	Discount Received		100·00
	Being final adjustment of creditors through payments by J. Halden, Ltd.		
	J. Halden, Capital Account[3]	1,000·00	
	J. Halden, Ltd., Collection Account . .		1,000·00
	Being cash drawn against net collection by J. Halden, Ltd.		

[1] This is made up of the Capital Account of J. Halden after adjusting debtors and creditors, i.e. the 'net' assets taken over.

[2] This will be charged against profit prior to incorporation.

[3] See ([1]) on p. 23170.

JOURNAL—(*contd.*)

19.9		£p	£p
May 31	J. Halden, Capital[1]	10,916·88	
	J. Halden, Ltd.		8,500·00
	J. Halden, Ltd. Collection[2] . . .		2,300·00
	J. Halden, Ltd. Interest[2]		116·88
	Being discharge of final balances by allotment of 8,500 shares of £1 each fully paid: £2,500 debentures at 96% and cash, £16·88 for balance of interest.		

[1] It will be observed that the vendor receives £11,916·88. This sum is accounted for as follows:

			£p
(*a*) Capital per Balance Sheet			12,000·00
Less loss on Bad Debts—	£		
Book Value of Debtors	6,720		
Less Provision	220		
	6,500		
Amount realized . .	6,300		
			200·00
			11,800·00
Add Interest on purchase price, *less* tax . . .			116·88
			£11,916·88

[2] The balance due to J. Halden after the allotment of shares is £2,416·88 discharged as follows:

		£p
(*a*) £2,500 Debentures at 96%		2,400·00
(*b*) Cash		16·88
		£2,416·88

A transfer of £100 might be made from Interest Account to Collection Account, bringing the latter up to £2,400 and the former down to £16·88 discharged respectively by Debentures and Cash (as above).

Profit Prior to Incorporation. A company cannot make profits nor incur losses prior to incorporation, so that where it is formed to take over a business from a date prior to its incorporation (usually being the date of the close of the last accounting period of the vendor concern) the profit or loss arising between the two dates must be kept quite apart from the profits or losses after incorporation. It may be noticed that the date of the certificate entitling the company to commence business (necessary in public companies) being purely a legal formality is quite immaterial to the present topic.

The vendor, in releasing his right to profit (a loss may be ignored at the moment), will normally require some compensation, either in the form of interest or an additional sum for goodwill. Therefore, it is first necessary to compute the amount of pre-incorporation profit, against which will be debited the interest (if any) payable to the vendor; if there still remains a balance of pre-incorporation profit, this is in the nature of a capital profit and not available for distribution amongst the members of the company.

Illustration 57

A company is incorporated to take over a business as and from 1st January 19.., the company being incorporated on 31st March 19.., followed in due course by the receipts of its certificate entitling it to commence business. The profit for the first year ended 31st December 19.., is £3,200 (before debiting interest to vendor), of which the proportion attributable to the three months ended 31st March is £600. The vendor is entitled to 10 per cent interest per annum on the purchase consideration of £14,000, up to the date of incorporation. Ignore Taxation.

ALLOCATION OF PROFIT

	Pre-Incorporation	Post-Incorporation	Total
	£	£	£
Profit	600	2,600	3,200
Less Interest to Vendor at 10% p.a. on £14,000 for 3 months: 1st Jan. 19.., to. 31st March. 19...	350		350
Balance	£250	£2,600	£2,850
Disposal	Capital Reserve	Available for Dividend	

Instead of receiving interest, the vendor may increase the purchase consideration by the estimated profit (if possible), so that the 'excess' figure will be automatically added to goodwill; therefore, the pre-incorporation profit will be credited not to a capital reserve, but to GOODWILL, so as to cancel the amount originally included therein representing estimated profit. It is extremely improbable that the *actual* profit will correspond with the estimated profit, hence there will almost invariably be a difference between the estimate and actual. This may, in case of a profit balance, belong to the purchasing company or to the vendor, according to agreement. The converse position would arise in case of a loss balance.

Illustration 58

Same facts as before, except that the purchase consideration is £14,600 without interest, and assuming that £14,000 represents book values of tangible assets at 1st January, journalize (without narrative) the opening

JOURNAL

	£	£
Assets	14,000	
Goodwill	600	
Vendor		14,600

entries of the purchasing company. Disposal of profit will be:

(a) Pre-incorporation profit, £600 will be transferred to Goodwill.
(b) Post-incorporation profit, £2,600 will be available for dividend.

The Goodwill Account will subsequently be eliminated thus:

JOURNAL

	£	£
Profit and Loss Account (Pre-Incorporation) . .	600	
Goodwill		600

Illustration 59

Show the treatment, assuming the same facts as in the preceding illustration, except that the ACTUAL pre-incorporation profit is £850; the total profit for the year remaining the same, £3,200.

ALLOCATION OF PROFIT

Pre-Incorporation £850	Post-Incorporation £2,350	Total £3,200

The pre-incorporation profit will be disposed of by transferring £600 thereof to the credit of Goodwill Account and £250 to the credit of capital reserve or, if the agreement so provides, to the credit of the vendor. The post-incorporation profit is available for dividend.

If there have been drawings on the part of the vendor, the balance payable to the vendor will be *pro tanto* reduced.

Loss Prior to Incorporation. Any loss prior to incorporation may be dealt with thus:

(a) debited against the profits after incorporation;
(b) debited to a special account headed 'Loss prior to Incorporation'; or
(c) debited to Goodwill Account.

The same principle in (b) and (c) applies as in the case of a profit prior to incorporation. If the purchase consideration is based upon the position as at the date of the Balance Sheet without reference to a subsequent loss, the vendor agreeing to forgo all question of profit and conversely being released from any loss, then logically the vendor ought to ALLOW interest to the purchaser, although this is obviously a very rare occurrence.

Illustration 60

A company sells its business to another as from 1st January 19.., the purchasing company being incorporated on the 31st March 19... The purchase consideration is £14,000, but as the parties are aware, there has been a loss during the three intervening months, it is agreed that the purchasing company will bear all the loss, subject to the vendor allowing interest at 10 per cent per annum for the period 1st January 19.., to 31st March 19.., on the purchase consideration. The loss for the year ended 31st December 19.., is £3,200 apart from interest, of which £600 is attributable to the pre-incorporation period.

ALLOCATION OF LOSS

	Pre-Incorporation	Post-Incorporation	Total
	£	£	£
Loss	600	2,600	3,200
Less Interest due from Vendor at 10% p.a. on £14,000 for 3 months to 31st March. 19...	350		350
	£250	£2,600	£2,850
Disposal	[1]Carried forward	[2]Carried forward	

[1] This item will be shown in the Balance Sheet as an 'asset' till written-off.
[2] This item will be shown in the Balance Sheet as an 'asset' till eliminated by subsequent profits.

Where no interest is to be calculated and the purchase price is to be reduced by the estimated loss of £600 (assuming the estimated losses to mature exactly into an actual loss of £600), there will be a provision made in the opening entries against which the loss will be debited.

Illustration 61

Same facts as in the preceding example, except that no interest is to be computed and the purchase consideration has been reduced by £600. Show the opening Journal entry.

JOURNAL

	£	£
Assets.	14,000	
Vendor		13,400
Provision[1]		600

[1] The 'profit' of £600 is illusory, as the value of the assets although appearing in the books at £14,000 is diminished by the loss of £600.

Disposal of loss will be:

(a) Pre-incorporation loss £600 will be offset against the Provision.

(b) Post-incorporation loss £2,600 will be carried forward till eliminated by subsequent profits.

The entry (a) will cancel the Provision credited in the opening entry.

If the loss were £850 instead of £600, the debit balance of £250 would be transferred either to the debit of vendor, if the agreement so provides, or to Loss prior to Incorporation Account.

Where interest is charged by the vendor, such interest will be an *additional* loss, so that using the figures already given the loss of £600 would be increased by £350 interest to £950, and be dealt with as a loss prior to incorporation.

If it should happen that there is a loss prior to incorporation and a profit after incorporation, the former may be set off against the latter, thus reducing the divisible profit.

Where the loss prior to incorporation is debited against goodwill, this is correct only if the amount of goodwill is at the opening a balancing figure, for if the *true* goodwill has already been debited, no subsequent losses can increase it, but rather the reverse.

Illustration 62

Same facts as previously, except that tangible assets at a book value of £14,000 are purchased for £15,800. Loss prior to incorporation is £600. Show opening Journal entry.

It is obvious that the goodwill figure in the opening entry is £1,800; but this is based upon the book values at 1st January. Yet at the time of incorporation the assets had fallen in value (apart from other fluctuations) by £600, leaving the true book value at £13,400; hence the goodwill is the purchase consideration (£15,800) less the true value of assets (£13,400); that is, £2,400. At the date of the opening entry the 1st January figures are entered thus:

JOURNAL

	£	£
Assets.	14,000	
Goodwill	1,800	
Vendor .		15,800

When the loss is ascertained at the end of the year, viz. £600, the amount will be transferred to the debit of goodwill, increasing it to £2,400.

If the opening entry is adjusted to cover the estimated loss at the date of purchase, it would be as follows:

JOURNAL

	£	£
Assets (old Book Value)	14,000	
Goodwill	2,400	
Vendor .		15,800
Provision		600

The debit for loss prior to incorporation will be offset against the provision £600, thereby eliminating it.

If the business had been acquired on the basis that the loss to 31st March 19.., was only £600 (and it turns out to be £1,000), then the extra loss of £400 must be transferred to Loss prior to Incorporation Account. This is justified because the purchasers contemplated the tangible assets to be £13,400 (paying £15,800 therefor), but the assets were £400 less than they imagined, for which, had they known it, they would have paid only £15,400.

Summary of Treatment of Profit Prior to Incorporation. 1. Where assets are taken over and paid for on the basis of the last Balance Sheet, the vendor taking the whole profit between the latter date and the date of the incorporation of the company, no charge being made for Goodwill.

2. Where the vendor increases the same price of the business to cover the whole of the profit indicated in the foregoing paragraph no charge being made for Goodwill.

3. Where the vendor surrenders the whole of the profit indicated in paragraph (1) and charges interest on the purchase price in lieu thereof, no charge being made for Goodwill.

4. Where, in addition to the purchase price, either with or without the addition of interest, the purchasing company is required to pay for Goodwill.

In the above instances the pre-incorporation profit will be (referring to each paragraph):

1. eliminated,
2. eliminated, and
3. the excess of profit over interest credited to Capital Reserve or, in the converse instance, debited to Loss prior to Incorporation Account or Goodwill Account.

As to (4) there will be a Goodwill Account opened, so that any excess interest over profit must be debited to Loss prior to Incorporation Account.

Where the pre-incorporation profit exceeds that estimated in fixing the purchase price, the excess will be credited to Capital Reserve; in the converse case, debited to Loss prior to Incorporation Account if paragraph (4) applies, otherwise Loss prior to Incorporation Account or Goodwill Account.

Similar principles, conversely treated, will apply to Loss prior to Incorporation.

Therefore, it is of vital importance to be acquainted with the DETAILS of the constitution of the PURCHASE CONSIDERATION.

Methods of Computing Profit Prior to Incorporation. 1. By the taking out of accounts, either with or without closing-off the books, whereby the actual profit or loss up to the date of incorporation is ascertained, such profit or loss being credited or debited to the vendor, or transferred on the lines already outlined. The simplest, but not always the most expedient, method is to close off the old books; the new books of the purchaser being opened with the assets as they exist at the date of incorporation, thus automatically including the results to that date; the difference between the assets acquired and purchase consideration being goodwill or reserve. If the purchase consideration EXCEEDS book values, the balancing item is a debit for goodwill; if it is LESS than book values, the balancing item is CAPITAL (or depreciation or asset) reserve. The accounts will then relate exclusively to the post-incorporation period, and adjustments for pre-incorporation profit or loss will not be required.

2. By taking the gross profit on a percentage basis of sales, and apportioning it into the 'pre' and 'post' periods on either TIME or SALES basis, the expenses against the gross profit being split according to the circumstances, viz.:

(i) Common charges:
(a) Fixed charges on actual facts or on a time basis, e.g. rates, insurance.
(b) Fluctuating charges on the basis appropriate thereto, e.g.:
   Bad debts according to the date they became bad or upon credit sales.
   Discount allowed and received according to the dates of allowance or the date the debts were incurred.
   Carriage out according to the dates of sales.

(ii) Non-common charges. These will be dealt with accordingly as they belong to the 'pre' or 'post' periods, and normally are not split, e.g. directors' fees, if the vendor is not a limited company these must exclusively belong to the 'post-incorporation' period. Similarly, formation expenses, although necessarily incurred in point of time prior to the incorporation of the company, will not be introduced into the books until the 'post-incorporation' period, as they are expended EXCLUSIVELY for the purchasing company. Thus, the procedure is:

(a) to apportion gross profit according to the sales prior to or after incorporation, or according to the respective periods prior to or after incorporation;
(b) to apportion the expenses according to the facts; leaving
(c) two profits and/or losses, viz. before and after incorporation.

Illustration 63

Perwick, Ltd., was incorporated on 1st April 19.., taking over a business as and from the preceding 1st January. The net sales for the year ended 31st December 19.., are £125,000, £25,000 of which were made during the three months ended 31st March 19...

The gross profit for the year is £40,000; general expenses are £26,000, and *include* directors' fees, £2,000; issued share capital is £60,000, in ordinary shares of £1 each fully paid.

It is decided to place £3,000 to reserve.

Show Profit and Loss Account, basing the apportionment of gross profit on sales. Ignore taxation and preliminary expenses.

PERWICK, LTD.

PROFIT AND LOSS ACCOUNT FOR THE YEAR ENDED
31ST DECEMBER 19..

		Pre-Incorporation	Post-Incorporation			Pre-Incorporation	Post-Incorporation
		£	£			£	£
General Expenses[1]		6,000	18,000	Gross Profit[2] . . . b/d		8,000	32,000
Directors' Fees			2,000				
Net Profit	c/d	2,000	12,000				
		£8,000	£32,000			£8,000	£32,000
Reserve			3,000	Net Profit b/d		2,000	12,000
Interest to Vendor		?					
Balance to Capital							
Reserve		2,000					
Balance	c/d		9,000				
		£2,000	£12,000			£2,000	£12,000
				Balance . . . b/d			9,000

[1] Apportioned on a time basis, i.e. 3:9.
[2] Apportioned on sales basis, i.e. 25:100.

Illustration 64

A company acquires a business as on 1st January 19.., it being incorporated on the 1st May 19... The first accounts are drawn up to the 30th September 19...

The gross profit is £5,600.

The general expenses are £1,422; directors' emoluments, £3,600 per annum; formation expenses, £150.

Rent to 30th June was £120 per annum, after which it was increased to £300 per annum.

Salary of the manager, who upon incorporation of the company was made a director, was £1,800 per annum (since incorporation included in directors' fees above).

Show Profit and Loss Account, assuming that the net sales were £82,000, the monthly average of which for the first four months of 19.. being one-half of that of the remaining period. The commodity earned a uniform profit. Interest and tax may be ignored.

PROFIT AND LOSS ACCOUNT FOR THE NINE MONTHS ENDED
30TH SEPTEMBER 19..

		Pre-Incorporation	Post-Incorporation				Pre-Incorporation	Post-Incorporation
		£	£				£	£
General Expenses (b)		632	790	Gross Profit (a) .	.	b/d	1,600	4,000
Rent (c)		40	95					
Manager's Salary		600						
Directors' Fees (d)			1,500					
Formation Expenses (e)			150					
Capital Reserve (or Goodwill)		328						
Balance	c/d		1,465					
		£1,600	£4,000				£1,600	£4,000
				Balance .	.	b/d		1,465

(a) The profit is apportioned in the ratio of $2:5$.

> If the first four months sales be represented by 1
> then subsequent sales will be represented by 2,
> but as the number of months in first period is four
> and in the second five, the ratio is computed thus—
>
> $$\text{Pre-incorporation} = 1 \times 4 = \quad 4 = 2$$
> $$\text{Post-incorporation} = 2 \times 5 = 10 = 5$$
>
> $$\overline{14 \quad 7}$$

(b) In absence of information, apportioned on time basis, i.e. $4:5$.

(c) 4 months at £10 a month = £40 (to 1st May 19..).

     2 months at £10 a month, plus 3 months at £25 a month = £95 (to 30th Sept. 19..).

(d) Directors' emoluments, five months (to 30th Sept. 19..), at £300 a month.

(e) Strictly, to Appropriation Account. Formation expenses may, alternatively, be written-off
against pre-incorporation profits.

Illustration 65

X, Ltd., was incorporated on 1st July 19.., and acquired from Y as and
from 1st January 19... the business carried on by him. The purchase price
of the fixed assets and goodwill was defined by the agreement as a sum
equal to 75 per cent of the profits of the business for twenty years from 1st
January 19.., payment to be made each year on the ascertainment of the
sum due.

The following were the balances as on 31st December 19.., after
closing the Trading Account.

Debits		£	Credits	£
Debtors		600	Share Capital	1,200
Stock at cost		750	Creditors	1,150
Bank		2,900	Profit for the year *after* providing	
Preliminary Expenses . .		200	for Corporation Tax and charg-	
Directors' Fees . . .		300	ing all other expenses allowable	
			under Purchase Agreement .	2,400
		£4,750		£4,750

Write off one-quarter of the Preliminary Expenses and set out *draft* Balance Sheet as on 31st December 19..; and Profit and Loss Appropriation Account, showing profit prior to incorporation.

X, LTD.

Draft PROFIT AND LOSS APPROPRIATION ACCOUNT FOR THE YEAR ENDED 31ST DECEMBER 19..

	1 £	2 £		1 £	2 £
Preliminary Expenses . . .		50	Net Profit	1,200	900
Balance	1,200	850			
	£1,200	£900		£1,200	£900

[1] Profit prior to incorporation.

[2] Profit since incorporation.

Draft BALANCE SHEET AS AT 31ST DECEMBER 19..

	£	£		£	£
Share Capital . . .		1,200	Bank	2,900	
Capital Reserve—Profit			Debtors. . . .	600	
prior to Incorporation		1,200	Stock . . .	750	
Profit and Loss Account .		850			4,250
			Fixed Assets and Good-		
Creditors—			**will . . . .**		**1,800**
General . . .	1,150		Preliminary Expenses	200	
Vendor . . .	**1,800**		*Less* written-off .	50	150
		2,950			
		£6,200			£6,200

Notes. (*a*) The amount of £1,800 is the sum payable for the acquisition of Fixed Assets and Goodwill, arrived by taking three-quarters of the profit of the company for the year £2,400. The student must note that the basic figure is not £2,100, i.e. £2,400 *less* Directors' Fees £300, because the question clearly states otherwise; further, if the new company could charge up Directors' Fees indiscriminately it could deprive the Vendor of *any* sum for the Fixed Assets and Goodwill by utilizing all the profits of the company in payment of Directors' Fees.

(*b*) The apportionment of profit prior to incorporation is upon a time basis, i.e.:

	£	£
Prior to incorporation, one-half of £2,400 . . .		1,200
Subsequent to incorporation, one-half of £2,400 . .	1,200	
Less Directors' Fees	300	
		900
		£2,100

(*c*) As a matter of prudence a Reserve may be created to cover the sum of £1,800 payable to the Vendor by first utilizing the profit prior to incorporation of £1,200 and the sum of £600 out of profits subsequent to incorporation.

(*d*) It is assumed that Corporation Tax is 'allowable' as the question states: . . . after providing for Corporation Tax and charging all *other* expenses allowable.'

Apportionment of Shares between Vendors. Difficulties sometimes arise in the division of shares received from a purchasing company in the lack of agreement between the vendors.

Where partners are vendors, the problem is so to apportion the shares in the new company as to preserve the original positions of the partners as enjoyed in the partnership, viz. (a) to maintain the same divisibility of profits; and (b) to preserve the same priority as to the right of repayment of capital.

The rules may be summarized, ignoring taxation:

1. Where a partner has made a loan or advance to the partnership, he should take a first preference share with dividend at the same rate as interest on the loan.[1]

2. [2]Surplus capital second preference share with or without dividend right.[1]

(a) If no interest on capital—no dividend.

(b) If interest on capital—same rate of dividend as the interest paid in the partnership.

The above share to be preferential as to capital, the share in (1) having priority over the share in (2).[1]

3. The balance of all shares in profit-and-loss ratios.

4. Partnership salaries as before.

Where the capitals of the partners are proportionate to profit-sharing, the *whole* of the share capital of the company will be so divided, it being immaterial whether interest on capital in the partnership was charged or not.

Where taxation comes up for consideration—as in most cases it undoubtedly will—the above rules are modified so as to give the directors their income from the company in the form of directors' remuneration and not as dividends. This point is illustrated on p. 23182 *et seq.*

Illustration 66

A, B, and C are in partnership, sharing profits in the ratio of 2:2:1 after providing for interest on capital at 5 per cent per annum, and salaries of £1,200 to B and £1,150 to C. They decide to form a limited company to take over the business. The assets and liabilities are to be taken over at book values with the exception of goodwill, the value of which is to be taken at an increase of £5,000. The capitals of A, B, and C at the date of purchase by the limited company were £8,000, £6,000, and £3,500.

Show how you would deal with the allocation of capital of the partners in the new company so as to preserve the same rights as between themselves as obtained in the partnership.

1. The capitals of the partners in the business are not proportional to their shares in profits and losses.

---

[1] Alternatively, instead of first and second preference shares, debentures may be issued for (1) and preference shares for (2).

[2] See p. 23181.

2. The Capital Account after writing-up assets will be as follows:

	A	B	C
	£	£	£
Capitals	8,000	6,000	3,500
Add Increase in Assets in ratio 2:2:1	2,000	2,000	1,000
Revised Capitals	£10,000	£8,000	£4,500

3. If the capitals were in profit-sharing ratios, and assuming C's capital to be in the same proportion to the total capital as his share of profit, the relative excess capitals would be as follows:

	A	B	C
	£	£	£
Capitals as above	10,000	8,000	4,500
Less Capitals in the Profit-sharing ratio	8,000	8,000	4,000
Surplus Capital held by A and C over B	2,000		500
As between A and C profits are divided in proportion of 2:1. Assuming, therefore, C's surplus Capital of £500 to represent one-third, the Capitals would be	1,000		500
Surplus Capital of A over C	£1,000		

In the event of a winding-up therefore, A should receive £1,000 before B and C are repaid anything. The next £1,500 should be shared by A and C in the ratio of 2:1, and the balance between A, B, and C in the ratio of 2:2:1.

4. (*a*) In order that the ultimate net profit shall continue to be shared in the proportions of 2:2:1, ordinary shares must be issued to the partners in those proportions in respect of part of their capital.

(*b*) To equate the rights of the partners as to interest on capital, preference shares carrying 5 per cent per annum interest may be issued for the balance of the respective capitals.

(*c*) The priorities as to repayment of capital attaching to the various classes of shares must be made to conform to the present rights of the partners in regard to payment of capitals and loans in the partnership.

5. Capital may thus be issued:

(i) £1,000 5 per cent 'A' cumulative preference shares of £1 each, issued to A in respect of his absolute surplus of capital, such shares to have priority over all other shares as to repayment of capital in the event of liquidation.

(ii) £1,000 5 per cent 'B' cumulative preference shares of £1 each to be issued to A and £500 5 per cent 'B' cumulative preference shares to be issued to C in respect of their surplus capital over that of B, such shares to rank *pari passu* with 'A' preference shares as to dividend and next after the 'A' preference shares as to repayment of capital in the event of liquidation.

(iii) None of the above preference shares to be entitled to share in any surplus of assets remaining on a winding-up, except to the extent of all arrears of preference dividend due on such shares.

(iv) Ordinary shares, ranking for dividend and repayment of capital after all preference shares, and carrying the right to participate in any surplus of assets on a winding-up to be issued as follows: A, £8,000; B, £8,000; C, £4,000.

(v) Directors' salaries of £1,200 and £1,150 per annum to be paid to B and C respectively to take place of the salaries hitherto paid to them.

(vi) The distribution of profits in the partnership and the company respectively is illustrated by the following statements (using the foregoing data).

Profits assumed, £7,225.

	PARTNERSHIP			COMPANY			
	A	B	C		A	B	C
	£	£	£		£	£	£
Interest on Capital—				5% 'A' Preference Share Dividend	50		
5% on £10,000	500						
5% on £8,000		400		5% 'B' Preference Share Dividend	50		25
5% on £4,500			225	Directors' Remuneration		1,200	1,150
Salaries		1,200	1,150				
Balance, 2:2:1	1,500	1,500	750	[See below]	100	1,200	1,175
				Dividends on: Ordinary Shares	1,900	1,900	950
	£2,000	£3,100	£2,125		£2,000	£3,100	£2,125

In order to reduce Corporation and Advance Corporation Taxes the directors could treat the ordinary dividend as remuneration and thereby obtain maximum benefits of their personal tax allowances.

Divisible profits could, therefore, be distributed as directors' remuneration[1] as follows:

[1] Prior to 1st April 1969, the allowable charge for remuneration of directors of a close company was, in respect of three working proprietors, £10,000. On and after 1st April 1969, the various limits on allowable remuneration of directors ceased to have effect. Although, however, the restriction on the amount allowable for Corporation Tax purposes for directors' remuneration has been removed, it remains a basic tax rule that directors' remuneration will only be allowed where the amount charged is reasonable and has been incurred wholly and exclusively for purposes of the company's business.

	A	B	C
	£	£	£
Apportionment (as above)	100	1,200	1,175
Balance, 2:2:1 Additional Remuneration . .	1,900	1,900	950
	£2,000	£3,100	£2,125

1. Company, whereby B is to have £5,000 as director's fee:

	A	B	C
	£	£	£
Directors' Remuneration and Preference Dividends	3,900	5,000	3,075
Dividends: Ordinary Shares at 2½% . {A £8,000, B 8,000, C 4,000}	200	200	100
	£4,100	£5,200	£3,175

2. Company, whereby the whole of the profit, except for preference dividends and B's director's fee £1,200 and C's director's fee £1,150, is to be paid in dividends on Ordinary Shares:

	A	B	C
	£	£	£
Apportionment (see p. 23182) . . .	100	1,200	1,175
Dividends: Ordinary Shares at 50% . {A £8,000, B 8,000, C 4,000}	[1]4,000	[1]4,000	[1]2,000
	£4,100	£5,200	£3,175

[1] Alternatively, these sums might be treated as additional director's fees.

In a winding-up, should there be a loss, it would be charged first against the ordinary shares, then against the 'B' Preference shares and any balance, lastly, against the 'A' Preference shares. The comparative position between the partnership and the limited company is shown in the following illustrations.

Illustration 67

Assuming that the new company went into immediate liquidation and that the assets produced £21,000, there would be a loss of £1,500 (i.e. £22,500–£21,000) which would be borne as follows:

	PARTNERSHIP				LIMITED COMPANY		
	A	B	C		A	B	C
	£	£	£		£	£	£
Capital	10,000	8,000	4,500	Ordinary Shares	8,000	8,000	4,000
Loss 2:2:1	600	600	300	Less Loss	600	600	300
					7,400	7,400	3,700
				'B' Preference Shares	1,000		500
				'A' Preference Shares	1,000		
Repay	£9,400	£7,400	£4,200	Repay	£9,400	£7,400	£4,200

Illustration 68

If the assets produced £2,100 only, involving a loss of £20,400.

	PARTNERSHIP				LIMITED COMPANY		
	A	B	C		A	B	C
	£	£	£		£	£	£
Capital	10,000	8,000	4,500	Ordinary Shares	8,000	8,000	4,000
Loss 2:2:1	8,160	8,160	4,080	Less Loss	8,000	8,000	4,000
	Repay	Due	Repay		—	—	—
	£1,840	£160	£420				
Advantage (+) or disadvantage (−) compared with Company	+£107	−£160	+£53	'B' Preference Shares	1,000	—	500
				Less Balance of Loss (£20,400–£20,000)	267		133
					733	—	367
				'A' Preference Shares	1,000	—	—
				Repay	£1,733	nil	£367

Illustration 69

If the loss on liquidation is £21,900, the assets producing £600 only.

	PARTNERSHIP				LIMITED COMPANY		
	A	B	C		A	B	C
	£	£	£		£	£	£
Capital	10,000	8,000	4,500	Ordinary Shares as above	—	—	—
Loss 2:2:1	8,760	8,760	4,380	'B' Preference Shares	1,000	—	500
	Repay	Due	Repay	Less Loss	1,000	—	500
	£1,240	£760	£120		—	—	—
Advantage on a disadvantage as above	+£640	−£760	+£120	'A' Preference Shares	1,000	—	—
				Less Balance of Loss (£21,900–£21,500)	400	—	—
				Repay	£600	nil	nil

Thus B with the lowest relative capital, gains materially in the company at the expense of A and C, whilst the capital loss of A is much heavier than that of C.

Had the two preference shares been of the same status in a liquidation, the position would have been:

	A	B	C
	£	£	£
Ordinary Shares as above	—	—	—
Preference Shares 'A' and 'B'	2,000		500
Less balance of loss (£21,900 − £20,000) shared 20 : 5	1,520		380
Repay	£380	*Nil*	£120

Debtors' and Creditors' Suspense Accounts. Where, as is usual, the purchasing company collects debts as agent for the vendor and out of the proceeds pays the creditors on behalf of the vendor the procedure is to open Suspense Accounts for both debtors and creditors as they stand in the books at the date of the transfer, the *contras* therefor being the Debtors and Creditors Accounts.

The Ledgers will be continued in the ordinary way, but all receipts, together with allowances, discounts, and returns, must be separately dealt with, and this procedure may be facilitated by the employment of separate columns in the Cash Book. Alternatively, the balances are entered on a separate schedule against which the receipts or payments with discounts and the like are placed, thus showing the balances outstanding, if any, at the end of the financial year.

The double entry will, therefore, be as follows:

1. **For Debtors:**

Debit Sundry Debtors balances
    (or Total Account) in
    Ledger
  Credit Debtors' Suspense Account ⎬ for opening balances.

Debit Cash   (a) ⎫ (a) for cash received from debtors.
Debit Debtors' Suspense Account (b) ⎬ (b) for allowances, etc., to debtors.
  Credit Sundry Debtors Accounts (c) ⎭ (c) for cash and allowances, etc. [i.e. total of
    (a) and (b).]

Debit Debtors' Suspense Account ⎫
  Credit Vendor ⎬ for cash received from debtors.

Entries will be made by way of memorandum in the Schedule for an appropriate adjustment to be made in the total account (if any).

The vendor thus becomes a creditor for cash received by the purchasing company in respect of the debts due to the vendor, just as if he had himself collected the cash from his debtors and remitted the proceeds to the purchasing company.

2. **For Creditors** (reverse to those outlined in respect of debtors[1])—

[1] Creditors substituted for Debtors.

The vendor thus becomes a debtor for the cash paid to his creditors by the purchasing company.

The balance of the cash collected, less paid, will represent the amount due to or by the vendor arising from the debtors and creditors, subject to any collection expenses. The balances of the Suspense Accounts will be equal to the balances of debtors and creditors existing at the date of purchase still remaining in the Ledgers.

Where allowances are made to debtors it is important to debit them to the Debtors' Suspense Account, not being losses of the purchasing company, and where allowances are granted by creditors the amounts thereof should be credited to the Creditors' Suspense Account. In the event of there being a commission given by the vendor to the purchasing company in respect of collection, the entry should not intrude upon those required for the transactions already enumerated; the amount will, before settlement of the balance due to or by the vendor (or at the end of the financial period, if such settlement has not already taken place), be debited to the vendor and credited to Commission Account.

The entries in respect of creditors will conform to the same principles.

Illustration 70

A, Ltd., in taking over the business of A, agrees to collect the debtors at a commission of 5 per cent on net cash collected. The usual discount may be allowed to the debtors. Assuming that the discounts allowed are in order, write up the necessary Ledger Accounts from the following information:

	£
Debtors outstanding at the date of transfer . . .	2,560
Cash collected by A, Ltd, during the past financial year .	1,200
Discounts allowed in respect of the above do. . .	42

The balance due to vendor to be discharged at the end of each financial year as follows: one-half in cash; one-quarter in shares of £1 each fully paid of the new company at a premium of £0·25; and the balance in 9 per cent Treasury Loan, the price of which may be assumed to be 95.

Calculate to nearest £.

SUNDRY DEBTORS

		£				£
Balances . . .		2,560	Cash . . .			1,200
			Discount allowed . .			42
			Balances . . .	c/d		1,318
		£2,560				£2,560
Balances . . .	b/d	1,318				

DEBTORS' SUSPENSE

		£				£
Discount allowed . .		42	*Sundry Debtors* . .			2,560
Vendor . . .		1,200				
Balances . . .	c/d	1,318				
		£2,560				£2,560
			Balances . . .	b/d		1,318

Items in *italics* are opening balances.

CASH

		£				£
Sundry Debtors . . .		1,200		Vendor		570
				Vendor *re* £300 9% Treasury		
				Loan		285
				Balance	c/d	345
		£1,200				£1,200
Balance . . .	b/d	345				

VENDOR

	£			£
Commission on Cash Col-			**Debtors' Suspense Account:**	
lected	60		**Cash collected from Debtors**	**1,200**
Cash	570			
£300 3% Treasury Loan pur-				
chased	285			
Allotment Account . .	285			
	£1,200			£1,200

ALLOTMENT

	£		£
Share Capital Account .	228	Vendor	285
Share Premium . .	57		
	£285		£285

SHARE CAPITAL

				£
			Allotment Account . .	228

SHARE PREMIUM

				£
			Allotment Account . .	57

COMMISSION

				£
			Vendor	60

The Debtors' and the Debtors' Suspense Accounts are reflective and will not appear in the Balance Sheet.

The cash balance of £345 is accounted for thus:

	£
Commission	60
Share Capital	228
Premium on Shares	57
Total	£345

Several different methods are employed to separate the receipts from the old debtors from those arising from the new debtors.

The most important are:

1. The 'Schedule' method whereby receipts are separately scheduled.

2. The separate Cash Book column method, whereby two separate columns are used, one for receipts from old debtors and another for receipts from new debtors.

3. The separate Ledger column method, whereby two columns are ruled on each side of the Ledger, one for old debts and the receipts therefrom, and another for new debts and the receipts therefrom.

Elimination Process where All Assets and Liabilities are not Taken Over. The identical problem in connection with the opening entries of a purchaser will apply in a limited company where part only of the assets are acquired, but *all* the assets and liabilities—including those not taken over—remain in the books. A Vendor Account will be opened and debited with the purchase price payable to the vendor, and except for the fact that the capital introduced into the purchasing company's business will appear in the form of share capital will be dealt with as illustrated in connection with Partnership Accounts—see p. 2287 *et seq.*

Illustration 71

The Balance Sheet of B was:

	£		£
Capital	1,000	Sundry Assets	1,050
Bank Overdraft . . .	200	Stock	100
Creditors	250	*Debtors*	300
	£1,450		£1,450

B, Ltd., a new company, agrees to acquire the above business, taking over assets, except debtors, and liabilities except bank overdraft, the purchase consideration being £1,230. Show the opening entries in Ledger form, assuming that the same books are continued. B subscribes £1,500 to the new company, and is allotted 1,500 shares of £1 each fully paid.

[The items in italics are the 'eliminating' accounts.]

CASH

		£				£
Share Capital . . .		1,500	Vendor . . .			1,230
			Balance	c/d		270
		£1,500				£1,500
Balance	b/d	270				

VENDOR

		£			£
Cash		1,230	B Capital . . .		1,000
Debtors . . .		300	Bank . . .		200
			Goodwill . . .		330
		£1,530			£1,530

SHARE CAPITAL

					£
			Cash		1,500

B. CAPITAL

	£			£
Vendor	1,000	Balance	b/d	1,000

BANK

	£			£
Vendor	200	Balance	b/d	200

CREDITORS

				£
		Balances	b/d	250

DEBTORS

		£			£
Balances	b/d	300	Vendor		300

SUNDRY ASSETS

		£			
Balances	b/d	1,050	. . . .		

STOCK

			£				
Balance . . .	b/d		100		•		

GOODWILL

		£			
Vendor		330			

As a result of the above entries, the immediate position is as follows:

	Dr. £	Cr. £
Cash	270	
Share Capital		1,500
Creditors		250
Sundry Assets	1,050	
Stock	100	
Goodwill[1]	330	
	£1,750	£1,750

Where the new company is not to take over debtors—as in the preceding illustration—but nevertheless is to COLLECT them as agent for the vendor, it is clear that the asset cannot be struck out by an eliminating entry in the ordinary way, because the Debtors' Accounts must be continued as usual; yet Vendor must be debited, as the debts are not *acquired* by the purchasing company. This situation is met by the following entry:

Debit Vendor [as before].
Credit Debtors' *Suspense* [instead of debtors].

The effect of this is that the Vendor Account is properly adjusted, and although the debtors' balances formally remain in the books, they are offset by the Debtors' Suspense Account. The foregoing Trial Balance would be exactly as shown, with the addition of a debit for debtors of £300 and a credit for Debtors' Suspense Account of £300.

When the £300 is collected, cash will be debited and debtors credited; Debtors' Suspense Account debited and vendor credited. The result will

[1] Goodwill is arrived at as follows:

	£	£
Purchase Consideration		1,230
Less Net Assets, i.e.:		
Sundry Assets	1,150	
Less Creditors	250	
		900
Goodwill . . .		£330

be to clear the original Debtor's Accounts and the Debtors' Suspense Account, leaving £300 due to vendor.

These principles may have to be applied to questions which embody other distinct principles, e.g. where the assets taken over are to be revalued or where complicated capital adjustments between the vendor partners arise. The following example is illustrative of this type of problem.

Illustration 72

The Balance Sheet of A and B, who share profits 3:2 and are entitled to interest on capital at 5 per cent per annum, is as follows:

BALANCE SHEET

	£		£
Creditors	800	Sundry Assets	4,100
Capitals—		Debtors	1,200
A . . . £3,200		Investments	700
B . . . 2,000			
	5,200		
	£6,000		£6,000

They decide to convert their business to a limited company, the sole shareholders to be A and B. The purchase agreement provides:

1. That the debtors, investments, and creditors are not to be taken over, but the debtors collected and the creditors paid out of such proceeds by the company as agents for the firm.

2. That the purchase consideration is £5,000, to be settled in 4,000 5 per cent preference shares of £1 each fully paid and the balance in ordinary shares of £0·50 each fully paid in the new company.

In addition to the above, A and B subscribe equally for 500 preference shares and 1,000 ordinary shares.

The same books are employed by the new company, the latter revaluing the assets taken over at £4,300.

Show Ledger entries relative to the above in the books of the limited company, ignoring preliminary expenses.

CREDITORS

						£
				Balances	b/d	800

SUNDRY ASSETS

		£			
Balances	b/d	4,100			
Vendors—Appreciation of Assets . . .		200			

INVESTMENTS

			£					£
Balance	. . .	b/d	700		Vendors	. . .		700

CAPITALS[1]

			A	B				A	B
			£	£				£	£
Vendors	.		3,200	2,000	Balances	. .	b/d	3,200	2,000

VENDORS[1]

	£		£
Debtors' Suspense Account	1,200	Creditors' Suspense Account	800
Investments . . .	700	Capital Accounts—	
Preference Share Capital		A . . .	3,200
Account .	4,000	B . . .	2,000
Ordinary Share Capital		Appreciation of Assets	200
Account . . .	1,000	Goodwill Account . .	700
	£6,900		£6,900

DEBTORS

			£					
Balances	. . .	b/d	1,200					

GOODWILL

			£			
Vendors.	. .		700			

CASH

	£		
Preference Share Capital			
Account .	500		
Ordinary Share Capital			
Account . .	500		

DEBTORS' SUSPENSE

							£
				Vendors	. . .		1,200

[1] The Capital Accounts and the contents of the Vendors' Account may be merged in one account, the transfers of £3,200 and £2,000 then being unnecessary.

CREDITORS' SUSPENSE

		£				
Vendors. . . .		800				

SHARE CAPITALS

						Pre-ference	Ordi-nary
						£	£
				Vendors . . .		4,000	1,000
				Cash . . .		500	500

The amount of goodwill is the excess of the purchase consideration £5,000 over the value of the assets as revalued at £4,300.

The Trial Balance will now be:

TRIAL BALANCE

		£	£
	Creditors		*800* (1)
(5)	Goodwill	700	
(6)	Sundry Assets	4,300	
(7)	Debtors.	1,200	
	Preference Share Capital . .		4,500 (2)
	Ordinary Share Capital . .		1,500 (3)
(8)	*Creditors' Suspense* . . .	*800*	
(9)	Cash	1,000	
	Debtors Suspense		1,200 (4)
		£8,000	£8,000

The opening Journal entries if new books had been opened in the ordinary way would, ignoring narratives, be as follows:

JOURNAL

		£	£
(5)	Goodwill	700	
(6)	Sundry Asset	4,300	
(7)	Debtors.	1,200	
(8)	Creditors' Suspense . . .	800	
	Debtors' Suspense . . .		1,200 (4)
	Creditors		800 (1)
	Vendors		5,000
	Vendors	5,000	
	Preference Share Capital . .		4,000 (2)
	Ordinary Share Capital . .		1,000 (3)
(9)	Cash	1,000	
	Preference Share Capital . .		500 (2)
	Ordinary Share Capital . .		500 (3)

The numbers in parentheses refer to the appropriate items in each set of figures.

The results arising from the foregoing Journal entries are precisely the same as those disclosed in the above Trial Balance.

Illustration 73

The Trial Balance of P, Ltd., on 31st December 19.., is as follows:

TRIAL BALANCE, 31ST DECEMBER 19..

	£	£
V. Capital		8,250
Sundry Assets	10,300	
Sundry Liabilities		1,400
Profit and Loss Account		650
	£10,300	£10,300

The Trial Balance of P, Ltd., on 31st December 19.., is as follows:

The purchase consideration was £13,500, payable in 12,500 shares of £1 each, fully paid, and £1,000 in cash. The date from which the new company was to take over was 1st January 19... The debtors and creditors at that date were £3,000 and £1,200, which were not taken over but collected, and out of the proceeds the liabilities paid by the new company, the balance being paid to the vendor. No entries had been made in respect of the above transactions, except that the vendor had been debited with £1,000 paid to him in part discharge of the purchase consideration, and £1,750 out of the £1,800 due on debt collection after payment of creditors.

As on 1st January 19.., the assets taken over were reduced in value by £700.

Show adjusting entries in Journal form, ignoring narratives and interest, and assuming that all the debts and liabilities of the vendor have been paid; and prepare new Trial Balance.

The Capital Account of the vendor *before* the payments of £1,000 and £1,750 was £11,000, so that the net assets acquired were £9,200, as follows:

	£	£
Capital		11,000
Less Debtors. . . .	3,000	
Less Creditors . . .	1,200	
		1,800
Net Assets		£9,200

The purchase price being £13,500, Goodwill would, but for the adjustment of £700 in respect of sundry assets, be £4,300, but the latter sum must be *increased* to £5,000, and the sundry assets reduced by £700.

The adjusting entries, ignoring narratives, are:

	£	£
Goodwill	5,000	
Sundry Assets		700
Vendor		4,300
Vendor	12,500	
Share Capital		12,500

The Vendor's Account is:

VENDOR

		£			£
Cash		1,000	Balance . . . b/d		11,000
"		1,750			
Balance (per question) . c/d		8,250			
		£11,000			£11,000
Share Capital Account .		12,500	Balance . b/d		8,250
Balance . . . c/d		50	Goodwill . . .		4,300
		£12,550			£12,550
			Balance . . . b/d		50

The balance still remaining in favour of the vendor represents the excess of collections (£3,000) over payments to creditors (£1,200), and to vendor (£1,750).

The Trial Balance will now be:

TRIAL BALANCE, 31ST DECEMBER 19..

	£	£
Vendor		50
Sundry Assets [£10,300 − £700] . . .	9,600	
Sundry Liabilities		1,400
Profit and Loss Account . . .		650
Goodwill	5,000	
Share Capital		12,500
	£14,600	£14,600

If the Debtors' and Creditors' Suspense Accounts had been opened, they would have appeared as follows:

DEBTORS' SUSPENSE

	£		£
Vendor (Collection) Account . .	3,000	Vendor	3,000

CREDITORS' SUSPENSE

	£		£
Vendor . . .	1,200	Vendor (Collection) Account . . .	1,200

The Vendor's Accounts would appear thus:

VENDOR (PURCHASE OF BUSINESS)

	£			£
Debtors' Suspense Account	3,000	Balance . . .	b/d	11,000
Cash . . .	1,000	Creditors' Suspense Account		1,200
Share Capital Account	12,500	Goodwill . . .		4,300
	£16,500			£16,500

VENDOR (COLLECTION)

		£			£
Creditors' Suspense Account (cash paid) .		1,200	Debtors' Suspense Account (cash collected) . .		3,000
Cash		1,750			
Balance . . .	c/d	50			
		£3,000			£3,000
			Balance . . .	b/d	50

[The cash received from debtors and paid to creditors will be entered in the Cash Book and posted to the personal accounts in the ordinary way.]

The use of the Suspense Accounts may be dispensed with and the debtors and creditors left in the books without the raising of the Suspense Accounts (and the corresponding adjustments in the Purchase of Business Account). The balance of the latter account, therefore, is left 'open' until the vendors' debtors and creditors have been finally disposed of.

The cash received and paid will be dealt on the usual lines, either by inclusion in the new owner's cash and bank transactions or preferably by the use of a separate banking account opened for the purpose of dealing with the vendor's debtors and creditors; the final figure will then be paid to, or received from, the vendor, and dealt with through the Purchase of Business Account (or if closed off, by transfer to Vendor Account through the latter account).

Illustration 74

The summarized Balance Sheet of X is as follows:

BALANCE SHEET

	£		£
Creditors	1,000	Debtors	1,300
Accruals	120	Assets (to be retained by Vendor) .	1,100
Capital—X	4,000	Assets (to be taken over by Purchaser)	2,720
	£5,120		£5,120

Creditors and debtors are to be paid and received on behalf of X by the purchaser. At the end of the first year all the debts, except £40, have been collected in full and the creditors fully discharged. The purchase consideration is £3,800 to include goodwill £1,200, the balance to remain on loan till the debtors and creditors are cleared. With full agreement, the debts of £40 are written-off. The same books are continued in use by the purchaser.

Assuming that there are no transactions undertaken by the purchaser (in order to avoid obscuring the accounting factor arising from the above) show the accounts if: (1) Suspense Accounts were opened; (2) no Suspense Accounts were opened.

1.

PURCHASE OF BUSINESS ACCOUNT

		£			£
Debtors' Suspense		1,300	Creditors' Suspense		1,000
Assets retained by Vendor		1,100	Capital—X		4,000
Balance	c/d	3,800	Goodwill		1,200
		£6,200			£6,200
Vendor		3,800	Balance	b/d	3,800

DEBTORS AND CREDITORS

	Drs. £	Crs. £			Drs. £	Crs. £
Balances	1,300		Balances			1,000
Cash		1,000	Cash		1,260	
			Bad Debts		40	
	£1,300	£1,000			£1,300	£1,000

DEBTORS' AND CREDITORS' SUSPENSE

	£	£		£	£
Purchase of Business Account		1,000	Purchase of Business Account	1,300	
Bad Debts	40		Balance to Vendor		1,000
Balance to Vendor	1,260				
	£1,300	£1,000		£1,300	£1,000

VENDOR'S COLLECTION ACCOUNT

		£			£
Creditors' Suspense		1,000	Debtors' Suspense		1,260
Balance	c/d	260			
		£1,260			£1,260
Vendor		260	Balance	b/d	260

VENDOR

		£			£
Balance . . . c/d		4,060	Purchase of Business Account		3,800
			Vendor's Collection Account		260
		£4,060			£4,060
			Balance . . . b/d		4,060

CASH

		£			£
Debtors—X . . .		1,260	Creditors—X . . .		1,000
			Balance . . . b/d		260
		£1,260			£1,260
Balance . . . b/d		260			

TRIAL BALANCE

	£	£
Goodwill	1,200	
Cash (re X)	260	
Vendor		4,060
Assets	2,720	
Accruals		120
	£4,180	£4,180

2.

PURCHASE OF BUSINESS ACCOUNT

		£			£
Assets		1,000	Capital		4,000
Balance . . . c/d		4,100	Goodwill		1,200
		£5,200			£5,200
Debtors		40	Balance . . . b/d		4,100
Balance . . . c/d		4,060			
		£4,100			£4,100
			Balance . . . c/d		4,060

DEBTORS AND CREDITORS

	Drs. £	Crs. £		Drs. £	Crs. £
Balances . .	1,300		Balances . .		1,000
Cash—X . .		1,000	Cash—X . .	1,260	
			Purchase of Business Account .	40	
	£1,300	£1,000		£1,300	£1,000

VENDOR

					Purchase of Business Account . . .	£ 4,060

CASH

Debtors—X . . .		£ 1,260	Creditors—X . . . Balance	c/d	£ 1,000 260
		£1,260			£1,260
Balance	b/d	260			

The Trial Balance will be as on p. 23198.

Construction of Acquisition Entries. Examination papers frequently include complicated questions on the entries relative to acquisition of assets by a company; and no length of textual explanation can be an effective substitute for the practical exposition of the procedure required. In order to assist the student, three typical problems are set out and worked through.

Illustration 75

Coome & Co. sold their business on 15th January 19.., to Martin, Ltd., the latter being incorporated on that date. The purchaser is to take over as and from 1st January 19.., at which date the assets comprised the following:

	£
Buildings.	3,000
Fixtures	670
Debtors	4,200
Stock	1,800
Bank	700
Creditors.	1,300
Rates prepaid	30

The purchase agreement contained the following material clauses:

1. The creditors are to be *paid* by the vendors.
2. The trade debtors and bank balance are to be *retained* by the vendors, but the purchasers are to collect the debtors for a commission of 5 per cent on cash collected.
3. The purchase consideration is to be £7,000, to be discharged by: (*a*) a cash payment of £1,000; (*b*) an allotment of 3,000 preference shares of £1 each fully paid; and (*c*) an allotment of 4,000 ordinary shares of £1 each £0·75 paid; the amounts collected (less commission) to be applied at the end of December 19.., in making the ordinary shares fully paid, the balance over (if any) to be paid to the vendors on the same date.

The company issued 5,000 8 per cent £1 preference shares at a premium of £0·10, and, in addition, by the end of December the shares were called to the extent of £0·75. One preference shareholder holding 400 had paid all his calls in advance, whilst a shareholder with 600 was in arrear for the previous call of £0·10.

The general expenses included £200 for underwriting commission, which was discharged by the issue of 200 ordinary shares of £1 each fully paid at par, with an option to purchase a further 250 ordinary shares of £1 each at £1·25 within the next three years.[1]

The cash collected by the company on behalf of the vendors was £2,300; discounts allowed, £100.

The following balances, apart from those from the foregoing matters, were shown in the books of Martin, Ltd., on 31st December 19...

	£
Purchases	20,430
Sales	24,090
Purchases Returns	320
Discounts (on *all* Debtors)	400
Preliminary Expenses	100
General Expenses	1,410
Rates (on account of the year to 31st March next, of £120—same as the previous year)	100
Debtors (New and *Old*)	7,300
Creditors	2,180
Cash	3,355
	£59,685

Prepare Trial Balance at 31st December 19...

Illustration 76

Several involved entries are necessary before any attempt can be made at constructing the Trial Balance; but the student must be particularly careful to avoid altering the cash balance, as this is the true balance. In other words, the entries in respect of cash have *already* been recorded.

	£	£
(a) Goodwill (balancing figure)	1,500	
(b) Buildings	3,000	
(c) Fixtures	670	
Debtors	4,200	
(d) Stock	1,800	
(e) Rates Prepaid	30	
Debtors' Suspense		4,200
Vendors		7,000
	£11,200	£11,200

Items marked (a), (b), (c), (d), and (e) will appear as above in the Trial Balance.

The item of debtors will be superseded by the closing debtors as shown in the list of balances.

[1] This option must be noted on the Balance Sheet (see p. 2338).

As previously explained, the vendor will finally be credited with cash collected, and the debtors reduced by the cash and discount (the balances remaining being included in the end balances of debtors already shown in the list of balances).

Accordingly, the figure of Debtors' Suspense (£4,200) will be reduced by £2,400 (i.e. cash collected £2,300, plus discounts allowed £100), leaving £1,800 for the Trial Balance. Consequently, the vendors become creditors for £2,300, the difference of £100 being accounted for by the debit to the vendors for discounts allowed, but of this credit, £2,300, the sum of £115 is the commission to the purchaser for the collection, leaving £2,185 finally due to the vendors and £115 to be credited to Commission Account. As the question indicates, the balance at the end of the year due to the vendors is to be applied: (1) to make the ordinary shares allotted fully paid (upon which £0·75 per share has been credited as per the vending agreement), and (2) final balance to be paid in cash to the vendors.

The sum of £2,185 will be disposed of as follows:

(1) 4,000 at £0·25 (to bring the Ordinary Shares of
   £0·75 called and paid to £1 fully paid) . . = £1,000 [to be shown in Trial Balance] Ordinary Share Capital.

(2) Balance to Vendors . . . . . = £1,185 which already having been paid, will not be shown in the Trial Balance as its effect is to reduce the cash balance, and the ACTUAL cash balance at 31st Dec., 19.., is shown in the list of balances.

As a result, therefore, of these adjustments, the following will appear in the Trial Balance:

			£
(f) Debtors' Suspense	.	Cr.	1,800
(g) Commission	.	Cr.	115
(see below) (k) Ordinary Share Capital	.	Cr.	1,000

It will be noticed that of the original credit item of £4,200 appearing in Debtors' Suspense Account, the combined sum of £2,915 (f, g, k) has been accounted for, the difference of £1,285 being made up of (1) cash paid as above, £1,185, and (2) Discounts Account credited, £100 (not being the purchasing company's loss).

The amount of £7,000 has been discharged in cash, £3,000 in preference shares and £3,000 in ordinary shares (i.e. 4,000 ordinary shares of £1 each, £0·75 paid).

Share Capital and Premiums. 5,000 preference shares at a premium of £0·10 are called up to the extent of £0·75, so that the preference share capital will appear:

	£	£
(h) 5,000 Preference Shares at £0·75	3,750	
(i) Vendors' Shares (as above), 3,000 at £1 . . .	3,000	
	——— Cr.	6,750
(j) Premium on Shares, 5,000 at £0·10	Cr.	500
(k) 4,000 Ordinary Shares at £0·75	3,000	
Plus Amounts collected, applied as above . .	1,000	
	——— Cr.	4,000

In addition, a shareholder with 400 Preference Shares has paid all his calls in advance, all of which will have been duly absorbed, save the last call of £0·25, so that he is a creditor for 400 at £0·25 = £100. Further, there are calls in arrear of 600 at £0·10 = £60.

Hence, the Trial Balance must include the above, viz.:

		£	£
(l) Calls in advance	Cr.		100
(m) Calls in arrear	Dr.	60	

There has been incurred an expense of £200 (included in the balances presented) discharged by an allotment of ordinary shares of £1 each fully paid, the latter only requiring insertion into the Trial Balance, thus:

		£
(n) Ordinary Share Capital	Cr.	200

[The amount of £200 included in general expenses must be separated and shown in Balance Sheet till written-off.]

Lastly, as the discount includes the sum of £100, which properly is chargeable to the vendors, there must be a credit inserted therefrom, and entered in the Trial Balance.

		£
(o) Discounts Account	Cr.	100

The figures in the list may now be totalled, to which will be added the accounts lettered (a–o) in the preceding paragraphs.

TRIAL BALANCE, 31ST DECEMBER 19..

		Total	Debits	Credits
	£	£	£	£
Total per List .		59,685		
Less Credits—				
Sales .	24,090			
Purchase Returns	320			
Creditors .	2,180	26,590	33,095	26,590
	Debits	Credits		
Plus (a) Goodwill .	1,500			
(b) Buildings .	3,000			
(c) Fixtures .	670			
(d) Stock .	1,800			
(e) Rates .	30			
(f) Debtors' Suspense .		1,800		
(g) Commission .		115		
(h) Preference Share Capital .		3,750		
(i) Preference Share Capital (Vendors) .		3,000		
(j) Premium on Preference Shares .		500		
(k) Ordinary Share Capital (Vendors) .		4,000		
(l) Calls in Advance .		100		
(m) Calls in Arrear .	60			
(n) Ordinary Share Capital (Underwriters) .		200		
(o) Discounts .		100		
	£7,060	£13,565	7,060	13,565
			£40,155	£40,155

The process of preparing **final** accounts calls for no comment, save that there will be required an adjustment for profit prior to incorporation, and the underwriting commission must be shown separately in the Balance Sheet.

The following illustration is somewhat involved, and requires a thorough knowledge of the principles outlined and a capacity to adapt them to the particular circumstances.

Examination Problem

A and B were partners sharing profits and losses in the ratio of 20:17, and closed their books yearly at 31st December.

On 1st May 19.., A & B, Ltd., was incorporated to acquire the above business as and from the preceding 1st January.

The purchase agreement provides:

1. Purchase consideration: 6,000 preference shares, £1 each fully paid; 2,400 ordinary shares, £0·25 each fully paid.

2. Vendors to retain cash, and to entrust the company with the collection of debtors and the discharge of creditors, any balance till final clearance to be retained in a separate account.

3. Each of the vendors to subscribe in cash for one-half of the balance of the authorized capital, 850 preference shares and 200 ordinary shares.

The Articles of Association appoint A and B sole directors, with fees of £200 per month each.

The accounts have been continued in the books without a break since 1st January 19.., and no entries arising from the formation of the company or its acquisition of the business have been made.

Ignoring tax, prepare final accounts to the 30th September 19.., from the following Trial Balance and information:

TRIAL BALANCE

	£	£
A: Capital on 1st January 19..		3,000
B: Capital on 1st January 19..		2,860
A: Drawings during Period	750	
B: Drawings during Period	800	
A and B *re* Shares		900
Buildings	4,800	
Creditors (£1,500 owing at 1st January 19.., ALL paid)		700
Debtors (£1,000 due at 1st January 19.., £100 still outstanding)	1,050	
Preliminary Expenses	150	
Plant and Machinery (Balance at 1st January 19.., £1,200)	1,500	
Furniture and Fittings (Balance at 1st January 19.., £360	460	
Purchase and Sales	2,000	11,200
Wages [charge to Trading Account]	1,800	
Stock	500	
Bank (Balance at 1st January 19.., £500)	3,500	
Sundry Expenses	1,350	
	£18,660	£18,660

A and B agree to take the preference shares for their capitals at 1st January 19...

The average of the monthly sales (the company sells a commodity at a fixed price) for the first four months of 19.. was one-half of the remainder of the period, and the expenditure each month on items in the Profit and Loss Account was constant.

Write off £72 depreciation from plant and machinery, and all the preliminary expenses. Stock at 30th September 19.., is valued at £800.

In addition to preparing final accounts, show (1) the Journal entries necessary to put the books in order; and (2) the respective shareholdings of the vendor partners.

(*Adapted from Institute of Chartered Accountants' Final.*)

Solution

JOURNAL

19..		£	£
May 1	Capital—A	3,000	
	B	2,860	
	Purchase of Business Account . . .		5,860
	Being transfer of capitals at 1st January 19..		
	Goodwill	740	
	Purchase of Business Account . . .		740
	Being cost of goodwill of business acquired.		
	Purchase of Business Account	6,600	
	Preference Share Capital		6,000
	Ordinary Share Capital		600
	Being issue of shares [detailed] in satisfaction of purchase price as per agreement.		
	A and B	900	
	Preference Share Capital		850
	Ordinary Share Capital		50
	Being issue of shares [detailed] per cash received and allotments made.		
Sept. 30	Vendors[1]	100	
	Debtors' Suspense		100
	Being adjustment for firm debtors not taken over still remaining in books.		

[1] See Note 2, p. 23208.

[The following redrafted Trial Balance—arising from the Journal entries and postings—would in examination work be superimposed upon the examination paper Trial Balance, as time would not permit of the slightest unnecessary writing.]

REDRAFTED TRIAL BALANCE, 30TH SEPTEMBER 19..

	£	£
A: Capital		***
B: Capital		***
A: Drawings	750	
B: Drawings	800	
A and B *re* Shares		***
Buildings	4,800	
Creditors		700
Debtors	1,050	
Preliminary Expenses	150	
Plant and Machinery	1,500	
Furniture and Fittings	460	
Purchases and Sales	2,000	11,200
Wages	1,800	
Stock	500	
Bank	3,500	
Sundry Expenses	1,350	
Goodwill	740	
Preference Share Capital		*6,850*
Ordinary Share Capital		*650*
Vendors	*100*	
Debtors' Suspense		*100*
	£19,500	£19,500

Note. The asterisks *** represent original accounts that have now disappeared, the new items being in italics.

The next step is to proceed to the final accounts, dealing carefully with directors' fees (against which the withdrawals of A and B will be debited) and the question of profit prior to incorporation, leaving the apportionment of shareholding of preference shares (£6,850) and ordinary shares, £650 (2,600 of £0·25 each), till the last.

Note. The profit is apportioned on a 'turnover' basis, as clearly indicated in the question. The question in effect states that the turnover in each of the first four months is half that in the following five months, so that the respective ratios of TOTAL turnover may be very simply computed by assuming sales for *each* month in the pre-incorporation period to be *one* unit, in which case the sales for each month in the post-incorporation period will be *two* units. Hence the total turnover in the two periods is:

	Months	Units		Fractions
Pre-incorporation period	4	× 1	= 4	$\frac{2}{7}$
Post-incorporation period	5	× 2	= 10	$\frac{5}{7}$
			14	

TRADING AND PROFIT AND LOSS ACCOUNT FOR THE NINE MONTHS ENDED 30TH SEPTEMBER 19..

	£	£		£	£
Stock		500	Sales		11,200
Purchases . . .		2,000	Stock		800
Wages . . .		1,800			
Gross Profit . . c/d		7,700			
		£12,000			£12,000

		Pre-Incorporation [4 mos.]	Post-Incorporation [5 mos.]		Pre-Incorporation [4 mos.]	Post-Incorporation [5 mos.]
Expenses . £1,350				Gross Profit . b/d	($\frac{4}{9}$) 2,200	($\frac{5}{9}$) 5,500
Depreciation . 72						
£1,422		632	790			
Directors' Fees . .			2,000			
Preliminary Expenses[1] .			150			
Capital Reserve . .		1,568				
Net Profit . .			2,560			
		£2,200	£5,500		£2,200	£5,500

[1] More accurately to the Appropriation Account.

BALANCE SHEET AS AT 30TH SEPTEMBER 19..

	£	£		£	£
Capital and Surplus:			*Fixed Assets at cost:*		
Share Capital, Authorized and Issued:			Buildings . . .		4,800
6,850 Preference Shares of £1 each, fully paid . .	6,850		Plant and Machinery .	1,200	
2,600 Ordinary Shares of £0·25 each, fully paid .	650		Add Purchases . .	300	
		7,500		1,500	
Capital Reserve . .		1,568	Less Depreciation .	72	
Profit and Loss Account		2,560			1,428
			Furniture and Fittings .		460
		11,628	Goodwill . . .		740
Current Liabilities:					1,428
Trade Creditors . .	700		*Current Assets:*		
Directors' Fees (see note 1) .	450		Stock . . .	800	
		1,150	Sundry Debtors . £1,050		
			Less Debtors' Suspense Account 100		
				950	
			Vendor (see note 2, p. 23208)	100	
			Cash at Bank . .	3,500	
					5,350
		£12,778			£12,778

Notes. 1. This is arrived at by the £2,000 (debited to Profit and Loss Account) *less* the debit of drawings of £550 (in Trial Balance), the respective accounts being:

	A	B	Total
	£	£	£
Directors' Fees for *five* mos. at £200 per mo.	1,000	1,000	2,000
Less Drawings	750	800	1,550
Cr. Balances	£250	£200	£450

2. The Suspense Accounts would be opened at the date of taking over but as the amount due to the Vendors (Bank £500 and Debtors £1,000) and due from Vendors (Creditors £1,500) are equal and have been cleared up save for the balance of Debtors £100, an entry is made for the latter item only.

The allocation of share capital will be thus:

	A	B	Total
	£	£	£
Capital	3,000	2,860	5,860
Profit on Sale [divided 20:17]	400	340	740
Cash Subscribed	450	450	900
Total to be allotted	£3,850	£3,650	£7,500

PREFERENCE SHARES

	A	B	Total
	£	£	£
Capital	3,000	2,860	5,860
Cash Application	425	425	850
Balance in Profit and Loss ratio [20:17] to make up total Preference Share Capital [to nearest whole number].	76	64	140
Total	£3,501	£3,349	£6,850

ORDINARY SHARES

	A		B		Total	
	No.	£p	No.	£p	No.	£p
Cash Application	100	25·00	100	25·00	200	50·00
Balance in Profit and Loss ratio to make up total Ordinary Share Capital [to nearest whole number]	1,297	324·25	1,103	275·75	2,400	600·00
Total	1,397	£349·25	1,203	£300·75	2,600	£650·00

SUMMARY

	A		B		Total	
	£p	£p	£p	£p	£p	£p
Total Amount due . .		3,850·00		3,650·00		7,500·00
Allotments in £'s—						
Preference Shares .	3,501·00		3,349·00		6,850·00	
Ordinary Shares . .	349·25		300·75		650·00	
		3,850·25		3,649·75		7,500·00
Balance, settled in Cash .	[due from A]	£0·25	[due to B]	£0·25		—

With regard to the allotment of ordinary shares, the obviously practical method would be to allot (apart from the cash subscriptions):

A: 1,300 shares of £0·25 = £325 instead of 1,297 shares of £0·25 each
                       = £324·25

B: 1,100 shares of £0·25 = £275 instead of 1,103 shares of £0·25 each
                       = £275·75

This would entail a further payment by A to B for three 'extra' shares of £0·25 = £0·75, leaving a final adjustment of £1 in cash.

In the latter event, in order to preserve round numbers of shares, A would be allotted 3,500 instead of 3,501 preference shares, and B 3,350 instead of 3,349 preference shares, the division of shares being thus:

	A		B	
	No.	£	No.	£
Preference Shares	3,500	3,500	3,350	3,350
Ordinary Shares	1,400	350	1,200	300
Total		£3,850		£3,650

The above allocation will avoid any cash payment between A and B, as the former will receive one preference less than the allocation shown on p. 23208 instead of paying B £1.

Illustration 77

On 1st January 19.., A sells his business to Jones, Ltd., the latter taking over all assets and liabilities, the purchase consideration being £3,000 payable equally in cash and shares of £1 each fully paid. A sum of £500 on account has been paid to A during the year ended 31st December 19.., but no other entries have been made.

A's Balance Sheet, at the time of the sale, was as follows:

BALANCE SHEET AS AT 1ST JANUARY 19..

	£		£
Creditors	900	Sundry Fixed Assets	1,500
Capital	2,200	Debtors	1,400
		Stock	200
	£3,100		£3,100

Sundry Fixed Assets are to be revalued at £1,270.

In addition to the matters arising out of the above, there are the following balances in the books of Jones, Ltd., at 31st December 19..:

BALANCES

	£
Share Capital	5,000
A (Vendor)	1,700
Debtors	1,250
Sundry Fixed Assets	1,500
Stock	200
Purchases	4,800
Sales	5,300
Creditors	430
Cash in Bank	4,680

Prepare Trial Balance at 31st December 19...

TRIAL BALANCE

		£	£
Goodwill		1,030	
Share Capital			6,500
A (Vendor)	[1]		1,000
Debtors		1,250	
Sundry Fixed Assets		1,270	
Stock		200	
Purchases		4,800	
Sales			5,300
Creditors			430
Bank		4,680	
		£13,230	£13,230

[1] A is still a creditor for £1,000 to be paid in cash.

The necessary adjusting entries would be:

JOURNAL

19..		£	£
Jan. 1	Goodwill	1,030	
	Sundry Fixed Assets		230
	Vendor		800
	Being adjustment of accounts in accordance with purchase agreement dated ...., and revaluation of fixed assets.		
	Vendor	1,500	
	Share Capital		1,500
	Being allotment of 1,500 shares of £1 each fully paid to vendor, in part discharge of liability to him as per directors' resolution dated .... *vide* Minute Book, p.		

SECTION H. DIVISIBLE PROFITS AND FINAL ACCOUNTS

The existence of profits is a necessary factor before a dividend can be paid; in other words, there must be an excess of income over expenditure. The legal requirements (which differ considerably from the accounting requirements) may be summarized thus:

1. Subject to the undermentioned rules, the Articles must be adhered to, and in the absence of contrary restrictions the directors may make suitable reserves for contingencies and other proper purposes as laid down in Clause 117 of Table A (1948).

2. There is no need to provide for depreciation on FIXED assets, the authority therefor being contained in the judgement delivered in *Verner* v. *General Commercial Trust.* As a result, 'Fixed assets may be sunk and lost, and yet the excess of current receipts over current payments may be divided, but FLOATING or CIRCULATING capital must be maintained'.

Provision must be made, however, for the upkeep, that is, the depreciation, of FLOATING assets. (Articles may provide for depreciation of BOTH type of assets.)

Thus, broadly, divisible profits are the excess of current income over current appropriate expenses remaining after charging depreciation of floating assets.

3. The divisible profit of the current year is usually not to be reduced by losses incurred in the past, unless the directors decide otherwise; but regard must be had to the nature of the business, the amount and nature of the loss. (*Ammonia Soda Co.* v. *Chamberlain.*)

4. Goodwill for the purpose of determination of profits is a FIXED asset. (*Wilmer* v. *McNamara.*)

5. Profits arising from forfeited shares are available for dividends, unless the Articles FORBID (*Hilder* v. *Dexter*); unless the company has adopted the DOUBLE ACCOUNT System when these profits are irrevocably

'Capital', the distribution of which is, notwithstanding Articles, forbidden. (*Wall* v. *London and Provincial Trust.*)

6. Where goodwill (and probably any other FIXED asset) has been written-off, the amount, if reasonable, and if the proceeding is not contrary to the constitution of the company, may be recredited to Profit and Loss Account, unless it appears that the item has been irrevocably written-off. (*Stapley* v. *Read Bros.*)

7. Where a capital profit has accrued to the company, it is necessary, before such profit is available for dividend, that three conditions shall be fulfilled: (*a*) The profit must be REALIZED; (*b*) a surplus must exist after a REVALUATION of ALL assets; (*c*) there must be nothing in the Articles of the company forbidding such distribution. (In other words, the capital profit, when realized, must be used to write down all assets to their fair value, only the balance remaining being distributable.) These restrictions, however, only apply to CASH dividends, or other releases of ASSETS: a bonus Share dividend may be paid out of unrealized profits if the articles permit (*Foster* v. *New Trinidad Lake Asphalte Co.; Lubbock* v. *British Bank of South America*).

8. The profit in (7) is never available for dividend if it is on an 'original' asset (*Foster* v. *New Trinidad Lake Asphalte Co.*).

9. The requirements appertaining to item (7) do not apply to revenue profits (*City of Glasgow Bank* v. *McKinnon*), that is, they may be *unrealized*, and no surplus of assets may remain after revaluation.

10. Profit may be said to be the increase in net assets which has taken place during the period in question, due allowance being made for any capital introduced into or taken out of the business in the meanwhile (*re Spanish Prospecting Co.*).

11. Whenever the rights of third parties intervene, profit MUST be strictly ascertained, and in the absence of special stipulations *actual* profit is to be taken (*re Spanish Prospecting Co.*).

12. Preliminary expenses may be charged to capital, i.e. retained as a debit balance (*Bale* v. *Cleland*), and shown as such in the Balance Sheet, but the item *may* be written-off.

13. It was laid down in *re Crabtree* that *depreciation of* trade machinery must be provided for in ascertaining profit, but this case had reference to the claim of an executor of a partner against the surviving partners, and hence has no bearing on divisible profits of a *limited company*.

14. Profits, though accrued and earned, may still not be wholly available for, or divisible among, ordinary shareholders, because:

(*a*) The Articles may require an allocation of a proportion to reserve.

(*b*) A proportion may be payable to prior shareholders, including the payment of arrears of cumulative preference dividends or even to 'outside' parties, e.g. managers' commission, income bondholders.

(*c*) A proportion may have to be 'laid aside' during the currency of the debenture liability, thus tying up a certain amount of profits for several years; hence these profits are divisible eventually, but not immediately.

15. Profits from subsidiary companies must not be credited to Profit and Loss Account, unless the profit has been received by way of dividend,

nor need losses be debited thereto unless the holding company has become liable in law for the amount thereof. Profit of a subsidiary arising before acquisition must be credited by the holding company as a Capital Reserve.

16. A distinction must be made between:

(a) Trading profits.   (c) Divisible profits.
(b) Net profits.

Thus: (a) trading profits usually exclude the increments (less expenses) of a non-trading nature, e.g. capital profits, dividends from companies; but, on the other hand, allocations to reserve, taxation, and capital losses are excluded from the debit.

(b) Net profits will include all sources of income less all expenses for the current year, except taxation and other appropriations, e.g. sinking funds built up in connection with redemption of debentures.

(c) Divisible profits are net profits reduced by the appropriations above mentioned, less any *debit* balance of previous years if the directors so DECIDE, but usually not otherwise. (See (3), p. 23211.)

Where directors are entitled to remuneration based upon net profits, it is a matter of construction whether they are entitled to the proportion before or after charging up such remuneration; if 'before', it is strictly an appropriation; if 'after', a charge, e.g. if the profits are £11,000, the directors being entitled to 10 per cent thereof; if the construction of the agreement requires the remuneration to be on profits remaining after charging such remuneration, the amount is $\frac{1}{11} \times £11,000 = £1,000$ (leaving net profits 'after' £10,000), this being a *charge*. Otherwise, the directors are entitled to $\frac{1}{10} \times £11,000$, i.e. £1,100 (leaving £9,900), this being an *appropriation*. Where directors are entitled to a proportion of profits based upon DIVIDENDS, the usual practice is to show the amount payable to the directors thereunder as an appropriation.

Practice is fairly uniform in writing-off discount on debentures and preliminary expenses to the Profit and Loss Appropriation Account.

Such expenses are of a capital nature, incurred not so much in the course of earning profits as prior to and necessary for the earning of future profits.

The phrase 'profits available for dividends' is one often met with in practice, and its precise significance affects not only members but creditors, e.g. debenture holders where they are entitled to a proportion of 'profits available for dividends'. Such profits are not 'available' *merely* because a profit during the period has been earned (*re Long Acre Press*), because the directors are entitled: (1) to make suitable reserves; and (2) to write off past losses (though not always BOUND so to do).

The result may be to leave no profits 'available'.

17. A revaluation involving an increase of net assets may, subject to the Articles, be used to extinguish or reduce a debit balance to Profit and Loss (and so allow subsequent profits to be distributed). This procedure is one which is considered undesirable.

Capital Reserve. It is important to observe the circumstances which require the creation of a Capital Reserve. They are:

1. [Usually] profit prior to incorporation. (See p. 23170 *et seq.*).

2. The credit balance of Capital Reduction Account in a scheme of reduction of capital.

3. Capital profits:

  (*a*) Where there is a profit on realization of an *original* asset.

  (*b*) Where there is a profit on realization of a fixed asset, but no surplus remains on the revaluation of the other assets.

  (*c*) Where there is an *unrealized* accretion in the value of a fixed asset.

4. Capital profits, as mentioned hereunder, where the Articles *forbid* distribution by way of cash dividends:

  (*a*) Premiums on Debentures.

  (*b*) Profits on Forfeited Shares or Surrendered Shares.

  (*c*) Profit on Redemption of Debentures.

5. Under Sect. 58, Companies Act 1948, the heading of the account being Capital Redemption Reserve Fund. (See p. 23147.)

6. Share Premium Account.

7. The excess of net assets over purchase price on the acquisition of a business.[1]

As regards (4), notwithstanding any provisions in the Articles, the profits therein enumerated cannot be distributed if the company has adopted the **Double Account System** (*Wall* v. *London and Provincial Trust*).

Profit and Loss Appropriation Account. The Appropriation Account is the final section of the Profit and Loss Account to which is carried the balance from the main Profit and Loss Account, representing the profit or loss for the current year.

By its utilization, particularly necessary in the case of limited companies, items representing appropriations of, rather than charges against, profits are eliminated from the main Profit and Loss Account, enabling it to exhibit the true result of the year's operations.

The Appropriation Account will thus include the balance of Profit and Loss Account brought forward, the result of the current year's operations brought down, and all items representing appropriations of profit: transfer to reserve, dividends, amounts written-off goodwill, etc. Similarly, withdrawals from reserves and provisions no longer required should be credited to the Appropriation Account.

---

[1] If the value of the net assets taken over is discharged by the issue of shares of a lesser amount or value, the excess is often regarded as Share Premium, just as if the net assets taken over were cash subscriptions; e.g. if X, Ltd., issues 20,000 shares of £1 each fully paid at a premium of £0·25, the cash receivable will be £25,000, Share Capital being credited with £20,000 and Share Premium with £5,000.

If the company takes over the net assets (excluding goodwill) of £25,000 (say assets £30,000 *less* liabilities £5,000), the effect is similar to that in the preceding paragraph, the company acquiring the same amount of net assets (although differing in detail); viz. £25,000 for an issue of 20,000 shares of £1 each fully paid. (See also p. 2389.)

Illustration 78

Two typical Appropriation Accounts are appended.

Students should carefully compare them, as in practice there is very little uniformity of layout.

PROFIT AND LOSS APPROPRIATION ACCOUNT

(Previous Year) £		£	£	(Previous Year) £		£
—	Reserve for increased replacement costs		15,000	140,000	Balance brought forward from last year	120,000
50,000	General Reserve		25,000		Balance brought down from Profit and Loss Account	300,000
	Dividends (gross) for the year:			260,000		
	Paid:				Transfer from Dividend Reserve	20,000
	6% Preference Shares, half-year to	£		—	Provisions no longer required	10,000
50,000	30th June	50,000		—		
	Ordinary Stock, interim dividend 5%	40,000				
—			90,000			
	Proposed: 6% Preference Shares, half-year to					
50,000	31st Dec.	50,000				
130,000	Ordinary Stock, final dividend 25%	200,000				
			340,000			
120,000	Balance carried to Balance Sheet		70,000			
£400,000			£450,000	£400,000		£450,000

PROFIT AND LOSS APPROPRIATION ACCOUNT

	£	£	(Previous Year) £
Balance brought forward from last year		90,000	100,000
Net Profit for the year brought down		210,000	150,000
		300,000	£250,000
Less: Dividends (gross):			
Interim 10% (paid 30th June)	50,000		—
Final 20% (proposed)	100,000		100,000
	150,000		100,000
Appropriations recommended by the Directors:			
General Reserve	100,000		50,000
Staff Pension Fund	20,000		10,000
		270,000	£160,000
Balance carried to Balance Sheet		£30,000	£90,000

It should be noted that, although legally an appropriation of profits, Corporation Tax is often charged in the Profit and Loss Account and not in the Appropriation Account.

Agreements for additional remuneration by way of Share of Profits. A frequent form of remunerating responsible officials of a company is to give, in addition to a fixed salary, a share of profit. In order to define the position clearly, a written agreement should be drawn up between the parties providing for:

(*a*) Commencement and period of the agreement with special regard to the conditions of service, termination of service before the expiry of the fixed period, and the position arising from illness or death of the official.

(*b*) How and when the extra remuneration shall be paid.

(*c*) The precise basis of computing the extra remuneration, that is, the exact meaning of the word 'profit'.

The following points call for precise determination:

(i) Is the profit to be net trading profit or net profit (i.e. including all other forms of profit, e.g. dividends receivable) or net profit available for dividend, in which case the Directors could quite properly under Table A,[1] or where articles provided, make suitable allocations to reserve or against contingencies, or write off Discount on Debentures, Goodwill, etc., and choose not to regard the surplus as available for dividend until a past loss had been overtaken (*re Long Acre Press*); on the other hand the company might be under a contractual obligation to set aside a certain amount of profit each year toward building up a Sinking Fund for Debenture Redemption.

The profit might include transfers from Reserves, exceptional and non recurring gains, etc.

Furthermore, even where NET PROFIT is taken as the basis it would seem that *all* profit should be brought in, not only Revenue but Capital Profit (*re Spanish Prospecting Co.*).

(ii) In respect of depreciation, the question arises as to what asset is to be written down and how. Where, however, no specific reference is made it would seem that depreciation of fixed (probably excluding Goodwill) and wasting assets should be provided for on the fixed instalment method in preference to diminishing balance method which would throw a heavier burden in the early years of the life of the assets. (*Edwards* v. *Saunton Hotels.*)

(iii) Unless agreed otherwise, Corporation Tax (still regarded in law as an appropriation of profit) is not chargeable against net profit.

(iv) In the absence of clear agreement to the contrary, the extra remuneration is *not* to be charged against net profit for the purpose of arriving at such extra remuneration (*Edwards* v. *Saunton Hotels*); if, therefore, the extra remuneration is one tenth of net profit, it is exactly that, not one-eleventh as if the extra remuneration had to be charged in arriving at the net profit upon which the extra remuneration is based.

Managers' and Directors' Commissions. This type of problem is frequent in the examinations, and the following illustration should be worked through carefully.

[1] Companies Act 1948.

Illustration 79

You are appointed auditor of the A1 Trading Co., Ltd., and the following account is submitted to you:

PROFIT AND LOSS ACCOUNT FOR THE YEAR ENDED
31ST DECEMBER 19..

	£			£
Office and Administration Expenses	14,983	Balance from Trading Account	b/d	66,973
Travelling and Distribution Expenses	20,395	Dividends on Investments (gross)		4,983
Corporation Tax	4,260	Transfer Fees		274
Interest on Debentures (gross)	4,200			
Directors' Emoluments	4,000			
Preliminary Expenses	1,600			
Depreciation of Plant	3,400			
Transfer to Pension Fund	2,000			
Transfer to Debenture Redemption Fund	700			
Net Profit	16,692			
	£72,230			£72,230
				16,692

The Pension Fund is the property of the company, and the amounts allocated thereto at the discretion of the directors, but subject to the final approval of the shareholders.

The managing director's agreement entitles him to a commission of 5 per cent of the profits before charging his commission, but after charging directors' commission; and the Articles of Association provide for a commission payable to directors of $1\frac{1}{2}$ per cent on the maximum amount which could be distributed by way of dividends out of the net profit of the year.

Show the amount due to the directors and managing director respectively, showing in detail how the figures are arrived at.

The agreement should and probably will, define the term 'profits'. The term 'profits', in absence of definition in the agreement, will comprise all the sources of revenue, *less* proper charges incurred in earning the revenue. As the term used above is 'profits', not 'trading profits', all the credit items on the Profit and Loss Account will be included; if, however, the basis of commission was 'trading profits', the *gross* dividends will be excluded.

Subject to agreement: as appropriations of profits, preliminary expenses, pension fund contribution, debenture redemption fund transfer and taxation (*Johnstone* v. *Chestergate Hat Co.*) are added to the profit for the purpose of the managing director's commission, while depreciation, if (as is assumed) properly written-off on the 'straight line' method, is a charge.

Since the Articles themselves give the directors their commission, it would appear that this is additional remuneration, and so must be charged before arriving at 'profits', for the purpose of the managing director's commission.

Net profits available for dividend would appear to mean the amount available after charging the managing director's commission, and appropriating such profits as are necessary for meeting preliminary expenses and pension fund. The balance shown in the accounts is the maximum amount available for gross dividends.

The Profit and Loss Account must be adjusted as follows:

COMPUTATION OF PROFITS

		£
Balance per Accounts		16,692
Add Corporation Tax		4,260
,, Preliminary Expenses		1,600
,, Transfer to Pension Fund		2,000
,, ,, ,, Debenture Redemption Fund		700
		25,252
Deduct Directors' Commission (below) y		232
Profits		£25,020
Managing Director's Commission, 5% x		£1,251

COMPUTATION OF 'PROFITS AVAILABLE FOR DIVIDEND'

	£
Balance per Accounts	16,692
Deduct Managing Directors' Commission (as above) . . .	1,251
	£15,441
Directors' Commission, 1½% thereon	£232

It is assumed that the managing director's commission is not to be computed on the profits *after* charging his commission, and therefore the calculation is based upon the profits *before* such charge is made.

Calculation:

Let

x = Managing Director's Commission
y = Directors' Commission

Then

$$x = \frac{5}{100}\left\{25,252 - \frac{1\frac{1}{2}}{100}(16,692 - x)\right\}$$

$$= \frac{1}{20}\left\{25,252 - \left(\frac{50,076 - 3x}{200}\right)\right\}$$

$\therefore$

$$20x = 25,252 - \left(\frac{50,076 - 3x}{200}\right)$$

Hence,

$$x = \underline{\underline{£1,251}}$$

By substitution, y can now be computed:

$$y = \frac{1\frac{1}{2}}{100}(16,692 - x)$$

$$= \frac{3}{200}(16,692 - 1,251)$$

$$= \frac{3}{200}(15,441)$$

Hence,

$$y = \underline{\underline{£232}}$$

Notes. 1. If the managing director's commission is to be computed on the profits *after* charging both commissions, the calculation will be as shown in (i) below.

2. If the directors' commission is also to be computed on the profits *after* charging both commissions, the calculations will be as shown in (ii) below.

(i) Let x = Managing director's Commission in £'s

                       y = Directors' Commission in £'s

(a)
$$x = \frac{5}{100}(25{,}252 - x - y)$$

$$20x = 25{,}252 - x - y$$
$$21x = 25{,}252 - y$$
$$y = 25{,}252 - 21x$$

(b)
$$y = \frac{1\frac{1}{2}}{100}(16{,}692 - x - y)$$

$$= \frac{3}{200}(16{,}692 - x - y)$$

$$200y = 50{,}076 - 3x - 3y$$
$$203y = 50{,}076 - 3x$$

Substitute for y the foregoing figures in italics.

$$50{,}076 - 3x = 203(25{,}252 - 21x)$$
$$= 5{,}126{,}156 - 4{,}263x$$
$$4{,}260x = 5{,}076{,}080$$
$$x = \underline{\underline{£1{,}191 \cdot 57}}$$

Substituting £1,191·57 for x in (b):

(ii)
$$y = \frac{1\frac{1}{2}}{100}(16{,}692 - x - y)$$

$$= \frac{3}{200}(16{,}692 - 1{,}191 \cdot 57 - y)$$

$$y = \underline{\underline{£229 \cdot 07}}$$

[*Alternative to* (ii), *substituting* £1,191·57 *for* x *in the foregoing figures in italics in* (i) (a):

$$y = 25{,}252 - 21x$$
$$= 25{,}252 - 21 \times 1{,}191 \cdot 57$$
$$= 25{,}252 - 25{,}022 \cdot 97$$
$$y = \underline{\underline{£229 \cdot 03}}]$$

The £0·04 *difference arises by reason of the fact that* £1,191·57 *is to the nearest second decimal place, i.e. to the nearest new penny.*

The statements of commission are:

	£p	£p
Managing Director's Commission:		
Profits (as adjusted).		25,252·00
Less Managing Director's Commission (*x*). .	1,191·57	
Directors' Commission (y) . . .	229·07	
		1,420·64
		£23,831·36

5% thereon £1,191·57

	£p	£p
Directors' Commission		
Profits		16,692·00
Less Managing Director's Commission (x). . .	1,191·57	
Directors' Commission (y) . . .	229·07	
		1,420·64
		£15,271·36

1½ thereon = £229·07

Illustration 80

Components Ltd. employ a manager who is entitled to a commission of 10 per cent, in addition to a salary of £2,500 per annum, on 'the sum available for distribution arising in each year'.

The Profit and Loss Account for the Company's first year of trading (the year ended 31st March, 19.1) is as follows:

		£		£
General Expenses		4,582	By Gross Profit . . .	40,000
Staff Bonus		1,500	Investment Income	
Corporation Tax . . .		8,000	(including tax credit) . .	4,500
Depreciation		1,000	Deposit Interest (gross) . .	100
Manager's Salary . .	£2,500			
Manager's Commission . .	500			
		3,000		
Net Profit		26,518		
		£44,600		£44,600

Compute the Commission due to the Manager (who has no shares in the company) assuming that the agreement as to commission makes no further reference to the basis and manner of computation, except that his commission, but *not* his salary, is to be charged for the purpose of arriving at his commission.

Capital allowance is £600.

In the absence of further details in the agreement:

1. Depreciation should be computed on the 'straight line' method, sufficient to extinguish the assets or reduce them to estimated realizable value at the end of their effective life. (*Edwards* v. *Saunton Hotels.*) It is assumed that depreciation is on this basis.

2. Taxation is an appropriation of and not a charge against profits and will be added back to the net profit. (*Johnstone* v. *Chestergate Hat Manufacturing Co.*)

3. The manager will be entitled to one-eleventh of the profit as adjusted.

4. Included in the item for manager's salary and commission is £500 which it is assumed is a payment or credit on account of the commission due for the year ended 31st March 19.1.

5. The articles of association are assumed not to contain any restrictive definition of sums available for distribution.

6. The question of the treatment of previous years' losses does not arise as the business is in its first year.

Computation:

		£
Net Profit		26,518
Manager's Salary and Commission		3,000
Corporation Tax per accounts		8,000
		£37,518

$$\tfrac{1}{11} \times £37,518 = £3,411 \text{ (which is 10\% of £34,107)}$$

The sum now due, therefore, is £3,411 − £500 paid or credited on account = £2,911.

Illustration 81

Assuming the same facts, except that the commission is based on profit *before* charging such commission as well as salary, the commission will be 10 per cent of £37,518 = £3,752.

This is the correct basis as far as commission is concerned in the absence of an agreement to the contrary.

Illustration 82

Same facts as stated in Illustration 80, except that in addition to commission being charged (but not salary) Corporation Tax at 40 per cent is to be charged for the purpose of arriving at the profit on which the manager's commission is payable. It may be assumed that the general expenses are all admissible for tax purposes:

Let C = Commission; and T = Corporation Tax.
$C = \tfrac{1}{11}(37,518 - T)$ (see p. 23222).
$T = \tfrac{2}{5}(30,918 - C)$ (see p. 23222).

The computations for Commission and Corporation Tax are:

	Commission	Corporation Tax
	£	£
Net Profit	26,518	26,518
Manager's Commission paid (or credited)	500	500
Manager's Salary	2,500	—
Depreciation	—	1,000
Corporation Tax	8,000	8,000
	37,518	36,018
Less Taxed Dividends . . .		4,500
		31,518
Capital Allowances . . .		600
		30,918
Corporation Tax . . .	T	
Commission . . .		C
	£37,518 − T	£30,918 − C

[The deposit Interest computed on the basis of Case III, Sch. D, is included in arriving at the total Corporation Tax liability.]

$$C = \tfrac{1}{11}(37,518 - T)$$
$$C = \tfrac{1}{11}[37,518 - \tfrac{2}{5}(30,918 - C)]$$

$$11C = \left[37,518 - \left(\frac{61,836 - 2C}{5}\right) \right] \quad \text{or} \quad 11C = 37,518 - \frac{61,836 - 2C}{5}$$

$$
\begin{aligned}
55C &= 187,590 - 61,836 + 2C & &= 37,518 - 12,367\cdot2 + \tfrac{2}{5}C \\
55C &= 125,754 + 2C & &= 25,150\cdot8 + \tfrac{2}{5}C \\
53C &= 125,754 & 55C &= 125,754 + 2C \\
\therefore\ C &= £2,373 & 53C &= 125,754 \\
& & \therefore\ C &= £2,373
\end{aligned}
$$

Corporation Tax payable is—

	£
Profit, as adjusted	30,918
Less Manager's Commission . . .	2,373
	£28,545

Corporation Tax at 40% thereon = £11,418

Manager is, therefore, entitled to $\tfrac{1}{11}$ £(37,518 − 11,418)
$$= \tfrac{1}{11} \times £26,100$$
$$= £2,373 = 10\% \text{ of } £23,727^{*}$$

Manager receives 2,373 − £500 paid to him on account = £1,873

* The item of £23,727 is arrived at thus—

	£
Profit	37,518
Less Corporation Tax . . .	11,518
	26,100
Less Commission	2,373
	£23,727

If Corporation Tax were calculated—as the ascertainment of either Tax or Commission gives the figure for the other, there is no need to compute BOTH—the calculation is:

Let
then,
$$T = \text{Corporation Tax}$$
$$T = \tfrac{2}{5}(30,918 - C) \qquad C = \tfrac{1}{11}(37,518 - T)$$
$$5T = 61,836 - \tfrac{2}{11}(37,518 - T)$$
$$= 61,836 - 6,822 + \tfrac{2}{11}T$$
$$= 55,014 + \tfrac{2}{11}T$$
$$55T = 605,154 + 2T$$
$$53T = 605,154$$
$$\therefore\ T = £11,418$$

Payment of Interest on Construction Capital. In the ordinary course of affairs, no dividends may be paid unless such dividends are paid out of profits: interest on debentures (being a charge) is, however, payable whether profits are earned or not. Where a company raises share capital and out of the proceeds defrays the expenses of the construction of any works or buildings or provision of plant which cannot be made profitable for a lengthened period, the company may pay interest on so much of that share capital as is paid up for the period, and may charge to capital the sum so paid by way of interest, provided that the restrictions imposed by Sect. 65 of the Companies Act 1948, are complied with, viz:

Authority for the payment must be given by the Articles *or* by special resolution, *and* must, in addition, have been previously sanctioned by the Department of Trade, who shall determine the period, which in *no* case shall continue beyond the close of the half-year next after the half-year during which the works or buildings have been actually completed or plant provided.

The rate of interest shall in no case exceed 4 per cent per annum or such *other* rate as may for the time being be fixed by the order of the Treasury (such order being laid before both Houses of Parliament) and the payment shall not operate as a reduction of the amount paid up on the shares in respect of which it is paid.

The *accounts* of the company shall show the share capital *on* which, and the rate *at* which, interest has been paid out of capital during the period to which the accounts relate.

The above section is **not** confined to *new* companies, and in every case before sanctioning any such payment the Department of Trade may appoint a person to inquire into the circumstances and charge the expense of the inquiry to the company, which may be required to give security for the payment of the cost of the inquiry.

Illustration 83

The formalities completed and the Department of Trade sanction granted, a company pays on 6,000 shares of £1 each fully paid interest at 5 per cent per annum for one year. Show Journal entries, taking Income Tax at 40%.

JOURNAL

	£	£
Interest on Construction Capital	300	
Members (Interest on Construction Capital) .		300
Being interest on 6,000 shares of £1 each fully paid at 5% per annum, per articles, Department of Trade sanction, and directors' resolution dated .... *vide* Minute Book, p.		
Asset(s)[1].	300	
Interest on Construction Capital . . .		300
Being transfer to asset(s) of interest on construction capital.		
Members (Interest on Construction Capital) . .	300	
Cash		180
Income Tax		120
Being payment of interest due *less* tax.		

[1] Apportioned where necessary amongst the various fixed assets, based as far as possible on the actual capital employed in the construction of each particular fixed asset.

The interest so paid is 'capitalized', that is to say, it is treated as part of the cost of construction, being added thereto (similarly to the legal expenses of acquiring property or brokers' charges on purchasing invest-ments).

So far as income tax is concerned, the payment is not a capital payment, and income tax must be deducted in the ordinary way.

The same rule applies, *mutatis mutandis*, to interest to 'Construction Debentures', so that the company may adopt the same procedure if it decides to finance the construction by way of debentures in preference to shares. (*Hinds* v. *Buenos Ayres Tramways Co.*)

Table A. References have been made throughout to Table A, and as the matters contained therein are of extreme importance, the vital clauses, in so far as they relate to accounts, are summarized below (the clauses being those in the 1948 Act):

Clause 15. The Directors may from time to time make calls subject to there being not more than one call made in any calendar month: no call must exceed 25 per cent of the nominal value of the share: at least 14 days' notice of the call must be given.

Clause 18. If a call is not paid by the day appointed the person from whom it is due shall be liable to pay interest at 5 per cent per annum, but the Directors may waive payment of such interest wholly or in part.

Clause 20. The Directors may, on the issue of shares, differentiate between the holders as to the amount of calls to be paid and the times of payment.

Clause 21. If a call is paid in advance the directors may pay interest thereon, but the rate shall not exceed 5 per cent (6 per cent under the 1929 Act) without the consent of the Company in General Meeting.

Clause 33.
Clause 34. } The directors have power to forfeit shares for non-payment of calls by resolution after giving 14 days' notice of such intention.
Clause 35.

Clause 40. The Company may by Ordinary Resolution convert paid-up Shares into Stock, and reconvert Stock into paid-up Shares of any denomination.

Clause 44. The Company may by Ordinary Resolution increase the Share Capital.

Clause 45. The Company may by Ordinary Resolution:

(a) Consolidate and divide all or any of its Share Capital into Shares of larger amount.

(b) Subdivide all or any of its existing Shares into Shares of smaller amount, subject to the provisions of Sect. 61 (1) (d), Companies Act 1948.

(c) Cancel any Shares which, at the date of the resolution have not been taken or agreed to be taken by any person.

Clause 46. The Company may by Special Resolution reduce its Share Capital, any Capital Redemption Reserve Fund, or any Share Premium Account in any manner and with, and subject to, any incident authorized and consent required by law.

Clause 58. At any General Meeting a vote shall be decided by a show of hands: a poll may be demanded by the chairman or at least three members present in person or by proxy, or even by one, or two, if they represent not less than one-tenth of the total voting rights of all the members having a right to vote at the meeting or hold shares in the company conferring a right to vote at the meeting, being shares on which an aggregate sum has been paid up equal to not less than one-tenth of the total sum paid on all the shares conferring this right.

Clause 62. On a show of hands every member present in person shall have one vote. On a poll every member shall have one vote for each Share of which he is the holder.

Clause 76. The remuneration of the Directors, which shall be deemed to accrue from day to day, shall be determined by the Company in General Meeting [if none voted, no remuneration]. [By Clause 108 the Managing Director's remuneration shall be fixed by the Directors.]

Clause 77. No share qualification is required unless fixed by the Company in General Meeting.

Clause 79. The amounts borrowed, for the Company's business, by the Directors (other than capital and temporary overdrafts) shall at no time exceed the nominal amount of the issued Share Capital of the Company without the sanction of the Company in General Meeting.

Clause 114. The Company in General Meeting may declare dividends, but no dividend shall exceed the amount recommended by the Directors.

Clause 115. The Directors may from time to time pay to the members such interim dividends as appear to the Directors to be justified by the profits of the Company.

Clause 116. No dividend shall be paid otherwise than out of profits.

Clause 117. The Directors may set aside out of profits any reserves they think proper.

Clause 118.[1] Subject to the rights of persons, if any, entitled to shares with special rights, all dividends shall be payable on the amounts PAID UP [according to the dates paid unless the terms of issue provide for shares to rank for dividend from a particular date] on the shares (Calls in Advance *whilst bearing interest* do not rank for dividend).

Illustration 84

The following facts are ascertained from the books of Prosperity, Ltd.:

The ordinary shares had been issued at a premium of £0·20 on 31st May 19.. 20,000 preference shares had been redeemed at par out of profits on 30th June 19.. and the half-year's dividend on the preference shares had been paid to that date, and an interim of 2 per cent actual on the ordinary shares had been declared and paid on 25th December 19...
On 20th December, 1,200 shares were forfeited for failure to pay calls (due on 30th June) of £0·50 a share, and 200 were reissued as fully paid for £0·75 a share on the same day as the forfeiture.

A member holding 800 ordinary shares with calls in arrear of £0·50 a share had been charged and had paid interest for the half-year to 31st December 19.., in accordance with the rate chargeable under Table A (which the company had adopted).

The investments of which £40,000 were listed on a recognized Stock Exchange were revalued at the previous 31st December and taken in the Balance Sheet at £45,000.

The debentures had been issued in 1st January 19.., at a discount of 10 per cent, and on 30th June 19.., £20,000 were redeemed at par out of current profits and cancelled. Interest on debentures had been paid to 30th June 19... All the shares were £1 shares. The preference shares are fully paid and the Directors proposed to pay the half-year's dividend thereon to 31st December.

In addition to the accounts arising out of the above, the following balance; are extracted from the books of the Company on 31st December 19..:

	£		£
6% Debentures	34,000	Profit and Loss (*Cr.*)	29,000
Plant and Machinery	38,000	Gross Profit (from Trading	
Stock at 31st December 19..	28,675	Account)	60,000
Debtors	115,000	General Expenses	62,000
Investments at Cost	50,000	Debenture Interest	1,800
Creditors	49,000	Ordinary Share Capital fully	
Dividend Received	2,600	paid	50,000
Bank (*Dr.*)	9,863	7% Redeemable Preference	
		Share Capital fully paid	50,000

---

[1] If this clause has been eliminated by the Articles and no other provision has been made, dividends will be payable on the NOMINAL value.

No entries have been made in reference to the shares forfeited and reissued.

The investments at 31st December 19.., were revalued at £49,200, and are to be taken in the Balance Sheet at that figure.

No Debenture Redemption Fund has been created.

The Profit and Loss balance is the balance of the preceding year's profit, after the adjustment required for the redemption of the preference shares, and the balance standing to the credit of Preference Share Capital Account is that after the redemption mentioned in the question has been carried out.

£3,000 had been debited to the Trading Account in respect of depreciation for the year. The Plant and Machinery Account balance of £38,000 is the written-down value. Depreciation provided prior to the current year amounts to £5,000.

Prepare Profit and Loss Account and Balance Sheet in respect of the year to 31st December 19... Ignore Tax.

[It is advisable to draw up a Trial Balance.]

The Trial Balance at 31st December 19.., is:

TRIAL BALANCE

	£	£
Ledger Accounts as shown		
6% Debentures		34,000
Plant and Machinery	38,000	
Stock-in-trade	28,675	
Debtors	115,000	
Investments (*see h below*)	50,000	
Bank	9,863	
Creditors		49,000
Dividends Received		2,600
Debenture Interest	1,800	
Profit and Loss Account		29,000
Gross Profit		60,000
General Expenses	62,000	
Ordinary Share Capital (*see j below*)		50,000
7% Redeemable Preference Share Capital	•	50,000
	305,338	274,600
*Balances **not** shown in Ledger Accounts presented*		
(*a*) Dividends: Preference	2,450	
(*b*) ,, Ordinary	972	
(*c*) Capital Redemption Reserve Fund		20,000
(*d*) Premium on Shares Forfeited		50
(*e*) Share Premium		10,000
(*f*) Calls in Arrear	400	
(*g*) Interest on Calls in Arrear		10
(*h*) Investment Provision		5,000
(*i*) Forfeited Shares		500
(*j*) Ordinary Share Capital, Shares Forfeited	1,000	
	£310,160	£310,160

Adjustments must be made in respect of: (*a*) investment provision; (*b*) debenture interest accrued; (*c*) debenture discount, for the preparation of the Profit and Loss Account, as follows:

JOURNAL

	£	£
(a) Investment Provision	4,200	
Profit and Loss Appropriation Account . .		4,200
[Bring provision back to £800.]		
(b) Debenture Interest	1,200	
Sundry Debenture Holders . . .		1,200
[Interest at 6% per annum on £40,000 debentures, for half-year ended 31st December, 19..]		
(c) Debenture Discount	6,000	
6% Debentures		6,000
[Adjustment of omission of entry to Debenture Discount Account.]		

The bank balance (£9,863) is not affected by any of the adjustments, being the correct figure, all bank entries having been made.

The debentures originally issued were £60,000 and the discount thereon £6,000; as £20,000 have been redeemed the debentures outstanding are £40,000, so that a transfer is required as in (c) above. The non-record of the debenture discount does not disturb the *agreement* of the Trial Balance.

The items not shown in the Ledger Accounts presented are arrived at as follows:

(a) *Dividend on Preference Shares.*

7% for half-year on £70,000 = £2,450.

(b) *Dividend on Ordinary Shares.* This is computed on paid-up capital—as the company has adopted Table A—of 49,000 shares, i.e. 50,000 less 1,000.

	£
2% on 48,200 Ordinary Shares of £1 each fully paid =	964
2% on 800 Ordinary Shares of £1 each £0·50 paid =	8
	£972

[If the 1,200 shares had been forfeited *after* the payment of the dividend, the latter would have been £980, arrived at as follows:

	£
2% on 48,000 Ordinary Shares of £1 each *fully* paid =	960
2% on 2,000 Ordinary Shares of £1 each £0·50 paid =	20
	£980

If the 200 shares out of the 1,200 forfeited *before* the payment of the dividend had not been reissued until *after* the payment of the dividend, the latter would have been £968, arrived at as follows:

	£
2% on 48,000 Ordinary Shares of £1 each *fully* paid =	960
2% on 800 Ordinary Shares of £1 each £0·50 paid =	8
	£968]

(c) *Capital Redemption Reserve Fund.* This represents the profits applied in the redemption of redeemable preference shares.

(d) *Premium on Share Forfeited.*

(e) *Share Premium Account.*

(f) *Calls in Arrear.*

(i) *Forfeited Shares.*

(j) *Ordinary Share Capital.*

(Accounts in explanation of (d), (e), (f), (i), and (j) are appended.)

ORDINARY SHARE CAPITAL

19..			£	19..			£
Dec. 20	Forfeited Shares Account	c/d	1,200	June 30	Balance	b/d	50,000
31	Balance		49,000	Dec. 20	Forfeited Shares reissued		200
			£50,200				£50,200
				19..			
				Jan. 1	Balance	b/d	49,000

SHARE PREMIUM

19..			£	19..			£
Dec. 31	Balance	c/d	10,000	June 30	Cash		10,000
			£10,000				£10,000
				19..			
				Jan. 1	Balance	b/d	10,000

CALLS

19..		£	19..			£
June 30	Ordinary Share Capital Account	25,000	June 30	Cash		24,000
				Calls in Arrear Account		1,000
		£25,000				£25,000

CALLS IN ARREAR

19..			£	19..			£
June 30	Calls Account		1,000	Dec. 20	Forfeited Shares Account		600
				,, 31	Balance	c/d	400
			£1,000				£1,000
19..							
Jan. 1	Balance	b/d	400				

FORFEITED SHARES

19..			£	19..			£
Dec. 20	Calls in Arrear Account		600	Dec. 20	Ordinary Share Capital Account		1,200
	Ordinary Share Capital Account		200		Cash		150
	Premium on Shares Forfeited Account		50				
31	Balance	c/d	500				
			£1,350				£1,350
				19..			
				Jan. 1	Balance	b/d	500

PREMIUM ON SHARES FORFEITED

				19.. Dec. 20	Forfeited Shares Account		£ 50

(g) *Interest on Calls in Arrear.*
   5% for half-year on £400 = £10.
(h) *Investment Provision.* It is clear that there must be a provision of £5,000 in the books offsetting the item of £50,000 investments AT COST. An adjustment of £4,200 is required. (See Journal entry (a), p. 23227.)

PROFIT AND LOSS ACCOUNT FOR THE YEAR ENDED
31ST DECEMBER 19..

		£			£
General Expenses		62,000	Gross Profit . . . b/d		63,000*
Balance . . . . c/d		1,000			
		£63,000			£63,000
Depreciation .		3,000	Balance† . . . b/d		1,000
Directors' Emoluments		?	Dividends Received .		2,600
Debenture Interest[1] .		3,000	Interest on Calls in Arrear		10
			Balance . . . c/d		2,390
		£6,000			£6,000
Balance, being Loss for the year b/d		2,390	Investment Provision no longer		
Capital Redemption Reserve Fund[2] .		20,000	required . . .		4,200
Dividends:			Balance from previous year[2] .		49,000
Paid					
Preference, half-year to 30th June .		2,450			
Ordinary Interim 2% actual Proposed:		972			
Preference, half-year to 31st December		1,750			
Balance carried to Balance Sheet .		25,638			
		£53,200			£53,200

---

* Per question £60,000 plus Depreciation £3,000.
† The published account would start with this balance.
[1] The item of £3,000 Debenture Interest is computed as follows:

	£
Debenture Interest on £60,000 @ 6% per annum for half-year to 30th June 19..	1,800
Debenture Interest on £40,000 @ 6% per annum for half-year to 31st December 19..	1,200
	£3,000

[2] The balance forward *before* transfer to Capital Redemption Reserve Fund of £20,000 must have been £49,000. The items in italics account for item of £29,000 in the Trial Balance.

See p. 23231 for Balance Sheet.

Illustration 85

The authorized capital of Sellers, Ltd., is £500,000, consisting of 25,000 cumulative preference shares of £1 each and 250,000 ordinary shares of £1 each. The balances appearing in the books on 31st December 19.2, were as shown on p. 23230.

DEBITS

	£
Investments in U.K. Subsidiary Company at Cost—Ordinary Shares £20,000, Debentures £20,000	40,000
Purchases	501,150
Packing Wages	25,000
Stock at 1st January 19.2	160,500
Delivery Expenses	43,330
Charges Paid against Consignments Unsold	1,750
Salaries, Travelling Expenses, and Commission	69,750
Rent, Rates, and General Expenses	34,500
Bad Debts written off	250
Freight and Carriage Inwards	2,500
Bills Paid against Consignments not finally dealt with	60,000
Preference Dividend: Half-year to 30th June 19.2, gross, paid 10th July	6,000
Commission on Issue of Debentures: Balance as on 1st January, 19.2	2,500
Balance at Bankers	65,000
Bills Receivable	3,750
Debenture Interest: Half-year to 30th June 19.2, gross, paid 10th July	5,600
Trade Debtors	55,000
Freehold Property at Cost	426,250
Furniture, Fixtures, and Fittings at Cost *less* Depreciation (£10,000)	50,000

CREDITS

	£
Corporation Tax (agreed liability year ended 31/12/19.1)	35,000
Sales	792,000
Sales *ex* Consignments not finally dealt with	52,000
Dividends and Interest received, gross on 31st July—	
Ordinary Shares	2,400
Debentures	1,600
Profit and Loss Account	35,000
General Reserve (Revenue)	55,150
Shares Issued—	
6% Preference (200,000)	200,000
Ordinary (200,000, £0·75 called up)	150,000
8% First Mortgage Debentures, secured on Freehold Properties	140,000
Sundry Consignors: Balances on Account Sales	20,000
Subsidiary Company: Current Account	2,000
Trade Creditors	61,680
Commission on Sales *ex* Consignments	6,000

[*Note.* Ignore Tax on Dividends.]

Prepare Trading and Profit and Loss Account for the year ended 31st December 19.2, and Balance Sheet as on that date, after taking into account the following:

(*a*) The value of the stock on 31st December 19.2, was £155,000 and, in addition, there were stocks unsold in store ex sundry consignments invoiced *pro forma* at £20,000.

(*b*) The directors are entitled to £4,000 per annum remuneration; directors' fees of £1,000 were paid by the subsidiary company and, in addition, the managing director was paid the sum of £500 due under his employment agreement with that company.

(*c*) Bills receivable for £1,500, maturing after 31st December 19.2, had been discounted with the bank.

(*d*) Rent of warehouse at £1,000 a year had been paid for the half-year

PROSPERITY LIMITED

Balance Sheet as at 31st December 19..

	£	£	£		£	£	£
Capital and Surplus—				**Fixed Assets—**			
Share Capital:				Plant and Machinery at cost		46,000	
Authorized	?			Less Accumulated Depreciation		8,000	38,000
Issued:							
50,000 7% Redeemable Preference Shares of £1 each, fully paid (? earliest and latest date of redemption and whether must be redeemed in any event or at the option of the company and the amount (if any) of the premium payable on redemption)		50,000		**Current Assets—**			
				Stock-in-Trade		28,675	
				Debtors		115,000	
49,000 Ordinary Shares of £1 each	49,000			Investments at Cost:			
Less Calls in Arrear	400	48,600		Quoted (Market Value ?)	£40,000	50,000	
			98,600	Unquoted	10,000		
				Cash at Bank		9,863	203,538
Capital Reserves:[1]				Debenture Discount[3]			6,000
Capital Redemption Reserve Fund	20,000						
Share Premium Account	10,000						
Forfeited Shares[2]	500						
Premium on Forfeited Shares[3]	50	30,550					
Profit and Loss Account		25,638					
			154,788				
6% Debentures (? secured)			40,000				
Provision—							
Depreciation of Investments			800				
Current Liabilities—				} Directors.			
Trade Creditors	49,000						
Debenture Interest	1,200						
Proposed Preference Dividend	1,750		51,950				
			£247,538				**£247,538**

[1] Capital and revenue reserves need no longer be distinguished it may, however, still be helpful to distinguish the two kinds of reserve.

[2] 1,000 shares at £0·50 [i.e. application and allotment, excluding premium].

[3] The Premium on Shares Forfeited Account may be transferred to reserve or utilized to write off debenture discount.

[4] It would be advisable to write off a proportion of the debenture discount as one-third of the debentures have been redeemed.

SELLERS LIMITED

BALANCE SHEET AS AT 31ST DECEMBER 19.2

	£	£	£
Capital and Surplus—			
Share Capital:			
Authorized:			
250,000 6% Cumulative Preference Shares of £1 each		250,000	
250,000 Ordinary Shares of £1 each		250,000	
		£500,000	
Issued:			
200,000 6% Cumulative Preference Shares of £1 each, fully paid	200,000		
200,000 Ordinary Shares of £1 each £0·75 paid	150,000		
		350,000	
Revenue Reserves:			
General	55,150		
Profit and Loss Account	55,970		
		111,120	
			461,120
8% First Mortgage Debentures			140,000
Corporation Tax—Accounting Year ended 31st December 19.2			43,150
Current Liabilities—			
Trade Creditors		61,680	
Sundry Consignors:	£		
Balances on Account Sales	20,000		
Resales made (see note 4)	52,000	72,000	
Directors' Fees		4,000	
Rent accrued		500	
Debenture Interest (secured)		5,600	
Subsidiary Company on Current Account		2,000	
Corporation Tax—Accounting Year ended 31st December 19.1		35,000	
Proposed Preference Dividend (gross)		6,000	
Proposed Ordinary Dividend (gross)		20,000	
			206,780
Note. There is a contingent liability in respect of Bills discounted of £1,500.			
			£851,050

	£	£
Fixed Assets—		
Freehold Property at cost	60,000	426,250
Furniture, Fixtures, and Fittings at cost	15,000	45,000
Less Accumulated Depreciation		
		471,250
Investment in and Amount owing by Subsidiary—		
Shares at cost	20,000	
Debentures at cost	20,000	
		40,000
Current Assets—		
Stock	155,000	
Trade Debtors, *less* Provision (£2,750)	52,250	
Charges Paid against Consignments unsold	1,750	
Bills met against Consignments (see note 4)	60,000	
Rates Paid in Advance	800	
Bills Receivable	3,750	
Balance at Bankers	65,000	
		338,550
Commission on Issue of Debentures—		
Balance 1st January 19.2	2,500	
Less written-off during year	1,250	
		1,250
		£851,050

} Directors.

Notes:

1. Much of the detail shown under Current Assets and Liabilities would not be published.
2. Corresponding 19.1 figures are required in the published accounts.
3. Since there is a subsidiary company, group accounts will be required (see next chapter).
4. Part of these items could probably be set off against each other.

to 30th June 19.2; and rates amounting to £1,600 for half-year to 31st March 19.3, had been paid on 30th November 19.2.

(e) A provision of 5 per cent of trade debtors is to be created for bad and doubtful debts.

(f) Depreciation of furniture, fixtures, and fittings is to be provided for at 10 per cent on the written-down value.

(g) Corporation Tax of £43,150 is to be provided on the 19.2 profits.

(h) £1,250 is to be written-off Commission on Issue of Debentures Account.

(i) Provision is to be made for the half-year's dividend to 31st December 19.2, on the preference shares and for a first and final ordinary dividend of 10 per cent. The Articles are silent concerning payments of dividends but the appropriate provisions of Table A have been excluded.

TRADING AND PROFIT AND LOSS ACCOUNT FOR THE
YEAR ENDED 31ST DECEMBER 19.2..

	£		£
Stock, 1st January 19.2.	160,500	Sales	792,000
Purchases	501,150	Stock, 31st December 19.2.	155,000
Freight and Carriage Inward	2,500		
Gross Profit c/d	282,850		
	£947,000		£947,000
Rent, Rates, and General Expenses[1]	34,200	Gross Profit b/d	282,850
Packing Wages	25,000	Commission on Sales ex Consign-	
Delivery Expenses	43,330	ments	6,000
Salaries, Travelling Expenses, and Commission	69,750		
Bad Debts	3,000		
Balance c/d	113,570		
	£288,850		£288,850
Debenture Interest	11,200	Balance[4] b/d	113,570
Directors' Emoluments[2]	4,000	Franked Investment Income	
Depreciation	5,000	Unquoted Investment	2,400
Corporation Tax on current profits	43,150	Debenture Interest from Subsidiary company	1,600
Balance c/d	54,220		
	£117,570		£117,570
Commission on Issue of Debentures	1,250	Balance, 1st January 19.2	35,000
Preference Dividends: Paid £6,000 Proposed 6,000	12,000	Net Profit for the year b/d	54,220
Proposed Ordinary Dividend[3] 20,000	32,000		
Balance carried to Balance Sheet	55,970		
	£89,220		£89,220

[1] £34,500 per Trial Balance plus Rent accruing £500, less Rates in advance £800.
[2] A note will be required on the following lines:
In addition to the amount shown above, £1,500 was paid by a subsidiary company. In the published account further details would be required concerning directors' remuneration.
[3] Because the Articles are silent and the appropriate provisions of Table A have been excluded, the proposed ordinary dividend is computed on the basis of the nominal value of the issued ordinary share capital (see p. 23225).
[4] The published account would start with this balance.

Illustration 86

Included in the Trial Balance of a company at 31st December 19.2, were the following items:

7% Preference Share Capital, £1 fully paid	60,000
Ordinary Share Capital, £1 called	30,000
Debenture Interest, half-year to 30th June 19.2, gross (paid 4th July)	3,150
Preference Dividend, half-year to 30th June 19.2, (paid 4th July)	2,100
Calls in arrear (Ordinary shares: 600 at £0·25)	150
Provision for Corporation Tax (on previous year's profits)	12,000
Income Tax Account—debit	70
7% Debentures	90,000
Dividend received 24th December from trade investment in I.M. Backing (Britain) Ltd., including imputed tax credit	550
Loan interest received 6th December, gross	175
Net Profit	26,651
Profit and Loss Account—Balance at 1st January 19.2—credit	2,642
ACT[1]—(£1,400 Pref. Div.; £220 Trade Div.)	1,620

Included in the matters requiring consideration in the preparation of the final accounts were:

(a) Debenture Interest for the half-year to 31st December had not been paid.

(b) Preference Dividend for the half-year to 31st December is to be provided for.

(c) Ordinary Dividend of 10 per cent for the year on the paid-up ordinary share capital is to be recommended.

(d) Estimated Corporation Tax on the current year's profits is £13,400.

The provision appearing in the Trial Balance is the exact amount required to meet the Corporation Tax liability payable on the following day (1st January).

Assuming Income Tax at 40 per cent, prepare the Profit and Loss Appropriation Account for the year, making such adjustments as you consider necessary.

[1] Advance Corporation Tax.

PROFIT AND LOSS APPROPRIATION ACCOUNT
FOR THE YEAR ENDED 31ST DECEMBER 19.2

	£		£
Debenture Interest (gross)	6,300	Profit b/d	26,651
Net Profit for the year c/d	21,076	Investment Income—	
		Trade (including Tax Credit)	550
		Loan Interest (gross)	175
	£27,376		£27,376
Taxation—			
(1) Corporation Tax £13,400		Balance b/f	2,642
(2) On Franked Investment		Net Profit for the year b/d	21,076
Income 220			
	13,620		
Preference dividend paid			
for half-year to 30th June 19.2	2,100		
Proposed Dividends—			
Preference Dividend for the			
half-year to date	2,100		
Ordinary dividend of 10% for			
the year to date	2,985		
Balance c/f	2,913		
	£23,718		£23,718

Notes. 1. On 4th July the preference dividend of £2,100 for the half-year to 30th June 19.2 was paid and the ACT due of £1,400 would have been remitted to the Collector of Taxes on 14th October 19.2 (i.e. payment fell within return period three months ended 30th September 19.2). Similarly the half-year's net debenture interest of £1,890 was paid on 4th July and the Income Tax due under S.54 Income and Corporation Taxes Act 1970 of £1,260 would also have been remitted on 14th October 19.2.

In respect of the dividends proposed the amounts payable have been shown and these amounts would be similarly shown in the Balance Sheet under Current Liabilities. Liability to ACT arises only when a dividend is paid, and the amount thereof would appear as a separate current liability. A similar sum would either appear as a deferred asset or be deducted from Deferred Tax Account (if there is one). The debenture interest for the half year to 31st December 19.2, is at 31st December DUE and PAYABLE in which case there is a current liability of £1,890 net to Debenture holders and £1,260 Income Tax to the Inland Revenue.

The debit balance on Income Tax Account is the £70 suffered on the loan interest received which though in a different return period may be carried forward for set-off against the Income Tax of £1,260 due to be retained on payment of debenture interest for the half-year to 31st December, and therefore the Income Tax S.54 liability is £1,260 less £70 = £1,190 which will be included under Current Liabilities in the Balance Sheet. In the case of published accounts, the £1,190 would not require to appear separately but could be included with sundry creditors.

The Tax Credit of £220 on the Franked Investment Income, i.e. the dividend received from I.M. Backing (Britain) Ltd. is shown in the Profit and Loss Appropriation Account

2. It will be seen that the provision for taxation in the Balance Sheet at 31st December 19.2, will appear as follows:

(a) A current liability of £12,000 in respect of the accounting year ended 31st December 19.1, and payable the following day 1st January 19.3; and

(b) A provision for Corporation Tax on the profits of the accounting year ended 31st December 19.2, estimated at £13,400 and payable on 1st January 19.4. The provision would be shown as a separate item in the balance sheet immediately above Current Liabilities showing date due for payment.

(c) A current liability of £3,390 for ACT on proposed dividends.

(d) A deferred asset of ACT recoverable of £4,790 (i.e. £3,390 + ACT on Preference Dividend paid £1,400).

3. The ordinary dividend is 10 per cent on the paid-up capital, i.e. £30,000 called *less* £150 calls in arrear.

Published Accounts. The annual accounts sent to the members and debenture-holders of a company will usually consist of:

(a) Profit and Loss Account (and Appropriation Account);
(b) Balance Sheet;
(c) Auditors' Report;
(d) Directors' Report.

Usually, the notice convening the Annual General Meeting is sent with the accounts and in most cases a copy of the Chairman's Speech or Statement is attached.

No two sets of accounts are exactly alike, and the student should take every opportunity of studying the published accounts of public companies.

Illustration 87

The following is the Trial Balance at the end of the sixth financial year of a purely hypothetical company, Furnico Ltd., together with additional notes necessary for the preparation of final accounts. A set of accounts are prepared in vertical form suitable for publication, complying with the requirements of the Companies Acts 1948 to 1976. An unqualified Report of the Auditors and a Report of the Directors are appended. Both these reports have been framed to accord with the requirements of the Companies Acts, and in the case of the Report of the Directors certain information has been assumed merely for illustrative purposes. Income Tax, where appropriate, has been calculated at 40%.

A notice convening the Annual General Meeting of Furnico Ltd. precedes the final accounts, as is common practice today.

Furnico Ltd., a company registered in England, manufactures and deals in household furniture and has an Authorized Capital of £800,000 divided into 400,000 8 per cent preference shares and 400,000 ordinary shares, all of £1 each.

The Trial Balance at 31st December 19.2, was as follows:

	£	£
Investments at cost:		
200,000 Ordinary shares of £0·25 each in a subsidiary company (Plenishings Ltd.), fully paid	50,000	
25,000 6% Debentures in the subsidiary company	25,000	
25,000 Ordinary shares of £1 each £0·75 paid, in an associated company (Furni-Units Ltd.)	18,750	
Freehold Land and Buildings at cost	230,000	
Leasehold Land and Buildings at cost	280,000	
Goodwill at cost	15,000	
Plant and Machinery at cost	150,000	
Preliminary Expenses	2,000	
Ground Rent, half-year to 30th June 19.2, paid 4th July 19.2 (gross)	2,000	
Debenture Interest, half-year to 30th June 19.2, paid 6th July 19.2 (gross)	2,400	
Preference Dividend, half-year to 30th June 19.2, paid 21st July 19.2	12,000	
Subsidiary Company's Current Account	500	
Balance at Bank	20,100	
Discount on Debentures	4,000	
Advertising Account	6,000	
Trade Debtors	50,000	
Administration Salaries	26,500	
Auditors' Remuneration	1,500	
Selling Expenses	18,500	
General Expenses	4,000	
Corporation Tax Account		14,500
Stock in Hand	80,000	
Depreciation Provisions—		
Leasehold Property		60,000
Plant and Machinery		30,000
6% First Mortgage Debentures		80,000
Trade Creditors		37,800
Issued Share Capital—		
300,000 8% Preference shares of £1 each, fully paid		300,000
300,000 Ordinary shares of £1 each, fully paid		300,000
General Reserve		15,000
Profit and Loss Account—balance as at 1st January 19.2		15,000
Trading Account (balance)		150,050
Debenture Interest received 6th December 19.2 from subsidiary company (gross)		1,500
Investment Income received 3rd March, 19.2 (including Tax Credit)		5,000
Income Tax Account	600	
Advance Corporation Tax (ACT)	10,000	
	£1,008,850	£1,008,850

The following matters are to be taken into account:

(a) The amount shown against Salaries includes remuneration in respect of two of Furnico Ltd's three directors, viz., £4,500 for Chairman's salary, and £4,750 for fees of one other director who also received £200 as director's fees from the subsidiary company. The third director is entitled to fees amounting to £1,500, but he has waived his rights thereto.

(b) A provision of 2 per cent of Trade Debtors is to be made for Doubtful Debts.

(c) Depreciation Provisions are to be increased as follows:

Leasehold Property	£5,600
Plant and Machinery	£6,000

The company's Leasehold Land and Buildings comprise:

Long leases	£210,000	
Short leases	70,000	
		£280,000

The company's Freehold and Leasehold Land and Buildings were professionally valued on 20th December 19.2, at £650,000.

(d) The balance on Corporation Tax Account represents the amount provided in respect of the profits for the accounting year ended 31st December 19.1. The liability for that year has now been agreed at £15,000, and £16,000 is to be provided for Corporation Tax on the current year's profits.

(e) Provision is to be made for the half-year's dividends to 31st December on the Preference shares, and for a first and final ordinary dividend of 10 per cent. Related ACT to be taken into account.

(f) One-half of Preliminary Expenses is to be written-off.

(g) The company's Stock in Hand has been valued by the officials of the company at the lower of cost and net realizable value. This has been usual practice of the company in valuing stock over a number of years.

(h) The turnover of Furnico Ltd. for 19.2 was £475,500 in respect of furniture sales, and excludes inter-company sales. Products to the value of £158,000 were exported during 19.2 to various overseas countries.

(i) The 6 per cent First Mortgage Debentures are payable at par on 31st December 19.9. These debentures were issued at a discount of 5 per cent.

(j) The debit balance on the Advertising Account represents expenditure on a special long-term advertising campaign.

(k) General Expenses comprises:

	£
Pension paid to former director	1,000
Auditors' taxation fee	220
Auditors' travelling expenses	80
Sundries	2,700
	£4,000

(l) Plenishings Ltd., the subsidiary company of Furnico Ltd., was incorporated in Scotland. Plenishings Ltd. has issued 300,000 shares of £0·25 each of the same class as those held by Furnico Ltd. For some years past, Plenishings Ltd. have been unable to pay a dividend.

(m) Investment income, £5,000, is derived from a dividend of 12% + Tax Credit received in respect of the company's holdings of 25,000 Ordinary Shares of £1 each (£0·75 paid) in its associated company Furni-units Ltd. The Articles of Association of Furni-Units Ltd. provides that dividends are payable in proportion to the nominal value of the shares.

(n) Furni-Units Ltd. is a company registered in Scotland associated with Furnico Ltd. Furni-Units Ltd. has issued 100,000 Ordinary Shares of £1 each and these shares are not quoted on any Stock Exchange. On the basis of the last audited accounts of Furni-Units Ltd., the Profit and Loss Account balance is £18,000 of which £10,000 was accumulated since Furnico Ltd. acquired its investment in Furni-Units Ltd.

From the accounts of Furni-Units Ltd. sent to Furnico Ltd. during 19.2 it has been ascertained that Furnico Ltd.'s share of the profits of Furni-Units Ltd. for 19.2 is £14,500 before tax and £8,000 after tax.

Furnico Ltd does not hold any other class of shares in Furni-Units Ltd.

(o) ACT companies:

—Paid on Preference Dividend to 30th June 19.2	£8,000
—on Franked Investment Income from Furni-Units	£2,000
	£10,000

N.B. The £8,000 is recoverable from the Corporation Tax due for year to 31st December 19.1.

FURNICO LTD.
NOTICE CONVENING
THE ANNUAL GENERAL MEETING 19.3

Notice is hereby given that the sixth Annual General Meeting of the members of the Company will be held on Thursday, 24th April 19.3 at 3.0 p.m. at the Woodchoppers Hall, London:

1. To receive and adopt the Accounts for the year ended 31st December 19.2, together with the Reports of the Directors and Auditors thereon.

2. To confirm and declare dividends on the Preference shares and ordinary shares.

3. To re-elect a Director.

4. To re-appoint and fix the remuneration of the Auditors.

5. To transact other ordinary business of the Company.

By Order of the Board:

I. TALLBOY
Secretary

Woodcraft Works
London
1st April 19.3

Note.

1. Only the holders of Ordinary shares (except as afterwards provided) are entitled to attend and vote at the Meeting.

2. Any member of the Company entitled to attend and vote at the

Annual General Meeting may appoint a proxy or proxies, to attend and vote instead of him and such proxy/proxies need not be a Member/Members of the Company.

3. There will be available for inspection at the registered office of the Company, Woodcraft Works, London, during usual business hours on any weekday (except Saturdays) until the date of the Annual General Meeting:

(i) The properly indexed Register of each Director's, and his family's, interests in the shares of the Company and in the shares and debentures of the Subsidiary Company.

(ii) Copies of each Director's current service contract with the Company.

The above will be made available for inspection at the place of the Annual General Meeting for at least fifteen minutes prior to the Meeting and also during the entire tenure of the Meeting.

Any person entitled to attend the Annual General Meeting will on request be supplied, within ten days thereafter, with a copy of the Directors' Interests mentioned in 3 (i) above showing the required information in respect of the twelve months prior to the date of this Notice.

FURNICO LTD.

PROFIT AND LOSS ACCOUNT FOR THE YEAR ENDED 31ST DECEMBER 19.2

Corresponding figures for the year ended 31st December, 19.1

	£	£	£
TURNOVER FOR YEAR			
Home		£317,500	
Export		158,000	
			£475,500
TRADING PROFIT FOR YEAR BEFORE CORPORATION TAX			£84,650[1]
After crediting:			
Debenture Interest from Subsidiary Company (gross)		£1,500	
Income from Unquoted Investments (including Tax Credit)		5,000	
		£6,500	
And after charging:			
Directors' Emoluments:			
Fees	£4,950		
Other Emoluments	4,500		
	9,450		
Less Fees paid by Subsidiary Company	200		
	9,250		
Pension paid to former Director	1,000		
		10,250	
Auditors' Remuneration		1,580	
Depreciation:			
Leasehold Property	£5,600		
Plant and Machinery	6,000		
		11,600	
Debenture Interest (gross)		4,800	
		£28,230	
Less TAXATION—			
(1) CORPORATION TAX		£16,000	
(2) on Franked Investment Income		2,000	
			18,000
NET PROFIT FOR YEAR AFTER CORPORATION TAX			£66,650
Add Balance brought forward		15,000	
Less: Underprovision for Corporation Tax—			
Accounting Year to 31st December 19.1		500	
			14,500
			£81,150
Deduct Appropriations:			
Transfer to General Reserve		£10,000	
Preliminary Expenses written-off		1,000	
Dividends paid and proposed:			
Paid—Preference Dividend for half-year to 30th June 19.2		12,000	
Proposed—Preference Dividend for half-year to 31st December 19.2		12,000	
Ordinary dividend of 10% for year		30,000	
			65,000
BALANCE CARRIED FORWARD			£16,150

[1] See p. 23249 for computation of this figure.

FURNICO LTD.

BALANCE SHEET AS AT 31st DECEMBER 19.2

CAPITAL EMPLOYED	Authorized £	Issued and paid up £	£
PREFERENCE CAPITAL			
400,000 8% Preference Shares of £1 each	400,000	300,000	300,000
ORDINARY CAPITAL			
400,000 Ordinary Shares of £1 each	400,000	300,000	300,000
REVENUE RESERVES			
General		25,000	
Profit and Loss Account		16,150	
			41,150
CORPORATION TAX—Accounting Year to 31st December 19.2			16,000
			£657,150

Corresponding figures as at 31st December, 19.1

EMPLOYMENT OF CAPITAL	Cost or Valuation £	Depre-ciation £	£
FIXED ASSETS			
Goodwill, at cost	15,000		15,000
Freehold Land and Buildings at cost	230,000		230,000
Leasehold Land and Buildings, at cost	280,000	65,600	214,400
Plant and Machinery	150,000	36,000	114,000
	£675,000	£101,600	£573,400
Less LONG-TERM LIABILITIES			
6% First Mortgage Debentures			80,000
			493,400
Unquoted Investments at cost			18,750
			512,150
INTERESTS IN SUBSIDIARY			
Shares		50,000	
Debentures		25,000	
Current Account		500	75,500
			587,650
CURRENT ASSETS			
Stock-in-Trade	80,000		
Trade Debtors, less provision for Doubtful Debts	49,000		
Balance at Bank	20,100		
		149,100	
CURRENT LIABILITIES			
Trade Creditors	38,960[1]		
Debenture Interest (net)	1,440		
Ground Rent (net)	1,200		
Corporation Tax—Accounting Year to 31st December 19.1	7,000		
Provision for Preference Dividend—Half-year	12,000		
Provision for Ordinary Dividend	30,000		
Advance Corporation Tax on Dividends	28,000[2]		
(proposed dividends are subject to confirmation)		118,600	
WORKING CAPITAL			30,500
ASSETS WHICH ARE NEITHER FIXED NOR CURRENT			
Preliminary Expenses—			
Balance at 1st January 19.2		2,000	
Less Written-off during year		1,000	
		1,000	
Discount on Debentures		4,000	
Deferred Revenue Expenditure (Advertising)		6,000	
Recoverable Advance Corporation Tax		28,000[2]	39,000
			£657,150

C. HAIR
T. ABLE
} Directors

[1] Includes £1,160 in respect of Income Tax; see p. 23250.

[2] Proposed Dividends £42,000 × $\frac{40}{60}$ (Rate of Income Tax 40%).

Statement of Source and Application of Funds

	£	£
Source of funds		
Profit before tax and dividends paid		31,650
Adjustments for items not involving the movement of funds:		
Transfer to General Reserve	10,000	
Depreciation	11,600	
Preliminary Expenses written off	1,000	22,600
Total generated from operations		54,250
Application of funds	£	
Dividends paid	12,000	
Taxation	18,500	
Further Investment in Subsidiary	10,000	
Deferred Expenditure	6,000	46,500
		7,750
Increase/decrease in working capital	£	
Increase in Current Assets	7,100	
Decrease in Current Liabilities	650	7,750

Funds statements are prepared by comparing last year's accounts with this year's, and this example, as last year's figures are not shown, is by way of illustration only.

NOTES ON PROFIT AND LOSS ACCOUNT (part of submitted set of accounts):

1. *Turnover:*
Turnover is stated at the total amount received and receivable by the Company for goods sold during the year but excluding inter-Company sales.

2. Particulars of Directors' Emoluments under Sect. 6 of the Companies Act 1967:

(a)	Description	Number
	Chairman's Emoluments:	
	£4,500	1
	Directors' Emoluments:	
	Exceeding £2,500 but not exceeding £5,000 a year . . .	2
	Director's Emoluments Waived:	
	£1,500	1

(b) Emoluments of highest paid director which exceed those of the Chairman—£4,750.

3. *Interest on Loans:*

Amount of interest on loans maturing within five years—Nil
Other interest:
Debenture Interest (gross) £4,800

NOTES ON BALANCE SHEET (part of submitted set of accounts):

1. No provision has been made for depreciation of Freehold Land and Buildings.
2. Trading Stocks are valued at the lower of cost and net realizable value on bases and methods consistently applied over many years.

3. *Land and Buildings:*

The Company's land and buildings which are held leasehold consist of the following—

Land and Buildings held on leases with more than 50 years to run .	£210,000
Land and Buildings held on leases with less than 50 years to run .	70,000
	£280,000

4. *Interest in Subsidiaries:*

Subsidiary's Name	Country in which registered	Class of share held	Proportion of nominal value of the issued shares of that class
Plenishings Ltd.	Scotland	Ordinary shares of £0·25 each	66⅔%

5. Statement of identities and places of incorporation of companies not subsidiaries whose shares the Company holds and particulars of these shares—

Name of Associate Company	Country in which registered	Class of share held	Proportion of nominal value of the shares issued of that class
Furni-Units Ltd.	Scotland	Ordinary shares of £1 each	25%

6. *Unquoted Investments at Cost:*

The Company's unquoted investments, cost £18,750, represent the Company's holding of 25,000 Ordinary shares of £1 each (£0·75 paid) in the Associated Company, Furni-Units Ltd., regarding which the following information is given:

	£
(a) aggregate income for the year from the investment including Tax Credit	5,000
(b) this Company's share of profits of Furni-Units Ltd. arising in that company's Accounts sent by it during this company's financial year	
(i) before tax	12,750
(ii) after tax	8,000
(c) this Company's share of undistributed profits of Furni-Units Ltd. since the time the investment was acquired	2,500
(d) Furni-Units Ltd. has not incurred any losses since the date of this Company's investment therein.	

7. There is a contingent liability of £6,250 in respect of uncalled capital on shares forming part of the Unquoted Investments of the Company.

8. *Loan Capital*—This comprises £80,000 6% First Mortgage Debentures redeemable at par on 31st December 19.9.

9. *Company Status*—The Company is not a 'close company'.

FURNICO LTD.

REPORT OF THE AUDITORS TO THE MEMBERS

The adjoining Accounts have been prepared under the historical cost convention. These Accounts, together with the notes thereon, give, in our opinion, a true and fair view of the Company's affairs as at 31st December 19.2 and of the Company's profit and source and application of funds for the year ended on that date, according to the previously stated convention and comply with the Companies Acts 1948 and 1967.

A. LERT & Co.

CHARTERED ACCOUNTANTS

Auditors

1 TICK STREET,
LONDON
16*th March* 19.3

FURNICO LTD.

REPORT OF THE DIRECTORS

The directors have pleasure in presenting their Annual Report with the Accounts for the year ended 31st December 19.2.

Trading Results and Appropriations

The trading profit for the year before Corporation Tax amounted to £84,650, and after providing £18,000 for Corporation Tax the net profit for the year was £66,650, which is a record in the Company's history. Adding the balance of unappropriated profit brought forward of £15,000 *less* £500 in respect of Corporation Tax under-provided on the previous year's profit, the profit available for distribution is £81,150. Out of this amount, a dividend on the 300,000 8% Preference £1 Shares for the half-year ended 30th June 19.2 of £12,000 was paid on 21st July 19.2, and the Advance Corporation Tax due thereon of £8,000 was remitted to the Inland Revenue.

The profit remaining is	£69,150
The directors recommend that this be dealt with as follows:	
Transfer to General Reserve . .	£10,000
Amount written-off Preliminary Expense	1,000
The payment of the Preference Dividend for the half-year ended 31st December 19.2	12,000
The payment of a first and final Ordinary Dividend for the year of 10% . .	30,000
	£53,000
Leaving a balance unappropriated to be carried forward of	£16,150

Principal Activities

The Company is principally engaged in the manufacture and distribution to wholesalers, both at home and in certain overseas countries, of high quality household furniture. During the last quarter of the year a new outlet for sales of the Company's products in Sweden and France was secured, and, whilst at the outset certain marketing difficulties were encountered, these have been resolved and the results are proving to be highly satisfactory.

The production of fibre-glass furniture was introduced in May 19.2, and fibre-glass chairs and tables were marketed at the beginning of August. The results up to the end of the year have proved to be disappointing but it is considered too early to determine fully the success or otherwise of this venture. It is hoped that a sales campaign to be introduced early next year in Germany and France will prove successful.

[*Note.* Mention, if at all, of the year's activities will usually be brief, as the Report will generally be accompanied by the Chairman's Review.]

Investment in Subsidiary Company

The Company has for the past three years held 200,000 fully-paid Ordinary £0.25 Shares in Plenishings Ltd. The entire Issued Share Capital of Plenishings Ltd. comprises 300,000 fully-paid Ordinary £0·25 shares. The Company also holds £25,000 6% Debentures in Plenishings Ltd. Whilst the debenture interest has always been timely received, the net trading results of the subsidiary have been so poor that it has, as yet, been unable to pay a dividend. Plenishings Ltd. manufactures fabrics, mainly, and a new low-cost production process was introduced during November 19.2; it is anticipated that this, together with changes in fabric designs which have now been introduced, will prove to be much more rewarding.

Investment in Associated Company

The Company's holdings of 25,000 Ordinary shares of £1 each (£0·75 paid) in Furni-Units Ltd. still proves to be a highly successful investment. Furni-Units Ltd., which specializes in the manufacture and distribution of built-in furniture units, extended its range in October 19.1, with great success, and as a result a dividend of 12% + Tax Credit was paid on 3rd March 19.2. This dividend, in accordance with Furni-Units Ltd.'s Articles of Association, was paid on the nominal value of the shares. The nominal value of each share is £1 on which £0·75 has been paid.

Directors

The following are the names of the directors of the Company at the date of this Report, all of whom held office throughout the Company's financial year just ended:

C. Hair (*Chairman*), T. Able, C. Tee.

E. Adnuff retired as a director on 31st March 19.2, after six years of distinguished service with the Company.

C. Tee retires from the Board in accordance with the Company's Articles of Association and, being eligible, offers himself for re-election.

Directors' Interest in Shares

(a) Details of the interests of each director, and of his family interests, in Share Capital of the Company at the beginning and end of 19.2 are as follows:

| | Preference Shares | | Ordinary Shares | |
	Number	Amount £	Number	Amount £
C. Hair	5,000	5,000	10,000	10,000
T. Able	2,000	2,000	4,000	4,000
C. Tee	1,000	1,000	2,000	2,000

(b) Details of the interests of each director, and of his family interests, in the Share Capital and Debentures of the Company's subsidiary Plenishings Ltd. at the beginning and end of 19.2 are as follows:

| | Ordinary Shares | | 6% Debentures | |
	Number	Amount £	Number	Amount £
C. Hair	2,000	500	1,000	1,000
T. Able	1,000	250	Nil	
C. Tee	1,000	250	Nil	

Director's Contact

T. Able has entered into a contract with the Company whereby the Company has the sole right to exploit all new furniture designs created by T. Able. T. Able has exceptional talents and experience in this field of work, and in terms of the contract was paid a fee of £4,750 in respect of his services for the year.

Turnover and Profit

The Company's principal class of business is the manufacture and distribution of household furniture. The Company also, on a small scale, manufactures shop fittings to specifications supplied by customers.

Details of the turnover of each class of business and the extent to which, in the opinion of the directors, the carrying on of each class of business contributed to the profit of the company for the year before taxation are as follows:

Class of Business	Turnover for 19.2 £	Profit for 19.2 before Taxation £
Manufacture of Household Furniture	460,300	80,500
Manufacture of Shop Fittings	15,200	4,150
	£475,500	£84,650

Exports

The value of goods exported by the Company from the United Kingdom during 19.2 amounted to £158,000.

Freehold and Leasehold Land and Buildings

The Company's Freehold and Leasehold Land and Buildings which appear in the Balance Sheet at 31st December 19..2, at the net book value of £444,400 were professionally valued on 20th December 19.2, by A. S. Sayer & Co., Valuers, and the market value thereof was estimated at £650,000.

Employees and their Remuneration

The average number of persons employed by the Company within the United Kingdom in each week during 19.2 was 104, and their aggregate gross remuneration for the year was £118,875.

Political and Charitable Contributions

During 19.2 the Company made payments totalling £120 to various political organizations. No amount in excess of £50 was given to any one political organization.

Charitable donations during 19.2 amounted to £68.

Auditors

Messrs. A. Lert & Co., the Company's auditors, are willing to continue in office and offer themselves for re-selection in terms of S.14(1) of the Companies Act 1976.

On behalf of the Board

C. HAIR

Chairman

WOODCRAFT WORKS
LONDON
1*st April* 19.3

Notes (NOT part of submitted set of accounts)

1. The commencing Trading Profit figure of £84,650 in the published Profit and Loss Account is arrived at as follows:

		£
Trading Account balance per Trial Balance		150,050
Deduct Items which do not require to be disclosed in the published accounts:		
Administration Salaries	£17,250	
Selling Expenses	18,500	
General Expenses	2,920	
Ground Rent (gross)	4,000	
Provision for Doubtful Debts	1,000	
		43,670
Adjusted Trading Profit		£106,380
Further adjustments in respect of items which require to be disclosed but which have been shown inset:		
Add Debenture Interest from Subsidiary Company (gross)	£1,500	
Income from Unquoted Investments (including Tax Credit)	5,000	
		6,500
		£112,880
Less Directors' Emoluments	£10,250	
Auditors' Remuneration	1,580	
Depreciation	11,600	
Debenture Interest (gross)	4,800	
		28,230
Trading Profit per Published Accounts		£84,650

2. To assist the reader in following the Income Tax accounting entries concerning Furnico Ltd., the following Income Tax Account is submitted as being appropriate to record the Income Tax position, both for quarterly settlement purposes and for Income Tax year-end purposes. Full narratives are shown merely for explanatory purposes.

FURNICO LTD.

GENERAL LEDGER

INCOME TAX ACCOUNT

Dr.	£		Cr. £
19.2		**19.2**	
Oct. 14 Bank— Income Tax remitted to Collector of Taxes	1,760	July 4 Ground Rent Account— Income Tax retained on payment of Ground Rent for half-year to 30th June £2,000 at 40%	800
Dec. 6 Debenture Interest Received Account— Income Tax suffered on debenture interest received from Plenishings Ltd, £1,500 at 40%	600[1]	July 6 Debenture Interest Account— Income Tax retained on payment of debenture interest for half-year to 30th June £2,400 at 40%	960
Dec. 31 Balance c/d— Income Tax due in respect of Ground Rent and debenture interest due and payable £800 + £960 less Income Tax suffered on debenture interest received £600	1,160	Dec. 31 Ground Rent Account— Income Tax in respect of ground rent due and payable for half year to 31st December £2,000 at 40%	800
		Debenture Interest Account— Income Tax in respect of debenture interest due and payable for half-year to 31st December £2,400 at 40%	960
	£3,520		£3,520
		19.3 Jan. 1 Balance b/d	£1,160[2]

The modern trend in published accounts is to give as much material information as possible in as clear a way as possible. Many companies have experimented with new methods of layout and presentation in an attempt to make the accounts more easily understood by the general public, e.g. 'cutting the cake' illustrations to show what proportion of the company's revenue has gone on purchase of raw materials, wages, dividends, taxation, etc.; the use of 'conversational' language, and so on. For examination purposes, the student is advised to keep to the more usual methods of drafting the Balance Sheet and Accounts, remembering that whatever method of presentation is adopted, they must be clear and lucid and give a true and fair view and, of course, comply with the Companies Acts, 1948 to 1976.

A further illustration will be found at the end of the next chapter, incorporating presentation of group accounts.

[1] The £600 debit balance represents the balance appearing in the Trial Balance at 31st December 19.2, at which stage no provision had been made for the amounts due and payable for the half-year to 31st December 19.2, in respect of ground rent and debenture interest.

[2] The £1,160 has been included with Trade Creditors in the balance sheet.

SECTION I. DIVIDENDS

A dividend is a division of the profits of a company amongst the members. A dividend cannot be paid unless there are (1) profits and (2) a 'declaration'.

A dividend may be classified from different aspects:

1. 'Time', i.e. interim or final.
2. 'Priority', i.e. preference, ordinary, deferred.
3. 'Amount', i.e. fixed rate of fluctuating.
4. 'Form', i.e.:
   (a) Cash.   (c) Bonus.
   (b) Scrip or specie.
5. 'Sanction', i.e. where a dividend may be paid on declaration by directors, or where, as is usual with ordinary dividends, the sanction of the company in general meeting is required.

The following points are essential to a proper understanding of accounting treatment of dividends:

1. (a) An interim dividend may be paid if in the *bona fida* opinion of the directors such a payment is justified, subject to any contrary provision in the Articles. If Table A has been adopted, Clause 115 authorizes such a payment. At any time before its payment, an interim dividend may be cancelled.

(b) A final dividend on shares, other than on those carrying a fixed rate (usually preference shares) may be RECOMMENDED by the directors, but must be SANCTIONED by the company in general meeting.

Position of Preference Shares. Directors are not compelled to pay dividends of any kind. It is within their reasonable discretion (subject to the Articles) to build up adequate reserves. If Clause 117 of Table A has not been excluded, the directors may, before recommending *any* dividend, set aside out of the profits of the company such proper reserves for meeting contingencies or for equalizing dividends, or for any other proper purpose, invested inside or outside the business, as they think fit.

2. Even though a share is a preferred or preference share, it carries no *right* to a dividend (unlike debenture interest) unless the profits have been *earned* and the directors or the company sanctions the payment. The right is not an absolute one: it is at best relative. It merely ensures that a holder of such a share is to be paid a dividend in priority to those holding shares of a lower grade; but unless the share is a [1]*cumulative* preference share, such right of priority is confined to the particular year under consideration. Hence a non-cumulative preference share carries no right to have previous years' omissions made good. Thus, if a company has paid no dividends during a period of, say, four years followed by a successful year, the preference shareholder will obtain priority only for the *current* year's dividend, even though the fifth year's profits are more than sufficient to

[1] Unless the articles either state otherwise or are repugnant thereto, a preference share is *prima facie* cumulative; that is, it has the right to have any arrears of dividends paid out of future profits before any other class of share can receive a dividend.

make up for the 'dividendless' years. If, however, the preference shares are cumulative, the holder *is* entitled to receive not necessarily five years' dividends, but to prevent any dividend being paid on a lower grade share unless and until the whole of the five years' dividends are paid to him. Yet, despite this very valuable privilege, the participation in profits is merely a DIVIDEND, and becomes an ENFORCEABLE DEBT against the company only upon its DECLARATION and, where required, after the sanction of the company has been given.

3. With regard to amount, except that a 'fixed' class is restricted to the fixed rate, the *quantum* of the dividend is dependent upon the amount of profits, after making suitable provision for depreciation, Corporation Tax, sinking fund contribution, if necessary, the financial resources of the company, the general business conditions ruling and the normal business requirements of the company.

Position of Partly-paid Shares. The position of partly-paid shares is, as regards dividends:

(*a*) The dividend is payable on the nominal, called-up, or paid-up, amount, according to the provisions of the ARTICLES.

(*b*) If no provision thereon is contained in the Articles, and Table A provisions relating to dividends have not been excluded, and therefore by implication INCLUDED, the dividend is to be based upon the PAID-UP amount according to dates paid, and calls in advance whilst BEARING interest are not to be included for such purpose.

(*c*) If the Articles are silent on the matter and the appropriate provisions of Table A have been EXCLUDED, the basis of the dividend is the NOMINAL amount of the share.

(*d*) The question whether holders of newly issued shares may receive current dividends depends upon the terms of issue, one method being to preclude a payment of a dividend in respect of profits arising in the financial year of issue, but to allow interest on the amounts paid up within the year, although should the issue be made very early in the financial year the terms usually permit the shares to rank for dividend on the full amount paid—as if paid at the commencement of the year.

4. The dividend may be paid—as is usual—by cash (in practice by dividend warrant), but the company may distribute another form of asset, viz. shares it HOLDS. In this connection, it is necessary to observe two very important matters: (*a*) the company actually *distributes* some sort of assets, thus diminishing them to the extent of the dividend; (*b*) a member is entitled to be paid CASH, unless the Articles OTHERWISE provide.

This distribution must be very clearly differentiated from the BONUS Share dividend—commonly called the capitalization of reserves, It would, it may be mentioned, be much more accurate to describe the procedure as the capitalization of reserves and PROFITS. This matter receives consideration on p. 23255.

Dividends. Dividends are no longer declared 'gross' or 'free of tax'. The rate prescribed is payable to shareholders. However, advance corporation tax (ACT) is payable by the company as described at p. 2356.

e.g. J. Brown holds £1,000 8% preference shares and 10,000 ordinary shares of £1 each, fully paid, in an industrial concern which declared an ordinary dividend of 12%. Income Tax is at rate of 30%.

He would be paid £80 on the preference shares and £1,200 on the ordinary. The amount of his 'tax credit' would be as follows:

(a) On preference dividend

$$\frac{30}{70} \times £80 \quad \text{i.e.} \quad £34 \cdot 28$$

(b) On ordinary dividend

$$\frac{30}{70} \times £1,200 \quad \text{i.e.} \quad £514 \cdot 28$$

The amount of ACT paid by the company would include the £548·56 in respect of J. Brown, and would be available for deduction from the agreed Corporation Tax liability on the profits of the year for which the dividends were paid.

Treatment of dividends in accounts will be dealt with under three headings: (a) Cash dividends; (b) Bonus Share dividends (see p. 23255); and (c) Scrip dividends (see p. 23266).

Cash dividends

The Companies Act 1967, required the aggregate amount of dividends paid and proposed to be shown separately in the Profit and Loss Account and the aggregate amount which is recommended for distribution by way of dividend to be shown separately in the Balance Sheet (Sch. 3, paras 12 (1) (h) and 8 (1) (e). It is important to note that a dividend is regarded as having been paid on the date when it became due and payable, namely the date when the dividend was declared.

Illustration 88

For simplicity assume the following:

Proposed ordinary dividend of £600. Income Tax 40 per cent.[1] Show Journal entries without narrations.

Profit and Loss Appropriation Account	Dr. £600	
To Ordinary Dividend payable Account		£600

For published account purposes, the entries at this stage could be shown:

1. In the Profit and Loss Appropriation Account as:

Proposed ordinary dividend of ?% gross . . . £600

In accordance with the Statement of Standard Accounting Practice in respect of dividends paid or proposed the amount of ACT should be

---

[1] ACT rate equivalent 40/60 ths.

shown as follows:

(a) Balance Sheet

Current Liability	
Advance Corporation Tax	£400[1]
Deferred Asset	
Recoverable Advance Corporation Tax	£400

(b) Profit and Loss Appropriation Account
If the ACT is considered irrecoverable, shown thus:

Irrecoverable Advance Corporation Tax	£400

The Journal Entries are:

Deferred Asset Account (ACT)	Dr. 400	
To Advance Corporation Tax Account		£400

If (b) above applies the Dr. is

Profit and Loss Appropriation Account (ACT)	Dr. 400

When the ordinary dividend is paid the Journal entries are:

Ordinary Dividend Payable A/C	Dr. £600	
To Bank		£600

When the ACT is remitted to the Inland Revenue (actually to the Collector of Taxes) the Journal entry is—

ACT account	Dr. £400	
To Bank		£400

Participating Preference Shares. There are innumerable ways of participating in the profits of the company, particularly where a share, although preferential as to dividends—with or without being cumulative—also carries a right to a further dividend; thus Beauchamp Pellets, Ltd., may have participating preference shares—cumulative to 8 per cent, with the right to have a further 2 per cent maximum non-cumulative—if and when the ordinary shares have received 10 per cent dividend.

Illustration 89

Assume that the profits after Corporation Tax are £6,000 and there are 20,000 8 per cent cumulative participating preference shares, with participating right to 2 per cent after the payment of a dividend of 10 per cent on the ordinary shares (15,000): all fully-paid £1 shares. The preference dividends are paid half-yearly. The balance on Profit and Loss Account brought forward is £1500.

Show Profit and Loss Appropriation Account in vertical form, taking Income Tax at 40 per cent.

[1] i.e. $\frac{40}{60} \times £600 = £400$

PROFIT AND LOSS APPROPRIATION ACCOUNT

	£	£
Profit for year after Corporation Tax		6,000
Add Balance brought forward		1,500
		7,500
Deduct Appropriations:		
Dividends for year:		
Paid—		
Preference dividend for first half-year to	800	
Proposed—		
Preference dividend for second half-year to	800	
Ordinary dividend of 10% for year	1,500	
Participating preference dividend of 2% for year . . .	400	
		3,500
Balance carried forward		£4,000

(*Note.* ACT is assumed to be recoverable and does not affect profit.)

Illustration 90

If the foregoing participating right attached to preference shares (£20,000) is, say, 50 per cent of the dividends received by the holders of ordinary shares (£15,000) over and above 10 per cent, and the ordinary dividend is 20 per cent, then the latter would be £3,000; and the extra dividend to the preference shareholders $3\frac{3}{4}$ per cent—that is, half of the *excess* the ordinary shareholders receive over 10 per cent. As they receive 20 per cent (£3,000), the 'excess' dividend is 10 per cent (£1,500), of which the preference shareholders receive half (£750), which expressed in terms of a percentage is $3\frac{3}{4}$ per cent (£750 = $3\frac{3}{4}$ per cent of £20,000). It is important to observe that the preference shareholders obtain half of such surplus and *not* a dividend on half the excess **rate,** which would be 5 per cent instead of $3\frac{3}{4}$ per cent. ACT will be payable on the dividends.

Bonus Share Dividends. Where a company has accumulated a large Reserve out of profits, instead of distributing such profits by way of cash dividend, it may distribute bonus shares in respect of a part or all of such reserve.

Apart from the fact that a capital profit not realized is not available for a cash distribution, there are many circumstances preventing or rendering undesirable an actual distribution of cash or other assets by way of dividend (see p. 23199).

1. In a private company, if all the members are really 'working part-ners', the earnings may be used, provided all the legal requirements are carried out, to increase the remuneration of such members.

2. In all cases, consideration must be given to the liquid position of the company, not only as the date of the intended dividend, but in the near future. Installation of new machinery and extension of works may be required, in addition to other possible calls upon the liquid funds of the company; whilst the present assets may be 'frozen', e.g. in fixed assets,

most of which, owing to changing fashions, may have to be scrapped to meet the changed circumstances—radio concern changing over to television—large sums may be locked up in 'Shares in and Loans to Subsidiary Companies'; large stocks, which technically are comparatively liquid assets, may be held on a falling market. Proposed changes of a fiscal nature may necessitate large 'cash reserves', thus constraining the company to keep its cash intact; it being an elementary maxim that no borrowing should be made in order to pay a dividend. Again, a sinking fund set aside for debenture redemption represents undistributed profits, although the investment against it may have been sold and utilized to redeem the debentures, so that a bonus dividend may well be made from the sinking fund now 'free'.

BONUS SHARES

Advantages and Disadvantages. The advantages and disadvantages of an issue of bonus shares are briefly summarized (a) as regards the company, and (b) as regards the shareholders.

(a) *The Company's Viewpoint.* (i) Profits can be distributed without any distribution of the company's assets, or reduction of the additional working capital created by those profits.[1]

(ii) If dividends are not largely increased, the distribution of profits over a larger number of shares will reduce the rate of dividend paid. This may be considered expedient to conceal from workers the fact that high dividends are being paid, or to bring the rate more into line with the capital employed in the business.

(iii) If the company is to maintain the same rate of dividend it must earn larger profits, unless it modifies its reserve policy.

(b) *The Shareholder's Viewpoint.* (i) Income Tax and Capital Gains Tax may be payable on a bonus share distribution.[2]

(ii) Unless the company makes increased profits, the fall in rate of dividend or depletion of reserves will cause the market price per share to fall—though the total value of the large holding may be greater.

(iii) Speculative dealings in the shares may be caused.

4. A bonus issue of debentures or redeemable preference shares ranks as a distribution, and so also will payments of interest or dividends. An issue of irredeemable bonus shares, however, unless related to a previous repayment, does not rank as a distribution. It should be appreciated that distributions are chargeable to Advance Corporation Tax, and in the hands of the recipients (the shareholders), distributions include the Tax Credit.

---

[1] Where share capital has been repaid after 6th April 1965, and a bonus issue of non-redeemable share capital has been subsequently made—in 1966/67 or later—then the lesser of the two amounts is deemed to be a distribution.

[2] As a distribution represents income in the hands of the recipient, Income Tax will be charged in appropriate cases, even on capital dividends which were formerly tax free. The Tax Credit element of the dividend will be added to the amount received for tax computation purposes. The Tax Credit will be deducted as a payment on account of the tax liability computed.

5. If the bonus is applied in reducing or extinguishing the uncalled Capital (e.g. making shares of £1 each, £0·75 paid into fully-paid £1 shares) there is a distinct tangible benefit to the shareholder and therefore the amount is taxable.

A bonus share dividend is merely a book entry effected by a transfer from General Reserve or Profit and Loss Apropriation Account to Share Capital—each shareholder receiving a share certificate proportionate to his holding—instead of cash. Thus, if the share capital is £8,000 in fully-paid ordinary shares of £1 each and £3,000 is transferred thereto, each shareholder will have the right to an allotment of three new shares for every eight old shares that he holds. He is usually given the option of taking up the shares or selling his right of allotment to another person, that is, 'renouncing'.

As shareholders are entitled to CASH dividends, the sanction of the Articles or special resolution is required for *any* dividend otherwise than in cash, whether it is: (*a*) an actual distribution of other assets; or (*b*) a 'notional' distribution by way of a bonus share dividend.

Although the issue of bonus shares to ordinary shareholders is generally regarded as a 'book entry', it may confer a substantial advantage to such holders where there are preference shares which carry a right in a winding-up to share *pari passu* in a surplus, as the bonus issue, by absorbing such part of the reserves of the company as is necessary for such purpose, diminishes the 'surplus'. In other words, such 'surplus' has been utilized solely to increase the claims of the ordinary shareholders by the additions of the relevant amount of reserves.

It should be noted that distributions in respect of share capital made on the winding-up of companies are NOT regarded as distributions for taxation purposes.

Illustration 91

The net assets of a company are £65,000, represented by Preference Share Capital £20,000, Ordinary Share Capital £30,000 (all shares being fully-paid up) and Reserves £15,000. The preference shares carry the right to participate *pari passu* in a surplus *in a winding-up.*

If the company went into liquidation and assuming the net proceeds £65,000, the division could be:

	Preference £	Ordinary £
Share Capital	20,000	30,000
Add Surplus £15,000 ⅖	6,000 ⅗	9,000
	£26,000	£39,000

Thus the division is simple when both classes of shares rank *pari passu.* The ratio of preference to ordinary shares is reflected in the division of the amount realized.

If, however, the reserves had been capitalized by way of bonus shares, the preference shares would obtain £20,000 and the ordinary shares £45,000. There would be no surplus, as prior to liquidation the ordinary share capital had become £45,000 by the transfer of the reserves of £15,000, thus increasing the original ordinary share capital from £30,000 to £45,000.

A result disadvantageous to the preference shareholders would arise if: (a) the preference shareholders had no priority in a winding-up and (b) there was a substantial loss in the realization of the assets.

Illustration 92

If the net assets in the preceding example realized only £15,000, the preference shares could receive:

(a) If there had been **no** bonus issue of £15,000,

$$\frac{20,000}{30,000} \times £15,000 = £10,000$$

(b) if there had been a bonus issue of £15,000,

$$\frac{20,000}{45,000} \times £15,000 = £6,667$$

If the bonus shares issued carried full voting rights the effect might be to reduce the actual or potential voting power of the preference shareholders. Usually, however, the bonus shares would be 'non-voting', although in view of the present attitude of institutional investors (e.g. insurance companies) the non-voting shares seem to be on the way out.

In most companies, the preference shares carry no voting power except in certain circumstances, e.g. dividend in arrear for six months or other stated period. The latent power is important where the company is in difficulty, and should not be ignored merely because it is, in most instances, not likely to have to be used.

The effect on the rights of the preference shareholders as a result of the bonus issue may be such as to require the approval of the preference shareholders under Sect. 72, Companies Act 1948, or according to the specific provisions (if any) of the Memorandum of Association. This is a difficult legal point and would require the guidance of the company's legal advisers.

Unless the bonus involves the disclosure for the first time of a hidden or secret reserve, there is no monetary gain to the shareholder. The price of the share is based upon earning power, and consequently the mere book entry is, as such, not a magic wand to augment the resources of the company or its earning capacity; and the original holder of 50 shares, now increased, say, to 70, will, just as before, be entitled only to his share of distributable profits. Thus his *rate* of dividend on his 70 will be less than that on his original 50. Hence the market price per share, seeing that it yields a lower *rate*, will tend to decrease proportionately. By the issue of bonus shares there is a large book capital laying claim to the earnings of the company. In many instances the position of a shareholder is likely to be prejudiced, because his holding of 50 shares may become 55 (e.g. in a '1 for 10' distribution), the total value of which will be the same as his original 50, but in the market the holding becomes an 'odd lot' and may, as a consequence, fetch a lower price than a round number like 50. Even if he sells 50, he is still left with five, which is an 'odd lot'.

The bonus nowadays is generally taken as an indication that the effective rate of dividend will probably be paid (i.e. the same *rate* on *increased* capital).

It may be necessary to INCREASE the NOMINAL capital to cover the bonus shares issue, e.g. if the issued share capital is £10,000, the bonus share dividend 6,000 £1 fully-paid shares and the nominal capital £13,000, it will be necessary to increase the latter. No capital duty is payable on the issue of bonus shares.

Book-keeping Entries

Upon sanction of the dividend:

(1) Debit Profit and Loss Appropriation Account [or Reserve].
    Credit Bonus Share Dividend Account.

Upon the issue of the shares:

(2) Debit Bonus Share Dividend Account.
    Credit Share Capital Account.

In addition, the return of allotments must be filed with the Registrar of Companies; certificates issued; the Register of Members adjusted, and the appropriate minutes recorded. The Balance Sheet and the Annual Return will show the amended share capital.

Illustration 93

X, Ltd., declares a bonus share dividend (out of reserve) of 100 per cent, the share capital being 30,000 shares of £1 each fully paid. Show Journal entries.

JOURNAL

	£	£
Reserve	30,000	
Bonus Share Dividend		30,000
Being bonus dividend of 100% sanctioned by resolution of the company in general meeting held [Date]		
Bonus Share Dividend	30,000	
Share Capital		30,000
Being utilization of bonus dividend in increasing the issued share capital as sanctioned by the company in general meeting held [Date]		

The utilization of a bonus share dividend for the purpose of discharging calls on shares involves the following entries:

(a) If Call Account is opened:

   (1) *Debit Call Account.*
      Credit Share Capital Account.
   (2) Debit Profit and Loss Appropriation Account [or Reserve].
      Credit Bonus Share Dividend Account.
   (3) *Debit Bonus Share Dividend Account.*
      Credit Call Account.

(b) If Call Account is NOT opened:

   (1) Debit Profit and Loss Appropriation Account [or Reserve].
      Credit Bonus Share Dividend Account.
   (2) *Debit Bonus Share Dividend Account.*
      Credit Share Capital Account.

Items in italics cancel out, leaving a final result of:

      Debit Profit and Loss Appropriation Account [or Reserve].
      Credit Share Capital Account.

From the above, it will be perceived that the balance of Profit and Loss Appropriation Account is reduced by the amount by which the share capital is increased, the latter being in the form of a greater **sum paid up** on the same number of shares already issued, instead of a greater **number** of shares occasioned by the issue of bonus shares.

Illustration 94

Stanbury, Ltd., has 10,000 shares of £1 each, £0·60 called and paid, and after passing the necessary resolutions, declares a bonus dividend in the form of paying up the £0·40 uncalled on the shares. Show Journal entries.

JOURNAL

	£	£
Final Call	4,000	
Share Capital		4,000
Being call of £0·40 a share on 10,000 shares per resolution of directors, *vide* Minute Book, p.		
Profit and Loss Appropriation	4,000	
Bonus share Dividend		4,000
Being bonus dividend sanctioned by resolution of the company in general meeting held [Date]		
Bonus Share Dividend	4,000	
Final Call		4,000
Being utilization of bonus dividend in payment of final call as sanctioned by the company in general meeting held [Date]		

Where a bonus dividend is to be applied in the issue of share capital at a premium, the following entries are required:

(a) If Call Account is opened:

   (1) *Debit Call Account.*
       Credit Share Capital Account (amount to be credited).
       Credit Share Premium Account (premium).
   (2) Debit Profit and Loss Appropriation Account [or Reserve].
       Credit Bonus Share Dividend Account.
   (3) *Debit Bonus Share Dividend Account.*
       Credit Call Account.

(b) If Call Account is NOT opened:

   (1) Debit Profit and Loss Appropriation Account [or Reserve].
       Credit Bonus Share Dividend Account.
   (2) *Debit Bonus Share Dividend Account.*
       Credit Share Capital Account (amount to be credited).
       Credit Share Premium Account (premium).

Items in italics cancel out, leaving a final result of—

   Debit Profit and Loss Appropriation Account [or Reserve].
   Credit Share Capital Account.
   Credit Share Premium Account.

Illustration 95

Wycoller Ltd., has an issued capital of 20,000 shares of £1 each, £0·87½ paid, and resolutions are passed whereby a bonus dividend is declared: (a) to make the shares fully-paid; (b) to issue a further 5,000 shares of £1 each fully paid—that is, one for every four held—at £1·50 each; and (c) to pay a cash dividend of 20 per cent per annum for the year on the augmented capital after taking into account an interim of 8 per cent already paid (on the old capital).

The company's Articles provide for dividends on the *paid-up* capital. The profits available for dividend are £12,000.

Show the necessary Journal entries, employing Call Account for (a) only. The entries for the interim dividend are not required.

It will be noticed that no mention is made of the NOMINAL share capital, hence a very necessary preliminary assumption must be made and STATED in the answer, viz.: 'Assumed that either the nominal capital at the date of the resolution was at least £25,000, or it has been validly increased to that sum.'

JOURNAL

		£	£
Final Call		2,500	
Share Capital			2,500
Being, etc.			
Profit and Loss Appropriation Account[1] . .		10,000	
Bonus Share Dividend			10,000
Being, etc.			
Bonus Share Dividend		2,500	
Final Call			2,500
Being, etc.			
Bonus Share Dividend		7,500	
Share Capital			5,000
Share Premium			2,500
Being issue of ordinary shares of £1 each fully paid at £1·50 each to the shareholders in the ratio of one new share for every four held, sanctioned by the company in general meeting.			
Profit and Loss Appropriation Account . . .		3,600	
Dividend			3,600
Being final dividend, making with the interim dividend of 8%, 20% per annum, on 25,000 shares of £1 each fully paid sanctioned by the company in general meeting.			
Dividend		3,600	
Advance Corporation Tax		2,400	
Cash			6,000
Being payment of amount due to shareholders in respect of final dividend and payment of Advance Corporation Tax at say $\frac{40}{60}$ ths on final dividend paid.			

[1] £2,500 relates to the first part [making the partly paid shares fully paid] and £7,500 to the bonus *issue*. [The entries may be separately recorded.]

The final dividend is computed as follows:

	£
As the TOTAL Dividend for the year is 20% on £25,000, it equals . .	5,000
Less Interim Dividend of[2] 8% on 20,000 shares, £0·87½ called and paid $[\frac{8}{100}\times£17,500]$	1,400
Final Dividend =	£3,600

Illustration 96

A company issued 25,000 7 per cent Redeemable Preference Shares of £1 each at par. At 30th June 19.., the shares are to be redeemed at £1·10 a share and for the purpose of assisting the redemption 15,000 Ordinary

---

[2] The question does not state that the interim was AT THE RATE OF 8 per cent, but a PAYMENT of 8 per cent.

Shares of £1 each were issued at par. On the above date 1,000 of the Redeemable Preference Shares had been forfeited for non-payment of the last call of £0·25, 800 of which had been reissued as fully paid for £0·60 a share. The balance of Profit and Loss Account was £12,100 and the General Reserve £3,000. On the same day as the redemption took place a Bonus Share Dividend was declared of £12,500.

Show the Ledger balances as on 30th June 19.., and the Ledger entries relating to the redemption of the Preference Shares, the issue of the Ordinary Shares, and the Bonus Shares.

7% REDEEMABLE PREFERENCE SHARE CAPITAL

		£				£
Sundry Members . .		24,800		Balance	b/d	24,800

ORDINARY SHARE CAPITAL

		£			£
Balance . . .	c/d	27,500	Cash		15,000
			Bonus Share Dividend Account . .		12,500
		£27,500			£27,500
			Balance	b/d	27,500

FORFEITED SHARES

		£				£
Reserve		150		Balance	b/d	150

PREMIUM ON SHARES REISSUED

		£				£
Bonus Share Dividend .		280		Balance	b/d	280

PROFIT AND LOSS APPROPRIATION

	£				£
Sundry Members—Premium	2,480		Balance	b/d	12,100
Capital Redemption Reserve Fund . . .	9,620				
	£12,100				£12,100

SUNDRY MEMBERS

		£			£
Cash	. . . . . .	27,280	7% Redeemable Preference Share Capital . .		24,800
			Profit and Loss Appropriation Account—Premium on Redemption .		2,480
		£27,280			£27,280

CAPITAL REDEMPTION RESERVE FUND

		£			£
Bonus Share Dividend Account . . .		**9,800**	Profit and Loss Appropriation Account .		9,620
			Reserve		180
		£9,800			£9,800

RESERVE

		£				£
Capital Redemption Reserve Fund . . .		180	Balance . . .	b/d		3,000
Bonus Share Dividend		**2,420**	Forfeited Shares . .			150
Balance . . .	c/d	550				
		£3,150				£3,150
			Balance . . .	b/d		550

BONUS SHARE DIVIDEND

		£			£
Ordinary Share Capital	.	**12,500**	**Capital Redemption Reserve Fund** . . .		**9,800**
			Reserve . . .		**2,420**
			Reserve . . .		
			Premium on Shares Reissued . . .		280
		£12,500			**£12,500**

Alternatively, the Premium on Shares Reissued Account could be left intact and the Reserve Account used to the extent of a further £280, bringing down the balance of £270 (instead of £550).

CASH

		£			£
Balance (Capital) . .	b/d	25,230	Sundry Members—Redemption of 24,800 Shares of £1 each at £1·10 a Share		27,280
,, (Profit and Loss)	b/d	15,100			
Ordinary Share Capital Account . .		15,000	Balance . . .		28,050
		£55,330			£55,330
Balance . . .	b/d	28,050			

Where Preference Shares have been redeemed the Capital Redemption Reserve Fund may be utilized in paying up unissued shares (whether there has been a fresh issue of shares or not). The new issue of shares for CASH was £15,000, so that £9,800 must be transferred from undistributed profits to Capital Redemption Reserve Fund. As the balance of Profit and Loss Appropriation Account is, after the charge for premium, only £9,620, a further £180 will be transferred from Reserve to Capital Redemption Reserve Fund, bringing it up to £9,800, which may now be used towards the issue of fully-paid Bonus Shares of £12,500, the difference of £2,700 coming from Reserve £2,420 and Premium on Shares Reissued £280.

The balance on Forfeited Shares Account may be transferred to reserve, there being no possibility of the issue of the remaining 200 Preference Shares.

The opening balances are in italics, the redemption entries in ordinary type, and the Bonus Share entries in heavy type.

The Cash Account is inserted to assist the student in balancing the accounts.

Company distributions are liable to ACT. Distributions are defined in the Income and Corporation Taxes Act 1970 (as amended). For present purposes, it may be noted that distribution includes dividends paid on share capital and also capital dividends. However, also included are other items which formerly were not liable to Tax. For example, any distribution to shareholders out of company assets, whether in cash or not, is classed as a taxable distribution unless it is, in fact, a repayment of share capital or is made for a new consideration. Also included in this category are certain 'repayments of share capital' which have been preceded by a bonus issue; the bonus issue, up to the amount of the share capital previously repaid, is regarded as a distribution and thus taxable. Further, where share capital is repaid, and a bonus issue is made, or if there is a repayment, accompanied by a bonus issue, the bonus issue, up to the amount of the share capital repaid, is treated as a distribution. The issue of bonus redeemable Preference Shares and Bonus Debentures or loan stock are regarded as distributions.

In the case of close companies, loan interest paid to a participator or his associate in excess of a certain amount (which amount itself is excluded) is treated as a distribution. The amount which is excluded, i.e. not treated as a distribution, is an amount equal to interest at 12 per cent on the smaller of: (i) the total loans on which interest is paid, and (ii) the issued share capital plus the share premium account, if any.

It should be mentioned that in respect of the quarterly accounting to the Collector of Taxes relating to distributions, etc. (see p. 2359), the amount of ACT due thereon and remitted with the Return should be in respect of distribution, etc., made in actual cash. Consequently, where a taxable bonus issue of shares has been made, details thereof should be included in the Return made within 14 days after the relevant return period, but the tax is not due on this date. A notice of assessment is later issued by the Inland Revenue, and the Advance Corporation Tax liability is due for payment within 14 days after the date of issue of the assessment.

SCRIP DIVIDENDS

Financial companies frequently distribute dividends in the form of shares or debentures in other companies received for underwriting or for placing shares. ACT is payable thereon.

As has been mentioned previously, a member of a company is entitled to be paid in **cash,** unless the articles as originally framed or as altered by special resolution state otherwise. (*Hoole* v. *G.W.R.: Wood* v. *Odessa Waterworks Co.*)

Book-keeping entries are:

(1) Debit Profit and Loss Appropriation Account [or Reserve].
   Credit Dividend Account (or Scrip Dividend Account).

(2) Debit Dividend Account (or Scrip Dividend Account).
   Credit Investment Account.

A practical difficulty arising in scrip dividends is the apportionment of the investments distributed amongst the shareholders and the consequent trouble in dealing with the fractions.

If there is a book profit on the distribution (e.g. a £10 dividend is distributed by a scrip of shares of 10 shares of £1 each where less than par or at a premium over cost), such profit should be transferred to Investment Reserve, unless *all* the investments have been distributed or sold; or if not, so much as is required to revalue the remaining shares at nil.

A Capital Reserve may be used to *issue* shares, but not to *distribute* assets, whether Cash or Investments or any other form of assets.

Illustration 97

The Balance Sheet of Investments, Ltd., is:

BALANCE SHEET AS AT ....

	£		£
Issued Capital:		Sundry Assets . . .	110,000
100,000 Ordinary Shares of £1		12,500 Shares in X, Ltd. at Cost	25,000
each (fully paid) . .	100,000		
Profit and Loss Account . .	35,000		
	£135,000		£135,000

It is resolved at the general meeting that a dividend of 20 per cent be paid, to be satisfied by the issue of 10,000 shares in X, Ltd., at the market value of £2. Assume that the cost of the shares is £2 each.[1] Show Journal entries and write up the Investment Account in the books of Investments, Ltd., to give effect to the foregoing resolution. State the number of shares in X, Ltd., distributed to the holder of ten ordinary shares in Investments, Ltd.

JOURNAL

		£	£
Profit and Loss Appropriation		20,000	
Scrip Dividend			20,000
Being dividend of 20% sanctioned as per resolution dated			
Scrip Dividend		20,000	
Shares in X, Ltd.			20,000
Being satisfaction of the dividend by transfer of 10,000 fully-paid shares in X, Ltd. as per resolution dated			

The effect of the dividend is that every holder of ten ordinary shares in Investments, Ltd., will receive one share in X, Ltd.

The Investment Account will be as follows:

SHARES IN X, LTD.

		Nominal	Capital			Nominal	Capital
		£	£			£	£
Balance . . .	b/d	12,500	25,000	Dividend . .		10,000	20,000
				Balance . . .	c/d	2,500	5,000
		£12,500	£25,000			£12,500	£25,000
Balance . . .	b/d	2,500	5,000				

¹ A liability to ACT will not arise where assets distributed represent an exchange of assets at market value.

In the case of a scrip dividend, the company may have a profit or loss on book value, as the transaction may be looked upon as analogous to a sale, inasmuch as the dividend (being a liability) is discharged by the transfer of shares. It is usual, however, to credit the profit, if any, to Reserve, and to charge any loss to Profit and Loss Appropriation Account or Reserve.

Illustration 98

Where a Loss. In reference to the preceding illustration, assume that all the shares were distributed in satisfaction of the dividend at a value of £1·60 a share. The Journal entries are similar to those above. The distribution will be on the basis of one share for every eight held in ordinary shares of the company. The Investment Account will be as follows:

SHARES IN X, LTD.

		Nominal	Capital			Nominal	Capital
		£	£			£	£
Balance	b/d	12,500	25,000	Dividend Account		12,500	20,000
				Profit and Loss Appropriation Account [or Reserve][1]			
							5,000
		£12,500	£25,000			£12,500	£25,000

[1] i.e. loss of £0·40 a share on 12,500 shares [difference between 'sale' £1·60 and cost £2].

Arrangements will have to be made in respect of fractional shares.

Illustration 99

Where a Profit. The share capital of a company is 40,000 shares of £1 each, £0·75 paid. A dividend is paid in the form of shares held by the company as an asset, shown in the books as 5,000 shares of £1 each fully paid at cost price (£1·10). The present value of the shares is £1·50 a share, and a 10 per cent scrip dividend is paid. Table A is adopted, and the necessary resolution in respect of the dividend has been passed. Show Ledger Accounts.

DIVIDEND

	£		£
Shares in .... Ltd. at £1·50 each	3,000	Profit and Loss Appropriation Account [or Reserve]	3,000

SHARES IN .... LTD.

		Nominal	Capital			Nominal	Capital
		£	£			£	£
Balance	b/d	5,000	5,500	Dividend Account	c/d	2,000	3,000
Reserve—Profit on Appropriation of Shares to Dividend				Balance		3,000	3,300
			800				
		£5,000	£6,300			£5,000	£6,300
Balance	b/d	3,000	3,300				

RESERVE

						£
				Shares in ......Ltd.[1]		800

[1] i.e. gain of £0·40 a share on 2,000 shares [difference between 'sale' £1·50 and cost £1·10].

Dividends accruing on the investment and transfer costs are ignored. If the company agreed to pay such costs, the amount thereof would be charged to the reserve.

The three relative positions in regard to dividends may be thus shown. Tax ignored.

Illustration 100

BALANCE SHEET

	£		£
Share Capital	10,000	Sundry Assets. . . .	7,000
Profit and Loss Account . .	5,000	Investments	5,000
Creditors.	2,000	Cash	5,000
	£17,000		£17,000

1. Result of CASH dividend of 50 per cent:

BALANCE SHEET

	£		£
Share Capital	10,000	Sundry Assets. . . .	7,000
Profit and Loss Account . .	Nil	Investments	5,000
Creditors.	2,000	Cash	Nil
	£12,000		£12,000

2. Result of SCRIP dividend of 50 per cent:

BALANCE SHEET

	£		£
Share Capital	10,000	Sundry Assets. . . .	7,000
Profit and Loss Account . .	Nil	Investments	Nil
Creditors.	2,000	Cash	5,000
	£12,000		£12,000

3. Result of BONUS SHARE dividend of 50 per cent (or 1 for 2):

BALANCE SHEET

	£		£
Share Capital	15,000	Sundry Assets. . . .	7,000
Profit and Loss Account . .	Nil	Investments	5,000
Creditors.	2,000	Cash	5,000
	£17,000		£17,000

It will be observed that (3) Balance Sheet position is similar to, though differing in form from, the original; whilst (1) and (2) Balance Sheet positions show a reduction in assets of £5,000, thus weakening the position of creditors thereby.

There will be stamp duty of £0·50 per cent on £5,000 in (3) if the NOMINAL capital prior to the issue of bonus shares was £10,000 only.

Obviously, the 50 per cent dividend may be composed of two or all the elements above, say 20 per cent in cash, 25 per cent bonus shares, and 5 per cent script dividend.

Summary of Treatment of Fractional Shares. (a) Odd shares may be sold and the proceeds divided amongst the shareholders entitled to the fractions.

(b) A fractional certificate may be issued conferring the right to a share certificate if surrendered with sufficient other fractional certificates to make up a full share within a specified time.

(c) Arrangements may be made between the various shareholders for the purchase of the shares making up the fractions.

(d) Fractions may be avoided by the issue of partly-paid shares, or shares of a low denomination.

Dividends Paid Direct to Bankers. A practice has grown up of paying dividend warrants direct to the banking account of the shareholder (on the necessary authority of the holder being given). As the number of banking institutions is comparatively small, an important economy is effected, because ONE warrant will be paid to each bank representing all the dividends payable to shareholders (on their authority) who have banking accounts with the particular bank, the latter 'distributing' the amount amongst its various customers.

Illustration 101

Thus, if a company has, say, twenty shareholders, and, in response to the request of the company, eighteen of them signed the form of authorization enabling the company to pay to their bank direct; and assuming eleven have accounts with Barclays (head office or branches) and seven with Midland Bank (head office or branches), the company would need to prepare four warrants only, as follows:

(1) Barclays (total Dividends to members banking with Barclays)	11
(2) Midland (total Dividends to members banking with Midland)	7
(3) Individual Member	1
(4) Individual Member	1
	20

Separate Dividend Banking Account. Where the amount of the dividend and numbers of dividend warrants are large, the total amount is transferred to a Dividend Bank Account, the dividend warrants being paid therefrom, the debit balance of which (if any) will equal the balance of unpaid dividends. After a lapse of a reasonable period, such an account will be closed and the balance transferred to the general Bank Account or to a Deposit Account available for the payment of the warrants when presented.

The entries upon the transfer of the cash to the Dividend Bank Account are:

(1) Debit Profit and Loss Appropriation Account
    Credit Dividend Account } for proposed dividend.

(2) Debit Dividend Bank (or Banking) Account
    Credit General Bank Account } for proposed dividend.

(3) Debit Deferred Asset (ACT)
    Credit Advance Corporation Tax Account } for ACT on dividend due and payable

(4) Debit Dividend Account
    Credit Dividend Bank (or Banking) Account } for payments of dividend warrants.

If after the lapse of a reasonable time dividend warrants are outstanding, the amount is transferred back to the general Bank Account or to a Deposit Account, by a transfer as follows:

(1) Debit (General) Bank or Deposit Account.
    Credit Dividend Bank Account.

When after this transfer any of the outstanding warrants are presented, the payment will be made out of the general Bank or Deposit Account, the entry being:

Debit Dividend Account.
Credit (General) Bank or Deposit Account.

Companies may take power in their Articles to forfeit unclaimed dividends after a specified time, but where a Stock Exchange quotation is desired unclaimed dividends must not be forfeited before the claim becomes statute-barred. Any unpaid balance of a dividend should appear on both sides of the Balance Sheet. On the liabilities side the total of unclaimed dividends will appear as 'Unclaimed Dividends' and the corresponding entry on the assets side will be 'Cash at Bank on Dividend Account'.

If and when any outstanding dividend is forfeited,[1] the entries are:

(1) Debit Dividend Account.
    Credit Reserve (or Profit and Loss Appropriation Account).

(2) Debit (General) Bank Account.
    Credit Deposit Account.

---

[1] In the carrying out of the power of forfeiture, the Directors must act in a strictly constitutional manner, so that the forfeiture, which is a *stricti juris* matter, must be carried out by proper resolution of Directors or otherwise in accordance with the Articles. Striking out from the Balance Sheet of an amount due to a member, of itself, has no legal consequence except that its elimination would be equivalent to a cessation of acknowledgement of indebtedness for the purpose of the Limitation Act 1975.

No transfer in (2) is required if previously the unpaid dividends were retransferred to general Bank Account.

Alternately, the balance of Dividend Account may be transferred to an Unclaimed Dividend Account, and (on forfeiture of dividend) the balance transferred to Reserve or Profit and Loss Appropriation Account.

Illustration 102

Warren Dawlish & Co., Ltd., has an issued share capital of £200,000 in ordinary share of £1 each fully paid, and makes up its accounts annually to 30th September.

On 30th September 19.8, the following balances (*inter alia*) appear in the books.

	£
Profit and Loss Account	37,351 Cr.
Dividend No. 6	160 Cr.
Dividend No. 7	1,212 Cr.
Unclaimed Dividends	527 Cr.
Dividend Banking Account [i.e. *Dividends Nos. 6 and 7*]	1,372 Dr.
Deposit Account—*re* Unclaimed Dividends	527 Dr.

On 10th January 19.9, a dividend, No. 8 of 16 per cent, was declared for the year ended 30th September 19.8, warrants being dispatched the following day. During the year ended 30th September 19.9, the following warrants were duly presented for payment: Dividend No. 2, £27; No. 6, £124; No. 7, £1,108; No. 8, £31,196; and on 30th September 19.9, the balances on Dividends Nos. 6 and 7 were transferred to Unclaimed Dividends Account.

Show Ledger Accounts in respect of the dividends.

DIVIDENDS

		No. 6	No. 7				No. 6	No. 7
19.9 Sept. 30	Sundries (Dividend Banking Account) Unclaimed Dividends Account	£ 124 36	£ 1,108 104	19.8 Sept. 30	Balances	b/d	£ 160	£ 1,212
		£160	£1,212				£160	£1,212

DIVIDEND NO. 8

			£				£
19.9 Sept. 30	Sundries (Dividend Banking Account) Balance	c/d	31,196 804	19.9 Jan. 10	Profit and Loss Appropriation Account		32,000
			£32,000				£32,000
				19.9 Oct. 1	Balance	b/d	804

UNCLAIMED DIVIDENDS

19.9 Sept. 30	Sundries (Dividend Banking Account)	c/d	£ 27	19.8 Sept. 30	Balance	b/d	£ 527
	Balance	c/d	640	19.9 Sept. 30	Dividend No. 6 Account		36
					Dividend No. 7 Account		104
			£667				£667
				19.9 Oct. 1	Balance	b/d	640

DIVIDEND BANKING ACCOUNT

19.8 Sept. 30	Balance	b/d	£ 1,372	19.9 Sept. 30	Dividend No. 2		£ 27
19.9 Jan. 10	(General) Bank Account[1]		32,000		Dividend No. 6		124
Sept. 30	Deposit Account		27		Dividend No. 7		1,108
					Dividend No. 8		31,196
					Deposit Account—		
					Re Dividend No. 6		36
					Re Dividend No. 7		104
					Balance	c/d	804
			£33,399				£33,399
19.9 Oct. 1	Balance	b/d	804				

[1] i.e. 16 per cent on 200,000 shares.

DEPOSIT

19.8 Sept. 30	Balance	b/d	£ 527	19.9 Sept. 30	Dividend Banking Account	c/d	£ 27
19.9 Sept. 30	Dividend Banking Account (No. 6)		36		Balance	c/d	640
	Dividend Banking Account (No. 7)		104				
			£667				£667
19.9 Oct. 1	Balance	b/d	640				

Notes. When the old dividend warrants *re* Dividend No. 2 are paid the amount is transferred from the Deposit Account to the Dividend Banking Account, and the actual payment made out of the latter account and debited to Unclaimed Dividends Account. As the Dividend Banking Account at the commencement (£1,372) is reflective of Dividends Nos. 6 and 7, the payments out of this Banking Account are debited to Dividends No. 6 and No. 7 Account; then when the final balances thereon are 'lifted' to Unclaimed Dividends Account there must be a corresponding transfer from Dividend Banking Account to Deposit Account.

Whenever the unclaimed dividends are written-off as profit, the amount represented thereby will be transferred from the Deposit Account to the General Bank Account.

Actually the company would require production and verification before the warrants in respect of Dividend No. 2 were paid, as such warrants would be considered 'stale'.

Opening entries are in italics.

If the payment of £27 is not utilized out of the Deposit Account, the Deposit Account would be the opening balance of £527 and an 'in' transfer of £113 instead of £140, leaving the balances the same. The method shown in the text is considered preferable so as to keep identified each transfer from Dividend Banking Account to the Deposit Account.

The effect of the Dividend No. 8 should be carefully noted. In this case a 16 per cent dividend was declared on 10th January 19.9. Thus the *actual* dividend payable to the shareholders is 16 per cent, and this amounts to £32,000. However, assuming Income Tax at 40 per cent the company is due to pay Advance Corporation Tax (ACT) of £21,333$\frac{1}{3}$ ($\frac{40}{60} \times$ £32,000). The £21,333$\frac{1}{3}$ will have been credited to ACT account and will be due to be remitted to the Collector of Taxes within approximately 3 months of date dividend paid; when remitted, Bank will be credited and ACT account debited.

Dividend Equalization Fund or Reserve. This is a reserve built up out of profits for the purpose of attempting to maintain a steady and unfailing yearly dividend. It is an 'internal' reserve, an appropriation of profits of a voluntary nature, for a specific purpose. Entries in Journal form are:

(1) On creation of Reserve—
      Profit and Loss Appropriation Account.   *Dr.*
        To Dividend Equalization Reserve.

(2) On utilization—
      Dividend Equalization Reserve.   *Dr.*
        To Dividend Account.

(3) On declaration—
      ACT Account (deferred asset)   *Dr.*
        To ACT Account (currently liability)

(4) On payment—
      Dividend Account   *Dr.*
        To Bank.

SECTION J. RECONSTRUCTIONS, AMALGAMATIONS, AND ABSORPTIONS

Before proceeding with the accounting records arising out of the above, it is important that the precise meaning attached to the terms be understood. An amalgamation in its broadest conception means the combination of two (or more) companies into one by:

1. An absorption of one concern by another, the procedure in which is to wind-up the former (known as absorption); or

2. A formation of an entirely new company to acquire the separate concerns, necessitating the winding-up of the latter. This procedure is known as an amalgamation (in its narrower sense).

3. The formation of a holding company to acquire the SHARES in the concerns in question, in which case not only is a new company formed, but the constituent companies remain.

4. The exchange of shares of one company with those of another, in which case the old companies remain unchanged and, as contrasted with (3), no new company is formed, the merging process being effected by an exchange of shares, e.g. Y company acquires a block of shares in Z company, the latter at the same time acquiring a block of shares in Y company.

A reconstruction, the purpose of which will be noted shortly, may take the form of an internal reorganization of capital or the inauguration of a new company, the latter acquiring the assets and assuming the liabilities of the former company, the second procedure often being designated an external reconstruction.

The various positions may be illustrated by reference to two imaginary companies, Y and Z.

(a) If an amalgamation takes place, there are two liquidations (i.e. Y and Z) and the formation of a new company, say, W.

(b) If an absorption takes place, there is one liquidation (say, Y) and no new company formed.

(c) If an amalgamation takes place by means of a holding company there is no liquidation, but (unless such company is already in existence) a formation of a new company.

(d) If an amalgamation takes place by means of share exchange, there is neither liquidation nor formation involved.

(e) If there is an external reconstruction, there is a liquidation, say, of Y, superseded by the formation of a new company, say, W.

There are thus:

    (i) *Two* liquidations and *a* formation = AMALGAMATION.
    (ii) *One* liquidation and *no* formation = ABSORPTION.
    (iii) *No* liquidation and *a* formation   = NEW HOLDING COMPANY.
    (iv) *No* liquidation and *no* formation = SHARE EXCHANGE.
    (v) *One* liquidation and *a* formation = EXTERNAL RECONSTRUCTION.

Having noted what may be called the 'mechanical' side of these mergers, it is necessary to remind the student of the 'legal' side, and careful reference should be made to the subject-matter in a law textbook.

The chief objects of amalgamation are:

1. To eliminate or minimize competition.

2. To pool resources, whether financial or technical, facilitating the best utilization of staff, and development of research.

3. To effect general economies in (a) production, (b) use and power of capital, (c) selling, (d) distribution, and (e) general overheads through centralization and closing down unprofitable and redundant sections.

4. To create a more powerful economic unit to control markets, supplies of materials; to effect purchases on a larger scale and, consequently, at generally lower prices and on more advantageous terms; to combat the demands of trade unions, and to exercise more political influence in commercial matters, e.g. as to tariffs, etc.; to create by the augmentation of the issued capital a larger market for share dealings and the raising of further capital.

The objections to amalgamations are:

1. Anti-social factors involving exploitation of the public, creating monopolistic conditions of price inflation, withholding of supplies, creation of artificial shortages and, in wartime, the danger to the State through adherence to Cartel arrangements.

2. Political objections from Trade Unions.

3. Disappearance of the small trader and therewith the loss of the personal element.

4. The danger of amalgamation of businesses which are best left in their present form and structure.

5. The possible loss of valuable goodwill through disappearance of the names of old proprietors, although the utilization of the Holding Company will largely overcome this.

6. Over-centralization involving loss of control, lack of cohesion in management, unwillingness of directors and high executives to lose their 'sovereignty'.

7. Over-capitalization through the watering of capital by promoters and vendors (this applies particularly to extravagant prices paid for goodwill of businesses purchased in boom periods).

8. Scope is given to unscrupulous promoters.

The fact may also be mentioned that nationalization of large units of industry is facilitated by prior amalgamations, but this is a matter which depends upon the political inclination of the individual.

For taxation purposes, where there has been a company reconstruction and within two years after the reconstruction at least 75 per cent of the trade belongs to the same persons as belonged to that percentage within one year before the reconstruction, the trade is treated on the 'continuing basis', i.e. it is NOT treated as a ceasing and commencing trade. However, in these circumstances the successor company can utilize any unrelieved capital allowances and trading losses of the predecessor company.

Complex Capital Gains Tax problems can arise regarding company reorganizations, amalgamations and reconstructions. However, in respect of share exchange transactions, i.e. where new shareholdings are issued in exchange for old shareholdings, a disposal and acquisition is deemed not to have taken place; the new shareholding is regarded as the same asset acquired when the old shareholding was acquired. Most of the problems ensuing from the Capital Gains Tax concern the shareholders as individual taxpayers, and consequently no further reference will be made to this tax in this chapter.

The above objects may be reached by the operation of an entirely new and substituted company; or by an absorption; or by the formation of a holding company, or by an exchange of shares. In the second case the stronger usually takes over the weaker.

In reconstruction, which, as has been already stated, may be: (a) external, involving a winding-up, and a new company being formed; or (b) internal, not involving winding-up, the objects are:

(i) Compromise with creditors (including debenture-holders).

(ii) Compromise with members by alteration of various rights between each class, usually involving the writing down of the amount of share capital (as in a reduction of capital, which is a special form of reconstruction).

(iii) The raising of further capital from members, obviously only where shares are fully paid, as if they are partly paid a call will be made in the ordinary way.

(iv) Alteration of domicile (external reconstruction).

(v) Alteration of Memorandum.

(vi) Decentralization whereby mere sections, branches, or departments become self-contained units.

It is important that the student should observe whether the reconstruction has become necessary or is merely advisable. A necessary reconstruction almost invariably involves the alteration of rights, or the imposition of some sacrifice, temporary or permanent on both members and creditors.

Before proceeding with the principles involved in merger and reconstruction operations, it may be here remarked that examination questions in this department of accounting are very popular—at least with the examiners; and a very thorough comprehension of the principles and rules is imperative. The questions may be broadly divided into two types:

(a) The 'mechanical' or mere book-keeping problem.

(b) The 'diagnosis and cure' or 'accounting' problem.

The latter problems are infinitely more difficult than the former, involving, as they do, not only the knowledge of the mere book-keeping entries, but a wide knowledge of business affairs, business psychology, finance, and even political and technical matters. The book-keeping entries will first be disposed of.

Closing Entries on Liquidation. 1. Debit Realization Account with assets other than fictitious assets taken over; credit the individual Asset Accounts.

2. Debit provisions like bad debts provision (which, although deducted from assets, are CREDIT balances); credit Realization Account.

3. Debit liabilities and *if taken over* credit Realization Account. If to be *paid* by the company, liabilities will remain untransferred in the books, and upon payment the accounts will be debited and cash credited. The above term 'liabilities' includes debentures.

4. Debit purchasing company and credit Realization Account with the purchase consideration, the ascertainment of which being frequently the most difficult part of the problem.

5. Debit Realization Account with expenses of realization; credit cash.

6. Debit cash, shares, or other assets paid in discharge of the purchase consideration; credit the purchasing company.

7. The balance of Realization Account will be closed by a transfer to Sundry Members' Account.

(a) If a profit: debit Realization Account; credit sundry members.

(b) If a loss: debit sundry members; credit Realization Account.

8. Debit share capital and credit sundry members with share capital.

9. Debit general reserve (and other accounts of undistributed profits); credit sundry members.

10. Debit sundry members and credit fictitious assets, including debit balance on Profit and Loss Account.

11. Debit sundry members and credit cash, shares, or other assets as paid to them (according to circumstances), remembering that cash may already be diminished by the payment of liabilities and expenses of realization.

Where there are different classes of members, the transfers will vary according to the nature of the items and the particular rights of each class, so that it will be essential to have separate Members' Accounts for each class, e.g. preference, ordinary, deferred.

The following points may arise (numbers in parentheses refer to the foregoing entries):

1. Where cash is not taken over—and usually the arrangement is for cash to be retained by the acquired company—the purchase consideration being accordingly diminished, no entry will be required, the balance remaining in the Cash Book. Where certain assets are not acquired by the purchasing company but sold piecemeal, the selling company will debit them to a separate Realization Account in the ordinary way; or by leaving the assets untransferred, crediting them with cash received, and transferring the balance of each separate asset to Realization Account as representing a profit or loss on each asset disposed of. Where the selling company has sufficient cash to pay creditors, the purchase consideration will usually be based on assets only.

2. Where debentures are to be redeemed at a premium by the *purchasing* company, the alternative methods may be:

(*a*) Debit debentures; credit Realization Account, ignoring all considerations of premium, as the acquired company is relieved entirely of its burden, the amount of which will normally appear in the books at the nominal value.

(*b*) Where the selling company receive the cash from the purchasing company, the debentures will not be transferred to Realization Account, as in (*a*), but as follows: debit Realization Account and credit debentures with the premium.

Alternatively, the entries in (2*b*) may be effected through the Debenture-holders' Account.

3. Any profits or losses connected with the discharge of liabilities will be: (*a*) in case of profits, debited to liabilities and credited to Realization Account; and (*b*) in case of losses, debited to Realization Account and credited to the liabilities.

The disposition of certain items appearing in the books of the absorbed company requires careful consideration.

As will be remembered assets and liabilities taken over will be dealt with through the transfer to Realization Account, but such debit items that appear as assets will, if they are fictitious, e.g. Discount on Debentures, Preliminary Expenses and Profit and Loss Account (if the losses have exceeded gains) be transferred to the debit of Sundry Members, and credit items like Share Capital and Profit and Loss Account will be transferred to the credit of Sundry Members.

It is, however, the items described as Reserves, Provisions and Funds that give the most trouble, but the principle is simple. Is the item a liability, or an undistributed profit (i.e. a provision or a reserve)? Or does it include both? If a liability, it will be either taken over or discharged. In the former case it will be transferred to Realization Account; in the latter case it will be paid off in the ordinary way. If, however, the item is undistributed profit it will be transferred to Sundry Members.

In addition, items which are provisions against loss or depreciation of assets are similar to liabilities (except that they cannot, as such, be taken over by the absorbing company, although the latter could introduce into their opening entries exactly the same provision figure). Therefore they are equivalent to a liability no longer required as the assets in respect of which they were created will be taken over by the absorbing company, so that they will be transferred to Realization Account. Typical of such items are Amortization Funds, Bad Debts Provisions, Depreciation Funds, Leasehold Redemption Funds.

Where items partake of both liabilities and undistributed profit, e.g. Workmen's Compensation Fund, that part representing liability will be dealt with in the way mentioned above, that is, if taken over will be credited to Realization, or if paid off, will be dealt with as for any other liability paid, i.e. credit to Cash or Bank. It is important to understand that items like that will have been built up normally as provisions for likely liabilities, and if excessive, will be a secret reserve, but the true nature must be ascertained and dealt with on a sale of the company.

The four fundamental rules are:

1. If provision for a liability not required, the credit is to Realization Account.

2. If undistributed profit, the credit is to Sundry Members.

3. If a 'mixed' fund, the credit will be (a) to Realization Account as to the part representing a liability (or provision against loss or depreciation of an asset), and (b) to Sundry Members as to the part representing undistributed profit.

4. If a debit balance of Profit and Loss or a fictitious asset the debit will be to Sundry Members.

The following is a summary of the treatment of Reserves, Provisions and Funds:

Credit Balance	Nature	Treatment
1. General Reserve	Undistributed profit	Credit Sundry Members.
2. Provision	Provision for loss—equivalent to liability	Credit Realization Account (liability not maturing).
3. Leasehold Redemption	Provision for depreciation equivalent to liability	Do.

4. Debenture Redemption	Undistributed profit (held back in accordance with Debenture Trust Deed).	Credit Sundry Members.
5. Rehabilitation Fund	Provision for meeting expenses of deferred repairs, renewals, additions, replacements.	Credit Sundry Members for the Capital portion of replacements of and additions to Assets, e.g. Plant. Credit Realization Account for the Revenue portion, e.g. repairs and renewals.
6. Workmen's Profit Sharing Fund	Liability to work-people	If taken over, Credit Realization Account; if paid off (as probable), credit Cash or Bank.
7. Insurance Funds: Fire, Marine, Workmen's Compensation	Undistributed profit and Liability (The excess of the Fund over Liabilities (b) will be undistributed profit (a).)	(a) Credit Sundry Members (b) As in (6).
8. Contingencies Reserve	As 7.	As 7.
9. Capital Reserve	Profit not of a distributable nature	Credit Sundry Members.

Illustration 103

[*External Reconstruction.*] G, Ltd., agrees to reconstruct by forming a new company, G (New), Ltd., to which the business is sold, the purchase consideration therefor being the issue of 100,000 shares of £1 each, credited as £0·25 per share paid. For the purpose of sale, sundry assets are to be valued at £40,000.

The Balance Sheet of G, Ltd., at the date of sale was as follows:

G, Ltd., Balance Sheet as at ....

	£		£
Authorized and Issued Share Capital	55,000	Sundry Assets . . .	62,000
Liabilities	15,000	Profit and Loss Account . .	8,000
	£70,000		£70,000

Assuming that the liabilities are taken over by G (New), Ltd., close the books of G, Ltd., ignoring realization expenses.

REALIZATION ACCOUNT

	£		£
Sundry Assets[1]	62,000	Sundry Creditors[1]	15,000
		G (New), Ltd.: Purchase	
		Consideration	25,000
		Loss on Realization	22,000
	£62,000		£62,000

SUNDRY MEMBERS

	£		£
Profit and Loss Account[1]	8,000	Balance[1]	55,000
Loss on Realization	22,000		
Shares in G (New), Ltd.	25,000		
	£55,000		£55,000

[1] Inserted direct from Balance Sheet.

[2]G (New), LTD.

	£		£
Realization Account	25,000	Shares	25,000

[2]SHARES IN G (New), LTD.

	£		£
G (New), Ltd.	25,000	Sundry Members	25,000

[2] In examination work these accounts may be dispensed with.

Competing Claims of Members. Where there are several classes of members, their rights as between themselves depend upon the *Memorandum and Articles of Association*. Where no specific reference is made therein, the rights are dependent upon circumstances.

1. Where preference shares have priority as to repayment of Capital in a winding up, calls must be made on shares of a junior class (e.g. ordinary share) if not fully paid, in order to meet the preference priority.

2. It may happen that of shares of the same class some may be fully paid, some partly paid and/or some with calls in advance. The latter are treated as *debts* and must be paid off before the others and, where necessary, calls made on the partly paid shareholders.

Where there are calls in arrear the holders thereof are not entitled to any share in a distribution until the non-defaulting shareholders have been paid sufficient to equate the position, that is, to make all the shares (of the same class), the same amount paid up.

In practice, a full call will not usually be necessary, but only sufficient to enable such dividend to be paid on the full-paid shares as will leave all the shares of the same class with the same amount paid up.

3. If there is a preference as to dividends, it is *prima facie* cumulative, but on a winding up, in the absence of some provision in the Articles to the contrary, the preference shareholders do not become entitled to payment of the arrears of preference dividends, except where already declared before the liquidation commences (*re Crichton Oil Co.*). [The right may, however, arise if, on a true construction of the Articles by the Court, such right is clearly indicated or intended (*re Walter Symons*).]

Where arrears are payable, they are calculated up to the date of winding up and not to the date of payment; and by reason of the liquidation the sum is a capital repayment, (*re Dominion Tar & Chemical Co.*). If, however, the Memorandum or Articles entitle the preference shareholders to the arrears of preference dividend, they will be entitled thereto unless the clause is qualified by special words, e.g. dividends DUE, in which case the preference shareholders would not be entitled to the arrears, unless dividends have been DECLARED before the commencement of the winding up (*re Crichton's Oil Co.*).

4. Where preference shareholders are entitled to priority of repayment of capital, they are not entitled to share *pari passu* with ordinary shareholders in a surplus unless expressly authorized by the Articles. The onus is on the preference shareholders to prove that they have such a right.

Where the rights of preference shares as to profits or capital, either directly or by inference through reference to other classes of shares, are *not* defined, the legal position appears to be different from that in *Scottish Insurance Corporation* v. *Wilson's & Clyde Coal Co., Ltd.*, and *re Isle of Thanet Electricity Supply*, where the rights *were* defined.

In *re Marshall Bros. (Belfast)*, it was held that the rule of construction that express rights negative any further rights (i.e. further rights cannot be implied) applies *only* to instances where preference rights are attached thereto in the Memorandum or Articles of Association or in the terms of issue.

A further refinement is that the case brings back the rule of distinguishing between capital and profit in a liquidation (as contrasted with the rule of extinguished identity), the distinction being a necessary one where the company is a going concern. In other words, in the circumstances the distinction between capital and profit is continued in, and not submerged by, the commencement of liquidation.

The case of *re Marshall Bros.* decided[1]:

1. That the capital reserve was divisible *pari passu* amongst *all* the shareholders, preference and ordinary; and
2. The uncapitalized profit was divisible amongst the ordinary shareholders only.

The barest minimum right attached to a preference share, viz. priority

[1] This case is thought to be unsound and unlikely to be supported in the English Courts.

as to dividends, would appear quite sufficient to preclude *any* further right (unless expressly defined) to participation in any of the surplus assets of the company, hence it is only in respect of surplus *capital* assets that a preference shareholder could establish a claim, by implication, to participate in a surplus in a liquidation.

The members, however, may agree to take shares instead of a cash payment, so that it is immaterial what profit or loss on realization arises, as the DEBIT to each class of member is fixed at the outset; but as the Realization Account must be closed, the balance will be split according to the balances on the accounts of the members, thus constituting merely a balancing item.

Illustration 104

[*External Reconstruction.*] The Balance Sheet of D, Ltd., is as follows:

D, LTD., BALANCE SHEET AS AT ………

	£		£	£
Authorized and Issued Share Capital—		Fixed Assets—		
50,000 6½% Preference Shares of £1 each, fully paid	50,000	Patents . . .	24,500	
60,000 Ordinary Shares of £1 each,		Freehold Property . .	60,000	84,500
fully paid	60,000	Current Assets—		
5% Debentures . . £10,000		Cash . . .	500	
Add Interest accrued . 2,000		Debtors . . .	12,000	
	12,000	Stock . . .	18,000	
Creditors.	8,000			30,500
		Profit and Loss . .		15,000
	£130,000			£130,000

The following scheme was passed and sanctioned:

1. X. Ltd., to be formed to take over the business.
2. One share of £0·50 fully paid in the new company to be issued for every three ordinary shares in the old company.
3. Three shares of £0·50 fully paid in the new company to be issued for every five preference shares in the old company.
4. Debenture-holders to be paid in full by X, Ltd.
5. The creditors to receive 80 per cent of the sums due to them in fully-paid shares of £0·50 in the new company in full settlement.
6. Patents and Profit and Loss Account to be written-off.
7. Arrears of preference divided to be cleared by issuing one £0·50 fully-paid preference share in X, Ltd. for every twenty held.
8. Any balance available by the scheme to be used in writing down the freehold property.

Show closing and opening Journal entries. Ignore expenses.

D, Ltd., Journal

	£	£
Realization Account	90,500	
Freehold Property		60,000
Stock		18,000
Debtors		12,000
Cash		500
Being sundry assets taken over by X, Ltd., in accordance with reconstruction scheme.		
5% Debentures	12,000	
Realization Account		12,000
Being debentures taken over, etc.		
X, Ltd.	32,650	
Realization Account		32,650
Being purchase consideration under reconstruction scheme.		
Preference Share Capital	50,000	
Ordinary Share Capital	60,000	
Sundry Members		110,000
Being share capitals transferred to sundry members.		
Reconstruction Account	45,850	
Realization Account		45,850
Being loss on realization.		
Shares in X, Ltd.	32,650	
X, Ltd.		32,650
Being discharge of purchase consideration.		
Sundry Members (Preference) . . .	16,250	
,, ,, (Ordinary)	10,000	
Creditors	6,400	
Shares in X, Ltd.		32,650
Being discharge of liability under reconstruction scheme.		
Reconstruction Account	1,250	
Sundry Members (Preference) . .		1,250
Being discharge of arrears of preference dividends by distribution of one share for 20 preference shares under scheme of reconstruction.		
Reconstruction Account	39,500	
Patents		24,500
Profit and Loss Account . . .		15,000
Being debit balances written-off under scheme of recon- struction.		
Sundry Creditors	1,600	
Reconstruction Account . . .		1,600
Being amount written-off sundry creditors under recon- struction scheme.		
Sundry Members (Preference) . . .	35,000	
Sundry Members (Ordinary) . . .	50,000	
Reconstruction Account . . .		85,000
Being balance of Reconstruction Account written-off to sundry members.		

The more important Ledger accounts are:

SUNDRY MEMBERS

	Preference	Ordinary			Preference	Ordinary
	£	£			£	£
Reconstruction Account	35,000[1]	50,000[1]	Share Capital Account		50,000	60,000
Shares in X, Ltd.	16,250	10,000	Reconstruction Account		1,250[1]	
	£51,250	£60,000			£51,250	£60,000

As the transfer to sundry members is merely a balancing figure the transfers from the Share Capital Accounts may be made to one account for Sundry Members, thus:

SUNDRY MEMBERS

		£			£
Reconstruction Account		85,000	Share Capital Accounts:		
Shares in X, Ltd.:			Preference		50,000
Preference Shareholders		16,250	Ordinary		60,000
Ordinary Shareholders		10,000	Reconstruction Account		1,250
		£111,250			£111,250

RECONSTRUCTION ACCOUNT

		£				£
Preference Shareholders[1]		1,250	Sundry Creditors			1,600
Sundry items written-off		39,500	Sundry Members—			
Realization Account		**45,850**	Preference	35,000[1]		
			Ordinary	50,000[1]		
						85,000
		£86,600				£86,600

[1] As the transfer to sundry members is merely a balancing figure, a frequent practice is to transfer the amount written-off share capitals to Reconstruction Account without employing the account for Sundry Members. This would avoid the transfers above indicated, whilst the Journal entries in respect of the shares paid to members and the share capital transfers would be modified accordingly.

REALIZATION ACCOUNT

		£			£
Sundry Assets		90,500	5% Debentures of X, Ltd.		12,000
			X, Ltd.—Purchase Consideration		32,650
			Reconstruction Account		**45,850**
		£90,500			£90,500

CREDITORS

	£		£
Reconstruction Account	1,600	Balances	8,000
Shares in X, Ltd. . .	6,400		
	£8,000		£8,000

X, LTD.

	£		£
Realization Account . .	32,650	Shares . . : .	32,650

SHARES IN X, LTD.

	£		£
X, Ltd.	32,650	Sundry Members—	
		Preference . . .	16,250
		Ordinary . . .	10,000
		Creditors . . :	6,400
	£32,650		£32,650

If all the adjustments appear in one account, e.g. the Realization Account, the transfer of £85,000 to the debits of Sundry Members would be arrived at thus:

REALIZATION ACCOUNT

	£			£
Sundry Assets . . .	90,500	5% Debentures . . .		12,000
Preference Shareholders .	1,250	Sundry Creditors . .		1,600
Sundry items written-off:		X, Ltd.: Purchase Consideration		32,650
[Patents and Profit and Loss		Sundry Members:		
Account] . . .	39,500	Preference . .	35,000	
		Ordinary . .	50,000	
				85,000
	£131,250			£131,250

As a result the transfer previously shown in heavy type would not be necessary.

ALTERNATIVE METHOD.

RECONSTRUCTION ACCOUNT

	£		£
Preference Shareholders . .	1,250	Share Capital Accounts wiritten-	
Sundry items written-off .	39,500	off—	
Realization Account . . :	45,850	Preference . . .	35,000
		Ordinary . . .	50,000
		Sundry Creditors . . .	1,600
	£86,600		£86,600

¹SHARE CAPITALS

	Preference	Ordinary		Preference	Ordinary
	£	£		£	£
Reconstruction Account	35,000	50,000	Balances Reconstruction Account	50,000	60,000
Shares in X, Ltd.	16,250	10,000		1,250	
	£51,250	£60,000		£51,250	£60,000

¹ In the alternative method these accounts take the place of Sundry Members Account. [See p. 23285.]

The purchase consideration is arrived at as follows:

		Shares @ £0·50 each	£
Shares to be issued to:			
(1) Ordinary Shareholders		20,000	10,000
(2) Preference Shareholders:	*Shares*		
(a) for Capital	30,000		
(b) for 'Arrears' of Dividends	2,500	32,500	16,250
(3) Creditors (80% of £8,000 = £6,400)		12,800	6,400
Total		65,300	£32,650

The opening Journal entries for X, Ltd. are:

	£	£
Freehold Property¹	14,150	
Stock	18,000	
Debtors	12,000	
Cash	500	
Debenture Holders of D, Ltd.		12,000
D, Ltd. (Vendor)		32,650
Being sundry assets and debenture taken over and purchase consideration as per agreement dated........ .		
D, Ltd. (Vendor)	32,650	
Share Capital		32,650
Being discharge of purchase consideration by allotment of 65,300 shares of £0·50 each, fully paid, as per agreement and directors' resolution, *vide* Minute Book, p.		

¹ This is a balancing figure (see paragraph 8 in question). It reflects the loss on realization of the old company £45,850 as the book value of the property in the old books is £60,000 and in the new books £14,150.

Share Fractions. It may not be possible to give an exact allotment owing to fractions arising from the basis of the exchange; thus, assuming an exchange of 7 shares in the new company for every 4 in the old, Y, a member holding 25 ordinaries, would theoretically be entitled to $\frac{7}{4} \times 25$ shares in the purchasing company, or $43\frac{3}{4}$ shares. But, as fractions of shares cannot be issued, the usual procedure is either:

1. to sell the shares not capable of allotment and divide the proceeds amongst those entitled to the fractions, or,

2. payment of cash to cover the original shares not divisible into whole shares, on the basis of market price of the shares to be allotted or on the basis of the paid-up value of either the exchanged share or the new shares, or

3. to issue—in big-scale share exchanges—fractional certificates. The holder may then:

(*a*) sell them,
(*b*) buy sufficient to make up a 'full' share, or
(*c*) pay cash to make his fractions 'full'.

Before this can be carried out, a full list of members must be prepared, because, although the TOTAL exchange will probably obviate fractions, it is very unlikely that the individual exchanges will.

Illustration 105

The Issued Share Capital of Beer, Ltd. is £10,000, that of Skittles, Ltd. £4,000, all divided into shares of £1 each, fully paid.

It is arranged that Beer, Ltd. should take over the shares of Skittles, Ltd. by issuing shares (of £1 each fully paid) to the shareholders of the latter company on the basis of their respective values, viz.; Beer, Ltd. £1·60, and Skittles, Ltd. £1.

The shareholders all hold shares capable of exact exchanges, i.e. 8 or multiples of 8, totalling 3,560, except 5 shareholders holding respectively A 23, B 74, C 100, D 118, and E 125.

Show how the exchange will be dealt with in the books of Beer, Ltd., including fractions.

DIVISION

	Original Shares		Shares in Beer, Ltd.	
Sundry shareholders holding 8 or multiples of 8	3,560		$\frac{5}{8} \times 3,560$	2,225
Other holdings—				
A		23	$\frac{5}{8} \times$ 23	$14\frac{3}{8}$
B		74	$\frac{5}{8} \times$ 74	$46\frac{1}{4}$
C		100	$\frac{5}{8} \times$ 100	$62\frac{1}{2}$
D		118	$\frac{5}{8} \times$ 118	$73\frac{3}{4}$
E	440	125	$\frac{5}{8} \times$ 125	$78\frac{1}{8}$
	4,000			2,498
			Fractions	2
				2,500

The number of shares to be issued by Beer, Ltd., is $\frac{20}{32}$ ($\frac{5}{8}$) of $4,000 = 2,500$. Ignoring other factors that would probably exist, this puts the shareholders of Skittles, Ltd., in the same positions as before, viz.:

4,000 Shares (Skittle, Ltd.) at par = 4,000
2,500 " (Beer, Ltd.) at £1·60 = 4,000

The amount due to 'other' shareholders for fractions may be discharged:

1. By Cash payments amounting to £2, e.g. to (A) £0·375 etc.
2. By Cash equivalent to shareholding, i.e. $\frac{8}{5} \times £2 = £3·20$ e.g. to holder of 23 shares $\frac{5}{8} \times £0·375 = £0·60$ (the arithmetic equivalent of holding $\frac{3}{8}$ of a share worth £1·60).
3. Cash payments on unexchangeable shares, i.e. 2 @ £1 = £2.

Thus the purchase consideration would be the allotment of 2,498 shares plus Cash payments amounting to : (a) £2 or (b) £3·20 being £1·60 a share for 2 shares.

Alternatively, the shares could be divided by 8, leaving the undivisible shares as fractions and discharging the latter by the above method.
This would be:

	Original Shares	Exchangeable Multiple of 8	Balance not Exchanged	Shares in Beer, Ltd.
Sundry shareholders	3,560	3,560		2,225
Other shareholders—				
A . . . 23		16	7	10
B . . . 74		72	2	45
C . . . 100		96	4	60
D . . . 118		112	6	70
E . . . 125		120	5	75
	440	—	416	
	4,000	3,976	24	2,485

This would result in issuing 2,485 shares in Beer Ltd., to shareholders of Skittles, Ltd., and cash payments of:

(a) £24, as above (e.g. £7 to A, etc.).
(b) £38·40, i.e. $\frac{8}{5} \times$ £24 (i.e. £1·60 for each unexchanged share) thus—

		£p
A would receive Cash .	. . . . .	11·20
B ,, ,,	. . . . .	3·20
C ,, ,,	. . . . .	6·40
D ,, ,,	. . . . .	9·60
E ,, ,,	. . . . .	8·00
		£38·40

(c) as in (a). No difference arises here because the shares of both companies are £1 fully paid.

Thus, the purchase consideration would be the allotment of 2,485 shares and cash payments amounting to (a) £24 or (b) £38·4, being 24 unexchangeable shares of £1·60 each.

Illustration 106

[*Absorption.*] Hebden, Ltd., sells its business to Bridge, Ltd., the latter to take over the assets at book values and pay creditors; *in addition*, it is to pay Hebden, Ltd., £100 towards redemption of its debentures at a premium of 10 per cent. The payment of purchase price is to be £2,000 in shares of £1 each at par and the balance in cash.

BALANCE SHEET (HEBDEN, LTD.)

	£			£
Issued Capital	3,000	Sundry Assets		5,200
Profit and Loss Account . .	300	Debtors . . . £1,700		
Creditors	2,450	*Less* Provision . 150		
Debentures	1,000			1,550
	£6,750			£6,750

Show entries in the books of Hebden, Ltd.

Ignore realization expenses and the question of the possible increase of the nominal capital of Bridge, Ltd.

Entries in Ledger form in the books of Hebden, Ltd.:

REALIZATION ACCOUNT

	£		£
Sundry Assets . . .	5,200	Bad Debts Provision . .	150
Debtors . . .	1,700	Creditors . . .	2,450
Premium on Debentures .	100	Bridge, Ltd., Purchase Con-	
Profit on Realization . .	150	sideration . . .	4,550
	£7,150		£7,150

BRIDGE, LTD.

	£		£
Realization Account . .	4,550	Shares	2,000
		Cash	2,550
	£4,550		£4,550

DEBENTURES

	£		£
Cash	1,100	Balance . . . b/d	1,000
		Premium . . .	100
	£1,100		£1,100

SUNDRY MEMBERS

	£		£
Cash[1]	1,450	Share Capital . .	3,000
Shares[1]	2,000	Profit and Loss Account .	300
		Realization Account:	
		Profit . . .	150
	£3,450		£3,450

[1] See note (²) on p. 23292.

CASH

	£		£
Bridge, Ltd. . . .	2,550	Debentures . . .	1,100
		Sundry Members . .	1,450
	£2,550		£2,550

SHARES

	£		£
Bridge, Ltd. . . .	2,000	Sundry Members . .	2,000

If the debentures plus premium had been formally taken over by Bridge, Ltd., the purchase consideration would have been reduced by £1,100, and the vendor company would have been relieved of its liability accordingly. This would have had the effect of reducing the cash receipt from £2,550 to £1,450 and eliminating the payment to the debenture-holders. The Debenture Account of £1,100 would accordingly have been credited to Realization Account. Alternatively, the debit for the premium would not have been made and the original balance of £1,000 been credited to the Realization Account. In both methods the relief to the vending company is £1,000.

The opening Journal entries of the company are:

	(1) Where the Cash is paid to Vendor Company to discharge debt			(2) Where the Liability is formally taken over		
		£	£		£	£
Sundry Assets[1]	Dr.	5,200		Dr.	5,200	
Debtors	Dr.	1,700		Dr.	1,700	
Premium on Debentures (or Goodwill)	Dr.	100		Dr.	100	
Creditors			2,450			2,450
Debenture Holders of Hebden, Ltd.						1,100
Hebden, Ltd.			4,550			3,450
Being assets and liabilities taken over and purchase consideration as per agreement dated						
Debenture Holders of Hebden Ltd.				Dr.	1,100	
Hebden, Ltd.	Dr.	4,550		Dr.	3,450	
Cash			2,550			2,550
Share Capital			2,000			2,000
Being discharge of purchase consideration.						
		£11,550	£11,550		£11,550	£11,550

[1] Assumed that the purchasing company ignores the bad debts provision of Hebden, Ltd.
[2] Each member of Hebden, Ltd., will receive:
   (1) 2 shares in Bridge, Ltd., for 3 held in Hebden, Ltd.
   (2) £0·48⅓ in cash for every one share held in Hebden, Ltd., i.e.:

$$\frac{1,450}{3,000} \times £1 = £0·48\tfrac{1}{3}$$

Illustration 107

[*Absorption.*] X, Ltd., agrees to take over, Y, Ltd.

The issued share capital of Y, Ltd., is 10,000 shares of £2 each, £1 paid, market value £4·75, reserves are £25,000.

X, Ltd., has an issued share capital of 20,000 shares of £3 each, £2·50 paid, market value £10; reserves are £90,000.

The purchase consideration is the exchange of 2 shares in X, Ltd., for 5 in Y, Ltd.; fractions total to 15 shares, which X, Ltd., agrees to pay in cash on market-value basis of shares.

Show the closing entries of Y, Ltd., and the opening entries of X, Ltd., in respect of the above acquisition.

The question should occasion no difficulty if it be remembered that share capital and reserves (meaning, by the latter, surplus of undivided profits) must be reflective of assets less liabilities or 'net' assets. The details of the latter are not available, so that one must substitute the term 'net' assets for assets and liabilities, the amount represented thereby equalling the sum of capital and reserves; thus, if assets are £2,000 and liabilities £400, the 'net' assets must be £1,600, which will be reflected in, say, share capital £1,150; reserves, £450.

Hence, it is immaterial in which form the Balance Sheet position is shown, subject to the qualification that if share capital, reserves, and creditors *are* given, the gross assets are the sum of three, the 'net' assets being the latter minus creditors. Thus, in the above, if the figure of £400 liability is disclosed, the balancing figure is gross assets, £2,000.

Closing entries in Ledger form in the books of Y, Ltd., are:

REALIZATION ACCOUNT

	£		£
Sundry 'Net' Assets . .	35,000	Purchasing Co. (X, Ltd.):	
Profit on Realization .	5,000	Shares . £39,850[1]	
		Cash . . 150[1]	
			40,000
	£40,000		£40,000

[1] Posted direct to Sundry Members.

SUNDRY MEMBERS

	£		£
Shares	39,850	Share Capital . . .	10,000
Cash	150	Reserves. . . .	25,000
		Profit on Realization . .	5,000
	£40,000		£40,000

Opening entries in Journal form in the books of X, Ltd., are:

JOURNAL

	£p	£p
Goodwill	5,000·00	
Sundry 'Net' Assets	35,000·00	
Y, Ltd.		40,000·00
Being sundry 'net' assets and goodwill acquired from Y, Ltd., as per purchase agreement dated		
Y, Ltd.	40,000·00	
Share Capital		9,962·50
Share Premium[1]		29,887·50
Bank		150·00
Being allotment of £3,985 shares of £3 each, credited as £2·50 paid, premium thereon, cash paid for fractions; as per directors' resolution dated ...., *vide* Minute Book, p.		

[1] 3,985 shares at [£10−£2·50].

Purchase consideration = 2 shares for every 5, i.e.
$$= 4,000 \text{ shares for } 10,000 \text{ (the total shares in Y, Ltd.)}$$
$$= 4,000 \times £10 \text{ (market price of X, Ltd. Shares)}$$
$$= £40,000$$

Discharged in:		£	
Cash for fractions	15 at £10	150	
Shares	3,985 at £10	39,850	£40,000

Alternatively, goodwill may be debited and Share Premium credited with £7,500, to bring up goodwill to £12,500 to correspond with the market capitalization of the shares computed as follows:

	£
10,000 shares valued at £4·75 each .	47,500
Represented by 'net' assets	35,000
Goodwill	£12,500

Illustration 107

[*Absorption*.] The following are the summarized Balance Sheets of X, Ltd., and Y, Ltd.:

BALANCE SHEETS AS AT ....

	X, Ltd.	Y, Ltd.		X, Ltd.	Y, Ltd.
	£	£		£	£
Authorized and Issued Share Capital	50,000	20,000	Sundry Assets	45,000	34,000
Profit and Loss Account	3,000		Shares, Y, Ltd.	20,000	
Creditors	12,000	5,000	Loan, Y, Ltd.	10,000	
Loan, H, Ltd.	10,000		Profit and Loss Account		1,000
Loan, X, Ltd.		10,000			
	£75,000	£35,000		£75,000	£35,000

H, Ltd. (a holding company), owns the whole of the share capital of X, Ltd., the latter owning the whole of the share capital of Y, Ltd.

X and Y, Ltd., is formed to acquire the sundry assets and creditors of X, Ltd., and Y, Ltd., the sundry assets being revalued at £40,000 and £21,000 for X, Ltd., and Y, Ltd., respectively. The amount of loan due to X, Ltd., is to be discharged in shares in the new company, the debt due to H, Ltd., to be similarly discharged. Show the closing Journal entries of X, Ltd., and Y, Ltd., and the opening Journal entries of the new company. Ignore narratives, stamp duties, etc.

X, LTD., JOURNAL

	£	£
Profit and Loss Account	3,000	
Share Capital	50,000	
H. Ltd. [Sole Shareholder]		53,000
Realization Account	45,000	
Sundry Assets		45,000
Creditors	12,000	
Realization Account		12,000
X and Y, Ltd.	28,000	
Realization Account		28,000
Realization Account	14,000	
Liquidator, Y, Ltd.[1]	**6,000**	
Shares in Y, Ltd.		20,000
Liquidator, Y, Ltd.[1]	**10,000**	
Loan, Y, Ltd.		10,000

[1] See Y, LTD., JOURNAL on p. 23296.

X, Ltd., Journal—(contd.)

	£	£
Shares in X and Y, Ltd.	44,000	
X and Y, Ltd.		28,000
Liquidator, Y, Ltd.[1]		**16,000**
H. Ltd. [Sole Shareholder]	19,000	
Realization Account		19,000
H. Ltd. [Sole Shareholder]	34,000	
do. [Loan Account]	10,000	
Shares in X and Y, Ltd.		44,000

[1] See Y, Ltd., Journal below.

Y, Ltd., Journal

	£	£
Share Capital	20,000	
Profit and Loss Account		1,000
X, Ltd. [Sole Shareholder] . .		19,000
Realization Account	34,000	
Sundry Assets		34,000
Creditors	5,000	
Realization Account		5,000
X and Y, Ltd.	16,000	
Realization Account		16,000
X, Ltd. [Sole Shareholder]	13,000	
Realization Account		13,000
Shares in X and Y, Ltd.	16,000	
X and Y, Ltd.		16,000
X, Ltd. [Sole Shareholder][1]	**6,000**	
X, Ltd. [Loan Account][1]	**10,000**	
Shares in X and Y, Ltd.		16,000

[1] See X, Ltd., Journal on p. 23295.

The opening Journal entries of X and Y, Ltd., are:

X AND Y, LTD., JOURNAL

	£	£
Sundry Assets.)	40,000	
do. (Y, Ltd.)	21,000	
Creditors (X, Ltd.)		12,000
do. (Y, Ltd.)		5,000
Vendor (X, Ltd.)		28,000
do. (Y, Ltd.)		16,000
Vendor (X, Ltd.)	28,000	
,, (Y, Ltd.)	16,000	
Share Capital		44,000

Notes. 1. The liquidator of Y, Ltd., will hand over to the liquidator of X, Ltd. (sole shareholder), the net proceeds of the liquidation; and this must be done before the process of winding up X, Ltd. can be contemplated.

2. The reader will find the solution simpler if he writes up the Ledger accounts.

Illustration 109

X, Ltd., agreed to acquire the business of Y, Ltd. The issued share capital, creditors and debit balance of Profit and Loss Account were, respectively, £30,000 (in £1 shares, £0·50 paid), £3,500, and £12,200. The shareholders of Y, Ltd., agreed to take shares in X, Ltd., on the basis of such shares being worth £1·25 each, and the shares in Y, Ltd., £0·37½ each. (Shares in X, Ltd., are £1 fully paid.)

Show opening Journal entries, assuming that X, Ltd., revalues the acquired assets at 90 per cent of the book values appearing in the books of Y, Ltd. Ignore fractions of shares and stamp duties.

JOURNAL

	£	£
Goodwill	6,830	
Sundry Assets[1]	19,170	
Creditors		3,500
Y, Ltd.		22,500
Being business acquired from Y, Ltd. as per purchase agreement dated		
Y, Ltd.	22,500	
Share Capital[2]		18,000
Share Premium		4,500
Being allotment of 18,000 shares of £1 each fully paid at £1·25 each as per purchase agreement dated		

[1,2] See notes on p. 23298.

Illustration 110

[*Amalgamation.*] Arundel, Ltd., and Warwick, Ltd., agree upon an amalgamation. Their Balance Sheets are:

BALANCE SHEETS

	Arundel, Ltd.	Warwick, Ltd.		Arundel, Ltd.	Warwick, Ltd.
	£	£		£	£
Authorized and Issued Share Capital of £1			Furniture, etc.	3,000	2,100
			Debtors	4,800	6,000
Shares fully paid	10,000	8,000	Bank	6,120	4,080
Reserve		500	Profit and Loss Account		
Profit and Loss Account		1,200	count	380	
Sundry Creditors	4,300	2,480			
	£14,300	£12,180		£14,300	£12,180

The assets of Arundel, Ltd., are to be taken at book values, except furniture, which is to be written down by £1,020; those of Warwick, Ltd., are to be taken at book values, except that the debtors are to be considered worth £3,300. The share capital of the combined company is to be 8,000 preference shares of £1 each fully paid, and ordinary shares of £0·50 each fully paid. The allocation of the shares is equal, except that the surplus capital of Arundel, Ltd., is to be satisfied in preference shares.

---

[1] The sundry assets entered into the books of X, Ltd., are:

	£
Share Capital	30,000
Creditors	3,500
	33,500
Less Profit and Loss Account	12,200
Book values of sundry assets in the books of Y, Ltd.	21,300
Less depreciation 10 per cent	2,130
	£19,170

[2] The shares allotted are 18,000, arrived at as follows:

$$60,000 \times \frac{37\frac{1}{2}}{125}$$

It will be seen that, ignoring expenses, the shareholders of Y, Ltd. obtain, by the acceptance of shares in X, Ltd., the same money equivalent as selling the shares at the current market value, thus:

(a) 60,000 shares in Y, Ltd., at £0·37½ = £22,500
(b) 18,000 shares in X, Ltd., at £1·25   = £22,500

It may be deemed desirable to set off the share premium against goodwill.

Show the Balance Sheet of the new company, and the details of the exchange of shares.

The capital of the new company will be as follows:

	Arundel, Ltd.		Warwick, Ltd.		New Company	
	£	£	£	£	£	£
Assets—						
Furniture, etc. . . .	1,980		2,100		4,080	
Debtors	4,800		6,000		10,800	
Bank . . .	6,120		4,080		10,200	
		12,900		12,180		25,080
Liabilities—						
Sundry Creditors . .	4,300		2,480		6,780	
Bad Debts Provision . .	Nil		2,700		2,700	
		4,300		5,180		9,480
Net Capital . . .		£8,600		£7,000		£15,600

This would be satisfied in shares as follows:

	Arundel, Ltd.	Warwick, Ltd.	New Company
	£	£	£	£
Preference Shares of £1 each, fully paid—				
(a) For surplus	1,600			
(b) Balance equally . .	3,200			
		4,800	3,200	8,000
Ordinary Shares of £0·50 each, fully paid		[1]3,800	[1]3,800	7,600
		£8,600	£7,000	£15,600

The exchange of shares is:

ARUNDEL, LTD.—
4,800 New Company Preference Shares (£1)
7,600 New Company Ordinary Shares (£0·50) } for   10,000 Shares in Old Company

i.e.   12 New Company Preference Shares (£1)
19 New Company Ordinary Shares (£0·50) } for every   25   ,,   ,,

WARWICK, LTD.—
3,200 New Company Preference Shares (£1)
7,600 New Company Ordinary Shares (£0·50) } for   8,000 Shares in Old Company

i.e.   16 New Company Preference Shares (£1)[2]
38 New Company Ordinary Shares (£0·50)[3] } for every   40   ,,   ,,

[1] 7,600 *Shares.*
[2] Or 2 for 5.
[3] Or 19 for 20.

BALANCE SHEET—NEW COMPANY

	£			£
Authorized Capital . . .	?	Furniture . . .		4,080
		Debtors . .	£10,800	
Issued Share Capital—		*Less* Bad Debts		
8,000 Preference Shares of £1		Provision .	2,700	
each fully paid . . .	8,000			8,100
15,200 Ordinary Shares of		Bank		10,200
£0·50 each fully paid . .	7,600			
Creditors	6,780			
	£22,380			£22,380

In all probability it will not be possible to divide the shares exactly so that fractional certificates may have to be given. See p. 23288.

Where companies each holding shares in other company amalgamate, a statement must be prepared which will be built up on the lines of a Consolidated Balance Sheet prepared in connection with Holding Companies. (See Chapter 24.)

Illustration 111

The following are the abridged Balance Sheets of Further, Ltd., and More, Ltd.:

BALANCE SHEETS

	Further, Ltd.	More, Ltd.		Further, Ltd.	More, Ltd.
	£	£		£	£
Issued Share Capital .	8,000	3,000	Sundry Assets . .	11,200	4,000
Profit and Loss Account	1,500		Goodwill . . .	800	1,000
Creditors .	2,500	2,500	Profit and Loss Account .		500
	£12,000	£5,500		£12,000	£5,500

Further, Ltd., holds 2,000 shares in More, Ltd., at cost £400, and More, Ltd., holds 1,000 shares in Further, Ltd., at cost £1,400—in each case included in Sundry Assets.

The shares of Further, Ltd., are of £1 and fully paid; the shares of More, Ltd., are of £0·50 and *all are £0·30 called and paid*. The two companies agree on an amalgamation on the basis that:

1. A new company is to be formed called Furthermore, Ltd.;
2. The goodwill values are: (*a*) Further, Ltd., £3,000, and (*b*) More, Ltd., £500;
3. The shares which each company holds in the other are to be valued at book value having regard to the goodwill valuations in (2);
4. The new shares are to be of a nominal value of £0·25 and to be credited as £0·20 paid.

Prepare: (i) new combined Balance Sheet resulting from the merger; (ii) Schedule showing fully the shareholdings therein attributable to the shareholders of Further, Ltd., and More, Ltd.

All costs, etc., are to be ignored.

The position arising out of the above can be best shown in a preliminary summary statement, thus:

	Further, Ltd.	More, Ltd.	Further- more, Ltd.
	£	£	£
Sundry Assets	11,200	4,000	
Less Shares at cost	400	1,400	
	10,800	2,600	13,400
Goodwill as revised	3,000	500	3,500
Liquidator of—			
More, Ltd.	413		
Further, Ltd.		1,464	
	14,213	4,564	16,900
Deduct Creditors	2,500	2,500	5,000
	11,713	2,064	11,900
Less Due to Liquidators of—			
More, Ltd.—$\frac{1}{8}$	1,464		
Further, Ltd.—$\frac{1}{5}$		413	
Due to Shareholders other than Further, Ltd., and More, Ltd.	£10,249	£1,651	£11,900

The computation arriving at the items £413 and £1,464 is as follows:

The Liquidator of Further, Ltd., has 'net' assets (excluding the value of the holding in More, Ltd.) of £11,300, i.e. £10,800 + £3,000 less £2,500. To this must be added the value of the holding in More, Ltd. This holding is 2,000 shares. The total *number* of the shares of More, Ltd., is 10,000. The nominal value of £0·50 is not material in arriving at this figure; the criterion is the *paid-up* value of £0·30. Hence, the item of £3,000 representing the share capital of More, Ltd., in full detail is 10,000 shares of £0·50 each, £0·30 called and paid equals £3,000.

Arising from these facts, it is clear that Further, Ltd., owns one-fifth of the equity of More, Ltd., as it holds 2,000 shares out of the 10,000, so that whatever may be the value of the equity of More, Ltd., Further, Ltd., gets one-fifth; but the value of such equity cannot be determined until the value of the equity of Further, Ltd., is known as More, Ltd., has, through its shareholding in Further, Ltd., an interest therein. Such interest is one-eighth as More, Ltd., owns 1,000 shares of £1 each fully paid (out of 8,000) of Further, Ltd.

Consequently, it is seen that Further, Ltd., owns *one-fifth* of More, Ltd., and the latter owns one-eighth of Further, Ltd.

The position of the liquidator of each company can now be clarified and it is immaterial which company is taken first.

As the position of the liquidator of Further, Ltd., has already been mentioned, this company will be used as the basis of the required computation.

The Liquidator has already £11,300 of net assets to which must be added the value of the holding in More Ltd. This is one-fifth of the equity of the latter company. Hence the total is £11,300 + $\frac{1}{5}$M (letter M symbolizes the equity of More, Ltd.). But what is the worth of M? It is £600 (excluding its proportion of Further, Ltd., i.e. £2,600 + £500 − £2,500) plus the value of the holding in Further, Ltd. As its holding in Further, Ltd., is one-eighth, M's total is £600 plus $\frac{1}{8}$F (letting F symbolize the equity of Further, Ltd.).

Thus
$$F = 11,300 + \tfrac{1}{5}M \text{ and } M = 600 + \tfrac{1}{8}F.$$
$$\therefore \quad = 11,300 + \tfrac{1}{5}(600 + \tfrac{1}{8}F)$$
$$= 11,300 + 120 + \tfrac{1}{40}F$$
$$= 11,420 + \tfrac{1}{40}F$$
$$\therefore \; 40F = 456,800 + F$$
$$\therefore \; 39F = 456,800$$
$$\therefore \quad F = 11,713 \text{ to nearest £.}$$

Therefore, the value of F's holding in M is £11,713 *less* £11,300 = £413.

The liquidator of Further, Ltd., will bring into account £413, thus bringing the equity of that company to £11,713; but as More, Ltd., owns one-eighth thereof, £1,464 is attributable to the latter company.

The liquidator of More, Ltd., will bring into account the aforesaid £1,464, thus bringing the equity of that company to £2,064 [£600 'other' net assets plus £1,464], but as Further, Ltd., owns one-fifth thereof, £413 is attributable to the latter company.

[The item of £1,464 can be proved by proceeding to work out the value of M, thus:
$$M = 600 + \tfrac{1}{8}F, \text{ but } F = 11,300 + \tfrac{1}{5}M.$$

Substituting for F $(11,300 + \tfrac{1}{5}M)$

$$M = 600 + \tfrac{1}{8}(11,300 + \tfrac{1}{5}M)$$
$$\therefore \; 8M = 4,800 + 11,300 + \tfrac{1}{5}M$$
$$= 16,100 + \tfrac{1}{5}M$$
$$\therefore \; 40M = 80,500 + M$$
$$\therefore \; 39M = 80,500$$
$$\therefore \quad M = 2,064 \text{ to nearest £.}$$

Therefore the value of M's holding in F is £2,064 less £600 = £1,464.]

The basis of exchange is (after cancelling the inter-company shareholdings):

	Original Shares	Cancelled Shares	Balance of General Shareholders	New Company Equity for General Shareholders £	Share of £0·25 Each £0·20 Paid
Further, Ltd.	8,000	less 1,000 (owned by More, Ltd.)	7,000	10,249	51,245
More, Ltd.	10,000	less 2,000 (owned by Further, Ltd.)	8,000	1,651	8,255
				£11,900	59,500

The general shareholders of Further, Ltd., will receive for their 7,000 shares of £1 each fully paid, 51,245 shares of £0·20 each, £0·20 paid, in Furthermore, Ltd.; and the general shareholders of More, Ltd., for their 8,000 shares of £0·50 each £0·30 paid, 8,255 shares of £0·25 each, £0·20 paid. Provision would obviously have to be made for fractions (exactly how many, will depend upon the composition of the shareholding) but approximately in the case of Further, Ltd., the share exchange would be 7 new for 1 old, absorbing 49,000, leaving 2,245 to be dealt with by means of fractions; and in the case of More, Ltd., the share exchange would be 1 new for 1 old, leaving 255 to be dealt with by means of fractions.

The abridged Balance Sheet resultant on the amalgamation will be:

FURTHERMORE, LTD.

	£		£
Issued Share Capital—		Sundry Assets	13,400
59,500 Shares of £0·25 each,		Goodwill	3,500
£0·20 paid	11,900		
Creditors	5,000		
	£16,900		£16,900

If the fractions are to be dealt with by payment of the cash equivalent £0·20 [not £0·25], the liabilities side would be modified accordingly; the undermentioned details taking the place of Share capital £11,900:

Shares of £0·25 (£0·20 paid) to be Allotted			Cash Payable		
		£			£
Further, Ltd. . . .	49,000 =	9,800	2,245 Shares at £0·20 . .		449
More, Ltd. . . .	8,000 =	1,600	255 Shares at £0·20 . .		51
	57,000 =	£11,400	2,500		£500

The abridged Balance Sheet will then be:

FURTHERMORE, LTD.

		£		£
Issued Share Capital—			Sundry Assets	13,500
57,000 Shares of £0·25 each,			Goodwill	3,500
£0·20 paid		11,400		
Amalgamation Creditors—				
Liquidator				
Further, Ltd. . .	£449			
More, Ltd. . . .	51			
		500		
Creditors		5,000		
		£16,900		£16,900

Relief from Capital and Transfer Stamp Duty. Where a new company is formed for the acquisition of other companies, or there is a reconstruction of an existing company, or an amalgamation for such purpose, there may be claimed relief from the *ad valorem* capital duty (Sect. 55, Finance Act 1927,[1] as amended by Sect. 31 Finance Act 1928, Sect 41 Finance Act 1930) and Sect 59 (7), Sch. 22 pt V Finance Act 1973.

The conditions laid down for exemption are:

(*a*) that the company whose shares or undertaking are being acquired shall have either its place of effective management or its registered office in a member State;

(*b*) that the consideration for the acquisition (ignoring such part thereof as consists of liabilities assumed or discharged by the acquiring company) shall consist either wholly of the issue of shares, or of the issue of shares plus a cash payment not exceeding 10% of the nominal value of those shares;

(*c*) in the case of a merger by exchange of shares—

    (i) that the transaction brings the acquiring company's beneficial ownership of shares in the acquired company to 75% or more of the latter's issued share capital, or further increases the existing shareholding beyond 75%; and

    (ii) that the consideration shares are issued *pro rata* to the holders of shares in the acquired company.

(*d*) in the case of an acquisition of the undertaking (or part of it) of another company, that the consideration shares are issued either to that company or to the holders of shares in that company.

The benefit of the exemption is lost in the case of a merger by exchange of shares if the 75% shareholding is not maintained for 5 years or if within that period any of the shares, which are held by the acquiring company immediately after the exempted transaction, are disposed of except in either case as part of a further restructuring operation which is itself an exempt transaction or in the course of the winding up of the acquiring company.

Increase of Capital Following a Reduction as a Result of Losses

Where the nominal capital of a capital company is reduced as a result of losses sustained, any subsequent increase in its issued capital within 4 years of the reduction is to be charged with Capital Duty only if and to the extent that the total of that and any previous increases since the reduction exceeds the reduction.

---

[1] To constitute an issue of shares for the purpose of Sect. 55, Finance Act 1927, the *legal* title must pass, so that where through the exercise of the right of renunciation given in the allotment letters so many allottees renounced that the shareholders who first became the registered holders in the transferee company represented less than 90 per cent of the shareholders of the transferor company, the Court decided that the procedure was not an 'issue' to enable the transferee company to obtain relief (*Oswald Tillotson, Ltd.* v. *C.I.R.*). Where the offeror company is virtually composed of the same members who own 90 per cent of the shares in the offeree company the Court has refused to allow the minority shareholders' shares to be expropriated by the offering company. *In re Bugle Press, Ltd.* (1960).

The introduction of Capital Duty has in general no effect on liability to either fixed or *ad valorem* Conveyance or Transfer duty. The only exception concerns the sale otherwise than as part of an undertaking of such things as know-how, patents, copyrights or trade-marks in consideration of the issue of shares: such a transaction will be chargeable to Capital Duty, but the instrument conveying or transferring the know-how, etc, to the company issuing the shares will be exempt from Conveyance or Transfer on sale duty.

The relief is given by way of reduction, that is, for the purposes of charging the capital duty of £1 per £100 or part of £100 on the issued capital, such capital is considered as being reduced by:

(*a*) An amount equal to the issued share capital of the vending subsidiary company; or

(*b*) Where only *part* of the undertaking of the vending company is acquired, by that proportion of the issued share capital of the vending company which the portion of the undertaking acquired bears to the whole undertaking; or

(*c*) If the shares issued as consideration are credited as *partly* paid up, only the amount credited as paid up is available for relief, if this is less than the amount computed in (*a*) and (*b*).

In order to obtain the benefit or relief from the capital or stamp duty:

1. In the case of an existing acquiring company, the resolution increasing its nominal capital must state the purpose of such increase;
2. In the case of a newly-formed acquiring company, its Memorandum of Association must contain as one of its objects the acquisition of the undertaking (or part) of the vendor company or of shares therein.

The reliefs granted will be cancelled and the correct duties charged (plus interest at 5 per cent per annum) if:

(*a*) It is found subsequently that any material particular in the claim is untrue;

(*b*) The conditions are not fulfilled;

(*c*) Within two years (except arising from reconstruction, amalgamation or liquidation):

(i) the vending company parts with the shares issued to it, or
(i) the holding company parts with the shares acquired by it.

(*d*) As stated earlier in the case of a merger by exchange of shares if the 75% holding is not maintained for 5 years:

If the undertaking is taken over, then it is immaterial whether the shares given in exchange are allotted to the existing company or to its shareholders; but if the undertaking is not taken over but *shares* acquired therein, then the allotment of the shares exchanged must be to the *holders* of the shares in the existing company. If the allotment is to the existing *undertaking* itself no relief is available (*Murex* v. *C.I.R.*).

Illustration 112

X, Ltd., is formed with a Nominal Capital of £20,000 to take over the undertaking of Y, Ltd. The issued share capital of Y, Ltd., is £15,000 in £1 shares.

Assuming that the purchase consideration wholly discharged in fully-paid shares is: (a) £18,000, (b) £12,000, show relief in respect of capital duty available to X, Ltd.

(a) The *relief* is £1 per cent of £15,000.
(b) The *relief* is £1 per cent of £12,000.

If X, Ltd., had similarly acquired from members of Y, Ltd., 90 per cent[1] of their shares (Y, Ltd., remaining in existence), the relief would be: (a) £13,500 [i.e. 90 per cent of £15,000]; (b) £12,000.[2]

Illustration 113

Z, Ltd., has a Nominal Capital of £20,000, half of which is issued and fully paid. For the purpose of acquiring 75 per cent[2] of the undertaking of R, Ltd. (Issued Capital, £17,000), Z, Ltd., increased its Nominal Capital by £15,000. The purchase consideration is £13,000 payable in 16,000 £1 shares credited as £0·75 paid and £1,000 in cash.

Show the relief available from payment of Capital Duty.

	£
For the purpose of £1 per cent Capital Duty, the Share Capital issued by Z, Ltd., of	12,000
is reduced by	
(a) 75 per cent of the issued capital of R, Ltd., £12,750; or	
(b) The amount credited as partly paid on 16,000 shares £0·75 paid, issued as purchase consideration, i.e. £12,000 whichever is *less*	12,000
∴ Capital Duty payable is	Nil

Illustration 114

[*Internal Reconstruction.*] The Balance Sheet of Dunster, Ltd., at 31st December 19.., is as follows:

---

[1] See Sect. 209, Companies Act 1948, *re* power to acquire shares of dissenting minority when scheme approved by shareholders of not less than 90 per cent in value.

[2] A compulsory transfer under Sect. 209 is not regarded for stamp-duty purposes as a conveyance or transfer on sale and therefore no *ad valorem* duty is payable thereon, but merely the nominal £0·50 stamp. *Ridge Nominees* v. *C.I.R.* (1961).

BALANCE SHEET AS AT 31 DECEMBER 19..

	£		£
Authorized and Issued Share		Sundry Assets . . .	154,000
Capital: 80,000 Shares of		Investments . . .	3,000
£1 each fully paid . .	80,000	Profit and Loss Account .	106,000
Debentures . . £130,000			
Plus Interest (gross) 8,000			
	138,000		
Creditors . . .	45,000		
	£263,000		£263,000

The following reconstruction is passed and duly sanctioned.

1. Each share is to be subdivided into twenty fully-paid ordinary shares of £0·05 each.

2. After such subdivision, each shareholder shall surrender to the company 95 per cent of his holdings, for reissue to debenture-holders and creditors, as necessary, and the balance cancelled.

3. Of those surrendered, 460,000 shares of £0·05 each shall be converted into participating preference shares of £0·05 each fully paid.

4. The claims of the debenture-holders shall be reduced by £0·83$\frac{1}{3}$ in the £; in consideration therefor the debenture-holders shall *also* receive participating preference shares to the value of £0·16$\frac{2}{3}$ in the £ upon their claims as at 31st December 19...

5. The claims of the creditors to be reduced to £0·20 in the £, to be satisfied by the issue of ordinary shares of £0·05 each *ex* the shares surrendered.

6. The shares surrendered and not reissued to be cancelled.

Set out Journal entries and resultant Balance Sheet assuming that the amounts of the assets are unaltered. The merits of the scheme may be ignored.

It is advisable in a question of this nature to construct a rough tabular statement and therefrom compile the revised Balance Sheet; then proceed to the Journal entries. (See below.)

(*a*) The members lose 95 per cent of their capital, viz. £76,000, leaving them with £4,000 in shares.

(*b*) The debenture-holders lose £0·66$\frac{2}{3}$ in the £, because they receive back in another form £0·16$\frac{2}{3}$ out of their £0·83$\frac{1}{3}$ loss, thus $\frac{2}{3} \times £138,000 = £92,000$ is a gain to the company, leaving the debenture-holders with $\frac{1}{3} \times £138,000$, viz. £46,000, in:

			£
Preference Shares .	.	.	23,000
Debentures .	.	.	23,000
			£46,000

(c) The creditors lose $\frac{4}{5} \times$ £45,000, that is, a gain to the company of £36,000, the creditors being allotted £9,000 of ordinary shares. There is thus a total gain to the company of £204,000, which is utilized in eliminating the adverse balance of profit and loss of £106,000, leaving a reserve of £98,000.

Old Balance Sheet Items	Total	New Ordinary Shares	Participating Preference Shares	Debentures	Profit
	£	£	£	£	£
Share Capital	80,000	4,000			76,000
Debentures	138,000		23,000	23,000	92,000
Creditors	45,000	9,000			36,000
Total	263,000	13,000	23,000	23,000	204,000
Elimination of Profit and Loss Account .	106,000				
Reserve	98,000				204,000

The resultant Balance Sheet will be:

DUNSTER, LTD.,[1] BALANCE SHEET AS AT 31ST DECEMBER 19 . .

	£		£
Authorized and Issued Share Capital—		Sundry Assets . . .	154,000[2]
		Investments	3,000[2]
80,000 Ordinary Shares of £1 each fully paid reduced (as sanctioned by the Court) to—			
260,000 Ordinary Shares of £0·05 each fully paid .	13,000[3]		
460,000 Participating Preference Shares of £0·05 each fully paid	23,000[3]		
Reserve	98,000[3]		
Debentures	23,000[3]		
	£157,000		£157,000

[1] (And reduced) if the Court orders.

[2] Per original Balance Sheet.

[3] From the statement on this page, accounting for the remaining figures in the original Balance Sheet.

It will be of material assistance if the student prepares rough Ledger Accounts, because many of the entries in the Journal deal with balances of accounts.

JOURNAL

	£	£
Share Capital (Old)	80,000	
Ordinary Share Capital . . .		80,000
Being subdivision of 80,000 shares of £1 each fully paid into 1,600,000 shares of £0·05 each fully paid pursuant to scheme passed by special resolution dated ...., confirmed by Court Order dated ...., *vide* Minute Book, p.		
Ordinary Share Capital	76,000	
Surrendered Shares		76,000
Being surrender of 96% of ordinary shares, viz. 1,520,000 to be dealt with in accordance with scheme.		
Debentures	107,000	
Interest on Debentures	8,000	
General Creditors	45,000	
Reconstruction Account . . .		160,000
Being reduction of £0·83⅓ in £ on the rights of debenture-holders and surrender of the rights of unsecured creditors.		
Surrendered Shares	76,000	
Participating Preference Share Capital . .		23,000
Ordinary Share Capital . . .		9,000
Reconstruction Account . . .		44,000
Being issue of 460,000 participating preference shares of £0·05 each fully paid (into which 460,000 of the surrendered shares have been converted) and 180,000 ordinary shares of £0·05 each fully paid (£0·20 in £), and cancellation of shares surrendered and not reissued as per scheme.		
Reconstruction Account	204,000	
Profit and Loss Account . . .		106,000
Reserve		98,000
Being cancellation of profit and loss balance and creation of reserve in pursuance of reconstruction scheme.		

Illustration 115

[*Internal Reconstruction.*] The following is the Balance Sheet of S. M., Ltd.:

BALANCE SHEET AS AT 1ST JANUARY 19..

	£		£
Authorized and Issued Capital:		Sundry Assets	15,000
20,000 Ordinary Shares of £1		Investment on Workmen's Com-	
fully paid	20,000	pensation Fund	3,000
18,000 7% Preference Shares		Property:	
of £1 fully paid . . .	18,000	London . . £16,000	
'A' 6% Debentures (secured on		Manchester . . 12,000	
London Property) . .	3,000		28,000
'B' 6% Debentures (secured on		Profit and Loss Account . .	4,000
Manchester Property) . .	3,500		
Workmen's Compensation			
Fund:			
London . . £2,000			
Manchester . 1,000			
	3,000		
Creditors.	2,500		
	£50,000		£50,000

A scheme was duly prepared and sanctioned, whereby:

(a) Ordinary shares were to be reduced to £0·10.

(b) Preference shares were to be reduced to £0·80.

(c) Debenture-holders forgo their interest (£520), which is included among sundry creditors.

(d) 'B' debenture-holders agreed to take over the Manchester property at £5,000; to accept an allotment of 3,000 £0·10 ordinary shares at par; and upon their forming a company called M.P., Ltd., to take over the Manchester property, they allotted S.M., Ltd., 1,800 £1 shares fully paid at par.

(e) The Manchester Workman's Compensation Fund disclosed the fact that there were liabilities of £200. In consequence, the investments and the fund were realized to the extent of the balance, the investment realizing a profit of 10 per cent on book value, and the proceeds used for part payment of the creditors.

(f) The sundry assets were to be written down by £9,000, any balance to be applied as to three-quarters in writing down the London property, one-quarter to a capital reserve.

Show Journal entries covering these steps.

	£	£
Ordinary Share Capital	18,000	
7% Preference Share Capital	3,600	
Sundry Creditors (Debenture Interest) . . .	520	
Workmen's Compensation Fund (Manchester) . .	880	
Capital Reduction Account		23,000
Being reduction of capital, viz. 20,000 ordinary shares of £1 each to £0·10 each; 7% preference shares of £1 each to £0·80 each; cancellation of debenture interest; and elimination of proportion of workmen's compensation fund in pursuance of scheme of reduction as per special resolution ...., confirmed by Court Order dated ...., *vide* Minute Book, p.		
Capital Reduction Account	23,000	
Manchester Property		7,000
Sundry Assets		9,000
Profit and Loss Account		4,000
London Property		2,250
Capital Reserve		750
Being assets written down in pursuance of scheme of reduction.		
'B' Debenture-holders	5,000	
Manchester Property		5,000
Being transfer of Manchester Property at valuation in pursuance of scheme of reduction.		
'B' Debenture-holders	300	
Ordinary Share Capital		300
Being allotment of ordinary shares in part settlement of liability to debenture-holders.		
'B' Debentures	3,500	
Investment (Shares in M.P., Ltd.)	1,800	
'B' Debenture-holders		5,300
Being discharge of balance by investments and transfer from 'B' Debentures Account.		
Cash	880	
Workmen's Compensation Investment, Manchester ,		800
Workmen's Compensation Fund, Manchester		80
Being amount received from workmen's compensation fund investments and transfer of profit thereon to fund.		
Creditors	880	
Cash		880
Being part payment of liability to creditors.		

DRAFT BALANCE SHEET AS AT 1st JANUARY 19..

	£	£		£	£
Authorized Share Capital—			Sundry Assets . .	15,000	
Ordinary Shares—200,000 of			Less written off by Order of		
£0·10 each . . .		20,000	Court	9,000	
7% Preference Shares—					6,000
22,500 of £0·80 each . .		18,000	Investments on Workmen's		
			Compensation Funds—		
		£38,000	London .	2,000	
			Manchester . . .	200	
					2,200
Issued Share Capital—			Shares in M.P., Ltd., at Cost		1,800
Ordinary Shares—23,000 of			London Property	16,000	
£0·10 each fully paid .		2,300	Less written off by Order of		
7% Preference Shares—			Court	2,250	
18,000 of £0·80 each fully paid		14,400			13,750
Capital Reserve . .		750			
'A' 6% Debentures (secured on					
London Property) . .		3,000			
Workmen's Compensation					
Funds—					
London . . .	2,000				
Manchester . . .	200				
		2,200			
Creditors . . .		1,100			
		£23,750			£23,750

It will usually be advisable to prepare rough 'working' accounts for the more difficult and involved entries, thus:

Rough Accounts:

W.C.F. INVESTMENTS (M/c)

		£			£
Balance	.	1,000	Sale . .		800
			Balance . .		200
Balance[1]	.	200			

'B' DEBENTURE-HOLDERS

	£			£
M/c Property	5,000	'B' Debentures		3,500
Ordy. Share		Investment A/c		1,800
Capital .	300			

W.C. FUND

		£			£
Capital Reduc-			Balance	.	1,000
tion .		880	Profit	.	80
Balance	.	200			
			Balance[1] .	.	200

CREDITORS

		£			£
Capital Re-			Balance		2,500
duction .		520			
Cash .		880			
Balance .		1,100			
			Balance .	.	1,100

[1] The balances may be transferred to General Investments and Liabilities respectively.

The form in which the reconstruction is to be carried out involves a consideration of variable premises, most of which are omitted from examination questions. It is therefore essential that, in addition to the submission of the formal answer in the light of the circumstances and facts disclosed, suitable comments should be made.

Principles Underlying Reconstruction

1. The scheme should be clear cut, easily understood by laymen and non-controversial.

2. No attempt should be made to put through an unjust and unfair scheme.

3. The scheme should avoid the setting off of one class of members against another.

4. Whatever proposals are made, the essence of them is the earning power of the company. All members, even debenture-holders, are dependent for their income on the company's earnings.

5. Latest figures of actual earnings should be given, supplemented by careful and honest estimates of future earning power.

6. No class of members should be called upon to make sacrifices for the benefit of another class except where absolute necessity dictates, e.g. if there is no prospect within a reasonable time of paying dividends to ordinary shareholders except at the expense of the preference shareholders, the latter should not generally be called upon to sacrifice their Capital and/or Income. The ordinary shareholder is assumed to know the risk attaching to his holding. On the other hand if, taking a long-term view, the position is such that there is little prospect of the preference shareholder receiving dividends, then some adjustment will be called for, particularly as the ordinary shareholder should not be called upon to renounce for all time his prospect of receiving dividends.

7. Regard must be had to real as distinct from apparent sacrifices, and a cut in the capitals of both preference and ordinary shares would give the latter an advantage over the former unless the preference shareholders were compensated.

8. No change should take place in the respective positions except where unavoidable, e.g. generally speaking a preference shareholder will want to remain as such and not become an ordinary shareholder, and conversely, so that:

(9) Contractual rights and priorities should be maintained as far as possible.

The matters likely to call for practical attention in problems of this nature are:

1. Whether the reconstruction should be 'internal' or 'external'.

2. Whether the company's affairs have reached stability, so that another reconstruction in the future may be avoided.

3. The respective rights of the various classes of members as to:

(a) Capital repayment in a winding up.
(b) Dividends.
(c) VOTING powers.

4. A careful consideration of the proposed alterations in so far as they are likely to affect the rights of *members*, having regard to the possibility of a refusal by a class to acquiesce.

5. Where the reconstruction involves some sacrifice on the part of *creditors*, including debenture-holders, the proposals which are likely to meet with their approval must be carefully considered; whether, for instance, they will be likely to agree to a composition for cash, or for cash and shares, or for shares only.

6. In all cases, especially where the immediate trouble is the shortage of working capital, the question of raising the additional capital will require consideration.

7. Involved in the scheme may be the reorganization of the business and technical side of the company, together with a possible reconstitution of the size and personnel of the Board of Directors. The desirability of the appointment of a new chairman may call for consideration.

8. In order to ascertain the amount to be written off against members (and possibly creditors), the assets and liabilities will be revalued, so that the company can start with a 'clean slate'. This obviously will necessitate not only the revision of book values of assets and liabilities, but the complete elimination of such debit balances as are not in the nature of assets, examples of which are preliminary expenses and profit-and-loss balance.

Accounting Aspects of Reconstruction. The chief matters that directly concern accounting work are those relating to the reconstitution of the share capital, and the revision of the values of the assets and liabilities. After the advice of the accountant has been sought as to the opportuneness and method of reconstruction, having regard to all the circumstances, assets (the valuation of which may require the services of technical experts) will be adjusted accordingly. When the revised capital balance has been struck, the task of the accountant is to evolve an *effective* scheme which is fair and just as between all parties, particularly as regards the division of future profits of the company; this being difficult if the profits are likely to be subject to extensive fluctuations. The particular aspects, at all events for examination purposes, which will require careful consideration are:

1. The position of each class of member as regards potential dividends.
2. The position of each class of member in the event of liquidation.
3. The treatment of 'arrears' (if any) on cumulative preference shares.
4. The position of: (1) debenture-holders, having regard to the nature and value of their security, and (2) creditors.
5. The particular assets and liabilities chosen to be adjusted.[1]
6. The practical point of allotting a reasonably large number of shares (even if of low denomination), and the exchange basis such as to avoid so far as is possible the use of shares fractions.
7. The gearing of the reconstituted Share Capital.
8. The resultant voting power.

Speaking generally, unless the earning capacity of the company has become permanently impaired, it is neither just nor reasonable that the

---

[1] If Plant is written down, it will lighten the burden of the depreciation charge until such time as the Plant requires replacement, whilst a reduction of an interest bearing liability will lighten the burden of the interest charge.

preference shareholders should suffer a reduction in the amounts receivable in dividends. The preference shareholder has taken shares of this class upon the understanding that he should have a prior right to dividend over that possessed by the ordinary shareholder, but without right to further participation in the profit. In order to keep faith, it is the duty of the company to preserve this right as far as possible. It must be borne in mind, however, that usually the control of the company lies with the ordinary shareholders, who would have the power to withhold dividends from the preference shareholders until the adverse balance of profit and loss has been made good out of future profits. As a result, the preference shareholders are generally quite willing to accept a curtailment of some rights in return for the prospect of dividend being paid to them in the very near future.

Another matter which will tend to create an accommodating spirit amongst the preference shareholders is the fact that often the only alternative to the reconstruction is liquidation. The latter will usually involve losses owing to forced sale, such losses being borne entirely by the preference shareholders if the position is so serious that the capital of the ordinary shareholders is already lost.

The important point from the dividend aspect is that so far as the ordinary shareholders are concerned (assuming two classes only, viz. preference and ordinary), it is quite immaterial at what book value the shares appear in the books of the company, as the true value depends upon the annuity value or yield basis, so that if, after reconstruction, they are still entitled to all the SURPLUS profits, or the same proportion as before, their dividend position is unimpaired.

The position of the ordinary shareholder is unaffected as regards dividends if:

1. There is no alteration in *amount, rate,* **or** *priority* **of the preference shares.**

2. No other class of shareholders is admitted into the participation of the 'equity' of the ordinary shareholders, or if such right already exists, it remains unchanged.

Any **diminution** of the foregoing rights will benefit the ordinary shareholders.

A share will be just as valuable if it obtains an annual dividend of, say, £0·05 whether it is denominated and credited in the company's books at £10 or £1 of £0·25, or even £0·01, inasmuch it proves the SAME annuity in each case.

Where debenture-holders suffer a reduction in the amount of interest they receive from the company, whether in rate or book value of the debentures, the burden on the company will be correspondingly reduced, thus benefiting its members.

Illustration 116

The issued share capital of Eldwick, Ltd., is 10,000 6 per cent preference shares and 20,000 ordinary shares, all of £1 each, fully paid. The net assets are £13,000, and the debit balance of Profit and Loss Account is £17,000.

Assuming that the company has 'turned the corner' and ignoring other considerations, e.g. liquid position of the company, it is obvious that it is to the advantage of the company as a whole to reconstruct by a thorough revaluation and, as a necessary concomitant, the reorganization of the capital, so as to enable the company to resume payment of dividends at an early date.

If the net assets are, upon revaluation considered to be worth £11,000 only, this involves a capital loss of £19,000, made up as follows:

		£
(i) Reduced Value of Assets	. .	2,000
(ii) Elimination of Fictitious Asset	. .	17,000
		£19,000

If it is agreed to charge this up to the ordinary shareholders, leaving them with £1,000 of capital instead of £20,000, it is immaterial whether that capital is in the form of 1,000 shares of £1 each, fully paid, or 20,000 shares of £0·05 each, fully paid, for their 'equity' will remain unaltered. The preference shareholders appear to be sufferers in one sense, as the capital security is diminished as compared with the position when there was no debit balance on Profit and Loss Account, yet the mere formality of bringing down the position to 'rock bottom' makes the real security neither worse nor better than immediately before the reconstruction. The damage was done during the period prior to the inauguration of the scheme. Actually, their comparative position in a winding-up *vis-à-vis* the ordinary shareholder may be strengthened. From a dividend point of view, their position is that they are still entitled to their annual dividend of 6 per cent on their *unaltered* share capital before the ordinary shareholders can possibly participate in the profits.

As regards the ordinary shareholders, the priorities ranking in front of them are still the same, hence their share in the surplus of the divisible profits is not jeopardized by the writing down of £20,000 to £1,000.

If the company in the year after reconstruction earns (and distributes) £1,100, the preference shareholders will receive £600, leaving £500 for the ordinary shareholders. This will be distributed as follows:

	£
(a) Assuming that no reconstruction took place—2½% on 20,000 £1 shares	500
(b) Assuming the reconstruction resulted in the Ordinary Shares being written down to—	
(1) 20,000 shares of £0·05 each—£0·02½ a share, or 50% on 20,000 £0·05 shares	500
(2) 1,000 shares of £1 each—£0·50 a share, or 50% on 1,000 £1 shares	500

Assuming, further, that $7\frac{1}{2}$ per cent yield would be required on an ordinary share of this class, the valuations are:

£

(a) $\dfrac{2\frac{1}{2}}{7\frac{1}{2}} \times £1$ $= £0\cdot33\frac{1}{3}$ on 20,000 £1 shares   .   6,666·66$\frac{1}{3}$

(b) (1) $\dfrac{50}{7\frac{1}{2}} \times £0\cdot05 = £0\cdot33\frac{1}{3}$ on 20,000 £0·05 shares   .   6,666·66$\frac{1}{3}$

(2) $\dfrac{50}{7\frac{1}{2}} \times £1$ $= £6\cdot66\frac{1}{3}$ on 1,000 £1 shares   .   .   6,666·66$\frac{1}{3}$

If the 'arrears' of cumulative preference dividends are to be brought into account in the reconstruction, the position of the ordinary shareholders is generally adversely affected (assuming that they are not compensated in other directions), because:

1. If the 'arrears' of cumulative preference dividends are converted into preference shares, more of the profits will be 'charged' to meet the dividend on the increased number of preference share; but against this the RATE per cent payable on the preference shares may be reduced, the consequences of which will be to offset, wholly or in part, the increased 'charge'.

2. If such 'arrears' are converted into ordinary shares, it results in the proportion of surplus profits, payable to ordinary shareholders, being reduced in consequence of the increased number of participants, but this will hasten the time when the ordinary shareholders will receive dividends because the 'arrears' of preference dividends are no longer in the way.

3. If the 'arrears' are converted into Income Certificates there will be an increased charge not only for interest, but for providing a Sinking Fund for their redemption. The latter, however, becomes 'free' when the certificates have been redeemed.

Briefly, the ordinary shareholders benefit to the extent of obtaining an early participation in dividends, but sacrifice some proportion thereof by having them curtailed to the extent required to pay dividends on the shares issued to the preference shareholders in cancellation of the 'arrears' of their dividends.

Before proceeding further, it is important to note that in the majority of reconstructions, only part of the 'arrears' are given in the shares, the preference shareholders sacrificing the remainder.

Illustration 117

Taking the facts as in the previous illustration, the arrears on the 6 per cent preference shares (assumed to be cumulative) are, say, £2,400, that is, no dividends have been paid on these shares for four years, and the capital is reorganized by debiting the whole of the capital loss to the ordinary shareholders by reducing the nominal value of £0·05. The 'arrears' are to be cancelled, and in lieu thereof the preference shareholders are to be allotted four new ordinary shares of £0·05 each for five preference shares.

Ignoring the treatment of 'arrears', the revised position would be:

		£
10,000 6% Preference Shares of £1 fully paid	. .	10,000
20,000 Ordinary Shares of £0·05 each fully paid	. .	1,000
		£11,000

This figure is represented by Net Assets at their revised
value—£11,000, as against £13,000 previously.

As there are to be created further ordinary shares to the extent of 8,000 of £0·05 each ($\frac{4}{5}$ of 10,000) and no book liability exists for the 'arrears' (not being a real liability), the issue will involve either an increase (by writing up the assets) or a diminution of the ordinary share capital. If the ordinary shareholders are to surrender the required amount to cover the £400, they will suffer by having less 'equity' in the surplus, as they retain £600 only of their £1,000. On the other hand, the matter may be adjusted by reference to the assets, the latter being reduced not by £2,000 as mentioned, but by £1,600 only. This will leave the ordinary capital at £1,400 (£1,000 for the ordinary shareholders and £400 for the preference shareholders in respect of the 'arrears' of dividends). In the first case, the surplus profit available for the old ordinary shareholders is $\frac{6}{10}$, whereas in the second it is $\frac{10}{14}$ or $\frac{5}{7}$, the detrimental effect of the former as compared with the latter being $\frac{4}{35}$ (the difference between $\frac{5}{7}$ and $\frac{6}{10}$) of the surplus profits.

The usual practice is to obtain an approximate valuation of tangible assets; to ascertain the effect on share capital; and, if necessary, to effect an equitable readjustment of capital by an adjustment of the valuation of goodwill. The viewpoint of winding up must be briefly considered, and this will be dealt with on p. 23320 *et seq.*

Other arrangements may be entered into with reference to the arrears, e.g. £400 may be allotted in preference shares, or split between the preference shares and ordinaries, or an entirely new class of share created, say, preferred ordinary ranking for dividends after the preference, but before the ordinary shares. To deal with each possible arrangement is impossible in a work of this description, but the principles involved are the same, viz. (1) what amount of profit will be required to meet the dividend of the prior classes of shares; and (2) what amount (not merely rate) of dividend will be available to the lower-grade shares.

The position may be compared by taking three alternatives:

(*a*) Where the 'arrears' are given to the preference shares in *preference* shares.

(*b*) As in (*a*), except that *ordinary* shares are allotted.

(*c*) Where the 'arrears' are split into equal parts of preference and ordinary, the increase of £400 being borne by the present holders of ordinary shares.

The Balance Sheets will be thus:

	(a) £	(b) £	(c) £		(a) [1]£	(b) [1]£	(c) [2]£
Preference Shares—				Net Assets .	11,400	11,400	11,000
Old .	10,000	10,000	10,000				
New .	400		200				
Ordinary Shares—							
Old .	1,000	1,000	600				
New .		400	200				
	£11,400	£11,400	£11,000		£11,400	£11,400	£11,000

[1] i.e. £11,000 (as shown on p. 23316) plus £400.
[2] £11,000 only, £400 being taken from the old ordinary shareholders.
[3] £1,000 less £400 given to preference shareholders.

The respective positions may be illustrated thus:

	(a) £	(b) £	(c) £
Profits (say)	1,100	1,100	1,100
Amount required to meet Preference Dividends of 6%	624	600	612
Surplus . .	£476	£500	£488

DISTRIBUTION OF PROFITS

	(a) £	(b) £	(c) £
Old Preference Shareholders as holders of—			
(i) New Preference Shares . .	624	600	612
(ii) New Ordinary Shares in respect of 'Arrears'		(x) 143	(y) 122
Old Ordinary Shareholders as holders of New Ordinary Shares . . .	476	(x) 357	(y) 366
	£1,100	£1,100	£1,100

(x) Respectively $\dfrac{400}{1,400}$ and $\dfrac{1,000}{1,400}$ of £500.   (y) Respectively $\dfrac{200}{800}$ and $\dfrac{600}{800}$ of £488.

It has been assumed so far that the preference shareholders have a preference as to dividends, and according to the arrangements shown above, they not only suffer no abridgement of this privilege, but they obtain a return on their 'arrears'. Thus they obtain the income equivalent to actually receiving the amount of the 'arrears', and reinvesting it in some form or other, whilst at the same time their capital position suffers no contraction.

If they have no preference as to *capital* and are, therefore, on the same level as the ordinaries, it might be considered that they ought to share a due proportion of the capital loss. If this is to effected, it might be done by reducing the share capital by proportionate amounts; but in order to preserve to them the same amount of dividend, the rate of dividend would have to be considerably increased. This is usually a very unwise procedure. Consequently, a new class of share might be created of comparatively small dimensions and given to the preference shareholders, entitling them to dividends, requisite to bring the return to that originally obtained; with a small participation in the surplus, after payment of a certain rate to the ordinary shareholders, to compensate them for loss of priority of dividend; alternatively, the preference shareholders may be induced to take new preference shares reduced in rate and a comparatively small number of ordinary shares, the incentive offered being that, whilst the preference shareholders will receive less as preference dividend, they will receive more of the ultimate surplus profits.

Winding-up Aspect of Reconstructions. The problem raised by this aspect differs materially from that previously dealt with in reference to the prospective yield on the shareholding as reconstituted. Here the assets and their probable realization are a matter of primary importance; whereas, whilst the company is dividend-producing, the mere book denomination of the share is of secondary importance.

Where the preference shareholders have no priority as to capital, they stand on the same footing as the ordinary shareholders, so that if the respective capitals are revised, it can be readily seen that the greater the proportion of capital, the greater the return. Further, if the preference shareholders have the right to share in a surplus in the winding up (which they do not possess preferential as to capital unless the articles expressly so state) such surplus will be divisible proportionately to capitals.

Where the preference share capital remains *unaltered*, and the holders possess no right to share in a surplus in the winding up, the position is simple. The preference shareholders obtain the same undiminished right of return of capital, but thereafter everything belongs to the ordinary shareholders.

Where the preference shareholders have the right to participate in a capital surplus arising in a winding up, the important matters for them are:

1. preserving their original capital;
2. the sharing of the SURPLUS.

So far as relates to the ordinary shareholders, they are concerned first, in the repayment of their capitals, so that the smaller the preference share capital the greater is the possibility of a repayment to them; whilst, secondly, they are concerned in obtaining the return of their ORIGINAL capital (if possible), so that, in addition to being interested in cutting down the amount of preference share capital, they wish to see their own capital as large as possible, because after payment of the preference share capital, they will receive all the remaining surplus up to the extent of their *revised* capital, and the higher the relative proportion of the ordinary capital to the preference capital the more favourable is the ordinary shareholder's position. Where the preference shareholders have the right to participate in the surplus, the same principle applies (as mentioned on p. 23320).

Illustration 118

The share capital of X, Ltd., is 2,000 preference shares and 2,000 ordinary shares all of £1 each fully paid. The preference have priority and participation rights in winding up. Assuming that the assets realize (on liquidation) £3,200, show in columnar form the respective positions assuming (1) no reconstruction, (2*a*) a reconstruction by which the preference shares were cut down by £500 and the ordinary shares by £1,000, (2*b*) a reconstruction by which the preference shares were cut down by nil and the ordinary shares by £1,500.

	(1)		(2a)		(2b)	
	Preference	Ordinary	Preference	Ordinary	Preference	Ordinary
	£	£	£	£	£	£
Repayment of Capitals—						
Preference	2,000		1,500		2,000	
Ordinary . . .		1,200		1,000		500
Surplus (*pari passu*) .	Nil	Nil	420	280	560	140
	£2,000	£1,200	£1,920	£1,280	£2,560	£640

Illustration 119

X, Ltd., has a share capital of 5,000 7 per cent preference shares and 5,000 ordinary shares, all of £1 each fully paid. There is a capital loss of £4,000, of which £1,000 is to be borne by the preference shareholders and the balance by the ordinary shareholders. On liquidation the assets realize £15,000 after all expenses and creditors have been paid. The profits were: Years 1, 2, 3, and 4, £300, £350, £600, and £1,000·respectively.

Set out in tabular form the respective positions of the two classes of shares, contrasting them: (1) assuming no reconstruction; (2) on the basis of the above reconstruction.

(i) Where the preference shares are non-cumulative and without preference as to repayment of capital, or right to participate in surplus (all profits have been paid in dividends):

Yearly Profits and Dividends, and Repayment of Capitals	Total		(1) Preference		(1) Ordinary		Total		(2) Preference		(2) Ordinary	
	£	£	£	£	£	£	£	£	£	£	£	£	£
Dividends—													
Year 1 . . .	¹300		Nil		Nil				280		20		
„ 2 . . .	350		350		300				280		70		
„ 3 . . .	600		350		250				280		320		
„ 4 . . .	1,000	2,250	350	1,050	650	1,200	2,250		280	1,120	720	1,130	
Repayment of Capitals—													
Preference .	5,000			5,000			4,000			4,000			
Ordinary .	5,000				5,000						2,000		
Surplus to Ordinary .	5,000				5,000						9,000		
		15,000				10,000	11,000					11,000	
	£	17,250	£	6,050	£	11,200	£17,250		£	5,120	£	12,130	

¹ It is assumed that the directors decide not to recommend the payment of the preference dividend in this year inasmuch as the profits do not wholly cover it. If £300 [i.e. 6% on the preference shares] was paid there would be no dividend on the ordinary shares in Year 2.

(ii) Where the preference shares are cumulative and without preference as to repayment of capital, or right to participate in surplus (all profits have been paid in dividends):

Yearly Profits and Dividends; and Repayment of Capitals	Total		(1) Preference		(1) Ordinary		Total		(2) Preference		(2) Ordinary	
	£	£	£	£	£	£	£	£	£	£	£	£	£
Dividends—													
Year 1 . . .	300		Nil		Nil				280		20		
„ 2 . . .	350		350		Nil				280		70		
„ 3 . . .	600		¹700		200				280		320		
„ 4 . . .	1,000	2,250	350	1,400	650	850	2,250		280	1,120	720	1,130	
Repayment of Capitals—													
As in (1)		15,000		5,000		10,000	15,000			4,000		11,000	
	£	17,250	£	6,400	£	10,850	£17,250		£	5,120	£	12,130	

¹ Assumed arrears cleared in Year 3.

(iii) Where the preference shares are cumulative without preference as to repayment of capital or right to participate in surplus, but the right to have 'arrears' paid on dissolution. (No dividends have been paid):

Yearly Profits and Repayment of Capitals		Total	(1) Preference		Ordinary		Total	(2) Preference		Ordinary	
	£	£	£	£	£	£	£	£	£	£	£
Dividends—											
Year 1	300			Nil		Nil			Nil		Nil
„ 2	350			Nil		Nil			Nil		Nil
„ 3	600			Nil		Nil			Nil		Nil
„ 4	1,000			Nil		Nil			Nil		Nil
	£2,250										
Repayment of Capitals—											
Preference 'Arrears'		1,400	1,400				1,120	1,120			
Preference Capital		5,000	5,000	6,400			4,000	4,000	5,120		
Ordinary		5,000			5,000		2,000			2,000	
Surplus to Ordinary		5,850			5,850	10,850	10,130			10,130	12,130
	¹£ 17,250		£ 6,400		£ 10,850	£17,250		£ 5,120		£ 12,130	

¹ For the purpose of comparison the sum of £17,250 has been taken as the amount available for distribution in the dissolution, i.e. £15,000 and £2,250 profits which have not been distributed.

It is assumed that 'surplus' covers both that of capital and of revenue.

(iv) Where the preference shares are non-cumulative, with preference as to repayment of capital, together with the right to participate in surplus (all profits have been paid in dividends):

Yearly Profits and Dividends; and Repayment of Capitals	Total	(1) Preference		Ordinary		Total	(2) Preference		Ordinary	
	£	£	£	£	£	£	£	£	£	£
Dividends (as in i)	2,250		1,050		1,200	2,250		1,120		1,130
Repayment of Capitals—										
Preference	5,000	5,000				4,000	4,000			
Ordinary	5,000			5,000		2,000			2,000	
Surplus (pari passu)	5,000	2,500		2,500		9,000	6,000		3,000	
			7,500		7,500			10,000		5,000
	£17,250		£8,550		£8,700	£17,250		£11,120		£6,130

(v) Where the preference shares are cumulative, with preference as to repayment of capital, together with the right to participate in surplus (all profits have been paid in dividends):

Yearly Profits and Dividends; and Repayment of Capitals	Total	(1)		Total	(2)	
		Preference	Ordinary		Preference	Ordinary
	£	£	£	£	£	£
Dividends (as in ii).	2,250	1,400	850	2,250	1,120	1,130
Repayment of Capitals (as in iv)	15,000	7,500	7,500	15,000	10,000	5,000
	£17,250	£8,900	£8,350	£17,250	£11,120	£6,130

(vi) Where the preference shares are cumulative without preference as to repayment of capital or right to participate in a CAPITAL surplus, but the right to have 'arrears' paid on dissolution, together with REVENUE surplus. (No dividends have been paid):

Yearly Profits and Repayment of Capitals	Total	(1)				Total	(2)			
		Preference		Ordinary			Preference		Ordinary	
	£	£	£	£	£	£	£	£	£	£
Dividends—										
Year 1 . .	300									
„ 2 . .	350									
„ 3 . .	600									
„ 4 . .	1,000		Nil		Nil		Nil		Nil	
	£2,250									
Repayment of Capitals—										
Preference 'Arrears' .	1,400	1,400				1,120	1,120			
Preference Capital .	5,000	5,000				4,000	4,000			
Revenue Surplus to Preference .	850	850				1,130	1,130			
			7,250					6,250		
Ordinary .	5,000			5,000		2,000			2,000	
Surplus to Ordinary .	5,000			5,000	10,000	9,000			9,000	11,000
	£ 17,250	£ 7,250		£ 10,000		£17,250	£ 6,250		£ 11,000	

It should be noted that in the circumstances outlined the fact that there is sufficient to pay both the preference and the ordinary capitals in full obviously gives no advantage to the former even if they have a preference as to repayment of capital, but the distinctions have been made to explain the principles involved.

The principles outlined are just the same, even if the 'arrears' of cumulative preference dividends are compounded in the form of share capital, the amounts receivable depending upon the results on the relative capitals remaining for the preference and ordinary shareholders.

Where there is a new class of share introduced, and even if there are several grades of shares already existing, e.g. preference, ordinary, and deferred, although the detail may become involved, the above principles are nevertheless applicable.

The difficulties of reconciling the conflicting positions arising in respect of dividends and capital repayments in a winding-up are often considerable, seeing that rights to dividends (particularly as regards ordinary shareholders) do not depend necessarily on book value of shareholdings, whilst the repayment right in a winding-up depend primarily upon the proportions of book value of shareholdings of various classes. In practice, most weight is given to the 'going concern' aspect, i.e. dividends being of more importance than the winding-up rights.

It is important to remember, therefore, that regard must be had to:

1. Dividend aspect.
2. Winding-up aspect according to:

(a) Whether preference shareholders have a right to priority in repayment of capital or not.

(b) Whether the preference shareholders have the right to participate in surplus assets remaining after payment of costs, liabilities and repayment of capitals.

(c) Whether the 'arrears' of cumulative preference dividends are to be paid and, if so, in what priority.

The question as to whether the reorganization involves the issue of partly paid shares is important, particularly from the winding-up aspect.

In both cases, the range of profits and the possibility of the assets realizing an amount: (a) insufficient, (b) sufficient to repay original capitals; and in (b) the possibility of a small or large surplus over the *original* capital must be considered, as must the nature of the surplus.

It should be clear to the student that surplus means the amount remaining after payment of (1) *all* costs and expenses; (2) creditors, including DEBENTURE holders; (3) book values of share capitals (i.e. as they exist at the commencement of winding-up).

It may be mentioned in connection with the dividend aspect, that the greater the amount of reduction of capital applied against fixed assets, the less will be the charge in the future for depreciation, thus enhancing the amount of profits; although the reflex action will take place when such fixed assets are to be replaced, when the depreciation charge will considerably increase.

In dealing with the above examples, it has not been thought necessary to repeat the fact of the importance of VOTING rights (mentioned on p. 23313), but this is an exceedingly important matter.

In examination problems, the student will have neither time nor opportunity to deal in detail with all phases already outlined; but he will be expected to pay prime attention to the dividend aspect, with a brief reference to the winding-up position, as this is comparatively less important than the former; yet an understanding of the guiding principles of the latter should be known.

As a matter of practice, it is quite impossible to view the winding-up position with certainty, the contingencies being so very numerous and frequently utterly incapable of even an approximate prognostication.

It is, therefore, a matter of importance not only to bestow great care in the formulation of the scheme of reconstruction, but to choose carefully the opportune time. The necessity for the latter precaution may cause a delay not only of weeks, but of months, before a fair, equitable, and workable scheme can be prepared so as to meet with the approval of all interested parties.

Illustration 120

A company has passed through a period of heavy losses and, in the opinion of the directors after full consideration, the time to deal with the reconstruction has arrived. Its Balance Sheet at 30th June 19.8 may be summarized as follows:

BALANCE SHEET AS AT 30TH JUNE 19.8

	£		£
Share Capital Authorized and Issued—		Goodwill at Cost . . .	10,000
100,000 6% Cumulative Preference Shares of £1 each	100,000	Works and Plant at Cost, *less* Depreciation . . .	110,000
£130,000 Ordinary Shares of £1 each . . .	130,000	Stock, Work in Progress, Book Debts, Cash, *less* Trade Liabilities . . .	31,000
(*Note*. The cumulative dividend on the Preference Shares has been paid up to 31st December 19.6.)		Profit and Loss Account . .	79,000
	£230,000		£230,000

Each share (both preference and ordinary) carries one vote. On a liquidation the cumulative preference share capital is repayable at par plus any 'arrears' of dividend, and ALL surplus goes to the ordinary shareholders.

It is *believed* that the net profits in future will *average* £12,000 per annum. The floating assets, less liabilities, are considered to be worth the book figure of £31,000; goodwill is considered valueless; works and plant are revalued at £101,500.

A recapitalization being desired, you are requested to reframe the Balance Sheet as it would appear after giving effect to such recapitalization (involving a reduction in the nominal amount of the issued share capital) as you consider would be likely to commend itself to both the preference and the ordinary shareholders. Show how the right of each class would be altered under the scheme you propose.

The company desires to avoid the creation of a *new* class of shares.

Before dealing with the scheme, the student will observe that the words in italics are important, and it will be advisable to preface the answer by stating the assumptions that there is sound justification for the belief, and that the yearly profits will not fluctuate unduly from the average of £12,000.

The question confines the scope by reason of the statement that:

1. The preference capital is repayable at par, plus 'arrears'.

2. The ordinary shareholders are entitled to any surplus.

3. The preference shareholders have priority in the winding-up.

4. The scheme is to provide for some diminution of the nominal value of the preference shares, as well as the ordinary shares.

5. No new class of shares is to be created.

On the other hand, the question contains no information as to the possibility of the company requiring additional working capital, nor the amount and security of the creditors. This may be commented on, but ignored in the working of the problem.

REFRAMED BALANCE SHEET AS AT 30TH JUNE 19.8

	£		£
Authorized Share Capital—		Works and Plant at Cost, *less*	
100,000 7% Preference Shares		Depreciation, *less* amounts	
of £0·87½ each . . .	87,500	written off under Scheme .	101,500
712,500 Ordinary Shares of		Stock, Work in Progress, Book	
£0·20 each . . .	142,500	Debts, Cash, *less* Trade	
		Liabilities	31,000
Issued Share Capital—			
100,000 7% Preference Shares			
of £0·87½ each fully paid .			
(a)	87,500		
180,000 Ordinary Shares of			
£0·20 each fully paid (b)	36,000		
5% Income Certificate of £0·30			
each . . . . (c)	9,000		
	£132,500		£132,500

The preference shareholders will receive:

		£
1. One new 7% Preference Share of £0·87½ fully paid in exchange for one old Preference Share	= 100,000 at £0·87½	87,500 (a)
2. One new Ordinary Share of £0·20 fully paid for two old Preference Shares .	$= \dfrac{100,000}{2} = 50,000$ at £0·20	10,000 (b)
3. Three 5% Income Certificates of £0·30 each for every ten old Preference Shares for 1½ years' 'arrears' [£9,000]	$= \frac{3}{10} \times 100,000 = 30,000$ at £0·30	9,000 (c)

The ordinary shareholders will receive:

		£
One new Ordinary Share of £0·20 fully paid for one old Ordinary Share	= 130,000 at £0·20	26,000 (b)

Alternatively, the following scheme might be suggested.
The preference shareholders will receive:

£

1. One new 8% Preference Share of £1 fully paid for two old Preference Shares $. = \dfrac{100,000}{2} = 50,000$ at £1 — 50,000

2. One new Ordinary Share of £0·37½ each fully paid for two old Preference Shares $. = \dfrac{100,000}{2} = 50,000$ at £0·37½ — 18,570

3. One 5% Income Certificate of £0·30 for two old Preference Shares $. . = \dfrac{100,000}{2} = 50,000$ at £0·30 — 15,000

The ordinary shareholders will receive:

One new Ordinary Share of £0·37½ fully paid in exchange for one old Ordinary Share $. = 130,000$ at £0·37½ — 48,750

The position of the shareholders before and after the scheme may be contrasted, as well as the relative position as between alternative schemes with reference to the profits of £12,000 indicated in the question, on the lines shown in the succeeding illustration.

Illustration 121

Z, Ltd., proposes the following scheme of reconstruction:

The issued share capital is to be reduced by £110,339 by (a) writing £0·25 off each 8 per cent £1 cumulative preference (participating) share, each reduced preference share to be subdivided into one *non-cumulative* 8 per cent preference share of £0·50 fully paid and one ordinary share of £0·25 fully paid; (b) by writing £0·75 off each of the £1 ordinary shares. The preference dividends in 'arrears' for nine years are to be cancelled.

The preference shareholders are at present entitled to 25 per cent of surplus profits after payment of: (a) their 8 per cent cumulative dividend; (b) 20 per cent of remaining profits to a fund for redeeming certain certificates issued some years ago in lieu of three year's preference dividend 'arrears'; and (c) 10 per cent on the ordinary shares. Under the scheme, 20 per cent of remaining profits to fund in (b) above is to be continued.

The Balance Sheet (abridged) before the scheme is as follows:

BALANCE SHEET

	£		£
Issued Share Capital—		Sundry 'Net' Assets . .	347,114
8% Cumulative Preference Participating Shares of £1 each fully paid . . .	299,993		
Ordinary Shares of £1 each fully paid . . .	47,121		
	£347,114		£347,114

You are required (A) to show the Balance Sheet after the scheme has been sanctioned; and (B) to make brief comments on the scheme itself. Ignore the winding-up aspect, and nominal capital.

(A) BALANCE SHEET (*after* RECONSTRUCTION)

	£p		£p
Issued Share Capital—		Sundry 'Net' Assets	236,775·00
8% Non-cumulative Preference			
Shares of £0·50 each fully paid.	149,996·50		
Ordinary Shares of £0·25 each			
fully paid—			
£p			
[Allotted to Old Preference			
Shareholders] 74,998·25[1]			
Allotted to Old Ordinary			
Shareholders] 11,780·25[2]	86,778·50		
	£236,775·00		£236,775·00

(B) The following points emerge from the scheme:

1. The preference shareholders sacrifice nine years' dividends and relinquish a substantial claim on future profits.

2. Although the rate of dividend remains the same, the preferential right of the preference shares to dividends is reduced by exactly half.

3. The preference shareholders lose entirely their cumulative and (for what they are worth) their participating rights.

4. As against the above, the preference shareholders are given over 86 per cent of the 'equity' of the business which will tend to compensate them for the relinquishment of the participating rights. In fact, the scheme clearly separates the 'preferential' from the 'equity' rights and simplifies the position.

5. The old ordinary shareholders have less preference capital ranking in front of them for dividend, but as a result of the scheme have less than 14 per cent of the equity of the business.

6. The scheme releases for payment to ordinary shareholders future profits, as otherwise they would be charged with the nine years' 'arrears' of preference dividends, together with the current preference dividends on £299,993, as against £149,996·50.

7. As the proportion set aside for certificate redemption is increased (as shown below) the **current** divisible profits are reduced, but this allocation will cease when the amount required to pay off the certificates had been raised.

In short, the old preference shareholders forgo all claims based on the past, but secure the substantial and major share of the 'equity'; whilst the old ordinary shareholders, in consideration of obtaining dividends at an early stage, sacrifice in favour of the old preference shareholders the bulk of their 'equity'.

The effects of the scheme may be gauged by assuming divisible profits of £10,000, £30,000, and £50,000. The comparative positions would be:

[1] Proportion of 'equity' = 86% approximately.
[2] Proportion of 'equity' = 14% approximately.

Profits	Old Preference Shareholders		Old Ordinary Shareholders	
	Before Scheme	After Scheme	Before Scheme	After Scheme
£	£	£	£	£
10,000	10,000	10,000[1]	Nil	Nil
*[2]30,000	(a) 24,022	(b) 24,445	(a) 4,778	(b) 1,955
50,000	28,022	38,273	16,778	4,127

* These amounts are arrived at as follows:

POSITION *before* SCHEME

		Preference Shareholders	Ordinary Shareholders
	£	£	£
Profits	30,000		
Less 8% Dividend on Preference Shares	24,000		
	6,000	24,000	
Less 20% Provision for Certificate Redemption . . . [2]	1,200		
	4,800		
Less 10% Dividend on Ordinary Shares	4,712		4,712
	88		
Divisible— £			
25% thereof for Preference Shareholders . 22		22	
75% thereof for Ordinary Shareholders . 66			66
—	88		
		£24,022	£4,778

[1] Allowing nothing for provision for redemption of certificates. The calculations are made upon the assumption that the preference shares were £300,000, the difference of 7 being signatories' shares.

[2] The total profits divided before the scheme were £28,800 (see (a) above), and after the scheme £26,400 (see (b) above), the diminution of £2,400 arising from the increased allocation to Certificate Redemption Fund (as shown above and on p. 23331).

POSITION *after* SCHEME

		Old Preference Shareholders	Old Ordinary Shareholders
	£	£	£
Profits	30,000		
Less 8% Dividend on 299,993 Preference Shares of £0·50 each	12,000	12,000	
	18,000		
Less 20% Provision for Certificate Redemption . . . [1]	3,600		
	14,400		
Payable as Dividend on Ordinary Shares—			
(i) 299,993 of £0·25 each £12,445		12,445	
(ii) 47,121 of £0·25 each 1,955			1,955
	14,400		
		£24,445	£1,955

[1] See note 2, p. 23330.

Calculations based actually upon 300,000 shares (see note 1, p. 23330).

The profits available for distribution to the ordinary shareholders are divisible in the proportion of 299,993:47,121.

The calculation for the division of the profits of £50,000 will be similarly made.

In all cases the resultant voting power must be carefully noted.

Examination Problem

The following reconstruction scheme is approved by a majority of the shareholders of a public company with a capital of £600,000 in fully-paid shares of £1 each.

A new company is to be formed, to take over the entire undertaking of the original company, with a capital of £600,000 in shares of £0·50 each. Original shareholders are to have the right to apply for five shares in the new company, paid up to the extent of £0·40 per share, for every three shares of the old company. Cash creditors, amounting to £30,000 are to be paid off, and the costs of the scheme, £3,000, are to be paid by the new company.

Assume that, in due course, all the original shareholders applied for, and were allotted, the shares in the new company to which they were entitled, a call of £0·05 per share was made, and the creditors and costs were paid as arranged.

Show:

(i) The issued share capital of the new company as it will appear on the Balance Sheet.
(ii) The reserve, if any, available for writing down assets.
(iii) The cash available for the new company.

(*Adapted from Institute of Chartered Accountants Inter.*)

			£
(i) Issued Share Capital—			
1,000,000 shares of £0·50 each, £0·45 paid			450,000

	£	£
(ii) Capital Reserve—		
Paid-up value of shares in old company ['net' assets]		600,000
Less shares issued in exchange, 1,000,000 credited with £0·40 paid	400,000	
costs of scheme	3,000	
		403,000
Amount available for writing down assets.		£197,000

		£
(iii) Cash available for new company—		
Call, 1,000,000 shares, £0·05 each		50,000
Less creditors paid off	30,000	
costs of scheme .	3,000	
		33,000
Net cash available		£17,000

[The above question will be answered easily if the entries are journalized and posted to rough Ledger Accounts.]

Amalgamations. From the point of view of investors and shareholders affected by an amalgamation or absorption the usual 'acid tests' applied are directed to comparisons as between pre-merger and post-merger:

1. Amount of net assets attributable to each share;
2. Yield-earning and dividend to each share (and as a result comparing the resultant 'cover');
3. Voting power to each share;
4. The relative gearing of the share;
5. Position in a winding up;
6. Capital Gains Tax position.

Miscellaneous. Many difficulties may arise in practice, even in the case of comparatively simple amalgamations, and the following are probably the more important matters which must be considered:

1. The method most likely to receive the requisite approval of members, e.g. approval of 90 per cent in value required before compulsory share acquisition powers of Section 209, Companies Act 1948 operate, special resolution only required to authorize liquidator to accept shares, etc. in consideration for transfer of business or property under Section 287.
2. The taxation advantages and disadvantages of the various methods.
3. The 'freezing' of revenue reserves as pre-acquisition profits. Where a holding company is to acquire the share capitals of two or more existing companies, all reserves of the latter will be frozen (except possibly for

profits earned subsequent to a prior takeover date as from which the shares are acquired) but the reserves of one of the existing companies can remain free if it becomes the holding company and, if desired, sells its undertaking to a new subsidiary company in exchange for shares.

4. The requirement of Section 56, Companies Act 1948, for a company where applicable, to raise a Share Premium Account whether its shares are issued for cash *or, otherwise* (vide *Henry Head & Co. Ltd.* v. *Ropner Holdings, Ltd.*, where a holding company which had acquired subsidiaries by an exchange of shares had to create a Share Premium Account equal to the difference between the nominal value of the shares it issued and the true value of the assets acquired as represented by the shares of the subsidiary companies). This treatment results in an automatic freezing of pre-acquisition profits.

SECTION K: THE COMPANIES ACTS 1980 AND 1981

Companies Act 1980

The Act which contains 90 sections and four schedules was brought about in part by the second directive on company law by the European Economic Community.

Shareholders' rights generally (and particularly minority holders) are further protected as are those of prospective shareholders. Directors' powers are further controlled and the misuse of inside information is recognised and curbed. The rights and interests of employees are recognised in sections 46 and 74.

There are two types of companies[1] public and private, and these are further described as follows.

A. *Public companies*

A company is 'public' if it has (a) a minimum of two (formerly seven) members; (b) liability limited to the amount of its share capital; (c) declared in its memorandum of association that it is a public company; (d) registered as such and (e) its name ending with the expression 'public limited company' (p.l.c.).

The minimum authorised and issued capital is £50,000, at least 25% of which must be paid up. Any share premiums must be paid up in full. An important duty is imposed on the directors to call an extraordinary general meeting to decide the future of a company the net assets of which fall to half or less of the called up shares.

No dividend can be paid unless net realised profits exceed net unrealised losses, and interim accounts may require to be prepared to justify this situation and these must be submitted to the registrar of companies.

---

[1] No companies limited by guarantee may now be formed with a share capital.

B. *Private companies*

These are companies registered under the Acts which are not public companies. The minimum membership is also two but there is now no restriction on the maximum (formerly 50).

Such a company is unable to offer shares to the public, direct or indirect. Dividends however may be paid out of net realised profits, ignoring net unrealised losses. Interim accounts may require to be produced to justify this situation.

Share Capital. The main provisions of the 1980 Act concerning share capital include the following matters:

1. The powers of directors to issue shares up to the authorised limit has been removed. Such a decision must now be made at a general meeting.
2. Pre-emptive rights are now conferred by law on existing equity shareholders in the case of a further issue of equity shares.
3. Sec 57 of the Companies Act 1948 is now repealed and shares may not now be issued at a discount.
4. Allotments for non-cash considerations are strictly controlled in terms of Sec 23.
5. Procedures regarding the variation of class rights are contained in Secs 32 and 33.

Distribution of Profits. A distribution is defined in Sec 45(2) (as amended by the 1981 Act) as meaning every description of distribution of a company's assests to members of the company, whether in cash or otherwise, except distributions made by way of—

(*a*) an issue of shares as fully or partly paid bonus shares;
(*b*) the redemption of preference shares out of the proceeds of a fresh issue of shares made for the purposes of the redemption and the payment of any premium on their redemption out of the company's share premium account;
(*c*) the reduction of share capital by extinguishing or reducing the liability of any of the members on any of its shares in respect of share capital not paid up or by paying off paid up share capital; and
(*d*) a distribution of assets to members of the company on its winding up.

The basic rule is that distributions must be paid out of available profits, Sec 39.

In the case of a public company a distribution can only be made where, after the distribution, the net assets are not less than the share capital and undistributable reserves (which are defined in Sec 40(2) as amended by the Companies Act 1981).

If the most recently completed accounts contravene these rulings (i.e. for both public and private companies) in respect of a proposed distribution, interim accounts require to be prepared and additionally in the case of a public company must comply with other requirements including filing same with the registrar.

In the case of investment companies a distribution of realised net profits may, however, be made provided after so doing the assets are at least one and a half times the liabilities (Sec 41).

Realised profits of insurance companies are dealt with in Sec 42.

Directors of the Company. Further legislation or amending legislation is detailed in Part 1V of the act and includes the following:

(a) Any agreement for the employment of a director for more than five years must be approved in general meeting.

(b) The Sec 26 Companies Act 1967 requirement to maintain a register of contracts of employment of directors within the United Kingdom has been expanded to include service contracts of the company's directors with its subsidiaries and service contracts which require directors to work mainly abroad.

(c) In terms of Sec 48, no property worth more than the lower of either (a) £50,000 or (b) 10% of the company's net assets can be transferred to or from a director or connected person unless agreed beforehand at a general meeting of the company. A 'connected person' includes a spouse, a child, a company where the director controls more than 20% of the voting power or equity and other persons detailed in Sec 64. Transfers of property of less than £1,000 are exempt.

(d) Sec 49 prohibits loans or guarantees on behalf of directors except in limited circumstances detailed in Sec 50 and in the case of a relevant company (i.e. a public company or a private company which is a member of group containing a public company) further prohibits quasi-loans to directors or connected persons unless the quasi-loan does not exceed £1,000 and is repayable within two months. A 'quasi-loan' would include for example the payment by a company of private debts (including credit card facilities) of one of its directors or his relatives and other connected persons.

The limited circumstances referred to where loans are permitted include (a) advances to directors to meet future company expenditure, full particulars of which must be disclosed at a general meeting and in the case of a relevant company the maximum permitted advance is £10,000 and (b) loans to directors where this is in the normal course of the company's business (i.e. as a Moneylender) and normal terms for repayment are agreed. In the case of a relevant company which is not a recognised banker the limit is £50,000. It should be further noted that favourable terms can be granted for house-purchase or improvements (maximum £50,000) if like facilities are available to the money-lending company's ordinary employees.

(e) Directors now have a statutory obligation to have regard to the interests of the company's employees as well as shareholders, Sec 46(1).

(f) Any material interest of any director in any material transaction, arrangement or agreement must now be disclosed in the annual accounts.

(g) The Act widens the definition of a 'director' to include any person (other than a professional adviser) with whose directions and instructions the directors of a company are accustomed to act. Such person is described as a 'shadow director' and must reveal any interest in contracts, transactions or arrangements with the company (Sec 63). Details of his service contract must also be open to inspection by the company's members.

Inside Dealing (Part V of the Act). An 'insider' is an individual (excluding a corporate body) who is or has been in the past six months connected with a company and is—

(a) a director of the company or related company;

(b) an officer or employee of the company or related company or occupies a position involving a professional or business connection with the company or related company where it may reasonably be assumed confidential information is available (described in Sec 73(1) as 'unpublished price sensitive information') which may affect the value of securities and which ought not to be disclosed except for the proper performance of his functions.

Insider dealing occurs when unpublished price sensitive information leads to the buying or selling of securities in a company and is dealt with in Sec 68. The significant features of the legislation where the price of a company's securities has been affected by unpublished information known to an insider are as follows:

(a) The insider shall not deal on a recognised stock exchange in securities of his own company.

(b) The insider, who by virtue of his position is privy to confidential price sensitive information concerning another company, is disqualified from dealing on a recognised stock exchange in the securities of that other company.

(c) Where another individual has knowingly received information, direct or indirect, from an insider concerning a company's securities no dealings are permitted by that individual.

(d) In the case of unpublished information concerning a take-over bid which is price sensitive, no individual party to the take-over shall deal in the securities of that company in another capacity; nor shall any other individual so deal where he has knowingly obtained such information.

(e) None of the information held in the aforementioned cases shall be relayed to any other person (this includes a corporate body) where it would be reasonable to assume that person would deal in the company's securities.

Sec 68(8) lists some specific exceptions to these rules where insiders are acting in good faith and where the making of a profit is not the prime motivating force.

Sec 69 prohibits the misuse of information concerning company securities obtained by Crown servants.

Under the terms of Sec 70 dealings through an off-market are subject to the same legislation as deals through a recognised stock exchange.

The two remaining points worthy of particular comment concern the following amended legislation:

(a) The powers of a company will now include powers to make provision for the benefit of employees (past and present) on the cessation or transfer of the whole or part of the business (Sec 74)—taken in conjunction with the duty of caring for employees' interests generally, referred to earlier, this represents an important recognition of the rights of employees.

(b) So far as the shareholders are concerned any member can now petition the court if he considers the company's affairs are being conducted in a manner unfairly prejudicial to some part of the members (including at least himself).

If the court considers the petition is justified it may make an order

   (i) to regulate the further conduct of the company's affairs;
  (ii) to restrain the doing or continuing of any act which was the reason for the complaint;
 (iii) to authorise civil proceedings to be brought in the name and on behalf of the company by such persons and on such terms as it directs;
 (iv) to provide for the purchase of the shares of any members by other members or by the company itself and in the latter case to reduce the company's capital accordingly.

The Companies Act 1981

The most important amendments of this Act involve, except in circumstances referred to later, an entirely new Schedule 8 to be substituted for the existing Schedule 8 to the Companies Act 1948 and sets out two balance sheet and four profit and loss account formats.

Once a company selects a format this must be adhered to rigidly unless a good cause for departure is shown. All headings listed must be shown (in the order laid down) unless there are no amounts in the current or previous year for any heading. There is however some scope for adjustment of items with Arabic numbers (see later).

The new statutory provisions are in compliance with European Economic Community regulations and are reproduced in full as follows:

Balance Sheet Formats

Format 1

A. Called up share capital not paid (1)

B. Fixed assets
   I   Intangible assets
      1. Development costs
      2. Concessions, patents, licences, trade marks and similar rights and assets (2)
      3. Goodwill (3)
      4. Payments on account
   II   Tangible assets
      1. Land and buildings
      2. Plant and machinery
      3. Fixtures, fittings, tools and equipment
      4. Payments on account and assets in course of construction

   III Investments
1. Shares in group companies
2. Loans to group companies
3. Shares in related companies
4. Loans to related companies
5. Other investments other than loans
6. Other loans
7. Own shares (4)

C. Current assets
    I Stocks
1. Raw materials and consumables
2. Work in progress
3. Finished goods and goods for resale
4. Payments on account
   II Debtors (5)
1. Trade debtors
2. Amounts owed by group companies
3. Amounts owed by related companies
4. Other debtors
5. Called up share capital not paid (1)
6. Prepayments and accrued income (6)
   III Investments
1. Shares in group companies
2. Own shares (4)
3. Other investments
   IV Cash at bank and in hand

D. Prepayments and accrued income (6)

E. Creditors: amounts falling due within one year
1. Debenture loans (7)
2. Bank loans and overdrafts
3. Payments received on account (8)
4. Trade creditors
5. Bills of exchange payable
6. Amounts owed to group companies
7. Amounts owed to related companies
8. Other creditors including taxation and social security (9)
9. Accruals and deferred income (10)

F. Net current assets (liabilities) (11)

G. Total assets less current liabilities

H. Creditors: amounts falling due after more than one year
1. Debenture loans (7)
2. Bank loans and overdrafts
3. Payments received on account (8)
4. Trade creditors

5. Bills of exchange payable
6. Amounts owed to group companies
7. Amounts owed to related companies
8. Other creditors including taxation and social security (9)
9. Accruals and deferred income (10)

I.   Provisions for liabilities and charges
    1. Pensions and similar obligations
    2. Taxation, including deferred taxation
    3. Other provisions

J.   Accruals and deferred income (10)

K.   Capital and reserves
    I   Called up share capital (12)
    II   Share premium account
    III Revaluation reserve
    IV Other reserves
        1. Capital redemption reserve
        2. Reserve for own shares
        3. Reserves provided for by the articles of association
        4. Other reserves
    V   Profit and loss account

Balance Sheet Formats

Format 2

ASSETS

A.   Called up share capital not paid (1)

B.   Fixed assets
    I   Intangible assets
        1. Development costs
        2. Concessions, patents, licences, trade marks and similar rights and assets (2)
        3. Goodwill (3)
        4. Payment on account
    II Tangible assets
        1. Land and buildings
        2. Plant and machinery
        3. Fixtures, fittings, tools and equipment
        4. Payments on account and assets in course of construction
    III Investments
        1. Shares in group companies
        2. Loans to group companies
        3. Shares in related companies
        4. Loans to related companies
        5. Other investments other than loans
        6. Other loans
        7. Own shares (4)

C.　Current assets
    I   Stocks
        1. Raw materials and consumables
        2. Work in progress
        3. Finished goods and goods for resale
        4. Payments on account
    II   Debtors (5)
        1. Trade debtors
        2. Amounts owed by group companies
        3. Amounts owed by related companies
        4. Other debtors
        5. Called up share capital not paid (1)
        6. Prepayments and accrued income (6)
    III Investments
        1. Shares in group companies
        2. Own shares (4)
        3. Other investments
    IV Cash at bank and in hand

D.　Prepayments and accrued income (6)

LIABILITIES

A.　Capital and reserves
    I   Called up share capital (12)
    II   Share premium account
    III Revaluation reserve
    IV Other reserves
        1. Capital redemption reserve
        2. Reserve for own shares
        3. Reserves provided for by the articles of association
        4. Other reserves
    V   Profit and loss account

B.　Provisions for liabilities and charges
        1. Pensions and similar obligations
        2. Taxation including deferred taxation
        3. Other provisions

C.　Creditors (13)
        1. Debenture loans (7)
        2. Bank loans and overdrafts
        3. Payments received on account (8)
        4. Trade creditors
        5. Bills of exchange payable
        6. Amounts owed to group companies
        7. Amounts owed to related companies
        8. Other creditors including taxation and social security (9
        9. Accruals and deferred income (10)

D.　Accruals and deferred income (10)

Notes on the balance sheet formats

(1) *Called up share capital not paid*
   (Formats 1 and 2, items A and C.II.5.)
   This item may be shown in either of the two positions given in Formats 1 and 2.

(2) *Concessions, patents, licences, trade marks and similar rights and assets*
   (Formats 1 and 2, item B.I.2.)
   Amounts in respect of assets shall only be included in a company's balance sheet under this item if either—
   (*a*) the assets were acquired for valuable consideration and are not required to be shown under goodwill; or
   (*b*) the assets in question were created by the company itself.

(3) *Goodwill*
   (Formats 1 and 2, item B.I.3.)
   Amounts representing goodwill shall only be included to the extent that the goodwill was acquired for valuable consideration.

(4) *Own shares*
   (Formats 1 and 2, items B.III.7 and C.III.2.)
   The nominal value of the shares held shall be shown separately.

(5) *Debtors*
   (Formats 1 and 2, items C.II.1 to 6.)
   The amount falling due after more than one year shall be shown separately for each item included under debtors.

(6) *Prepayments and accrued income*
   (Formats 1 and 2, items C.II.6 and D.)
   This item may be shown in either of the two positions given in Formats 1 and 2.

(7) *Debenture loans*
   (Format 1, items E.1 and H.1 and Format 2, item C.1.)
   The amount of any convertible loans shall be shown separately.

(8) *Payments received on account*
   (Format 1, items E.3 and H.3 and Format 2, item C.3.)
   Payments received on account of orders shall be shown for each of these items in so far as they are not shown as deductions from stocks.

(9) *Other creditors including taxation and social security*
   (Format 1, items E.8 and H.8 and Format 2, item C.8.)
   The amount for creditors in respect of taxation and social security shall be shown separately from the amount for other creditors.

(10) *Accruals and deferred income*
(Format 1, items E.9, H.9 and J and Format 2, items C.9 and D.)
The two positions given for this item in Format 1 at E.9 and H.9 are an alternative to the position at J, but if the item is not shown in a position corresponding to that at J it may be shown in either or both of the other two positions (as the case may require).
The two positions given for this item in Format 2 are alternatives.

(11) *Net current assets* (*liabilities*)
(Format 1, item F.)
In determining the amount to be shown for this item any amounts shown under "prepayments and accrued income" shall be taken into account wherever shown.

(12) *Called up share capital*
(Format 1, item K.I and Format 2, item A.I.)
The amount of allotted share capital and the amount of called up share capital which has been paid up shall be shown separately.

(13) *Creditors*
(Format 2, items C.1 to 9.)
Amounts falling due within one year and after one year shall be shown separately for each of these items and their aggregate shall be shown separately for all of these items.

Profit and loss account formats

Format 1

(see note (17) below)

1. Turnover
2. Cost of sales (14)
3. Gross profit or loss
4. Distribution costs (14)
5. Administrative expenses (14)
6. Other operating income
7. Income from shares in group companies
8. Income from shares in related companies
9. Income from other fixed asset investments (15)
10. Other interest receivable and similar income (15)
11. Amounts written off investments
12. Interest payable and similar charges (16)
13. Tax on profit or loss on ordinary activities
14. Profit or loss on ordinary activities after taxation
15. Extraordinary income
16. Extraordinary charges
17. Extraordinary profit or loss
18. Tax on extraordinary profit or loss
19. Other taxes not shown under the above items
20. Profit or loss for the financial year

Profit and loss account formats

Format 2

1. Turnover
2. Change in stocks of finished goods and in work progress
3. Own work capitalised
4. Other operating income
5. (*a*) Raw materials and consumables
   (*b*) Other external charges
6. Staff costs:
   (*a*) wages and salaries
   (*b*) social security costs
   (*c*) other pension costs
7. (*a*) Depreciation and other amounts written off tangible and intangible fixed assets
   (*b*) Exceptional amounts written off current assets
8. Other operating charges
9. Income from shares in group companies
10. Income from shares in related companies
11. Income from other fixed asset investments (*15*)
12. Other interest receivable and similar income (*15*)
13. Amounts written off investments
14. Interest payable and similar charges (*16*)
15. Tax on profit or loss on ordinary activities
16. Profit or loss on ordinary activities after taxation
17. Extraordinary income
18. Extraordinary charges
19. Extraordinary profit or loss
20. Tax on extraordinary profit or loss
21. Other taxes not shown under the above items
22. Profit or loss for the financial year

Profit and loss account formats

Format 3

(see note (*17*) below)

A. Charges

1. Cost of sales (*14*)
2. Distribution costs (*14*)
3. Administrative expenses (*14*)
4. Amounts written off investments
5. Interest payable and similar charges (*16*)
6. Tax on profit or loss on ordinary activities
7. Profit or loss on ordinary activities after taxation
8. Extraordinary charges
9. Tax on extraordinary profit or loss
10. Other taxes not shown under the above items
11. Profit or loss for the financial year

B. Income

1. Turnover
2. Other operating income
3. Income from shares in group companies
4. Income from shares in related companies
5. Income from other fixed asset investments (15)
6. Other interest receivable and similar income (15)
7. Profit or loss on ordinary activities after taxation
8. Extraordinary income
9. Profit or loss for the financial year

Profit and loss account formats

Format 4

A. Charges

1. Reduction in stocks of finished goods and in work in progress
2. (a) Raw materials and consumables
   (b) Other external charges
3. Staff costs:
   (a) wages and salaries
   (b) social security costs
   (c) other pension costs
4. (a) Depreciation and other amounts written off tangible and intangible fixed assets
   (b) Exceptional amounts written off current assets
5. Other operating charges
6. Amounts written off investments
7. Interest payable and similar charges (16)
8. Tax on profit or loss on ordinary activities
9. Profit or loss on ordinary activities after taxation
10. Extraordinary charges
11. Tax on extraordinary profit or loss
12. Other taxes not shown under the above items
13. Profit or loss for the financial year

B. Income

1. Turnover
2. Increase in stocks of finished goods and in work in progress
3. Own work capitalised
4. Other operating income
5. Income from shares in group companies
6. Income from shares in related companies
7. Income from other fixed asset investments (15)
8. Other interest receivable and similar income (15)
9. Profit or loss on ordinary activities after taxation
10. Extraordinary income
11. Profit or loss for the financial year

Notes on the profit and loss account formats

(*14*) *Cost of sales: distribution costs: administration expenses*
(Format 1, items 2, 4 and 5 and Format 3, items A.1, 2 and 3.)
These items shall be stated after taking into account any necessary provisions for depreciation or diminution in value of assets.

(*15*) *Income from other fixed asset investments: other interest receivable and similar income*
(Format 1, items 9 and 10: Format 2, items 11 and 12: Format 3, items B.5 and 6: Format 4, items B.7 and 8.)
Income and interest derived from group companies shall be shown separately from income and interest derived from other sources.

(*16*) *Interest payable and similar charges*
(Format 1, item 12: Format 2, item 14: Format 3, item A.5: Format 4, item A.7.)
The amount payable to group companies shall be shown separately.

(*17*) *Formats 1 and 3*
The amount of any provisions for depreciation and diminution in value of tangible and intangible fixed assets falling to be shown under items 7(*a*) and A.4(*a*) respectively in Formats 2 and 4 shall be disclosed in a note to the accounts in any case where the profit and loss account is prepared by reference to Format 1 or Format 3.

Additional items may be inserted or further details provided. Assets, however, may not be set against liabilities nor income against expenditure. As indicated earlier in the formats shown, items with Arabic numbers may be re-arranged where in the directors' opinion this is more suitable for the business concerned. They may also be combined but the details must be shown in the notes attached to the accounts unless the amounts involved are immaterial (Sch 1 Part 1 Sec A items 3(3) and (4)).

Every profit and loss account of a company shall show separately as additional items—

(*a*) any amount set aside or proposed to be set aside to, or withdrawn or proposed to be withdrawn from, reserves; and
(*b*) the aggregate amount of any dividends paid and proposed.

A company's balance sheet or profit and loss account may include an item representing or covering the amount of any asset or liability, income or expenditure not otherwise covered by any of the items listed in the format adopted, but the following shall not be treated as assets in any company's balance sheet—

(*a*) preliminary expenses;
(*b*) expenses of and commission on any issue of shares or debentures; and
(*c*) costs of research.

Fixed assets are defined as those used by a company on a continuing basis. All other assets are current assets. There are no longer assets which are neither fixed nor current.

Investments not intended for resale are fixed assets and movements on same must be shown.

SSAP 9[1] requires details of stocks to be shown and it will be noted this is now incorporated in Statute.

The detail of creditors to be shown is a new requirement and instead of the heading 'Current liabilities' there is to be inserted 'Creditors; amounts falling due within one year'. Similar details require to be given of creditors due after one year.

It must be stressed that the overriding requirement of the accounts giving a 'true and fair view' applies and if the prescribed format does not do so in any particular case, the directors must depart from the statutory form in order to give the required 'true and fair view'. For full details see Sec 1 of the 1981 Act which replaces and extends Sec 149 of the 1948 Act.

Statutory Accounting Principles. Five Accounting Principles are contained in Sch 1 Part 11 para 10–14 which are reproduced in full:

10. The company shall be presumed to be carrying on business as a going concern.

11. Accounting policies shall be applied consistently from one financial year to the next.

12. The amount of any item shall be determined on a prudent basis, and in particular—

(a) only profits realised at the balance sheet date shall be included in the profit and loss account; and

(b) all liabilities and losses which have arisen or are likely to arise in respect of the financial year to which the accounts relate or a previous financial year shall be taken into account, including those which only become apparent between the balance sheet date and the date on which it is signed on behalf of the board of directors in pursuance of section 155 of this Act.

13. All income and charges relating to the financial year to which the accounts relate shall be taken into account, without regard to the date of receipt or payment.

14. In determining the aggregate amount of any item the amount of each individual asset or liability that falls to be taken into account shall be determined separately.

However in terms of para 15 if it appears to be directors of a company that there are special reasons for departing from any of the principles stated above in preparing the company's accounts in respect of any financial year they may do so but particulars of the departure, the reasons for it and its effect shall be given in a note to the accounts.

[1] See p. 0532 *et seq.*

It will be noted that paras 10, 11 and 13 give statutory authority to the principles set out in SSAP 2.

Historical Cost Accounting. Sch 1 Part 11 paras 17 to 21 deal with fixed assets which under the historical cost convention will be shown at purchase price or cost of production.[1] Provisions for depreciation shall be made in respect of wasting assets so as to write them off over their useful life.

In the case of fixed investments of the kind shown earlier at B111 of the balance sheet formats, provision may be made for any reduction in value and if so the amount must be disclosed in the profit and loss account or in a note attached to the accounts.

A permanent fall in the value of any fixed asset must be provided for and shown in the profit and loss account or in a note attached to the accounts.

Where in these two cases, the reasons for the provisions cease to apply the overprovision must be written back and likewise shown separately (para 19(3)).

Sch 1 Part 11 paras 22 and 23 deal with current assets which should be valued at the lower of purchase price or cost of production[1] and net realisable value.

Para 27 deals with the valuation of stocks and fungible assets (including investments) on the basis of (a) First in, first out (FIFO), (b) Last in, first out (LIFO), (c) A weighted average price or (d) Any similar method. Fungible assets are assets which are largely indistinguishable one from another (e.g. large quantities of similar items). Subsections 4 and 5 impose a duty on the directors of a company to disclose by way of a note attached to the accounts any material difference between the value placed on any asset in terms of the regulations aforementioned and either the current cost or replacement cost at the date of the balance sheet.

Alternative Cost Accounting. Sch 1 Part 11 paras 29 to 34. Under these regulations, intangible fixed assets may be valued under current cost conventions and additionally in the case of intangible fixed assets may be shown at a market value determined at their most recent valuation.

Depreciation will be calculated on the alternative values but only the depreciation on the historical cost need be shown provided the difference is separately reported in the profit and loss account or in a note attached thereto.

Investments shown at B111 in the standard format may be shown at market value or at an appropriate valuation of the directors, showing in the latter case, the methods and reasons for same.

Investments shown at C111 may be included at current costs as may stocks.

In all cases however (except stocks), information must be provided on

---

[1] Cost of production includes direct costs and may include indirect production cost and interest charges (shown separately). Distribution costs should not be included.

the balance sheet or in a note attached which will enable the historical cost (as earlier described) to be established.

Any surplus or deficit arising due to the alternative method of valuation must be shown separately in the balance sheet and can only later be reduced or transferred to profit and loss account in prescribed circumstances (para 34(4)).

Notes to the Accounts. These are detailed in Sch 1 Part 111 paras 35 to 57 and include the following:

(a) The accounting policies adopted must be stated in the preparation of the profit and loss account and balance sheet, including the policies in the depreciation and diminution in value of assets (para 36).

(b) Any contingent right to the allotment of shares in the company (para 40).

(c) Shares issued during the year (para 39).

(d) Debentures issued during the year (para 41).

(e) Movements in fixed assets (para 42).

(f) Any security to creditors (para 48(4)).

(g) All guarantees and financial commitments (para 50).

(h) Interest on loans and overdrafts, income from listed investments; net rents from land (if material); auditors fees and expenses (para 53).

(i) United Kingdom taxation.

(j) Turnover of different classes of business and the directors' estimate of the profit or loss from each class (para 55).

(k) Average number of employees by categories and the aggregate amount of wages and salaries and related costs (para 56).

(l) Any extraordinary transactions (para 57).

Group Accounts. Sch 1 Part 1V paras 59 to 68 deal with the preparation of group accounts which must comply with the new Schedule 8. As with individual companies the requirement to give a true and fair view overrides the accounting requirements. If the accounting period of a subsidiary differs from the holding company, the group accounts should deal with the balance sheet of the subsidiary as at the end of its most recent financial year before that of the holding company and with its profit and loss account for that year.

Provided a consolidated profit and loss account is prepared, the holding company is exempt from presenting its own profit and loss account.

Accounting Exemptions. Certain exemptions are granted to small and medium size companies which in terms of S.8 are as follows:

	Small company	Medium Size Company
Turnover not exceeding	£1,400,000	£5,750,000
Balance sheet total not exceeding	£ 700,000	£2,800,000
Average number of persons employed (on a weekly basis) not exceeding	50	250

The exemptions which do not apply in the case of:

  (*a*) a public company
  (*b*) a banking, shipping or insurance company
  (*c*) a member of an ineligible group which is defined as a group containing
      (1) a company ineligible under (*a*) or (*b*)
      (2) a body corporate (other than a company) which has power to offer shares or debentures to the public or
      (3) a body corporate (other than a company) which is either a recognised bank or licensed institution within the meaning of the Banking Act 1979 or an insurance company within the meaning of the Insurance Companies Act 1974

are as follows:

Small Company Exemptions. The following modifications are allowed in the accounts delivered to the registrar:

  (1) Balance Sheet—only the items in the format which have a letter or Roman number need be shown—Sec 6(3).
  (2) The profit and loss account is not required—Sec 6(2)(b).
  (3) The only notes to the accounts which are required are on: accounting policies; share capital; substantial investments in other corporate bodies; aggregate creditors due after more than five years; secured creditors; ultimate holding companies and loans to directors and officers Sec 6(5).

If not appearing in the balance sheet, the following should be included in the notes:

  (*a*) total debtors due after more than one year;
  (*b*) where format 2 is adopted, total creditors due within one year and total after one year.
  (4) A report by directors is not required, Sec 6(6).
  (5) A special report by auditors is required, Sec 7(4).

Medium Size Company Exemptions. Modifications are permitted as follows:

  (*a*) A number of items may be combined as profit or loss:
      (1) Format 1—Items 1, 2, 3 and 6 .
      (2) Format 2—Items 1 to 5
      (3) Format 3—Items A1, B1 and B2
      (4) Format 4—Items A1, A2, and B1 to B4
  (*b*) There is no need to disclose turnover nor analysis of same.

The balance sheet delivered to the registrar must be signed by two directors (unless there is only one) and there must be a statement that they have relied on the exemptions granted on appropriate grounds (i.e. small or medium company).

A holding company is entitled to the benefit of the exemptions for individual accounts only to the extent that consolidated group figures comply with the exemption rules.

Dormant Companies. A company is 'dormant' if there has been no significant transaction during the period concerned. Auditors need not be appointed if the prescribed procedures are followed, Sec 12(1) to (5).

Banking, Insurance and Shipping Companies. Such companies may prepare accounts and group accounts in accordance with existing statute prior to the 1981 Act (Sch 2 paras 1 and 2).

Investment Companies. Sch 1 para 34 concerning revaluation reserves does not apply to Investment Companies. Reduction in the value of fixed investments need not be charged to profit and loss account. However, any distributions, which reduce the company's net assets to less than its called up share capital and undistributable reserves must be disclosed (Sch 1 Part V para 72).

Overseas Companies. The former exemptions regarding reports and information to be supplied to the registrar have been withdrawn.

Publication of Accounts. The regulations have been further tightened so that

(*a*) When a company publishes full accounts the audit report must also be published. A holding company publishing its own accounts must also publish group accounts.

(*b*) When abridged accounts are published a statement must be attached as to whether full accounts have been filed with the registrar and whether an auditors' report has been given and whether this was qualified.

Company Names and Business Names. In order to reduce the burden of checking names the registrar is now only obliged to refuse to register a name which is the same as that of an existing registered company. A name will be the same for this purpose despite minor difference detailed in S22(3).

The Register of Business Names Act 1916 has been repealed, the onus being placed on persons dealing with an unincorporated business to satisfy themselves that they know with whom they are dealing. However, more onerous requirements are placed on businesses to reveal (on letter heads, invoices etc) details of all partners in the business. Secs 28–30.

Merger Relief. The case of Shearer v Bercain in 1980 established that merger accounting was illegal. The 1981 Act now gives relief however in certain circumstances from the requirement under Sec 56 Companies Act 1948 to create a share premium account, e.g. where a company acquires (or reaches) a holding of 90% in the equity of another company by an exchange of shares, there is no need to account for share premium. Secs 36–41 provide full details.

Financial Assistance for Acquisition of Own Shares. In terms of Sec 42(1) and (2) it is illegal in general terms for a company or its subsidiaries to provide financial assistance to any person to acquire shares in the company or its holding company.

There are however various exceptions to the rule e.g. where the company is in the lending business or where the assistance is to employees who are not directors.

Purchase and Redemption by a Company of its Own Shares. This is an important change in legislation and the principal effect is that without affecting the authorised capital, a company which is empowered by its articles to do so, may purchase its own shares either on or off market. An off market purchase is one made either without a recognised stock exchange or on a recognised stock exchange but not subject to a marketing arrangement.

A special resolution is required for an off-market purchase. An ordinary resolution is sufficient for a market purchase, a copy of which must be passed to the registrar within fifteen days.

A private company may, if authorised by its articles, make a payment out of capital for the redemption or purchase of its own shares. Secs 45/46.

In all cases of purchase of shares a return must be made to the registrar giving details of same within twenty-eight days of purchase.

Disclosure of Interest. Part 14 Secs 74–77 deal with this matter.

The basic provision is that any person who has an interest of 5% or more of the share capital of a public company must declare that interest in writing to the company. Persons acting together must also disclose their interest and the Department of Trade's power to investigate ownership is strengthened.

SECTION L: OTHER STATEMENTS OF STANDARD ACCOUNTING PRACTICE

Current Cost Accounting. Statement of Standard Accounting Practice 1/16 concerns current cost accounting. This Statement has caused considerable controversy in the British business community and indeed it has frequently been openly challenged. Of course arguments about how best to account for inflation are by no means new. There can be no final and absolute answer to the problem but this does not imply that the search to find one should be abandoned. Nevertheless where inflation falls to a more acceptable level it becomes less important to the business fraternity to produce financial statements which take account of inflation.

One problem experienced by large groups is that where reports have to be presented to shareholders resident in different countries different information is required for each country, otherwise results may be misinterpreted because of the lack of international uniformity in accounting standards. Whatever the difficulties experienced to comply with SSAP 1/16 some companies have surmounted them by omitting from published accounts any current cost statements. This is a most unsatisfactory state of affairs. Where rules exist they should be supported. First of all, however, the rules should be operable. The main objective of all annual financial statements is to give a true and fair view of the financial position. Where inflation is high, historical cost accounting does not meet the requirement of a true and fair view. It is imperative that the accounting profession produce a statement of standard accounting practice on inflation accounting which can justify appropriate penalties being imposed on companies which fail to comply with the standards. SSAP 1/16 is lengthy and on the assumption that this will be superseded in the fairly short term only certain paragraphs are reproduced hereunder (original paragraph numbering has been retained).

1. This Standard applies to most listed companies and other large entities whose annual financial statements are intended to give a true and fair view of the financial position and profit or loss.

5. The basic objective of current cost accounts is to provide more useful information than that available from historical cost accounts alone for the guidance of the management of the business, the shareholders and others on such matters as:

(a) the financial viability of the business;
(b) return on investment;
(c) pricing policy, cost control and distribution decisions; and
(d) gearing.

III. STANDARD ACCOUNTING PRACTICE

Scope

46. This Standard applies to all annual financial statements intended to give a true and fair view of the financial position and profit or loss other than those of entities falling within the categories listed below:

(a) entities which do not have any class of share or loan capital listed on The Stock Exchange and satisfy at least two of the following three criteria:
  (i) they have a turnover of less than £5,000,000 per annum;
  (ii) their balance sheet total at the commencement of the relevant accounting period is less than £2,500,000 as shown in the historical cost accounts; and
  (iii) the average number of their employees is less than 250;
(b) wholly owned subsidiaries of companies or other entities where the parent is registered in the UK. This exemption does not apply where the parent is exempted under (c) or (d) below;
(c) (i) authorised insurers;
  (ii) property investment and dealing entities, with the exception of such entities as hold the properties of another entity within the group to which this Standard does apply; and
  (iii) investment trust companies, unit trusts and other similar long-term investment entities; and
(d) entities whose long-term primary financial objective is other than to

achieve an operating profit (before interest on borrowing); such entities may include charities, building societies, friendly societies, trade unions and pension funds.

Where an entity exempted under (c) or (d) above has subsidiaries which are not themselves exempted under these sections and which collectively exceed the limit in (a) above, the group accounts should include consolidated current cost information in respect of such subsidiaries.

47. Annual financial statements of entities coming within the scope of the Standard should include, in addition to historical cost accounts or historical cost information, current cost accounts prepared in accordance with this Standard. The current cost accounts should contain a profit and loss account and balance sheet, together with explanatory notes, disclosing the information set out in paragraphs 55–59.

The Current Cost Profit and Loss Account

49. The current cost operating profit is derived by making the following main adjustments to the historical cost trading profit (before interest on net borrowing) to allow for the impact of price changes on the funds needed to maintain the net operating assets:

(a) in relation to fixed assets, a depreciation adjustment being the difference between the proportion of their value to the business consumed in the period and the depreciation calculated on the historical cost basis;

(b) in relation to working capital:

    (i) a cost of sales adjustment being the difference between the value to the business and the historical cost of stock consumed in the period; and

    (ii) an adjustment based on monetary working capital.

50. Where a proportion of the net operating assets is financed by net borrowing, a gearing adjustment is required in arriving at the current cost profit attributable to the shareholders. This should be calculated by:

(a) expressing net borrowing as a proportion of the net operating assets using average figures for the year from the current cost balance sheets; and

(b) multiplying the total of the charges or credits made to allow for the impact of the price changes on the net operating assets of the business by the proportion determined at (a).

This adjustment, normally a credit, could be a debit if prices fall.

52. The treatment within the current cost profit and loss account of gains and losses on asset disposals, extraordinary and exceptional items, prior year items, income from associates, group consolidation adjustments, minority interests and the translation of foreign currencies should, where practicable, be consistent with the definitions of profit set out in this Standard. Where this is impracticable the treatment adopted should be disclosed in a note to the current cost accounts.

The Current Cost Balance Sheet

53. Assets and liabilities should be included in the balance sheet, as far as practicable, on the following bases:

(a) *Land and buildings, plant and machinery and stocks subject to a cost of sales adjustment*—at their value to the business.

(b) *Investments in associated companies*—either at the applicable proportion of the associated companies' net assets stated under this Standard or, where such information is not readily available, at directors' best estimate thereof. Allowance for premium or discount on acquisition should be made as stated under (e) below.

(c) *Other investments (excluding those treated as current assets)*—at directors' valuation. Where the investment is listed and the directors' valuation is materially different from mid-market value, the basis of valuation and the reasons for the difference should be stated.

(d) *Intangible assets (excluding goodwill)*—at the best estimate of their value to the business.

(e) *Goodwill (premium or discount) arising on consolidation.*

(f) *Current assets, other than those subject to a cost of sales adjustment*—on the historical cost basis.

(g) *All liabilities*—on the historical cost basis.

Contents of Accounts

Profit and Loss Account

55. The current cost profit and loss account should show (not necessarily in this order):

(a) the current cost operating profit or loss;

(b) interest/income relating to the net borrowing on which the gearing adjustment has been based;

(c) the gearing adjustment;

(d) taxation;

(e) extraordinary items; and

(f) current cost profit or loss (after tax) attributable to shareholders.

56. A reconciliation should be provided between the current cost operating profit and the profit or loss before charging interest and taxation calculated on the historical cost basis giving the respective amounts of the following:

(a) depreciation adjustment;

(b) cost of sales adjustment;

(c) monetary working capital adjustment and, where appropriate, interest relating to monetary working capital; and

(d) other material adjustments made to profits calculated on the historical cost basis when determining current cost operating profit.

The adjustments for cost of sales and monetary working capital may be combined.

Notes to the Accounts

58. The notes attached to the current cost accounts should describe the bases and methods adopted in preparing the accounts particularly in relation to:

(*a*) the value to the business of fixed assets and the depreciation thereon;

(*b*) the value to the business of stock and work in progress and the cost of sales adjustment;

(*c*) the monetary working capital adjustment;

(*d*) the gearing adjustment;

(*e*) the basis of translating foreign currencies and dealing with translation differences arising;

. (*f*) other material adjustments to the historical cost information; and

(*g*) the corresponding amounts.

Group Accounts

60. A company which is the parent company of a group and which is required to produce current cost group accounts should produce such group accounts in accordance with the principles set out in this Standard. It need not, however, produce current cost accounts for itself as a single company where historical cost accounts are the main accounts.

Date from which Effective

63. The accounting practices set out in this Standard should be adopted as soon as possible. They should be regarded as standard for annual financial statements relating to accounting periods starting on or after 1st January 1980.

Accounting for Post Balance Sheet Events. Statement of Standard Accounting Practice 1/17 concerns accounting for post balance sheet events and is largely reproduced hereunder:

I. EXPLANATORY NOTE

1. Events arising after the balance sheet date need to be reflected in financial statements if they provide additional evidence of conditions that existed at the balance sheet date and materially affect the amounts to be included.

2. To prevent financial statements from being misleading, disclosure needs to be made by way of notes of other material events arising after the balance sheet date which provide evidence of conditions not existing at the balance sheet date. Disclosure is required where this information is necessary for a proper understanding of the financial position.

3. A post balance sheet event for the purpose of this standard is an event which occurs between the balance sheet date and the date on which

the financial statements are approved by the board of directors. It is not intended that the preliminary consideration of a matter which may lead to a decision by the board of directors in the future should fall within the scope of this standard.

4. Events which occur after the date on which the financial statements are approved by the board of directors do not come within the scope of this standard. If such events are material the directors should consider publishing the relevant information so that users of financial statements are not misled.

5. The process involved in the approval of financial statements by the directors will vary depending on the management structure and procedures followed in preparing and finalising financial statements. However, the date of approval will normally be the date of the board meeting at which the financial statements are formally approved, or, in respect of unincorporated enterprises, the corresponding date. In respect of group accounts, the date of approval is the date the group accounts are formally approved by the board of directors of the holding company.

Classification of Post Balance Sheet Events

6. Events occurring after the balance sheet date may be classified into two categories: "adjusting events" and "non-adjusting events".

7. Adjusting events are events which provide additional evidence relating to conditions existing at the balance sheet date. They require changes in amounts to be included in financial statements. Examples of adjusting events are given in the appendix.

8. Some events occurring after the balance sheet date, such as a deterioration in the operating results and in the financial position may indicate a need to consider whether it is appropriate to use the going concern concept in the preparation of financial statements. Consequently these may fall to be treated as adjusting events.

9. Non-adjusting events are events which arise after the balance sheet date and concern conditions which did not exist at that time. Consequently they do not result in changes in amounts in financial statements. They may, however, be of such materiality that their disclosure is required by way of notes to ensure that financial statements are not misleading. Examples of non-adjusting events which may require disclosure are given in the appendix.

10. Disclosure would be required of the reversal or maturity after the year end of transactions entered into before the year end, the substance of which was primarily to alter the appearance of the company's balance sheet. Such alterations include those commonly known as "window dressing".

11. There are certain post balance sheet events which, because of statutory requirements or customary accounting practice, are reflected in financial statements and so fall to be treated as adjusting events. These include proposed dividends, amounts appropriated to reserves, the effects of changes in taxation and dividends receivable from subsidiary and associated companies.

Disclosure in Financial Statements

12. Separate disclosure of adjusting events is not normally required as they do no more than provide additional evidence in support of items in financial statements.

13. In determining which non-adjusting events are of sufficient materiality to require disclosure, regard should be had to all matters which are necessary to enable users of financial statements to assess the financial position.

III. STANDARD ACCOUNTING PRACTICE

21. Financial statements should be prepared on the basis of conditions existing at the balance sheet date.

22. A material post balance sheet event requires changes in the amounts to be included in financial statements where:

(a) it is an adjusting event; or

(b) it indicates that application of the going concern concept to the whole or a material part of the company is not appropriate.

23. A material post balance sheet event should be disclosed where:

(a) it is a non-adjusting event of such materiality that its non-disclosure would affect the ability of the users of financial statements to reach a proper understanding of the financial position; or

(b) it is the reversal or maturity after the year end of a transaction entered into before the year end, the substance of which was primarily to alter the appearance of the company's balance sheet.

24. In respect of each post balance sheet event which is required to be disclosed under paragraph 23 above, the following information should be stated by way of notes in financial statements:

(a) the nature of the event; and

(b) an estimate of the financial effect, or a statement that it is not practicable to make such an estimate.

25. The estimate of the financial effect should be disclosed before taking account of taxation, and the taxation implications should be explained where necessary for a proper understanding of the financial position.

26. The date on which the financial statements are approved by the board of directors should be disclosed in the financial statements.

Date from which Effective

27. The accounting practices set out in this statement should be adopted as soon as possible and regarded as standard in respect of financial statements relating to accounting periods beginning on or after September 1, 1980.

APPENDIX

This appendix is for general guidance and does not form part of the Statement of Standard Accounting Practice. The examples are merely illustrative and the lists are not exhaustive.

ADJUSTING EVENTS

The following are examples of post balance sheet events which normally should be classified as adjusting events:

(a) Fixed Assets. The subsequent determination of the purchase price or of the proceeds of sale of assets purchased or sold before the year end.

(b) Property. A valuation which provides evidence of a permanent diminution in value.

(c) Investments. The receipt of a copy of the financial statements or other information in respect of an unlisted company which provides evidence of a permanent diminution in the value of a long term investment.

(d) Stocks and work in progress.

    (i) The receipt of proceeds of sales after the balance sheet date or other evidence concerning the net realisable value of stocks.

    (ii) The receipt of evidence that the previous estimate of accrued profit on a long term contract was materially inaccurate.

(e) Debtors. The renegotiation of amounts owing by debtors, or the insolvency of a debtor.

(f) Dividends receivable. The declaration of dividends by subsidiaries and associated companies relating to periods prior to the balance sheet date of the holding company.

(g) Taxation. The receipt of information regarding rates of taxation.

(h) Claims. Amounts received or receivable in respect of insurance claims which were in the course of negotiation at the balance sheet date.

(i) Discoveries. The discovery of errors or frauds which show that the financial statements were incorrect.

NON-ADJUSTING EVENTS

The following are examples of post balance sheet events which normally should be classified as non-adjusting events:

(a) Mergers and acquisitions.

(b) Reconstruction and proposed reconstructions.

(c) Issues of shares and debentures.

(d) Purchases and sales of fixed assets and investments.

(e) Losses of fixed assets or stocks as a result of a catastrophe such as fire or flood.

(f) Opening new trading activities or extending existing trading activities.

(g) Closing a significant part of the trading activities if this was not anticipated at the year end.

(h) Decline in the value of property and investments held as fixed assets, if it can be demonstrated that the decline occurred after the year end.

(i) Changes in rates of foreign exchange.

(j) Government action, such as nationalisation.

(k) Strikes and other labour disputes.

(l) Augmentation of pension benefits.

Accounting for Contingencies. Statement of Standard Accounting Practice 1/18 concerns accounting for contingencies. Selected paragraphs from the Statement are reproduced hereunder and the original paragraph numbering has been retained.

I. EXPLANATORY NOTE

1. The term contingency used in this statement is applied to a condition which exists at the balance sheet date, where the outcome will be confirmed only on the occurrence or non-occurrence of one or more uncertain future events. It is not intended that uncertainties connected with accounting estimates should fall within the scope of this statement, for example the lives of fixed assets, the amount of bad debts, the net realisable value of inventories, the expected outcome of long term contracts or the valuation of properties and foreign currency balances.

2. Contingencies existing at the balance sheet date should be taken into consideration when preparing financial statements. Estimates of the outcome and of the financial effect of contingencies should be made by the board of directors of the company. These estimates will be based on consideration of information available up to the date on which the financial statements are approved by the board of directors and will include a review of events occurring after the balance sheet date. As an example, in the case of a substantial legal claim against a company, the factors to be considered would include the progress of the claim at the date on which the financial statements are approved, the opinion of legal experts or other advisers and the experience of the company in similar cases.

4. Existing conventions preclude contingent gains from being accrued in financial statements. The existence of a contingent gain should be disclosed only if it is probable that the gain will be realised. When the realisation of the gain becomes reasonably certain, then such a gain is not a contingency and accrual is appropriate.

III. STANDARD ACCOUNTING PRACTICE

15. A material contingent loss should be accrued in financial statements where it is probable that a future event will confirm a loss which can be estimated with reasonable accuracy at the date on which the financial statements are approved by the board of directors.

16. A material contingent loss not accrued under paragraph 15 above should be disclosed except where the possibility of loss is remote.

17. Contingent gains should not be accrued in financial statements. A material contingent gain should be disclosed in financial statements only if it is probable that the gain will be realised.

18. In respect of each contingency which is required to be disclosed under paragraphs 16 and 17 above, the following information should be stated by way of notes in financial statements:

(a) the nature of the contingency; and
(b) the uncertainties which are expected to affect the ultimate outcome; and
(c) a prudent estimate of the financial effect, made at the date on which the financial statements are approved by the board of directors; or a statement that is not practicable to make such an estimate.

19. Where there is disclosure of an estimate of the financial effect of a contingency, the amount disclosed should be the potential financial effect. In the case of a contingent loss, this should be reduced by:

(a) any amounts accrued; and
(b) the amounts of any components where the possibility of loss is remote.

The net amount only need be disclosed.

20. The estimate of the financial effect should be disclosed before taking account of taxation, and the taxation implications of a contingency crystallising should be explained where necessary for a proper understanding of the financial position.

21. Where both the nature of, and the uncertainties which affect, a contingency in respect of an individual transaction are common to a large number of similar transactions, the financial effect of the contingency need not be individually estimated but may be based on the group of similar transactions. In these circumstances the separate contingencies need not be individually disclosed.

Date from which Effective

22. The accounting practices set out in this statement should be adopted as soon as possible and regarded as standard in respect of financial statements relating to accounting periods beginning on or after September 1, 1980.

CHAPTER 24

HOLDING COMPANIES

It has been seen in connection with Company Accounts that one form of merger takes place by the medium of the Holding Company. The procedure, it will be remembered, is not to acquire the ASSETS with or without LIABILITIES of the absorbed company, but its SHARES. The separate entity of the absorbed company remains undisturbed, the acquiring company paying out, or discharging in other ways, the claims of the shareholders of the absorbed company. Consequently, no entries are required in the financial books of the latter company, as the transaction merely involves the transfer of shares from the old shareholders to the new holder (the acquiring company) with the consequent alterations in the Register of Members.

Definition of Holding Company and Subsidiary Company. Section 154, Companies Act 1948, states:

1. For the purposes of this Act, *a company shall*, subject to the provisions of subsection (3) of this section, *be deemed to be a subsidiary of another if, but only if*:

   (*a*) *That other either:*
      (i) *Is a member of it and controls the composition of its board of directors*; *or*
      (ii) *Holds more than half in nominal value of its equity share capital*; *or*
   (*b*) *The first-mentioned company is a subsidiary of any company which is that other's subsidiary.*

2. For the purposes of the foregoing subsection, the composition of a company's board of directors shall be deemed to be controlled by another company if, but only if, that other company by the exercise of some power exercisable by it without the consent or concurrence of any other person can appoint or remove the holders of all or a majority of the directorships; but for the purposes of this provision that other company shall be deemed to have power to appoint to a directorship with respect to which any of the following conditions is satisfied, that is to say:

   (*a*) That a person cannot be appointed thereto without the exercise in his favour by that other company of such a power as aforesaid; or
   (*b*) That a person's appointment thereto follows necessarily from his appointment as director of that other company; or
   (*c*) That the directorship is held by that other company itself or by a subsidiary of it.

3. In determining whether one company is a subsidiary of another:

   (*a*) Any shares held or power exercisable by that other in a fiduciary capacity shall be treated as not held or exercisable by it:
   (*b*) Subject to the two following paragraphs, any shares held or power exercisable:

      (i) By any person as a nominee for that other (except where that other is concerned only in a fiduciary capacity); or
      (ii) By, or by a nominee for, a subsidiary of that other, not being a subsidiary which is concerned only in a fiduciary capacity;

   shall be treated as held or exercisable by that other;
   (*c*) Any shares held or power exercisable by any person by virtue of the provisions of any debentures of the first-mentioned company or of a trust deed for securing any issue of such debentures shall be disregarded;
   (*d*) Any shares held or power exercisable by, or by a nominee for, that other or its subsidiary (not being held or exercisable as mentioned in the first foregoing paragraph) shall

2401

be treated as not held or exerisable by that other if the ordinary business of that other or its subsidiary, as the case may be, includes the lending of money and the shares are held or power is exercisable as aforesaid by way of security only for the purposes of a transaction entered into in the ordinary course of that business.

4. For the purposes of this Act, *a company shall be deemed to be another's holding company if, but only if, that other is its subsidiary.*

5. In this section, the expression 'company' includes any body corporate, and *the expression 'equity share capital' means, in relation to a company, its issued share capital excluding any part thereof which, neither as respects dividends nor as respects capital, carries any right to participate beyond a specified amount in a distribution.*

In determining the question whether a company holds more than half of the equity share capital of another, any such shares in the latter held by a *nominee* or *subsidiary* of the former, e.g. if X, Ltd., owns shares in Y, Ltd., any shares therein not directly owned by X, Ltd., but through its nominee or subsidiary, will be deemed to be a holding of X, Ltd., just as if X, Ltd., had such shares in its *own* name.

In regard to (5) above, preference shares with **any** participation rights (either as to dividends or even only as to surplus assets remaining in a winding-up after all the share capital has been repaid) will be considered for the purpose of the above Section as equity share capital.

From this, it will be seen that, before a subsidiary/holding company relationship can exist, there must, subject to direct and indirect holdings and control, be beneficial ownership of more than one-half in nominal value of the equity share capital or share ownership combined with power to control the composition of the board of directors. The definition, however, embraces sub-subsidiaries and other companies where the requisite share-ownership or power of control is held by two or more companies in a group. To constitute equity share capital, there must be the right to participate without limit in a distribution of a dividend *and/or* capital.

Advantages and Disadvantages of Holding Companies. The advantages are:

1. Preservation of separate entities, thus avoiding the sacrifice of the goodwill of the subsidiary company.

2. Different accounting periods may be used where in the opinion of the directors there are good reasons for doing so, although otherwise as will be seen later Section 153 of the Companies Act 1948, requires the same period to be used for the holding company and its subsidiaries to facilitate the preparation of group accounts.

3. Losses of a subsidiary company previously incurred may be carried forward for Corporation Tax purposes together with capital allowances, if any, and normal assessments continued in the ordinary ways whereas by an ordinary amalgamation the absorbed company no longer being an entity, would sacrifice such right (but see p. 2416).

This must now be considered in relation to Sect. 154 Income and Corporation Taxes Act 1970 and Sect. 17, Finance Act 1971, where the continuing basis (i.e. preceding year) of assessment will, notwithstanding the amalgamation, continue where:

(*a*) a COMPANY is the vendor of the business, and
(*b*) at ANY time within TWO years of the change at least 75 per cent

of the business belongs to the same persons as those to whom it belonged at any time WITHIN ONE year of the change.

4. Clear results of the operations and of the financial position of each constituent part are easily ascertained by the management, although the Consolidated Balance Sheet will disclose only matters that relate to the group as a whole.

5. By the simple expedient of selling shares in the subsidiary, the holding company can release its control or indeed the whole of its interest in the subsidiary.

6. Where a subsidiary is operating at a loss, or is otherwise unsatisfactory, its closure or sale is simpler than if it was merely a departmentalized part of a business into which it had been absorbed or merged.

The disadvantages are (in addition to those attendant upon *any* amalgamation):

1. Danger of fraudulent flotation and manipulation.

2. Danger of oppression of minority shareholders.

3. Lack of information to HOLDING COMPANY members as to the real worth of the investments in the subsidiary companies, although this is now obviated to some extent by the compulsory submission of group accounts.

4. Favouritism. One section may be allowed to sell at exorbitant prices to another section; advancement of money to a constituent company at excessive interest, or conversely, at unremunerative interest or without security.

5. Resulting from (4), the position of creditors and other members of the subsidiary company may be jeopardized.

6. Excessive Directors' Fees. Several or all directors of the holding company may join the Board and receive excessive fees from the subsidiary company.

7. Accounting difficulties, e.g. in dealing with the valuation of stocks and proper recording of inter-company transactions.

8. Where the subsidiary company is quoted on the Stock Exchange, the limited number of minority shares may prevent a 'free' market in the shares.

9. It is difficult to appraise the true earning capacity of subsidiary companies.

10. Profits and losses of individual subsidiary companies are not usually disclosed, although under the Companies Acts 1948 to 1976, Balance Sheet and accounts will have to be filed with the Registrar.

Creation of the Holding Company. The Holding Company may come into existence:

(*a*) Entirely as a new company to acquire all of a majority of the shares in: (i) new companies and/or (ii) existing companies, for either (1) Cash and/or (2) Shares exchange.

(*b*) By an already existing company forming new companies or taking over existing companies by way of development and expansion.

Particularly as regard new companies formed, the purpose may be: (*a*) to oust weaker rivals, (*b*) to 'departmentalize' activities, e.g. formation of companies in particular areas (including overseas) or with limited functions such as supplying raw materials, manufacturing, carrying out repair work marketing the finished products or in exceptional cases, to carry out all the operational functions.

· A particular difficulty arises where shares are acquired from shareholders of existing companies (as distinct from those formed by the Holding Company where all the shares in the new companies can be acquired) by reason of the inability to acquire all the shares of the existing companies, as some shareholders will not or cannot sell their shares. These shareholders form, almost invariably, a minority, and the terms majority (or controlling) interest and minority (or outside) interest are used to denote the shareholding of the Holding Company and the other shareholders respectively.

It has been seen that the essential factor is that the company holding shares in other companies: (a) does so deliberately to obtain control and (b) does, in fact, exercise directly or indirectly such control of the activities of those other companies.

The law has laid down certain minimum requirements in order to bring companies within the rules appertaining to Holding Companies and Subsidiary Companies, but in order to exercise undoubted and paramount control a Holding Company ought (from the business point of view) to be in a position to force through an extraordinary and special resolution—which requires a majority of not less than three-quarters of the shareholders entitled to vote (and voting) at a meeting called for the purpose of passing such a resolution, so that effective voting power is essential. On the other hand, companies (even if not Holding Companies as defined by the Companies Act 1948) do dominate the destinies of companies in which they have substantial holdings, although well below 50 per cent as: (1) many, in fact most, shareholders neither attend meetings nor trouble to fill up a proxy form, (2) even if they do attend they may not cast their vote, (3) they may be at variance with other shareholders when important issues arise so that the voting power of the substantial shareholder often scores over the divided votes of the other shareholders, and (4) many shareholders follow the lead of the big shareholder.

Book-keeping Entries in the Holding Company. On the purchase of the shares the acquiring company (holding company) will debit Shares in Subsidiary Company Account and credit Cash, Share Capital, or Debentures Account, according to the manner in which the claims of the shareholders of the absorbed company are satisfied.

With regards to dividends received by the holding company from a subsidiary company, only the dividends out of *profits made after the date of the purchase by the holding company* can be credited to the Profit and Loss Account of the latter.

Illustration 1

The following is the Balance Sheet in abridged form of S, Ltd., all the shares of which are purchased at the date of the Balance Sheet by H, Ltd., for £9,000.

S, LTD., BALANCE SHEET

	£		£
Share Capital (£1) . . .	3,000	Sundry Assets . . .	10,000
Reserve	3,300		
Profit and Loss Account . .	2,700		
Creditors . . .	1,000		
	£10,000		£10,000

Although, in law, the holding company has acquired *shares*, the accounting must have regard to net assets acquired. These are £10,000 assets, *less* creditors £1,000. This balance is reflected in share capital £3,000 and undistributed profits of £6,000, so that whenever the latter are paid out in dividends, the receipt in the books of the holding company must be treated as a return of the purchase price; this can readily be seen it is assumed that on the day following the purchase this has been done. The Balance Sheet will be:

S, LTD., BALANCE SHEET

	£		£
Share Capital . . .	3,000	Sundry Assets . . .	4,000
Creditors	1,000		
	£4,000		£4,000

The Investment Account of the holding company would appear thus:

SHARES IN SUBSIDIARY COMPANY

		£			£
Cash for Purchase of 3,000 Shares of £1 each at £3 a share . . .		9,000	Dividend received in respect of Profit prior to Purchase		6,000
			Balance . . . c/d		3,000
		£9,000			£9,000
Balance . . . b/d		3,000			

Dividends from a subsidiary company out of its profits earned *subsequent* to the purchase of the shares by the holding company will be credited to Profit and Loss Account in the books of the latter.

In regard to losses, these may have been incurred before or after the purchase by the holding company. The losses incurred prior to the purchase by the holding company would normally be taken into account in estimating the value of the shares acquired, so that all subsequent profits may be properly credited, upon the payment of dividends, in the books of the holding company. In regard to losses incurred since the date of the acquisition by the holding company, it is usual to create a provision therefor in the books of the latter and show it as a deduction from the investment in the Balance Sheet.

It is an unsound practice to bring into account the profit of the subsidiary otherwise than by way of dividends received, but if this is done the amount should be shown separately in the Balance Sheet of the holding company.

Illustration 2

On 1st April 19.2, Holdings, Ltd., purchase 18,000 ordinary shares of £1 each fully paid in Sub, Ltd., at £2·25 a share. On 31st December 19.2 the latter company paid a dividend of 75 per cent, together with a bonus share dividend of 'one for three'.

The Profit and Loss Appropriation Account of Sub, Ltd., was in credit as follows:

		£
19.1 Dec. 1	Balance brought forward	20,000
19.2 Nov. 30	Profit for the Year brought down . . .	12,000
		£32,000

The issued share capital of Sub, Ltd., was £20,000 in ordinary shares of £1 each fully paid.

Ignoring Taxation and narratives, show the Journal entries of Holdings, Ltd., in respect of the cash and bonus dividends on the shares held in Sub, Ltd.

1. CASH DIVIDEND:

In all cases of this type it must be decided whether the dividend is to be considered as being paid out of current profits, or out of the balance of Profit and Loss Account brought forward, or partly out of each. Depending upon this consideration, the entries will be:

(a) Current profits utilized as far as possible (this solution is based on the principle that dividends are paid, in the absence of other information, out of the latest available profits).

JOURNAL

		£	£
19.2 Dec. 31	Cash	13,500	
	Investment (or Shares) in Sub, Ltd. . .		6,300
	Dividends Receivable		7,200

The above dividend is partly capital and partly income, the latter being $\frac{8}{12}$ of 90 per cent of £12,000, representing the accruing income from the date of purchase (1st April 19.2) to the end of the financial year (30th November 19.2) on 18,000 shares, being 90 per cent of the issued share capital of Sub, Ltd.

The apportionment is analogous to that required in Executorship Accounts and, strictly, should be calculated in days, i.e. $\frac{245}{365}$ of 90 per cent of £12,000.

(*b*) If paid out of the balance of Profit and Loss Account, the whole of the dividend will be credited to the Investment Account.

(*c*) The third alternative is to split the dividend between the balance forward and the current year's profit in proportion to their respective amounts, so that as far as Holdings' 90 per cent share of the £15,000 dividend is concerned, the allocation is:

Balance Forward $\qquad$ $90\% \times \dfrac{20,000}{32,000} \times £15,000 = £8,437 \cdot 50$

Current Profit $\qquad$ $90\% \times \dfrac{12,000}{32,000} \times £15,000 = £5,062 \cdot 50$

As, however, the latter is for the year to 30th November and the shares were purchased on 1st April, only eight-twelfths of this can be regarded as income. The entries will therefore be:

JOURNAL

19.2 Dec. 31			£	£
	Cash		13,500	
	Investment in Sub, Ltd.			10,125
	Dividends Receivable			3,375
	$[\frac{2}{3} \times £5,062 \cdot 50]$			

2. BONUS DIVIDEND:

As to the bonus share dividend, the numerical holding is increased from 18,000 to 24,000 shares, but the true value of the equity remains unchanged. No journal entry is therefore required, the only entry in the books being in the nominal column of the Investment Account in respect of the additional shares. Even if all the **bonus** shares are sold, there will be no profit unless the net proceeds of the latter exceed one-quarter of the cost of the original holding after deduction of that part of the dividend which is a return of the outlay: that is, the bonus shares sold realize three-quarters of the original net cost per share. thus, taking the entries made in (1*a*), the original net cost of the shares—18,000 at £2·25 each— is £40,500 *less* the proportion of the dividend £6,300, making £34,200. On 18,000 shares, this gives a net cost per share of £1·90, but taking the bonus issue into account, on 24,000 shares, a net cost per share of £1·425, so that before any profit can be made the bonus shares must realize three-quarters of the original net cost per share, i.e. $\frac{3}{4}$ of £1·90 = £1·425.

Illustration 3

K, Ltd., on 1st August 19.., purchased 25,000 6 per cent cumulative preference shares and 1,000 ordinary shares (all £1 each, fully paid) at £1·10 and £3 respectively in D, Ltd.

The Balance sheet of D, Ltd., at 30th November 19.., showed Profit and Loss Account in credit as follows:

	£
Profit brought forward	1,600
Profit for year .	3,600

The issued share capital of D, Ltd., was 30,000 preference and 2,000 ordinary shares.

At the annual general meeting, the members approved the following recommendations of the Directors:

1. Payment of two years' Preference Dividend to date.
2. Payment of Ordinary Dividend of 75 per cent.

Draft Journal entries, ignoring narratives and taxation, to record the receipt of these dividends in the books of K, Ltd.

The position on 1st August 19.. (acquisition date) is:

	Total £		Applicable to Preference £		Ordinary £
Profit brought forward .	1,600	Year's Dividend	1,800		
Proportion of profit for year accruing— $\frac{8}{12}$ of £3,600 .	2,400	8 months' Dividend	1,200	Balance	1,000
	£4,000		£3,000		£1,000

K. Ltd., proportion—		
Preference—$\frac{25}{30}$.	£2,500	
Ordinary—$\frac{1}{2}$.		£500

These last figures represent the capital proportion of the first dividends received by K, Ltd., from D, Ltd., and will therefore be credited to the Investment Account. The excess of the dividends received over these amounts will be credited to Dividends Receivable.

JOURNAL

	£	£
Cash (2 years' dividend on 25,000 Preference Shares) . .	3,000	
D, Ltd. Preference Shares Investment		2,500
Dividends Receivable		500
Cash (75% on 1,000 Ordinary Shares)	750	
D, Ltd. Ordinary Shares Investment		500
Dividends Receivable		250

Note. This is the most prudent solution, but the alternative methods described in the previous illustration may be used.

Sometimes holding companies bring into their accounts all the profits or losses of their subsidiaries—although not legally compelled to do so, and, indeed, as mentioned, it is an unsound policy—treating the subsidiaries as debtors for profits and crediting a *separate* account called 'Profit and Losses of Subsidiary Companies Account', or 'Subsidiary Companies Revenue Account', losses being treated conversely. On the receipt of dividends by the holding company, cash will be debited and the Subsidiaries Profits Account credited.

Illustration 4

Sub, Ltd., in its first year loses £5,000; in its second year makes a profit of £12,000 and pays a dividend of £6,000. Show Journal entries, without narratives, in the books of the holding company, assuming that the latter company brings into account profits or losses of the subsidiary company; and that the whole of the share capital of Sub, Ltd., is held by the holding company.

JOURNAL

		£	£
Year 1	Profits and Losses of Subsidiary Companies . .	5,000	
	Sub, Ltd., Profit Account		5,000
2	Sub, Ltd., Profit Account	12,000	
	Profits and Losses of Subsidiary Companies .		12,000
	Cash	6,000	
	Sub, Ltd., Profit Account		6,000

The result is to show the Profits and Losses of Subsidiary Companies Account in credit for £7,000, £6,000 of which is received in cash, £1,000 being a debit balance on Sub, Ltd., Profits Account. The Profits and Losses of Subsidiary Companies Account is usually closed off to Profit and Loss Account.

Where, as is usual, there have been inter-company transactions, all UNREALIZED profits must be reserved for or eliminated. The most frequent example of this occurs where a subsidiary company sells goods to the holding company or to another subsidiary at a profit to itself. In the books of the selling company the profit on the sale will be brought into its accounts, thus showing a profit to the group as a whole, although the goods may not have been sold to outsiders. Hence the necessity for a reserve in respect of such unrealized profit. Obviously, if the buying company has sold the goods no adjustment is entailed.

Group Accounts. It will be obvious that the entries outlined in the previous pages appearing in the final accounts—i.e. an Investment in Subsidiary Account at cost in the Balance Sheet and a credit to Profit and Loss Account in respect of dividends received—will give very inadequate information to the members of the holding company. For this reason, the submission of group accounts is made compulsory by the Companies Act 1948. Thus, Section 150 of the Act states:

(1) Where at the end of its financial year a company has subsidiaries, accounts or statements (in this Act referred to as 'group accounts') dealing as hereinafter mentioned with the state of affairs and profit or loss of the company, and the subsidiaries shall, subject to the next following

subsection, be laid before the company in general meeting when the company's own Balance Sheet and Profit and Loss Account are so laid.

(2) Notwithstanding anything in the foregoing subsection:

(a) Group accounts shall not be required where the company is at the end of its financial year the wholly owned subsidiary of another body corporate incorporated in Great Britain; and

(b) Group accounts need not deal with a subsidiary of the company if the company's directors are of opinion that:

(i) It is impracticable, or would be of no real value to members of the company, in view of the insignificant amounts involved, or would involve expense or delay out of proportion to the value to members of the company; or

(ii) The result would be misleading, or harmful to the business of the company or any of its subsidiaries; or

(iii) The business of the holding company and that of the subsidiary are so different that they cannot reasonably be treated as a single undertaking;

and, if the directors are of such an opinion about each of the company's subsidiaries, group accounts shall not be required:

Provided that the approval of the Department of Trade shall be required for not dealing in group accounts with a subsidiary on the grounds that the result would be harmful or on the ground of the difference between the business of the holding company and that of the subsidiary.

(4) For the purpose of this section a body corporate shall be deemed to be the wholly owned subsidiary of another if it has no members except that other and that other's wholly owned subsidiaries and its or their nominees.

Moreover, it is provided in Section 152 as amended by C.A. 1976 Sch. 2:

(1) The group accounts of a holding company prepared under S.1 C.A. 1976 (taken with S.150 of this Act) shall give a true and fair view of the state of affairs and profit or loss of the company and the subsidiaries dealt with thereby as a whole, so far as concerns members of the company.

(3) Without predice to subsection (1) of this section, the group accounts if prepared as consolidated accounts, shall comply with the requirements of the Eighth schedule to this act,[1] so far as applicable thereto, and if not so prepared shall give the same or equivalent information.

Provided that the Department of Trade may on the application or with the consent of a company's directors, modify the said requirements in relation to that company for the purpose of adapting them to the circumstances of the company.

Form of the Group Accounts. Having laid down the information which is to be given, the Act allows some latitude to the Directors in deciding how the information should be presented to the members, the relative section is:

151.—(1) Subject to the next following subsection, the group accounts of a holding company prepared under S.1 C.A. 1976 (taken with S.150 of this Act) shall be consolidated accounts comprising:

(a) A consolidated Balance Sheet dealing with the state of affairs of the company and all the subsidiaries to be dealt with in group accounts:

(b) A consolidated Profit and Loss Account dealing with the profit or loss of the company and those subsidiaries.

---

[1] This may now be regarded as Schedule 2 of the Companies Act 1967.

(2) If the company's directors are of the opinion that it is better for the purpose:

(a) Of presenting the same or equivalent information about the state of affairs and profit or loss of the company and those subsidiaries; and

(b) Of so presenting it that it may be readily appreciated by the company's members;

the group accounts may be prepared in a form other than that required by the foregoing subsection, and in particular may consist of more than one set of consolidated accounts dealing respectively with the company and one group of subsidiaries and with other groups of subsidiaries, or of separate accounts dealing with each of the subsidiaries, or of statements expanding the information about the subsidiaries in the company's own accounts, or any combination of those forms.

(3) The group accounts may be wholly or partly incorporated in the company's own Balance Sheet and Profit and Loss Account.

In connection with the last subsection, the following subsection of Sect. 149 may be noted:

(5) Subsections (1) and (2) of this section [which require the Balance Sheet and Profit and Loss Account to give a true and fair view of the state of affairs and profit or loss respectively, and require compliance with the eighth Schedule][1] shall not apply to a company's profit and loss account, if:

(a) The company has subsidiaries: and

(b) The profit and loss account is framed as a consolidated profit and loss account dealing with all or any of the company's subsidiaries as well as the company, and:

(i) **Complies with the requirements of this Act relating to consolidated profit and loss accounts; and**

(ii) **Shows how much of the consolidated profit or loss for the financial year is dealt with in the accounts of the company.[2]**

Thus a consolidated Profit and Loss Account may be substituted for a separate Profit and Loss Account of the Holding Company.

Financial Year of the Group. Since group accounts have to be prepared, it is obviously preferable from the accountancy point of view that the financial years of all the companies in the group should coincide. From the directors' point of view, however, there may be good reasons against it, the most common probably being the increase of tax liabilities on an adjustment of the accounting period. Section 153 of the Act therefore provides:

A holding company's directors shall secure that, except where in their opinion there are good reasons against it, the financial year of each of its subsidiaries shall coincide with the company's own financial year.

Any necessary changes will be made in terms of S.3 C.A. 1976 which provides for the amendment of a company's accounting reference period (see p. 2310) by notification in prescribed form to the Registrar. The notification will normally be given during the period which is to be altered, but can in the case of a group be given after same, provided (a) the purpose of the amendment is to bring the accounting reference dates of the various companies in the group into line, *and* (b) the time limit for laying the accounts before the company in general meeting and delivery of same to the Registrar has not expired (see p. 2311).

---

[1] See footnote on previous page.
[2] See pp. 2487 and 2488.

On the other hand, by Section 151(2):

Where the financial year of a subsidiary does not coincide with that of the holding company, the group accounts shall, unless the Department of Trade on the application or with the consent of the holding company's directors otherwise direct, deal with the subsidiary's state of affairs as at the end of its financial year ending with or last before that of the holding company, and with the subsidiary's profit or loss for that financial year.

The directors of the holding company, moreover, are required to annex to the accounts a statement showing:

(a) The reasons why they consider that the subsidiaries' financial years should not end with that of the holding company.

(b) The dates on which the subsidiaries' financial years ending last before that of the company respectively ended or the earliest and latest of those dates. (Schedule 2 Part II, paragraphs 15 (6) and 22.)

Accounts of the Holding Company. The provisions of Part 1 of Schedule 2 to the Companies Act 1967 have been considered in the previous chapter. The following modifications of and additions to those requirements in respect of a company's own accounts are contained in Part II of the Schedule:

15.—(1) This paragraph shall apply where the company is a holding company, whether or not it is itself a subsidiary of another body corporate.

(2) The aggregate amount of assets consisting of shares in, or amounts owing (whether on account of a loan or otherwise) from, the company's subsidiaries, distinguishing shares from indebtedness, shall be set out in the Balance Sheet separately from all the other assets of the company, and the aggregate amount of indebtedness (whether on account of a loan or otherwise) to the company's subsidiaries shall be so set out separately from all its other liabilities and—

(a) The references in Part I of this Schedule to the company's investments (except those in paragraphs II (6B) and 12 (4)) shall not include investments in its subsidiaries required by this paragraph to be separately set out; and

(b) Paragraph 5, sub-paragraph (1) (a) of paragraph 12, and sub-paragraph (2) of paragraph 14 of this Schedule shall not apply in relation to fixed assets consisting of interests in the company's subsidiaries.

(3) There shall be shown by way of note on the Balance Sheet or in a statement or report annexed thereto the number, description and amount of the shares in and debentures of the company held by its subsidiaries or their nominees, but excluding any of those shares or debentures in the case of which the subsidiary is concerned as personal representative or in the case of which it is concerned as trustee and neither the company nor any subsidiary thereof is beneficially interested under the trust, otherwise than by way of security only for the purposes of a transaction entered into by it in the ordinary course of a business which includes the lending of money.

(4) Where group accounts are not submitted, there shall be annexed to the Balance Sheet a statement showing:

(a) The reasons why subsidiaries are not dealt with in group accounts;

(b) The net aggregate amount, so far as it concerns members of the holding company and is not dealt with in the company's accounts, of the subsidiaries' profits after deducting the subsidiaries' losses (or vice versa)—

(i) For the respective financial years of the subsidiaries ending with or during the financial year of the company; and

(ii) For their previous financial years since they respectively became the holding company's subsidiary;

(c) The net aggregate amount of the subsidiaries' profits after deducting the subsidiaries' losses (or vice versa):

(i) For the respective financial years of the subsidiaries ending with or during the financial year of the company; and

(ii) For their other financial years since they respectively became the holding company's subsidiary;

so far as those profits are dealt with, or provision is made for those losses, in the company's accounts;

(d) Any qualifications contained in the report of the auditors of the subsidiaries on their accounts for their respective financial years ending as aforesaid, and any note or saving contained in those accounts to call attention to a matter which, apart from the note or saving, would properly have been referred to in such a qualification, in so far as the matter which is the subject of the qualification or note is not covered by the company's own accounts and is material from the point of view of its members;

or, in so far as the information required by this sub-paragraph is not obtainable, a statement that it is not obtainable.

Provided that the Department of Trade may, on the application or with the consent of the company's directors, direct that in relation to any subsidiary this sub-paragraph shall not apply or shall apply only to such extent as may be provided by the direction.

(5) Paragraphs (b) and (c) of the last foregoing sub-paragraph shall apply only to profits and losses of a subsidiary which may properly be treated in the holding company's accounts as revenue profits or losses, and the profits or losses attributable to any shares in a subsidiary for the time being held by the holding company or any other of its subsidiaries shall not (for that or any other purpose) be treated as aforesaid so far as they are profits or losses for the period before the date on or as from which the shares were acquired by the company or any of its subsidiaries, except that they may in a proper case be so treated where:

(a) The company is itself the subsidiary of another body corporate; and
(b) The shares were acquired from that body corporate or a subsidiary of it;

and for the purpose of determining whether any profits or losses are to be treated as profits or losses for the said period the profit or loss for any financial year of the subsidiary may, if it is not practicable to apportion it with reasonable accuracy by reference to the facts, be treated as accruing from day to day during that year and be apportioned accordingly.

(6) Where group accounts are not submitted there shall be annexed to the Balance Sheet a statement showing, in relation to the subsidiaries (if any) whose financial years did not end with that of the company:

(a) The reasons why the company's directors consider that the subsidiaries' financial years should not end with that of the company; and
(b) The dates on which the subsidiaries' financial years ending last before that of the company respectively ended or the earliest and latest of those dates.

16.—(1) The Balance Sheet of a company which is a subsidiary of another body corporate, whether or not it is itself a holding company, shall show the aggregate amount of its indebtedness to all bodies corporate of which it is a subsidiary or a fellow subsidiary and the aggregate amount of the indebtedness of all such bodies corporate to it, distinguishing in each case between indebtedness in respect of debentures and otherwise, and the aggregate amount of assets consisting of shares in fellow subsidiaries.

(2) For the purposes of this paragraph, a company shall be deemed to be a fellow subsidiary of another body corporate if both are subsidiaries of the same body corporate but neither is the other's.

Consolidated Accounts. The remaining section of Part II of Schedule 2 deal with the consolidated amounts of a holding company and its subsidiaries as follows:

17. Subject to the following paragraphs of the Part of this Schedule, the consolidated Balance Sheet and Profit and Loss Account shall combine the information contained in the separate balance sheets and profit and loss accounts of the holding company and of the subsidiaries dealt with by the consolidated accounts, but with such adjustments (if any) as the directors of the holding company think necessary.

18. Subject as aforesaid and to Part III of this Schedule [which contains exceptions for certain classes of company, e.g. banking, discount and assurance companies] the consolidated accounts shall, in giving the said information, comply, so far as practicable, with the requirements of this Act and the Companies Act 1967 as if they were the accounts of an actual company.

19. Sections one hundred and ninety-six and one hundred and ninety-seven of this Act and sections four and six to eight of the Companies Act 1967 [which contain provisions for the disclosure of loans to and remuneration, etc., of directors] shall not, by virtue of the two last foregoing paragraphs, apply for the purpose of the consolidated accounts.[1]

20. Paragraph 7 of this Schedule [which requires disclosure in respect of increases and decreases in reserves and provisions] shall not apply for the purpose of any consolidated accounts laid before a company with the first Balance Sheet so laid after the coming into force of this Act.

21. In relation to any subsidiaries of the holding company *not* dealt with by the consolidated accounts:

(*a*) Sub-paragraphs (2) and (3) of paragraph 15 of this Schedule [concerning the separate statements of assets consisting of shares, etc., in subsidiaries and a statement of shares and debentures held by subsidiaries] shall apply for the purpose of those accounts as if those accounts were the accounts of an actual company of which they were subsidiaries; and

(*b*) There shall be annexed the like statement as is required by sub-paragraph (4) of that paragraph where there are no group accounts (see p. 2412), but as if references therein to the holding company's accounts were references to the consolidated accounts.

22. In relation to any subsidiaries (whether or not dealt with by the consolidated accounts], whose financial years did not end with that of the company, there shall be annexed the like statement as is required by sub-paragraph (6) of paragraph 15 of this Schedule where there are no group accounts (see p. 2413).

Miscellaneous. Extracts from the Companies Acts to be noted:

1948.—*Section 156* (as amended by C.A. 1976). The profit and loss account of a company prepared under S.1 C.A. 1976 and, so far as not incorporated in the balance sheet or profit and loss account, any group accounts of a holding company prepared under that section taken with S. 150 of this Act shall be annexed to the Balance Sheet and approved by the board of directors before the Balance Sheet is signed on their behalf, and the Auditors' Report shall be attached thereto.

1967.—*Section 14(3)* (*Extract*): [The auditors shall state in their report]—

Whether in their opinion the group accounts have been properly prepared in accordance with the provisions of the Companies Acts 1948 and 1967, and whether in their opinion a true and fair view is given of the state of affairs and profit or loss of the company and its subsidiaries dealt with thereby, so far as concerns members of the company subject to the non-disclosure of any matters (to be indicated in the report) which by virtue of Part III of Schedule 2 are not required to be disclosed.

Schedule 2 Part III, paragraph 26 [which states exceptions for special classes of company]—

Where a company entitled to the benefit of any provision contained in this Part of this Schedule is a holding company, the reference in Part II of this Schedule to consolidated accounts complying with the requirements of this Act shall, in relation to consolidated accounts of that company, be construed as referring to those requirements in so far only as they apply to the separate accounts of that company.

Summary. It has been deemed necessary to give the provisions of the Companies Acts 1948 to 1976 in detail. To assist the student, however, the following summary of the main points is given:

1. Group Accounts in one form or another must be submitted to the members of the holding company.

[1]See footnote[1] to p. 2346.

2. Such accounts must deal with and give a true and fair view of affairs and profit or loss of the group as a whole, as far as concerns members of the holding company.

3. Primarily, the group accounts should consist of a Consolidated Balance Sheet and Consolidated Profit and Loss Account combining the information contained in the separate balance sheets and profit and loss accounts of the constituent companies, with such adjustments (if any) as the directors of the holding company think necessary.

4. If, however, the directors consider that the same or equivalent information would be better presented or more readily appreciated by the members of the company in another form, they may do so, and in particular they may present:

(a) Consolidated accounts dealing with
  (i) the Company and one group of subsidiaries,
  (ii) other groups of subsidiaries.
(b) Separate accounts dealing with each of the subsidiaries.
(c) Statements expanding the information about the subsidiaries in the company's own accounts.
(d) Any combination of these forms.

In addition, group accounts may be wholly or partly incorporated in the company's own Balance Sheet and Profit and Loss Account.

5. Consolidated accounts must comply with the provisions of the Companies Acts as if they were the accounts of an actual company. Group accounts, if not prepared as consolidated accounts, must nevertheless give the same or equivalent information.

6. Group accounts are not required when the holding company is itself the wholly owned subsidiary of another body corporate incorporated in Great Britain.

7. A subsidiary may be excluded from group accounts in certain circumstances (Companies Act 1948, Sect. 150 (2b)). When any of the subsidiaries are so excluded, or when no group accounts are presented, the directors are required to annex to the holding company's accounts:

(a) A statement giving the reasons for the exclusion.
(b) Certain information detailed in paragraph 15 (4) of Part II, Schedule 2.

8. Unless the directors consider that there are good reasons against it, the financial year of each subsidiary must coincide with that of the holding company. Where it does not, the financial year of the subsidiary to be taken is stated in Sect. 152 (2). Also the directors must give their reasons and certain information (Schedule 2, Part II, paragraphs 15 (6) and 22).

Despite the alternative methods already described, it will probably be found in the majority of cases that the best way of presenting group accounts is in the form of a Consolidated Balance Sheet and a Consolidated Profit and Loss Account. The preparation of these accounts will therefore be described in detail. It may be noted that, whilst the principles are comparatively easy to understand, many difficult and complicated problems are bound to arise in practice which will only be solved in the light of experience.

Group Taxation Relief. For Corporation Tax purposes, 'group relief' may be obtained in respect of the trading loss of a member of the same group, all the constituents companies of which are resident in the United Kingdom. Companies are members of the same group if one company is the subsidiary of another company, or both these companies are subsidiaries of a third company. For the purpose of group relief a company is a subsidiary of another company if that other company holds directly or indirectly at least 75 per cent of the ordinary share capital of the first company (compare this with the definition of a subsidiary company for accounting purposes wherefor the ordinary share capital holding is 'more than half'—see p. 2401). Group relief is available only where a member company, called the 'surrendering company', has incurred a trading loss, and another member company having made a trading profit, and called the 'claimant company', claims, with the consent of the surrendering company, to set off wholly or partly, the loss incurred by the surrendering company. A claim for group relief must be made within two years after the end of the surrendering company's accounting period to which the claim relates. Set off is allowable only in respect of an accounting period, or part thereof, corresponding with the claimant company's accounting period. If the accounting periods of the companies concerned do not coincide, group relief is restricted to the smaller of the claimant company's profits or the surrendering company's losses for the corresponding accounting period.

A payment made by a claimant company, and qualifying for group relief, is not allowed as a deduction in computing the profits of the claimant company for Corporation Tax purposes. Similarly, the amount received by the surrendering company is not liable to Corporation Tax. However, the claimant company can set off the amount allowed for group relief against its total profits of the accounting period AFTER deducting trading losses, capital allowances, and charges on income[1] for that accounting period and previous accounting periods, but BEFORE deduction of trading losses and capital allowances from subsequent accounting periods. The payment referred to will be that sometimes made by the claimant company to the surrendering company in compensation for relinquishing the loss which would otherwise have been available for carry-forward. Such a payment should be made particularly where the surrendering company is not a wholly-owned subsidiary within the group, otherwise the minority shareholders would suffer the loss of a claim for relief against future taxable profits.

Group relief is also available to companies in a consortium whereby five or fewer companies own directly the entire ordinary share capital of a trading company or the same number of companies wholly own a holding company which in turn holds 90 per cent of the ordinary share capital of a

---

[1] Charges on income comprise any yearly interest, annuity or other annual payment all of which are payable under deduction of Income Tax.

trading company. For such a claim to be effective the trading company must be the surrendering company and any claimant company must be a member of the consortium.

Group Income. Normally, where a company pays a dividend or makes annual payments advance corporation tax (ACT) on the dividends and Income Tax deducted at the standard rate from the annual charges must be remitted to the Collector of Taxes. However, in respect of a group of companies resident on the United Kingdom, a paying member company and a receiving member company may jointly elect that the paying member company may pay dividends without paying ACT and annual payments gross, i.e. without deduction of Income Tax. Such payments, for taxation purposes, are termed 'group income'. To obtain group relief the paying company must either: (i) be a subsidiary company of the receiving company (both these companies may be subsidiaries of another company); or (ii) be a trading company, in which case the receiving company must be a member of a consortium. For these purposes a consortium comprises five or fewer resident companies who between them own at least 75 per cent (and each such company owns at least 5 per cent) of the ordinary share capital of the paying trading company.

Irrespective of any joint election in force, a company may notify the Collector that it does not want the election to take effect for specified dividends. This action may be expedient where, for example, the fund from which the subsidiary company pays the dividend comprises income liable to Corporation Tax and also franked investment income in which circumstances, from the group viewpoint, it may be more appropriate for the subsidiary company to pay ACT on so much of the dividend as will enable full set off to be made against the Tax Credit element of its Franked Investment Income. The parent company in turn will then be able to set off the tax credit on the part-dividend received against ACT due on any of its own dividends paid or other distributions made. A similar election may be made in respect of annual payments.

Statement of Standard Accounting Practice. Statement of Standard Accounting Practice No. 1/14 deals with the presentation of group accounts for a group of companies. The following extract sets out the Standard Accounting Practice only (original paragraph numbering has been retained):

Standard Accounting Practice

Consolidated financial statements

15. A holding company should prepare group accounts in the form of a single set of consolidated financial statements covering the holding company and its subsidiary companies, at home and overseas. The only exceptions to this practice are in the circumstances set out in paragraphs 19 to 22 below. A description of the bases on which subsidiary companies have been dealt with in the group accounts should be given.

Uniform accounting policies

16. Uniform group accounting policies should be followed by a holding company in preparing its consolidated financial statements. Where such group accounting policies are not adopted in the financial statements of a subsidiary, appropriate adjustments should be made in the consolidated financial statements. In exceptional cases where this is impracticable, different accounting policies may be used provided they are generally acceptable and there is disclosure of :

(a) the different accounting policies used:

(b) an indication of the amounts of the assets and liabilities involved, and where practicable an indication of the effect on results and net assets of the adoption of policies different from those of the group;

(c) the reasons for the different treatment.

Group accounting periods and dates

17. For the purposes of consolidated financial statements the financial statements of all subsidiaries should wherever practicable be prepared:

(a) to the same accounting date; and

(b) for identical accounting periods as the holding company.

18. If a subsidiary does not prepare its formal financial statements to the same date as the holding company and if it is not practicable to use for consolidation purposes special financial statements drawn up to the same date as those of the holding company (Department of Trade or other Government consent having been obtained as necessary), appropriate adjustments should be made to the consolidated financial statements for any abnormal transactions in the intervening period. The following additional information should be given for each principal subsidiary with a different accounting date:

(a) its name; and

(b) its accounting date; and

(c) the reason for using a different accounting date.

Where the accounting period of a principal subsidiary was of a different length from that of the holding company the accounting period involved should be stated.

Exclusion of subsidiaries from group accounts and consolidation

19. Group accounts need not be prepared, unless required by law, where the holding company itself is at the end of its financial year a wholly-owned subsidiary.

20. When a company is not a wholly-owned subsidiary and it does not prepare group accounts dealing with all its subsidiaries for one of the other reasons permitted under the Companies Acts, the reason for the exclusion of any subsidiary must be stated. Consideration will need to be given to whether the resulting financial statements give a true and fair view of the position of the group as a whole.

21. A subsidiary should be excluded from consolidation if:

(a) its activities are so dissimilar from those of other companies within the group that consolidated financial statements would be misleading and that information for the holding company's shareholders and other users of the statements would be better provided by presenting separate financial statements for such a subsidiary; or

(b) the holding company, although owning directly or through other subsidiaries more than half the equity share capital of the subsidiary, either:

(i) does not own share capital carrying more than half the votes; or

(ii) has contractual or other restrictions imposed on its ability to appoint the majority of the Board of Directors; or

(c) the subsidiary operates under severe restrictions which significantly impair control by the holding company over the subsidiary's assets and operations for the foreseeable future; or

(d) control is intended to be temporary.

22. If a group prepares group accounts in a form other than consolidated financial statements in circumstances different from those set out in paragraph 21, the onus is on the directors to justify and state the reasons for reaching the conclusion that the resulting group accounts give a fairer view of the financial position of the group as a whole. Similar considerations apply where consolidated financial statements are prepared dealing with a subsidiary which comes within the scope of the circumstances set out in paragraph 21.

Accounting treatment of subsidiaries excluded from consolidation

23. Where a subsidiary is excluded from consolidation on the grounds set out in paragraph 21 (a) because of dissimilar activities, the group accounts should include separate financial statements for that subsidiary. They may be combined with the financial statements of other subsidiaries with similar operations, if appropriate. The separate financial statements should include the following information:

(a) a note of the holding company's interest;

(b) particulars of intra-group balances;

(c) the nature of transactions with the rest of the group; and

(d) a reconciliation with the amount included in the consolidated financial statements for the group's investment in the subsidiary which should be stated under the equity method of accounting.

24. Where a subsidiary is excluded from consolidation on the grounds of lack of effective control as set out in paragraph 21 (b), it should be dealt with in the consolidated financial statements: either

(a) under the equity method of accounting if in all other respects it satisfies the criteria for treatment as an associated company under SSAP 1; or, if these conditions are not met,

(b) as an investment at cost or valuation less any provision required.

In either event, separate financial information about it should be included in the group accounts to meet the requirements of the Companies Acts.

25. Where a subsidiary is excluded from consolidation on the grounds set out in paragraph 21 (c), because of severe restrictions, the amount of the group's investment in the subsidiary should be stated in the consolidated balance sheet at the amount at which it would have been included under the equity method of accounting at the date the restrictions came into force. No further accruals should be made for its profits or losses. However, if the amount at which the investment is stated in the consolidated financial statements on this basis has been impaired by a decline in value of the investment (other than temporarily), provision for the loss should be made through the consolidated profit and loss account. For this purpose, investments should be considered individually and not in the aggregate.

26. Where a subsidiary is excluded from consolidation on the grounds set out in paragraph 21 (c) the following information should be disclosed in the group accounts:

(a) its net assets;

(b) its profits or losses for the period;

(c) any amounts included in the consolidated profit and loss account in respect of:

(i) dividends received;

(ii) writing down of the investment.

27. Where a subsidiary is excluded from consolidation on the grounds set out in paragraph 21 (d) that control is intended to be temporary, the temporary investment in the subsidiary should be stated in the consolidated balance sheet as a current asset at the lower of cost and net realizable value.

Disclosure in respect of subsidiaries from consolidation

28. In respect of subsidiaries excluded from consolidation, the following information should be disclosed in the group accounts:

(a) the reasons for excluding a subsidiary from consolidation;

(b) the names of the principal subsidiaries excluded;

(c) any premium or discount on acquisition (in comparison with the fair value of assets acquired) to the extent not written off; and

(d) any further detailed information required by the Companies Acts.

Changes in composition of the group

29. When subsidiaries are purchased, the purchase consideration should be allocated between the underlying net tangible and intangible assets other than goodwill on the basis of the fair value to the acquiring company. If this is not done by means of adjusting the values in the books of the acquired company, it should be done on consolidation. Any

difference between the purchase consideration and the value ascribed to net tangible assets and identifiable intangible assets such as trademarks, patents or development expenditure, will represent premium or discount on acquisition.

30. In the case of material additions to or disposals from the group, the consolidated financial statements should contain sufficient information about the results of the subsidiaries acquired or sold to enable shareholders to appreciate the effect on the consolidated results.

31. Where there is a material disposal, the consolidated profit and loss account should include:

(a) the subsidiary's results up to the date of disposal; and

(b) the gain of loss on the sale of the investment, being the difference at the time of the sale between:

(i) the proceeds of the sale; and

(ii) the holding company's share of its net assets together with any premium (less any amounts written off) or discount on acquisition.

Effective date of acquisition or disposal

32. The effective date for accounting for both acquisition and disposal of a subsidiary should be the earlier of:

(a) the date on which consideration passes; or

(b) the date on which an offer becomes or is declared unconditional.

This applies even if the acquiring company has the right under the agreement to share in the profits of the acquired business from an earlier date.

Disclosure of principal subsidiaries

33. The names of the principal subsidiaries should be disclosed in the group accounts, showing for each of these subsidiaries:

(a) the proportion of the nominal value of the issued share of each class held by the group; and

(b) an indication of the nature of its business.

Outside or minority interests

34. Outside or minority interests in the share capital and reserves of companies consolidated should be disclosed as a separate amount in the consolidated balance sheet and should not be shown as part of the shareholders' funds; debit balances should be recognized only if there is a binding obligation on minority shareholders to make good losses incurred which they are able to meet.

35. Similarly, the profits or losses of such companies attributable to outside interests should be shown separately in the consolidated profit and loss account after arriving at group profit or loss after tax but before extraordinary items. Minority interests in extraordinary items should be

deducted from the related amounts in the consolidated profit and loss account.

Restrictions on distributions

36. If there are significant restrictions on the ability of the holding company to distribute the retained profits of the group (other than those shown as non-distributable) because of statutory, contractual or exchange control restrictions the extent of the restrictions should be indicated.

PREPARATION OF THE CONSOLIDATED BALANCE SHEET

The holding company and its subsidiaries are considered as a whole economic unit, all the assets and liabilities of the various companies being aggregated. The Consolidated Balance Sheet must be compiled as if it were the Balance Sheet of an actual company and therefore, as regards the published result, many of the provisions of the Companies Acts will apply as if it were a single Balance Sheet.

The consolidated accounts may be compared with those of a concern having a head office and several branches as described in an earlier chapter and to a certain extent the same principles will apply, although the analogy cannot be pressed too far. The basic principle underlying the preparation of the Consolidated Balance Sheet is that all 'internal' items or inter-company balances appearing of course on opposite sides of the respective Balance Sheets) must be eliminated, the result showing the assets and liabilities of the group as a whole in relation to the outside world. The simplest example of this is in respect of the holding of shares in a subsidiary (hereinafter referred to as S) by the holding company (H), the item appearing on the assets side of H and, as share capital, on the liabilities side of S, thus:

Illustration 5

H acquired all the shares of S on 30th June 19.., for £2,000. From the following skeleton Balance Sheets prepare the Consolidated Balance Sheet at 30 June 19...

BALANCE SHEETS AS AT 30TH JUNE 19..

	H	S		H	S
	£	£		£	£
Share Capital—			Sundry Assets	6,500	2,500
£1 fully paid	5,000	2,000	Shares in S at cost	2,000	
Profit and Loss Account	1,500	—			
Creditors	2,000	500			
	£8,500	£2,500		£8,500	£2,500

CONSOLIDATED BALANCE SHEET

	£		£
Share Capital	5,000	Sundry Assets	
Profit and Loss Account . .	1,500	[£6,500 + £2,500] . . .	9,000
Creditors [£2,000 + £500] . .	2,500		
	£9,000		£9,000

The items in heavy print, being internals, are eliminated, the remainder being aggregated, or, in other words, the item 'Shares in S' is eliminated from the assets side of the H Balance Sheet and the assets and liabilities of S, which it represents, are substituted.

Pre-acquisition Profits and Losses. It will be noticed that in the illustration above, the Profit and Loss Account of S is shown as nil, for the sake of simplicity. This will rarely be the case in practice, as there will usually be undistributed profits (or losses) at the date of acquisition of shares, reflected in reserves and in the balance of Profit and Loss Account and in an increase in the net assets of the company. As was stated in the early part of this chapter, such profits must be regarded as capital by the holding company since they will be taken into account in fixing the purchase price. Thus, in the Consolidated Balance Sheet preparation, all reserves and profits (or losses) existing at the date of acquisition must be set off against the purchase price of the shares and will consequently not appear in the Balance Sheet itself.

Illustration 6

Assuming the same facts as in the previous illustration, except that the shares cost £2,300, the Sundry Assets of H and S being £6,200 and £2,800 respectively, and £200 and £100 standing to the credit of the Profit and Loss Account and Reserve respectively of S, show the Consolidated Balance Sheet.

CONSOLIDATED BALANCE SHEET

	H	S	Adjust-ments	Total		H	S	Adjust-ments	Total
	£	£	£	£		£	£	£	£
Share Capital .	5,000	**2,000**	− 2,000	5,000	Sundry Assets	6,200	2,800		9,000
Reserve . .		**100**	− 100		Shares in S				
Profit and Loss	1,500	**200**	− 200	1,500	at cost	**2,300**		− 2,300	
Creditors .	2,000	500		2,500					
	£8,500	£2,800	−£2,300	£9,000		£8,500	£2,800	−£2,300	£9,000

Illustration 7

Assuming the same facts as above, except that the Share Capital of S (all acquired) was £2,600, the Profit and Loss Account of S being £300 in debit and the Reserve nil, show the Consolidated Balance Sheet.

CONSOLIDATED BALANCE SHEET

	H	S	Adjust-ments	Total		H	S	Adjust-ments	Total
	£	£	£	£		£	£	£	£
Share Capital	5,000	2,600	− 2,600	5,000	Sundry Assets	6,200	2,800		9,000
Profit and Loss	1,500			1,500	Shares in S	2,300		− 2,300	
Creditors	2,000	500		2,500	Profit and Loss		300	− 300	
	£8,500	£3,100	−£2,600	£9,000		£8,500	£3,100	−£2,600	£9,000

Equity. The net worth of a concern is sometimes referred to as the equity of the concern. The equity can be calculated either by taking the net assets or by taking share capital, reserves and profit-and-loss balance. Thus the equity of S (above) is £2,300—net asset (£2,800 *less* £500) or capital *less* loss (£2,600 *less* £300).

Goodwill or Cost of Control. In all the illustrations so far, the cost of the shares in S has been equal to the equity, so that a straight elimination has been possible in preparing the Consolidated Balance Sheet. It often happens, however, that the the cost of the shares differs from the equity of S. If the cost is greater, this is, in the absence of other information, taken as indicating the unrecorded or undervalued goodwill of S. Such excess will therefore appear in the Consolidated Balance Sheet as Goodwill or Cost of Control.[1]

Illustration 8

H acquired all the shares of S on 30th June 19.., for £2,600, the Balance Sheets being as follows. Show the Consolidated Balance Sheet.

BALANCE SHEETS AS AT 30TH JUNE 19..

	H	S		H	S
	£	£		£	£
Share Capital	5,000	2,000	Sundry Assets	5,900	2,800
Profit and Loss	1,500	300	Shares in S	2,600	
Creditors	2,000	500			
	£8,500	£2,800		£8,500	£2,800

[1] Other terms are in use, e.g. Excess of Cost of Shares over Par Value and Accumulated Profit and Reserves at date of acquisition.

CONSOLIDATED BALANCE SHEET

	H	S	Adjustments	Total		H	S	Adjustments	Total
	£	£	£	£		£	£	£	£
Share Capital	5,000	2,000	− 2,000	5,000	Sundry Assets	5,900	2,800		8,700
Profit and Loss	1,500	300	− 300	1,500	Shares in S	2,600		− 2,600	
Creditors	2,000	500		2,500	Goodwill			+ 300	300
	£8,500	£2,800	−£2,300	£9,000		£8,500	£2,800	−£2,300	£9,000

As there are only £2,000 Share Capital and £300 pre-acquisition profits to set off against the purchase price £2,600, the remaining £300 is carried out into the Consolidated Balance Sheet as Goodwill.

Where, on the other hand, the purchase price of the shares is *less* than the equity of S, this is in normal circumstances taken as indicative of negative goodwill (i.e. 'Badwill') and the difference will appear on the liabilities side of the Consolidated Balance Sheet as Capital Reserve.[1]

CONSOLIDATED BALANCE SHEET

	H	S	Adjustments	Total		H	S	Adjustments	Total
	£	£	£	£		£	£	£	£
Share Capital	5,000	2,000	− 2,000	5,000	Sundry Assets	6,300	2,800		9,100
Profit and Loss	1,500	300	− 300	1,500	Shares in S	2,200		− 2,200	
Creditors	2,000	500		2,500					
Capital Reserve			+ 100	100					
	£8,500	£2,800	−£2,200	£9,100		£8,500	£2,800	−2,200	£9,100

Illustration 9

Assuming the same facts as above, except that the cost of shares was £2,200, Sundry Assets of H being £6,300, show the Consolidated Balance sheet.

The goodwill already appearing in the individual Balance Sheets of the constituent companies will remain unaffected by the adjustments and will appear in aggregate in the Consolidated Balance Sheet, unless it is considered advisable to utilize the whole or part of the Capital Reserve in extinguishing or reducing it. (But in examination work this should not be done unless clearly instructed or special circumstances warrant it.)

---

[1] Some accountants take the view that such a credit to Capital Reserve is illogical, as the assets virtually acquired should be shown at cost; e.g. if the cost of the shares acquired is £2,600, represented by net assets £2,700, the former figure is the correct figure of cost and not £2,700 assets with a Capital Reserve of £100.

Further consideration of what has so far been called Goodwill will show that the excess of the purchase price over the net assets acquired may in fact be apportioned between:

1. Unrecorded or undervalued goodwill, and
2. Cost of control,

for the price paid for all of the majority of the shares in a company carrying with them control of the company will usually be greater than that for a small number of shares carrying no power of control. No attempt is often made to differentiate between the two, the excess being shown as Goodwill and/or Cost of Control. If the premium paid is the measurement of the true goodwill based on super-profits, it can be described as such, but, where:

(a) There are no super-profits, or
(b) The premium exceeds that based thereon,

it is strictly cost of control. The 'excess' premium may be well worthwhile because of:

(i) The resultant economies,
(ii) The elimination of competition,
(iii) The prevention of acquisition of control by rivals.

Therefore, the distinction must be based upon the facts of the case and, if the profit-level is such as to justify the premium paid for the shares, the proper description is goodwill, otherwise it is cost of control (see note on p. 2424).

In addition it must be remembered that the excess cost may be reflected in an undervaluation of assets other than goodwill or in an overstatement of liabilities. In order to show a true and fair view of the state of affairs in the Consolidated Balance Sheet, the correct treatment in this case is to adjust the assets and/or liabilities concerned to their correct value when preparing the Balance Sheet.

The converse position where the cost of the shares is less than their apparent value, which has so far been described as Capital Reserve, may on further consideration of the facts be due to:

1. Over-valuation of assets and/or understatement of liabilities. The book value will be adjusted in the Consolidated Balance Sheet, thus reducing the Capital Reserve.

2. The company in which the shares are acquired earning profits less than normal in that type of business. There is thus an element of negative goodwill which will be put to Capital Reserve, which, as stated on p. 2425, may be wholly or partly set off against goodwill.

3. A share exchange, the cost of shares in S being shown at the nominal value of the shares in H exchanged therefor, which is less than the actual value (H gives (say) shares of £0·50 worth £0·90 for shares in S worth £0·60), the investment in S being shown at cost based on the nominal (£0·50 value). In the Consolidated Balance Sheet the difference will be

shown as Capital Reserve. In the books of H the correct treatment is to raise a Share Premium Account with the excess of the market over the nominal value of the shares, the investment in S being increased accordingly.

4. The shares in S being acquired cheaply through special circumstances, e.g. slump conditions, forced selling, temporary diffculties of S. Thus, the £1 shares of S may be bought for, say, £0·75 while they are worth £0·85 on book values. If it is decided that the latter are overvalued, or that there is an element of 'Badwill', adjustments will be required as in (1) and (2) above respectively; otherwise, in contrast to (3), there is an apparent profit on acquisition, but the prudent course would be to put this to Capital Reserve.

Where, as will be considered in greater detail later, H does not acquire all the shares in S, but say 75 per cent thereof, it will be clear that the goodwill figure described above will represent a proportion only of the total goodwill of S, the remainder attaching to the other 25 per cent of the shares held by the Minority Shareholders. The question therefore arises whether, in the Consolidated Balance Sheet, the goodwill should be written up to its true value by adding to the (in this case) three-quarters interest of H, the one-quarter interest of the Minority Shareholders, a corresponding entry being made on the liabilities side of the Consolidated Balance Sheet to show this latter one-quarter interest. It is contended that since all the other assets are shown in the Consolidated Balance Sheet in full and not merely to the extent of H's proportion, it is only logical to deal similarly with goodwill. The better practice, however, is not to do this, since goodwill should be shown at cost and not at an inflated figure. It should be noted that this question applies only to Goodwill proper and not to Cost of Control, the latter obviously attaching entirely to the large bulk of shares which carry with them the power of control, and in no respect to the small minority interest.

In dealing with Goodwill and Capital Reserve in advanced problems, it may be necessary to prepare two schedules:

1. Dealing with the difference between the cost of shares and the par value, and
2. Dealing with the pre-acquisition profits and losses.

Alternatively the schedules may be:

(a) Dealing with losses prior to acquisition and excess of cost of shares over par value, and
(b) Dealing with profits prior to acquisition and excess of par value of shares over cost.

Illustration 10

H acquires 60,000 shares in S at a cost of £50,000 and 30,000 shares in R at a cost of £55,000, the pre-acquisition loss of S being £6,000 and the pre-acquisition profit of R being £10,000. All the shares are fully-paid £1 shares. There is no minority interest.

The two schedules are:

(1) GOODWILL (or Cost of Control)

	S £	R £	Total £
Cost of Acquisition . . .	50,000	55,000	105,000
Par Value	60,000	30,000	90,000
	−£10,000	+£25,000	+£15,000

(2) CAPITAL RESERVE

	S £	R £	Total £
Pre-acquisition Profit . . .		10,000	10,000
Pre-acquisition Loss . . .	−6,000		− 6,000
			£4,000

There is thus a debit on Goodwill of £15,000 and a credit on Capital Reserve of £4,000; the latter would normally be set off against the former, leaving a net balance of Goodwill of £11,000.

The main disadvantage of this arrangement is that there may be both debit and credit items in each schedule, whereas, as will be seen in the alternative method, this likely confusion is avoided; thus:

(a) (Debit) GOODWILL (or cost of Control)

	S £	R £	Total £
Cost of Acquisition . . .		55,000	
Par Value		30,000	
Pre-acquisition Loss . . .	6,000		
	£6,000	£25,000	£31,000

(b) (Credit) CAPITAL RESERVE

	S £	R £	Total £
Par Value	60,000		
Cost of Acquisition . . .	50,000		
Pre-acquisition Profit . . .		10,000	
	£10,000	£10,000	£20,000

The credit of £20,000 is set off against the debit of £31,000, leaving a net debit of Goodwill of £11,000. This method not only avoids plus and minus signs but also it avoids a credit appearing in Goodwill and a debit in Capital Reserve (see items in previous illustration of −£10,000 in Goodwill and −£6,000 in Capital Reserve).

Inter-company Balances. The fact that all internal items or inter-company balances must be eliminated in the preparation of the Consolidated Balance Sheet has already been stated. These will include:

1. Share Capital—the elimination of the share capital of S against H's investment in S has already been shown. Conversely, as will be described in greater detail later, any shares in H held by S must also be eliminated against the share capital of H, which of course appears in the Consolidated Balance Sheet as the share capital of the group.
2. Debentures of one company held by another.
3. Loans to one company by another.
4. Current Accounts.

These adjustments present no difficulty, it merely being a question of setting off an asset in one Balance Sheet against a liability in another. Thus, if on the liabilities side of H's Balance Sheet appears Debentures £10,000 and the assets side of S's Balance Sheet shows that S holds £3,000 thereof, the net figure in the Consolidated Balance Sheet will be Debentures £7,000. Again, if Sundry Debtors of H include S £400, then Sundry Creditors of S must include H £400; the £400's will be eliminated and only the outside debtors and creditors shown in the Consolidated Balance Sheet.

Contingent Liabilities. In their own balance sheets the constituent companies will show contingent liabilities in the normal way by means of a note. When preparing the Consolidated Balance Sheet, such liabilities must be divided into: (i) internal and (ii) external. The latter will continue in the Consolidated Balance Sheet as notes, but the former will usually appear in the Consolidated Balance Sheet itself as actual liabilities, so that a note is unnecessary.

The two most common items of this type are:

1. Bills of Exchange—where, for instance, S has issued bills to H which has discounted them. S will show Bills Payable amongst its liabilities and there will be a note to H's Balance Sheet in respect of the contingent liability on bills discounted. In the Consolidated Balance Sheet, Bills Payable will appear as a liability of the group.

Illustration 11

The Balance Sheet of S shows Bills Payable of £6,000. All these were issued to H, in whose Balance Sheet appear the following:

> Bills Receivable (from S), £2,000.
> *Note.* There is a contingent liability on Bills discounted of £9,000 (£4,000 of which are from S).

How would these items appear in the Consolidated Balance Sheet!

The £2,000 of S's bills held by H will be set off against Bills Payable £6,000 (being internal transactions), the remaining £4,000 being shown on the Consolidated Balance Sheet as a liability. There will be a note to the

Consolidated Balance Sheet in respect of H's contingent liability on bills discounted of £5,000 (i.e. excluding S's bills discounted which appear as an actual liability,)

2. Guarantees by one company in the group in respect of another—where, for instance, H guarantees certain liabilities of S. As in (1), these will appear in the Consolidated Balance Sheet as actual liabilities of the group, so that a note is unnecessary.

Minority Interests. In all the illustrations so far, H has acquired all the shares in S, i.e. H has had a 100 per cent holding and the question of a minority interest does not therefore arise. It may be objected on purely technical grounds that H, being a separate legal person (but only ONE) cannot constitute (no more than an individual can) the sole shareholder of S. This situation is, however, met by H holding all the shares in S except one which is allotted to a nominee (usually a director) of H. If, however, H (directly or through nominee(s)) has less than a 100 per cent holding in S, say 80 per cent, there will be a minority interest in respect of the remaining (20 per cent) issued share capital held by shareholders outside the group. In the preparation of the Consolidated Balance Sheet the principles already outlined will again be followed. All the assets and liabilities of the constituent companies will be aggregated, but the minority shareholders must be shown as Creditors on the liabilities side in respect of their interest. The latter will consist of their share of: (a) Share Capital, (b) Reserves, and (c) Profit and Loss balance (the total of these being equal to the net assets). Obviously, in making the necessary adjustments for the Consolidated Balance Sheet in respect of H's holding, only its due proportion of profits, etc. (e.g. 80 per cent), will be taken into account. As far as the minority shareholders are concerned, there will be no need to make the sharp contrast between pre- and post-acquisition profits required in respect of H's holding, their interest not being affected thereby.

Illustration 12

H acquired 80 per cent of the shares of S on the 30th June 19.., for £2,700, when the profit and loss of the latter was in credit for £800. From the following Balance Sheets prepare the Consolidated Balance Sheet.

BALANCE SHEETS AS AT 30TH JUNE 19..

	H	S		H	S
	£	£		£	£
Share Capital—			Sundry Assets	2,000	2,600
£1 fully paid	3,000	2,000	Debtors	1,300	900
Profit and Loss	1,000	800	Bills Receivable		500
Creditors	1,500	1,200	Shares in S	2,700	
Bills Payable (in favour of S)	500				
	£6,000	£4,000		£6,000	£4,000

CONSOLIDATED BALANCE SHEET

	H	S	Adjustments	Total		H	S	Adjustments	Total
	£	£	£	£		£	£	£	£
Share Capital .	3,000	2,000	− 1,600 − 400	3,000	Sundry Assets .	2,000	2,600		4,600
Profit and Loss	1,000	800	− 640 − 160	1,000	Debtors .	1,300	900		2,200
					Bills Receivable .		500	− 500	
Creditors .	1,500	1,200		2,700	Shares in S .	2,700		− 500 ⎫ − 1,600 ⎬ − 640 ⎭ − 460	
Bills Payable .	500		− 500						
Minority Interest .			+ 400 + 160	560[1]	Goodwill (or Cost of Control)			+ 460	460[2]
	£6,000	£4,000	−£2,740	£7,260		£6,000	£4,000	−£2,740	£7,260

[1] The Minority Interest is—
   20% of Share Capital (£2,000) plus Profit and Loss (£800), i.e. £2,800 = £560

[2] The Goodwill (or Cost of Control) is proved as follows—	£	£
Cost of 1,600 Shares		2,700
Less Share Capital (80% of £2,000)	1,600	
Profit and Loss (80% of £800)	640	
		2,240
		£ 460

An objection is sometimes raised against this method of preparing a Consolidated Balance Sheet where the holding of H is less than 100 per cent on the grounds that the assets and liabilities of S appear in full in the Consolidated Balance Sheet although H (or the group) has not a 100 per cent share therein. Nevertheless, H does control them and it is usually considered that they are best shown as group figures with the minority interest shown separately. The alternative would be to take H's proportion of each asset and liability only, so that no entry for minority interest would be required, but it is rarely used in practice.

Illustration 13

H owns 4,000 shares in A, 3,000 shares in B, and B owns 5,000 shares in A. The issued share capital of A and B (both subsidiaries of H) are £10,000 and £5,000 respectively, all in £1 shares fully paid. There are no Preference Shares.

The profits of A and B for the year ended 31st December 19.., are £1,500 and £2,000 respectively. Show the amounts attributed to Minority Interests, ignoring Taxation.

	£	£
Minority Interest in the profit of—		
A: 10 per cent of £1,500.		150
B: 40 per cent of £2,000	800	
20 per cent of £1,500 (see below)	300	
		1,100

Thus, Minority shareholders own 40 per cent of B's profit and 30 per cent of A's profit.

The Minority Interest of B is 40 per cent, but as B has a 50 per cent interest in A, the Minority Interest of the former company must (indirectly) therefore be 40 per cent of the share of profit B will get from A, i.e. 50 per cent; therefore, the proportion of profit attributable to the Minority Interest of B as regards A's profit is 40 per cent of 50 per cent, i.e. 20 per cent.

This can be seen clearly if it is assumed that the profit of A is fully distributed, thus:

A			B		
Holder	Shares	Profit	Holder	Shares	Profit
		£			£
H	4,000	600	H	3,000	1,650
B	5,000	750			
Minority . . .	1,000	150	Minority . . .	2,000	1,100
					(See
		1,500			above)
Less to B . . .		750			
	10,000	£750		5,000	£2,750[1]

[1] Profit £2,000, plus dividend from A of £750, equals £2,750.

Illustration 14

From the following details, prepare schedule showing Minority Interests to be brought into the Consolidated Balance Sheet. All shares are £1 each, fully paid.

No entries have been made in the books of any of the companies for proportion of profit or dividend attributable to them from their holdings in the other companies. Ignore taxation.

	Sub-sidiary A	Sub-sidiary B
	£	£
Ordinary Shares	8,000	5,000
5% Preference Shares	3,000	—
Ordinary Shares in Subsidiaries held by—		
H.	4,800	3,000
B.	1,200	—
Outsiders	2,000	2,000
Preference Shares held by—		
H	1,500	—
B.	500	—
Outsiders	1,000	—
The profits are	1,600	*Loss* 900

Show the Minority Interests, bringing into account the current year's arrear of Cumulative Preference Dividend. Workings to nearest £.

		£			Minority Interest £
Preference Dividend—					
Outsiders	1,000 at 5%	50			50
H	1,500 at 5%	75			
B (see below)	500 at 5%	25			
		£150			

		£			
Profits—					
A: Profit		1,600			
Less Preference Dividend		150			
		£1,450	Minority Interests, 25%.	£363	
			Interest in A of Minority Share-		
			holders of B—40% of 15%		
B: Loss		900	equals 6%[1]	87	
Less Preference Dividend (see above)		25			450
		£875			
			Minority Interests, 40%		350

It would not be correct to show the Minority Interests as a net figure of £150; each heading should be shown, particularly as the item of £350 does not represent anything more than what is analogous to a contingent asset.

As, in fact, A has Minority Shareholders of 25 per cent only, it would seem a better way to show, as an offset, the item of £87 against the loss of £350, because it is, in fact, the Minority Interests of B (as regards B's share of A's profit). Thus:

	£		£
A: Profit (as shown above)	1,450	Minority Interests—25% of £1,450	363
of which 15% is attributable to B	218		
	£1,232		
B: Loss (as shown above)	875		
Less Share of A's Profit	218		
	£657	Minority Interests—40% of £657	263

Although the former method is usually employed, the latter method, which is theoretically correct, should be mentioned in any examination problem relating to the above subject matter.

Thus, it can be seen that the effect is to show figures of £363 and £263 instead of £450 and £350.

Post-acquisition Profits and Losses. So far the Consolidated Balance Sheet has been prepared at the date of acquisition of shares in S, so that all reserves and profit-and-loss balance of S relate to the pre-acquisition period. Such reserves and profit or loss balance are, in the preparation of the Consolidated Balance Sheet, divided into: (a) H's proportion, which having been adjusted against the cost of the shares S, appears in the Consolidated Balance Sheet either in the Capital Reserve of Goodwill figure, and (b) minority shareholders' proportion which in the Consolidated Balance Sheet is added to the minority interest. Post-acquisition profits (or losses) and increases (or decreases) in reserves must similarly be

---

[1] As B owns 1,200 shares in A, it is entitled to 15 per cent (£$\frac{1200}{8000}$) of £1,450, but the Minority Shareholders have 40 per cent interest in B, hence their proportion of A's profit is 40 per cent of 15 per cent of £1,450.

split between H and minority shareholders; but while the latter are added to (*or deducted from*) the minority interest as above, the former will appear in the Consolidated Balance Sheet in the actual profit and loss or reserve figure. Thus, where the balance sheets are given at some date after the date of acquisition, it will be necessary, as far as H's proportion is concerned, to apportion reserves and profit and loss between the pre- and post-acquisition periods.

The rule whereby the pre-acquisition profit of a subsidiary attributable to a holding company must be considered as capital, not only conforms to sound accounting practice, but is afforded recognition by the Companies Acts 1948 and 1967. So far, however, as concerns the Minority Shareholders of a subsidiary, it is immaterial whether or not their proportion of the profit has been earned before or after the date of the acquisition of the shares in the subsidiary by the holding company.

Illustration 15

Assuming the same facts as in Illustration 12, on p. 2430, except that the date of acquisition of the shares was one year before the date of the Balance Sheets and at that date the credit balance of profit and loss of S was £600, £200 having been earned since, show Consolidated Balance Sheet.

CONSOLIDATED BALANCE SHEET

	H	S	Adjust-ments	Total		H	S	Adjust-ments	Total
	£	£	£	£		£	£	£	£
Share Capital	3,000	2,000	− 1,600	3,000	Sundry Assets	2,000	2,600		4,600
			− 400		Debtors.	1,300	900		2,200
Profit and Loss	1,000	800	− 480	1,160	Bills Receiv-able		500	− 500	
			− 160		Shares in S	2,700		− 1,600	
Creditors	1,500	1,200		2,700				− 480	
Bills Payable	500		− 500					− 620	
Minority Inter-ests			+ 400	560	Goodwill (or Cost of Control)			+ 620	620[2]
			+ 160						
	£6,000	£4,000	−£2,580	£7,420		£6,000	£4,000	−£2,580	£7,420

(For [1] and [2] see footnotes on p. 2435.)

Where the shares are acquired during the financial year of S and no accounts are drawn up to that date, the current year's profits must be apportioned, in the absence of other information, on a time basis.

Illustration 16

Had the shares been acquired in the previous illustration on the 1st January 19.., the profit of £200 of S for the year to 30th June 19.. would, in the absence of other data, be split as to £100 pre- and £100 post-acquisition. Thus, 80 per cent of £700, i.e. £560, would be adjusted against the cost of shares in S, 80 per cent of £100, i.e. £80, would be left in Profit and Loss, making with H's £1,000 a total of £1,080, and 20 per cent of £800, i.e. £160, would be added to minority interests, as before.

Preference Shares of Subsidiary. When the share capital of S consists of Preference as well as Ordinary shares:

1. If they are all held by H no difficulty arises, the normal elimination being required.

2. If some or all are held by outside shareholders the minority interest will be increased accordingly. The treatment will depend on the rights attaching to the shares as defined in the Memorandum and Articles of Association of the particular company. The term 'Preference Share' has a wide meaning and the principles already outlined in the previous chapter must be applied. The following factors must be considered:

(a) Rights as to Capital on a liquidation—if there is a right to priority of repayment, the full amount must be added to minority interest, otherwise they will be treated as ordinary shares.

(b) Rights as to dividend—where there is no right to priority, they will usually be treated as ordinary shares where there is such a right it must be taken into account, and if it is cumulative, any arrears should be provided for by adjusting the Profit and Loss Balance and increasing the minority interest. In regard to such arrears, there is of course no legal liability until the preference dividends are declared. If, however, the right is cumulative, arrears will have to be met before any dividend can be paid on the ordinary shares, and most accountants consider it preferable to make an adjustment for them. Alternatively, the matter could be dealt with in a note on the Consolidated Balance Sheet (see p. 2460 (9)).

(c) Rights as to participation in profits beyond a fixed amount—where such a right exists it must be taken into account, since the balance of profit available to the ordinary shares is thereby reduced.

3. In the books of S, if the shares are allotted to H as the original shareholder, the entries will be the same as if they had been allotted to an individual. If, on the other hand, H acquires the shares from the existing

---

[1] The minority interest is unchanged, since it is not in any way concerned with the date of acquisition by H.

[2] Goodwill is greater than in Illustration 12 on p. 2431 by 80% of £200, i.e. £160, the Profit and Loss figure being correspondingly increased. The Goodwill figure is proved as follows:

	£	£
Cost of 1,600 Shares		2,700
Less nominal value of Shares	1,600	
80% of pre-acquisition Profit (£600)	480	
		2,080
		£620

shareholders, no entries are required in the books of S, the necessary alterations being made in the usual way on the transfer of shares in the register of members, etc.

It must be remembered that in all cases where there are Preference Shares, the exact treatment will depend upon the facts in each particular instance.

SUMMARY OF RULES OF CONSOLIDATION

The basic principles of the preparation of the Consolidated Balance Sheet have now been outlined. Before proceeding with more intricate problems where there are several subsidiaries or where shares in the holding company are held by one or more of the subsidiaries and so on, the following summary of the more important factors is given:

1. All inter-company indebtedness and profits (and losses) must be eliminated, including in the former share capital, debentures, loans and current accounts. The share capital of H, however, remains except that it is reduced by any of the shares that are held by S.

2. Pre-acquisition profits and losses must be capitalized, such profits being in effect a reduction of the purchase price, thus reducing Goodwill or Cost of Control, or increasing Capital Reserve. Losses will have a converse result.

3. The interest of the minority shareholders in S will require adjustment for their share of Share Capital, Reserves, Profits and/or Losses. The sharp distinction required in (2) does not arise in regard to the minority interest.[1]

4. Elimination of unrealized profit or inter-company transaction to the extent of H's holding.

5. Subject to these adjustments, all the assets and liabilities of the constituent companies will be aggregated under common headings.

METHODS OF CONSOLIDATED BALANCE SHEET PREPARATION

As long as effect is given to the principles outlined, the method used in the preparation of the Consolidated Balance Sheet is of little importance and will depend to some extent on individual preference. The following methods are in use:

1. Employment of an adjustment column on each side of the draft Consolidated Balance Sheet (as has been done in all the illustrations so far). There will thus be four columns (where there is one S) on each side,

---

[1] There may be losses of subsidiaries which more than extinguish their issued capital, so that the Minority Shareholders' equity is in debit, but this is not a recoverable debt and should be separately shown as a deduction from the Group Reserves or Capital. If, indeed a subsidiary is insolvent, it is usual to leave such company's Balance Sheet and Profit and Loss Account out of the Consolidation.

viz.: (1) H, (2) S, (3) Adjustments, (4) Total. Variations of this method are:

(a) To use plus and minus signs in the adjustment column.

(b) To split the adjustment column into Dr. and Cr.

(c) To eliminate complete in the adjustment column such items as shares in S, transferring the balance in that column to Goodwill or Capital Reserve and carrying out the final figure from there.

(d) Not to make the balancing transfer as in (c) but to extend the balance immediately with appropriate marking, e.g. G for Goodwill, M for Minority Interest, etc.

2. Aggregation of the various items in the individual balance sheets in one column, the requisite transfer being made from/to these totals, the net result being extended into a final column. Thus, inter-company balances are eliminated by straight contra subtraction; pre-acquisition profits are transferred to Capital Reserve, from which the outside shareholders' proportion is transferred to Minority Interest, and so on. Variations of this method are:

(a) To make the net adjustment direct from the totals of the appropriate assets and liabilities.

(b) To employ a special column of eliminations.

3. Preparation of a Schedule of Adjustments from which the Consolidated Balance Sheet is compiled.

4. Employment of a journal, the journal entries being 'posted' into an adjustment column just as if the Consolidated Balance Sheet were part of an actual double-entry account. (In practice and in complicated examination problems, this procedure will be absolutely necessary. It may be mentioned here that in some of the recent examinations the journal entries would without any further work earn the bulk of the marks; indeed, in one recent question merely to write out the balance sheets in columnar form and the final aggregated figures would take at least half an hour.)

A comparison of these methods is given below. Journal entries will be illustrated in greater detail later in this chapter.

Illustration 17

The Balance Sheets of H, Ltd., and S, Ltd., are:

BALANCE SHEETS AS AT 31ST OCTOBER 19.2

	H, Ltd.	S, Ltd.		H. Ltd.	S, Ltd.
	£	£		£	£
Share Capital (£1 fully paid)	2,000	500	Sundry Assets	2,000	1,300
Reserve (at 1st Nov. 19.1)	300	100	Shares in S, Ltd at cost	2,300	
Profit and Loss Account Balance, 1st Nov. 19.1 £600	£300				
Plus Profit for Year 400	100				
	1,000	400			
Creditors	1,000	300			
	£4,300	£1,300		£4,300	£1,300

H, Ltd., has an 80 per cent interest in S, Ltd., acquired half-way through the financial year. Included in sundry assets of H, Ltd., is £300 loan to subsidiary company (shown in the latter's Balance Sheet as creditors). Sundry assets of the subsidiary company include fittings of £400 to be revalued at £500 as at 1st November 19.1, being over-depreciation adjustment. It may be assumed that the profits are uniformly earned. Prepare Consolidated Balance Sheet.

(1a)

CONSOLIDATED BALANCE SHEET OF H, LTD., AND ITS SUBSIDIARY, S, LTD., AS AT 31ST OCTOBER 19.2

	H, Ltd.	S, ltd.	Adjustments	Total		H, Ltd.	S, Ltd.	Adjustments	Total
	£	£	£	£		£	£	£	£
Share Capital	2,000	500	(a) −500	2,000	Sundry Assets	2,000	1,300	(e) +100 −300	3,100
Reserve	300	100	(b) −100	300					
Profit and Loss Account	600	300	(c) −300	600	Shares in S, Ltd.	2,300		(f) −2,300 +1,460	1,460
Profit for Year	400	100	(d) −60	440	Goodwill				
Minority Share-Holders (as per Schedule in (3))			+220	220					
Creditors	1,000	300	−300	1,000					
	£4,300	£1,300	−£1,040	£4,560		£4,300	£1,300	−£1,040	£4,560

Note. The lettered references are to the Schedule given in (3) on p. 2441. Where there is no Schedule the adjustments will be given in detail as in previous illustrations in this chapter.

Alternatively—(1b) [See also p. 2440]

CONSOLIDATED BALANCE SHEET OF H, LTD., AND ITS SUBSIDIARY, S, LTD., AS AT 31ST OCTOBER 19.2

Liabilities side

	H	S	Adjustments Dr.	Adjustments Cr.	Total
	£	£	£	£	£
Share Capital	2,000	500	(a) 400		2,000
Reserve	300	100	(b) 100		300
P. & L. Balance	600	300	(c) 20 / (m) 80		600
Profit for Year	400	100	(i) 240 / (f) 60		440
Creditors	1,000	300			1,000
Minority Interests:					
Share Capital			(l) 10 / (g) 10	(b) 100	
Reserve			(e) 40	(c) 20	
P. & L. Balance			(d) 300	(i) 60	220
Profit for Year				(f) 10 / (g) 10	
Increase of Assets				(h) 20	
	£4,300	£1,300	£1,260	£220	£4,560
				{£1,040}	

Assets side

	H	S	Adjustments Dr.	Adjustments Cr.	Total
	£	£	£	£	£
Sundry Assets	2,000	1,300	(h) 20 / (j) 80	(d) 300	3,100
Shares in S	2,300			(a) 400 / (k) 1,900	300
Goodwill			(k) 1,900	(l) 80 / (e) 40 / (j) 80 / (m) 240	1,460
	£4,300	£1,300	£2,000	£3,040	£4,560
				{£1,040}	

(2)

Consolidated Balance Sheet of H, Ltd., and its Subsidiary, S, Ltd., as at 31st October 19.2

	£	£			£	£
Share Capital (H)		2,000	Sundry Assets—		2,000	
Capital Reserve—			H		2,000	
Reserve of S at date of acquisition	100		S £1,300			
Pre-acquisition Profit	350		*Less* Contra 300			
Increase of Assets	100			1,000		
	—		Increase to C.R. 100			
	550				1,100	3,100
Less M.I. 20%	110					
	440		Goodwill—			
Deducted Contra	440		Cost of Shares		2,300	
			Nominal Share Capital			
General Reserve—			—S £500			
H	300		*Less* M.I. 20% 100			
S £100					400	
Less Transfer to C.R. 100					1,900	
	—		*Less* C.R. Contra		440	1,460
		300				
Profit and Loss Account—						
H Balance	600					
Profit for Year	400					
	1,000					
S Balance £300						
Profit for Year 100						
	400					
Transfer to C.R. 350						
Post-acquisition Profit 50						
Less M.I. 20% 10						
	40					
		1,040				
Creditors—						
H	1,000					
S £300						
Less Contra 300						
	—					
		1,000				
Minority Interests—						
Share Capital	100					
Capital Reserve	110					
Profit and Loss	10					
		220				
		£4,560				£4,560

Note. M.I. = Minority Interest. C.R. = Capital Reserve.

	H, Ltd. (80%)	Minority Shareholders S, Ltd. (20%)
	£	£
Share Capital.	400	100 (a)
Balance of Profit and Loss Account	240	60 (c)
Profit to date of purchase of Shares by H, Ltd.	40	10 (d)
Increase of Sundry Assets	80	20 (e)
Reserve.	80	20 (b)
	840	210
Goodwill	1,460	
	£2,300 (f)	210
Profit since purchase of Shares by H, Ltd.	40	10 (d)
		£220

The reference letters are to the Consolidated Balance Sheet in (1a) on p. 2438.

4. A full Journal illustration will be given in Illustration 22 on pp. 2453–2457. The entries will, however, be the same as those shown in the Dr. and Cr. adjustments in (1) on p. 2439, thus for item (a):

	£	£
Share Capital of S	400	
Shares in S		400

Many of the individual entries may be consolidated in the journal, thus for items (a) and (k)—

	£	£
Goodwill	1,900	
Share Capital of S	400	
Shares in S		2,300

Profits and Dividends of Subsidiaries. The alternative treatment of the profits of subsidiaries in the books of the holding company was considered in the early pages of this chapter and it will be remembered that it is sometimes the practice to 'take up' such profits whether dividends are declared by S or not. Where this practice obtains, a Profit of Subsidiaries Account is debited with H's proportion of the profits and a Profits and Losses of Subsidiaries Account (which may be closed off to Profit and

Loss Account) credited. When a dividend is paid, cash is debited and the Profit of Subsidiary Account credited. The effect of these alternatives on the Consolidated Balance Sheet is now considered:

1. Where not taken up, the position is straightforward, as has been shown in all the illustrations so far. After the necessary adjustments for pre-acquisition profits, minority interest, etc., the profits of H and S are added and extended into the total column.

2. Where the profits have been taken up, H's proportion will be already included in H's profit balance and, therefore, in the Consolidated Balance Sheet H's proportion of S's profit balance must be eliminated against the balance of Profit of Subsidiary Account in H's Balance Sheet.

Where dividends are paid out of pre-acquisition profits, they must be adjusted against the cost of the shares in S. Where paid out of post-acquisition profits, the ultimate result in the Consolidated Balance Sheet is unchanged since H's profit balance, increased by the receipt of the dividend, is added to S's profit balance which has been decreased by a like amount. The treatment of dividends in the consolidated accounts is dealt with fully on pp. 2458 and 2462 *et seq*.

Group Consisting of more than One Subsidiary. Where H holds shares in more than one subsidiary, no particular difficulty arises and there will be no departure from the principles already given. The goodwill or cost of control must be asscertained for each company and then the normal adjustments, eliminations, and aggregation will take place.

Illustration 18

From the following skeleton Balance Sheets and the information given, prepare the Consolidated Balance Sheet. Ignore tax.

BALANCE SHEET AS AT 31ST DECEMBER 19. .

	H, Ltd.	S, Ltd.	Y, Ltd.		H, Ltd.	S, Ltd.	Y, Ltd.
	£	£	£		£	£	£
Share Capital—				Sundry Assets	1,350	1,500	1,200
£1 fully paid	3,000	1,000	800	Profit of S Account	450		
Profit and Loss	100	200	300	900 Shares in S at cost	1,200		
Profit for Year	800	300	100	600 Shares in Y at cost	900		
	£3,900	£1,500	£1,200		£3,900	£1,500	£1,200

1. The credit balance of Profit and Loss Account of Y, Ltd., was £300 when the shares therein were acquired by H, Ltd., but the whole of the profits of S, Ltd., have been earned since acquisition of its shares by H, Ltd.

2. It was the practice of H, Ltd., to take up in its books its proportion of the profits of S, Ltd.

3. Y, Ltd., had during the year to 31st December 19.., declared and paid a dividend of £80, reducing the profit for the year from £180 to £100.

CONSOLIDATED BALANCE SHEET OF H, LTD., AND ITS SUBSIDIARIES AS AT 31ST DECEMBER 19..

	H, Ltd.	S, Ltd.	Y, Ltd.	Adjustments	Total
	£	£	£	£	
Share Capital	3,000	1,000	800	(a) − 1,800	3,000
P. & L.	100	200	300	(b) − 825	975
Profit for Year	800	300	100		
Minority Interest				(a) + 300 } (b) + 150 }	450
	£3,900	£1,500	£1,200	−£2,175	£4,425

	H, Ltd.	S, Ltd.	Y, Ltd.	Adjustments	Total
	£	£	£	£	£
Sundry Assets	1,350	1,500	1,200		4,050
Profit of S A/c	450			(b) − 450	
Shares in S	1,200			(a) − 900 } (a) − 600 }	300 } G¹
Shares in Y	900			(b) − 225	75 } G¹
	£3,900	£1,500	£1,200	−£2,175	£4,425

¹ G = Goodwill.

(a) Elimination of Share Capitals:

	Total £		H £		M.I. £
S	1,000	(90%)	900	(10%)	100
Y	800	(75%)	600	(25%)	200
	£1,800		£1,500		£300

(b) Elimination of Profit and Loss:

	Balance £	Profit for Year £	Against Cost of Shares £	Profit of S Account		Interest of H in P. and L. £	M.I.	£
S	200			(90)	180		(10%)	20
Y	300		(75%) 225				(25%)	75
S		300		(90%)	270		(10%)	30
Y		100				(75%) 75	(25%)	25 (a)
	£500¹	£400¹	£225		£450	£75¹		£150

	S £	Y £	Total £
G (Goodwill) is:			
Cost of Shares	1,200	900	2,100
Less Equity acquired:			
90% of Share Capital (£1,000)+Pre-acquisition Profit (nil)	900		
75% of Share Capital (£800)+Pre-acquisition Profit (£300)		825	1,725
	£300	£75	£375

The dividend paid by Y during the year can be ignored in the preparation of the Consolidated Balance Sheet, the adjustments being made to the remaining balance. The total profit of £180 is apportionable as to 25 per cent (£45) to Minority Interest and 75 per cent (£135) to H. As the minority shareholders have received 25 per cent of the dividend, i.e. £20, their interest shown in the Consolidated Balance Sheet will be confined to the balance, i.e. £45 less £20 = £25 (see (a) above). As to H's proportion of the dividend, this will be included in H's profit for the year and will thus appear in the Profit total for the group. The assumption that the dividend is included in H's profit is based on the fact that Shares in Y are shown in the Balance Sheet of H at cost. It must be remembered that only dividends paid out of post-acquisition profits may be regarded as revenue by H. If the dividend were paid out of the balance of Profit and Loss Account at the date of acquisition it would be of a capital nature and must be adjusted against the cost of the shares by crediting Shares in Y Account. In the Consolidated Balance Sheet this would alter the Goodwill figure accordingly.

Shares of Holding Company held by Subsidiary.

Although a company cannot hold its own shares, a subsidiary can hold shares in its holding company, so that, in fact, the latter does have an interest in its own shares. In this connection, however, the following section of the Companies Act 1948, should be noted:

¹£500 + £400 = £900 less £75 remaining in P. & L. makes the net adjustment of £825 shown in the C.B.S.

27.—(1) Except in the cases hereafter in this section mentioned, a body corporate cannot be a member of a company which is its holding company, and any allotment or transfer of shares in a company to its subsidiary shall be void.

(2) Nothing in this section shall apply where the subsidiary is concerned as personal representative, or where it is concerned as trustee, unless the holding company or a subsidiary thereof is beneficially interested under the trust and is not so interested only by way of security for the purposes of a transaction entered into by it in the ordinary course of a business which includes the lending of money.

(3) This section shall not prevent a subsidiary which is, at the commencement of this Act,[1] a member of its holding company, from continuing to be a member; but, subject to the last foregoing subsection, the subsidiary shall have no right to vote at meetings of the holding company or any class of members thereof.

(4) Subject to subsection (2) of this section, subsections (1) and (3) thereof shall apply in relation to a nominee for a body corporate which is subsidiary, as if reference in the said subsections (1) and (3) to such a body corporate included references to a nominee for it.

(5) In relation to a company limited by guarantee or unlimited which is a holding company, the reference in this section to shares, whether or not it has a share capital, shall be construed as including a reference to the interest of its members as such, whatever the form of that interest.

In preparing the Consolidated Balance Sheet in these circumstances, no difficulty arises when the Holding Company owns all the shares in the subsidiary, the normal adjustments being made. Where, however, there is a minority interest in the subsidiary, the work is more involved, for it will be seen that this interest is, as it were, twofold, viz. (*a*) in the equity of the subsidiary and (*b*) in the equity of the holding company by reason of the shares held in that company by the subsidiary. The most accurate way to compute the minority interest is to assume that all available profits are distributed at the date of the Consolidated Balance Sheet. The principle involved is shown by the following illustration:

BALANCE SHEETS

	H	S		H	S
	£	£		£	£
Share Capital £1 f.p.	500	100	Sundry Assets	480	90
Post-acquisition Profits	100	50	Shares in S (75)	120	
			Shares in H (50)		60
	£600	£150		£600	£150

In the normal way, the minority interest in S will be one-quarter of share capital and profits, i.e. £25 plus £12·50, but the latter figure takes no account of S's share of H's profits. The actual amount which would accrue to the minority shareholders if the whole £150 were distributed can be ascertained in the following way (to the nearest £):

[1] 1st July 1948.

	H	S	Outside Shareholders in S	in H
	£	£	£	£
Profits per Balance Sheet	100	50		
S's Profit distributed	+ 38	− 50	+ 12	
	138	—		
H's Profit distributed	− 138	+ 14		+ 124
	—	14		
S's Profit distributed	+ 10	− 14	+ 4	
	10	—		
H's Profit distributed	− 10	+ 1		+ 9
	—	1		
S's Profit distributed	+ 1	− 1		
	1	—		
H's Profit distributed	− 1			+ 1
Distribution	—	—	£16	£134

The algebraic calculation is:

Let H = total profits of H and S = total profits of S

Then $H = 100 + \frac{3}{4}S$, and $S = 50 + \frac{1}{10}H$

Thus $H = 100 + \frac{3}{4}(50 + \frac{1}{10}H) = \frac{150}{4} + 150 + \frac{3}{40}H$

∴ $40H = 4,000 + 1,500 + 3H$

∴ $37H = 5,500$

∴ $H = 149$ and $S = 50 + 15 = 65$.

Allocation of Profits—		H	S
Profits per Balance Sheet	. . .	£100	£50
Add $\frac{3}{4}$ of total profit of S	. . .	49	
$\frac{1}{10}$ of total profit of H	. . .		15
Total profits as above	. . .	149	65
Less amounts added above	. . . (a)	15	(b) 49
		£134	£16

$(a) = 10\% \times £149$; $(b) = 75\% \times £65$

The true minority interest in the profits is therefore as £16 opposed to £12·50.

Note. It is usual in practice to avoid the 'criss-cross' calculations and add to the minority shareholders of the subsidiary their proportion of the profit of the Holding Company, without the addition of its share of the profit of the subsidiary company, as if fully distributed.)

CONSOLIDATED BALANCE SHEET

		£			£
Share Capital . . .		450	Sundry Assets . . .		570
Profit and Loss Account . .		134	Goodwill . . .		55
Minority Interest—			[£180 − £75 − £50]		
Share Capital . .	£25				
Profit and Loss . .	16				
		41			
		£625			£625

Illustration 19

The Balance Sheets of H, Ltd., and S, Ltd., are:

BALANCE SHEETS

	H, Ltd.	S, Ltd.		H, Ltd.	S, Ltd.
Share Capital . . .	3,000	1,500	Sundry Assets . . .	1,300	1,550
Profit and Loss Account: Profit			1,200 Shares in S, Ltd. at cost	2,000[1]	
for Year . . .	300	200	100 Shares in H, Ltd. at cost		150[1]
	£3,300	£1,700		£3,300	£1,700

Prepare Consolidated Balance Sheet.

1. If the mutual purchases took place at the date of the above Balance Sheet—

CONSOLIDATED BALANCE SHEET OF H, LTD., AND ITS SUBSIDIARY,
S, LTD., AS AT............

	£	£		£	£
Share Capital . . .	3,000		Sundry Assets . . .		2,850
Less Shares held by S, Ltd. .	100		Goodwill . . .	850	
		2,900	Less Reserve per contra . .	167	683[1]
Reserve—					
Proportion of Profits attributable					
to H, Ltd., as at.........	167[1]				
Less Contra . . .	167				
Profit and Loss Account (H, Ltd.)		290			
Minority Shareholders—					
Share Capital . .	300				
Profit and Loss Account. .	43				
		343			
		£3,533			£3,533

[1] Goodwill = Cost of Shares £2,150, less Nominal Value of Shares £1,300, less Profit £167. (See p. 2448.) Of the total of the Profit and Loss Accounts of £500, £457 is applicable to H, Ltd., and H, Ltd.'s own account should be shown as £290 (i.e. £300 less $\frac{1}{30}$th bought in by the Group), leaving £167 to be carried to Capital Reserve.

2. If they took place at the start of the accounting period:

CONSOLIDATED BALANCE SHEET OF H, LTD., AND ITS SUBSIDIARY,
S, LTD., AS AT............

	£	£		£	£
Share Capital . . .	3,000		Sundry Assets . . .		2,850
Less Shares held by S, Ltd.	100		Goodwill . . .		850[1]
		2,900			
Profit and Loss Account—					
(H, Ltd.) . . .	300				
(S, Ltd.) . . .	157				
		457			
Minority Shareholders—					
Share Capital . . .	300				
Profit and Loss Account .	43				
		343			
		£3,700			£3,700

[1] Goodwill = £2,150 − £1,300.

In the second case, all the profits are earned after the acquisition of the shares and so no deduction is made from the £850 goodwill figure. The proportion of the combined profits of H, Ltd., and S, Ltd., for the year applicable to the shareholders of H, Ltd., is £457. The precise split in this figure between H, Ltd., and S, Ltd., is somewhat academic. A division on a complete distribution of profits can be worked out by simple arithmetic as £289 to H, Ltd., and £159 to S, Ltd., but it seems rather doubtful whether there is any merit in showing such a split. It seems better to leave H, Ltd.'s account at its actual figure of £300 and to carry the adjustment in S, Ltd.'s figure.

The calculations are:

$$H = 300 + \tfrac{4}{5}S$$
$$S = 200 + \tfrac{1}{30}H \qquad (1)$$
$$5H = 1,500 + 4(200 + \tfrac{1}{30}H)$$
$$H = £473$$

and
$$S = 200 + \tfrac{1}{30}(473) \qquad (1)$$
$$= £216$$

Allocation of Profits:

	H, Ltd.	S, Ltd.
	£	£
Balances per Accounts	300	200
Add $\tfrac{12}{15}$ of £216	173	
,, $\tfrac{1}{30}$ of £473		16
	473	216
Less $\tfrac{12}{15}$ of £216		173
,, $\tfrac{1}{30}$ of £473	16	
Balance, H, Ltd.'s Interest therein . . .	£457	
Proportion attributable to Minority Shareholders [$\tfrac{1}{5}$ of £216] .		£43

Alternative Method:

	H, Ltd.	S, Ltd.
	£	£
Sundry Assets	1,300	1,550
Goodwill	800	50
	2,100	1,600
Equity $\frac{4}{5}$ of £1,716	1,373	
$\frac{1}{30}$ of £3,473		116
[See below]	3,473	1,716
Less Proportion due to S, Ltd. (Share Capital £100 + Profits £16)	116	
Less Proportion due to H, Ltd. (Share Capital £1,200 + Profits £173)		1,373
(*a*) Share Capital £2,900 plus Profit £457; (*b*) Share Capital £300 plus Profit £43.	(*a*) £3,357	£343

The calculations are—

$$S = £1,600 + \tfrac{1}{30}H$$

$$H = £2,100 + \tfrac{4}{5}S$$

The results are—

$$S = £1,716$$

$$H = £3,473$$

Part-sale of Holding in Subsidiary. When H disposes of part of its holding in S and the holding/subsidiary company relationship continues, the usual principles will be followed, but consideration must be given to the particular circumstances of each individual case.

Illustration 20

From the following abridged Balance Sheets and information, prepare draft Consolidated Balance Sheet. Ignore Tax.

BALANCE SHEETS AS AT 31ST DECEMBER 19..

	H, Ltd.		S, Ltd.			H, Ltd.	S, Ltd.
		£		£		£	£
Share Capital—					Sundry Assets	23,000	9,050
£1 fully paid		20,000		5,000	Shares in S at cost—		
Reserve		2,000		500	3,000 at £2	6,000	
Profit and Loss—							
At 1st Jan.							
19..	3,000		1,000				
Profit for Year	800		800				
Dividend from							
S	200		1,800				
		4,000					
Less Dividend			250	1,550			
Creditors		3,000		2,000			
		£29,000		£9,050		£29,000	£9,050

H had acquired 4,000 shares in S at £2 per share on the 1st January 19.., and sold 1,000 of them at the same price on the 1st October 19... On the 1st July 19.., an interim dividend of 5 per cent was paid by S.

CONSOLIDATED BALANCE SHEET OF H, LTD., AND ITS SUBSIDIARY, S, LTD., AS AT 31ST DECEMBER 19. .

	H, Ltd.	S, Ltd.	Adjust- ments	Total		H, Ltd.	S, Ltd.	Adjust- ments	Total
	£	£	£	£		£	£	£	£
Share Capital	20,000	5,000	− 5,000	20,000	Sundry	23,000	9,050		32,050
Reserve	2,000	500	− 500	2,000	Assets				
P. & L.					Shares in S	6,000		− 3,900	
Balance	3,000	1,000	− 1,000	3,000				− 2,100	
Profit, etc.,									
for Year	1,000	550	− 220	1,330	Goodwill			+ 2,100	2,100
Creditors	3,000	2,000		5,000					
Minority In-									
terest			+ 2,820	2,820					
[See note (a)]	£29,000	£9,050	−£3,900	£34,150		£29,000	£9,050	−£3,900	£34,150

It is assumed (from the treatment of the dividend in the books of H) that the interim dividend was paid out of profits for the year to 31st December 19...

The only effect of the holding of the 1,000 additional shares for a part of the year is that H receives a greater proportion of the interim dividend than it would otherwise have done. When H bought the 4,000 shares for £8,000, the position was:

	£		£
Cost of Shares			8,000
Share Capital of S	5,000		
Reserve	500		
Profit and Loss Account	1,000		
	£6,500	80% acquired =	5,200
Goodwill (or Cost of Control)			2,800

As ¼ of the holding has been sold and the shares comprising it carry with them their share of the Goodwill, the deduction to be made is   700

Per Consolidated Balance Sheet above   £2,100

Note (a). Minority Interest is $\frac{2}{5} \times £(5,000 + 500 + 1,000 + 550)$ £2,820

Unless it is indicated that special circumstances apply, the procedure to be followed is to assume that the sale is accompanied by the same circumstances as if H had no controlling interest. A sale, therefore, on 1st October would be cum div. and consequently there would be no apportionment of the profits of S to date of sale, with the result that H would get no benefit from the holding of the 1,000 shares beyond the interim dividend paid before the date of sale.

If the dividend was paid out of the opening balance of Profit and Loss Account, £200 would be deducted from the cost of the shares and deleted from H's Profit and Loss Account with consequent reduction in Goodwill and re-allocation of the profit for the year.

It might well be that the whole of the shares were sold to one buyer, in which case H (particularly as it controls S) might stipulate for some other arrangement regarding retention of a portion of the profits for the year to 31st December 19.., attachable to the holding of the 1,000 shares, e.g. H to have four-fifths of the profits to the date of sale and three-fifths thereafter.

If the thousand shares had been sold at £1·75 each, involving a loss of £0·25 a share, the loss of £250 might be added to Cost of Control (but not Goodwill), as the book value of the holding would be £6,250. On the other hand, H might make the necessary adjustments in its books. If the latter decided to write down its holdings by £250, the Consolidated Balance Sheet would be as before, as far as Goodwill or Cost of Control is concerned. From the accounting point of view, the prudent course would be for H to make a provision for Subsidiary Company Investment Loss, leaving the investment in its books at £6,250 and showing in the Consolidated Balance Sheet, Goodwill or Cost of Control £2,350 (£2,100 as before, plus £250) *less* Provision £250.

Illustration 21

From the following skeleton Balance Sheets and information, prepare Consolidated Balance Sheet as at 31st December 19...

BALANCE SHEETS AS AT 31ST DECEMBER 19..

	H, Ltd.	S, Ltd.		H, Ltd.	S, ltd.
	£	£		£	£
Share Capital	5,000	1,000	Sundry Assets	4,650	1,600
Investment Reserve	150		Shares in S—		
Profit and Loss:			600 at Cost	900	
At 1st Jan. 19..	300	360			
Profit for Year	100	240			
	£5,550	£1,600		£5,550	£1,600

H bought 800 shares in S at £1·50 per share when the Profit and Loss Account of the latter stood at £220, and sold 200 of them on 30th June, 19.., at £2·25 per share, crediting the £0·75 per share profit on sale to an Investment Reserve.

CONSOLIDATED BALANCE SHEET OF H, LTD., AND ITS SUBSIDIARY, S, LTD., AS AT 31ST DECEMBER 19. .

	H, Ltd.	S, Ltd.	Adjustments	Total		H, ltd.	S, Ltd.	Adjustments	Total
	£	£	£	£		£	£	£	£
Share Capital £1 f.p.	5,000	1,000	−1,000	5,000	Sundry Assets	4,650	1,600		6,250
Inv. Reserve	150			150	Shares in S	900		− 732[4]	168[5]
Profit and Loss—									
Balance	300	360	− 276[1]	384 }					
Profit for Year	100	240	− 96[2]	244 }					
Minority Interest			+ 640[3]	640					
	£5,550	£1,600	− £732	£6,418		£5,550	£1,600	−£732	£6,418

[1] M.I. $\frac{2}{5} \times$ £360 = £144; H $\frac{3}{5} \times$ £220 = £132 against cost of shares.
[2] M.I. $\frac{2}{5} \times$ £240 = £96.
[3] Share Capital £400 + [1]£144 + [2]£96.
[4] Share Capital £600 + [1]£132.
[5] Goodwill.

Alternatively, the position may be shown in detail as follows, allowing the present consolidated Balance Sheet to be linked up with the previous one:

CONSOLIDATED BALANCE SHEET OF H, LTD., AND ITS SUBSIDIARY, S, LTD., AS AT 31ST DECEMBER 19. .

	£	£	£		£	£	£
Share Capital			5,000	Sundry Assets—			
Capital Reserve—				H		4,650	
Pre-acquisition Profit		220		S		1,600	
Less Minority Interest $\frac{1}{5}$		44					6,250
				Goodwill at cost—			
Deducted contra		£176		Cost of 800 Shares		1,200	
				Less Share Capital	800		
Investment Reserve (see 4 below)			150	„ Capital Reserve	176		
Profit and Loss Account—						976	
H Balance, 1st Jan. 19. .		300					
Profit for Year		100				224	
			400	Deduct applicable to 200			
				Shares sold—			
				Sale Price	450		
S Balance, 1st Jan. 19. .	360			Less Investment Reserve	150		
Less to Capital Reserve	220					300	
	140						
Profit to 30th June 19. .	120			Less Share Capital £. £200			
	260			$\frac{1}{5}$ Original Capital			
				Reserve to Minority Interest			
Less Minority Interest—				contra 44			
Original $\frac{2}{5}$ £52					244		
New (re Sale) $\frac{1}{5}$ 52						56	168
	104						
		156					
Profit to 31st Dec. 19. . 120							
Less Minority Interest $\frac{2}{5}$ 48							
		72	628				
Minority Interest—							
Share Capital		400					
Capital Reserve $\frac{1}{5}$		44					
Do. Sale from Goodwill contra		44					
Profit and Loss Account		152					
			640				
			£6,418				£6,418

Notes. 1. Assumed that the profit of S was earned evenly during the year.

2. The Goodwill figures are taken to be in respect of ordinary Goodwill, for which there is no account in the books of S—that is to say, that no account is taken of any amount paid by H on the original purchase for an 80 per cent control, nor of any amount received by H on the subsequent sale for relinquishing its 75 per cent majority.

3. Apart from the considerations in (2), Goodwill is shown at cost (in respect of 800 shares *less* ¼ (in respect of 200 shares sold). It is apparent from the price of the sale on 30th June that the value of Goodwill has considerably increased. Goodwill might therefore be written up to its new valuation, in order to show the correct figure, with consequent adjustments on the liabilities side to the interest of H and the minority shareholders. It is, however, the usual practice to show Goodwill at cost and not to revalue it.

4. The Investment Reserve of £150 is made up of £52 in respect of profits of S applicable to 200 shares sold, from the date of purchase to date of sale (this figure is shown in the Consolidated Balance Sheet as being transferred out of Profit and Loss Account to Minority Interest), and £98 received in respect of additional Goodwill. If Goodwill were revalued as indicated in (3) above, this £98 would be dealt with in the revaluation. If no revaluation is made, it is considered better not to deduct it from the Goodwill figure in the Consolidated Balance Sheet, since if that were done, a secret reserve would be created.

Journal Entries. The tendency in professional examinations is towards intricate and detailed problems in Holding Company accounts and, therefore, a candidate must be able to avoid confusion in preparing the Consolidated Balance Sheet. For this reason, the method of adjustment by means of additions, subtractions and contras is not recommended except in the simpler problems. The most satisfactory method is that using columns for the balance sheet figures of each of the constituent companies with a column for the preliminary aggregation of those figures, followed, on each side of the balance sheet, by three columns for: (*a*) debit adjustments, (*b*) credit adjustments, and (*c*) final aggregation respectively. In very complicated cases, it will often be necessary to write up the adjustment columns from a set of journal entries. Since the aggregation columns are merely a matter of copy-work or of addition and subtraction, it is contended that the presentation of the correct journal entries will earn a very large proportion of the marks allotted to the question, and in fact the formal copy-work, etc., will take time out of all proportion to the number of marks it can possibly earn.

Illustration 22

From the Balance Sheets and information given below, prepare Consolidated Balance Sheet, showing Journal entries for the adjustments.

BALANCE SHEETS AS AT 31ST DECEMBER 19.. '

	Great, Ltd.	Medium, Ltd.	Small, Ltd.
	£	£	£
Share Capital: £1 fully paid	100,000	50,000	20,000
Reserve	20,000	6,000	
Profit and Loss	10,000	10,000	
Debentures	40,000		
Creditors	4,000	8,000	5,000
Bills Payable			1,000
Loan from Medium			2,000
Loan from Small	1,500		
Provision re Subsidiaries	1,500		
	£177,000	£74,000	£28,000
Sundry Fixed Assets	97,300	30,400	9,200
Goodwill		15,000	
Shares at cost—			
Medium, 40,000	46,000		
Small, 20,000	17,000		
Debentures at cost: Great, £10,000		9,500	
Stock	9,000	9,000	11,000
Debtors and Cash	7,000	7,000	2,300
Bills Receivable	700		
Loan to Great			1,500
Loan to Small		2,000	
Development Expenditure		1,100	
Profit and Loss			4,000
	£177,000	£74,000	£28,000

1. The shares in Medium were acquired some years previously when the Reserve and Profit and Loss Account of that company stood at £6,000 and £5,500 respectively.

2. The shares in Small were acquired at the date of the above Balance Sheets, the price being adjusted so as to take into account the fact that the fixed assets of that company were worth £2,500 more than book value.

3. The Bills Payable in the Balance Sheet of Small had all been issued to Great, and there was a note in the latter's Balance Sheet of a contingent liability of £300 in respect of bills discounted.

4. The provision re subsidiaries in the Balance Sheet of Great arose in respect of:

(a) £1,100 for unrealized profit on goods costing Great £3,900 which had been sold to Small for £5,000 at which figure they were included in the latter's Balance Sheet, none having been sold.

(b) £400 in respect of Development Expenditure of Medium to be written off.

5. The debentures of Great appearing in the Balance Sheet of Medium had been purchased in the open market.

JOURNAL

	£	£
Share Capital of Medium	50,000	
Share in Medium		40,000
Minority Interest		10,000
Allocation of share capital of Medium between Great and outside shareholders.		
Goodwill	6,000	
Shares in Medium		6,000
Excess of cost of shares over nominal value.		
Share Capital of Small	20,000	
Shares in Small		17,000
Capital Reserve		3,000
Excess of nominal value of shares of Small (all held by Great) over cost.		
Reserve of Medium	6,000	
Profit and Loss of Medium	5,500	
Capital Reserve		9,200
Minority Interest		2,300
Allocation of pre-acquisition reserve and profit and loss balance between Great and outside shareholders in ratio of 4:1.		
Debentures of Great	10,000	
Debentures in Great		9,500
Capital Reserve		400
Minority Interest		100
Elimination of inter-company holding and allocation of 'profit' between Great and outside shareholders.		
Bills Payable (Small)	700	
Bills Receivable (Great)		700
Elimination of inter-company holding.		
Loan from Medium	2,000	
Loan from Small	1,500	
Loan to Small		2,000
Loan to Great		1,500
Elimination of inter-company loans.		
Provision re Subsidiaries	1,500	
Minority Interest	100	
Stock		1,100
Development Expenditure		500
Elimination of unrealized profit from Stock and writing off of Development expenditure. (*Note.* Since Great provided £400, it is assumed that £500 is to be written off, outside shareholders bearing their one-fifth proportion.)		

JOURNAL (*contd.*)

	£	£
Sundry Fixed Assets	2,500	
Capital Reserve		2,500
Unrecorded undervaluation of assets of Small taken into account in fixing price of shares.		
Goodwill	4,000	
Profit and Loss Account of Small . . .		4,000
Debit balance at date of acquisition.		
Profit and Loss Account of Medium . . .	900	
Minority Interest		900
One-fifth share of post-acquisition profits (£10,000 − £5,500).		
Capital Reserve	10,000	
Goodwill		10,000
Elimination of items added to Goodwill in above entries against Capital Reserve.		

Note. The balance of Capital Reserve, which is £5,100, might also be used to write down the Goodwill figure of Medium to £9,900.

Summary of Goodwill and Capital Reserve from above entries.

GOODWILL

	£	£
Per Balance Sheet of Medium		15,000
Add re Medium (excess over par of cost)	6,000	
,, Small (pre-acquisition loss) . . .	4,000	
		10,000
		25,000
Less Transfer from Capital Reserve		10,000
Per Consolidated Balance Sheet		15,000

CAPITAL RESERVE

	£	£
Re Medium (pre-acquisition profits) . . .	9,200	
,, Small (excess of par over cost)	3,000	
,, Debentures of Great	400	
,, Sundry Fixed Assets of Small	2,500	
		15,100
Less Transfer to Goodwill		10,000
Per Consolidated Balance Sheet		£5,100

Consolidated Balance Sheet of Great, Ltd., and its Subsidiaries as at 31st December 19..

Liabilities / Capital

	Great, Ltd.	Medium, Ltd.	Small, Ltd.	Total	Adjustments Dr.	Adjustments Cr.	Total
	£	£	£	£	£	£	£
Share Capital	100,000	50,000	20,000	170,000	50,000 / 20,000		100,000
Reserve	20,000	6,000		26,000	6,000		20,000
Profit and Loss	10,000	10,000		20,000	5,500 / 900	3,000	13,600
Debentures	40,000			40,000	10,000	9,200	30,000
Creditors	4,000	8,000	5,000	17,000			17,000
Bills Payable			1,000	1,000	700	400	300
Loan from Medium			2,000	2,000	2,000		
Loan from Small	1,500			1,500	1,500	2,500	
Provision re Subsidiaries	1,500			1,500	1,500	10,000	
Capital Reserve						2,300 / 100 / 900	5,100
Minority Interest					10,000 / 100		13,200
	£177,000	£74,000	£28,000	£279,000	£108,200	£28,400	£199,200
					£79,800		

Assets

	Great, Ltd.	Medium, Ltd.	Small, Ltd.	Total	Adjustments Dr.	Adjustments Cr.	Total
	£	£	£	£	£	£	£
Sundry Fixed Assets	97,300	30,400	9,200	136,900	2,500		139,400
Goodwill		15,000		15,000	6,000 / 4,000	10,000 / 40,000	15,000
Shares in Medium	46,000			46,000		6,000	
Shares in Small	17,000			17,000		17,000	
Debentures in Great		9,500		9,500		9,500	
Stock	9,000	9,000	11,000	29,000		1,100	27,900
Debtors and Cash	7,000	7,000	2,300	16,300			16,300
Bills Receivable	700			700		700	
Loan to Great			1,500	1,500		1,500	
Loan to Small		2,000		2,000		2,000	
Development Expenditure		1,100		1,100		500	600
Profit and Loss			4,000	4,000		4,000	
	£177,000	£74,000	£28,000	£279,000	£12,500	£92,300	£199,200
						£79,800	

CONSOLIDATED PROFIT AND LOSS ADJUSTMENTS

After aggregating the various debits and credits of the constituent companies' Profit and Loss and Appropriation Accounts under their appropriate headings, adjustments will be required, of which the following are the most important:

1. The transfer of *profit or loss of subsidiaries* attributable to the Holding Company's shares applicable to the period *prior* to acquisition of shares, the transfer being to the credit of the cost of the shares for profit or to the debit thereof for loss, the net effect of which is to decrease Goodwill or increase Capital Reserve in the case of profit, or conversely for loss.

2. The transfer to the credit of Minority Shareholders in respect of the proportion of the *subsidiaries' profits* attributable to them; or to the debit in case of *loss*. As already indicated in this chapter, the Minority Shareholders cannot legally become liable to the Holding Company for such share of loss, not even if such share of loss exceeds their paid-up capital, owing to the principle of limited liability, so that the most favoured opinion is that such sum should be featured as a contingent asset (analogous to Short Workings in Royalty Accounts) or deducted from the Reserves or Share Capital of the Holding Company, being, of course, clearly described in the Consolidated Balance Sheet.

3. The *elimination of internal items*, e.g. dividends and interest arising within the Group. If the Holding Company has already passed through its books its proportion of the proposed dividends from subsidiaries, there will be a cancellation of both sides of the Consolidated Profit and Loss Account, and similarly in the Consolidated Balance Sheet for such proposed dividends receivable and payable. The remaining parts of the proposed dividends will be transferred to the credit of Minority Shareholders.

If such proposed dividends have not been dealt with in the books of the Holding Company, a cancellation will be made by reducing the dividends debit in the Consolidated Profit and Loss Account and the Proposed Dividends item on the liabilities side of the Consolidated Balance Sheet. [Alternatively, the unentered Dividends Receivable may be introduced as an asset and as a profit (as if the Holding Company had actually entered them in its books and then cancelled them).]

Except where an election for group relief is in force, advance corporation tax (ACT) is payable on dividends paid, and subsidiaries paying dividends will debit Dividends Payable Account with the amount paid and the ACT Recoverable Account with the ACT paid.[1] Conversely, the Holding Company will credit Dividends Receivable Account with the amount of dividend received plus Tax Credit and debit Profit and Loss Account with the same value of Tax. Consequently, on consolidation the

---

[1] Where the basic rate of tax is for example 33%, the advance corporation tax is obtained from the formula $33/67 \times$ dividend paid. The ACT must be paid to the Collector in about three months from date of payment of a dividend but will be deducted from corporation tax due in about 19 months.

amounts of dividends paid by the subsidiaries will eliminate the dividend received (credit) and Tax (debit) in the Holding Company's Accounts.

Similarly, unless an election for group relief is in force in respect of charges on income,[1] Income Tax is deductible from payments thereof, e.g. Debenture Interest, both the receiving and the paying companies will have entered the item in their respective books on a gross basis (after transferring the relevant Income Tax thereon to Income Tax), so that again there will be an elimination of both the gross interest debited and the gross interest credited, no adjustment being required for Income Tax because the same amount of Income Tax has been debited (by the receiving company) and credited (by the paying company).

If the interest is due but has not been paid, the debtor company will have already charged the accrual gross to its Profit and Loss Account and credited a liability for the 'net' sum payable, and credit Income Tax with the Income Tax thereon. If the receiving company has brought such interest into its books, there will be an eliminating transfer of both 'net' payable and receivable sums in the Consolidated Balance Sheet, but no adjustment for Income Tax, assuming that the receiving company had dealt correctly with sum receivable by debiting the 'net' interest as an asset and debiting Income Tax with the Income Tax thereon and crediting Profit and Loss with the gross amount.

If the receiving company has *not* brought such interest into its books, it can be brought in and taken out 'net', or the 'net' liability in the Consolidated Balance Sheet can be debited and the interest charged in the Consolidated Profit and Loss Account credited, the Income Tax thereon being debited to Income Tax and interest account credited. In other words, there will be a credit to interest charged of the gross sum, and (i) a debit to Income Tax (both in the Consolidated Profit and Loss Account) and (ii) a debit to the liability for the 'net' interest payable in the Consolidated Balance Sheet.

Where elections for group relief ARE in force in respect of dividends and charges on income, the paying Subsidiary Company (or the paying Trading Company in the case of a consortium) is relieved of the requirement to deduct Income Tax and account for ACT. Consequently no adjustment will be required in respect thereof for consolidation purposes.

4. Where the Holding Company has taken up the *whole* of its proportion of the PROFITS of the subsidiaries, this will require elimination, as the total Group profit is already in the Consolidated Profit and Loss Account.

5. *Transfer of goods* within the group will require eliminating from the sales and purchases side of the Consolidated Profit and Loss Account (although the sales and purchase items will not appear in the published accounts).

6. Any *profit on sales* made by one member of the group to the other is not true profit, except where realized, so that the profit on the unsold goods will require eliminating. This is required whether it is the Holding Company that sells to a subsidiary or *vice versa*, the elimination being the

[1]See page 2358 *re* charges on income.

cost price of the goods remaining unsold (from the asset in the Consolidated Balance Sheet and from the Trading Profit in the Consolidated Profit and Loss Account), the difference being the profit on sale representing the proportion attributable to the Minority Shareholders, the profit remaining to the Holding Company where the sale is by it to a subsidiary, but the profit remaining in respect of a sale from the subsidiary to the Holding Company ensures to the benefit of the Minority Shareholders. Many accountants consider that even where there is a Minority Interest the whole of the cost should be eliminated as the 'paper' profit is wholly artificial. Goods bought by a member and resold to another member (both at a profit) and remaining unsold should not carry any profit at all.

7. Where a *fixed asset is sold at a profit or loss* by a member of a group to another member, the position is similar to that in (6). It is generally agreed that the adjustments required are such as to restore the position in the accounts as if the sale had not been made, and this will involve, not only the cancellation of the profit or loss on the transfer, but the amendment of the *depreciation charge* if it has been based on the *transfer* value.

8. Where there are *foreign subsidiaries*, adjustments may be required to deal with any special factors in foreign taxes, particularly where a special tax is levied on distributed dividends, including tax on distributions to non-resident holders.

9. Where a subsidiary is acquired which has arrears of *cumulative preference dividends*, such arrears may be dealt with:

(a) By way of 'note' only, no accounting entries being made in the Consolidated Accounts, but when such arrears are paid they must be treated, as far as possible, as arising out of pre-acquisition reserves of the subsidiary and, if the latter are not sufficient, from the post-acquisition profit of the subsidiary; or

(b) By accounting entries in the Consolidated Accounts to bring the gross amount of arrears into liability to Minority Shareholders and as an addition to Goodwill or deduction from Capital Reserve. When the arrears are paid, they will be dealt with as in (a), that is, out of pre-acquisition reserves of the subsidiary, as far as possible and, if not sufficient, from the post-acquisition profit of the subsidiary and applied to *increase* Goodwill or *decrease* Capital Reserve.

Where some of the preference shares of the subsidiary have been acquired by the Holding Company, the same rule will apply to the remainder *not acquired*.

10. Where a *Holding Company writes off* the whole or part of the *cost of the shares* acquired in a subsidiary, the write-off should be cancelled (thus increasing the profit and likewise increasing goodwill (or decreasing Capital Reserve); or it may remain undisturbed, but the amount of profit so applied must be disclosed in the Consolidated Accounts.

11. Where a subsidiary issues bonus shares out of accumulated profit, it is important as regards the Holding Company to distinguish between the pre- and post-acquisition profits utilized in the process.

If pre-acquisition profits are used, no adjustment in the Consolidated

Accounts is required, as such profits have been brought into account on acquisition (in reducing Goodwill or Cost of Control) and the amount of such accumulated profits will now appear in the Balance Sheet of the subsidiary in another form, i.e. as Share Capital.

The capitalization normally involves the permanent freezing of the amount used by removing it from the distributable class to the undistributable class, but in this case the position is unaltered because before the capitalization took place the amount had already, in effect, been capitalized by crediting it to Goodwill or Cost of Control.

If, however, the capitalization is made out of post-acquisition profits (whether as the ordinary balance of Profit and Loss Account or as any other separate revenue reserve) an adjustment is required, as otherwise the total of such accumulated post-acquisition profits shown in the Consolidated Balance Sheet would exceed the maximum amount that could be paid to the shareholders of the holding company. In other words, such sum has become permanently frozen, so that a transfer to a Capital Reserve is required.

The Holding Company might adjust its asset item of Shares in Subsidiary to the extent of the profit so used, but it could not correspondingly credit its Profit and Loss Account (and so make the amount available for its shareholders dividends); hence, it would credit a Capital Reserve in its own books, giving the same result as in the preceding paragraph.

12. At the date of the consolidation, differences may occur between the debit against one member of the group and credit in favour of another, e.g. Cash or Goods in Transit; interest or charges for work done recorded in one subsidiary and not in another, and such other differences commonly met with in dealing with branches. The adjustments will be required on the lines normally adopted in Branch Accounts (with the same need for care in dealing with the unrealized profits).

13. Where on the purchase of its shares fixed assets of a subsidiary are acquired on the basis of a revalued figure, and the amended values are not given effect to in the books of a subsidiary, an adjustment for the relevant distribution is required in the Consolidated Accounts as follows:

Debit Consolidated Profit and Loss Account; and

Credit Fixed Asset for the consequent additional depreciation in respect of the increased value of the fixed asset; and conversely in respect of decreased value of the fixed asset.

Illustration 23

X, Ltd., acquired 80 per cent of the share capital of S, Ltd., and in arriving at the price to be paid therefor Plant which stood in the books of S, Ltd., at £6,000 was revalued at £8,000; and the Fixtures which stood in the books of S, Ltd., at £2,000 were revalued at £1,500.

The Balance Sheet of S, Ltd., showed the above asset (on the non-revalued basis) at the end of the following year:

	£
Plant, less depreciation (i.e. 10 per cent depreciation)	5,400
Fixtures, less depreciation (i.e. 5 per cent depreciation) . . .	1,900

Show the adjusting entries for depreciation arising from the now recorded revaluations.

Plant: additional depreciation—10 per cent of £2,000.
Fixtures: reduced depreciation—5 per cent of £500.

Adjusting Journal entries[1]:

[1] On the acquisition of the shares of S, Ltd., the adjustment figures would be brought into account, thus:

		£	£
Debit Plant	. . . . . .	2,000	
Credit Fixtures	. . . . .		500
„ Cost of Shares, 80 per cent of £1,500	. .		1,200
Minority Shareholders, 20 per cent of £1,500	. .		300

JOURNAL

	£	£
Consolidated Profit and Loss Account . . .	200	
Plant (or Plant Depreciation Fund) . . .		200
Being increased depreciation charge arising from increase in valuation of plant by £2,000.		
Fixtures (or Fixtures Depreciation Fund) . . .	25	
Consolidated Profit and Loss Account . . .		25
Being decreased depreciation charge arising from decrease in valuation of fixtures by £500.		

Such adjustments affect the total consolidated profit in which the minority shareholders have 20 per cent interest; hence the adjustments must be made before ascertaining the proportion of profit of the subsidiary attributable to minority shareholders.

14. When a company acquires shares in a subsidiary company, and subsequently a dividend is paid out of pre-acquisition profits, such dividend received by the acquiring company is *pro tanto* a credit to the cost price of the shares acquired and must be regarded as a capital receipt and credited to Shares in Subsidiary Company (see pp. 2408 and 2409).

As the net assets acquired will be *pro tanto* represented by preacquisition profit remaining undistributed at the date the shares of the subsidiary company were acquired and paid for as part of the purchase price, any release by way of dividend reduces the remaining assets accordingly, and so in effect such dividend represents a partial return of the purchase price.

Whether dividend is paid or not will be immaterial to the Goodwill on Capital Reserve arising from the difference between the Cost of Shares acquired and the net assets (i.e. Share Capital plus Reserve) acquired.

Illustration 24

When H, Ltd., acquired its 80 per cent holdings in S, Ltd., the abridged Balance Sheets were:

	H, Ltd. £	S, Ltd. £		H, Ltd. £	S, Ltd. £
Share Capital (£1) . . .	50,000	20,000	Shares in S, Ltd. (16,000) .	40,000	
Revenue Reserves . . .	25,000	14,000	Sundry Net Assets .	25,000	27,000
			Cash at Bank . . .	10,000	7,000
	£75,000	£34,000		£75,000	£34,000

Forthwith, a dividend of 30 per cent was paid by S, Ltd.

Show essential Ledger Accounts and Consolidated Balance Sheet (ignoring tax).

COST OF SHARES

		£				£
Cash	. . .	40,000	Dividend . . .			4,800
			Balance . . .	c/d		35,200
		£40,000				£40,000
Balance . . .	b/d	35,200	Share Capital . .			16,000
			Revenue Reserve: Pre-acquisition Profit, 80% of (£14,000–£6,000) .			6,400
			Goodwill . . .			12,800
		£35,200				£35,200

MINORITY SHAREHOLDERS

		£				£
Balance	c/d	5,600	Share Capital . . .			4,000
			Revenue Reserve 20% of (£14,000–£6,000) . .			1,600
		£5,600				£5,600
			Balance	b/d		5,600

GOODWILL

	£			
Cost of Shares . .	12,800			

REVENUE RESERVE—S, LTD.

	£		£
Dividend H, Ltd. £4,800		Balance . . .	14,000
Dividend S, Ltd. 1,200	6,000		
Cost of Shares 80% .	6,400		
Minority Shareholders 20%	1,600		
	£14,000		£14,000

CONSOLIDATED BALANCE SHEET

	£		£
Share Capital . . .	50,000	Goodwill . . .	12,800
Revenue Reserve—H, Ltd. .	25,000	Net Sundry Assets . .	52,000
Minority Shareholders .	5,600	Bank	15,800
	£80,600		£80,600

If no dividend had been paid, the sole difference to the aggregate of assets would be the amount of dividend, £1,200, paid to the minority shareholders; that is, cash and minority shareholders would be £1,200 more than if no dividend had been paid. The Goodwill item is unchanged.

CONSOLIDATED BALANCE SHEET

	£	£		£	£
Share Capital . . .		50,000	Goodwill—		
Revenue Reserve H, Ltd. .		25,000	Cost of Shares . .	40,000	
Revenue Reserve S, Ltd. .	14,000		Less Nominal: 80% of		
Less Contra . . .	11,200		£20,000 . .	16,000	
	2,800			24,000	
Less Minority Shareholders .	2,800	—	Less 80% of £14,000 .	11,200	
					12,800
Minority Shareholders Share			Net Sundry Assets . .		52,000
Capital 20% of £20,000. .	4,000		Bank		17,000
Revenue Reserve 20% of £14,000	2,800				
		6,800			
		£81,800			£81,800

		(a) Where dividend is paid		(b) Where no dividend is paid
		£		£
Cost of Shares . . .		40,000	Cost of Shares . . .	40,000
Less Dividend . . .		4,800	Less Nominal Value of Shares .	16,000
		35,200		24,000
Less Nominal Value of Shares .		16,000	Less 80% of Revenue Reserve of	
		19,200	£14,000	11,200
Less 80% Revenue Reserve of S, Ltd., per Balance Sheet . . . £14,000				
Less Dividends—				
H, Ltd. £4,800				
M.I. 1,200				
6,000				
£8,000				
80% thereof		6,400		
Goodwill		£12,800	Goodwill	£12,800

	(a)			(b)	
	H, Ltd.	S, Ltd.		H, Ltd.	S, Ltd.
	£	£		£	£
Bank . .	10,000	7,000		10,000	7,000
Div. received .	4,800				
Div. paid H, Ltd.		£4,800			
Div. paid S, Ltd.		1,200			
		6,000			
	£14,800	£1,000 = £15,800		£10,000	£7,000 = £17,000

15. *Derived profits.* A subsidiary company itself may hold shares in another subsidiary and the former may not be wholly owned by the holding company, so that there are minority shareholders who will be entitled not only to their proportion of profit arising in the subsidiary of which they are shareholders, but also for their proportion of profit of such

company which it derives from its holding in another subsidiary; thus H has two subsidiaries: A and B; but A also owns shares in B.

A, therefore, will have its **own** profit, plus its *proportion* of the profit of **B**, hence the minority shareholders of **A** obtained their due proportion of the profits of two companies.

It is important to keep in mind the fact that as all profits and reserves existing at the date of acquisition must 'disappear', i.e. by crediting the Cost of Shares acquired (or direct to Goodwill) and by crediting the minority shareholders, such profits of B in existence when A acquired its shares therein will not come into the Profit and Loss Account of A, so that the minority shareholders of **A must not be credited with any share of pre-acquisition profit of B.** The rule may be simply stated:

When shares are acquired in a subsidiary or fellow subsidiary, whether the acquiring company is itself the holding company or its subsidiary, the **pre-acquisition profit and reserves** must wholly be transferred out, i.e.:

(i) To Cost of Shares of the *acquiring* company; and
(ii) To minority shareholders of the company *acquired*.

Students usually find much difficulty in calculating the 'derived' profits, but the following basic rules should be helpful:

1. Ascertain the date of acquisition of the shares of a fellow subsidiary, commencing with one that has not acquired shares in another subsidiary, and the profit attributable, either as ascertained or apportioned thereto, will be apportioned to the acquiring company on the usual lines as between pre-acquisition and post-acquisition, the former being used against the cost of shares acquired and the latter diverted to the Profit and Loss Account of the acquiring company as 'derived' profit.

2. If the acquiring company is itself acquired by another fellow subsidiary (or the Parent) the **dates** of the **respective acquisitions** determine the treatment of the profit of the former, which will be made up of its 'own' normal trading profit and the *derived* profit arising from its holding in the company it has acquired as and from such acquisition date.

As regards the *own* or *direct* profit, this will be dealt with in the ordinary way in apportioning it between pre-acquisition and post-acquisition, but the *derived* profit will be dealt with as follows:

(a) If its own shares have been acquired by another company **before** it acquired shares of a fellow subsidiary, the **whole** of the *derived* profit will be post-acquisition profit.

(b) If the date referred to in (a) is **after,** then such *derived* profit will be apportioned as to:

(i) such part of the *derived* profit accruing as arises **between** the date the acquiring company acquired its shares and the date such acquiring company was itself acquired will be pre-acquisition profit.

(ii) such part of the *derived* profit accruing as arises **since** the date that such acquiring company was itself acquired will be post-acquisition profit.

Illustration 25

X, Ltd., acquired all the shares in Y, Ltd., on 1st April 19.3, and the profit accruing to it **since** the acquisition is (say) £750 for the nine months ended 31st December 19.3 (the profit for the full year being £1,000). H, Ltd., acquired all the shares in X, Ltd., in 19.1.

The whole of the *derived* profit of X, Ltd., viz. £750, is post-acquisition profit in respect of H, Ltd.

If, however, H, Ltd., acquired such shares on 1st October 19.3, the *derived* profit of £750 must be divided into:

	£
(a) Pre-acquisition (1st April to 30th September) . .	500
(b) Post-acquisition (1st October to 31st December) .	250

If there were minority shareholders, the profit as mentioned above would be that remaining after the deduction required for the proportion attributable to such minority shareholders.

Illustration 26

A, Ltd., acquired its shareholding of 10 per cent in B, Ltd., when the latter's Profit and Loss Account balance was in debit £600. **Later,** H, Ltd., acquired 80 per cent of the shares in A, Ltd., and on the same day acquired 60 per cent of the shares in B, Ltd., when the Profit and Loss Account balances of those companies stood at a credit of £2,000 and a debit of £1,000 respectively.

Show statement of how the present credit balances in the Profit and Loss Account of £3000 and £2,400 for A, Ltd., and B, Ltd., respectively will be dealt with.

STATEMENT OF ALLOCATION OF THE PROFIT OF A, LTD., AND B, LTD.

	A, Ltd. Profit own £	derive £				B, Ltd. Profit £	Total £
Profit and Loss Account balance . .	3,000					2,400	5,400
Transfer from B, Ltd. (post-acquisition profit)		300					
Minority Interest . .	600	60				720	1,380
	2,400	240				1,680	4,020
Pre-acquisition profit or loss . .			A, Ltd.—10 per cent of £600 (loss) . .	£60			
H, Ltd.—80 per cent (profit) . .	1,600		H, Ltd.—60 per cent of £1,000 (loss) . .	600			
H, Ltd.—80 per cent (loss)		32[1]				660	908
	800	272				2,340[2]	3,112
			Post-acquisition Profit—proportion transferred to A, Ltd. . . .			300	
Post-acquisition profit of H, Ltd. . .	£800	£272[1]				£2,040	£3,112

[1] See footnote on p. 2467.
[2] Note that the pre-acquisition losses must be added.

Illustration 27

The following acquisitions of share capital took place at the end of each related year.

| | | | PROFIT AND LOSS ACCOUNT BALANCES AT ACQUISITION DATES | | |
		Year	B, Ltd.	C, Ltd.	D, Ltd.
			£	£	£
H, Ltd.	70 per cent of D, Ltd.	1			− 2,000
H, Ltd.	60 per cent of B, Ltd.	2	3,000		− 600
B, Ltd.	15 per cent of D, Ltd.	3			200
B, Ltd.	10 per cent of C, Ltd.	4		600	300
C, Ltd.	5 per cent of D, Ltd.	5			800
H, Ltd.	80 per cent of C, Ltd.	6		4,000	900
Present Balances of Profit and Loss		7	£8,000	£2,400	£1,000

[1] The only matter that is likely to harass the reader is in respect of the allocation of the *derived* profit of A, Ltd., which is explained thus:

H, Ltd., acquired its shares in A, Ltd., at a date **after** A, Ltd., acquired its shares in B, Ltd., and the starting point is the latter date. At that date, the Profit and Loss Account of B, Ltd., was in debit £600 so that it has earned £3,000 since; hence £60 is the pre-acquisition loss of A, Ltd., and does not enter into its Profit and Loss Account, but is added to the Cost of Shares (Goodwill), and £300 is available to A, Ltd. (as A, Ltd. owns 10 per cent of B, Ltd.), which would be distributable by A, Ltd., in the ordinary way. As, however, H, Ltd., has in the meantime acquired its 80 per cent holding in A, Ltd., such part of the £300 *derived* profit (after crediting the minority shareholders with £60—20 per cent of £300), that is, £240, must now be split up as to pre-acquisition and post-acquisition. Now, at the date that H, Ltd., acquired its 80 per cent holding in A, Ltd., the loss of B, Ltd., had increased by £400 (£40 attributable to A, Ltd.) and the profit earned since was £3,400 (£340 attributable to A, Ltd.); hence the pre-acquisition **loss** attributable to H, Ltd., by reason of its holding in A, Ltd., is **£32** (80 per cent of £40) and the post-acquisition **profit** is **£272** (80 per cent of £340), thus accounting for its share of the *derived* profit of £240.

Had H, Ltd., acquired its shares in A, Ltd., **before** the latter acquired its shares in B, Ltd., the allocation above would not be required, because at the date that A, Ltd., became entitled to its share of the profit of B, Ltd., H, Ltd., was **already** a shareholder of A, Ltd.; hence all the profit falling to A, Ltd., from B, Ltd., would be regarded, for the purposes of H, Ltd., as all post-acquisition.

The present Profit and Loss Account balances are £3,000 plus £2,400 c = £5,400
This is accounted for as follows:

	£
(1) Available profit attributable to H, Ltd.: £800 + £272 + £2,040	3,112
(2) Goodwill (Cr.): £1,600 less (Dr.) [£32 + £60 + £600]	908
(3) Minority Shareholders: £600 + £60 + £720	1,380
	£5,400

The derived profit of A, Ltd., may be dealt with thus:

| | | Divided between | | |
		A, Ltd.	H, Ltd.	Minority
		£	£	£
Debit balance of B, Ltd., at the date of purchase by H, Ltd., of shares in B, Ltd.	£1,000			
Less debit balance of B, Ltd., at date of purchase by A, Ltd., of shares in B, Ltd.	600*			
	£400	Dr. 40	Dr. 32	Dr. 8
Profit of B, Ltd., earned since H, Ltd., acquired its shares in A, Ltd.	£3,400	Cr. 340	Cr. 272	Cr. 68
		£300	£240	£60

* 10 per cent of £600 (£60) is the pre-acquisition loss existing when A, Ltd., bought its shares in B, Ltd., and hence never appears in A, Ltd.'s Profit and Loss Account.

H, Ltd., has no Profit and Loss balance; there are no preference or ordinary dividends, paid or proposed.

Prepare statement showing how the present combined Profit and Loss Account credit balance of £11,400 will be dealt with in the Consolidated Accounts.

Statement of Profits of the Group

Per Accounts	H, Ltd. £	B, Ltd. 'Derived' £	B, Ltd. 'Own' £	'Derived' £	C, Ltd.	C, Ltd. 'Own' £	'Derived' £	D, Ltd. £	Total £
D, Ltd.	2,100	120	8,000	10*		2,400		1,000	11,400
C, Ltd., 'own'	1,280	180							
C, Ltd., 'derived'	4	1							
B, Ltd., 'own'	3,000								
B, Ltd., 'derived'	181								
		301							
	(o)								
Less Minority Shareholders	40 per cent	120	3,200	1		240		100	(1) 3,661
		181	4,800	9		2,160		900	7,739
				10 per cent		10 per cent		10 per cent	
Less Pre-acquisition profit, or Pre-acquisition loss	B, Ltd. (g)	120	(m) 1,800	4	(i) 3,200	3,260	C, Ltd. (a) 40	1,330	(2) 3,734
	H, Ltd. (l)	181	3,000	5	60	1,100	B, Ltd. (c) 30	2,230	
		181	3,000				H, Ltd. (e) 1,400		
Less Post-acquisition profit, or post-acquisition loss	H, Ltd.	181	(n) 3,000	5	(h) 180	1,100	C, Ltd. (b) 10	2,100	(3) 4,005
		—	—	—	(j) 1,280	—	B, Ltd. (d) 120	—	
	(3) £4,005						H, Ltd. (f) 2,100		

SUMMARY—

		£
(1) Minority Shareholders		3,661
(2) Cost of Shares		3,734
(3) Profit since acquisition, to Consolidated Balance Sheet		4,005
		£11,400

* (Having regard to its insignificance the item of £10 would in practice be ignored.)

Notes—

1. **D, Ltd.** Profit and Loss Account—
   - (a) C, Ltd., acquired shares when the credit balance of D, Ltd., was
   - (b) Profit of D, Ltd., earned since acquisition by C, Ltd. (£1,000—£800)
2.
   - (c) B, Ltd., acquired shares when the credit balance of D, Ltd., was
   - (d) Profit of D, Ltd., earned since acquisition by B, Ltd. (£1,000—£200)
3.
   - (e) H, Ltd. acquired shares when the debit balance of D, Ltd., was
   - (f) Profit of D, Ltd., earned since acquisition by H, Ltd. (£2,000+£1,000)
4. **C, Ltd.** Profit and Loss Account (own direct profit)—
   - (g) B, Ltd., acquired shares when the credit balance of C, Ltd., was
   - (h) Profit of C, Ltd., earned since acquisition by B, Ltd. (£2,400—£600)

	£	Proportion	£
	800	5 per cent	40
	200	5 per cent	10
	200	15 per cent	30
	800	15 per cent	120
	−2,000	70 per cent	−1,400
	3,000	70 per cent	2,100
	600	10 per cent	60
	1,800	10 per cent	180

(i) H, Ltd., acquired shares when the credit balance of C, Ltd., was 4,000   80 per cent   3,200

(j) Loss of C, Ltd., incurred since acquisition by H, Ltd. (£4,000—£2,400) . . . . . −1,600   80 per cent   −1,220

5. **C. Ltd.,** Profit and Loss Account (derived profit):

The profit accruing to C, Ltd., is the post-acquisition profit of D, Ltd.,' attributable to C, Ltd.'s holding in D, Ltd. (See 1(b) p. 2469) = £10

£

(k) B, Ltd., acquired shares in C, Ltd., when the profit of D, Ltd., was £300, but such profit had since grown to £800 when C, Ltd., acquired shares in D, Ltd. Hence, as B, Ltd., was already a shareholder in C, Ltd., when C, Ltd., acquired its shares in D, Ltd., the whole of the derived profit ascribable to B, Ltd., is post-acquisition profit (10 per cent of £10) 1

(l) H, Ltd., acquired shares in C, Ltd., when the profit of D, Ltd., was £900, but when C, Ltd., acquired its shares in D, Ltd., the profit was £800; therefore H, Ltd., acquired shares in C, Ltd., within the period in which C, Ltd., became entitled to 5 per cent of the profit thereof (i.e. 5 per cent of £200. See 1(b).) The intervening profit of D, Ltd., is £100 (i.e. from £800 to £900) before H, Ltd., acquired its shares in C, Ltd., and 5 per cent of £100 (i.e. from £900 to £1,000) since such acquisition.

Hence pre-acquisition profit as regards H, Ltd., is 80 per cent of £5 (5 per cent of £100) 4

Post-acquisition profit as regards H, Ltd., is 80 per cent of £5 (5 per cent of £100) 4

6. **B. Ltd.,** Profit and Loss Account (own direct profit):   £   Proportion

(m) H, Ltd., acquired shares when the credit balance of B, Ltd., was 3,000   60 per cent   1,800

(n) Profit of B, Ltd., earned since acquisition by H, Ltd. (£8,000—£3,000) 5,000   60 per cent   3,000

(o) B, Ltd., Profit and Loss Account (derived profit):

As H, Ltd., acquired shares in B, Ltd., before any of the acquisitions were made by B, Ltd., in the other companies the whole of the profit of £301, ascribable to H, Ltd., is post-acquisition profit to H, Ltd. 301   60 per cent   181

If H, Ltd., had acquired its shares in B, Ltd., at a later period instead of the second year the structure of the statement would be materially altered but the treatment of the direct profit would create no difficulty. It would, however, be necessary to examine the derived profit of B, Ltd., having regard to the date of the acquisition of the shares of B, Ltd., by H, Ltd.; for example, the treatment of £120, one of the derived profit items of B, Ltd., would be as shown hereunder (ignoring the direct profit of B, Ltd.) if H, Ltd., had acquired the shares of B, Ltd. say at the end of year 5.

Reference to Note 2(d) will show that the free profit available to B, Ltd., commenced at the end of year 3, when the credit balance of D, Ltd.'s Profit and Loss Account stood at £200 and had since grown to £1,000, i.e. by £800, of which the proportion ascribable to B, Ltd., is 15 per cent thereof, i.e. £120. H, Ltd., however, did not become a shareholder in B, Ltd., until a date subsequent to the commencement of the date when part of D, Ltd.'s profit became available to B, Ltd., and therefore the intervening profit, i.e. that falling before the date of the acquisition of shares in B, Ltd., by H, Ltd. (i.e. between the earlier and the later date) or such proportion of it (where there are minority shareholders) will be regarded as a pre-acquisition profit of H, Ltd.

The profit of D, Ltd., at this later date (i.e. when H, Ltd., became a shareholder in B, Ltd.) had grown from £200 to £800 (i.e. £600), and then later (after the acquisition of the shares of B, Ltd., by H, Ltd.) by a further £200, to reach the present balance of £1,000.

Therefore the profit of £120 (i.e. 15 per cent of £800) attributable to B, Ltd., is divisible as regards H, Ltd.:

(1) 15 per cent of £600 Pre-acquisition

(2) 15 per cent of £200 Post-acquisition

£
90
30
£120

Hence the item in the 'derived' profit column of B, Ltd., will be:

(a) £90 (less minority shareholders' 40 per cent £36)

(b) £30 (less minority shareholders' 40 per cent £12)

£
54   Pre-acquisition
18   Post-acquisition
£72

The amended derived profit column of B, Ltd., would be:

£
As shown 120
" " 181
301
Less Minority Shareholders—40 per cent 120
181
Less Pre-acquisition profit (as above) 54
Balance Post-acquisition profit to H, Ltd. (i.e. **£18**+60 per cent of £180+£1 (**£181**)) £127

Illustration 28

The summarized Balance Sheets of a group at 31st December, Year 59, were:

	Senior, Ltd. £	Major, Ltd. £	Minor, Ltd. £
Sundry Assets	240,000	27,850	30,000
Investments—			
In Major, Ltd. (30,000 shares)	24,000		
In Minor, Ltd., *less* £1,000 dividend credited			
(16,000 shares)		19,000	
Revenue Account		5,150	
	£264,000	£52,000	£30,000
	£	£	£
Share Capital—			
Ordinary shares of £1 each . . .	200,000	40,000	24,000
Revenue Reserves and Surplus . .	24,000		2,000
Creditors	40,000	12,000	4,000
	£264,000	£52,000	£30,000

Major, Ltd., acquired two-thirds interest in Minor, Ltd., in Year 47, when the credit balance on Revenue Account in Minor, Ltd.'s books was £2,400.

Senior, Ltd., acquired three-quarters interest in Major, Ltd., in Year 50, when the Revenue Account as shown in Major, Ltd.'s books was in debit to the extent of £4,000 and that in Minor, Ltd.'s books showed a credit balance of £1,800.

On the acquisition date, the directors of Senior, Ltd., considered the assets of Major, Ltd., to be overvalued to the extent of £3,000, but no adjustment was made in books of Major, Ltd.

In the Year 47, Major, Ltd., credited a sum of £1,000, being a portion of a dividend received from Minor, Ltd., paid out of pre-acquisition profits, to Investiment Account.

Prepare Consolidated Balance Sheet, showing working figures.

COST OF CONTROL—

		Major, Ltd. £		Minor, Ltd. £	Total
	£		£		
Cost of shares acquired		24,000		19,000	
Less Nominal Value	30,000		16,000		
Less ¾ Depreciation					
Provision (a) of					
£3,000 . £2,250		(c)			
Pre-acquisition Loss					
(b) . 2,550 4,800		25,200 Profit 600	16,600		
		Cr. £1,200		Dr. £2,400	Dr. £1,200

MINORITY SHAREHOLDERS—

		£		£	
Share Capital	(¼)	10,000	(⅓)	8,000	
(a) *Less* ¼ Depreciation Provision .	750				
Profit and Loss . . (Dr.)	1,104	1,854	(Cr.)	667	
		£8,146		£8,667	£16,813

DRAFT CONSOLIDATED PROFIT AND LOSS ACCOUNTS

	Senior, Ltd. £		Major, Ltd. £		Minor, Ltd. £	Total £
Per Accounts	24,000	(Loss)	− 5,150		2,000	20,850
Less **Transfer**		(See note) 4 (b))	733			
			− 4,417			
Less Minority Shareholder			($\frac{1}{4}$) 1,104	($\frac{1}{3}$)	667	437
			− 3,313		1,333	21,287
Cost of Shares		(b)	2,550	(c)	600	1,950
Transfer to Major, Ltd.					733	
	£24,000		£763		—	£23,237

DRAFT CONSOLIDATED BALANCE SHEET
AS AT 31ST DECEMBER YEAR 59

	£			£
Share Capital	200,000	Sundry Assets (per question)	£297,850	
Profit and Loss	23,237	Less Revaluation Depreciation (a)	3,000	
Minority Shareholders	16,813			294,850
Creditors	56,000	Cost of Control		1,200
	£296,050			£296,050

Notes.

The problem is straightforward, except that relating to the pre-acquisition profit attributable to Senior, Ltd., by reason of the profit arising to Major, Ltd., through the latter's holding of shares in Minor, Ltd.

The procedure best followed is to deal with the 'terminal' company first, as follows:

1. Deduct the profit attributable to the minority shareholders (in this case $\frac{1}{3}$): this leaves the balance to the majority holder Major, Ltd.

2. This profit, however, is not 'available' profit, as the proportion attributable to Major, Ltd., arose **prior** to the acquisition by Major, Ltd., of Minor, Ltd.'s shares (at this stage the fact that Senior, Ltd., is a member of Major, Ltd., or will become so later (as here) can be completely ignored).

At the acquisition date the credit balance of profit and loss of Minor, Ltd., was £2,400, of which £1,600 is pre-acquisition profit of Major, Ltd., but the latter took the dividend of £1,000 (being its $\frac{2}{3}$ share of £1,500 dividend) leaving £600 (per statement) to be credited to the cost of shares.

3. The balance, post-acquisition profit, now 'goes over' to the intermediate company, Major, Ltd., to swell its own profit or (as in this case) to diminish the loss. This brings the loss down to £4,417 (subject to the minority shareholders). Now follows the most troublesome part, i.e. the treatment of the 'derived' profit.

4. The position to be ascertained is the 'profit' (or loss) position at the date that Senior, Ltd., comes on the scene, i.e. in Year 50.

This should be dealt with in two parts, viz:

(a) Major, Ltd.'s 'own' profit or loss. This was in debit £4,000, that is £3,000 so far as Senior, Ltd., is concerned ($\frac{3}{4}$ holding).

(b) Major, Ltd.'s 'derived' profit or loss. This was a credit of £733 which, as it were, commenced to accrue to Major, Ltd., in Year 47, but Senior, Ltd., did not come on the scene till some time **after,** i.e. in Year 50, so whilst the minority interest is not concerned with the date of "entry" of Senior, Ltd., yet the intervening 'derived' profit contained in £733 is, so far as concerns Senior, Ltd., the post-acquisition portion of the 'derived' profit. This is £2,000 *less* the profit of Minor, Ltd., up to the date of Major, Ltd.'s acquisition, viz. £1,800: that is, £200 of which $\frac{2}{3}$ is attributable to Senior, Ltd.

The destination of the profits of Minor, Ltd., is therefore:

	Total £	Major, Ltd. £	Minority Share- holders £
(i) Accumulation profit on Major, Ltd., acquisition (£2,400−£1,500)	900	600	300
(ii) Post-acquisition profit £1,100 divided into:			
(a) Before Senior, Ltd., became a member of Major, Ltd. (£1,800−£900) .	900	600	300
(b) Since Senior, Ltd., became a member of Major, Ltd. (£2,000−£1,800) .	200	133	67
	£2,000	£1,333	£667

5. The figure of £1,104 can be proved thus:

Major, Ltd.	Pre- Acquisi- tion £	Post- Acquisi- tion £	Total £
Profit (*Loss*)	−4,000	−1,150	−5150
,, ex Major, Ltd.	600	133	733
	−3,400	−1,017	−4,417
Minority Shareholders ($\frac{1}{4}$)	850	($\frac{1}{4}$) 254	1,104
Balance	−£2,550	−£763	−£3,313

Illustration 29

From the Balance Sheets and information given below, prepare Consolidated Balance Sheet.

BALANCE SHEETS AS AT 31ST DECEMBER 19 .

	H	S		H	S
	£	£		£	£
Share Capital—			Sundry Assets . .	8,000	1,200
£1 fully paid . .	10,000	2,000	Stock	6,100	2,400
Profit and Loss . .	4,000	1,200	Debtors . . .	1,300	1,700
Reserve . . .	1,000	600	Bills Receivable . .	100	
Creditors . . .	2,000	1,200	Shares in S—		
Bills Payable . .		300	1,500 at Cost .	1,500	
	£17,000	£5,300		£17,000	£5,300

1. All the profit of S has been earned since the shares were acquired by H, but there was already the Reserve of £600 at that date.

2. The bills accepted by S are all in favour of H, which has discounted £200 of them.

3. Sundry assets of S are under-valued by £200.

4. The stock of H includes £500 bought from S at a profit to the latter of 25 per cent on cost.

CONSOLIDATED BALANCE SHEET
AS AT 31ST DECEMBER 19..

	H	S	Adjustments	Total		H	S	Adjustments	Total
	£	£	£	£		£	£	£	£
Share Capital	10,000	2,000	(a) − 1,500 (b) − 500	10,000	Sundry Assets	8,000	1,200	(h) + 200	9,400
Profit & Loss	4,000	1,200	(c) − 75 (d) − 300	4,825	Stock	6,100	2,400	(c) − 75	8,425
					Debtors	1,300	1,700		3,000
Reserve	1,000	600	(e) − 150 − 450	1,000	Bills Receivable	100		(g) − 100	
Creditors	2,000	1,200		3,200	Shares in S	1,500		(a) − 1,500	
Bills Payable		300	(g) − 100	200					
Minority Interest			(b) + 500 (d) + 300 (e) + 150 (h) + 50	1,000					
Capital Reserve			(f) + 450 (h) + 150	600					
	£17,000	£5,300	−£1,475	£20,825		£17,000	£5,300	−£1,475	£20,825

Notes. (1) The adjustments have been lettered to facilitate reference.

(2) Item (c) represents the elimination of H's proportion of the unrealized profit on the sale of goods, i.e. 75 per cent of 20 per cent of £500 [or 25 per cent of £400]. It will be noticed that the adjustment is made to H's share of S's profit, so that the £300 transferred to Minority Interest includes their £25 proportion.

(3) Minority Interest is 25 per cent of (Share Capital + Profit and Loss + Reserve + Under-valuation of Sundry Assets) = 25 per cent of £(2,000 + £1,200 + £600 + £200) = 25 per cent of £4,000. [See (b), (d), (e), and (h).]

(4) Capital Reserve is:

	£	£
Share Capital of S	2,000	
Reserve	600	
Under-valuation of Assets	200	
	£2,800	
		75% thereof = 2,100
Cost of Shares		1,500
Capital Reserve		£600

Illustration 30

H holds 6,000 shares and £3,200 Debentures of S, the dates of acquisition being 1st March 19.1, and 1st January 19.1 respectively. All the shares are of £0·50 each, fully paid. The cost price of the shares was £0·70 per share and the Debentures par.

The accounts relate to the first year of the company. There was an interim dividend declared by S of 10 per cent, followed by a final proposed dividend of 16 per cent, H proposing a dividend of 15 per cent.

The abridged final accounts of H and S were as follows:

BALANCE SHEET AS AT 31ST DECEMBER 19.1

	H	S		H	S
	£	£		£	£
Share Capital	10,000	5,000	Sundry Assets	9,163	11,961
Profit and Loss Account	2,423	561	Shares in S at cost	4,200	
Debentures (5%)		4,000	Debentures of S at cost	3,200	
Corporation Tax Provision	3,200	1,500	Dividend Receivable (from S)	480	
Debenture Interest accrued			Debenture Interest Receivable		
(gross)		100	(gross)	80	
Proposed Dividend	1,500	800			
	£17,123	£11,961		£17,123	£11,961

PROFIT AND LOSS ACCOUNT
FOR THE YEAR ENDED 31ST DECEMBER 19.1

	H	S		H	S
	£	£		£	£
Directors' Remuneration	8,000	4,500	Trading Profit	14,183	8,061
Debenture Interest (gross)		200	Debenture Interest (gross)	160	
Net Profit c/d	7,123	3,361	Dividends	780	
	£15,123	£8,061		£15,123	£8,061
Corporation Tax on profits			Net Profit b/d	7,123	3,361
for year	3,200	1,500			
Dividend paid		500			
Dividend proposed	1,500	800			
Balance to Balance Sheet	2,423	561			
	£7,123	£3,361		£7,123	£3,361

Prepare Consolidated Balance Sheet and Consolidated Profit and Loss Account. Ignore advance corporation and income taxes. (The word 'Ltd.' is omitted for reasons of space.)

CONSOLIDATED BALANCE SHEET OF H AND S AS AT 31ST DECEMBER 19.1

	Aggregate of H & S £	Adjustments Dr. £	Adjustments Cr. £	Total £
Share Capital	15,000	3,000 / 2,000		10,000
Profit and Loss Account	2,984	410		2,574
Debentures (5%)	4,000	3,200		800
Debenture Interest accrued (gross)	100	80		20
Proposed dividend	2,300	480 / 320		1,500
Corporation Tax Provision	4,700			4,700
Minority Interest—				
Share Capital of S			2,000	
Proposed Dividend of S			320	
Profit for Year of S ($\frac{1}{3}\times£561$)			224	2,544
	£29,084	£9,490	£2,544	£22,138
		2,544		
		£6,946		

	Aggregate of H & S £	Adjustments Dr. £	Adjustments Cr. £	Total £
Sundry Assets	21,124			21,124
Shares in S	4,200		3,000 / 186 / 1,014	
Debentures of S	3,200		3,200	
Dividend Receivable	480		480	
Debenture Interest Receivable	80		80	
Goodwill		1,014		1,014
	£29,084	£1,014	£7,960	£22,138
			1,014	
			£6,946	

Note. The proportion of profit accruing at 1st March, 19.1, is $\frac{1}{3}\times\frac{3}{4}\times£3,361$ less Corporation Tax £1,500 equals $\frac{1}{10}$ of £1,861.

CONSOLIDATED PROFIT AND LOSS ACCOUNT FOR THE YEAR ENDED 31ST DECEMBER 19.1

Debit side

	Aggregate of H & S £	Adjustments Dr. £	Adjustments Cr. £	Total £
Directors' Remuneration	12,500			12,500
Debenture Interest	200		160	40
Net Profit c/d	10,484		780	9,704
	£23,184		£940	£22,244
Corporation Tax on profits for Year	4,700		300	4,700
Dividend Paid	500		200	
Dividend Proposed	2,300		480	1,500
Pre-acquisition Profit accruing at date of acquisition of S Shares attributable to H.		186	320	186
Dividends Paid and Proposed to Minority Interest		200 320		520
Balance of Profit of S attributable to Minority Interest		224		224
Balance to Consolidated Balance Sheet	2,984		410	2,574
	£10,484	930	1,710	£9,704
		930		
			£780	

Credit side

	Aggregate of H & S £	Adjustments Dr. £	Adjustments Cr. £	Total £
Trading Profit	22,244			22,244
Debenture Interest	160	160		
Dividends	780	300 480		
	£23,184	£940		£22,244
Net Profit b/d	10,484	780		9,704
	£10,484	780	—	£9,704
		£780		

Illustration 31

The following are the abridged final accounts of H and S:

BALANCE SHEET AS AT 31ST DECEMBER 19.9

	H	S		H	S
	£	£		£	£
Share Capital—£1 f.p.	10,000	5,000	Sundry Assets	36,700	7,100
Revenue Reserve	5,000	3,500	Stock	4,000	4,500
Profit and Loss Account	5,000	4,000	Shares in S at cost	6,300	
Creditors	7,000	3,500	H Debentures at cost		6,400
Debentures 4%	20,000	1,000	Discount on Debentures	1,000	
Proposed Dividend	1,000	1,000			
	£48,000	£18,000		£48,000	£18,000

PROFIT AND LOSS ACCOUNT
FOR THE YEAR ENDED 31ST DECEMBER 19.9

	H	S		H	S
Directors' Remuneration	3,000	2,000	Trading Profit	8,000	9,260
Depreciation	1,000	1,500	Debenture Interest		280
Debenture Interest	800	40	Dividend received	800	
Net Profit c/d	4,000	6,000			
	£8,800	£9,540		£8,800	£9,540
Dividends paid	500	1,000	Balance from last year	2,500	1,500
Proposed Dividends	1,000	1,000	Net Profit b/d	4,000	6,000
Transfer to Reserve		1,500			
Balance to Balance Sheet	5,000	4,000			
	£6,500	£7,500		£6,500	£7,500

H holds 4,000 shares in S, bought when the credit balance on the Profit and Loss Account of S was £125 and Revenue Reserves were £2,000. On 1st January 19.9 H issued £20,000 debentures at a discount of 5 per cent and S was allotted (for cash) £2,000; on 1st March 19.9 S purchased £5,000 of the debentures of H for £4,500. H has sold goods to S for £500 (cost £450), all of which remains unsold.

Prepare Consolidated Balance Sheet and Consolidated Profit and Loss Account, assuming that all dividends to H are to be regarded as being paid out of current profit of S, ignoring taxation and accruing interest on the Debentures at the date of purchase by S, and assuming that the proposed dividend of S had *not* been brought into the books of H at 31st December 19.9. (See p. 2479.)

Consolidated Balance Sheet of H and S as at 31st December 19.9

Equity and Liabilities

	Aggregate of H & S	Adjustments Dr	Adjustments Cr	Total
	£	£	£	£
Share Capital £1 f.p.	15,000	(a) 4,000 (b) 1,000 (h) 1,600		10,000
Revenue Reserve	8,500	(j) 700 (i) 50 (**X**) **140**	(c) 250	6,200
Capital Reserve				200[3]
Profit and Loss Account	9,000	(e) 7,000		8,860[4]
Debentures (4%)	21,000			14,000
Creditors	10,500			10,500
Proposed Dividend	2,000	(s) 800 (o) 200	(b) 1,000 (f) 700 (i) 70 (o) 50 (**q**) **800**	1,000
Minority Interest				2,820[5]
	£66,000	15,490 · 3,070	3,070	£53,580
		£12,420	£12,420	

Assets

	Aggregate of H & S	Adjustments Dr	Adjustments Cr	Total
	£	£	£	£
Sundry Assets	43,800			43,800
Stock	8,500		(**k**) **40**	8,460
Shares in S at cost	6,300		(a) 4,000 (h) 1,600	
H Debentures at cost	6,400	(c) 250	(i) 100 (v) 600	
Discount on Debentures		(d) 350	(e) 7,000	
Dividend Receivable	1,000	(f) 70		720[2]
Goodwill		(a) 800 (v) 600	(d) 350 (s) 800	600[1]
	£66,000	£2,070	14,490	£53,580
			£12,420	

Note. Items in ordinary type are transfers within the Consolidated Balance Sheet; items in heavy type are transfers as between the Consolidated Balance Sheet and Consolidated Profit and Loss Account.

CONSOLIDATED PROFIT AND LOSS ACCOUNT OF H AND S FOR THE YEAR ENDED 31ST DECEMBER 19.9

Debit side

	Aggregate of H & S	Adjustments Dr.	Adjustments Cr.	Total
	£	£	£	£
Directors' Remuneration	5,000			5,000
Depreciation	2,500		(m) 280	2,500
Debenture Interest	840			560
Minority Interest		(q) 1,200	(T) 840 (z) 1,200	1,200
Net Profit applicable to members of H c/d	10,000		2,320 / 1,200	7,960
	£18,340	£1,200	£1,120	£17,220
Transfer to Reserve	1,500		(q) 300 (p) 800	1,200
Dividend paid	1,500		(s) 200 (q) 200 (X) 140	500
Proposed dividend	2,000			1,000
Balance to Balance Sheet	9,000			8,860
	£14,000	—	£2,440	£11,560

Credit side

	Aggregate of H & S	Adjustments Dr.	Adjustments Cr.	Total
	£	£	£	£
Trading Profit	17,260	(k) 40 (m) 280 (p) 800 (s) 800	(m) 800	17,220
Debenture Interest	280			
Dividend Received	800			
Dividend Receivable				
	£18,340	1,920 / 800	£800	£17,220
		£1,120		
Balance from last year	4,000	(t) 100 (q) 300		3,600
Net Profit b/d	10,000	(T) 840 (z) 1,200		7,960
	£14,000	£2,440	—	£11,560

Note. Items in italics are transfers within the Consolidated Profit and Loss Account.

See footnotes on p. 2481.

ALTERNATIVE METHODS OF PRESENTATION

Once the principles underlying preparation of consolidated accounts are fully understood, no difficulty should arise with the alternative methods allowed in Section 151 of the Companies Act 1948. It will be remembered that one of these is to present separate consolidated accounts for a particular group of subsidiaries.

Illustration 32

From the following Balance Sheets prepare Consolidated Balance Sheet of X and Y:

BALANCE SHEETS

	H	X	Y		H	X	Y
	£	£	£		£	£	£
Share Capital	55,000	20,000	10,000	Sundry Assets	26,000	36,000	22,000
Profit and Loss	5,000	12,000	10,000	Shares in—			
Debentures			5,000	X (15,000)	20,000		
Creditors—				Y (9,000)	10,000		
Sundry		1,000	1,000	X Loan	4,000		
Y		1,000		Debtors—			
H Loan		4,000		Sundry		2,000	3,000
				X			1,000
	£60,000	£38,000	£26,000		£60,000	£38,000	£26,000

CONSOLIDATED BALANCE SHEET OF X AND Y, SUBSIDIARIES OF H

	£	£		£
Interest of H—			Sundry Assets	58,000
Share Capital	24,000		Sundry Debtors	5,000
Profit and Loss	18,000			
Loan (X)	4,000			
		46,000		
Minority Interest				
Share Capital	6,000			
Profit and Loss	4,000			
		10,000		
Debentures		5,000		
Sundry Creditors		2,000		
		£63,000		£63,000

Notes to illustration on p. 2480.

[1] Goodwill is cost of shares £6,300 less Nominal Capital, £4,000, and proportion of Reserve and Profit and Loss Account at acquisition, £1,600 and £100 respectively.

[2] Discount on Debentures is 5 per cent of £13,000 Debentures of H held outside the Group, i.e. £650, plus the discount applicable to the minority shareholders' proportion of the Debentures held by S, i.e. one-fifth of 5 per cent of £7,000, i.e. £70.

[3] The profit on the £5,000 Debentures bought on 1st March is £500 less £250 dealt with as Discount on Debentures. Of the balance of £250, one-fifth is due to the minority interest.

[4] Profit and Loss Account is made up of H £5,000, plus four-fifths of S (£4,000 less pre-acquisition profits £125) and four-fifths of S's proposed dividend, less four-fifths of H's unrealized profit of £50.

[5] The minority interest is Share Capital £1,000, Reserve £700, Profit and Loss Account £800 (Profit of the year £1,200 plus balance brought forward £300, less included in Reserve £300 and dividends paid and proposed £400). Proposed Dividend £200, Discount on Debentures £70 (see [2] above) and Profit on Debentures £50 (see [3] above). In the Consolidated Profit and Loss Account, the minority interest has been charged in arriving at the net profit of the year applicable to the members of H, so that the position is shown so far as it concerns those members.

The allocation of Capital and Profit is:

						H	M.I.
Share Capital—X:	.	.	.	.	£20,000	£15,000	£5,000
Y:	.	.	.	.	10,000	9,000	1,000
						£24,000	£6,000
Profit and Loss—X:.	.	.	.	.	£12,000	£9,000	£3,000
Y:	.				10,000	9,000	1,000
						£18,000	£4,000

Illustration 33

From the following details, prepare consolidated accounts. The shares in S
were acquired by H on the 1st April prior to the date of the following
accounts:

BALANCE SHEETS AS AT 31ST MARCH 19. .

	H	S		H	S
	£	£		£	£
Share Capital: £1 fully paid	5,000	1,600	Sundry Assets	9,684	4,420
Profit and Loss Account	1,846	1,220	Shares in S: 1,200 at Cost	1,850	
Creditors	3,254	512	Dividend Receivable from S	120	
Provision for Corporation Tax	1,554	928			
Proposed Dividend		160			
	£11,654	£4,420		£11,654	£4,420

PROFIT AND LOSS AND APPROPRIATION ACCOUNTS
FOR THE YEAR ENDED 31ST MARCH 19. .

	H	S		H	S
	£	£		£	£
Expenses	2,300	1,920	Trading Profit	4,580	3,428
Profit c/d	2,400	1,508	Dividend from S	120	
	£4,700	£3,428		£4,700	£3,428
Corporation Tax on Current Profits	1,554	928	Balance from previous year	1,000	800
Proposed Dividend		160	Profit for Year b/d	2,400	1,508
Balance	1,846	1,220			
	£3,400	£2,308		£3,400	£2,308

The accounts are shown on p. 2484.

Illustration 34

From the following figures, prepare a Consolidated Profit and Loss Account of a Holding Company for the year 19.9.

	Holding Company	Subsidiaries			Associated Company D
		A	B	C	
	£	£	£	£	£
Trading Profit, 19.9	120,000	18,000	10,200	4,500	92,000
Investment Income	10,000				22,000
Profit on Sale of Buildings				1,000	
Dividends received (on 19.8 account)—					
From A	2,000				
„ B	1,500				
Profits brought forward, 1st January 19.9	15,000	20,000	2,500	200	22,500
	£148,500	£38,000	£12,700	£5,700	£136,500
Depreciation	9,000	1,000	800	800	12,000
Directors' Fees	18,000		2,000	2,000	10,000
Loss on Sale of Investments	15,500				
Debenture Interest	8,500		2,500		3,000
Dividends—					
Ordinary (on 19.8 account)	20,000	4,000	1,500		
Preference (Interim, 19.9)	7,500			2,000	4,000
Corporation Tax on Current Profits	52,000	11,000	3,900	650	77,000
Balances	18,000	22,000	2,000	250	30,500
	£148,500	£38,000	£12,700	£5,700	£136,500
Share Capital Issued—					
Ordinary: Total	300,000	80,000	40,000	15,000	100,000
Holding Company shareholding		40,000	40,000	10,000	40,000
Preference (held outside Group)	200,000			80,000	150,000

CONSOLIDATED BALANCE SHEET OF H AND ITS SUBSIDIARIES

	H	S	Adjustment	Total
	£	£	£	£
Share Capital	5,000	1,600	(a) −1,200 (b) − 400 (x) − 905	5,000
Profit and Loss Account	1,846	1,220		2,161
Creditors	3,254	512		3,766
Corporation Tax	1,554	928	(a) − 120	2,482
Proposed Dividend		160	(d) − 40	
Minority Interest—				
Share Capital			(b) + 400	
Dividend			(d) + 40	
Profit and Loss Account			(i) + 305	745[1]
	£11,654	£4,420	−£1,920	£14,154

	H	S	Adjustment	Total
	£	£	£	£
Sundry Assets	9,684	4,420		14,104
Shares in S	1,850		(a) −1,200 (e) − 650	
Dividend	120		(c) − 120	
Goodwill			(e) + 650 (f) − 600	50
	£11,654	£4,420	−£1,920	£14,154

[1] The equity of minority shareholders is:

		£			or	£
Share Capital of S		1,600			Share Capital of S	1,600
P. and L. Balance of S.		800			Profit and Loss of S	1,220
Profit for Year	1,508					£2,820
Less Taxation	928				¼ thereof	705
		580			Dividend ¼ × £160	40
		£2,980				£745
¼ thereof		£745				

CONSOLIDATED PROFIT AND LOSS AND APPROPRIATION ACCOUNT

	H	S	Adjustments	Total		H	S	Adjustments	Total
	£	£	£	£		£	£	£	£
Expenses	2,300	1,920	(g) − 120	4,220	Trading Profit	4,580	3,428		8,008
Profit	2,400	1,508		3,788	Dividend	120		(h) 120	
	£4,700	£3,428	−£120	£8,008		£4,700	£3,428	−£120	£8,008
Corporation Tax on current profits	1,554	928	(h) + 120	2,482	Balance from previous Year	1,000	800	(f) − 600	1,200
Dividends—		160		40	Profit for Year	2,400	1,508	(g) − 120	3,788
Balance— H	1,846	1,220	(f) − 600 } (x)	2,161					
			(i) − 305						
			(i) + 305						
M.I.				305					
	£3,400	£2,308	−£720	£4,988		£3,400	£2,308	−£720	£4,988

CONSOLIDATED PROFIT AND LOSS ACCOUNT OF HOLDING COMPANY AND ITS SUBSIDIARIES FOR THE YEAR 19.9

	£	£		£	£
Depreciation		11,600	Trading Profit		152,700
Directors' Fees		22,000	Investment Income		10,000
Loss on Sale of Investments		15,500	Profit on Sale of Buildings		1,000
Debenture Interest		11,000			
Corporation Tax on Current Profits		67,550			
Combined Net Profit for Year c/d		36,050			
		£163,700			£163,700

	£	£		£	£
			Net Profit b/d		36,050
Dividends for 19.9 payable by Holding Company—			*Less* Outside Shareholders—		
Preference:			Int. 19.9 Pref. Div. C paid	2,000	
Interim paid	7,500		Undistributed Profit for Year	3,050[1]	
Final not yet paid	7,500	15,000			5,050
Proposed Ordinary		?			31,000
Balance of Undistributed Profits—			Balance from 19.8	37,700	
Holding Company	10,500[4]		*Less* 19.8 Ordinary Dividends paid to outside Shareholders—		
Interest of Holding Company in Subsidiaries	13,000[3]		A £2,000		
		23,500	Holding Co. 20,000		
				22,000	
					15,700
			Less Minority Interest in undistributed Balance £10,200		
			Less Dividend paid by A 2,000		
				8,200[2]	
					7,500
		£38,500			£38,500

Notes.

(1) The allocation of undistributed profit is—

	A	£	B	C	Minority Shareholders	Holding Company
			£	£		
Balance per Accounts	22,000		2,000	250		
Less brought forward		£20,000	2,500	200	*Minority Shareholders*	*Holding Company*
„ Ord. Div., 19.8		4,000	1,500			
		16,000	1,000		£	£
	6,000		1,000	50		
Minority Shareholders	3,000		—	50 =	3,050[1]	
Holding Company	£3,000		£1,000	— =		4,000
Balances forward as above	16,000		1,000	200		
Minority Shareholders	8,000		—	200 =	8,200[2]	
Holding Company	£8,000		£1,000	— =		9,000
					£11,250	£13,000[3]
						£24,250[5]

The total profit balances (per accounts) are—

		£	
H.		18,000	
	Less Pref. Div. unpaid	7,500	£10,500[4]
A.		22,000	
B.		2,000	
C.		250	
			£24,250[5]

(2) In Company C there are insufficient profits to cover the final Preference Dividend, so that in the meantime the balance forward must be regarded as belonging to outside shareholders (i.e. the preference shareholders of C.) Actually at the end of 19.8 the Holding Company has a two-thirds interest in the £200 balance of C, but it loses this interest in 19.9 in favour of the preference shareholders. Whether the full outstanding dividend should be provided for in the accounts of C, resulting in a debit balance on its Profit and Loss Account, is a moot point.

(3) Associated Company—see p. 2493.

Holding Company's Profit and Loss Account framed as a Consolidated Profit and Loss Account. By Sect. 149, Companies Act 1948 (see pp. 2331 and 2411, a Holding Company is empowered to issue its own Profit and Loss Account framed as a Consolidated Profit and Loss Account. In order to comply with Subsect. 5 (b) (ii), the Holding company must deduct from the Consolidated Profit and Loss Account such amount thereof attributed to it as is retained by a subsidiary and carried forward in its accounts, i.e. not distributed.

This deduction will bring the profit for the relevant year to the *same* as that revealed by its own Profit and Loss Account.

The adjustment merely affects the particular year being *currently* dealt with, so that the amount of the profit of the **Holding** Company forward from a previous year, its proposed dividend, allocations and balance forward will be dealt with in the ordinary way and carried to the Balance Sheet of the Holding Company and not Consolidated Account.

Although in the case of large groups complications will inevitably arise, nevertheless the basic principle is simple.

1. The Consolidated Profit and Loss Account must first be prepared in the ordinary way and the balance forward will appear in the Consolidated Balance Sheet.

2. Instead of this Consolidated Profit and Loss, the Holding Company presents what is in effect its own Profit and Loss Account (which will have been prepared in conjunction with its *own* Balance Sheet) in another form.

3. The Consolidated Profit and Loss Account is taken as the primary basis, but will require amending because it includes (subject to the Minority Interest) the total profit of **all** the companies of the Group. In the absence of special factors, from such combined profit is deducted the subsidiaries' *undistributed* profits of the current period attributed to the Holding Company, to bring such combined total down to that of the Holding Company; if, however, the Holding Company has received dividends from the subsidiaries and taken them into account as income, then the *excess* of the profit of the subsidiaries attributable to the Holding Company over the dividends paid to it will represent the appropriate profit *retained*, and this sum falls to be deducted from the Consolidated Profit and Loss Account. (It will be remembered that a dividend paid by a subsidiary to the Holding Company will be eliminated in the Group Consolidated Profit and Loss Account, i.e. the dividend receivable is a *contra* to the dividend paid after charging up Minority Interest, if any, with the amount appropriate thereto.)

4. The consolidated statement will be completed by the addition to the current profit of the Parent Company its own carry forward *less* dividends paid (and proposed) thereout.

Illustration 35

H. Ltd., owns 60 per cent of the share capital of S, Ltd., the shares being acquired on 1st January, and the Profit and Loss Accounts for the first year to 31st December are:

	£			£
H, Ltd. Trading profit	3,000	S, Ltd. Trading profit	. .	2,800
Dividend from S, Ltd. .	600	Dividend payable	. .	1,000
Forward	£3,600			£1,800

The Profit and Loss Account of H, Ltd., framed as a Consolidated Profit and Loss Account for the year ended 31st December will be:

	£
Consolidated Profit (£3,000 + £2,800)	5,800
Less Profit of S, Ltd., attributable to Minority Shareholders—40 per cent of £2,800	1,120
(Consolidated Profit attributable to H, Ltd.)	4,680
Less Profit attributable to H, Ltd., undistributed (retained) by S, Ltd.—60 per cent of £1,800	1,080
Balance—Profit of H, Ltd., for the year [agreeing with the balance of the Profit and Loss Account of H, Ltd.]	£3,600

The Consolidated Profit and Loss Account would normally be:

	£
Consolidated Profit	4,680
Minority Shareholders—£1,120, less Dividend £400	720
Accounting for the items £3,600 and £1,800 [To Consolidated Balance Sheet]	£5,400

It should be emphasized that the adjustment made involves no double entry. Instead of publishing the two sets of accounts relating to H, Ltd., **and** the group, that is, the Profit and Loss Account of H, Ltd., in its **ordinary** form, and the Consolidated Profit and Loss Account, the latter is not presented to the shareholder, but only the former, in a **different** form from the normal, as a Consolidated Statement. This is done by first using the Consolidated Profit and Loss Account, and secondly, by deducting therefrom such profits of the subsidiary as are attributable to H, Ltd., and not yet distributed, that is, the profit retained by the subsidiary company.

The following gives figures as appropriate to the situation:

	S, Ltd. £	H, Ltd. £	M. I. £
Profit	2,800	1,680 (60%)	1,120 (40%)
Dividend	1,000	600 (60%)	400 (40%)
Balance undistributed . .	£1,800	£1,080	£720

Illustration 36

The following are the Profit and Loss Accounts of H, Ltd., and its subsidiaries A, Ltd., and B, Ltd., for the year ended 31st December. H, Ltd., own 60 per cent and 80 per cent of the share capital of A, Ltd., and B, Ltd., respectively, the acquisitions having been made several years ago.

PROFIT AND LOSS ACCOUNTS FOR THE YEAR ENDED 31ST DECEMBER

	H, Ltd. £	A, Ltd. £	B, Ltd. £			H, Ltd. £	A, Ltd. £	B, Ltd. £
Directors' Fees .	8,000	3,000	2,000	Trading Profits .		38,000	19,000	22,000
Depreciation .	4,000	2,000	1,000	Dividends				
Corporation Tax .	12,000	7,000	9,000	General . £2,000				1,000
Profit for year (c/d)	22,400	7,000	11,000	A. Ltd. . 2,400				
				B, Ltd. . 4,000		8,400		
	£46,400	£19,000	£23,000			£46,400	£19,000	£23,000
Dividends .	16,000	4,000	5,000	Profit for year (b/d)		22,400	7,000	11,000
Reserve . .	5,000	1,500	2,000	Balance forward				
Balance . .	4,800	3,500	7,750	(from previous year) .		3,400	2,000	3,750
	£25,800	£9,000	£14,750			£25,800	£9,000	£14,750

Apart from dividends paid out of current profits and brought into the books of H, Ltd., there are no inter-company adjustments. Prepare the Consolidated Profit and Loss Account of H, Ltd., framed as a Consolidated Profit and Loss Account.

CONSOLIDATED PROFIT AND LOSS ACCOUNT FOR THE YEAR ENDED 31ST DECEMBER

	£	£
Trading Profit for the year		79,000
Gross Income from General Investments . .		3,000
		82,000
Less Directors' Fees	13,000	
Depreciation	7,000	
		20,000
Profit for the year before Corporation Tax . .		62,000
Less Corporation Tax on current profits . .		28,000
Profit for the year after Corporation Tax .		34,000
Less Proportion of profit attributable to Minority Shareholders		5,000
Profit of Group for the year . . .		29,000
Less undistributed Profit of Subsidiaries applicable to Group (See (i))		6,600
Profit for year of H, Ltd., per Profit and Loss Account of H, Ltd.		22,400
Add Balance brought forward . . .		3,400
		25,800

Less Appropriations—
Reserve 5,000
Dividend 16,000
                                              ─────── 21,000

Balance carried forward . . . . . £4,800[1]

(i) STATEMENT OF PROFIT

	A, Ltd. £		B, Ltd. £
Profit for the year after Corporation Tax	7,000		11,000
Less Dividends	4,000		5,000
Balances not distributed (i.e. retained)	£3,000		£6,000
Attributable to H, Ltd. 60 per cent	£1,800	80 per cent	£4,800
	(See (iii))		(See (iii))

£6,600

SHAREHOLDERS

	A, Ltd. £		B, Ltd. £
Proportion of Profit 40% of £7,000	2,800	20% of £11,000	2,200
Less Dividend	1,600		1,000
	£1,200		£1,200
	(See (iii))		(See (iii))

(iii) STATEMENT OF PROFIT

	A, Ltd. £	Attributable to— H, Ltd. (60%) £	Minority (40%) £
Profit	7,000	4,200	2,800
Dividend	4,000	2,400	1,600
Undistributed (a)	£3,000	£1,800	£1,200
		(See (i))	(See (ii))

	B, Ltd. £	H, Ltd. (80%) £	Minority (20%) £
Profit	11,000	8,800	2,200
Dividend	5,000	4,000	1,000
Undistributed (b)	£6,000	£4,800	£1,200
		(See (i))	(See (ii))
Totals (a) + (b)	£9,000	£6,600	£2,400

───

[1] This amount will appear in the Balance Sheet of H, Ltd.

The Consolidated Balance Sheet will contain the profit, as shown in the Consolidated Statement, of £29,000, plus the proportion of the profit of A, Ltd., and B, Ltd., brought forward attributable to H, Ltd., and the Minority Shareholders respectively, the Consolidated Statement showing the Profit and Loss position of **H, Ltd.,** only (in the form set out therein), and the balance forward so shown will appear in the Balance Sheet of **H, Ltd.**

For the purpose of arithmetical check, a form of reconcilation may be prepared thus:

Balances of Profit and Loss Accounts at end:

	£	£
£4,800 + £3,500 + £7,750		16,050
Add Transfers to Reserve, A, Ltd., and B, Ltd. (£1,500 + £2,000)		3,500
		19,550
Less Undistributed Profits		
H, Ltd. :	6,600	
Minority Shareholders (£1,200 + £1,200)	2,400	
Balance of Profit and Loss Accounts of A, Ltd., and B, Ltd., forward from previous year (£2,000 + £3,750)	5,750	
		14,750
Balance per Consolidated Statement		£4,800

Note. In presenting the accounts as above (Sect. 149 (5), Companies Act 1948), the omission of details of Directors' Emoluments, Pensions, etc., and (in Consolidated Balance Sheet) Loans to Directors as required by Sects. 196 and 197 Companies Act 1948, and Sects. 6, 7 and 8 Companies Act 1967 (Para 19, Schedule 2 to Companies Act, 1967) is not permissible; and the Profit and Loss Account must show how much of the consolidated profit is dealt with in the accounts of the Holding Company. (See p. 2346.)

Plurality of Acquisitions by Parent Company. Where a Parent Company makes several purchases of shares of a subsidiary during a year regard must be had to the date of each purchase, so as to ascertain the portion of the year's profit or loss accruing at such date.

As with most problems relating to Group Accounts, there exist alternative methods of procedure. The simplest procedure is:

1. At the end of the accounting period the proportion of the minority interests will be known and therefore this will be deducted from the Subsidiary Company's profit after Corporation Tax (and after the usual appropriations, e.g. transfers to Reserve and Preference Dividends (if any)).

2. The balance remaining is the Parent Company's profit, but it is not 'free', as there is proportion that was accruing at the date of each acquisition (i.e. pre-acquisition profit) which must be used against the Cost of the Shares (or its equivalent, as several methods are adopted to arrive at the same final result).

In ascertaining the pre-acquisition profit attributable to the Parent, each purchase should be taken independently, as if it were the *sole* purchase, and calculation made of the accruing profit based on that individual purchase. In order to prove the resultant 'free' (i.e. post-acquisition) profit, a total column is desirable showing the profit attributable to each (separate) holding, to subdivide this figure into 'before' and 'after' according to each date of purchase.

Illustration 37

The share capital of Y, Ltd., consists of 10,000 shares of £1 each fully paid. X, Ltd., acquired that company's shares as below:

19.9						
Jan. 1	.	.	.	.	.	2,000
Apr. 1	.	.	.	.	.	1,000
May 1	.	.	.	.	.	1,500
Sept. 1	.	.	.	.	.	500
Dec. 1	.	.	.	.	.	2,500
						7,500

The profit of Y, Ltd., for the year ended 31st December 19.9 is £2,400. Show the profit attributable to Y, Ltd., as to: (a) pre-acquisition and (b) post-acquisition.

	£
Profit of Y, Ltd.	2,400
Less Minority Interests 25 per cent . . .	600
Profit of Y, Ltd., attributable to X, Ltd. . . .	£1,800

SCHEDULE OF PROFIT ATTRIBUTABLE TO X, LTD., AND ITS ALLOCATION

19.9	Shares acquired	Fraction	Attributable Profit	Months accruing at date of Purchase	Pre-acquisition Profit	Months since Date of Purchase	Post-acquisition Profit
			£		£		£
Jan. 1	2,000	$\frac{1}{5}$	480	0	—	12	480
Apr. 1 . . .	1,000	$\frac{1}{10}$	240	3	60	9	180
May 1 . . .	1,500	$\frac{3}{20}$	360	4	120	8	240
Sept. 1 . .	500	$\frac{1}{20}$	120	8	80	4	40
Dec. 1	2,500	$\frac{1}{4}$	600	11	550	1	50
	7,500	$=\frac{3}{4}$	1,800	[(a)+(b)]	(a) £810		(b) £990
Minority Interests . .	2,500	$\frac{1}{4}$	600				
	10,000		£2,400				

Therefore, in preparing the group accounts, the credit of £2,400 will be *disposed of* as follows:

	£
(1) Credit to Cost of Shares (or Capital Reserve) . .	810
(2) Credit to Minority Interests . . .	600
(3) Balance unappropriated forward	990
	£2,400

Although X, Ltd., did not become a Holding Company in relation to Y, Ltd. (in absence of special circumstances, e.g. ability to control Y, Ltd., otherwise than through its shareholding) till 1st December, 19.9, it is clearly so at 31st December 19.9.

Alternative calculation:

X, Ltd.

	Profit (for each sub-period) £	Shares acquired	Pre-acquisition £	Post-acquisition £	Minority Interests	Minority Interests £	Minority Shares
Apr. 1	600	2,000		$\frac{2}{10}$ 120	$\frac{8}{10}$	480	8,000
		+1,000	60		$-\frac{1}{8}\times480$	60	−1,000
		3,000				420	7,000
May 1	200			$\frac{3}{10}$ 60	$\frac{7}{10}$		
						560	
		+1,500	120		$-\frac{15}{70}\times560$	120	−1,500
		4,500				440	5,500
Sept. 1	800			$\frac{45}{100}$ 360	$\frac{55}{100}$	440	
						880	
		+ 500	80		$-\frac{5}{55}\times880$	80	− 500
		5,000				800	5,000
Dec. 1	600			$\frac{50}{100}$ 300	$\frac{50}{100}$	300	
						1,100	
		2,500	550		$-\frac{25}{50}\times1,100$	550	−2,500
		7,500				550	2,500
Dec. 31	200	—		$\frac{75}{100}$ 150	$\frac{25}{100}$	50	—
	£2,400	7,500	£810	£990		£600	2,500

Note. The figures shown in italics are the releases of the share of the accumulated profit attributable to the Minority Interests on the acquisition of the appropriate shares therefrom, e.g. immediately prior to 1st September, 19.9, the Minority Interests were 5,500 [10,000 = 4,500 already acquired by X, Ltd.]; on the latter date 500 shares are sold to X, Ltd., there is a release to X, Ltd., of $\frac{500}{5,500} = \frac{5}{55} \times £880$.

Associated Company.[1] Although the term is often employed to indicate a subsidiary, it is more commonly meant to indicate:

1. A company associated with another through mutual shareholdings insufficient to make either a holding company or a subsidiary.

2. A company which has close trade associations with another.

3. A company in which another company has a substantial holding of shares without constituting legal control.

4. A company which is controlled by substantially the same individuals controlling another, e.g. A and B are the sole shareholders in both C, Ltd., and D, Ltd. These companies are associated companies.

---

[1] See p. 24103 for SSAP 1/1 Accounting for Associated Companies.

PUBLISHED CONSOLIDATED ACCOUNTS

In examination work there will be no time usually to rewrite the consolidated accounts which have been prepared in draft form in one of the ways
outlined in this chapter; in practice, of course, this will be done and from
the fair copy the accounts will be prepared for publication. It will be
remembered that the latter must comply in most respects with the
requirements of the Companies Acts 1948 to 1976 as if they were the
accounts of an actual company.

The following additional points should be noted:

1. Whenever on consolidation a difficulty is encountered in the treatment
of an item, it should be remembered that the primary object is to show a
true and fair view of the state of affairs of the Group from the viewpoint
of the members of the Parent company.

2. Although the Acts require the consolidated accounts to show the
contents of the individual companies' accounts, the Directors are authorized to make such adjustments as they consider necessary. Thus, a
pre-acquisition revenue reserve of a subsidiary becomes, and should be
shown as, a capital reserve or as a deduction from Goodwill.

3. As shown in pp. 2426, 2462 and 2474, adjustments may be required
for assets or liabilities the book values of which differ considerably from
their portion of the purchase price. When such adjustments are not made
in the books of the subsidiary, it may be necessary on consolidation, in the
case of fixed assets, to make a provision for depreciation different from
that made in the subsidiary's accounts. It will facilitate matters if the
books of the subsidiary are adjusted to correspond with the depreciation
charge in the consolidated accounts.

4. Apart from the adjustments mentioned in (3), fixed assets are usually
consolidated at cost to the various subsidiary companies, less aggregate
depreciation since date of acquisition by each of those companies. Some
accountants, however, prefer to take the net book amount valuation (i.e.
cost less depreciation) at the date of acquisition, plus subsequent additions
at cost, less accumulated depreciation since acquisition.

5. When any change is made by a subsidiary in its reserves (e.g. by
capitalization in bonus shares) this can have no effect on the consolidated
assets and liabilities,[1] but is merely a matter for adjustment in the group
reserves.

Where, as is permitted by Section 151 (3) of the Companies Act 1948,
the group accounts are incorporated in the holding company's own
Balance Sheet and Profit and Loss Account, the latter account will be
similar to that already outlined in the previous chapter except that (1)
each item will be subdivided into (a) Holding Company and (b) Subsidiaries, the total being extended into a final column; (2) the balance of
the account will be split between (a) minority shareholders of subsidiaries,

[1] But see p. 2462.

(b) Holding Company's profit, and (c) Holding Company's proportion of subsidiaries' profits.

In all cases, except for the first accounts laid before the company after the coming into force of the Companies Act 1948, the corresponding figures for the previous year's accounts (including Balance Sheet) must be shown against each item.

For the auditor's report on group accounts, see Section. 14 (3) of the Companies Act 1967, an extract of which is reproduced on p. 2414.

Illustration 38

The Profit and Loss Accounts for the year ending 31st March 19.9 and Balance Sheets at the date of H, Ltd.,[1] and its subsidiaries, S, Ltd., and T, Ltd., are:

PROFIT AND LOSS ACCOUNTS

	H, Ltd.	S, Ltd.	T. Ltd.		H, Ltd.	S, Ltd.	T, Ltd.
	£	£	£		£	£	£
Debenture Interest		400	320	Trading Profits	21,330	10,810	8,594
Directors' Fees	4,000	1,000	1,000	Dividends on Investments	1,000	1,000	820
Corporation Tax on current profits	11,520	4,370	3,825	Interest on Debentures in S, Ltd.	240		
Advance Corporation Tax on Franked Income	330	330	270	Dividends— S, Ltd.	2,400		
Net Profit, after Corporation Tax (c/d)	9,970	5,710	3,999	T, Ltd.: Preference	400		
				Ordinary	450		
	£25,820	£11,810	£9,414		£25,820	£11,810	£9,414
Dividends—				Balance (b/d)	9,970	5,710	3,999
Preference Dividend;				Balance forward, 1st			
Paid			300	April, 19.8	5,930	4,500	2,756
Proposed			300				
Ordinary Dividend:							
Proposed	10,000	3,000	500				
Balance	5,900	7,210	5,655				
	£15,900	£10,210	£6,755		£15,900	£10,210	£6,755

[1] Group relief in respect of Advance Corporation Tax on inter-group dividends has been granted.

BALANCE SHEETS

	H, Ltd.	S, Ltd.	T, Ltd.		H, Ltd.	S, Ltd.	T, Ltd.
	£	£	£		£	£	£
SHARE CAPITAL (£1 each, fully paid)				FIXED ASSETS AT COST			
5% Preference			12,000	Land and Buildings	11,000	22,000	12,000
Ordinary	100,000	30,000	10,000	Plant and Other	33,000	13,000	4,000
				SUBSIDIARY COMPANIES			
				24,000 shares in S, Ltd., at cost	31,000		
				£6,000 4% Debentures in S, Ltd.	6,000		
REVENUE RESERVES							
General	10,000	6,000	4,500	8,000 5% Preference Shares in T, Ltd.	8,000		
Profit and Loss	5,900	7,210	5,655	9,000 Ordinary Shares in T, Ltd.	11,000		
				CURRENT ASSETS			
				Cash at Bank	15,522	9,700	15,951
				Debtors	17,300	11,100	6,000
				Bills Receivable	1,000	900	
LONG TERM LIABILITY				Investments (quoted)	11,000	9,000	8,000
4% Debentures (Secured)		10,000	8,000	Stock	6,000	5,000	4,000
				Dividends Receivable			
				S, Ltd.	2,400		
				T, Ltd.— Preference	200		
CURRENT LIABILITIES				Ordinary	450		
Creditors	10,527	8,938	3,998				
Bills Payable	1,000		1,000				
Corporation Tax	11,520	4,370	3,825	DEFERRED ASSET			
ADVANCE CORPORATION TAX	4,925	1,182	222	Recoverable Advance Corporation Tax			49
Proposed Dividends							
Preference			300				
Ordinary	10,000	3,000	500				
	£153,872	£70,700	£50,000		£153,872	£70,700	£50,000

In the Balance sheet of S, Ltd., is a Note as follows:

Contingent Liability for Bills Discounted, £1,200.

The shares of S, Ltd., were acquired on 1st April 19.7, when the Profit and Loss Account was £4,500 (credit) and the General Reserve £6,000.

The shares in T, Ltd., were acquired on 1st January 19.5, when the Profit and Loss Account was £2,500 and the General Reserve £3,000.

Included in Debtors and Creditors are inter-company items: S, Ltd., owes T, Ltd., £800 and H, Ltd., owes S, Ltd., £300. H, Ltd., bought goods from S, Ltd., for £6,000 (cost to S, Ltd., £4,500) of which H, Ltd., has sold some for £5,500 at a profit on the cost to H, Ltd., of 10 per cent. Proposed dividends: H, Ltd., 10 per cent; S. Ltd., 10 per cent; T, Ltd. Preference (half-year) and Ordinary 5 per cent; H, Ltd., has two bills payable to S, Ltd., £800 and £200, the former having been discounted by S, Ltd. In addition, S, Ltd., has bills receivable in the ordinary course of business for £1,100, of which £400 have been discounted. T, Ltd., has one bill payable of £1,000 outstanding, being an acceptance to H, Ltd.

Prepare Consolidated Profit and Loss Account for the year ended 31st March 19.9, and Balance Sheet at that date, and show consolidating Journal entries.

CONSOLIDATED PROFIT AND LOSS ACCOUNT OF H, LTD., AND ITS SUBSIDIARIES FOR THE YEAR ENDED 31ST MARCH 19.9

[*Note.* For the benefit of readers who prefer to prepare the draft consolidated accounts by making the adjustments in columnar form, in addition to the formal schedules, such adjustments are shown in the consolidated accounts in columnar form.]

	£	
Trading Profit for the year.		40,734
Less Elimination of inter-company unrealized profit		200
		40,534
Dividend on Investments		2,820
		43,354
Less Debenture Interest	£480	
Directors' Fees	6,000	
		6,480
Net Profit of Group for year before Corporation Tax		36,874
Less Corporation Tax on current profits	£19,715	
Tax on Franked Investment Income	930	
		20,645
Net Profit of Group for year after Corporation Tax		16,229
Less Preference Dividends of T, Ltd., payable to Minority Shareholders		200
Net Profit of Group for year after Corporation Tax and outside Preference Shareholders' Dividend		16,029
Less proportion thereof attributable to Minority Shareholders		1,482
Net Surplus of Group, attributable to H, Ltd., for year		14,547
Add Balance of Profit and Loss attributable to Group brought forward		6,160
		20,707
Less proposed Ordinary Dividend for year		10,000
Balance, per Consolidated Balance Sheet		10,707

CALCULATION OF MINORITY SHAREHOLDERS' (ORDINARY) PROPORTION OF THE PROFIT FOR THE YEAR

	S, Ltd		T, Ltd.		
	£	£	£	£	£
Trading Profit		10,810		8,594	
Dividend on Investments		1,000		820	
		11,810		9,414	
Less Debenture Interest	400		320		
Directors' Fees	1,000		1,000		
Corporation Tax	4,370		3,825		
Tax on Franked Investment Income	330		270		
Preference Dividend	6,100		600		
		6,100			6,015
		£5,710			£3,399
$\frac{6}{30}$ thereof		£1,142	$\frac{10}{16}$ thereof		£340

CARRY FORWARD AT 1ST APRIL 19.8

			£
S, Ltd. (Balance at date of acquisition of Shares by H, Ltd.)	$\frac{24}{30} \times £4,500$	£3,600	4,500
Less pre-acquisition profit to H, Ltd.	$\frac{6}{30} \times £4,500$	900	
Minority Shareholders			4,500

per Profit and Loss account of S, Ltd.

		£
T, Ltd. (Balance at date of acquisition of Shares by H, Ltd.)		2,500
Add subsequent profit (less dividends paid)		256
		2,756

per Profit and Loss account of T, Ltd.

Less Pre-acquisition profit to H, Ltd.	$\frac{9}{10} \times 2,500$	£2,250	
Post-acquisition profit to H, Ltd.	$\frac{9}{10} \times £256$	230	
Minority Shareholders	$\frac{1}{10} \times £2,756$	276	
		£2,756	

CONSOLIDATED PROFIT AND LOSS ACCOUNT FOR THE YEAR ENDED 31ST MARCH 19.9 (Alternative Method)

Debit side

	Aggregate £	Consolidation Adjustments Dr £	Consolidation Adjustments Cr £	£
Debenture Interest (Gross)	720		(a) 240	480
Directors' Fees	6,000			6,000
Corporation Tax on current profits	19,715			19,715
Tax on Franked Investment Income	930			930
Dividends				
Preference paid	300		(c) 200	100
Preference proposed	300		(c) 200	100
Ordinary proposed	13,500		(c) 2,850 (j) 600 (k) 50	10,000
Minority Shareholders, Ordinary		(h) 1,482	(b) 8,058	1,482
Balance forward	18,765	1,482 / 10,716 Contra	12,198	10,707
	£60,230	£12,198	£12,198	£49,514

Credit side

	Aggregate £	Consolidation Adjustments Dr £	Consolidation Adjustments Cr £	£
Trading Profits	40,734	(g) 200		40,534
Dividends on Investments	2,820			2,820
Debenture Interest (Gross)	240	(a) 240		
Inter-company Dividends	3,250	(c) 3,250		
Balance forward 1st April 19.8	13,186	(d) 3,600 (e) 2,250 (f) 276 (i) 900		6,160
		10,716	10,716 Contra	
	£60,230	£10,716	£10,716	£49,514

Note. The Consolidated Adjustments are shown in the above Consolidated Accounts by way of **alternative** construction and in constructing such Consolidated Accounts they may be ignored. They are introduced for the purpose of guidance for students who prefer this alternative method.

Consolidated Balance Sheet at 31st March 19.9

Liabilities / Capital

	Aggregate £	Consolidating Adjustments Dr £	Consolidating Adjustments Cr £	Consolidated Total £
Issued Share Capital—				
5% Preference	12,000	(t) 4,000 ; (o) 8,000		
Ordinary	140,000	(o) 24,000 ; (z) 9,000 ; (z) 7,000		100,000
Revenue reserves	20,500	(d) 4,800 ; (e) 2,700 ; (x) 11,200 ; (y) 450		11,350
Capital Reserve			(q) 4,350	4,350
Profit and Loss Account	18,765	(b) 8,058		10,707
4% Debentures (secured)	18,000	(o) 6,000		12,000
Current Liabilities				
Creditors	23,463	(r) 1,100		22,363
Bills Payable	2,000	(s) 1,200		800
Corporation Tax	19,715			19,715
Advance Corporation Tax	6,329			6,329
Proposed Dividends	13,800	(j) 600 ; (k) 50 ; (t) 3,050 ; (u) 100	(v) 4,000 ; (u) 100 ; (z) 7,000 ; (f) 276 ; (h) 1,482 ; (i) 1,900 ; (x) 1,200 ; (y) 450	10,000
Minority Shareholders				
Preference				Contra
Ordinary				11,308
			19,758	
		£81,308	61,550	
	£274,572	£81,308	£81,308	£213,022

Assets

	Aggregate £	Consolidating Adjustments Dr £	Consolidating Adjustments Cr £	Consolidated Total £
Fixed Assets				
Land and Buildings at Cost	45,000			45,000
Plant and other Fixed Assets	50,000			50,000
Subsidiary Companies	56,000	(m) 56,000	(m) 56,000 ; (d) 8,400	—
Cost of Shares (e) £2,700 (e) £2,250		(q) 4,350	(e) 4,950 ; (o) 47,000	
Current Assets				
Cash at Bank	41,173			41,173
Debtors	34,400		(r) 1,100	33,300
Bills Receivable	1,900		(s) 1,200	700
Investments	28,000			28,000
Stocks	15,000		(g) 200	14,800
Dividends Receivable	3,050		(t) 3,050	—
Deferred Asset				
Advance Corporation Tax Recoverable	49			49
			Contra	
		60,350	121,900	
		61,550		
	£274,572	£121,900	£121,900	£213,022

JOURNAL

	£	£
Goodwill	56,000	
Shares in S, Ltd.		31,000
Preference Shares in T, Ltd. . . .		8,000
Ordinary Shares in T, Ltd. . . .		11,000
Debentures in S, Ltd.		6,000
Shares in S, Ltd.	24,000	
Preference Shares in T, Ltd.. . . .	8,000	
Ordinary Shares in T, Ltd. . . .	9,000	
Debentures in S, Ltd.	6,000	
Goodwill		47,000
General Reserve of S, Ltd. ($\frac{24}{30}$ of £6,000) .	4,800	
Profit and Loss Account of S, Ltd. ($\frac{24}{30}$ of £4,500) .	3,600	
Goodwill		8,400
General Reserve of T, Ltd. ($\frac{9}{10}$ of £3,000) .	2,700	
Profit and Loss Account of T, Ltd. ($\frac{9}{10}$ of £2,500) .	2,250	
Goodwill		4,950
Creditors S, Ltd.	800	
Creditors H, Ltd.	300	
Debtors T, Ltd.		800
Debtors S, Ltd.		300
Bills Payable H, Ltd.	200	
Bills Receivable T, Ltd.		200
Bills Payable H, Ltd.	1,000	
Bills Receivable S, Ltd.		1,000
Consolidated Trading Account . . .	200	
Stock ($\frac{24}{30}$ of $\frac{1000}{6000}$ of £1,500)		200
Debenture Interest H, Ltd. . . .	240	
Debenture Interest S, Ltd. . . .		240
Dividend Receivable by H, Ltd., from Subsidiaries:		
on Shares in S, Ltd.. . . .	2,400	
on Preference Shares in T, Ltd. . .	400	
on Ordinary Shares in T, Ltd. . .	450	
Dividend payable by S, Ltd. ($\frac{24}{30}$ of £3,000)		2,400
Preference Dividend paid and payable by T, Ltd. ($\frac{8}{12}$ of £600)		400
Ordinary Dividend payable by T, Ltd. ($\frac{9}{10}$ of £500)		450
Share Capital of S, Ltd. ($\frac{6}{30}$ of £30,000) . .	6,000	
General Reserve of S, Ltd. ($\frac{6}{30}$ of £6,000) . .	1,200	
Profit and Loss Account of S, Ltd. ($\frac{6}{30}$ of £4,500) .	900	
Consolidated Profit and Loss Account of S, Ltd.—		
Profit for year ($\frac{6}{30}$ of £5,710) . . .	1,142	
To Minority Shareholders		9,242

JOURNAL (*contd.*)

	£	£
Ordinary Share Capital of T, Ltd. ($\frac{1}{10}$ of £10,000) .	1,000	
General Reserve of T, Ltd. ($\frac{1}{10}$ of £4,500) . .	450	
Profit and Loss Account of T, Ltd. ($\frac{1}{10}$ of £2,756) .	276	
Consolidated Profit and Loss Account of T, Ltd—		
Profit for year ($\frac{1}{10}$ of £3,399)	340	
Minority Shareholders		2,066
Preference Share Capital of T, Ltd.	4,000	
Preference Dividend of T, Ltd.	100	
Minority Shareholders		4,100
Goodwill	4,350	
Capital Reserve		4,350

	H, Ltd. £		S, Ltd. £		T, Ltd. £	Total £
Profit and Loss Account—balance forward at						
1st April 19.8 . . .	5,930		4,500		2,756	13,186
Less Minority Shareholders . .		$\frac{6}{30}$	900	$\frac{1}{10}$	276	1,176[1]
	5,930		3,600		2,480	12,010
Less Pre-acquisition Profits						
Capital Reserve . . .	$\frac{24}{30} \times £4,500$	3,600		$\frac{9}{10} \times £2,500$	2,250	5,850[2]
	£5,930		£ —		£230	£6,160

[1] See (*f*) and (*i*) in Consolidated Profit and Loss Account and Consolidated Balance Sheet.
[2] See (*d*) and (*e*) in Consolidated Profit and Loss Account and Consolidated Balance Sheet.

Schedules:

SUMMARY OF THE DISPOSAL OF THE AGGREGATE AMOUNT FORWARD FROM 1ST APRIL 19.8

		£
Total	(*Cr.*)	13,186
Minority Shareholders	(*Cr.*)	1,176
Capital Reserve	(*Cr.*)	5,850
Balance H, Ltd.—£5,930, plus T, Ltd., £230 . .	(*Cr.*)	6,160
		£13,186

CAPITAL RESERVE

	S, Ltd. £	T, Ltd. £	Total £
Share Capital—Ordinary	24,000	9,000	33,000
General Reserve	4,800	2,700	7,500
Profit and Loss	3,600	2,250	5,850
	32,400	13,950	46,350
Less Cost of Shares acquired . .	31,000	11,000	42,000
	£1,400	£2,950	£4,350

Minority Shareholders (Ordinary)

	£	£	£
Share Capital	6,000	1,000	7,000
General Reserve	1,200	450	1,650
Profit and Loss Account forward . . .	900	276	1,176
Profit and Loss Account current . . .	1,142	340	1,482
	£9,242	£2,066	£11,308

Accounting for Associated Companies. Statement of Standard Accounting Practice 1/1 concerns accounting for associated companies and selected paragraphs are reproduced hereunder. Original paragraph numbering has been retained.

I—EXPLANATORY NOTE

1. Statement of Standard Accounting Practice 1 "Accounting for the Results of Associated Companies" (SSAP 1) was issued in January 1971 to introduce a standard accounting treatment for investments in companies, the policies of which, although they are not subsidiaries of the investing company, are subject to significant influence by the investing company.

2. It is generally accepted accounting practice for a company not to take credit in its own (i.e. non-consolidated) profit and loss account and balance sheet for its share of the profits of other companies which have not been declared as dividends. The view is taken that the inclusion of undistributed profits would ignore the separate legal status of the entities concerned and, as regards the investing company, be contrary to the practice of not taking credit for investment income until it is received or receivable.

3. However, where a company conducts an important part of its business through the medium of other companies, the mere disclosure of dividend income (or mere inclusion of dividend income alone) from these companies is unlikely to be sufficient to give adequate information regarding the sources of their income and the manner in which their funds are being employed.

9. This SSAP is intended to apply to companies incorporated under the Companies Acts. The principles laid down in it are, nevertheless, applicable to financial statements of any entity, whether incorporated or not, which invests in another entity or entities.

10. In some cases, partnerships or non-corporate joint ventures can have features which justify accounting for a proportionate share of individual assets and liabilities as well as profits or losses.

II—DEFINITION OF TERMS

13. An *associated company* is a company not being a subsidiary of the investing group or company in which:

(a) the interest of the investing group or company is effectively that of a partner in a joint venture or consortium and the investing group or company is in a position to exercise a significant influence over the company in which the investment is made; or

(b) the interest of the investing group or company is for the long term and is substantial and, having regard to the disposition of the other shareholdings, the investing group or company is in a position to exercise a significant influence over the company in which the investment is made.

Significant influence over a company essentially involves participation in the financial and operating policy decisions of that company (including dividend policy) but not necessarily control of those policies. Representation on the board of directors is indicative of such participation, but will neither necessarily give conclusive evidence of it nor be the only method by which the investing company may participate in policy decisions.

III—STANDARD ACCOUNTING PRACTICE

Bases of accounting for associated companies

18. Income from investments of a company or its subsidiaries in associated companies should be brought into account on the following bases:

(a) *In the investing company's own financial statements;* dividends received and receivable.

(b) *In the investing group's consolidated financial statements (or the equivalent prepared in accordance with paragraphs 24 and 35 below):* the investing group's share of profits less losses of associated companies.

These bases need not be applied to interests in partnerships or non-corporate joint ventures where such arrangements have features which justify accounting for a proportionate share of individual assets and liabilities as well as profits or losses.

Profit and loss account items

19. *Profit before tax.* The investing group should include in its consolidated financial statements the aggregate of its share of before-tax profits less losses of associated companies. This item should be shown separately and suitably described, for example as "share of profits less losses of associated companies".

20. *Taxation.* The tax attributed to the share of profits of associated companies should be disclosed separately within the group tax charge in the consolidated financial statements.

21. *Extraordinary items.* The investing group's share of aggregate extraordinary items dealt with in the associated companies' financial statements should be included with the group's extraordinary items to the extent that the group's share of the items involved would be classified.

22. *Net profit retained by associated companies.* The investing group's share of aggregate net profits less losses retained by associated companies should be shown separately in the financial statements of the investing group.

23. *Other items.* The investing group should not include its share of associated companies' items such as turnover and depreciation in the aggregate amounts of these items disclosed in its consolidated financial statements. If the results of one or more associated companies are so material in the context of the financial statements of the investing group that more detailed information about them would assist in giving a true and fair view, this information should be given by separate disclosure of the total turnover of the associated companies concerned, their total depreciation charges, their total profits less losses before taxation and the amount of such profits less losses attributable to the investing group. In judging materiality regard should be had not merely to the group's share of the net profit of an associated company but also to the scale of its operations in relation to those of the group.

24. Except where it is a wholly owned subsidiary, an investing company which does not prepare consolidated financial statements should show the information required by paragraphs 19 to 23 of this SSAP by preparing a separate profit and loss account or by adding the information in supplementary form to its own profit and loss account in such a way that its share of the profits of the associated companies is not treated as realised for the purposes of the Companies Acts 1948 to 1981. (References in this SSAP to investing groups and consolidated financial statements are to be taken as embracing this information in the case of investing companies which do not have subsidiaries or which do not otherwise prepare consolidated financial statements.)

Balance sheet items

25. *Investing company's interests in associated companies.* Unless shown at a valuation, the amount at which the investing company's interests in associated companies should be shown in the investing company's own financial statements is the cost of the investment less any amounts written off.

26. *Investing group's interests in associated companies.* The amount at which the investing group's interests in associated companies should be shown in the consolidated balance sheet is the total of:

(*a*) the investing group's share of the net assets other than goodwill of the associated companies stated, where possible, after attributing fair values to the net assets at the time of acquisition of the interest in the associated companies, and

(*b*) the investing group's share of any goodwill in the associated companies' own financial statements, together with

(*c*) the premium paid (or discount) on the acquisition of the interests in the associated companies in so far as it has not already been written off or amortised.

Item (*a*) should be disclosed separately but items (*b*) and (*c*) may be shown as one aggregate amount.

27. *Loans to associated companies.* The total of loans to associated companies from the group should be separately disclosed in the consolidated financial statements.

28. *Loans from associated companies.* The total of loans from associated companies to the group should be separately disclosed in the consolidated financial statements.

29. *Trading balances.* Balances arising from unsettled normal trading transactions between the associated companies and the investing group should be included under current assets or liabilities as appropriate, with separate disclosure if material in the context of the financial statements of the investing group.

30. *Other items.* More detailed information about the associated companies' tangible and intangible assets and liabilities should be given if the interests in the associated companies are so material in the context of the financial statements of the investing group that more detailed information about them would assist in giving a true and fair view. In judging materiality, regard should be had not merely to the net carrying amount of the investment in an associated company, but also to the scale of its operations in relation to those of the group.

31. *Accumulated reserves.* The investing group's share of the post-acquisition accumulated reserves of associated companies and any movements therein should be disclosed in the consolidated financial statements. In arriving at the amount to be disclosed, it will also be necessary to take account of and disclose movements on associated companies' reserves which have not arisen from amounts passing through the profit and loss account, for example surpluses on revaluation of fixed assets. If the accumulated reserves of associated companies overseas would be subject to further tax on distribution, this should be made clear.

32. *Permanent impairment in value.* Where there has been permanent impairment in the value of any goodwill (including any premium paid) attributable to an investment in an associated company, it should be written down, and the amount written off in the accounting period separately disclosed. Because an impairment in the value of the underlying net assets would normally be reflected in the books of the associated company, further provision against the investing group's share of these net assets should not usually be necessary.

33. *Deficiency of net assets.* Where an associated company has a deficiency of net assets but is still regarded as a long-term investment it will usually be supported by its shareholders (either by way of loans or by way of an agreement, either formal or informal, to support it). In these circumstances, the investing group should reflect its share of the deficiency of net assets in its consolidated financial statements.

34. *Investment in an unincorporated entity.* Where an investment is made in an unincorporated entity, a liability could arise which would be in excess of that resulting from taking account only of the investing group's share of net assets of the associated company (e.g., as a result of joint and several liability in a partnership). In such circumstances it may be necessary to consider whether it would be prudent either to include an additional provision, or to recognise a contingent liability for this excess.

35. Except where it is a wholly owned subsidiary, an investing company which does not prepare consolidated financial statements should show the

information required by paragraphs 25 to 34 of this SSAP by preparing a separate balance sheet or by adding the information in supplementary form to its own balance sheet.

Inclusion of the results of associated companies in the consolidated financial statements of the investing group

36. The financial statements used for the purpose of including the results of associated companies should be either conterminous with those of the investing group or made up to a date which is either not more than six months before, or shortly after, the date of the financial statements of the investing group. In relation to associated companies which are listed on a recognised stock exchange, only published financial information should be disclosed in the financial statements of the investing group.

37. Before incorporating the results of an associated company based on financial statements issued before completion of those of the investing group, care should be taken to ensure that the later information has not materially affected the view shown by the financial statements of the associated company. If financial statements not conterminous with those of the investing group are used and the effect is material the facts and the dates of year-ends should be disclosed.

38. Where the interest of the investing group or company in any company other than a subsidiary is not effectively that of a partner in a joint venture or consortium and the investing group or company holds 20 per cent or more of the equity voting rights of that company but does not account for that company as an associated company, details of the accounting treatment adopted, and the reason for doing so, should be stated by way of note to the financial statements. In those cases where disclosure of the reason would be harmful to the business, the directors may omit the information, after consultation with their auditors (in a comparable manner to that permitted by the Companies Acts for subsidiaries where the disclosure would be harmful to the business except that Department of Trade approval would not be required in this case). Conversely, where the investing group or company holds less than 20 per cent of the equity voting rights of a company but accounts for that company as an associate, the basis on which significant influence is exercised should be stated.

Accounting adjustments

39. Wherever the effect is material, adjustments similar to those adopted for the purpose of presenting consolidated financial statements should be made to exclude from the investing group's consolidated financial statements such items as unrealised profits on stocks transferred to or from associated companies and to achieve reasonable consistency with the accounting policies adopted by the investing group.

Restrictions on distribution

40. If there are significant restrictions on the ability of an associated company to distribute its retained profits (other than those shown as

non-distributable) because of statutory, contractual or exchange control restrictions, the extent of the restrictions should be indicated.

Minority interests

41. Where the investment in an associated company is held by a subsidiary in which there are minority interests, the minority interests shown in the consolidated financial statements of the group should include the minority share of the subsidiary's interest in the results and net assets of the associated company.

Investments by associated companies

42. Where an associated company itself has subsidiary or associated companies, the results and net assets to be dealt with in the investing group's consolidated financial statements are its attributable proportion of the results and net assets of the group (including the appropriate proportion of the results and net assets of its associated companies) of which the associated company is the holding company.

Loss of status as associated company

43. When an investment in a company ceases to fall within the definition of an associated company, it should be stated in the consolidated balance sheet of the investing group at the carrying amount under the equity method at that date. However, the carrying value should be adjusted if dividends are subsequently paid out of profits earned prior to the change of status. Provision should be made against the investment if there has been any impairment in value.

Effective date of acquisition or disposal

44. The effective date for both acquisition and disposal of an interest, or any portion of an interest, in an associated company should be the earlier of:

(a) the date on which consideration passes; or
(b) the date on which an offer becomes unconditional.

This applies even if the acquiring company has the right under the agreement to share in the profits of the acquired business from an earlier date.

Corresponding amounts

50. On first introducing the amended standard method of accounting set out in this SSAP the corresponding amounts for the preceding period should be appropriately stated on a comparable basis.

Date from which effective

51. The amended method of accounting for associated companies set out in this SSAP should be adopted as soon as possible and regarded as standard in respect of financial statements relating to accounting periods starting on or after 1 January 1982.

CHAPTER 25

DOUBLE ACCOUNT SYSTEM

THIS is the name given to the method of presenting the published accounts of certain companies, usually of the public utilities type. It is not meant to indicate a special system of book-keeping, and all companies adopting this system of presenting their accounts keep their books on the ordinary double-entry principles.

The system, which applied chiefly to Railways, Gas and Electric Lighting companies, all of which are now State-owned, is not in everyday use, except that many Water Companies still draw up their published accounts thereunder.

This chapter, therefore, will be confined to general principles only.

The General Principles. Under the double account system, the Balance Sheet is in two parts, viz.:

1. The Receipts and Expenditure on Capital Account.
2. The General Balance Sheet.

The first part, that is, the Receipts and Expenditure on Capital Account, deals with the funds raised and fixed assets acquired. On the credit side appears the cash received from the issue of stock, shares, debentures, and *loans*, together with any premiums thereon. Discounts on these items, if any, are usually deducted from the premiums, and the net figure carried out. On the debit side are shown the various fixed assets purchased out of the capital moneys, including loans raised.

Although (except for the provision of Sect. 57 of the Companies Act 1948) limited companies may not issue shares at a discount, the special Acts under which 'Double Account' companies are incorporated usually permit the issue of stock and shares at a discount, under certain conditions, even though such issue may be an original issue of the stock or shares in question.

The balance of the Capital Account (or, in the case of electrical undertakings, the totals of the respective sides) is carried down and shown as a separate item in the General Balance Sheet. As the items in the Receipts and Expenditure on Capital Account are shown on the same sides as they actually appear in the books, the *balancing* item in the Capital Account appears on the SAME side in the General Balance Sheet, as will the totals if carried down, because the items in the General Balance Sheet are on the same sides as are adopted by other companies; e.g. if the capital moneys received amount to £1,000 and expenditure thereout is £750, there is a credit balance of £250 which will appear upon the liabilities side of the General Balance Sheet, i.e. the 'debit side', the balancing figure being on that side of the Receipts and Expenditure on Capital Account. The Receipts and Expenditure on Capital Account is generally shown in columnar form, there being three columns on each side, the first presenting the totals up to the time of the commencement of

2501

the accounting period, the second the amount spent or raised during the accounting period, and the third the total of the first two columns.

The General Balance Sheet deals with the remaining assets and liabilities which may be considered as floating capital. It will usually be found to contain reserves and depreciation funds (if any) which have been built up out of profits.

The difference between the presentation of the accounts of companies operating under the double account system and those drawn up in the usual way (designated by way of contrast as the single account system) is shown clearly in the following illustration.

Illustration 1

1. Double Account system:

CAPITAL ACCOUNT

	£		£
Fixed Assets (detailed) .	41,000	Ordinary Stock . .	50,000
Balance . . .	9,000		
	£50,000		£50,000

GENERAL BALANCE SHEET

	£		£
Balance of Capital Account .	9,000	Stocks and Stores . . .	8,500
Revenue Account . . .	3,000	Cash at Bank	5,500
Depreciation Fund . . .	2,000		
	£14,000		£14,000

2. Single Account system:

BALANCE SHEET

	£		£
Ordinary Stock . . .	50,000	Fixed Assets (detailed) £41,000	
Profit and Loss Account . .	3,000	Less Depreciation 2,000	
			39,000
		Stocks and Stores . .	8,500
		Cash at Bank	5,500
	£53,000		£53,000

The characteristic features of the system are:

1. The assets purchased remain in the books at the cost price and are not written down, so that:

2. Depreciation is provided for by the creation of reserves and others funds which appear on the liabilities side of the General Balance Sheet.

3. Loans and debentures are considered as 'capital', and consistent with this procedure, loan and debenture interest are debited to Revenue *Appropriation* Account, like dividends.

4. Discounts and Premiums on Capital Stock and Debentures are permanently retained as Capital items.

5. Renewals are provided for out of current revenue.

6. Accounts, particularly in the case of railways, are supported by voluminous statistical returns.

7. The Balance Sheet is presented in two parts. *Capital* Receipts and Expenditure the balance of which is carried down into the Balance Sheet (*a*) if the Receipts exceed Expenditure to the left hand and (*b*) if Expenditure exceeds Receipts to the right hand.

The system comes in for criticism on the following grounds:

(i) That inasmuch as assets remain at cost in the Capital Account, the Balance Sheet does not show the true position. Against this is to be stated that, whilst the system permits the permanent inclusion of assets at cost, the practice is to build up depreciation and other funds to cover obsolescence, and wear-and-tear of the asset.

(ii) That included in the Capital Account is expenditure on fictitious assets, e.g. expenditure in connection with the promotion of Parliamentary Bills—even those in opposition to rival schemes and preliminary expenses; but the same criticism is applicable under the Single Account system.

(iii) That included in the capital are assets which have a very short life.

(iv) That inasmuch as renewals are charged to revenue, involving perhaps, little or no expenditure in some years and very heavy expenditure in others, each year's profits (or losses) are incorrectly stated. On the other hand, by proper division by way of renewal funds a just proportion can be debited to revenue, so that revenue will be charged with an amount approximating to the depreciation incurred *during* the life of the asset. Particular attention will have to be paid to this question in the early years of a company, because actual renewals will be very small.

(v) That the precise determination of the amount properly chargeable to revenue in respect of renewals is difficult or impossible to calculate.

(vi) Lack of understanding of the accounts by the general public.

Replacements. The treatment of replacements, especially where improvements are effected, often causes great perplexity in the mind of the student. The main point is that once an asset appears in the Receipts and Expenditure on Capital Account it is never shown at a less figure (e.g. in respect of sale or depreciation), although it may be increased.

CHAPTER 26

STOCK EXCHANGE TRANSACTIONS—INVESTMENT ACCOUNTS—VALUATION OF SHARES— INVESTMENT TRUSTS AND UNIT TRUSTS

THE problems arising out of Stock Exchange transactions may be dealt with in the following sequence:

1. Purchase and sale of investments.
2. Treatment of dividends and interest.
3. Brokers' Accounts.

Purchase and Sale of Investments. Where investments are purchased on the Stock Exchange, it is the practice to charge the buyer with brokerage (based on an official scale), stamp duty, transfer duty, registration fee, and the cost of the contract stamp. There are often additional stamp duties in the case of a company incorporated abroad, e.g. South Africa. The only expenses to the seller are the brokerage and the contract stamp, both of which are payable on every Stock Exchange transaction, whether a purchase or a sale. In the case of a sale, the expenses (brokerage and contract stamp) are *deducted* from the proceeds of realization of the investment.

Although the treatment and practice of the Stock Exchange is outside the scope of this book, the following observations are given so far as is necessary to enable the student to understand the calculations of Investment Accounts.

The operations on the Stock Exchange are carried on by its members who are either dealers—who actually buy or sell investments—or brokers, who merely act as intermediaries between the dealers and the public.

The price quoted by a dealer to the broker is not a single, but a double price, the one at which he is prepared to buy and the other to sell, as upon an inquiry from the broker he is not aware whether the latter wishes to buy or sell for his client. The lower figure is obviously the *dealer's buying price*, the higher his *selling price*, the difference being the 'TURN'.

Job lines or odd lots (as market terms them) are blocks of shares other than in round figures (such as 50 or 100). They are expensive to buy, and on sale are likely to fetch poor prices.

The investor, except in the case of certain classes of stocks, pays for his purchase and receives cash in respect of his sales at the end of the 'Account'. There are twenty-four Accounts to the year, most of them being of fortnightly duration, the remainder being of three weeks.

Contract Stamps. For any purchase *or sale* of securities carried out for the general public, a proper contract must be rendered by the broker doing the business. Such contract must be properly stamped.

Book-keeping Entries. If the question of interest and dividend be ignored, the entries in the books of the investor are: (*a*) debit Investment Account and credit broker with the total cost in case of purchase; (*b*) debit broker and credit Investment Account with the net proceeds in case of a sale. Where the investment has been sold there will be a debit balance in the Investment Account if a loss has been incurred, which will be transferred to Profit and Loss Account or reserve; in case of a profit, the entries will be reverse to the above. In case of partial sale, the profit or loss thereon will be transferred in the manner to be indicated, and the balance of the investment at cost brought down at the end of the accounting period.

DIVIDENDS AND INTEREST

Difficulties arise, however, by reason of the fact that the buyer of an investment normally acquires the right to the next dividend, i.e. it is 'cum dividend' unless the investment is purchased 'ex dividend', so that in almost every case a part of the purchase price includes a portion of the accruing dividend. Hence, the dividend received after purchase is in reality not all income, but a part recoupment of the capital outlay, and a proportion should be credited to the cost of the investment. The same principle applies on a sale 'cum dividend'. In this case, part of the sale price is in reality income.

In order to overcome this difficulty, the Investment Account is ruled with two columns on each side, one for capital and the other for income, and the following rules apply.

1. Upon a purchase cum dividend being made, that part of the purchase price which relates to the dividend accruing *from* the date of the last dividend (or in the case of companies from the date of the last accounting period) to the date of purchase is debited in the income column; the balance in the capital column.

2. Upon a sale cum dividend, that part of the sale price which relates to the dividend accruing [as in (1)] is credited in the income column; the balance in the capital column.

Illustration 1

X buys 1,000 $7\frac{1}{2}$ per cent preference shares on 30th April at £1·10 cum dividend. Dividends are due on 1st January and 1st July. Ignoring expenses of purchase and taxation, show the Investment Account from 30 April until 1st July.

INVESTMENT

			Income	Capital				Income	Capital
			£p	£p				£p	£p
19 . . April 30	Purchase (de- tails), 1,000 $7\frac{1}{2}$% Prefer- ence Shares . 4 Months' Dividend .		 25	 1,075	19 . . July 1	Dividend for half year to date . .		 37·50	

On purchase, 4 months' accruing dividend included in the price, i.e. four-sixths of £37·50, is debited in the income column. The net credit to income is £12·50, being the dividend for the two months, 1st May to 30th June, i.e. two-sixths of £37·50.

Conversely, in regard to sales, the whole proceeds are treated as capital, save for the dividend accruing for the period elapsing between the date of the last dividend and the date of sale.

Illustration 2

Assuming that the shares in the previous illustration were sold on 31st July at £1·02$\frac{1}{2}$ cum dividend, show the entries in the Investment Account relating to the sale.

INVESTMENT

		Income £	Capital £	19.. July 31		Income £p	Capital £p
					Sale (details), 1,000 7$\frac{1}{2}$% Preference Shares 1 Month's Dividend[1]	6·25	1,018·75

[1] At the date of sale there is one month's dividend included in the price, i.e. $\frac{1}{6}$ of £37·50.

In the case of fixed-income stocks the price goes ex dividend usually BEFORE the dividend date, and the price reduction consequent upon the quotation being 'ex' and not 'cum' is the FULL period's dividend. It is important to realize the significance of this because the proceeds due to capital are too small by the interest accruing during the period elapsing between the sale and the dividend date, whilst income will obtain the FULL period's income in spite of the sale of the security before the expiry of such period. Similarly, upon a purchase ex dividend the capital cost is too small and income will receive the *first* dividend at the expiry of the succeeding period, although the investment was purchased BEFORE the commencement of such period.

In order to adjust the position arising out of the above, the procedure is as follows:

1. Upon a purchase ex dividend that part of the dividend which arises in the period elapsing between the date of purchase and that of the dividend is debited in the capital column and credited in the income column.

2. Upon a sale ex dividend, that part of the dividend which arises in the period elapsing between the date of the sale and that of the dividend is credited in the capital column and the balance in the income column.

It should be noted that upon a sale ex dividend, the SELLER receives and retains the forthcoming dividend, the sale price having been reduced by such dividend. Further, the sale ex dividend is a sale 'ex' the WHOLE dividend not merely the accruing dividend, hence the receipt by capital is too small, thus necessitating the above apportionment.

Illustration 3

X sells £1,000 6 per cent Government Stock at par. How will the seller and buyer respectively deal with the transaction? Dividends are due on 1st June and 1st December.

Suppose for simplicity the 'true' value of the stock *without* dividend is always at par, then the price 'cum dividend' would be (ignoring tax):

									£
On Dec.	1	.	.	.	.	.	.	.	100
,, Jan.	1	.	.	.	.	.	.	.	$100\frac{1}{2}$
,, Feb.	1	.	.	.	.	.	.	.	101
,, March	1	.	.	.	.	.	.	.	$101\frac{1}{2}$
,, April	1	.	.	.	.	.	.	.	102
,, May	1	.	.	.	.	.	.	.	$102\frac{1}{2}$
,, ,,	30	.	(Just prior to the dividend.)					.	103

On 1st May or thereabouts the stock would be marked x.d (i.e. ex dividend) and will therefore be reduced by the FULL half-year's dividend of[1] £3, leaving the x.d. price at $99\frac{1}{2}$. Suppose the holder sold on that date he would still receive his £$102\frac{1}{2}$, but in the form of the sale price £$99\frac{1}{2}$ and dividend received a month later £3, whereas the true price is £100, and income accruing amounts to £2·50. In order, therefore, to make the accounts correct, upon the receipt of the dividend of £3, income column will be credited with £2·50 and capital column with £0·50, bringing the total capital credit to £100, i.e. par, and leaving income with a credit of £2·50.

The amount £0·50 is that part of the dividend arising in the period elapsing between the date of sale (1st May) and the due date of the dividend (1st June), i.e. one month on £100 at 6 per cent per annum. As the stock is sold, income is entitled only to five months' dividend (1st December to 1st May), i.e. five months on £100 at 6 per cent per annum = £2·50, and the apportionment of income is that sum, the accounts show the true state of affairs.

Conversely as regards the buyer, it is clear that the true purchase price is £100, therefore he could debit £0·50 in the capital column and credit income column.

On 1st December the buyer will have held the stock for seven months, so that the credit to income should amount to £3·50. This, in effect, is made up as follows: (*a*) the above £0·50 transferred, and (*b*) the £3 received on 1st December in respect of the half-yearly dividend. In other words, the buyer entirely misses the dividend for the month of May, but his purchase price is reduced accordingly. It will be seen that the 'marking down' unduly deflates the true price by the dividend due between the marking x.d. and the date on which the dividend is paid—in the above instance, one month.

The accruing interest to be brought down where a sale x.d. has taken place is ascertained as follows:

1. Interest from the date of the last payment to the date of balancing the account on the part retained and interest from the date of the last payment to the date of sale on the part sold; or

[1] For the present purpose advance corporation tax is ignored.

2. Interest from the date of the last payment to the date of balancing the account on the part retained, plus interest from the date of the last payment to the date of the next payment on the part sold, *less* the interest from the date of sale to the date of the next payment on the part sold; or

3. Interest from the date of the last payment to the date of balancing the account of the part retained and the part sold ex dividend, *less* interest on the latter from the date of balancing the account back to the date of the sale ex dividend.

Illustration 4

A buys £10,000 3 per cent Government Stock at 85 on 5th October 19.8, and sells £6,000 at 84 on 28th March 19.9. Interest dates are 5th October, 5th January, 5th April, and 5th July. Accounts are to be made up to 31st March 19.9. Show Ledger Account in respect of the above, ignoring taxation, brokerage, etc. Applying method (1) above:

(*a*) Interest to date of the balancing the account on the part retained, i.e. £4,000 at 3 per cent per annum for 85 days.

$$\tfrac{85}{90} \times £30 \qquad\qquad\qquad\qquad \begin{array}{r} £p \\ 28 \cdot 33\tfrac{1}{3} \end{array}$$

		£p
$\frac{85}{90} \times £30$		28·33⅓
Add one quarter's Interest on £6,000 at 3% per annum	£45	
Less $\frac{8}{90} \times £45$	4	
		41·00
		£69·33⅓

(*b*) Interest on £4,000 plus £6,000, i.e. £10,000 at 3 per cent per annum for 85 days.

	£p
$\frac{85}{90} \times £75$	70·83⅓
Less Interest on £6,000 at 3% per annum for 3 days, $\frac{3}{90} \times £45$	1·50
	£69·33⅓

The balance retained is $\frac{4}{10} \times £8,500$		£3,400

The loss on realization is:

Cost of £6,000, i.e. $\frac{6}{10}$ of £8,500	£5,100	
Less Sale	5,044	
		£56

The interest is as follows:

	£p
On £10,000 from 6 Oct., 19.8 to 5 Jan., 19.9	75·00
On £10,000 from 6 Jan., 19.9 to 28 March, 19.9 $\frac{82}{90} \times £75$	68·33⅓
On £4,000 from 29 March, 19.9 to 31 March, 19.9 $\frac{3}{90} \times £30$	1·00
	£144·33⅓

The same result is obtained by applying rules shown in paragraphs (2) and (3).

GOVERNMENT STOCK

Debit

Date	Particulars		Nominal £	Income £p	Capital £
19.8 Oct. 5	Cash: Purchase at 85		10,000		8,500
19.9 Mar. 31	Interest on Investments Account			144·33⅓	
			£10,000	£144·33⅓	£8,500
19.9 April 1	Balance	b/d	4,000	69·33⅓	3,400
	"	b/d		4·00	

Credit

Date	Particulars		Nominal £	Income £p	Capital £
19.9 Jan. 5	Interest for quarter year to date			75·00	
Mar. 28	Cash: Sale at 84	c/d	6,000		5,040
	Interest on £6,000 sold Ex. Div. Mar. 28 to April 5 [$\frac{8}{60} \times £45$]				4
	Balance, Interest, Accruing on £6,000 from Jan. 6 to Mar. 28 [$\frac{82}{60} \times £45$][1]	c/d		41·00	
31	Interest Accruing on £4,000 from Jan. 6 to Mar. 31 [$\frac{85}{60} \times £30$]	c/d		28·33⅓	
	Loss on Sale				56
	Balance, Stock [$\frac{4}{10} \times £8,500$]	c/d	4,000		3,400
			£10,000	£144·33⅓	£8,500

[1] According to rule in paragraph (1) on p. 2604.

If the remaining stock is sold on 5th April 19.9, at 86, the account will be closed thus:

GOVERNMENT STOCK

			Interest	Capital				Interest	Capital
			£p	£				£	£
19.9 April 1	Balance . .	b/d	69·33⅓	3,400	19.9 April 5	Interest on £10,000 at 3% p.a. for quarter to date .		75	
	,, . .	b/d	4·00						
5	Profit on Sale . Interest on Investments Account[1] .		1·66⅔	40		Cash—Sale of £4,000 Stock at 86 . .			3,440
			£75·00	£3,440				£75	£3,440

[1] The above amount is Interest on £4,000 at 3 per cent per annum for 5 days, i.e. $\frac{5}{90} \times £30$.

If part only is sold, say £1,000, the remaining balance would be brought down at $\frac{3,000}{4,000} \times £3,400 \left(\text{or } \frac{3,000}{10,111} \times £8,500 \right) = £2,550$.

Illustration 5

On 1st June 19.9, Scarsdale Investment Trust, Ltd., held £10,000 6 per cent Queensmania Stock standing in the books at £9,560. Interest is payable on 31st July and 31st January. On 1st September 19.9, a further £5,000 of the stock was bought at 98 cum dividend and on 1st January 19.0 a further £4,000 of the stock was bought at 97 x.d.

On 31st March 19.0 £8,000 of the stock was sold at 101 c.d. and on 15th June 19.0 £6,000 of the stock was bought at 99½ x.d., and on 30th June, £2,000 of the stock was sold at 99½ x.d. Show the Investment Account for the period ending 30th June 19.0.

Ignore Advance Corporation Tax and Expenses.

The amount to credit of Interest Account, £915, is made up as follows:

	£
£	
10,000—1 June to 1 Sept., 3 months at 6% p.a.	150·00
15,000—1 Sept. to 1 Jan., 4 months at 6% p.a.	300·00
19,000—1 Jan. to 31 Mar., 3 months at 6% p.a.	285·00
11,000—1 April to 15 June, 2½ months at 6% p.a. . . .	137·50
[2] 17,000—15 June to 30 June, ½ month at 6% p.a.	42·50
	£915·00

Where many investments are held, a schedule will be prepared showing the cost price and current price of each investment. Care must be exercised in the compilation of the current price because the market price, except where quoted x.d., will include the accrued and accruing dividend or interest.

[2] £17,000 is the nominal amount of Stock held until the very last day of the period when £2,000 was sold, leaving £15,000.

6% QUEENSMANIA STOCK

Date	Particulars		Nominal	Income	Capital
19.9 June 1	Balance	b/d	£ 10,000	£	£ 9,560
	Balance, accruing interest for four months			200	
Sept. 1	Cash: Purchase at 98 Cum. Div., £4,900		5,000		4,875
	Capital				
	Income 1 month (Aug. 1 to Sept. 1)			25	
19.0 Jan. 1	Cash: Purchases at 97 Ex. Div., £3,880		4,000		3,880
	Interest transferred to Contra (Jan. 1 to Jan. 31)				20
June 15	Cash Purchase at 99¼ Ex. Div., £5,970		6,000		5,970
	Capital				
	Interest transferred to Contra (June 15 to July 31)[2]				45
30	Interest Account			915	
	Profit and Loss Account: Profit on Sale				260
	Transfer from Contra			10	
			£25,000	£1,150	£24,610
19.0 July 1	Balance	b/d	15,000	255	14,610

Date	Particulars		Nominal	Income	Capital
19.9 July 31	Half year's Interest to date		£	£ 300	£
19.0 Jan. 1	Transfer from Contra			20	
31	Interest on £15,000 at 6% p.a. for half year £8,080			450	
Mar. 31	Cash: Sale at 101 Cum. Div., £8,080		8,000		8,000
	Capital				
	Income 2 months, Feb. 1 to March 31			80	
June 15	Transfer from Contra			45	
30	Cash: Sale at 99½ Ex. Div., £2,000		2,000		1,990
	Capital				
	Interest: 1 month June 30 to July 31, to Contra				10
	Balance, Accruing Interest £275[1] Less Adjustment 20	c/d		255	
	Balance Capital— 15000/25000 × £24,350	c/d	15,000		14,610
			£25,000	£1,150	£24,610

[1] The balance of Interest is calculated:
Interest from last payment to balancing the account, £11,000 × 5/12 × 6/100 on the part retained and the part sold Ex Div., i.e. £10,000 plus £5,000 plus £4,000, less £8,000
Add Interest on £2,000 from the date of balancing the account back to the date of the sale Ex div.

£
275.
nil
———
275

30
10   20
———
£255

[2] The £30 adjustment is required as the transfer of £45 is for 1½ months to 31st July, whereas the period relates to ½ month to 30th June, i.e. £15
Deduct Interest on £2,000 sale on 30th June (£10) added to income and charged to capital and charged to income on 31st July when the half-year's interest is paid

Where there are several operations in one investment the average cost of the balance remaining is taken into account, the balance of the capital column being transferred as a profit or loss to Profit and Loss on Investment Account.

The most cautious rule to adopt is:

1. To treat each transaction as a separate one in case of **loss.**
2. To treat the transactions as a whole in case of **gain.**

Illustration 6

G. Ambler held the following investments on 1st January 19..:

	Cost	Sold during Year for
	£p	£p
£500 5% Japanese Bonds	70·65	90·60
100 Beautility Furniture Ordinary	169·43	221·20
100 Bleachers' Ordinary	105·17	113·40
100 Courtney Pope Ordinary	115·18	
20 International Nickels	180·55	
500 Black and Blue Ordinary	139·17	50·49
		(250 only)
During the year he purchased:		
200 Charterhouse Investment Ordinary	139·17	
500 Amalgamated Bankets	94·90	

All the above are after dealing with Brokerage (as per Broker's Contract Notes).

The object of the transactions was gain by way of appreciation. Ignoring expenses and dividends, prepare Investments Trading Account. (See p. 2610.)

Brokers' Account. The main entries in the broker's books are:

Upon a purchase for a client:

1. Debit Client with:
   (a) Cost of Security purchased, and
   (b) Brokers' Commission thereon; and
   Credit Dealer with (a), and Commission Account with (b).

2. Debit Client with:
   (a) Contract Stamp and Credit Contract Stamps Account;
   (b) Transfer Duty and Credit Transfer Stamps Account;
   (c) Registration fee and credit cash.

Upon a sale for a client:

1. Debit dealer with:

   (a) Cost of Security sold, and Credit Commission Account with (b) Broker's Commission thereon and credit client with the net excess of (a) over (b).

In practice a Contract Journal will be employed for the entries for purchases and sales.

INVESTMENTS TRADING ACCOUNT

Debit side

		£p	£p
Opening Stocks—			
£500 5% Japanese Bonds		70·65	
100 Beautility Furniture Ordinary		169·43	
100 Bleachers' Ordinary		105·17	
100 Courtney Pope Ordinary		115·18	
20 International Nickels		180·55	
500 Black and Blue Ordinary	b/f	139·17	780·15
Purchases—			
200 Charterhouse Investment Ordinary			139·17
500 Amalgamated Bankers			94·90
Net Profit (per Contra)			61·16
			£1,075·38
Opening Stocks—	b/d		
100 Courtney Pope Ordinary		115·18	
20 International Nickels		180·55	
250 Black and Blue Ordinary		69·59	
200 Charterhouse Investment Ordinary		139·17	
500 Amalgamated Bankets		94·90	599·39

Credit side

		Loss £p	Gain £p	Gain £p	£p
Sales—					
£500 Japanese Bonds			19·95		90·60
100 Beautility Furniture Ordinary			51·77		221·20
100 Bleachers' Ordinary			8·53		113·70
250 Black and Blue Ordinary		19·09		80·25	50·49
Net Profit		19·99			
		61·16			
		£80·25	£80·25	£80·25	
Closing Stocks	c/f				599·39
					£1,075·38

Note. The treatment of the sale of half the holding of 500 Black and Blue is: Cost of 250 = ½ × £139·17 = £69·58 as against price realized therefor £50·49. As regards the profit on sale of part of a holding, it may be dealt with on similar lines or used to 'average down' the remaining part, thus not bringing into credit any profit till the original outlay is recovered, e.g. assuming 50 Courtney Pope Ordinary Shares were sold for £70, the profit would be £70 – £57·59 [i.e. ½ × £115·18], viz £12·41 and £57·59 brought down, the sale price of £70 to reduce the cost of the unsold part to £45·17. When the remaining shares are sold, the final result will be the same, as shown below (assuming the sale price thereof at £60)—

(1) Where profit credited on each sale:

				£p
Sale of 50 (1st Sale)		£70	Profit	12·42
Sale of 50 (2nd Sale)		60	Profit	2·41

(2) Where no profit credited till original capital recouped:

				£p
1st Sale		£70	Profit	nil
2nd Sale		60	Profit	14·83	[£60 – £45·17]

[i.e. Sales £130 – Cost, £115·18]

Illustration 7

A Broker carried out the following instructions for clients:

From A. Purchase of 200 T, Ltd., at £0·72½.
 „ A. Purchase of 100 B, Ltd., at £0·80.
 „ B. Sale of 200 I, Ltd., at £5.
 „ C. Purchase of 1,000 C, Ltd., at £0·10.
   Sale of 500 K, Ltd., at £0·60.

CONTRACT JOURNAL

Date	Name of Party	Description of Security	Price		Name of Party	Description of Security	Com- mission	
			£p	£p			£p	£p
	A	200 T, Ltd .	0·72½	146·81	Dealer		1.81	145·00
	A	100 B, Ltd	0·80	81·00	Dealer		1·00	80·00
	Dealer		5·00	1,000·00	B	200 I, Ltd.	12·50	987·50
	C	1,000 C, Ltd.	0·10	101·25	Dealer		1·25	100·00
	Dealer		0·00	300·00	C	500 K, Ltd. .	3·75	296·25
				£1,629·06			£20·31	£1,608·75
				(1)			(2)	(3)

Note: £20·31 = 1¼ per cent of £1,625 (£145 + £80 + £1,000 + £100 + £300)

(1) Each item debited to dealer or client.
(2) Total posted to credit of Commission Account.
(3) Each item credited to dealer or client.

The registration fees, transfer duties and contract stamps may be incorporated in the Contract Journal but are often put through a Fees and Stamp Journal (debt to client: credit to cash for Registration fees and respective stamp accounts for Transfer Duties and Contract Stamps).

In the case of a reinvestment order, i.e. a purchase and sale of a security (not being the *same* Stock or Share) though the same broker in the same account, the broker is *permitted* to charge a reduced commission, viz. one-half on the transaction attracting the smaller consideration, or, if necessary, on part of the larger bargain.

In the foregoing transaction the broker may charge a reduced commission on both £80 and £100 of not less than £0·50 each.

Illustration 8

The commission permissible on a reinvestment is shown at the top of p. 2612.

There will be entries in connection with collecting dividends for clients where securities have been *purchased* cum dividend and the dividend paid before registration of transfer; and collecting dividends from clients where in similar circumstances a client has *sold* securities; cost of split transfers, etc., but these are straightforward and call for no special mention here.

	£	£p
Sale of £1,000 Government Stock at par		1,000·00
Less Commission—⅜% on Stock		3·75
		£996·25
Reinvested in—		
Purchase of 600 Shares at £1		600·00
Add Commission at 1¼%	7·50	
Less ½ Commission—£600 Stock		
[i.e. ³⁄₁₆% on £600]	1·13	
		6·37
		£606·37

If total accounts are employed, the normal subdivisions of Bought and Sales Ledger will be impracticable as clients and dealers will be buyers and sellers so that the Ledger will be subdivided into: (a) Clients and (b) Dealers.

VALUATION OF SHARES

One of the most perplexing problems that confront accountancy students is that of shares. The underlying principles are by no means difficult, but their application calls for a considerable knowledge of technical points.

Shares, as the student will be fully aware, are of varying classes, and the appellation ascribed thereto is by no means an unerring guide to their true nature. The types are usually classified into preference (or preferred), ordinary and deferred; but it is impossible to measure their characteristics, qualities or defects unless detailed information is at hand which discloses to what extent the shares are covered in relation to capital and revenue, quite apart from voting rights and other important factors. A preference share, for instance, may be cumulative or non-cumulative; it may be a participating preference share, i.e. in addition to entitling the holder to the prior right to dividend at a fixed rate, it carries the right to participate further in the distributable profits of the company.

Ordinary shares are usually distinguished from preference shares in that they carry no priorities as to dividends and/or capital, obtaining (subject of course to suitable allocations to reserves) the right to the remaining profits, when they are distributed.

A detailed consideration of all the shades of difference between each class is impossible in this work; and attention will be given to the more usual significance involved in the terms employed.

The necessity for a valuation arises, *inter alia*, in the following circumstances.

1. For capital transfer tax purposes.
2. For amalgamation and absorption schemes.
3. For the valuation of the assets of the Balance Sheet of Trust and Finance Companies.

4. For security margin purposes, e.g. where a bank lends money on the security of shares.

5. For the discharge of debts and liabilities, in exceptional cases.

6. For equilibrium purposes where it is necessary to avoid having too great a proportion of any one type of share.

7. For the valuation of a 'Fixed' Trust unit.

8. Purchasing shares for control.

9. For estimating the 'break-up' value, e.g. where a mining company has exhausted its payable ore reserves and contemplates winding up.

In most instances, the valuation will be readily ascertained from the published price where the securities are quoted or dealt in on the recognized Stock Exchanges. Where, however, the securities either:

(a) are rarely dealt in on the Stock Exchange,
(b) are not quoted or dealt in at all,

recourse must be had to the preparation of a valuation.

In practice, an infinite number of technical points and market factors will affect the true valuation of shares, particularly as more than one factor may be operative at the same time.

Income Basis.[1] It is clear that the normal purpose of the contemplated purchase is to provide for the buyer an annuity; for his outlay he will expect a yearly income return, great or small, stable or fluctuating, but nevertheless some sort of return commensurate with the price paid therefor. In other words, the investment is made, primarily at all events, with a view to providing a recurring income. Apart from the fact that he may cherish a hope that when the time arrives for selling he will be able to secure a profit, the purchaser's object in making the purchase is to secure, as already stated, a recurring income; he is prepared to risk fluctuation and even the possibility that in any one year (or even years) no income at all will be forthcoming; but all the same, he expects income, again hoping that it will, as time goes on, tend to increase rather than decrease.

To the ordinary shareholder, the benefits (sometimes illusory) of stability and comparative certainty supposed to be inherent in the preference share do not appeal. The same principle of valuation exists for both classes of shares—preference and ordinary—although the considerations affecting the yield required differ considerably.

This fundamental point will now be stated and illustrated.

The value of a share is arrived at by taking the rate of annual return divided by the return expected and multiplied by the par or paid-up amount of the share upon which the dividend is based, without taking into account any accruing dividend. This sounds a very forbidding calculation, but it is not such an alarming proposition after all, as can now be seen.

For simplicity, take three companies all paying 30 per cent dividend on their ordinary share of £1, and all of the class whereby an investor expects (say) 12 per cent annual return on his outlay; but the first company's

---

[1] The percentage returns in this section are inclusive of Tax Credit.

shares are fully paid and the second and third £0·50 paid. The second
company has adopted Table A, and the third company's articles state that
dividends are payable on the nominal value. The share valuation would
be:

$$\text{Company 1 } \frac{30}{12} \times £1 \quad = £2·50$$

$$\text{Company 2 } \frac{30}{12} \times £0·50 = £1·25$$

$$\text{Company 3 } \frac{30}{12} \times £1 \quad = £2·50$$

The calculation in the case of the second company is based upon the
paid-up value by reason of the fact that Table A stipulates that dividends
are payable on the paid-up value of a share. The above prices, it will be
seen, are sufficient to give the purchaser his expected 12 per cent on the
basis of a 30 per cent dividend. For example, Jones buys 1,000 shares in
company number 1 costing £2,500. He therefore receives, assuming no
change in the future, £300, which is 12 per cent on £2,500.

The circumstances may be such that when the purchaser acquires his
share the dividend has just become payable, so that shortly after the
purchase he would receive his £300 by way of dividend (and thus a
part-return of his capital outlay). Hence, in these circumstances, the price
would be for 1,000 shares £2,500 plus £300 = £2,800. When he receives
his £300 dividend, the purchaser is left with a net cost of £2,500, being the
true cost of his shares according to the facts indicated.

The position may be symbolized as follows:

The estimated price of a share ex dividend is

$$\frac{\text{Yield}}{\text{Risk}} \times \text{Basic denominator of share.}$$

For example, a company has shares of £0·25 each fully paid, the rate of
dividend being 45 per cent and the expected yield 9 per cent. The ex
dividend price will be therefore:

$$\frac{45}{9} \times £0·25 = £1·25.$$

Before proceeding to the next and probably most difficult stage, it may
be a matter of interest to know the calculation in the case of American
Common Stocks where (as is usual) stocks are of no par value, so that
dividends cannot be expressed in terms of a percentage, but in terms of
dollars and/or cents.

The symbolized calculation is:

$$\frac{100}{\text{Risk}} \times \text{Dividend in terms of dollars.}$$

For example, Amplifiers, Inc., pay $16 dividend annually and the yield expected is (say) 10 per cent. The estimated price ex divided is

$$\frac{100}{10} \times \$16 = \$160$$

It will therefore be clear that, inasmuch as there is a yearly return amounting to $16 for an expenditure of $160, the expected yield is attained.

So far, it has been postulated that a share attracts a certain yield—the investor, that is, requires or expects a minimum yearly return from the investment he has made. This minimum yield is not a static figure; it varies considerably at different times and is therefore a somewhat fluctuating, although extremely important factor. Despite this, its determination is founded upon certain fixed principles. It is clear, for example, that at any time—taking two extreme cases—the yield on British Banks' Stocks will always be considerably less than that obtained on a silver mine situated in Mexico. No expert knowledge of investments is necessary to indicate the overwhelming superiority of the quality of the former over the latter. What, then, are the determinants of yield? In order words, what determines the status of investments?

There are four points of importance which require stressing in order to answer this question satisfactorily. The first is that yields generally vary directly with ruling rates of interest; that is to say, that in times of cheap money—which predicate low rates of interest—yields will tend all round to be much less than in times of dear money—which predicate high rates of interest. The search for a yield more satisfactory than that obtaining in the case of, say, British Government Securities will tend to create a demand for other investments, thus forcing up their prices and tending, therefore, to reduce the yield therefrom.

The second is that temporary and transient features often tend to obscure true values, e.g. forced sales.

Rumours favourable or adverse, particularly those concerning pending takeover bids, periods of intense activity or extreme sluggishness, market manipulations; these and many more causes may, in a short-term period, have the effect of creating a state of disequilibrium.

The third is that many investments are priced at a figure bearing no relationship to yield, either being gambling counters, or exceptional 'bell wether' stocks (the well-known United States Steel Corporation is an excellent example of that type) or shares which offer alluring prospects for the future, although they may be making no profits or actually losing money, for example, gold-mining companies and, more recently, companies with direct or indirect interests in Canadian oil.

The fourth is that certain shares may be priced purely on the prospects of a liquidation value, that is, on the basis of what they are likely to return by way of capital, the question of yield not entering into the question, except that if the process of liquidation is likely to be protracted, allowance must be made for the loss of dividend or interest the investor would otherwise receive.

The following are the chief factors affecting the yield required on ordinary shares:

1. The estimated annual return, having regard to the nature of the business and status of the business and directors, and the risk involved. this return requirement will itself be influenced by general market conditions and ruling rates of interest. It is a significant fact that the investor will pay *more* attention to dividends than to earnings so that, *ceteris paribus*, two similar companies may be paying the same dividends on greatly differing earnings, yet the prices of the shares of each company will tend to approximate to each other (unless influenced by other factors).

2. The trend of profits having regard to the capital required in the business. The mere size of profits earned without taking into account the real capital employed affords no guide in determining yield.

3. Stability of earnings: the company with stable earnings as compared with the company whose earnings are highly fluctuating will command a superior status, other things being equal. In this connection, it is important to remember that the management factor—involving the question of ability and integrity—is vital. Particularly important is this factor in a small company as, to take one example only, unscrupulous directors might be able to alter the articles of association so as to increase their remuneration and thereby bring down the amount of future profits. The latter point naturally leads to the next, namely,

4. Voting rights of members and the degree of power possessed by the executive. For instance, the latter may own more than 50 per cent of the whole voting strength: even if less, it may effectively exert a decisive influence.

5. The reliability of profit, and Balance Sheet disclosure. The current Balance Sheet should be capable of being linked-up with the preceding one, and the profit disclosed reconciled therewith. The separation of abnormal from normal profits and losses, and the further classification of assets and liabilities, including provisions for taxation, etc., is important.

6. The prospects of a company may be sufficiently bright to induce an investor to remain content with a small yield. The prospects may take the form of an early resumption of dividends, capitalization of reserves, or the possibility of the company requiring more capital and offering members the right of subscription on 'bonus terms'. It is true that, unless future earnings increase, the value of the shares will tend proportionately to decrease; for instance, if the share capital was doubled, there being double the quantity of 'share claims' on earnings, the price of the shares would tend to fall to approximately half that obtaining before the further issue was made. Despite this, the advantages arising from this procedure are sometimes considerable (however, depending on the circumstances, bonus issues, or proportions thereof, may be regarded as company distributions and as such liable to Income Tax Schedule F; also in the hands of the recipients such bonus issues, or proportions thereof, may, on subsequent disposal, be liable to Capital Gains Tax) and may in practice more than compensate for a comparatively small formal yield.

Theoretically, if the company's profits do not rise by reason of the further issue, there will be a loss to the investor.

This may be illustrated simply as follows (ignoring taxation):

A company pays 10 per cent annually, the yield being 5 per cent. The price of a £1 share fully paid will therefore be:

$$\frac{10}{5} \times £1 = £2 \text{ x.d.}$$

The company decides to offer to its shareholders one share for two at £1. As the company now has in issue three shares for every two (before the issue), unless the earnings rise, the dividends in future will be $6\frac{2}{3}$ per cent only ($\frac{2}{3}$ of 10 per cent) and therefore the price will be:

$$\frac{6\frac{2}{3}}{5} \times £1 = £1 \cdot 33\frac{1}{3} \text{ x.d.}$$

Therefore, the shareholder, assuming he took up the shares offered, will lose. This is clearly discernible by assuming that A has 100 shares in the above imaginary company. Before the issue, the value of his holding is:

$$100 \times £2 = £200 \text{ x.d.}$$

When he has taken up his further shares, namely, 50 at £1, he has 150 shares worth £1·33$\frac{1}{3}$ each, equals £200. Thus, despite having paid in to the company £50, he is receiving no more in the aggregate by way of dividends than he did prior to the issue, so that he incurs a loss on the transaction. But in practice it does not work out like that, because, given normal circumstances, it will generally be assumed that a company will be able to utilize profitably its extra capital. If, therefore, in future, the above company will be still able to maintain its 10 per cent rate, the value of the new shares will be £2 thus making the value of 150 shares £300. Hence the benefit attaching to the original 100 shares held before the further issue is £50. This can be seen as follows:

	£
100 Shares at £2 . . .	200
Add Cost of 50 Shares at £1 . .	50
	250
Profit	50
150 Shares at £2 . . .	£300

There is thus a profit of £50 in terms of the original 100 shares; and the 'rights' are worth £1 per new share.

7. The financial position of the company will also influence yield, in that the investor must consider such questions as reserves, liquidity of capital, quantity of goodwill, wastage of assets, etc.

8. Technical market factors; for example, whether a share is cum div. or

ex div., rates of exchange as affecting price of foreign shares, flight of capital, quantum of shares held, etc.

9. The latter point may be illustrated by reference to *Short and another v. Treasury Commissioners* where the question of the valuation of shares taken over by the Government was the subject of arbitration, the Treasury's valuation being £1·46¼ and the Arbitrator's £2·08¾. The former was taken as being the fair price as it was that quoted on the Stock Exchange, the value being that, in the opinion of the Treasury, as between willing buyer and willing seller. The Stock Exchange price was considered by two shareholders as being a depressed price, whereas on a fair valuation the shares were considered to be worth £2·08¾ (as per the Arbitrator's view based upon fair earning capacity). The shareholders maintained that Stock Exchange values did not appraise the correct position.

The court's decision was that whilst the Stock Exchange quotation was the best criterion normally, yet it was not conclusive and might be displaced by evidence affecting the value, the reasoning being:

'If an *individual* shareholder in a company owns such a number of shares in any company as gives him effective control of the company's affairs, it may well be that the value to be attributed to that holding upon a sale of it as a separate transaction is a figure greater than the sum arrived at by multiplying the number of his shares by the market value for the time being of a single share. In such a case a shareholder in question has got, and is able to sell, something more than a mere parcel of shares'.

The two claimants, the court held, had not such a holding as confers an effective control of the company's affairs. In other words, the shares had no 'control' value and the court dismissed the claim for the payment of £2·08¾ per share. This generally indicates the undesirability of acquiring a minority holding in a company.

10. The nature of the capital structure; for example, the ratio of ordinary shares to preference shares. This ratio is of the greatest importance, as in a period of increasing prosperity a company with few ordinary shares in relation to preference shares may raise sharply the dividends on its ordinaries which would tend to increase enormously in value under these circumstances.

11. The effect of death or sale of shares by any member with large and influential holding, particularly as regards continuity of management and contacts.

12. The fact that in non-quoted shares no free market exists.

13. General economic conditions; prospects of a particular trade or industry.

14. Inauguration of Sinking Fund for redeeming redeemable preference shares, or continuing acquisitions of fixed assets secured by borrowing on Mortgage Debentures, necessitating increasing use of profits to build up Debenture Redemption Fund.

15. Political, financial and other external factors.

Where a valuation of ordinary shares is required in the case of the death of a member of a private company, if the deceased held a controlling interest therein within seven (formerly five) years of his or her death, such valuation would follow the somewhat involved procedure laid down by Sect. 55, Finance Act 1940.[1] The valuation would be made, not by reference to dividends, but total assets, otherwise the basis would be:

1. The amount and stability of profits (averages over a reasonably indicative period) adjusted to give effect to matters known or likely to affect profits.
2. Dividends.
3. Reserve appropriations.
4. Capital—both as to amount and structure.
5. Risk involved. Normal yield expected from shares of companies of a similar nature would be deducible from the shares of such companies quoted or dealt in on the Stock Exchange.
6. The utilization of the formula:

$$\frac{dividends}{yield} \qquad \frac{par \; (or \; paid \; up)}{amount \; of \; share.}$$

Obviously, even if the deceased had not a controlling interest, the effects (if any) of the death would require consideration. Normally the effect would be negligible unless the holding, without necessarily being controlling, were substantial.

Equity or 'Net Assets' Basis. The procedure of arriving at the value of a share employed in the equity method is simply to estimate what the assets, *less* liabilities, are worth, i.e. the 'net' assets—allowing for a probable loss or possible profit on book values—the balance being available for shareholders. Included in the liabilities may be debentures, debenture interest, expenses outstanding, and possibly preference dividends if the articles of association stipulate for payment of 'arrears' in a winding up.

If there is one class of share, say ordinary share capital, or even preference and ordinary share capital where the holders of the former have no priority as to capital, the balance available over the total number of shares will represent the value of such shares.

[1] Sect 55, Finance Act 1940, does not apply if the shares were actually dealt in on any recognized Stock Exchange within twelve months before the date of death, and subject to certain reliefs as laid down by Sect. 28, Finance Act 1954, in appropriate circumstances. Sect. 66, Finance Act 1960, gives an important relief in that it virtually abolishes, in the case of ordinary trading companies, the break-up value basis of valuation and substitutes the going-concern basis.

Illustration 9

BALANCE SHEET

	£		£
Share Capital—		Sundry Assets . . .	51,000
10,000 6% Preference Shares of		Discount on Debentures . .	1,000
£1 each fully paid . . .	10,000	Preliminary Expenses . . .	3,000
30,000 Ordinary Shares of £1 each		Profit and Loss Account . .	6,000
fully paid	30,000		
	40,000		
General Reserve	2,000		
Debenture Redemption Fund .	3,000		
7% Debentures . . .	5,000		
Depreciation Fund . . .	1,000		
Sundry Creditors . . .	10,000		
£	61,000	£	61,000

It may be assumed that the assets are worth their book value, that debenture interest for one year is owing, and that the dividends on the preference shares are two years in 'arrear'. Show the approximate valuation of the shares, ignoring tax.

Solution 9

Find the 'net' assets, and in so doing care must be exercised in dealing with reserves. The debenture redemption fund is not a liability, but a portion of the undistributed profits (or in this case a deduction from the loss) and exists as such in accordance with the terms of the debenture deed.

Although it is of no moment here, the student should be familiar with the two alternative methods of arriving at 'net' assets[1]:

(a) Assets			51,000
Less Liabilities—7% Debentures	5,000		
Depreciation Fund . . .	1,000		
Sundry Creditors . . .	10,000	16,000	
			35,000
Less Debenture Interest owing			350
'Net' Assets			£34,650
(b) Share Capital	40,000		
Reserve	2,000		
Debenture Redemption Fund	3,000		
		45,000	
Less Profit and Loss Account . . .	6,000		
„ Discount on Debentures . . .	1,000		
„ Preliminary Expenses . . .	3,000		
		10,000	
			35,000
Less Debenture Interest owing . . .			350
'Net' Assets			£34,650

[1] See p. 3142.

If the preference shares are preferential as to capital they have the first 'charge' on the assets, and as there are ample assets, they are fully covered. In the absence of further participation rights, they are worth £1 each.

The 'net' assets available for the ordinary shares are:

		£
Balance as above	. . . .	34,650
Less Preference Shares	. . . . . .	10,000
'Net' Assets	. . . .	£24,650

Hence, the ordinary shares worth $\dfrac{£24,650}{£30,000} = £0·82\frac{1}{6}$ each.

Should the preference shares be on the same basis as the ordinary shares for capital repayment purposes (merely having the right to dividends only in priority to the ordinary shares) then the value of all the shares $= \dfrac{£34,650}{£40,000} = £0·86\frac{5}{8}$ each.

If the '*arrears*' *of dividends* are to be repaid to the preference shareholders in a winding-up as well as capital in priority, then the valuations will appear as under:

		£
'Net' Assets	. . . .	34,650

Of which preference shareholders will take:

	£	
Capital	10,000	
Plus Preference Dividends (2 years at 6% per annum on £10,000, ignoring Tax)	1,200	
		11,200
Balance to Ordinary Shareholders		£23,450

The preference shares, cum div., are therefore worth $\dfrac{£11,200}{£10,000} = £1·12$ each, and the ordinary shares are worth $\dfrac{£23,450}{£30,000} = £0·78\frac{1}{6}$ each.

Lastly, if the 'arrears of dividends are payable as in the preceding example, but WITHOUT priority as to capital, the result will be as follows:

		£
'Net' Assets	. . . .	34,650
Less Preference dividend	. . . . . .	1,200
		£33,450

The value of all the shares will be $\dfrac{£33,450}{£40,000} = £0·83\frac{5}{8}$, to which will be added $\dfrac{£1,200}{£10,000}$ per share for dividend for preference shareholders = £0·12.

Hence, preference shares are worth £0·83$\frac{5}{8}$ + £0·12 = £0·95$\frac{5}{8}$ each.

Ordinary shares are worth £0·83$\frac{5}{8}$ each.

Even if the equity basis were adopted, there would be many subsidiary matters calling for consideration, e.g. the ratio of fixed and floating assets and their valuation; the proportion of assets acquired at a period of high inflation; the rate of profits earned and the consistency thereof; the rate of development of the business; the trend of profits IN RELATION TO CAPITAL REQUIREMENTS; the effect of events between the last Balance Sheet and the date of the required valuation. Further, in case of death or transfer, it should always be the subject of inquiry as to the effect, if any, upon the prospects and earning capacity, of the substitution of the new holder for the old, as even in large companies the personnel of the directorate counts very considerably.

It need hardly be stressed that when a company is: (*a*) known to be at the end of its life, or (*b*) likely to be taken over on an asset basis by another company, the valuation will be on the above-mentioned basis, even if quoted on the Stock Exchange, because the market value will naturally be based on the break-up basis.

Illustration 10

Using the 'income' basis in Illustration 11 on p. 2620, and assuming that 25 per cent dividend is payable, find the probable approximate value which could be placed on the ordinary shares.

It will be seen that no visible reserves exist, but there may be secret or undisclosed reserves; if none exist, it would appear that dividends have been distributed fully in the past. This, together with the result for the current year (unless accounted for by special circumstances) may tend to require a slightly higher risk than would otherwise be the case. It is assumed that 8 per cent represents a fair return on the class of share in question.

The valuation of the ordinary shares is £$\frac{25}{8}$ = £3·12$\frac{1}{2}$. If the dividend has been declared (or the market is reasonably certain that it will be declared shortly) the price will be £3·12$\frac{1}{2}$ + £0·25.[1] = £3·37$\frac{1}{2}$.

Assuming that 8 per cent is a fair return, the purchaser of 1,000 of these shares cum div. would pay:

	£
1,000 at £3·37$\frac{1}{2}$	3,375
Less Dividend receivable . . .	250
Net Cost	£3,125

His yearly dividend (assuming no change of circumstances) will be £250, i.e. 1,000 at £0·25, hence he receives an annual return of £250 for his net outlay of £3,125 which is exactly 8 per cent.

[1] 25 per cent of £1 = £0·25, ignoring tax.

Illustration 11

Two companies, A and B, are assumed to be exactly on the same footing, not only as to assets, liabilities, and reserves, but also as to all other factors except that the arrangement of the share capital differs.

The share capital of each company is £10,500 in fully paid shares of £1 each, constituted as follows:

A	£	B	£
10,000 6% Preference Shares . . .	10,000	1,000 6% Preference Shares . . .	1,000
500 Ordinary Shares . . .	500	9,500 Ordinary Shares . . .	9,500

The ordinary shares of the companies may be taken to represent a somewhat speculative industrial risk and the market yield is 8 per cent.

The companies' profits and distributions are: 19.1, £1,960; and 19.2, £630.

Estimate the approximate probable prices of the ordinary shares of the companies, ignoring all facts other than those stated above.

The approximate probable prices are:

	A		B	
	19.1	19.2	19.1	19.2
	£	£	£	£
Profits	1,960	630	1,960	630
Less 6% Preference Dividend . .	600	600	60	60
Available for Ordinary Shares .	£1,360	£30	£1,900	£570
Dividends	272%	6%	20%	6%
Price [x.d.]	$£\frac{272}{8} = £34$	$£\frac{6}{8} = £0.75$	$£\frac{20}{8} = £2.50$	$£\frac{6}{8} = £0.75$

It will be seen that, although the profits are the same in both companies, the fluctuations in the prices of the ordinary shares are great. The company having the smaller proportion of ordinary or equity shares is A, and such shares will stand very high in relation to the ordinary OR equity shares of the other company in a PROSPEROUS period and fall very steeply in a SLUMP period. Hence, the 'high geared' equity shares (i.e. the preference shares are high in proportion to the ordinary shares) will rise rapidly in a period of prosperity and fall rapidly in a period of depression, as in (A), whilst 'low geared' equity shares (i.e. the preference shares are low in proportion to the ordinary shares) will rise more slowly in a period of prosperity, and suffer a more gradual fall in a period of depression, as in (B).

Valuation of Preference Shares. The holder of preference shares seeks security as to capital (and with that in view he will be anxious to see that if a winding up ever arises the preference shares have priority over ordinary shares); and secondly, security as to dividends, and from this angle the purchaser will be very much concerned with the rate of dividend payable as well as the question of whether the shares are cumulative or non-cumulative. The preference share is of a precarious nature as will be gathered from the following reasons:

1. They may be non-cumulative.

2. Even where they are cumulative, the preference shareholder is not *guaranteed* an assured annual return on his share. For that matter, nor is a debenture-holder, but the latter's interest does constitute a *charge* upon the profits, and is not merely an *appropriation* of them.

3. The amount represented by the yearly dividend is a *maximum* return.

4. Even if the company has ample earnings, the valuation will be largely affected by ruling rates of interest. For instance, a purchaser of preference shares may be prepared to pay £1·50 for a £1 6 per cent preference share. Such a share will bring the holder, in ordinary circumstances, a return of 4 per cent per annum, but should rates of interest become harder, a preference share of the type that formerly yielded 4 per cent might be required to yield, say, 6 per cent, thus involving a decline in the share value of £1 or so. This possibility of a decline is not as remote as might appear at first sight, even in the highest-grade companies, as recent events have shown. There is also the danger that preference shares purchased at a big premium might be repaid by the company to the holder at par—or even less—by reason of the company being wound up, and although, it should be observed, the Coal Nationalization Act sought to preserve the value of the preference shares of collieries by using the yardstick of dividends and not liquidation, stock exchange or repayment value, yet it has been judicially decided that the Directors may (and, indeed, ought to) pay-off surplus Preference Capital, whether liquidation is contemplated or not (*Scottish Insurance Corporation* v. *Wilson's & Clyde Coal Co., Ltd.*, and *re Chatterley-Whitfield Collieries, Ltd.*).

Illustration 12

The following are Balance Sheets of two well-established companies:

BALANCE SHEETS

	H, Ltd.	S, Ltd.		H, Ltd.	S, Ltd.
	£	£		£	£
Issued Capital (all £1 fully paid—			Freehold and Leasehold Properties at Cost, *less* Depreciation	67,200	14,755
50,000 5½% Preference Shares	50,000		Plant and Machinery at Cost, *less* Depreciation	12,300	3,711
100,000 Ordinary Shares	100,000		Fixtures, Furniture, and Fittings at Cost, *less* Depreciation	3,400	1,730
30,000 Ordinary Shares		30,000	Patents at Cost	8,000	
Profit and Loss Account	27,183	3,280	Debtors	5,200	7,388
Creditors	23,000	8,250	Stock	54,358	11,210
			Bank	19,725	2,736
			Shares in S, Ltd., at Cost	30,000	
	£200,183	£41,530		£200,183	£41,530

The preference shares are cumulative, non-participating, with priority as to repayment in a winding up. The capitals have remained unchanged throughout the history of the companies and ample depreciation has been written off assets, including leaseholds.

S, Ltd. is a subsidiary company of H, Ltd., which owns the *whole* of the Share Capital.

The profits (excluding dividends received by H, Ltd., from its holding in S, Ltd.) were:

	H, Ltd. £	S, Ltd. £
19.3	14,200	3,700
19.4	12,700	4,200
19.5	18,100	1,800
19.6	11,000	1,400
19.7	26,000	3,700
19.8	23,000	5,600
19.9	28,000	6,900
	£133,000	£27,300
	Average = £19,000	Average = £3,900

A similar company's ordinary shares quoted on the Stock Exchange are round about par, its latest dividend being 6 per cent. The same company's 6 per cent preference shares are quoted at £1·20. (This company may be assumed to be fairly comparable with H, Ltd., and S, Ltd.)

You are asked to give your view as to the fair value of the shares of H, Ltd., as the directors contemplate receiving an offer for the purchase of such shares from a rival company. [Ignore Tax.]

The preference shares will be dealt with first.

The combined average profits for the seven years are sufficient to pay the preference dividend over eight times, and in the *worst* year, namely, 19.6, the profits covered the preference dividends over four times.

The preference capital is covered by the combined net assets of the companies more than three and a half times. The net liquid assets of the companies are more than sufficient to cover the preference capital.

As the yield on a preference share of this type appears to be about 5 per cent, the approximate value of the preference shares is:

$$\frac{5\frac{1}{2}}{5} \times £1 = £1 \cdot 10 \text{ ex div.}$$

As to the ordinary shares:

The combined average annual profits available for the ordinary shareholders are:

	£
Holding Company	19,000
Les Preference Dividend	2,750
	16,250
Subsidiary Company	3,900
	20,150
of which, say, 40%[1] is a fair allocation to Reserve, say . .	8,150
Available for Dividend on Ordinary Shares of 12% . .	£12,000

As normally the expected yield on ordinary shares of a similar company is 6 per cent, the valuation of the ordinary shares of the company under inquiry is:

$$\frac{12}{6} \times £1 = £2 \text{ a share, ex div.}$$

The following procedure will be a further test of the valuation:
The capitalized value of the ordinary shares is:

$$\frac{100}{6} \times £12,000 = £200,000$$

$$= £2 \text{ a share, ex div.}$$

The net tangible assets of the company are:

	£	£
Holding Company	170,183	
Less Creditors	23,000	
		147,183
Subsidiary Company	41,530	
Less Creditors	8,250	
		33,280
		£180,463

	£
Valuation of Preference Shares:	
50,000 × £1·10	55,000
Valuation of Ordinary Shares:	
100,000 × £2	200,000
	255,000
Net tangible Assets	180,463
Excess, being estimated Goodwill	£74,537

[1] A company is expected to allocate a substantial proportion of its profits to reserve nowadays. In practice, the amount would be affected by the charge for taxation.

The number of years' purchase of average profits of the two companies is:

$$\frac{74,537}{22,900} = \text{say } 3 \cdot 25 \text{ years.}$$

From the dividend aspect, the stability of dividend cover is the vital criterion. Such cover must be measured by reference, not only to an average, but to the company's most disastrous year. This is so, even if the preference shares are cumulative, and the more so if noncumulative. The sole point of difference between them is that, in the case of the former, they will be entitled to receive the 'arrears' before the ordinary shares are restored to the dividend list. The preference shareholder can only rely upon the result in any *one* year, because a surplus of a year's trading is generally available for the ordinary shareholders, and it is no answer that prudent directors will (or should) set aside a portion of a year's earnings to reserve.

In short, neither the normal nor abnormal years form the true guide, but the subnormal years. Violent fluctuations, though tending to maintain average, make it thoroughly unreliable as a measuring rod for stability.

Illustration 13

Steadfast, Ltd., and Erratic, Ltd., are two companies, each having a 6 per cent Preference Share Capital of £50,000 in fully-paid £1 shares. [Thus the preference dividend required is £3,000 per annum.] The following table shows the earnings and cover for the last six years.

Year	STEADFAST, LTD.			ERRATIC, LTD.		
	Net Earnings	Times Covered	Deviation from Average	Net Earnings	Times Covered	Deviation from Average
	£			£		
19.4	+15,000	5·00	·00	+93,000	31·00	26·00
19.5	+14,100	4·70	·30	+24,000	8·00	3·00
19.6	+16,500	5·50	·50	−4,500	−1·50	6·50
19.7	+14,250	4·75	·25	−27,000	−9·00	14·00
19.8	+15,750	5·25	·25	−10,500	−3·50	8·50
19.9	+14,400	4·80	·20	+15·000	5·00	·00
	£90,000	(b) 30·00	(a) 1·50	£90,000	(b) 30·00	(a) 58·00

Average annual deviation $\left[\dfrac{a}{6}\right]$ . . . (c) ·25 (c) 9·67

Average cover $\left[\dfrac{b}{6}\right]$ . . . . (d) 5·00 (d) 5·00

Coefficient of dispersion $\left[\dfrac{c}{d}\right]$ . . . ·05 1·93

It will be seen that the coefficient in Steadfast, Ltd., is comparatively very small, and signifies a far greater degree of uniformity and stability than is the case of Erratic, Ltd.

The degree of stability of dividends will indicate the measure of risk attached to a preference share; and subject thereto, its value will tend to be in inverse ratio to the ruling rate of interest. For example, a 6 per cent £1 fully-paid preference share, adequately covered, may be priced to yield, say, 4 per cent. The price may, therefore, be expected to be around £1·50 = ($\frac{6}{4}$ × £1) but as interest rates increase, so will the required yield, and hence the price will decrease in ratio. As with ordinary shares, the preference share yield will be greater in the case of a speculative company than in the case of a sounder concern; but so far as the preference share is concerned, not only the nature of the company's activities, but also the degree of stability must be taken into account.

In interpreting the coefficient of dispersion, it is necessary to inquire into special factors, e.g. differing stages of development, whilst the longer the period employed for comparison, the more reliable, in the absence of special factors, will be the deduction.

When dealing with cover, it is essential to bear in mind that the amount required to pay the dividend on prior preference shares must be deducted from the net earnings in gauging the cover for the junior preference shares; whilst the 'gearing' principle (as shown on p. 2623) is applicable.

Illustration 14

A company has three classes of preference shares—1st, 2nd, and 3rd—requiring a yearly dividend of £1,000, £3,000, and £1,500 respectively. Assuming the company's yearly profit to be £6,000, show the cover of each class of preference share.

Share	Balance of Profits	Required for Dividend	Times Covered	Balance
	£	£		£
1st Preference	6,000	1,000	6	(a) 5,000
2nd Preference	(a) 5,000	3,000	1$\frac{2}{3}$	(b) 2,000
3rd Preference	(b) 2,000	1,500	1$\frac{1}{3}$	(c) 500
Available for Ordinary Shareholders	(c) 500			

Finally, even where the preference dividend is amply covered, as to both earnings and stability, the preference shareholder is usually precluded by the Articles of the company from receiving more than the normal value of the share in a winding up; so that, theoretically at all events, a preference shareholder may lose the premium paid for the share in the event of the liquidation of the company.

Sale of Bonus Shares. There will be no profit on the sale of bonus shares until the holder has received therefor an amount exceeding the proportion of the original net cost as represented by the subjoined formula:

$$\frac{\text{Bonus shares}}{\text{Old shares} + \text{bonus shares}} \times \text{Net cost of old shares.}$$

Illustration 15

A purchased 18,000 shares at £2·25 each cum dividend, and received: (1) a cash dividend of £0·35 a share and (2) a bonus share dividend of 'one for three'. Write up the Ledger Account relating to the treatment of the bonus shares, assuming that they were sold at £1·42½ a share. Ignore tax and expenses.

SHARES IN ...., LTD.

		Nominal	Price	£				Nominal	Price	£
			£p						£p	
Purchase .		18,000	[1]1·90	34,200	Sale .			6,000	1·42¼	8,550
Bonus .					Balance .	c/d		18,000	1·42½	25,650
Share										
Dividend .		6,000								
		24,000		£34,200				24,000		£34,200
Balance .	b/d	18,000	1·42½	25,650						

[1] Cost £2·25, less dividend £0·35.

The amount of £8,550 is:

$$\frac{\text{Bonus shares (6,000)}}{\text{Old shares (18,000)} + \text{bonus shares (6,000)}} \times £34,200$$

i.e. ¼ × £34,200   = £8,550

As the sale price of three-quarters of the original cost price of the shares [viz. ¾ × £1·90] is £1·42½, the investor has neither profit nor loss, for he has his original number of shares worth £25,650 and cash £8,550, amounting to £34,200, being the net cost of his original holding.

Sale of Bonus Rights. Where a company increases its issued share capital, giving the shareholders the right to apply for the new shares in a fixed proportion, many shareholders do not wish to increase their holdings and prefer to sell the 'rights' for cash.

The approximate value of such 'right' is arrived at as follows:

(a) Add to the market price of the old shares the cost of the new shares.

(b) Divide the result obtained in (a) by the **total** number of shares now held.

(c) Deduct the result obtained in (b) from the market or cum bonus quotations, giving the approximate value of the 'right'.

Illustration 16

A company whose shares stand at £1·40 cum bonus offers shareholders the right to apply for two new shares at £1·05 each for every five held. show the approximate value of the 'right'.

			£
(a) Old shareholding	. . . . .	5 × £1·40 =	7·00
New shareholding	. . . . .	2 × £1·05 =	2·10
		7	9·10
(b) £9·10 divided by 7	. . . .		1·30
(c) Market value £1·40, less £1·30 is the approximate value of the 'right'	. . . . . .		0·10

Alternatively, the calculation is as follows:

$$\frac{\text{New shares}}{\text{Total shares}} \times (\text{cum bonus price minus new issue price to shareholders})$$

i.e. $\frac{2}{7} \times (£1·40 - £1·05) = £0·10$

Calculation of the 'ex-capital' price of a share after a scrip of a free issue to the ordinary shareholders:

The pre-scrip issue price has to be deflated in proportion to the issue of ordinary shares and, as well, a deduction from the pre-scrip issue must be made in order to take account of the right to the issue of preference shares which disappears when the share in question is quoted 'ex capital'.

Illustration 17

X, Ltd., issues a one-for-four scrip issue to the ordinary shareholder in ordinary shares and a one-for-thirteen scrip issue in $4\frac{1}{2}$ per cent preference shares. The price of the ordinary shares at the date of scrip issue was £1·47$\frac{1}{2}$.

The 'ex cap' price is to assume a holding of 52 ordinary shares—52 because this is the lowest common denominator of 4 and 13. The calculation is then as follows:

	£
52 at date of issue £1·47$\frac{1}{2}$	76·70
Less 4 new Preference Shares say £0·71$\frac{1}{4}$ (see note) . . . (i.e. 1 for 13)	2·85
	73·85
Add 13 new Ordinary Shares . . . . . . (i.e. 1 for 4)	nil
Value of 65 ordinary shares	73·85

Value per ordinary share £$\frac{73·85}{65}$ £1·13$\frac{8}{13}$

The above illustration is taken from an actual market issue; in fact, the price of the ordinary shares rose by £0·06$\frac{5}{13}$ on the first day on which they went 'ex capital', their closing price being £1·20 and that of the preference shares £0·70

(*Note.* This price would be the estimated market price, having regard to the status of the company, whether dividend is cumulative or non-cumulative, number of times preference dividend covered, rights in a winding-up, general level of interest rates, market conditions, etc.)

Published Accounts. Study of published accounts of limited companies shows that the degree of disclosure of the less-enlightened is that dictated by legal compulsions; and there is a marked reluctance to discard the reticent attitude of former years.

With the moral persuasion of the Institute of Chartered Accountants, the Statements of Standard Accounting Practice issued by the leading accountancy bodies and the further legal requirements of the Companies Acts 1948 to 1976, much progress has been made to give the shareholders much fuller and better-arranged information concerning the results of companies' operations and financial state.

INVESTMENT TRUSTS AND UNIT TRUSTS

Investments trusts, together with unit trusts, form a group of financial intermediaries whose main function is to enable investors to spread their risks and to obtain the advantage of professional management of their investments. Both investment trusts and unit trusts have this in common: that they generally hold the shares of a wide range of companies, and thus the purchaser of shares (or units) in the trust spreads his funds in small amounts over a large number of expertly selected investments. There are important distinctions between the two types of trust, however, the main difference being that an investment trust is not really a trust at all but a limited company operating under the Companies Acts 1948 to 1976, whereas a unit trust operates under a trust deed. On pp. 2640 and 2641 a tabular comparison between an investment trust and a unit trust is shown.

Investment Trusts

An investment trust raises its capital by issuing shares to the public in the normal way, and utilizes the funds so obtained to invest in other securities. The investments are varied in order to obtain the maximum return possible. There is often a close link with the new-issue market in such a manner that some investment trust companies underwrite issues of securities which they intend to acquire themselves as permanent investments. In this way, the trusts can obtain securities on very favourable terms. A large number of investment trusts are of Scottish origin, the movement having its main origins in Dundee and Edinburgh towards the end of the nineteenth century after the Companies Act 1862, introduced the principle of limited liability for joint stock companies. Certain investment trusts confine themselves to particular industries or to particular countries, while others spread their funds over several industries and countries. Some trusts specialize in investments in North American companies.

The following extract from the Radcliffe 'Report on the Working of the Monetary System' gives an indication of the nature and extent of the investments made by investment trusts:

'The funds of investment trusts are normally invested in securities that are readily marketable on the Stock Exchange, but since they are willing to remain long-term holders many of them hold unquoted investments or investments in which there is a very limited market. Some would be prepared to take a block of shares in a company with a capital of £50,000 or less if they thought well of its prospects, and would make investments down to £2,000, while others would regard an investment of £20,000 as the lower limit. . . .One or two of the trusts are linked with companies which specialize in nursing small firms to the stage at which a Stock Exchange flotation is possible. There are also some small firms which are jointly owned by a group of associated investment trusts. In those cases the trusts will be represented on the board and may exercise effective control. In general, however, they seek representation only if it seems necessary in order to protect their investment.

The normal method of acquiring unquoted securities is by a placing, either directly or through a broker or issuing house. Investments trusts also underwrite quoted securities and may simply subscribe for the stock which they are asked to underwrite. They are thus an important element in the machinery of the new issue market.'

Investment trusts distribute dividends annually out of the income they receive from their investment assets after allowing for expenses of administration and allocations to reserves. Expenses of administration normally amount to approximately one-third to one-half per cent of the investment trust company's capital. Government statistics reveal that at the end of 1965 the combined assets of some 335 investment trusts had a market value of over £3,000m.

The law and practice relating to the content and form of the published accounts of limited companies is dealt with in Chapter 23, and these apply to investment trust companies.

The Companies Act, 1948, required a distinction to be made between trade and other investments in the Profit and Loss Account. The Companies Act 1967, however, requires that the Profit and Loss Account must show income from investments, distinguishing between income from quoted and unquoted investments (Companies Act 1967, 2 Sch. 12 (1) (g)). Normally, the amounts brought into the credit of the Profit and Loss Account will include tax credit (see Chapter 23 C, Companies and Advance Corporation Tax, etc.). In the case of an ordinary trading company the requirements of Schedule 2 to the Companies Act 1967, in respect of disclosure in Profit and Loss Account of income from investments could be readily satisfied by a simple entry such as the following (Tax being disregarded for present purposes):

Extract from Profit and Loss Account:

	19.9 £	19.8 £
Investment Income:		
From Quoted Investments	x	x
From Unquoted Investments	x	x
	£x	£x

In the case of an investment trust company, however, there would usually be a rather more elaborate treatment of income from investments in the Revenue Account (as the Profit and Loss Account of an investment trust company is conventionally termed), and details should normally be shown by way of note.

Examples of the treatment of investment income in the Revenue Account of two well-known British investment trust companies indicate the similarities and the differences which can arise in the accounts of different companies:

INVESTMENT TRUST COMPANY (A)

Extract from Revenue Account:

	19.8 £	19.7 £
Gross Income:		
Dividends and Interest (1)	x	x

Relative Explanatory Note to Revenue Account

	19.8 £	19.7 £
Note (1)—Dividends and Interest, including estimated Double Taxation Relief:		
Quoted Investments	x	x
Unquoted Investments	x	x
	£x	£x

INVESTMENT TRUST COMPANY (B)

Extract from Revenue Account:

	19.8 £	19.7 £
1. Income—Note (1)		
Interest and Dividends (excluding Double Tax Relief claims):		
Franked	x	x
Unfranked	x	x
	£x	£x

Relative Explanatory Note to Revenue Account:

	19.8 £	19.7 £
Note (1)		
Interest and Dividends (excluding Double Tax Relief Claims) have been received from Investments as follows—		
Quoted on British Stock Exchanges	x	x
Quoted on Other Stock Exchanges	x	x
Unquoted on Other Stock Exchanges	x	x
Investment Funds on Deposit	x	x
	£x	£x

Comparison of these two extracts immediately reveals differences in treatment of certain items, e.g. in the Revenue Account of Company (A) investment income was indicated as including estimated Double Taxation Relief, whereas in the Revenue Account of Company (B) investment income was shown as excluding Double Taxation Relief Claims. Consequently where a uniform disclosure of investment income is not commonly accepted and used, meaningful comparisons cannot readily be made. However in August 1968, the Institute of Chartered Accountants in England and Wales issued a Recommendation of the treatment of investments in the accounts of investment trust companies. Because of Scotland's historic association with the investment trust movement, the English Institute sought the views of the Scottish Institute before issuing the Recommendation. The Scottish Institute was in general agreement with the Recommendation, but several fundamental points of difference arose concerning Balance Sheet disclosures.

C.A. Recommendations.[1] The following are the English Recommendations concerning the Revenue Account (apparently the Scottish Institute are in agreement with the general terms of these):

In order to present a true and fair view and to comply with the requirements of Schedule 2 the following items should be shown separately in the revenue accounts:

(a) Income from (i) quoted investments and (ii) unquoted investments including, in the case of income from overseas investments, the amount before overseas withholding taxes but after all overseas indirect taxes. The amount of franked investment income comprised in the total, gross of income tax, should be disclosed by way of note or otherwise;

---

[1] The following notes relate to the English C.A. Recommendation:

(a) References to 'Capital Gains Tax' are to Corporation Tax on Capital Gains, the rate of which in the case of investment trust companies approved under Section 37 of the Finance Act 1965 as amended, is limited to the rate of Capital Gains tax payable by an individual.

(b) Unless otherwise stated, references are to Schedule 2 to the Companies Act 1967, being the form of Schedule 8 to the Companies Act 1948 as amended by Schedule 1 to the Companies Act 1967.

(c) The final Recommendations only are stated here; preliminary discussions contained in the statements of both Institutes have been omitted. In consequence the paragraph numbering in the English Institute's Recommendation is the same as that shown in the full statement.

(d) interest received from sources other than investments, e.g. bank deposit interest;

(e) other income, e.g. underwriting commission, (where the company is obliged to take up shares, through the issue being under subscribed, it is normal for the commission received to be deducted from the cost of the shares);

(f) expenses of management distinguishing between directors' emoluments and other expenses;

(g) interest payable (i) on short-term loans and to bankers, and (ii) on long-term loans and on debentures;

(h) taxation based on revenue brought into account, stating:
   (i) the amount of United Kingdom corporation tax,
   from which should be deducted:
   (ii) the relief for overseas taxation
   leaving:
   (iii) The amount of United Kingdom corporation tax after overseas taxation relief,
   to which should be added:
   (iv) the amount of overseas taxation
   and
   (v) tax on any surplus of franked investment income, as reduced by any relief for management expenses, charges on income, etc.

Balance Sheet. The following are the English recommendations concerning the Balance Sheet:

10. Investments held by investment trust companies should be regarded as fixed assets.[1] They should preferably be stated in the balance sheet at either:

(a) Cost (or revaluation at a past date) with a note of the market value; or
(b) Market value (including the value as estimated by the directors in the case of unquoted investments).

11. For the purpose of calculating the market value of quoted investments it is appropriate to take middle market price but in any event the basis used should be defined.

12. Paragraph 8 (3) of Schedule 2 requires that quoted investments shall distinguish between those quoted on a recognized stock exchange and those quoted elsewhere. Furthermore, the investments must be stated in a way that enables the accounts to show a true and fair view. In the context, notwithstanding that many overseas quoted investments are also quoted on United Kingdom stock exchanges, the distinction for the purposes of paragraph 8 (3) of Schedule 2 should be made according to the location of the principal market for the shares.

13. If a capital surplus is realized which gives rise to a chargeable gain the capital gains tax thereon should be charged to the account to which the surplus itself is credited.

14. When investments are written up in the accounts on a revaluation (at current market value or otherwise) an estimate should be made of the tax on any chargable gain which would have arisen on a simultaneous sale of the assets at the amount at which they are stated. The estimated amount of this potential liability should either be (a) charged against the surplus on revaluation and credited to a deferred taxation account or (b) shown by way of note and continue to be so shown. There may be circumstances in which the former treatment is the more appropriate. If the latter treatment is adopted, it should be made clear that no provision has been made in the accounts for such potential liability.

15. Where investments are stated in the balance sheet at cost, with a note of market value, the note should include an estimate of any capital gains tax which would have arisen if all the investments had been disposed of simultaneously at the values noted.

16. There should be a note on the accounts stating whether or not the company is approved as an 'investment trust' under section 37 of the Finance Act 1965, as amended. If it is so approved it would be appropriate for the note to mention, in connexion with any entry or note made in accordance with paragraphs 14 and 15 above, that the holders of ordinary shares at the appropriate time after the realization of gains by the company would be personally entitled to relief from capital gains tax on the subsequent disposal of their shares.

17. With effect from 7 April 1965, the premium on investment currency has not been recoverable on that part of any sale proceeds which must be surrendered to the Bank of England (currently 25 per cent) at the official rate of exchange. Any revaluation of such investments, whether written into the balance sheet or stated by way of note, should take account of the whole of the premium, and this basis should be stated. The potential loss on realization represented by the fraction of the premium which is liable to surrender is for accounting purposes similar in nature to capital gains tax arising on a disposal, and procedures in line with those recommended in paragraphs 14 and 15 above should be followed, with necessary adaptations in wording. The estimate of capital gains tax for the purpose of paragraphs 14 and 15 above should then be based on the net value of the investments concerned, after deducting the part of the currency premium which is liable to surrender.

The following is the Scottish Institute's summary of those Balance Sheet matters where their approach differs from that of the English Institute:

1. Investment trust companies should not be considered as fundamentally different from commercial companies: they have the same basic objectives and like commercial concerns they manage their assets for the purpose of producing a growing income for their shareholders.

2. The accounts of investment trust companies should be prepared on a 'going concern' basis, as is done by commercial concerns, and not on a 'break up' basis.

3. Such accounts should give shareholders and other interested parties sufficient information to enable them to form a reasonable view of the affairs of the company.

---

[1] See p. 2649 for SSAP 1/19 Accounting for Investment Properties.

4. The accounts of individual investment trust companies should be drawn up so as to allow valid comparisons with the accounts of other investment trust companies, particularly in regard to 'capital employed'.

5. The most meaningful figure to show in the balance sheet as an asset in respect of investments is market value, taking middle market price at balance sheet date for quoted investments and the directors' valuation for unquoted investments.

6. An approximation of the potential corporation tax liability on unrealized surpluses arising from the valuation of investments should be made.

7. A provision should *not* be made in the balance sheet for this potential liability but it should be disclosed by way of note. Such note (or the director's report) could also usefully include the amount per share of this liability and an estimate of the capital gain per share which would have been apportioned to shareholders free of future taxation if this liability had in fact arisen.

8. For investments in premium currencies the whole premium should be brought into account in arriving at the balance sheet valuation: the amount of the premium which would have to be surrendered if these investments were disposed of should be shown by way of note as in the case of potential tax liability.

9. A standard procedure should be evolved for treating loans in premium currencies: the committee's preference is given in the immediately preceding section.

Note.—the published accounts of a British investment trust company are shown on p. 2643.

Unit Trusts

The unit trust movement has advanced rapidly in recent years probably for the reason that, despite more stringent controls effected as regards setting up and management of such trusts, there are little or no restrictions on advertisements in connexion with them, and units can be purchased readily by small investors. Investment trusts, as already explained, are limited companies and as such are obliged to conform with the legalities of the Companies Acts 1948 to 1976. Units trusts, on the other hand, are actual trusts which are governed by the Trustee Acts[1], by the Prevention of Fraud (Investments) Act 1958, and by the terms of their trust deeds which are in effect legal agreements between the trustees and the trust managers. Before a unit trust can come into operation, the terms of the trust deed must receive approval by the Department of Trade. The main responsibilities of trustees appointed under the trust deed generally are:

(a) To acquire paid-up capital invested in terms of the trust deed.
(b) To ensure adherence to the provisions of the trust deed.
(c) To verify the basis of calculating the buying and selling prices.
(d) To approve all advertisements relating to the unit trust.
(e) To ensure that an adequate reserve fund is set up to meet contingencies.

The Department of Trade regulations concerning unit trusts operate very much in favour of the investors' interest. Indeed, the Department is empowered to ensure that the managers appointed under the trust deed are sufficiently experienced to carry out their responsibilities. The trustees of most unit trusts usually comprise banks and/or insurance companies. The day-to-day management of unit trusts is conducted by experts,

[1] See p. 2641 for information concerning the Trustee Investments Act 1961.

approved by the Department of Trade, and supervised by the trustees in accordance with the terms of the trust deed. To invest in a unit trust, application may be made to the trust managers either direct by completing one of the advertisements which appear regularly in the press or through a banker, stockbroker, solicitor or accountant. A minimum number of units is usually stipulated for initial investment, the value of which is generally stipulated for initial investment, the value of which is generally not less than £50. The amount of minimum subscription required is usually determined by the nature of the unit trust itself.

Generally, a unit-holder's investment in a unit trust is spread over a wide range of securities and the unit-holder obtains a distribution both of risk and of prospects which it would normally be impossible for him to secure in any other way. The securities held by the unit trust are called 'underlying' securities and the total holding is referred to collectively as a 'portfolio'. Some unit trusts, however, are speculative in nature and investments are made in specialized industries in the United Kingdom or overseas. Such unit trusts, aiming at minimizing management costs, often require initial investments of large sums of money of four-figure dimensions. However, unit trusts with general investments portfolios have proved attractive to the small investor, who is often more intent in securing a fairly safe investment. A considerable number of large unit trust concerns operate linked unit trust and life assurance schemes, and many also operate regular savings plans whereby holdings can be built up by regular payments often on a monthly or quarterly basis.

Where a linked unit trust and life assurance scheme is operated, a relatively small part of each trust is utilized to provide life assurance cover for the investor, but Income Tax relief is obtained on the entire amount invested in such units, thus making them particularly attractive. Some schemes guarantee against a fall in prices: if at the time of death, units are worth less than the amount contributed the companies make up the difference.

A unit trust can be of the cash fund type or the appropriation type. In the cash fund type, all monies subscribed on the sale of units are paid direct into the unit fund and thereafter investments are purchased. In the appropriation type, the managers in the first place act as principals and, having first purchased the relative investments, have these appropriated to the fund in exchange for units which are then offered for sale to the public. Most unit trusts formed in recent years have been of the cash fund type.

The expenses of managing unit trusts are met from the amounts invested by the unit-holders. By law, management expenses must not exceed $13\frac{1}{4}$ per cent of the amount invested. The rate charged must be spread over a 20-year period, and the method of so doing is usually left to the discretion of the managers. A fairly high initial charge is usually made (about 5 per cent); a much smaller charge (about $\frac{1}{2}$ per cent), but so as not to exceed $13\frac{1}{4}$ per cent, is levied over the ensuing 19 years often in the form of a half-yearly service charge. The rate charged can be less than $13\frac{1}{4}$ per cent and often is in the case of speculative unit trusts, as already mentioned. One great advantage of unit trust over investment trusts is that whereas in the case of investment trusts marketability problems can often arise, unit trusts are always freely marketable because the unit trust managers are responsible for selling units or buying them back from the investors whenever so requested.

In order to bring a unit trust into line with modern practice and to incorporate the latest requirements of the Department of Trade, Supplemental Trust Deeds are normally executed by the Trustees and Managers and approved by the Department of Trade. Copies of Trust Deeds and any Supplemental Trust Deeds can be inspected during normal business hours at trust offices, or copies may be purchased for a small charge. (*Note.* The half-yearly published accounts of a British unit trust are shown on p. 2647.)

Taxation Aspects. For taxation purposes an investment company is defined as 'any company whose business consists wholly or mainly in the making of investments, and the principal part of whose income is derived therefrom'. Like any other company, the total profits of an investment company resident in the United Kingdom are liable to Corporation Tax. Normally trading companies pay Corporation Tax on trading profits after deducting allowable expenses. Investment companies, however, receive most of their income under deduction of taxation and consequently allowable management expenses are deductible in computing profits liable to Corporation Tax. The management expenses do not include expenses which are deductible in computing income for Schedule A (Rents from Property) purposes. If the management expenses of an accounting period together with allowable 'charges on income'[1] paid during that period cannot be wholly allowed by way of deduction in that period, the unallowed balance may be carried forward to and allowed in a later accounting period. Alternatively a claim may be made to set off the unallowed balance of management expenses against taxation suffered on a surplus of 'franked investment income'.[2] A similar relief may be claimed in respect of charges on income which exceed the profits chargeable to Corporation Tax. Capital Allowances are, as in the case of normal trading companies, deductible as expenses of the accounting period. Where, however, the full amount of capital allowances cannot be allowed in an accounting period, the unallowed balance is treated as a management expense and may be allowed against profits of a future accounting period or periods or against a surplus of franked investment income or against capital gains of the accounting period.

Shareholders in an approved investment company do not pay Capital Gains Tax on gains which have already been taxed in the hands of the investment company. An approved investment company must satisfy the following conditions:

(i) The company must not be a 'close company'.[3]

(ii) The company's income must be derived wholly or mainly from shares or securities.

(iii) The company must not hold shares or securities in a company

---

[1] See p. 2358.　[2] See p. 2363.　[3] See p. 2374.

which amount to more than 15 per cent in value of the whole of the investment company's investments. This does not apply to shares or securities held in another investment company or a company which would qualify as such except that its shares or securities are not quoted on a recognized stock exchange in the United Kingdom.

(iv) The company's shares or securities, or any class of them, must be quoted on a recognized Stock Exchange in the United Kingdom.

(v) The company, by its Memorandum or Articles of Association, is prohibited from distributing as dividends, capital gains arising from the disposal of investments.

(vi) The company, in respect of any accounting period, does not retain more than 15 per cent of income derived from shares and securities.

Condition (iii) does not apply to shares or securities acquired before 6th April 1965, which on that date represented not more than 25 per cent in value of the investment company's investments, or to shares or securities acquired either before or after 6th April 1965, which when acquired represented not more than 15 per cent in value of the investing company's investments, provided that in either case no additional relevant shares or securities are acquired. An additional acquisition, for the purpose, means the acquisition of new shares or securities in exchange for consideration, but does not include share or security exchanges which may take place in the case of amalgamations of companies.

The rate of Corporation Tax payable by an approved investment company on any chargeable gains of an accounting period is the current rate of Capital Gains Tax applicable to an individual and not the current rate of Corporation Tax normally applied to companies.

The excess of an investment company's chargeable gains over the allowable losses after deduction of tax on the net gain are apportioned to the various classes of shareholders. However, shareholders can set off their proportion of the company's chargeable gains against their own liability by deduction from the proceeds of shares subsequently sold by them. Certificates showing the Capital Gains Tax position are issued to shareholders annually. For example, if shares purchased for £1 each are sold at £2·50 each and the accumulated proportion of chargeable gains is £0·25, the effective net sales price is £2·50 *less* £0·25 (or £2·25), and Capital Gains Tax is due on £2·25 *less* £1 (or £1·25).

An authorized unit trust is treated for Corporation Tax purposes in the same way as an investment company. Authorization is obtained from the Department of Trade.

For Capital Gains Tax purposes a unit-holder in an authorized unit trust does not pay tax on gains which have already been taxed in the hands of the unit trust. The net gains realized by a unit trust in an accounting period are apportioned among the unit-holders.

In respect of an investment trust and a unit trust, net gains realized in an accounting period are the gains realized *less* losses for that period and *less* any unrelieved losses brought forward from previous periods and also *less* tax payable on those net gains. The amount apportioned to a shareholder or unit-holder can be added to the cost of the shares or units when calculating liability to tax on disposal of the shares or units. A notice is sent to each shareholder or unit-holder showing the total net gains for the period and the amount thereof apportioned to each.

INVESTMENT TRUST AND UNIT TRUST COMPARED

INVESTMENT TRUST

Incorporated under the Companies Acts 1948 and 1967, and regulated by its Memorandum and Association.

Share Capital may be geared as in normal companies; thus there may be ordinary and preference shareholders. Debentures may also be issued. Prospectus and minimum subscription required before business permitted to commence. Managed by directors of the company.

Shareholders are entitled to attend and vote at Annual General Meetings.

Shares are bought and sold through stockbrokers. Transfer can be effected by means of Stock Transfer Form.

Prices of shares are determined by the market prices of the relevant types of shares quoted on the Stock Exchange.

Shares purchased must normally be paid for in full at date of acquisition.

Management expenses are not controlled by legislation and directors' remuneration is, in theory, determined by the shareholders.

Dividends on fixed capital are paid according to the fixed rates specified. Ordinary dividends may be high, in total anyway, because under Capital Gains Tax 85 per cent of investment income must be distributed for a company to qualify as an investment trust. The general policy, however, is to plough back a certain proportion of distributable profits to reserve.

UNIT TRUST

Incorporated under a trust deed conforming with the Trustee Acts and the Prevention of Fraud (Investments) Act 1958, and regulated by the Department of Trade.

Trust deed involves the trustee, usually a bank or insurance company which holds the securities; the settlors, viz. the managers of the trust and the beneficiaries, viz. members of the public who invest in the trust. Trustees must have minimum paid-up capital of £500,000.

Unit-holders have no proprietorship rights and are not entitled to attend trust meetings.

Units are bought and sold through the trust managers. Application to purchase may be made direct to managers or through a bank, solicitor, broker, accountant. Sales are effected by managers within a short time of simple notification from unit-holder.

Prices of units are determined by the trust managers in accordance with formula laid down by the Department of Trade.

In certain unit trusts unit-holdings may be built up by a regular saving scheme.

Management expenses are restricted to a maximum of $13\frac{1}{4}$ per cent over a 20-year period. Trustees' and managers' remuneration is determined by the trust deed and/or supplemental trust deeds.

Taxation legislation provides that all investment income is deemed to be taxable in the hands of the unit-holders in the year the investment income is received by the trust. Consequently most unit trusts distribute all available profits.

INVESTMENT TRUST	UNIT TRUST
Company is liable to pay Corporation Tax on profits.	Unit trust is liable to pay Corporation Tax on profits.
Company is liable for Capital Gains Tax in respect of investments sold at a profit (computed at the Personal Rate).	Unit trust is liable for Capital Gains Tax in respect of investments sold at a profit (computed at the Personal Rate).
Certificates are issued to shareholders showing the company's net capital gains for each accounting period allocated to each type of share held on specified dates and shareholders are entitled, where shares are sold, to add these amounts per share to either their prices at 6th April 1965, or later leading to acquisition date. These amounts can then be set off against the shareholders' Capital Gains Tax Computations by deducting them from the prices realized.	Certificates are issued to unit-holders showing the trust's net capital gains for each accounting period allocated to the unit-holders, and showing related middle market price rates. Unit-holders are entitled, where units are sold, to add appropriate amounts to their market prices at 6th April 1965, or cost prices, if later. These amounts can then be set off against the shareholders' Capital Gains Tax Computations by deducting them from the prices realized.

TRUSTEE INVESTMENTS ACT 1961

This Act provides that trustees who wish to invest in equities, i.e. ordinary shares, are required to divide the fund into two equal portions—Part I and II, the 'narrower-range' portion, to be invested only in specified types of fixed-interest securities; and Part III the 'wider-range' portion, which can be invested in securities, such as equities, outside the narrower range.

The first Schedule to the Act as extended by the Trustee Investments (Additional Powers) Order 1964 and various other enactments, specifies in Part I: **Narrower-Range Investments not requiring advice.** These comprise National Savings Certificates; National Development Bonds; Post Office Savings Bank deposits; deposits in Ordinary Departments of Trustee Savings Banks.

In part II the **Narrower-Range Investments requiring advice** include chiefly:

1. British Government Stocks; fixed-interest stocks of British Commonwealth Governments, local and public authorities, nationalized industries and those issued in Britian by the International Bank;
2. Stock and mortgage loans of British local authorities;
3. Debentures issued by a British company provided that the issued share capital is not less than £1-million and a dividend has been paid on all its shares in each of the preceding five years;
4. Deposits in Special Investment Departments of Trustee Savings Banks;
5 Deposits in a designated Building Society;
6. Mortgages of freehold property in England, Wales and Northern Ireland and leasehold property in these countries with not less than 60 years to run, and in loans on heritable security in Scotland.
7. Perpetual rent charges in England, Wales and Northern Ireland, and feu-duties or ground annuals in Scotland.

In Part III the **Wider-Range Investments** include:

(*a*) Any securities in a United Kingdom company not falling within the list in Part II. These comprise preference shares and equities, provided that the company has issued capital of not less than £1-million and has paid a dividend in each of the preceding five years;

(*b*) Shares in a designated building society;

(*c*) Units or other shares in a unit trust authorized by the Department of Trade.

Part of all the wider-range fund can be invested in narrower-range investments but not vice versa. Once the division is made, the two funds have to be kept separate.

In the exercise of his powers of investment, a trustee has to consider the need for diversification and the suitability of the trust investment. Unless he himself is an investment expert, he may not invest in anything but Defence Bonds, National Savings Certificates and Post Office or Trustee Savings Banks or bank deposits without securing the advice, confirmed in writing, of 'a person who is reasonably believed by the trustee to be qualified by his ability in and practical experience of financial matters'. The trustee also has to obtain and consider the advice of the expert at such intervals as appear to the trustee to be appropriate.

Notes

(i) On 15th May 1964, Defence Bonds were replaced by National Development Bonds which, in turn, were replaced, on 1st April 1968, by British Saving Bonds.

(ii) On 1st October 1969, the Post Office Saving Bank was renamed the National Saving Bank.

ILLUSTRATION OF PUBLISHED ACCOUNTS OF AN INVESTMENT TRUST COMPANY[1]

REVENUE ACCOUNT

For the year ended 30th November 19.7

	Notes	19.7 £	19.7 £	19.6 £	19.6 £
Gross Revenue	1				
Franked investment income			2,702,062		2,422,273
Unfranked investment income					
United Kingdom			16,058		67,523
Overseas			399,584		314,275
Interest on short term deposits			278,625		159,643
Underwriting Commission			19,819		19,565
			3,416,148		2,983,279
Expenses					
Management expenses		174,312		103,085	
Directors' fees	2	12,500		12,500	
Auditors' remuneration		3,538		3,322	
			190,350		118,907
			3,225,798		2,864,372
Interest Charges	3		89,282		36,939
Net revenue before taxation			3,136,516		2,827,433
Taxation	4		1,162,990		1,058,502
Revenue after taxation			1,973,526		1,768,931
Dividends					
On 4¾% preference stock	5	24,771		24,771	
On 5% preference stock	5	31,500		31,500	
			56,271		56,271
Earned on ordinary stock			1,917,255		1,712,660
per unit of 25p		(3·954p)		(2·532p)	
On ordinary stock units of 25p					
Interim: 1·15p per unit (19.6: 1·08p)		557,589		523,649	
Proposed Final: 2·72p per unit (19.6: 2·37p)		1,318,819		1,149,118	
			1,876,408		1,672,767
			40,847		39,893
Taxation adjustments			452		456
Unappropriated revenue			41,299		40,349
Balance brought forward from last year			2,270,989		2,230,640
Balance carried forward			£2,312,288		£2,270,989

[1] In this illustration and on the following one of a unit trust, only the published accounts themselves and certain relevant notes are shown. In fact, other details would be included with the published accounts, e.g. the Directors' Report, Auditors' Report, trust details, trust portfolio and additional information for shareholders and unit-holders.

STOCK EXCHANGE TRANSACTIONS, ETC.

BALANCE SHEET

as at 30th November 19.7

	Notes	19.7 £	19.7 £	19.6 £	19.6 £
Investments at valuation	6				
Quoted:					
In Great Britain		51,380,230		31,114,904	
Abroad		13,037,707		12,797,341	
			64,417,937		43,912,245
Unquoted:					
In Great Britain		567,155		1,226,500	
Abroad		127,665		87,527	
			694,820		1,314,027
			65,112,757		45,226,272
Subsidiary Companies	7				
Shares		2		1	
Current account		329		368	
			331		369
Current Assets					
Sales for future settlement		57,090		80,356	
Short term deposits		4,478,722		2,803,596	
Cash with banks		16,358		127,798	
		4,552,170		3,011,750	
Less: Current liabilities					
Creditors		19,536		11,711	
Bank overdraft		30,810			
Purchases for future settlement		141,483		3,153	
Debenture interest accrued		2,833		2,833	
Dollar loan interest accrued		20,225		—	
Provision for taxation	8	487,759		94,095	
Provision for dividends	9	1,346,955		1,177,254	
		2,049,601		1,289,046	
Net current assets			2,502,569		1,722,704
Capital employed			£67,615,657		£46,949,345
Financed as follows:					
Debenture debt and dollar loan	10				
4¼% debenture stock 1984/90		800,000		800,000	
U.S. dollar loan 1982		1,376,425		—	
			2,176,425		800,000
Capital: authorised and issued					
4¾% cumulative preference stock	5	745,000		745,000	
5% cumulative preference stock	5	900,000		900,000	
Ordinary stock (in units of 25p)		12,121,500		12,121,500	
Reserves					
Capital—share premium		108,500		108,500	
general	11	49,251,944		30,003,356	
Revenue Account		2,312,288		2,270,989	
Ordinary Stockholders' interest			63,794,232		44,504,345
			£67,615,657		£46,949,345

.... Director

.... Director

NOTES ON THE ACCOUNTS

Accounting Policies

(a) Investment income and interest are included in revenue on the date on which they are received. All income is stated gross. Imputation tax credits are shown in the charge for taxation.

Overseas income at rates of exchange ruling when remitted.

Provision is made for all outstanding expenses and accrued interest payable.

(b) Quoted investments are valued at middle market prices and unquoted investments at a valuation determined by the Directors. The full investment currency premium is added to valuations where applicable.

(c) Assets and liabilities denominated in overseas currencies are converted into sterling at rates of exchange ruling at the close of the Company's financial year.

(d) Gains and losses on the disposal of investments, together with provisions for taxation on chargeable gains, are dealt with through General Capital Reserve.

1. Gross Revenue

	19.7	19.6
Income received from unquoted investments was as follows:		
Franked	£13,399	£6,077
Unfranked—United Kingdom	6,806	20,588
Overseas	4,342	3,706
	£24,547	£30,371

2. Directors' fees

The Chairman, who is the highest paid Director	£3,500	£3,500
Number of other Directors (in range £0–£2,500)	4	4

3. Interest charges (gross)

On Bank overdraft	£2,476	£2,939
On 4¼% Debenture Stock 1984/90 (See Note 10)	34,000	34,000
On Dollar Loan—repayable within 5 years	52,806	—
	£89,282	£36,939

4. Taxation

Corporation Tax at 52% (52%)	£239,000	£212,500
Less: relief for overseas tax	53,532	38,543
	£185,468	£173,957
Overseas Tax	52,532	38,899
Tax suffered on franked income	924,990	845,646
	£1,162,990	£1,058,502

Provision has not been made for advance corporation tax on the dividends proposed in these accounts as, in the opinion of the directors, such tax will be fully relieved. (See Note 8 below).

A provision of £384,948 (19.6: nil) for taxation on net chargeable gains arising from the realisation of investments during the year has been made as shown in Note 11.

5. Preference Stocks

Under the provisions of the Finance Act 1972, dividends on the 4¾% and 5% cumulative preference stocks of the Company are paid at annual rates of 3·325% and 3·5% respectively and carry imputed tax credits calculated with reference to the basic rate of income tax at the time of payment.

6. Investments at valuation

The full investment currency premium of 38% (19.6: 39¼%) amounting to £3,850,334 (19.6: £3,672,887) is included in the valuation of overseas investments and currencies and takes into account the sum of £3,501 (19.6: nil), being the premium on the amount by which the valuation of the dollar loan portfolio exceeds the dollar loan liability.

The reduction during the year in the value of unquoted investments in Great Britain largely arises from the public quotation obtained by A. B. Sea (Oils) Ltd.

7. Investment in subsidiary companies

The wholly owned subsidiary companies are Sydney Investments (Australia) Ltd., which is registered in Australia, and Investment Management Ltd., which is registered in England. The accounts of these companies have not been consolidated because of the insignificant amounts involved. The book value of the investment in each case is only £1.

The U.K. subsidiary formed during the year has not traded.

The running expenses of the Australian subsidiary amounting to £4,018 (19.6:£3,947) have been met by payment of a service fee which is included in the Company's expenses of management.

8. Taxation (Balance Sheet)

The provision for taxation is the estimated total liability to United Kingdom taxes, less relief due in respect of income tax and overseas tax suffered by deduction from unfranked investment income, payable 1st September 19.8. A nominal liability to Advance Corporation Tax amounting to £198,000 (19.6:£125,000) existed on 30th November 19.7 in respect of the final ordinary dividend provided on that date. No provision has been made for the sum as the liability will be eliminated by tax credits on franked investment income received before the dividend is paid.

9. Provision for dividends

	19.7	19.6
Preference—for half year to date	£28,136	£28,136
Ordinary—proposed final for year	1,318,819	1,149,118
	£1,346,955	£1,177,254

10. 4¼% Debenture Stock 1984/90 and dollar loan

(a) The Debenture stock is to be repaid at par on 1st November 1990 but it may be redeemed in whole, or in part, any time after 1st November 1984 on the Company giving two months' notice.

(b) The dollar loan represents amounts drawn down—U.S. $2,500,000 (19.6:nil)—against a Multi-currency loan facility of U.S. $4,000,000 repayable on 7th April 1982, or earlier at the option of the Company. It is secured on specific investments denominated in U.S. dollars.

11. General capital reserve

Balance at 30th November 19.6		£18,352,520
Add: net profit on investments realised during year		3,226,080
		£21,578,600
Deduct: expenses of formation of subsidiary company, written off	£188	
expenses relating to negotiation of dollar loan agreement	1,328	
provision for tax on net chargeable gains of the year	384,948	
		386,464
Balance at 30th November 19.7		£21,192,136

The figures shown in the Balance Sheet are arrived at as follows:—

	19.7	19.6
General capital reserve as above	£21,192,136	£18,352,520
Unrealised appreciation on investments held at year-end	28,059,808	11,650,836
	£49,251,944	£30,003,356

Unrealised appreciation includes the sum of £23,883,665 (19.6:£6,583,065) which is taxable if realised (see Note 12 (c)).

12. Contingent Liabilities

There are contingent liabilities in respect of:

(a) uncalled capital amounting to £147,100 (19.6:£97,703) on shares held as investments.

(b) surrender of 25% of the investment currency premium applicable to overseas investments and currencies. In the event of such investments held at 30th November 19.7 being realised thereafter at the valuation incorporated in the accounts the surrender of premium would have amounted to £962,583 (19.6:£918,222). The requirement to surrender 25% of the investment currency premium on sales of premium worthy securities has been subsequently removed with effect from 1st January 19.8.

(c) tax on chargeable gains. In the event of all investments held at 30th November 19.7 being realised thereafter at the valuation incorporated in the accounts the liability, after allowing for the loss of dollar premium as shown above, would have been approximately £3,805,000 (19.6:£985,000).

Sources and Applications of Funds

	19.7 £'000s	19.6 £'000s
Sources		
Revenue before tax	3,136	2,827
Sale of Investments		
United Kingdom	5,991	6,509
Overseas	1,965	2,375
Foreign currency loans raised	1,376	—
Currency differences—realised	9	9
unrealised	105	—
	12,582	11,720

Applications			
Purchase of Investments			
United Kingdom	5,045		5,424
Overseas	3,276		2,990
Dividends paid	1,763		1,656
Taxation paid	1,155		1,185
		11,239	11,255
Increase/Decrease in Liquidity		1,343	465
Increase in Sales for Future Settlement	46		(177)
Increase in Creditors	(166)		684
	(120)		507
Movement in net liquid funds:			
Increase in short term deposits	1,568		422
Decrease in cash with banks	(105)		(464)
	1.463		(42)
		1,343	465

Capital gains Tax

In so far as a gain or loss on a disposal falls to be computed under reference to market values of the Company's stocks at 6th April 1965, these were as follows:

4¼% debenture stock 1984/90	£68·60
4¼% debenture stock 1984/90 (ranking for interest from 1/4/65)	£71·30
4¾% cumulative preference stock units of £1	63p
5% cumulative preference stock units of £1	71·5 p
Ordinary stock units of 25p	62·5 p

ILLUSTRATION OF PUBLISHED ACCOUNTS OF A UNIT TRUST

The Trust's accounts for the six months ended 15th April 19.9

Income Account	£	£	Group 1	£ per unit
Gross Income				
Franked		1,587,882		·0030
Unfranked	259,062		·0005	
Less: Corporation tax (Provided at 45%)	116,578		·0002	
		142,484		·0003
		1,730,366		·0033
Equalization receivable on creation of units		44,316		—
		1,774,682		·0033
Management charge payable in accordance with Clause 13(A) of the trust deed	119,020		·0002	
Less: Relief from taxation	53,559		·0001	
		65,461		·0001
		1,709,221		·0032
Related tax credits		655,001		·0012
		1,054,220		·0020
Balance brought forward	7,109		—	
Add: Adjustment to previous distributions	12,378		—	
	19,487		—	
Less: Balance carried forward	12,126			
		7,361		—
Amount to be distributed on 1st June 19.9		£1,061,581		·0020

Capital Account   £

Value of the Trust fund on 15th October 19.8	107,075,779
Amount vested on creation of units: For Securities	248,012
For Cash	7,577,554
	7,825,566
	114,901,345
Investment sold: Realized profit	2,045,872
Appreciation thereon brought to account on 15th October 19.8	2,026,910
Surplus realized since 15th October 19.8	18,962
Provision for taxation on Capital Gains	482,581
	463,619
	114,437,726
Unrealized appreciation in the value of the portfolio since 15th October 19.8	6,295,910
Value of the Trust fund on 15th April 19.9	**£120,733,636**

Distribution per unit

	group 1	group 2
Group 1—Units purchased before: 16th October 19.8	£	£
Group 2—Units purchased: 16th October 19.8 to 15th April 19.9		
Dividends—Payable	·002000000	·000946862
—Equalisation	—	·001053138
Total per unit to be paid on 1 June 19.9	·002000000	·002000000
Related tax credit	·001404254	·000664817

Equalization is the accrued income included in the price of units purchased during the distribution period which, after averaging, is refunded as part of a unitholder's first distribution, giving the same net rate on all units. As a capital repayment it is not liable to tax but must be deducted from the cost of the units for capital gain tax purposes.

Notes to the Accounts
 1. The bid price per unit (ex-distribution) on 16th April 19.0 was £0·22$\frac{11}{12}$.
 2. The tax voucher shows net gains of £0·002121408 per unit. For further details see Tax Matters below.
 3. There were 530,790,425 units in creation on 15th April 19.9.

Tax Matters (Note referred to in Notes to the Account)
 The imputed tax credit on your distribution is 41·25 per cent. If you are a unitholder or hold a Monthly Investment Plan the amount of the distribution plus tax credit shown on the voucher should be entered on your tax return, and if you are entitled to do so you may claim repayment of tax up to the amount of the tax credit through your Inspector of Taxes. You will not be taxed again on your distribution unless you are liable to higher rates of tax. When you come to dispose of your holding of Units you will be able to reduce the long-term gains (on which tax is payable) by the amount of any 'net gains' apportioned to your holding of units. 'Net gains' are gains less losses on the changing of investments within the unit trust after deduction of the tax payable by the unit trust. Any such 'net gains' appropriate to your holding would be recorded on your tax voucher, which should be retained along with the contract notes or other purchase records.
 The middle price on 6th April 1965 on which capital tax calculations may be based was £0·14$\frac{3}{8}$. As from 16th April 19.9 and until 15th November 19.9 the 1965 valuation, adjusted for all net gains certifications, is £0·14950775.

Accounting for Investment Properties. Statement of Standard Accounting Practice 1/19 concerns accounting for Investment Properties and is largely reproduced hereunder.

PART I—EXPLANATORY NOTE

1. Under the accounting requirements of SSAP 12 "Accounting for Depreciation", fixed assets are generally subject to annual depreciation charges to reflect on a systematic basis the wearing out, consumption or other loss of value whether arising from use, effluxion of time or obsolescence through technology and market changes. Under those requirements it is also accepted that an increase in the value of such a fixed asset does not generally remove the necessity of charge depreciation to reflect on a systematic basis the consumption of the asset.

2. A different treatment is, however, required where a significant proportion of the fixed assets of an enterprise is held not for consumption in the business operations but as investments, the disposal of which would not materially affect any manufacturing or trading operations of the enterprise. In such a case the current value of these investments, and changes in that current value, are of prime importance rather than a calculation of systematic annual depreciation. Consequently, for the proper appreciation of the financial position, a different accounting treatment is considered appropriate for fixed assets held as investments (called in this standard "investment properties").

3. Investment properties may be held by a company which holds investments as part of its business such as an investment trust or a property investment company.

4. Investment properties may also be held by a company whose main business is not the holding of investments.

5. Where an investment property is held on a lease with a relatively short unexpired term, it is necessary to recognise the annual depreciation in the financial statements to avoid the situation whereby a short lease is amortised against the investment revaluation reserve whilst the rentals are taken to the profit and loss account.

6. This statement requires investment properties to be included in the balance sheet at open market value. The statement does not require the valuation to be made by qualified or independent valuers; but (in paragraph 12) calls for disclosure of the names or qualifications of the valuers, the bases used by them and whether the person making the valuation is an employee or officer of the company. However, where investment properties represent a substantial proportion of the total assets of a major enterprise (e.g., a listed company) the valuation thereof would normally be carried out:

(*a*) annually by persons holding a recognised professional qualification and having recent post-qualification experience in the location and category of the properties concerned; and

(*b*) at least every five years by an external valuer.

PART II—DEFINITION OF TERMS

7. For the purposes of this statement, but subject to the exceptions in paragraph 8 below, an *investment property* is an interest in land and/or buildings:

(*a*) in respect of which construction work and development have been completed and

(*b*) which is held for its investment potential, any rental income being negotiated at arm's length.

8. The following are exceptions from the definition:

(*a*) A property which is owned and occupied by a company for its own purposes is not an investment property.

(*b*) A property let to and occupied by another group company is not an investment property for the purposes of its own accounts or the group accounts.

PART III—STANDARD ACCOUNTING PRACTICE

9. This statement does not apply to investment properties owned by charities.

10. Investment properties should not be subject to periodic charges for depreciation on the basis set out in SSAP 12, except for properties held on lease which should be depreciated on the basis set out in SSAP 12 at least over the period when the unexpired term is 20 years or less.

11. Investment properties should be included in the balance sheet at their open market value.

12. The names of the persons making the valuation, or particulars of their qualifications, should be disclosed together with the bases of valuation used by them. If a person making a valuation is an employee or officer of the company or group which ownes the property this fact should be disclosed.

13. Subject to paragraph 14 below, changes in the value of investment properties should not be taken to the profit and loss account but should be disclosed as a movement on an investment revaluation reserve, unless the total of the investment revaluation reserve is insufficient to cover a deficit, in which case the amount by which the deficit exceeds the amount in the investment revaluation reserve should be charged in the profit and loss account. In the special circumstances of investment trust companies and of property unit trusts it may not be appropriate to deal with such deficits in the profit and loss account. In such cases they should be shown prominently in the financial statements.

14. Paragraph 13 does not apply to the financial statements of pension funds and the long-term business of insurance companies where changes in value are dealt with in the relevant fund account.

15. The carrying value of investment properties and the investment revaluation reserve should be displayed prominently in the financial statements.

Date from which effective

16. The accounting and disclosure requirements in this statement should be adopted as soon as possible and regarded as standard in respect of financial statements relating to accounting periods starting on or after 1 July 1981.

CHAPTER 27

INSURANCE CLAIMS

Loss of Profit Insurance. This type of insurance, sometimes called 'consequential loss', has for its purpose the indemnification of the insured for losses arising from the suspension, wholly or in part, of the activities of the business caused by fire. Policies vary considerably according to circumstances applicable to the particular business, but the following conditions are generally contained in the policy:

1. The period of indemnity is fixed in the policy.

2. The basis of compensation is computed by reference to a percentage which the turnover is supposed to earn. This percentage multiplied by the amount of turnover reduced or lost as a result of the fire gives the amount of the claim, subject to certain amendments and limitations arising out of the 'special circumstances clause' and the 'average proviso', to be mentioned later.

3. (a) The percentage is calculated on the trading results of the **last accounting period** as follows:

$$\frac{\text{Net Profits} + \textit{Insured} \text{ Standing Charges}}{\text{Turnover}} \times 100$$

It will be noted that this percentage is, broadly, the rate of Gross Profit for the last **accounting** period and it is the **ONLY** occasion when reference is made to the figures for the last accounting period.

Where there is a Net Loss instead of a Net Profit, the formula above will be amended as follows:

$$\frac{\textit{Insured} \text{ Standing Charges} - \text{Net Loss}}{\text{Turnover}} \times 100$$

(b) The reduced turnover is the turnover of the period of interruption following the fire (but not exceeding the period of indemnity) as compared with the turnover of the **corresponding period** of the **year immediately preceding** the fire, technically described as the *standard* turnover. For instance, if a fire occurred on 31st January 19.8, and the period of indemnity was for three months, a comparison would be made of the turnover for February, March, and April 19.8, with those of February, March and April 19.7, in order to arrive at the 'reduced' turnover.

4. The insurance company will not generally undertake a consequential loss risk unless there is also, in addition, an admission of liability for loss of property by fire.

5. Although a period is fixed as in (1), the liability of the insurance company will not extend beyond the period of interruption, i.e. the period subsequent to the fire during which the diminished activities arising from the fire continue; for example, though the period of indemnity might be fixed for six months, if the interruption of normal business be for only two months, the liability of the insurance company will be for the latter period and NOT six months.

6. There is usually a clause for indemnity to cover an increase in Cost of Working (i.e. an increase of insured standing charges due to the fire), for the sole purpose of 'avoiding' or reducing the reduction in turnover (that is, in effect, trying to increase the turnover) which, but for this additional cost, would have taken place, or would have been maintained, during the period in consequence of the damage. There are, however, certain limitations—where all the insurable standing charges are not covered by the policy then a proportion only of the claim will be allowed, viz.:

$$\frac{\text{Net Profit} + \text{INSURED Standing Charges}}{\text{Net Profit} + \text{ALL Insurable Standing Charges}}$$

Furthermore, the claim can never exceed the sum produced by applying the rate of Gross Profit (as calculated in 3 (a)) to the amount of reduction in turnover thereby 'avoided', that is, the maximum saving of liability of the insurer.

From such a claim for increased cost of working, as computed above, will be deducted any savings in insured standing charges that may have been thereby effected.

7. There is usually included in the policy what is known as the SPECIAL CIRCUMSTANCES CLAUSE, which states 'that such adjustment shall be made as may be necessary to provide for the trend of the business and for variations in or special circumstances affecting the business either before or after the damage, or which would have affected the business had the damage not occurred, so that the figures thus adjusted shall represent as nearly as may be reasonably practicable the results which, but for the damage, would have been obtained during the relative period after the damage'. This clause may, therefore, affect the calculations for the Rate of Gross Profit, reduced turnover, and increase in cost of workings.

8. AVERAGE PROVISO. By such a clause, a final limitation to the claim will arise if 'the sum insured by the policy be *less* than the sum produced by applying the rate of gross profit (as computed in 3 (a)) to the annual turnover (i.e. turnover for the 12 months IMMEDIATELY BEFORE the date of the fire), the amount payable shall be proportionately reduced'. For example, if the rate of Gross Profit is 30 per cent, the annual turnover £20,000, and the amount insured £5,000, the effect of this most important proviso is to reduce proportionately the sum that would (but for the proviso) be payable; that is, to pay only:

$$\frac{\text{Amount Insured}}{\text{rate of Gross Profit} \times \text{Annual Turnover}} = \frac{£5,000}{30\% \text{ of } £20,000}$$

$$= \tfrac{5}{6} \text{ of the claim.}$$

This, it must be emphasized, is a limiting clause, and the insurance company's liabilities will be restricted to the normal claim or the amount as reduced by the average proviso, whichever is the smaller.

Whilst the subject, simple in principle, may involve considerable complex computations, students will find little trouble if they remember the following points when preparing a claim:

(a) Fixing the period of the claim by taking the period of indemnity or the period of interruption, whichever is the smaller.

(b) Ascertaining the 'short' or reduced turnover.

(c) Calculating the rate of gross profit based on the last **accounting** period preceding the fire.

(d) Computing the gross profit lost by applying (c) to (b).

(e) Adding thereto increased Cost of Working, bearing in mind the two restrictions as mentioned in (6).

(f) Deducting any savings in insured standing charges.

(g) Applying, if required, any amendments to the foregoing arising out of the 'special circumstances clause'.

(h) Finally, ascertaining if the circumstances call for the application of the 'average proviso', and applying it, if necessary, in reduction of the claim.

Illustration 1

Z was insured for consequential loss. A fire occurred on 31st March 19.., and as a result there was a diminished turnover (as compared with the corresponding months of the preceding year) of £10,000; the insured was insured for a period which adequately covered the dislocation period, and no special factors existed.

The accounts for last accounting (or financial) period, of a year to 31st January 19.., showed a net profit of £2,000 after debiting standing charges (all insured), £3,000, the turnover being £50,000.

Show particulars of claim.

[The accounting period comes into the calculation *solely* in order to find the *rate of gross profit.*]

$$\text{The Rate of Gross Profit} = \frac{£2,000 + £3,000}{£50,000} \times 100 = 10 \text{ per cent}$$

Loss of Turnover   £10,000

Loss of Gross Profit—10 per cent thereof   Claim £1,000

Illustration 2

Assume the same facts as those in the previous illustration, except that the amount insured was £2,400 and that the turnover for the year immediately preceding the fire (Annual Turnover) was £32,000.

In order to see if the average proviso applies, the rate (already ascertained by reference to the accounting period) is applied to the Annual Turnover. The amount so ascertained is:

$$10 \text{ per cent of } £32,000 = £3,200$$

As, however, the amount of gross profit is insured only for £2,400, the proviso operates so as to reduce the claim proportionately. Therefore, the amended claim is:

$$\frac{2,400}{3,200} \times £1,000 = £750$$

Illustration 3

From the following information compute Consequential Loss claim:

Financial year ends 31st December with Turnover of £200,000.
Fire takes place 1st June following.
Period of interruption: 1st June to 1st November.
Period of indemnity: 6 months.
Net Profit £12,000, plus *Insured* Standing Charges £24,000 = 18 per cent rate of Gross Profit. $[\frac{36}{200} \times 100]$.
Sum Insured £36,300.
Uninsured Standing Charges £2,000.
Standard Turnover, i.e. for corresponding months (1st June to 1st November) in the year preceding the fire, £75,000.
Turnover in period of interruption £22,500.
Annual Turnover (i.e. twelve months preceding the fire) £220,000.
Increase of Cost of Working £4,000, with a saving of insured standing charges £1,500.
Reduced Turnover avoided through Increase in Cost of Working £10,000, i.e. but for this expenditure the turnover after the fire would have been only £12,500.
Owing to reasons acceptable to the insurer, the 'special circumstances' clause stipulates for:

(i) increase of Turnover (Standard and Annual) by 10 per cent;
(ii) increase of rate of Gross Profit from 18 per cent to 20 per cent.

COMPUTATION OF CLAIM

	£
Loss of Gross Profit:	
Turnover in Standard period	75,000
Add agreed increase of 10 per cent	7,500
= Adjusted Standard Turnover	82,500
Less Actual turnover during period of interruption (period of indemnity of six months being adequate)	22,500
Reduced Turnover	£60,000

	£	£
Agreed Rate of Gross Profit thereon = 20 per cent		
Loss of Gross Profit		12,000
Increase in Cost of Working	4,000	

Apportionment by reason of uninsured standing charges—

$$\frac{\text{Net Profit} + \text{Insured Standing Charges}}{\text{Net Profit} + \text{All Standing Charges}} = \frac{12,000 + 24,000}{12,000 + 26,000}$$

$$= \frac{36}{38} = \qquad £3,789$$

The sum produced by applying the rate of adjusted Gross Profit to the amount of the reduction in Turnover avoided—£10,000 at 20 per cent.

	£
Therefore limited to [See (a) in next illustration]	2,000
	14,000
Less saving in Insured Standing Charges [see (b) in next illustration]	1,500
	£12,000

Average proviso

The adjusted rate of Gross Profit applied to the adjusted Annual Turnover is 20 per cent of £242,000 = £48,400, which is more than the amount **insured** (£36,300), so that the average clause applies.

$$\frac{\text{Amount Insured}}{\underset{\text{Rate of Gross Profit} \times \text{Annual Turnover}}{\text{(adjusted)} \qquad\qquad \text{(adjusted)}}}$$

$$= \frac{36,300}{20\% \text{ of } (220,000 + (10\%) \text{ i.e. } 22,000)} = \frac{36,300}{48,400} = \frac{3}{4} \text{ (or 75 per cent)}$$

Hence the amount payable under the policy is

75 per cent of £12,500 = £9,375

Illustration 4

If, in relation to the preceding illustration, there had been no adjustments in the 'special circumstances' clause, i.e. the rate of Gross Profit remaining at 18 per cent and the turnover at the original figure of £200,000, the claim would be:

	£
Loss of Profit 18 per cent of £75,000 − £22,500 = 18 per cent of £52,500	9,450
Increase in Cost of Working *less* Savings in Insured Standing Charges (£1,800 − £1,500) (See (*a*) and (*b*) in preceding illustration)	300
	£9,750

Average proviso

$$\frac{36,300}{18\% \text{ of } 220,000} = \frac{36,300}{39,600} = \frac{11}{12} \text{ (or 91·67 per cent)}$$

Hence the amount payable under the policy is 91·67 per cent of £9,750 =   £8,938

The additional benefit arising from the 'special circumstance' clause (raising the rate of Gross Profit and Standard Turnover) without the average proviso is £12,500 − £9,750 = £2,750; by applying the 'special circumstances' clause the benefit that would have so arisen has been substantially reduced by the operation of the 'average' clause, as the claim is £9,375 instead of £8,938.

This result arises from the fact that in relation to the adjusted circumstances the cover by the amount insured is made grossly inadequate. The combined effect of the increases both of Turnover and Gross Profit has imperilled the amount insured (representing the limit of liability to the insurer). Cover of £36,300 on a turnover of £200,000 carrying a Gross Profit of 18 per cent is a very different proposition from £36,300 cover on a turnover of £242,000 carrying a Gross Profit of 20 per cent.

Loss of Stock Claims. Subject to verification of facts an insurance company will, in consideration of a premium, agree to indemnify a trader in respect of loss of stock by fire or other causes.

Where it is not possible to verify the actual stock lost, a frequent plan is to construct a 'Trading Account' assuming a given rate of gross profit earned on sales and therefrom compute the stock at end, that is, the stock (on the assumption given) that would be in existence but for the cause of the loss of stock, e.g. fire.

In the examinations the percentage results usually 'work out' in round sums, but the practical aspect should (in a note) be commented on in asnwering this type of question. Apart from the fact that, in practice, the exact percentage result will rarely arise, except, for instance, in slow-moving and expensive lines (motor cars, jewellery) and nearly so in branded and fixed-price goods (e.g. patent medicines, cigarettes), many factors will arise to upset the percentage result, such as:

1. End season sales at 'cut' prices.
2. Goods likely to perish or deteriorate after a short period sold off at reduced prices.
3. Circumstances requiring goods to be purchased locally to fulfil urgent orders.
4. Changes beyond executive control, e.g. in the tobacco trade where the increase of duty is passed on to retailer without permitting of retail price to be increased by more than the extra duty.
5. Pilferage.

In preparing a claim for submission to an insurance company in respect of stock lost by fire where a 'Trading Account' is to be constructed, the following information would be required:

(a) Basis of previous stocktakings, particularly as regards consistency of valuation.

(b) The stock value at the date of the last Balance Sheet (or nearer date, e.g. where accounts are prepared periodically and stock actually taken or based on reliable estimates).

(c) The total purchases of goods from the date used in (b) to the date of the fire, care being taken to exclude therefrom goods invoiced but not delivered to the premises where the fire has occurred.

(d) The total sales of goods for the period indicated in (c).

(e) The value of stock salvaged.

(f) The average rate of gross profit made in recent years, having regard to any factor likely to render such average rate unreliable, e.g. change in nature and type of goods sold; effect of price controls and orders; variations in wholesale prices not yet adjusted to consumer; and variations of rate of gross profit, e.g. through wholesale price increase exactly passed on to consumer, or owing to the preponderance of sales of one class of goods carrying a gross profit rate higher or lower than another class, in a short-term period, that is where the incidence of sales per month or other short period, as between articles giving highly differential rates of gross profit, is subject to variation, e.g. in the month of January sales of goods carrying a low rate of gross profit might be at their peak, whilst those with a high rate of gross profit might be at their 'low', owing to seasonal influences.

In addition, the precise terms of the policy would have to be examined, particularly as regards the 'average clause', which would operate to the disadvantage of the insured if he was not fully covered. If the value of the stock was, say £10,000 and the insured was covered for £8,000 then the average clause could operate so that the insured could claim only for eight-tenths of his loss, even if it was less than £8,000.

Illustration 5

A fire occurred on the premises of a merchant on 25th July 19... The value of the stock salved was £170.

The books disclosed that on 1st March 19.., the stock was valued at £4,020; the net purchases to the date of the fire amounting to £25,180, and the net sales to £32,000.

The average gross profits for the last three years (the agreed basis) were 15 per cent on sales. Prepare claim.

TRADING ACCOUNT FOR THE PERIOD 1ST MARCH TO
25TH JULY 19..

19..		£	19..		£
Mar. 1	Stock . . .	4,020	July 25	. Sales. (Net	32,000
July 25	Purchases (Net) . .	25,180		Stock	2,000
	Gross Profit . . .	4,800			
		£34,000			£34,000

FIRE CLAIM

	£
Loss of Stock per Trading Account .	2,000
Less Value of Salvage . . .	170
Balance due from Insurance Company	£1,830

Notes. (a) There may be a special clauses in the insurance policy to which the claim must adhere. The insurance company are entitled to replace the actual stock which, owing to falling prices, may be less than £1,830 in value.

(b) The fact that a uniform gross profit of 15 per cent on sales is earned every year does not necessarily indicate that such a uniformity exists in every section of the business or is uniformly earned during every part of the year; e.g. using simple figures, a 20 per cent rate may be earned during the first half of the year and 10 per cent for the second half.

If the question had stated that the average gross profits for the last three years were $\frac{3}{17}$ on cost of goods sold, it would merely be necessary to translate the fraction in terms of *sales*, i.e. $\frac{3}{20} = 15$ per cent.

It may be noted that the same principle is applied in stock estimating systems. If there had been no fire, the statement of the approximate stock for the period, assuming it to be for one month, would be as follows:

ESTIMATE OF STOCK

		19.. March			19.. April		19.. May	
		£	£		£	£	£	£
Balance at commencement	b/f	4,020		b/f	2,000			
Purchases (net)		25,180	29,200					
Sales (net)		32,000						
Less Gross Profit		4,800	27,200					
Balance at end	c/f		£2,000					

The figures for the succeeding months will be inserted in due course.

Illustration 6

On 15th June 19.9, the premises of Beech and Pine were destroyed by fire, but sufficient records were saved from which the following particulars were ascertained:

	£
Stock at Cost, 1st January 19.8	7,350
Stock at Cost, 31st December 19.8	7,960
Purchases, less Returns, year ended 31st December 19.8	39,800
Sales, less Returns, year ended 31st December 19.8	48,700
Purchases, less Returns, 1st January 19.9, to 15th June 19.9	16,200
Sales, less Returns, 1st January 19.9, to 15th June 19.9	23,120

In valuing the stock for the Balance Sheet at 31st December 19.8, £230 had been written off certain stock which was a poor selling line, having cost £690. A portion of these goods were sold in March 19.9, at a loss of £25 on original cost of £345. The remainder of this stock was now estimated to be worth the original cost. Subject to the above exception, gross profit had remained at a uniform rate throughout.

The Stock salvaged was £580.

Show the amount of the claim.

Rate of Gross Profit based upon the accounts for the year ended 31st December 19.8:

	£	£
Sales, less Returns		48,700
Less Opening Stock	7,350	
,, Purchases, less Returns	39,800	
	47,150	
Less Closing Stock (31st December 19.8)	7,960	
		39,190
		9,510
Add amount of Stock written off at 31st Dec. 19.8		230
Gross Profit on normal Sales—20%		£9,740

Value of Stock 15th June 19.9, based on sales from 1st January 19.9 to 15th June 19.9.

	Normal £	Abnormal £	
Sales	22,800	320	
Gross Profit—20% on normal Sales	4,560	90	(see (3))
Cost of Sales	£18,240	£230	
Stock, 31st December 19.8	7,500	460	
Purchases	16,200	—	
	23,700	460	
Less Cost of Sales	18,240	230	
	5,460	230	
Add Old Stock	345	115	(Appreciation) (see (3))
	5,805	£345	
Less Salvage	580		
Value of Stock for claim	£5,225		

Notes. 1. For the purpose of ascertaining normal Gross Profit, the depreciation of the abnormal Stock must be eliminated.

2. When the account is built up, the total commencing Stock must be split as between:

	£
(a) 'Normal'	7,500
(b) 'Abnormal' [£690 − £230]	460
Balance Sheet, 31st December, 19.8	£7,960

[3]. In regard to the 'abnormal' Stock, it is obvious that half was 'cleared' for £320, showing a profit (in terms of the written down value at 31st December, 19.8) of £90; thus:

	Stock Sold £		Stock Unsold £	Total £
Cost Price	345		345	690
Less Written off, 31st Dec. 19.8	115		115	230
	230		230	£460
Sale	320	Appreciation	115	
Profit	£90	Stock, 15th June 19.9	£345	

4. The question arises as to whether the restoration of the £115 written off is justified, seeing that such Stock is *still* unsold at 15th June 19.9 and would, therefore, be a matter requiring a satisfactory explanation to the insurance company.

5. It is assumed that the write-off of £230 made in December 19.8, was applicable uniformly to the whole of the abnormal Stock, and these goods were in units of equal value.

Book-keeping Entries. The amount of the agreed claim will be debited to the insurance company and

(a) Stock lost—credited to Trading Account.

(b) Expenses in connection with the claim and of repairing DAMAGED assets—credited to the appropriate expense accounts (thus eliminating or reducing the debit against expenses incurred).

(c) Assets lost—credited to assets accounts and the balance of:

1. a loss debited to Loss of Asset Account;
2. a profit credited to Profit and Loss Account or Reserve.

Salved stock, if retained by the insured, will be debited to a Salved Stock Account and credited to the Trading Account. As the LOSS (i.e. the difference between the true value and salved value) has been debited to the insurance company and credited to Trading Account (see (a) *supra*), the latter account is in credit for the same amount of stock as if no loss had occurred.

If such salved stock is taken over by the insurance company, there will be a correspondingly increased loss to the insured which will augment the amount of the claim in (a), so that the full loss will be included in the claim and credited to Trading Account; hence the entries in the foregoing will not arise.

Illustration 7

Importers, Ltd., suffered loss by fire. Claims made against and admitted by Credential Insurance Co., Ltd., and expenditure, were:

			£		£		£
Loss of profits	.	. claimed	6,000	admitted	4,000		
Stock Damaged	.	. ,,	4,000	,,	2,000		
Stock Destroyed	.	. ,,	5,000	,,	4,000		
Building Damaged	.	. ,,	1,200	,,	1,000	repairs cost	1,100
Fittings Destroyed	.	. ,,	1,000	,,	900	renewal cost	950
Fire Expenses	.	. ,,	80	,,	80	cost	80
			£17,280		£11,980		

The amounts claimed and admitted for loss of profits were half in respect of loss of profits in 19.7 and 19.8, and half in respect of advertising expenditure, put to suspense in 19.6, which it was proposed to write off equally in 19.7, 19.8, and 19.9, and which had been rendered partly useless.

Renewals of fittings (which originally cost £800 and had not been written down) and repairs to buildings were completed by and paid for on 31st December 19.7; the expenses were also paid on that date.

Show by Journal entries the records that should be made in the books of Importers, Ltd., at the end of 19.7.

JOURNAL

	£	£
Stock Destroyed	5,000	
,, Damaged	4,000	
Trading Account		9,000
Being value of stock transferred.		
Credential Insurance Co., Ltd.	11,980	
Profit and Loss Account		1,000
,, ,, Suspense		1,000
Advertising Suspense		2,000
Stock Damaged		2,000
Stock Destroyed		4,000
Buildings		1,000
Fittings		900
Fire expenses		80
Being sundry claims admitted by insurance campany.		
Profit and Loss Account	3,100	
Stock Damaged		2,000
Stock Destroyed		1,000
Buildings		100
Being claims re stock and excess of repairs not admitted and now written off.		
Salvaged Stock	?	
Profit and Loss Account		?
Being valuation of damaged stock.		

Notes. 1. The Profit and Loss Suspense Account should be carried forward and credited in 19.8.

2. Advertising Suspense should be written off as early as practicable.

3. Cash received will be credited to the Insurance Co., and that paid for repairs debited to Buildings and Fittings Accounts respectively.

4. There is a profit on fittings of £100 which may be transferred to reserve.

Own Insurance. Large companies often prefer to carry a proportion of risk themselves, thus reducing the amount payable in respect of insurance premiums. It is highly desirable, however, to allocate a certain proportion of the profits for the purpose of providing a fund that can be used should a loss (which is not fully covered by insurance) occur. As cash will be required to acquire an asset in substitution for the one destroyed, such reserve is usually invested in good marketable securities. Much depends on chance as to the success of one's own insurance, as a loss may be incurred in the very early stages of the building up of the fund. It should not be forgotten that any loss chargeable to the fund will be the book value less depreciation, e.g. a car has a book value of £600 on 1st January 19.8, and it is totally destroyed on 31st December 19.9; it can be discerned immediately that the real loss is somewhat less than £600; as the car will have diminished in value by use and obsolescence. If £262 represents the depreciation, then the amount of the loss is only £338.

Illustration 8

Scarsdale Motor Co., Ltd., insured its motors for four-fifths of their value, providing for the uncovered risk by a yearly appropriation to an insurance reserve of 10 per cent of one-fifth of the written-down value, commencing at the beginning of the FIRST year. At 1st January 19.9, the balance of Motor Account (after providing for depreciation at the rate of 10 per cent per annum on the diminishing balance) is £100,000, the insurance reserve having been credited with four annual contributions totalling £9,434. The reserve has been invested in £12,560 7 per cent Loan at 70, 75, 78, and 80 in respective years.

On 30th September 19.9, an accident occurred causing a total loss of one of the motors, standing in the books at the **commencement of the first year** at £2,743 to nearest £. A cheque was received from the insurance company for £1,584, being the agreed sum due under the claim, *less* 1 per cent commission. The motor is not to be replaced, and on 31st December 19.9, the fifth contribution is made to the insurance reserve and the required sum invested in 7 per cent Loan at 85. There have been no additions to, or sales of, motors within the foregoing period. Brokerage and interest may be ignored. Show Journal entries without narratives, dealing with the claim and the fifth appropriation to the insurance reserve, assuming no other changes in the Motor Account. All calculations are to be made to the nearest £.

JOURNAL

19.9		£	£
Sept. 30	Motor Loss Account	2,000	
	Motor Account		2,000
	Depreciation Account	150	
	Motor Loss Account		150
	Insurance Company	1,600	
	Insurance Reserve[1]	400	
	Motor Loss Account		1,850
	General Reserve[1]		120
	Insurance Reserve[1]		30
	Profit and Loss Account	16	
	Insurance Company (1% of £1,600) . . .		16
Dec. 31	Depreciation	9,800	
	Motor Account		9,800
	Profit and Loss Account	1,764	
	Insurance Reserve		1,764
	Insurance Reserve Investment	1,394	
	Broker		1,394

[1] The insurance company, according to the question, indemnifies the insured for the book value of the lost motor at the commencement of the year of loss. Thus, four-fifths of the depreciation (£120) written off represents a profit, which will be transferred to general reserve. The remaining one-fifth depreciation (£30) will be transferred to the credit of insurance reserve.

Note. The written down value of the motor lost at 30th September 19.9, was £2,000, *less* £150 (10 per cent on £2,000 for nine months) = £1,850, of which one-fifth (£370) is applicable to the Motor Company.

The depreciation at 31st December 19.9, is arrived at as follows:

	£
Motor Account at 1st January 19.9	100,000
Less Motor at written down value . . .	2,000
	£98,000
10 per cent for year	£9,800

The transfer to Insurance Reserve is computed as follows:

	£
Book Value of Motors at 31st December 19.9 . .	98,000
Less Depreciation	9,800
Balance at 31st December 19.9, *after* depreciation .	£88,200

The risk carried by the motor company $= \frac{1}{5} \times £88,200 = £17,640$.
Annual allocation is 10 per cent of risk $= 10\% \times £17,640 = £1,764$.
The cash to be invested is arrived at as follows:

The investment at 1st January 19.9, was built up in the three preceding years by investing a similar amount in 7 per cent Loan at the prices indicated in the question, representing the annual allocations to the Insurance Reserve. It will be seen that each year 10 per cent of one-fifth of the Motor Account is transferred to the latter account. The allocations are as shown on the next page.

The Investment Account as at 1st January, 19.9 will be as follows:

INVESTMENT

			Nominal						
19.9 Jan. 1	Balance .	b/d	£ 12,560	£ 9,434					

The Insurance Reserve Account will be as follows:

INSURANCE RESERVE

19.9				£	19.9			b/d	£
Sept. 30	Sundries . .			400	Jan. 1	Balance . . .	b/d		9,434
Dec. 31	Balance. . . .	c/d	10,828	Sept. 30	Sundries . . .			30
					Dec. 31	Transfer from Profit and Loss Account . .			1,764
				£11,228					£11,228
					19.0 Jan. 1	Balance . . .	b/d		10,828

The amount, therefore, to be invested is £10,828 *less* £9,434 = £1,394.

MOTOR

Year			£	Year			£	Allocation to Insurance Reserve	Nominal Amount Invested
1	Cash		137,174	1	Depreciation		13,717	$\frac{1}{50} \times 137,174 = \frac{£}{2,743}$	$2,743 \times \frac{100}{70} = \frac{£}{3,919}$
					Balance	c/d	123,457		
			£137,174				£137,174		
2	Balance	b/d	123,457	2	Depreciation		12,346	$\frac{1}{50} \times 123,457 = 2,469$	$2,469 \times \frac{100}{75} = 3,292$
					Balance	c/d	111,111		
			£123,457				£123,457		
3	Balance	b/d	111,111	3	Depreciation		11,111	$\frac{1}{50} \times 111,111 = 2,222$	$2,222 \times \frac{100}{78} = 2,849$
					Balance	c/d	100,000		
			£111,111				£111,111		
4	Balance	b/d	100,000	4	Motor Loss Account		2,000	$\frac{1}{50} \times 100,000 = 2,000$	$2,000 \times \frac{100}{80} = 2,500$
					Depreciation		9,800		
					Balance	c/d	88,200		
			£100,000				£100,000		
5	Balance	b/d	88,200						£12,560

Total Reserve at the beginning of the 4th Year £9,434

$\frac{1}{50} \times 88,200 =$ £1,764

¹ i.e. 1st January 19.9.

This sum invested will buy $£1,394 \times \frac{100}{85}$ Nominal 7 per cent Loan = £1,640; hence, the Investment Account as at 1st January 19.0 will be as follows:

INVESTMENT

			Nominal					
19.9			£	£				
Jan. 1	Balance	b/d	12,560	9,434				
Dec. 31	Broker	.	1,640	1,394				
			£14,200	£10,828				

Note. The fifth contribution has been made (in accordance with the question) on 31st December 19.9, not 1st January 19.0.

Compensation Claims. Claims may arise:

1. By acquisition of premises by local authorities for the purposes of widening of streets, slum clearance, purchase of property for new buildings, etc., resulting in:

2. Removal expenses.

3. Increased rental.

4. Damage (or loss) in respect of fittings and fixtures.

6. Loss in connection with the sale, removal of or damage to stock and other assets.

6. Increased cost of new leases or loss of value of unexpired portion of lease.

7. Loss of goodwill.

8. Loss in connection with discontinued use of old address, e.g. discarding advertising blocks containing old address.

9. Possible inability to complete contracts within the stipulated period.

10. Loss of sub-rentals.

The claim may or may not be increased by interest till settlement.

CHAPTER 28

BANKRUPTCY

A person who is in financial difficulties usually finds it necessary to call his creditors together; whereupon he will, unless other arrangements are made, either have to execute a deed of arrangement, or will be formally adjudicated bankrupt. The law requires certain evidences of unwillingness or inability to pay creditors before the formality (with resultant disabilities) of bankruptcy can be imposed upon the debtor, although it should be remembered that the sole fact of inability to pay debts as they arise, i.e. insolvency, is not synonymous with bankruptcy, inasmuch as a certain procedure must be followed before a state of bankruptcy can exist.

The importance of the subject from an accounting point of view lies in the necessity for the preparation of a Statement of Affairs, Deficiency Account, and the accounts for winding up the affairs of the bankrupt. The law relating to bankruptcy will be considered only in so far as it is relevant to the accountancy aspect.

Statement of Affairs. The debtor (who invariably invokes professional assistance) must prepare a Statement of Affairs, setting out the assets and liabilities in a certain form which will be dealt with in detail later, together with a further statement explaining how the present position has been arrived at, called the Deficiency or Surplus Account.

The details may assume somewhat formidable proportions, but the principle involved is extremely simple, and once the elementary rules are thoroughly assimilated, no difficulty should be experienced in the working of examination problems on this subject. The procedure is as follows:

1. A rough statement should be prepared with assets on the right-hand side and liabilities on the left, in ordinary two-sided Balance Sheet form.

2. Each item must appear on the *same* side in the Statement of Affairs or Deficiency Account as it appears in the rough Balance Sheet.

The estimated value of each asset will appear on the right-hand side of the Statement of Affairs.

The estimated amount of each liability will appear on the left-hand side of the Statement of Affairs.

The estimated loss (the excess of the book value over estimated realizable value of an asset, or the increase in the amount of liability over the book value) will appear on the right-hand side of the Deficiency Account.

The estimated gain (the excess of estimated realizable value over the book value of an asset, or the decrease in the amount of liability over the book value) will appear on the left-hand side of the Deficiency Account.

3. Any item not in the rough balance sheet must appear both in the Statement of Affairs and in the Deficiency Account, but on reverse sides; in other words, there must be double entry therefor.

4. The Capital Account must be accounted for in the Deficiency Account on the same side as it appears in the Balance Sheet. Certain

adjustments are required in connection with the Capital Account, as will be noticed presently, but the rule herein will, nevertheless, be followed.

5. The balance of the Statement of Affairs and Deficiency Account will be equal and closed by a cross transfer.

These rules may be summarized:

(a) Every item in the Balance Sheet must be accounted for directly or indirectly on the corresponding side of the Statement of Affairs or the Deficiency account.

(b) Any item not in the Balance Sheet must directly or indirectly appear both in the Statement of Affairs on the one side and in the Deficiency Account on the opposite side.

It should be noted that there is a fixed layout in which bankruptcy accounts are presented, as shown in detail on p. 2822. In the first few examples the layout is, for convenience, only approximately adhered to, so that the principles may be fully explained.

Illustration 1

The following is the Balance Sheet of XY as it appears on the 31st December 19..:

BALANCE SHEET

	£		£
Sundry Creditors (c) . . .	600	Sundry Debtors (b) . . .	1,000
Loan (c)	55	Stock (a)	150
Capital (d)	495		
	£1,150		£1,150

The debtors are estimated to produce £325 and stock £180. The creditors and loan-holders have no special rights.

Prepare in *rough* outline the Statement of Affairs and Deficiency Account for submission to the creditors.

STATEMENT OF AFFAIRS

	£		£
Unsecured Creditors (c) . .	655	Stock (a)	180
		Debtors (b) . . .	325
			505
		Deficiency (e) . . .	150
	£655		£655

DEFICIENCY ACCOUNT

	£		£
Capital . . . (d)	495	Bad Debts . . . (b)	675
Appreciation of Stock . (a)	30		
Deficiency as per Statement of Affairs . . (e)	150		
	£675		£675

It will be observed that each item in the Balance Sheet is duly accounted for on its proper side, the only item likely to cause trouble being that of stock. The Balance Sheet shows the item of £150 on right-hand side, but being worth £180 the latter value must be shown in the Statement of Affairs on right-hand side, so that in order that the two statements will 'balance' £30 will be shown on the LEFT-hand of the Deficiency Account. The balance on each of the accounts will be reflective and closed by a transfer (item marked 'e'). The sides of the Statement of Affairs are similar to those of a Balance Sheet, whilst those of the Deficiency Account are opposite to those of a Profit and Loss Account, so that the left-hand side of the Deficiency Account is GAIN, and the right-hand side is LOSS.

Where, as is required by law, the capital at a date prior to the Statement of Affairs has to be ascertained, the intervening movement of capital must be traced, but, as already mentioned, the same principle applies, viz. that the capital balance in some form or other must appear on the same side of the Deficiency Account as it appears in the Balance Sheet from which the Statement of Affairs and the Deficiency Account are prepared.

Illustration 2

Assume the same facts as in the previous illustration, and in addition the question states that a year ago the debtor's capital was £2,100; his profits (*less* losses) being £400, and his drawings £2,005. Now, it is clear that the left-hand item of £495 (present capital per Balance Sheet) must be accounted for, i.e. a net left hand of £495: hence it is necessary to key up the intervening figures, thus:

LEFT HAND	£	£	RIGHT HAND
Old Capital . . .	2,100		
Add profits . . .	400		
		2,500	
Less Drawings . . .		2.005	
Net left-hand Balance . .		£495	

All that requires to be done is to substitute the details above for £495, taking care that the latter item is not actually inserted in addition to the substituted figure. The above affects only the Deficiency Account, which therefore will be:

DEFICIENCY ACCOUNT

		£			£
Capital	(d)[1]	2,100	Drawings . . . (d)		2,005
Profits	(d)	400	Bad Debts . . . (d)		675
Appreciation of Stock	(a)	30			
Deficiency as per State-					
ment of Affairs	(e)	150			
		£2,680			£2,680

[1] The phrase used in the official form is: 'Excess of assets over liabilities on . .'

The items marked (d) (italicized) simply replace the single item 'left hand' of £495.

The preparation of these accounts, although essentially the same in principle, is not quite so simple when—as almost invariably happens— there are different grades of creditors. For the moment, it will suffice to say that, where a creditor holds property of the debtor as security, he is able to utilize it; and may claim against the estate of the bankrupt for the balance if the security falls short of the debt, but must surrender the surplus to the estate if the security exceeds the debt due. Certain other creditors have the right to be paid in priority to the ordinary or unsecured creditors. These creditors are known as preferential creditors. On pp. 2809–10 a full list is given and illustrated; but the principle of dealing with the unsecured and preferential creditors will first be shown.

Illustration 3

X, who has been adjudicated a bankrupt, shows the following assets and liabilities (put in Balance Sheet form). The figures in parenthesis on the assets side show the estimated realizable value of the respective assets.

X—BALANCE SHEET

	£		£	Estimated to produce £
Creditors	2,300	Debtors (h) . . .	1,500	(1,200)
Bank Overdraft . . .	520	Stock	430	(300)
Loan secured by Mortgage		Cash (a)	25	(25)
on buildings . . .	1,000	Buildings (g) . . .	1,560	(1,100)
Capital	295	Goodwill (c) . . .	500	(Nil)
		Patent (d) . . .	100	(230)
	£4,115		£4,115	

Of the creditors, £360 are preferential; the bank has no security. The capital of X three years ago was £1,000, his losses for the last two years being £705, and the profit for the year prior thereto, £700. His drawings over the period of three years were £700.

Prepare Statement of Affairs and Deficiency Account.

The important points to observe are:

(*a*) The capital (see previous illustration) will not appear as £295 in the Deficiency Account, but as follows:

	£		£
Capital	1,000	Losses	705
Profit	700	Drawings	700
	£1,700		£1,405

(*b*) The item of buildings £1,560 would, in the ordinary course, be shown as follows:

> Statement of Affairs—right hand . . £1,100 (estimated realizable worth)
> Deficiency Account do. . . 460 (estimated loss on realization)

As, however, it is security, it is shown in the Statement of Affairs in a different form (but having the same effect on the balancing result) as a DEDUCTION from the left-hand item—LOAN ON MORTGAGE.

(*c*) The preferential creditors are included in the £2,300, which is a left-hand item, and hence £2,300 must be accounted for as follows:

	£	£
Unsecured Creditors—		
Sundry Creditors	2,300	
Less Preferential Creditors . . .	360	
		1,940
Bank		520
		£2,460

The preferential creditors are shown in short (but not carried into the total column) on the left hand, but as they have the first right to the free assets they are DEDUCTED from the estimated value of the free assets.

STATEMENT OF AFFAIRS

Liabilities	£	£	*Assets*	£
			Cash (*a*)	25
Unsecured Creditors (*e*) .		2,460	Stock (*b*)	300
Loan (*f*) . . .	1,000		Goodwill (*c*) . . .	—
Less Buildings (*g*) .	1,100		Patent (*d*)	230
			Debtors (*h*) . . .	1,200
Surplus to *Contra* .	£100[1]		Surplus per *Contra* . .	100[1]
				1,855
			Deduct Preferential Creditors .	
Preferential Creditors (*e*)	£		(*e*) per *Contra* . .	360
deducted *Contra* .	360			1,495
			Deficiency	965
		£2,460		£2,460

[1] See note [1] on p. 2806.

DEFICIENCY ACCOUNT

	£			£
Capital	1000	Business Loss		705
Profits	700	Bad Debts (h)		300
Appreciation of Patent	130	Depreciation of Stock (b)		130
Deficiency as per State-		Depreciation of Buildings (g)		460[1]
ment of Affairs	965	Depreciation of Goodwill (c)		500
		Drawings		700
	£2,795			£2,795

[1] If reference be made to the Balance Sheet it will be seen that Buildings £1,560 right hand, and Loan £1,000 left hand = £560 net right hand. This is reflected in items[1]: i.e. £100 Surplus of Security over debt right hand, *plus* £460 in Deficiency Account (for loss of value on buildings) = £560 right hand.

(e) The Creditors in Balance Sheet left hand are reflected in the above £2,460 left hand and £360 right hand deduction = £2,820 (i.e. Creditors, £2,300 + Bank Overdraft, £520).

Sometimes, in addition to there being a first mortgage on property, there is a second mortgage. In this case, the surplus, if any, of the security available for the first mortgagee is not brought over to the free assets, but deducted from the loan of the second mortgagee.

The treatment is dealt with below, the whole of the illustration being concentrated on this particular point.

Illustration 4

From the following particulars prepare a Statement of Affairs and Deficiency Account.

							Estimated Value
						£	£
Unsecured Creditors	.	.	.	.	.	1,800	
Preferential Creditors	.		.	.	.	200	
Loan First Mortgage	.	.	.	.	.	1,000	
Loan Second Mortgage	.	.	.	.	.	300	
Sundry Assets	.	.	.	.	.	2,000	(1,010)
Buildings (Security for the Mortgages)	.	.	.	1,500	(1,130)

The capital three years ago was £2,500, business losses being £1,400, gambling losses £60, drawings £840.

The rough Balance Sheet is as follows:

	£		£
Sundry Creditors	2,000	Sundry Assets	2,000
Loan creditors:		Buildings	1,500
1st Mortgage	1,000		
2nd Mortgage	300		
Capital	200		
	£3,500		£3,500

STATEMENT OF AFFAIRS

	£		£
Unsecured Creditors . . .	1,800	Sundry Assets	1,010
Fully Secured Creditor— £		*Deduct* Preferential Creditors	
First Mortgage . . 1,000		per *Contra*	200
Less Buildings . . 1,130			
			810
Surplus, as below . £130		Deficiency	1,160
Partly Secured Creditor—			
Second Mortgage . 300			
Less Surplus from Fully			
Secured Creditor[1] . 130			
	170		
Preferential Creditors			
Deducted *Contra* . . 200			
	£1,970		£1,970

[1] The item of £130, surplus from the security of the first mortgage, is *deducted* from the left-hand item of partly secured creditor. It can be seen that the loans in the Balance Sheet left hand are £1,300, and the security in the Balance Sheet right hand is £1,500.

These are reflected in the Statement of Affairs left hand . . .	£170
And Deficiency Account right hand	370
Net right hand	£200

DEFICIENCY ACCOUNT

	£		£
Capital	*2,500*	*Business Losses* . .	*1,400*
Deficiency as per State-		Depreciation of Assets .	990
ment of Affairs . .	1,160	Depreciation of Buildings .	370
		Drawings . .	*840*
		Gambling Losses . .	*60*
	£3,660		£3,660

The items in the Deficiency Account in italics represent the Capital item of £200 in the rough Balance Sheet on p. 2806.

It will be obvious that not only the business position, but also the private position will have to be brought into account; but so long as the two capitals in the Deficiency Account are kept separate the problem presents no new difficulties.

Illustration 5

Y, as a result of being in financial difficulties, disclosed the following position in regard to his affairs, at the date of the Receiving Order.

(a) Business

BALANCE SHEET

	£		£	Estimated to Produce £
Creditors	1,600	Stock	200	40
Preferential Creditors . .	150	Debtors—		
Loan on Mortgage (secured		Good	810	810
on Property) . . .	1,200	Doubtful . . .	500	200
Bills Payable . . .	600	Bad	600	Nil
Capital	620	Cash . . .	10	10
		Property . . .	1,800	1,700
		Bills Receivable . .	250	210
	£4,170		£4,170	

Three years ago, his business capital was £1,000; profits and drawings during the period were, respectively, £1,100 and £1,480.

Contingent liability for bill discounted, £300 expected to rank for £80.

(b) Private

BALANCE SHEET

	£		£	Estimated to Produce £
Capital	1,600	Furniture . . .	600	500
		Life Policy . . .	1,000	700
	£1,600		£1,600	

Prepare Statement of Affairs and Deficiency Account.

STATEMENT OF AFFAIRS

Liabilities		£	Assets		£
Unsecured Creditors . . .		2,200	Cash		10
	£		Stock		40
Creditors fully secured . 1,200			Furniture		500
Less Property : . . 1,700			Life Policy		700
			Book Debts—		
Surplus to *Contra* . £500			Good		810
			Doubtful . . £500		
Bills Discounted[1] . . £300			Bad 600		
				£1,100	
Estimated to rank . . .		80			
Preferential Creditors De-			Estimated to Produce . .		200
ducted *Contra* . . . £150			Bills of Exchange . . .		210
		2,280	Surplus per *Contra* . . .		500
Surplus		540			2,970
			Deduct Preferential Creditors per		
			Contra		150
		£2,820			£2,820

[1] See note [1] under.

DEFICIENCY ACCOUNT

			£			£
Business—				Bad Debts . . .		900
Capital . .	(a)		1,000	Depreciation of Stock .		160
Net Profit . .	(a)		1,100	Depreciation of Property .		100
Private—				Depreciation of Life Policy		300
Capital . .			1,600	Depreciation of Furniture .		100
				Loss on Bills Receivable .		40
				Loss on Bills Discounted[1] .		80
				Drawings . .	(a)	1,480
				Surplus as per Statement		
				of Affairs . .		540
			£3,700			£3,700

(a) £1,000 + £1,100 − £1,480 = £620, Capital per Business Balance Sheet.

[1] The item £80 must be introduced by 'double entry.'

The following are the classes of unsecured creditors:

Pre-Preferential Debts. (a) In the case of a deceased insolvent estate, reasonable funeral and testamentary expenses.

(b) Money belonging to a Friendly Society or Trustee Savings Bank in possession of Bankrupt as its officer.

(c) Proper expenses incurred by a Trustee under Deed of Arrangement avoided by bankruptcy of the debtor.

Preferential Creditors (Sect. 33, Bankruptcy Act 1914, as amended by Sect. 115, Companies Act 1947, and Sect. 456, Companies Act 1948 and under other Statutes, most recently the Social Security Acts 1973 and 1975 and Insolvency Act 1976).

1. Local rates which have become due and payable within the twelve months *preceding* the Receiving Order.

2. Assessed taxes up to the 5th April *preceding* the Receiving Order, not exceeding one year.

3. Wages and salaries of a clerk or servant, workman or labourer for four months (not exceeding £800) accrued before Receiving Order, including holiday and sickness pay.

4. Where a labourer in husbandry has contracted for wages in a lump sum, the whole or a part of such sum, as the court may decide to be due, proportionate to the time of service expired.

5. Contributions under the Social Security Acts payable during the twelve months prior to the date of the Receiving Order. This extends to redundancy fund contributions.

6. Compensation under Reinstatement in Civil Employment Act 1944,[1] not exceeding £200 for any individual.

7. Value Added Tax, due in the twelve months prior to the Receiving Order.

8. P.A.Y.E. deductions by an employer (*less* refunds to employees) arising during the twelve months prior to the Receiving Order.

9. Compensation under the National Services Act 1948,[1] or the Reinstatement in Civil Employment Act 1950,[1] not exceeding £50 for any individual.

10. All accrued holiday pay payable to any clerk, servant, workman or labourer (or in case of death to his or her legal personal representative) on the termination of his or her employment before, or because of, the Receiving Order.

11. Under the Workmen's Compensation Act 1925,[1] any sum due in respect of compensation, the liability wherefor accrued before the date of the Receiving Order, in satisfaction of a right which arose in respect of employment before 5th July 1948.

12. Levies under the Betting and Gaming Duties Act 1972, which have become due and payable within the twelve months preceding the Receiving Order.

The mere fact of obtaining judgement or a garnishee order does not enable the creditor to rank preferentially.

In reference to assessed taxes, the Inland Revenue is preferential for one year prior to the making of the Receiving Order; thus, if a Receiving Order were made on 15th March 19.9, the liability for 19.8–19.9 is *not* preferential as it has not arisen. The Revenue may select any year and is not limited to the last fiscal year ended before the Receiving Order. In regard to Corporation Tax in the case of companies, which is assessed by reference to an accounting period and not to a fiscal year, the Revenue

---

[1] Such claims are given preferential status but are now of little practical importance.

may select any one such period ended prior to the relevant date (see *In re Pratt*).

In addition, there is the right of the landlord to recover by distress rent outstanding in respect of the period, not exceeding six months prior to adjudication (date debtor declared bankrupt).

Should the landlord distrain within three months of the *Receiving Order*, the preferential debts constitute a first charge on the goods or the proceeds of sale thereof, the landlord being subrogated to the rights of the creditors preferred. Therefore, should the assets be insufficient to pay *all* the preferential debts and the rent accrued (not exceeding the aforesaid six months) the landlord's claim will be limited to such sum as remains after paying off the preferential debts.

Deferred Creditors. In bankruptcy the following are deferred:

1. Money lent by a married woman to her husband for use in his trade or business as a sole trader or *otherwise*,[1] and money lent by a married man to his wife for use in her trade or business. Any loan made before marriage is not affected.

2. Loans to a firm where the lender is to receive a share of profits or a rate of interest varying with profits; or money paid for goodwill in consideration for a share of profits.

3. Beneficiaries claiming under a covenant made in consideration of marriage for the future payment of money, or to settle after-acquired property (where the covenant has become void against a Trustee in Bankruptcy).

4. Interest on debts in excess of 5 per cent, but only when ALL creditors have been paid. (This position does not apply in liquidation, although they are often included in the unsecured creditors in the Statement of Affairs.)

When all debts and claims for interest have been paid in full, interest at 4 per cent per annum from the date of the Receiving Order to the date of the final payment on such debts is payable, or proportionately if the surplus is not sufficient to pay 4 per cent. Should there still be a surplus after the payment of the full interest, it belongs to the debtor.

Deferred creditors do not become entitled to any dividend at all until the unsecured creditors have received payment in full; hence it is probably best to include them in a note on the Statement of Affairs so that, if they are of material amount, the balance available for the ordinary unsecured creditors is not normally reduced. If there is any surplus, the deferred creditors will rank against it to the full extent of their debts before any return is made to the debtor.

Secured Creditors. A secured creditor is one holding a mortgage, charge, or lien on the **property** of the **debtor** or any part thereof, as security for any debt due to him from the **debtor.**

---

[1] The words 'or otherwise' are *ejusdem generis*; therefore if the loan by wife is to firm of which she is a partner, or where she lends money to her husband for purposes not connected with his trade, the above rule does not apply.

Such creditors are entitled to satisfy the debt owing to them fully or in part out of the property held by them before any distribution to the unsecured creditors. Where the security is insufficient to discharge the whole debt, the secured creditor ranks as an unsecured creditor for the balance. Where the security is more than sufficient the surplus must be handed over to the estate.

Where the creditor holds security given by a *third* party, he is as regards the Bankrupt Estate UNSECURED, and after receipt of the final dividend will apply the security towards making up the balance of his debt.

Schedules. It must be observed that the items appearing in the Statement of Affairs are found from different schedules which are required by law to be extracted, just as the item 'Sundry Debtors' in an ordinary Balance Sheet is found from a schedule of debtors drawn up for the purpose.

The schedules are:

A. Unsecured creditors.
B. Creditors fully secured.
C. Creditors partly secured.
D. Liabilities on bills discounted.
E. Contingent or other liabilities (including deferred debts).
F. Creditors for rent recoverable by distress.
G. Preferential creditors for rates, taxes, and wages.
H. Property.
I. Debts due to the estate.
J. Bills of exchange on hand.
K. Deficiency (or Surplus) Account.

In the official form **all** liabilities must be included in the Gross Liabilities column, whether secured, preferential, unsecured or deferred (and even if secured wholly or in part by a third party, e.g. a guarantor). (This column is 'memo' only and as it does not form an essential part of the formal construction of the Statement of Affairs it has been omitted from the preceding explanatory illustrations.)

A question of more advanced type is now presented.

Illustration 6

A Receiving Order was made against X on the 15th March 19.8. The following details were disclosed.

Creditors with security—

		£	
(1) Northern Bank, secured by hypothecation of stock valued at £15,000		10,000	
(2) Loan on Mortgage, with Interest		8,000	
The Premises which are mortgaged value at		11,000	(estimated to realize £9,200)
(3) Trade Creditors		4,000	
Holding Life Policy of X	2,000		
Holding Life Policy of Mrs. X	1,000		

	£
Other Creditors: Unsecured . . .	12,000
Preferential: Income Tax, Sch. D.—	
19.6–19.7, Arrears . .	700
19.7–19.8 (Loss) . . .	nil
19.8–19.9 . . .	460
Rates accrued due . . .	400
Wages, preferential . . .	35
Other Stock	2,200
Book Debts—Good	3,000
Doubtful and Bad . .	6,000 (estimated to realize £3,100)
Bills Receivable discounted . . .	1,200 (expected to rank £200)

At 31st December 19.5, his capital was £12,605. Trading has subsequently shown a loss of £8,000. Drawings (including a debit for Income Tax) £3,000. Except for book debts and premises, assets are estimated to realize book values. Prepare Statement of Affairs and Deficiency Account.

Before proceeding to prepare the Statement of Affairs, it is essential to draft the rough Balance Sheets.

BUSINESS BALANCE SHEET

		£			£
Bank		10,000	Stock		15,000
Loan on Mortgage . . .		8,000	,, ...		2,200
Trade Creditors. . . .		16,000	Book Debts		9,000
Expense Creditors—			Premises		11,000
Income Tax . .	£1,160				
Rates . . .	400				
Wages . . .	35				
		1,595			
Capital		1,605			
		£37,200			£37,200

PRIVATE BALANCE SHEET

	£			£
Capital	2,000		Life Policy . .	2,000

The creditors amounting to £35,595 require analysis, as follows:

CREDITORS	£	£
Fully Secured Creditors—Bank	10,000	
Mortgage	8,000	
		18,000
Partly Secured Creditors		4,000
Preferential Creditors—Rates	[1]400	
Wages	35	
Income Tax (19.6–19.7)	[2]700	
		1,135
Unsecured Creditors		12,000
Non-provable Income Tax (because in 19.8–19.9 Y is not carrying on business)		460
		£35,595

The item of £460 represents a gain and therefore is a 'left-hand' item in the Deficiency Account; but as the question states that the drawings include Income Tax, the item will be deducted from the right-hand item of drawings, viz. £3,000 − £460 = £2,540.

It must now be noted that in the Statement of Affairs there is a further column for gross liabilities into which **all liabilities,** whatever the nature, must be inserted. This column is only of a supplementary nature. Its inclusion has been deferred until this illustration so as not to confuse the fundamental principle of construction.

The wife is a deferred creditor (see p. 2811).

K—DEFICIENCY (OR SURPLUS) ACCOUNT

	£		£
Excess of Assets over Liabilities on the 31st Dec. 19.5—		Net Loss arising from Business	8,000
Business	12,605	Bad Debts as per Schedule I	2,900
Private	2,000	Depreciation of Premises	1,800
Deficiency as per Statement of Affairs	835	Household and Personal Expenses	2,540
		Loss on Bills Discounted	200
	£15,440		£15,440

[1] Had the item been rent it would not have been preferential, but recoverable by distress.
[2] Had this been 19.7–19.8 the liability would not have been preferential.

STATEMENT OF AFFAIRS

Gross Liabilities	Liabilities		Expected to Rank	Assets		Estimated to Produce
£			£			£
12,000	Unsecured Creditors as per List (A)		12,000	Stock as per List (H)		2,200
18,000	Creditors fully secured as per List (B)	£18,000		Book Debts as per List (I)—		3,000
	Estimated Value of Securities	24,200		Good	?	
		£6,200		Doubtful	?	
	Surplus to contra			Bad		
					£6,000	
4,000	Creditors partly secured as per list (C)	£4,000		Estimated to Produce		3,100
	Less Estimated Value of Securities	2,000	2,000	Surplus from contra		6,200
1,200	Bills Receivable discounted as per List (D)	£1,200	200			14,500
1,135	Expected to Rank Preferential Creditors per Lists (F) & (G)	£1,135		Deduct Preferential Creditors per contra		1,135
	Deducted Contra					13,365
				Deficiency explained in Statement K		835
¹36,335			£14,200			£14,200

¹ £35,595 (as shown opposite) – £460 + £1,200.

(a) Non-provable debt included in Balance Sheet.
(b) Liability for Bills Discounted not included in Balance Sheet.

Illustration 7

The firm Hard and Upp file their petition and you are asked to draw up a Statement of Affairs and Deficiency Account as at 31st December 19.9 from the following information:

	£		£
Sundry Assets	61,092	Estimated to produce	47,300
Unsecured Creditors	53,635		

The Capital Accounts (excluding their Current Accounts) at 31st December 19.9 are £10,000.

The drawings are £1,400 per annum (£800 for Hard and £600 for Upp).

Trading results are, after charging £500 per annum interest on Capital and £200 per annum in respect of Partnership Salary (Upp):

			£
19.5	.	Profit	1,300
19.6	.	Profit	400
19.7	.	Loss	1,600
19.8	.	Profit	200
19.9	.	Loss	3,000

On 1st January 19.5, Upp had introduced into the business further cash amounting to £2,000, which has been duly credited to his Capital Account.

The Capital (composed of the fixed Capital of £10,000 *and* the balance of the current accounts) is £7,457, which will be made up of £10,000 Capital (Credit) and Current Accounts, (Debit) £2,543 (see p. 2817).

The rough Balance Sheet is:

	£		£
Creditors	53,635	Sundry Assets	61,092
Capitals	10,000	Current Accounts	2,543

The effective Capital is therefore £7,457 and this item is a left-hand item to be accounted for on the same side in the Deficiency Account as shown on p. 2818 as follows:

Capital (1st Jan. 19.9)	.	.	(a)	Loss, year ended 31st Dec. 19.9	.	(b)
				Personal Drawings, 31st Dec. 19.9.		(c)

The Capital and Current Accounts as at 1st January 19.9 are:

	£	£	£	£
Capital Accounts, 1st Jan. 19.5				8,000
Addition. 19.5				2,000
Capital Accounts				10,000
Current Accounts, 1st Jan. 19.5 . . .			3,657	
Less Loss, 19.7	1,600			
Drawings 4 years, 31st Dec. 19.8 . .	5,600			
		7,200		
Deduct—				
Profit, 19.5	1,300			
Profit, 19.6	400			
Profit, 19.8	200			
Interest on Capital for 4 years ended 31st Dec. 19.8	2,000			
Partner's Salary for 4 years ended 31st December 19.8	800			
		4,700		
			2,500	
(As below)				1,157
At 1st January 19.9				11,157 (*a*)
Less Loss, 19.9		3,000		
Deduct Interest on Capitals for 19.9 . .	500			
Partner's Salary for 19.9 . . .	200			
		700		
			2,300 Dr.	(*b*)
Less Drawings for 19.9			1,400	
				Dr. 3,700 (*c*)
Capital and Current Accounts, 31st December 19.9				£7,457

The composition of this total is—		£
Capital Accounts	Cr.	10,000
Current Accounts	Dr.	2,543
(As above)		£7,457

The combined Current Account need not be built up in detail, but it is given below for guidance.

	£		CURRENT ACCOUNT	£
Drawings . . .	1,400	19.5	Opening . . .	3,657
Closing . . .	4,257		Salary and Interest . .	700
			Profit . . .	1,300
Drawings . . .	1,400	19.6	Opening . . .	4,257
Closing . . .	3,957		Salary and Interest .	700
			Profit . . .	400
Loss	1,600	19.7	Opening . . .	3,957
Drawings . . .	1,400		Salary and Interest .	700
Closing. . . .	1,657			
Drawings . . .	1,400	19.8	Opening . . .	1,657
Closing . . .	1,157		Salary and Interest	700
			Profit . . .	200
		19.9	Opening . . .	1,157

HARD AND UPP

STATEMENT OF AFFAIRS, 31ST DECEMBER 19.9

Gross Liabilities		Expected to Rank		Estimated to Produce
£ 53,635	Unsecured Creditors . .	£ 53,635	Sundry Assets . . . . Deficiency subject to Costs . .	£ 47,300 6,335
£53,635		£53,635		£53,635

DEFICIENCY ACCOUNT

	£			£
Excess of Assets over Liabilities at 1st January 19.9 . . (a)	11,157	**Loss for Year ended 31st December 19.9 . . . (b)**		**2,300**
Deficiency per Statement of Affairs	6,335	**Personal Drawings . . (c)**		**1,400**
		Loss and Expenses— Sundry Assets . . .		13,792
	£17,492			£17,492

The Current Account for 19.9 is—	£		£
Drawings . . .	1,400	Opening	1,157
Loss	3,000	Salary and Interest . .	700
		Closing . . .	2,543
	£4,400		£4,400

Firm Bankruptcy. The position dealt with so far has been confined to a sole trader. Where, however, there is a firm bankruptcy the problems are a little more complicated. It should be remembered that Statement of Affairs will be required both for the firm and for its constituent members. Subject to certain exceptions, the private creditors have recourse only to the private estate, and the partnership creditors to the firm estate, generally referred to as the joint estate. Another confusing point arises where joint property is pledged as security for a private debt of one of the partners, in which case the private creditor is not a secured creditor, because he has not obtained the property of the debtor as security, but that of the joint estate. Examples are shown to illustrate the principles involved.

Illustration 8

A and B are partners and the position is as follows:

BALANCE SHEETS
Firm

	£			£
Creditors	600	Stock		300
		Debtors		100
		A £120		
		B 80		
				200
	£600			£600

A

	£		£
Creditors	250	Furniture	300
Surplus	30	Sundry Assets	100
Firm	120		
	£400		400

B

	£		£
Creditors	900	Furniture	600
Firm	80	Life Policy	250
		Deficiency	130
	£980		£980

It is assumed that all assets are worth book value save that stock is estimated to realize £140. Prepare draft Statements of Affairs and Joint Deficiency Account.

STATEMENTS OF AFFAIRS
Joint

			£
Creditors	600	Stock	140
		Debtors	100
		Sundry Assets (A's Estate) . .	150
			390
		Deficiency	210
	£600		£600

A

	£			£
Creditors	250	Furniture	300
Surplus	150	Sundry Assets . . .	100
	£400			£400

B

	£			£
Creditors	900	Furniture	600
		Life Policy	250
		Deficiency	50
	£900			£900

Joint Deficiency Account

	£			£
A—Surplus	150	Excess of Liabilities over Assets of—	
Deficiency as per Statement of Affairs	210	A £120	
		B £80	200
		Depreciation of Stock . . .	160
	£360			£360

Each Statement of Affairs is separately compiled and each deficiency or surplus is separately ascertained. Any surplus introduced from a separate estate to the joint estate (not being in the original Balance Sheet of the firm) must have its double entry. It has already been stated that as regards creditors, each 'set' proves against the particular debtor, i.e. separate against separate, joint against joint, but it should be observed that the surplus of A, i.e. £150, is now available for the joint creditors.

Where in a partnership a partner has given security for a firm debt, the joint estate has first claim on such security: any surplus goes to the separate estate of that partner, the reverse applying when joint property is given as security to separate creditors.

Illustration 9

The creditors are:

		£				£
Joint	. . .	3,000	Assets	.	. .	1,600
A	. . .	500	,,	.	. .	400
B	. . .	600	,,	.	. .	640

The £640 asset of B has been placed as security for a loan of £500 to the firm included in the figure £3,000. The joint assets are estimated to realize £1,800. Prepare Statement of Affairs.

STATEMENT OF AFFAIRS
JOINT

	£		£
Unsecured Creditors . . .	3,000	Assets	1,800
		Deficiency	1,200
	£3,000		£3,000

A

	£		£
Creditors	500	Assets	400
		Deficiency	100
	£500		£500

B

	£		£
Creditors	600	Surplus from Security held by Joint Creditors . .	440
		Deficiency	160
	£600		£600

The joint creditor of £500 would get (with the other joint creditors) £0·60 in the £ dividend = £300, i.e. $\frac{18}{30} \times$ £500. Hence, there is a shortage of £200. He recoups this from the £640 asset of B, leaving still a surplus of £440 which is now available for B's creditors.

This may be further proved as follows. The joint creditor has £640 security of B against the partnership debt £500, leaving £140 surplus. This dividend £300 received from the joint estate is now due to B's separate estate, since the £500 debt has been satisfied in full. B's estate thus receives £440 from the asset £640.

Statutory Forms. The two principal forms required by statute to be completed are here shown:

1. Statement of Affairs in Bankruptcy.
2. Statement K, deficiency (or Surplus) Account.

These are set out on the following pages.

Trustee's Accounts and Remuneration. The trustee in Bankruptcy must keep detailed accounts of his receipts and payments in the prescribed form of cash book. If the debtor's business is carried on, a Trading Account must be kept on a cash basis.

THE BANKRUPTCY ACTS 1914 AND 1926
STATEMENT OF AFFAIRS

In the High Court of Justice.

IN BANKRUPTCY.   No.   of 19. .

Re..

TO THE DEBTOR.—You are required to fill up, carefully and accurately, this sheet, and such of the several sheets, A, B, C, D, E, F, G, H, I, J, and K, as are applicable showing the state of your affairs on the day on which the Receiving Order was made against you, viz., the   day of   19... Such sheets, when filled up, will constitute your Statement of Affairs, and must be verified by oath or declaration.

Gross Liabilities	Liabilities (as stated and estimated by Debtor)	Expected to Rank	Assets (as stated and estimated by Debtor)	Estimated to produce
		£		£
	Unsecured Creditors as per List (A) £		Property as per list (H), viz.—	
			(a) Cash at Bankers	
	Creditors fully secured, as per list (B) . . .		(b) Cash in hand	
	Estimated value of securities . . .		(c) Cash deposited with Solicitor for Costs of Petition . .	
			(d) Stock-in-trade (cost £)	
	Surplus		(e) Machinery . .	
	Less amount thereof carried to sheet (C) .		(f) Trade fixtures, fittings, utensils, &c. .	
			(g) Farming stock .	
	Balance thereof to contra . . .		(h) Growing crops and tenant right .	
			(i) Furniture . .	
	Creditors partly secured, as per list (C) .		(j) Life policies . .	
	Less estimated value of securities . .		(k) Stocks and Shares . .	
			(l) Reversionary and other interests under Wills .	
			(m) Other property, viz.—	
	Liabilities on Bills discounted other than Debtor's own acceptances for value, as per list (D), viz.—			
	On Accommodation Bills as Drawer, Acceptor, or		Total as per list (H) .	
			Book Debts as per list (I), viz.—	
	Indorser . . £		Good . . .	£
	On other Bills as Drawer or Indorser . . £		Doubtful . . .	
			Bad . . .	
	£			£
	Of which it is expected will rank against the estate for dividend		Estimated to produce .	
	Contingent or other Liabilities as per list (E) . £		Bills of Exchange or other similar securities on hand as per list (J) . . . £	
	Of which it is expected will rank against the estate for dividend £		Estimated to produce .	
	Creditors for rent, &c., recoverable by distress, as per list (F) . .		Surplus from securities in the hands of Creditors fully secured (per contra)	
	Creditors for rates, taxes, wages, &c., payable in full, as per list (G) .			£
	Sheriff's charges payable under sec. 41 of the Act, estimated at . .		Deduct Creditors for distrainable rent, and for preferential rates, taxes, wages, sheriff's charges, &c. (per contra)	
	Deducted contra . .			£
	[1] Surplus explained in Statement (K)		Deficiency explained in Statement (K) . . .	
£	£			£

1 Strike out words which do not apply.

LIST "K"—DEFICIENCY (OR SURPLUS) ACCOUNT

	£	£		£	£
Excess of Assets over Liabilities on the[1] .... day of ....19...... (if any)			Excess of Liabilities over Assets on the[1] .... day of ....19...... (if any)		
Net Profit (if any) arising from carrying on business from the .... day of ....19......, to date of Receiving Order, after deducting usual Trade Expenses			Net loss (if any) arising from carrying on business from the .... day of ....19......, to date of Receiving Order, after charging against Profits the usual Trade Expenses		
Income or profit from other sources (if any) since the[1] .... day of ....19......			Bad Debts (if any) as per Schedule 'I'[2]		
Gifts from relations and others			Depreciation of stock-in-trade		
			Depreciation of machinery		
			Depreciation of trade fixtures, fittings, &c.		
			Expenses incurred since the .... day of ....19......, other than usual Trade Expenses, viz., Household and personal expenses of self and[3]		
			[4]Other Losses and Expenses (if any)—		
			....		
			....		
			....		
[6]Deficiency as per Statement of Affairs (if any)			[5]Surplus as per Statement of Affairs (if any)		
Total amount to be accounted for[6]	£		Total amount accounted for[6]	£	

NOTES.—
[1] This date should be twelve months before date of Receiving Order, or such **other time** as Official Receiver may have fixed.
[2] This schedule must show when debts were contracted.
[3] Add 'wife and children' (if any), stating number of latter.
[4] Here add particulars of other losses or expenses (if any), including liabilities (if any) for which no consideration received.
[5] Strike out words which do not apply.
[6] These figures should agree.

Lists 'A', 'B', etc., mentioned above contain the details of the figures set down in the Statement of Affairs and Deficiency Account. Where any of the lists 'A' to 'J' are blank, list 'L' will be substituted therefor, as below.

Signature..................... Dated..................19......

List 'L'

(In substitution for such of the Sheets named 'A—J', as will have to be returned blank.)

LIST	PARTICULARS AS PER FRONT SHEET	DEBTOR'S REMARKS

The Trustee's remuneration is fixed by the creditors or the Committee of Inspection, and must be by way of a percentage on realizations and a percentage on dividends to unsecured creditors, including preferential creditors and secured creditors to the extent that their security is insufficient so that they rank as unsecured for the balance.

CHAPTER 29

LIQUIDATION

LIQUIDATION is the term used to signify the process of winding up a company and thereby bringing to an end its corporate life. When a company is ordered by the Court to be wound up compulsorily, it is necessary to prepare a Statement of Affairs for submission to the creditors of the company.

The principles already outlined relative to bankruptcy, subject to certain modifications of detail, apply to limited companies in compulsory liquidation.

The main points of difference are:

1. A limited company may have issued debentures giving a floating charge. Such a position is impossible in the case of an individual.
2. The position in relation to shareholders (in liquidation called contributories), which cannot arise in the case of a private individual.
3. The Deficiency Account contains a considerable amount of detail (whereas in bankruptcy such account merely contains the net loss or profit) and the period covered is three years prior to the winding-up order or as the Official Receiver directs, or from the formation of the company if the latter is within three years of the order; on the other hand, the Deficiency Account in bankruptcy commences at a date twelve months prior to the receiving order unless the Official Receiver otherwise orders.

The forms now required vary in layout as compared with the old forms (and with those required in bankruptcy), but the principle of preparation is unchanged.

It should be noted that Preferential Creditors rank before Debentures with a floating charge.

The forms will include profits and losses of the period prior to the date of the Statement of Affairs (which will link up with the opening surplus or deficiency on Profit and Loss), and the gains or losses arising from estimated realizable values, and the liabilities as compared with the Balance Sheet figures forming the basis of the Statement of Affairs will be dealt with on the same principle (although differing in form) as in Bankruptcy.

The balance of estimated surplus or deficiency as regards unsecured creditors is automatically the difference between Gross Assets and Gross Liabilities, so that the Schedule of Gross Assets is a 'memo' Schedule.

The following example illustrates the layout referred to above.

Illustration 1

On 1st April 19.9, a compulsory order for winding up was made against Y, Ltd., the following particulars being disclosed:

			(Estimated to Produce)
	£	£	£
Cash in hand		5	5
Debtors		200	180
Land and Buildings		3,000	2,400
Fixtures		1,000	1,000
Unsecured Creditors	1,000		
Debentures—			
Fixed (secured on Land and			
Buildings	2,100		
Floating	500		
Preferential Creditors	300		
Share Capital (£1 fully paid)	16,000		

Estimated liability for bills discounted £300, estimated to rank at £300. Contingent liabilities (*re* legal costs) £600, estimated to rank at £600.

The company was formed on the 1st October 19.7, and has made losses of £15,695.

Prepare Statement of Affairs and Deficiency Account.

The rough Balance Sheet is:

		£			£
Share Capital		16,000	Assets (as per question)		4,205
Creditors		3,900	Profit and Loss Account		15,695
		£19,900			£19,900

The items of £300 and £600 would appear as footnotes in the Balance Sheet of the company, and when brought into the statements will require 'Double Entry'.

The question of Debenture Interest has been ignored in this illustration, but the rule in reference thereto is that Debenture Interest is payable up to and including the date of repayment of the Debenture *in the case of a company which is* SOLVENT, otherwise interest ceases at the commencement of the liquidation.

Unpaid calls on shares are brought into the Statement of Affairs at the estimated realizable *amount,* a balance being entered in the Deficiency Account as an item contributing to the deficiency, i.e. as a loss.

The nominal amount of unpaid capital liable to be called up is **not** shown as an asset, but indicated by way of note at the foot of the Statement of Affairs.

[See Statement of Affairs on p. 2903.]

STATEMENT AS TO THE AFFAIRS OF Y LIMITED

on the 1st April 19.9, the date of the Winding-up Order, showing assets
at estimated realizable values and liabilities expected to rank.

	(a) Estimated Realizable Values £	(b) Due to Secured Creditors £	(c) Deficiency Ranking as Unsecured £	Surplus carried to last column £	Estimated Realizable Values £
Assets not specifically pledged—					
Cash on Hand					5
Debtors					180
Fixtures					1,000
Assets Specifically Pledged—					
Freehold Property	2,400	2,100	—	300	
Estimated surplus from Assets specifically pledged					300
Estimated Total Assets available for Preferential Creditors, Debenture-holders secured by a Floating Charge, and Unsecured Creditors					1,485

SUMMARY OF GROSS ASSETS	£
Gross Realizable Value of Assets specially charged	2,400
Other Assets	1,185
Gross Assets	£3,585

Gross Liabilities £	LIABILITIES	
	Secured Creditors to extent to which claims are estimated to be covered by Assets specifically pledged (item (a) or (b) above, whichever is the less)	
2,100	[Insert in 'Gross Liabilities' column only]	—
300	Preferential Creditors	300
	Estimated Balance of Assets available for Debenture-holders secured by a floating charge, and Unsecured Creditors	1,185
500	Debenture-holders secured by a floating charge	500
	Estimated Surplus as regards Debenture-holders	685
	Unsecured Creditors— £	
1,000	Trade Accounts 1,000	
600	Contingent Liabilities (re legal costs) 600	
300	Contingent Liabilities (Bills discounted) 300	
		1,900
£4,800	Estimated Deficiency as regards Creditors being difference between—	
	£	
	Gross Assets 3,585	
	Gross Liabilities 4,800	
		1,215
	Issued and Called-up Capital: 16,000 shares of £1 each	16,000
	Estimated Deficiency as regards Members	£17,215

DEFICIENCY OR SURPLUS ACCOUNT	£
Items contributing to Deficiency or reducing Surplus—	
Net Trading losses (after charging items shown in note below)	15,695[1]
Estimated losses now written off	620
Other items contributing to Deficiency or reducing Surplus—	
Contingent Liabilities (re legal costs)	600
Contingent Liabilities (Bills discounted)	300
Deficiency as shown by Statement	£17,215

[1] Details in prescribed form are required to be shown separately.
[Note. As to Net Trading Profits and Losses (see form on p. 2924).]

The following example illustrates the position when shares are partly paid:

Illustration 2

BALANCE SHEET

	£		£
Share Capital (£1 each £0·50 called)	5,000	Sundry Assets	4,100
Calls in Advance	200	Calls in Arrear . . .	300
Creditors	2,000	Profit and Loss Account . .	2,800
	£7,200		£7,200

Sundry Assets are estimated to produce £3,000.

The calls are irrecoverable. The creditors include preferential creditors of £300. Prepare Statement of Affairs and Deficiency Account.

STATEMENT OF AFFAIRS ON.....................................19..

Gross Liabilities £			Estimated Realizable Value £
	Assets not specifically pledged—		
	Sundry.		3,000
	Unpaid Calls.		nil
	SUMMARY OF GROSS ASSETS	£	
	Sundry	3,000	
	Gross Assets	£3,000	
	Estimated Total Assets available for Preferential Creditors, Debenture-holders secured by a floating charge and Unsecured Creditors		3,000
	LIABILITIES		
300	Preferential Creditors		300
	Estimated balance of Assets available for Debenture-holders secured by a floating charge and unsecured creditors . .		2,700
1,700	Unsecured Creditors		1,700
	Estimated Surplus as regards Creditors—	£	
	Gross Assets	3,000	
£2,000	Gross Liabilities	2,000	
			1,000
	Issued and Called-up Capital—		
	10,000 Shares of £ each, £0·50 called		5,000
	Estimated Deficiency as regards members . .		£4,000

DEFICIENCY OR SURPLUS ACCOUNT

	£
Items contributing to Deficiency (or reducing Surplus)—	
Trading Losses (to be shown in prescribed detail) . .	2,800
Losses now written off	1,100
Calls irrecoverable	300
Items reducing Deficiency (or Contributing to Surplus)—	4,200
Calls in Advance	200
Deficiency as shown by Statement	£4,000

Preferential Creditors. The liquidator must, so far as he can, pay the preferential creditors and follow, broadly, on the same lines as in Bankruptcy (see p. 2809), except that the date by reference to which priority is to be ascertained (i.e. the relevant date) is that of the resolution to wind up if a voluntary liquidation, or, in the case of a compulsory winding up, the date of the appointment or first appointment of the provisional liquidator if one is appointed, otherwise the date of the Court Order (*vide* Sect. 319, Companies Act 1948).

(Exception: if the Compulsory Order is made where the company is *already* in process of being wound up voluntarily, the relevant date is the date of the resolution to wind up voluntarily.)

The clauses relating to National Insurance contributions and compensation under the Social Security Acts, will not rank for preferential treatment if the company is being wound up voluntarily MERELY FOR THE PURPOSES of reconstruction or of amalgamation with another company. But where any payment has been made to any clerk, servant, workman or labourer in employment of a company, on account of wages or salary, or accrued holiday pay, out of money advanced by some person for that purpose, that person has a similar right of priority in respect of the money so advanced and paid out, that is, he is subrogated to the rights of the persons so paid.

(The above paragraph is not applicable to Bankruptcy.)

Liquidator's Final Account. In all liquidations, a liquidator must prepare in statutory form a statement of his receipts and payments made up to the date of his application for release.[1]

The preparation of a Liquidator's Cash Account calls for no detailed explanation, but the following matters should be noted:

1. There is no double entry required.
2. The items should follow the order of the official form.

Preferential creditors are paid before debenture-holders with a floating charge, whilst debenture-holders with a fixed charge will receive payment out of the proceeds of their security, unless the latter is insufficient for that purpose, in which case the balance owing will rank as an unsecured liability (unless the charge is floating as well as fixed in which case the liability ranks after the preferential liabilities have been paid in full).

3. The rights of various classes of shareholders (particularly if there is a surplus) require careful consideration. [See pp. 23281 and 23320 *et seq.*]
4. The calculation of the remuneration.
5. The form of cash book for liquidation differs from that required for bankruptcies.[2] The main outlines of the forms are given below, so that point (4) only requires further explanation.

As to (4), the remuneration is fixed by the Court in a compulsory, and by agreement in a voluntary winding up, usually upon a double basis, viz. as a percentage of receipts by the liquidator and dividends to unsecured creditors. There is little difficulty with the former, but the latter requires

---

[1] The student is referred to a legal work for further detail on this subject.
[2] A statement of the receipts and payments must be furnished by a trustee in bankruptcy.

care because the liquidator (or trustee) obtains the sum upon the amount PAID so that if there is insufficient to pay the creditors in full and the liquidator, both must suffer abatement.

Illustration 3

A liquidator has £11,220 to pay £20,000 creditors. After he has received his commission on collections, he is entitled to a further 2 per cent on dividends paid.

If he pays £100 he receives £2, thus absorbing £102. Hence, he receives $\frac{2}{102} \times £11,220 = £220$, leaving £11,000 for distribution.

Illustration 4

The following are the balances of X, Ltd., which decided to wind up voluntarily on 1st January 19...

BALANCE SHEET

	£		£	Estimated to Produce £
Share Capital (£1 fully paid) .	2,000	Cash	60	
Creditors	4,900	Stock	1,700	1,680
(including £210 preferential)		Debtors	4,790	4,495
		Profit and Loss Account .	350	
	£6,900		£6,900	

The liquidator's remuneration is to be 4 per cent on amounts collected and 2 per cent on dividends paid to unsecured creditors. Liquidation expenses are £40. Show Liquidator's Cash Account (calculate to nearest £).

LIQUIDATOR'S CASH ACCOUNT

Receipts	£	£	Payments	£	£
Balance . .		60	Law Costs . . .	?	
Sale of Assets—			Auctioneer's Charges	?	
Stock . .	1,680		Incidental Expenses	?	40
Debtors . .	4,495		Liquidator's Remuneration—		
		6,175	4% on Amounts Collected	247	
			2% on Dividends to Unsecured Creditors[1]	98	
					345
			Preferential Creditors[2] .		210
			Dividend of £1 in £ to Unsecured Creditors .		4,690
			Return to Contributories—		
			£0·475 in £ on 2,000 Shares of £1 each, fully paid . .		950
		£6,235			£6,235

[1] Where there are mutual debts, e.g. A owes the Company £500 and is owed by it £100, the remuneration will be based on the 'net' or set-off figure, i.e. £400, and not on the debt due to the Company, £500. (See continuation at foot of p. 2907.)

[2] These include preferential creditors, and also secured creditors to the extent that their security is insufficient to cover their claims so that they rank as unsecured for the balance.

Collection of Calls. Where shares are partly paid, the liquidator will make a call in order to pay off liabilities as far as possible and so adjust the position between the contributories (i.e. shareholders) as between themselves.

Where practicable, a liquidator will attempt to avoid making a call greater than is really required, as otherwise there may be entailed a return to the contributories upon whom the call was made. If a call of £0·50 will settle the list of contributories, it would involve a corresponding return to the contributories upon whom the call was made if the actual call was greater than £0·50, e.g. if it were £0·60 a return of £0·10 would be required.

The same principles apply where more than two classes of contributories have to be dealt with.

Illustration 5

The cash remaining in the hands of the liquidator prior to making the return to contributories (before making calls) is £3,500. The issued share capital is 10,000 preference shares of £1 each fully paid (with priority as to capital), 10,000 ordinary shares of £1 each, £0·75 paid, and 20,000 ordinary share of £1 each, £0·50 paid. Show Liquidator's Cash Account.

The loss suffered by the contributories is ascertained by taking the deficiency and dividing it by the issued share capital (on the assumption that the latter is FULLY PAID).

BALANCE SHEET

	£		£
Preference Shares . . .	10,000	Cash	3,500
Ordinary Shares—		DEFICIENCY	24,000
10,000 (£0·75 paid) . .	7,500		
20,000 (£0·50 paid) . .	10,000		
	£27,500		£27,500

Loss per ordinary share is therefore:

$$\frac{\text{Deficiency}}{\text{FULLY PAID Ordinary Capital}} \quad \text{i.e.} \quad \frac{24,000}{30,000} \times £1 = £0·80 \text{ per ordinary share}$$

Footnote [1] to p. 2906 (*continued*)

Where there is insufficient cash left to pay the unsecured creditors in *full*, the calculation will not be 2 per cent thereof, but $\frac{2}{102}$, e.g. assuming the unsecured creditors to be £4,690 and after all obligations have been discharged (save that of the Liquidator's 'Dividend' Remuneration of 2 per cent) there is a cash balance of £2,870·28, the respective payments to the liquidator and unsecured creditors will be—

Liquidator . . $\frac{2}{102} \times £2,870·28 = £56·28$
Unsecured creditors $\frac{100}{102} \times £2,870·28 = £2,814$

The liquidator thus receives 2 per cent of £2,814.

Preferential creditors are 'unsecured' for the purpose of calculating the liquidator's remuneration.

LIQUIDATOR'S CASH ACCOUNT

	£		£
Balance . .	3,500	Preference Shareholders .	10,000
Proceeds of Calls—			
Ordinary Shares:			
10,000 at £0·05	500		
20,000 at £0·30	6,000		
	£10,000		£10,000

In all the above instances no return was made to the ordinary shareholders, but if they have paid in previous calls more than their loss per share they will be entitled to a return, computed on the principles outlined.

If a contributory fails to pay his calls in full, whether by insolvency or otherwise, he is thereby debarred from participation in any return to contributories, until the other contributors have been paid sufficient to make all the shares the same amount paid up.

Where there is a third grade of share, e.g. Deferred Share, the rule already explained will be applied subject to these modifications:

1. Ascertain if there is any of the deferred capital (however small) remaining. If the deficiency is *less* then the fully paid deferred capital, part of such capital remains. If so, the prior classes of shares will receive their capitals back as existing and the question of any priority of payment of capital as between themselves, e.g. preference shares and ordinary shares, does not arise; so that:

(*a*) Apply the previous rules for ascertaining the loss to be sustained (*deferred* share capital being substituted for *ordinary* share capital).

(*b*) Pay out cash to the preference and/or ordinary shares (i) in full if fully called and paid (ii) if not, to the extent called and paid.

2. If such deferred capital is entirely exhausted—

(*a*) Make such calls as are required to make any such deferred capital fully paid.

(*b*) *Reduce* Deficiency by the amount of such fully called and paid Deferred Share Capital.

(*c*) Apply the rule previously outlined to ascertain the loss on the *Ordinary* Share Capital and proceed accordingly.

Illustration 6

The position in Balance Sheet form of Dick Hudson, Ltd., immediately prior to dealing with the repayment to members is as shown at the top of p. 2909.

Preference have priority over ordinary; and ordinary have priority over deferred as regards repayment of capital.

Show Liquidator's Cash Account.

Ascertain the position of the Deferred Share Capital, e.g. whether or not *any* capital remains. On the basis of these being fully called and paid, the deficiency per share would be arrived at as follows:

$$\frac{2,700 \text{ (Deficiency)}}{3,000 \text{ (fully paid Deferred Capital)}} \times £0·10 = £0·09.$$

BALANCE SHEET

	£		£
1,000 6% Preference Shares of £1 each, fully paid	1,000	Cash at Bank	4,700
2,000 Ordinary Shares of £1 each, fully paid	2,000	Deficiency	2,700
2,000 Ordinary Shares of £1 each, £0·75 paid	1,500		
3,000 Ordinary Shares of £1 each, £0·30 paid	900		
10,000 Deferred Shares of £0·10 each, fully paid	1,000		
20,000 Deferred Shares of £0·10 each, £0·05 paid	1,000		
	£7,400		£7,400

The prior Share Capitals are therefore intact and can be paid out per Balance Sheet: and the loss for the Deferred Shareholders is £0·09 a share producing a repayment of £0·01 per share to the fully paid Deferred shareholders and requiring the calling up of £0·04 per share on the partly paid Deferred shareholders.

LIQUIDATOR'S CASH ACCOUNT

	£		£
Balance	4,700	Repayment of Capitals	
Proceeds of Call—		1,000 Preference (£1)	1,000
20,000 Deferred Shares at £0·04 per share	800	2,000 Ordinary (£1)	2,000
		2,000 Ordinary (£0·75)	1,500
		3,000 Ordinary (£0·30)	900
		10,000 Deferred (£0·01)	100
	£5,500		£5,500

Illustration 7

Same facts as before, except that cash is £3,000, and the deficiency £4,400, show Liquidator's Cash Account.

As the deficiency in the second illustration *exceeds* the FULLY PAID Deferred Share Capital, all such Capital is lost: nevertheless, the call of £0·05 a share on the 20,000 Deferred Share Capital will be made *and* the deficiency corresponding with the fully paid Deferred Share Capital will be reduced. For the sake of clarity, the position arising as a result of these operations is shown:

	£		£
Capital (excluding deferred) [first four items in above Balance Sheet]	5,400	Cash at Bank [£3,000 + £1,000]	4,000
		Deficiency [£4,400 − £3,000]	1,400
	£5,400		£5,400

The Deferred Share Capital being lost, the loss per ordinary shareholder is required. This is:

$$\frac{1,400 \text{ (Deficiency)}}{7,000 \text{ (Fully paid ordinary capital)}} \times £1 = £0.20 \text{ a share.}$$

LIQUIDATOR'S CASH ACCOUNT

	£		£
Balance	3,000	Repayment of Capitals—	
Proceeds of Calls—		1,000 Preference (£1) .	1,000
20,000 Deferred Shares		2,000 Ordinary (£0·80)[1] .	1,600
at £0·05 per Share .	1,000	2,000 Ordinary (£0·55)[1] .	1,100
		3,000 Ordinary (£0·10)[1] .	300
	£4,000		£4,000

[1] As the loss per Ordinary Share is £0·20, the repayments to the ordinary shareholders will be the amount paid, *less* £0·20 per share, viz. £0·80, £0·55, and £0·10 for the fully paid, £0·75 paid and £0·30 paid respectively.

Where there are no arrears of a call made by a Liquidator the problem of the treatment of a defaulting shareholder will not arise, because, where the loss is equivalent to the same amount per share as the uncalled portion, there will be a repayment *equal* to the called-up amount of the fully paid shares; thus, if there are 2,000 shares of £1 each, fully paid, and 1,000 shares of £1 each, £0·70 paid, and the deficiency is £0·70 per share, the former will receive repayment of £0.30 per share and the latter nothing.

Should the deficiency mentioned above be a *lesser* figure, even the partly called and paid share will obtain a repayment; thus, if the deficiency is £0·60 per share there will be a repayment of £0·40 per share and £0·10 per share respectively for the fully paid and partly paid shareholders.

Should the deficiency be a *greater* figure a call will be made to cover the deficiency, and as a result there would be no repayment to the partly called and paid shareholders; thus, if the deficiency per share is £0·95, there will be a repayment of £0·05 to the fully paid shareholders and a call of £0·25 upon the partly called and paid shareholders to bring their loss of £0·70 per share to £0·95.

Illustration 8

The liquidator has in hand £5,725 after payment of all costs and creditors, but before collecting from the deferred shareholders £0·05 per share on their 10,000 shares of £0·10 (£0·05 previously called and paid).

The ordinary share capital is:

4,000 Shares of £1 each fully paid.

5,000 Shares of £1 each £0·75 called and paid (except arrears of a previous call of £0·125 per Share on 1,000 Shares).

1,000 Shares of £1 each, £0·10 called and paid.

The loss per Ordinary share is £0·15, so that the fully paid ordinary shareholders are entitled to a repayment of £0·85 per share, the £0·75

called *and paid* to £0·60 per share; but the ordinary shareholders who
have paid £0·10 per share only must pay in £0·05 per share (to bring their
loss to £0·15 per share).

LIQUIDATOR'S CASH ACCOUNT

	£		£
Balance of Proceeds	5,725	Repayment of Capitals—	
Deferred Shares—		4,000 Ordinary Shares,	
Call of £0·05 per Share		£0·85	3,400
on 10,000 Shares	500	4,000 Ordinary Shares	
Ordinary Shares—		£0·60	2,400
Call of £0·05 per Share		1,000 Ordinary Shares	
on 1,000 Shares	50	£0·475	475
		[i.e. £0·60 *less* Call un-	
		paid £0·125]	
	£6,275		£6,275

The deficiency of £0·15 is arrived at as follows:

	£		£
Share Capital—		Cash	5,725
Ordinary £1 (4,000)	4,000	Deficiency	2,500
Ordinary £0·75 (4,000)	3,000		
Ordinary £0·625 (1,000)	625[1]		
Ordinary £0·10 (1,000)	100		
Deferred £0·05 (10,000)	500		
	£8,225		£8,225

	£
[1] 1,000 at £0·75 called	750
Less Call in arrear	125
	£625

When the call on the deferred is received, the Cash is £6,225 and the Share Capital £8,725;
but as the Deferred Capital (now £1,000) is entirely lost, this is eliminated and the deficiency
reduced to £1,500, so that the loss to the ordinary shareholders is:

$$\frac{1,500 \ \text{(Deficiency)}}{10,000 \ \text{(fully-paid Ordinary Capital)}} \times £1 = £0·15 \ \text{per Ordinary Share}$$

Illustration 9

X, Ltd., is in liquidation, and after payment of all expenses and creditors
in full there remains a surplus of £3,850 excluding calls in arrears.
  The issued share capital is:

2,000 Preference Shares of £1 each fully paid, having priority over Ordinary and Deferred
    Shares.
5,000 Ordinary Shares of £1 each, fully paid ⎫ having priority over
5,000 Ordinary Shares of £1 each, £0·75 paid ⎭ Deferred Shares
2,000 Deferred Shares of £1 each, £0·60 paid.

A contributor holding 1,000 ordinary shares, £0·75 called, failed to contribute further to the assets of the company to the extent of his unpaid call of £0·10 a share. Show Liquidator's Cash Account.

LIQUIDATOR'S CASH ACCOUNT

	£			£
Balance (details on lines of previous illustrations) .	3,850	Preference Shareholders .		2,000
Proceeds of Calls—		Ordinary Shareholders		
Deferred Shares:		5,000 at £0·40 . .		2,000
2,000 at £0·40 . .	800	4,000 at £0·15 . .		600
		1,000 at £0·05[1] . .		50
	£4,650			£4,650

[1] 1,000 shares at £0·15—£0·10 call in arrears.

The loss per share is £0·60 arrived at as follows:

	£		£
Preference Share Capital .	2,000	Cash . . .	3,850
Ordinary Share Capital .	8,750	Call in Arrear .	100
		Call due from Deferred .	800
		Deficiency . .	6,000
	£10,750		£10,750

$$\therefore \text{Loss} = \frac{6,000}{10,000} \times £1 = £0·60$$

Calls in Advance. Where calls have been paid in advance, the amounts receivable from contributories will be correspondingly less; and when the loss per share is ascertained the amount so paid in advance must first be returned in addition to that receivable in common with the remaining contributories.

Illustration 10

The position of Z, Ltd., in liquidation, in Balance Sheet form, before the adjustment for contributories is:

BALANCE SHEET

	£		£
Share Capital issued—		Cash	1,260
1,000 £1, fully paid . . .	1,000	DEFICIENCY	400
1,000 £1, £0·60 paid . . .	600		
Calls in advance—			
400 at £0·15 . . .	60		
	£1,660		£1,660

Show the Liquidator's Cash Account.

Each contributory loses £0·20 a share, i.e. $\dfrac{400}{2,000} \times £1$.

LIQUIDATOR'S CASH ACCOUNT

	£		£
Balance	1,260	Repayment of Calls in advance—	
		400 at £0·15 . .	60
		Shareholders—	
		1,000 at £0·80 . .	800
		1,000 at £0·40 . .	400
	£1,260		£1,260

Illustration 11

On 30th June 19.., the liquidator of X, Ltd., having a share capital issued of 5,000 preference shares of £1 each fully paid *without* priority as to capital, 8,000 ordinary shares of £1 each, £0·90 paid, and 12,000 ordinary shares of £1 each, £0·75 paid, had a cash balance £1,645.

A dividend to the unsecured creditors of £0·625 in the £ had already been paid as well as the amount due to the preferential creditor.

By 31st December 19.., he had realized the remaining assets, amounting to £3,100, of which 2,000 was in respect of secured creditors of £1,400. All the costs of liquidation were £270.

The creditors, other than the *secured* creditors, were:

	£
Trade Creditors	4,548
Gas Board for Gas supplied	14
Salary of Clerk for six months	714
Directors' Fees for four months	200

Prepare Liquidator's Final Receipts and Payments Account.

LIQUIDATOR'S RECEIPTS AND PAYMENTS ACCOUNT

		£			£
Balance . . .	b/d	1,645	Secured Creditors . .		1,400
Realization of Assets:			Liquidation Costs . .		270
General . . .		1,100	Dividend of £0·375 in £ to		
Re Secured Creditors .		2,000	the Unsecured Creditors—		
			£0·375 in £ on		
			£5,000[1] . .		1,875
			Balance	c/d	1,200
		£4,745			£4,745
Balance . . .	b/d	1,200	Preference Shareholders—		
Proceeds of Calls—			5,000 at £0·20 . .		1,000
Ordinary Shares 12,000			Ordinary Shareholders—		
at £0·05 . .		600	8,000 at £0·20 . .		800
		£1,800			£1,800

[1] See footnote on p. 2914.

The loss per share is £0·80, computed as follows:

$$\frac{\text{Deficiency}}{\text{FULLY-PAID}} = (a) \frac{20,000}{25,000} \times £1 = £0·80$$

Share Capital

(a) This is shown by preparing rough Balance Sheet, thus:

(Rough) BALANCE SHEET

	£		£
Share Capital issued—		Cash (after payment of Costs and	
5,000 Preference £1,		Creditors)	1,200
fully paid . .	5,000	DEFICIENCY	20,000
8,000 Ordinary £1,			
£0·90 paid . .	7,200		
12,000 Ordinary £1,			
£0·75 paid . .	9,000		
	£21,200		£21,000

Receiver for Debenture-holders. A Receiver is an independent person appointed by the Court or an individual or group of individuals, to take possession of certain property for protective purposes, or receive income and profits therefrom and apply them as required.

Most appointments arise by order of Court, e.g. Receiver *pendente lite*, but a mortgagee has power to appoint a Receiver without the intervention of the Court, under the Law of Property Act 1925, Sects. 101 and 109 (subject to certain exceptions).

A Receiver for Debenture-holders may be appointed if the Debentures confer that power on the Debenture-holders when their power of sale arises, as defined in the Debenture. If no such power is contained in Debentures, application must be made to the Court for the appointment of a Receiver.

In the case of Receiver appointed by the Court, accounts will be made up in such form and at such times as the Court may direct.

In regard to a Receiver for Debenture-holders, he may be given power to carry on the business of the company in respect of whose Debentures he has been appointed, in which case he is called Receiver and Manager.

Under the Companies Act 1948 (Sects. 366 and 367), neither a body corporate nor an undischarged bankrupt can act as Receiver or Manager. Where a receiver or manager is appointed in respect of the whole or

---

[1] The unsecured creditors are;

	£
Trade Creditors	4,548
Gas Board	14
Balance of Salary to Clerk* . . .	238
Directors' Fees	200
	£5,000

*The Clerk is entitled to be regarded as a preferential creditor for four months (not exceeding £800) = $\frac{4}{6} \times £714 = £476$, hence the balance of £238 (being £714 less £476) ranks as unsecured.

substantially the whole of the property of an English company on behalf of holders of debentures secured by a floating charge, then:

(a) The Receiver must forthwith send notice to the *company* of his appointment.[1]

(b) There shall within fourteen days of the notice (or extended time if allowed by the Receiver or Court) be made out and submitted to the Receiver a statement in prescribed form as to the affairs of the Company; and

(c) The Receiver must within two months after receipt of such statement send a copy of the statement to the Court and the Registrar of Companies and also a summary of the statement to the latter (accompanied in both cases by such comments as he thinks fit); to the company a copy of such comments or, if he makes none, a notice to that effect, and to any Trustees for Debenture-holders on whose behalf he was appointed and to all Debenture-holders a copy of such summary (Sect. 372).

The Receiver must forward an abstract in the prescribed form of his Receipts and Payments within two months after the expiration of twelve months from the date of his appointment, every subsequent twelve months and on ceasing to act, to

(a) Registrar of Companies.
(b) Trustees for Debenture-holders.
(c) All Debenture-holders (so far as he is aware of their addresses).
(d) The Company (Sect. 372).

The abstract must show, in the case of the yearly return, the receipts and payments for the said period of twelve months; in that on ceasing to act, the receipts and payments from the end of the last twelve-month period to the date of his ceasing to act, *and* the aggregate amounts of his receipts and payments during all preceding periods since his appointment.

The Court may extend the period of two months for delivery of the abstract (Sect. 372).

Such duty of the Receiver to render proper accounts includes the vouching of such accounts.

The statement required to be submitted to the Receiver must:

(a) Show details of assets, debts and liabilities of the company.

(b) Show names, residences and occupations of its creditors, securities given, the dates securities given and such other information as may be prescribed.

(c) Be verified by affidavit of one or more directors and the secretary of the company at the date of the Receiver's appointment, or past or present officers of the company, or those taking part in the formation of the company within *one* year before the date of the Receiver's appointment, or past or present employees of the company within the said year capable

---

[1] Under the Companies Act 1948, Sect. 102, the person making or obtaining (from the Court) the appointment must notify the Registrar of Companies within seven days of the appointment.

(in the opinion of the Receiver) of giving the information required, or present officers or employees (or those who have been within the said year) of a *company* which is (or within the said twelve months was) an officer of the company to which the statement relates (Sect. 373).

A Receiver appointed out of Court may apply to the Court for directions.

A Receiver appointed out of Court is personally liable on contracts entered into with him unless the contract otherwise provides, subject to the right of indemnity. The Court has power to fix the remuneration of a Receiver appointed out of Court (Sect. 371) bringing the position [in the above respect] of the Receiver appointed under an instrument in line with that of a Receiver appointed by the Court.

If the proceeds of sale of the property comprised in the charge in favour of Debenture-holders with a *floating* charge are insufficient to meet fully the claims of such Debenture-holders, the sums available are to be applied in the following order:

1. Cost of realization.
2. Others costs, including the remuneration of the Receiver.
3. Costs and expenses of the Debenture Trust Deed (including the remuneration of the Trustees under the Deed if the Trust Deed provides that such remuneration be a first charge on the amounts realized from the debenture-holders' security).
4. Plantiff's costs of action.
5. Preferential creditors.[1]
6. Debenture-holders.

(*re Glyncorrwg Colliery Company.*)

Illustration 12

Below is the Balance Sheet (abridged) of Y, Ltd., at 31st December 19.9.

The mortgage was secured on the real property and the debentures which had been issued were secured by a floating charge on the assets of the company.

The company being in a precarious condition, a receiver was appointed by the debenture-holders: a liquidator was also appointed. The mortgagees realized their security for £4,000.

The receiver seized certain of the assets amounting to £37,000 and sold them for £34,000. The bank had the guarantees of the directors totalling £2,000, in addition to their life policies amounting to £3,000. The directors duly honoured their obligation to the bank. The balance of the assets realized five-sixths of their book value. The respective costs and remuneration of the receiver and liquidator were £600 and £400. The preference shareholders were entitled to be repaid £1 in the £ in priority to ordinary shareholders.

Prepare Receipts and Payments Account of the receiver and liquidator.

---

[1] The date by reference to which priority is to be ascertained is the date of the appointment.

BALANCE SHEET

	£		£
Issued Share Capital—		Sundry Assets . . .	52,900
10,000 Preference		Preliminary Expenses . .	1,000
Shares of £1 each,		Profit and Loss Account . .	3,350
fully paid	10,000	Real Property	5,000
10,000 Ordinary			
Shares of £1 each,			
fully paid . . £10,000			
5,000 Ordinary			
Shares of £1 each,			
£0·85 paid . . 4,250	14,250		
6% Debentures . . .	25,000		
Loan on Mortgage . . .	3,000		
Bank (No. 1) Ac-			
count . . Cr. £7,200			
Less Bank (No. 2)			
Account : . Dr. 2,000			
	5,200		
Trade Creditors. . . .	2,800		
Commissioners of In-			
land Revenue—			
Corporation Tax: Accounting			
Year ended 31st Dec.—			
19.6 , . £1,500			
19.7 . . 500			
	2,000		
	£62,250		£62,250

RECEIVER'S RECEIPTS AND PAYMENTS ACCOUNT

	£		£
Sale of Assets (specified)	34,000	Costs . . . £ ?	
Surplus from Mortgagees[1]	1,000	Remuneration . ?	
			600
		Preferential Creditors—	
		Corporation Tax Ac-	
		counting Year ended	
		31st Dec. 19.6 . .	1,500
		Debenture Holders	25,000
		Balance to Liquidator .	7,900
	£35,000		£35,000

[1] It is not stated whether this is 'net', after deduction of realization expenses. The proceeds should be entered 'gross' and the costs thereof entered as payments.

LIQUIDATOR'S RECEIPTS AND PAYMENTS ACCOUNT

		£		£		£
Receiver	.	7,900	Costs . . £ ?			
Sundry Assets	.	13,250	Remuneration . ?			
						400
			Unsecured Creditors in			
			full (as per Schedule)	.		8,500
			Preference Shareholders	.		10,000
			Balance . .	.	c/d	2,250
		£21,150				£21,150
Balance	b/d	2,250	Ordinary Shareholders—			
			10,000 at £0·20 .	.		2,000
			5,000 at £0·05 .	.		250
			[£0·20 − £0·15]			
		£2,250				£2,250

Schedule of Unsecured Creditors

	£
Commissioners of Inland Revenue:	
Corporation Tax Accounting Year ended 31st Dec.	
19.7 (subject to adjustment)	500
Bank £5,200, *less* Guarantees and Life Policies £5,000	200
Directors	5,000
Trade Creditors	2,800
	£8,500

The loss on each share is £0·80 calculated in the ordinary way.

[*Note.*] If there is a balance remaining on hand, it must be paid to the Companies Liquidation Account at the Bank of England before dissolution of the company.

Settling the List of Contributories. *Contributions by 'B' Contributories.* The liquidator may call upon the 'B' contributories (in case of default by the 'A' contributories) to pay in money to meet the debt and costs in respect of debts existing at the date they ceased to be members. The 'B' contributories are those contributories who have ceased to be members within one year from the date of the commencement of the liquidation, the 'A' contributories being the present member.

Illustration 13

In a liquidation which commenced on 1st February 19.9 the unsecured creditors were £13,000.

The following are the material details of the contributories appearing on the 'B' list:

	No. of Shares	Date of Ceasing to be Member	Creditors Out-standing at Date of Ceasing to be Member
			£
A	1,000	1st August 19.8	500
B	1,500	1st September 19.8	750
C	300	1st October 19.8	800
D	200	15th December 19.8	950

The above creditors had received no payment at the date of the liquidation.

The shares are of £1 each, £0·60 paid.

Assuming that the contributories on the 'A' list completely default, and that the liquidator realizes a further £1,148·33, show the amount of the dividend to the unsecured creditors. Ignore expenses, costs, and remuneration of the liquidator.

The 'B' contributories duly fulfil their obligations.

STATEMENT OF LIABILITY OF 'B' CONTRIBUTORIES

Creditors Outstanding		A		B		C		D		Cash
		Shares	£	Shares	£	Shares	£	Shares	£	£
		1,000		1,500		300		200		
		£								
(1) . . .	500	(a)	166·67		250·00		50·00		33·33	500·00
(2) . . .	250				187·50		37·50		25·00	250·00
(3) . . .	50						30.00		20·00	50·00
(4) . . .	150	(b)							1·67	1·67
Total . . .	£950									
										£801·67

Notes. (a) The liability in each case is in proportion to the shareholding as at the date of ceasing to be members in respect of debts outstanding on that date, e.g. in (a) the liability of each 'B' contributory is $\frac{10}{30}$; $\frac{15}{30}$; $\frac{3}{30}$; and $\frac{2}{30}$ of £500.

(b) Although the amount required to be contributed solely by D appears to be £150 (the others not being liable because they were not members at the 15th December 19.8, the date of the extra £150 outstanding) yet the sum claimable from him is £1·67, inasmuch as his maximum liability to the company is £80, being £0·40 in £ on 200 shares; and having already contributed £78·33 [items 1, 2, and 3] he can be called upon to pay only £1·67.

[This illustration is continued on p. 2922.]

STATEMENT as to the affairs of..

on the...19.., the
and liabilities expected to rank.

	Estimated Realizable Values £
ASSETS NOT SPECIFICALLY PLEDGED (as per List 'A')	
Balance at Bank	
Cash in hand	
Marketable Securities	
Bills Receivable	
Trade Debtors	
Loans and Advances	
Unpaid Calls	
Stock-in-Trade	
Work in Progress	
....	
....	
Freehold Property	
Leasehold Property	
Plant and Machinery	
Furniture, Fittings, Utensils, etc.	
Patents, Trade Marks, etc.	
Investments other than marketable securities	
Other property, viz:	
....	
....	
....	

	(a) Estimated Realizable Values	(b) Due to Secured Creditors	(c) Deficiency Ranking as Unsecured (see next page)	Surplus carried to last column
ASSETS SPECIFICALLY PLEDGED (as per List 'B')				
	£	£	£	£
Freehold Property				
....				
....				
....				
	£	£	£	£

Estimated surplus from Assets specifically pledged . . . . .

ESTIMATED TOTAL ASSETS AVAILABLE FOR PREFERENTIAL CREDITORS, DEBENTURE-HOLDERS SECURED BY A FLOATING CHARGE, AND UNSECURED CREDITORS*
(carried forward to next page) . . . . . £

SUMMARY OF GROSS ASSETS   (d) £

Gross realizable value of assets specifically pledged . .
Other Assets . . . .

     GROSS ASSETS . . . . £

...., Limited....

date $\dfrac{\text{of the Winding-up Order}}{\text{directed by the Official Receiver}}$ showing assets at estimated realizable values

---

ESTIMATED TOTAL ASSETS AVAILABLE FOR PREFERENTIAL CREDITORS, DEBENTURE-
HOLDERS SECURED BY A FLOATING CHARGE, AND UNSECURED CREDITORS*
(brought forward from preceding page) . . . . .

(e)   LIABILITIES
Gross   (to be deducted from surplus or added to deficiency,
Liabilities   as the case may be)
SECURED CREDITORS (as per list 'B') to extent to which claims are
    estimated to be covered by Assets specifically pledged (item (a)
    or (b) on preceding page, whichever is the less)
            [Insert in 'Gross Liabilities' column only.]
PREFERENTIAL CREDITORS (as per List 'C'). . . . .

ESTIMATED BALANCE of assets available for Debenture-holders secured
    by a floating charge, and Unsecured Creditors* . . .
DEBENTURE-HOLDERS secured by a floating charge (as per list 'D')

ESTIMATED SURPLUS/DEFICIENCY as regards Debenture-holders*   £
UNSECURED CREDITORS (as per List 'E')—   £
        Estimated unsecured balance of claims of Creditors
            partly secured on specific assets, brought from
            preceding page (c) . . . . .
        Trade Accounts . . . . .
        Bills Payable . . . . .
        Outstanding Expenses . . . . .
        ....
        ....
        Contingent Liabilities (state nature)—
        ....
        ....

ESTIMATED SURPLUS/DEFICIENCY AS REGARDS CREDITORS*
    being difference between: £
            GROSS ASSETS brought from preceding page (d)
                        and
            GROSS LIABILITIES as per column (e) . . .

£

ISSUED AND CALLED-UP CAPITAL
............preference shares of............each . . .
............called-up (as per List 'F') . . .
............ordinary shares of............each
............called-up (as per List 'G') . . .
....
....

ESTIMATED SURPLUS/DEFICIENCY AS REGARDS MEMBERS* (as per List
    List 'H') . . . .   £

---

* These figures must be read subject to the following notes:
    1. (f) There is no unpaid capital liable to be called up or
        (g) The nominal amount of unpaid capital liable to be called up is   Strike out
            £   estimated to produce £   which is/is not (f) or (g)
            charged in favour of Debenture-holders.
    2. The estimates are subject to costs of the winding-up and to any
        surplus or deficiency on trading pending realization of the Assets.

It may be noted that C's maximum liability is £0·40 in £ on 300 shares, viz. £120, so that whatever be the amount of the creditors in item 3, the liquidator could have claimed from C only £32·50, i.e. £120 less already contributed £87·50 [items 1 and 2].

The cash received into the *general* funds of the company is £801·67, which together with £1,148·33 makes £1,950 available for unsecured creditors of £13,000, i.e. £0·15 in £.

Statutory Forms. The most important statutory forms in liquidation are:

1. Statement of Affairs and Deficiency Account in Compulsory Liquidation.

2. Declaration of Solvency embodying a Statement of Assets and Liabilities in a Member's Voluntary Winding-up. (See Sect. 283, Companies Act 1948.)

3. Statement of Liquidator's Receipts and Payments.

4. Liquidator's Statement of Accounts (when the property of the company has been disposed of).

Forms (1) and (2) are reproduced on pp. 2920–1 and 2923–5.

DECLARATION OF SOLVENCY

We, ...

....

....

....

of..

....

....

....

(a) 'all the'
or 'the maj-
ority of the'
as the case
may be.

being (a)..Directors of..............................

.... Limited,

do solemnly and sincerely declare that we have made a full inquiry into the

affairs of this company, and that, having done so, we have formed the opinion

that this company will be able to pay its debts in full within a period of

(b) Insert
a period of
months not
exceeding
twelve.

(b)...............................months, from the commencement........ of the winding-up,

and we append a statement of the company's assets and liabilities as

at..19.. being the latest

practicable date before the making of this declaration. And we make this

solemn declaration, conscientiously believing the same to be true, and by

virtue of the provisions of the Statutory Declarations Act 1835.

Declared at...

the........day of...

One thousand nine hundred and ....

...........................before me. ....

....

(c) or Notary
Public or
Justice of the
Peace

(c) A Commisioner for Oaths.

Statement as at...19..

showing Assets at estimated realizable values and Liabilities expected to rank

---

ASSETS AND LIABILITIES	Estimated to Realize or to Rank for Payment (to nearest £)
ASSETS:	£
Balance at Bank	
Cash in hand	
Marketable Securities	
Bills Receivable	
Trade Debtors	
Loans and Advances	
Unpaid Calls	
Stock-in-Trade	
Work in Progress	
....	
....	
....	
Freehold Property	
Leasehold Property	
Plant and Machinery	
Furniture, Fittings, Utensils, etc.	
Patents, Trade Marks, etc.	
Investments other than marketable securities	
Other property, viz.:	
....	
....	
....	
Estimated realizable value of Assets	£

LIABILITIES:
Secured on specific assets, viz.:   £
....
Secured by Floating Charge(s)
Estimated Cost of Liquidation and other expenses including
    interest accruing until payment of debts in full
Unsecured Creditors (amounts estimated to   £   £
    rank for payment)—
        Trade accounts
        Bills Payable
        Accrued Expenses
        Other Liabilities:
        ....

        ....

        Estimated Surplus after paying Debts in full   .   .   .   .   £

Remarks:

List 'H'—Deficiency or Surplus Account

The period covered by this Account must commence on a date not less than three years before the date of the winding-up order (or the date directed by the Official Receiver) or, if the company has not been incorporated for the whole of that period, the date of formation of the company, unless the Official Receiver otherwise agrees.

ITEMS CONTRIBUTING TO DEFICIENCY (OR REDUCING SURPLUS):

1. Excess (if any) of Capital and Liabilities over Assets on the ....19...... as shown by Balance Sheet (copy annexed)
2. Gross dividends and bonuses declared during the period from ....19...... to the date of the Statement
3. Net trading losses (after charging items shown in note below) for the same period
4. Losses other than trading losses written off or for which provision has been made in the books during the same period
5. Estimated losses now written off or for which provision has been made for the purpose of preparing the Statement (give particulars or annex schedule)
6. Other items contributing to Deficiency or reducing Surplus:

   ....

ITEMS REDUCING DEFICIENCY (OR CONTRIBUTING TO SURPLUS):

7. Excess (if any) of Assets over Capital and Liabilities on the ....19...... as shown on the Balance Sheet (copy annexed)
8. Net trading profits (after charging items shown in note below) for the period from the ....19...... to the date of the Statement
9. Profits and income other than trading profits during the same period (give particulars or annex schedule)
10. Other items reducing Deficiency or contributing to Surplus:

    ....

    DEFICIENCY/SURPLUS as shown by Statement

NOTE AS TO NET TRADING PROFITS AND LOSSES:

Particulars are to be inserted here (so far as applicable) of the items mentioned below which are to be taken into account in arriving at the amount of net trading profits or losses shown in this Account:

   Provisions for depreciation, renewals, or diminution in value of fixed assets
   Charges for United Kingdom taxation
   Interest on debentures and other fixed loans
   Payments to directors made by the company and required by law to be disclosed in the accounts
   Exceptional or non-recurring expenditure:

Less: Exceptional or non-recurring receipts:
   ....

   Balance, being other trading profits or losses

   Net trading profits or losses as shown   Deficiency or Surplus Account above

Signature   Dated   19

The differences of detail between the Deficiency Account in bankruptcy and compulsory liquidation are:

	BANKRUPTCY	COMPULSORY LIQUIDATION
Commencing item	Excess of Assets over Liabilities [or conversely]	Excess of Assets over Capital and Liabilities (or *vice versa*).
Date of commencing item	*One* year before the Receiving Order—or as Official Receiver otherwise orders.	*Three* years before the Winding-up Order, or as the Official Receiver directs, where the company has been in existence for at least a period of three years, otherwise from the date of formation, unless the Official Receiver otherwise directs.
Details	(a) *Net* Profit (or Loss). (b) Other profits (or losses) including those arising out of the valuations of Assets and Liabilities in the Statement of Affairs.	See form on p. 2924.

So far as the details in the Statement of Affairs are concerned, Debentures will not occur in Bankruptcy; nor Deferred Debts in Liquidation.

Liquidator Carrying on Business. When the liquidator carries on the company's business, he must keep a trading account and cash book including all receipts and payments. Costs and expenses properly incurred in the course of the liquidation are payable in priority to the liquidator's remuneration. Taxation arising by reason of the business being carried on by the liquidator is included in this class of expense and the Crown therefore takes priority to the liquidator (*In re Beni-Felkai Mining Co., Ltd.*). This priority must be distinguished from the preferential claim for taxation due at the commencement of the winding up which falls within the general class of preferential creditors referred to earlier in this chapter and which rank after the liquidator's remuneration.

CHAPTER 30

MANUFACTURING ACCOUNTS

In previous chapters, no reference has been made to the preparation of the final accounts of a manufacturer.

These accounts will, in addition to the Trading and Profit and Loss, contain a separate section from which will be ascertained the cost of manufacture of the goods or articles. Such information will be prepared on the usual double-entry lines, and in almost all well-organized concerns will be linked up with an efficient costing system. The limits of space will not permit of any detailed explanation of Cost Accounts, embodying, as they do, an exceptional number of technical features; so that no reference will be made thereto except in so far as is required to make the present chapter comprehensible.

The 'Manufacturing Account' is the account employed to show the cost of manufacture or production: and, ignoring for the present the question of quantities or units produced, the rules for compilation may be summarized thus:

1. The cost of goods consumed is ascertained by means of inset figures or a separate sub-account containing: (a) commencing stock of raw materials; (b) raw materials purchased; (c) carriage of raw materials; less (d) closing stock of raw materials; and (e) by-products and/or rejected raw material. The items (a), (b), (c) are debits, and (d), (e) are credits posted in the usual way from the Ledger Accounts. Unfortunately, students tend to lose sight of the essentially simple factors, especially where the credit item takes the form of a deduction instead of being presented in the familiar way.

2. To the total of (1) are added the wages of employees whose work is such that it is directly identified with manufacture, such expenditure being known as direct wages. The total now presented is the **prime cost.** It may here be stated that authorities on this subject hold divergent views on the precise meaning of the term, some maintaining that depreciation of machinery may be justifiably included in the prime cost; but on this and other controversial topics the student is advised to conform to the orthodox method, making such comments as are desirable in connection with the controversial points—unless, indeed, an opinion is definitely called for.

3. To the prime cost are added the factory[1] or works or indirect expenses of manufacture, which will include some or all of the following, according to circumstances:

Works power, rent, rates, heating, lighting, depreciation of machinery (connected with manufacture), works internal transport, works manager's salary, proportion of directors' remuneration, proportion of cost of experiment, repairs to works, storekeeping, and other indirect wages. The total now presented is the gross **works cost of manufacture.**

---

[1] Alternatively described as Factory Overhead.

4. The partly finished goods or work in progress, as distinct from completely manufactured goods, must now be brought into account. The work in progress at the commencement of the period will be debited and work in progress at close of the period will be credited (and debited to Work-in-progress Account) OR the two figures may be shown in inset form, the net difference of which will be either added to or deducted from the total as ascertained in (3). The difference, as mentioned, will be deducted where it reflects an INCREASE of work in progress at the close over that at the commencement, and added where it reflects a DECREASE. The result arising from this entry gives the **net works cost of manufacture.**

5. Where there are by-products or rejected material, the amount thereof (usually at estimated realizable value) is deducted before arriving at the net works cost of manufacture. The deduction will be made either from the raw materials purchased or from the gross cost according to circumstances.

The net works cost of manufacture will be transferred to the Trading Account and will be treated therein just as goods purchased in the case of a non-manufacturing concern. The Trading and Profit and Loss Account may be prepared on the usual lines or a further subdivision thereof made, e.g. in three sections:

(a) The administration expenses are added to the works cost of manufacture in order to obtain the total cost of manufacture.

(b) This section, which is the Trading Account, commences with the stock of FINISHED goods at the commencement of the period, to which is added the total of (a); the credit side includes sales of finished goods and stock of finished goods at the end of the period, the balance giving the gross profit on goods sold (or gross loss).

(c) The balance on (b) is carried down into this final section and the selling and distribution expenses are debited, leaving the net result of the period. This is the ordinary Profit and Loss Account.

Quantities. Where quantities of goods enter into the question, it is necessary to observe the following general principles:

1. Columns to record quantities should be ruled.
2. Quantities of goods will be compiled on the ordinary principle, viz. the commencing quantity plus that received should equal the quantity transferred or sold plus that remaining on hand at the close.
3. Quantities of raw materials and work in progress will appear only in the Manufacturing Account, but quantities of FINISHED goods may appear in both the Manufacturing and the Trading Account.
4. Where, as is frequently the case, incomplete data is furnished in the question, it is necessary to piece together such links of information disclosed, and to this end, unless the facts in the question definitely state otherwise or the inferences are inconsistent therewith, the student should assume that the opening and closing stocks are values on a uniform basis. This applies particularly to stock or finished goods.

In the vast majority of cases the information required to disclose quantities, although incomplete, is such that the required figure is ascertainable by building up the accounts in skeleton form. The varieties of problems are so numerous that no rule can be enunciated to cover them, and constant practice is necessary to enable a student to become proficient in readily perceiving the connecting links.

As an extremely simple example, a question may disclose the fact that 1,000 units have been sold at £2 each; that the opening and closing stocks of finished goods were 200 and 100 units respectively valued at £1·50 each. This will automatically disclose the fact that apart from exceptional circumstances the influx of finished goods is 900 units from the manufacturing section, this being the balancing figure of quantities.

This aspect of Manufacturing Accounts is important, and several illustrations will follow in order that the student may become thoroughly familiar with the method of obtaining complete accounts from incomplete data.

5. Where this is a discrepancy in quantitative results, the amount thereof should be shown as a separate item so that the quantity columns balance.

Illustration 1

The following items appear in the Trial Balance of a company as at 30th June 19 . . :

	Dr. £		Dr. £	Cr. £
Stock, 1st January 19 . .—		Depreciation (contd.)—		
Finished Goods (1,600		Factory and Buildings	400	
tons)	16,380	Lease of City Office	500	
Work in Progress	1,000	Factory Wages	156,000	
Raw Materials	8,640	Overhead	12,000	
Chemicals	390	Sales (35,400 tons)		400,000
Purchases—		Carriage Outwards	2,320	
Raw Materials	142,620	Salaries	22,400	
Chemicals (net price)	12,370	General Expenses	18,310	
Depreciation—		Trade Discounts on Materials		3,400
Plant	16,000	Cash Discounts allowed	5,100	

Stock, 30th June 19 . . : Finished Goods, 1,200 tons, £12,380.
Raw Materials, £6,860; Work in Progress, £2,000; Chemicals, £760.

Prepare accounts of the results of the operations for the half-year ended 30th June 19 . . . (See p. 3004.)

It will be observed that the Trading Account in this illustration has been debited with actual cost, but the practice frequently obtains to charge up trading with the 'outside' cost, that is, the cost as if the finished goods had been purchased from suppliers instead of being manufactured in the proprietor's own factory.

Manufacturing, Trading, and Profit and Loss Accounts for the Half-year ended 30th June 19 . .

Dr.

	£	£
Stock—Raw Materials (Opening)		8,640
Purchases	142,620	
Less Trade Discount	3,400	139,220
		147,860
Less Stock (Closing)		6,860
Raw Materials consumed		141,000
Stock—Chemicals (Opening)	390	
Purchases	12,370	12,760
Less Stock (Closing)	760	12,000
		153,000
Deduct Work in Progress—		
Closing	2,000	
Less Opening	1,000	1,000
		152,000
Factory Wages		156,000
Factory Overhead		12,000
Power		?
Depreciation—		
Machinery and Plant	16,000	
Factory and Buildings	400	16,400
		£336,400

	Tons	£
Stock—Finished Goods . . b/d	1,600	16,380
Transfer of Finished Goods from Factory . . c/d	35,000	336,400
Gross Profit		59,600
	36,600	**£412,380**

	£	£
Salaries		22,400
General Expenses		18,310
Carriage Outwards		2,320
Discounts		5,100
Depreciation—		
Lease of City Office		500
Net Profit		10,970
		£59,600

Cr.

	£	£
Cost of Manufacture		
35,000 tons at £9·61 per ton [1] . . c/d		336,400
		£336,400

	Tons	£
Sales	35,400	400,000
Stock . . b/d	1,200	12,380
	36,600	**£412,380**

	£
Gross Profit . . b/d	59,600
	£59,600

[1] This quantity figure constitutes the connecting link for quantities of finished goods.

The principle is similar, but there will be required additionally:

1. A transfer from the Manufacturing Account to Profit and Loss Account in respect of Manufacturing Profit (or possibly Loss), thus: if a profit:

Debit Manufacturing Account.
Credit Profit and Loss Account.

If a loss:

Debit Profit and Loss Account.
Credit Manufacturing Account.

2. An adjustment for **unsold** finished stock in the selling department (or trading section), because until the goods are sold there is no real profit, although internal profit may have arisen as a result of the transfers of finished goods at loaded prices from the manufacturing section to the trading section. These adjustments are dealt with below.

3. Where, in addition to trading in goods manufactured in one's own factory, similar goods have to be purchased from others, the cost will be charged to Trading Account in the ordinary way. This point is illustrated on p. 3007.

Illustration 2

One hundred units of goods are manufactured at a cost of £2, all of which are transferred to Selling Department at £2·50 a unit. Selling Department expenses are £0·20 a unit sold. Sales are £110, representing a selling price of £2·75 a unit.

Show Manufacturing Account and Profit and Loss Account of Selling Department as appear in the Ledger.

MANUFACTURING ACCOUNT

	Units	£		Units	£
Cost . . .	100	200	Transfer to Selling Department . .	100	250
Profit and Loss Account . . .		50			
	100	£250		100	£250

SELLING DEPARTMENT
PROFIT AND LOSS ACCOUNT

	Units	£		Units	£
Transfer from Manufacturing Account .	100	250	Sales . . .	40	110
Selling Expenses .		8	Stock at 'Cost' . .	60	150
Profit and Loss Account . .		2			
	100	£260		100	£260

GENERAL PROFIT AND LOSS ACCOUNT

		£				£
Provision for Profit on Unsold Stock	[1]	30		Transfer—Profit from: Manufacturing Account		50
Balance—Profit		22		Selling Department		2
		£52				£52

[1] This is arrived at by taking 60 units at £0·50 [i.e. a loaded price £2·50 *less* true price £2]; or taking one-fifth of £150 as the loading is 25 per cent of cost, which is 20 per cent of selling price. Both calculations give £30.

If the manager is to take a proportion of the profits of the Manufacturing Department, it is part of the cost, so that the true cost will be increased by the amount given to the manager. To take an exaggerated supposition, if the manager took ALL the profit the true cost would be £250, i.e. £2·50 a unit, so that the 'loading' over true price is nil. Hence there will be no provision for profit on unsold stock, and the credit to General Profit and Loss Account disappears, the £50 being credited to the personal account of the manager.

It will be seen, therefore, that the *greater* the proportion of manufacturing profit given to the manager, the *lesser* is the loading.

Illustration 3

The same facts as in the preceding illustration, except that the manager is to be credited with 20 per cent of the profit of the Manufacturing Department. Show the accounts.

The manufacturing profit will be £40 only, £10 being transferred to the credit of the Manager. The Selling Department Profit and Loss Account remains unaffected.

GENERAL PROFIT AND LOSS ACCOUNT

	£			£
Provision for Profit on Unsold Stock[1]	24		Transfer Profit from—Manufacturing Account	40
Balance—Profit	18		Selling Department	2
	£42			£42

[1] This is arrived at by taking 60 units at £0·50, *less* one-fifth, that is, 60 at £0·40, or £24. It is clear that the true cost of 100 units is £210, viz. £2·10 each, as against the internal invoice price of £2·50, disclosing a loading of £0·40.

The results can readily be proved by the following rough account built up by ignoring the loading:

PROFIT AND LOSS ACCOUNT

	Units	£		Units	£
Cost	100	200	Sales	40	110
Manager's Commission		10	Stock[2]	60	126
Selling Expenses		8			
Balance—Profit		18			
	100	£236		100	£236

[2] This is arrived at by taking 60 at £2·10; or $\frac{60}{100} \times £210$.

Illustration 4

A company has three departments: mill, factory, and selling. The goods manufactured by the mill are invoiced to the factory at 20 per cent on mill cost, and the factory sells to the Selling Department at a profit of 10 per cent on factory cost. From the following details prepare ledger accounts:

	£
Cost of Goods (Mill)	50,000
Opening Stock of Mill Goods in Factory at 'loaded' price	6,540
Closing Stock of Mill Goods in Factory at 'loaded' price	12,540
Other Purchases and Expenses of Factory	13,500
Selling Department Expenses	5,650
Closing Stock of Factory Goods in Selling Department at 'loaded' price	22,275
Opening Stock of Factory goods in Selling Department	nil
Sales	65,625

MILL MANUFACTURING ACCOUNT

	£		£
Cost	50,000	Transfer to Factory	60,000
General Profit and Loss Account	10,000		
	£60,000		£60,000

FACTORY MANUFACTURING ACCOUNT

		£		£
Goods—			Transfer to Selling Department	74,250
Stock (Opening)	6,540			
Purchases	60,000			
	66,540			
Less Stock (Closing)	12,540			
		54,000		
Other Purchases and Expenses		13,500		
		67,500		
General Profit and Loss Account		6,750		
		£74,250		£74,250

SELLING DEPARTMENT
PROFIT AND LOSS ACCOUNT

	£		£
Transfer from Factory	74,250	Sales	65,625
Selling Department—Expenses	5,650	Stock at 'Cost'	22,275
General Profit and Loss Account	8,000		
	£87,900		£87,900

GENERAL PROFIT AND LOSS ACCOUNT

	£		£
Provision for increase of Mill Stock in Factory $\frac{1}{6} \times £6,000$ [£12,540 − £6,540].	1,000	Profit— Mill . . .	10,000
		Factory . . .	6,750
Provision for increase of Factory Stock in Selling Department: $\frac{1}{11} \times £22,275$ . .	2,025	Selling Department .	8,000
Provision for increase of Mill Stock in Selling Department (a) . . .	2,700		
Balance—Profit . .	19,025		
	£24,750		£24,750

(a) The computation is as follows:

The true cost of Factory Goods (for which a provision has been created) is £22,275 *less* $\frac{1}{11}$ thereof = £20,250.

But the true cost of Factory Goods is made up of the following:

	£
Mill Goods	54,000
Other Goods, etc.. . .	13,500
	£67,500

This shows a ratio of 4 : 1, thus for every £1 of Factory Cost, four-fifths represents Mill Goods at loaded price; hence $\frac{4}{5} \times £20,250$ is attributable to Mill Goods at the cost to the Factory, that is, at loaded price. This amounts to £16,200. As this figure includes mill profit, it is necessary to create a provision for its elimination of $\frac{1}{6}$ of £16,200 = £2,700.

[The final provision may be arrived at, alternatively, by taking the increase of goods in Selling Department, dividing it by the total transfer value from factory, and multiplying by the loading of Mill Goods in factory. Thus—

$$\frac{\text{Increase of goods}}{\text{Transfer value from factory}} \times \text{Mill loading in factory}$$

i.e.

$$\frac{22,275}{74,250} \times \frac{54,000}{6} = \tfrac{3}{10} \times 9,000 = £2,700.]$$

It is clear that the loading on £54,000 is £9,000, so that if there is no increase of factory stock in the Selling Department, no provision is necessary; if, on the other hand, no sales were made, there would be an increase of factory stock in the Selling Department of all the factory goods, so that the whole of the loading of £9,000 would require to be provided for. As in the above case the increase of factory goods in Selling Department is three-tenths, the provision is $\frac{3}{10} \times £9,000 = £2,700$.

Illustration 5

M, Ltd., has two departments, one manufacturing, the other merchanting. Stocks are issued from a central store to both departments. You are required to compile quantitative and financial Manufacturing and Trading Accounts per the Ledger to show the profit or loss on each department from the following figures:

	Quantity in lb	£
Stock of Raw Materials in stores at beginning of year .	5,680	852
Purchases	250,080	38,554
Stores issued:		
Manufacturing Department	152,640	
Merchanting Department	100,000	
Works Charges—		
Materials		3,000
Wages		4,000
Expenses		1,500
Depreciation		1,000
Stock of Manufactured Goods of year	10,040	4,016
Stocks at close of year—		
Raw Materials in Stores	3,120	481
Manufactured Goods in Manufacturing Dept. .	2,680	1,072
General Expenses:		
Manufacturing Department		2,100
Merchanting Department		900
Buying expenses to be apportioned on the basis of the quantities respectively used in each Dept. . . .		2,000
Sales:		
Manufacturing		44,884
Merchanting		17,500
Sales of Waste Products by Manufacturing Dept. . .	50,080	834

Interest on capital at 5 per cent per annum to be charged to each department on the basis of capital employed, namely, £20,000 and £16,000 respectively.

STORES ACCOUNT

	Lb.	Cost per lb.				Lb.	Cost per lb.	
		£p	£				£	£p
Stock of Raw Materials:	5,680	0·15	852·00		Issues—Merchanting Department:	100,000		15,407·30
Purchases:	250,080	0·15416	38,554·00		Manufacturing Department:	152,640		23,517·70
					Stock of Raw Materials: c/d	3,120	0·15416	481·00
	255,760		£ 39,406·00			255,760		£ 39,406·00
Stock of Raw Materials b/d	3,120	0·15416	481·00					

It is assumed that stocks are issued proportionately to materials used and to the departments on the basis of 'first in, first out'. Thus the 5,680 lb. are first issued, proportionately to materials used.

The buying expenses are to be apportioned between the departments in the ratio of materials used, so that the total could be charged to Stock Account and the issues would then be loaded in the correct proportions.

PROFIT AND LOSS ACCOUNT

			£				£
Balance	. . .	c/d	6,849	Net Profit— Manufacturing	£		
				Dept. . .	5,447·94	b/d	
				Less Loss— Merchanting			
				Dept[1] . .	398·94	b/d	
							5,049
				Interest on Capital	. .		1,800
			£6,849				£6,849
				Balance	. . .	b/d	6,849

[1] From p. 3012.

Manufacturing Account

	Lb.	£p			Lb.	£p
Issue of Raw Materials	152,640	23,517·70	Sales of Waste Products		50,080	834·00
Works Materials		3,000·00	Production of Stock	c/d	102,560	33,392·06
Wages		4,000·00				
Expenses		1,500·00				
Depreciation		1,000·00				
Buying Expenses $\frac{152640}{152640} \times £2,000$		1,208·36				
	152,640	£34,226·06			152,640	£34,226·06

Manufactured Stock Account

		Lb.	£p			Lb.	£p
Stock of Finished Materials	b/d	10,040	4,016·00	Stock of Finished Materials		2,680	1,072·00
Cost of Production		102,560	33,392·06	Cost of Sales to Trading Account[1]	c/d	109,920	36,336·06
		112,600	£37,408·06			112,600	£37,408·06

[1] To p. 3012.

TRADING ACCOUNT

		Merchanting Department	Manufacturing Department			Merchanting Department	Manufacturing Department
		£	£			£	£
Cost of Sales—					Sales[1]	17,500·00	44,884·00
Issue of Goods	£15,407·30				Loss[1] . . . c/d	398·94	
Buying Expenses $\frac{1000}{252640} \times £2,000$	791·64						
	b/d	16,198·94	36,336·06				
General Expenses .		900·00	2,100·00				
Interest on Capital .		800·00	1,000·00				
Profit[1] . .	c/d		5,447·94				
		£17,898·94	£44,884·00			£17,898·94	£44,884·00

[1] To p. 3010.

Illustration 6

Four companies entered into a pooling agreement under which they were to pay into a joint account their profits of each year.

The amount of the joint pool was to be applied first in making good the amount of any deficit of a member and then the balance was to be divided among all the members in proportion to their share capital.

The results of the first year of the arrangement were:

	A	B	C	D
	£	£	£	£
Share Capital	160,000	150,000	120,000	270,000
Sales	45,000	62,000	32,000	140,000
Opening Stock	4,000	6,000	9,000	20,000
Closing Stock	5,000	8,000	4,000	16,000
Purchases	19,000	33,000	18,000	80,000
Expenses	15,000	23,000	13,000	37,000

Make up the Pool account showing the amounts each member will pay in or draw out.

Another company, E, is invited to join the Pool, its profits are £16,000 on a share capital of £300,000.

Calculate what benefit, if any, there would be to E if it joined the Pool on the assumption that, if E joins, economies amounting to £9,000 a year can be made in the expenses of the five companies.

STATEMENT OF PROFITS

	A		B		C		D	
	£	£	£	£	£	£	£	£
Sales		45,000		62,000		32,000		140,000
Less Opening Stock	4,000		6,000		9,000		20,000	
Purchases	19,000		33,000		18,000		80,000	
	23,000		39,000		27,000		100,000	
Closing Stock	5,000		8,000		4,000		16,000	
	18,000		31,000		23,000		84,000	
Expenses	15,000	33,000	23,000	54,000	13,000	36,000	37,000	121,000
	Profit	£12,000	Profit	£8,000	*Loss*	£4,000	Profit	£19,000

Total Profits (net)	£35,000
Total Share Capital	£700,000
Percentage on Capital	5%

POOL ACCOUNT

	£		£
Deficit—C	4,000	Profits:	
Balance, divisible proportion to Capital—		A	12,000
A $\frac{160,000}{700,000} \times £35,000$ [5% on £160,000]	8,000	B	8,000
		D	19,000
B $\frac{150,000}{700,000} \times £35,000$ [5% on £150,000]	7,500		
C $\frac{120,000}{700,000} \times £35,000$ [5% on £120,000]	6,000		
D $\frac{270,000}{700,000} \times £35,000$ [5% on £270,000]	13,500		
	£39,000		£39,000

A, therefore, pays in net £4,000, B £500, and D £5,500, making a total of £10,000 which C draws out.

If E joins the Pool, the total capital and profits will be:

	Capital £	Profit £
A, B, C, and D . . .	700,000	35,000
Add E . . .	300,000	16,000
,, Economies .		9,000
	£1,000,000	£60,000 [6% on total Capital]

E's share of the total profits will be:

£

$$\frac{300}{1,000} \times £60,000 \quad . \qquad . \qquad . \qquad . \qquad 18,000$$

Deduct E's existing profit 16,000

Benefit to E by joining Pool . . . £2,000

Note—The previous return on E's Capital was . . $5\frac{1}{3}$% (16,000 on £300,000)
Under the Pool it will be . . . 6 (18,000 on £300,000)

Gain . . . . . . $\frac{2}{3}$%

Gain of $\frac{2}{3}$% on £300,000 = £2,000

[In practice, the item of expenses would be segregated into Manufacturing, Administrative, Selling and Distribution Expenses.]

Illustration 7

The following summary is prepared from the accounts of the Packing Manufacturers, Ltd., for the year 19 . . :

	£
Material consumed	30,000
Wages of Operatives	12,100
Overhead Expenses	8,000
	50,100
Net Profit	4,900
Sales	£55,000

The following material facts exist:

1. The year is a normal year.

2. All operatives are paid on the basis of 44-hour week of which 4 hours are taken up each Saturday morning for general clearing up and maintenance.

3. The materials used vary considerably in quality and price.

4. A small portion of the materials purchased is merchanted and sold at a profit of 5 per cent on cost.

5. No special sales staff is employed on this portion of the company's business.

6. The sales of merchanted goods are £6,300; and the costs applicable thereto £100.

Prepare statement showing results of: (a) manufacturing and (b) merchanting.

	£	£	£
Manufacturing:			
Materials consumed	30,000		
Less Cost of Merchanted Goods:			
$\frac{20}{21} \times £6,300$	6,000		
		24,000	
Wages of Operatives	12,100		
Less value of time on Clearing up and Maintenance:			
$\frac{1}{11} \times £12,100$	1,100		
		11,000	
Overhead Expenses	8,000		
Add Labour Cost as above	1,100		
	9,100		
Less Proportion attributable to Merchanting	100		
		9,000	
		44,000	
Sales			48,700
Net Profit		4,700	
		£48,700	£48,700
Merchanting:			
Cost of Goods		6,000	
Attachable Expenses		100	
		6,100	
Sales			6,300
Net Profit		200	
		£6,300	£6,300

Note. (i) It is assumed that a uniform percentage of profit will arise from all the jobs undertaken.

(ii) A satisfactory statement is impossible in the absence of separation of overheads, e.g. into Manufacturing, Administration, Selling, and Distribution.

Illustration 8

Plastics, Ltd., manufacture their products through two processes, 1 and 2.

The output of process 1 is transferred to process 2 at a price which shows process 1 a profit of $33\frac{1}{3}$ per cent on cost; and the output of process 2 is transferred to the Selling Department at a price which shows process 2 a profit of 25 per cent on cost.

The following information is provided for the year ended 31st December 19..

	Process 1	Process 2
	£	£
Stock, 1st January 19...	210	90
Materials used	800	700
Direct Labour	1,000	914
Overhead	300	184
Stock, 31st December 19..	180	128

The above stocks are those which have passed through the process and are valued at *prime cost* to the process concerned.

The stock of finished goods in the Selling Department (which handles no 'outside' goods) at 1st January 19.., and 31st December 19.., was £620 and £800 respectively.

Sales during the year ended 31st December 19.., were £6,086.

The Provisions for unrealized profit included in the stock valuation at the commencement of the year were: Process 2, £16; Finished Goods, £214.

The manager of process 2 is entitled to 20 per cent of the net profit of his department before charging such percentage.

Assuming that all the stock at 1st January 19.. (commencement of the year), had been sold during the year, show Process Accounts and a Trading Account together with a *pro forma* composite memorandum account proving the trading profit as shown in the Trading Account.

PROCESS ACCOUNTS
FOR THE YEAR ENDED 31ST DECEMBER 19..

	Process 1		Process 2			Process 1	Process 2
	£	£	£	£		£	£
Stock Opening		210		90	Transfer to Process 2	2,840	
Materials used	800		700		Transfer to Trading		
Direct Labour	1,000		914		Account		5,750
Process 1			2,840				
Prime Cost	1,800		4,454				
Overhead	300		184				
		2,100		4,638			
		2,310		4,728			
Less Stock, Closing		180		128			
		2,130		4,600			
Manager's Commission			230				
Profit		710	920				
				1,150			
		£2,840		£5,750		£2,840	£5,750

TRADING ACCOUNT
FOR THE YEAR ENDED 31ST DECEMBER 19..

		£			£
Stock, Opening		620	Sales		6,086
Finished Goods from Process 2		5,750	Stock, Closing		800
Gross Profit c/d		516			
		£6,886			£6,886
Provision for unrealized Profit, Closing: c/f			Gross Profit b/d		516
Process 2	£20		Provision for unrealized Profit, Opening: b/f		
Finished Goods	230		Process 2	£16	
		250	Finished Goods	214	
Trading Profit		496			230
		£746			£746

Calculation of closing Provision— £
Process 2 Stock:

25 per cent of $\frac{2,840}{4,454}$ of £128 20

Finished Goods—
80 per cent of 20 per cent of £800 . . . 128

25 per cent of $\frac{2,840}{4,454}$ of (£800 − £160)[1] 102

————
230
————
£250
————

MEMO. ACCOUNT

	Pro-cess 1	Pro-cess 2		Pro-cess 1	Pro-cess 2
	£	£		£	£
Stock, Opening	210	(a) 74	Transfer	2,130	
Materials used	800	700	Transfer c/d		4,124
Direct Labour	1,000	914			
Process 2		2,130			
Overhead	300	184			
	2,310	4,002			
Less Stock, Closing	180	(b) 108			
	2,130	3,894			
Manager's Commission		230			
	£2,130	£4,124		£2,130	£4,124
Stock, Opening		(c) 406	Sales		6,086
Finished Goods b/d		4,124	Stock, Closing		(d) 570
Gross Profit		2,126			
		£6,656			£6,656

Profit per Accounts— £
Process 1 . . . 710
Process 2 . . . 920
Trading . . . 496

As per Memo. . . £2,126

(a) Stock at cost, £90 − £16 [Opening Provision].
(b) Stock at cost, £128 − £20 [Closing Provision].
(c) Stock at cost, £620 − £214 [Opening Provision].
(d) Stock at cost, £800 − £230 [Closing Provision].

Examination Problem

XYZCo., Ltd., manufactures lemon squash. Prepare from the following balances and records Manufacturing, Trading and Profit and Loss Accounts, showing in them such percentages and figures per case as will furnish costing information and facilitate periodical comparisons.

---

[1] i.e. $\frac{2,840}{4,454} \times$ (£800 − $\frac{1}{5}$ of £800), being the proportion of Process 2 cost before adding either the company's 80 per cent or the manager's 20 per cent of the profit added thereto.

Stocks at cost on 1st January 19. .—		£
Bottled Lemon Squash	. . . .	2,112
Ingredients	. . . .	4,784
Bottles, etc.	. . . .	1,226
Purchases:		
Ingredients .	. . . .	10,432
Bottles, etc.	. . . .	3,128
Factory Wages .	. . . .	5,120
Factory Expenses	. . . .	628
Factory Rent .	. . . .	594
Carriage Inwards	. . . .	382
Distributing Charges	. . . .	522
Office Salaries and Expenses	. . . . . — .	2,080
Selling Expenses	. . . .	904
Stocks at cost on 30th June 19. .—		
Ingredients .	. . . .	3,775
Bottles, etc.	. . . .	1,007
Sales	. . . .	26,294

The stock of bottled lemon squash on 30th June 19. ., was 12,500 cases; 7,000 cases produced during the period had been invoiced out at £1,824 and treated as sales, but were still held by customers on sale or return on 30th June 19. . . .

Messina lemons purchased at £1·20 a case during the year 19. . have been found unsuitable for manufacture; the sales include 1,260 cases of these lemons sold during the period at £0·90 a case, and 180 cases were still in stock on 30th June 19. ., when the net realizable value was £0·80 a case.

100,000 cases of bottled lemon squash were produced during the six months.

(*Adapted from Institute of Chartered Accountants, Final.*)

Solution

It is essential that the lemons unsuitable for the manufacture of lemon squash which were sold should be treated separately. A Lemon Trading Account should be opened and the profit or loss on these dealings separately ascertained. The Ledger account would appear as follows:

LEMON TRADING ACCOUNT

	Cases	£		Cases	£
Stock eliminated from Production Account [See note *b*]	1,440	1,728	Lemons Sold . . Stock of Lemons . Loss transferred to Profit and Loss Account . .	1,260 180	1,134 144 450
	1,440	£1,728		1,440	£1,728

SALES ACCOUNT (*d*)

		£			£
Lemons Sold		1,134	Sales (as per question)		26,294
Lemon Squash on Sale or Return . .	c/d	1,824			
Profit and Loss Account .		23,336			
		£26,294			£26,294
			Balance	b/d	1,824

The balance of £1,824 is deducted from debtors in the Balance Sheet.
See p. 3019 for Manufacturing, Trading, and Profit and Loss Account.

XYZCO., LTD.
Manufacturing, Trading and Profit and Loss Account for the Six Months ended 30th June 19..

	£	£	% on Manufacturing Cost £	Cost per Case £	£			Cost per Case £	£
(a) Stock of Ingredients, 1st January 19..	4,784					Manufacturing Cost of 100,000 Cases	c/d	0·200	20,000
Add Purchases	10,432								
	15,216								
Less Cost of Lemons unsuitable for manufacture	1,728								
	13,488								
(b) Less Stock, 30th June 19..	3,559	9,929							
Stock of Bottles, etc.— 1st January 19..	1,226								
Add Purchases	3,128								
	4,354								
Less Stock, 30th June 19..	1,007	3,347							
Carriage Inwards		382							
Materials Consumed			68·29	0·137	13,658				
Factory Wages			25·60	0·051	5,120				
Factory Expenses			3·14	0·006	628				
Factory Rent [Rates ?]			2·97	0·006	594				
			100·00	0·200	£20,000			0·200	£20,000
			Cases						
Stock, 1st Jan. 19..			10,560		2,112		b/d		
Manufacturing Cost (x) [see p. 3020]			100,000		20,000				
			110,560		22,112				
(c) Less Stock, 30th June 19..			19,500		3,900	Sales		0·256	23,336
Cost of Cases Sold			91,060	0·200	18,212				
Gross Profit	c/d			0·056	5,124				
				0·256	£23,336			0·256	£23,336

(a) As has been stated above, the dealings in unsuitable lemons must be entirely eliminated from the Production Account. The stock of ingredients (£3,775) includes such lemons at cost, hence a deduction therefrom of 180 cases of lemons at £1·20 [i.e. cost] is required, whatever the latter are now worth, so that the stock of ingredients will be as follows:

		£
Stock as per question	. . . . . .	3,775
Less 180 cases of Lemons at £1·20 per case	. .	216
Balance .	. . . .	£3,559

The current net realizable value of the 180 cases is included in the Lemon Trading Account.

(b) The unsuitable lemons were originally included at cost in the purchases; but as these do not now form part of the cost of production, they must be eliminated at cost and debited to Lemon Trading Account, which shows the dealings in unsuitable lemons.

(c) The closing stock of 12,500 cases must be supplemented by the stock of cases out on sale or return, the latter having been deleted from Sales. [See Sales Account (d).]

(d) The Sales figure given includes goods out on sale or return and unsuitable lemons, both of which must be deleted. (See accounts above.)

(e) No mention is made in the question of the cost of the cases, but it is assumed that such is included in the phrase 'bottles, etc.'.

[Alternatively, the goods sent out on Sale or Return may be retained in the Trading Account and a provision created for the unearned profit. This provision will be £424, being £1,824 *less* Cost £1,400. The latter is 7,000 at £0·20 a case. Thus the gross profit will be increased by £424 to £5,548, but as the provision will be deducted in the Profit and Loss section, the net profit will remain unchanged. The Stock on hand (neither sold nor out on Sale or Return) will be £2,500. Sales will be increased by £1,824 to £25,160.]

The account will then read (from part on p. 3019 marked x):

	£		£
Stock, 1st Jan. 19.. . .	2,112	**Sales and deliveries on Sale or**	
Manufacturing Cost . .	20,000	**Return**	25,160
	22,112		
Less **Stock, 30th June, 19**.. .	2,500		
Cost of Sales . . .	**19,612**		
Gross Profit c/d . .	**5,548**		
	£25,160		£25,160

	£		£
Office Salaries . . .	2,080	**Gross Profit** b/d . . .	**5,548**
Distributing Charges . .	522	*Less* **Provision on 7,000**	
Selling Expenses . .	904	**Cases on Sale or Return** .	**424**
Loss on Lemons sold .	450		
Net profit for half-year c/f .	1,168		
	£5,124		£5,124

Alternative figures are in heavy type.

X Y Z Co., Ltd.

		£			£
Office Salaries . . .		2,080	Gross Profit . . .	b/d	5,124
Distributing Charges .		522			
Selling Expenses . .		904			
Loss on Lemons sold .		450			
Net Profit for Half Year .	c/f	1,168			
		£5,124			£5,124

Examination Problem

Coinop, Ltd. sets up at selected sites automatic vending machines which, on insertion of a coin, issue either chocolate in bars or fruit drinks. Bars of chocolate are sold at $2\frac{1}{2}$p each; fruit drinks at 5p a cup. Under the terms of the agreement with the site owner, Coinop Ltd. pays a fixed rental of £5 per week together with a further rental payable after but in respect of the year to 31st March 19.4, of 2 per cent of the takings in that year in the case of chocolates, and 5 per cent in the case of fruit drinks. To increase its sales, it negotiated with six distributors the rental of machines, dealing only in fruit drinks, to them at a rental of 10 per cent of takings. In addition, Coinop Ltd. will supply the drinks at cost plus 5 per cent. The chocolate is bought at $1\frac{1}{2}$p a bar and the fruit drinks at $2\frac{1}{2}$p per cup.

The under-mentioned balances have been extracted from the books for the year ended 31st March 19.4:

	£
Purchase of 100 Machines	5,000
Purchase of Bars of Chocolate	22,500
Purchase of Cups of Fruit Drinks	62,500
Amounts Collected from Machines and Uncollected Cash . .	87,462
Cost of Installing Machines on Sites	400
Wages of Collectors and Service Men	15,960
Maintenance of Machines	5,120
Administration Costs	6,420
Fixed Rentals Paid	10,400
Rentals from Distributors	7,500

The following further information and instructions have been supplied:

	1st April 19.3	31st March 19.4
1. Uncollected Cash	Nil	£35
Stock in Machines at Last Collections Preceding	4,200 bars	1,900 bars
Stock in Machines at Last Collections ceding	1,400 cups	4,000 cups
Stock at Head Office	10,000 bars	12,000 bars
Stock at Head Office	3,000 cups	2,000 cups

2. Costs of installation are to be written off to Profit and Loss Account.

3. Machines, 40 of which were on sites and 60 in hands of distributors, are to be depreciated at 20 per cent on cost.

4. The rentals received from distributors are to be credited to Trading Account.

5. It is estimated that the uncollected cash represents 600 bars of chocolate and 400 cups of fruit drinks.

You are required to prepare:

(a) a Trading Account for the year distinguishing between sales of chocolate and fruit drinks; and

(b) a Profit and Loss Account for the year. Workings to nearest £.

(*Adapted from Institute of Chartered Accountants, Final*)

COINOP, LTD

TRADING ACCOUNT

FOR THE YEAR ENDED 31ST MARCH 19.4

	Units Bars	Units Cups	Total £	Chocolate (Bars) £	Fruit Drinks (Cups) £		Sales (b)—	Units Bars	Units Cups	Total £	Chocolate (Bars) £	Fruit Drinks (Cups) £
Cost of Goods Sold during year (a)	1,500,900	2,498,800					At Sites	1,500,900	998,800	87,462	37,522	49,940
Maintenance of Machines (c)			84,984	22,514	62,470		Distributors		1,500,000	39,375		39,375
			5,120	1,920	3,200		Rentals from Distributors	1,500,900	2,498,800	7,500		7,500
Rentals paid (d)—												
Variable			3,247	750	2,497							
Fixed			10,400	2,080	8,320							
Depreciation (e)			1,000	240	760							
Gross Profit to Profit and Loss Account			29,586	10,018	19,568							
			£134,337	£37,522	£96,815					£134,337	£37,522	£96,815

COINOP LTD.

PROFIT AND LOSS ACCOUNT

FOR THE YEAR ENDED 31ST MARCH 19.4

	Total £	Chocolate (Bars) £	Fruit Drinks (Cups) £			Total £	Chocolate (Bars) £	Fruit Drinks (Cups) £
Cost of Installing Machines in Sites (f)	400	32	368		Gross Profit b/d	29,586	10,018	19,568
Wages of Collectors and Service Men (g)	15,960	6,892	9,068					
Administration Costs (h)	6,420	1,807	4,613					
Net Profit for Year	6,806	1,287	5,519					
	£29,586	£10,018	£19,568			£29,586	£10,018	£19,568

Notes.

(a) Number and Cost of Goods Sold during year are computed thus:

		Bars			Cups
Stocks at 1st April 19.3:					
In Machines	4,200			1,400	
Head Office	10,000	14,200		3,000	4,400
Purchases $\frac{£22,500}{1\frac{1}{2}p}$		1,500,000	$\frac{£62,500}{2\frac{1}{2}p}$		2,500,000
		1,514,200			2,504,400
Less Stocks at 31st March 19.4:					
In Machines (1900–60)	1,300		(4,000–400)	3,600	
Head Office	12,000	13,300		2,000	5,600
		1,500,900			2,498,800
	at 1½p	£22,514		at 2½p	£62,470

(b) (i) Sales are calculated thus:

	Bars		Cups
No. of units sold as in (a) above.	1,500,900		2,498,800
Less Units sold to distributors [see (ii) below]			1,500,000
	1,500,900		998,800
at 2½p	£37,522	at 5p	£49,940

The stock in the machines at the end is stated to be 'at last collections preceding 31st March 19.4.' Thus the uncollected cash in the machines at 31st March 19.4, represents the value of the sales effected after stocktaking date. The stocks at end must be reduced by the sales which have been rightly treated as sales but also included in stock. Therefore the stocks of chocolate must be reduced by 600 bars and the stocks of fruit drinks by 400 cups.

(ii) Number and Selling Price of Units Sold to Distributors are calculated thus:

Rentals received from distributors amount to £7,500 which is 10 per cent of takings. The takings are therefore £75,000, and the number of units sold by distributors are $\frac{£75,000}{5p}$ = 1,500,000. The selling price to distributors is therefore 1,500,000 at 2½p+5% = £39,375. Alternatively, the sales of fruit drinks to distributors may be calculated thus:

	% £	Number £	Cost £
Purchases of Fruit Drinks	100	2,500,000	62,500
Distributors	60	1,500,000	37,500
Sites	40	1,000,000	25,000
	100	2,500,000	£62,500

Sales to distributors:

1,500,000 at £(37,500 + 5% of 37,500) = £39,375

(c) Maintenance of machines has been apportioned between the products on a usage basis. It is assumed that maintenance is carried out in respect of all machines and not only on those at Coinop, Ltd.'s own sites.

	Bars	Cups
Total no. of sales	1,500,900	2,498,800
Ratio of apportionment, say . . .	15	25
$\frac{15}{40}$ of £5,120	£1,920	
$\frac{25}{40}$ of £5,120		£3,200

(d) Rentals are allocated and apportioned to the products thus—
Further Rentals accrued—

	Bars	Cups	
2% of takings at our sites (£37,522)	£750	.	
5% of takings at our sites (£49,940) .		£2,497	
	£750	£2,497	£3,247

The variable rental accrued may be allocated to the products direct, but the fixed rental must be apportioned. Apportionment is made by area occupied by the products in the machines and it is estimated that four bars of chocolate occupy the same space as one cup of fruit drink. On this basis the apportionment of fixed rentals is as follows:

	Bars	Cups
	£	£
$\frac{1}{5}$ of £10,400	2,080	
$\frac{4}{5}$ of £10,400		8,320

Machines in hands of distributors are not taken into account in this instance as no rental is received in respect of these.

(e) Depreciation is calculated and apportioned to the products thus:

Cost of 100 machines . .	£5,000
Depreciation—20% on cost	£1,000

As 60 machines are in the hands of distributors, and sell only fruit drinks, £600 of the depreciation may be allocated direct. The remaining £400 is apportioned on a usage basis. Total allocation and apportionment is as follows:

	Bars	Cups
	£	£
$\frac{6}{10}$ of depreciation allocated direct		600
$\frac{4}{10}$ of depreciation apportioned in the ratio		
1,500,900 : 998,800, say 15 : 10 . . .	240	160
	£240	£760

(f) Six-tenths of the installation charges may be allocated direct to the fruit drinks as 60 machines are in the hands of distributors. The remaining four-tenths is apportioned by area occupied by the products. As in (d) above, it is assumed that four bars of chocolate occupy the same space as one cup of fruit drink. The allocation and apportionment is therefore as follows:

	Bars	Cups
	£	£
$\frac{6}{10}$ of installation charges allocated direct . . .		240
$\frac{4}{10}$ of installation charges apportioned in the ratio 15 : 10 as		
before	32	128
	£32	£368

(g) Wages of collectors and service men are apportioned on the basis of amounts collected from machines, i.e., £37,522:£49,940, say 38:50. Apportionment is as follows:

	Bars £	Cups £
$\frac{38}{88}$ of £15,960 .	6.892	
$\frac{50}{88}$ of £15,960 .		9,068

(h) Administration costs are apportioned on the basis of *total* turnover (including rentals), i.e., £37,522:£96,815, say 38:97.

	Bars £	Cups £
$\frac{38}{135}$ of £6,420 .	1,807	
$\frac{97}{135}$ of £6,420 .		4,613

CHAPTER 31

MANAGEMENT ACCOUNTING, AIDS AND TECHNIQUES

SECTION A: INTRODUCTION

MANAGEMENT accounting is a very comprehensive subject, the treatment of which, even in textbooks that deal with it in depth, is liable to attract criticism in certain authoritative quarters. The difficulties (and perhaps risks) involved in dealing with the subject in a general accountancy book are therefore much greater. Consequently, it should be stressed that the topics contained in this chapter are neither exhaustive nor intended to be so, but are merely a selection of those aspects of the subject that are important from the examination viewpoint. Management accounting is so closely related to cost accounting that a fairly comprehensive knowledge of the latter is a prerequisite of the former; only two aspects of cost accounting are briefly outlined, here viz. budgetary control and marginal costing.

In order to determine how the management accounting function can best contribute to the successful operation of a business concern, it is essential to have a clear understanding of the management function. The main processes of management involve: (i) forecasting, (ii) planning, (iii) organizing, (iv) motivating, (v) co-ordinating, (vi) control, and (vii) communication. As there are a number of splendid books available dealing in detail with the various processes and the main facets of management, it is considered undesirable to deal at length with the management function in a book of this nature. It is, however, intended to show in a concise manner the valuable role which management accounting can play in contributing to the success of the various processes.

Forecasting. Although business forecasting is now recognized as a technique of modern management, it is as well to emphasize that businessmen have always made forecasts, whether on an intuitive basis or on the basis of a methodical study of known facts. It has become apparent nowadays, particularly in the case of large-scale undertakings, that a reliable system of forecasting is a prerequisite of business success. The need for a scientific method of forecasting has been largely influenced by the following factors:

(i) The importance attached to exporting goods, and, as a result of the many problems arising therefrom, the importance of looking ahead much more intently.

(ii) The greater likelihood of machinery and plant becoming obsolete because of the acceleration in the rate of introduction of improved methods and machines. The increasing part being played in business by electronic computers often necessitates changes of business plans.

(iii) The difficulties in managing ever-growing business organizations, and in particular coping with the demands of highly organized labour forces in matters such as greater assurance of security of employment and prosperity in the long term.

3101

(iv) The increasing number of mergers and take-over bids which necessitates reliable forecasting to minimize the risks and uncertainties involved.

Forecasts may be prepared in respect of: (a) Sales; (b) Production; (c) Production, Selling and Distribution, Administration, Research and Development Costs; (d) Capital Expenditure; (e) Cash; (f) Profit and Loss Account; (g) Balance Sheet.

In considering forecasts, due regard must be made to the key and the limiting factors.

The key factor is that aspect of the business as a whole which predominates to such an extent that all other forecasts are influenced by it. In most businesses the key factor is the probability of effecting sales. However, there are trades and industries in which sales to not constitute the key factor, and there are extraordinary situations experienced by other trades and industries when sales cease to be the key factor. In the short term the level of activity cannot exceed the capacity of the business. Occasions may arise when shortages of resources rather than of orders may prevent development and expansion. **A limiting factor** is any restriction on any aspect of a business which may affect profit maximization. Even where there would appear to be no limiting factor, there is always a maximum activity level beyond which a business cannot operate efficiently because of the limitation of human beings. One of the main reasons for the existence of a large number of apparently successful small- and medium-sized firms alongside much larger concerns is the scarcity of skilled managers capable of planning, controlling, co-ordinating and motivating giant concerns.

Planning. Once all the required forecasts have been prepared, adjusted, and agreed from the overall viewpoints of: (a) profitability, (b) production capacity of plant, and (c) sufficiency of working capacity, a plan of action, may be prepared. A plan of action (or planning) is basically a method of setting down in a logical sequence the various forecast activities of each aspect of a business as one integrated whole. The plan will often be drawn up in both statistical and financial terms to cover all aspects of the company's operations, and will deal with all the facilities, human and material, that will be needed to achieve the desired results. Such plans are usually expressed in the form of budgets. (See budgetary control on page 3157).

Organizing. In any business concern it is the responsibility of top-level management to ensure that there is a carefully defined policy laid down whereby there is at all times a specific plan of action relating to men, material and machines. Organizing is that aspect of laid-down policy which is concerned with personnel. A framework should be established, known as an organization chart, where personnel and their responsibilities and the various lines of authority are clearly set down. Often a great deal of time has to be spent in establishing a suitable organization chart.

Probably several experimental charts will be put into operation before a final one can be prepared. Where this is done, it is essential to advise all personnel concerned of the nature of the chart currently in operation, otherwise great uncertainty may arise, with the possibility that any so-called final chart may be regarded with disdain. In preparing a sound organization chart the first step is to demarcate and define clearly in writing every position in the business concern. This necessitates dividing the work first into broad groups, departments, sections or divisions, next into principal functions, then into sub-functions, and so on. The amount of detailed analysis which will be carried out will be determined by many factors, because no single type of organization is necessarily the best for every undertaking even within the same industry.

The nature of the business and the quality of personnel will, of course, greatly influence the organization structure. It should, however, be stressed that the structure must be examined fairly frequently by top-level management to ensure that the fundamental principles of organization are being observed.

As a general rule in most business concerns there will be a body of men—normally the board of directors—who direct the concern in the accomplishment of predetermined objectives. The body of men is often referred to as top management (although this strictly is incorrect as the term is an abstract one). One of these men is often appointed as the managing director whose responsibility it is to ensure that the laid-down policies of the board are effected. To this end, the principal functions of the business concern are subdivided and allocated to top executives who are accountable therefore to the managing director. In turn, all other executives are given responsibilities in such a manner as will ensure that no responsibility is left unassigned and that the burden of responsibilities is fairly shared at each level of authority.

It should be noted that authority and responsibility must go hand in hand, and consequently an individual cannot be held responsible where he does not have the relevant authority over subordinates. On the other hand, an individual given responsibility is accountable to his superior for the exercise of that authority, because authority always entails responsibility. The responsibility of a superior for the actions of his subordinate is absolute. Having used his authority to get a job done, the superior must take full and absolute responsibility for that work as though he had performed it himself. This rule is sometimes referred to as the principle of **Responsibility for Supervision.**

In a business concern, each subordinate must know the superior to whom he is responsible, and should generally be responsible to one superior only—that is, there should be unity of command. Clear and direct lines of formal authority running from the top to the bottom of the organizational structure should be drawn and depicted in the organization chart. **The Scalar Principle** is said to be observed where such a simple, clear and direct chain of authority has been created. Where the Scalar Principle is not observed, there is danger of overlapping authority and divided responsibility resulting in confusion, discord and inefficiency. The number of subordinates which a superior can effectively supervise is determined, *inter alia*, by the nature of the business and the personal qualities of the supervisors and the subordinates. Broadly, however, the span of control should be limited to five or six subordinates performing work which interlocks. The greater the number of subordinates the greater the number of relationships and points of contact between the subordinates, and the more difficult it is to correlate their work.

The following is an extract from an organization chart which depicts the relationship of the Office Manager to the other executives in an imaginary business.

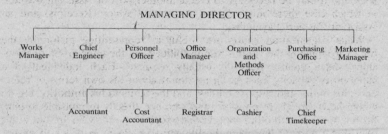

In this particular case, the Office Manager, as is common, reports directly to the Managing Director; his immediate subordinates, to whom he delegates certain authority and duties, are the Accountant, Cost Accountant, Registrar, Cashier and Chief Timekeeper. These officials are said to be in direct or line relationship.

According to the chart, the Personnel Officer and the Organization and Methods Officer of this business are also answerable directly to the Managing Director. This is generally the most satisfactory arrangement though it is not uncommon for these officials to be subordinate to the Office Manager. Where the Office Manager has no authority over these two officials, he will generally have a functional relationship with them and therefore will require to work in close collaboration with them on many matters. Such relationships are often denoted on the chart by broken lines.

The following chart suggests possible lines of authority and spans of control of the executives and supervisors in an office:

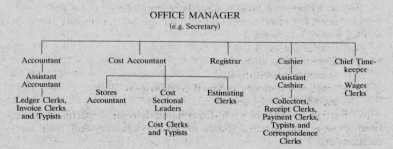

In this hypothetical case, the line of authority runs directly from the Office Manager to the most junior clerk. A Cost Clerk, for example, may be answerable directly to his Sectional Leader who, in turn, would be responsible to the Cost Accountant. Observe that the Cost Sectional Leaders are in a lateral relationship to each other, with the Cost Accountant as their common superior.

There would appear to be sufficient work for the Accountant, Cost Accountant and Cashier to employ continuously and economically their own typing staff. A centralized typing-pool is often more efficient.

The span of control, in the case of the Cashier, would appear to be too wide and it may be necessary to create another post of Assistant Cashier, in which case there might be an Assistant Cashier (Receipts) and an Assistant Cashier (Payments).

While organization charts are useful in representing pictorially the broad grouping of the various responsibilities and the inter-group relationships, much greater detail is usually required. Each individual in a supervisory capacity must be in no doubt about his own terms of reference, his duties and responsibilities, and the limits to his authority, e.g. to whom he is directly responsible, and who are directly responsible to him; his relationship with other supervisors, executives, etc., who are not in his own direct vertical line of authority, must be clear. In order to ensure maximum co-operation and co-ordination in translating the common policy into a programme of action, all specialist, functional and lateral relationships must also be clearly defined and described in writing. Diagonal lines on a chart do not provide this information as they merely indicate that there is a relationship between two executives.

Since it is necessary for each executive to have adequate knowledge of the responsibilities of other executives, whether or not he has any lateral or functional relationships with them, it is usually advisable to collate all the data relating to the organizational structure in the form of a loose-leaf book, usually called the Organizational Manual. This may comprise:

(i) Organizational charts and notes on the general framework of the business;

(ii) main divisions and subdivisions of the business;

(iii) schedule relating to the heads of departments showing—

   (a) the exact title of each position;

   (b) to whom each head is directly responsible;

   (c) normal duties, responsibility and levels of authority, fully described and clearly defined;

   (d) special duties, if any;

   (e) limitations to authority;

   (f) immediate subordinates;

   (g) functional contacts and staff relationships, if any;

   (h) membership of committees;

(iv) Further analysis of each division, subdivision, department or section, showing the detailed duties of all subordinates and their inter-relationship.

The amount of detail included will vary considerably between one business and another. Many authorities claim that the main responsibilities should be stated in general terms only in order to leave the executive with plenty of scope for initiative, for it is feared that if the duties are specified in too great detail, extensive and frequent amendments may be necessary.

Motivating. The object in any business concern in motivating personnel is to ensure that each employee carries out his allocated duties with maximum effect. No doubt the strongest motivator is often the financial incentive, but this by itself has clearly been proved in practice to be dependent upon other factors or conditions. A large number of the working population is more concerned in finding happiness, satisfaction and contentment at work than high remuneration with the absence of these conditions. This, of course, is not surprising when it is realized that each person during his working life spends on average approximately one-third of his waking hours at his place of work. Consequently it should be the aim of the top management, through the managers, to create an atmosphere of mutual trust and belief in a worthwhile common task if they are to get the most out of employees. Some positive motivation methods are as follows—

1. Providing employees with information necessary for a clear understanding of all matters that directly affect them, in order to secure and maintain their interest, to develop loyalty and to imbue them with a sense of participation and responsibility.
2. Establishing an equitable basis of work allocation, and framing just, objective and impartial disciplinary rules that will create confidence in and respect for superiors, and raise the level of morale.
3. Providing a sympathetic outlet for grievances so as to prevent frustration and avoid an atmosphere of discord.
4. Installing a fair and just system of remuneration related, where practicable, to output by an acceptable incentive scheme.
5. Laying down a rational and enlightened policy of promotion, and establishing training schemes that will provide employees with opportunities for self-development and advancement.
6. Introducing retirement and welfare schemes to create a feeling of security of tenure.
7. Establishing schemes for consultation so as to provide a means of exchanging viewpoints that will foster a sense of group harmony.

Co-ordinating. Co-ordinating in business terms means the inter-relating of the various functions and activities of a business in one complete working unit in such a manner that maximum efficiency and profitability are attained. A business concern of any magnitude cannot operate successfully where it consists of a series of different departments operating independently and without any cohesive plan. In large-scale undertakings the co-ordination process is often controlled by a separate department within the organization, and normally the co-ordination required is achieved by a system of budgetary control.

Control. Control embraces the checks applied in all activities of a business to ascertain that the management policies and plans are being implemented, and if they are not, to ensure that corrective action is taken. In particular, control information, from which comparisons may be made of actual with plan, is derived from the accounting and costing records. Effective control should not only bring to light any wastes, inefficiencies, losses or weaknesses, but should also ensure that timely measures are taken to rectify these and, further, to prevent any recurrence. Such control can be achieved only through the organizational structure, i.e. by individuals according to their specific functions and responsibilities. The major fields of activity in which control may be effected are those relating to material, production, quality, marketing, personnel, cost, reporting and finance.

Communication. Communicating in the business sense refers to the transmission of instructions and information, whether verbally, in writing or by means of signs or signals, to and from the business concern's own personnel, customers, suppliers and others. In order to gain the confidence of employees, to obtain their full co-operation, and thus achieve greater efficiency, modern practice is to keep all personnel informed of company activities, generally through the medium of a monthly bulletin.

The effectiveness of a management accountant can be gauged from his ability to provide meaningful and timely financial and other reports to the right managers. In general, this ability cannot be readily attained; indeed, a very considerable amount of technical knowledge, experience and skill is required in preparation of appropriate and easily comprehensible reports from which correct inferences can be drawn by the recipients that will enable them to make decisions. Not only must consideration be given to the recipient's position in the business, and to his technical, business and accounting knowledge, but also the purpose for which the reports themselves are primarily intended must be clearly understood.

Routine reports are prepared at regular intervals, e.g. daily, weekly, four-weekly, quarterly or annually. Special reports are prepared as and when required. The type of information required differs widely between the various managerial grades, and its extent is largely determined by the nature of the organization. A charge-hand, for example, normally requires information regarding his own sphere of authority only, and consequently to be of use to him it must include considerable detail. A managing director, however, requires information relating to the whole organization presented to him in condensed form, with all unimportant details omitted but all essentials shown in readily assimilable form.

Apart from the generally accepted rôle of the management accountant in communication, viz. the presentation of accounting information to management, he can render a most important service by appraising the efficacy of the whole system of communications, both internal and external, in operation in the business organization. It is strongly recommended that up-to-date information concerning new communications equipment produced by the various specialist manufacturers should constantly be obtained. In fairly large businesses this no doubt will be the responsibility of an Organization and Methods Department. Nevertheless, the management accountant should always be searching for improved means of communication with a view to minimizing costs and at the same time improving the service.

Of the various media of communication, verbal, i.e. the conveying of instructions, orders, requests, information etc. by means of the human voice can, in certain circumstances, be the most effective and also the most desirable. Furthermore, some form of verbal contact within a business concern will always be necessary. Sometimes, however, verbal communication is impracticable, and consequently in order to convey information, instructions etc. to a large number of employees simultaneously (or almost) a much more effective system must be used. This may be achieved by means of loudspeakers, by printed or duplicated circulars, or by recording tapes. Because of the high cost of employing stenographers and typists, consideration should be given to the use of dictating machines and standard letters. The costs of printing should be compared with those of duplicating. The effectiveness of the existing external telephone system should be carefully studied; many systems could be made much more effective by the installation of automatic branch exchanges and by the use of night service facilities. The Post Office will provide very useful information relating to suitable telephone systems and facilities. Consideration should also be given to the transmission of internal information by devices such as gravity chutes, conveyor belts and pneumatic tubes. Photocopying equipment, once installed, often proves to be almost indispensable because of the saving in typing and checking time, for if the original is error-free there is no danger of a faulty copy. Stencil cutting machines are available, at relatively low cost, which will produce excellently cut stencils from printed or duplicated originals. Again, provided that the originals are error free the newly cut stencils will not require to be checked. The risk of error inherent in any manual-labour system can be reduced by the numerous machines that are obtainable, the cost of which can be recovered over a fairly short period of time. The use of modern accounting machines, computers and computer service bureaux will often warrant investigation. Sorting machines, mail franking, folding, sealing or opening machines can be cost-reducing investments.

The foregoing suggestions are by no means exhaustive; they should, however, be sufficient to indicate that the service which can be given by the management accountant in the field of communication systems alone can be very extensive.

SECTION B: INTERPRETATION OF ACCOUNTS

By 'interpretation of accounts' is meant the explanation and amplification of and translation into clear and simple form of the data presented by the Profit and Loss Account and Balance Sheet of a business; to make such deductions and draw such inferences as may be possible therefrom as to its operations, financial position, and prospects.

The examination of the Profit and Loss Account and Balance Sheet may arise:

1. For a special objective, e.g. for the purpose of agreeing profits for taxation purposes or to enable an intending lender, e.g. a banker, to decide whether or not to lend.
2. For a restricted objective, e.g. criticism of form, content and conformity to law of published accounts.
3. To assess and interpret results of one year's operations.
4. To assess and interpret results for a period of years:
   (a) broadly, by way of further explanation of (3), and
   (b) in detail, with some special object in view.

In practice, the most frequent form of interpretation is that arising under (3) where the professional accountancy and financial periodicals make analyses and give interpretations of them, although the professional accountancy publications lean more to criticism of content and form rather than attempting interpretation.

The financial periodicals do not confine themselves necessarily to the requirements of (3) and often attempt a very broad interpretation under (4).

It will be recognized that in many instances full and complete detail will be available which will enable a comprehensive analysis and interpretation to be given, and problems that arise in the examination comprise those where considerable detail is available (although not necessarily complete) and those where full detail is *not* available (as in published accounts).

The main headings are now dealt with separately.

1. **Special Objective.** Emphasis will be laid on the particular points relative to the inquiry and purpose.

The circumstances involving such inquiries are:

1. On sale of a business.
2. On the admission of a partner.
3. On a potential investor being desirous of purchasing a block of shares.
4. On the proposed acquisition by a company of a business.
5. On a creditor or potential creditor, including a banker or a debenture-holder, being desirous of ascertaining what security is available for the advance or liability.

In circumstances (1) and (2), naturally the inquiry is chiefly directed to ascertaining to what extent the true position is actually better than the Balance Sheet disclosure, e.g. existence of secret reserve.

In circumstances (3) and (4) affecting a buyer, the reverse position obtains, the inquiry being weighted in ascertaining to what extent the true position is actually worse than the Balance Sheet disclosure, e.g. overvaluation of assets, including inadequate provision for depreciation.

In circumstance (5) the adequacy of the security is the chief consideration, particularly as to the likely position in the case of a forced realization of those assets that are 'free' and those mortgaged or charged in favour of other creditors, so that he can measure the risk involved if he has to take secondary security or rank with unsecured creditors if no security is available.

Included in the enquiry will be, in cases (1) to (4), a consideration of earning capacity and goodwill; whilst in (5) it will be the capacity to earn sufficient income to pay the interest (or other reward) on the loan, and it would obviously not be sufficient unless the amount so required was covered by a very ample margin.

In all cases regard will be had to the liquid position, security of tenure, and the general trend of the company's profit and achievement.

Analysis of Components of a Balance Sheet. It is important that a student should be able to analyse and break down each component element in a Balance Sheet, that is, to consider it in detail and in relation to other items. The analysis (in summary form) of each item is now considered in the case of a limited company.

Liabilities Side

1. *Share Capital.* Class of shares; issued at par, premium or discount; uncalled up Capital; paid up Capital. Calls in advance; calls in arrear; interest and security for latter. Redeemable preference shares; rate and redemption (earliest and latest date and at what price); arrears of preference dividends; expropriation rights. Founder's shares. Forfeiture of shares: profit on reissue of forfeited shares.

Table A (Articles) *re* dividends; position as to dividends and winding up and generally respective rights and priorities; Lien; Nominal capital; uncalled Capital (charged). Reserve Capital, from (shares with distinctive numbers, stock, units of stock); expenses of issue. Share capital is *not* synonymous with *real* capital employed.

2. *Debentures.* Nature; naked; charged (fixed and/or floating—if so, on what). Issued at par, premium or discount and how treated. Redemption by drawings, by purchase in open market or fixed date or piecemeal— when and what price; treatment of profit or loss on redemption. Sinking Fund; convertible, when and how. Interest; cover, margin of security. Own debentures redeemed reissuable; company's borrowing powers.

3. *Creditors.* Trade; expenses (accrued and accruing). Lien; set-off; statute-barred. Discounts and other deductions. Class; secured or unsecured—former shown separately—details of charge. Loan creditors. Subsidiary companies separate. Taxation provision separate; also Bank and other short-term borrowing separate. Contingent liabilities. Capital expenditure authorized by directors but not contracted for.

4. *Bills Payable.* Separate; accommodation bills; maturities.

5. *Bank Loans, Overdrafts, etc.* Separate. Security; interest. Purpose. Repayment. Limits on borrowing. If Cash in same bank, terms *re* set-off. Rates of interest.

6. *Reserves.* Purpose. Segregate from provisions. Whether represented by earmarked, readily realizable securities (Reserve Fund). Increase and

source; decrease and how utilized. Capital Reserves separate from Revenue Reserves (although not required by Companies Act 1967).

7. *Capital Redemption Reserve Fund.* Consistent with nominal amount of preference shares redeemed without use of proceeds of new issue. Bonus shares.

8. *Provisions.* Purpose; commitments, contingencies, diminution of assets; ascertainable specific requirements. Taxations provision, with basis, separate.

9. *Profit and Loss Account.* Connect with balance forward; addition of current profit or deduction of current loss. Dividends, Reserves and other appropriations; taxation. Transfers from Reserves. Profits earned in relation to: (*a*) share capital and (*b*) capital employed and comparison thereof with previous years.

Assets Side

1. *Land and Buildings.* valuation; revaluation, names of valuers and basis used; subdivided freehold, long (50 years or over), or short leasehold. If leasehold, unexpired years; amortization; dilapidations; renewal; compensation. Location; site factors; size and capacity. Treatment of additions; improvements. Free or secured.

2. *Plant and Machinery.* Cost; additions; sales. Depreciation; obsolete plant. Reconciliation with plant register. Free or secured.

3. *Patents, Trademarks etc.* How acquired; origin or transfer. Life. Effectiveness (reflecting true value). Depreciation. Fees.

4. *Loose Tools.* Revaluation.

5. *Fixtures and Fittings.* Cost; additions; sales. Depreciation. Renewals.

6. *Stock.* Subdivision: Raw materials, work in progress, finished goods, stock out on consignment, sale or return; in Transit. Expenses stock (e.g. advertising material). Stock records; valuation; consistent treatment; by, when, or how taken, valued and certified. Free or Secured. Elimination of unearned profit on sale—price variations (e.g. Branches, goods from subsidiaries, etc.). No profit on finished goods or work in progress, and on latter, reasonable loading for overheads. On long-term contracts, treatment according to proximity of completion; contract terms. Conservative treatment of old and 'sticky' stock.

7. *Debtors.* Total accounts. Home or foreign; if latter, currency or sterling debt; forward exchange contract, Nature. Realizability. Provision for bad and doubtful debts; discounts; set-offs and contras. Exclusion of 'internal' debts: Proprietor, directors. Branch accounts. Loans to directors separate. Loans to subsidiary companies separate. Security; interest; repayments.

8. *Bills Receivable.* Amount and maturities; parties to Bills; provision for dishonoured Bills. Contingent Liability for Bills discounted. Nature and purpose.

9. *Investments.* Subsidiaries separate. General investment policy. Dividends. Purchases and sales cum or ex div. Recent sales or purchases. Earmarked for special purpose (e.g. sinking fund); dividend accruing to the fund or other special purpose. Free or secured; degree of realizability.

Fixed or current asset. Quoted or unquoted; market value of quoted (quoted now includes trade investments); cost and aggregate amounts written-off unquoted and details of income receivable and share of profits in respect of equity shares. Contingent liability for uncalled capital. Tax reserve certificates separate as current asset; interest accruing only when certificate surrendered before Balance Sheet is signed.

10. *Goodwill.* Purchase. Valuation consistent with profit capacity. Write-offs, how dealt with; write-backs, how dealt with. No Balance Sheet inclusion for 'created' as distinct from purchased goodwill.

11. *Fictitious Assets.* Expenses of issue of shares and debentures, discount on same. Separate items.

Bankers and the Balance Sheet. The Banker in lending must aim at protecting the amount he lends and the interest payments, so that the dominating factors are the security and realizability of the loan and the borrower's ability to pay regularly the interest; hence the purpose and duration of the loan and the security available are of prime importance, as well as the standing, integrity and business record of the borrower, and the inherent soundness to which he proposes to lend money he will consider:

1. The reliability of the Balance Sheet and the extent to which it is truly representative of the financial position.

2. Fixed and current assets—exclusion of fictitious and intangible items, and to what extent 'free' or 'encumbered'.

3. Working Capital.

4. Amount and realizability of investments; such as may be considered 'quick assets', like British Government securities, may be considered as falling under (3).

5. Particular of all liabilities, including taxation; whether and to what extent and under what conditions liabilities are secured on specific assets.

6. Consideration of specific assets, e.g. debtors, stock, work in progress.

7. The amount of drawings, if a sole trader or partnership, or directors' fees and dividends if a limited company.

8. Existence and nature of contingent liabilities, e.g. calls on shares, forward purchases, etc.; secret reserves.

9. Depreciation provision (the condition and modernness of the plant, etc.; but this, as such, would not be ascertainable from the Balance Sheet).

10. Profit-earning capacity of the business.

As distinct from a prospective buyer of the business or of its shares, the Banker will pay close attention to the estimated 'break-up' value of assets in a forced realization rather than 'fair value as a going concern'.

The Balance Sheet submitted would have to be 'up to date' reflecting the position at the time of the loan negotiations.

Illustration 1

Field and Meadow, Ltd., desires to obtain from its bankers a loan of £20,000. The Balance Sheet representing the current position is as shown below.

You are asked by the bankers to investigate and report.

BALANCE SHEET

	£		£
Authorized and Issued Share Capital		Goodwill	25,000
60,000 Shares of £1 each, fully paid	60,000	Leasehold Premises (at Cost) . .	22,000
Profit and Loss Account . .	1,550	Plant and Machinery (at Cost, *less*	
8% Debentures (Redeemable)—		Depreciation)	8,300
180 of £100 each	18,000	Investments and Loans (at Cost, *less*	
Sundry Creditors.	18,000	Provision)	14,100
Bank Overdraft	2,000	Stock and Work in Progress. . .	6,300
		Sundry Debtors, *less* Provision for Bad	
		and Doubtful Debts. . . .	23,750
		Cash on hand	100
	£99,550		£99,550

Show the basic features of a report on the position, including those matters on which it is desirable to have fuller information.

It may be assumed that the bankers are satisfied about the general prospects of the business and the purpose of the proposed loan.

The main headings of the Report would be:

1. The net asset position is £36,550, excluding goodwill and depreciation of the leasehold premises.

2. Assuming that the investments and loans are not such as can be counted as liquid or near-liquid assets, the working capital at £12,150 appears to be adequate, notwithstanding the unsatisfactory cash position. The size of the stock and work in progress is low as compared with the debtors, which seems to indicate either an exceptionally low level of stock, or that the company does not require heavy stocks, or that the debtors position is unsound by reason of overdue accounts, or by long credit facilities given by the company.

3. No provision by way of sinking fund is being made for the redemption of the debentures, and, although there are investments and loans, these fall short of the debenture debt and do not provide a satisfactory basis for ensuring debenture redemption, although assuming their reasonable liquidity, they would at the current date partly meet the redemption, but in that event the item would be ruled out of the category of current assets.

4. The amount standing to the credit of the Profit and Loss Account is small and no general reserve exists; this may signify a low earning capacity (which may be attributable to a weak liquid position which it is intended to remedy by the loan now asked for) or an abnormally high distribution of profits signifying a disregard for careful husbanding of resources.

The specific detailed inquiry would be directed to the following matters:

(*a*) Analysis of the recent (Manufacturing) Trading and Profit and Loss Accounts with particular attention to turnover, gross and net profit, directors' fees, dividends.

(*b*) The date of redemption of the debentures, and the price of redemption; inspection of debentures, nature of charges (if any) they carry on the company's assets.

(c) Detailed particulars of investments and loans; in respect of the former whether or not they are fully paid; present market value of investments; in respect of loans, to whom and on what terms; when repayable. Realizability of both investments and loans. In view of the poor liquid position, why loans should be made by the company.

(d) The date and terms of the lease, including the tenure.

(e) General condition of the plant and machinery; whether any obsolete.

(f) Separate examination of Stock (there should be both Raw Materials and Finished Goods) and work in progress; its valuation, particularly as to whether work in progress and finished goods include profit (not yet earned) or selling and distribution charges.

(g) Examination of schedule of book debts to see if there are any debts irrecoverable and if the provision is adequate.

(h) Examination of the schedule of creditors with particular regard to the period of credit, overdue liabilities including any which may be pressing by reason of actual or contemplated legal proceedings; whether it includes *all* liabilities, including adequate provision for taxation and arrears of debenture interest.

(i) General examination of the recent trend in relation to availability of labour supplies of goods and continued likelihood of sales being maintained or increased.

Subject to the information arising from the above inquiries being satisfactory and proper security being given by the company (together with personal guarantees by the directors), the Report would be sufficiently favourable to enable the Bank to view sympathetically the request for a further loan of £20,000.

[In practice, the numerous inquiries would be made and dealt with prior to the drafting of the Report, so that a firm conclusion could be arrived at. In examinations, in the absence of exact data, the general principles should be stated and the queries set out; but it will not usually be possible to do more than suggest a tentative recommendation. It is sometimes objected that all the detail should be given, enabling the candidate to come to a firm conclusion; but, apart from considerations of space, a candidate's knowledge of the subject can be tested by the setting of the 'inexact' question.]

2. Restricted Objectives

As this calls for criticism of form, content and conformity with law, it will be necessary to apply a knowledge of accounting principles and company law, which subjects have already been dealt with elsewhere in this book.

3. Results of One Year's Operations

The interpretation of the results of the year's operations of companies from published accounts must be confined to the necessarily abridged detail contained therein, without access to, or means of obtaining further information, except that given in the Chairman's review. Such interpretation will take the form of explanation of and comment on the past year's results and the financial position at the end of the year, with such deductions as are possible in relation to the profit trend of the past few years.

In this connection, the usual comments in the press are confined to summarizing the year's profit, tax, allocation to reserves; stating the chief Balance Sheet changes; rate of profit earned and dividends declared; and broadly commenting thereon.

Where the published accounts are drawn up clearly, reliable interpretation is possible and the true profit, its disposition and its resultant influence on the Balance Sheet can be ascertained.

The Profit and Loss Account must show the turnover for the year, the normal trading results, abnormal and unusual items, income from trade investments, depreciation, auditors' and directors' remuneration, provision for taxation and transfers to and from Reserves. Where a holding company is concerned, a group Profit and Loss Account built upon similar lines is required, subject to certain exceptions. The information given in the Profit and Loss Account is generally insufficient to reveal anything as to efficiency and detailed overheads.

The Balance Sheet must show certain minimum detail (see p. 2332), (including, where applicable, a Group Balance Sheet, subject to certain exceptions), and the following matters will usually be the subject of comparison and comment:

1. Adequacy of the working capital, and arising therefrom the strength or weakness of the cash position.

2. The relative proportions of the fixed and liquid assets.

There are frequently some special or unusual matters requiring comment, e.g. charging to Profit and Loss Account items properly belonging to Profit and Loss Appropriation Account, e.g. Debenture Redemption Fund Contribution; or charging to the latter account items being neither charges to, nor appropriation of, profit, e.g. payments made to an Amortization Policy.

3. The adequacy of the provision for depreciation.

4. The provision for taxation based upon the current year's results.

5. The existence of and alterations to general reserves.

6. Consistency of accounting methods.

7. The general overall picture of the current Balance Sheet.

In all the above, comparison with preceding years' accounts will be made, together with such inferences arising therefrom as may be possible, reflecting management ability and policy.

4. Interpretation of Results over a Period of Years

In a long-term interpretation the line of approach is to explain the broad trends of the business, without giving undue attention to yearly variations, except where special circumstances otherwise demand.

From the inferences that can be made reliably, some measure of forecast is usually possible, but allowance will have to be made for those factors which might affect appreciably a short-term comparison (e.g. transition from war to peace production) as distinct from those factors which might affect appreciably the long-term position. The long-term factors may be deep-seated and fundamental, so as to exercise a permanent influence on the earning capacity of the business; or merely superficial and not sufficient to alter materially former earning-power.

Even in the most comprehensive set of published accounts much conjecture is inevitable, often involving contradictory interpretations by commentators, but many points of obscurity are often clarified and explained by the Chairman's review, particularly those factors which cannot be revealed by an examination and analysis of the published accounts.

The following are the general inferences to be drawn from the examination of a series of yearly published accounts:

1. Depreciation written-off approximating to capital expenditure—a fair inference is that fixed assets are being maintained, but factors lacking in coming to a definite conclusion are: (*a*) adequacy of rate, (*b*) depreciation method adopted, and (*c*) degree of obsolescence.

2. If profits do not vary considerably from one year to another a fair inference is that the business is stable, but factors lacking are; (*a*) whether so-called stability arises from deliberate policy of using or creating secret reserves; (*b*) the volume of sales and rate of gross earnings; (*c*) the consistency of stock valuations.

3. A progressively increasing amount of fixed assets without a corresponding increase in net profit—a fair inference is that the assets are not paying their way, either because selling prices have not been adjusted to cover their enhanced cost, or through lack of full employment of such assets, e.g. short time, or assets employed with a short life with frequent replacements (particularly in periods of rising prices, e.g. second-hand vehicles).

4. Where short-term liabilities, e.g. Bank Loans or Bank overdraft, do not decrease or actually increase, a fair inference is that the company's position continues to be sufficiently unattractive to support a 'funding' operation by the issue of shares or debentures; if related to a constant or growing amount of fixed assets, and not compensated for by a corresponding increase in liquid assets, the company's position is likely to become vulnerable. Reference will have to be made to the profits earned, and, unless these are declining, the position may reveal a tendency to overdistribute dividends or to the utilization of the major part of retained profit in extending the acquisition of fixed assets or the increasing of the volume of credit business (or extended period of credit to customers) in extent greater than the financial position warrants. Other changes in policy may be indicated, i.e. transference from cash or normal credit sales to hire-purchase sales (itself often evidence of financial weakness). The position may be reflective of continued decline in profit capacity (or actual losses) but this would be apparent from the examination of the published accounts.

5. Where trade creditors (including adequate provision for taxation) are increasing as compared with debtors, a fair inference is that the company

is overtrading. Where, in the past, under the heading of creditors were included 'credit balances' (like General Reserves), the practical effect was to create a secret reserve which might (and often did) cover periods of declining profits.

6. Capital issues should normally, after due time for their utilization, be reflected in a corresponding increase of net profit and volume of business. If not, a fair inference is that the financial position is deteriorating, unless the issue is mainly for 'funding' short-term liabilities (if for reducing liability to Bank, the issue would be followed by the elimination of the charge for Bank Interest or redeeming wholly or in part debentures and/or other prior charges, by the elimination or reduction in Debenture and/or Loan Interest).

7. Where dividend *rates* are maintained, with regular and reasonable appropriations to Reserve, a fair inference is that the business is being conducted on sound lines, particularly if there appears to be adequate provision for depreciation, and the fixed assets are not being unduly increased and the ratio of liquid assets to current liabilities is maintained.[1]

8. Where the working capital is declining, a fair inference is that the business is declining, or, if the fixed assets are unduly increasing, that the business is becoming 'top heavy' and unstable on its foundations.

9. Should the liquid assets and profit be increasing consistently, it may be fairly inferred that the business is expanding (but it may have been financed by borrowing on Loan or Share Capital so that the rate of dividend might not be correspondingly increased). If, however, the profits are increasing without a rateable increase in the liquid assets it may indicate any or all of the following factors; (*a*) higher profit margins; (*b*) quicker rate of turnover; (*c*) quicker discharge of current liabilities, or a utilization of profit for expansion of fixed assets or reduction of long-term liabilities.

When a Holding Company's accounts are published, they now have to be supported by Group Accounts of such Holding Company and its subsidiaries, so that much of the guesswork of the past is now avoided. Recent publications of Group Accounts have disclosed for the first time the real position of the group as a whole particularly as regards combined profits, directors' remuneration and combined assets and liabilities. Apart from the disclosure of the main facts, the compulsory consolidation of group accounts (at one common terminal date) has eliminated many abuses, e.g. where one holding company (which drew up its accounts at a date different from that of its subsidiary) borrowed £4,000,000 from its subsidiary and repaid it to the subsidiary the day following the terminal date of its own accounts, so that the Balance Sheets both of the holding company and its subsidiary showed the same amount (approximately) of 'Cash at Bank'. In certain circumstances, an examination of the Balance Sheet together with the Profit and Loss Account will be required, not

---

[1] The rate must be considered in the light of any Bonus Share issue, e.g. if a Bonus Share issue has been made in ratio of '1 for 2' and the old rate was 15 per cent. The equivalent rate after the Bonus issue is 10 per cent.

merely for formal and legal correctness, but for the purpose of ascertaining the real content (viewed from a particular angle according to the objective in question).

This work of examination will usually be undertaken in detail, going further than that of dealing with the normal published accounts of companies; and therefore much that is surmise in the latter will be classified and explained as a result of inquiry and investigation of the actual accounts.

Working Capital. It is essential that at any time a business should be in a position of stabilized solvency, that is, in a position to pay its debts as they arise, and in addition to take advantage of such business opportunities as may occur and to meet any contingencies that may be reasonably visualized.

It will be realized in this connection that a business may have a large surplus of assets over liabilities, but if such assets are in the main fixed, there will probably be great difficulty in finding the ready cash to meet current liabilities without having recourse to borrowing (on the security of the fixed assets).

Working capital may be defined as the excess of current and liquid assets over current liabilities requisite in a business, having regard to reasonable provision for contingencies, so as to enable it to conduct its operations normally and free from financial embarassment, and to avoid losses consequent upon incurring commitments beyond its capacity in the ordinary course of events.

The definition must be construed very broadly; many businesses are conducted quite successfully on a very small margin of working capital, indeed in some cases there is a deficiency, i.e. more current liabilities than current and liquid assets. The facts and circumstances of each case must be considered. Thus, it will be possible to carry on business with a small margin or even a deficiency in a case where goods are sold for cash, whilst being bought on credit terms, or where the sale credit period is shorter than the purchase credit period.

On the other hand, the position may be the reverse to such favourable circumstances; and the gap may be covered by short-term financing, bank overdrafts, and bills of exchange. Yet, merely having the advantage of a credit period of being able to finance sales does not necessarily bespeak the existence of working capital. As long as there exists a reserve of strength in the form of assets which can be converted into cash without undue delay or loss, a lack of working capital will not be detrimental to the business. Many businesses, particularly small ones, work 'from hand to mouth', but without the reserve of strength required to meet special circumstances.

The assets which are included in working capital may be briefly classified as follows:

1. Liquid—Cash in hand, cash at bank, readily realizable investments.
2. Near liquid—Bank deposits where long notice of withdrawal is required, investments which are not so readily realizable as those in (1).

3. Other current assets which may be classified under (1) or (2) according to the particular facts—debtors, bills receivable, stocks.

Any investment or cash which is held for a *specific* purpose must be excluded, for instance, where part is a sinking fund or pension fund. Moreover, the investments should be such as are convertible into cash without undue difficulty, i.e. those which are quoted or dealt in on the Stock Exchange and enjoy a reasonably good market; investments in private companies, trade investments, investments in subsidiaries could not be included in the constitution of working capital. Similarly, bills of exchange should be readily convertible and should be short-term in tenor and such as are received as *normal* payments from customers (and not substitutions for normal cheque payments).

From these 'working' assets will be deducted the current liabilities and commitments of a short-term nature, including creditors, bills payable, bank overdrafts, current expenses and tax including P.A.Y.E. Provided that the tax liability is, as it ought to be, included, Tax Reserve Certificates are quite properly regarded as part of the working capital, since in effect so much of the tax liability as is covered by these certificates can be regarded as having been discharged.

In attempting to estimate the amount of working capital required in a business, the following points will be considered:

1. The normal average period of credit given to and allowed by the business.

2. The amount of stock that is required to feed the business. The rapidity of turnover will be a vital element, e.g. normally a motor-car vendor might have to hold a car in stock for, say, three months, but a retail tobacconist would be likely to hold his stock for no more than a few days. Hence it is desirable to compute the cost of estimated sales for the year and divide by the estimated number of times the stock is likely to be turned over.

3. Provision for meeting the peak load of expenses, having regard to the amount of cash in hand or at bank, or other credit facilities available. In this connection the differential period of credit given and allowed is an important factor. In certain parts of the year heavy expenses, e.g. tax, will have to be paid (out of proportion to the *average* expenses) so that the marginal credit position cannot be ignored. If, for instance, debtors are allowed three months credit, but creditors allow only fourteen days, the gap must be provided for, particularly if at the same time heavy expenses coincide with payments for goods bought in a 'buying' season, i.e. where the purchase of goods cannot be spread evenly. This gap will be even wider if a period of time must elapse before these heavy purchases are translated into actual sales, e.g. because of time required in manufacturing the finished product, and even more so if extended credit is given to customers.

4. The running expenses of the business will have to be estimated and, subject to factors contained in (3), spread over the year.

5. The credit-worthiness of the business will be a great factor in

covering any gap in the working capital, as upon this will depend the extent to which recourse can be had to short-term borrowing, e.g. through a temporary overdraft.

It is therefore important to examine the effect of the year's operations, not merely from the angle of the variation of the total capital structure but from that of the *working* capital structure.

An examination not only of the Balance Sheet, but of the Trading and Profit and Loss Account (and Appropriation Account) must be made to connect the opening and closing working capital by means of Variation Statements.

Variation Statements. The object of these statements is to show how the various components of a Balance Sheet have varied from the comparable components in a previous Balance Sheet and to show the reasons therefor.

There are almost an infinite number of possible variations, but the principle involved is the same, viz. to ascertain the particular variation and then to explain how it arises. These variations are (*inter alia*):

1. Increase or Decrease of Liquid Assets;
2. Increase or Decrease of Working Capital;
3. Increase or Decrease of Fixed Assets;
4. Increase or Decrease of Surplus.

The statement constructed is often described as a 'Statement of Variation in Funds and Application of such Funds', often cryptically referred to as a 'Where got where gone' statement.

Therefore, the procedure to be adopted will vary according to the particular information **sought**, the details of which will vary accordingly. Once the principle is learned there is no need to commit any set of rules to memory.

For example, the build up of the statement to connect opening and closing working capital will be the opening working capital, plus:

(*a*) Profit, before the debits of a non-financial nature, such as depreciation, loss on sale of fixed assets and transfers to General Reserve, and before credits of a similar nature such as profit on sale of fixed assets and transfers from General Reserve to Profit and Loss Account.

(*b*) Increase of loans, debentures, share capital and realizations of fixed assets from which will be deducted.

(*c*) Reductions of items indicated in (*b*).

To take one simple illustration: If, say, the fixed assets have increased during a financial year, then it is necessary not only to state the variation of the fixed assets, but to show the source from which such an increase has arisen.

BALANCE SHEETS

	19.8 £	19.9 £		19.8 £	19.9 £
Share Capital	10,000	12,000	Liquid Assets	9,500	9,700
Profit and Loss Account	6,000	7,500	Fixed Assets	8,000	12,000
Depreciation Provision	500	800			
Creditors	1,000	1,400			
	£17,500	£21,700		£17,500	£21,700

There have been no sales of fixed assets nor dividends paid. Prepare Statement of Variation as to:

Increase in *fixed* assets and the source thereof.

Statement of Increase of Fixed Assets and Source thereof:

		£
(a) Increase of Fixed Assets		4,000

(b) Source of increase:

		£	
(a) Decrease of Working Capital:			
(i) Increase in creditors	£400		
(ii) *Less* Increase in liquid assets	200		
		200	
(b) Profit for year		1,500	
(c) Increase in Depreciation Provision		300	
(d) Increase in Share Capital		2,000	
		£4,000	

Illustration 3

BALANCE SHEETS

	31/3/19.8 £	31/3/19.9 £		31/3/19.8 £	31/3/19.9 £
Share Capital	10,000	11,000	Current Assets	19,700	50.300
Profit and Loss Account	7,000	2,000	Fixed Assets	3,300	14,500
Depreciation Provision		300	Goodwill	2,000	1,500
Current Liabilities	8,000	53,000			
	£25,000	£66,300		£25,000	£66,300

PROFIT AND LOSS APPROPRIATION ACCOUNT
FOR THE YEAR ENDED 31ST MARCH 19.9

	£		£
Goodwill written off (a)	500	Net Profit	100
Depreciation	300	Balance forward	7,000
Dividend	2,500	Goodwill	2,000
Taxation	3,800		
Balance to Balance Sheet	2,000		
	£9,100		£9,100

(a) Assumed to be a charge against, and not an appropriation of, profit.

Prepare Variation of Working Capital Statement.

Variation of Working Capital Statement:

	£
Excess of Current Assets over Current Liabilities at 31/3/19.8	11,700
Excess of Current *Liabilities* over Current *Assets* at 31/3/19.9	2,700
Decrease in Working Capital	£14,400

The amount of Working Capital has been employed thus:

	£	£
Increase in Fixed Assets		11,200
Profit .	2,100	
Less Dividend	£2,500	
Taxation	3,800	
	6,300	
Diminution in own Reserve	−4,200	
Less Shares issued	1,000	
		3,200
Diminution in available Reserve	£3,200	£14,400

Briefly, the Working Capital has been 'consumed':

	£	£
(a) By diminished profit after tax and dividends.	4,200	
Less Capital raised	1,000	
		3,200
(b) ,, Increase in Fixed Assets		11,200
		£14,400

Briefly, therefore, the liquidity has been run down by £14,400, accountable as follows: £11,200 has gone into Fixed Assets and profit overspent by £4,200, *less* Capital raised £1,000.

The real position is worse; taking into account the year's profit of only £2,100, the company has had to meet the tax bill of £3,800, thus showing an effective loss of £1,700, which position is made even more unsatisfactory by a dividend payment of £2,500, thus showing an overspending of £4,200.

Ignoring introductions of further capital, debentures, etc., it can therefore be seen that:

(a) any capital expenditure which exceeds retainable profit plus depreciation of fixed assets must be at the expense of Working Capital; and

(b) any capital expenditure plus any diminution in retainable profit (i.e. effective loss) *less* depreciation of Fixed Assets must be likewise at the expense of Working Capital.

A student is often perplexed by the statement that an increase in current assets (and working capital) is the sum of (a) retainable profit plus (b) depreciation of fixed assets.

A simple situation may be taken by assuming all the profits are converted into cash, and the Balance Sheets at the two comparable dates are:

BALANCE SHEETS

	(1)	(2)		(1)	(2)
	£	£		£	£
Capital	10,000	10,000	Cash	12,000	16,000
Profit and Loss Account .	11,000	14,000	Fixed Assets (after writing off Depreciation of (£1,000) .	9,000	8,000
	£21,000	£24,000		£21,000	£24,000

		£
The increase in working capital is		4,000

Accounted for as follows:
(i) Profit	£3,000	
(ii) Depreciation	1,000	
		£4,000

That is, the £3,000 profit is reflected in:
	£
(i) Increase of Working Capital [Cash, in this illustration] . .	4,000
(ii) Decrease of Fixed Assets	1,000
	£3,000

Thus the profit of £4,000, without taking into account depreciation, would be reflected in an increase of Working Capital £4,000, but whilst this latter increase remains, £1,000 of profit has been used to write down Fixed Assets.

Illustration 4

	19.8	19.9
	£	£
Net Liquid Resources	5,200	5,900
Fixed Assets	3,000	2,800
	£8,200	£8,700
Share Capital	5,000	5,000
Profit and Loss	3,200	3,700*
	£8,200	£8,700

* After depreciation, £200.

The increase in the Net Liquid Resources (£5,900–£5,200) of £700 is made up of (a) profit of £500 (£3,700–£3,200) plus depreciation £200.

In general terms, any capital expenditure in that year should, in order to maintain working capital, be confined to £700, any additional expenditure being by way of permanent financing (share capital) or long-term borrowing.

The foregoing illustration serves merely as a guide to the general principle. The composition of the item net liquid assets is important because: (a) the assets themselves will not necessarily be mainly cash on hand and at Bank, as they will also comprise debtors, stock, etc., and (b) there will be current liabilities falling to be deducted, so that there may result a minus 'cash' position.

	19.8 £	19.9 £	+ or − £
Stock	4,200	5,700 +	1,500
Debtors	7,900	8,300 +	400
Bank	1,000	− −	1,000
	13,100	14,000 +	900
Current Trade Liabilities	8,300	7,100 −	1,200
Bank Overdraft.	—	600 +	600
	£4,800	£6,300 +	£1,500

Assuming there were no non-financial transactions, except a depreciation charge of £400, the profit after such charge would be £1,100.

The 'Cash' position may be tabulated as follows:

	£	£
Increase of Stock and Debtors		1,900
Decrease of Current Trade Liabilities		1,200
		3,100
Net Profit	1,100	
Depreciation	400	
		1,500
Decrease of 'Cash' Resources		£1,600

This is reflected in the conversion of the opening item Cash at Bank £1,000 into the closing item Bank Overdraft £600.

Illustration 6

TRADING AND PROFIT AND LOSS ACCOUNTS

		19.8 £	19.9 £			19.8 £	19.9 £
Stock		21,000	24,000	Sales		137,000	162,000
Purchases		93,000	107,000	Stock		24,000	28,000
Gross Profit	c/d	47,000	59,000				
		£161,000	£190,000			£161,000	£190,000
General Expenses		31,000	38,500	Gross Profit	b/d	47,000	59,000
Depreciation		4,000	3,500				
Net Profit	c/d	12,000	17,000				
		£47,000	£59,000			£47,000	£59,000
Taxation		9,600	12,000	Balance	b/f	4,200	1,000
General Reserve		3,000	1,000	Net Profit	b/d	12,000	17,000
Dividends		2,000	3,000				
Goodwill written off		600	400				
Balance	c/f	1,000	1,600				
		£16,200	£18,000			£16,200	£18,000

BALANCE SHEETS

	19.8	19.9		19.8		19.9	
	£	£		£	£	£	£
Issued Capital	50,000	50,000	Fixed Assets	60,100		58,100	
Profit and Loss	1,000	1,600	Additions	2,000		14,400	
General Reserve	4,500	5,500					
Debentures	20,000	25,000		62,100		72,500	
Current Liabilities	23,000	29,500	Depreciation	4,000		3,500	
Provision for Taxation	12,100	17,500			58,100		69,000
			Current Assets		46,500		54,500
			Preliminary Expenses		1,000		1,000
			Goodwill		5,000		4,600
	£110,600	£129,100			£110,600		£129,100

Set out the variations in Capital and Surpluses, showing the connection between the two.

Summary of Change during 19.9:

		19.8	19.9	
		£	£	£
Liquid Assets		46,500	54,500+	8,000
Current Liabilities		35,100	47,000+	11,900
Net Liquid Resources	(a)	£11,400	£7,500−	£3,900
Fixed Assets		58,100	69,000+	10,900
Debentures		20,000	25,000+	5,000
Net Fixed Assets	(b)	£38,100	£44,000+	£5,900
Capital Employed	(a)+(b)	£49,500	£51,500+	£2,000

Reconciliation:

		19.8	19.9	
		£	£	£
Issued capital		50,000	50,000	—
Profit and Loss		1,000	1,600+	600
General Reserve		4,500	5,500+	1,000
		55,500	57,100+	1,600
Less Preliminary Expenses		1,000	1,000	
„ Goodwill		5,000	4,600−	400
		£49,500	£51,500+	£2,000

Statement of Source of Increase of Capital:

	£	
Increase of Credit Balance of Profit and Loss	3,600	(d)
General Reserve	1,000	
Goodwill w/o	400	
	5,000	
Less Dividend	3,000	(c)
Increase	£2,000	

Statement of Source of Decrease of Net Liquid Resources:

	£	£	
Addition to Fixed Assets		14,400	
Dividend		3,000	(c)
		17,400	
Less Increase of Credit Balance of Profit and Loss	3,600		(d)
„ General Reserve	1,000		
„ Goodwill w/o	400		
„ Debentures Issued	5,000		
„ Depreciation	3,500		
		13,500	
Decrease		£3,900	

[The increases of Profit and Loss shown in the Balance Sheet is the excess of (d) over (c).]

Changes in Assets:

	£
Increase of Liquid Assets	8,000
Increase of Fixed Assets	10,900
Total Increase of Assets	£18,900

Source of Increase:

	£	£
Creditors:		
Liquid (Current) Liabilities		11,900
Fixed (non-Current) Liabilities		5,000
Total Increase in Creditors		16,900
Profits:		
Increase of Profit and Loss	3,600	
General Reserve	1,000	
Goodwill w/o	400	
	5,000	
Less Dividend	3,000	2,000
		£18,900

Thus, additions to fixed assets of £10,900 have used up the additional loans of £5,000, and have been financed by: (a) an increase of *current* liabilities of £3,900; and (b) the profit of £2,000.

The additions to the liquid assets are £8,000 reflected in an increase of £11,900 in current liabilities, thus leaving an increase of £3,900 to finance partially the fixed assets.

The fixed assets increase (before depreciation) is £14,400 which is compensated by the addition of depreciation of £3,500 in the schedule of profit.

Preparation of Working Capital Statement. The question of working capital, with emphasis on the liquid cash position, is particularly important in the early stages of a business, as there will probably be rapid expansion until normal factors operate.

A schedule will be prepared to estimate the monthly or weekly inflow and outflow of cash, the former comprising cash sales and receipts from debtors, the latter cash purchases and payments to creditors and of overheads. The payments to creditors are likely to be abnormal for a short period by reason of the necessity for building up minimum stocks (subject to any extended credit given by suppliers), but unless the business is working at a loss or expansion is too rapid, the liquid position will improve.

If there is a deficiency in any week or month, that is, an excess of payments over receipts and cash in hand and at bank, its amount is the minimum working capital required, and where there is a deficiency in more than one period, the highest individual figure will be taken.

In dealing with the foregoing, due regard must be had to contingencies and to periodical payments such as taxation. Unless these are considered a business may be showing an apparent amplitude of working Capital which may be unjustifiably used for further development.

Illustration 7

X, Y and Z are considering the formation of a company for manufacturing and selling a certain commodity and submit the following information to you:

(a) Cost of Factory £32,000; the vendor agreeing to accept one-quarter of the purchase price in 9 per cent Mortgage Debentures in the proposed company.

(b) Cost of installing Plant, etc., expected to be £9,000, all payable in cash within one month of the formation of the company.

(c) The prime cost of the commodity produced expected to be £0·25 for labour and £0·50 for materials, the latter being purchased on terms for payment in the month following delivery. [In the first month the labour charge worked out at £0·50 instead of £0·25, but the selling price was not amended, the extra cost being regarded as abnormal.]

(d) The selling price expected to show $33\frac{1}{3}$ per cent gross profit on prime cost, and sales expected:

	Units		Units
First month . . .	2,400	Third month . . .	3,200
Second month . .	2,800	Subsequent months .	3,200

One-quarter of such sales expected to be for cash, balance on credit for settlement month following sale.

(e) It is estimated that a stock of raw materials, totalling £6,000, and 1,600 units of finished goods will be required at the commencement of trading and these levels will be maintained.

(*f*) Overhead charges expected to be £400 per month payable in cash during the month, increasing at the end of the third month by 25 per cent.

(*g*) A margin of £1,000 is to be allowed over and above the minimum cash requirements (to nearest even thousand pounds), it being assumed that the credit terms will be strictly adhered to and no short-term finance will be used.

(*h*) Preliminary expenses expected to be £1,800 payable in cash immediately the company is formed.

(*i*) The share capital to be in the proportion of four-fifths in ordinary shares of £1 each (issued at £1·20 payable in full on allotment) and one-fifth in 6 per cent redeemable preference shares of £1 each at par (payable in full on allotment) and redeemable at par by equal annual drawings over 16 years.

In consideration of services rendered, etc., an allotment is to be made to X, Y and Z equally at par to the extent of one-sixteenth of the ordinary share capital to be in issue.

(*j*) Preliminary expenses are to be written off against share premium. You are required: (i) to compute the capital required and its division into the various classes; and (ii) to submit a *pro forma* Balance Sheet (showing how you arrive at the figures you use), assuming the foregoing arrangements have been carried out and the estimates realized, as at the end of six months' trading (which commenced immediately the company was formed). Ignore taxation and depreciation.

Capital required:

	£	£
Factory	32,000	
Less 9% Mortgage Debenture	8,000	
		24,000
Installation		9,000
Preliminary Expenses		1,800
Stock: Raw Materials	6,000	
Finished Goods, 1,600 units at, say, £0·75	1,200	
		7,200
		42,000
Working Capital	1,000	
Add Margin	1,000	
		2,000
		£44,000

Division:

	£
6% Redeemable Preference Shares	8,000
30,000 Ordinary Shares of £1 each issued at £1·20 per share	36,000

[Premium on shares, £6,000; Ordinary Share Capital, £30,000.]

CASH

	£		£
Receipts of Share Capital	44,000	Payments—	
Trading Receipts	15,600	Capital per Schedule	42,000
		Trading Payments	15,200
		Balance	2,400
	£59,600		£59,600

ORDINARY SHARE CAPITAL

	£		£
		Cash	30,000
		X, Y, and Z	2,000
			£32,000

PRELIMINARY EXPENSES

	£		£
Cash	1,800	Share Premium	3,800
Share Capital	2,000		
	£3,800		£3,800

SHARE PREMIUM

	£		£
Preliminary Expenses	3,800	Cash	6,000
Balance	2,200		
	£6,000		£6,000

TRADING AND PROFIT AND LOSS ACCOUNT

	£	£		£	£
Costs—(See p. 3131)			Sales—		
Cash	15,200		Cash		4,500
Creditors	1,600		Credit[1]	11,100	
		16,800	Debtors[2]	2,400	
Mortgage Interest		360			13,500
Net Profit		840			
		£18,000			£18,000

[1] Months 1–5, Cash received.
[2] Month 6, receivable in Month 7.

X, Y, AND Z, LTD.

PRO FORMA BALANCE SHEET AT ....

	£		£		£	£
Authorized Share Capital .				Fixed Assets, at Cost—		
Issued Share Capital—				Factory	32,000	
8,000 6% Redeemable				Installation . . .	9,000	
Preference Shares of						41,000
£1 each, fully paid				Liquid Assets—		
(redeemable by equal				Cash	2,400	
annual drawings over				Debtors	2,400	
16 years) . . .	8,000			Stocks	7,200	
32,000 Ordinary Shares						12,000
of £1 each, fully paid .	32,000					
		40,000				
Share Premium Account .	6,000					
Less Preliminary Expenses written off .	3,800					
		2,200				
Profit and Loss Account .		840				
			43,040			
9% Mortgage Debentures (secured on Fixed Assets) . .			8,000			
Current Liabilities—						
Trade Creditors .	1,600					
Interest on Debentures .	360					
			1,960			
			£53,000			£53,000

The number of shares taken up by X, Y, and Z is 2,000 being one-sixteenth of the shares in issue, 32,000. If the shares to be taken up are one-sixteenth of the shares *already* in issue, the number would be $\frac{1}{16}$ of 30,000 = 1,875.

Statement of Working Capital

Month	Raw Materials		Wages		Over-head Charges	Total	Cash Sales		Credit Sales		Total	Deficiency	Surplus
	Units	£	Units	£	£	£	Units	£	Units	£	£	£	£
1	2,400	1,200	2,400	(a) 1,200	400	1,600	600	600	1,800	1,800	600	1,000	200
2	2,800	1,400	2,800	700	400	2,300	700	700	2,100	2,100	2,500		300
3	3,200	1,600	3,200	800	400	2,600	800	800	2,400	2,400	2,900		300
4	3,200	1,600	3,200	800	500	2,900	800	800	2,400	2,400	3,200		300
5	3,200	1,600	3,200	800	500	2,900	800	800	2,400	2,400	3,200		300
6	3,200	1,600	3,200	800	500	2,900	800	800	2,400	2,400	3,200		300
		£7,400		£5,100	£2,700	£15,200		£4,500		£11,100	£15,600	£1,000	£1,400

Proof of Profit:

		£
Excess of Receipts over Payments in Trading (£1,400 − £1,000)	.	400
Excess of Debtors over Creditors (£2,400 − £1,600)	.	800
		1,200
Less Debenture Interest provision	.	360
Net Profit	.	£840

Proof of Gross Profit:

	£	£	£
Sales per Profit and Loss	.	.	18,000
Less Cost per Profit and Loss	.	16,800	
Deduct Overhead Charges	2,700		
Abnormal Wages (see (a) above)	600		
		3,300	13,500
Gross Profit, being 33⅓ per cent on £13,500			£4,500

(i.e. Net Profit of £840+£360+£2,700+£600)

Illustration 8

From the particulars given below, prepare Quarterly statement of X, Co. Ltd.:

	30th June	30 Sept.	31st Dec.
	£	£	£
Freehold Premises	5,000	5,000	5,000
Plant and Machinery.	4,200	4,500	4,500
Fixtures and Fittings.	1,800	1,800	1,800
Motor Vehicles	800	800	800
Goodwill	3,000	3,000	3,000
Cash at Bank	1,050	850	1,460
Debtors	4,200	5,400	4,840
Stock	8,100	9,250	8,560
Current Liabilities	1,700	3,100	1,800
Bank Loan	2,000	2,000	2,000
Taxation.	2,300	(see below)	(see below)
Mortgage on Freehold Premises	2,000	2,000	2,000
Additional Plant		300	
Purchases		17,150	13,710
Sales		20,000	18,000
Depreciation—			
Plant and Machinery		160	60
Fixtures and Fittings		40	40
Motor Vehicles		20	20

Taxation to be built up at 45 per cent (estimated to cover Corporation Tax) on profit for each quarter.

X Co., Ltd. Quarterly Statement

	30th June		+	–	30th Sept.		+	–	31st Dec.	
	£	£	£	£	£	£	£	£	£	£
FIXED CAPITAL—										
Freehold Premises		5,000				5,000				5,000
Plant and Machinery		4,200	300	160		4,340		60		4,280
Fixtures and Fittings		1,800		40		1,760		40		1,720
Motor Vehicles		800		20		780		20		760
Goodwill		3,000				3,000				3,000
		14,800	300	220		14,880		120		14,760
Less Mortgage on Freehold Premises		2,000				2,000				2,000
		£12,800	£300	£220		£12,880		£120		£12,760
WORKING CAPITAL—										
Cash and Bank		1,050		200		850	610			1,460
Debtors		4,200	1,200			5,400		560		4,840
Stock		8,100	1,150			9,250		690		8,560
		13,350	2,350	200		15,500	610	1,250		14,860
Less Current Creditors	1,700		1,400		3,100			1,800	1,300	
,, Bank Loan	2,000				2,000				2,000	
,, Taxation	2,300		374		2,674		468		3,142	
	6,000					7,774				6,442
		£7,350	£576	£200		£7,726	£142	£550		£8,418
SUMMARY—										
Net Fixed Capital		12,800	300	220		12,880		120		12,760
Working Capital		7,350	576	200		7,726	142	550		8,418
		£20,150	876	£420		£20,606	142	£430		£21,178
			420				430			
[See Note *re* Taxation]			+£456				+£572			

CALCULATION OF STOCKS:

	£	£		£	£
Opening Stock	8,100			9,250	
Purchases	17,150			13,710	
Gross Profit (25% of Cost of Sales)					
(20% of Sales) (a)	4,000		(b)	3,600	
		29,250			26,560
Net Sales for Quarter		20,000			18,000
Estimated Stock at end of Quarter		£9,250			£8,560

$$(a)\ \tfrac{1}{4}\times(25,250-9,250)=£4,000 \qquad (b)\ \tfrac{1}{4}\times(22,960-8,560)=£3,600$$

Taxation

(i) Quarter ended 30th September. Increase of £374 (£2,674 – £2,300).

(ii) Quarter ended 31st December. Increase of £468 (£3,142 – £2,674).

(i) $£374-\tfrac{58}{45}\times£456$ or $\tfrac{45}{100}(456+374)=\tfrac{45}{100}\times£830$.

(ii) $£468=\tfrac{58}{45}\times£572$ or $\tfrac{45}{100}(572+468)=\tfrac{45}{100}\times£1,040$.

Illustration 9

The Gross Profit of Y, Ltd., for the year ended 30th September, 19.8, was £2,500, made up of:

	£
Sales	10,000
Cost of Sales	7,500
Gross Profit	2,500

As and from 1st October 19.8, selling prices were increased by 20 per cent and the company's organization was reviewed and improved. The Gross Profit for the year ended 30th September 19.9, was £6,750 made up of:

	£
Sales	18,000
Cost of Sales. . . .	11,250
Gross Profit	6,750

Show the various factors contributing to the increase in the Gross Profit from £2,500 to £6,750, i.e. £4,250.

Increase in VOLUME of Sales (to ascertain ratio of increase):

		Alternative Calculation
	£	£
Sales for year ended 30th September 19.9 . . .	18,000	18,000
Price factor $\frac{1}{6}$	3,000	
	15,000	
Sales for previous year at 19.8–19.9 prices . .	10,000	
$10,000 \times \frac{120}{100}$		12,000
Increase in Volume in terms of adjusted 19.9 prices .	£5,000	£6,000

This equals **50 per cent increase,** so that the Cost of Sales should normally be correspondingly increased.

Increase in Gross Profit arising from improvement in organization:

Cost of Sales for year ended 30th September 19.9, $\frac{150}{100}$ of £7,500 (at 19.7–19.8 rates plus 50 per cent increase) .	£11,250
Actual cost for year ended 30th September 19.9 . .	11,250
	—

Increase in Gross Profit attributable to price increase:

Sales for year ended 30th September 19.9, at 19.7–19.8 rates, $\frac{150}{100} \times £10,000$	£15,000	
20 per cent thereof		3,000

Increase of Gross Profit attributable to increased volume:

Increase in Volume of Sales for the year ended 30th September 19.9, 50 per cent of £10,000 . .	£5,000	
Gross Profit thereon[1] 25 per cent . . .		1,250
Increase in Gross Profit in 19.8–19.9 . . .		£4,250

It will be observed that there is no efficiency improvement, as the Cost of Sales has moved proportionately to increase of volume. If the Cost of

[1] 19.7–19.8 Rate of Gross Profit is $\dfrac{£2,500}{£10,000} = 25$ per cent.

Sales had been, say, £10,800, the Gross Profit would have been increased by £450 through improvement in efficiency.[1]

As students experience difficulty with this type of problem, the following explanations are made:

Assume that the 19.7–19.8 price per unit of sale is £1. The volume in 19.7–19.8 was, therefore, 10,000. As the price has increased by 20 per cent, i.e. to £1·20, the number of units sold must of $\frac{100}{120}$ £18,000, or 15,000, so that the break-down is:

19.7–19.8 volume	. 10,000	At £1·20 each.	. 12,000	
Increased volume				
19.8–19.9 .	. 5,000	At £1·20 each.	. 6,000	
	15,000		18,000	£18,000

The increase in volume, therefore, is 50 per cent (and the Cost of Sales adjusted will be $\frac{150}{100}$ of £7,500 = £11,250).

The principle familiar to students in Standard Costing should now be applied (as with Materials used to obtain price and usage variances).

1. *Price factor.* On every unit sold there is £0·20 'extra' and as 15,000 units are sold there is a 'price' gain of £3,000.

2. *Volume factor.* As the price factor has been dealt with, comparison should be made (at **old** price) with the previous year as regards volume. The 19.7–19.8 volume was 10,000 at £1, so that this is a comparison of 'like with like'.

The increased volume for 19.8–19.9 is, however, 5,000 and at 19.7–19.8 prices would have earned 25 per cent thereon, or £1,250.

The following illustrate in alternative ways the above results:

(1)

				Sub-division of 19.8–19.9 Increase due to—	
	19.8–19.9 £	19.7–19.8 £	Increase £	Price £	Volume £
Sales	18,000	10,000	8,000	3,000	5,000
Cost of Sales adjusted to sales	11,250	7,500	3,750		3,750
Gross Profit	£6,750	£2,500	£4,250	£3,000	£1,250

(2) 19.7–19.8

				19.8–19.9 Increase due to—	
			Volume	Price	Total 19.8–19.9
	£		£	£	£
Sales 10,000 at £1	10,000	Sales 5,000 at £1	5,000	Sales 15,000 at	18,000
Cost of Sales	7,500	Cost of Sales (50% of £7,500)	3,750	£0·20 3,000	11,250
Gross Profit	£2,500		£1,250	£3,000	£6,750

Balance Sheet Interpretation by Comparative Columns. In order to obtain useful results, it is advisable to compare a present Balance Sheet with those drawn up in the past; and this is usually and most conveniently done by tabulating the main groups of figures and converting them into index figures. Therefrom will be deduced the various changes and their

[1] This assumes the price factor in the cost of goods has gone up proportionately to the selling price, but if the increase was higher, there would be an efficiency factor, as, notwithstanding the disproportionate increase in the price of the goods purchased, the total cost has not increased disproportionately; in fact it is exactly the same.

significance, such changes being reconciled with the yearly amount of profits (or losses) disclosed in the published Balance Sheets. The question of interpretation has already been dealt with and this paragraph is confined merely to ratios and indices.

The general principles may now be demonstrated by the employment of the following two Balance Sheets in abridged form.

BALANCE SHEET AS AT 31ST DECEMBER

	19.1 £	19.2 £		19.1 £	19.2 £
Share Capital—			Fixed Assets—		
Preference	12,500	13,500	Goodwill	6,000	6,000
Ordinary	10,000	10,000	Buildings	9,000	8,700
General Reserve	10,000	11,000	Plant and Machinery	5,000	7,200
Profit and Loss Account	8,200	9,550		20,000	21,900
	40,700	44,050	Current Assets—		
Debentures (secured on Buildings)	8,000	5,000	Stock	2,000	9,000
Current Liabilities—			Debtors	12,100	7,700
Creditors: Trade	17,000	18,000	Prepayments	300	200
Expenses	300	250	Investments—		
Bills Payable	2,000	4,500	Government Securities	8,400	4,700
			General	8,000	12,000
			Cash in Bank	7,200	11,300
			Development and Research Account	10,000	5,000
	£68,000	£71,800		£68,000	£71,800

Show (1) Comparative Balance Sheets in tabular form.
(2) Variations in the main groups of Assets and Liabilities.

COMPARATIVE BALANCE SHEETS AS AT 31ST DECEMBER

		19.1		19.2	Increase or Decrease of Groups £
Current Assets[1]—	£		£		
Bank	7,200		11,300		
Debtors	12,100		7,700		
Prepayments	300		200		
Stock	2,000		9,000		
Investments[2]	16,400		16,700		
		38,000		44,900	+6,900
Less Current Liabilities—					
Creditors: Trade	17,000		18,000		
Expenses	300		250		
Bills Payable	2,000		4,500		
		19,300		22,750	+3,450
Fixed Assets—		18,700		22,150	+3,450
Buildings	£9,000		£8,700		
Less Debentures	8,000		5,000		
	1,000		3,700		
Plant and Machinery	5,000		7,200		
		6,000		10,900	+4,900
Net Tangible Assets		24,700		33,050	+8,350
Intangible Assets—					
Goodwill	6,000		6,000		
Development and Research Account	10,000		5,000		
		16,000		11,000	−5,000
		£40,700		£44,050	+£3,350

[1] These may be further subdivided into liquid and non-liquid assets.
[2] Assumed that the general investments are marketable.

Represented by:

Capital—	£	£		£	£	£
Preference Shares	12,500			£13,500		
Ordinary Shares	10,000			10,000		
Undistributed Profits—		22,500			23,500	+ 1,000
Reserve	10,000			£11,000		
Profit and Loss Account	8,200			9,550		
		18,200			20,550	+ 2,350
		£40,700			£44,050	+£3,350

The foregoing variations may be expressed in the following form:

CURRENT ASSETS AND CURRENT LIABILITIES

	Assets	Liabilities	Balance	
			Surplus	Deficiency
	£	£	£	
19.1	38,000	19,300	18,700	
19.2	44,900	22,750	22,150	

[The variations in fixed assets and fixed liabilities may be similarly shown.]

The variations may be shown in terms of a ratio of the surplus of current assets over current liabilities (or conversely), thus:

	Ratio		Index [using 19.1 as 100]
19.1	197	i.e. $\dfrac{38,000}{19,300} \times 100$	100
19.2	197	i.e. $\dfrac{44,900}{22,750} \times 100$	100
			$\left[\text{i.e. } \dfrac{197}{197} \times 100\right]$

The ratio and index in 19.3 would be, assuming that the current assets and current liabilities were £33,140 and £21,500, as follows:

	Ratio		Index [using 19.1 as 100]
19.3	154	i.e. $\dfrac{33,140}{21,500} \times 100$	78
			$\left[\text{i.e. } \dfrac{154}{197} \times 100\right]$

The ratios and indices in 19.4, 19.5, 19.6, and 19.7 would be, on the basis of the following figures, as below:

	19.4	19.5	19.6	19.7
	£	£	£	£
Current Assets	39,500	42,200	35,000	32,500
Current Liabilities	22,000	20,750	23,500	27,001

	Ratio		Index [using 19.1 as 100]

19.4   180   i.e. $\dfrac{39,500}{22,000} \times 100$ 91

$$\left[\text{i.e. } \frac{180}{197} \times 100 \right]$$

19.5   203   i.e. $\dfrac{42,200}{20,750} \times 100$ 103

$$\left[\text{i.e. } \frac{203}{197} \times 100 \right]$$

19.6   149   i.e. $\dfrac{35,000}{23,500} \times 100$ 76

$$\left[\text{i.e. } \frac{149}{197} \times 100 \right]$$

19.7   119   i.e. $\dfrac{32,150}{27,000} \times 100$ 60

$$\left[\text{i.e. } \frac{119}{197} \times 100 \right]$$

SECTION C. BALANCE-SHEET CRITICISM AND ACCOUNTING RATIOS

Problems are frequently set in connection with limited company Balance Sheets calling for criticism, in so far as they relate to the proper compliance with legal requirements. Such criticisms call for a thorough knowledge of what may be termed the 'published accounts provisions' of the Companies Acts 1948 to 1976. The questions put before the student may contain, in addition, points that are common to all Balance Sheet questions, e.g. heading, sequence, and classification of items: construction and interpretation.

The Balance Sheet (Illustration 10) on p. 3139 is such a problem.

Suggest such suitable amendments as you consider are required, assuming that there is no question as to the accuracy of the figures presented.

(*Adapted from Institute of Chartered Accountants' Final.*)

1. Form:

(*a*) Heading should be Balance Sheet at, as at, or as on, 31st December 19 . . .

(*b*) The layout of the Balance Sheet requires amendment to accord with Schedule 2 of the Companies Act 1967. Assets and liabilities should be grouped under appropriate headings, e.g. Fixed Assets, Current Assets, etc. The general headings 'Assets' and 'Liabilities' are then unnecessary.

(*c*) Sundry debtors should not include sundry debit balances, as these may be purely fictitious assets, and in any case may be of such a nature as to require disclosure under Schedule 2 of the Companies Act 1967, whilst deducted therefrom should be the provision for debtors now merged with the item 'Sundry creditors, including reserve for debtors'.

(*d*) Calls in arrear are usually deducted from share capital.

Illustration 10

X Ltd. Balance Sheet for Year to 31st December 19..

Liabilities	£	£	Assets	£
Capital—			Sundry Debtors and Sundry Debit Balances	57,050
100,000 7% Redeemable Preference Shares of £1 each fully paid	£100,000		Stock-in-trade	37,200
50,000 Ordinary Shares of £1 each	50,000		Cash	1,000
		150,000	Buildings, Plant, Goodwill, Patents, etc.	97,300
Debenture Stock at Issue Price of 95		19,000	Preliminary Expenses	8,200
Bank Overdraft		14,000	Loans to Directors	18,400
Sundry Creditors, Reserves, and Credit Balances, including Reserve for Debtors		110,100	Investments and Loans in Subsidiary Companies *less* Repayments and Loans from Subsidiary Companies	110,250
Profit and Loss Account *less* Corporation tax		36,550	Calls in Arrear	250
		£329,650		£329,650

(See pp. 3138 and 3140.)

(*e*) The item of creditors includes reserves and credit balances, which may be true liabilities requiring separate disclosure and classification as to class of creditors and provisions under Schedule 2 of the Companies Act 1967, or may represent part of the undistributed profits of the company.

(*f*) The Profit and Loss Account should be linked up with the balance brought forward from the preceding year.

2. Legal Requirements

Assets (except investments) should be grouped under Fixed Assets, Current Assets and Assets which are Neither Fixed nor Current.

(*a*) *Buildings, Plant, Goodwill, Patents, etc.* The two latter items must be stated separately from the former, provided that their amount can be ascertained either from: (i) books of the company; (ii) contract of sale; or (iii) document relating to stamp duty.

The basis of valuation of fixed assets must be stated (e.g. cost or valuation, *less* accumulated depreciation).

If any of the fixed assets: (i) are shown at valuation, the amount and year of valuation must be disclosed; (ii) have been valued during the year, the names or qualifications of the valuers and the basis of valuation must be disclosed.

The total amount of Goodwill, Trade-marks, and Patents may be shown under one heading (not necessarily separately).

The items comprised in the 'etc.' must be dealt with and, if necessary, shown separately.

(*b*) *Loans to Directors.* Illegal unless covered by the exemptions laid down by Sect. 190 of the Companies Act 1948. Former exempt private companies are no longer excluded from the effect of Sect. 190. If advances or repayments have been made during the year, the Balance Sheet must show the total advances or repayments; and in the case of loans made prior to the period to which the accounts relate which are still outstanding, the amount thereof must be shown.

(*c*) *Investments.* The law requires to be shown separately: (i) invest-ments in, (ii) loans to, (iii) loans from, subsidiary companies, (iv) unquoted equity share capital investments, (v) quoted investments, (vi) unquoted investments with the valuations required by Part I of Schedule 2 to the Companies Act 1967. The amount of £110,250 will be increased by the loan from the subsidiary company and the latter shown separately as a liability. Any contingent liability for unpaid calls should be shown by way of note.

(*d*) *Capital.* Details of the nominal capital are required.

(*e*) *Redeemable Preference Shares.* There must be stated the earliest and latest dates on which the company has power to redeem these shares, and whether they must be redeemed in any event or are liable to be redeemed at the option of X, Ltd., and a note of the amount (if any) of the premium payable on redemption.

(*f*) *Calls in arrear*, as mentioned, are usually deducted from the share capital, although the method adopted in the above Balance Sheet does not infringe any legal principle.

(g) *Debenture Stock.* The item requires fuller description, e.g. 8 per cent Debenture Stock. The debenture stock should be shown at £20,000, and the debenture discount disclosed separately as an asset till written off. If the Debenture Stock (as is probable) is secured on the assets of the company (unless secured by operation of law), this fact should be stated, although there is no obligation to specify the particular asset charged. If any debentures have been redeemed, but are available for reissue, particulars thereof must be shown. Any accruing interest should be added to the liability, and not shown amongst *other credit balances.*

(h) The basis of computation of any amount set aside for United Kingdom Corporation Tax must be stated.

(i) In addition to the criticism made in paragraph (1), the general nature of the liabilities should be shown, particularly as regards Provisions, and the Reserves shown separately although Capital Reserves and Revenue Reserves need not separately be disclosed.

(f) The Balance Sheet must be signed by two of the directors, and the Auditors' Report and Directors' Report must be annexed to the Balance Sheet; a Profit and Loss Account is also required.

(k) Corresponding figures required for preceding year.

(l) Group Accounts or alternative information on Subsidiaries is required.

In the absence of further information, it is not possible to enter into greater detail.

3. Interpretation

Information concerning the profit of the year and the utilization of reserves is not disclosed in the Balance Sheet (e.g. as to depreciation, provision for tax, etc.); nor is the manner of its appropriation shown.

In order to obtain a fair comparison preceding years' Balance Sheets and Accounts should be available.

Accounting Ratios. Accounting ratios are relationships between figures, expressed as ratios. To be meaningful, however, certain figures or groups of figures must be related to other specially selected figures or groups of figures. A certain degree of skill is required in computing meaningful ratios because their usefulness is limited. All ratios are not always necessary or informative, and in preparing them the accountant must bear in mind the nature of the organization, the type of product and the organization structure. The effective use of ratios in a business can be maximized by calculating, on the basis of past figures and experience, standard or average ratios with which relevant ratios for the current period may be compared, trends noted, investigated and accounted for. Note carefully that generally there are no standard ratios which can be applied to all types of organizations, and that ratios in isolation are virtually useless. To be of value, they must be compared with corresponding ratios of other periods, and in certain cases with those of other organizations in the same industry.

Bearing these points in mind, the following ratios are in common usage:

Balance Sheet Ratios

1. **Equity to Total Capital Employed.** This ratio indicates how much of the total capital employed has been provided by the ordinary shareholders. 'Total capital employed' is not uniformly interpreted: sometimes the term is applied to the aggregate of the issued share capital, reserves, debentures and other long-term liabilities (this can alternatively be expressed as 'total assets *less* current liabilities') and sometimes it is applied to the total assets actually employed. To obviate any ambiguity, it is recommended that the term 'capital employed' should never be used with qualification. It is suggested that the term 'total capital employed' be used to mean total assets employed, and 'net capital employed' or 'net worth' or 'net assets' be used to mean total assets *less* current liabilities.

This point is considered to be important and consequently the following simple illustration is intended to clarify the position:

BALANCE SHEET
£

	£		£
Issued Share Capital:			
Ordinary	100,000	Fixed assets . . .	150,000
Preference	40,000	Current assets . . .	90,000
Reserves and Surplus . .	30,000		
Debentures . . .	10,000		
Current Liabilities . . .	60,000		
	£240,000		£240,000

		£
(*a*) Total Capital Employed		£240,000

(*b*) Net Capital Employed or Net Worth or Net Assets:		
Total Assets	£240,000	
Less: Current Liabilities	60,000	
		£180.000

(*c*) Net Capital Employed attributable to Proprietors		
(i.e. Ordinary Shareholders and Preference Shareholders):		
Ordinary	£100,000	
Preference	40,000	
Reserves and Surplus	30,000	
		£170,000

or alternatively:			
Total Assets		£240,000	
Less: Current Liabilities . . .	£60,000		
Debentures . . .	10,000		
		70,000	
			£170,000

(d) Net Capital Employed attributable to providers of Long-term Capital:

Ordinary	£100,000	
Preference	40,000	
Reserves and Surplus	30,000	
Debentures	10,000	
		£180,000

or alternatively:

Total Assets	£240,000	
Less: Current Liabilities	60,000	
		£180,000

Note that this is the same as (b)

(e) Net Capital Employed attributable to Equity Shareholders:

Ordinary	£100,000	
Reserves and Surplus	30,000	
		£130,000

or alternatively:

Total Assets		£240,000
Less: Preference	£40,000	
Debentures	10,000	
Current Liabilities	60,000	
	110,000	
		£130,000

(f) Net Capital Employed attributable to Preference Shareholders:

Preference	£40,000

or alternatively:

Total Assets		£240,000
Less: Ordinary	£100,000	
Reserves and Surplus	30,000	
Debentures	10,000	
Current Liabilities	60,000	
	200,000	
		£40,000

(g) Net Capital employed attributable to Debenture Holders:

Debentures	£10,000

or alternatively:

Total Assets		£240,000
Less: Ordinary	£100,000	
Preference	40,000	
Reserves and Surplus	30,000	
Curennt Liabilities	60,000	
	230,000	
		£10,000

Note. In this illustration it has been assumed that the equity applies to the ordinary shareholders only, and consequently the Reserves and Surplus £30,000 is attributable solely to the ordinary shareholders. Where, however, the preference shareholders participated in the profits in excess of the nominal rate, then an appropriate apportionment of the £30,000 would be required. The importance of qualifying the term 'capital employed' should now be fully appreciated.

In this instance, the ratio of Equity to Total Capital Employed is

$$100,000 : 240,000 = 1 : 2 \cdot 4.$$

2. **Fixed Interest Shares plus Long-term Liabilities to Equity.** This is otherwise known as the Gearing Ratio. Where the amount of the fixed-interest, etc. exceeds the amount of equity the company is said to be highly geared. If the reverse is the case the company is low geared (see p. 2623).

3. **Current Assets to Current Liabilities.** This is more commonly known as the Current Ratio or the Working Capital Ratio. This ratio shows whether a business is declining in its financial strength or whether it is growing vigorously. It also indicates the extent to which current assets are available to meet current liabilities as and when they become due. Before too much reliance is placed on this ratio, however, many factors should be considered, especially the values attached to stocks and work in progress. In order to withstand a sudden reduction in the period of credit granted by creditors, or the shock of a bad debt of substantial amount a safe margin of working capital should be maintained. A 2:1 ratio is often associated with the current ratio as a standard. Normally, however, this cannot be regarded seriously, as a safe ratio can be determined only in accordance with the particular circumstances. Where the ratio is too high the indication would be that inefficient use is being made of working capital, e.g. stock levels are too high and/or the period of credit granted to debtors is too great.

4. **Liquid Assets to Current Liabilities.** This ratio is more often referred to as the Liquid Ratio, or Quick Ratio or Acid Test. Difficulty may arise here in determining which assets and liabilities are to be taken into account. Generally, however, current assets which are not readily realizable are excluded, as are also current liabilities the payment of which could not be readily demanded, e.g. taxation liabilities due, say, nine months hence.

5. **Stock to Working Capital.** Stocks of raw materials and finished goods, and work in progress are the least liquid items, and consequently the amount of working capital tied up therein should be carefully controlled. A comparison periodically of the ratio of each category to working capital is generally desirable.

6. **Fixed Assets to Long-term Liabilities.** Because long-term liabilities such as debentures are normally secured on fixed assets (and particularly

land and buildings), this ratio is of particular interest to prospective long-term liability holders. The ratio generally must be at least 2:1, otherwise the cover is deemed to be inadequate.

7. **Net Capital Employed (Attributable to Proprietors) to Fixed Assets.** This ratio indicates the extent to which the shareholders' interest is represented by fixed assets. Generally the shareholders should have substantial interest in fixed assets, free from any encumbrances thereon. However, in the case of land and buildings, which generally tend to appreciate in value, it is considered that these should be financed by debentures or mortgages. This is particularly so in manufacturing and trading concerns, otherwise the undesirable situation arises that part of risk capital is invested in relatively non-risk investments, and consequently capital is not being used to optimum advantage. Obviously, no hard-and-fast rules can be laid down as to the ideal ratio in this respect but any prior charges on fixed assets must be taken into account otherwise this ratio will provide misleading information.

8. **Net Capital Employed (Attributable to Proprietors) to Total Liabilities.** Total liabilities in this context comprise the aggregate of long-term liabilities and current liabilities, i.e. share capital and reserves are excluded because these represent the net capital employed. It will be seen, therefore, that the net capital employed plus 'total liabilities' equals total assets, and consequently this ratio, more commonly referred to as the Proprietorship Ratio, indicates the extent to which the total assets are being financed by shareholders and by creditors.

It must be emphasized that accounting ratios should be inter-related as appropriate, and should not be interpreted in isolation. In other words, interpretations concerning any particular facet of a business undertaking should be made only after all relevant ratios and other factors relating to that facet have been considered. Obviously, for example, ratios (7) and (8) should be inter-related in order to obtain the most meaningful results.

Profit and Loss Account Ratios

To facilitate comparisons either with budgeted figures or with actual figures of the corresponding period of the previous year, each item shown in profit statements presented to management should be expressed as a percentage generally of net sales. In addition, the following profit-and-loss account ratios are more commonly used in practice:

1. **Gross Profit to Sales.** This ratio, known as the Gross Profit Ratio, is probably the most used in practice, particularly in wholesale and retail trading concerns where it is a reliable guide to the adequacy of selling prices and the efficiency of stock control. Fluctuations in the Gross Profit Ratio may be accounted for by one or more of the following reasons:

(a) Stock losses due to abnormal depreciation, obsolescence or pilferage.

(b) Variation in the proportion of different classes of goods bought and sold, e.g. a decrease in gross profit may result from discontinuance of a highly profitable line, an increase in the rate of Purchase Tax, or an increase in the proportion of low-margin, price-controlled utility goods sold.

(c) Changes in buying policy or in purchase price of materials.

(d) Changes in profit margins.

(e) Changes in personnel and the basis of their remuneration.

(f) Changes in carriage rates.

(g) Changes in the degree of production efficiency.

(h) Changes in the volume of output.

(i) Changes in the basis of valuation of stock or work in progress.

2. **Stock Ratios.** 'Stock' embraces raw materials, consumable stores, component parts, containers, work in progress and finished goods. The sooner stocks are turned over, i.e. used in the next process or sold, the less is the risk from pilferage, wastage and obsolescence. In order that the working capital tied up in stocks may be minimized, and also to ensure that production delays are avoided a stock-control system must be operated. Whatever system of stock control is operated, a maximum and minimum stock-level for each class of goods will be required and re-order levels established. In arriving at the minimum stock levels, many factors require consideration: the normal delivery time of supplies; storage space; terms of purchase and bulk buying discounts; the availability of same goods from other suppliers in cases of emergency; the availability of substitute where appropriate; imminent changes in purchase prices.

The value of stocks held by most manufacturing and trading concerns is generally such that it would be imprudent not to have an effective method and procedure of controlling stocks. The cost of control may be great, but there is generally no cheap or easy method of achieving what is desired. Elaborate records must often be kept, and continuous stock-taking will be required so that every item of stock is checked at least, say, once a month. Whatever basis of valuing stocks is used the same should be uniformly adopted from period to period.

In applying ratios to stocks, it must be especially remembered that these are to be regarded as indicators only, and that they are not substitutes for efficiency either of the personnel involved or of the control system. Some stock ratios are:

(a) Raw materials to total sales.

(b) Work in progress to total sales.

(c) Raw materials to total purchases.

(d) Finished goods to total sales.

Ratios (a), (b) and (c) indicate, particularly where a specified number of months stock supply is normally kept on hand, the production efficiency of the undertaking. Ratio (d) indicates the rate of stock-turn, and normally the quicker the stock of finished goods can be turned over the better, because sales are being effected and, in consequence, profits should be maximized. Several methods can be adopted to arrive at the stock-turn ratio, but generally the more realistic is to take the cost of sales figure and the average stock figure. In this way, a like-with-like relationship is achieved because normally stock figures are valued at cost. In the case of retail trade business only, finished goods stock may be valued at selling price, and the relationship to total sales established in order to avoid any distortion in the ratio caused by fluctuating gross-profit margins. To arrive at the average stock-value figure (whatever the basis of valuation) it is important that stock should be taken on the same day in each period—at the beginning, middle or end. The stock value should be annually and divided by either 12 or 13 (depending upon the number of periods adopted) to arrive at the average. This method of valuation is more reliable than calculating the mean of the opening and closing stocks of the period.

Balance Sheet and Profit and Loss Account Ratios

1. **Net Sales to Net Capital Employed.** This ratio, used to measure the efficiency of the use of capital, can be regarded as a general indicator only, and consequently undue fluctuations thereof can be determined only from a further breakdown of the ratio of net sales to certain of the various items contained in the net capital employed figure.

2. **Net Sales to Equity Interest.** Equity interest means the ordinary share capital plus reserves attaching to the ordinary shareholders. This ratio indicates the turnover rate—or activity, as it is sometimes called—on the net capital employed attributable to the ordinary shareholders. Generally, the greater the turnover of net capital the greater the profit. A low rate indicates that the business is under-trading, i.e. making insufficient use of the productive and selling capacity available. On the other hand, a high rate might indicate that the business was over-trading, i.e. conducting a greater volume of trade than it is financially safe to do. Net sales may also be expressed as a ratio to any asset or group of assets to determine their turnover rate, e.g. to total capital employed, tangible fixed assets and current assets.

3. **Net Sales to Debtors.** This ratio determines the period of credit allowed to debtors. Debtors normally pay more promptly during periods of prosperity, and less so during periods of recession. The higher this ratio the less period of credit taken by debtors. For example, if the normal period of credit is one month then ideally the ratio should be 12:1. However, this is by no means always experienced in practice, and where difficulty in collecting debts is encountered incentives are often given by way of cash discounts for payments within specified time limits.

4. **Net Sales to Working Capital.** This ratio measures the efficiency of the employment of working capital. As has been stressed previously, this ratio like most others should not be used in isolation.

5. **Net Purchases to Creditors.** This ratio determines the period of credit taken by the organization in paying creditors. As with the net sales to debtors ratio, there should be a relationship between the normal period of credit granted by suppliers and the ratio. If the ratio is increasing, it is

possible that this is as a result of difficulty experienced in meeting accounts as they become due. If this is the case, valuable cash discounts will inevitably be lost.

6. **Net Operating Profit to Total Tangible Assets.** This ratio denotes the net profitability of the tangible capital employed from all sources. To be meaningful a consistent basis should be adopted and applied in computing both the amount of the net profit and the amount of the net capital employed. In computing net operating profit for comparison purposes exceptional and non-recurring items and all appropriations should be excluded. Losses or gains from the disposal of capital assets should also be eliminated. Whilst the earning of profits should not be regarded as the sole purpose of any business concern, it is nevertheless the yardstick by which the efficiency or otherwise of the management is gauged by shareholders. Consequently, this ratio is often referred to as the primary ratio.

The net operating profit may also be related to the total capital employed or to the net capital employed attributable either to the ordinary shareholders or to the preference shareholders. Where the return on net capital employed attributable to the ordinary shareholders is computed, interest paid to other providers of long-term capital, e.g. preference shareholders and debenture-holders must be charged. Whether or not goodwill and other intangibles should be included in capital depends on the purpose of the computation. However, because appropriations in general are eliminated in arriving at the net profit, by the same token, any amounts written off intangibles should be disregarded. If goodwill has been paid for on the acquisition of the business, and represents an under-valuation of the assets, the sum paid for goodwill may be regarded as part of the capital employed. However, where goodwill can be regarded as the purchase price of a number of years' super profits, it may be advisable to exclude this item in the computation of capital employed.

7. **Further Earning Ratios.** Generally speaking, shareholders are concerned only with the return which they receive on their investments with business undertakings; consequently the earnings ratios are often of prime importance to them. This aspect should highlight that all of the ratios previously considered are more often used for management accounting purposes only. The more common earnings ratio are:

(a) Ordinary Dividend to Ordinary Share Capital.
(b) Preference Dividend to Preference Share Capital.

These ratio are normally expressed as percentages. Generally, a fixed percentage rate applies in respect of preference shares.

(c) *Profit Retained to Total Net Profit.* This ratio denotes the dividend policy of the company and also the growth prospects of the company and, in consequence, the growth value of shares held therein. If the company policy is to develop or expand, the most economic source of capital is the company's own profits.

(d) *Dividend Cover.* The ratios of earnings to preference and ordinary dividends indicate the extent of the risks involved as far as both preference and ordinary shareholders are concerned. As with other ratios, there can be no standards for the dividend cover ratio, but generally the preference dividend should be covered at least twice by the amount of earnings otherwise the risk element might be considered too high.

Before equity-holders, i.e. ordinary shareholders and participating preference shareholders, can share in distributable profits, debenture holders are entitled to receive their fixed-interest payment (otherwise they might foreclose), and non-participating preference shareholders must receive their fixed dividends or part thereof if a dividend is declared. The relationship between the total net distributable profits and the amounts due to each class of holders, viz. debenture, participating preference and equity, is known as 'times covered'—this means the number of times that the interest or dividend is covered by earnings.

(e) *Price-earnings Ratio (P/E Ratio).* This ratio, which is now widely used by investors because of the interest shown in the earnings made by business undertakings rather than in their actual distributions, relates the market price of shares to the earnings of those shares. The P/E has been widely used in the U.S.A. for some years. When Corporation Tax, introduced by the Finance Act, 1965, replaced Income Tax and Profits Tax on U.K. company profits, the system of company taxation in the U.S.A. and U.K. was more comparable and so P/E ratios became fashionable in the U.K. particularly for comparisons of investments in both countries. Assume 100,000 ordinary shares of £1 each; earnings after all charges and Corporation Tax £20,000; market value of 1 ordinary share £1·75. P/E ratio is:

$$\frac{\text{Market Price of Share}}{\text{Earnings per Share}} = \frac{1 \cdot 75}{\dfrac{20,000}{100,000}} = 1 \cdot 75 \times 5 = 8 \cdot 75.$$

The following illustration is given to show how certain of the aforementioned ratios would be computed:

Illustration 12

The following is the trial balance at 31st December, 19.2, of Twotoone Co Ltd.:

	£ 000s
Stocks at 31st December, 19.2	300
Sales for Year	3,000
Bank Overdraft (temporary)	200
Trade Debtors	400
Reserves	140
Debentures	100
Trade Creditors	500
Ordinary Share Capital	1,500
Cash	200
Fixed Assets	1,700
Cost of Sales	2,200
Interest Paid	40
Bills Receivable	300
Income from Investments	140
Temporary Investments	500
Corporation Tax—	
Accounting Year to 31st December 19.2	60

From the foregoing balances produce a financial statement and a revenue statement to facilitate the computation of the following ratios and compute them: (i) acid test; (ii) current; (iii) proprietorship; (iv) gearing; (v) primary; (vi) equity turnover; (vii) stock turnover; (viii) trade debtors turnover.

Solution

TWOTOONE CO. LTD.

FINANCIAL STATEMENT AS AT 31ST DECEMBER 19.2

		£
		000s
Liquid Assets		
Cash .		200
Temporary Investments		500
Bills Receivable		300
Trade Debtors		400
		1,400

Current Liabilities	£	
	000s	
Trade Creditors	500	
Bank Overdraft (temporary)	200	
		700

Safety margin	700
Other Current Assets	
Stocks at 31st December, 19.2	300
NET WORKING CAPITAL	£1,000 (A)

Fixed Assets	1,700
Deduct Long-term Liabilities—Debentures	100
NET FIXED CAPITAL	£1,600 (B)

NET CAPITAL EMPLOYED (A)+(B)	£2,600

	£
	000s
Ordinary Share Capital	1,500
Reserves	140
Net Profit—Year ended 31st December 19.2	900
Corporation Tax—Accounting Year to 31st December 19.2	60
NET CAPITAL EMPLOYED Attributable to Shareholders	£2,600

REVENUE STATEMENT
YEAR ENDED 31ST DECEMBER 19.2

	£ 000s
Sales for year	3,000
Less Cost of Sales.	2,200
NET OPERATING PROFIT	800
Add Income from Investments.	140
	940
Less Interest paid	40
NET PROFIT for year	£900

(i) Acid Test (or Liquid Ratio or Quick Ratio) $= \dfrac{\text{Liquid Assets}}{\text{Current Liabilities}} = \dfrac{1400}{700} = 2:1$

(ii) Current Ratio (or Working Capital Ratio) $= \dfrac{\text{Current Assets}}{\text{Current Liabilities}} = \dfrac{1700}{700} = 2\cdot4:1$

(iii) Proprietorship Ratio $= \dfrac{\text{Net Capital employed (Shareholders)}}{\text{Total Liabilities}} = \dfrac{2600}{800} = 3\cdot25:1$

(iv) Gearing Ratio $= \dfrac{\text{Long-term Liabilities}}{\text{Ordinary Share Capital}} = \dfrac{100}{1500} = 1:15$

(v) Primary Ratio $= \dfrac{\text{Net Operating Profit}}{\text{Total Tangible Assets}^1} \times 100 = \dfrac{800}{3400} \times 100 = 23\cdot5\%$

(vi) Equity Turnover Ratio (or Equity Activity Ratio) $= \dfrac{\text{Net Sales}}{\text{Equity Interest}} \times 100 = \dfrac{3000}{2600} \times 100 = 115\cdot4\%$

(vii) Stock Turnover $= \dfrac{\text{Cost of Sales}}{\text{Average Stock}^2} = \dfrac{2200}{300} = 7\cdot3:1$

(viii) Trade Debtors Turnover $= \dfrac{\text{Net Sales}}{\text{Trade Debtors}^3} = \dfrac{3000}{700} = 4\cdot29$

Priority Percentages. Priority percentages is a term used to denote a method of presenting the distributability of the profits of a company among the different classes of prior capital, ordinary shares and reserves. The profits available to each class are expressed as a percentage of the total available profits.

For example, assume that the profits of a company after general charges and Corporation Tax are £1,000,000 and that these are distributable as follows:

Debenture holders	.	£100,000 (gross)
Preference shareholders	.	£100,000
Ordinary shareholders	.	£300,000
Reserve . . .	.	£500,000

[1] Total Tangible Assets (£000's) = Liquid Assets £1,400 + Other Current Assets £300 + Fixed Assets £1,700 = £3,400.

[2] The average stock figure should ideally be computed (see p. 3147). In the absence of appropriate information the year-end stock figure (the only stock figure given) has been taken.

[3] This includes Bills Receivable £300 (000's).

The tabulation of the foregoing may be made thus:

Distributability of Profits			Percentage of Total Profits	Priority Percentages
		£		
Debenture Interest	(gross)	100,000	10	0–10
Preference Dividend	.	100,000	10	10–20
Ordinary Dividend	.	300,000	30	20–50
Reserve	.	500,000	50	50–100
		£1,000,000	100	

Debenture interest and Preference dividend together require 20 per cent of total profit. Ordinary dividend requires 30 per cent of the remaining 80 per cent, so that Ordinary dividend is covered $\frac{80}{30}$ or $2\frac{2}{3}$ times.

Since 50 per cent of the profit has been retained in reserve, the profits could fall by 50 per cent before uncovering the Ordinary dividend; by 80 per cent before affecting the Preference dividend and by 90 per cent before endangering the Debenture interest.

Assuming, however, that profits remaining at £1,000,000 with the Debenture interest absorbing £300,000, Preference dividend £300,000 and Ordinary dividend £250,000, the priority percentages may be expressed:

Net Profits	Debentures	Preference Dividend	Ordinary Dividend	Reserve
£1,000,000	0–30	30–60	60–85	85–100

Notice the effect of a fall of only 15 per cent in profits: the Ordinary dividend would be endangered. A fall of just over 40 per cent would endanger the Preference dividend and one of about 72 per cent would begin to eat into Debenture interest.

Many other accounting ratios are in common use and it would be impracticable in a book of this nature to consider in detail the various situations where they can be used to advantage. Generally, however, they are an effective tool of the management accountant in the provision of information and data needed to assist in the planning, policy making and the controlling of the day-to-day activities of a business. Ratios are also often used in costing, budgetary control and standard costing. In particular, the management accountant can employ ratios to assist in determining the efficiency of such management policies as those relating to production control and the detection of waste, losses, defective work, idle plant and bottlenecks of all type; purchasing, store-keeping, material control and material usage; personnel selection, labour supervision and labour output; publicity and advertising, selling and distribution methods; scientific research and development; organization and the control of delegated responsibility; provision of essential information to shareholders, trade federations and the parent company.

SECTION D. TAKEOVER BIDS

General. A take-over bid is an attempt to gain control of a company by making an offer to purchase shares therein either by a direct approach to the ordinary shareholders or by placing the proposals before the directors of the company for subsequent communication to the shareholders. Any person can purchase shares in a public company and can also sell the shares which he holds or, in some cases, will hold. Consequently, companies have been taken over by persons (and this has included companies) whose only interest in acquiring control was to sell out ultimately, and often quite soon, at a capital profit. New company controllers quite frequently entered into a 'lease-back' arrangement with a finance house or an insurance company whereby owned business premises taken over were sold to the finance house or the insurance company on condition that the vendors obtained a 99 years' lease of the premises concerned. In this way, the purchasers acquired a sound investment and the vendors frequently obtained a tax-free capital profit. Because of the normal tendency for land and buildings to appreciate considerably in value and of the practice of showing such fixed assets in balance sheets at historical cost, the capital profit reaped on the sale of business premises alone often enabled the take-over company to recoup most if not all of the actual cost of the take-over. This motive for a take-over bid is, however, not so popular nowadays because under the Finance Act, 1965, such capital profits are liable to Capital Gains Tax.

Method of Gaining Control. In order to gain control of a company, it is necessary merely to acquire more than half in nominal value of the company's equity share capital. From the take-over company's viewpoint and also from that of the minority shareholders, i.e. those shareholders who either did not sell out to the take-over company or received no offer therefrom, this type of take-over can lead to considerable trouble. In particular, under Sect. 72 of the Companies Act 1948, where shareholders' rights are varied the holders of not less in the aggregate than 15 per cent of the class of shares involved may apply to the court to have the variation cancelled, and where this action is taken the variation cannot be effected unless and until it is confirmed by the court. Further, under Sect. 210 of the 1948 Act, where the court is satisfied on the instigation of minority shareholders, that oppression of the minority has taken place, an order may be made regulating the conduct of the future affairs of the company or for the purchase of any members' shares by the company or by other members, and where the company is required to purchase shares the capital will be reduced accordingly. Generally, therefore, it is preferable that a complete take-over be made, in which circumstances the take-over offer is conditional on acceptance by a specified majority of shareholders, normally 90 per cent. If a 90 per cent acceptance is obtained, then under Sect. 209 of the 1948 Act, the take-over company is empowered to acquire the shares of the shareholders dissenting from the scheme or contract approved by the majority.

Legislative Controls. Under the Fair Trading Act 1973 as amended, the Department of Trade is empowered to refer to the Monopolies Commission any proposed merger which it considers would operate against the public interest. In particular the Department has power to request the Monopolies Commission to investigate any merger which: (a) involves the take-over of total assets in excess of £5 million, or (b) creates or intensifies a monopoly, i.e. a one-third market, in the supply of goods or services in the United Kingdom. Further, by the Industry Act 1971, the I.R.C. may promote or assist the re-organization or development of any United Kingdom industry and if requested by the Secretary of State, may establish or develop any United Kingdom industrial enterprise. Because the I.R.C. has public funds at its disposal, it can have an influential effect on any proposed merger in which it participates. It was to be expected that such financial power in the hands of a Government-sponsored organization would attract considerable criticism with regard primarily to the proposed mergers in which it had become involved, and secondly the amount of public finance which had been defrayed in order to achieve its objects.

The City Code. The ethics of some past take-over negotiations have left much to be desired, and this in spite of the guidelines laid down in 1959 by the City Working Party which comprised representatives of the Issuing Houses Association, the Accepting Houses Committee, the Association of Investment Trust Companies, the British Insurance Association, the Committee of London Clearing Bankers, the Confederation of British Industry, the National Association of Pension Funds and The Stock Exchange. Certain merchant bank advisers came into disrepute because of the parts which they played in take-over activities that were outside the spirit of the guidelines (more commonly known as the 'Queensberry Rules'). These rules were brought up to date in 1963 as the 'Revised Notes on Company Amalgamations and Mergers', but some merchant bankers often advised clients on how best to circumvent them, and were left to do so unchallenged; the Stock Exchange seldom exercised its power to suspend share quotations of any of the companies involved. In July 1967, however, as a direct result of the Metal Industries affair,[1] such a furore ensued in the City and elsewhere that the Stock Exchange Council, supported by the Governor of the Bank of England, had the City Working Party reconvened and a Panel on Take-overs was set up under Sir Humphrey Mynors. The City Working Party were firmly of the opinion that a voluntary self-imposed discipline was much preferable to government control, and so that 'City Code on Take-overs and Mergers' was devised, and published in March 1968. The Code was revised in April 1969 and again in April 1976, in the light of the year's experience.

---

[1] In July 1967, Thorn Electrical made a £15·5 million bid for Metal Industries. Aberdare Holdings however, in a straight fight with Thorn obtained 52½ per cent of M.I. In order to swamp Aberdare's effective control, the directors of M.I., on the advice of their merchant bankers, issued a block of shares of Thorn, who, by making a higher bid, gained 'victory'. The issue of the block of shares to Thorn was made by M.I.'s directors without consulting the majority of M.I. shareholders.

The Code begins by setting out general principles of conduct to be observed in take-over bids. In particular, the directors of both the offeror company and the offeree company must act in the best interests of their own shareholders, and should provide them with sufficient evidence, facts and opinions, and also sufficient time to enable them to make an assessment and a decision. There are thirty-five Rules, some precise and others merely guidance on the application of the general principles. It would be inappropriate to consider here the Code Rules in detail, but the most important one as far as accountants are concerned is Rule 16, which concerns profit forecasts and asset valuations. The directors concerned are finally responsible for profit forecasts and asset valuations; but in arriving at these, accounting-bases and calculations for profit forecasts must be examined and reported on by the auditors or consultant accountants, and asset revaluations should be supported by the opinion of independent professional experts, and the basis of valuation clearly stated.

C.A. Institute's Recommendations. To coincide with the publication of the revised edition of the City Code,[1] the Council of the Institute of Chartered Accountants in England and Wales in consultation with the Council of the Institute of Chartered Accountants of Scotland (and after discussion with the Panel on Take-over and Mergers) issued a 'Statement in Accountants' Reports on Profit Forecasts'. The following are brief notes on this Statement:

1. Reporting accountants, whether they are consultant accountants or in fact the company auditors, should in their report take care to avoid giving any impression that they are in any way confirming, underwriting, guaranteeing or otherwise accepting responsibility for the ultimate accuracy and realization of forecasts—this is the full responsibility of the directors and should be signified as such in any relevant circular.

2. In accordance with the Code, the accounting-bases and calculations for profit forecasts must be examined and reported on by the auditors or consultant accountants, referred to collectively as 'reporting accountants'. For the purposes of their review the main points to be considered by the reporting accountants are:

(a) The nature and background of the company's business.
(b) The accounting practices normally followed by the company.
(c) The assumptions on which the forecasts are based.
(d) The procedures followed by the company for preparing forecasts.

The Statement sets out in some detail each of the foregoing points. With regard to point (a), mention is made of factors requiring particular attention, viz. the bases: (i) of valuing stock and work in progress, (ii) of taking credit for profits and providing for losses on long-term contracts,

---

[1] Copies of the City Code may be obtained from The Secretary, Issuing Houses Association, Roman Wall House, 1–2 Crutched Friars, LONDON, EC3N 2NJ and copies of the C.A. Statement may be obtained from The Institute of Chartered Accountants in England and Wales, Moorgate Place, London.

and (iii) of calculating depreciation charges; the accounting treatment: (i) of research and development expenditure, (ii) of exceptional items, and (iii) of taxation and investment grants.

3. The accountants' report, addressed to the directors, will cover the following matters, where appropriate:

(a) The fact that they have carried out a review of the accounting bases and calculations on which the profit forecasts have been based.

(b) Specific identification of the forecasts and documents to which the report refers.

(c) If, as will usually be the case, they have not carried out an audit of estimated results for expired periods, a statement to that effect.

(d) Whether in their opinion the forecasts have been properly compiled on the basis of the assumptions made by the board of directors, as set out in the circular, and are presented on a basis consistent with the accounting practices normally adopted by the company.

If the reporting accountants have reason for material reservations about the accounting bases and calculations for the forecasts, or if they have reason to consider them inconsistent with the stated assumptions, they should qualify their report accordingly.

The accountants' report must, to accord with the Code, be accompanied by a statement by the directors that the accountants have given and not withdrawn their consent to publication of their report. Before giving such consent, the accountants should examine the whole text of the directors' circular to ensure that their report is appropriate thereto.

The following is the Institute's suggested form of an unqualified accountants' report:

To the directors of X, Ltd.

We have reviewed the accounting bases and calculations for the profit forecasts of X, Ltd. (for which the directors are solely responsible) for the periods . . . set out on pages . . . of this circular. The forecasts include results shown by unaudited interim accounts for the period . . . In our opinion the forecasts, so far as the accounting bases and calculations are concerned, have been properly compiled on the footing of the assumptions made by the Board set out on page . . . of this circular [and separately reported on by Messrs . . . on page[1]] and are presented on a basis consistent with the accounting practices normally adopted by the company.

Finally, regarding the Code as a whole, the City Working Party stated that a code administered by the Panel would possess a degree of flexibility and speed in action that would be difficult to achieve by any more legalistic procedures imposed by statute. To be more fully effective, however, and also to be a reasonable substitute for what would have been inevitably enforced government regulations, the Panel would require to have penal power, and this is not mentioned in the City Code. The power has, however, been subsequently granted to the Panel, and when in any take-over or merger a breach of Code is referred to the Panel an offender may, after due hearing and right of appeal, be censured either privately or

---

[1] i.e., the merchant bank or other adviser, if any.

publicly, and in extreme cases be precluded temporarily or permanently from participating in any future take-over or merger.

SECTION E. BUDGETARY CONTROL

A budget is defined in the Institute of Cost and Management Accountants' 1974 edition of *Terminology of Management and Financial Accountancy* as a 'financial and/or quantitative statement, prepared and approved prior to a defined period, of the policy to be pursued during that period for the purpose of attaining a given objective. It may include income, expenditure and the employment of capital'. The I.C.M.A. definition of budgetary control is 'the establishment of budgets relating to the responsibilities of executives to the requirements of a policy, and the continuous comparison of actual with budgeted results either to secure by individual action the objective of that policy or to provide a basis for its revision'.

Budgetary control, therefore, relates to the use of budgets as control devices whereby predetermined plans or standards, output, income and expenditure are compared with actual attainment so that, if necessary, corrective action may be taken before it is too late. Normally, what are known as sectional budgets are prepared for each separate function of an organization, e.g. production, administration, selling and distribution, and these sectional budgets are aggregated in a master budget which can be expressed in the form of a budgeted profit-and-loss account and balance sheet. The effectiveness of a budgetary control system depends on the ability of those concerned to ensure that appropriate remedial action is taken when departures are revealed.

Objectives. The main objectives of a budgetary control system are:

1. to assist directors or managers to plan the future policy of the organization;
2. to provide clearly-defined targets of output, income and expenditure for each section or function of the organization;
3. to promote co-operation and co-ordination among directors or managers in the attainment of pre-determined targets;
4. to indicate the financial requirements, normally month by month, and the sources from which the required finances are to be obtained.

Clearly, therefore, no system of budgetary control will be effective unless managers at all levels are prepared to accept the discipline which must necessarily be imposed. In setting targets, levels should be sought that will motivate staff rather than discourage them.

Basic Requirements. Before a budgetary control system is installed, the following requirements should be satisfied:

1. First and foremost, there should be a clear organization chart showing in detail the position, authority and responsibility of each executive, and the activities for which he is responsible.
2. There should be clearly defined policies and objectives.

3. There should be sufficient information available for the purpose of preparing each sectional budget.

4. There should be complete co-operation between executives, and each executive should take part in the preparation of the budget for which he will be held primarily responsible. Furthermore, the agreement of each executive should be obtained in writing before the budgets are put into operation.

5. There should be a logical sequence in the preparation of the various sectional budgets leading up to that of the master budget.

6. There should be established a standard procedure of reporting whereby budget variances will be readily ascertained and communicated to those responsible so that immediate action can be taken.

7. There should be an accounts classification system and a well devised and appropriate financial and cost accounting system.

Preparation of Information. Each executive compiles, in respect of the department or function for which he is responsible, an estimate of the operations for the ensuing budget period (for instance the sales director will be required to produce estimates of budgeted sales in terms of units and money values).

It will be apparent that certain departmental budgets can be prepared only after necessary information is supplied by certain other departments. In particular, the production budget cannot be prepared until the esti-mated sales figures are available, because it must be ascertained that the production required to meet estimated sales can be achieved. The finance department, too, must know the plans of all departments before it can prepare a statement of budgeted cash receipts and disbursements.

Since there must be a logical sequence in preparing the various sectional budgets, a procedure should be set up to ensure the proper arrangement of the estimates of these departments. Often a senior member of the accounting staff will act as budget controller, and will advise on the preparation of their budgets and collate them into the master budget. Such a system, however, sometimes imposes an undue strain on the co-ordinating ability of the budget controller; the formation of a budget committee may overcome this defect. Such a committee may be composed of the managing director, the budget controller and heads of main departments. Greater co-ordination should thereby be achieved, but there is always the tendency that, in committee, certain matters of little concern to individual members will be discussed, with the result that the time available for each member to put forward all matters relating to his department is curtailed. In consequence, some large organizations prepare a budget manual which sets out in detail the procedures to be followed in the preparation of budgets, the responsibilities of those involved, the routine and, in many cases, specimen forms and reports together with information as to their uses and functions. A timetable showing the dates by which the budgeting procedures should be finalized is also normally provided.

Continuous comparison of budgets with actual performance must be made, in order to ascertain whether or not efficiency is being maintained: this is the function of the cost department. The accounts classification, which is a prerequisite of any successful system of budgetary control, should be compiled by this department on the basis of the organization structure. Budget variances may thus be recorded against the various divisions as shown by the budget. It is not the duty of the cost department to take executive remedial action on their findings but rather to provide accurate information in such a form as will be readily and correctly interpreted by departmental managers and others concerned.

Presentation of Information. Prescribed minimum information showing comparisons of actual and budgeted figures should be presented in time for any necessary remedial action to be promptly taken. The periods covered should be clearly stated, and the regularity of presentation should be pre-determined. For example, in some instances, monthly information may suffice; in others, weekly or even daily presentation may be desirable. Each report should be presented in such a form as will:

(i) be most suited and useful to the recipient;
(ii) show only those costs which are within the control of the recipient;
(iii) show clearly the variances from the budget, together with notes explaining how the variances have arisen. In particular, controllable variances should be clearly distinguished from those that are beyond the control of the sectional head, e.g. variances due to faulty budgeting or to external economic influences.

Use of Information. The function of the cost accountant or budget controller is to present timely comparative statements showing budgeted and actual figures, variances from budget and the causes thereof. Management's role in budgetary control is to determine:

(i) whether each variance is justified according to the circumstances;
(ii) whether adverse or unfavourable variances can be remedied;
(iii) whether favourable variances can be maintained.

Flexible Budgets. A fixed budget provides a satisfactory basis for control purposes where each production department operates at exactly the rate of activity planned. This, however, seldom occurs in practice. It is virtually impossible to compare actual costs for one rate of activity with budgeted costs at another rate. It will be appreciated that while some costs vary with the volume of production, others do not. Consequently, by ascertaining which costs are fixed, which are variable and which are semi-variable, it is possible to develop flexible budgets for each department of a business concern. A flexible budget indicates the anticipated costs for any given level of departmental activity.

Flexible budgets are used mainly for the control of production costs where there is a more direct relationship between costs and volume of production. They are sometimes used to control distribution and administration costs, but many of these, e.g. advertising, building and maintenance costs are determined by managerial decisions rather than by the level of production.

Budget Period. The length of any budget period depends upon the nature of the budget itself. General rules cannot be laid down as to the period of time that a budget should cover. However, it may be said that, generally, the longer the period involved the less reliable the figures ascertained. In determining a suitable budget period consideration will be given to the product involved, the general economic situation, and the business concern's share of the market. For purposes of control, the period itself should be divided into several shorter periods. For instance, if it is one year, this may be divided into three four-monthly, twelve monthly, or thirteen four-weekly control periods. The shorter the control period the sooner current matters may be reported to management; in this way the task of effective management control is made easier. Several different control periods related to different costs will probably be operated within one business concern. Certain costs will be more effectively controlled daily, others weekly and others monthly.

Accounts Classification Code. The preparation and presentation of comparative statements and control information will normally form part of the duties of the cost accountant, who should ensure that a suitable method of accounts classification and coding is installed. A variety of methods of such classification and coding exists, but generally a numbering system as opposed to a lettering system is more flexible and thus more popular. The system will be compiled on the basis of the organization structure, and should cover all aspects of the business; costs should be classified and coded relative to the various departments involved. All business transactions can thus be recorded systematically according to standard laid-down procedures thereby facilitating the early preparation of meaningful accounts showing budget figures, actual figures, variances between budgeted and actual and, where appropriate, related comparative figures. Budget reports prepared by the cost accounting section are submitted at regular pre-determined intervals to the departmental managers. The budget report sent to any manager should concern only those costs which are within his control. Variances from budget should be clearly shown. In particular, controllable variances should be highlighted in the report, and brief explanatory notes given concerning them.

Advantages of Budgetary Control. The advantages that may be derived from a properly exercised system of budgetary control are as follows:

1. Sales and production may be co-ordinated by estimating sales and by planned production to meet those sales.

2. A profitable sales and production programme may be formulated by ascertaining the lines of goods most desirable to reconcile a well-conceived sales programme with a well-balanced production programme.

3. Control of expenditure may be achieved by:

   (a) the preparation by each department of estimated expenditure requirements for the budget period, and the agreement of these with the budget controller, budget committee or board of directors as the case may be;

(b) the prohibition of expenditure in excess of that estimated unless properly authorized;

(c) a stipulation that each department must submit monthly reports showing comparisons between budgeted expenditure and actual expenditure.

4. A financial programme may be formulated. It is possible that the cash resources may be scarce even although the profits earned are high, and consequently it is essential to plan cash resources in order that necessary funds will be available when most needed, and also the borrowing and investment may be properly timed. The financial programme will comprise estimates of cash receipts based on the sales programme, and cash disbursements based on the production and expense estimates. Capital receipts and expenditure must also be taken into account. Cash receipts, therefore, might consist of amounts received from debtors, proceeds from sales of fixed assets, proceeds from a fresh issue of capital, or investment income received. Cash disbursements might consist of payments to creditors in respect of direct materials, payments for direct labour (i.e. wages), payments in respect of production overhead, selling and administration costs, dividend payments, taxation payments and capital payments.

5. All the activities of the organization may be co-ordinated as a result of:

(i) each department's preparing an estimate of its activities for the ensuing budget period;

(ii) these estimates being studied by departmental heads, the budget officer or committee and the board of directors;

(iii) the proposed activities of each department being compared with the activities of the others.

6. A budgeted Profit and Loss Account and Balance Sheet may be prepared and appropriate plans formulated from them to make possible the attainment of the estimated financial results.

Budget Reports. In budgetary control, preparation of the various budgets is only the first step; actual costs must be recorded, related to the budgets, and the **causes of variation** ascertained. Budget reports are then sent to the appropriate managerial grades responsible for completing the technique of budgetary control by **taking action** to correct any adverse trends disclosed.

Budget reports should be presented in the most useful manner. The basic requirements are:

1. They must be presented **regularly and promptly.** The **cost of compilation** must not be overlooked. In some cases, monthly presentation may suffice; in others, weekly, whilst in others daily presentation may be desirable.

2. Each report should embrace only those items of expense which are within the control of the recipient. A good working plan is to send it to the person immediately responsible and also a copy to his immediate superior.

3. Each must clearly show the **variance from the budget:** suitable explanatory notes are usually helpful.

The difference may be caused by price, quantity or volume variations from budget. The controllable variances must, in particular, be emphasized in the reports.

4. A report must be in the **form most suited and useful to the recipient.** Thus quantities, with or without values, are often most useful to a foreman for control purposes.

A system of Budgetary Control is often supplemented by a system of Standard Costing which is defined by the ICMA as 'a pre-determined cost calculated in relation to a prescribed set of working conditions correlated to technical specifications and scientific measurement of materials and labour to the prices and wage rates expected to apply during the period to which the standard cost is intended to relate with an addition of an appropriate share of Budgeted Overhead. Its main purposes are to provide bases for control through variance accounting for the valuation of stocks and work-in-progress and in exceptional cases for fixing selling prices.'

	BUDGET	ACTUAL	VARIANCE Adverse	VARIANCE Favourable	% OF BUDGET Adverse	% OF BUDGET Favourable	CAUSE OF VARIANCE Price	CAUSE OF VARIANCE Quantity
	£	£	£	£	%	%	£	£
Direct Material								
Product A	6,000	6,600	600		10·0		190	10
Product B	9,000	9,000	—	—	—	—		
Product C	3,000	2,850		150		5·0		50
Direct Labour								
Product A	10,500	10,800	300		2·9			100 (Note 1)
Product B	10,500	10,200		300		2·9	90	10
Product C	4,500	4,650	150		3·3		50	
Production Overhead								
Product A	2,400	2,469	69		2·9	} 2·9 (Note 2)		
Product B	3,000	2,913		87	2·9			
Product C	1,200	1,239	39		3·33			
Production Cost	£50,100	£50,721	£1,158	£537	2·3	1·1		

PRODUCT ANALYSIS

| PRODUCT | BUDGET | ACTUAL | VARIANCE | | % OF BUDGET | |
			Adverse	Favourable	Adverse	Favourable
	£	£	£	£	%	%
A	18,900	19,869	969		5·1	
B	22,500	22,113		387		1·7
C	8,700	8,739	189	150	2·2	1·7
Production Cost	£50,100	£50,721	£1,158	£537	2·3	1·1

Notes:

1. This adverse quantity variance was caused by the use of a large quantity of poor-quality material bought from ....

2. Production overhead is here recovered as a percentage of direct labour cost. A separate budget report would compare actual and budgeted production overhead in detail.

SECTION F. MARGINAL COSTING

Marginal costing is a method of costing whereby fixed costs, which are related to time and not to production, are excluded from cost comparisons.

The marginal cost per unit is the amount at any given volume of output by which aggregate costs are changed if the volume of output is increased or decreased by one unit. In consequence, marginal cost comprises only those costs which fluctuate with the volume of production, viz., labour, materials and variable overheads.

Fixed costs are incurred whether or not goods are being produced. It follows, therefore, that any excess of the selling price of goods over the marginal costs will contribute to the fixed costs. This excess is known as the GROSS MARGIN or CONTRIBUTION.

Where the gross margin is sufficient to cover the fixed costs only, break-even point (B.E.P.) has been reached, i.e. a profit has not been made, nor has a loss been incurred.

It is common practice for certain businesses to fix the selling prices of some commodities above the marginal cost, but below total cost, in order to strengthen goodwill or to use these prices as 'loss leaders' with the aim of attracting customers to other normal priced goods.

During a depression or at times when similar exceptional circumstances prevail, a business may be faced with the alternatives of closing down or selling its products at a price below total cost. Before making a policy decision, however, it should consider the following matters:

1. Whether the marginal product or job costs as disclosed by the current costing system are reliable;

2. Whether the emergency is likely to be short-lived or of relatively long duration;

3. Whether skilled operators are likely to be available later if they are dismissed now;

4. The extent to which valuable plant will deteriorate if the factory is closed down;

5. Whether, if an order at a price below total normal cost is declined, it will pass to a competitor with the possibility that the customer's future orders will be lost;

6. Whether prices of labour and materials are likely to change during the term of the contract.

Break-even Chart. A break-even chart is a chart on which is plotted the relationship of either total costs to sales or of fixed costs to gross margin. The level of activity at which neither a profit nor a loss is shown is called the break-even point (B.E.P.).

To prepare a break-even chart, it is necessary to draw up budgets of sales and variable cost at different levels of productive capacity, based on past records and anticipated price fluctuations with particular reference to labour rates, costs of raw materials and market conditions. Once prepared, the chart will disclose the profitability or otherwise of a business at various levels of activity and appropriate management decisions may be determined therefrom. A specimen break-even chart is shown in Fig. 1:

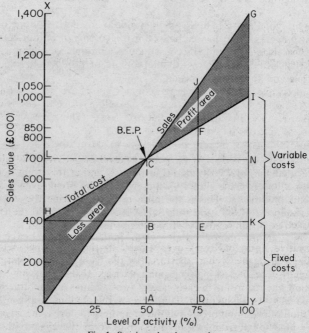

Fig. 1. Specimen break-even chart.

Notes to Chart (*Fig. 1*)

100 PER CENT ACTIVITY. When the business is working at 100 per cent level of activity the sales value if £1,400,000 (line YG), the analysis of which is as follows:

			£
Fixed Cost (Line YK)			400,000
Variable Cost or Marginal Cost (Line KI) .	£1,000,000		
Less	400,000		
			600,000
Net Profit (Line IG)	£1,400,000		
Less	1,000,000		
			400,000
Sales Value (Line YG).			£1,400,000

The gross margin, i.e. sales *less* marginal cost, is £800,000 or twice the amount of fixed cost.

75 PER CENT ACTIVITY. When the level of activity decreases the sales value and marginal cost also decrease, as will the gross margin. At 75 per cent level of activity the gross margin is reduced to £600,000 as follows:

		£
Sales Value (Line DJ)		1,050,000
Less Variable Cost or Marginal Cost (Line EF) .	£850,000	
Less	400,000	
		450,000
Gross Margin		£600,000
Comprising—		
Net Profit (Line FJ)	£1,050,000	
Less.	850,000	
		200,000
Fixed Cost (Line DE)		400,000
		£600,000

50 PER CENT ACTIVITY. At 50 per cent level of activity, the sales line OG intersects the total cost line HI at point C and at this point neither a profit nor a loss is made. Point C, therefore, is the break-even point.

MARGIN OF SAFETY. This is the term used to describe the volume of sales between the B.E.P. and total sales. It is represented in the chart in the area CGN or alternatively within the level of activity AY.

Alternative Form of Break-even Chart. In the foregoing method of preparing a break-even chart the fact that the fixed costs are first plotted on the chart necessitates, in ascertaining variable costs at varying levels of production, the recording in each case of two readings and subtracting one (the fixed costs) from the other. To overcome the obvious disadvantages of this method of presentation, and at the same time to derive the advantages of being able to ascertain required readings from the chart without the necessity of further calculation, and to establish the gross margin at any level of activity, an alternative method may be used. This method involves the plotting on the chart of the variable costs first, and then drawing the fixed costs line above and parallel to the variable costs line. The following illustration uses the two methods of preparation of break-even charts for purposes of comparison.

Illustration 13

The following figures relate to the manufacturing operations of a business for its financial year just ended:

	£
Sales	2,000,000
Direct Wages	300,000
Direct Materials	810,000
Variable Costs	400,000

Prepare a break-even chart from these figures and determine therefrom the break-even point.

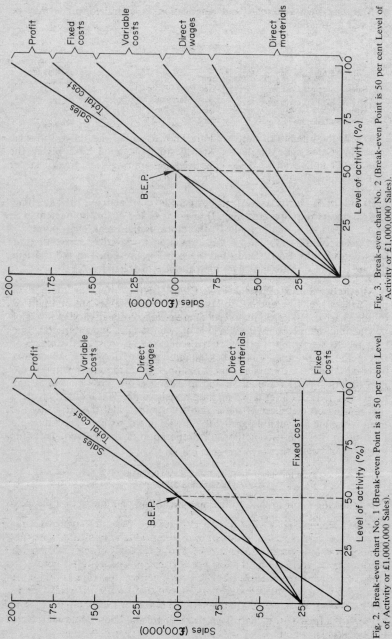

Fig. 2. Break-even chart No. 1 (Break-even Point is at 50 per cent Level of Activity or £1,000,000 Sales).

Fig. 3. Break-even chart No. 2 (Break-even Point is 50 per cent Level of Activity or £1,000,000 Sales).

Marginal Cost Formulae and Applications. General formulae may be derived as follows:

Total Cost	= Variable Cost + Fixed Cost
Marginal Cost	= Variable Cost
Marginal Cost + Fixed Cost + Profit	= Sales
Sales − Marginal Cost − Fixed Cost	= Profit
Sales − Marginal Cost	= Fixed Cost + Profit
Gross Margin	= Sales − Marginal Cost
Gross Margin	= Fixed Cost + Profit
Gross Margin − Fixed Costs	= Profit

Where the number of units sold are known, any of the above formulae involving Sales and Marginal Cost will still hold good by applying the number of units sold to the selling price per unit and marginal cost per unit respectively.

Illustration 14

Assuming the following:

	£
Selling Price per Unit .	10
Marginal Cost per Unit	6
Total Fixed Cost	2,000

Calculate: (*a*) the number of units which require to be sold in order: (i) to break even, (ii) to make a profit of £20,000; and (*b*) the profit made if 40,000 units are produced and sold.

Solution

(*a*) Let x = number of units
   (i) x (Selling Price per unit − Marginal Cost Per Unit) = Fixed Cost + Profit
   But at break-even point profit is nil
   ∴ $x(£10 − £6) = £2,000$
   ∴ $x = £500$ units
   (ii) Using same formula as in (i)
   ∴ $x(£10 − £6) = £2,000 + £20,000$
   ∴ $x = 5,500$ units
(*b*) Using the same formula as in (i) and with $x = 40,000$ units
   ∴ $40,000(£10 − £6) = £2,000 + P$
   ∴ $£160,000 − £2,000 = P$
   ∴ $P = £158,000$

Profit Volume (P/V) Ratio. The P/V ratio is generally expressed as a percentage, and is useful in determining the profitability of total sales of a number of different products which cannot readily be analysed into the various units produced and sold. For this reason it should be noted that the ratio is unfortunately named, because neither the volume of output nor sales is taken into consideration; indeed, the ratio is arrived at simply by expressing the gross margin (or contribution) as a percentage of sales, i.e. $\dfrac{\text{Gross Margin}}{\text{Sales}} \times 100$.

Example

		£
Sales		100,000
Marginal Costs		60,000
Gross Margin (or Contribution)		40,000

$$\text{P/V Ratio} = \frac{£40,000}{£100,000} \times 100 = 40\%$$

Where sales and marginal costs are in direct proportion the P/V ratio is the same at all levels of output, and in such circumstances the gross margin can readily be calculated at all levels of output because by simple proportion:

$$\text{Gross Margin} = \text{Sales} \times \text{P/V ratio}.$$

The useful application of the P/V Ratio may be seen from the following:

Illustration 15

These are the operating results of a business at normal output level:

Sales											£150,000
Less Fixed Costs						£40,000	
Variable Costs						102,000	
											142,000
Profit											£8,000

Calculate the sales at which the business: (i) breaks even, and (ii) makes a profit of £24,000. Assume that the selling price and the relationship of variable costs to output remain static.

Solution

Sales										£150,000
Less Variable Costs									102,000
Gross Margin or Contribution							48,000
Less Fixed Costs									40,000
Profit										£8,000

(i) P/V Ratio

$$= \frac{£48,000}{£150,000} \times 100$$

$$= 32\%$$

∴ Break-even value of sales

$$= \frac{\text{Fixed Costs}}{\text{P/V Ratio}}$$

$$= \frac{£40,000}{32} \times 100$$

$$= £125,000$$

(ii) Gross Margin

$$= \text{Fixed Costs} + \text{Profit}$$
$$= £40,000 + £24,000$$
$$= £64,000$$

∴ Value of Sales producing a Gross Margin of £64,000

$$= \frac{£64,000}{32} \times 100$$
$$= £200,000$$

Break-even charts can be useful guides to management in relating costs and profits to different levels of activity. However, as with most other useful management tools and techniques, the information derived from charts should not be viewed in isolation. From the illustrations, it may have been noted that in every case it has been assumed that at all selected levels of activity and output fixed costs have remained static, and variable or marginal costs have varied in direct proportion to sales. In practice this is very often not the case; fixed costs are normally only fixed within a certain limited range of production, and variable or marginal costs per unit and selling prices per unit are not always static at all levels of output. Indeed there is seldom anything static about cost because many factors tend to affect it. Consequently, decision-making information should be extracted from break-even charts only from within the limits of the activity on which the charts have been prepared.

SECTION G. MECHANICAL AIDS IN ACCOUNTING

There is a growing use of mechanical devices in accounting routine and therefore it is necessary for the student to be familiar with those mainly in everyday use. The benefits from their use are considerable, provided that they are fully, efficiently and adequately employed. The full benefits will not ensue if:

1. They are not operated by properly trained staff;
2. There is insufficient work to keep the machinery fully employed;
3. There is no corresponding efficiency in dealing with the work of the machines, where the ledger sheets are not arranged in proper sequence, or where the work of the operator is interrupted by having to replace one ledger by another, or where the material to be worked on is not within easy reach of the machine;
4. The quantity of work involved is too small to justify the considerable outlay, i.e. on the purchase and upkeep of the machine, particularly where the labour-saving is trivial;
5. There is inefficiency in organization.

Good organization is required to obviate:

(a) Dangers arising from the cards or loose leaves being lost, destroyed, misplaced or fraudulently substituted. No handwriting on the sheets tends to increase the latter risk.

(b) Original errors being undetected, as such errors will percolate automatically through the whole of the records based thereon and will not generally be discovered by the failure of one set of books to balance with another.

Office machinery can be divided into:

(i) Direct machinery, which is employed in the performing of the actual accounting entries, including statistical and financial records.

(ii) Indirect machinery, which is ancillary to the direct machinery and of great assistance in preparing for or the checking of accounting entries.

(iii) Auxiliary equipment, comprising the numerous devices and machines of use generally in the office routine.

Examples of (i): Burroughs posting machines; National accounting machines, Hollerith (and Powers) tabulating and sorting machines, book-keeping typewriters (from which can be prepared, in one operation, the ledger entry, daybook entry, statement of account and other records, e.g. proof sheets for daily balancing).

Examples of (ii): Elliott Fisher invoicing machines, comptometers, adding and calculating machines, carbotypes.

Examples of (iii): duplicating machines, Addressographs, typewriters, internal telephones, postal frankers, letter openers and sealers, signographs, dictating machines, dictographs, time recording machines, cheque protectors, numbering and coin-sorting machines, photostats.[1]

In addition, there can be added the more familiar types of machine and equipment like perforating machines, stamp affixers, cash registers, filing cabinets, and many others.

Advantages of Mechanized Accounting. 1. Saving of time and labour resulting in reduction of wages for office administration.

2. Increase of accuracy in routine work, and elimination of errors.

3. Greater legibility, neatness, and accuracy of recording.

4. Assists division of labour.

5. Records can be kept always up to date, enabling quick dispatch of invoices, statements, etc., and the speedier preparation of periodic and annual accounts.

6. Facilitates, in conjunction with total accounts, daily Trial Balances and balancing generally.

7. Constant flow of subsidiary records (as the slip system or its equivalent is used for posting, etc.).

8. As original records will be made in duplicate (or triplicate), needless effort of time and labour avoided on copy work (and 'reading over'), thus enabling interested departments to have their 'copy' in good time.

9. In very large concerns the reduction of routine staff will free a certain amount of floor space.

10. Facilitation of extraction of supplementary data, e.g. financial, costing, budgetary, statistical.

Disadvantages. (a) Too much reliance upon the automatic accuracy of some of the direct machinery.

---

[1] These machines, which enable photographs of documents—probates, wills, accounts, plans, etc.—to be taken quickly and the negatives stored in a small space, are extremely useful and were invaluable in the last war.

(*b*) The danger arising from a mistake of the person using a machine for the 'original' record, as this will travel right through all records and would not be discovered by an 'out of balance' discrepancy as in manual work.

(*c*) The danger of the operator becoming 'mechanical' in ways and outlook.

(*d*) The high initial cost and upkeep.

(*e*) Possibility of fraud through fraudulent use of loose leaves and substitution of fictitious accounts without any guidance through examination of handwriting.

(*f*) Waste through inefficient use and neglect of upkeep of equipment.

Objective Accounting. Operations frequently arise involving the question as to whether they are to be regarded as part of a whole, or whether they are to be regarded as separate. In other words, whether the operations are joint or severable.

Sometimes there is clear external evidence of intention; sometimes no indication is available as to the intentions of the parties involved, in fact, in many instances, even the parties themselves have no clear conception of what their intentions were.

In the absence of information, treatment should be on the basis of reasonable inference, having regard to changed circumstances, lapse of time, etc., and where no equal tenable solutions are available, the most conservative aspect should be taken.

The transactions in question may be simultaneous or resultant. As examples, the following may be said to give rise to a consideration of whether they are to be considered as one or several:

(i) X purchases a business and, in addition, purchases the business property. (A simultaneous transaction.)

(ii) X purchases the business *only* mentioned in (i) and later purchases the property (a resultant transaction.)

(iii) X as in (i) buys the property and adjacent property at the same time as the business is acquired.

(iv) As in (iii) acquiring such property at a later date.

(v) An underwriter is allotted shares in part payment of underwriting and also acquires shares by 'firm' underwriting.

(vi) X is a debenture-holder (with others) in a company which goes into liquidation. X, with his co-debenture-holders, takes over the security and forms a syndicate which later they sell.

(vii) X is paid a debt in foreign currency which he decides to hold, and later acquires further units of that foreign currency.

(viii) X buys shares in a company and later acquires further shares in that company.

In many cases, in practice, the need for a decision does not arise, but when it does, as for instance where there are third-party interests, all the facts of the particular case will call for consideration.

In connection with 'Objective Accounting', mention may be made of the growing tendency to departmentalize the profit or loss of a business in order to obtain greater efficiency and cut out unprofitable sections. For the profit of the business may be regarded in its simplest form as the accretion of net assets over a period, while subdivision of the business into separate departments—buying, manufacturing, selling, repairing (without going into great detail)—might reveal a profit in one and a loss in another.

The Economic Year. The tendency during recent years has been to move the accounting year of businesses from the calendar year to the economic year, that is one commencing and ending with the business activities at their lowest ebb.

At the end of such a period the stock will be at the lowest, the cash at the highest (unless the period of credit is long) and the peak of sales over, thus enabling accounts for the year to be built up quickly and accurately. Where the period of credit given to customers is short, say, a month, accounts may be drawn up to the date of the expiry of such period.

The year end will be at the end of a natural period, e.g. the completion of a harvest of a farmer; end of the Christmas trade of a poultry business or at the end of a period dictated by business convenience, e.g. clearance sales after Christmas or Whitsuntide sales; after delivery of fireworks by fireworks manufacturer.

It may well be that a business may have more than one 'season' or be engaged in several activities with different peaks and slack periods. In such cases, a decision will have to be taken on the balance of advantage as regards *final* accounts; but interim accounts may be prepared for each relevant period (for each department).

It will often happen, particularly in manufacturing concerns, that the buying season supervenes, so that, although it does not weaken the validity of the argument in favour of the accounting terminal date being at the end of the peak season, the advantage arising through having a peak cash and a nadir of stock will be offset by the increase of new stock bought and creditors therefor.

SECTION H. ELECTRONIC DATA PROCESSING (E.D.P.)

The term E.D.P. is used to describe a system of processing data by means of electronically powered machines. These machines are called computers, and work at enormous speeds and with great accuracy once they are set up by qualified personnel. Computers are now extensively used in industry, commerce, transport, communications and administration.

There are two types of computers—(i) the analog computer, and (ii) the digital computer. The analog computer deals with the measurement of quantities, lengths, volumes, degrees, etc., and is generally used in the technical and scientific fields: it therefore falls outside the scope of this present book. The digital computer, like the abacus which was used for calculating-purposes from the beginning of recorded history until the end of the sixteenth century (and still in use in parts of the Far East), handles numbers as distinct units and is therefore appropriate to work of an accounting nature.

Components of a Computer. An electronic computer, whether analog or digital, has five basic components or units:

1. Input Unit.
2. Storage or Memory Unit.
3. Arithmetical or Logical Unit.
4. Control Unit.
5. Output Unit.

Since the analog computer is not being considered here, the following details concerning the five units of an electronic computer relate to the digital computer.

Input Unit. In technical terms, 'input' applies to data which is fed into a computer for processing. The three commonest media used for processing data are punched paper tape, punched cards and magnetic tape. The medium used is determined:

(i) by the use to which the data is to be put;
(ii) by the required degree of permanency of information;
(iii) by the volume of work involved.

Where a particular calculation is required, once-only punched paper tape might be most suitable. Where information will be required for continual use, the most suitable media might be punched cards. Where speed of input processing is of paramount importance owing to the volume of work involved, magnetic tape will probably be selected since the speed at which the computer reads magnetic tape can be many times greater than that at which it reads punched paper tape or punched cards.

Paper tape is a continuous roll of specially prepared paper in which are punched round holes, the number of holes across the width depending upon the paper tape selected. Paper tape may be obtained in 5, 6, 7 or 8 'channels'; this means that the number of holes which can be punched per row depends upon the number of 'channels' available. The great disadvantage of paper tape, apart from its fragility, is that a wrong punching cannot be rectified. Consequently, before processing in the computer, the punched paper tape must be checked on a verifier.

The reading by the computer of punched paper tapes is done either by the use of a light source opposite a photo-electric cell or by a metal brush in contact, through the punched holes, with a metal plate. Whichever method is used the computer can detect, read and transcribe at high speed.

A punched card consists of a rectangular-shaped card normally with 80 'fields' or columns with rectangular holes being punched in the appropriate columns in accordance with a code. As with punched paper tape, punched cards must be checked on a verifier before they are processed further. The chief disadvantage of punched cards is their bulkiness and in consequence the amount of storage space which they require. Their chief advantages are that they are much less fragile than punched paper tape, for a wrongly punched card can easily be replaced, and even after punching can easily be revised and brought up to date.

Magnetic tape consists of a thin layer of magnetic substance (ferro oxide) between two layers of plastic. Normally, the tape is half an inch wide and is so designed that it can record up to 800 signals to the linear inch. Since data can be transferred to magnetic tape at enormous speeds most modern computers are equipped to transcribe automatically information from punched paper tape or punched cards on to magnetic tape. Magnetic tape is, of course, much more expensive than paper tape.

Storage or Memory Unit. The storage or memory unit which houses the data and program required for processing is generally an essential part of any computer system. The program in current use is kept in this unit, and relevant data is fed from the input unit either for temporary retention or for collation with other data and subsequent delivery to the arithmetical and logical unit.

Arithmetical and Logical Unit. The arithmetical and logical unit, as the name implies, carries out the necessary arithmetical calculations and the logical tests in order to determine whether a number is positive or negative and whether two numbers are the same. From the information gained the program may be modified if necessary. The data is ultimately transferred back to the storage or memory unit.

Control Unit. The control unit is directly linked to the storage or memory unit and in accordance with the program stored therein directs, modifies where necessary, and controls the sequence, timing and flow of the operations of the other units of the computer system.

Output Unit. The output unit removes the appropriate data from the storage or memory unit and generally produces it in two different forms: where the information is required to be re-processed by computer, then it may be produced on tape or punched cards; where the information is for immediate use, then it will generally have been transcribed and will be in printed form. Certain computer systems have a visual display unit which can show graphs, charts, drawings, tables and accounts, and these can be photographed if required.

The arithmetical and logical unit effects all subtraction, multiplication and division operations by a systemized adding operation. The calculations are done, briefly, as follows:

SUBTRACTION. This is effected by adding complements. For example, a computer in order to 'subtract' 3 from 7 actually:

(i) adds to 7 the complement of 3 which, taking 10 as a base, is 7, thus giving 14, and

(ii) discards the 1 in the 'tens' column, leaving 4 as the correct answer.

This is equivalent to the following procedure, more readily understood:

$$7 - 3 = 7 + (10 - 3) - 10$$
$$= 7 + 7 - 10$$
$$= 14 - 10$$
$$= 4$$

MULTIPLICATION. Multiplication is achieved by repeated addition. For example, to multiply 8 by 5, 8 is added to 8 four times thus:

$$8 \times 5 = 8 + 8 + 8 + 8 + 8 = 40$$

DIVISION. Division is achieved, in effect, by repeated subtraction. For example, to divide 20 by 5, the computer continues to subtract 5 until the remainder is less than 5. The answer (that is, the quotient) is the number of times 5 has already been subtracted thus:

1st subtraction $20 - 5 = 15$
2nd subtraction $15 - 5 = 10$
3rd subtraction $10 - 5 = 5$
4th subtraction $5 - 5 = 0$

Since four subtractions are required, the quotient is 4.

As already stated, the computer does not, in fact subtract one number from another but produces the necessary result by an addition operation:

1st subtraction $20 - 5 = 20 + (10 - 5) - 10 = 15$
2nd subtraction $15 - 5 = 15 + (10 - 5) - 10 = 10$
3rd subtraction $10 - 5 = 10 + (10 - 5) - 10 = 5$
4th subtraction $5 - 5 = 5 + (10 - 5) - 10 = 0$

Uses of the Computer. Computers vary in size, adaptability, capability and design. They range from the small electronic calculators many of which are in use today to the giants which are mostly owned by a government, a university, an industrial combine (particularly in the electrical and engineering sector), or a commercial combine (particularly in the insurance, banking and finance group). The following is a very brief summary of the general range of the commercial use of computers:

1. Management accounting and statistics, embracing all accounting and statistical work involved in the running of business concerns.

2. Production control.

3. Stock control, including maintenance of stores records and replenishing of stocks.

4. Invoicing and billing.

5. Payroll procedure—related records such as labour cost allocation, production analysis, labour statistics and personnel records can be handled simultaneously with the payroll procedure.

6. Bank accounting—many special-purpose electronic systems exist to sort and handle all cheques and maintain details of customers' accounts.

7. Airline reservations—computers are used to provide up-to-the-minute information regarding airline scheduled flights.

Systems Analysis and Programming. In practice the differentiation between systems analysis and programming varies; in fact, in some cases, no distinction is made. Generally, however, systems analysis means the detailed examination of a job and the drawing up of a plan as to how it may be done by computer. Programming involves the plan development, designed in detail by the systems analyst, to suit the particular computer, including its translation into a usable form for the computer.

Computers are not brains, and therefore they must be given detailed instructions in order to carry out their function. There are few companies where systems and procedures are sufficiently detailed for electronic requirements, and consequently it is necessary to smooth out the various links in the system at the point of application to the computer. The process has to be carried much further when installing a computer than, for example, when installing a machine system. The studies preliminary to the installation of a computer often require up to two years or more for one application. The first application generally takes the longest time.

Programming utilizes flow charts which follow an operation right through from beginning to end, showing every possibility and providing a route or flow to cover every case. Computers can answer binary questions only, i.e. questions with two possible answers, and before any program is finalized it must be carefully tested on the computer and any errors rectified.

Microcomputers. One of the spin-offs of the space programme is the benefit to industry and commerce of the great advances in microprocessor technology. Because in space programmes all equipment must be fitted in to a capsule so the number of electronic circuits which are containable in one device has been increased dramatically. By photographic and etching processes microcircuits are created on a slice of silicon, a non-metalic element. After testing the slice is divided into microcircuit chips which are mounted on the final component with connecting wires. The present day silicon chip is a low-cost, reliable and flexible control device and in large-scale integration a single silicon chip can contain over 250,000 components. As a consequence computers are nowadays both considerably smaller and cheaper and thus many companies and firms which until recently could never have considered computerization can now afford to purchase a computer. The opportunities for accountants, and this probably applies more to those in professional practice, to use computers to produce clients' financial statements and accounts is greater than ever before. Further, this facility is not necessarily restricted to the bigger practice firms. Microcomputers cut the cost of computer power and thus the microcomputer does not have to be in operation all day in order to be economic. Other significant advantages of microcomputers are that they generally do not need specialized staff to operate them and they, unlike other computers which require complex air conditioning and dust-free environment, can be operated satisfactorily virtually anywhere.

SECTION I. INVESTMENT APPRAISAL

Investment Appraisal, or Investment Analysis as it is sometimes called, is a means of assessing whether capital expended on a project would show a satisfactory rate of return to an undertaking, either absolutely or when compared with expenditure on alternative projects, and of indicating the optimum time to invest.

Complex Problem. Many factors require consideration before additional capital is invested in a business undertaking, and certain information must be ascertained. Eg., all or some of the following might be appropriate:

- (a) Initial outlay.
- (b) Duration of project.
- (c) Residual value.
- (d) Annual running costs.
- (e) Source and cost of capital to be invested.

Cash Flow. The initial step in appraising a capital investment project is to calculate the expected cash flow year by year from the project over its life. The cash flow in any year is the difference between the actual income and expenditure attributable to the project. In the first year, the cash flow will often be negative, i.e. expenditure will exceed income, owing to the initial heavy expenditure. In later years cash flow should become positive, i.e. income will exceed expenditure, because of the decline in capital expenditure and the achievement of a return on the project.

Payback Period. This is a technique of ascertaining the number of years which it takes an investment to earn a surplus (cash flow), i.e. profit before charging depreciation, to repay the additional capital and outlay involved.

Illustration 15

Assume capital expenditure of £45,000 to be incurred on alternative projects A and B, with cash flows expected from each as follows:

Year No.	Project A Cash Flow £	Project B Cash Flow £
1	15,000	(1,000)[1]
2	10,000	3,800
3	6,000	4,200
4	5,000	6,000
5	4,000	8,800
6	3,500	11,000
7	1,500	12,200
	45,000	45,000
8	1,200	7,800
9	800	3,000
10	200	800
	47,200	56,600

[1] Brackets indicate a negative cash flow, i.e. a cash outflow.

Whilst from the above it is apparent that both Project A and project B can 'payback' the initial outlay by the end of the seventh year, it is also apparent, overall, Project B is more profitable. This, therefore, is the serious deficiency of the Payback Method, where speed of recovery of the initial capital outlay is the sole concern, and where, in consequence, it is possible that the least profitable project is selected because it has the shortest payback period. If payback period criteria alone are used to appraise projects, then faulty investment decisions will frequently be made.

Discounted Cash Flow. Sums received at different dates are not comparable unless the interest element is taken into consideration. For example, £1,000 receivable now is worth more than £1,000 in one year from now. This is simply because £1,000 invested now should earn interest or profits and so accumulate to more than £1,000 one year hence. The net present value (NPV) of a capital project is the sum of the present values of yearly cash flows during the life of the project; the NPV varies with the rate of return used to discount the cash flow.

Illustration 16

Assume that £1,000 is receivable one year from now and the current rate of interest is 10 per cent per annum.

Since the interest on £1,000 amounts to £100 at the end of one year:
  £1,000 invested now produced £1,100 in one year;
  $\therefore$ £1,000 is the present value (PV) of £1,100 at the end of one year;
  $\therefore \dfrac{1,000}{1,100} \times 100$, £909, is the PV of £1,000 at the end of one year.

In other words, if £1,000 is due at the end of one year, then its value at present is £909 assuming a rate of interest of 10 per cent per annum.

To find the present value of £1 due at the end of one year, the formula employed is:

$$\frac{1}{1+i} \times 1, \text{ or, simply } \frac{1}{1+i}$$

where i represents the interest earned on £1 in one year.

It follows that the PV of any sum expressed in £s due at the end of one year at 10 per cent per annum can be found by multiplying that sum by 0·909. This figure 0·909 is known as the PV Index (or PV Factor, or Profitability Index) of £1 due at the end of one year with interest accruing at 10 per cent per annum.

The formula for the PV of £1 due at the end of two or more years is $\dfrac{1}{(1+i)} n$, where n represents the number of years at the end of which the sum is payable. In actuarial work $\dfrac{1}{(1+i)} n$ is denoted by V^n.

Tables are available from which the PV index or factor can be obtained for the present value of £1 due at the end of any number of years from, say, 1 to 100 at the more common rates of interest.

A knowledge of the mathematics above is not a prerequisite for the application of the Discounted Cash flow (DCF) technique. The Present Value Section of compound interest tables gives the data from which to derive the required amounts.

The cash flow, once ascertained must be valued on present-day terms. Two methods of discounting cash flow popular in industry today are the Yield or Rate of Return method, and the Present Value Method.

Yield or Rate of Return Method. With this method the cash flow is discounted at the annual rate of compound interest which will make the NPV of the project equal to the capital amount invested. In order to find the required rate of discount reference should be made to compound interest tables. Suitable Tables may be purchased, but for present purposes a Table is given on page 3187 showing the present value of 1 for 1 to 15 years ahead at rates of interest of 5 per cent to 20 per cent.

At this point it should be stressed that no project of importance should be evaluated without account having been taken of taxation and relevant investment grants. The full implications of these will be considered later in this chapter. Meantime consider the following project:

Project. A machine which costs £1,000 will, it is estimated, enable a company to earn annual cash flows of £100, £200, £300, £400 and £500, at which stage the useful life of the machine is terminated and there is no residual value. Find the rate of interest which equates the NPV and the initial capital value of the machine.

Method. Unfortunately there is no formula to ascertain the required answer. The desired rate of interest must be found by empirical methods, i.e. by trial and error. However, this is not such an arduous task as it may seem at first sight. By referring to the appropriate compound interest table, it will generally be found that the required rate of interest will be determined after two or three attempts.

First, set down the years and the expected cash flows as follows:

Year	Cash Flow
	£
1	100
2	200
3	300
4	400
5	500

Next, remembering that the total present value of NPV should in this case be equal to £1,000 and that the project runs for five years, it follows in this case that the arithmetic average present value is around $\frac{£1,000}{5}$, or £200. Consequently, the task is much simplified by reference to the Table on p. 3187 in order to ascertain at which rate of interest £300 three years from now (the cash flow of the year 3 which is the middle or average of the five-year project) equals a present value of £200. Remember of course, that this is an approximation only, but nevertheless a starting point.

Let $x =$ the present value of 1 due 3 years hence;
thus $300x = 200$
and $\therefore$ $x = \dfrac{200}{300} = 0.667$.

Referring now to the Present Value Table, we see that this represents a rate of discount of 14 per cent. The computation may now be continued as follows:

Year	Cash Flow	Discount Rate	Present Value
	£	14%	£
1	100	0·877	87·70
2	200	0·769	153·80
3	300	0·675	202·50
4	400	0·592	236·80
5	500	0·519	259·50
	£1,500		£940·30

It can be seen that the NPV of £940·30 falls short of the required £1,000 by £59·70. Consequently, a lower rate of discount is required; let us try 12 per cent.

Year	Cash Flow	Discount Rate	Present Value
	£	12%	£
1	100	0·893	89·30
2	200	0·797	159·40
3	300	0·712	213·60
4	400	0·636	254·40
5	500	0·567	283·50
	£1,500		£1,000·20

Disregarding the excess of 0·20, it may be stated that the total cash flow over the five-year period is equivalent now, that is the present, to £1,000. As £1,000 is the initial cost of the machine, it means that 12 per cent is the rate of discount which equates the total cash flow and the initial capital outlay. It follows that this capital project produces a return of 12 per cent per annum.

Interpolation Method. For examination purposes an extract from appropriate Present Value Tables will normally be provided where a set question involves the use of the DCF technique in the solution. In such circumstances, therefore, the examinee is expected to utilize the appropriate rates from those provided. Because of the importance of the time factor in examinations it would be both unreasonable and unthinkable to waste time in arriving at appropriate discount rates by what could be a fairly long-drawn-out process of elimination, although such a procedure no doubt should be employed in practice: a much quicker method must therefore be adopted. One that is considered to be sufficiently accurate for this purpose is the interpolation method. With this method, two discount rates with a fairly wide divergence, for example 10 per cent and 15 per cent, may be used, and provided that the lower rate is in fact too low and the higher too high a fairly accurate rate of interest can be determined. Assuming the same data as stated in the illustration immediately preceding, and that the interpolation method is employed, using 10 per cent and 15 per cent rates, the position would be as follows:

Year	Cash Flow	Discount Rate	Present Value	Discount Rate	Present Value
	£	10%	£	15%	£
0	(1,000)	1·000	(1,000)	1·000	(1,000)
1	100	0·909	91	0·870	87
2	200	0·826	165	0·756	151
3	300	0·751	225	0·658	197
4	400	0·683	273	0·572	229
5	500	0·621	311	0·497	249

Total Outflow   £(1,000)   £(1,000)
Total Inflow   £1,065   £913

It should be stated that the interpolation method can be applied here because the 10 per cent rate is too low and the 15 per cent too high. The actual rate lies somewhere between and can be found by interpolation as follows:

The difference between the two rates is 5 per cent, and a proportion of this difference related to the differences in the total present values is added to the 10 per cent rate thus:

$$10\% + \left(\frac{1,065 - 1,000}{1,065 - 1,000 + 1,000 - 913} \times 5\% \right)$$

$$= 10\% + \left(\frac{65}{152} \times 5\% \right)$$

$$= 12\% \text{ approx.}$$

This is the rate arrived at previously. It will be readily appreciated, however, that with the first method a considerable number of computations based on rates selected at random may have been necessary before arriving at the required discount rate.

The interpolation formula given above may be applied in examinations without any need to check the reasoning behind it. However, the following general reasoning is offered to show the logicality of the calculations. With the 10 per cent discount rate, the total inflow exceeds the total outflow by £65. With the 15 per cent discount rate, the total outflow exceeds the total inflow by £87. Thus the total difference is £65 + £87 = £152, and consequently the difference of 5% in the discount rates used = £152.

In order to find the actual discount rates, the 10 per cent discount rate must be increased so that the £65 excess is eliminated. By simple proportion the increase is thus $\frac{65}{152}$nds of 5 per cent. Therefore, the approximate annual rate is $10\% + \frac{65}{152} \times 5\%$) which, as already stated, equals 12 per cent.

Present Value Method. The Yield or Rate of Return Method was seen to be a method of discounting the yearly cash flows at a rate necessary to arrive at a predetermined NPV of nil. The Present Value Method, on the other hand, is a method of discounting yearly cash flows at the business concern's cost of finance, or required rate of return. Given a business concern's cost of finance, a project's cash flow in any year can be discounted to find its present value. If the resulting NPV is negative, the project is unfavourable since it does not yield the required rate of interest. If the resulting NPV is positive, then the profits are expected to be more valuable than the outlays, and to that extent the project is favourable.

In order to take account of reducing earnings when assessing capital projects, a rate of return higher than anticipated may be set so that allowance can be made for the effect of inflation. This, however, is normally inadvisable since inflation can be expected to have a similar effect on both revenue and expenditure.

The following illustration shows the similarity between the two methods under consideration. Normally, the initial outlay is shown as the first item in the Table, and this method will be adopted hereafter.

Assume that an item of plant costs £1,400 and gives cash flows as shown in column (a). The discount rate applied is 14 per cent.

Year	(a) Cash Flow £	(b) Discount Rate 14%	(a)×(b) Present Value £
0	(1,400)	1·000	(1,400·00)
1	450	0·877	394·70
2	411	0·769	316·10
3	376	0·675	253·80
4	330	0·592	195·40
5	242	0·519	125·60
6	185	0·456	84·40
7	75	0·400	30·00
	£669		NPV £ NIL

From this illustration it is seen that by discounting the cash flow at 14 per cent per annum the NPV is nil. Had the discount rate used been greater than 14 per cent the NPV would have been negative; had it been less than 14 per cent the NPV would have been positive. Consequently the project is acceptable if the required rate of return is 14 per cent or less. This conclusion applies to the Yield Method and the Present Value Method.

In the foregoing problem the application of either method would lead to the same decision being made to whether the capital project should be accepted or rejected. Each method has its advantages and disadvantages. The Yield Method is more difficult in practice because the required rate of discount can only be arrived at by trial and error. However, this method has the advantage that the project's yield can be calculated even if the required rate of return has not been decided. Whichever method is applied will depend on the circumstances; if various alternatives are under consideration the Present Value Method will probably be preferable. For examination work, the Interpolation Method should be adopted.

Taxation and Investment Grants. In appraising capital investment projects the effect thereon of taxation and investment grants should be taken fully into account. Taxation will comprise, in respect of limited companies, Corporation Tax and Capital Allowances, and in respect of sole traders and partnerships, Income Tax and Capital Allowances. The appraisal of capital investment projects of limited companies will be considered here, but the principles involved may be adapted to projects of other business concerns.

The investment grants now in force may be payable irrespective of the taxation position of companies. Where applicable, investment grants are deemed to reduce the cost of an investment by the amount of the grant.

Illustration 17

The following are details relating to a proposed capital investment project:

New Plant and Machinery cost	£5,000
Investment Grant (Development Area)	45 per cent
Writing Down Allowance	20 per cent
Expected Life	10 years
Expected Scrap Value	Nil

Assume: (i) that the investment grant will be paid in the year following that in which the investment is made, i.e. in year 1; and (ii) that the rate of Corporation Tax for all years is $42\frac{1}{2}$ per cent. Prepare a DCF computation.

For the foregoing illustration, discount rates of 14 per cent and 16 per cent were also applied. With a rate of 14 per cent the NPV was $-107 \cdot 90$, which indicated that the rate was too low; a 16 per cent rate showed a NPV of $+66 \cdot 40$, which indicated that the rate was too high. The true rate lies somewhere between 14 per cent and 16 per cent. For practical purposes the rate may be taken as 15 per cent.[1]

The rate of return of 15 per cent is after allowing for Corporation Tax. This rate is equivalent to an external gross return of 15 per cent $\times 100/58\frac{3}{4}$ or $25 \cdot 53$ per cent with Income Tax at the standard rate of $41\frac{1}{4}$ per cent.

It is important to note that the return of 15 per cent per annum is not earned on the whole amount of the initial investment of £5,000 throughout its life.

[1] Students should, for practice, find the discount rate by interpolation using rates, say, of 12 per cent and 18 per cent.

DCP COMPUTATION

Year	(a) Capital Expenditure	(b) Investment Grant	(c) Gross Profits before Tax and Depreciation	(d) Corporation Tax of 42½% on previous year's profits (c)×42½%	(e) Writing Down Allowances in respect of previous year's profits	(f) Corporation Tax saved by Annual Allowances (e)×42½%	(g) Corporation Tax payable (d)−(f)	(h) Cash Flow after Corporation Tax (c)−(g)	(i) Discount Factors for 15%	(j) Discounted Value of Col. (h)
	£	£	£	£	£	£	£	£		£
0	5,000							(5,000)	1·000	(5,000)
1		2,250	1,250		550	234	(234)	3,734	0·870	3,248·60
2			1,100	531	440	187	344	756	0·756	571·50
3			825	468	352	150	318	507	0·658	333·60
4			780	351	282	120	231	549	0·572	314·00
5			695	332	225	96	236	459	0·497	228·10
6			580	295	180	77	218	362	0·432	156·40
7			420	247	144	61	186	234	0·376	87·90
8			220	179	115	49	130	90	0·327	29·40
9			150	94	92	39	55	95	0·284	26·90
10			40	64	74	31	33	7	0·247	1·70
11				17	296*	126	(109)	109	0·215	23·40
	5,000	2,250	6,060	2,578	2,750	1,170	1,408	1,902		21·50

* Balancing Allowance. Amounts in parentheses are negative.

What it indicates is that a net after-tax rate of return of 15 per cent is earned on the amount remaining invested in the project from year to year.

TABLE SHOWING PRESENT VALUES OF 1

From 1 to 15 Years ahead at Rates of Interest of 5% to 20%

Years Ahead	5%	6%	7%	8%	9%	10%	11%	12%
Now	1·000	1·000	1·000	1·000	1·000	1·000	1·000	1·000
1	0·952	0·943	0·935	0·926	0·917	0·909	0·901	0·893
2	0·907	0·890	0·873	0·857	0·842	0·826	0·812	0·797
3	0·864	0·840	0·816	0·794	0·772	0·751	0·731	0·712
4	0·823	0·792	0·763	0·735	0·708	0·683	0·659	0·636
5	0·784	0·747	0·713	0·681	0·650	0·621	0·593	0·567
6	0·746	0·705	0·666	0·630	0·596	0·564	0·535	0·507
7	0·711	0·665	0·623	0·583	0·547	0·513	0·482	0·452
8	0·677	0·627	0·582	0·540	0·502	0·467	0·434	0·404
9	0·645	0·592	0·544	0·500	0·460	0·424	0·391	0·361
10	0·614	0·558	0·508	0·463	0·422	0·386	0·352	0·322
11	0·585	0·527	0·475	0·429	0·388	0·350	0·317	0·287
12	0·557	0·497	0·444	0·397	0·356	0·319	0·286	0·257
13	0·530	0·469	0·415	0·368	0·326	0·290	0·258	0·229
14	0·505	0·442	0·388	0·340	0·299	0·263	0·232	0·205
15	0·481	0·417	0·362	0·315	0·275	0·239	0·209	0·183

Years Ahead	13%	14%	15%	16%	17%	18%	19%	20%
Now	1·000	1·000	1·000	1·000	1·000	1·000	1·000	1·000
1	0·885	0·877	0·870	0·862	0·855	0·847	0·840	0·833
2	0·783	0·769	0·756	0·743	0·731	0·718	0·706	0·694
3	0·693	0·675	0·658	0·641	0·624	0·609	0·593	0·579
4	0·613	0·592	0·572	0·552	0·534	0·516	0·499	0·482
5	0·543	0·519	0·497	0·476	0·456	0·437	0·419	0·402
6	0·480	0·456	0·432	0·410	0·390	0·370	0·352	0·335
7	0·425	0·400	0·376	0·354	0·333	0·314	0·296	0·279
8	0·376	0·351	0·327	0·305	0·285	0·266	0·249	0·233
9	0·333	0·308	0·284	0·263	0·243	0·225	0·209	0·194
10	0·295	0·270	0·247	0·227	0·208	0·191	0·176	0·162
11	0·261	0·237	0·215	0·195	0·178	0·162	0·148	0·135
12	0·231	0·208	0·187	0·168	0·152	0·137	0·124	0·112
13	0·204	0·182	0·163	0·145	0·130	0·116	0·104	0·093
14	0·181	0·160	0·141	0·125	0·111	0·099	0·088	0·078
15	0·160	0·140	0·123	0·108	0·095	0·084	0·074	0·065

SECTION J. OPERATIONAL RESEARCH (O.R.)

General. Operational Research, O.R. as it is usually abbreviated, is the application of scientific processes in the solving of the complex operational problems that arise within organizations.

In the application of the O.R. technique, all significant factors in a problem are identified and their interaction is ascertained; these factors are measured in order to assess their relative importance. From all the amassed information the problem then is reduced to the preparation of a chart showing procedures currently in use and those proposed to be adopted under changed conditions.

O.R. technique can be applied in such problems as production planning, inventory control, labour control and payroll analysis, sales analysis, queuing, etc.

Many of the significant factors of a problem can be expressed mathematically. In fact, most of the techniques involved in O.R. have a mathematical or statistical basis, and consequently O.R. is sometimes defined as a scientific method of providing managers with a logical and quantitative basis for decision making. Where O.R. is employed to solve complex managerial problems the O.R. team may comprise, for example, an engineer, an economist, an industrial psychologist, a mathematician and an accountant. The field of O.R. and that of accounting overlap only within very limited sectors. Wherever they do overlap, O.R. is complementary to, and not a substitute for, accounting techniques.

Inter-relationships of Techniques. There is, apparently, some difference of opinion in modern industry regarding the various techniques used in O.R. and the relationship that exists between one technique and another. Whatever the differences of opinion and the reason therefor, it can safely be stated that the sequence of an O.R. project is: (i) to formulate the problem; (ii) to construct a scientific or mathematical model representing the problem; (iii) to obtain a solution from the model; (iv) to test the model and solution; (v) to establish controls over the solution; (vi) to implement the solution.

Bearing in mind the controversy that exists over the inter-relationship of O.R. techniques, the following list shows what are often regarded as these inter-related techniques:

1. *Linear Programming*, which embraces the following:
   (*a*) Simplex Method.
   (*b*) Transportation Technique.
   (*c*) Convex Programming.
   (*d*) Dynamic Programming.
2. *Network Analysis*, which embraces the following:
   (*a*) Line of Balance.
   (*b*) Critical Path Analysis (CPA) or, as it is often termed, Critical Path Method (CPM).
   (*c*) Programme Evaluation and Review Technique (PERT).
   (*d*) Resource Allocation in Multi Project Scheduling (RAMPS).

Linear Programming

Linear programming is a mathematical method of planning an operation so as to utilize limited resources to best advantage. ('Linear' simply means 'proportional'; thus, if 1 lb of a commodity costs £1, 10 lb will cost £10.)

Management is continually being confronted with some aspects of the basic business problem of how to devise the maximum use from limited resources under certain conditions or constraints, and how to combine these resources in such a way that the stated objective is achieved. Linear programming can be a most serviceable tool to management in delineating or limiting the boundaries of probability. It can be applied in providing solutions to many business problems, and in particular it can assist in ascertaining:

(i) the product mix that will maximize sales or minimize costs;
(ii) the most economical use of labour and production sources;
(iii) the most profitable basis of machine loading;
(iv) the most economical use of labour and production resources.

Simplex Method. This method of linear programming is suitable where the variable factors in a business problem bear a straight-line relationship one to another, i.e. where the equations representing the data in the problem when represented on a graph produce a straight line.

The procedure is to plot these equations on the same graph and then to manipulate the figures within the matrix until the optimum or maximum position is found.

Transportation Technique. This technique may be applied in solving a linear programming problem where the data are expressed in terms of one kind of unit only, thus leading to a readier solution. It is particularly suited to problems involving the selection of the optimum method of distributing orders from a number of despatch points to a number of destinations.

Convex Programming. This technique is a further development of simplex linear programming, and is used where the equations representing the problems are of the second or higher degree. In such cases, for example where unit-cost changes with volume, the variables will follow a curve rather than a straight line.

Dynamic Programming. This technique may be applied to the solution of problems where decisions must be made at distinct stages in order to achieve an optimum allocation of resources; it is particularly useful in multi-stage decision processes involving probability.

Network Analysis

General. Network analysis is a method of planning the undertaking of a project in such a way that by the preparation in a logical fashion of a network diagram of the detailed activities to be undertaken, inter-relation of these activities can be planned and controlled so as to complete the project at the earliest possible date and lowest cost.

In the early stages these techniques were closely identified with large-scale construction and civil engineering projects, but they are now frequently employed in the installation of data processing systems and in research and development projects. When network analysis is used in connection with the latter, electronic computers are generally also used because of the frequent scheduling and programming revisions involving the complete re-allocation of resources.

The basic procedure in preparing a network analysis is to record in detail the various activities, events and operations to be performed, to arrange the events and operations in a logical sequence and to allot a number to each event.

An event is a specified accomplishment in the programme; it is clearly definable, and is reached and passed in an instant of time. An activity is a time-consuming link between related events. The events should be joined by lines or arrows to indicate sequence and the time allowance for each activity should be inserted.

Line of Balance (LOB). Various types of flow, process and operations charts have been used extensively for many years in industry to schedule and progress work. The modern network analysis techniques are merely extensions and developments of tried and tested management tools.

While flow process and operation charts are useful in providing a rough check on the progress of work and the sequence of operations, they cannot pinpoint bottlenecks in production. The LOB technique was developed to overcome this deficiency and involves a chart so prepared as to show the relationship between work progress and delivery deadlines thus highlighting bottlenecks that could hold up entire operations.

Critical Path Analysis or Method (CPA or CPM). In any network, the duration of the project is determined by the longest path in the network. The longest path is termed the 'critical path', and the activities involved are known as 'critical activities'. They are so termed because any delay with the activities in this path will delay the completion of the project by the same time. Conversely, any saving of time on the critical path will accelerate completion date, whereas a saving of time on all other paths will not affect it. Consequently, the attention of management will be directed towards the critical path in order to eliminate bottlenecks.

Figure 4 is an illustration of a very simple network diagram:

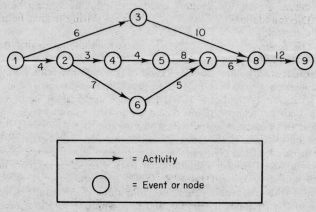

Fig. 4. A simple network diagram.

In this network there are three paths:

1. 1—3—8—9, and the time involved is $6 + 10 + 12 = 28$.

2. 1—2—4—5—7—8—9, and the time involved is
$4 + 3 + 4 + 8 + 6 + 12 = 37$.

3. 1—2—6—7—8—9 and the time involved is $4 + 7 + 5 + 6 + 12 = 34$.

The critical path, therefore, is path 2, where the total time involved is 37. (Note that the time involved may be any unit of time, e.g. hours, days, weeks, months, etc.)

It will be seen that the time in critical path 2 exceeds that for paths 1 and 3 by 9 and 3 respectively. This difference in time between non-critical paths and critical paths is known as 'slack' or 'float'.

The critical path can change where reductions in time are made in the current critical path or increases in time in the current non-critical paths. For example, if the time involved in activity 5—7 could be reduced to 4, the total time involved in path 2 would become 33 and, in consequence, path 3 with a total time of 34 would be the new critical path.

The preparation of a complex network diagram is an involved operation requiring the co-operation, under the direction of the operational research executive, of the other technicians concerned.

In a relatively simple project such as the building of a house, the preparation of a network diagram calls for a high degree of skill and knowledge. Assume, for example, that the only activities necessary for the building of a house are as follows:

(a) Obtain bricks
(b) Obtain timber
(c) Obtain electrics
(d) Obtain piping and sanitary ware
(e) Dig foundations
(f) Concreting
(g) Dig drains
(h) Lay drains
(i) Erect shell to first floor
(j) Joists
(k) Complete shell
(l) Roof timber
(m) Wiring to ground floor
(n) Plumbing to ground floor
(o) Wiring to first floor
(p) Glazing
(q) Plumbing to first floor
(r) Roof tiling
(s) Plasterwork
(t) Paint work

Many of the 20 activities listed above can be done concurrently. For instance, whilst the foundations are being dug the bricks and timber, at least, can be ordered. The wiring and plumbing work may also be carried out at the same time. Of course, it will be evident that certain activities cannot be undertaken until certain others are effected, e.g. roof tiling cannot be commenced until the shell has been completed and the roof timbers affixed.

The network diagram in Fig. 5 has been devised for building the house:

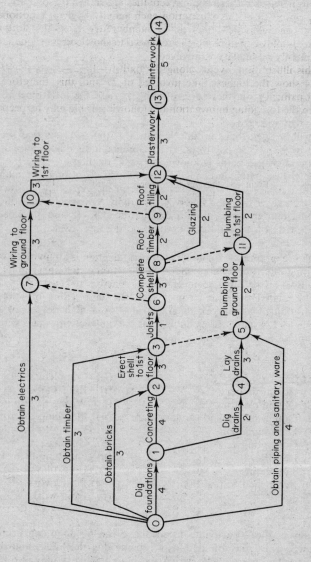

Fig. 5. A network diagram divised for building the house.

In this network diagram the 20 activities are shown by solid arrows, and for the purposes of this illustration each activity is given a notional time number. The activities meet at 15 numbered events; the dotted lines indicate dummy activities which are drawn to show correct sequencing and consequently no activity is involved.

In this illustration, events along the path 0—1—2—3—6—8—9—12—13—14 show the highest time involved of 27 and, this, therefore, is the critical path.

From the foregoing information the following Table may be prepared:

TABLE

Path	Event	Previous Event	Time	Earliest Time	Latest Time	Slack
A	14	13	5	17	27	10
	13	12	3	12	22	10
	12	10	3	9	19	10
	10	7	3	6	16	10
	7	0	3	3	13	10
B	14	13	5	19	27	8
	13	12	3	14	22	8
	12	9	2	11	19	8
	9	8	2	9	17	8
	8	6	3	7	15	8
	6	3	1	4	12	8
	3	0	3	3	11	8
C	14	13	5	22	27	5
	13	12	3	17	22	5
	12	9	2	14	19	5
	9	8	2	12	17	5
	8	6	3	10	15	5
	6	3	1	7	12	5
	3	2	3	6	11	5
	2	0	3	3	8	5
D	14	13	5	27	27	0
	13	12	3	22	22	0
	12	9	2	19	19	0
	9	8	2	17	17	0
	8	6	3	15	15	0
	6	3	1	12	12	0
	3	2	3	11	11	0
	2	1	4	8	8	0
	1	0	4	4	4	0
E	14	13	5	25	27	2
	13	12	3	20	22	2
	12	8	2	17	19	2
	8	6	3	15	17	2
	6	3	1	12	14	2
	3	2	3	11	13	2
	2	1	4	8	10	2
	1	0	4	4	6	2

Path	Event	Previous Event	Time	Earliest Time	Latest Time	Slack
F	14	13	5	21	27	6
	13	12	3	16	22	6
	12	11	2	13	19	6
	11	5	2	11	17	6
	5	4	3	9	15	6
	4	1	2	6	12	6
	1	0	4	4	10	6
G	14	13	5	16	27	11
	13	12	3	11	22	11
	12	11	2	8	19	11
	11	5	2	6	17	11
	5	0	4	4	15	11

There are seven paths through the network in this illustration. For the sake of convenience these paths have been lettered A, B, C, D, E, F, and G. As has already been stated, the critical path is that path which shown the longest time required for completion, in this case Path D in the tabulation.

The 'Latest Time' column indicates the latest time at which an event can occur. On the critical path the latest time at which events can occur coincides with the earliest time at which events can occur. On non-critical paths the latest time at which events can occur are, of course, related to the relevant times and events on the critical path.

Where a reduction in completion time of the project is contemplated, efforts to this end should be concentrated on reducing the critical-path time.

It is important to realize that the CPA technique takes account of the optimum use of resources from the time aspect only; the financial implications are not taken into account.

Program Evaluation and Review Technique (PERT). This technique was adopted independently by the U.S. Navy to schedule, progress and ensure completion on the target date of the Polaris building programme. Whilst PERT and CPA were developed independently and for different purposes, their subsequent development has been along similar lines and they are now basically the same (in fact, the terms are now often used interchangeably).

Resource Allocation and Multi Project Scheduling (RAMPS). This technique was developed by an American company and is more recent than CPA or PERT. Basically it involves a system of allocating resources by means of network diagrams whereby the best allocation of resources over various projects and the optimum level of the resources may be estimated by management.

CHAPTER 32

MISCELLANEOUS

Foreign Exchange. In businesses involving numerous transactions in foreign currency it is necessary to distinguish those payable in *sterling* (although invoiced in foreign currency) from those payable in *foreign currency*. Hence, the former will be entered in the books in the usual way, the foreign currency equivalent where applicable entered by way of Memorandum only. As to the transactions involving receipts and payments in terms of foreign currency, the Day Books and Ledgers will be ruled with two columns on each side, one for foreign currency and one for sterling. The invoices will be entered in the foreign currency column and converted into sterling at parity or other suitable rate. Alternatively, the sterling column may be completed by insertion of the actual sterling figure when the payment is made. Unless the latter method is adopted, there will usually be a difference between the sterling figure so converted and that arising upon payment, such difference being transferred to a Difference on Exchange Account or Profit and Loss on Exchange Account.

In many instances, a trade will enter into a forward exchange contract whereby a banker arranges to supply sterling for foreign currency or *vice versa* at a rate of exchange determined, not at the time the delivery of the sterling or foreign currency is made, but at the time the **arrangement** is made, e.g. an English trader may have sold goods to a French trader, payment for which is to be made in three months' time. The former may assure himself of the precise amount of sterling he is to receive at the end of three months by entering into a forward exchange contract with his banker *immediately*, under which the latter undertakes to acquire French francs and supply sterling at the date required at a rate of exchange fixed at the date of making the arrangement.

In order to ascertain the true position in these circumstances, the trader should convert the foreign currency at the ruling rate of exchange as if the position had not been secured by the forward exchange transaction; and record the difference arising from the forward exchange transaction, thus affording information both as to (i) the profit or loss that would have resulted if no forward exchange transaction had taken place; and as to (ii) the profit of loss on the forward exchange contract.

Where there are numerous accounts involving foreign currency, the provision for loss (if any) may be made by taking the *total* sterling value against the *total* currency value, thus dealing with the situation as a whole instead of considering separately each individual balance.

Illustration 1

Addingham sold goods to Montreux Frères payable in francs. The invoice amounted to 12,750 francs, the rate of exchange being 8.50 to £. Upon remittance the banker credited Addingham with the proceeds of the francs, the sterling equivalent being £1,508·88, i.e. 12,750 francs at 8.45 to £.

No arrangement had been made for forward exchange.

Show the Ledger Account of Montreux Frères in the seller's book.

MONTREUX FRÈRES

	Francs	Rate	Sterling		Francs	Rate	Sterling
			£p				£p
Goods . .	12,750	8·50	1,500·00	Remittance	12,750	8·45	1,508·88
Profit and Loss on Exchange Account .			8·88				
	12,750		£1,508·88		12,750		£1,508·88

Normally, the ultimate difference in exchange will be ascertained at the end of the accounting period.

Illustration 2

Same facts as above, except that Montreux Frères pay by two remittances of 4,000 francs at 8·55 and 8,750 at 8·48.

Show the Ledger Account of Montreux Frères in the seller's books.

MONTREUX FRÈRES

	Francs	Rate	Sterling		Francs	Rate	Sterling
			£p				£p
Goods . .	12,750	8·50	1,500·00	Remittance .	4,000	8·55	(a) 467·84
				Remittance .	8,750	8·48	(b) 1,031·84
				Profit and Loss on Exchange Account			0·32
	12,750		£1,500·00		12,750		£1,500·00

If the difference in exchange were transferred on the occasion of each remittance, the foregoing account would show: (a) a loss of £2·75, and (b) a profit of £2·43. Similar principles apply where the English trader is a debtor.

Illustration 3

The Paris agents of a London firm, having collected certain moneys on behalf of their principals from French debtors, have in hand a sum of 42,500 francs. In the London books this amount of currency is converted into sterling at 8·50 to £.

On instructions, the agents purchase 1,600 French 8 per cent bonds of 25·00 francs each (nominal) at $99\frac{1}{2}$ per cent, of which they sell 960 bonds at 102 per cent, remitting the proceeds to their principals, the rate of exchange being 8·48 to £.

Shortly afterwards the London firm make up their books, the then current rate of exchange being 8·50 to £. Show the accounts the London

PARIS AGENTS

		Francs	Rate	Sterling				Francs	Rate	Sterling
Balance	b/d	42,500	8·50	£p 5,000·00	Purchase of Bonds			39,800	8·48	£p 4,693·40
Sale of Bonds		24,960	8·48	2,943·40	Cash			24,960	8·48	2,943·40
Profit on Exchange			8·48	11·05	Balance		c/d	2,700	8·50	317·65
		67,460		£7,954·45				67,460		7,954·45
Balance	b/d	2,700	8·50	317·65						

FRENCH EIGHT PER CENT BONDS

		No.	Nominal Francs	Price Francs	Rate	Sterling			No.	Nominal Francs	Price Francs	Rate	Sterling
Purchase of Bonds		1,600	40,000	39,800	8·48	£p 4,693·40	Sale of Bonds		960	24,000	24,960	8·48	£p 2,943·40
Profit on Bonds				1,080	8·48	127·36	Balance	c/d	640	16,000	15,920	8·48	1,877·36
		1,600	40,000	40,880		£4,820·76			1,600	40,000	40,880		£4,820·76
Balance	b/d	640	16,000	15,920	8·48	1,877·36	Balance	c/d	640	16,000	15,920	8·50	1,872·94
							Loss on Exchange						4·42
		640	16,000	15,920		£1,877·36			640	16,000	15,920		£1,877·36
Balance	b/d	640	16,000	15,920	8·50	£1,872·94							

[1] The net result is a profit of £122·94, i.e. £127·36 less £4·42. The amount of £4·42 is a loss of $\frac{0\cdot92}{8\cdot50}$ of £1,877·36.

[2] The proportion of Bonds at cost (ignoring market value), viz $\frac{64}{160}$ of 39,800 francs = 15,920 francs. [See Note 3, p. 3204.]

If the detail shown in p. 3201 is not required, the account may be constructed as follows:

FRENCH EIGHT PER CENT BONDS

	No.	Nominal Francs	Sterling		No.	Nominal Francs	Sterling
Purchases	1,600	40,000	£p 4,693·40	Sale	960	24,000	£p 2,943·40
Profit			122·94	Balance ... c/d	640[1]	16,000	1,872·94
	1,600	40,000	£4,816·34		1,600	40,000	£4,816·34
Balance ... b/d	640	16,000	1,872·94				

[1] i.e. $\frac{64}{160}$ of 39,800 francs at 8·50 = 15,920 francs at 8·50

NOTES. If the shares had been valued at *par*, the balance would be $\frac{64}{160}$ of 40,000 = 16,000 francs at 8·50.

2. If the valuation in (1) had been made *ignoring* rate of exchange, the balance would be 16,000 francs at 8·48.

3. If the shares had been valued at *cost*, ignoring rate of exchange, the balance would be $\frac{64}{160}$ [i.e. $\frac{2}{5}$] of £4,693·40 = £1,877·36. This is the same as $\frac{2}{5}$ of 39,800 francs at 8·48, as shown in the French Eight per Cent Bonds Account marked [2] on page 3203.

firm would keep to record these transactions, disclosing the profits or losses on the investment and on the foreign exchange fluctuations. Ignore expenses.

Forward Exchange. If the trader had entered into a forward exchange transaction with the banker, the position would be modified according to the rate so arranged. The accounting entries would be the same as previously outlined, together with those necessary to record the profit or loss by reason of having covered in advance the conversion of his foreign currency. The entries may therefore be summarized.

1. Debit Foreign Currency Suspense Account in sterling at the rate ruling at the date of receipt and credit customer therewith.

2. Credit or debit the customer so far as relates to the particular remittance to close the account, transferring the amount to Profit and Loss on Exchange Account.

So far as the entries are similar to those outlined in the case where the trader has not entered into a forward exchange transaction except that in (1) the debit is to Foreign Currency Suspense Account instead of cash or bank.

3. Debit bank and credit Foreign Currency Suspense Account with the proceeds of the foreign currency at the rate of exchange *previously* agreed upon between the trader and the banker when the forward exchange transaction was negotiated.

4. Close the Foreign Currency Suspense Account to Profit or Loss on Forward Exchange Account.

Illustration 4

Serra Frères owe Johnson 17,000 francs, rate of exchange upon the date of sale being 8·50 francs to £. On the same date Johnson entered into a forward exchange contract at 8·25 to £. When Serra Frères remitted the rate of exchange was 8·75 to £. Show accounts in Johnson's books. (See p. 3206.)

Superannuation Schemes. Many businesses now have in operation schemes whereby superannuation and pensions are provided for when employees retire at a certain age. In order to provide against hardship in the case of a person dying or ceasing to be employed, arrangements are made for payment of a lump sum to the estate of the deceased, or to the ex-employee.

The schemes vary considerably in detail and in a great number of cases arrangements are made with leading assurance offices whereby in consideration of an annual premium, the liability for implementing the scheme is taken over by the assurance office.

Where the employer elects to take responsibility himself without arrangements with an assurance office the accounting will vary, as stated, but the essential principle is the same, viz. by having a nucleus fund of income-bearing investments, followed by annual or other periodical contributions by both employer and employees, a reasonably certain income

SERRA FRÈRES

	Francs	Rate	Sterling		Francs	Rate	Sterling
			£p				£p
Goods	17,000	8·50	2,000·00	Remittance	17,000	8·75	1,942·86
				Profit and Loss on Exchange Account			57·14
	17,000		£2,000·00		17,000		£2,000·00

BANK

	Francs	Rate	Sterling				
			£p				
Foreign Currency Suspense Account			2,060·61				

FOREIGN CURRENCY SUSPENSE

	Francs	Rate	Sterling		Francs	Rate	Sterling
			£p				£p
Serra Frères	17,000	8·75	1,942·86	Bank	17,000	8·25	2,060·61
Profit and Loss on Forward Exchange Account			117·75				
	17,000		£2,060·61		17,000		£2,060·61

is derived from which to provide the payments and augment the fund. Special arrangements are required in the early years of a scheme for the older employees who will not have the opportunity to pay in for a sufficiently long period of years to benefit.

Perodically, a revaluation will be taken of the actuarial risk involved (similar to the actuarial valuation of an assurance company) and the fund adjusted accordingly.

The contributions made by employers and employees under, and in accordance with, a scheme approved by the Inland Revenue under Sect. 208., Income and Corporation Taxes Act 1970 (abbreviated to T.A. 1970) will be allowed as admissible charges against their respective profits for taxation purposes. To obtain such approval, the main conditions are:

1. The Superannuation Fund is created under a Trust that is irrevocable and trustees appointed.
2. The *sole* (or main) object is to provide superannuation for employees (widows, children, or dependants).
3. The employer contributes to the fund.
4. The scheme is recognized both by the employer and employees.

Application for official approval must be made *in writing* by the trustees of the fund before the end of the year of assessment, supported by a certified copy of the Trust Deed and two copies of the rules agreed thereunder. Investment income of an approved fund is exempted from Tax.

Illustration 5

Under the rules of the Engee Company Staff Superannuation Fund a member, when he becomes superannuated, is entitled to an annuity, based on the amount standing to his credit.

The Annuity and General Funds are kept separate, and interest received on investments is apportioned between the funds in proportion to the mean of the opening and closing balance for the year (*before* crediting such interest). Any surplus (or deficiency) on the Annuity funds enures to (or has to be borne by), the General Fund, and for this purpose a valuation of the liabilities for the annuities is made every three years.

From the following data show the Annuity Fund and General Fund for the years 19.7 and 19.8.

Ignore Tax deductions or repayments.

	19.7 £	19.8 £
Balance at 1st January 19.7—		
Annuity Fund, £9,000		
General Fund, £87,000		
Interest on Investments	5,000	5,400
Contributions of Employer and Employees	9,000	8,200
Payments to Annuitants	1,000	1,200
Amounts standing to the credit of Employees who became super-		
annuated during the year	3,000	2,200

A valuation was taken on 31st December 19.7, and showed the liability for current annuities at £12,000.

ANNUITY FUND

19.7 Dec. 31			£	19.7 Jan. 1		b/d	£ 9,000
	Cash—Annuitants		1,000		Balance		
	Balance, per Valuation	c/d	12,000	Dec. 31	General Fund, re Employees Superannuated		3,000
					Interest on Investments ($\frac{1}{10}$)		500
					General Fund for Deficiency		500
			£13,000				£13,000
19.8 Dec. 31	Cash—Annuitants		1,200	19.8 Jan. 1	Balance	b/d	12,000
	Balance	c/d	13,600	Dec. 31	General Fund, re Employees Superannuated		2,200
					Interest on Investments ($\frac{1}{6}$)		600
			£14,800				£14,800
				19.9 Jan. 1	Balance	b/d	13,600

GENERAL FUND

19.7 Dec. 31			£	19.7 Jan. 1		b/d	£ 87,000
	Annuity Fund— Transfer thereto for Superannuated Employees		3,000		Balance		
				Dec. 31	Contributions		9,000
	Annuity Fund— Transfer re Deficiency		500		Interest on Investments ($\frac{9}{10}$)		4,500
	Balance	c/d	97,000				
			£100,500				£100,500
19.8 Dec. 31	Annuity Fund— Transfer thereto for Superannuated Employees		2,200	19.8 Jan. 1	Balance	b/d	97,000
				Dec. 31	Contributions		8,200
	Balance	c/d	107,800		Interest on Investments ($\frac{8}{9}$)		4,800
			£110,000				£110,000
				19.9 Jan. 1	Balance	b/d	107,800

Note. *Apportionment of Interest:*

	ANNUITY FUND 19.7 £		19.8 £		GENERAL FUND 19.7 £		19.8 £
Opening	9,000		12,000		87,000		97,000
Closing (9,000 +3,000−1,000)	11,000	(12,000+2,200 −1,200)	13,000	(87,000+9,000 −3,000)	93,000	(97,000+8,200 −2,200)	103,000
	2)20,000		2)25,000		2)180,000		2)200,000
Mean	£10,000		£12,500		£90,000		£100,000
	(a)		(c)		(b)		(d)

19.7   *Interest* $= \dfrac{a}{a+b} \times 5{,}000$

$$= \dfrac{10}{100} \times 5{,}000 = £500$$

$Interest = \dfrac{b}{a+b} \times 5{,}000$

$$= \dfrac{90}{100} \times 5{,}000 = £4{,}500$$

19.8   *Interest* $= \dfrac{c}{c+d} \times 5{,}400$

$$= \dfrac{12\frac{1}{2}}{112\frac{1}{2}} \left(\tfrac{1}{9}\right) \times 5{,}400 = £600$$

$Interest = \dfrac{d}{c+d} \times 5{,}400$

$$= \dfrac{100}{112\frac{1}{2}} \left(\tfrac{8}{9}\right) \times 5{,}400 = £4{,}800$$

Illustration 6

The Superannuation Fund of Elbee Co., Ltd., commenced in 19.1 under an approved Trust Deed. All employees thereunder are to benefit. In order that due recognition should be given to length of service *prior* to the formation of the fund the company undertook to form a Reserve Fund to provide a nucleus for claims arising through the death or retirement of members who had been in the company's employment prior to 19.1. The estimated liability on this account at 1st January 19.8 was £70,000.

The following balances appeared in the books at 31st December 19.8.

	£
Contributors' Account (Balance, 1st January 19.8)	23,400
Employees' Contributions	7400
Company's Contributions	5600
Amount contributed by Company from Reserve Fund in respect of deceased employees' services prior to 19.1	3300
Claims and Withdrawals	4100
Interest on Investments (Tax credit 40%)	960
Printing and Stationery	200
Revenue Account (*Cr.*), 1st January 19.8	1,000
Investments at Cost	36,000
Cash at Bank	1,360

Interest on employee's balances amounting to £950 is to be provided out of Revenue Account; company's contributions of £600 in respect of employees who have left are to be surrendered and credited to Revenue Account under the scheme. Provision is to be made for audit of £210. Ignore tax charges at one-quarter of standard rate on withdrawals.

1. Calculate the company's liability on Reserve Fund as at 31st December 19.8, after crediting interest amounting to £2,750 on the balance of the account at the commencement of the year.

2. Prepare Revenue Account and Contributors' Account for the year to, and Balance Sheet as at, 31st December 19.8.

(1) *In Company's books:*	£
Reserve Fund, 1st January 19.8	70,000
Add Interest thereon	2,750
	72,750
Less Contribution to Superannuation Fund	3,300
Balance, 31st December 19.8	£69,450

(2) *In the books of the Trust:*

CONTRIBUTORS' ACCOUNT

19.8			£	19.8			£
Dec. 31	Cash—			Jan. 1	Balance . . . b/d		23,400
	Claims and With-			Dec. 31	Contributions—		
	drawals . .		4,100		Employees . .		7,400
	Revenue Account—				Company . .		5,600
	Transfer thereto for				Reserve Fund .		3,300
	Company's Contribu-				Revenue Account—		
	tion for Employees		600		Transfer therefrom		
	Balance . . . c/d		35,950		for Interest on Em-		
					ployees' Balances .		950
			£40,650				£40,650
				19.9			
				Jan. 1	Balance . . . b/d		35,950

REVENUE ACCOUNT

19.8			£	19.8			£
Dec. 31	Printing and Stationery .		200	Jan. 1	Balance . . . b/d		1,000
	Contributors' Account			Dec. 31	Interest on Investments—		
	Transfer thereto for				Net . . .		960
	Interest . . .		950		Tax recoverable:		
	Audit . . .		210		£1,600 at 40% .		640
	Balance . . . c/d		1,840		Contributors' Acct.—		
					Transfer therefrom for		
					Contributions sur-		
					rendered . .		600
			£3,200				£3,200
				Jan. 1	Balance . . . b/d		1,840

BALANCE SHEET AS AT 31ST DECEMBER 19.

		£			£
Contributors' Account . .		35,950	Investments at Cost . . .		36,000
Revenue Account . . .		1,840	[Market Value?]		
Reserve Fund . . .		69,450	Inland Revenue . .		640
Provision for Audit . . .		210	Cash at Bank . . .		1,360
			Company . . .		69,450
		£107,450			£107,450

Illustration 7

The Rules of a Staff Superannuation Scheme are:

1. Equal contributions by employer and member (to be credited to members' accounts).

2. The payment to a member, on retirement through age or infirmity, of an annuity *actuarially* calculated to be a value equal to the amount standing to his credit at the end of the year in which he retires.

3. The payment, to the personal representatives of a member who dies in service, of the amount standing to his credit at the *end* of the year in which the *death occurs.*

4. The payment to a contributor who leaves for any reason other than

age or infirmity, of the amount of his contributions up to the time he leaves and interest thereon credited up to the end of the *preceding* year; and the transfer of the balance on the account of such a member to the Stabilization Account.

5. The interest earned in each year to be credited to the individual members' accounts and the Annuity Fund in proportion to the balances thereof at the *beginning* of the year.

6. Fluctuations in the value of investments to be ignored, but profits and losses realized to be carried to the Stabilization Account.

7. The actuarial valuation of current annuities every three years and a transfer from (or to) the Stabilization Account to (or from) the Annuity Fund of the amount, if any, by which the valuation exceeds or is less than the Annuity Fund.

8. A supplementary contribution to the Stabilization Account of the amount, if any, required by that account to enable any necessary transfer to be made to the Annuity fund.

The Trial.Balance of the scheme at 31st December 19.. is:

	£	£
Contributors' Accounts (1st January 19..)		121,000
Annuity Fund		11,000
Contributions of Employer and Members		13,388
Investments (value at 31st December 19.., £145,221)	144,000	
Balance at Bank.	4,989	
Interest		4,752
Profit on Realization of Investments		109
Payments to Annuitants	1,260	
	£150,249	£150,249

A valuation as on 31st December 19.., showed the liability for current annuities to be £12,600.

The credit balances included in Contributors' Accounts on 1st January 19.. and members' contributions during the year of: (i) members who became entitled to annuities, (ii) members who died in the service, and (iii) members who left the service for reasons other than age or infirmity were:

	Balances, 1st January 19.. £	Members' Contributions during Year £
(i)	1,550	30
(ii)	640	32
(iii)	880	48

No payments had been made in respect of (ii) or (iii) by the end of the year. Prepare the draft Annual Accounts of the scheme for the year ended 31st December 19.., and Balance Sheet as at that date. Ignore tax and make calculations to nearest £.

CONTRIBUTORS' ACCOUNT

19.. Dec. 31			£	£	19.. Jan. 1 Dec. 31			£
	Annuity Fund for retired Members:				Jan. 1	Balance	b/d	121,000
	Bal., 1st Jan. 19..		1,550		Dec. 31	Contributions		13,388
	Interest (3·6%)		56			Interest (3·6%)		4,356
	Contributions during year		60					
				1,666				
	Decreased Members:							
	Bal., 1st Jan. 19..		640					
	Interest (3·6%)		23					
	Contributions during year		64					
				727				
	Ex-employee Mem- bers:							
	Contributions during year		48					
	Bal., 1st Jan. 19..		440					
				488				
	Stabilization A/c:							
	Interest on £880 (3·6%)			32				
	Employer's Con- tributions			488				
	Balance	c/d		135,343				
				£138,744				£138,744
					19.. Jan. 1	Balance	b/d	135,343

ANNUITY FUND

19.. Dec. 31			£	19.. Jan. 1 Dec. 31			£
	Cash—Annuitants		1,260	Jan. 1	Balance	b/d	11,000
	Balance per Valuation	c/d	12,600	Dec. 31	Interest, 3·6%		396
					Transfer from Con- tributors' Accounts		1,666
					Transfer from Stabiliza- tion Account		798
			£13,860				£13,860
				19.. Jan. 1	Balance	b/d	12,600

STABILIZATION ACCOUNT

19.. Dec. 31		£	19.. Dec. 31		£
	Transfer to Annuity Fund	798		Profit on Sale of Invest- ments	109
				Transfers from Contribu- tors' Accounts	520
				Employer's Supplement- ary Contributions (due)	169
		£798			£798

BALANCE SHEET AT 31ST DECEMBER 19..

	£		£
Contributors' Accounts . .	135,343	Investments (Market value,	
Annuity Fund (per Valuation) .	12,600	£145,221). . . .	144,000
Creditors—		Employer—	
Deceased Members £727		Supplementary Contribu-	
Ex-employee Members 488		tions	169
		Cash at Bank . . .	4,989
	1,215		
	£149,158		£149,158

Note. There are three calls on the Fund:

(*a*) An annuity to each normally retiring member (the main object of the scheme);

(*b*) A payment out to the representatives of each deceased member, not an annuity, but a lump sum cash payment;

(*c*) A payment out to an employee who leaves his employment (otherwise than by age or infirmity).

Obviously the least advantage will be to members of Class (*c*), who have returned to them (with interest) only their *own* contributions.

Clearly, the Annuity Fund dealing with class (*a*) must be administered on strict lines (hence the necessity for a periodic revaluation of the liability for current annuities); the Contributor's Accounts will be used for dealing with classes (*b*) and (*c*) without affecting the Annuity Fund; as to new liabilities under class (*a*), these must be credited to the Annuity Fund (swelling the opening balance), the *actual* payments of annuities being debited against the Fund. The balance of this Fund will, pending the revaluation, be carried forward to the succeeding year.

On the revaluation, it may be that the balance is not adequate to meet the liabilities for current annuities, and therefore in case it is not (as in the question), a draft has to be made upon the Stabilization Account (in effect, a Suspense Account). If the Fund exceeds the liability, the benefit is carried to the Stabilization Account. The Stabilization Account is built up by special gains and the amount of the employer's contributions not repaid when members leave (Class (*c*)); but this account itself may prove insufficient to meet any draft on it for the Annuity Fund, hence calling for a supplementary contribution from the employer.

The Interest is £4,752, which is 3·6 per cent on the opening balances of the Contributor's Accounts and Annuity Fund (i.e. £121,000 + £11,000 = £132,000) calculated as follows—

$$\frac{4,752}{132,000} \times 100 = \frac{4,752}{1,320} = \frac{198}{55} = 3 \cdot 6\%$$

Interest to Class (*a*), 3·6% × £1,550 = £56

Interest to Class (*b*), 3·6% × £640 = £23.

The Contributors' Account is a 'total' account and there would be separate accounts for each contributor.

FARM ACCOUNTS

Several special features arise in farm accounts, although in practice many farmer's accounts are very crude and unreliable.

The chief points are:

1. Separate 'departmental' accounts for different activities, e.g. Dairy, Crops, Fruit and Livestock rearing (subdivided as required).

2. Systems of transfers as in commerical activities, e.g. as in a garage. Typical are:

Debit to Wages and Credit to Rents of Cottages for rent-free occupation of labourers[1];

Debit to Wages and Credit to Milk, etc. Accounts for subsistence of labourers; (and family of occupier if they assist in the farm activities)[1];

Debit to Drawings and Credit to Milk, etc. Accounts for subsistence of occupier.

Debit to various crop accounts and Credit to respective Field Accounts for cost of crops raised;

Debit to Calves Account and Credit to Cows Account for calves produced (similar for sheep, pigs, poultry).

The system of rotation of crops resulting in a number of fields lying 'fallow', occasionally sown with 'fallow crops', means that a number of fields are not in full production and, as there are expenses incurred in a fallow year, these are carried forward to the producing years *less* realization of fallow crops (if any).

Where, as is customary, many transactions are on a semi-barter or set-off system, an exchange register with supporting invoices (rarely given) is required to show the true 'gross', e.g. a heifer and two pigs might be exchanged for a bull, either without cash passing at all or for a net payment or receipt.

Highly organized farms keep statistical data and registers, but the typical small farmer does not trouble to keep these, except as registered by law, e.g. Milk Marketing Board, etc. and Agistment Register.

Occasionally, heavy expenditure may be incurred on seeds and fertilizers which will be spread over a period, whilst equipment will be dealt with in the usual manner.

Other special features exist, e.g. subsidies, valuation of livestock, compensation for loss in cases of destruction of animals ordered on account of disease, e.g. foot-and-mouth disease, cost of pest control.

Particular attention must be paid to adequate insurance, some of which are of especial importance to farmers, e.g. anthrax, loss of cattle through straying, etc. Some farmers do not (because of the high premium) insure tractors, but place to Reserve a certain sum each year to cover losses.

Two technical features of farm accounting are valuation of livestock and manurial rights, but these are for farm valuation experts.

---

[1] If farm is in charge of bailiff, similar entries would be made; and also analogous entries for Heat and Light (debit Wages; credit to Farm Heat and Light Account).

Illustration 8

CATTLE TRADING ACCOUNT FOR THE YEAR ENDED ....

	No.	£	£		No.	£	£
Opening Stock . .	500		42,000	Sales . . .	190		56,300
Purchases . . .	250		27,000	Cattle Slaughter (Sales			
Births . . 69				of Meat) . .	60	24,000	
Less Stillborn . 3	66			Sale of Hides . .		4,200	
—				Sales of Offal . .		3,600	
							31,800
Foodstuffs—				Sale of Carcases	4		170
Opening Stocks		800		Closing Stock .	562		?
Concentrates .		1,200					
Hay (transferred)		2,700					
Crop and Pasture							
(transferred). .		5,200					
		9,900					
Less Closing Stocks .		900					
			9,000				
Balance . . c/d			10,270				
	816		£88,270		816		£88,270
Labour (transferred) .			1,900	Balance . . b/d			10,270
Grinding . .			300				
Repairs . .			400				
Depreciation . .			350				
Insurance . .			150				
Allocation of General							
Expenses . .			2,000				
Profit on Cattle for							
Year to General							
Profit and Loss Ac-							
count . .			5,170				
			£10,270				£10,270

Notes. 1. Labour transferred—credited to Wages.

2. Repairs, Depreciation, and General Expenses transferred—credited to the respective accounts; this should include proportion of Rent, even if farm owned by the occupier. Rent Account will be debited in the first instance with the total rent, credit landlord, if rented; if not, the credit will be to owner-occupier, with basis of a fair letting value. (In fixing this figure, regard will be had to whether the farmer as 'tenant' is charged with cost of Repairs, Rates, etc.)

3. There should be a subsidiary account, if number and size of transactions warrant it, in respect of Sales of Meat, etc., a transfer being made to the debit representing the cost of cattle slaughtered. A further subdivision of Calves, Cows, etc., could be made, a transfer being necessary to debit of Calves, credit of Cows on birth.

4. Hay is transferred from Hay Account, except to the extent of Hay *purchased.*

5. Insurance is either transferred from General Insurance, or, as is likely, if separate insurance, directly charged.

The Ministry of Agriculture, Fisheries and Food have prepared excellent publications concerning Farm Management, Education, Finance and Statistics. Many of these are priced publications[1] and may be obtained from Her Majesty's Stationery Office bookshops; others are free, and single copies can be obtained only from the Ministry.[2] The free publica-

[1] Details of all of the publications prepared by the Ministry of Agriculture, Fisheries and Food are contained in Goverment Publications, Agricultural and Food, Sectional List No. 1.

[2] Free publications (single copies) specified in Sectional List No. 1 can be obtained only from the Ministry of Agriculture, Fisheries and Food (Publications), Tolcarne Drive, Pinner, Middlesex, HA5 2DT.

tions include the following Business Records Leaflets:

1. *Feed Recording:* Short Term Leaflet No. 49.
2. *Guide for the Completion of N.A.A.S./N.F.U.*[1] *Farm Business Records:* S.T.L. No. 50.
3. *Keeping Financial Records:* S.T.L. No. 48.
4. *Office Organization for Farm and Horticultural Businesses:* S.T.L. No. 47.

The N.A.A.S./N.F.U. Farm Business Records Book, available from N.F.U. Secretaries, is a nationally agreed system of farm recording. The Record Book is divided into three sections: (A) Physical Records; (B) Financial Records; (C) Variable costs for the Calculation of Gross Margins. The National Farmers' Union of Scotland assisted by the Department of Agriculture and Fisheries, the Scottish College of Agriculture and a working party of Accountants (comprising three members of the Scottish C.A. Institute and two members of the Association of Certified Accountants) introduced the Scottish Farm Business Records Book in 1965. The Scottish Record Book is divided into two parts—Part I: Basic and Physical Records; and Part II: Financial Summaries (Standard Form of Account). Both types of Record Books have been designed to cover as much detail and as many circumstances as possible; consequently, in the case of smaller farmers, only certain of the records will be applicable. It must be made clear:

(i) that it is the farmer himself (or a secretarial service employed by him) who is responsible for keeping the required records[2];

(ii) that generally the accountant will prepare the standard form of account and assist in completing other relevant records;

(iii) that a professional valuer will often be engaged to value livestock, crops and stores at the end of the financial year;

(iv) that a farm management adviser might use the accounts and records for analysis purposes and in order to advise the farmer on future policies and plans.

VENDOR'S GUARANTEES OF DEBTORS AND CREDITORS TAKEN OVER BY PURCHASER

A vendor may guarantee to the purchaser that:

(*a*) Debtors taken over will not produce less than a certain *minimum* sum and/or that

(*b*) Creditors taken over will be settled at a certain *maximum* sum.

---

[1] N.A.A.S. is the National Agricultural Advisory Service; N.F.U. is the National Farmers' Union.

[2] A scheme is operated by the U.K. Government whereby grants are paid to farmers for a period of three years towards the cost of keeping farm business records. Contributions attaching to eligibility for the grant are that the Records Book must be kept on behalf of the farmer by a secretarial services organization and a certificate must be submitted at the year end to the effect that the records have been so kept. Only one grant (for a three-year period) can be obtained.

The interpretation of such a guarantee is a *legal* matter (a fact that a candidate should always state) requiring guidance from a legal adviser. Subject to indicating this point, the candidate should work out the problem according to the following generally accepted principles:

1. If the guarantee is contained in one document, the inference is that it must be taken as a *whole* so that the purchaser cannot obtain benefit from (*a*) by reason of receiving more than the minimum and charge up the loss arising in (*b*) by reason of the creditors being settled at a higher figure, and vice versa.

2. Where a person is included in both the Debtors and Creditors and a part-settlement arises by set-off, the sum set off must be regarded, as the case may be, as a receipt or payment, e.g.—

X is a debtor for £50 and a Creditor for £20, paying on account £25; if the £20 is used as a set-off, the transaction is regarded as a receipt from X (debtor) £45 and a payment to X (creditor) £20, leaving a net balance as a Debtor of £5.

3. As, in general terms, a creditor may in absence of agreed appropriation, set off a payment against any particular item owing by a debtor, even a statute-barred debt, the purchaser would naturally credit receipts to debts incurred since the purchase of the business and not to the debt taken over, so that the guarantee should embody some safeguard to the vendor of the business in this respect, as well as in respect of bad debts by reason of negligence in collection.

Where the old ledgers are continued by the purchaser, schedules should be prepared showing precisely the amounts involved.

There is no need to separate cash received from, or paid to, debtors and creditors, but discounts, allowances, bad debts, etc. must be so kept.

A difficulty arises where a provision for bad debts and discounts exists, as the purchaser may choose to make a provision differing from that made by the vendor; but this is not logical, the true provision being the excess of book debts transferred over the *guaranteed* amount. (The nominal amounts of book debts in the Sales Ledger will not be disturbed.) Similar principles apply to creditors in respect of discounts.

Illustration 9

Vendor, on selling his business, undertook (in one agreement) that the debtors per the Sales Ledger amounting to £4,500 would realize £4,100, and the creditors per the Purchase Ledger amounting to £3,600 would be settled for £3,500.

The accounts revealed that the bad debts, discounts, etc., allowed the debtors were £480; and allowed by creditors £160.

State the amount due by the vendor in respect of his guarantee.

It is assumed that, in all respects, the purchaser of the business has carried out his part of the bargain, and that all the taken-over debtors and creditors have been fully dealt with, i.e. no outstandings remain.

The vendor is liable for £80, being the excess of the bad debts, etc., over the provision of £400 (£4,500–£4,100); but can claim the gain of £60 in respect of the profit on settlement of the creditors.

		£
The purchaser has lost by Bad Debts, etc.: £4,100−£4,020 the latter being cash received [£4,500−£480]	. =	80
The purchaser has gained by Discounts: £3,500−£3,440 the latter being cash paid [£3,600−£160]	. =	60
	Net	£20

If there were separate agreements (assuming they did not provide for the vendor claiming a gain on settlement of debtors or creditors), the vendor would be liable for £80 loss on debtors without being able to set off the gain on creditors.

EXAMINATION HINTS

The reader who has worked carefully through the text should find himself well equipped to deal successfully with the problems arising in the examinations. Unfortunately, candidates do not spend a sufficient amount of time really mastering one type of problem, invariably skimming over the text (and 'auditing' the illustrations instead of working them out), hoping to 'revise' during the last few weeks or days prior to the examination, such work usually being carried out in a frenzied effort to cover the whole ground in a very short period, and invariably succeeding only in creating a state of mental confusion.

No amount of exhortation and outlining a long list of rules will be of the slightest avail unless, during the period of his study, the student has succeeded in acquiring the rules by practice and experience. Most candidates have the benefit of the guidance afforded them by the several first-class correspondence courses, but usually candidates do not avail themselves fully of such help, particularly that given both in the study notes and through the corrected exercises or tests, which are invariably accompanied by carefully prepared models or solutions.

Hence, the rules given below are intended to remind the reader of the more important points to be observed, all of which have been brought to his notice during the course of his study. These rules are not exhaustive and merely set out the more fundamental points.

1. Scan the entire examination paper to see the full extent of it; this is most important. It is not unknown for an examination candidate to discover too late that another question appeared on the other side of a page.

2. Pay particular attention to the directions given concerning the number of questions to be attempted. In certain examinations the papers set are divided into sections and only a specified number of questions in each section is required to be attempted. It need hardly be mentioned that any solution submitted in excess of the required number will earn no additional marks and in fact will normally be entirely disregarded by the examiner. A further point worth mentioning in this connection is that the examiner 'draws the line', so to speak, after the required number of solutions; where excess answers have been submitted he does not mark all

and select the required number which gained the highest marks. Consequently, in these cases it could be that solutions disregarded by the examiner are those which have earned higher marks than others. The motto is READ THE INSTRUCTIONS CAREFULLY and ABIDE BY THEM.

3. The time factor in examinations must be mentioned because it is considered by the author to be of almost paramount importance; so many candidates have failed their examinations owing to an apparent unawareness of this. It may safely be said that an examiner, in appraising a candidate's paper, is concerned primarily in ascertaining whether or not the candidate has displayed a good overall knowledge of his subject. How can this be demonstrated by the candidate if he has failed to attempt all the required number of questions? It cannot be overstressed that the examination candidate must, in order to give a good account of himself, plan the exact number of minutes he can devote to the solution of each question and ADHERE STRICTLY TO THE PLAN. The following is submitted as a safe and workable examination time plan:

Most examinations state after each question the marks allotted. Assume the total marks to be 100 and the time allowed three hours. Reserve five minutes for scanning the paper and ten minutes for final revision of all your solutions. The net available time is thus three hours *less* fifteen minutes, or 165 minutes. Consequently, the time to be spent on attaining one mark is $165 \div 100 = 1 \cdot 65$ minutes. Once this, unit-mark time factor, has been ascertained, it is simply a matter of multiplying it by the number of marks assigned to each question. This formula should be applied to a question only when it is being attempted. Thus, a question carrying twenty marks should be assigned $1 \cdot 65$ minutes $\times 20 = 33$ minutes. Say, for example, that this question were attempted at 9.15 a.m., then mark boldly at the side of the question '9.48.'; that is time up for that question, and irrespective of the stage reached in the solution move on to another question and apply the same rules. Do not be tempted to deviate from your plan. Of course, you will probably complete certain answers with time to spare, but implement your plan to the final question. Any surplus time, apart from the ten minutes reserved for revision at the end, can be devoted to further work on incomplete solutions. Students are often unaware of the fact that the marks for the first half of each question are more easily earned than those for the second half. In short, it can be stated that out of a paper containing five questions to be answered it is far easier to secure 60 per cent for the whole paper by gaining twelve marks for each than by attempting three questions only and endeavouring to gain twenty marks for each.

4. Answers should be outlined in a concise and readily readable form. This will be a help to the candidate himself in revising his answer (and amending if necessary) and also will facilitate the work of the examiner (giving him a chance to award fair marks). The judicious use of showing a vital point in BLOCK letters will help.

5. Read the question carefully; it is not possible to generalize, but often it will help the student if he runs over the question broadly to see what the examiner WANTS THE CANDIDATE TO DO, before going into the matter in

detail. Frequently, the details are somewhat involved, and the candidate will often find it easier to make a start in the right direction, if he knows what the examiner is asking him to do.

6. The candidate must always remember that mere copy earns no marks, and as his objective is to gain in the *time available* as many marks as he possibly can in the aggregate, he must rigidly avoid wasting time in perfecting work which is not 'productive.' In this connection the examiner will not object to the employment of reasonable abbreviations so long as he knows what they mean.

7. It is the author's experience that candidates are singularly lacking in their knowledge of quick mental arithmetic, and they show a deplorable lack of practice in the exercise of this important factor, involving a very serious inroad into the time available to them in the examination. Where necessary, reasonable approximation may generally be made, but the *basis* of a computation or calculation, and the rough workings, MUST be shown.

8. In most examination problems, the candidate cannot gain anything like full marks unless he gives the necessary assumptions, comments and qualifications, and this applies with particular force to the 'inexact' type of question, where, deliberately or otherwise, the examiner is vague and ambiguous in the wording of his question. It is at times almost a mental feat to understand what is required. No objection can be raised to a question where the ambiguity merely related to the use of a single word, unless its employment makes the question difficult to understand, as the candidate is entitled in such circumstances to make reasonable assumptions and, having stated them, proceed with his answer accordingly. It must also be remembered that, in certain cases, the vague question is the best method of testing the candidate's ability. In general, however, it is submitted that the candidate is entitled to know what is required of him without having to tussle with ambiguity of language.

9. Where a problem involves a purely legal point, the answer should give effect to it. If the question gives facts which are identifiable with an established point of law (whether arising by Statute or Case law) the candidate must proceed accordingly, supporting his answer by reference to the Statute or decided case. Where, however, the point of law is one that is capable of different interpretations (in the absence of authority), the candidate should answer according to his view of such particular legal point, but emphasizing by way of note other possible solutions and indicating that in practice legal guidance might have to be obtained.

10. As is known, the examiner gives due credit for style, layout, knowledge of English, etc., and, therefore, the candidate should make his answers with due regard to these matters. Apart from this reason, the candidate should realize that it is in his own interest to pay particular attention to alignment and spacing. (Most candidates persist in placing writing too near to figures. There should be ample space, as often the candidate will find during the course of his answer that he requires one or more inset columns for his figures.)

11. In dealing with contentious matters a fair sense of neutrality should be observed, calling for a reasoned and balanced marshalling of the

arguments on both sides, expressed in language that is clear, concise, and relevant.

AWARD WINNING ACCOUNTS

Lindustries Limited, an industrial holding company with operating subsidiaries in the United Kingdom and abroad, was joint winner of the Accountant Annual Awards for 1977. Kind permission has been granted by Lindustries Limited to reproduce extracts from the award winning annual report and accounts. Due to shortage of space reproduction herein is restricted to two items from the Directors' Report, the full accounts and source and application of funds. Students will derive benefit from a study of the extracted data as follow:

(1) Turnover, Profit and Dividends

Group turnover, profit and dividends are shown in the consolidate profit and loss account. The turnover and profit for the year of each of the divisions of the Group is shown below together with the comparative figures for the 18 month financial period ended on 3 April 1976 and for the final 12 months of that period.

	12 months ended 2 April 1977 £000	12 months ended 3 April 1976 £000	18 months ended 3 April 1976 £000
Turnover			
Engineering	31,763	29,574	44,936
Polymer	14,856	11,537	17,790
Textile	19,693	14,894	22,389
Overseas	12,652	14,391	19,772
	78,964	70,396	104,887
Profit			
Engineering	2,247	1,670	2,059
Polymer	883	568	967
Textile	2,185	2,157	3,118
Overseas	1,207	1,054	1,555
	6,522	5,449	7,699
Investment income	186	50	88
Interest payable	(499)	(625)	(1,065)
Group profit	6,209	4,874	6,722

(2) Inflation Adjusted Accounts

As final agreement is still awaited on the manner in which accounts should be prepared to reflect the effects of inflation, the following information has been produced in accordance with the guidance of the Stock Exchange:

(a) The group profit of £6,209,000 for the financial year ended 2 April 1977 would be reduced to £1,866,000 on a current cost accounting basis by the elimination of stock holding gains of £3,386,000 and by an additional depreciation charge of £957,000 based on the current value of fixed assets other than property.

(b) The value to the business of the fixed assets other than property is calculated to be £15,179,000 compared with the net book value in the historic accounts of £7,358,000. No revaluation of the property, which is included in the historic accounts at a net book value of £9,846,000, has been attempted.

(c) The adjustment to current purchasing power of the net monetary items would give rise to a gain of £723,000, representing the diminution in real terms of the net monetary liabilities over the financial year.

Consolidated Profit and Loss Account for the financial year ended 2 April 1977
Lindustries Limited and subsidiary companies

	Notes	1977 12 months £000	1976 18 months £000
Turnover	2	78,964	104,887
Group profit	3	6,209	6,722
Share of profits of associated companies	6	396	309
Profit before taxation		6,605	7,031
Taxation	7	3,070	3,428
Profit after taxation		3,535	3,603
Attributable to minority interests		203	271
Profit attributable to Lindustries Limited before extraordinary items		3,332	3,332
Extraordinary items	8	(163)	652
Profit attributable to Lindustries Limited		3,169	3,984
Dividends	9	895	1,232
Profit for the year retained	10	2,274	2,752
Earnings per 25p ordinary share	11	17.6p	17.4p
Statement of retained profits			
Retained profit for the year		2,274	2,752
Retained profit at the beginning of the year:			
As previously reported		13,679	10,937
Prior year adjustment	12	755	745
As restated		14,434	11,682
Retained profit at the end of the year	21	16,708	14,434

Consolidated
Balance Sheet at 2 April 1977
Lindustries Limited and subsidiary companies

	Notes	1977 £000	1976 £0000
Assets employed			
Fixed assets	14	17,204	17,446
Investments	15	1,661	1,457
		18,865	18,903
Current assets:			
Stock	16	22,926	18,684
Debtors		17,991	15,525
Bank and cash balances		1,127	1,042
		42,044	35,251
Current liabilities:			
Creditors and accrued liabilities	17	14,930	12,498
Advance payments from customers		1,417	1,113
Bank overdrafts and short term loans		2,432	2,479
Taxation	18	2,180	2,069
Dividends		595	558
		21,554	18,717
Net current assets		20,490	16,534
		39,355	35,437
Deferred taxation	19	5,349	4,108
		34,006	31,329
Financed by			
Issued capital of Lindustries Limited	20	6,806	6,806
Reserves	21	21,511	19,246
		28,317	26,052
Debentures and term loans	22	5,201	4,568
Minority interests		488	709
		34,006	31,329

W. E. Luke, Director
P. A. Rippon, Director

ACCOUNTANCY

Parent Company
Balance Sheet at 2 April 1977
Lindustries Limited

	Notes	1977 £000	1976 £000
Assets employed			
Subsidiary companies	13	27,865	25,625
Fixed assets	14	1,008	1,127
Investments	15	28	42
Advance corporation tax recoverable	19	413	496
		29,314	27,290
Current assets:			
Debtors		49	62
		49	62
Current liabilities:			
Creditors and accrued liabilities		82	97
Bank overdraft and short term loans		1,085	1,737
Taxation	18	609	679
Dividends		595	558
		2,371	3,071
Net current liabilities		2,322	3,009
		26,992	24,281
Financed by			
Issued capital	20	6,806	6,806
Reserves	21	15,390	13,357
		22,196	20,163
Debentures and term loans	22	4,796	4,118
		26,992	24,281

W. E. Luke, Director
P. A. Rippon, Director

Notes on Accounts

1. **Accounting policies**

(a) *Basis of consolidation*

The consolidated accounts include the accounts of all the subsidiaries for the financial year ended 2 April 1977 and of principal associated companies in accordance with (b) below.

(b) *Associated companies*

The consolidated profit and loss account includes the Group's share of the results of the principal associated companies (note 6) and the reserves in the consolidated balance sheet include the Group's share of the post acquisition reserves of these companies (note 21). The figures are taken from the latest reliable accounts, some of which are unaudited and which are in respect of years ended on dates between 31 January 1977 and 2 April 1977. The remaining associated companies are not material and are treated as trade investments in the consolidated accounts.

(c) *Depreciation*

Depreciation is calculated in general on a straight line basis on cost or valuation. Freehold properties and long leasehold properties are depreciated at 2% per annum and short leasehold properties are amortized over the period of the lease. Depreciation on plant and equipment is at prescribed rates ranging from 5% to $33\frac{1}{3}$% per annum according to the expected life of the asset. Certain overseas companies calculate depreciation on a reducing balance basis in order to comply with local practice.

(d) *Tooling*

Expenditure on tooling, which is not directly recoverable from the customer, is written off in the year of purchase unless the tooling is expected to be in use for more than three years, in which case it is treated as plant and depreciated over three years.

(e) *Research and development*

Expenditure on research and development, which is not directly recoverable from the customer, is written off in the year in which it is incurred.

(f) *Stock and work in progress*

Stock and work in progress is valued at the lower of cost and net realisable value, after making due allowance for obsolete and slow moving items. Cost includes direct expenditure and the appropriate proportion of fixed and variable production overheads. The basis of valuation has been changed and the effect of this is explained in note 12.

(g) *Deferred taxation*

Provision is made for net tax deferred as a result of timing differences in the accounting and taxation treatment of depreciation, revaluation of properties, stock and certain provisions. Adjustments to the provision are made at the current rates of tax but the opening balance is not revalued to take account of any changes in rates of tax. The provision has been reduced by advance corporation tax recoverable against future liabilities.

(h) Grants

Government grants on the purchase of fixed assets are treated as deferred credits and transferred to profit and loss account over the expected useful lives of the assets concerned. Grants for revenue expenditure are credited to profit and loss account in the year in which the corresponding expenditure has been charged, provided the grant has been agreed.

(i) Foreign currencies

Assets and liabilities in foreign currencies are converted into sterling at rates of exchange ruling at the balance sheet date. Differences arising from changes in exchange rates are dealt with as follows:

(i) Those arising from normal trading transactions are dealt with in arriving at the Group profit.

(ii) Those arising from the conversion of foreign currency capital and reserves of subsidiary and associated companies are shown as extraordinary items in the consolidated profit and loss account (note 8).

	1977 12 months £000	1976 18 months £000

2. Turnover Turnover represents the sale of goods and services outside the Group.

3. Group profit The Group profit is shown after charging the following:

	1977 12 months £000	1976 18 months £000
Interest payable (note 4)	499	1,065
Auditors' remuneration (parent £10,000 – 1976 £8,150)	124	114
Depreciation	1,848	2,651
Emoluments of directors of Lindustries Limited (note 5)	116	198

and crediting the following:

Dividends from quoted trade investment	96	83
Other dividends and interest	90	5
	186	88

4. Interest payable

Debentures	142	233
Term loans	251	223
Bank overdrafts	106	609
	499	1,065

5. Emoluments of directors of Lindustries Limited

Fees	5	8
Other emoluments	97	139
Pension scheme contributions	10	20
Pensions	4	7
Compensation for loss of office	–	24
	116	198

Fees and other emoluments were paid as follows (1976 – annual rates):

The emoluments of the Chairman were £8,162 (1976 – £8,387) and of the highest paid director were £22,567 (1976 – £21,744). The table below shows the number of directors within the bands stated; also shown is the amount of tax at the rates ruling for 1976/77 at the top end of each band above £10,000 and the corresponding take-home pay based upon a married man without children and with no other income.

Emoluments	Tax	Take-home pay	1977 Number	1976 Number
£	£	£		
Not more than 2,500			3	5
2,501 to 5,000			1	2
7,501 to 10,000			1	1
10,001 to 12,500	5,270	7,230	–	1
12,501 to 15,000	6,991	8,009	1	1
15,001 to 17,500	8,811	8,689	3	2
17,501 to 20,000	10,686	9,314	–	–
20,001 to 22,500	12,674	9,826	–	1
22,501 to 25,000	14,749	10,251	1	1

6. Associated companies

Lindustries Limited's share of the profits of its principal associated companies has been incorporated in the consolidated profit and loss account as follows (note 1 (b)):

	1977 12 months £000	1976 18 months £000
Share of profits before tax	396	309
Taxation	135	101
	261	208
Extraordinary item – foreign exchange differences	70	8
	331	216
Dividends paid to Group companies	61	102
Profit for the year retained	270	114

On 2 October 1976 an associated company became a wholly owned subsidiary through the acquisition by the Group of the 50% shareholding not previously held.

7. Taxation

Based on profits for the year:

UK corporation tax at 52% (1976 52%)	1,284	2,488
Double taxation relief	(409)	(577)
	875	1,911
Overseas tax	867	879
Deferred taxation (note 1 (g))	1,236	618
	2,978	3,408

On share of profits of associated companies:

UK corporation tax	14	3
Overseas tax	121	98
	3,113	3,509

Adjustments in respect of previous periods:

UK corporation tax	(105)	(109)
Overseas tax	(2)	(60)
Deferred taxation (note 1 (g))	64	88
	3,070	3,428

8. Extraordinary items

Profit/(loss) on foreign exchange (note 1 (i))	(195)	652
Loss on U.S. dollar borrowings in Mexico resulting from devaluation of the peso, after deducting tax relief of £210,000 and minority interest of £85,000	(125)	—
Profit on redemption of debentures	157	—
	(163)	652

	1977 12 months £000	1976 18 months £000
9. Dividends		
Dividends paid, declared or proposed:		
Preference stock – 3·5% (1976 5·25%)	39	58
Preferred ordinary stock – 4·2% (1976 6·3%)	46	69
	85	127
Ordinary shares		
Interim paid 1·4p (1976 1st 1·2p; 2nd 2·0p)	258	589
Final proposed 3·0p (1976 2·8p)	552	516
	895	1,232
10. Profit for the year retained		
Lindustries Limited	2,033	1,009
Subsidiary companies	(29)	1,629
Associated companies	270	114
	2,274	2,752

11. Earnings per share

The calculation of earnings per 25p ordinary share is based on earnings of £3,247,000 (1976 (18 months) £3,205,000) and ordinary shares in issue at the year end of 18,422,031 (1976 18,422,031). The earnings figure is the profit attributable to Lindustries Limited before extraordinary items, £3,332,000 (1976 (18 months) £3,332,000), less preference and preferred ordinary dividends, £85,000 (1976 (18 months) £127,000).

12. Prior year adjustment

The basis of valuation of stock was changed at the beginning of the year to conform with the Statement of Standard Accounting Practice No. 9 by the inclusion of certain fixed overheads. The adjustment to the valuation of the opening stock is shown as a prior year adjustment in the profit and loss account. In resting the comparative figures for the eighteen months ended 3 April 1976 to reflect the changed basis of valuation, the profit has been increased by £10,000, and the retained profits at the beginning of the period have been increased by £745,000. The net adjustment of £755,000 has been added to the stock at 3 April 1976 in the balance sheet. In accordance with agreed practice these adjustment have no effect for taxation purposes.

13. Subsidiary companies

	1977 £000	1976 £000
Shares at cost less amounts written off	13,752	13,752
Amounts owing from subsidiaries	14,834	13,512
Dividends receivable	3,309	2,721
Amounts owing to subsidiaries	(4,030)	(4,360)
	27,865	25,625

14. Fixed assets

	Freehold property £000	Leasehold property Long leases £000	Leasehold property Short leases £000	Plant and equipment £000	Total £000
Group					
Cost or valuation:					
At 3 April 1976	8,019	3,087	136	19,124	30,366
Exchange rate adjustments	(88)		(3)	(338)	(429)
Capital expenditure	268	35	253	1,983	2,539
Disposals	(238)	(1)	(71)	(1,441)	(1,751)
At 2 April 1977	7,961	3,121	315	19,328	30,725

Accumulated depreciation:					
At 3 April 1976	1,175	181	46	11,518	12,920
Exchange rate adjustments	(17)	—	(3)	(175)	(195)
Charge for year	154	60	14	1,620	1,848
Disposals	(57)	—	(2)	(993)	(1,052)
At 2 April 1977	1,255	241	55	11,970	13,521
Net book value	6,706	2,880	260	7,358	17,204
Valuations incorporated above:					
1957	41	—	—	213	254
1968	2,282	—	—	—	2,282
1970	1,535	161	—	—	1,696
1972	291	—	—	—	291
1973	—	1,200	—	—	1,200
1976	93	—	—	—	93
	4,242	1,361	—	213	5,816
Accumulated depreciation	427	117	—	213	757
	3,815	1,244	—	—	5,059
Parent company					
Cost or valuation:					
At 3 April 1976	—	1,035	—	183	1,218
Transfers to Group companies	—	—	—	(183)	(183)
At 2 April 1977	—	1,035	—	—	1,035

Accumulated depreciation:

At 3 April 1976	—	6	85	91
Charge for year	—	21	—	21
Transfers to Group companies	—	—	(85)	(85)
	—	27	—	27
Net book value	—	1,008	—	1,008

	Group 1977 £000	Group 1976 £000	Parent 1977 £000	Parent 1976 £000
Associated companies				
Unquoted shareholdings at cost or valuation	255	318	—	—
Share of post acquisition reserves:				
At 3 April 1976	762	675	—	—
Profit for the year retained	270	114	—	—
Adjustment on associate becoming subsidiary	13	(27)	—	—
Group profit on stock eliminated	—	—	—	—
	1,300	1,080	28	42
Loans	57	73	—	—
	1,357	1,153	28	42
Trade investments				
At cost or valuation:				
Quoted shareholding (a)	301	301	—	—
Unquoted shareholdings (b)	3	3	—	—
	304	304	—	—
Total investments	1,661	1,457	28	42

(a) Market value	627	1,093
(b) Directors' valuations	3	3

The market value and directors' valuations shown above do not take account of any potential tax liability in the event of disposal.

16. Stock

Stock is classified as follows:

Raw materials and components	6,730	4,906
Work in progress	6,830	6,111
Finished goods	9,366	7,667
	22,926	18,684

See also note 12.

17. Creditors

Creditors include a deferred credit of £1,253,000 (1976 £1,302,000) in respect of grants received which will be transferred to the profit and loss account over the lives of the assets to which they relate (note 1(h)).

18. Taxation

U.K. and overseas tax payable before 1 April 1978	1,915	1,748	679
U.K. and overseas tax payable on and after 1 April 1978	265	321	—
	2,180	2,069	679

19. Deferred taxation

	Group 1977 £000	Group 1976 £000	Parent 1977 £000	Parent 1976 £000
Tax on excess of tax allowance on fixed assets over depreciation charged in the accounts	2,894	2,386	—	15
Estimated potential tax liability arising on the surplus on revaluation of properties	721	716	—	—
Stock appreciation relief	2,650	1,546	—	—
Tax relief on provisions made in the accounts which will be obtained when the expenditure is incurred, less liability on income which will be taxed when received	(503)	(29)	—	—
Advance corporation tax recoverable against future liabilities	(413)	(511)	(413)	(511)
	5,349	4,108	(413)	(496)

The debit balance of £413,000 (1976 £496,000) above is shown as advance corporation tax recoverable in the parent company balance sheet.

The period of deferment of the tax on stock appreciation relief is dependent upon future legislation and stock levels.

20. Share capital

	Authorised 1977 £000	Authorised 1976 £000	Issued 1977 £000	Issued 1976 £000
5% (now 3·5% plus tax credit) cumulative preference stock	1,100	1,100	1,100	1,100
6% (now 4·2% plus tax credit) non-cumulative preferred ordinary stock	1,100	1,100	1,100	1,100
Ordinary shares of 25p each	10,300	10,300	4,606	4,606
	12,500	12,500	6,806	6,806

Certain directors and senior officials of the Group held the following options:

(a) Exercisable after 4 February 1978 and before 4 February 1982 to subscribe for 575,000 ordinary shares of 25p at a price of 40p.

(b) Exercisable after 16 March 1980 and before 16 March 1984 to subscribe for 167,500 ordinary shares of 25p at a price of 67p.

21. Reserves

	Share premiums £000	Capital reserve £000	Retained profits £000	Total £000
Group				
At 3 April 1976				
Parent and subsidiaries	4,556	247	12,926	17,729
Associated companies	5	4	753	762
	4,561	251	13,679	18,491
Prior year adjustment (note 12)			755	755
	4,561	251	14,434	19,246
Movement during the year:				
Attributable to subsidiary liquidated		(9)	—	(9)
Profit for the year retained		—	2,274	2,274
At 2 April 1977	4,561	242	16,708	21,511
Parent and subsidiaries	4,556	238	15,672	20,466
Associated companies	5	4	1,036	1,045
	4,561	242	16,708	21,511
Parent				
At 3 April 1976	4,556	112	8,689	13,357
Profit for the year retained			2,033	2,033
At 2 April 1977	4,556	112	10,722	15,390

Retained profits of overseas subsidiary and associated companies of £5,518,000 (1976 £4,757,000) are subject to U.K. tax less double taxation relief if remitted to the U.K. by way of dividend.

	Group 1977 £000	Group 1976 £000	Parent 1977 £000	Parent 1976 £000
22. Debentures and term loans				
6¼% Debenture stock 1984/89 (secured)	2,157	2,488	2,157	2,488
Bank loans (unsecured), interest varying with inter-bank rates:				
Canadian $3m, repayable February 1984	1,655	1,630	1,655	1,630
U.S. $1.5m, repayable April 1981	872	—	872	—
U.S. $192,539, repayable November 1979	112	—	112	—
Department of Industry loan (unsecured), Interest at 10%, repayable June 1978–June 1982	405	450	—	—
	5,201	4,568	4,796	4,118
23. Commitments				
Not provided in accounts:				
Capital expenditure authorised by directors	1,651	525	—	—
Including capital expenditure contracted	1,310	292	—	—
24. Contingent liabilities				
Guarantees for bank and other loans	109	298	527	468
Notes receivable discounted	5	20	16	16
Uncalled share capital	9	9	—	—
Other claims	19	40	—	—
	142	367	543	484

The parent company has guaranteed annual payments of subsidiaries up to £127,000 (1976 – £89,000).

Source and application of funds

	1977 12 months £000	1976 18 months £000
Source of funds		
Profit before tax and extraordinary items less minority interests	6,402	6,760
Extraordinary items	(163)	652
	6,239	7,412
Adjustment for items not involving the movement of funds:		
Depreciation	1,848	2,651
Profits retained in associated companies	(270)	(114)
Exchange rate adjustments	259	54
Total generated from operations	8,076	10,003
Increase in term loans	939	150
Sales of fixed assets	699	351
	9,714	10,504
Application of funds		
Dividends	858	1,141
Tax Paid	1,718	2,099
Purchase of fixed assets	2,539	3,959
Increase (decrease) in investments in associates	(66)	26
Purchase of debentures	331	—
Decrease (increase) in minority interest	221	(275)
Other applications	9	(77)
	5,610	6,873
Increase in working capital	4,104	3,631
Comprising:		
Increase in net liquid funds:		
Increase in bank and cash balances	85	183
Decrease in bank overdrafts	47	1,831
	132	2,014
Increase (decrease) in stocks	4,242	(704)
Increase in debtors	2,466	1,901
Decrease (increase) in creditors	(2,432)	365
Decrease (increase) in advance payments	(304)	55
	4,104	3,631

INDEX

Aas v. *Benham*, 2207
Abridged double entry, 1121 *et seq.*
Absorption of companies, 23274 *et seq.*
Acceptor, *see* Bills of Exchange
Accommodation bills, 0620
Account sales, 1701, 1702
Accounting—
  mechanical aids, 3171
  objective, 3173
  ratio, 3141
Accounts—
  associations, 1201, *et seq.*
  classification code, 3160
  clubs, 1201
  doctor's, 1307
  farm, 3213
  interpretation of, 3108
  investment trusts, 2631
  liquidators', 2905 *et seq.*
  published, 23236–50
  real, personal and nominal, 0101
  superannuation, 3205, 3207
  unit trusts, 2636
Accounts current, 0401 *et seq.*
  change in rates of interest, 0410
  époque method, 0402, 0403, 0406
  periodic balance method, 0410
  products method, 0402, 0406
  red ink interest, 0402, 0410
Accruals, 0513 *et seq.*
Acquisition—
  entries (limited companies), 23155 *et seq.*, 23184, 23199, *et seq.*, 3216
Adjudication (bankruptcy), 2810
Adjustment—
  branch accounts, 1914, 1955 *et seq.*
  in final accounts, 0509 *et seq.*, 0565
  or total accounts, 1001
Administration charges, 1802
Admission of partner, 2260 *et seq.*
Advance Accounts, bills of exchange, 0631
Advance corporation tax, 2107, 2356–8, 2361–6, 2370, 2372–3, 23234–9, 23242, 23252–6, 23262, 23265–7, 23271, 23274, 2417, 2458, 2495–6, 24100, 3224, 3235
Advertisements (Hire-purchase) Act (1957), 2059

Agreements—
  for commission, 0305, 0561, 23216 *et seq.*
  of junior partners, 2243 *et seq.*
Aliquot parts, 0303
Allocation of expenses, 1802
Amalgamation of companies, 23274, *et seq.*
Ammonia Soda Co. v. *Chamberlain*, 23211
Amortization, *see* Depreciation
Annual General Meeting Notice, 23239
Annual return, 2318, 2321
Annuities—
  income tax, 2103
  partnership, 22147 *et seq*
Application and allotment, 2375 *et seq.*
Apportionment of shares between vendors, 23180 *et seq.*
Appropriation Account, 23213, 23214, 23259, 2467, 2477
  definition of, 0502
Arithmetic of Accountancy, 0301 *et seq.*
  aliquot parts, 0303
  average, 0310
  commission, 0305
  cost and selling price, 0302
  flat and redemption yield, 0309
  interest, 0312
  stocks and shares, 0306
Articles of Association, definition of, 2303
  (*see also* Table A)
Assets—
  depreciation of, 0701 *et seq.*
  fixed, floating and fictitious, 0579
  improvement, 0801
  in published Balanced Sheet, 23242
  life of, 0713
  tangible and intangible, 0579
  writing off, 0715
Assignment—
  of bill of exchange, 0602
  of life policies, 22114
Associated company, 2493
Associations, accounts of, 1201 *et seq.*

1

Assurance Accounts—
  special provisions in Companies Act, 2340, 2413
Auditors'—
  remuneration, 2340
  report, 2314–15, 2346, 23245, 2413
  rights, 2315, 2318
Authorized capital, 23144, 23224
Average, 0310
  clause, 2702
  due date, 0414 *et seq.*, 2215
  weighted, 0310
Award winning accounts, 3221–38

BAD Debts—
  Accounts, 0106, 0521, 0522
  amounts recovered, 0107
  Provision, 0521, 0522, 1103, 1122
Balance Sheet, 0502, 0505, 0578 *et seq.*, 2332 *et seq.*
  analysis, 3110 *et seq.*
  assets classified, 0579
  auditors' report, 2314–5, 2346, 23245
  bankers and, 3112
  combined, 1953, 1965
  consolidated, 2413 *et seq.*, 2433 *et seq.*, 2476
  contents of, 0578
  contingent liabilities, 0615, 0720
  criticism of, 3138
  directors' report and, 2312–14, 2346, 23245
  form of, 0580, 0581, 23242, 2493
  general survey of, 0581
  holding companies, 2413 *et seq.*, 2477
  interpretation of, 3108 *et seq.*, 3135
  limited companies, 23242, 2493
  preparation of, 0505
  provisions in, 0717 *et seq.*
  reserves in, 0717 *et seq.*
  sequence of items in, 0578, 23242
Balance Sheet Criticism and Accounting Ratios, 3138 *et seq.*
  accounting ratios, 3141 *et seq.*
  balance sheet ratios, 3138–45, 3147–48, 3150–51
  dividend cover, 3148
  form, 3138–40
  legal requirements, 3140–41
  price-earnings ratio, 3149
  priority percentages, 3151–52

Balance Sheet Criticism and Accounting Ratios (*contd.*)
  profit and loss ratios, 3145–47, 3147–49, 3150–51
Balancing methods (ledgers), 1004
Bale v. *Cleland*, 23212
Bank—
  interest, 0412, 0413
  overdrafts, 2106
  Statement, 0202
  Reconciliation Statements, 0201 *et seq.*
Bankruptcy—
  accounts of Trustee, 2821
  Acts (1924 and 1926), 2822
  adjudication, 2811
Betting and Gaming Duties Act 1972, 2810
  contingent liabilities, 2808
  deferred creditors, 2811
  Deficiency Account, 2801 *et seq.*, 2823
  'firm' bankruptcy, 2818 *et seq.*
  liquidation, compared, 2901, 2926
  preferential creditors, 2809
  pre-preferential creditors, 2809
  redundancy fund contributions, 2810
  remunerations of Trustee, 2821
  schedules, list of, 2812
  secured creditors, 2811
  Statement of Affairs, 2801 *et seq.*, 2822
  statutory forms, 2821
  unsecured creditors, 2804, 2809
Barrow v. *Barrow*, 2208
Beni-Felkai Mining Co. Ltd., In *re*, 2926
Betting and Gaming Duties Act 1972, 2810
Bills of Exchange, 0601 *et seq.*
  acceptors' books, 0606, 0609
  accommodation bills, 0620
  Act (1882), 0601, 0607, 0620
  advances against, 0630
  advantages of, 0604
  as security, 0636
  Banking and Financial Dealing Act (1971), 0607
Bill Books, 0627, 0629
Bills—
  Diary, 0630
  Discounted Register, 0629
  Payable Book, 0605, 0627, 0629
  Receivable Book 0605, 0627, 0629

Book-keeping entries, 0605 *et seq.*
cheque, definition of, 0601
creditor's books, 0607
days of grace, 0606
Day of Payment, 0607
debtor's books, 0605
definition of, 0601
discounting, 0607, 0617, 0620, 0632–3
dishonour, 0606, 0614
drawer's books, 0607
for collection, 0631
foreign bills, 0603, 0604
holder in due course, 0602
inland, 0603
Marginal Deposit Receipt, 0630
noting charges, 0614
promissory note, definition of, 0601
rebate on bills discounted, 0633
retiring, 0615
short, 0630
Special Margins Account, 0630
specimen, 0603, 0604
stamp duties, 0603
Bonus share dividends, 23255
received by holding company, 2407
Bonus shares, 23256
Book-keeping to Trial Balance, 0101 *et seq.*
bad debts, 0107
recovered, 0107
Cash Book, 0103
detection of errors, 0113
drawings, 0105
Journal, 0102
Ledger, 0101
Purchases Day Book or Journal, 0102
Purchases Returns Book or Journal, 0103
Sales Day Book or Journal, 0102
Sales Return Book or Journal, 0103
Trial Balance, 0107
Branch Accounts, 1901 *et seq.*
adjustments—
in Branch and Head Office Accounts, 1955
re price changes, 1939
stock, 1914, 1955
sundry, 1937
branch control, 1987
capital expenditure, 1986
charged out at selling price, 1913 *et seq.*

Branch Accounts (*contd.*)
debtors systems, 1902, 1904
departmental method, 1902
depreciation, 1935
difference in balance of stock, 1934
divisions, 1901
double-column method, 1925
double entry, 1949
expenses at branches, 1917
foreign branches, 1966 *et seq.*, 1985, 1986
foreign currency conversion, 1966 *et seq.*, 1974–7
goods—
in transit, 1919
invoiced at cost, 1902, 1910
invoiced at selling price, 1902, 1913, 1926
handling charges, 1921
head office books, 1985
inter-branch transfers, 1955
memorandum debtors, 1912
memorandum final accounts, 1906 *et seq.*
partnerships, 22203–6
price changes, 1939
profit and loss on exchange, 1977
recording assets and liabilities in head office books, 1985
returns, 1989
self-contained accounting, 1949, *et seq.*
stock and debtors systems, 1902, 1910
stock shortages, 1934
stores accounts, 1967
unrealized profit, 1955, 1962
Break-even Chart, 3165
Break-even Point, 3165
Brokerage—
on shares, 2601
voyage accounts, 0916–18
Brokers Transfer Form, 2331
Brown v. *de Tastet,* 2208
Budgetary Control, 3157 *et seq.*
Bugle Press Ltd., In *re* (1960), 23304

CALLS—
collection of, 2907
in advance, 2382, 2384, 23224
in arrear, 2383, 2384, 23224
interest on, 2384, 23224
Table A, 2382, 23224

Cancellation—
  of debentures, 23128 *et seq.*
  of shares, 23150, 23224
Capital—
  alterations, 23144, *et seq.,* 23224
  authorized, 23144, 23224
  called up, 2376
  consolidation of, 23144, 23224
  conversion of, 23144, 23212, 23224
  Fund Account, 1202
  increase and decrease, 23144, 23224
  interest on, 2212, 22140
  interest paid out of, 2333, 23222,
    23224
  issued, 2375 *et seq.*
  nominal, 2375, 23144
  redemption, 23147 *et seq.*
Redemption Reserve Fund, 23149,
  23214
  reduction of, 23150 *et seq.*
  reorganization of, 23155
  reserve, 0718, 2335, 23213
  stamp duty, relief from, 23304–5
  statement, 1119
  subdivision of, 23146
  subscribed, 2375 *et sq.*
  surplus, 23212
  working, 3118 *et seq.*
Capital and Revenue Expenditure,
  0801 *et seq*
  capital and revenue receipts, 0802
  capital expenses, 0801
  classification of expenditure, 0810
  deferred revenue expenditure, 0804
  improvements, 0801
  legal expenses, 0803
  repairs, 0803
  wages, 0803
Capital Transfer Tax, 2306
Carriage inwards and outwards, 0539
Cases, packing, 0901 *et seq.*
Cash—
  Book, 0103
  discount, 0104
  dividends, 23253
    received by holding company,
      2405, 2441
  float, 0208
  flow, 3179
  on delivery, 0914
  profits, 2230
  sales and purchases, 0103
'Cash' Basis, accounts on, 1201, 2230

Certificate—
  of incorporation, 2301
  to commence business, 23170
Charges, Register of, 2320, 2325
Chartered Company, 2308
Chatterley-Whitfield *re,* 2624
Cheque, definition of, 0601
Cheques—
  dishonoured, 0106, 0204
  uncleared, 0201
  unpresented, 0201
C.I.R. v. *Cock, Russell & Co., Ltd,*
  0537
City Code on takeovers, 3154–5
City of Glasgow Bank v. *McKinnon,*
  23212
Claims—
  compensation, 2715
  fire, 2703
  loss of profits insurance, 2701
  loss of stock, 2705
Close companies—
  associate, 2374
  definition, 2374
  director, 2374
  directors remuneration, 2374
  distributions, 2375
  participator, 2374
  special matters, 2374
  whole-time service director, 2374
  working proprietor, 2374
Clubs, accounts of, 1201 *et seq.*
C.O.D., 0914 *et seq.*
Coefficient of dispersion, 2628
Cohen Committee, report of, 2308,
  2332
Collateral security, 23111
Collection—
  Accounts, bills of exchange, 0630,
    0631
  of calls, 2907
Collins v. *Greyhound Racing Associa-*
  tion Ltd., 23157
Columnar Book-keeping, 1301
Commission—
  address, 0917
  agreements, 23220
  calculations, 0305
  del credere, 1702
  directors', 23216 *et seq*
  manager's, 0561, 23216, *et seq.*
  overriding, 23157
  shares on, 23110

Commission (*contd.*)
  underwriting, 23157
Companies—
  (Accounts) Regulations (1971), 2313,
    2314
  and Partnerships, compared, 2305
  associated, 2493
  types of, 2308
Companies Act (1947), 2306, 2332
Companies Act (1948)
  Sect.—
    27, 2445
    28, 2306
    51, 2375
    53, 23157
    54, 2339
    55, 2307
    56, 2334, 2399, 23333
    57, 2391, 23139, 2501
    58, 23147, 23214
    60, 2315
    61, 23224
    62, 23148
    65, 23223
    66, 23150
    72, 3153
    74, 23107
    86, 2318
    87, 2318
    90, 23112, 23114
    95, 2320
    102, 2915
    110, 2319
    124, 2319
    126, 2319
    128, 2319
    130, 2316, 2317
    145, 2319
    146, 2319
    149, 2333, 2346, 2411, 2487
    150, 2409, 2415
    151, 2410, 2494
    152, 2410, 2415
    153, 2402, 2411
    154, 2401
    155, 2314, 2333
    156, 2314, 2333, 2414
    157, 2312, 2314
    158, 2314
    163, 2346
    189, 2342
    190, 2341, 3140
    191, 2342

Companies Act (1948) (*contd.*)
    196, 2315, 2342–4, 2346, 2414
    197, 2341, 2346, 2414
    200, 2320
    209, 23306, 23332, 3153
    210, 3153
    283, 2922
    287, 23332
    319, 2905
    322, 23108
    366, 2914
    367, 2914
    371, 2916
    372, 2915
    373, 2916
    434, 2201
    436, 2311
Companies Act (1967)
  Sect.—
    1, 2310, 2312
    2, 2310
    3, 2310
    4, 2310
    5, 2311
    6, 2311, 2315, 2344–5, 2346,
        23243
    7, 2311, 2345
    8, 2311, 2315, 2345–6
    14, 2314, 23248
    16, 2312
    17, 2313
    18, 2313, 2314
    19, 2313, 2314
    20, 2313, 2314
    21, 2321
    22, 2313, 2314
    27–9, 2320
    31, 2312, 2313
    42, 2312
    51, 2321
  Schedule 2, 2313, 2332–40, 2346, 2360,
    2368, 2410–15, 3138, 3140
  Schedule 8, 2314, 2332, 2334, 2410,
    2411
Companies Act (1980) 23333–37
Companies Act (1981) 23337–51
Companies and Tax—
  advance corporation tax—*see* Cor-
    poration Tax
  annual payments received, 2359
  capital dividends, 2357
  charges on income, 2358
  collection of tax, 2359

Companies and Tax (*contd.*)
  debenture interest, 2358
  dividends paid, 2354, 2360
  dividends proposed, 2360
  dividends received, 2355, 2357
  interest on overdue tax, 2360
  loan interest, 2358n
  return period accounting (Form CT61), 2359
  notes in published accounts, 23243–4, 3227–38
  other distributions made, 2357
  other distributions received, 2357
  statutory accounts requirements, 2360
Comparative Balance Sheet, 3135 *et seq.*
Compensation claims, 2715
Consignment Accounts, 1701 *et seq.*
  accounts sales, 1701–2
  consignee's books, 1730
  consignor's book, 1702
  correction of errors, 1723
  cost price method, 1704, 1722
  del credere commission, 1702
  discounts and allowances, 1733
  invoice price method, 1711, 1720
  joint venture with, 1739
  loss of stock, 1707 *et seq.*
  memorandum column method, 1714
  profit and loss or exchange, 1728
  sale price method, 1711, 1720
  stock, 1706 *et seq.*
    loss, 1707–9
    unsold, 1706
Consolidated—
  Appropriation Account, 2458 *et seq.*, 2466, 2495
  Balance Sheet, preparation of, 2422, 2436, 2493
  Profit and Loss Account, preparation of, 2458 *et seq.*, 2495
Construction capital, interest on, 2334, 23222
Containers, 0901 *et seq.*
  reserve, 0905
  Trading Account, 0902
Contingent liabilities, 0615, 0720, 2338, 2429, 2808
Contingency—
  provision, 0720
  reserve, 0720

Contributories, list of, 2918
Control Account, 1001 *et seq.*
Conversion—
  of debentures into new debentures, 23139
  of debenture into shares, 23139
  of foreign currency, 1974
  of shares into stock, 23145
  of stock into shares, 23145
  to double entry, 1106
  to sterling, rules for, 1974 *et seq.*
Convex programming, 3189
Corporation tax—
  accounting for deferred taxation, 2367
  advance corporation tax, 2356, 2361–6, 2370, 2372
  basis of assessment, 2353
  capital allowances, 2355
  close companies, 2374
  companies chargeable, 2354
  computation of profits, 2355
  date of payment, 2356
  definition of terms, 2365
  directors remuneration, 2374
  dividends and other distributions, 2355, 2357
  financial year, 2353
  franked investment income, 2355, 2359, 2373
  income tax principles, 2355
  rate, 2353
  standard accounting practice, 2360–7
  statutory accounts requirements, 2360
  total profits, 2355
  yearly interest, 2355
Correction of errors, 1401 *et seq.*
  consignment accounts, 1723
Cost—
  and selling price, 0302
  of control, 2424, 2432
  of sales, 0542
  prime, 3001
Course of Dealing, 2201–2
Cover for dividend, 2625 *et seq.*
Crabtree, In *re*, 23212
Credit Sale Transactions, 2004
Creditors—
  deferred, 2811
  guaranteed by vendor, 3216
  preferential, 2809

Creditors (*contd.*)
　pre-preferential, 2809
　secured, 2811
　Suspense Account, 23185
　unsecured, 2804, 2812
Crichton, Oil Co., re, 23282
Critical Path Analysis (Method), 3190–94
Cross-holdings of companies, 23300
Cruikshank v. *Sutherland*, 2203, 2293
Current account, 2209, 2220
Current assets, 0579

DAILY balances, 0413
Day Book (or Journal)—
　C.O.D., 0914
　combined with Ledger, 1310 *et seq.*
　hire purchase, 2021
　purchases, 0102
　returns, 0103
　sales, 0102
Days of grace, 0607
Debenture holders—
　Receivers for, 2914
　Register of, 2320
Debentures, 23108 *et seq.*
　annual drawings, 23122
　book-keeping entries, 23113
　cancellation, 23128
　classification, 23108
　conversion, 23139
　definition, 23108
　expenses of issue, 2337, 23110
　fixed and floating charge, 23108
　insurance policy method, 23120
　interest on, 23112, 23128
　issue of, 23108, 23110, 23111
　own, 23127 *et seq.*
　premium, 23124
　purchase in open market, 23127
　redemption fund for, 23118–9
　redemption of, 23114, 23118, 23122
　sinking fund for, 0715, 23115
　tax on interest, 23113
Debtors—
　guaranteed by vendor, 3216
　provision, 1211 *et seq.*
　reserve, 1211 *et seq.*
　Suspense Account, 23185
Deferred—
　capital, 2909
　creditors, 2811

Deferred (*contd.*)
　payment, purchase by, 2058
　revenue expenditure, 0804
Deficiency Account—
　in bankruptcy, 2801 *et seq.*, 2823
　in liquidation, 2901 *et seq.*, 2924, 2926
Del credere commission, 1702
Departmental Accounts, 1801 *et seq.*
　administration charges, 1802
　allocation of expenses, 1802
　objects, 1801
　tabular statement, 1818
　Trading and Profit and Loss Account, 1806, 1810
　transfers, inter-departmental 1803
Depreciation, 0518, 0701 *et seq.*
　additions during year, 0520, 0703–4
　amortization, 0708
　annuity method, 0705
　causes, 0701
　definition, 0701
　depletion method, 0712
　digit method, 0704
　diminishing balance method, 0703
　distinction between depreciation and fluctuation, 0701
　efficiency hour rate, 0712
　fund or reserve, 0706
　general, 0518
　insurance policy method, 0708
　legal and commercial view, 0713
　life of asset, 0713
　machine hour rate, 0712
　maintenance and, 0701
　Plant Register, 0714
　progression, 0704
　renewals, 0713
　repairs, maintenance and depreciation fund or provision, 0711
　revaluation method, 0710
　sinking fund, 0706, 0714
　standard accounting practice, 0713–14
　straight line method, 0702
Detection of errors, 0113
Directors—
　commission paid to, 23216 *et seq.*
　register of, 2318, 2320
　remuneration of, 2315, 2341–6, 23224, 23243
　report of, 2312–14, 2345, 23245–8

Discount, 0523–0525
  bills, 0607, 0617, 0618, 0632–6
  cash, 0104
  companies, special provision in
    Companies Act, 2340, 2413
  provision, 0523
  trade, 0103
Discounted Cash Flow, 3180
Dishonour—
  of a bill, 0606, 0614
  of a cheque, 0106, 0204
Dissolution of Partnership, 22158 et
  seq.
Dividends, 23251 et seq.
  classification, 23251
  cover, 2627
  cum, 2602
  equalization fund, 23274
  equalization reserve, 23274
  ex, 2602
  interim, 23224, 23251
  proposed, 2337
Divisible profits and final accounts,
  23211 et seq.
Doctors' accounts, 1307 et seq.
Dominion Tar & Chemical Co., re,
  23282
Double Account system, 2501 et seq.
  Capital Account, 2502
  characteristics of, 2502
  depreciation in, 2503
  Receipts and Expenditure on Capital
    Account, 2501
  replacements, 2503
  'single account' system contrasted,
    2502
Double entry—
  abridged, 1121 et seq.
  conversion from single entry, 1106
  essentials of, 0101
Doubtful Debts provision, 0521
Drawing a bill, 0601
Drawings, 0105
  of partners, 2210
Duty stamps on bills, 0603
Dynamic programming, 3189

EARNINGS basis of share valuation,
  2613, 2619
Economic year, 3174
Edwards v. Saunton Hotels, 0702,
  23216
Efficiency hour rate, 0712

Effluxion of time, 0701
Electronic Data Processing, 3174 et
  seq.
Elimination process on acquisition—
  companies, 23188
  partnership, 2287 et seq.
Elliot v. Elliot, 22109 et seq.
Employers liability insurance, 0573
Endowment policy, 0708
  Account, 0709
Epoque method, accounts current,
  0402, 0403
Equalization fund for dividends, 23274
Equity, 2424
  basis of share valuation, 2619 et seq.
Errors—
  compensating, 0114
  correction of, 1401 et seq.
  in Trial Balance, 0113, 0114
  of—omission, 0113
    —commission, 0114
    —principle, 0114
Examination—
  hints, 3218–20
  procedure, 0549–64
Exchange—
  Control Act (1947), 2327
  foreign, 1966, 3201 et seq.
  forward, 3201, 3205
  profits and losses on consignment
    accounts, 1728 et seq.
Exempt private company, 2332
Expenditure, classification of, 0810
Expenses—
  accrued and accruing, 0513
  preliminary, 23155
  prepaid, 0510
  stock, 0517

Fair Trading Act (1973), 3154
Farm Accounts, 3213–6
Fictitious assets, 0579
Final accounts—
  adjustments, 0509
  debenture interest, 23112
  examination procedure, 0549
  functions of, 0501 et seq.
  limited company, 23225 et seq.
  rules for construction of, 0503 et seq.
Finance Act—
  (1910), (s. 74), 2327, 2330
  (1927), (s. 55), 23304
  (1928), (s. 31), 23304

Finance Act (*contd.*)
   (1930), (s. 41), 23304
   (1940), (s. 55), 2306, 2624
   (1954), (s. 28), 2619
   (1969), 2355, 2375
Finance, cost of 0575
Financial statement, 3127 *et seq.*
'Firm' bankruptcy, 2818 *et seq.*
Fixed assets, 0579
Flat yield, 0309 *et seq.*
Flexible budgets, 3159
Floating assets, 0579
Fluctuating exchange, 1966, 1971
Foreign—
   remittance, 1975
   revenue expenditure, 1968 *et seq.*
   Stores Accounts, 1967
Foreign bills of exchange, 0603 *et seq.*
Foreign Branch Accounts, 1966 *et seq.*
   branch records, 1966
   capital expenditure, 1968
   columnar Trial Balance, 1971
   combined accounts, 1982
Foreign Exchange, 3201 *et seq.*
   consignments, 1727 *et seq.*
   conversion rules, 1974–7
   currency suspense, 3206
   Difference on Exchange Account, 3201
   fluctuating, 1966, 1971
   forward exchange 3201, 3205
   memorandum currency column, 3202
   partnership accounts, 22206
   Profit and Loss on Exchange Account, 3201
   stable, 1966
Forfeited shares, 2392, *et seq.*
Forward Exchange, 3205
Foster v. *New Trinidad Lake Asphalte Co., Ltd.,* 23212
Fractional shares, 23270, 23288 *et seq.*
Fractions list, 23290
Fully paid shares converted into stock, 23145
Fund—
   amortization, 0708 *et seq.*
   capital, 1202, 1206
   depreciation, 0706
   reserve, 0719
   sinking, 0706

Garner v. *Murray,* rule in, 2204, 22171, 22172, 22200

Garwood v. *Poynter,* 2207
Gas Consumption Ledger, 1303
Gearing, high and low, 2623 *et seq.*
Glyncorrwg Collieries, In *re,* 2916
Goods—
   C.O.D., 0914
   in transit, 1919
   lost, 1919
   on approval, 0909
   on consignment, 1701
   on sale or return, 0909
   sent to branches, 1902 *et seq.*
Goodwill, 2264 *et seq.,* 22108, 23158, 23171, 2419
Gross—
   profit and gross loss, 0501
   profit, marginal, 0584
   works cost of manufacture, 3001
Group accounts, 2401 *et seq.*
Guarantee—
   of profits to partner, 2240
   recoupment, 2248
   vendor, 3216

HANDLING charges, branch accounts, 1921 *et seq.*
Head (Henry) & Co. Ltd v. *Ropner Holdings Ltd.,* 23333
Head Office branch accounts, 1901 *et seq.*
Hidden reserve, 0719
Hilder v. *Dexter,* 23211
Hill v. *Fearis,* 2264
Hinds v. *Buenos Aires Tramways Co., Ltd.,* 23224
Hire Purchase—
   Methods of financing, 2004
   treatment in final accounts, 2004
Hire Purchase Accounts, 2001 *et seq.*
   accounting methods, 2005
   adjustment accounts, 2020 *et seq.*
   Advertisements (Hire-purchase) Act (1957), 2059
   assignment, 2057
   Branch method—
      at cost price, 2017 *et seq.*
      at selling price, 2024 *et seq.*
      change in accounting method, 2039
   depreciation, 2051 *et seq.*
   goods out or stock method, 2017 *et seq.*

Hire Purchase Accounts (*contd.*)
  goods out or stock method (*contd.*)
    advantages and disadvantages of, 2028–9
  hire purchaser's books, 2048
  hire vendor's books, 2006 *et seq.*, 2059
  interest suspense method, 2008 *et seq.*
  Maintenance Suspense Account, 2043
  Memorandum Accounts, 2017 *et seq.*
  Methods in Hire Vendor's books summarized, 2029 *et seq.*
  ownership, 2001
  'possession', 2001
  post sales services, 2043 *et seq.*
  Purchaser's Books, 2048
  return, 2032 *et seq.*
  returns and repossessions, 2035
  Sales—
    contrasted with hire purchase, 2001, 2059
    for deferred payments, 2058
    Journal, 2021
    method, 2006
    with reserve, 2017
  stock schedule, 2022
Hire Purchase Act (1965), 2002–3, 2059,
Holder in due course, 0602
Holding Companies—
  accounts of, 2412 *et seq.*
  acquisition entries, 2404, 2422
  adjustments, 2458
  advantages, 2402–3
  alternative method of presenting group accounts, 2481
  arrears of preference dividend of subsidiary, 2460
  associated company, 2493
  auditor's report, 2414, 2495
  book-keeping entries, 2402 *et seq.*
  capital reserve, 2425
  Consolidated—
    accounts, 2413–14
    Appropriation Account, 2458 *et seq.*, 2487 *et seq.*
    Balance Sheet, preparation of, 2422 *et seq.*, 2436 *et seq.*, 2493
    Profit and Loss Account, 2458 *et seq.*, 2482 *et seq.*
  Consolidation Rules, 2414–5, 2436 *et seq.*

Holding Companies (*contd.*)
  Consolidation Rules (*contd.*)
    contingent liabilities, 2429
    cost of control, 2424
    creation of, 2403
    cross holdings, 23300, 2444 *et seq.*
    defined, 2401
    derived profits, 2464
    disadvantages, 2402–3
    dividends from subsidiaries, 2405, 2441 *et seq.*
    dividends from subsidiaries—
      bonus, 2407
      cash, 2406
    equity, 2424
    financial year of group, 2402, 2411
    goodwill, 2424
      computation of, 2426
    group accounts, 2409–11
      with more than one subsidiary, 2442
    group income, 2417
    group taxation relief, 2416
    inter-company balances, 2429, 2444
    Journal entries, 2453 *et seq.*
    minority—
      interests, 2430
      proportional method of computation, 2431
      shareholders, 2430
    part-sale of holding in subsidiary, 2449–53
    partial shareholding, 2430
    plurality of holdings, 2491
    post-acquisition, profits and losses, 2432, 2465, *et seq.*
    pre-acquisition profits and losses, 2423 *et seq.*
    preference shares of subsidiaries, 2435, 2460
    presentation of accounts, 2409 *et seq.*
    profits of subsidiaries, 2441
    published accounts, 2493
    rules for preparation of—
      Consolidates Balance Sheet, 2422, 2436 *et seq.*, 2493
      Consolidated Profit and Loss Account, 2458 *et seq.*, 2487
    shares in, held by subsidiary, 2444
    standard accounting practice, 2417
    statutory requirements, summary of, 2414

Holding Companies (*contd.*)
  subsidiary company—
    defined, 2401
    part-sale of holding in, 2449–52
    treatment of in Balance Sheet,
      2404, 2411
    unrealized profits, 2409, 2459
Hoole v. *G.W.R.,* 23266
Hotel book-keeping, 1305–7

IMPREST system, 0208
Improvements, 0801
Income—
  accrued and accruing, 0516
  and Expenditure Accounts, 1202
  investment, 2335, 2339
  unearned, 0515, 0516
Income Tax in relation to accounts,
  2101 *et seq.*
  adjustment of assessments, 2101 *et seq.*
  adjustment of profits, 2104, 2226
  allocation between partners, 2226,
    2227
  annual charges, 2358
  annuities, 2103
  basis of assessment, 2102
  business profits, 2102, 2226
  collection of tax, 2102–3
    at source, 2103
  Companies Act requirements, 2360
  current fiscal year, 2101
  dividends and annuities, 2107, 23253
  dividends and interest received, 2108
  due dates of payment, 2102
  fiscal year, 2101
  foreign income, 2102
  Income Tax Account, 23250
  interest payments, 2106
    received, 2108
  limited companies, 2357 *et seq.*
  partnership, 2226 *et seq.*
  P.A.Y.E., 0922, 2102
  payment of tax, 2103
  reserves in partnership, 2227
  royalty and deduction of tax, 1503
  Schedules, 2101
  split assessment, 2226
Income and Corporation Taxes Act
  (1970), 2374, 3207
Incorporation of company, 2301, 23155
Increase of authorized capital, 23144,
  23224
Index number, 3134 *et seq.*

Industry Act (1971), 3154
Inflation adjusted accounts, 3221
Inland bill, 0603
Inner reserve, 0719
Insolvency Act (1976), 2810
Institute of Charactered Accountants,
  recommendations of, 2634–6,
  3155–7
Insurance claims, 2701 *et seq.*
  average clause, 2702
  book-keeping entries, 2709
  compensation claims, 2715
  fire loss, 2707
  loss of profits insurance, 2701
  loss of stock claim, 2705
  own insurance, 2711
  rules for loss of profits claims, 2701–
    03
  salvaged stock, 2706–09
  'short' sales, 2703
Insurance policy—
  method of depreciation, 0708 *et seq.*
Interest—
  accruing, 0516
  as appropriation of profit, 2217
  compound, 0314
  in investment accounts, 2602
  on calls, 2382, 2383, 23224
  on construction capital, 2334, 23222
  on load, 0526–0529
  on own debentures, 23128 *et seq.*
  red ink, 0402
  Simple, 0312
  tax on, 2106 *et seq.*
  untaxed, 2108
Interim dividends, 23225, 23251
Interpretation of accounts, 3108 *et seq.*
Introduction of a partner, 22153
Investment appraisal, 3179 *et seq.*
Investment Trusts and Unit Trusts,
  2631 *et seq.*
  Comparison between, 2640–1
  investment trusts, 2631–6
  published accounts, 2643–48
  taxation aspects, 2638–40
  Trustee Investments Act (1961),
    2641–2
  unit trusts, 2636–8
Isle of Thanet Electricity Supply Co.,
  re, 23282
Issue of debentures, 23108, 23110,
  23111
  as collateral security, 23111

Issue of shares, 2375 *et seq.*

Johnstone v. *Chestergate Hat Manufacturing Co.*, 23217, 23220
Joint Stock Company, *see* Limited Company
Joint Venture—
    Accounts, 1601
    complete double entry books, 1609
    Consignment Account with, 1739 *et seq.*
    general rules, 1601
    interest, 1606
    Memorandum Account, 1601
    treatment of stock, 1602
Journal, 0102
    Goods on Approval, 0911, 0912, 0913
    Purchases, 0102
    Sales, 0102
    Share Transfer, 23106
    Transfer, 1003–4
Junior partners' agreements, 2242

LAW of Property Act (1925) (ss. 101 and 109), 2914
Law Reform (Limitation of Actions, etc.) Act (1954), 2204
Ledger, 0101, 0104, 0112
    combined with Day Book, 1310 *et seq.*
    gas consumption, 1303
    rental, 1303
    visitors', 1305–6
Lemon v. *Austin Friars Investment Trust*, 23108
Liabilities—
    contingent, 0615, 0720, 2338, 2429, 2808
Limited and ordinary partnerships contrasted, 22190
Limited Companies' Accounts, 2301, 2308 *et seq.*
    absorptions, 23274
    accounting, change in basis, 2340
    accounting records, 2310
    accounting reference period, 2310
    accounting reference date, 2310
    acquisition entries, 23155, 23160, 23199 *et seq.*, 23297 *et seq.*, 3216
    agreements for commission, 23216–7

Limited Companies' Accounts (*contd.*)
    allotment, 2375 *et seq.*
        letter, 2323
        particulars of, 23111
    alterations of capital, 23144 *et seq.*
    amalgamations, 23274, 23332
    annual return, 2319
    apportionment of shares between vendors, 23180 *et seq.*
    articles of association, 2303 (*see also* Table A)
    assets, 2335, 2338, 2347
    assurance companies, special provisions, 2340, 2413
    auditors, 2314
        remuneration of, 2340
        report of, 2314–5, 2346, 23245, 2495
        rights of, 2315, 2320
    authorized capital, 23144
    Balance Sheet, 2332, 23242
        circulation of, 2314
        documents to be attached to, 2314, 2333, 2346
        notes, 2338
        signature of, 2314, 2333
    bank loans and overdrafts, 2336
    banks, special provisions, 2333, 2340, 2413
    bonus shares, 23212, 23256
        advantages and disadvantages, 23256, 23257
        dividends on, 23255
    borrowing powers, 23224
    Brokers Transfer Form, 2331
    calls, 2376, 2382
    calls in advance and in arrear, 2382, 2383, 23224
    Capital (*see* Share Capital)
        commitments, 2338
        profit, distribution of, 23212
        Redemption Reserve Fund, 23147
        reserve, 0718, 23213, 2424 *et seq.*
    certificate—
        of incorporation, 2301
        to commence business, 23170
        where transfer not liable to stamp duty, 2330
    collateral security, 23111
    commissions, 23220
    Companies Acts (1947), (1948), (1967) and (1976) *see* Companies Act

Limited Companies' Accounts (*contd.*)
company taxation, 2353
comparison with partnership, 2305
competing claims of members, 23281 *et seq.*
construction capital, interest on 2334, 23222
contents of Balance Sheet, 2332
contingent liabilities, 0720, 2338
creditors' suspense account, 23185, *et seq.*
cross-holdings in reconstruction, 23300–23303
debentures, 2336, 23108 *et seq.*
  book-keeping entries, 23113
  cancellation of, 23128 *et seq.*
  classification of, 23108
  commission, 2337
  conversion, 23139
  debtors' suspense account, 23185 *et seq.*
  discount, 2336, 23110, 23122
  drawings, 23122
  expenses of issue, 2337, 23110
  fixed charge, 23108
  floating charge, 23108
  insurance policy method, 23120
  interest, 23112, 23128
  issue, 23108, 23110, 23111
    as collateral, 23111
    expenses, 23110
  mine redemption fund, 23144
  premium on, 23124
  purchase, 23127
  redemption of, 23114, 23118, 23122
    by annual drawings, 23122
    fund, 23115 *et seq.*
    reissue of redeemed, 2333, 2336
    repayment of maturity, 23115–8
    sinking fund, 0715, 23115
    stamp duty on, 23108
depreciation, 2335, 2340
Directors—
  Attendance Book, 2321
  duties to lay and deliver accounts, 2311
  emoluments of, 2315, 2341–6, 2348, 23224, 23243
  loans to, 2340
  payments to, 2341
  Register of, 2320
  Report of, 2312–14, 23245–8

Limited Companies' Accounts (*contd.*)
discount companies, special provisions, 2340, 2413
dividend—
  Bank Account, 23270
  Equalization Fund, 23274
  Equalization Reserve, 23274
dividends, 23225, 23251 *et seq.*
  arrears of preference, 2339, 23317
  bonus, 23212, 23255–7, 23269
  book-keeping entries, 23259–60, 23266
  cash, 23253, 23258, 23269
  fractions, 23270
  free of tax, 23252
  interim, 23225, 23251
  on participating preference shares, 23254
  on partly paid shares, 23225, 23251
  payment direct to bank, 23270
  preference shareholders, position of, 23251
  proposed, 2337, 2340
  scrip, 23266, 23269
  tax on, 2107, 2356
  through bankers, 23270
divisible profits, 23211 *et seq.*
  commissions, 23220
  constructions capital, interest on, 2334, 23222
  published accounts, 23241
elimination process of acquisition, 23188
emoluments of directors, 2315, 2341 *et seq.*, 2348, 23224, 23243
exempt private company, 2332
expenses, preliminary, 2337, 23155
final accounts, 23225 *et seq.*
foreign currencies, conversion of, 2338
forfeiture of shares, 2392, 2395
formation, 23155
fractional shares, 23270, 23288 *et seq.*
funds, provisions and reserves, 23279
general principles, 2301
goodwill, 2336, 23158 *et seq.*
holding company, 2401 *et seq.*
incorporation, 2301, 2310, 23155
increase of capital, 23144, 23224
interest—
  on calls in advance and in arrear,

Limited Companies' Accounts (*contd.*)
  interest (*contd.*)
      2382, 2384, 23229
      on construction capital, 2334, 23222
  investments, 2335, 2338, 2339, 2347
  issue of debentures, 23108, 23110, 23111
  issue of shares—
      at discount, 2337, 2391, 23101
      at par, 2375
      at premium, 2389, 2399
      by 'rights' issue, 2376–8
  liabilities, 2336
  liquidation, 23277 *et seq.*, 2901 *et seq.*
      fixed charge, 2902, 2905
      floating charge, 2901, 2905, 2915
  loans—
      to directors and officers, 2340
      to employees, 2339
  loss prior to incorporation, 23172
  members, 2302, 2318
      competing claims of, 23281
  Memorandum of Association, 2303, 23281
  Minute Book, 2319
  nominal capital, 23144, 23150, 23225
  notes to balance sheet and accounts, 2338, 2340
  notice convening meeting, 23239
  opening entries (*see* Aquisition Entries)
  option on shares, 2338
  over-subscription, 2386
  partnership contrasted, 2305
  patents, 2336
  payments to directors and officers, 2341
  preference shares—
      participating, 23254
      position *re* dividends, 23251, 23323 *et seq.*
      redeemable, 23147
      rights of, 23281
      valuation of, 2623
  preferential creditors, 2905
  preliminary expenses, 2337, 23155
  private company, 2306
      contrasted with public company, 2307
      exempt, 2332
  Profit and Loss—
      Account, 23207, 23229, 23233,

Limited Companies' Accounts (*contd.*)
  Profit and Loss (*contd.*)
      23241
      contents, 2339
      notes, 2340
      submission of, 2311
      Appropriation Account, 23207, 23214, 23229, 23233, 23235, 23241
      prior to incorporation, 23170, 23172, 23175
  proposed dividend, 2337
  prospectus, 23155
  provisions and reserves, 2334, 2337, 2339, 2347, 23213, 23279
  proxy, 23240
  public company, 2307
      compared with private company, 2307
  published accounts, 23236–50, 3221–38
  purchase consideration, 23157 *et seq.*
  Purchase of Business Account, 23196, 23197
  purchase of partnership business, 22179
  reconstruction, 23274 *et seq.*
      accounting aspect, 23314 *et seq.*
      acquisition of dissenting members' shares, 23306n
      claims of members, 23281
      closing entries on liquidation, 23277
      relief from stamp duty, 23304 *et seq.*
      underlying principles of, 23313
      winding-up aspect, 23320
  redeemable preference shares, 2333, 23147, 23263
  redemption of debentures, 23114, 23118, 23122
  reduction of capital, 23150 *et seq.*
  Register—
      of charges, 2318, 2320, 2325
      of debenture holders, 2318, 2321
      of Directors and Secretary, 2320
      of Directors' interests, 2320
      of members, 2318, 2324
      of share warrants, 2325
  Registrar of Companies, notice to, 2308, 2320, 2321, 23146, 23148, 23150, 23155
  registration of company, 23155
  reissue of forfeited shares, 2395

Limited Companies' Accounts (*contd.*)
  remuneration by share of profit, 23216 *et seq.*
  reorganization of capital, 23155
  report—
    auditors', 2314–15, 2346, 23245, 2413
    directors', 2312–14, 23245–8
  reserve liability, 2316
  reserves—
    and provisions, 2334, 2337, 2339, 2347, 23213, 23279
    dividend equalization, 23274
  return—
    annual, 2319
    of capital, 23153
  'rights' issue, 2376–8
  rulings and forms, 2322 *et seq.*
  secured liabilities, 2336, 2339
  share—
    fractional, 23270, 23288 *et seq.*
    premium, 2334, 2389, 2399
    register, 23106
    warrants, register of, 2325
  share capital—
    allotment, 2334, 2375
    allotment letter, 2323
    allotment sheet, 2386, 2389
    alterations, 23144, 23276
    application, 2376, 2386
    book-keeping entries, 2375 *et seq.*
    calls, 2375, 2382, 23224
      in advance and arrear, 2382–86, 23104, 23224
    cancellation of, 23150, 23224
    commission on shares, 2337, 23110, 23157
    consolidation of, 23147, 23224
    conversion of into stock, 23145–6, 23224
    decrease of, 23144
    discount on shares, 2337, 2391, 2310
    expenses of issue, 2337
    forfeited shares re-issued, 2395–8
    forfeiture, 2392 *et seq.*
    increase or decrease of autho-rized, 23144
    interest on calls, 2382–6, 23224
    issue at discount, 2391
    issue at premium, 2389
    notice of changes to Registrar, 23148

Limited Companies' Accounts (*contd.*)
  share capital (*contd.*)
    over-subscription, 2386
    participating preference shares, 23254
    preference shares, 23251, 23282, 23316
    premium account, share, 2334, 2389, 23100
    redeemable preference shares, 2333, 23147–9, 23263
    redemption of preference shares, 23147 *et seq.*
    reduction of, 23150, 23153
    reorganization of, 23155, 23274 *et seq.*
    return of cash to members, 23153
  shares, 2375
    calls on, 2382, 23224
    financial assistance for purchase of, 2339
    forfeiture, 2392
    into stock, conversion of, 23145
    numbering of, 23107
    option on, 2338
    over-subscription for, 2386
    subdivision of, 23146–7
    surrender of, 23103
  stamp duties, 23108, 23155–6, 23304
  statements and documents attached to, 2346
  statistical books, 2320
  statutory—
    books and documents, 2318
    declaration, 23156
    of solvency, 2923
    exceptions for banks, etc., 2333, 2340, 2413
    meeting, 2316
    report, 2316, 2320, 2321
    requirements (summary), 2346
  stock, 23144, 23224
    into shares, conversion of, 23144–5
    units, 23107, 23145
  Stock Transfer Act (1963), 2327–31
  Stock Transfer Form, 2328–9
  subsidiary company in balance sheet of parent, 2337
  surrender of shares, 23103
  Table A, 2319, 2321, 2382, 2384, 2392, 23104, 23145, 23147, 23154, 23211, 23216, 23224–5, 23233, 23251, 23252, 2614

Limited Companies' Accounts (*contd.*)
Taxation Account, 2104, 2108, 2110, 23250
taxation, basis of—
in balance sheet, 2338, 23242
in profit and loss account, 2339
trade marks, 2336
transfer—
form, 2326–7
register, 2324
true and fair view, 2333
turnover, 2313, 23241, 23243
types of companies, 2308
unclaimed dividends in, 23271 *et seq.*
underwriting commission, 23157
unlimited liability, 2305
vendors, 23110, 23180
apportionment of shares, 23180, 23208
voting, 23224, 23313, 23326
winding-up, 23274 *et seq.*
and liquidation, 2901 *et seq.*
aspect of reconstructions, 23320 *et seq.*
closing entries, 23277 *et seq.*
Limited partnership, 22189 *et seq.*
Act (1907), 2204, 2205, 22189–90, 2305
Line of Balance, 3190
Linear programming, 3188
Liquidation 2901 *et seq.*
and bankruptcy contrasted, 2901 *et seq.*, 2926
business carried on, 2926
calls in advance, 2912
closing entries, 23277 *et seq.*
collection of calls, 2907
compulsory and bankruptcy contrasted, 2926
contributories, 2918
creditors—
preferential, 2901, 2905
secured, 2901
unsecured, 2901
debenture interest, 2902
declaration of solvency, 2923
Deficiency Account, 2901 *et seq.*, 2924, 2926
Liquidator's—
Cash Acount, 2905 *et seq.*
Final Account, 2905 *et seq.*
remuneration, 2905
preferential creditors, 2901, 2905

Liquidation (*contd.*)
Receiver for debenture-holders, 2914–16
secured creditors, 2901
Statement of Affairs, 2901, 2920–1
statutory declaration of solvency, 2923
statutory forms, 2922
unsecured creditors, 2901
Loading, 1712, 3005
Loan Accounts—
interest on, 0526
of retired partners, 22104
Long Acre Press Ltd., In *re*, 23213, 23216
Loose Tools, 0566, 0711
Loss—
of profits insurance, 2701 *et seq.*
of stock claim, 2705
prior to incorporation, 23170
Lubbock v. *British Bank of South America*, 23212

McLeod v. *Dowling*, 2208, 2293
Management accounting, aids and techniques, 3101 *et seq.*
analysis of balance sheet components, 3110–12
bankers and the balance sheet, 3112–14
communication, 3107–8
comparative column interpretation, 3135–38
control, 3107
co-ordinating, 3106
definition, 3101
forecasting, 3101
interpretation of accounts, 3108
interpretation of results, 3115–18
key factor, 3102
limiting factor, 3102
motivating, 3106
organization chart, 3102, 3104–5
organizing, 3102
planning, 3102
processes of management, 3101
responsibility for supervision, 3103
restricted objectives, 3114
results of one year's operations, 3114–15
scalor principle, 3103
source of decrease of resources, 3125–6

Management accounting, aids and techniques (*contd.*)
source of increase of capital, 3125
special objective, 3109–14
variation statements, 3120
working capital, 3118–20, 3127–31
Managers' commission, 0561, 23216 *et seq.*
Manufacturing Accounts, 3001 *et seq.*
discrepancy in quantitative results, 3003
function, 3001
gross works cost of manufacture, 3001
managers' commission, 23216, 3006
net works cost of manufacture, 3002
overhead, 3001
pool accounts, 3013
prime cost, 3001
process account, 3015–7
quantities, 3002–3
Stores Account, 3009
treatment of profits on unsold stock, 3005 *et seq.*
work-in-progress, 3002
Marginal costing, 3165 *et seq.*
Marginal deposit receipt, 0630
Marginal Gross Profit, 0585
Marshall Bros. (Belfast), re, 23282
Mechanical aids in accounting, 3171 *et seq.*
Mechanized accounting, advantages and disadvantages of, 3172
Memorandum of Association, 2303
Microcomputers, 3178
Mine Redemption Funds, 23144
Minimum rent, royalties, 1501 *et seq.*
Minority—
interests, 2430
shareholders, 2430
Minute Book, 2319
Murex v. *C.I.R.,* 23305

National Insurance Contributions, 0540
Negotiable instruments, 0602
Net asset basis in share valuation, 2619 *et seq.*
Net profit and net loss, 0501
Network Analysis, 3189
Nominal accounts, 0101, 0105
Nominal capital—
decrease, 23144, 23150
increase, 23144, 23224

Nominal Ledger, 0104
Notice convening Annual General Meeting, 23239
Noting charges, 0614

OBJECTIVE accounting, 3173
Operational Research, 3187 *et seq.*
Ordinary shares, *see* Limited Companies' Accounts
valuation of, 2612
Oswald Tillotson, Ltd. v. *C.I.R.,* 23304
Outside interests, 2430
Outside shareholders, 2430
Overriding commission, 23157
Own debentures—
interest on, 23128 *et seq.*
purchase of, 23127 *et seq.*

PACKAGES, 0901 *et seq. (see also* Containers)
Participating preference shares, 23254
Partnership Accounts, 2201 *et seq.*
accounting provisions, 2201 *et seq.*
acquisition, 2281 *et seq.*
adjustment—
of 'cash' to 'earned' profits of new partner's capital account, 2274
of outgoing partner's account, 2296 *et seq.*
of profit-sharing ratios, 2227, 22137, 22148
of remaining partners' capitals to new profit ratio, 22117–19
admission of partner, 2260 *et seq.*
capital adjustment on, 2274 *et seq.*
during financial period, 2284
goodwill, 2264, 2267
revaluation of assets and liabilities, 2260–63
agreements, 2201, 2206, 2256 *et seq.*
alternative profit-sharing proposals, 2239
amalgamations, 2281
annuities, 22147 *et seq.*
purchase of, 22156–58
arrangements with creditors, 22200
assets and liabilities
not taken over, 2287
taken over, 22165
assignment of life policies, 22114
bad debts, adjustment for, 22100 *et seq.*
branches, 22103–106

Partnership Accounts (*contd.*)
Capital Accounts, 2208–9
  'cash' profits, 2230, 2232 *et seq.*
  change in constitution, 22153 *et seq.*
  change in profit ratio, 22137, 22155, 22168
  continuance of personnel, 22137 *et seq.*
  continuity, 22149
  contribution and purchase of share distinguished, 2271
  course of dealing, 2202, 2205
  Current Accounts, 2209, 22187
  death of a partner, 2293
  definition, 2201
  dissolution, 22158, 22187
  book-keeping entries, 22158 *et seq.*
  insolvency of partner, 2203, 22159, 22171 *et seq.*
    piecemeal payments, 22175–79
  distinction between contributions and purchase of share, 2271
  division of profits, 2202, 2257–60
  Drawings—
    Account, 2209
    restriction on, 2275
  elimination of assets not taken over, 2287 *et seq.*
  Elliott v. *Elliott*, 22109
  foreign exchange, 22206
  Garner v. *Murray*, 2204, 22172, 22174 *et seq.* 22194
  general principles, 2201
  goodwill, 22108, 2264
    premium method, 2267, 2269
    remaining undisturbed, 2270
  guarantee of profits, 2240 *et seq.*
  income tax, 2226 *et seq.*
  Interest—
    Accounts, 2210
    as proportion of profits, 2217
    in lieu of profits 22119
    on capital, 2212, 22140
    on drawings, 2210
    to outgoing partner, 22104, 22111
  junior partner's agreements, 2242 *et seq.*
  last Balance Sheet and retirement, 2297
  legal points, 2201–4, 2207
  life policies, assignment of, 22114
  limited company, partnership compared with, 2305

Partnership Accounts (*contd.*)
  limited partnership, 2204, 22189 *et seq.*
    compared with ordinary partnership, 22159 *et seq.*
  Loan Accounts, 2211, 22104
  maximum number of partners, 2201
  Memorandum Adjustment Statement, 2233, 2235, 2238, 22179
  Memorandum Revaluation Account, 2296, 22122, 22138
  outgoing partner, adjustments, 2293
  partners' salaries, 2212, 2239
  partners taking over assets and liabilities on dissolution, 22165–73
  payment on retirement based on profits, 22105
  payment to retired partner in lieu of goodwill, 22108
  piecemeal payments, 22175, 22178–9
  premiums—
    on entry of partners, 2269, 2270
    on life policies, 22114
  profit sharing, 2207 *et seq.*, 2239 *et seq.*
    ratio, effect of change in, 22137 *et seq.*
    readjustment of, 2227, 22155
  profit to outgoing partner, 2296
  profits in lieu of goodwill, 22108
  provision for payment to retiring partner, 22111
  purchase—
    and sale of partnership shares, 22126–34
    of annuity, 22151
  Purchase of Business Account, 2288–90
  receipts and expenditure account, 2254
  reconstruction, 22200
  recoupment of guaranteed share of profits, 2248 *et seq.*
  registration of name, 2201
  retired partner's balance as loan, 22104
  retirement—
    adjustment of capital on, 22117
    and admission, 22120 *et seq.*, 22155
    annuities on, 22147
    of partners, 2293 *et seq.*, 22155
    payments to retired partner based

Partnership Accounts (*contd.*)
  retirement (*contd.*)
    on profit, 22105
    share of profits in lieu of goodwill, 22108
  revaluation—
    on an admission, 2260 *et seq.*
    on a retirement, 22155 *et seq.*
  sale of business to comapny, 22179
    apportionment of shares between vendors, 23180
    vendor's guarantees of debtors and creditors, 3216
  salaries, partnes', 2210
  share of profit—
    in lieu of goodwill, 22108
    of outgoing partner, 2296–7, 22108
  shares of partnership bought and sold, 22126 *et seq.*
  single entry, 2256
  summary of legal points, 2205
  taking over of assets and liabilities on a dissolution, 22165
  valuations unaltered on an admission, 2262
  withdrawal of goods, 2211
Partnership Act (1890), 2201–4, 2208, 2305
  Section—
    19, 2202
    24, 2202
    33, 2208
    42, 2203, 2208
    43, 2203
    44, 2204
P.A.Y.E., accounting entries, 0922 *et seq.*, 2201
Percentages, 0301 *et seq.*, 0584
Periodic balance method, 0410
Personal accounts, 0101, 0105
PERT, 3194
Petty Cash Book, 0207 *et seq.*
  as double entry, 0208, 0210
  as memorandum book, 0210
  imprest system, 0208
Plant Registers, 0714
Pool accounts, 3013–4
Pratt, In *re*, 2811
Preference Shares, 23147, 23251, 2623
  participating, 23254
  redeemable, 23147–9, 23263
  valuation of, 2623 *et seq.*
Preferential creditors, 2809, 2905
Preliminary expenses, 2337, 23155

Premiums—
  debenture, 23124
  in partnership accounts, 2268
  life assurance, partnership, 22111, 22114 *et seq.*
Prepayments, 0510
Priority percentages, 3151
Private companies, 2306, 2307
Process accounts, 3015–7
Professional men—
  Cash profits, 2230, 2232 *et seq.*
  use of 100 per cent reserve on debtors, 1211
Profit and Loss Account, 0501 *et seq.*
  (*see also* Holding Companies and Limited Companies Accounts)
  accruals, 0513
  consolidated, methods of preparation, 2458 *et seq.*
  expenses, 0504
  prepayments, 0510
Profit and Loss Appropriation Account, 0502, 23214, 23255, 23259–61
Profits—
  available for dividends, 23211
  divisible, 23211
  loss of insurances, 2701
  prior to incorporation, 23170, 23175
Promissory note, 0601
Prospectus, 23155
Provisions, 0518, 0717, 0720 *et seq.*, 2334, 2337, 2339, 2347 (*see also* Reserves)
  contingency, 0702
Published Accounts, 23236–50, 3221–38
Purchase—
  C.O.D., 0914
  consideration, 23157
  of business account, 2287–92, 23164, 23196–7
  of debentures in open market, 23127
Purchases, 0538
  Day Book, 0102
  Ledger, 0113
  Returns Book, 0103

QUARTER days, 0513
Quarterly statements, 3132–3

RAMPS, 3188

Rates, 0572
Ratios, accounting, 3141 *et seq.*
Real accounts, 0101, 0104
Rebate on bills discounted, 0633
Receipts—
  and Expenditure Account, 1211, 2254
  treatment of debtors, 1211
  and Payments Accounts, 1201 *et seq.*
  from income and expenditure, 1207
  from receipts and expenditure, 1211
  Liquidator's, 2905
  Receiver's, 2918
Receiver for Debenture-holders, 2914
  accounts of, 2918
Reconstruction—
  accounting aspects, 23314–20
  methods of, 23274 *et seq.*
  objections to amalgamations, 23275
  objects of amalgamations, 23275
  principles of, 23313
  winding up aspects, 23320 *et seq.*
Recoupment—
  of guarantee in partnership, 2248
  of short workings, 1501
Redeemable preference shares, 23147, 23150, 23263
Redemption—
  of debentures, 23114, 23118, 23122
  yield, 0309 *et seq.*
Red ink interest, 0402, 0410
Reduction of capital, 23150, 23153
Registrar of Companies, 2320, 23146, 23148, 23150, 23155
Registration—
  of Business Names Act (1916), 2201, 22190, 2306
  of companies, 23155
Reinstatement in Civil Employment Acts, 2810
Relief from stamp duty, 23304
Remuneration—
  of auditors, 2340
  of directors, 2315, 2341–6, 2348, 23224, 23243
Renewals and replacements under double account system, 2503
Rental Ledger, 1303
Reorganization of capital, 23155, 23274
Repairs, 0803

Repayment of Capital, 23153
Report—
  Auditors', 2314–15, 2346, 23245, 2413
  Directors', 2312–14, 2346, 23245–8
  statutory, 2316 *et seq.*
Reserve—
  fund, 0720
  liability, 2315
Reserves, 0717 *et seq.*
  bad debts, 0512 *et seq.*, 1103, 1122
  capital, 0718, 2334, 23213–4
  contingent liabilities, reserves and provisions, 0720, 2334, 2337, 2338, 2339, 23279, 2429, 2808
  debtors, 1211 *et seq.*
  definition of, 0717, 2334
  discount, 0523
  dividend equalization, 23274
  general, 0718
  hidden, 0719
  inner, 0719
  revenue, 0718, 2334
  secret, 0719
  specific, 0719
Retirement of a bill, 0615
Return, Annual, 2319, 2321
Revenue—
  and capital expenditure, 0801
  reserves, 0718, 2334
Ridge Nominees v. *C.I.R.* (1962), 23306
'Rights' issues of shares, calculation of value, 2629
Rights of members in winding up, 23281, 23313–4, 23320
Royalty Accounts, 1501 *et seq.*
  book-keeping entries, 1503
  general principles, 1501, 1509
  Income Tax, 1503
  minimum rent, 1501 *et seq.*
  short-workings, 1501
  sub-royalties, 1510
  taxation and royalties receivable, 1509

SALARIES and wages, 0540, 0803
Sale—
  for deferred payments, 2058
  or return, 0909
  to limited company, 22179
Sales, 0540
  C.O.D., 0914 *et seq.*

Sales (*contd.*)
  cost of, 0542
  Day Book, 0102
  goods—
    on approval, 0909 *et seq.*
    on sale of return, 0909 *et seq.*
  Ledger, 0104
  Returns Book, 0103
Salvage, 2705 *et seq.*
Samples, 0574
Schemes of Reconstruction, 23274 *et seq.*
Scottish Insurance Corporation v. *Wilson's and Clyde Coal Co., Ltd.,* 23282, 2624
Scrip Dividends, 23266, 23270
Secret accounts, 1008
Secret reserve, 0719
Sectional balancing, 1001 *et seq.*
Selective Employment Tax, 0918
Self-balancing ledgers, 1001 *et seq.*
  adjustment accounts, 1005 *et seq.*
    construction of, 1001
  advantages, 1001
  analysis of subsidiary books, 1001
  Cash Book, 1002
  control accounts, 1001
  correction of errors, 1409 *et seq.*
  day books, 1003
  Journal, 1003
  Nominal Ledger Adjustment Account, 1006, 1007
  Purchases Ledger Adjustment Account, 1007
  Sales Ledger Adjustment Account, 1006
  Secret accounts, 1008
  total accounts—
    rules for construction of, 1002
    use of, 1008
Share—
  Capital, *see* Limited Companies Accounts
  premium account, 2334, 2389, 23100
Shares—
  and stocks, 0306
  bonus, 23212, 23256
  consolidation, 23147, 23224
  conversion into stock, 23145, 23224
  of ships, 0917
  ordinary valuation of, 2612
  preference, valuation of, 2623

Shares (*contd.*)
  subdivision of, 23146–7
Sharkey v. *Wernher,* 2212
Short and another v. *Treasury Commissioners,* 2618
Short bills, 0630
Shortworkings, 1501 *et seq.*
Simplex method, 3189
Single entry, 1101 *et seq.*
  abridged double-entry, 1121–3
  capital statements, 1119
  conversion to double entry, 1106 *et seq.*
  disadvantages of, 1118
  partnership accounts, 2256
  popular sense, 1105
  pure, 1101, 1105
  statement of affairs, 1103
  statement of profits, 1102
Sinking Fund
  debentures, 0714, 23115 *et seq.*
  investments, 0706, 0715
  method of depreciation, 0706
Social Security Acts 1973 and 1975, 2810
Societies, accounts of, 1201 *et seq.*
Sources and application of funds, 3120 *et seq.*
Spanish Prospecting Company, In *re.,* 23212, 23216
Special Margins Account, 0630
Specific reserve, 0719
Stable exchanges, 1966
Stamp Act, 2326
Stamp duties—
  bills, inland and foreign, 0603
  contract of sale, 23156, 2601
  limited companies, 2305, 2306, 23108, 23145, 23155, 23156, 23304
  limited partnerships, 22191
  relief from, 23304–6
Standard costing, 3162
Standing charges, 0585
Stapley v. *Read Bros. Ltd.,* 23212
Statement—
  of Affairs—
    bankruptcy, 2801 *et seq.,* 2822
    liquidation, 2901, 2920–1
    single entry, 1103
  of Profit, 1102
Statements of Standard Accounting Practice—
  1/5 Value Added Tax, 0922

Statements of Standard Accounting
Practice (*contd.*)
  1/8 Taxation in Company
    Accounts, 2360–7
  1/9 Stocks and Work-in-Progress,
    0532–7
  1/10 Source and Application of Funds,
    2348–53
  1/14 Group Accounts, 2417–22
  1/15 Accounting for Deferred Taxa-
    tion, 2367, 73
  1/16 Current Cost Accounting, 23351
  1/17 Accounting for Post Balance
    Sheet Events, 23355
  1/18 Accounting for Contingencies,
    23359
  1/19 Accounting for Investment
    Properties, 2649
Statistical and Statutory Books and
  Forms, 2318–22
  Allotment Letter 2323
  Annual Return, 2319, 2321
  bankruptcy, 2822 *et seq.*
  liquidation, 2919–25
  List of Members, 2318, 2324
  Minute Book, 2319
  Register—
    of Charges, 2320, 2325
    of Directors and Secretary, 2320
    of Directors' Interests, 2320
    of Members, 2318, 2324
    of Share Warrants, 2325
  Share Ledger, 2324
  Transfer—
    Form, 2326–7
    Register, 2324
Statutory—
  company, 2308
  meeting and report, 2316
Stewart v. *Gladstone,* 2208
Stock, 23144, 23224
  Attributable profit, 0536
  conversion into shares, 23144, 23224
  cost, 0535
  cost of conversion, 0535
  cost of purchase, 0535
  destroyed, 0552
  expenses, 0517
  foreseeable losses, 0536
  goods, 0529 *et seq.,* 0552
  in final accounts, 0503, 0504, 0529,
    0535
  joint venture, 1602

Stock (*contd.*)
  Long term contract, 0536
  lost on consignment, 1707 *et seq.*
  net realizable value, 0533, 0536
  replacement cost, 0533
  sold on consignment, 1706, 1718,
    1733
  units, 23107, 23145
  valuation, 0532
Stock Exchange (Completion of Bar-
  gains) Act 1976, 2304
Stock Exchange Transactions, 2601 *et
  seq.*
  book-keeping entries, 2601
  brokers' accounts, 2609
  contract stamps, 2601
  'cum dividend,' 2602
  dividends and interest, 2602 *et seq.*
  'ex dividend,' 2602
  purchases and sales, 2601
Stock Transfer Act (1963), 2327
Stock Transfer (Amendment of Forms)
  Order 1974, 2327
Stock Transfer Form, 2328–9
Stocken v. *Dawson,* 2208
Stocks and shares, 0306
  flat yield, 0309, 0310
  redemption yield, 0309, 0310
Stocktaking, 0530, 0531
Students Union, Accounts of, 1208
Sub-royalties, 1510
Subsidiary company, 2401
Sub-underwriting, 23157
Super-profits, 2266, 23158–60
Superannuation accounts, 3205 *et seq.*
Surrender value, 0708
Surrenders (Life Assurance), 0708
Suspense Accounts—
  correction of errors, 1401 *et seq.*
  creditors, 23185, 23186
  debtors, 23186
  hire purchase, 2008 *et seq.*

TABLE A 2319, 2321, 2382, 2384, 2392,
  23104, 23145, 23147, 23154, 23211,
  23216, 23224–5, 23233, 23251,
  23252, 2614
Table of present values, 3187
Tabular Book-keeping, 1301 *et seq.*
  combined Day Book and Ledger,
    1310
  Day Books or Journals, 1309

Tabular Book-keeping (*contd.*)
  Doctor's accounts, 1307
  Gas Consumption Ledger, 1303
  hotel book-keeping, 1305 *et seq.*
  Rental ledger, 1303
  transfers, 1309
  Visitors' Ledger, 1305
Take-over bids, 3153
  C.A. recommendations, 3155
  city code, 3154–5
  definition, 3153
  legislative controls, 3154
  method of gaining control, 3153
Taxation Account, 2101 *et seq.*, 2325,
  2360 *et seq.*, 23132, 23133
Terminology of Management and
  Financial Accounting, 3157
Tillotson (Oswald) Ltd. v. *C.I.R.,*
  23304,
Total accounts, 1001
Trade—
  charge, money order, 0914
  discount, 0102
Trading and Profit and Loss Account,
  0501 *et seq.*
  accruals, 0516
  adjustments, 0509, 0565–0571
  bad debts—
    provision, 0521, 0554
    treatment of, 0521 *et seq.*
  branches—
    memorandum, 1906 *et seq.*
    self-accounting, 1949 *et seq.*
  carriage inwards and outwards, 0539
  commission, 0561
  construction of rules for, 0503, 0508
  cost of sales, 0542
  debenture interest, 23112, 23128
  definition of, 0501
  departmental, 1804 *et seq.*
  depreciation, 0518, 0519, 0565
  discounts provisions, 0525, 0523
  examination procedure, 0549–0565,
    0581 *et seq.*
  expenses—
    accrued and accruing, 0513
    prepaid, 0510
    stock, 0517
  finance, cost of, 0575
  goods on approval, 0909
  income—
    accrued and accruing, 0516
    not yet earned, 0515

Trading and Profit and Loss Account,
    (*contd.*)
  load interest, 0526
  packages, treatment of, 0901 *et seq.*
  percentages, 0584–5, 1818
  prepayments, 0510
  provision—
    for bad and doubtful debts, 0521
    for discounts, 0523
  purchases, 0538
  rates, 0572
  rebates on bills discounted, 0633
  salaries, 0539, 0803
  sales, 0540
    cost of, 0542
  samples, 0575
  sequence of items in, 0577
  stock, 0503, 0517, 0529, 0532–7
    destroyed, 0552
    valuation, 0532
  stocktaking, 0530–1
  subdivision of, 0577
  transfers, 0528
  turnover, 0543
  unearned income, 0515
  valuation of stock, 0532
  Voyage Accounts, 0916 *et seq.*
  wages and salaries, 0539
Transfer—
  for nominal consideration, 2327
  form, 2326–7
  stamp duty, relief from 100 per cent,
    23304
Transportation technique, 3189
Trego v. *Hunt,* 2264
Trial Balance, 0107 *et seq.*
  errors not revealed in, 0113
Trimble and Bennett v. *Goldberg,* 2207
Turner v. *Major,* 2207
Turnover, 0543, 23241, 23243
  basis, profit apportioned on, 23206

UNCLAIMED dividends, 23271–2
Underwriting commission, 23157
Unearned income, 0515
Unrealized profits, 1803, 2409, 2436,
  2459, 3005 *et seq.*

VALUATION—
  of bonus rights, 2629
  of goodwill, 2278, 23158–60

VALUATION (*contd.*)
  of shares, 2612 *et seq.*
    bonus shares, 2628, 2629
    equity or net assets basis, 2619
    factors affecting yield, 2615
    gearing, 2623
    income basis, 2613–19
    net asset basis, 2619
    preference shares, 2623 *et seq.*
      coefficient of dispersion, 2628 *et seq.*
      dividend cover, 2627
      published accounts, 2631
      purposes of, 2612
  of stock, 0532
    for fire claim, 2705
    on joint venture, 1602
    unsold on consignment, 1706
Value Added Tax, 0918–22, 2201, 2810
Variation statements, 3120 *et seq.*
Vendors'—
  apportionment of share, 23180 *et seq.*, 23208
  guarantees of debtors and creditors, 3216 *et seq.*
Verner v. *General and Commercial Trust*, 23211
Visitors' Ledger, 1306
Voting power, 23224, 23313, 23326

Voyage Accounts, 0916–18

WAGES and salaries, 0539, 0803
Walker v. *Hirsch*, 2207
Wall v. *London and Provincial Trust*, 23212, 23214
Walter Symons, *re*, 23282
Watney v. *Wells*, 2202, 2207
Weighted average, 0310–12
Wilmer v. *McNamara*, 23211
Winding up, 23274 *et seq.*, 2901 *et seq.*
  aspect of reconstructions, 23320 *et seq.*
Wood v. *Odessa Waterworks*, 23266
Work-in-progress, 3002
Working capital, 3118 *et seq.*
  statement, preparation of, 3127
Working capital, 3118 *et seq.*
  statement, preparation of, 3127
Workmen's Compensation Act (1925), 2810
Worthington v. *Oceana Development Co. Ltd.*, 0537

YIELD—
  factors affecting, 2615
  flat, 0309 *et seq.*
  redemption, 0309 *et seq.*